AZ GR BRITAIN

BRITAIN

NORTHERN IRELAND

Handy Road Atlas

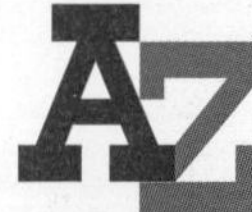

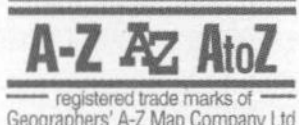

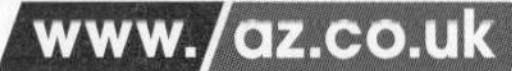

CW00708396

A-Z AZ AtoZ
registered trade marks of
Geographers' A-Z Map Company Ltd

www./az.co.uk

EDITION 23 2015
Copyright © Geographers' A-Z Map Company Ltd.
Telephone: 01732 781000 (Enquiries & Trade Sales)
01732 783422 (Retail Sales)
© Crown copyright and database rights 2014. Ordnance Survey 100017302.

Northern Ireland: This is Based upon Crown Copyright and is reproduced with
the permission of Land & Property Services under delegated authority from the
Controller of Her Majesty's Stationery Office, © Crown copyright and database
right 2014 PMLPA No 100508. The inclusion of parts or all of the Republic of
Ireland is by permission of the Government of Ireland who retain copyright in
the data used. © Ordnance Survey Ireland and Government of Ireland.

Land & Property Services
Paper Map Licensed Partner

ORDNANCE SURVEY
OF NORTHERN IRELAND

This is a registered Trade Mark of
Department of Finance and Personnel.

Motorway ≡M1
Autoroute
Autobahn

Motorway Under Construction
Autoroute en construction
Autobahn im Bau

Motorway Proposed
Autoroute prévue
Geplante Autobahn

Motorway Junctions with Numbers ≡4≡5
Unlimited Interchange ④ Limited Interchange ❺

Autoroute échangeur numéroté
Echangeur complet
Echangeur partiel
Autobahnanschlußstelle mit Nummer
Unbeschränkter Fahrtrichtungswechsel
Beschränkter Fahrtrichtungswechsel

Motorway Service Area ⑤
with access from one carriageway only ⑤

Aire de services d'autoroute
accessible d'un seul côté

Rastplatz oder Raststätte
Einbahn

Major Road Service Areas with 24 hour facilities

Primary Route ⑤ Class A Road ⑤

Aire de services sur route prioritaire ouverte 24h sur 24
Route à grande circulation   Route de type A

Raststätte durchgehend geöffnet
Hauptverkehrsstraße   A- Straße

Truckstop (selection of) ⑪
Sélection d'aire pour poids lourds
Auswahl von Fernfahrerrastplatz

Primary Route A40
Route à grande circulation
Hauptverkehrsstraße

Primary Route Junction with Number 4⬤
Echangeur numéroté
Hauptverkehrsstraßenkreuzung mit Nummer

Primary Route Destination DOVER
Route prioritaire, direction
Hauptverkehrsstraße Richtung

Dual Carriageways (A & B roads)
Route à double chaussées séparées (route A & B)
Zweispurige Schnellstraße (A- und B- Straßen)

Class A Road A129
Route de type A
A-Straße

Class B Road B177
Route de type B
B-Straße

Narrow Major Road (passing places)
Route prioritaire étroite (possibilité de dépassement)
Schmale Hauptverkehrsstraße (mit Überholmöglichkeit)

Major Roads Under Construction
Route prioritaire en construction
Hauptverkehrsstraße im Bau

Major Roads Proposed
Route prioritaire prévue
Geplante Hauptverkehrsstaße

Gradient 1:7 (14%) **& steeper** »
(Descent in direction of arrow)
Pente égale ou supérieure à 14% (dans le sens de la descente)
14% Steigung und steiler (in Pfeilrichtung)

Toll | Toll
Barrière de péage
Gebührenpflichtig

Dart Charge ©
www.gov.uk/highways/dartford

Park & Ride P+R
Parking avec Service Navette
Parken und Reisen

Mileage between markers ↘ 8 ↗
Distence en miles entre les flèches
Strecke zwischen Markierungen in Meilen

Airport ✈
Aéroport
Flughafen

Railway and Station ●
Voie ferrée et gare
Eisenbahnlinie und Bahnhof

Level Crossing and Tunnel ╳ ----
Passage à niveau et tunnel
Bahnübergang und Tunnel

River or Canal
Rivière ou canal
Fluß oder Kanal

County or Unitary Authority Boundary — · —
Limite de comté ou de division administrative
Grafschafts- oder Verwaltungsbezirksgrenze

National Boundary + — +
Frontière nationale
Landesgrenze

Built-up Area
Agglomération
Geschloßene Ortschaft

Town, Village or Hamlet ○
Ville, Village ou hameau
Stadt, Dorf oder Weiler

Wooded Area
Zone boisée
Waldgebiet

Spot Height in Feet · 813
Altitude (en pieds)
Höhe in Fuß

Height Above Sea Level 1,400'-2000' 427m-610m
Altitude par rapport au niveau de la mer 2000'+ 610m+
Höhe über Meeresspiegel

National Grid Reference (kilometres) ¹00
Coordonnées géographiques nationales (Kilomètres)
Nationale geographische Koordinaten (Kilometer)

Page Continuation
Suite à la page indiquée
Seitenfortsetzung **24**

Scale to Map Pages 1:316,800 = 5 miles to 1 inch / 3.1 km to 1 cm

0 1 2 3 4 5   10   15   20 Miles
0 1 2 3 4 5   10   15   20   25   30 Kilometres

Airfield
Terrain d'aviation
Flugplatz

Heliport
Héliport
Hubschrauberlandeplatz

Abbey, Church, Friary, Priory
Abbaye, église, monastère, prieuré
Abtei, Kirche, Mönchskloster, Kloster

Animal Collection
Ménagerie
Tiersammlung

Aquarium
Aquarium
Aquarium

Arboretum, Botanical Garden
Jardin Botanique
botanischer Garten

Aviary, Bird Garden
Volière
Voliere

Battle Site and Date
Champ de bataille et date
Schlachtfeld und Datum

Blue Flag Beach
Plage Pavillon Bleu
Blaue Flagge Strand

Bridge
Pont
Brücke

Castle (open to public)
Château (ouvert au public)
Schloß / Burg (für die Öffentlichkeit zugänglich)

Castle with Garden (open to public)
Château avec parc (ouvert au public)
Schloß mit Garten (für die Öffentlichkeit zugänglich)

Cathedral
Cathédrale
Kathedrale

Cidermaker
Cidrerie (fabrication)
Apfelwein Hersteller

Country Park
Parc régional
Landschaftspark

Distillery
Distillerie
Brennerei

Farm Park, Open Farm
Park Animalier
Bauernhof Park

Ferry (vehicular, sea)
(vehicular, river)
(foot only)
Bac (véhicules, mer)
(véhicules, rivière)
(piétons)
Fähre (auto, meer)
(auto, fluß)
(nur für Personen)

Fortress, Hill Fort
Château Fort
Festung

Garden (open to public)
Jardin (ouvert au public)
Garten (für die Öffentlichkeit zugänglich)

Golf Course
Terrain de golf
Golfplatz

Historic Building (open to public)
Monument historique (ouvert au public)
Historisches Gebäude (für die Öffentlichkeit zugänglich)

Historic Building with Garden (open to public)
Monument historique avec jardin (ouvert au public)
Historisches Gebäude mit Garten (für die Öffentlichkeit zugänglich)

Horse Racecourse
Hippodrome
Pferderennbahn

Industrial Monument
Monument Industrielle
Industriedenkmal

Leisure Park, Leisure Pool
Parc d'Attraction, Loisirs Piscine
Freizeitpark, Freizeit pool

Lighthouse
Phare
Leuchtturm

Mine, Cave
Mine, Grotte
Bergwerk, Höhle

Monument
Monument
Denkmal

Motor Racing Circuit
Circuit Automobile
Automobilrennbahn

Museum, Art Gallery
Musée
Museum, Galerie

National Park
Parc national
Nationalpark

National Trust Property
National Trust Property
National Trust- Eigentum

Nature Reserve or Bird Sanctuary
Réserve naturelle botanique ou ornithologique
Natur- oder Vogelschutzgebiet

Nature Trail or Forest Walk
Chemin forestier, piste verte
Naturpfad oder Waldweg

Place of Interest *Craft Centre* •
Site, curiosité
Sehenswürdigkeit

Prehistoric Monument
Monument Préhistorique
prähistorische Denkmal

Railway, Steam or Narrow Gauge
Chemin de fer, à vapeur ou à voie étroite
Eisenbahn, Dampf- oder Schmalspurbahn

Roman Remains
Vestiges Romains
römischen Ruinen

Theme Park
Centre de loisirs
Vergnügungspark

Tourist Information Centre (All year)
Office de Tourisme (ouvert toute l'année)
Touristeninformationen (ganzjährig geöffnet)
(Summer season only)
(été seulement)
(nur im Sommer geöffnet)

Viewpoint (360 degrees) (180 degrees)
Vue panoramique (360 degrés) (180 degrés)
Aussichtspunkt (360 Grade) (180 Grade)

Vineyard
Vignoble
Weinberg

Visitor Information Centre
Centre d'information touristique
Besucherzentrum

Wildlife Park
Réserve de faune
Wildpark

Windmill
Moulin à vent
Windmühle

Zoo or Safari Park
Parc ou réserve zoologique
Zoo oder Safari-Park

Please note: symbols have been enlarged for clarity

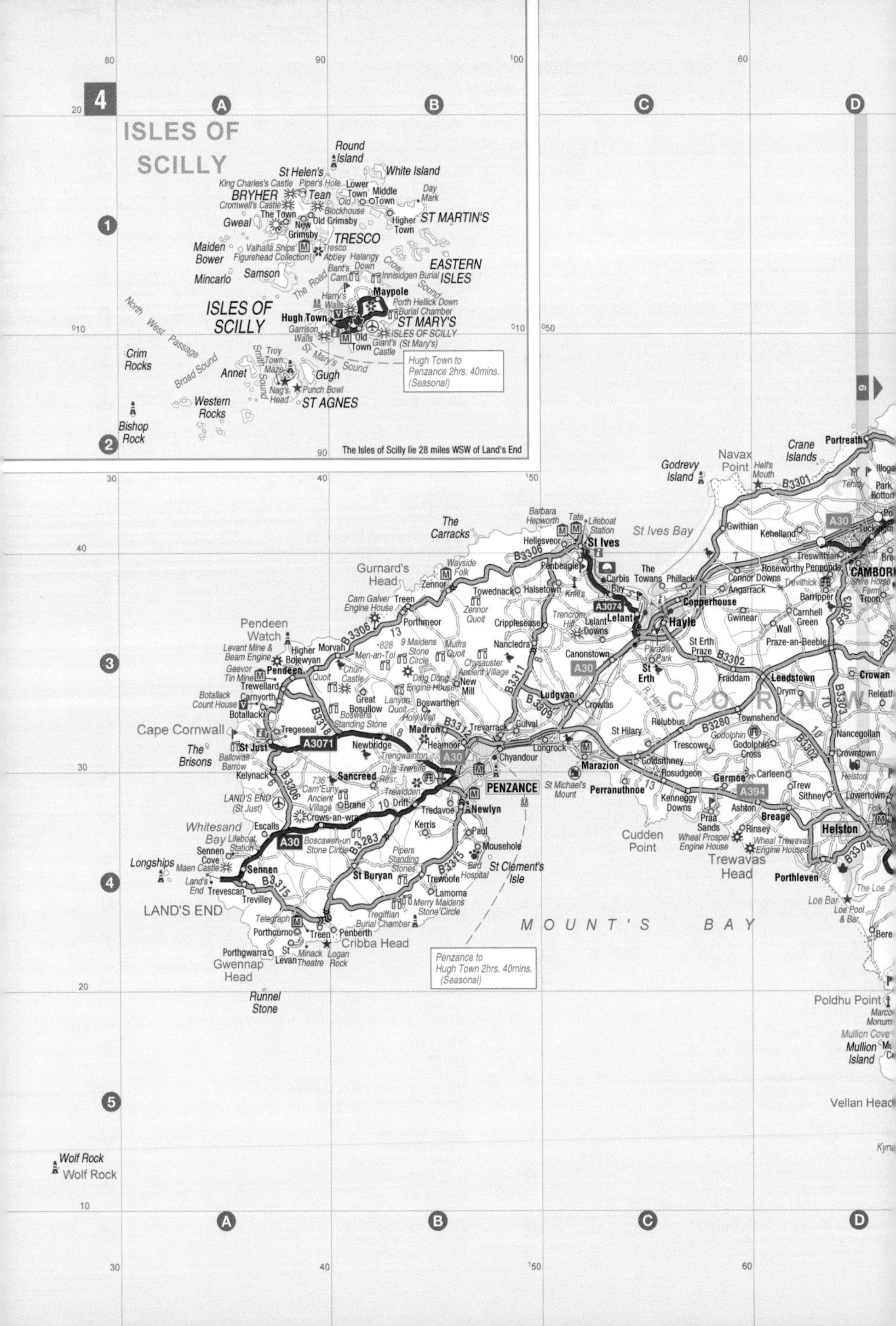
ISLES OF SCILLY
Round Island
White Island
St Helen's
Piper's Hole
King Charles's Castle
BRYHER
Tean
Lower Town
Middle Town
Day Mark
Cromwell's Castle
Old Blockhouse
The Town
Old Grimsby
New Grimsby
Higher Town
ST MARTIN'S
Gweal
TRESCO
Maiden Bower
Valhalla Ships Figurehead Collection
Tresco Abbey
Halangy Down
Bant's Carn
Innisidgen Burial
EASTERN ISLES
Crow Sound
Mincarlo
Samson
The Road
Maypole
Harry's Walls
Porth Hellick Down Burial Chamber
North West Passage
ISLES OF SCILLY
Hugh Town
ST MARY'S
Garrison Walls
Old Town
ISLES OF SCILLY (St Mary's)
Giant's Castle
Crim Rocks
Broad Sound
Troy Town Maze
Smith Sound
St Mary's Sound
Hugh Town to Penzance 2hrs. 40mins. (Seasonal)
Annet
Gugh
Nag's Head
Punch Bowl
Western Rocks
ST AGNES
Bishop Rock
The Isles of Scilly lie 28 miles WSW of Land's End
Crane Islands
Portreath
Godrevy Island
Navax Point
Hell's Mouth
B3301
Tehidy
Park Bottom
Barbara Hepworth
Tate
Lifeboat Station
The Carracks
St Ives
St Ives Bay
Gwithian
A30
Kehelland
Hellesveor
B3306
Treswithian
Penbeagle
The Towans
Phillack
Roseworthy
Penponds
CAMBORNE
Gurnard's Head
Wayside Folk
Zennor
Carbis Bay
Connor Downs
Trevithick
Angarrack
Towednack
Halsetown
Knill's
Zennor Quoit
Treen
Carn Galver Engine House
A3074
Copperhouse
Barripper
Lelant
Gwinear
Carnhell Green
Porthmeor
Cripplesease
Trencrom Hill
Lelant Downs
Hayle
Wall
Pendeen Watch
B3306
9 Maidens Stone Circle
Mulfra Quoit
Nancledra
St Erth Praze
Praze-an-Beeble
Levant Mine & Beam Engine
Higher Bojewyan
Morvah
Men-an-Tol
Paradise Park
B3302
Geevor Tin Mine
Pendeen
Chun Castle
Chysauster Ancient Village
Canonstown
St Erth
Fraddam
Leedstown
Crowan
Trewellard
Ding Dong Engine House
New Mill
B3311
A30
Drym
Carnyorth
Botallack Count House
Great Bosullow
Lanyon Quoit
Boswarthen
Ludgvan
CORNWALL
Botallack
Boswens Standing Stone
Holy Well
B3309
Crowlas
R. Hayle
Relubbus
B3318
Tregeseal
Madron
B3312
Trevarrack
Gulval
St Hilary
B3280
Townshend
Nancegollan
Cape Cornwall
St Just
A3071
Newbridge
Heamoor
Godolphin
Trescowe
Godolphin Cross
Crowntown
The Brisons
Ballowall Barrow
Trengwainton
A30
Chyandour
Longrock
Goldsithney
Kelynack
Drift Resr.
Trereife
Marazion
Rosudgeon
Germoe
Carleen
Helston
Sancreed
B3306
Carn Euny Ancient Village
Trewidden
PENZANCE
St Michael's Mount
Perranuthnoe
Kenneggy Downs
Trew
Sithney
LAND'S END (St Just)
Brane
Drift
Newlyn
A394
Lowertown
Ashton
Breage
Whitesand Bay
Escalls
Crows-an-wra
Tredavoe
Kerris
Praa Sands
Helston
Lifeboat Station
Boscawen-un Stone Circle
B3283
Paul
Cudden Point
Rinsey
Wheal Prosper Engine House
Wheal Trewavas Engine Houses
Sennen Cove
A30
Mousehole
Pipers Standing Stones
B3304
Longships
Maen Castle
Sennen
Bird Hospital
St Clement's Isle
Trewavas Head
Porthleven
Land's End
Trevescan
B3315
St Buryan
Trewoofe
B3315
Lamorna
The Loe
Treviley
Merry Maidens Stone Circle
Loe Bar
Loe Pool & Bar
LAND'S END
Tregiffian Burial Chamber
MOUNT'S BAY
Telegraph
Porthcurno
Treen
Penberth
Cribba Head
Porthgwarra
St Levan
Minack Theatre
Logan Rock
Penzance to Hugh Town 2hrs. 40mins. (Seasonal)
Gwennap Head
Runnel Stone
Poldhu Point
Mullion Cove
Mullion Island
Vellan Head
Wolf Rock
A
B
C
D
1
2
3
4
5
80
90
100
60
20
10
30
40
50

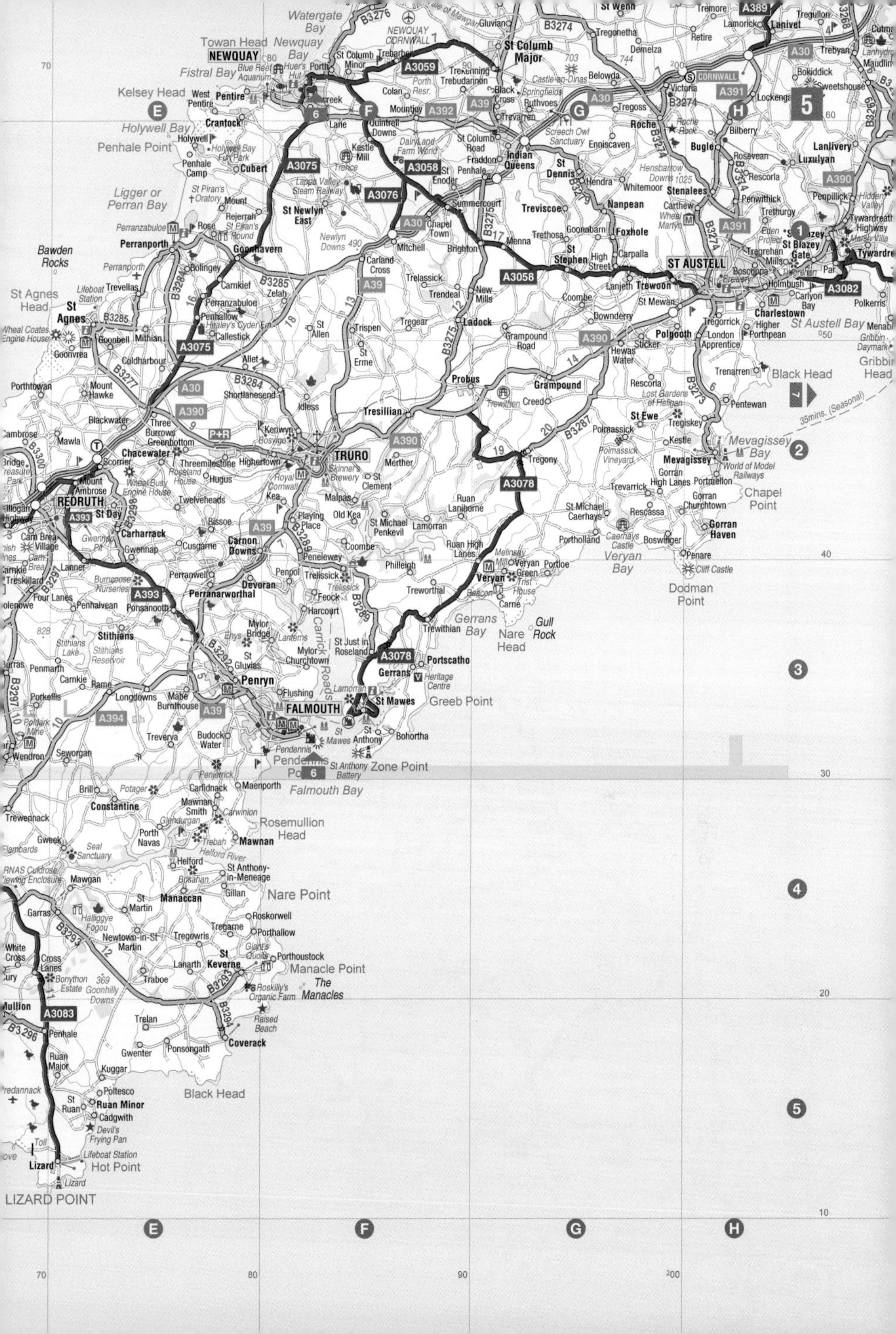

Watergate Bay
B3276
NEWQUAY CORNWALL
Gluvian
St Wenn
B3274
Tregonetha
Tremore
A389
Lamorick
Lanivet
Tregullon
Retire
Demelza
744
Towan Head
Newquay Bay
NEWQUAY
St Columb Minor
Trebarber
St Columb Major
703
200
CORNWALL
A30
Trebyan
Bokiddick
Sweetshouse
Fistral Bay
Blue Reef Aquarium
Huer's Hut
Porth
A3059
Trekenning
Tregenning
Castle-an-Dinas
Belowda
Victoria
Lanhydrock
Kelsey Head
West Pentire
Pentire
Colan
Porth Resr.
Trebudannon
Black Cross
Springfields
Ruthvoes
A30
Tregoss
B3274
A391
Lockengate
5
Crantock
E
Quintrell Downs
Mountjoy
A392
A39
Trevarren
G
Roche
Roche Rock
H
Holywell Bay
6
Lane
F
Dairy Land Farm World
St Columb Road
Screech Owl Sanctuary
Enniscaven
Bilberry
Bugle
Lanlivery
Holywell
Holywell Bay Fun Park
Kestle Mill
Trerice
Indian Queens
St Dennis
Penhale Point
Penhale Camp
Cubert
A3075
A3058
Fraddon
Penhale
St Enoder
Hendra
Hensbarrow Downs 1025
Whitemoor
Rosevean
Rescorla
Luxulyan
Lappa Valley Steam Railway
A3076
Summercourt
Stenalees
A390
Ligger or Perran Bay
St Piran's Oratory
Mount
St Newlyn East
Treviscoe
Nanpean
Penwithick
Penpillick
Carthew
Wheal Martyn
Trethurgy
Hidden Valley
Tywardreath
Rejerrah
St Piran's Round
Chapel Town
A30
Perranzabuloe
Rose
B3275
Trethosa
Goonabarn
Foxhole
A391
Eden Project
St Blazey
St Blazey Gate
Highway
Marsh Villa
Tywardreath
Bawden Rocks
Perranporth
Goonhavern
Newlyn Downs 490
Carland Cross
Mitchell
Brighton
17
Menna
St Stephen
High Street
Carpalla
ST AUSTELL
Tregrehan Mills
Par
Perranporth
Bolingey
B3285
Trelassick
A3058
Lanjeth
Trewoon
Boscoppa
Holmbush
A3082
St Agnes Head
Lifeboat Station
Trevellas
Carnkief
Zelah
A39
Trendeal
New Mills
Coombe
St Mewan
Carlyon Bay
Polkerris
St Agnes
B3285
Perranzabuloe
13
12
Downderry
Tregorrick
Charlestown
Wheal Coates Engine House
Goonbell
Mithian
Penhallow
Healey's Cyder Farm
18
St Allen
Trispen
Tregear
Ladock
Polgooth
London Apprentice
Higher Porthpean
St Austell Bay
Menabilly
Goonvrea
Callestick
A3075
St Erme
Grampound Road
A390
Hewas Water
Sticker
Gribbin Daymark
Coldharbour
Allet
14
Trenarren
Black Head
Gribbin Head
B3277
B3284
Probus
Grampound
Rescorla
Lost Gardens of Heligan
Porthtowan
Mount Hawke
A30
Shortlanesend
Trewithen
Creed
7
Pentewan
A390
Idless
Tresillian
St Ewe
Tregiskey
35mins. (Seasonal)
Blackwater
Three Burrows
9
Kenwyn
Bosvigo
20
B3287
Polmassick
Cambrose
Mawla
Greenbottom
P+R
A390
Polmassick Vineyard
Kestle
Mevagissey Bay
B3300
Chacewater
Scorrier
TRURO
Merther
19
Tregony
Mevagissey
World of Model Railways
2
Threemilestone
Highertown
Royal Cornwall
Skinner's Brewery
St Clement
Gorran High Lanes
Portmellon
Wheal Busy Engine House
Roseland House
Hugus
A3078
Trevarrick
Chapel Point
Mount Ambrose
REDRUTH
Twelveheads
Kea
Malpas
Old Kea
Ruan Lanihorne
St Michael Caerhays
Gorran Churchtown
St Day
A393
B3298
Bissoe
Playing Place
St Michael Penkevil
Lamorran
Rescassa
Gorran Haven
Carn Brea Village
Carharrack
Carnon Downs
A39
B3289
Coombe
Ruan High Lanes
Portholland
Caerhays Castle
Boswinger
Gwennap Pit
Gwennap
Cusgarne
Penelewey
Philleigh
Melinsey Mill
Veryan Bay
Penare
40
Lanner
Veryan
Green
Portloe
Cliff Castle
Treskillard
B3297
Burncoose Nurseries
Perranwell
Devoran
Penpol
Trelissick
Trist House
Dodman Point
Four Lanes
Penhalvean
A393
Ponsanooth
Perranarworthal
Feock
B3289
Treworthal
Carne
Harcourt
Beacon
Gull Rock
828
Stithians
Mylor Bridge
Enys
Lanterns
Carrick Roads
Trewithian
Gerrans Bay
Nare Head
Stithians Lake
Stithians Reservoir
St Gluvias
Mylor Churchtown
St Just in Roseland
A3078
Portscatho
Penmarth
B3292
Gerrans
Heritage Centre
3
Carnkie
Rame
Penryn
Flushing
Porkellis
Longdowns
Mabe Burnthouse
A39
Lamorran
St Mawes
Greeb Point
A394
FALMOUTH
Poldark Mine
Treverva
Budock Water
St Mawes
St Anthony
Bohortha
Wendron
Seworgan
Pendennis
St Anthony Battery
Zone Point
30
Penjerrick
Maenporth
Falmouth Bay
Brill
Potager
Carlidnack
Constantine
Mawnan Smith
Carwinion
Rosemullion Head
Trewennack
Glendurgan
Porth Navas
Trebah
Mawnan
Gweek
Seal Sanctuary
Helford River
Flambards
Helford
RNAS Culdrose Viewing Enclosure
Mawgan
Bosahan
St Anthony-in-Meneage
Gillan
Nare Point
4
St Martin
Manaccan
Garras
Halliggye Fogou
Roskorwell
Tregarne
Porthallow
B3293
Newtown-in-St Martin
Tregowris
Giant's Quoits
White Cross
12
St Keverne
Porthoustock
Manacle Point
Cross Lanes
Lanarth
Bonython Estate
Traboe
369
Goonhilly Downs
B3293
Roskilly's Organic Farm
The Manacles
20
Mullion
A3083
B3294
Raised Beach
Trelan
B3296
Penhale
Coverack
Ruan Major
Gwenter
Ponsongath
Kuggar
Poltesco
Black Head
Predannack
St Ruan
Ruan Minor
Cadgwith
5
Devil's Frying Pan
Toll
Lifeboat Station
Lizard
Hot Point
Lizard
LIZARD POINT
10
E
F
G
H
70
80
90
200

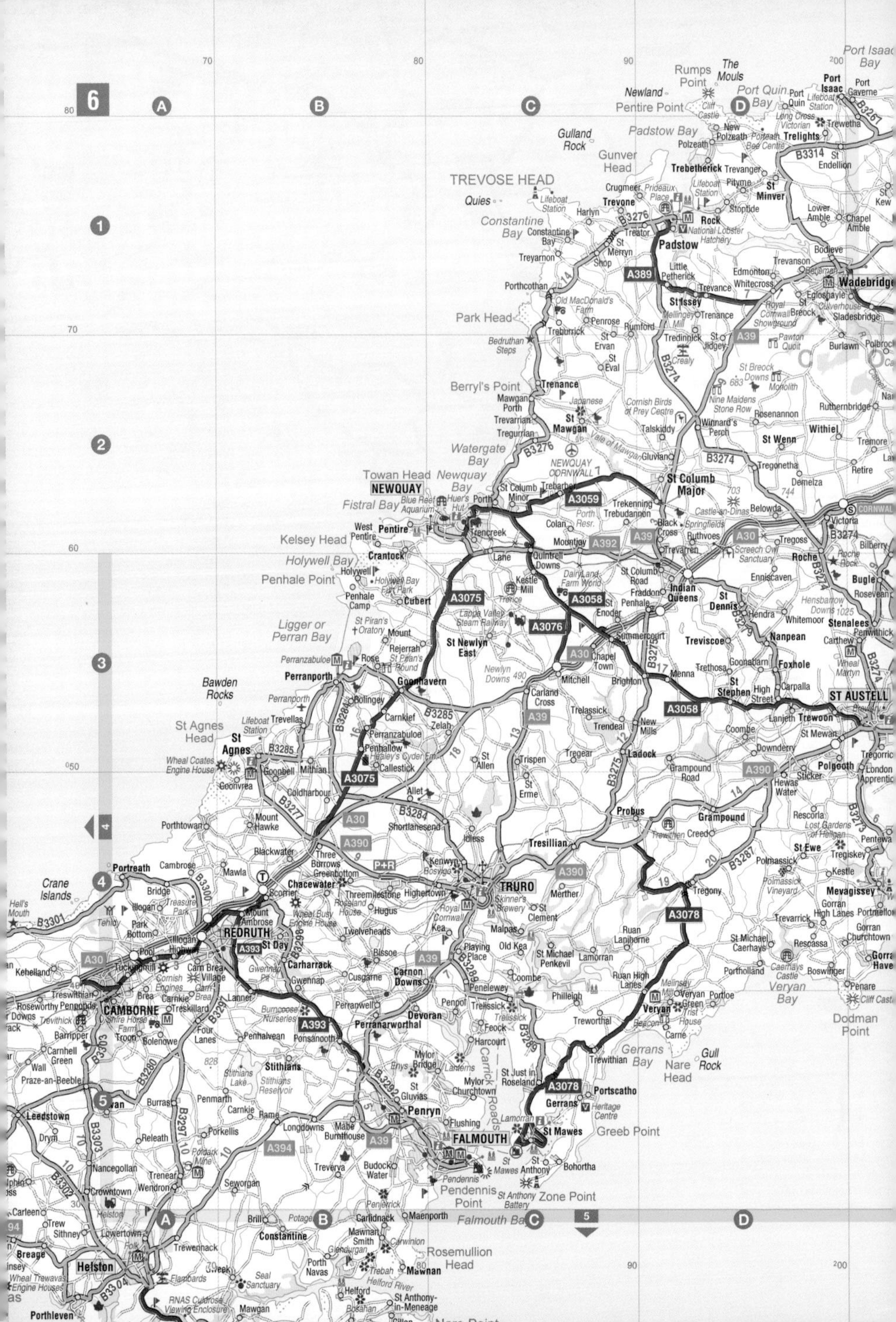

A
B
C
D
1
2
3
4
5
70
80
90
200
60
50
Port Isaac Bay
Rumps Point
The Mouls
Newland
Pentire Point
Port Quin Bay
Port Isaac
Port Gaverne
Padstow Bay
Polzeath
New Polzeath
Trelights
Trewetha
Gulland Rock
Gunver Head
TREVOSE HEAD
Quies
Lifeboat Station
Trebetherick
Trevanger
St Endellion
Crugmeer
Prideaux Place
Pityme
St Minver
St Kew
Trevone
Harlyn
Stoptide
Rock
Lower Amble
Chapel Amble
Constantine Bay
Treator
Padstow
National Lobster Hatchery
St Merryn
Shop
Treyarnon
Little Petherick
Bodieve
Edmonton
Whitecross
Trevanson
Wadebridge
Porthcothan
St Issey
Trevance
Egloshayle
Old MacDonald's Farm
Mellingey Mill
Trenance
Royal Cornwall Showground
St Breock
Sladesbridge
Park Head
Penrose
Rumford
Treburrick
St Ervan
Tredinnick
St Jidgey
Pawton Quoit
Burlawn
Bedruthan Steps
St Eval
Crealy
St Breock Downs
Monolith
Berryl's Point
Trenance
Nine Maidens Stone Row
Mawgan Porth
Japanese
Cornish Birds of Prey Centre
Rosenannon
Ruthernbridge
Trevarrian
St Mawgan
Talskiddy
Winnard's Perch
Tregurrian
Vale of Mawgan
St Wenn
Withiel
Tremore
Watergate Bay
NEWQUAY CORNWALL
Gluvian
B3274
Tregonetha
Retire
Towan Head
Newquay Bay
NEWQUAY
St Columb Minor
Trebarber
St Columb Major
Demelza
Fistral Bay
Blue Reef Aquarium
Huer's Hut
Porth
A3059
Trekenning
Trebudannon
Castle-an-Dinas
Belowda
Colan
Porth Resr.
Black Cross
Springfields
Victoria
West Pentire
Pentire
Trencreek
Kelsey Head
Mountjoy
A392
A39
Ruthvoes
A30
Tregoss
Bilberry
Crantock
Lane
Quintrell Downs
Trevarren
Screech Owl Sanctuary
Roche
Roche Rock
Holywell Bay
Holywell
Holywell Bay Fun Park
Dairy Land Farm World
St Columb Road
Indian Queens
Enniscaven
Bugle
Penhale Point
Kestle Mill
Fraddon
Penhale
Penhale Camp
Cubert
A3075
Trerice
A3058
St Enoder
St Dennis
Hensbarrow Downs
Roseveare
Lappa Valley Steam Railway
Hendra
Whitemoor
Stenalees
Ligger or Perran Bay
St Piran's Oratory
Mount
A3076
Summercourt
Treviscoe
Nanpean
Penwithick
St Newlyn East
Rejerrah
St Piran's Round
Chapel Town
Carthew
Perranzabuloe
Rose
Newlyn Downs
A30
Goonbarrow
Foxhole
Wheal Martyn
Bawden Rocks
Perranporth
Goonhavern
Mitchell
Brighton
Menna
Trethosa
Carpalla
Bolingey
St Stephen
High Street
ST AUSTELL
Perranporth
Carnkief
Carland Cross
A3058
Lanjeth
Trewoon
St Agnes Head
Lifeboat Station
Trevellas
B3285
Zelah
Trelassick
Trendeal
Coombe
St Mewan
St Agnes
Perranzabuloe
New Mills
Wheal Coates Engine House
B3285
Penhallow
Healey's Cyder Farm
St Allen
Tregear
Ladock
Downderry
Trispen
Goonbell
Mithian
Callestick
Grampound Road
Polgooth
Goonvrea
A3075
St Erme
A390
Sticker
Hewas Water
Tregorrick
London Apprentice
Coldharbour
Allet
B3277
Mount Hawke
A30
B3284
Probus
Grampound
Rescorla
Porthtowan
Shortlanesend
Trewithen
Creed
Lost Gardens of Heligan
A390
Idless
Tresillian
Pentewan
Blackwater
Three Burrows
Kenwyn
St Ewe
Tregiskey
Portreath
Cambrose
Mawla
Greenbottom
P+R
Bosvigo
Polmassick
Kestle
Crane Islands
Bridge
Chacewater
Threemilestone
Highertown
TRURO
A390
Merther
Tregony
Polmassick Vineyard
Mevagissey
Hell's Mouth
Scorrier
Illogan
Treasure Park
Rosland House
Royal Cornwall
Skinner's Brewery
St Clement
B3301
Tehidy
Mount Ambrose
Wheal Busy Engine House
Hugus
A3078
Gorran High Lanes
Portmellon
Park Bottom
REDRUTH
Illogan Highway
Twelveheads
Kea
Malpas
Ruan Lanihorne
Trevarrick
St Michael Caerhays
Gorran Churchtown
Pool
A393
St Day
Bissoe
Playing Place
Old Kea
St Michael Penkevil
Lamorran
Rescassa
A30
Tuckingmill
Cam Brea Village
Carharrack
A39
Carnon Downs
B3289
Portholland
Caerhays Castle
Boswinger
Gorran Haven
Kehelland
Cornish Engines
Carn Brea
Gwennap Pit
Gwennap
Cusgarne
Coombe
Ruan High Lanes
Veryan Bay
Treswithian
Penponds
Brea
Carnkie
Lanner
Penelewey
Philleigh
Melinsey Mill
Veryan Green
Portloe
Penare
Roseworthy
CAMBORNE
Treskillard
Burncoose Nurseries
Perranwell
Pencoj
Trelissick
Trist House
Cliff Castle
Downs
Trevithick
Shire Horse Farm
Devoran
Veryan
Dodman Point
Barripper
Troon
Bolenowe
Four Lanes
Penhalvean
A393
Ponsanooth
Perranarworthal
Feock
Beacon
Carne
Treworthal
Carnhell Green
B3303
B3280
Stithians Lake
Stithians
Mylor Bridge
Lanterns
Harcourt
Gerrans Bay
Gull Rock
Wall
Stithians Reservoir
Enys
B3292
St Gluvias
Carrick Roads
Mylor Churchtown
Trewithian
Nare Head
Praze-an-Beeble
St Just in Roseland
A3078
Portscatho
Penmarth
Carnkie
Rame
Penryn
Flushing
Gerrans
Heritage Centre
Leedstown
Burras
B3297
Longdowns
Mabe Burnthouse
Lamorran
St Mawes
Greeb Point
Drym
Releath
Porkellis
Poldark Mine
A394
A39
FALMOUTH
Nancegollan
Trenear
Seworgan
Treverva
Budock Water
Pendennis
St Mawes
St Anthony
Bohortha
Crowntown
Wendron
Pendennis Point
St Anthony Battery
Zone Point
Carleen
Helston
Penjerrick
Trew
Sithney
Lowertown
Brill
Potager
Constantine
Carlidnack
Maenporth
Falmouth Bay
Breage
Trewennack
Mawnan Smith
Glendurgan
Carwinion
Rosemullion Head
Wheal Trewavas Engine Houses
Helston
Flambards
Gweek
Seal Sanctuary
Porth Navas
Trebah
Mawnan
Helford River
RNAS Culdrose Viewing Enclosure
Porthleven
Mawgan
Helford
Bosahan
St Anthony-in-Meneage
Gillan

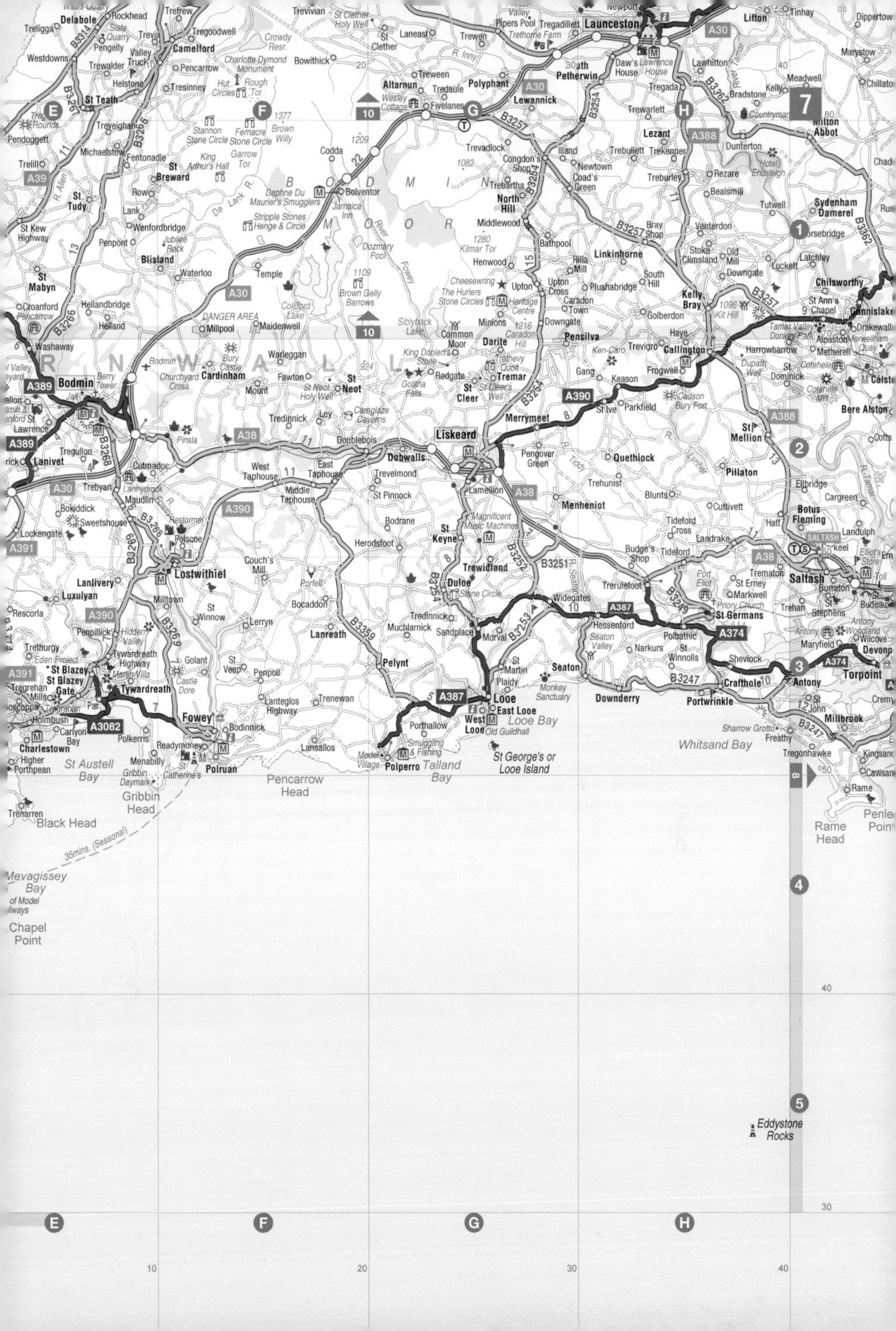

Delabole
Rockhead
Trefrew
Trevivian
St Clether Holy Well
Newport
Launceston
Lifton
Tinhay
Dippertown
Treligga
Slate Quarry
Trevia
Tregoodwell
Crowdy Resr.
St Clether
Laneast
Trewen
Pipers Pool
Tregadillett
Trethorne Farm
A30
Pengelly
Camelford
Valley Truckle
Charlotte Dymond Monument
Bowithick
R. Inny
Daw's House
Lawrence House
Lawhitton
Marystow
Westdowns
Trewalder
Pencarrow
Rough Tor
South Petherwin
Meadwell
Helstone
Tresinney
Hut Circles
Altarnun
Treween
Polyphant
Tregada
Kelly
Chillaton
St Teath
Wesley Cottage
Tredaule
Fivelanes
Lewannick
Bradstone
7
Milton Abbot
1377 Brown Willy
Trewarlett
Countryman
Treveighan
Stannon Stone Circle
Fernacre Stone Circle
B3257
Pendoggett
Michaelstow
1209
Trevadlock
Lezant
Dunterton
Fentonadle
King Arthur's Hall
Garrow Tor
Codda
Congdon's Shop
Illand
Trebullett
Trekenner
A388
Endsleigh
Trelill
St Breward
1082
Newtown
Coad's Green
Rezare
A39
B O D M I N M O O R
Trebartha
Treburley
Row
Bolventor
Daphne Du Maurier's Smugglers
Jamaica Inn
North Hill
Bealsmill
St Tudy
Lank
De Lank R.
Middlewood
Tutwell
Sydenham Damerel
Wenfordbridge
Stripple Stones Henge & Circle
Bray Shop
Venterdon
St Kew Highway
Penpont
Jubilee Rock
Dozmary Pool
River Fowey
1280 Kilmar Tor
Bathpool
Horsebridge
Blisland
Henwood
Rilla Mill
Linkinhorne
Stoke Climsland
Old Mill
Latchley
Waterloo
Temple
1109 Brown Gelly Barrows
Luckett
St Mabyn
Cheesewring
The Hurlers Stone Circles
Heritage Centre
Upton
Upton Cross
Plushabridge
South Hill
Downgate
Chilsworthy
A30
Colliford Lake
Caradon Town
Kelly Bray
1096 Kit Hill
St Ann's Chapel
Gunnislake
Croanford
Pencarrow
Hellandbridge
Helland
DANGER AREA
Millpool
Maidenwell
Siblyback Lake
Minions
1216 Caradon Hill
Golberdon
Tamar Valley Donkey Park
Drakewalls
Washaway
Bury Castle
Warleggan
Common Moor
Darite
Pensilva
Ken-Caro
Trevigro
Haye
Callington
Albaston
Metherell
Morwellham Quay
Harrowbarrow
Bodmin
Cardinham
Churchyard Cross
Fawton
924
King Doniert's Stone
Redgate
Trethevy Quoit
Tremar
Gang
Keason
Frogwell
Dupath Well
Cotehele
St Dominick
Calstock
A389
Berry Tower
Mount
St Neot Holy Well
St Neot
Golitha Falls
St Cleer
St Cleer's Well
A390
St Ive
Parkfield
Cadson Bury Fort
Cotehele Mill
Bere Alston
Lawrence
Tredinnick
Ley
Carnglaze Caverns
Merrymeet
A388
A389
Tregullon
Pinsla
A38
Doublebois
Liskeard
Pengover Green
St Mellion
Lanivet
Cutmadoc
West Taphouse
East Taphouse
Dobwalls
Quethiock
Pillaton
A30
Trebyan
Lanhydrock
Middle Taphouse
Trevelmond
St Pinnock
Lamellion
A38
Trehunist
Blunts
Ellbridge
Cargreen
Bokiddick
Maudlin
A390
Menheniot
Cuttivett
Botus Fleming
Sweetshouse
Restormel
Bodrane
St Keyne
Magnificent Music Machines
Tideford Cross
Hatt
Landulph
Lockengate
Polscoe
Herodsfoot
Landrake
SALTASH
A391
Couch's Mill
Trewidland
B3251
Budge's Shop
Tideford
A38
Lostwithiel
Porfell
Duloe
Stone Circle
Port Eliot
Trematon
St Erney
Saltash
Lanlivery
Trerulefoot
Markwell
Burraton
Luxulyan
Milltown
St Winnow
Bocaddon
Widegates
A387
Priory Church
Trehan
St Stephens
Rescorla
Lerryn
Lanreath
Tredinnick
Hessenford
St Germans
A390
Hidden Valley
B3359
Muchlarnick
Sandplace
Morval
A374
Antony
Woodland
Penpillick
Tywardreath Highway
Seaton Valley
Narkurs
Polbathic
Wilcove
Trethurgy
Eden Project
Golant
St Veep
Penpoll
Pelynt
St Martin
St Winnolls
Sheviock
Maryfield
Devonport
St Blazey
Marsh Villa
Castle Dore
Seaton
A374
Torpoint
A391
St Blazey Gate
Tywardreath
Plaidy
Monkey Sanctuary
Crafthole
Antony
Tregrehan Mills
Par
Lanteglos Highway
Trenewan
A387
Looe
B3247
Downderry
Portwinkle
St John
Cremyll
Holmbush
A3082
Fowey
Bodinnick
East Looe
Looe Bay
Millbrook
Carlyon Bay
Polkerris
Readymoney
Porthallow
West Looe
Old Guildhall
Sharrow Grotto
Freathy
B3247
Charlestown
Menabilly
Lansallos
Smuggling & Fishing
Model Village
Whitsand Bay
Tregonhawke
Kingsand
Higher Porthpean
St Austell Bay
Gribbin Daymark
St Catherine's
Polruan
Polperro
Talland Bay
St George's or Looe Island
Cawsand
Pencarrow Head
Rame
Gribbin Head
Trenarren
Black Head
Rame Head
Penlee Point
35mins. (Seasonal)
Mevagissey Bay
of Model Railways
Chapel Point
Eddystone Rocks
E
F
G
H
1
2
3
4
5
8
10
20
30
40

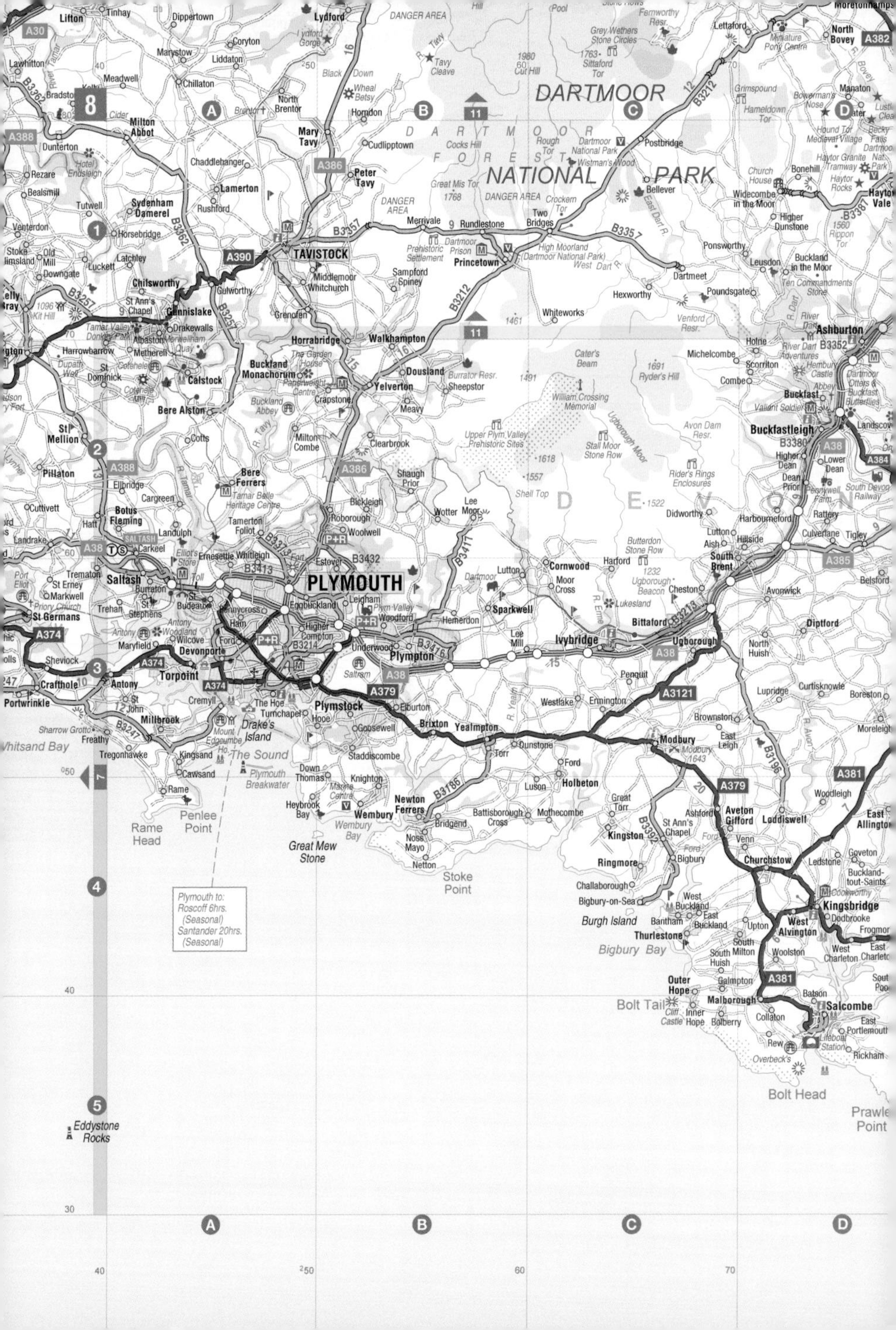

8
DARTMOOR
NATIONAL PARK
DARTMOOR FOREST
DANGER AREA
PLYMOUTH
TAVISTOCK
Lifton
Tinhay
Dippertown
Lydford
Lydford Gorge
Coryton
Marystow
Liddaton
Lewtrenchard
Chillaton
Meadwell
North Brentor
Brentor
Milton Abbot
Dunterton
Mary Tavy
Peter Tavy
Cudlipptown
Horndon
Wheal Betsy
Black Down
Tavy Cleave
Cut Hill
Cocks Hill
Great Mis Tor
Rough Tor
Chaddlehanger
Lamerton
Sydenham Damerel
Rushford
Horsebridge
Tutwell
Rezare
Bealsmill
Hotel Endsleigh
Latchley
Luckett
Chilsworthy
Gulworthy
Gunnislake
St Ann's Chapel
Kit Hill
Drakewalls
Albaston
Metherell
Harrowbarrow
Callington
St Dominick
Calstock
Cotehele
Bere Alston
Cotts
St Mellion
Pillaton
Botus Fleming
Landulph
Hatt
Cargreen
Bere Ferrers
Tamar Belle Heritage Centre
Tamerton Foliot
Ellbridge
Cuttivett
Landrake
Saltash
Carkeel
Ernesettle
Whitleigh
Trematon
St Erney
Markwell
Burraton
St Budeaux
Trehan
St Stephens
Port Eliot
St Germans
Antony
Antony Woodland
Wilcove
Maryfield
Devonport
Torpoint
Sheviock
Crafthole
Portwrinkle
St John
Millbrook
Cremyll
Mount Edgcumbe
Drake's Island
The Hoe
Turnchapel
Hooe
Plymstock
Goosewell
Staddiscombe
Down Thomas
Knighton
Heybrook Bay
Wembury
Wembury Bay
Great Mew Stone
The Sound
Plymouth Breakwater
Kingsand
Cawsand
Rame
Rame Head
Penlee Point
Freathy
Tregonhawke
Whitsand Bay
Sharrow Grotto
Eddystone Rocks
Plymouth to:
Roscoff 6hrs. (Seasonal)
Santander 20hrs. (Seasonal)
Middlemoor
Whitchurch
Grenofen
Horrabridge
Walkhampton
Buckland Monachorum
The Garden House
Buckland Abbey
Yelverton
Dousland
Crapstone
Meavy
Sheepstor
Burrator Resr.
Milton Combe
Clearbrook
Shaugh Prior
Bickleigh
Roborough
Woolwell
Estover
Leigham
Eggbuckland
Pennycross
Ham
Ford
Higher Compton
Underwood
Plympton
Woodford
Plym Valley
Saltram
Elburton
Brixton
Yealmpton
Dunstone
Torr
Newton Ferrers
Noss Mayo
Bridgend
Netton
Stoke Point
Battisborough Cross
Mothecombe
Luson
Holbeton
Ford
Sparkwell
Hemerdon
Lee Mill
Lutton
Cornwood
Moor Cross
Wotter
Lee Moor
Dartmoor Zoo
Ivybridge
Harford
Ugborough Beacon
Lukesland
Bittaford
Cheston
Ugborough
Penquit
Westlake
Ermington
Modbury
Brownston
East Leigh
Great Torr
Kingston
St Ann's Chapel
Bigbury
Ringmore
Challaborough
Bigbury-on-Sea
Burgh Island
Bigbury Bay
Bantham
West Buckland
East Buckland
Thurlestone
Outer Hope
Inner Hope
Bolt Tail
Galmpton
Malborough
Bolberry
South Huish
South Milton
Upton
Aveton Gifford
Ashford
Loddiswell
Venn
Churchstow
Ledstone
Kingsbridge
West Alvington
Dodbrooke
Woolston
West Charleton
East Charleton
Frogmore
Goveton
Buckland-tout-Saints
Woodleigh
East Allington
Salcombe
Batson
Collaton
Rew
Overbeck's
Lifeboat Station
East Portlemouth
Rickham
Bolt Head
Prawle Point
Moreleigh
Boreston
Curtisknowle
Lupridge
North Huish
Diptford
Avonwick
Belsford
South Brent
Aish
Lutton
Hillside
Harbourneford
Didworthy
Rattery
Tigley
Culverlane
Buckfastleigh
Higher Dean
Dean Prior
Lower Dean
Buckfast
Landscove
South Devon Railway
Ashburton
Holne
Scorriton
Michelcombe
Combe
River Dart Adventures
Hembury Castle
Dartmoor Otters & Buckfast Butterflies
Avon Dam Resr.
Rider's Rings Enclosures
Ryder's Hill
Cater's Beam
William Crossing Memorial
Stall Moor Stone Row
Ugborough Moor
Upper Plym Valley Prehistoric Sites
Shell Top
Butterdon Stone Row
Whiteworks
Hexworthy
Venford Resr.
Poundsgate
Dartmeet
Leusdon
Buckland in the Moor
Ten Commandments Stone
Ponsworthy
Higher Dunstone
Widecombe in the Moor
Church House
Bonehill
Haytor Rocks
Haytor Vale
Rippon Tor
Haytor Granite Tramway
Hound Tor Medieval Village
Becky Falls
Manaton
Bowerman's Nose
Hameldown Tor
Grimspound
North Bovey
Moretonhampstead
Miniature Pony Centre
Lettaford
Fernworthy Resr.
Grey Wethers Stone Circles
Sittaford Tor
Postbridge
Dartmoor National Park
Wistman's Wood
Bellever
Two Bridges
Crockern Tor
Princetown
High Moorland (Dartmoor National Park)
Dartmoor Prison
Rundlestone
Merrivale
Prehistoric Settlement
Sampford Spiney
Lustleigh
A30
A388
A390
A386
A374
A38
A379
A3121
A385
A384
A381
A382
B3362
B3257
B3357
B3212
B3413
B3373
B3432
B3417
B3416
B3214
B3247
B3186
B3392
B3196
B3213
B3380
B3352
B3387
P+R
A
B
C
D
1
2
3
4
5

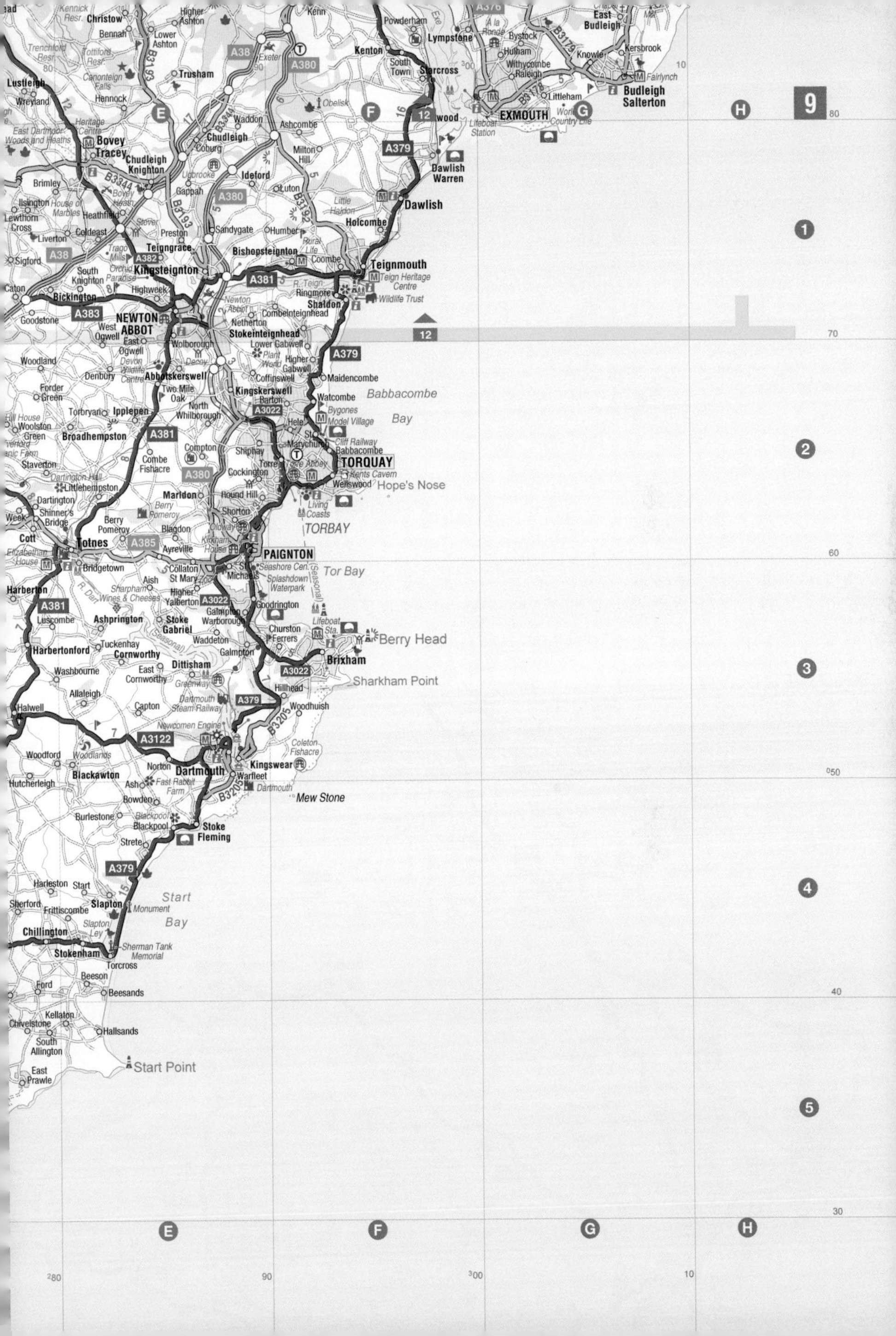

9
Christow
Kennick Resr.
Bennah
Higher Ashton
Lower Ashton
Kenn
Powderham
Lympstone
East Budleigh
Bystock
Hulham
Withycombe Raleigh
Knowle
Kersbrook
Fairlynch
Budleigh Salterton
Littleham
EXMOUTH
Lifeboat Station
World Country Life
Exeter
Kenton
South Town
Starcross
Trusham
Lustleigh
Wreyland
Trenchford Resr.
Tottiford Resr.
Canonteign Falls
Hennock
Heritage Centre
Bovey Tracey
East Dartmoor Woods and Heaths
Chudleigh
Chudleigh Knighton
Coburg
Waddon
Ashcombe
Obelisk
Ugbrooke
Ideford
Milton Hill
Luton
Gappah
Dawlish Warren
Dawlish
Little Haldon
Holcombe
Brimley
Ilsington
House of Marbles
Heathfield
Bovey Heath
Lewthorn Cross
Liverton
Coldeast
Stover
Preston
Sandygate
Humber
Rural Life
Teigngrace
Trago Mills
Orchid Paradise
Sigford
South Knighton
Kingsteignton
Bishopsteignton
Coombe
Teignmouth
Teign Heritage Centre
Caton
Bickington
Highweek
R. Teign
Ringmore
Shaldon
Wildlife Trust
Goodstone
NEWTON ABBOT
Newton Abbot
Netherton
Combeinteignhead
Stokeinteignhead
West Ogwell
East Ogwell
Wolborough
Decoy
Lower Gabwell
Plant World
Higher Gabwell
Woodland
Denbury
Devon Wildlife Centre
Abbotskerswell
Coffinswell
Maidencombe
Babbacombe Bay
Forder Green
Two Mile Oak
Kingskerswell
Barton
Watcombe
Bygones Model Village
Torbryan
Ipplepen
North Whilborough
Hele
Hill House
Woolston Green
Broadhempston
Shiphay
Marychurch
Cliff Railway
Babbacombe
Staverton
Combe Fishacre
Compton
Torre
Torre Abbey
TORQUAY
Kents Cavern
Dartington Hall
Littlehempston
Cockington
Wellswood
Hope's Nose
Dartington
Shinner's Bridge
Marldon
Hound Hill
Berry Pomeroy
Living Coasts
Shorton
TORBAY
Week
Cott
Blagdon
Oldway
Totnes
Elizabethan House
Ayreville
Kirkham House
PAIGNTON
Bridgetown
Aish
Collaton St Mary
St Michaels
Seashore Cen.
Splashdown Waterpark
Tor Bay
Harberton
R. Dart
Sharpham Wines & Cheeses
Higher Yalberton
Galmpton Warborough
Goodrington
Luscombe
Ashprington
Stoke Gabriel
Churston Ferrers
Lifeboat Sta.
Berry Head
Tuckenhay
Waddeton
Harbertonford
Cornworthy
Galmpton
Brixham
Washbourne
East Cornworthy
Dittisham
Greenway
Hillhead
Sharkham Point
Allaleigh
Dartmouth Steam Railway
Woodhuish
Halwell
Capton
Newcomen Engine
Coleton Fishacre
Woodford
Woodlands
Norton
Kingswear
Hutcherleigh
Blackawton
Dartmouth
Warfleet
Ash
Fast Rabbit Farm
Mew Stone
Bowden
Burlestone
Blackpool
Stoke Fleming
Strete
Harleston
Start
Start Bay
Sherford
Frittiscombe
Slapton
Monument
Slapton Ley
Chillington
Sherman Tank Memorial
Stokenham
Torcross
Beeson
Ford
Beesands
Kellaton
Chivelstone
Hallsands
South Allington
Start Point
East Prawle
A38
A380
A379
A381
A382
A383
A385
A3022
A3122
A376
B3193
B3344
B3192
B3179
B3178
B3205
E
F
G
H
1
2
3
4
5
12
80
70
60
50
40
30
280
90
300
10

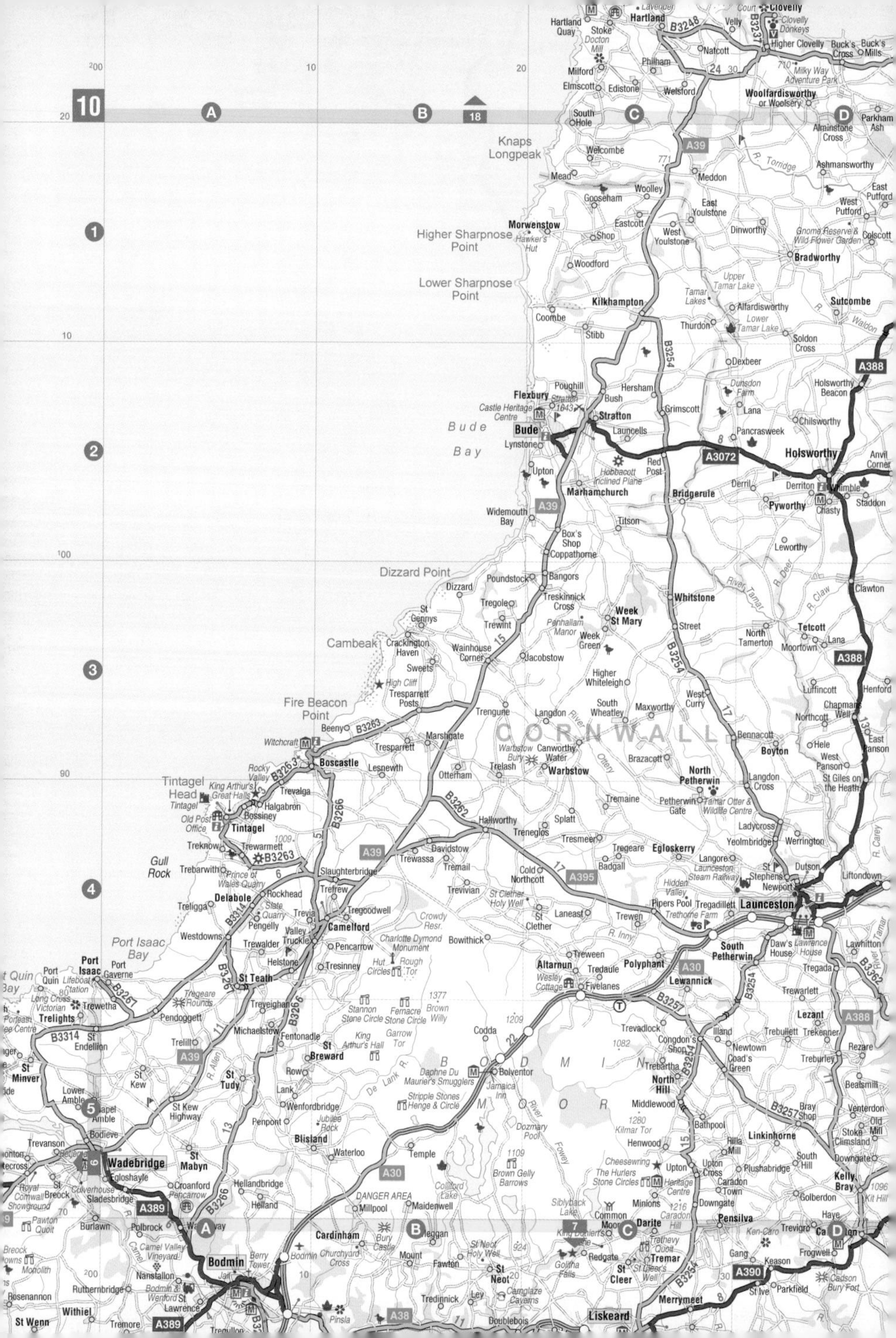
A
B
18
C
D
Hartland Quay
Stoke
Hartland
B3248
Velly
Clovelly
Clovelly Donkeys
B3237
Higher Clovelly
Buck's Cross
Buck's Mills
Docton Mill
Philham
Natcott
Milky Way Adventure Park
Milford
Elmscott
Edistone
Welsford
Woolfardisworthy or Woolsery
Parkham Ash
South Hole
Alminstone Cross
Knaps Longpeak
Welcombe
A39
R. Torridge
Ashmansworthy
Mead
Meddon
Woolley
Gooseham
East Youlstone
East Putford
West Putford
Morwenstow
Hawker's Hut
Eastcott
West Youlstone
Dinworthy
Gnome Reserve & Wild Flower Garden
Colscott
Higher Sharpnose Point
Shop
Bradworthy
Woodford
Upper Tamar Lake
Tamar Lakes
Lower Sharpnose Point
Kilkhampton
Alfardisworthy
Sutcombe
Coombe
Thurdon
Lower Tamar Lake
R. Waldon
Stibb
Soldon Cross
B3254
Dexbeer
A388
Dunsdon Farm
Holsworthy Beacon
Poughill
Hersham
Flexbury
Stratton 1643
Bush
Castle Heritage Centre
Stratton
Grimscott
Lana
Chilsworthy
Bude
Launcells
Pancrasweek
Bude Bay
Lynstone
A3072
Holsworthy
Anvil Corner
Red Post
Hobbacott Inclined Plane
Upton
Derril
Derriton
Whimble
Marhamchurch
Bridgerule
Pyworthy
Chasty
Staddon
Widemouth Bay
Titson
Box's Shop
Leworthy
Coppathorne
Dizzard Point
Bangors
Poundstock
Dizzard
River Tamar
R. Deer
Clawton
Treskinnick Cross
Whitstone
Tregole
Week St Mary
R. Claw
St Gennys
Trewint
Penhallam Manor
Street
Tetcott
Week Green
North Tamerton
Lana
Cambeak
Crackington Haven
Wainhouse Corner
Jacobstow
Moortown
Sweets
Higher Whiteleigh
High Cliff
Tresparrett Posts
West Curry
Luffincott
Henford
Fire Beacon Point
South Wheatley
Maxworthy
Chapmans Well
Trengune
Langdon
Beeny
B3263
CORNWALL
Northcott
Bennacott
East Panson
Marshgate
Boyton
Hele
Witchcraft
Tresparrett
Warbstow Bury
Canworthy Water
West Panson
Brazacott
Boscastle
Lesnewth
Otterham
Trelash
Warbstow
North Petherwin
Langdon Cross
St Giles on the Heath
Rocky Valley
King Arthur's Great Halls
Trevalga
Tintagel Head
Halgabron
B3262
Tremaine
Petherwin Gate
Tamar Otter & Wildlife Centre
Tintagel
Bossiney
B3266
Old Post Office
Hallworthy
Splatt
Treneglos
Ladycross
Tresmeer
Yeolmbridge
Werrington
Trewarmett
Treknow
Davidstow
Tregeare
Egloskerry
Langore
Gull Rock
Trebarwith
Prince of Wales Quarry
Trewassa
Tremail
Cold Northcott
Badgall
Launceston Steam Railway
Dutson
A395
St Stephens
Newport
Liftondown
Slaughterbridge
Hidden Valley
Delabole
Rockhead
Trefrew
Trevivian
St Clether Holy Well
Pipers Pool
Tregadillett
Launceston
Treligga
Slate Quarry
Trevia
Tregoodwell
Crowdy Resr.
St Clether
Laneast
Trethorne Farm
Pengelly
Camelford
Trewen
Westdowns
Valley Truckle
Charlotte Dymond Monument
Bowithick
R. Inny
South Petherwin
Daw's House
Lawrence House
Lawhitton
Port Isaac Bay
Trewalder
Pencarrow
Treween
Port Isaac
Port Gaverne
Helstone
Rough Tor
Altarnun
Tredaule
Polyphant
Lewannick
A30
Tregada
Port Quin
Lifeboat Station
St Teath
Tresinney
Hut Circles
Wesley Cottage
Fivelanes
B3257
B3362
Long Cross Victorian Gardens
Trewetha
B3267
Tregeare Rounds
Treveighan
Stannon Stone Circle
Fernacre Stone Circle
Brown Willy
Trewarlett
Trelights
Pendoggett
Michaelstow
Trevadlock
Lezant
Trekenner
A388
B3314
St Endellion
Trelill
Fentonadle
King Arthur's Hall
Garrow Tor
Codda
Congdon's Shop
Illand
Trebullett
Rezare
Newtown
Coad's Green
Treburley
St Minver
St Kew
Row
St Breward
BODMIN MOOR
Daphne Du Maurier's Smugglers
Bolventor
Trebartha
North Hill
St Tudy
Lank
Jamaica Inn
Beals Mill
Lower Amble
Chapel Amble
St Kew Highway
Wenfordbridge
Stripple Stones Henge & Circle
Dozmary Pool
Middlewood
Bray Shop
Venterdon
Old Mill
Jubilee Rock
Kilmar Tor
Bathpool
Stoke Climsland
Bodieve
Penpont
Rilla Mill
Henwood
Linkinhorne
Trevanson
Blisland
Waterloo
Temple
Downgate
St Mabyn
Wadebridge
Egloshayle
Brown Gelly Barrows
Cheesewring
Upton
Upton Cross
South Hill
Kelly Bray
A30
The Hurlers Stone Circles
Heritage Centre
Plushabridge
Caradon Town
Kit Hill
Royal Cornwall Showground
St Breock
Culverhouse
Croanford
Hellandbridge
Colliford Lake
Sladesbridge
Pencarrow
Helland
DANGER AREA
Siblyback Lake
Minions
Golberdon
A389
Maidenwell
Pawton Quoit
Millpool
Common Moor
Darite
Caradon Hill
Pensilva
Haye
Burlawn
Polbrock
Washaway
Cardinham
Bury Castle
Treslea
King Doniert's Stone
Trethevy Quoit
Ken-Caro
Trevigro
Callington
Camel Valley Vineyard
Breock Downs Monolith
Berry Tower
Bodmin
Churchyard Cross
Mount
St Neot Holy Well
Redgate
Tremar
Gang
Keason
Frogwell
Bodmin
Fawton
St Neot
Golitha Falls
St Cleer
St Cleer's Well
A390
Cadson Bury Fort
Nanstallon
Jail
Parkfield
Ruthernbridge
Bodmin & Wenford Rly
Canglaze Caverns
St Ive
Rosenannon
St Lawrence
Tredinnick
Ley
Merrymeet
Withiel
St Wenn
Tremore
Pinsla
A38
Doublebois
Liskeard
Tregullon

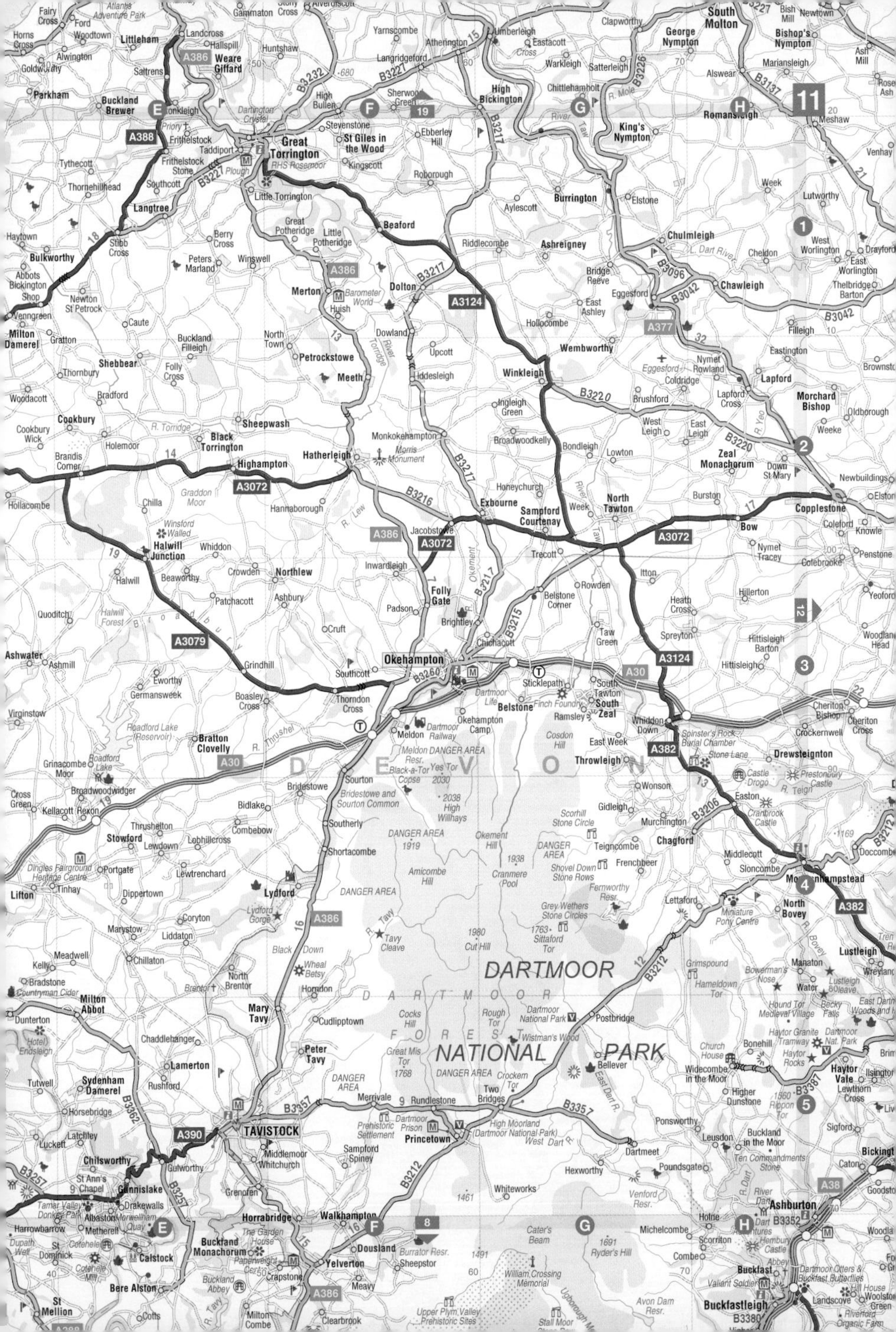

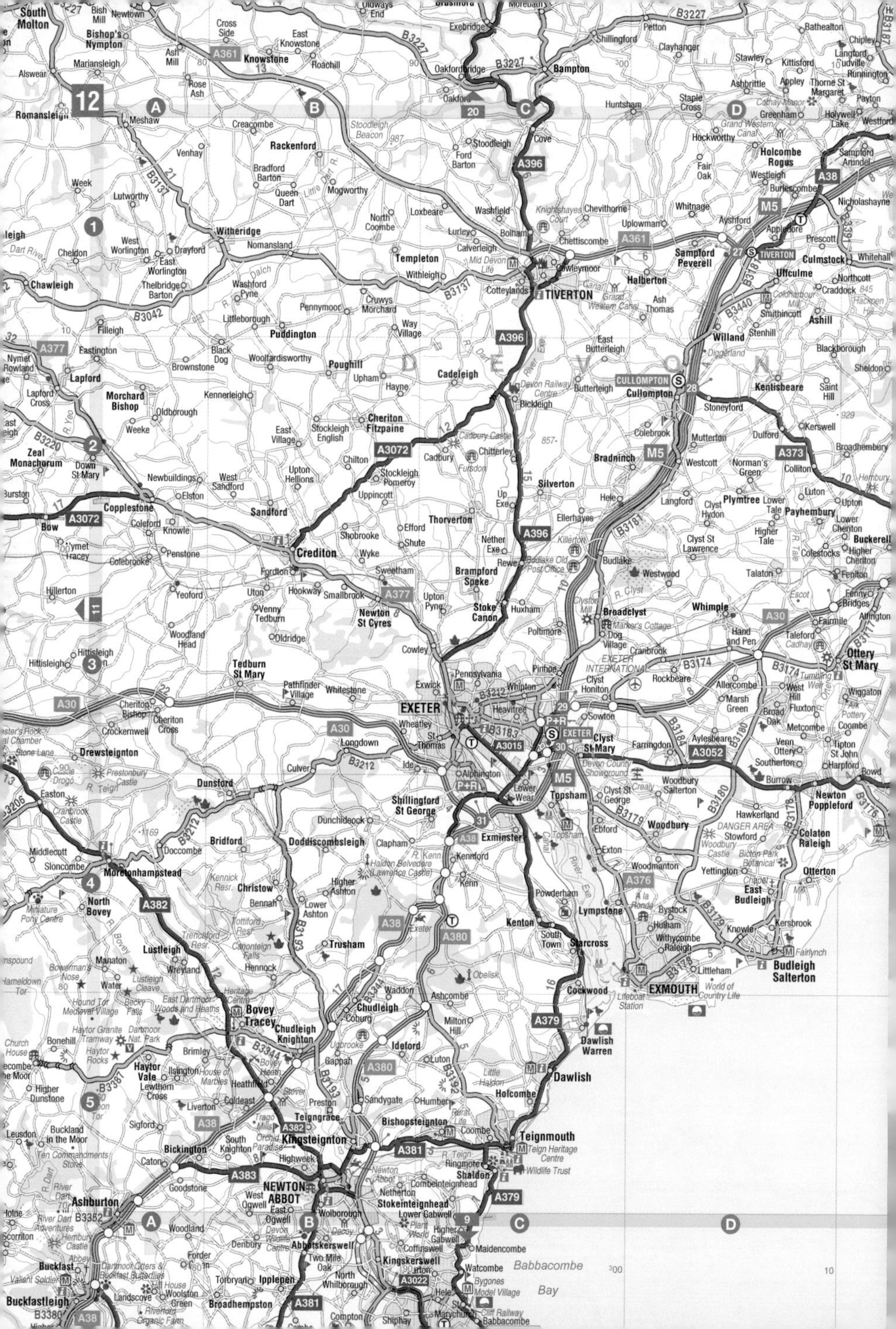
12
A
B
C
D
1
2
3
4
5
11
South Molton
Bish Mill
Newtown
Bishop's Nympton
Cross Side
East Knowstone
Knowstone
Roachill
Ash Mill
Rose Ash
Mariansleigh
Alswear
Romansleigh
Meshaw
Creacombe
Rackenford
Stoodleigh Beacon
Venhay
Bradford Barton
Queen Dart
Little Dart R.
Mogworthy
Week
Lutworthy
West Worlington
Drayford
East Worlington
Witheridge
Nomansland
Cheldon
Chawleigh
Thelbridge Barton
Washford Pyne
R. Dalch
Dart River
Oldways End
Exebridge
Morebath
Oakfordbridge
Oakford
Stoodleigh
Ford Barton
Cove
Bampton
Shillingford
Petton
Clayhanger
Huntsham
Staple Cross
Bathealton
Chipley
Stawley
Kittisford
Langford Budville
Runnington
Appley
Thorne St Margaret
Ashbrittle
Cothay Manor
Payton
Greenham
Holywell Lake
Westford
Grand Western Canal
Hockworthy
Holcombe Rogus
Sampford Arundel
Fair Oak
Westleigh
Burlescombe
Nicholashayne
Whitnage
Ayshford
Appledore
Prescott
Uplowman
Chevithorne
Knightshayes Court
Washfield
Loxbeare
North Coombe
Lurley
Bolham
Chettiscombe
Calverleigh
Templeton
Mid Devon Life
Withleigh
Cowleymoor
Cotteylands
TIVERTON
Sampford Peverell
Halberton
Ash Thomas
Culmstock
Whitehall
Uffculme
Northcott
Craddock
Coldharbour Mill
Smithincott
Ashill
Stenhill
Willand
Blackborough
Sheldon
Hackpen Hill
Diggerland
CULLOMPTON
Cullompton
Kentisbeare
Saint Hill
Stoneyford
Kerswell
Dulford
Broadhembury
Colebrook
Mutterton
Westcott
Bradninch
Norman's Green
Colliton
Hembury
Cruwys Morchard
Pennymoor
Way Village
Littleborough
Puddington
Filleigh
Black Dog
Brownstone
Woolfardisworthy
Poughill
Upham
Hayne
Cadeleigh
DEVON
Devon Railway Centre
Butterleigh
Bickleigh
East Butterleigh
Eastington
Nymet Rowland
Lapford
Lapford Cross
Morchard Bishop
Kennerleigh
Oldborough
Weeke
R. Yeo
Zeal Monachorum
Down St Mary
Burston
Bow
Nymet Tracey
Copplestone
Coleford
Knowle
Penstone
Colebrooke
Newbuildings
Elston
West Sandford
Sandford
Crediton
Fordton
Hookway
Smallbrook
Sweetham
East Village
Stockleigh English
Cheriton Fitzpaine
Cadbury Castle
Cadbury
Chitterley
Fursdon
Chilton
Upton Hellions
Stockleigh Pomeroy
Uppincott
Shobrooke
Efford
Shute
Wyke
Thorverton
Up Exe
Nether Exe
Silverton
Hele
Ellerhayes
Killerton
Budlake
Budlake Old Post Office
Rewe
Westwood
Langford
Plymtree
Clyst Hydon
Clyst St Lawrence
Lower Tale
Higher Tale
Payhembury
Lower Cheriton
Higher Cheriton
Buckerell
Colestocks
Talaton
Feniton
Luton
Upton
R. Tale
Hillerton
Yeoford
Uton
Venny Tedburn
Newton St Cyres
Brampford Speke
Upton Pyne
Stoke Canon
Huxham
Poltimore
Broadclyst
Clyst Mill
Marker's Cottage
Dog Village
Whimple
Escot
Fenny Bridges
Allington
Fairmile
Hand and Pen
Taleford
Cadhay
Ottery St Mary
Woodland Head
Oldridge
Cowley
Hittisleigh
Hittisleigh Cross
Tedburn St Mary
Pathfinder Village
Whitestone
Exwick
Pennsylvania
Whipton
Pinhoe
Cranbrook
EXETER INTERNATIONAL
Rockbeare
Allercombe
West Hill
Tumbling Weir
Wiggaton
Clyst Honiton
Sowton
Marsh Green
Broad Oak
Fluxton
Metcombe
Coombe
Venn Ottery
Tipton St John
Harpford
Otter Pottery
Cheriton Bishop
Cheriton Cross
Crockernwell
EXETER
Heavitree
Wheatley
St Thomas
Longdown
EXETER
Clyst St Mary
Farringdon
Aylesbeare
Devon County Showground
Southerton
Burrow
Bowd
Drewsteignton
Culver
Ide
Alphington
Castle Drogo
Prestonbury Castle
R. Teign
Dunsford
Easton
Cranbrook Castle
Shillingford St George
Lower Wear
Topsham
Clyst St George
Crealy
Woodbury Salterton
Newton Poppleford
Hawkerland
Colaton Raleigh
DANGER AREA
Stowford
Woodbury Castle
Bicton Park Botanical
Woodbury
Ebford
Exminster
Dunchideock
Doddiscombsleigh
Clapham
Kennford
Haldon Belvedere (Lawrence Castle)
Kenn
Exton
Woodmanton
Yettington
Otterton
Chapel
East Budleigh
Middlecott
Sloncombe
Moretonhampstead
Bridford
Doccombe
Kennick Resr.
Christow
Bennah
Higher Ashton
Lower Ashton
Powderham
Lympstone
A la Ronde
Bystock
Hulham
Withycombe Raleigh
Knowle
Kersbrook
Fairlynch
Budleigh Salterton
Littleham
EXMOUTH
World of Country Life
Lifeboat Station
North Bovey
Miniature Pony Centre
R. Bovey
Tottiford Resr.
Trenchford Resr.
Canonteign Falls
Trusham
Kenton
South Town
Starcross
Cockwood
Exeter
Obelisk
Lustleigh
Wreyland
Hennock
Manaton
Bowerman's Nose
Water
Lustleigh Cleave
Hamel Down Tor
Hound Tor Medieval Village
Becky Falls
East Dartmoor Woods and Heaths
Heritage Centre
Bovey Tracey
Chudleigh Knighton
Chudleigh
Coburg
Waddon
Ashcombe
Milton Hill
Ugbrooke
Ideford
Dawlish Warren
Church House
Bonehill
Haytor Granite Tramway
Haytor Rocks
Dartmoor Nat. Park
Haytor Vale
Ilsington
House of Marbles
Lewthorn Cross
Brimley
Bovey Heath
Heathfield
Gappah
Luton
Little Haldon
Dawlish
Holcombe
Higher Dunstone
Liverton
Coldeast
Stover
Preston
Sandygate
Humber
Rural Life
Trago Mills
Orchid Paradise
Teigngrace
Bishopsteignton
Coombe
Teignmouth
Teign Heritage Centre
Leusdon
Buckland in the Moor
Sigford
South Knighton
Kingsteignton
Bickington
Ten Commandments Stone
Highweek
Caton
R. Teign
Ringmore
Shaldon
Wildlife Trust
Goodstone
NEWTON ABBOT
Combeinteignhead
Netherton
Stokeinteignhead
Lower Gabwell
Higher Gabwell
Ashburton
River Dart Adventures
West Ogwell
East Ogwell
Devon Wildlife Centre
Wolborough
Decoy
Plant World
Woodland
Denbury
Abbotskerswell
Coffinswell
Maidencombe
Scorriton
Hembury Castle
Forder
Two Mile Oak
Kingskerswell
Babbacombe Bay
Buckfast
Buckfast Abbey
Valiant Soldier
Dartmoor Otters & Buckfast Butterflies
Torbryan
Ipplepen
North Whilborough
Watcombe
Bygones Model Village
Buckfastleigh
Landscove
Riverford Organic Farm
Fill House
Woolston Green
Broadhempston
Compton
Shiphay
Hele
Marychurch
Cliff Railway
Babbacombe
A361
A396
A377
A3072
A30
A3015
A3052
A373
A38
A376
A379
A380
A382
A383
A381
A3022
B3227
B3137
B3042
B3220
B3212
B3193
B3344
B3387
B3352
B3380
B3181
B3440
B3391
B3174
B3180
B3184
B3183
B3179
B3178
B3176
B3177
B3192
B3131
M5
P+R
TIVERTON
20
21
22
27
28
29
30
31
9

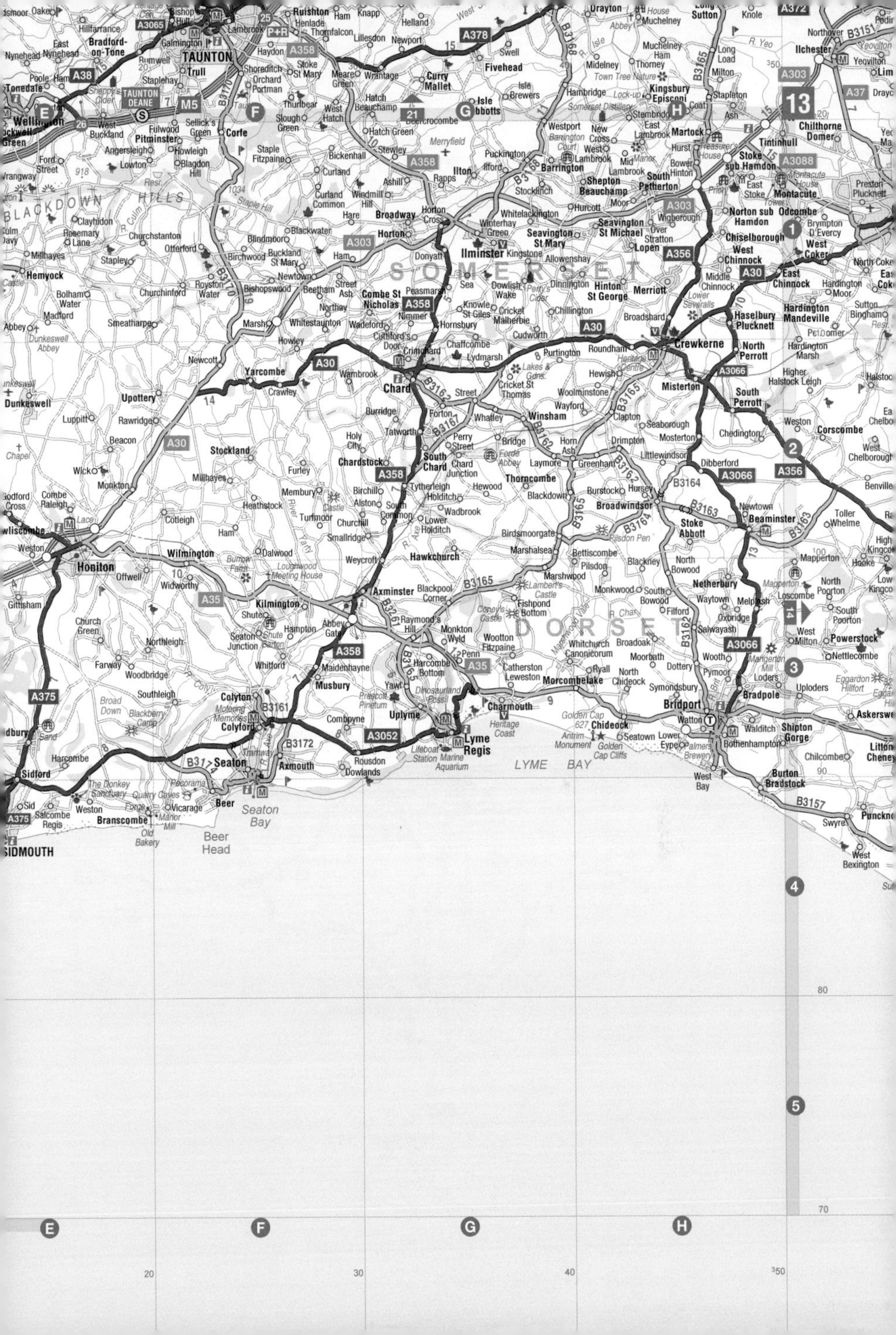

TAUNTON
Bishop's Hull
Lambrook
Ruishton
Henlade
Thornfalcon
Hillfarrance
Bradford-on-Tone
East Nynehead
Nynehead
Galmington
Rumwell
Haydon
Lillesdon
Newport
Helland
Knapp
Ham
Trull
Staplehay
Shoreditch
Orchard Portman
Stoke St Mary
Meare Green
Wrantage
Curry Mallet
Fivehead
Swell
Isle Brewers
Isle Abbotts
Poole
Tonedale
Wellington
TAUNTON DEANE
M5
A38
A3065
A358
A378
P+R
Thurlbear
West Hatch
Slough Green
Hatch Beauchamp
Beercrocombe
Hatch Green
Stewley
Bickenhall
Curland
Curland Common
Ashill
Windmill Hill
Broadway
Horton
Horton Cross
Rapps
Ilton
Puckington
Ilford
Stocklinch
Barrington
Merryfield
West Buckland
Fulwood
Pitminster
Sellick's Green
Corfe
Howleigh
Blagdon Hill
Angersleigh
Lowton
Staple Fitzpaine
Ford Street
Wrangway
BLACKDOWN HILLS
Clayhidon
Rosemary Lane
Churchstanton
Otterford
Culm Davy
Millhayes
Hemyock
Stapley
Blindmoor
Birchwood
Buckland St Mary
Blackwater
Hare
Newtown
Bishopswood
Royston Water
Churchinford
Bolham Water
Madford
Smeatharpe
Dunkeswell Abbey
Dunkeswell
Upottery
Newcott
Marsh
Whitestaunton
Howley
Yarcombe
Crawley
Wambrook
Chard
Street Ash
Beetham
Northay
Combe St Nicholas
Wadeford
Peasmarsh
Nimmer
Donyatt
Cuttiford's Door
Crimchard
Ilminster
Kingstone
Winterhay Green
Whitelackington
Seavington St Mary
Seavington St Michael
Dowlish Wake
Knowle St Giles
Cricket Malherbie
Hornsbury
Chaffcombe
Lydmarsh
Cudworth
Chillington
Dinnington
Hinton St George
Merriott
Allowenshay
Lopen
Over Stratton
Hurcott
Shepton Beauchamp
South Petherton
Wigborough
Drayton
Muchelney
Muchelney Ham
Midelney
Thorney
Long Sutton
Long Load
Kingsbury Episcopi
Hambridge
Westport
Stembridge
East Lambrook
West Lambrook
Mid Lambrook
New Cross
Martock
Hurst
Bower Hinton
Coat
Stapleton
Ash
Milton
Knole
Ilchester
Northover
Yeovilton
Chilthorne Domer
Tintinhull
Stoke sub Hamdon
Montacute
Odcombe
Norton sub Hamdon
Preston Plucknett
Brympton D'Evercy
Chiselborough
West Chinnock
Middle Chinnock
East Chinnock
West Coker
East Coker
North Coker
Hardington Moor
Hardington Mandeville
Haselbury Plucknett
Crewkerne
Roundham
Purtington
Broadshard
Lower Severalls
North Perrott
Misterton
South Perrott
Hardington Marsh
Higher Halstock Leigh
Halstock
Pendomer
Sutton Bingham
Chedington
Corscombe
Weston
West Chelborough
Benville
Mosterton
Seaborough
Drimpton
Littlewindsor
Dibberford
Clapton
Wayford
Woolminstone
Hewish
Winsham
Cricket St Thomas
Street
Forton
Whatley
Burridge
Tatworth
Holy City
Chardstock
South Chard
Perry Street
Chard Junction
Bridge
Forde Abbey
Thorncombe
Laymore
Horn Ash
Greenham
Blackdown
Burstock
Hursey
Broadwindsor
Stoke Abbott
Newtown
Beaminster
Toller Whelme
Tytherleigh
Holditch
Hewood
Wadbrook
Lower Holditch
Membury
Furley
Birchill
Alston
South Common
Churchill
Smallridge
Turfmoor
Weycroft
Hawkchurch
Birdsmoorgate
Marshalsea
Bettiscombe
Pilsdon
Pilsdon Pen
Blackney
North Bowood
South Bowood
Netherbury
Mapperton
Melplash
Loscombe
North Poorton
South Poorton
Axminster
Blackpool Corner
Marshwood
Lambert's Castle
Fishpond Bottom
Monkwood
Waytown
Oxbridge
Salwayash
Filford
Kilmington
Shute
Seaton Junction
Hampton
Abbey Gate
Raymond's Hill
Monkton Wyld
Wootton Fitzpaine
Whitchurch Canonicorum
Broadoak
Moorbath
Dottery
Wooth
Pymore
West Milton
Powerstock
Nettlecombe
Loders
Uploders
Eggardon Hillfort
Askerswell
Catherston Leweston
Ryall
North Chideock
Symondsbury
Morcombelake
Chideock
Seatown
Golden Cap
Bridport
Bradpole
Walditch
Shipton Gorge
Bothenhampton
Lower Eype
Watton
West Bay
Chilcombe
Burton Bradstock
Litton Cheney
Puncknowle
Swyre
West Bexington
B3157
Charmouth
Heritage Coast
Lyme Regis
Uplyme
Harcombe Bottom
Penn
Yawl
Maidenhayne
Musbury
Whitford
Combpyne
Rousdon
Dowlands
Axmouth
Colyton
Colyford
Seaton
Beer
Seaton Bay
Beer Head
Branscombe
Vicarage
Weston
Salcombe Regis
Sid
Sidford
SIDMOUTH
Harcombe
Farway
Woodbridge
Southleigh
Northleigh
Church Green
Gittisham
Honiton
Offwell
Wilmington
Widworthy
Dalwood
Stockland
Cotleigh
Heathstock
Ham
Millhayes
Monkton
Wick
Combe Raleigh
Godford Cross
Awliscombe
Weston
Lace
Beacon
Luppitt
Rawridge
Chapel
LYME BAY
SOMERSET
DORSET
A30
A303
A356
A3066
A3088
A37
A35
A375
A3052
B3161
B3172
B3174
B3165
B3162
B3167
B3164
B3163
B3168
B3170
B3151
B3261
13
14
E
F
G
H
1
2
3
4
5
20
30
40
350
70
80
90

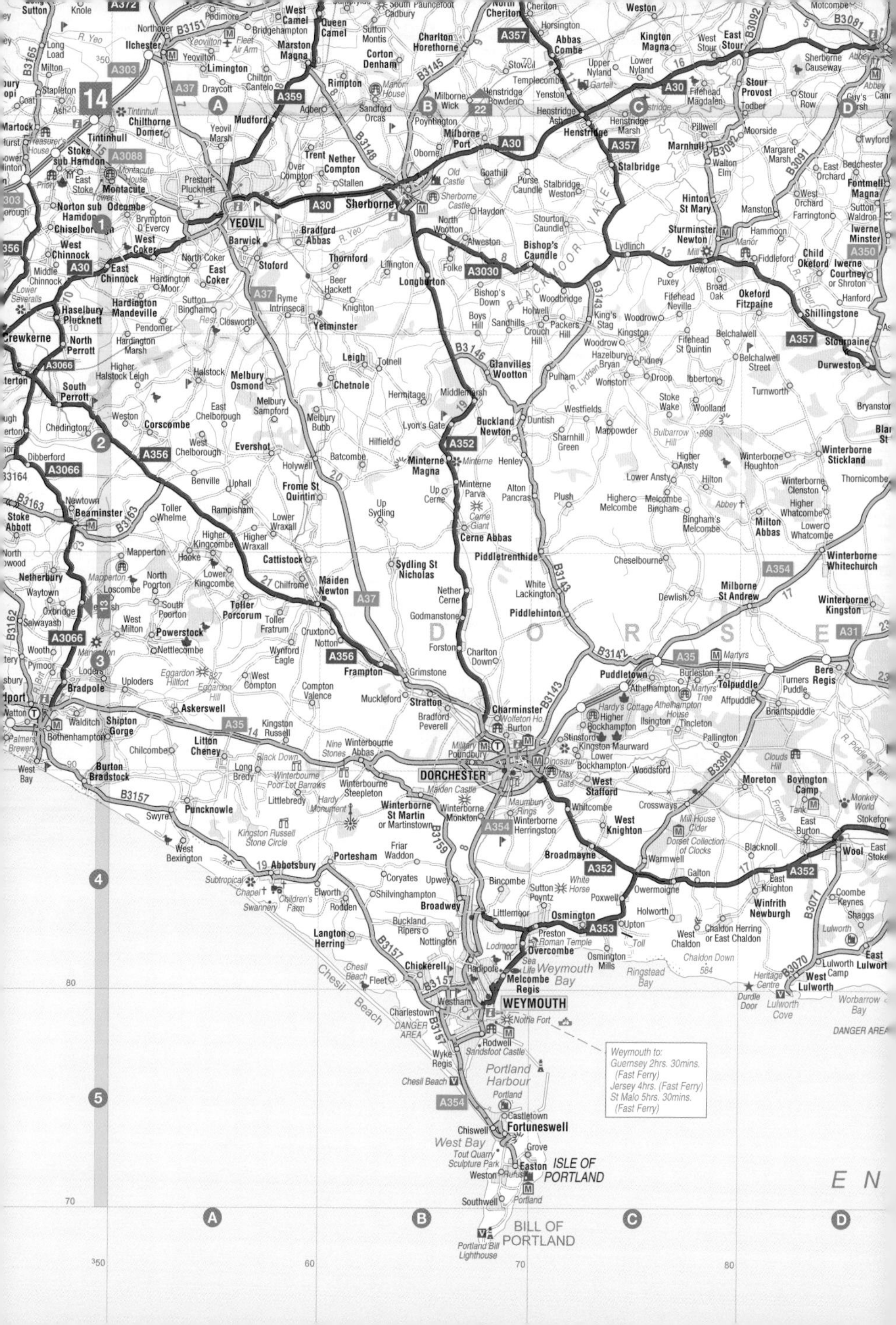

14
Sutton
Knole
A372
West Camel
Queen Camel
South Cadbury
North Cheriton
Cheriton
Weston
Motcombe
B3081
Northover
B3151
Podimore
Bridgehampton
Sutton Montis
Charlton Horethorne
A357
Abbas Combe
Horsington
Kingston Magna
West Stour
East Stour
B3092
Sherborne Causeway
Ilchester
Yeovilton
Fleet Air Arm
Marston Magna
Corton Denham
Upper Nyland
Lower Nyland
Stour Provost
Long Load
Limington
Chilton Cantelo
Rimpton
B3145
Stowell
Templecombe
A30
Fifehead Magdalen
Stour Row
Milton
A303
A37
Draycott
A359
Manor House
Milborne Wick
Henstridge Bowden
Yenston
Todber
Guy's Marsh
Stapleton
Tintinhull
Adber
Sandford Orcas
Henstridge Ash
Henstridge Marsh
Twyford
Martock
Chilthorne Domer
Mudford
Poyntington
Milborne Port
Henstridge
A357
Pillwell
Marnhull
Moorside
Treasurer's House
Tintinhull
Yeovil Marsh
Trent
Nether Compton
Oborne
Goathill
Stalbridge
Margaret Marsh
East Orchard
Bedchester
Stoke sub Hamdon
A3088
Over Compton
Stallen
Old Castle
Purse Caundle
Stalbridge Weston
Walton Elm
Fontmell Magna
East Stoke
Montacute
Preston Plucknett
Sherborne
Sherborne Castle
Haydon
Stourton Caundle
Hinton St Mary
West Orchard
Sutton Waldron
Norton sub Hamdon
Odcombe
Brympton D'Evercy
YEOVIL
Bradford Abbas
R. Yeo
North Wootton
Alweston
Bishop's Caundle
Sturminster Newton
Manston
Farrington
Iwerne Minster
Chiselborough
West Coker
Barwick
BLACKMOOR VALE
Lydlinch
Hammoon
A350
West Chinnock
North Coker
Thornford
Folke
A3030
Newton
Fiddleford
Child Okeford
Iwerne Courtney or Shroton
Middle Chinnock
A30
East Chinnock
East Coker
Stoford
Lillington
Longburton
Puxey
Broad Oak
Okeford Fitzpaine
Hardington Moor
Beer Hackett
Bishop's Down
Woodbridge
Fifehead Neville
Hanford
Lower Severalls
Haselbury Plucknett
Hardington Mandeville
Sutton Bingham
A37
Ryme Intrinseca
Knighton
Boys Hill
Holwell
King's Stag
Woodrow
Shillingstone
Pendomer
Closworth
Yetminster
Sandhills
Crouch Hill
Packers Hill
Kingston
Fifehead St Quintin
Belchalwell
Crewkerne
North Perrott
Hardington Marsh
B3146
Woodrow
Hazelbury Bryan
Pidney
A357
Stourpaine
Leigh
Totnell
Glanvilles Wootton
Belchalwell Street
Durweston
A3066
Higher Halstock Leigh
Halstock
Melbury Osmond
Chetnole
Pulham
Wonston
Droop
Ibberton
South Perrott
Hermitage
Middlemarsh
R. Lydden
Turnworth
Melbury Sampford
East Chelborough
Stoke Wake
Woolland
Bryanston
Weston
Corscombe
Melbury Bubb
Lyon's Gate
Buckland Newton
Duntish
Westfields
Chedington
West Chelborough
Mappowder
Bulbarrow Hill
Sharnhill Green
A352
Hilfield
Evershot
Batcombe
Minterne Magna
Minterne
Henley
Winterborne Houghton
Winterborne Stickland
Dibberford
A3066
A356
Holywell
Higher Ansty
Lower Ansty
Hilton
Thornicombe
B3164
Benville
Uphall
Frome St Quintin
Minterne Parva
Winterborne Clenston
Up Cerne
Alton Pancras
Plush
Higher Melcombe
Melcombe Bingham
Abbey
Newtown
Toller Whelme
Higher Whatcombe
B3163
Beaminster
Up Sydling
Cerne Giant
Bingham's Melcombe
Milton Abbas
Lower Whatcombe
Stoke Abbott
Rampisham
Lower Wraxall
B3163
Higher Kingcombe
Higher Wraxall
Cerne Abbas
North Poorton
Mapperton
Hooke
Cattistock
Piddletrenthide
Cheselbourne
Winterborne Whitechurch
Netherbury
Lower Kingcombe
Sydling St Nicholas
A354
Waytown
Loscombe
Chilfrome
Maiden Newton
White Lackington
Milborne St Andrew
Oxbridge
South Poorton
Toller Porcorum
Nether Cerne
Dewlish
Winterborne Kingston
B3162
Salwayash
West Milton
A37
Piddlehinton
A3066
Powerstock
Toller Fratrum
Godmanstone
A31
DORSET
Nettlecombe
Cruxton
Notton
Wooth
Mangerton
Wynford Eagle
Forston
Charlton Down
B3142
A35
Martyrs
Pymoor
A356
Bere Regis
Loders
Eggardon Hillfort
Frampton
Grimstone
Puddletown
Athelhampton
Burleston
Tolpuddle
Uploders
Eggardon Hill
West Compton
Compton Valence
Turners Puddle
Bradpole
Stratton
Affpuddle
Askerswell
Mucklesford
B3143
Charminster
Wolfeton Ho.
Hardy's Cottage
Athelhampton House
Martyrs' Tree
Briantspuddle
Bridport
Shipton Gorge
Bradford Peverell
Higher Bockhampton
Ilsington
Tincleton
Walditch
Kingston Russell
Burton
Bothenhampton
A35
Stinsford
Palmers Brewery
Chilcombe
Litton Cheney
Nine Stones
Winterbourne Abbas
Military Museum
Poundbury
Kingston Maurward
Lower Bockhampton
Pallington
West Bay
Long Bredy
Black Down
Dinosaur Museum
Clouds Hill
R. Piddle or Trent
Burton Bradstock
Winterbourne Poor Lot Barrows
Winterbourne Steepleton
DORCHESTER
Max Gate
West Stafford
Woodsford
Moreton
Bovington Camp
B3390
Littlebredy
Maiden Castle
B3157
Hardy Monument
Maumbury Rings
Winterborne Herringston
Whitcombe
Crossways
Tank Museum
Monkey World
Swyre
Puncknowle
Winterborne St Martin or Martinstown
Winterborne Monkton
A354
West Knighton
Mill House Cider
Dorset Collection of Clocks
East Burton
Stokeford
Kingston Russell Stone Circle
B3159
Broadmayne
Blacknoll
Wool
East Stoke
West Bexington
Abbotsbury
Portesham
Friar Waddon
Warmwell
A352
Galton
Subtropical Gardens
Chapel
Swannery
Children's Farm
Elworth
Rodden
Coryates
Shilvinghampton
Upwey
Bincombe
Broadwey
White Horse
Sutton Poyntz
Poxwell
Owermoigne
Holworth
East Knighton
Winfrith Newburgh
Coombe Keynes
Shaggs
B3071
Littlemoor
Osmington
A353
Upton
Chaldon Herring or East Chaldon
West Chaldon
Langton Herring
Buckland Ripers
Nottington
Preston
Roman Temple
Overcombe
Toll
Osmington Mills
Chaldon Down
Lulworth Castle
East Lulworth
Chesil Beach
Chickerell
Radipole
Lodmoor
Sea Life
Weymouth Bay
Ringstead Bay
B3070
Lulworth Camp
Fleet
B3157
Melcombe Regis
Heritage Centre
Durdle Door
West Lulworth
Lulworth Cove
Worbarrow Bay
Westham
WEYMOUTH
Charlestown
DANGER AREA
Nothe Fort
DANGER AREA
Rodwell
Sandsfoot Castle
Wyke Regis
Weymouth to:
Guernsey 2hrs. 30mins. (Fast Ferry)
Jersey 4hrs. (Fast Ferry)
St Malo 5hrs. 30mins. (Fast Ferry)
Portland Harbour
Chesil Beach
Portland
A354
Castletown
Chiswell
Fortuneswell
West Bay
Grove
Tout Quarry Sculpture Park
Easton
ISLE OF PORTLAND
Weston
Rufus
EN
Southwell
Portland
BILL OF PORTLAND
Portland Bill Lighthouse
A
B
C
D
1
2
3
4
5
350
60
70
80

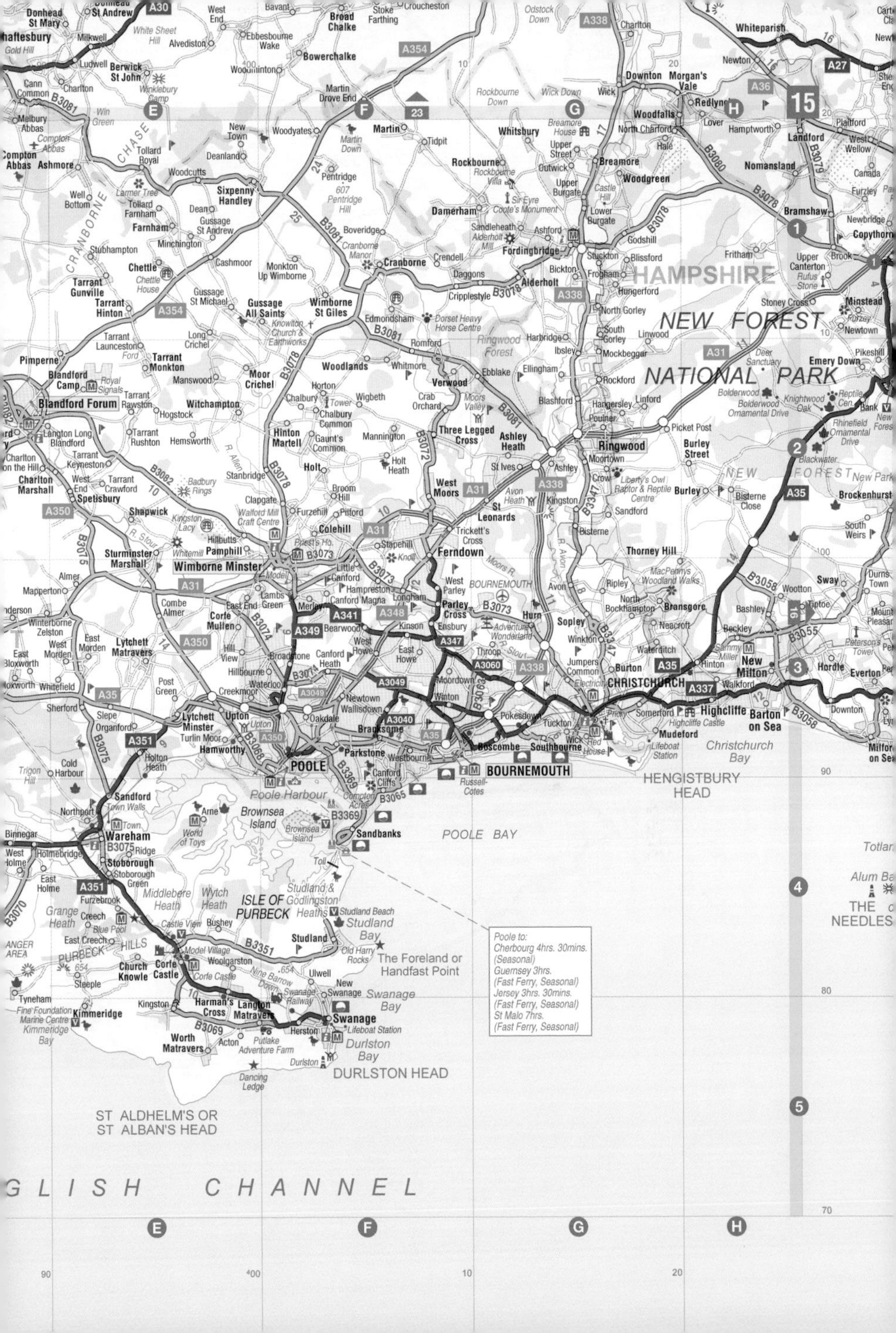

Donhead St Mary
St Andrew
A30
West End
Bavant
Broad Chalke
Stoke Farthing
Croucheston
Odstock Down
A338
Charlton
Whiteparish
Shaftesbury
Gold Hill
Milkwell
White Sheet Hill
Alvediston
Ebbesbourne Wake
A354
Bowerchalke
Newton
A27
Ludwell
Berwick St John
Woodminton
Downton
Morgan's Vale
Cann Common
Charlton
Winklebury Camp
Martin Drove End
Rockbourne Down
Wick Down
Wick
A36
Redlynch
15
B3081
Win Green
E
F
23
G
H
Melbury Abbas
Compton Abbas
New Town
Woodyates
Martin
Tidpit
Woodfalls
Lover
Hamptworth
Plaitford
Martin Down
Whitsbury
Breamore House
North Charford
Landford
West Wellow
Compton Abbas
Ashmore
Tollard Royal
Deanland
Upper Street
Hale
B3080
B3079
CHASE
Woodcutts
Rockbourne
Breamore
Nomansland
Pentridge
Rockbourne Villa
Outwick
Canada
Larmer Tree
Sixpenny Handley
607 Pentridge Hill
Upper Burgate
Woodgreen
Furzley
Well Bottom
Tollard Farnham
Dean
Damerham
Sir Eyre Coote's Monument
Castle Hill
Lower Burgate
B3078
Bramshaw
CRANBORNE
Farnham
Gussage St Andrew
B3081
Boveridge
Sandleheath
Alderholt Mill
Ashford
Godshill
Newbridge
Copythorne
Minchington
Cranborne Manor
Fordingbridge
1
Stubhampton
Cashmoor
Cranborne
Crendell
Stuckton
Blissford
Fritham
Upper Canterton
Brook
Chettle
Chettle House
Monkton Up Wimborne
Daggons
Bickton
Frogham
HAMPSHIRE
Rufus Stone
Tarrant Gunville
Cripplestyle
B3078
Alderholt
Hungerford
A338
Tarrant Hinton
A354
Gussage St Michael
Gussage All Saints
Wimborne St Giles
Edmondsham
Dorset Heavy Horse Centre
North Gorley
Stoney Cross
Minstead
NEW FOREST
Furzey
Tarrant Launceston
Ford
Long Crichel
Knowlton Church & Earthworks
B3081
Romford
Ringwood Forest
Harbridge
South Gorley
Linwood
Newtown
Pimperne
Tarrant Monkton
Woodlands
Whitmore
Ibsley
Mockbeggar
A31
Deer Sanctuary
Pikeshill
Emery Down
Blandford Camp
Royal Signals
Moor Crichel
Manswood
Verwood
Ebblake
Ellingham
NATIONAL PARK
Blandford Forum
Tarrant Rawston
Hogstock
Witchampton
Horton
Chalbury
Tower
Wigbeth
Crab Orchard
Moors Valley
Blashford
Rockford
Linford
Bolderwood
Bolderwood Ornamental Drive
Knightwood Oak
Reptile Cen.
Bank
Langton Long Blandford
Tarrant Rushton
Hemsworth
Chalbury Common
Hinton Martell
Gaunt's Common
Mannington
B3072
Three Legged Cross
Ashley Heath
Hangersley
Poulner
Picket Post
Rhinefield Ornamental Drive
New Forest
Tarrant Keyneston
Holt Heath
Ringwood
Burley Street
2
Charlton on the Hill
Charlton Marshall
West End
Tarrant Crawford
B3082
Stanbridge
Holt
West Moors
St Ives
Ashley
Moortown
Blackwater
Badbury Rings
B3078
Broom Hill
A31
Avon Heath
A338
Crow
Liberty's Owl Raptor & Reptile Centre
NEW FOREST
New Park
Spetisbury
Clapgate
Furzehill
Pilford
St Leonards
Kingston
B3347
Burley
Bisterne Close
A350
Shapwick
Walford Mill Craft Centre
Colehill
Sandford
A35
Brockenhurst
B3075
Kingston Lacy
R. Stour
Hillbutts
Priest's Ho.
A31
Stapehill
Trickett's Cross
Bisterne
South Weirs
Sturminster Marshall
Whitemill
Pamphill
B3073
Knoll
Ferndown
Thorney Hill
Wimborne Minster
Model
Little Canford
B3073
Moors R.
MacPenny's Woodland Walks
Durns Town
Almer
Sway
Mapperton
A31
Hampreston
West Parley
BOURNEMOUTH
Avon
Ripley
B3058
Wootton
Combe Almer
East End
Lambs Green
Canford Magna
Longham
Parley Cross
B3073
North Bockhampton
Bransgore
Bashley
Tiptoe
Mount Pleasant
Winterborne Zelston
Corfe Mullen
Merley
A341
A348
Hurn
Sopley
Neacroft
Beckley
16
Lytchett Matravers
A349
Bearwood
Kinson
Ensbury
Adventure Wonderland
Winkton
B3055
East Morden
West Morden
A350
Hill View
West Howe
A347
Throop
Waterditch
Sammy Miller
Peterson's Tower
East Bloxworth
Broadstone
Canford Heath
East Howe
A3060
A338
Jumpers Common
Burton
A35
Hinton
New Milton
Hordle
Everton
Hillbourne
B3074
Electricity
CHRISTCHURCH
3
Woxworth
Whitefield
Post Green
Creekmoor
Waterloo
A3049
Moordown
Walkford
A337
A35
A3049
Winton
Priory
Somerford
Highcliffe
Barton on Sea
Downton
Sherford
Slepe
Lytchett Minster
Upton
Newtown
Wallisdown
B3063
Pokesdown
Tuckton
Highcliffe Castle
B3058
Organford
Turlin Moor
Upton
A3040
Branksome
A35
Mudeford
Christchurch Bay
A351
Hamworthy
A350
Parkstone
Westbourne
Boscombe
Southbourne
Wick
Red House
Lifeboat Station
Milford on Sea
Holton Heath
B3068
POOLE
B3369
Canford Cliffs
BOURNEMOUTH
Russell-Cotes
HENGISTBURY HEAD
90
Trigon Hill
Cold Harbour
B3075
Poole Harbour
Compton Acres
B3065
Sandford
Town Walls
Arne
Brownsea Island
B3369
Northport
Town
World of Toys
Brownsea Island
Sandbanks
POOLE BAY
Binnegar
Wareham
B3075
Ridge
Totland
West Holme
Holmebridge
Toll
Stoborough
Stoborough Green
East Holme
Alum Bay
4
A351
Middlebere Heath
Wytch Heath
ISLE OF PURBECK
Studland & Godlingston Heaths
THE NEEDLES
B3070
Grange Heath
Furzebrook
Creech
Blue Pool
Castle View
Bushey
Studland Beach
Studland Bay
ANGER AREA
East Creech
PURBECK HILLS
B3351
Studland
Old Harry Rocks
The Foreland or Handfast Point
Model Village
Woolgarston
Church Knowle
Corfe Castle
Corfe Castle
Nine Barrow Down
654
Ulwell
Steeple
654
New Swanage
Swanage Bay
Tyneham
Swanage Railway
80
Fine Foundation Marine Centre
Kimmeridge
Kingston
Harman's Cross
Langton Matravers
Swanage
Kimmeridge Bay
B3069
Lifeboat Station
Herston
Worth Matravers
Acton
Putlake Adventure Farm
Durlston Bay
Durlston
Dancing Ledge
DURLSTON HEAD
Poole to:
Cherbourg 4hrs. 30mins. (Seasonal)
Guernsey 3hrs. (Fast Ferry, Seasonal)
Jersey 3hrs. 30mins. (Fast Ferry, Seasonal)
St Malo 7hrs. (Fast Ferry, Seasonal)
5
ST ALDHELM'S OR ST ALBAN'S HEAD
GLISH CHANNEL
70
E
F
G
H
90
400
10
20

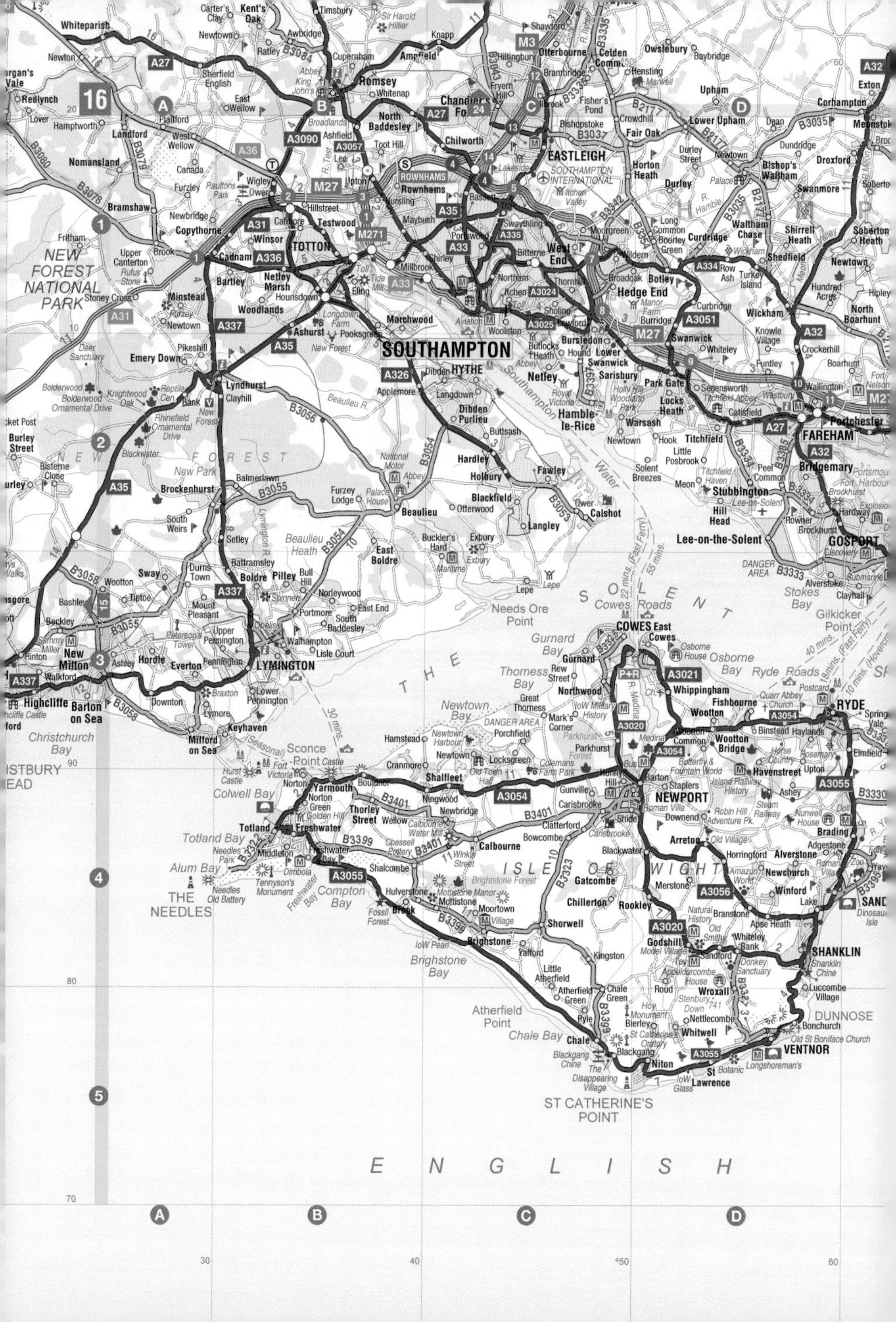

16
Whiteparish
Carter's Clay
Kent's Oak
Timsbury
Sir Harold Hillier
Shawford
Newtown
Awbridge
Knapp
M3
Newton
Ratley
B3084
Cupernham
Ampfield
Otterbourne
Colden Common
Owslebury
Baybridge
A27
Sherfield English
Abbey
King John's
Romsey
Whitenap
Hiltingbury
Brambridge
Hensting
Marwell
Morgan's Vale
Redlynch
East Wellow
Chandler's Ford
Fryern Hill
Fisher's Pond
Upham
Exton
Lover
Hamptworth
Plaitford
Broadlands
North Baddesley
Bishopstoke
Crowdhill
Lower Upham
Dean
Corhampton
Landford
West Wellow
Ashfield
A3090
A3057
Toot Hill
Chilworth
EASTLEIGH
Fair Oak
Durley Street
Newtown
Dundridge
Meonstoke
A36
Lee
SOUTHAMPTON INTERNATIONAL
Horton Heath
Bishop's Waltham
Droxford
Nomansland
Canada
ROWNHAMS
Rownhams
Lakeside
Durley
Palace
Swanmore
B3080
B3079
Furzley
Paultons Park
Wigley
Ower
M27
Upton
Nursling
Bassett
Itchen Valley
Soberton
B3078
Bramshaw
Newbridge
Hillstreet
Maybush
A35
Swaythling
Long Common
Boorley Green
Curdridge
Waltham Chase
Shirrell Heath
Soberton Heath
Copythorne
Testwood
A31
Winsor
M271
A335
Moorgreen
Wildern
Wickham
Fritham
TOTTON
A33
Bitterne
West End
Shedfield
Newtown
NEW FOREST NATIONAL PARK
Upper Canterton
Rufus Stone
Brook
Cadnam
A336
Shirley
Millbrook
Toll
Tide Mill
Northam
Broadoak
Botley
A334
Row Ash
Turkey Island
Hundred Acres
Stoney Cross
Bartley
Netley Marsh
Hounsdown
Eling
Thornhill
Hedge End
Hipley
Minstead
Furzey
Woodlands
Itchen
A3024
Sholing
Manor Farm
Curbridge
Burridge
North Boarhunt
A31
Newtown
A337
Longdown Farm
Ashurst
Pooksgreen
Marchwood
Aviation
Woolston
A3025
Lowford
A3051
Deer Sanctuary
Pikeshill
New Forest
SOUTHAMPTON
Butlocks Heath
Bursledon
Hound
Lower Swanwick
M27
Swanwick
Whiteley
Knowle Village
Crockerhill
Emery Down
A35
Abbey
Netley
Funtley
Boarhunt
Lyndhurst
A326
Dibden
HYTHE
Sarisbury
Park Gate
Fort Nelson
Bolderwood
Bolderwood Ornamental Drive
Knightwood Oak
Reptile Cen.
Bank
Clayhill
Applemore
Langdown
Royal Victoria
Holly Hill Woodland Park
Segensworth
Titchfield Abbey
Wallington
Westbury
Locks Heath
Catisfield
Portchester
Rhinefield Ornamental Drive
New Forest
Beaulieu R.
Dibden Purlieu
Hamble-le-Rice
A27
FAREHAM
Burley Street
Blackwater
Buttsash
Warsash
Newtown
Hook
Titchfield
A32
NEW FOREST
B3056
B3054
Southampton Water
Little Posbrook
Bridgemary
Portsmouth
New Park
National Motor
Hardley
Holbury
Fawley
Bisterne Close
Abbey
Solent Breezes
Titchfield Haven
Peel Common
Fort Harbour
Brookhurst
Burley
Balmerlawn
Brockenhurst
A35
B3055
Furzey Lodge
Palace House
Blackfield
Meon
Stubbington
Explosion
Beaulieu
Otterwood
Ower
Calshot
Lee-on-Solent
Hardway
South Weirs
Lymington R.
B3053
Hill Head
Rowner
Brockhurst
Langley
Setley
Beaulieu Heath
Buckler's Hard
Exbury
Lee-on-the-Solent
GOSPORT
Discovery
East Boldre
Maritime
DANGER AREA
B3333
Sway
Durns Town
Battramsley
Bull Hill
Submarine
B3058
Wootton
Boldre
Pilley
Lepe
Alverstoke
Tiptoe
Mount Pleasant
Spinners
Norleywood
Stokes Bay
Clayhall
Bashley
A337
East End
Portmore
SOLENT
Cowes Roads
Needs Ore Point
Beckley
South Baddesley
Gilkicker Point
Sammy Miller
Peterson's Tower
Upper Pennington
Obelisk
Walhampton
COWES
East Cowes
B3055
New Milton
Lisle Court
Gurnard Bay
Osborne House
Osborne Bay
Hinton
Ashley
Hordle
Everton
Pennington
LYMINGTON
Gurnard
Ryde Roads
Walkford
THE
Thorness Bay
Rew Street
A3021
Postcard
A337
Northwood
Whippingham
Quarr Abbey
Highcliffe
Barton on Sea
Downton
Braxton
Lower Pennington
Fishbourne
RYDE
Highcliffe Castle
B3058
Great Thorness
Wootton
A3054
Spring Vale
Lymore
Newtown Bay
IoW Military History
Mark's Corner
Binstead
Haylands
Christchurch Bay
Keyhaven
DANGER AREA
Porchfield
Wootton Common
Wootton Bridge
Hamstead
Newtown Harbour
Parkhurst Forest
A3020
Medina
Horse Country
Milford on Sea
Sconce Point
Castle
Newtown
Parkhurst
Havenstreet
Rosemary
Elmfield
HENGISTBURY HEAD
Cranmore
Locksgreen
Colemans Farm Park
A3054
Butterfly & Fountain World
Upton
Hurst Castle
Fort Victoria
Norton
Old Town Hall
Island Railway History
Colwell Bay
Yarmouth
Bouldnor
Shalfleet
Barton
Staplers
NEWPORT
Ashey
A3055
Norton Green
Golden Hill
A3054
Gunville
Carisbrooke
Roman Villa
Steam Railway
Thorley Street
Ningwood
Newbridge
B3401
Downend
Robin Hill Adventure Pk.
Nunwell House
Totland
Freshwater
Wellow
Calbourne Water Mill
Clatterford
Shide
Brading
Totland Bay
Needles Park
B3399
Chessell Pottery
Calbourne
Bowcombe
Carisbrooke
Arreton
Old Village
Adgestone
Middleton
Freshwater Bay
Winkle Street
Blackwater
Horringford
Alverstone
Alum Bay
Dimbola
A3055
Shalcombe
ISLE OF WIGHT
Amazon World
Newchurch
THE NEEDLES
Needles Old Battery
Tennyson's Monument
Freshwater Bay
Compton Bay
Hulverstone
Mottistone Manor
Mottistone
Brightstone Forest
Gatcombe
Merstone
A3056
Winford
Fossil Forest
Brook
Moortown Village
Chillerton
Rookley
Natural History
Branstone
Lake
SANDOWN
Dinosaur Isle
B3399
Brighstone
Shorwell
A3020
Godshill
Model Village
Toy
Old Smithy
Whiteley Bank
Apse Heath
IoW Pearl
Yafford
Kingston
Sandford
SHANKLIN
Shanklin Chine
Brighstone Bay
Donkey Sanctuary
Appuldurcombe House
Little Atherfield
Roud
Wroxall
Luccombe Village
Atherfield Green
Chale Green
Stenbury Down
Atherfield Point
Hoy Monument
Nettlecombe
DUNNOSE
Ryle
Bierley
Chale Bay
Chale
St Catherine's Oratory
Whitwell
Bonchurch
Old St Boniface Church
Blackgang Chine
Blackgang
A3055
VENTNOR
The Disappearing Village
Niton
IoW Glass
St Lawrence
Botanic
Longshoreman's
ST CATHERINE'S POINT
ENGLISH
A
B
C
D
30
40
50
60

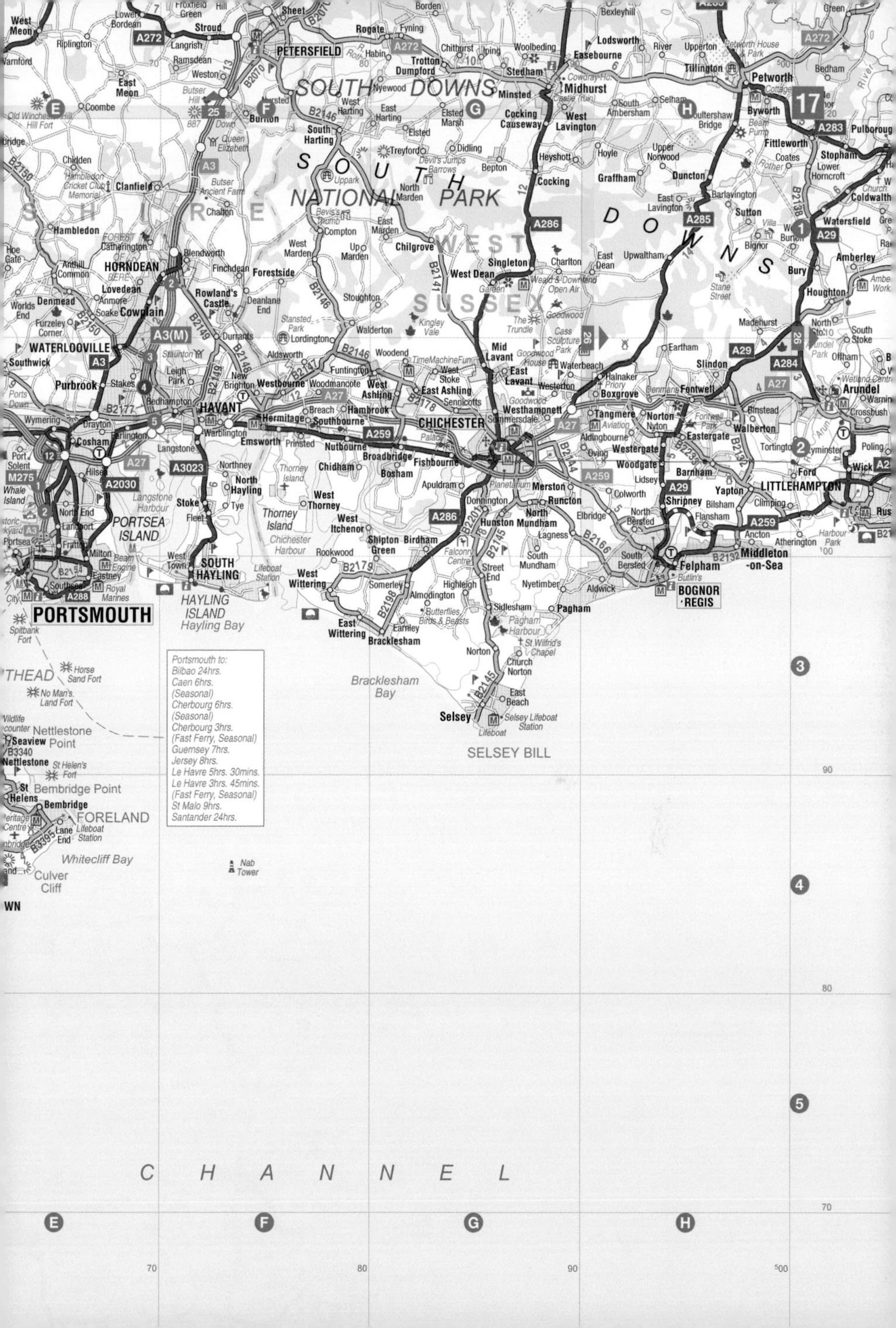

West Meon
Lower Bordean
Froxfield Green
Sheet
Borden
Bexleyhill
Green
Riplington
A272
Langrish
Stroud
PETERSFIELD
Rogate
Fyning
A272
Chithurst
Iping
Woolbeding
Lodsworth
River
Upperton
Petworth House & Park
A272
Warnford
Ramsdean
Habin
Trotton
Dumpford
Stedham
Easebourne
Tillington
Petworth
Bedham
Weston
Butser Hill
B2070
SOUTH DOWNS
Nyewood
Minsted
Midhurst
Cowdray Ho.
Byworth
17
East Meon
E
Coombe
25
F
Buriton
West Harting
East Harting
Elsted Marsh
G
Cocking Causeway
South Ambersham
Selham
H
Coultershaw Bridge
Beam Pump
A283
Pulborough
Old Winchester Hill Hill Fort
Queen Elizabeth
B2146
South Harting
Elsted
West Lavington
Fittleworth
Stopham
Treyford
Didling
Heyshott
Hoyle
Upper Norwood
Coates
Lower Horncroft
Chidden
A3
Devil's Jumps Barrows
Bepton
Rother
Hambledon Cricket Club Memorial
Clanfield
Butser Ancient Farm
S O U T H
Uppark
North Marden
Cocking
Graffham
Duncton
Barlavington
Coldwaltham
Chalton
NATIONAL PARK
East Lavington
Sutton
Waterfield
Hambledon
Bevis's Thumb
Compton
East Marden
A286
D O W N S
A285
Villa
Bignor
A29
Catherington
West Marden
Up Marden
Chilgrove
W E S T
East Dean
Upwaltham
Amberley
Blendworth
Singleton
Charlton
Bury
HORNDEAN
Finchdean
Forestside
B2141
West Dean
Weald & Downland Open Air
Anthill Common
Lovedean
Rowland's Castle
Deanlane End
Garden
Stane Street
Houghton
Denmead
Anmore
Soake
Cowplain
Stoughton
S U S S E X
Goodwood
Worlds End
B2150
B2149
B2146
Stansted Park
Kingley Vale
The Trundle
Cass Sculpture Park
Madehurst
North Stoke
South Stoke
Furzeley Corner
A3(M)
Durrants
Walderton
Lordington
26
26
Arundel Park
WATERLOOVILLE
Staunton
B2148
Aldsworth
Woodend
TimeMachineFun
Mid Lavant
Goodwood House
Waterbeach
Eartham
Slindon
A29
A284
Offham
Southwick
A3
Leigh Park
B2147
Funtington
West Stoke
East Lavant
Halnaker
Fontwell
A27
Wetland Centre
Purbrook
Stakes
New Brighton
Westbourne
Woodmancote
West Ashling
East Ashling
Westerton
Boxgrove
Denmans
Arundel
Ports Down
Bedhampton
HAVANT
A27
Sennicotts
Westhampnett
Tangmere
Norton
Binstead
B2177
Breach
Hambrook
B2178
Summersdale
Aviation
Nyton
Fontwell Park
Walberton
Crossbush
Wymering
Drayton
Hermitage
Southbourne
CHICHESTER
A27
Aldingbourne
Westergate
Eastergate
Tortington
Lyminster
Poling
Cosham
Farlington
Warblington
Emsworth
Prinsted
A259
Palace
Oving
Woodgate
Port Solent
M275
Hilsea
Langstone
A3023
Nutbourne
Broadbridge
Fishbourne
B2144
A259
Lidsey
Barnham
Ford
Wick
A2030
Northney
Thorney Island
Chidham
Bosham
Apuldram
Planetarium
Merston
Colworth
A29
Yapton
LITTLEHAMPTON
Whale Island
North End
North Hayling
Langstone Harbour
West Thorney
Donnington
Runcton
North Bersted
Shripney
Bilsham
Climping
Landport
PORTSEA ISLAND
Stoke
Tye
Thorney Island
West Itchenor
A286
Hunston
North Mundham
Elbridge
Flansham
A259
Fratton
Fleet
Chichester Harbour
Shipton Green
Birdham
B2201
Lagness
Ancton
Atherington
Harbour Park
Milton
Beam Engine
Rookwood
B2145
Falconry Centre
B2166
South Mundham
South Bersted
Felpham
B2132
Middleton-on-Sea
Southsea
Eastney
West Town
SOUTH HAYLING
Lifeboat Station
West Wittering
B2179
Street End
Aldwick
100
Royal Marines
A288
Somerley
Highleigh
Nyetimber
BOGNOR REGIS
Butlin's
PORTSMOUTH
HAYLING ISLAND
Hayling Bay
B2198
Almodington
Butterflies, Birds & Beasts
Sidlesham
Pagham
Spitbank Fort
East Wittering
Earnley
Bracklesham
Pagham Harbour
St Wilfrid's Chapel
Norton
Church Norton
3
Horse Sand Fort
THEAD
Bracklesham Bay
East Beach
No Man's Land Fort
B2145
Selsey
Selsey Lifeboat Station
Lifeboat
Nettlestone Point
Seaview
B3340
SELSEY BILL
Nettlestone
St Helen's Fort
90
St Helens
Bembridge Point
Bembridge
FORELAND
Lane End
Lifeboat Station
B3395
Whitecliff Bay
Nab Tower
4
Culver Cliff
WN
80
5
C H A N N E L
70
E
F
G
H
70
80
90
500

Portsmouth to:
Bilbao 24hrs.
Caen 6hrs.
(Seasonal)
Cherbourg 6hrs.
(Seasonal)
Cherbourg 3hrs.
(Fast Ferry, Seasonal)
Guernsey 7hrs.
Jersey 8hrs.
Le Havre 5hrs. 30mins.
Le Havre 3hrs. 45mins.
(Fast Ferry, Seasonal)
St Malo 9hrs.
Santander 24hrs.

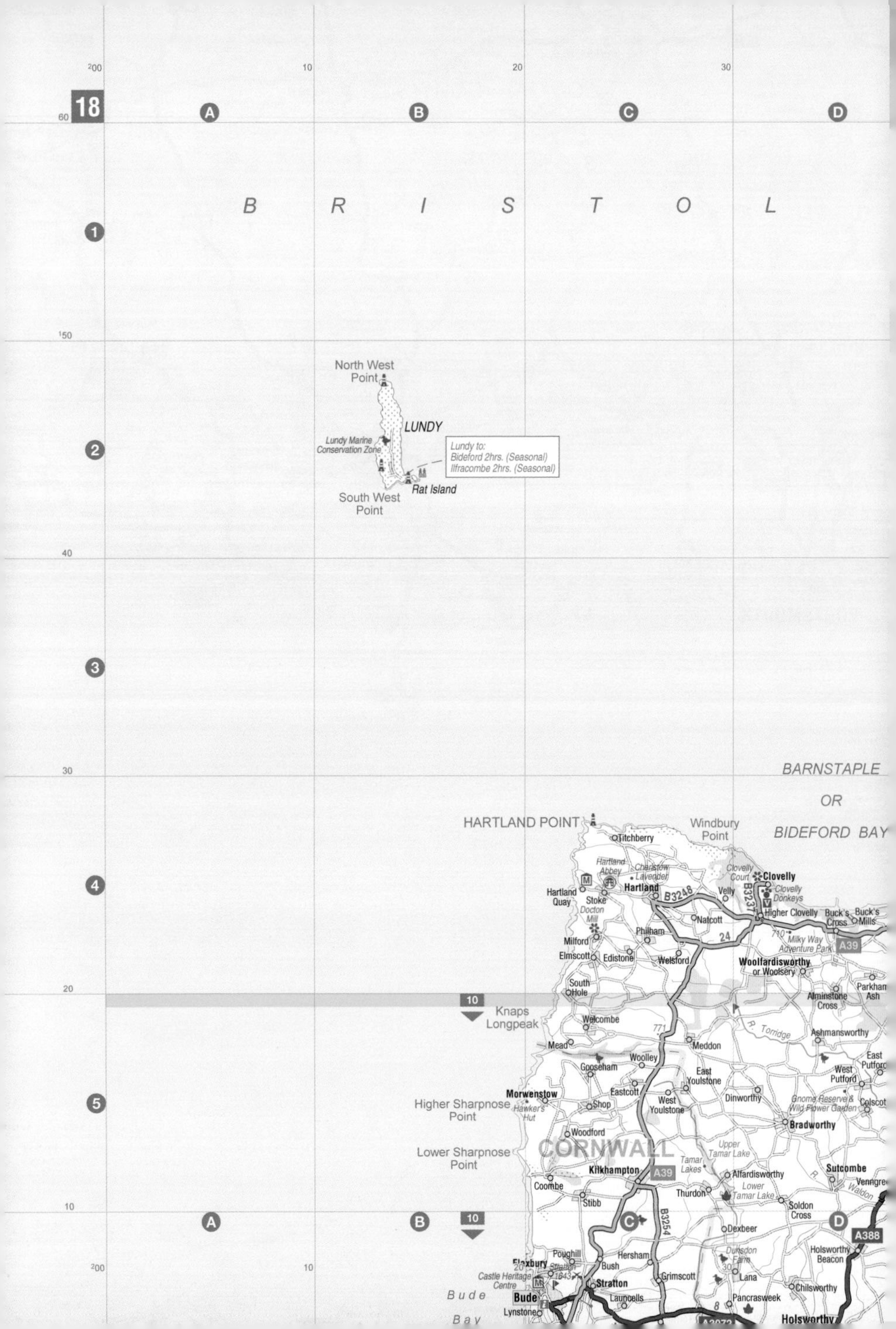
B R I S T O L
North West Point
LUNDY
Lundy Marine Conservation Zone
Lundy to:
Bideford 2hrs. (Seasonal)
Ilfracombe 2hrs. (Seasonal)
Rat Island
South West Point
BARNSTAPLE
OR
BIDEFORD BAY
HARTLAND POINT
Windbury Point
Titchberry
Hartland Abbey
Cheristow Lavender
Hartland
Clovelly Court
Clovelly
Clovelly Donkeys
Hartland Quay
Stoke
Docton Mill
B3248
Velly
B3237
Higher Clovelly
Buck's Cross
Buck's Mills
Natcott
Philham
Milky Way Adventure Park
A39
Milford
Elmscott
Edistone
Welsford
Woolfardisworthy or Woolsery
South Hole
Alminstone Cross
Parkham Ash
Knaps Longpeak
Welcombe
R. Torridge
Ashmansworthy
Mead
Meddon
Gooseham
Woolley
East Youlstone
West Putford
East Putford
Morwenstow
Hawker's Hut
Eastcott
Shop
West Youlstone
Dinworthy
Gnome Reserve & Wild Flower Garden
Colscott
Higher Sharpnose Point
Woodford
Bradworthy
Lower Sharpnose Point
CORNWALL
Upper Tamar Lake
Tamar Lakes
Kilkhampton
Sutcombe
Alfardisworthy
Vennngreen
Coombe
Thurdon
Lower Tamar Lake
Stibb
Soldon Cross
B3254
Dexbeer
A388
Poughill
Flexbury
Bush
Hersham
Dunsdon Farm
Holsworthy Beacon
Castle Heritage Centre
Stratton
Grimscott
Lana
Bude
Launcells
Chilsworthy
Pancrasweek
Lynstone
Bude Bay
Holsworthy
A3072

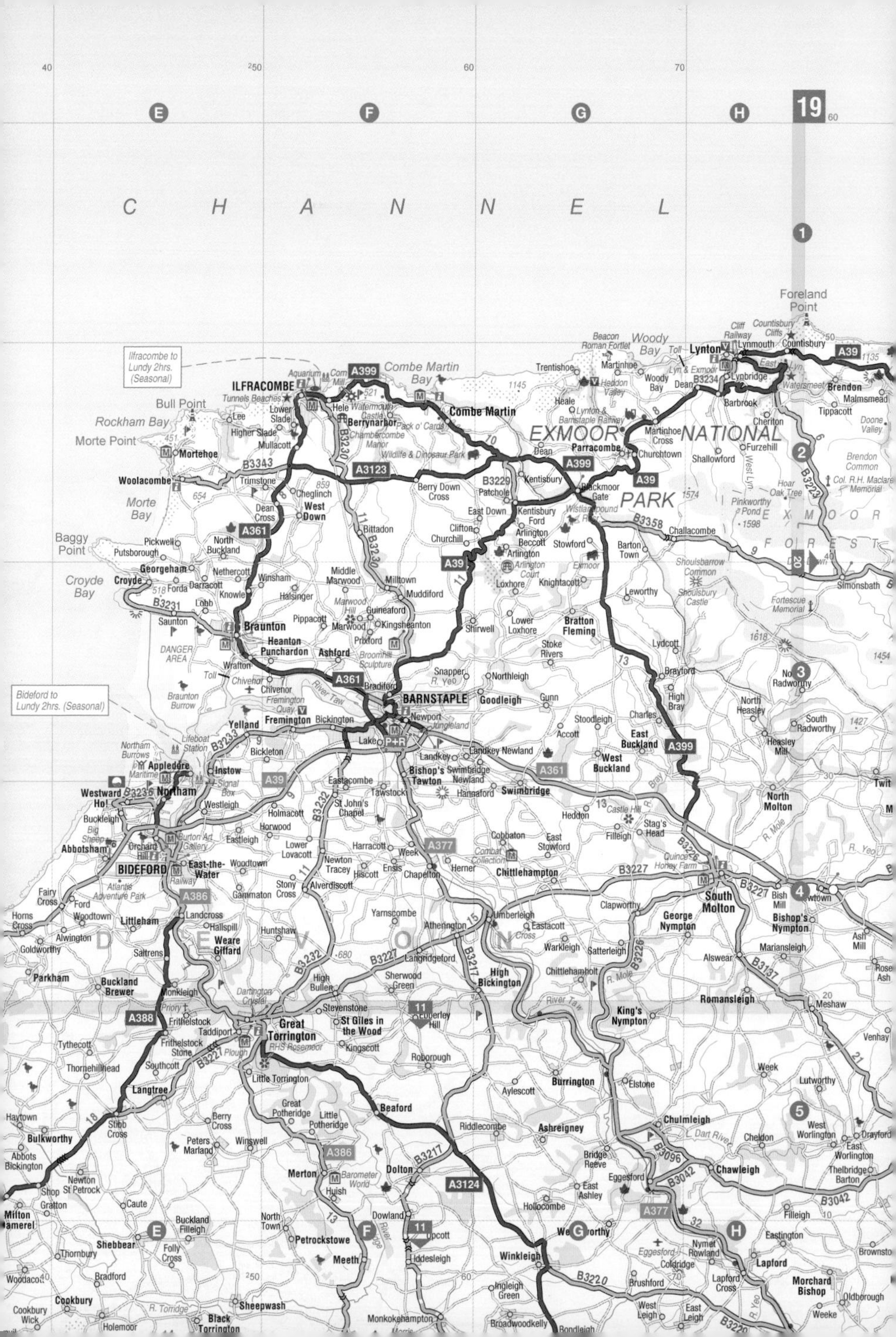

19
40
250
60
70
60
E
F
G
H
C H A N N E L
1
Foreland Point
Countisbury Cliffs
Cliff Railway
Countisbury
Lynmouth
Lynton
Woody Bay
Beacon Roman Fortlet
Toll
Lyn & Exmoor
Martinhoe
Trentishoe
Heddon Valley
Woody Bay
Dean
B3234
Lynbridge
East Lyn
Watersmeet
Brendon
Malmsmead
A39
1135
Barbrook
Cheriton
Tippacott
Doone Valley
Heale
Lynton & Barnstaple Railway
EXMOOR NATIONAL PARK
Martinhoe Cross
Parracombe
Churchtown
Furzehill
Shallowford
West Lyn
Brendon Common
Hoar Oak Tree
Col. R.H. Maclaren Memorial
B3223
2
Ilfracombe to Lundy 2hrs. (Seasonal)
ILFRACOMBE
Aquarium
Com Mill
A399
Combe Martin Bay
Tunnels Beaches
Bull Point
Rockham Bay
Morte Point
Lee
Lower Slade
Higher Slade
Mullacott
Hele
Watermouth Castle
Berrynarbor
Chambercombe Manor
Pack o' Cards
Combe Martin
Wildlife & Dinosaur Park
1145
Mortehoe
451
B3343
Woolacombe
Trimstone
A3123
Morte Bay
654
Dean Cross
Cheglinch
859
West Down
Berry Down Cross
B3229
Patchole
Kentisbury
Blackmoor Gate
A399
A39
1574
Pinkworthy Pond
1598
EXMOOR FOREST
Baggy Point
Putsborough
Pickwell
A361
North Buckland
East Down
Kentisbury Ford
Wistlandpound Rsvr
B3358
Challacombe
Clifton
Churchill
Arlington Beccott
Stowford
Barton Town
Arlington
Arlington Court
Shoulsbarrow Common
Simonsbath
Croyde Bay
Croyde
Georgeham
518
Forda
Nethercott
Darracott
Winsham
Knowle
Bittadon
B3230
Middle Marwood
Milltown
Muddiford
A39
Loxhore
Knightacott
Exmoor
Leworthy
Shoulsbury Castle
Fortescue Memorial
B3231
Lobb
Saunton
Braunton
Halsinger
Marwood Hill
Pippacott
Guineaford
Marwood
Kingsheanton
Prixford
Shirwell
Lower Loxhore
Bratton Fleming
Lydcott
1618
1454
DANGER AREA
Heanton Punchardon
Ashford
Broomhill Sculpture
Stoke Rivers
Wrafton
Toll
Chivenor
Chivenor
A361
Braunton Burrow
Fremington Quay
River Taw
Bradiford
Snapper
R. Yeo
Northleigh
Brayford
No Radworthy
3
Bideford to Lundy 2hrs. (Seasonal)
BARNSTAPLE
Goodleigh
Gunn
High Bray
North Heasley
South Radworthy
1427
Yelland
Fremington
Bickington
Newport
Jungleland
Stoodleigh
Charles
Accott
East Buckland
A399
Heasley Mill
Northam Burrows
Lifeboat Station
B3233
Bickleton
Lake
P+R
Landkey
Landkey Newland
West Buckland
A361
Appledore
Maritime
Instow
Signal Box
A39
Eastacombe
Bishop's Tawton
Swimbridge Newland
Bray
30
Twit
Westward Ho!
B3236
Northam
Westleigh
Tawstock
Hannaford
Swimbridge
North Molton
Buckleigh
Big Sheep
Holmacott
B3232
St John's Chapel
Heddon
Castle Hill
Stag's Head
Horwood
Filleigh
R. Mole
Abbotsham
Orchard Hill
Burton Art Gallery
Eastleigh
Lower Lovacott
Harracott
Week
A377
Cobbaton
Combat Collection
East Stowford
B3226
Quince Honey Farm
R. Yeo
BIDEFORD
East-the-Water
Railway
Woodtown
Newton Tracey
Hiscott
Ensis
Chapelton
Herner
Chittlehampton
B3227
Fairy Cross
Ford
Atlantis Adventure Park
A386
Stony Cross
Alverdiscott
Gammaton
South Molton
B3227
Bish Mill
4
Newtown
Horns Cross
Woodtown
Littleham
Landcross
Yarnscombe
Umberleigh
Clapworthy
George Nympton
Bishop's Nympton
Alwington
Hallspill
Huntshaw
Atherington
15
Eastacott
Cross
Ash Mill
D E V O N
Goldworthy
Weare Giffard
Warkleigh
Satterleigh
B3226
Mariansleigh
Saltrens
680
B3227
Langridgeford
B3217
Alswear
B3137
Rose Ash
Parkham
Buckland Brewer
High Bullen
Sherwood Green
High Bickington
Chittlehamholt
R. Mole
Monkleigh
Dartington Crystal
River Taw
Romansleigh
20
Meshaw
Priory
Stevenstone
11
Eworthy Hill
King's Nympton
A388
Frithelstock
Great Torrington
St Giles in the Wood
Venhay
Tythecott
Taddiport
RHS Rosemoor
Frithelstock Stone
Plough
B3227
Kingscott
Roborough
Thornehillhead
Southcott
21
Week
Little Torrington
Langtree
Aylescott
Burrington
Elstone
Lutworthy
Beaford
Great Potheridge
5
Haytown
18
Stibb Cross
Berry Cross
Little Potheridge
Riddlecombe
Ashreigney
Chulmleigh
West Worlington
Drayford
Bulkworthy
Peters Marland
Winswell
A386
L. Dart River
Cheldon
East Worlington
Abbots Bickington
Merton
Barometer World
B3217
Dolton
A3124
Bridge Reeve
B3096
Chawleigh
Thelbridge Barton
Newton St Petrock
Huish
East Ashley
Eggesford
B3042
Shop
Gratton
Caute
13
Dowland
Hollocombe
A377
B3042
Milton Damerel
Buckland Filleigh
North Town
11
Upcott
Wembworthy
32
Filleigh
Eastington
10
Shebbear
Petrockstowe
Eggesford
Nymet Rowland
Brownston
Thornbury
Folly Cross
Meeth
Iddesleigh
Winkleigh
Coldridge
Lapford
Woodacott
Bradford
250
60
B3220
Brushford
70
Lapford Cross
Morchard Bishop
Cookbury
Ingleigh Green
Oldborough
Cookbury Wick
R. Torridge
Black Torrington
Sheepwash
Monkokehampton
Broadwoodkelly
West Leigh
East Leigh
R. Yeo
Weeke
Holemoor
Bondleigh
B3220
20
40

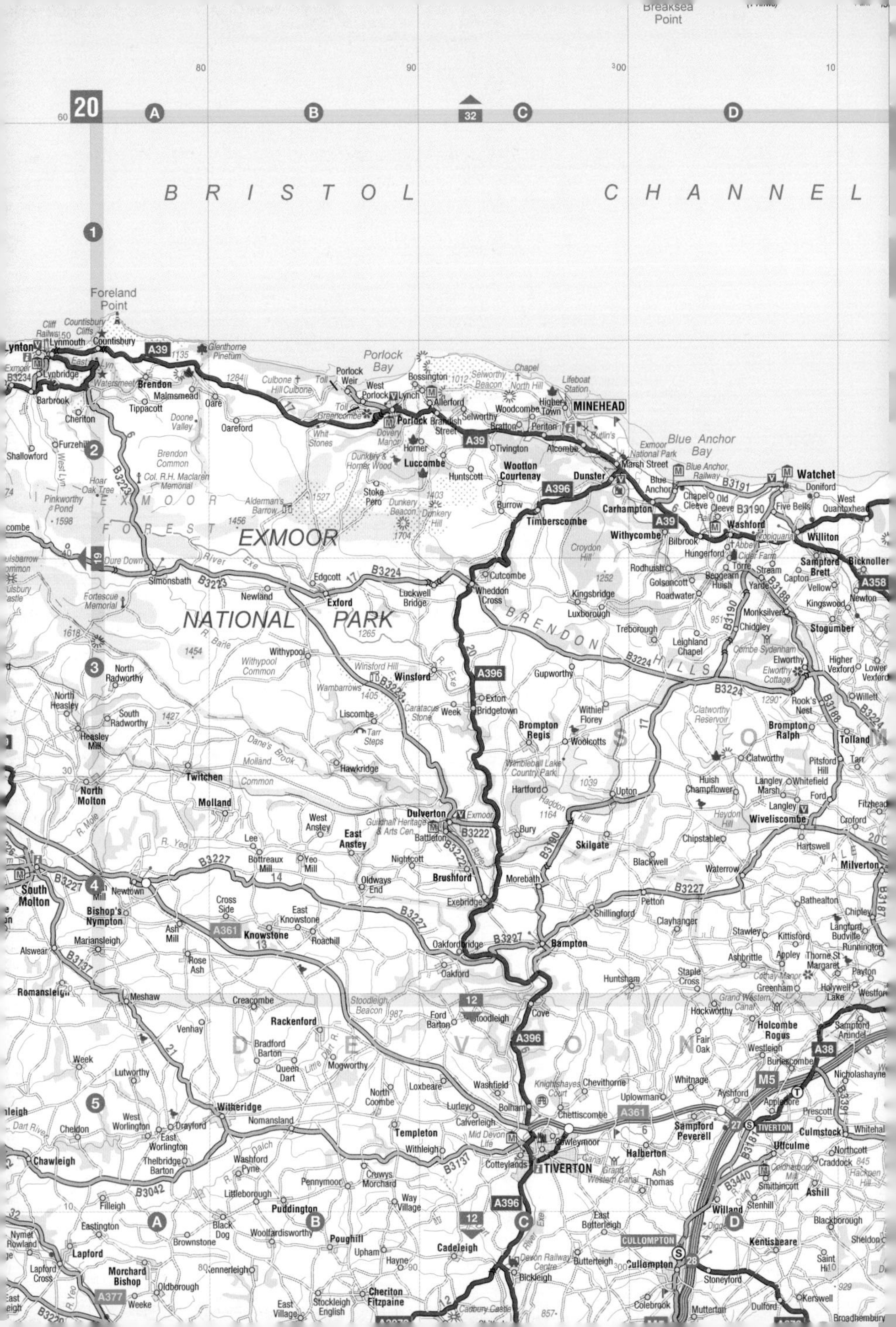

Breaksea Point
80
90
300
10
20
60
A
B
32
C
D
BRISTOL CHANNEL
1
Foreland Point
Cliff Railway
Countisbury Cliffs
Lynton
Lynmouth
Countisbury
A39
1135
Glenthorne Pinetum
Porlock Bay
Selworthy Beacon
Chapel
North Hill
Lifeboat Station
Exmoor
B3234
Lynbridge
East Lyn
Watersmeet
Brendon
Malmsmead
1284
Culbone Hill
Culbone
Toll
Porlock Weir
West Porlock
Lynch
Bossington
1012
Allerford
Selworthy
Woodcombe
Higher Town
MINEHEAD
Barbrook
Tippacott
Oare
Cheriton
Doone Valley
Oareford
Toll
Greencombe
Porlock
Brandish Street
Bratton
Periton
Butlin's
Whit Stones
Dovery Manor
Horner
A39
Tivington
Alcombe
Blue Anchor Bay
Exmoor National Park
Furzehill
Shallowford
West Lyn
2
Brendon Common
Col. R.H. Maclaren Memorial
Dunkery & Horner Wood
Luccombe
Huntscott
Wootton Courtenay
Dunster
Marsh Street
Blue Anchor Railway
Watchet
Doniford
Hoar Oak Tree
B3223
Pinkworthy Pond
EXMOOR FOREST
Alderman's Barrow
1527
Stoke Pero
Dunkery Beacon
1403
Dunkery Hill
A396
Blue Anchor
Chapel Cleeve
Old Cleeve
B3191
B3190
West Quantoxhead
Five Bells
1598
1456
Burrow
Timberscombe
Carhampton
A39
Washford
Williton
EXMOOR
1704
Withycombe
Bilbrook
Abbey
Dure Down
19
Croydon Hill
Hungerford
Cider Farm
Tropiquaria
Bicknoller
River Exe
Cutcombe
Rodhuish
Torre
Sampford Brett
A358
Simonsbath
B3223
Edgcott
B3224
Luckwell Bridge
Wheddon Cross
1252
Golsoncott
Beggearn Huish
Stream
Capton
Yellow
Fortescue Memorial
Newland
Exford
Kingsbridge
Roadwater
Yarde
B3188
Newton
NATIONAL PARK
Luxborough
Kingswood
1265
BRENDON
951
Monksilver
1618
R. Barle
Treborough
Chidgley
Stogumber
1454
Withypool
B3190
Leighland Chapel
Combe Sydenham
Withypool Common
Winsford Hill
Winsford
R. Exe
B3224
HILLS
Elworthy
Higher Vexford
Lower Vexford
3
North Radworthy
A396
Gupworthy
Elworthy Cottage
Wambarrows
B3223
1405
Caratacus Stone
B3224
1290
Rook's Nest
North Heasley
Exton
Week
Bridgetown
Withiel Florey
Clatworthy Reservoir
Willett
South Radworthy
1427
Liscombe
Brompton Regis
Brompton Ralph
Heasley Mill
Tarr Steps
Woolcotts
Tolland
Dane's Brook
Molland Common
Hawkridge
Wimbleball Lake Country Park
Clatworthy
Pitsford Hill
Tarr
30
Twitchen
1039
Hartford
Huish Champflower
Langley Marsh
Whitefield
North Molton
Upton
Ford
Molland
Haddon Hill
1164
Langley
Fitzhead
Dulverton
Exmoor
Heydon Hill
Wiveliscombe
Croford
West Anstey
Guildhall Heritage & Arts Cen.
B3222
Bury
R. Mole
East Anstey
Battleton
Skilgate
Chipstable
Hartswell
R. Yeo
Lee
B3190
Bottreaux Mill
Yeo Mill
Nightcott
Blackwell
Waterrow
Milverton
B3227
Morebath
South Molton
B3227
4
Newtown
14
Oldways End
Brushford
B3227
Bathealton
Bishop's Nympton
Cross Side
East Knowstone
B3227
Exebridge
Petton
Chipley
Shillingford
Clayhanger
Ash Mill
A361
Knowstone
Roachill
B3227
Stawley
Kittisford
Langford Budville
Mariansleigh
Oakfordbridge
Bampton
Alswear
13
Runnington
B3137
Rose Ash
Ashbrittle
Appley
Thorne St Margaret
Oakford
Staple Cross
Payton
Romansleigh
Huntsham
Cothay Manor
Greenham
Holywell Lake
Westford
Meshaw
Creacombe
Stoodleigh Beacon
12
Grand Western Canal
Rackenford
987
Ford Barton
Stoodleigh
Cove
Hockworthy
Holcombe Rogus
Sampford Arundel
Venhay
A396
Bradford Barton
DEVON
Fair Oak
A38
Westleigh
Week
Queen Dart
Little Dart R.
Mogworthy
Burlescombe
Lutworthy
21
Washfield
Whitnage
Nicholashayne
M5
Knightshayes Court
Chevithorne
North Coombe
Loxbeare
Ayshford
5
West Worlington
Witheridge
Lurley
Bolham
Uplowman
Appledore
Prescott
Nomansland
Chettiscombe
A361
Cheldon
Drayford
Calverleigh
Sampford Peverell
27
TIVERTON
Culmstock
Whitehall
Dart River
East Worlington
Templeton
Mid Devon Life
Cowleymoor
6
Halberton
Uffculme
Chawleigh
Thelbridge Barton
Washford Pyne
Withleigh
B3137
Cotteylands
TIVERTON
Grand Western Canal
Ash Thomas
Northcott
Craddock
845
Hackpen Hill
Pennymoor
Cruwys Morchard
B3440
Smithincott
B3042
Littleborough
Way Village
A396
Ashill
Filleigh
Puddington
Stenhill
Willand
10
Eastington
A
B
12
C
East Butterleigh
D
Blackborough
Black Dog
Woolfardisworthy
River Exe
CULLOMPTON
Brownstone
Poughill
Kentisbeare
Sheldon
Nymet Rowland
Lapford
Upham
Hayne
90
Cadeleigh
Devon Railway Centre
Butterleigh
300
Cullompton
28
Saint Hill
Lapford Cross
Morchard Bishop
80
Kennerleigh
Bickleigh
Stoneyford
R. Yeo
Oldborough
Cheriton Fitzpaine
929
A377
Weeke
East Village
Stockleigh English
Cadbury Castle
857
Colebrook
Mutterton
Dulford
Kerswell
Broadhembury

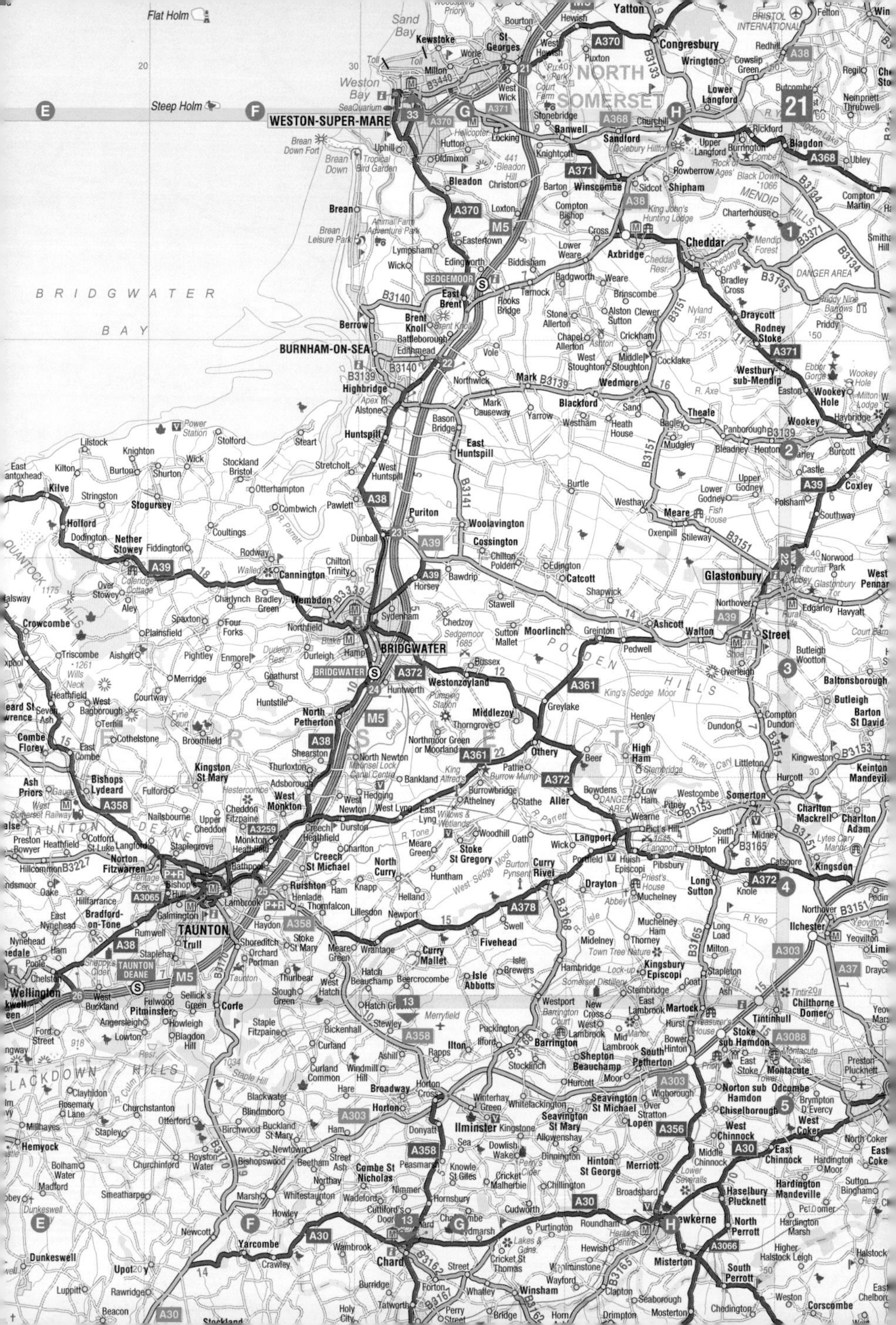

Flat Holm
Steep Holm
Sand Bay
Kewstoke
Weston Bay
WESTON-SUPER-MARE
SeaQuarium
Toll
Milton
Worle
St Georges
Hewish
West Hewish
Puxton
Yatton
Congresbury
Wrington
BRISTOL INTERNATIONAL
Felton
Redhill
Cowslip Green
Lower Langford
Butcombe
Regil
Nempnett Thrubwell
NORTH SOMERSET
Churchill
Banwell
Sandford
Locking
Hutton
Oldmixon
Uphill
Brean Down Fort
Brean Down
Tropical Bird Garden
Bleadon
Bleadon Hill
Christon
Knightcott
Dolebury Hillfort
Upper Langford
Burrington
Rickford
Blagdon
Blagdon Lake
Ubley
Rowberrow
Shipham
Sidcot
Winscombe
Barton
Black Down
MENDIP HILLS
Compton Martin
Compton Bishop
King John's Hunting Lodge
Charterhouse
Brean
Animal Farm Adventure Park
Brean Leisure Park
Loxton
Lympsham
Eastertown
Wick
Edingworth
Biddisham
Cross
Axbridge
Cheddar
Cheddar Resr.
Cheddar Gorge
Mendip Forest
Lower Weare
Weare
Badgworth
Bradley Cross
DANGER AREA
BRIDGWATER BAY
SEDGEMOOR
East Brent
Tarnock
Rooks Bridge
Brent Knoll
Berrow
Battleborough
Edithmead
BURNHAM-ON-SEA
Brinscombe
Stone Allerton
Alston Sutton
Clewer
Nyland Hill
Draycott
Rodney Stoke
Priddy Nine Barrows
Priddy
Chapel Allerton
Ashton
Crickham
West Stoughton
Middle Stoughton
Cocklake
Vole
Northwick
Mark
Wedmore
Westbury-sub-Mendip
Ebbor Gorge
Wookey Hole
Highbridge
Apex
Alstone
Mark Causeway
Blackford
Sand
Theale
Easton
Milton Lodge
Haybridge
Bason Bridge
Yarrow
Westham
Heath House
Bagley
Panborough
Wookey
Power Station
Stolford
Steart
Huntspill
East Huntspill
Mudgley
Bleadney
Henton
Burcott
Lilstock
Knighton
Wick
Stockland Bristol
Stretcholt
West Huntspill
Castle
East Quantoxhead
Kilton
Burton
Shurton
Otterhampton
Burtle
Upper Godney
Coxley
Kilve
Stringston
Stogursey
Combwich
Pawlett
Puriton
Westhay
Lower Godney
Polsham
Meare
Fish House
Southway
Holford
Dodington
Nether Stowey
Coultings
Dunball
Woolavington
Oxenpill
Stileway
QUANTOCK HILLS
Fiddington
Rodway
Cossington
Chilton Polden
Norwood Park
Walled
Cannington
Chilton Trinity
Edington
Catcott
Glastonbury
Tribunal
Abbey
Glastonbury Tor
West Pennard
Coleridge Cottage
Over Stowey
Aley
Charlynch
Bradley Green
Wembdon
Horsey
Bawdrip
Shapwick
Northover
Edgarley
Havyatt
Halsway
Crowcombe
Spaxton
Four Forks
Sydenham
Stawell
Chedzoy
Sedgemoor 1685
Sutton Mallet
Moorlinch
Greinton
Pedwell
Ashcott
Walton
Street
Court Barn
Plainsfield
Northfield
Blake
Hamp
BRIDGWATER
Triscombe
Aisholt
Pightley
Enmore
Durleigh Resr.
Durleigh
POLDEN HILLS
Butleigh Wootton
Wills Neck
Merridge
Goathurst
Bussex
Westonzoyland
Overleigh
Baltonsborough
Heathfield
West Bagborough
Courtway
Huntstile
Huntworth
Pumping Station
King's Sedge Moor
Butleigh
Seven Ash
Fyne Court
North Petherton
Middlezoy
Greylake
Henley
Barton St David
Combe Florey
Tetton
Cothelstone
Broomfield
Thorngrove
Compton Dundon
Dundon
East Combe
Shearston
Northmoor Green or Moorland
Othery
Beer
High Ham
Kingweston
Keinton Mandeville
Kingston St Mary
Thurloxton
North Newton
Maunsel Lock Canal Centre
King Alfred's
Pathe
Burrow Mump
Stembridge
River Cary
Littleton
Ash Priors
Bishops Lydeard
West Somerset Railway
Fulford
Hestercombe
Adsborough
Bankland
Hedging
Burrowbridge
Athelney
Stathe
Aller
Bowdens
Low Ham
Westcombe
Pitney
Somerton
Charlton Mackrell
Charlton Adam
Nailsbourne
Cheddon Fitzpaine
West Monkton
West Newton
West Lyng
East Lyng
Willows & Wetlands
R. Parrett
Wearne
Pict's Hill
Langport
Huish Episcopi
South Hill
Midney
Lytes Cary Manor
Upper Cheddon
Monkton Heathfield
Creech Heathfield
Durston
Woodhill
Oath
Wick
Upton
Preston Bowyer
Heathfield
Cotford St Luke
Langford
Staplegrove
Charlton
R. Tone
Meare Green
Stoke St Gregory
Burton Pynsent
Curry Rivel
Portfield
Pibsbury
Catsgore
Kingsdon
Hillcommon
Norton Fitzwarren
Creech St Michael
North Curry
Huntham
West Sedge Moor
Drayton
Priest's House
Muchelney
Abbey
Long Sutton
Knole
Oake
Bishop's Hull
Bathpool
Ruishton
Ham
Knapp
Helland
Northover
Yeovilton
Hillfarrance
Henlade
Thornfalcon
Lillesdon
Newport
Ilchester
East Nynehead
Bradford-on-Tone
Galmington
Haydon
Swell
Fivehead
R. Yeo
Nynehead
Rumwell
TAUNTON
Shoreditch
Trull
Stoke St Mary
Orchard Portman
Meare Green
Wrantage
Curry Mallet
Muchelney Ham
Thorney
Midelney
Town Tree Nature
Long Load
Milton
Staplehay
Kingsbury Episcopi
Sheppy's Cider
TAUNTON DEANE
Isle Brewers
Hambridge
Lock-up
Stapleton
Wellington
Chelston
Hatch Beauchamp
Beercrocombe
Isle Abbotts
Somerset Distillery
Coat
Ash
West Buckland
Thurlbear
Slough Green
West Hatch
Hatch Green
Merryfield
Stembridge
East Lambrook
Martock
Tintinhull
Chilthorne Domer
Fulwood
Pitminster
Sellick's Green
Corfe
Westport
Barrington Court
New Cross
West Lambrook
Mid Lambrook
Treasurer's House
Angersleigh
Howleigh
Blagdon Hill
Staple Fitzpaine
Bickenhall
Stewley
Puckington
Ilford
Barrington
Hurst
Bower Hinton
Stoke sub Hamdon
Lowton
Curland
Ilton
Rapps
Shepton Beauchamp
South Petherton
Montacute House
Preston Plucknett
Ford Street
Ashill
Stocklinch
Montacute
BLACKDOWN HILLS
Staple Hill
Curland Common
Windmill Hill
Moor
East Stoke
Clayhidon
R. Culm
Hare
Broadway
Horton Cross
Winterhay Green
Whitelackington
Hurcott
Wigborough
Norton sub Hamdon
Odcombe
Rosemary Lane
Churchstanton
Blackwater
Horton
Seavington St Michael
Seavington St Mary
Over Stratton
Lopen
Chiselborough
Brympton D'Evercy
Blindmoor
Ilminster
Kingstone
Millhayes
Otterford
Birchwood
Buckland St Mary
Donyatt
Allowenshay
West Chinnock
West Coker
Hemyock
Stapley
Ham
Newtown
Sea
Dowlish Wake
Perry's Cider
Dinnington
Hinton St George
Merriott
Middle Chinnock
East Chinnock
North Coker
East Coker
Bolham Water
Churchinford
Royston Water
Bishopswood
Beetham
Street Ash
Combe St Nicholas
Peasmarsh
Knowle St Giles
Cricket Malherbie
Chillington
Lower Severalls
Hardington Moor
Madford
Northay
Whitestaunton
Wadeford
Nimmer
Hornsbury
Broadshard
Haselbury Plucknett
Hardington Mandeville
Sutton Bingham
Smeatharpe
Marsh
Cuttiford's Door
Cudworth
Dunkeswell
Howley
Chard
Chaffcombe
Purtington
Roundham
Heritage Centre
Crewkerne
North Perrott
Pendomer
Hardington Marsh
Newcott
Yarcombe
Wambrook
Lakes & Gdns
Crewkerne
Hewish
Misterton
Higher Halstock Leigh
Halstock
Dunkeswell
Upottery
Crawley
Street
Cricket St Thomas
Winsham
Wayford
Clapton
South Perrott
Luppitt
Rawridge
Burridge
Forton
Whatley
Seaborough
Weston
Corscombe
Beacon
Stockland
Tatworth
Holy City
Perry Street
Bridge
Horn
Drimpton
Mosterton
Chedington
M5
A38
A39
A30
A303
A358
A370
A371
A372
A361
A378
A368
A3088
A3066
A3065
A3259
A37
A356
B3139
B3140
B3141
B3151
B3153
B3157
B3165
B3168
B3170
B3227
B3339
B3440
B3134
B3135
B3371
21

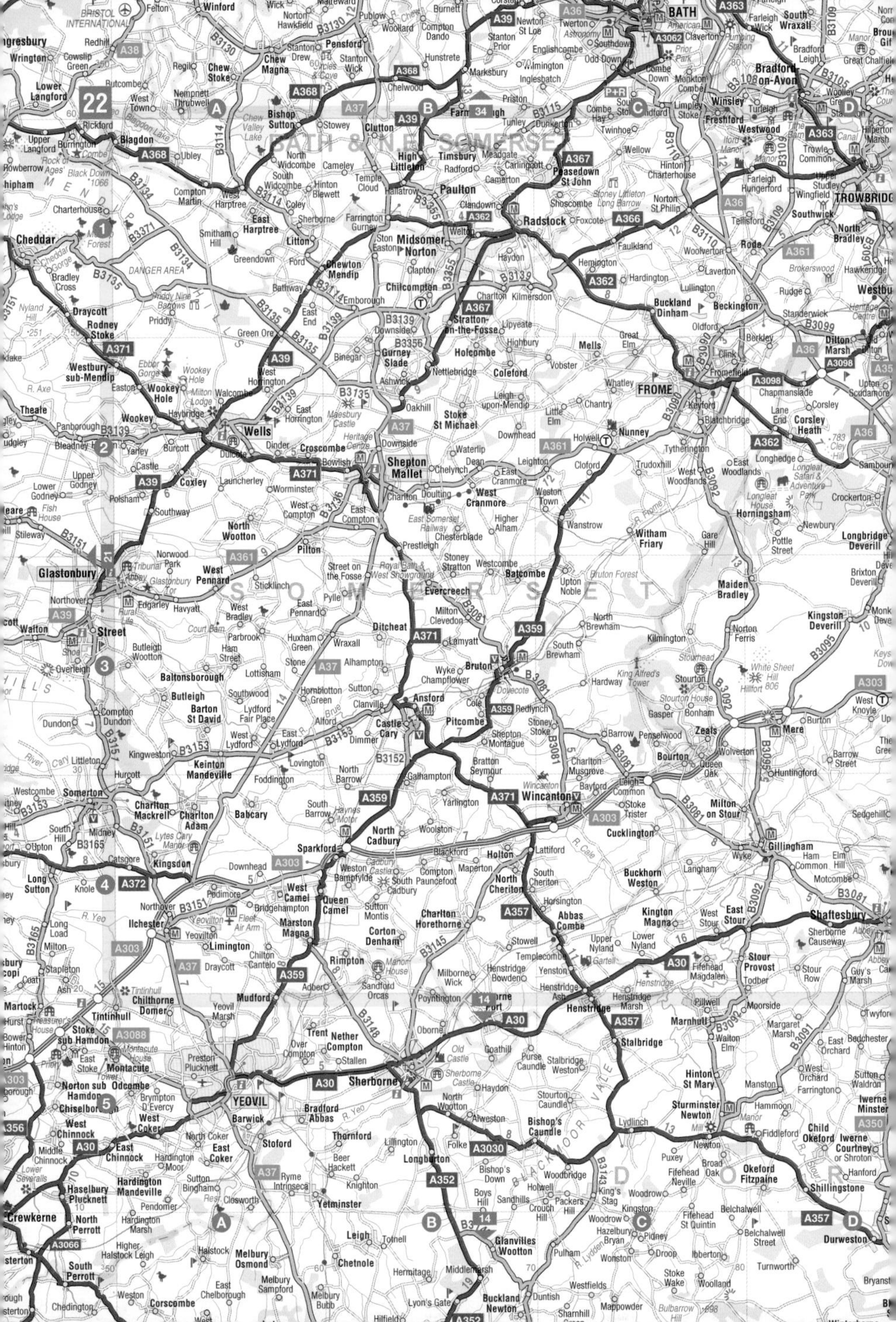

22
BRISTOL INTERNATIONAL
Felton
Winford
Wick
Norton Hawkfield
Pensford
Publow
Woollard
Burnett
Compton Dando
BATH
Twerton
Newton St Loe
Claverton
Farleigh Wick
South Wraxall
Redhill
Wrington
Cowslip Green
Regil
Chew Stoke
Chew Magna
Stanton Drew
Stanton Wick
Hunstrete
Stanton Prior
Marksbury
Englishcombe
Southdown
Odd Down
Combe Down
Monkton Combe
Bradford Leigh
Bradford-on-Avon
Lower Langford
Butcombe
Nempnett Thrubwell
West Town
Bishop Sutton
Stowey
Chelwood
Clutton
Farmborough
Priston
Wilmington
Inglesbatch
Tunley
Dunkerton
Combe Hay
Twinhoe
Limpley Stoke
Freshford
Winsley
Turleigh
Westwood
Upper Langford
Rickford
Burrington
Blagdon
Blagdon Lake
Chew Valley Lake
Ubley
BATH & N.E. SOMERSET
High Littleton
Timsbury
Meadgate
Carlingcott
Peasedown St John
Wellow
Hinton Charterhouse
Iford Manor
Trowle Common
Hilperton Marsh
Rowberrow
Rock of Ages
Black Down 1066
Shipham
North Widcombe
Cameley
Temple Cloud
Radford
Camerton
South Widcombe
Hinton Blewett
Compton Martin
West Harptree
Coley
Hallatrow
Paulton
Clandown
Shoscombe
Stoney Littleton Long Barrow
Norton St Philip
Farleigh Hungerford
Upper Studley
Wingfield
TROWBRIDGE
Charterhouse
MENDIP
East Harptree
Sherborne
Farrington Gurney
Radstock
Foxcote
Tellisford
Southwick
Cheddar
Mendip Forest
Smitham Hill
Litton
Ston Easton
Midsomer Norton
Welton
Haydon
Faulkland
Woolverton
Rode
North Bradley
Cheddar Gorge
Greendown
Ford
Clapton
Hemington
Hardington
Laverton
Brokerswood
Hawkeridge
Bradley Cross
DANGER AREA
Chewton Mendip
Chilcompton
Kilmersdon
Charlton
Lullington
Buckland Dinham
Beckington
Rudge
Westbury
Draycott
Nyland Hill
Priddy Nine Barrows
Priddy
Bathway
Emborough
East End
Downside
Stratton-on-the-Fosse
Lipyeate
Standerwick
Heritage Centre
Rodney Stoke
Green Ore
Gurney Slade
Holcombe
Highbury
Great Elm
Mells
Oldford
Berkley
Dilton Marsh
Westbury-sub-Mendip
Ebbor Gorge
Wookey Hole
Binegar
Nettlebridge
Coleford
Vobster
Clink
Fromefield
Chapmanslade
Upton Scudamore
R. Axe
Easton
Milton Lodge
Walcombe
West Horrington
Ashwick
Oakhill
Leigh-upon-Mendip
Whatley
FROME
Keyford
Lane End
Corsley
Theale
Wookey
Haybridge
Wells
East Horrington
Maesbury Castle
Stoke St Michael
Little Elm
Chantry
Nunney
Blatchbridge
Corsley Heath
Panborough
Bleadney
Yarley
Burcott
Dulcote
Dinder
Croscombe
Bowlish
Shepton Mallet
Downhead
Holwell
Tytherington
Longhedge
Cley Hill 783
Castle
Upper Godney
Lower Godney
Polsham
Coxley
Launcherley
Worminster
Chelynch
Doulting
Waterlip
Dean
East Cranmore
West Cranmore
Leighton
Cloford
Weston Town
Trudoxhill
West Woodlands
East Woodlands
Longleat Safari & Adventure Park
Longleat House
Crockerton
Sambourne
Southway
West Compton
East Compton
Charlton
East Somerset Railway
Chesterblade
Higher Alham
Wanstrow
Horningsham
Newbury
Fish House
North Wootton
Pilton
Prestleigh
Stoney Stratton
Westcombe
Witham Friary
Gare Hill
Pottle Street
Longbridge Deverill
Stileway
Norwood Park
West Pennard
Royal Bath & West Showground
Street on the Fosse
Batcombe
Upton Noble
Bruton Forest
Glastonbury
Tribunal
Abbey
Glastonbury Tor
Sticklinch
SOMERSET
Evercreech
Maiden Bradley
Brixton Deverill
Northover
Edgarley
Havyatt
East Pennard
Pylle
Milton Clevedon
North Brewham
Kingston Deverill
Walton
Street
West Bradley
Court Barn
Parbrook
Huxham Green
Wraxall
Ditcheat
Lamyatt
South Brewham
Kilmington
Norton Ferris
Butleigh Wootton
Ham Street
Alhampton
Wyke Champflower
Bruton
Stourhead
Overleigh
Lottisham
Stone
King Alfred's Tower
Hardway
Stourton
White Sheet Hill 806
Hillfort
Baltonsborough
Southwood
Hornblotton Green
Sutton
Ansford
Cole
Dovecote
Stourton House
West Knoyle
Butleigh
Barton St David
Lydford Fair Place
Alford
Clanville
Castle Cary
Pitcombe
Redlynch
Stoney Stoke
Gasper
Bonham
Zeals
Mere
Burton
Compton Dundon
Dundon
West Lydford
East Lydford
Dimmer
Shepton Montague
Barrow
Penselwood
Bourton
Wolverton
Kingweston
Lovington
Keinton Mandeville
Foddington
North Barrow
Galhampton
Bratton Seymour
Charlton Musgrove
Queen Oak
Barrow Street
Huntingford
Littleton
Hurcott
Somerton
Westcombe
South Barrow
Haynes Motor
Yarlington
Wincanton
Bayford
Leigh Common
Stoke Trister
Milton on Stour
Sedgehill
Charlton Mackrell
Charlton Adam
Babcary
North Cadbury
Woolston
Cucklington
Gillingham
Midney
Lytes Cary Manor
South Hill
Upton
Catsgore
Kingsdon
Sparkford
Blackford
Holton
Lattiford
Wyke
Ham Common
Elm Hill
Long Sutton
Knole
Downhead
Weston Bampfylde
Cadbury Castle
South Cadbury
Compton Pauncefoot
Maperton
North Cheriton
South Cheriton
Buckhorn Weston
Langham
Motcombe
Podimore
West Camel
Queen Camel
Bridgehampton
Sutton Montis
Charlton Horethorne
Horsington
Kington Magna
West Stour
East Stour
Shaftesbury
Long Load
Northover
Ilchester
Yeovilton
Fleet Air Arm
Marston Magna
Corton Denham
Abbas Combe
Upper Nyland
Lower Nyland
Sherborne Causeway
Milton
Limington
Chilton Cantelo
Rimpton
Stowell
Templecombe
Gartell
Fifehead Magdalen
Stour Provost
Stour Row
Guy's Marsh
Stapleton
Draycott
Tintinhull
Adber
Sandford Orcas
Manor House
Milborne Wick
Henstridge Bowden
Yenston
Henstridge
Todber
Martock
Chilthorne Domer
Mudford
Yeovil Marsh
Poyntington
Henstridge Ash
Henstridge Marsh
Pillwell
Moorside
Twyford
Treasurer's House
Tintinhull
Margaret Marsh
Stoke sub Hamdon
Trent
Nether Compton
Oborne
Stalbridge
Marnhull
Walton Elm
East Orchard
Bedchester
Montacute House
Over Compton
Goathill
Purse Caundle
Stalbridge Weston
Preston Plucknett
Stallen
Old Castle
Sherborne Castle
Hinton St Mary
West Orchard
Sutton Waldron
Norton sub Hamdon
Odcombe
Brympton D'Evercy
YEOVIL
Sherborne
Haydon
Stourton Caundle
Manston
Farrington
Chiselborough
West Coker
Barwick
Bradford Abbas
North Wootton
Alweston
Bishop's Caundle
Sturminster Newton
Hammoon
Iwerne Minster
West Chinnock
North Coker
East Coker
Thornford
Lillington
Folke
Lydlinch
Fiddleford
Child Okeford
Iwerne Courtney or Shroton
Middle Chinnock
East Chinnock
Hardington Moor
Stoford
Longburton
BLACKMOOR VALE
Newton
Lower Severalls
Haselbury Plucknett
Hardington Mandeville
Sutton Bingham
Ryme Intrinseca
Beer Hackett
Knighton
Bishop's Down
Woodbridge
Puxey
Fifehead Neville
Broad Oak
Okeford Fitzpaine
Hanford
Crewkerne
North Perrott
Pendomer
Closworth
Yetminster
Boys Hill
Sandhills
Holwell
Crouch Hill
King's Stag
Packers Hill
Woodrow
Kingston
Belchalwell
Shillingstone
Hardington Marsh
Fifehead St Quintin
Hazelbury Bryan
Pidney
Belchalwell Street
Durweston
Higher Halstock Leigh
Halstock
Melbury Osmond
Leigh
Totnell
Chetnole
Glanvilles Wootton
Pulham
Wonston
Droop
Ibberton
South Perrott
Melbury Sampford
Hermitage
Middlemarsh
Stoke Wake
Woolland
Turnworth
Weston
East Chelborough
Melbury Bubb
Lyon's Gate
Buckland Newton
Duntish
Westfields
Mappowder
Sharnhill
Bulbarrow Hill 898
Chedington
Corscombe
Hilfield
A36
A363
A39
A3062
A38
A368
A37
A362
A367
A366
A361
A371
A3098
A359
A303
A372
A357
A30
A3088
A3066
A352
A3030
A350
A356
B3114
B3130
B3134
B3135
B3139
B3151
B3153
B3157
B3165
B3355
B3356
B3081
B3092
B3095
B3099
B3109
B3110
B3115
B3145
B3148
B3143
B3091
B3105
B3108
B3090
B3098
B3136
B3152
B3371
B3350

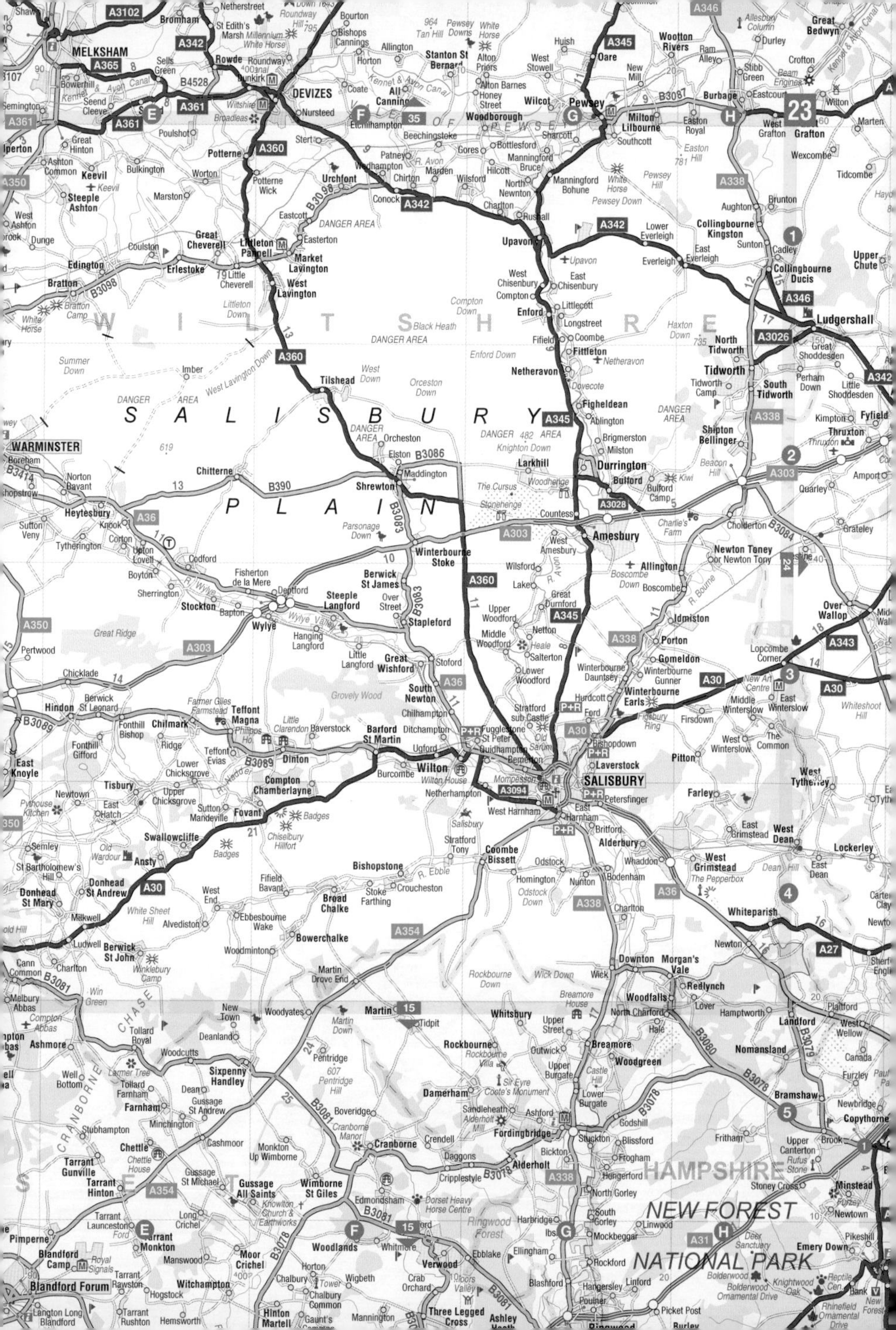

23
MELKSHAM
DEVIZES
Bromham
Netherstreet
St Edith's Marsh
Roundway Hill
Millennium White Horse
Bourton
Bishops Cannings
Allington
Horton
Pewsey Downs
White Horse
Tan Hill
Stanton St Bernard
Alton Priors
Alton Barnes
Honey Street
Huish
West Stowell
Oare
Wilcot
Pewsey
New Mill
Wootton Rivers
Ram Alley
Milton Lilbourne
Easton Royal
Burbage
Eastcourt
Stibb Green
Durley
Great Bedwyn
Crofton
Beam Engines
Wilton
Marten
West Grafton
Grafton
Wexcombe
Tidcombe
Allesbury Column
Rowde
Sells Green
Bowerhill
Seend Cleeve
Semington
Kennet & Avon Canal
Roundway
Coate
All Cannings
Nursteed
Broadleas
Etchilhampton
Beechingstoke
Woodborough
Vale of Pewsey
Sharcott
Southcott
Easton Hill
Poulshot
Stert
Patney
Gores
Bottlesford
Manningford Bruce
Great Hinton
Potterne
Potterne Wick
Bulkington
Worton
Wedhampton
Chirton
Marden
Wilsford
Hilcott
North Newnton
Manningford Bohune
White Horse
Pewsey Hill
Pewsey Down
Ashton Common
Keevil
Steeple Ashton
West Ashton
Marston
Urchfont
Conock
Charlton
Rushall
Upavon
Lower Everleigh
Everleigh
East Everleigh
Collingbourne Kingston
Aughton
Brunton
Sunton
Cadley
Collingbourne Ducis
Upper Chute
Dunge
Eastcott
Danger Area
Easterton
Great Cheverell
Coulston
Littleton Pannell
Market Lavington
Edington
Erlestoke
Little Cheverell
West Lavington
Bratton
Bratton Camp
White Horse
Littleton Down
West Chisenbury
East Chisenbury
Compton
Enford
Littlecott
Longstreet
Coombe
Fifield
Fittleton
Netheravon
Compton Down
Black Heath
Enford Down
Haxton Down
North Tidworth
Tidworth
Ludgershall
Great Shoddesden
Perham Down
Little Shoddesden
South Tidworth
Tidworth Camp
W I L T S H I R E
Summer Down
Imber
West Lavington Down
Tilshead
West Down
Orceston Down
Dovecote
Figheldean
Ablington
Danger Area
Shipton Bellinger
Kimpton
Fyfield
Thruxton
S A L I S B U R Y
P L A I N
WARMINSTER
Boreham
Norton Bavant
Heytesbury
Knook
Sutton Veny
Tytherington
Corton
Upton Lovell
Codford
Boyton
Sherrington
Chitterne
Orcheston
Elston
Maddington
Shrewton
Knighton Down
Larkhill
Brigmerston
Milston
Durrington
Bulford
Bulford Camp
Kiwi
Beacon Hill
Amport
Quarley
The Cursus
Woodhenge
Stonehenge
Countess
Amesbury
West Amesbury
Charlie's Farm
Cholderton
Grateley
Parsonage Down
Winterbourne Stoke
Wilsford
Lake
Newton Toney or Newton Tony
Allington
Boscombe Down
Boscombe
Fisherton de la Mere
Deptford
Stockton
Bapton
Wylye
Wylye Valley
Steeple Langford
Berwick St James
Over Street
Stapleford
Great Durnford
Upper Woodford
Middle Woodford
Heale
Netton
Salterton
Lower Woodford
Idmiston
Porton
Gomeldon
Over Wallop
Great Ridge
Pertwood
Hanging Langford
Little Langford
Great Wishford
Stoford
South Newton
Grovely Wood
Winterbourne Dauntsey
Winterbourne Gunner
Winterbourne Earls
Hurdcott
Lopcombe Corner
New Art Centre
Middle Winterslow
East Winterslow
Whiteshoot Hill
Chicklade
Hindon
Berwick St Leonard
Farmer Giles Farmstead
Teffont Magna
Fonthill Bishop
Chilmark
Ridge
Fonthill Gifford
Philipps Ho.
Little Clarendon
Baverstock
Barford St Martin
Chilhampton
Ditchampton
Fugglestone St Peter
Stratford sub Castle
Old Sarum
Ford
Figsbury Ring
Firsdown
West Winterslow
The Common
Teffont Evias
Lower Chicksgrove
Dinton
Ugford
Wilton
Quidhampton
Bemerton
Bishopdown
Laverstock
Pitton
West Tytherley
East Knoyle
Tisbury
Newtown
Upper Chicksgrove
Compton Chamberlayne
Burcombe
Wilton House
Netherhampton
Mompesson
SALISBURY
Petersfinger
Farley
Pythouse Kitchen
East Hatch
Sutton Mandeville
Fovant
Badges
West Harnham
East Harnham
Britford
Chiselbury Hillfort
Salisbury
Swallowcliffe
Semley
Old Wardour
Ansty
Badges
Stratford Tony
Coombe Bissett
Alderbury
East Grimstead
West Dean
Lockerley
St Bartholomew's Hill
Donhead St Andrew
Donhead St Mary
Bishopstone
Fifield Bavant
R. Ebble
Odstock
Homington
Whaddon
West Grimstead
The Pepperbox
Dean Hill
East Dean
West End
Croucheston
Stoke Farthing
Broad Chalke
Odstock Down
Nunton
Bodenham
Charlton
Milkwell
White Sheet Hill
Alvediston
Ebbesbourne Wake
Whiteparish
Ludwell
Berwick St John
Bowerchalke
Woodminton
Newton
Cann Common
Charlton
Winklebury Camp
Martin Drove End
Rockbourne Down
Wick Down
Wick
Downton
Morgan's Vale
Redlynch
Woodfalls
Lover
Hamptworth
Plaitford
Landford
West Wellow
Melbury Abbas
Win Green
Compton Abbas
Ashmore
New Town
Woodyates
Martin
Tidpit
Martin Down
Whitsbury
Breamore House
Upper Street
North Charford
Hale
Tollard Royal
Deanland
Rockbourne
Rockbourne Villa
Outwick
Breamore
Woodgreen
Nomansland
Canada
Well Bottom
Woodcutts
Larmer Tree
Sixpenny Handley
Pentridge
Pentridge Hill
Upper Burgate
Castle Hill
Furzley
Tollard Farnham
Farnham
Dean
Gussage St Andrew
Minchington
Damerham
Sir Eyre Coote's Monument
Lower Burgate
Godshill
Bramshaw
Newbridge
Copythorne
Stubhampton
Cranborne Chase
Boveridge
Cranborne Manor
Sandleheath
Alderholt Mill
Fordingbridge
Ashford
Stuckton
Blissford
Fritham
Upper Canterton
Brook
Rufus Stone
Chettle
Chettle House
Cashmoor
Monkton Up Wimborne
Cranborne
Crendell
Daggons
Bickton
Frogham
Tarrant Gunville
Gussage St Michael
Cripplestyle
Alderholt
Hungerford
HAMPSHIRE
Stoney Cross
Minstead
Furzey
Tarrant Hinton
Gussage All Saints
Wimborne St Giles
Edmondsham
Dorset Heavy Horse Centre
North Gorley
South Gorley
NEW FOREST
NATIONAL PARK
Newtown
Tarrant Launceston
Long Crichel
Knowlton Church & Earthworks
Ringwood Forest
Harbridge
Ibsley
Mockbeggar
Linwood
Deer Sanctuary
Pikeshill
Emery Down
Pimperne
Tarrant Monkton
Blandford Camp
Royal Signals
Manswood
Moor Crichel
Woodlands
Whitmore
Verwood
Ebblake
Ellingham
Rockford
Bolderwood
Knightwood Oak
Reptile Cen.
Blandford Forum
Tarrant Rawston
Witchampton
Hogstock
Horton
Chalbury
Tower
Wigbeth
Crab Orchard
Moors Valley
Blashford
Hangersley
Linford
Bolderwood Ornamental Drive
Bank
New Forest
Chalbury Common
Poulner
Picket Post
Rhinefield Ornamental Drive
Langton Long Blandford
Tarrant Rushton
Hemsworth
Hinton Martell
Gaunt's Common
Mannington
Three Legged Cross
Ashley Heath
Ringwood
Burley
A3102
A342
A365
A361
B4528
A360
A345
A346
A338
A342
B3098
A3026
A342
A360
A345
B3086
B390
B3083
A36
A303
A3028
A303
A360
B3414
A350
A338
A343
A30
A36
B3089
A3094
P+R
A30
A354
A338
A36
A27
B3081
B3080
B3079
B3078
B3078
A354
A338
A31
B3081
B3078
E
F
G
H
1
2
3
4
5
15
24
35

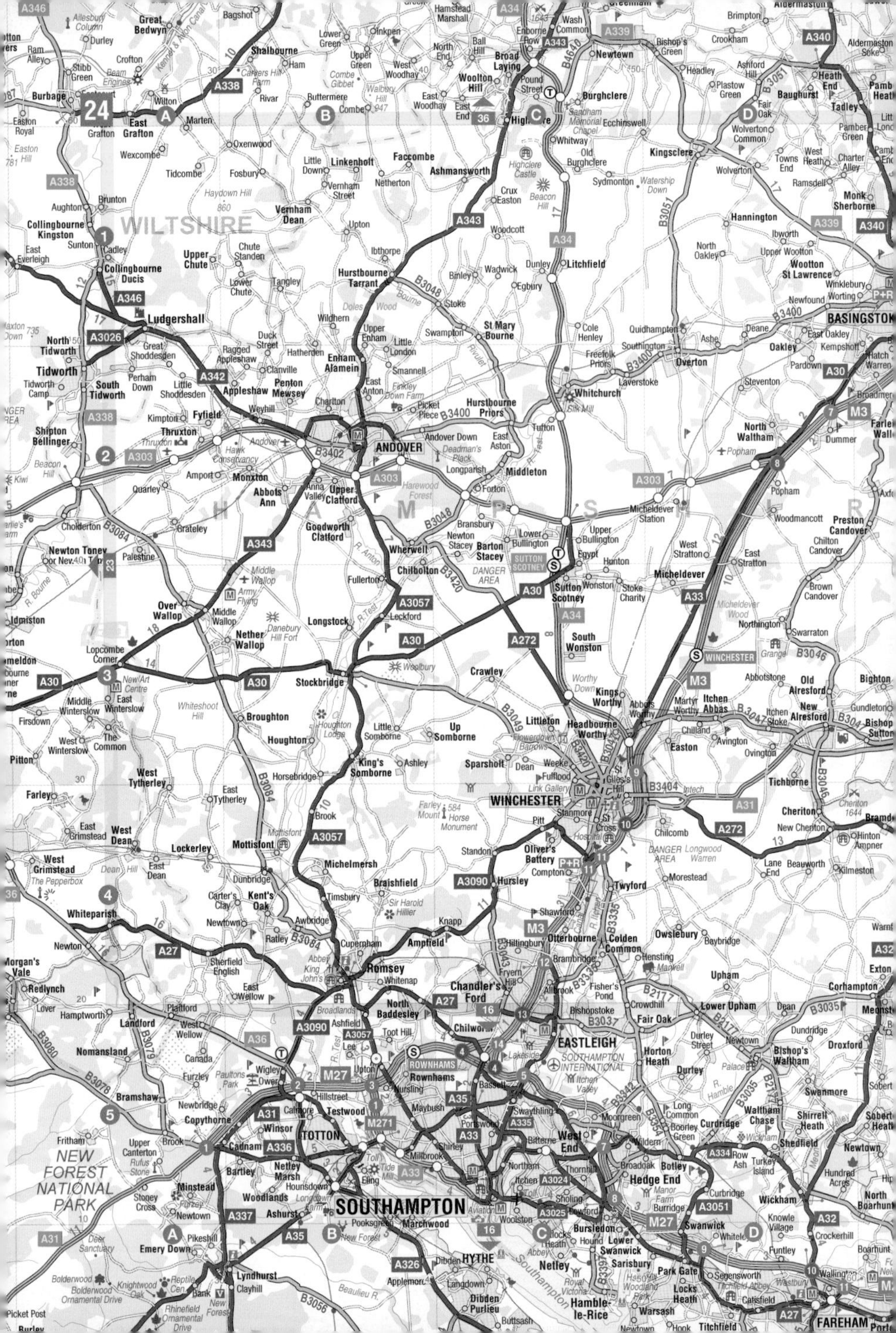
24
A346
Allesbury Column
Great Bedwyn
Bagshot
Durley
Shalbourne
Ham
Crofton
Beam Engines
Burbage
Wilton
A338
East Grafton
Grafton
Marten
Rivar
Easton Royal
Oxenwood
Wexcombe
Tidcombe
Fosbury
Haydown Hill
A338
Aughton
Brunton
WILTSHIRE
Collingbourne Kingston
Sunton
Cadley
East Everleigh
Collingbourne Ducis
A346
Ludgershall
North Tidworth
A3026
Tidworth
Tidworth Camp
South Tidworth
A338
Shipton Bellinger
Great Shoddesden
Perham Down
Little Shoddesden
A342
Ragged Appleshaw
Appleshaw
Clanville
Duck Street
Upper Chute
Chute Standen
Lower Chute
Tangley
Kimpton
Fyfield
Thruxton
Weyhill
Penton Mewsey
A303
Beacon Hill
Kiwi
Amport
Monxton
Quarley
Abbots Ann
Cholderton
B3084
Grateley
Palestine
Newton Toney
Idmiston
Over Wallop
Middle Wallop
Nether Wallop
A343
Lopcombe Corner
A30
Middle Winterslow
East Winterslow
Firsdown
West Winterslow
The Common
Pitton
West Tytherley
Farley
East Tytherley
East Grimstead
West Dean
West Grimstead
The Pepperbox
Lockerley
East Dean
Whiteparish
Newton
Morgan's Vale
Redlynch
A27
Sherfield English
Landford
Hamptworth
Plaitford
West Wellow
East Wellow
B3080
Nomansland
B3079
B3078
Bramshaw
Copythorne
Fritham
NEW FOREST NATIONAL PARK
Upper Canterton
Minstead
Stoney Cross
Newtown
Emery Down
A31
Lyndhurst
Bank
Clayhill
Bolderwood Ornamental Drive
Rhinefield Ornamental Drive
Picket Post
Burley
Lower Green
Inkpen
Upper Green
Combe Gibbet
West Woodhay
Buttermere
Combe
Walbury Hill 947
Hamstead Marshall
North End
Ball Hill
East Woodhay
East End
Woolton Hill
Broad Laying
Highclere
Faccombe
Little Down
Linkenholt
Vernham Street
Netherton
Ashmansworth
Vernham Dean
Upton
Ibthorpe
Hurstbourne Tarrant
A343
Crux Easton
Highclere Castle
Beacon Hill
Woodcott
Binley
Stoke
Wadwick
Egbury
Dunley
Litchfield
B3048
Wildhern
Upper Enham
Hatherden
Enham Alamein
Little London
Smannell
Swampton
St Mary Bourne
East Anton
Charlton
Picket Piece
B3400
Hurstbourne Priors
ANDOVER
Andover Down
East Aston
Longparish
Middleton
Forton
Anna Valley
Upper Clatford
Goodworth Clatford
Harewood Forest
Bransbury
Wherwell
Newton Stacey
Barton Stacey
Lower Bullington
Chilbolton
B3420
Fullerton
A3057
Leckford
Longstock
Danebury Hill Fort
A30
Stockbridge
Woolbury
Crawley
Broughton
Houghton
Houghton Lodge
Little Somborne
Up Somborne
King's Somborne
Ashley
Horsebridge
Sparsholt
Farley Mount
Horse Monument
Brook
A3057
Mottisfont
Michelmersh
Braishfield
Dunbridge
Kent's Oak
Carter's Clay
Timsbury
Newtown
Awbridge
Ratley
B3084
Cupernham
Ampfield
Knapp
Romsey
Abbey
King John's
Whitenap
North Baddesley
Chandler's Ford
A27
Broadlands
Ashfield
A3090
Toot Hill
Lee
Chilworth
Wigley
Ower
M27
Upton
Nursling
Rownhams
ROWNHAMS
Hillstreet
Calmore
Testwood
Winsor
TOTTON
Cadnam
A336
Netley Marsh
Bartley
Woodlands
Ashurst
A337
A35
Pooksgreen
Marchwood
SOUTHAMPTON
Millbrook
Shirley
Eling
Tide Mill
A33
A35
Maybush
Bassett
Portswood
Swaythling
A335
Aviation
HYTHE
Dibden
Applemore
A326
Langdown
Dibden Purlieu
Buttsash
B3056
Beaulieu R.
Greenham
Wash Common
Enborne Row
A343
A339
Newtown
Pound Street
Burghclere
Sandham Memorial Chapel
Ecchinswell
Whitway
Old Burghclere
Sydmonton
Watership Down
A34
Cole Henley
Freefolk Priors
Laverstoke
Whitchurch
Silk Mill
Tufton
Upper Bullington
Hunton
Egypt
SUTTON SCOTNEY
A30
Sutton Scotney
Wonston
Stoke Charity
A34
A272
South Wonston
Worthy Down
Kings Worthy
Abbots Worthy
Headbourne Worthy
Littleton
B3049
Flowerdown Barrows
Dean
Weeke
Fulflood
WINCHESTER
Stanmore
St Giles's Hill
St Cross
Pitt
Standon
Oliver's Battery
Compton
A3090
Hursley
Shawford
M3
Otterbourne
Hiltingbury
Colden Common
Brambridge
Fryern Hill
Allbrook
Bishopstoke
EASTLEIGH
SOUTHAMPTON INTERNATIONAL
Lakeside
Itchen Valley
Bitterne
West End
Northam
Itchen
A3024
Sholing
A3025
Woolston
Netley
Hound
Bursledon
Lowford
Hamble-le-Rice
Royal Victoria
Aldermaston
Brimpton
Crookham
Bishop's Green
Headley
Ashford Hill
B3051
Plastow Green
Heath End
Baughurst
Fair Oak
Tadley
A340
Wolverton Common
Kingsclere
Wolverton
Towns End
West Heath
Pamber Green
Charter Alley
Ramsdell
Monk Sherborne
B3051
Hannington
Ibworth
A339
North Oakley
Upper Wootton
Wootton St Lawrence
Winklebury
Worting
Newfound
B3400
Quidhampton
Ashe
Deane
Oakley
East Oakley
Kempshott
BASINGSTOKE
Southington
Overton
Pardown
A30
Steventon
M3
North Waltham
Dummer
Popham
A303
Micheldever Station
Woodmancott
Preston Candover
Chilton Candover
West Stratton
East Stratton
Micheldever
A33
Brown Candover
Micheldever Wood
Northington
Swarraton
Grange
B3046
WINCHESTER
M3
Abbotstone
Old Alresford
Martyr Worthy
Itchen Abbas
Itchen Stoke
New Alresford
B3047
Chilland
Avington
Easton
Ovington
Bighton
Gundleton
Bishop's Sutton
B3404
Intech
Tichborne
A31
A272
Cheriton
Chilcomb
New Cheriton
Hinton Ampner
Longwood Warren
DANGER AREA
Lane End
Beauworth
Kilmeston
Twyford
Morestead
B3335
Owslebury
Baybridge
Hensting
Marwell
Upham
Fisher's Pond
Exton
Corhampton
Meonstoke
Crowdhill
B2177
Fair Oak
Lower Upham
Dean
B3035
B3037
Horton Heath
Durley Street
Newtown
Dundridge
Droxford
Durley
Bishop's Waltham
Palace
B3354
B3342
Moorgreen
Long Common
Boorley Green
Curdridge
Waltham Chase
Swanmore
Shirrell Heath
Wickham
Shedfield
Wildern
Broadoak
Botley
Hedge End
A334
Row Ash
Turkey Island
Newtown
Hundred Acres
Manor Farm
Burridge
Curbridge
A3051
Wickham
Knowle Village
North Boarhunt
A32
M27
Swanwick
Whiteley
Crockerhill
Boarhunt
Lower Swanwick
Sarisbury
Funtley
Park Gate
Segensworth
Titchfield Abbey
Wallington
Locks Heath
Catisfield
Warsash
A27
FAREHAM
Titchfield
Hook

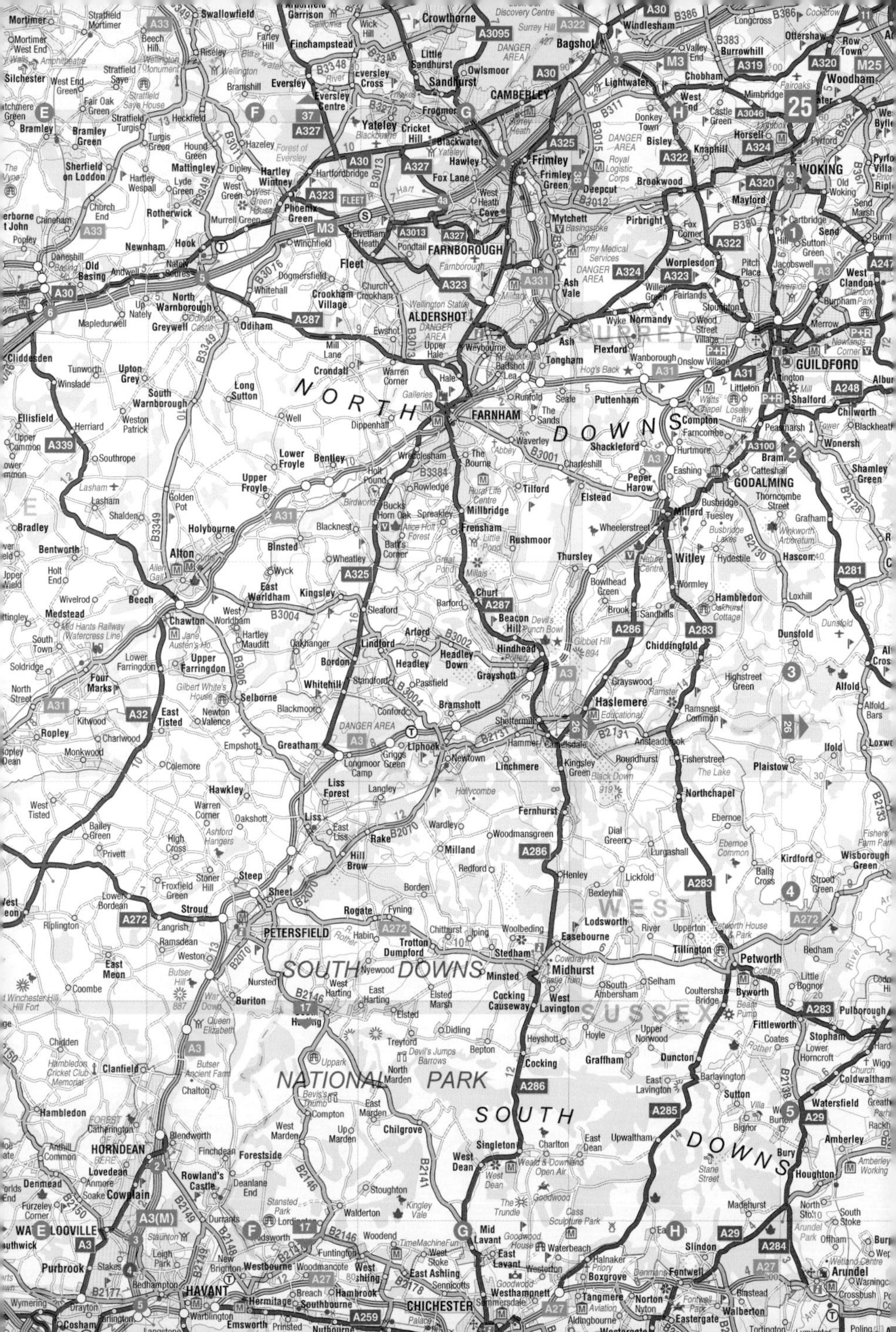

Mortimer
Stratfield Mortimer
Swallowfield
Crowthorne
Windlesham
Bagshot
Finchampstead
Little Sandhurst
Sandhurst
Owlsmoor
Silchester
Stratfield Saye
Eversley
Eversley Cross
Eversley Centre
CAMBERLEY
Lightwater
Chobham
Woodham
Bramley
Bramley Green
Heckfield
Yateley
Cricket Hill
Blackwater
Frogmore
Hawley
Frimley
Frimley Green
Knaphill
Horsell
WOKING
Sherfield on Loddon
Hartley Wintney
Hook
Phoenix Green
FLEET
Fleet
Fox Lane
Deepcut
Brookwood
Mayford
Rotherwick
Newnham
Old Basing
North Warnborough
Greywell
Odiham
Crookham Village
FARNBOROUGH
Mytchett
Pirbright
Worplesdon
Ash Vale
Ash
ALDERSHOT
Normandy
Flexford
Tongham
SURREY
GUILDFORD
Shalford
Chilworth
Cliddesden
Tunworth
Upton Grey
Winslade
Long Sutton
South Warnborough
Crondall
Puttenham
Seale
Compton
NORTH DOWNS
FARNHAM
Ellisfield
Herriard
Lower Froyle
Bentley
Upper Froyle
Wrecclesham
Shackleford
Peper Harow
GODALMING
Tilford
Elstead
Millbridge
Frensham
Rushmoor
Milford
Witley
Holybourne
Alton
Binsted
Kingsley
Thursley
Hambledon
Medstead
Chawton
East Worldham
Lindford
Bordon
Headley
Headley Down
Hindhead
Grayshott
Chiddingfold
Dunsfold
Alfold
Four Marks
Selborne
Haslemere
Ropley
East Tisted
Greatham
Liphook
Linchmere
Plaistow
Liss
Liss Forest
Rake
Fernhurst
Northchapel
Steep
Sheet
Stroud
PETERSFIELD
Rogate
WEST
Lodsworth
Midhurst
Easebourne
Petworth
Tillington
Kirdford
Wisborough Green
SOUTH DOWNS
East Meon
Buriton
Harting
Minsted
Cocking Causeway
West Lavington
SUSSEX
Fittleworth
Pulborough
Clanfield
NATIONAL PARK
Cocking
Graffham
Duncton
Sutton
HORNDEAN
Chilgrove
SOUTH
Singleton
West Dean
DOWNS
Amberley
Houghton
Cowplain
WATERLOOVILLE
Rowland's Castle
Mid Lavant
Slindon
Arundel
Purbrook
HAVANT
Westbourne
Emsworth
Fishbourne
CHICHESTER
East Ashling
Westhampnett
Boxgrove
Tangmere
Fontwell
Walberton
Cosham
Southbourne

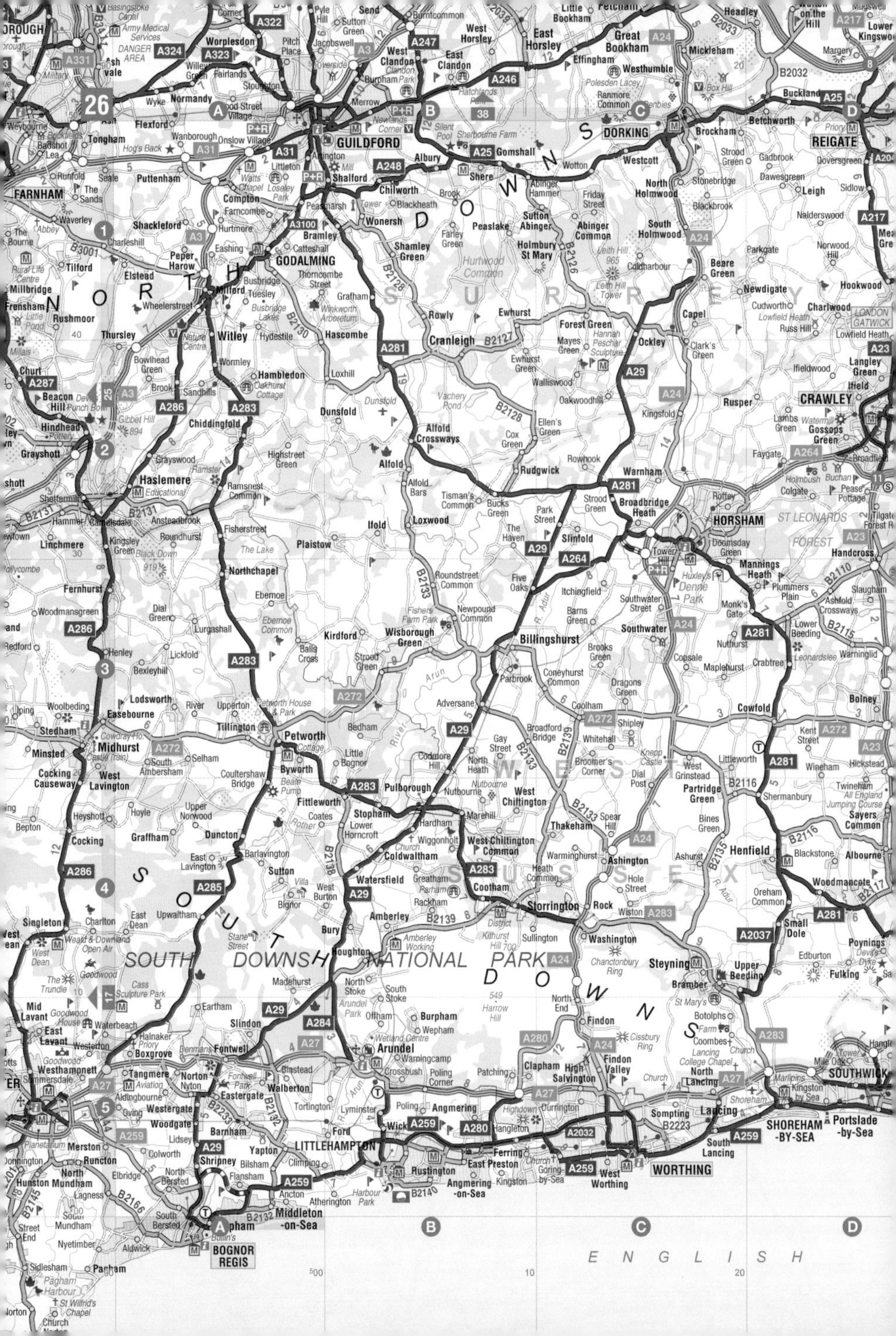

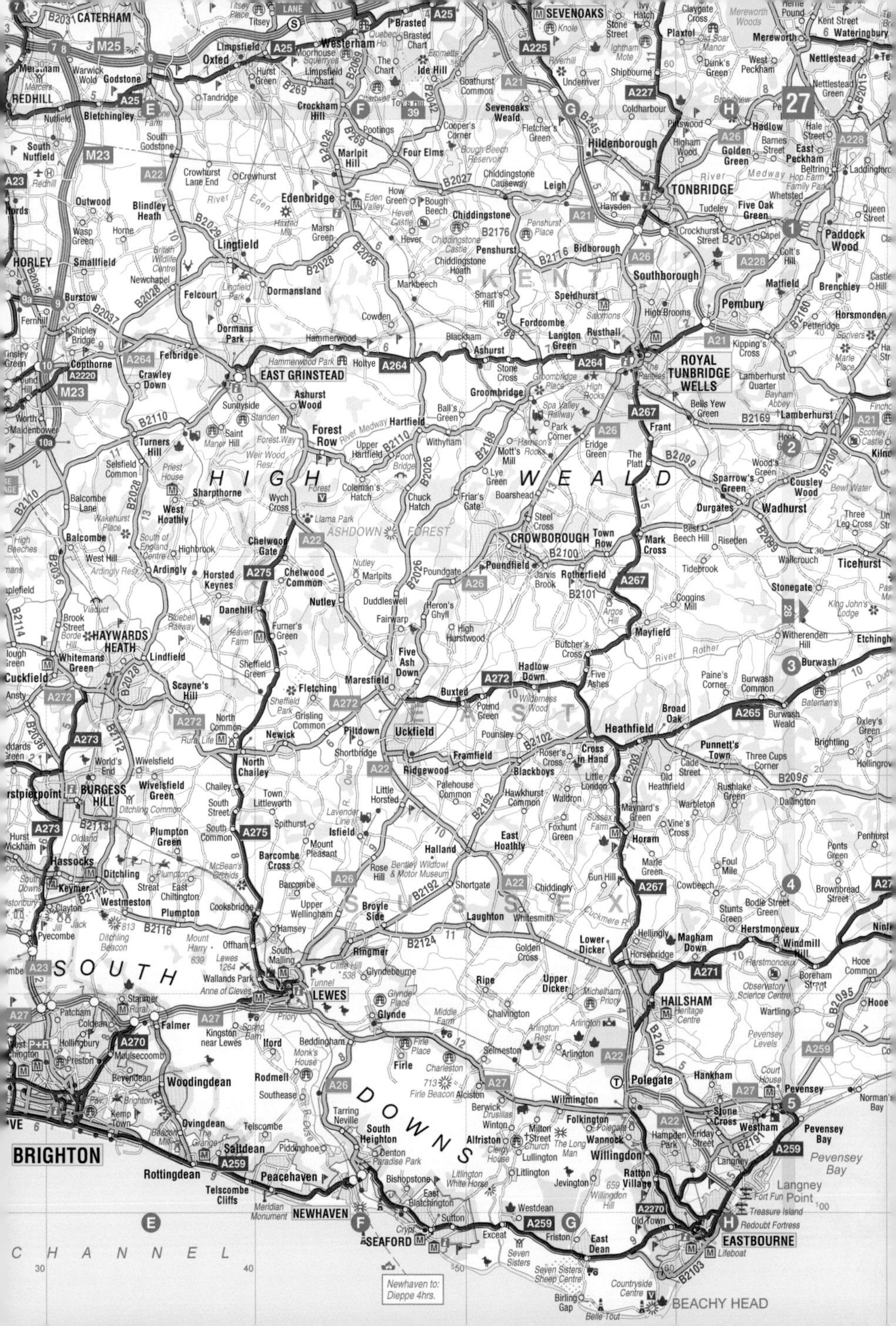
27
CATERHAM
M25
Oxted
Limpsfield
A25
Westerham
Brasted
SEVENOAKS
Knole
Stone Street
Ivy Hatch
Plaxtol
Mereworth
Kent Street
Wateringbury
Merstham
Godstone
REDHILL
Bletchingley
Tandridge
Crockham Hill
Ide Hill
Sevenoaks Weald
Hildenborough
Shipbourne
Nettlestead
Hadlow
South Nutfield
South Godstone
M23
A22
Four Elms
Marlpit Hill
Crowhurst
Edenbridge
Chiddingstone
Leigh
TONBRIDGE
Outwood
Blindley Heath
Hever
Penshurst
Bidborough
Five Oak Green
Paddock Wood
HORLEY
Smallfield
Lingfield
Markbeech
KENT
Southborough
Pembury
Brenchley
Horsmonden
Burstow
Felcourt
Dormansland
Speldhurst
Dormans Park
Fordcombe
Langton Green
Rusthall
Copthorne
Felbridge
Hammerwood
Holtye
A264
Ashurst
ROYAL TUNBRIDGE WELLS
Crawley Down
EAST GRINSTEAD
Ashurst Wood
Groombridge
Lamberhurst
Turners Hill
Forest Row
Hartfield
Withyham
Frant
Bells Yew Green
Saint Hill
HIGH WEALD
Sharpthorne
West Hoathly
Wych Cross
Coleman's Hatch
Chuck Hatch
Wadhurst
Balcombe
ASHDOWN FOREST
CROWBOROUGH
Mark Cross
Ticehurst
Chelwood Gate
Ardingly
Horsted Keynes
Chelwood Common
Nutley
Poundgate
Poundfield
Rotherfield
Stonegate
Danehill
Mayfield
HAYWARDS HEATH
Lindfield
Fairwarp
High Hurstwood
Burwash
Cuckfield
Five Ash Down
Hadlow Down
Scayne's Hill
Fletching
Maresfield
Buxted
EAST
Heathfield
Newick
Piltdown
Uckfield
Framfield
Cross in Hand
BURGESS HILL
Wivelsfield Green
North Chailey
Ridgewood
Blackboys
Punnett's Town
Chailey
Isfield
Horam
Hassocks
Ditchling
Plumpton Green
Barcombe Cross
Halland
East Hoathly
Keymer
Westmeston
Plumpton
SUSSEX
Laughton
Herstmonceux
SOUTH
Offham
Ringmer
Lower Dicker
Magham Down
Windmill Hill
LEWES
Glynde
Upper Dicker
HAILSHAM
Falmer
Iford
Firle
Woodingdean
Rodmell
Polegate
Hankham
Pevensey
DOWNS
Wilmington
Folkington
Westham
Pevensey Bay
BRIGHTON
Saltdean
Alfriston
Willingdon
Rottingdean
Peacehaven
NEWHAVEN
Seaford
East Dean
EASTBOURNE
Telscombe Cliffs
Exceat
Friston
BEACHY HEAD
CHANNEL
Newhaven to: Dieppe 4hrs.

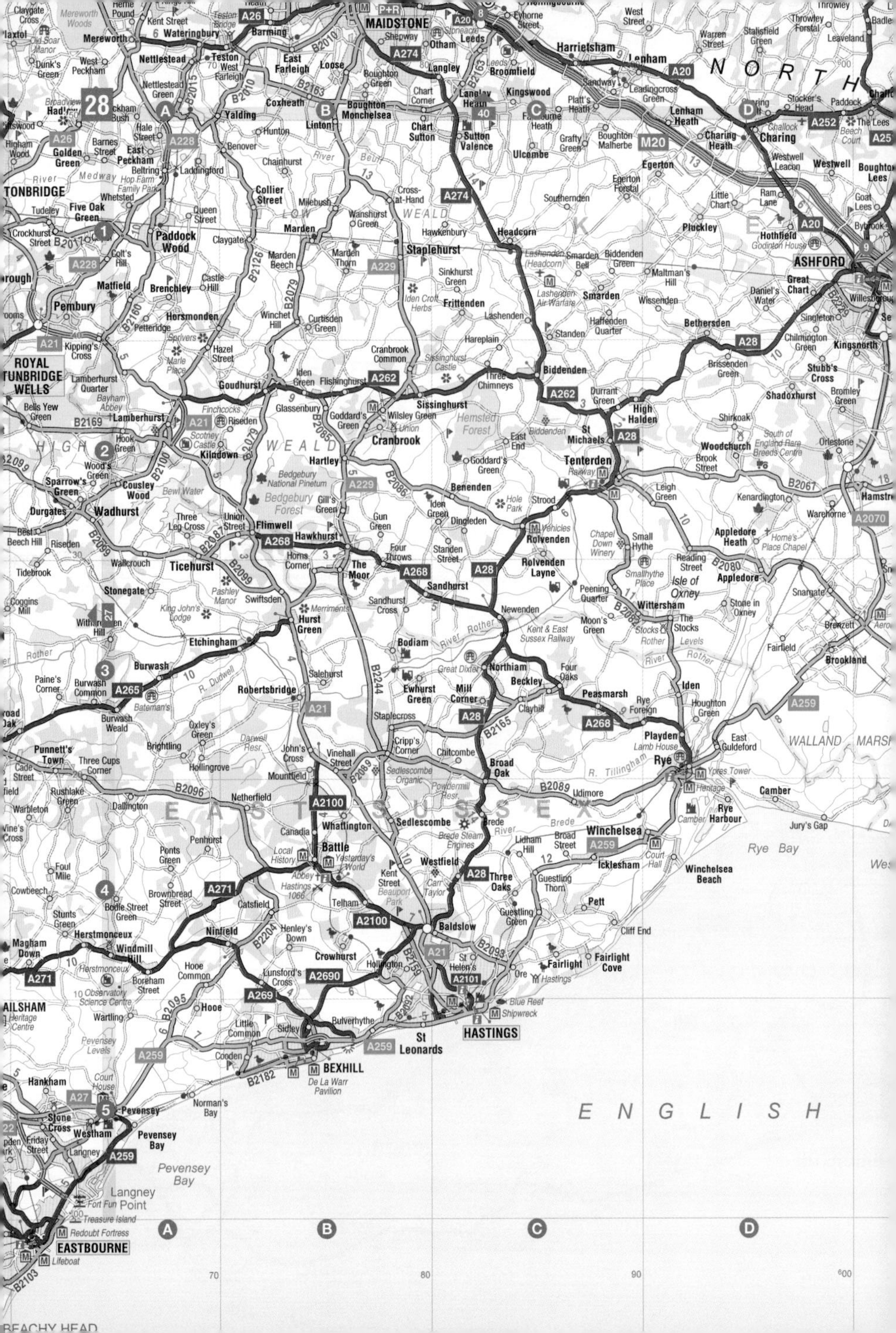

28
MAIDSTONE
P+R
A26
A20
8
Barming
Wateringbury
Mereworth
Kent Street
Teston
Nettlestead
West Peckham
Dunk's Green
Shepway
Otham
Leeds
Eyhorne Street
Harrietsham
Lenham
A20
N O R T H
West Street
Warren Street
Stalisfield Green
Throwley Forstal
Leaveland
East Farleigh
Loose
A274
Langley
Broomfield
Kingswood
Sandway
Leadingcross Green
Platt's Heath
Lenham Heath
Charing
Charing Heath
Stocker's Head
Paddock
A252
The Lees
Coxheath
Boughton Monchelsea
Linton
Chart Corner
Langley Heath
Chart Sutton
Sutton Valence
40
Ulcombe
Grafty Green
Boughton Malherbe
M20
Egerton
Egerton Forstal
Westwell Leacon
Westwell
Boughton Lees
Yalding
Hunton
Hale Street
A228
A26
Golden Green
East Peckham
Beltring
Hop Farm Family Park
Benover
Laddingford
Chainhurst
Collier Street
Medway
River Medway
TONBRIDGE
Five Oak Green
Tudeley
Whetsted
Queen Street
Milebush
Cross-at-Hand
Wanshurst Green
LOW WEALD
Southernden
Little Chart
Ram Lane
Goat Lees
Pluckley
Hothfield
Godinton House
A20
ASHFORD
Great Chart
Crockhurst Street
Paddock Wood
Claygate
Marden
Marden Thorn
Marden Beech
Staplehurst
A229
Hawkenbury
Headcorn
Lashenden (Headcorn)
Smarden Bell
Biddenden Green
Maltman's Hill
A228
Colt's Hill
Matfield
Brenchley
Castle Hill
Sinkhurst Green
Frittenden
Iden Croft Herbs
Lashenden Air Warfare
Smarden
Wissenden
Daniel's Water
Willesborough
Pembury
Horsmonden
Petteridge
Winchet Hill
Curtisden Green
Lashenden
Haffenden Quarter
Standen
Bethersden
Singleton
Chilmington Green
Kingsnorth
A21
Kipping's Cross
Sprivers
Marle Place
Hazel Street
Cranbrook Common
Hareplain
Sissinghurst Castle
A28
Brissenden Green
Stubb's Cross
ROYAL TUNBRIDGE WELLS
Lamberhurst Quarter
Bayham Abbey
Goudhurst
Iden Green
Flishinghurst
A262
Three Chimneys
Biddenden
A262
Durrant Green
High Halden
Shadoxhurst
Bromley Green
Bells Yew Green
B2169
Lamberhurst
Finchcocks
Riseden
Glassenbury
Goddard's Green
Sissinghurst
Wilsley Green
Union
Hemsted Forest
Biddenden
St Michaels
Shirkoak
A21
Scotney Castle
Kilndown
WEALD
Cranbrook
East End
A28
Woodchurch
South of England Rare Breeds Centre
Orlestone
HIGH
Hook Green
Wood's Green
Hartley
Goddard's Green
Tenterden
Railway
Brook Street
Sparrow's Green
Cousley Wood
Bewl Water
Bedgebury National Pinetum
Bedgebury Forest
A229
Gill's Green
B2086
Benenden
Hole Park
Strood
Leigh Green
B2067
Kenardington
Warehorne
A2070
Durgates
Wadhurst
Three Leg Cross
Union Street
Flimwell
Gun Green
Iden Green
Dingleden
Vehicles
Rolvenden
Chapel Down Winery
Small Hythe
Appledore Heath
Home's Place Chapel
Best Beech Hill
Riseden
B2099
A268
Hawkhurst
Horns Corner
Four Throws
Standen Street
Smallhythe Place
Reading Street
Isle of Oxney
Appledore
B2080
Tidebrook
Wallcrouch
Ticehurst
B2099
The Moor
A268
A28
Rolvenden Layne
Snargate
Stonegate
Pashley Manor
Swiftsden
Sandhurst
Peening Quarter
Wittersham
Stone in Oxney
Coggins Mill
King John's Lodge
Merriments
Sandhurst Cross
Newenden
The Stocks
Brenzett
27
Withered Hill
Hurst Green
Etchingham
Moon's Green
Kent & East Sussex Railway
Stocks
Rother Levels
Bodiam
River Rother
Fairfield
Rother
Burwash
R. Dudwell
Salehurst
Great Dixter
Northiam
Four Oaks
Brookland
Paine's Corner
Burwash Common
A265
Bateman's
Robertsbridge
B2244
Ewhurst Green
Mill Corner
Beckley
Peasmarsh
Iden
Houghton Green
A259
Burwash Weald
A21
Staplecross
A28
Clayhill
B2165
Rye Foreign
A268
Playden
Lamb House
East Guldeford
WALLAND MARSH
Oxley's Green
Brightling
Darwell Resr.
Cripp's Corner
Chitcombe
Broad Oak
Rye
Ypres Tower
Punnett's Town
Three Cups Corner
John's Cross
Vinehall Street
Hollingrove
Mountfield
Sedlescombe Organic
Powdermill Resr.
B2089
R. Tillingham
Udimore
Heritage
Camber
Cade Street
Rushlake Green
B2096
Netherfield
A2100
E A S T S U S S E X
Rye Harbour
Jury's Gap
Warbleton
Dallington
Whattington
Sedlescombe
Brede
Brede River
Winchelsea
Penhurst
Canadia
Battle
Local History
Yesterday's World
Brede Steam Engines
Lidham Hill
Broad Street
A259
Court Hall
Rye Bay
Ponts Green
Westfield
Icklesham
Winchelsea Beach
Foul Mile
Abbey
Hastings 1066
Kent Street
Beaufort Park
Carr Taylor
A28
Three Oaks
Guestling Thorn
Cowbeech
A271
Brownbread Street
Catsfield
Telham
Pett
Bodle Street Green
A2100
Baldslow
Guestling Green
Stunts Green
Herstmonceux
Ninfield
Henley's Down
Cliff End
Magham Down
Windmill Hill
Crowhurst
Hollington
A21
B2093
Fairlight
Fairlight Cove
A271
Herstmonceux
Hooe Common
Lunsford's Cross
A2690
St Helen's
A2101
Ore
Hastings
Observatory Science Centre
Boreham Street
A269
Blue Reef
AILSHAM
Heritage Centre
Hooe
B2095
B2092
Shipwreck
Wartling
Little Common
Sidley
Bulverhythe
HASTINGS
Pevensey Levels
St Leonards
A259
A259
Cooden
BEXHILL
B2182
De La Warr Pavilion
Hankham
Court House
A27
Norman's Bay
5
Pevensey
Stone Cross
Westham
Pevensey Bay
Friday Street
Langney
A259
ENGLISH
Pevensey Bay
Langney Point
Fort Fun
Treasure Island
Redoubt Fortress
EASTBOURNE
Lifeboat
B2103
BEACHY HEAD
A
B
C
D
1
2
3
4
5
70
80
90
600

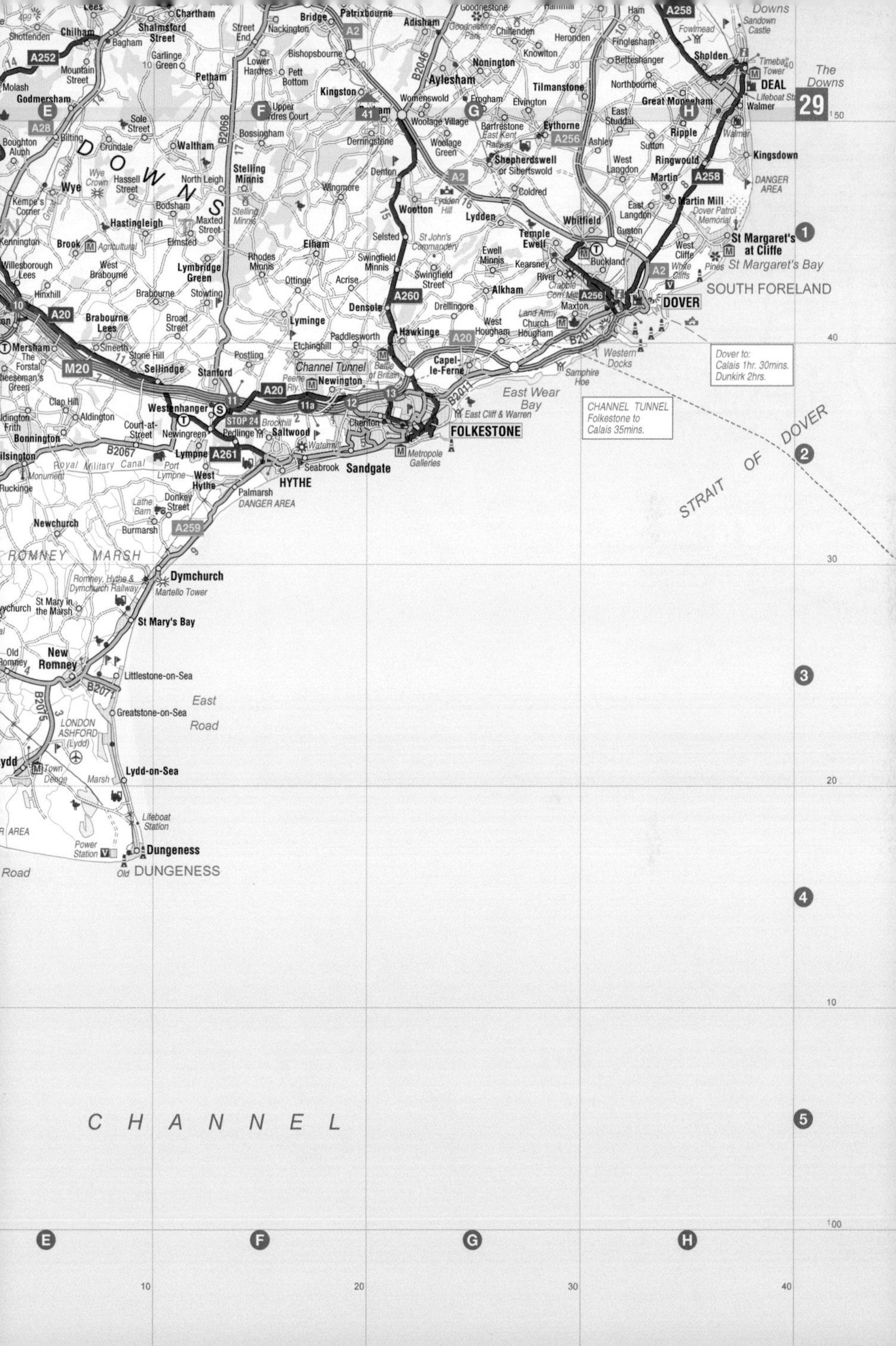

29
Lees
Chartham
Bridge
Patrixbourne
Goodnestone
Ham
A258
Downs
Sandown Castle
Shottenden
Chilham
Shalmsford Street
Street End
Nackington
A2
Adisham
Goodnestone Park
Chillenden
Heronden
Finglesham
Fowlmead
A252
Bagham
Garlinge Green
Lower Hardres
Bishopsbourne
Knowlton
Betteshanger
Sholden
Timeball Tower
Mountain Street
Petham
Pett Bottom
B2046
Aylesham
Nonington
The Downs
Molash
Godmersham
Kingston
Womenswold
Frogham
Tilmanstone
Northbourne
Great Mongeham
DEAL
Lifeboat Sta
Walmer
Upper Hardres Court
41
Woolage Village
Elvington
East Studdal
Barfrestone
Eythorne
A28
Sole Street
Bilting
Boughton Aluph
Crundale
Waltham
B2068
Bossingham
Derringstone
Woolage Green
East Kent Railway
A256
Ashley
Sutton
Ripple
DOWNS
Shepherdswell or Sibertswold
West Langdon
Ringwould
Kingsdown
Wye Crown
Hassell Street
North Leigh
Stelling Minnis
Denton
A2
Martin
A258
Wye
DANGER AREA
Kempe's Corner
Bodsham
Wingmore
Lydden Hill
Coldred
East Langdon
Martin Mill
Dover Patrol Memorial
Hastingleigh
Maxted Street
Elmsted
Wootton
Lydden
Whitfield
Kennington
Brook
Agricultural
Selsted
St John's Commandery
Temple Ewell
Guston
St Margaret's at Cliffe
St Margaret's Bay
Willesborough Lees
West Brabourne
Lymbridge Green
Rhodes Minnis
Elham
Swingfield Minnis
Ewell Minnis
Kearsney
Buckland
West Cliffe
White Cliffs
Pines
Hinxhill
Brabourne
Stowting
Ottinge
Acrise
Swingfield Street
Alkham
River
Crabble Corn Mill
A2
SOUTH FORELAND
A20
Brabourne Lees
Broad Street
Lyminge
Densole
A260
Drellingore
Maxton
A256
DOVER
Mersham
Smeeth
Stone Hill
Paddlesworth
Etchinghill
Hawkinge
West Hougham
Land Army
Church Hougham
A20
The Forstal
Sellindge
Postling
Channel Tunnel
Peene Rly.
Newington
Battle of Britain
Capel-le-Ferne
B2011
Western Docks
Dover to:
Calais 1hr. 30mins.
Dunkirk 2hrs.
M20
Stanford
Samphire Hoe
Cheeseman's Green
Clap Hill
Aldington
Westenhanger
A20
11a
12
13
East Wear Bay
CHANNEL TUNNEL
Folkestone to
Calais 35mins.
Aldington Frith
Court-at-Street
Newingreen
STOP 24
Pedlinge
Brockhill
Saltwood
Cheriton
East Cliff & Warren
FOLKESTONE
DOVER
Bonnington
B2067
Lympne
A261
Waterm
Metropole Galleries
OF
Bilsington
Royal Military Canal
Port Lympne
Seabrook
Sandgate
Monument
West Hythe
HYTHE
STRAIT
Ruckinge
Palmarsh
DANGER AREA
Lathe Barn
Donkey Street
Newchurch
Burmarsh
A259
ROMNEY MARSH
Dymchurch
Romney, Hythe & Dymchurch Railway
Martello Tower
St Mary in the Marsh
St Mary's Bay
Old Romney
New Romney
Littlestone-on-Sea
B2071
East Road
Greatstone-on-Sea
B2075
LONDON ASHFORD (Lydd)
Lydd
Town
Denge
Marsh
Lydd-on-Sea
Lifeboat Station
AREA
Power Station
Dungeness
Road
Old
DUNGENESS
CHANNEL
E
F
G
H
1
2
3
4
5
10
20
30
40
50
100

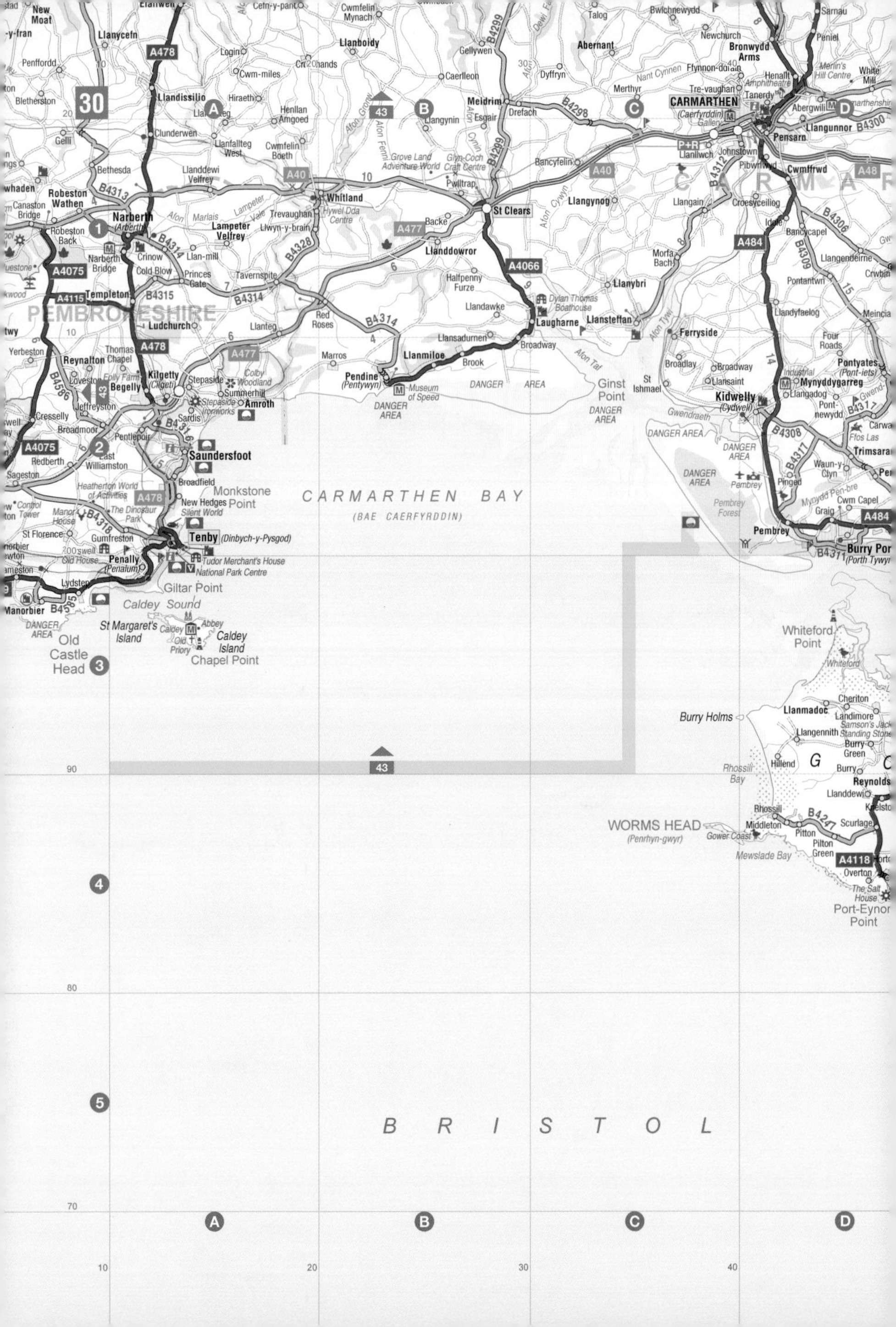
30
New Moat
Llanycefn
A478
Penffordd
Login
Cwm-miles
Llanboidy
Cwmfelin Mynach
Gellywen
Talog
Abernant
Bwlchnewydd
Newchurch
Bronwydd Arms
Sarnau
Peniel
Bletherston
Llandissilio
A
Hiraeth
Henllan Amgoed
43
B
Llangynin
Caerlleon
Meidrim
Drefach
Esgair
Dyffryn
Merthyr
C
Nant Cynnen
Ffynnon-ddrain
Tre-vaughan
CARMARTHEN
(Caerfyrddin)
Henallt
Amphitheatre
Merlin's Hill Centre
White Mill
Tanerdy
Abergwili
D
Llangunnor
B4300
Pensarn
Gelli
Clunderwen
Llanfallteg West
Cwmfelin Boeth
Afon Fenni
Grove Land Adventure World
Glyn-Coch Craft Centre
B4299
B4298
Bancyfelin
A40
P+R
Llanllwch
Johnstown
Pibwrlwyd
Cwmffrwd
A48
CARMA
Bethesda
Llanddewi Velfrey
A40
10
Pwlltrap
Robeston Wathen
B4313
Whitland
Hywel Dda Centre
St Clears
Afon Cywyn
Llangynog
Llangain
B4312
Croesyceiliog
Canaston Bridge
Narberth
(Arberth)
1
Afon Marlais
Lampeter Vale
Trevaughan
Llwyn-y-brain
Backe
Idole
Bancycapel
B4306
Robeston Back
Lampeter Velfrey
A477
A484
B4309
Llangendeirne
Narberth Bridge
Crinow
B4314
Llan-mill
B4328
Llanddowror
A4066
Morfa Bach
Crwbin
A4075
Cold Blow
Princes Gate
Tavernspite
6
Halfpenny Furze
Llanybri
Pontantwn
A4115
Templeton
B4315
B4314
7
Llandawke
Dylan Thomas Boathouse
15
PEMBROKESHIRE
Ludchurch
Red Roses
B4314
Laugharne
Llansteffan
Afon Tywi
Llandyfaelog
Meinciau
Llanteg
Ferryside
Four Roads
Yerbeston
Thomas Chapel
A478
A477
Marros
Llansadurnen
Broadway
Reynalton
Colby Woodland
Llanmiloe
Brook
Afon Taf
Broadlay
Broadway
Pontyates
(Pont-iets)
Loveston
Folly Farm
Kilgetty
(Cilgeti)
Stepaside
Pendine
(Pentywyn)
Museum of Speed
Llansaint
Industrial
Mynyddygarreg
B4586
Begelly
43
Summerhill
Stepaside Ironworks
Amroth
DANGER AREA
DANGER AREA
Ginst Point
DANGER AREA
St Ishmael
Kidwelly
(Cydweli)
Llangadog
Pont-newydd
Jeffreyston
Cresselly
Sardis
Gwendraeth
B4317
Broadmoor
Pentlepoir
B4316
DANGER AREA
B4308
Carway
Ffos Las
A4075
2
East Williamston
Saundersfoot
DANGER AREA
B4317
Trimsaran
Redberth
Waun-y-Clyn
Sageston
Broadfield
Monkstone Point
DANGER AREA
Pembrey
Pinged
Mynydd Pen-bre
Cwm Capel
Heatherton World of Activities
A478
CARMARTHEN BAY
(BAE CAERFYRDDIN)
Pembrey Forest
Graig
Control Tower
Manor House
B4318
The Dinosaur Park
New Hedges
Silent World
A484
St Florence
Gumfreston
Tenby (Dinbych-y-Pysgod)
Pembrey
Burry Port
(Porth Tywyn)
B4311
Penally
(Penalum)
Tudor Merchant's House
National Park Centre
Old House
Lydstep
Giltar Point
Manorbier
B4585
Caldey Sound
DANGER AREA
St Margaret's Island
Caldey
Abbey
Old Priory
Caldey Island
Chapel Point
Old Castle Head
3
Whiteford Point
Whiteford
Cheriton
Llanmadoc
Landimore
Burry Holms
Llangennith
Samson's Jack Standing Stone
Burry Green
Hillend
G
Rhossili Bay
Burry
Reynoldston
90
43
Llanddewi
Knelston
Rhossili
WORMS HEAD
(Penrhyn-gwyr)
Middleton
B4247
Scurlage
Gower Coast
Pitton
Pilton Green
Mewslade Bay
A4118
Horton
Overton
4
The Salt House
Port-Eynon Point
80
5
B R I S T O L
70
A
B
C
D
10
20
30
40

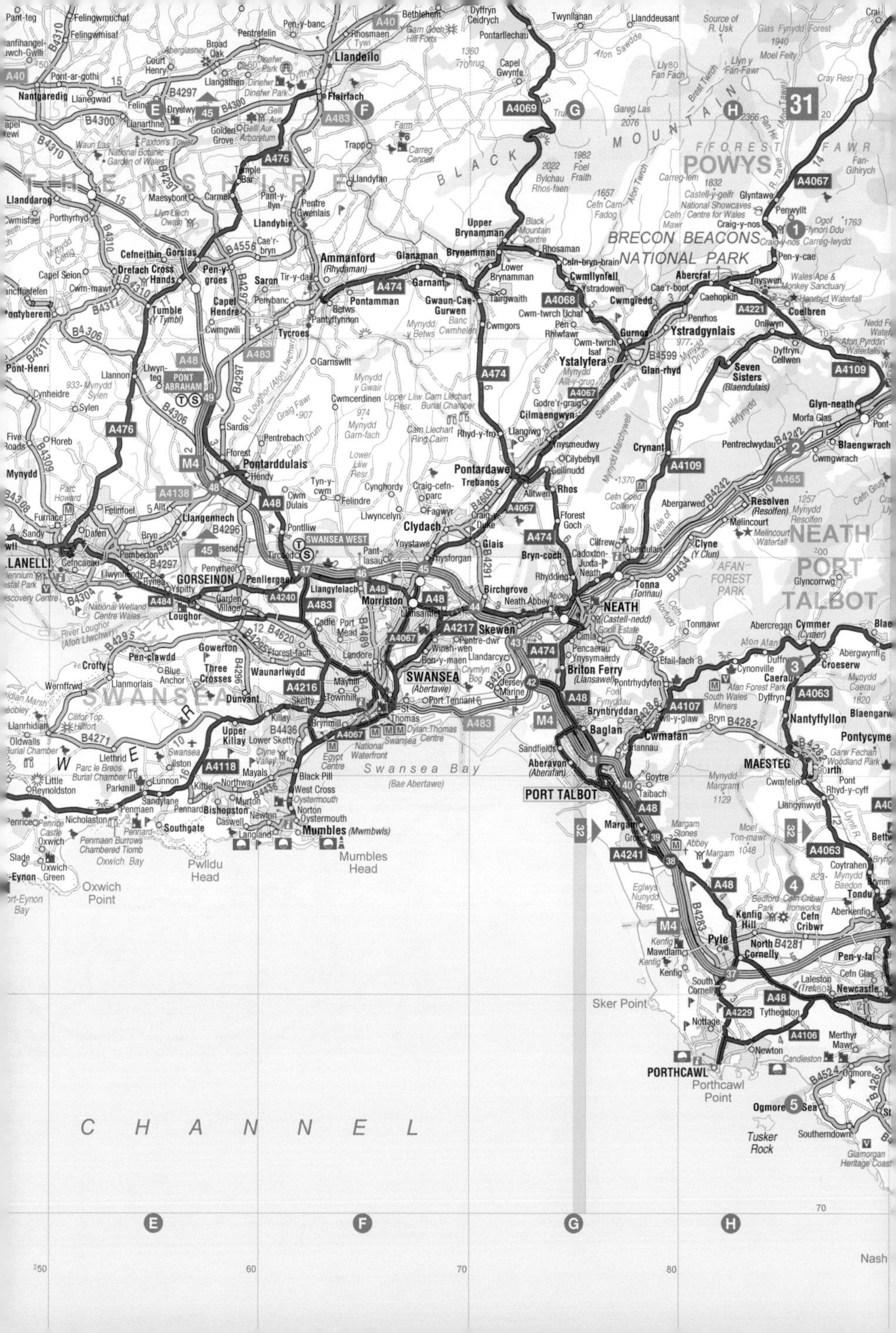

31
POWYS
BRECON BEACONS NATIONAL PARK
BLACK MOUNTAIN
FFOREST FAWR
NEATH PORT TALBOT
SWANSEA
CHANNEL
Llandeilo
Ammanford
Pontarddulais
Pontardawe
Ystalyfera
Ystradgynlais
Gorseinon
LLANELLI
Loughor
Morriston
SWANSEA
Skewen
NEATH
Briton Ferry
PORT TALBOT
MAESTEG
Pyle
PORTHCAWL
Mumbles
Swansea Bay
Oxwich Bay
Pwlldu Head
Mumbles Head
Porthcawl Point
Sker Point
Tusker Rock
E
F
G
H
50
60
70
80

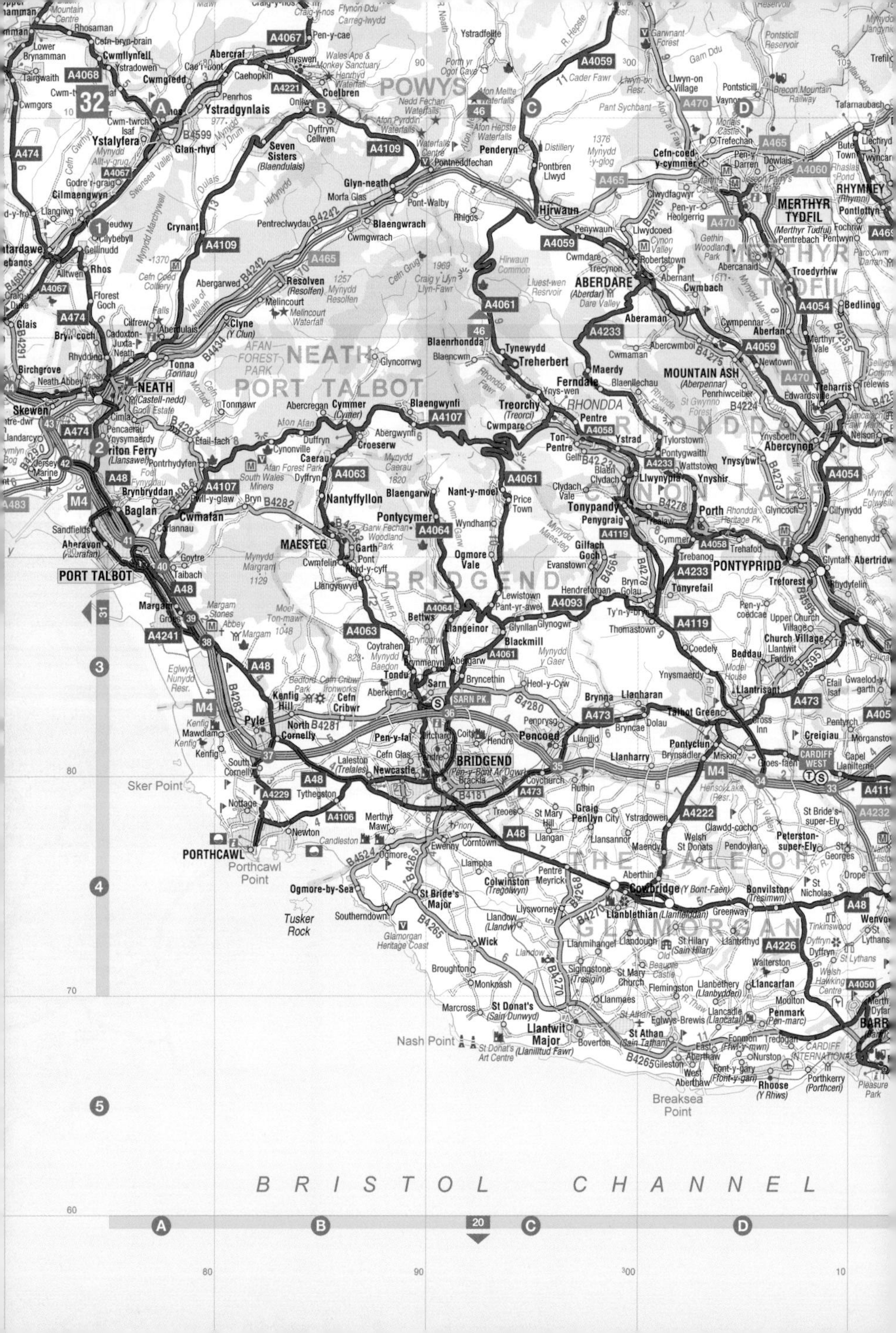
32
31
20
A
B
C
D
1
2
3
4
5
80
90
300
10
70
60
POWYS
NEATH
PORT TALBOT
BRIDGEND
RHONDDA
CYNON TAFF
MERTHYR
TYDFIL
THE VALE OF
GLAMORGAN
BRISTOL CHANNEL
NEATH
(Castell-nedd)
PORT TALBOT
MAESTEG
BRIDGEND
(Pen-y-Bont Ar Ogwr)
PORTHCAWL
ABERDARE
(Aberdar)
MOUNTAIN ASH
(Aberpennar)
PONTYPRIDD
MERTHYR
TYDFIL
(Merthyr Tudful)
RHYMNEY
(Rhymni)
Ystradgynlais
Ystalyfera
Glan-rhyd
Seven
Sisters
(Blaendulais)
Coelbren
Abercraf
Cwmllynfell
Lower
Brynamman
Rhosaman
Cefn-bryn-brain
Ystradowen
Cwmgiedd
Tairgwaith
Cwmgors
Cwm-twrch
Isaf
Godre'r-graig
Cilmaengwyn
Llangiwg
Rhos
Alltwen
Gellinudd
Cilybebyll
Fforest
Goch
Glais
Birchgrove
Neath Abbey
Skewen
Llandarcy
Jersey
Marine
Briton Ferry
(Llansawel)
Baglan
Sandfields
Aberavon
(Aberafan)
Cwmafan
Taibach
Goytre
Margam
Kenfig
Hill
Pyle
North
Cornelly
South
Cornelly
Sker Point
Nottage
Porthcawl
Point
Newton
Tythegston
Laleston
(Trelales)
Newcastle
Cefn Glas
Pen-y-fai
Cefn
Cribwr
Aberkenfig
Sarn
Tondu
Coytrahen
Bettws
Llangeinor
Blackmill
Glynllan
Glynogwr
Pant-yr-awel
Lewistown
Ogmore
Vale
Nant-y-moel
Price
Town
Wyndham
Pontycymer
Blaengarw
Nantyffyllon
Caerau
Croeserw
Cymmer
(Cymer)
Abercregan
Blaengwynfi
Abergwynfi
Duffryn
Cynonville
Pontrhydyfen
Efail-fach
Tonmawr
Tonna
(Tonnau)
Cadoxton-
Juxta-
Neath
Rhydding
Bryn-coch
Cilfrew
Aberdulais
Clyne
(Y Clun)
Resolven
(Resolfen)
Melincourt
Abergarwed
Crynant
Glyn-neath
Morfa Glas
Pont-Walby
Pontneddfechan
Rhigos
Blaengwrach
Cwmgwrach
Pentreclwydau
Glyncorrwg
Blaenrhondda
Blaencwm
Tynewydd
Treherbert
Treorchy
(Treorci)
Cwmparc
Ton-
Pentre
Pentre
Ystrad
Ferndale
Maerdy
Blaenllechau
Tylorstown
Pontygwaith
Wattstown
Ynyshir
Llwynypia
Tonypandy
Clydach
Vale
Penygraig
Porth
Trealaw
Cymmer
Trehafod
Trebanog
Tonyrefail
Gilfach
Goch
Evanstown
Hendreforgan
Bryn
Golau
Ty'n-y-bryn
Thomastown
Coedely
Beddau
Llantrisant
Talbot Green
Llanharan
Brynna
Llanharry
Pontyclun
Miskin
Groes-faen
Creigiau
Pencoed
Coychurch
Heol-y-Cyw
Bryncethin
Brynmenyn
Abergarw
Coity
Hendre
Brackla
Treoes
St Mary
Hill
Graig
Penllyn
Llangan
Ystradowen
Cowbridge
(Y Bont-Faen)
Llanblethian
Aberthin
Maendy
Welsh
St Donats
Pendoylan
Clawdd-coch
Peterston-
super-Ely
St Bride's-
super-Ely
Bonvilston
(Tresimwn)
St
Nicholas
Greenway
Llantrithyd
Walterston
Llancarfan
Moulton
Penmark
(Pen-marc)
Rhoose
(Y Rhws)
Porthkerry
(Porthceri)
Fonmon
East
Aberthaw
West
Aberthaw
Gileston
Breaksea
Point
St Athan
(Sain Tathan)
Eglwys-Brewis
Llantwit
Major
(Llanilltud Fawr)
Boverton
St Donat's
(Sain Dunwyd)
Marcross
Nash Point
Monknash
Broughton
Wick
Llandow
(Llandw)
Llysworney
Colwinston
(Tregolwyn)
Pentre
Meyrick
St Bride's
Major
Southerndown
Ogmore-by-Sea
Ogmore
Ewenny
Corntown
Llampha
Merthyr
Mawr
Candleston
Tusker
Rock
Glamorgan
Heritage Coast
Sigingstone
(Tresigin)
St Mary
Church
Flemingston
Llanbethery
(Llanbydderi)
Llanmaes
Llanmihangel
Llandough
St Hilary
(Sain Hilari)
Hirwaun
Penywaun
Cwmdare
Trecynon
Llwydcoed
Robertstown
Abernant
Cwmbach
Aberaman
Cwmaman
Abercwmboi
Penrhiwceiber
Abercynon
Ynysybwl
Ynysboeth
Treharris
Edwardsville
Aberfan
Troedyrhiw
Abercanaid
Pentrebach
Bedlinog
Penderyn
Pontbren
Llwyd
Cefn-coed-
y-cymmer
Pontsticill
Vaynor
Trefechan
Pen-y-
Darren
Dowlais
Llwyn-on
Village
Ystradfellte
Penrhos
Caehopkin
Onllwyn
Dyffryn
Cellwen
Pen-y-cae
Ynyswen
Craig-y-nos
Glyntaff
Treforest
Rhydyfelin
Church Village
Llantwit
Fardre
Efail
Isaf
Cross
Inn
Capel
Llanilterne
St
Georges
Drope
Wenvoe
St
Lythans
Dyffryn
Cilfynydd
Glyncoch
Senghenydd
Bute
Town
Llechryd
Tafarnaubach
Pontlottyn
Trefil
Nelson
Upper Church
Village
Pen-y-
coedcae
Bryncae
Dolau
Brynsadler
Llanilid
Ruthin
City
Llansannor
Llanmaes
Ynysmaerdy
M4
A48
A465
A470
A4059
A4061
A4063
A4107
A4109
A4067
A4068
A474
A4233
A4058
A4119
A4093
A473
A4222
A4226
A4229
A4106
A4054
A4060
A4221
A4241
A4064
CARDIFF
WEST
SARN PK.
CARDIFF
INTERNATIONAL

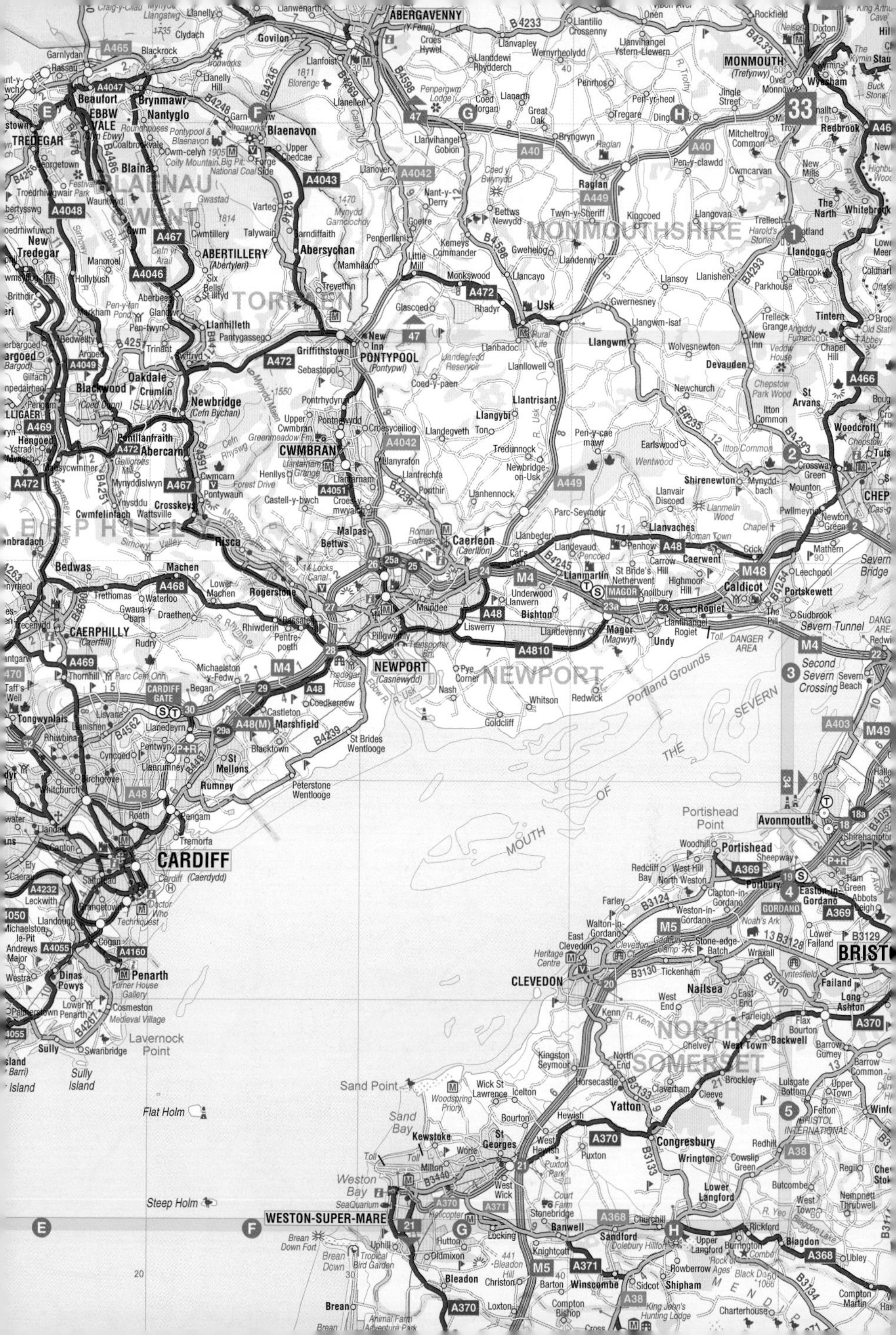
ABERGAVENNY
(Y Fenni)
Govilon
Clydach
Llanelly
Blackrock
Garnlydan
Beaufort
EBBW VALE
(Glyn Ebwy)
Brynmawr
Nantyglo
Blaenavon
Blaina
TREDEGAR
Georgetown
BLAENAU GWENT
Cwm
Cwmtillery
ABERTILLERY
(Abertyleri)
Abersychan
Talywain
Varteg
Garndiffaith
New Tredegar
Manmoel
Hollybush
Markham
Pen-twyn
Llanhilleth
Pantygasseg
Trinant
Oakdale
Crumlin
Blackwood
(Coed Duon)
ISLWYN
Newbridge
(Cefn Bychan)
Pontllanfraith
Abercarn
Hengoed
Maesycwmmer
Cwmcarn
Pontywaun
Crosskeys
Wattsville
Cwmfelinfach
Ynysddu
Risca
Bedwas
Machen
Trethomas
Lower Machen
Rogerstone
CAERPHILLY
(Caerffili)
Rudry
Draethen
Thornhill
Michaelston-y-Fedw
Began
CARDIFF GATE
Lisvane
Llanishen
Tongwynlais
Rhiwbina
Cyncoed
Pentwyn
Llanrumney
St Mellons
Rumney
Whitchurch
Birchgrove
Roath
Pengam
Tremorfa
CARDIFF
(Caerdydd)
Canton
Leckwith
Grangetown
Llandough
Cogan
Penarth
Dinas Powys
Lower Penarth
Cosmeston
Medieval Village
Sully
Swanbridge
Lavernock Point
Sully Island
Flat Holm
Steep Holm
TORFAEN
PONTYPOOL
(Pontypŵl)
Griffithstown
Sebastopol
New Inn
Trevethin
Pontrhydyrun
Upper Cwmbran
Pontnewydd
CWMBRAN
Croesyceiliog
Llantarnam
Henllys
Castell-y-bwch
Malpas
Bettws
Caerleon
(Caerllion)
NEWPORT
(Casnewydd)
Maindee
Pillgwenlly
Liswerry
Bassaleg
Rhiwderin
Castleton
Marshfield
Coedkernew
St Brides Wentlooge
Peterstone Wentlooge
Pye Corner
Nash
Goldcliff
Whitson
Redwick
Bishton
Llanwern
Underwood
Llanmartin
Magor
(Magwyr)
Undy
Rogiet
Caldicot
Portskewett
Caerwent
Penhow
Llanvaches
Llandevaud
Parc-Seymour
Shirenewton
Mynydd-bach
Mounton
Pwllmeyric
Crossway Green
Mathern
Sudbrook
Severn Tunnel
Second Severn Crossing
Severn Beach
Severn Bridge
Portland Grounds
THE SEVERN
MOUTH OF
Llanfrechfa
Ponthir
Llanhennock
Tredunnock
Llangybi
Llantrisant
Newbridge-on-Usk
Llandegveth
Coed-y-paen
Llanbadoc
Usk
Llangwm
Llansoy
Llanishen
Gwernesney
Llancayo
Rhadyr
Monkswood
Glascoed
Little Mill
Mamhilad
Goetre
Penperlleni
Kemeys Commander
Llanover
Llanfoist
Llanellen
Llanvihangel Gobion
Bryngwyn
Raglan
Twyn-y-Sheriff
Kingcoed
Llangovan
Llandenny
Gwehelog
MONMOUTHSHIRE
MONMOUTH
(Trefynwy)
Wyesham
Redbrook
Mitcheltroy Common
Penallt
Trellech
Llandogo
Catbrook
Parkhouse
Tintern
Chapel Hill
Devauden
Wolvesnewton
Newchurch
Itton Common
St Arvans
Woodcroft
Earlswood
Wentwood
Llanvair Discoed
Tregare
Great Oak
Llanarth
Coed Morgan
Clytha
Llantilio Crossenny
Llanvapley
Wernyrheolydd
Llanddewi Rhydderch
Llanvihangel Ystern-Llewern
Penrhos
Pen-yr-heol
Jingle Street
Rockfield
Dixton
Pen-y-clawdd
Cwmcarvan
New Mills
The Narth
Whitebrook
Portishead Point
Portishead
Avonmouth
Woodhill
Redcliff Bay
West Hill
North Weston
Sheepway
Portbury
Easton-in-Gordano
Pill
Ham Green
Abbots Leigh
Clapton-in-Gordano
Weston-in-Gordano
Walton-in-Gordano
Farley
East Clevedon
Clevedon
CLEVEDON
Tickenham
Nailsea
Wraxall
Failand
Long Ashton
Flax Bourton
Backwell
West Town
NORTH SOMERSET
Chelvey
Kenn
Kingston Seymour
North End
Horsecastle
Claverham
Brockley
Yatton
Cleeve
Congresbury
Wrington
Cowslip Green
Redhill
Felton
Lower Langford
Upper Langford
Burrington
Blagdon
Ubley
Rickford
Churchill
Sandford
Banwell
Winscombe
Sidcot
Shipham
Charterhouse
Compton Martin
Compton Bishop
Barton
Christon
Loxton
Bleadon
Hutton
Oldmixon
Locking
West Wick
St Georges
Worle
Milton
Kewstoke
Sand Bay
Sand Point
Wick St Lawrence
Icelton
Bourton
Hewish
Puxton
Weston Bay
WESTON-SUPER-MARE
Uphill
Brean Down
Brean
Butcombe
BRISTOL INTERNATIONAL
M4
M5
M48
M49
A48
A48(M)
A40
A4042
A4043
A449
A472
A466
A469
A467
A465
A468
A4810
A369
A370
A371
A368
A38
B4245
B4236
B4235
B4293
B3124
B3128
B3130
B3133
B3134

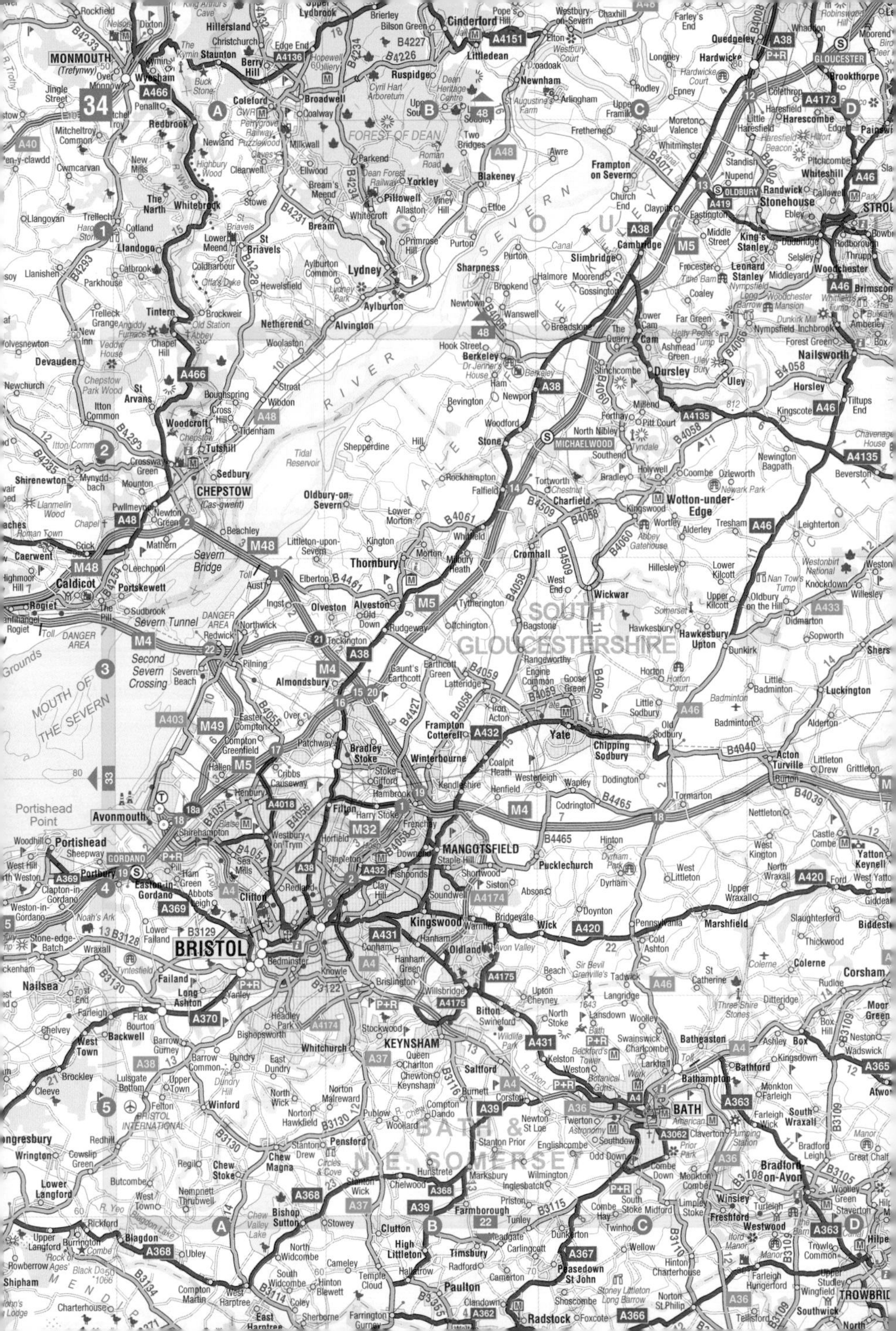
34
MONMOUTH
(Trefynwy)
Wyesham
Staunton
Coleford
Broadwell
Cinderford
Littledean
FOREST OF DEAN
Cyril Hart Arboretum
Dean Heritage Centre
Newnham
Arlingham
Quedgeley
Hardwicke
GLOUCESTER
Brookthorpe
Harescombe
Painswick
Frampton on Severn
Stonehouse
Randwick
Whiteshill
STROUD
Blakeney
Yorkley
Pillowell
Parkend
Bream
Lydney
Aylburton
Alvington
Whitebrook
Llandogo
St Briavels
Tintern
Chepstow Park Wood
St Arvans
Woodcroft
Tutshill
Sedbury
CHEPSTOW
(Cas-gwent)
Shirenewton
Caerwent
Caldicot
Portskewett
Rogiet
Severn Tunnel
Severn Bridge
Second Severn Crossing
MOUTH OF THE SEVERN
RIVER SEVERN
Sharpness
Slimbridge
Cambridge
Berkeley
Dursley
Cam
Uley
Nailsworth
Horsley
Kingscote
Woodchester
Leonard Stanley
King's Stanley
Stone
Wotton-under-Edge
Charfield
Cromhall
Thornbury
Oldbury-on-Severn
Alveston
Olveston
Wickwar
Hawkesbury Upton
SOUTH GLOUCESTERSHIRE
Almondsbury
Severn Beach
Pilning
Patchway
Bradley Stoke
Yate
Chipping Sodbury
Frampton Cotterell
Winterbourne
Acton Turville
Badminton
Luckington
Avonmouth
Portishead
Portishead Point
Portbury
Shirehampton
Filton
MANGOTSFIELD
Pucklechurch
Kingswood
Oldland
Wick
Marshfield
Colerne
Corsham
Box
BRISTOL
Bedminster
Clifton
Long Ashton
Nailsea
Backwell
Failand
Flax Bourton
Whitchurch
KEYNSHAM
Saltford
Bitton
BATH
Bathampton
Batheaston
Bathford
Combe Down
Bradford-on-Avon
Trowbridge
Freshford
Westwood
Winsley
BATH & N.E. SOMERSET
BRISTOL INTERNATIONAL
Winford
Chew Magna
Chew Stoke
Pensford
Bishop Sutton
Blagdon
Wrington
Congresbury
Lower Langford
Clutton
High Littleton
Timsbury
Paulton
Farmborough
Peasedown St John
Radstock
Dunkerton
West Harptree
East Harptree
Shipham
M4
M5
M32
M48
M49
A38
A4
A46
A420
A431
A432
A466
A48
A368
A369
A370
A37
A39
A36
A363
A367
A4174
A4175
B4058
B4465
B4040
B3130
B3115
A B C D
1 2 3 4 5
33
48

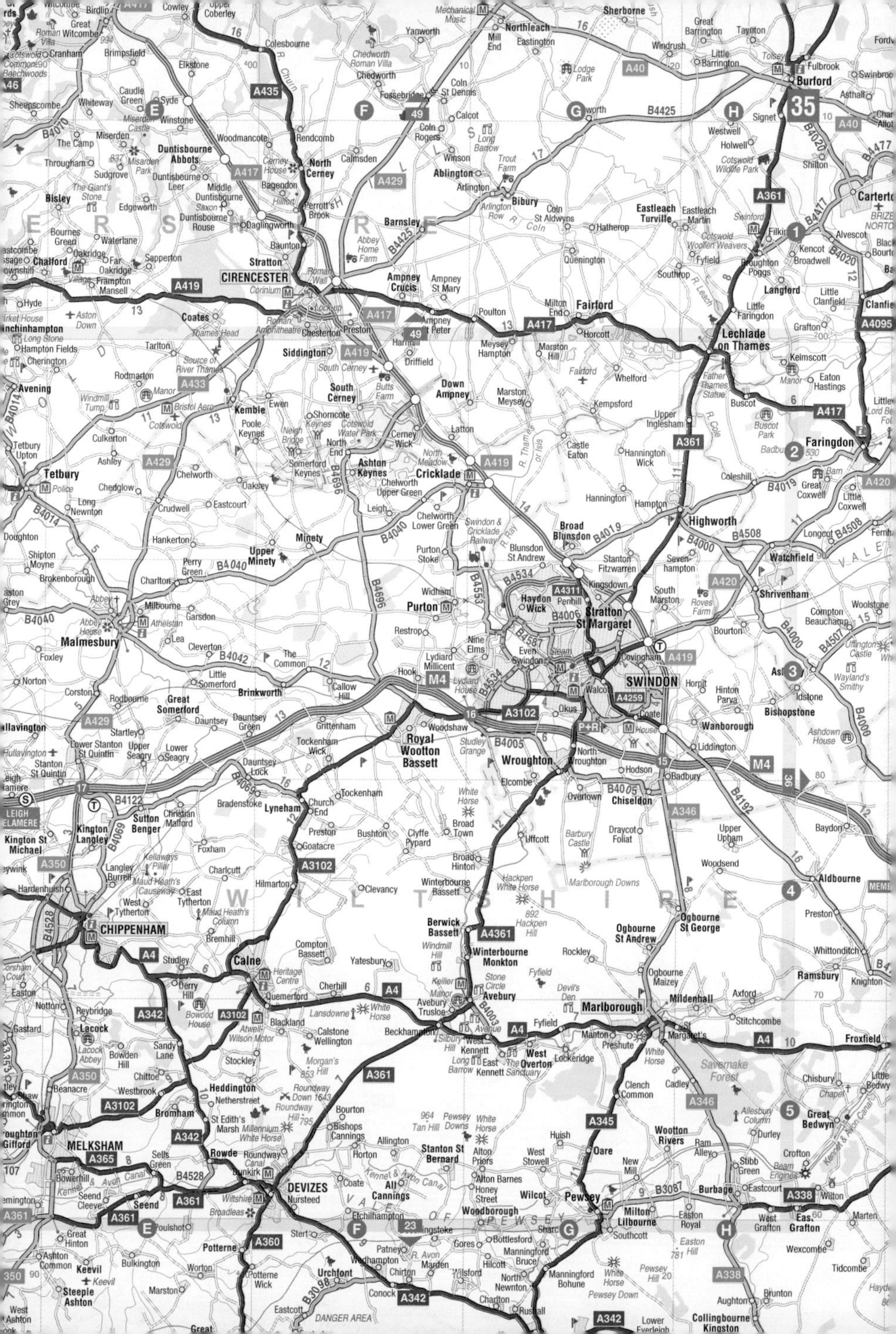

Birdlip
Cowley
Coberley
Great Witcombe
Cranham
Brimpsfield
Colesbourne
Elkstone
Caudle Green
Syde
Whiteway
Winstone
Miserden
Sheepscombe
The Camp
Woodmancote
Duntisbourne Abbots
Duntisbourne Leer
Middle Duntisbourne
Duntisbourne Rouse
Daglingworth
Throughham
Sudgrove
The Giant's Stone
Bisley
Edgeworth
Bournes Green
Waterlane
Oakridge
Far Oakridge
Sapperton
Chalford
Frampton Mansell
Rendcomb
North Cerney
Calmsden
Bagendon
Perrott's Brook
Baunton
Stratton
CIRENCESTER
Corinium
Chedworth Roman Villa
Chedworth
Fossebridge
Yanworth
Mechanical Music
Northleach
Mill End
Eastington
Sherborne
Great Barrington
Taynton
Windrush
Little Barrington
Burford
Fulbrook
Swinbrook
Asthall
Signet
Westwell
Holwell
Cotswold Wildlife Park
Shilton
Carterton
Brize Norton
Alvescot
Kencot
Broadwell
Filkins
Swinford
Broughton Poggs
Langford
Little Clanfield
Clanfield
Grafton
Kelmscott
Eaton Hastings
Buscot
Buscot Park
Faringdon
Coln St Dennis
Calcot
Coln Rogers
Long Barrow
Trout Farm
Winson
Ablington
Arlington
Arlington Row
Bibury
Coln St Aldwyns
Hatherop
Eastleach Turville
Eastleach Martin
Cotswold Woollen Weavers
Fyfield
Quenington
Southrop
Barnsley
Abbey Home Farm
Ampney Crucis
Ampney St Mary
Ampney St Peter
Harnhill
Driffield
Poulton
Milton End
Fairford
Horcott
Meysey Hampton
Marston Hill
Lechlade on Thames
Little Faringdon
Father Thames Statue
Whelford
Kempsford
Upper Inglesham
Coates
Thames Head
Roman Amphitheatre
Chesterton
Preston
Siddington
South Cerney
Butts Farm
Down Ampney
Marston Meysey
Tarlton
Source of River Thames
Hyde
Aston Down
Market House
Minchinhampton
Long Stone
Hampton Fields
Cherington
Rodmarton
Avening
Windmill Tump
Bristol Aero
Kemble
Ewen
Cotswold
Poole Keynes
Shorncote
Neigh Bridge
Cotswold Water Park
Somerford Keynes
North End
Cerney Wick
Latton
Ashton Keynes
Cricklade
North Meadow
Chelworth Upper Green
Chelworth Lower Green
Leigh
Castle Eaton
Hannington Wick
Hannington
Hampton
Highworth
Coleshill
Great Coxwell
Little Coxwell
Longcot
Fernham
Culkerton
Ashley
Tetbury Upton
Tetbury
Police
Chedglow
Chelworth
Oaksey
Long Newnton
Crudwell
Eastcourt
Doughton
Hankerton
Minety
Upper Minety
Swindon & Cricklade Railway
Purton Stoke
Broad Blunsdon
Blunsdon St Andrew
Stanton Fitzwarren
Sevenhampton
Watchfield
Shipton Moyne
Perry Green
Brokenborough
Charlton
Easton Grey
Milbourne
Garsdon
Abbey House
Athelstan
Malmesbury
Lea
Foxley
Cleverton
Widham
Purton
Restrop
Haydon Wick
Penhill
Kingsdown
Stratton St Margaret
South Marston
Roves Farm
Shrivenham
Compton Beauchamp
Woolstone
Uffington Castle
Wayland's Smithy
Bourton
Nine Elms
Lydiard Millicent
Lydiard House
Even Swindon
Steam
Covingham
SWINDON
Walcot
Okus
Coate
Hook
The Common
Little Somerford
Brinkworth
Callow Hill
Norton
Corston
Rodbourne
Great Somerford
Dauntsey
Dauntsey Green
Grittenham
Woodshaw
Royal Wootton Bassett
Studley Grange
Wroughton
North Wroughton
Hodson
Badbury
Chiseldon
Liddington
Wanborough
Hinton Parva
Horpit
Idstone
Bishopstone
Ashdown House
Hullavington
Startley
Lower Stanton St Quintin
Stanton St Quintin
Upper Seagry
Lower Seagry
Tockenham Wick
Dauntsey Lock
Leigh Delamere
Bradenstoke
Lyneham
Tockenham
Church End
Elcombe
Overtown
White Horse
Broad Town
Uffcott
Barbury Castle
Draycot Foliat
Upper Upham
Baydon
Kington Langley
Sutton Benger
Christian Malford
Kington St Michael
Foxham
Preston
Goatacre
Bushton
Clyffe Pypard
Broad Hinton
Woodsend
Aldbourne
Langley Burrell
Kellaways Pillar
Maud Heath's Causeway
Charlcutt
Hilmarton
Clevancy
Winterbourne Bassett
Hackpen White Horse
Marlborough Downs
Hardenhuish
East Tytherton
West Tytherton
Maud Heath's Column
CHIPPENHAM
Bremhill
Berwick Bassett
Hackpen Hill
Ogbourne St Andrew
Ogbourne St George
Preston
Whittonditch
Compton Bassett
Yatesbury
Windmill Hill
Winterbourne Monkton
Rockley
Studley
Calne
Heritage Centre
Derry Hill
Cherhill
Stone Circle
Avebury
Keiller Manor
Fyfield
Devil's Den
Ogbourne Maizey
Ramsbury
Knighton
Axford
Easton
Notton
Reybridge
Bowood House
Quemerford
Blackland
Lansdowne
White Horse
Avebury Trusloe
Marlborough
Mildenhall
Stitchcombe
Gastard
Lacock
Lacock Abbey
Bowden Hill
Sandy Lane
Atwell-Wilson Motor
Calstone Wellington
Beckhampton
Silbury Hill
West Kennett
Long Barrow
East Kennett
The Sanctuary
West Overton
Lockeridge
Manton
Preshute
St Margaret's
Savernake Forest
Froxfield
Chittoe
Stockley
Morgan's Hill
Beanacre
Westbrook
Heddington
Roundway Down 1643
Netherstreet
Roundway Hill
Clench Common
Cadley
Chisbury
Little Bedwyn
Shaw
Bromham
St Edith's Marsh
Millennium White Horse
Bourton
Bishops Cannings
Tan Hill
Pewsey Downs
White Horse
Allesbury Column
Great Bedwyn
Broughton Gifford
MELKSHAM
Sells Green
Rowde
Roundway
Allington
Horton
Stanton St Bernard
Alton Priors
Huish
West Stowell
Oare
Wootton Rivers
Ram Alley
Durley
Crofton
Beam Engines
Bowerhill
Kennet & Avon Canal
Seend Cleeve
Seend
Dunkirk
Wiltshire
DEVIZES
Nursteed
Coate
All Cannings
Alton Barnes
Honey Street
Woodborough
Wilcot
Pewsey
New Mill
Milton Lilbourne
Burbage
Stibb Green
Eastcourt
Wilton
Broadleas
Poulshot
Great Hinton
Etchilhampton
Vale of Pewsey
Stert
Sharcott
Southcott
Easton Royal
West Grafton
East Grafton
Marten
Potterne
Bulkington
Ashton Common
Keevil
Steeple Ashton
Worton
Potterne Wick
Urchfont
Wedhampton
Patney
Chirton
Marden
Gores
Bottlesford
Manningford Bruce
Hilcott
Wilsford
North Newnton
Manningford Bohune
Pewsey Hill
Pewsey Down
Easton Hill
Wexcombe
Tidcombe
Marston
Conock
Charlton
Rushall
Eastcott
DANGER AREA
Great
Lower Everleigh
Aughton
Brunton
Collingbourne Kingston
West Ashton
WILTSHIRE
A40
A417
A419
A429
A433
A435
A361
A420
A4095
A4311
A4259
A3102
A346
A350
A4361
A342
A4
A345
A365
A360
A338
B4425
B4019
B4508
B4000
B4040
B4042
B4014
B4696
B4553
B4534
B4006
B4587
B4005
B4192
B4069
B4122
B4528
B4003
B3087
M4
LEIGH DELAMERE

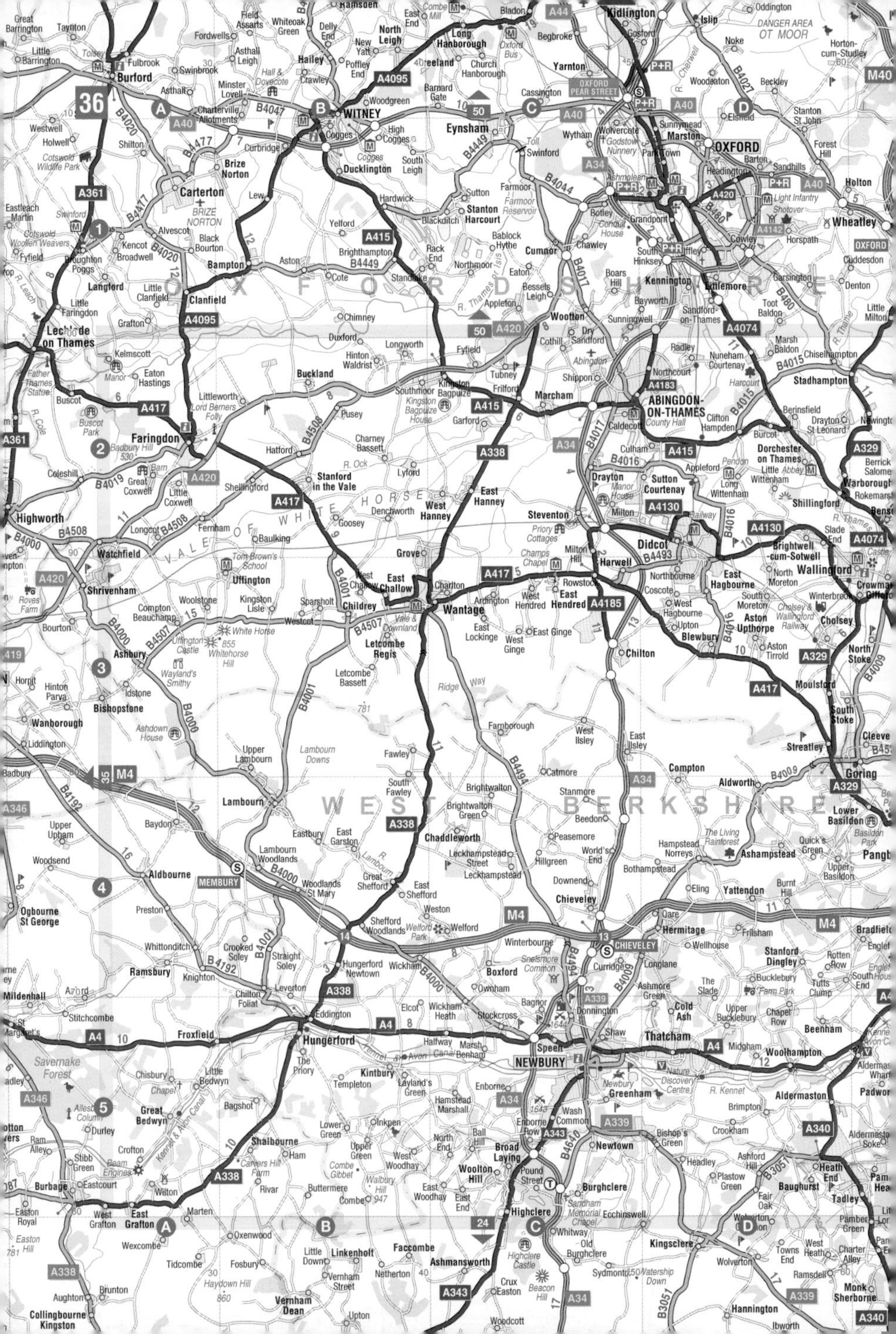

36
Great Barrington
Taynton
Little Barrington
Tolsey
Fulbrook
Burford
Field Assarts
Fordwells
Asthall Leigh
Swinbrook
Asthall
Minster Lovell
Hall & Dovecote
Charterville Allotments
Whiteoak Green
Ramsden
Delly End
New Yatt
North Leigh
East End
Combe Mill
Hailey
Poffley End
Crawley
Long Hanborough
Freeland
Church Hanborough
Oxford Bus
Bladon
Begbroke
Kidlington
Gosford
Yarnton
Islip
Oddington
DANGER AREA
OT MOOR
Noke
Horton-cum-Studley
Woodeaton
Beckley
Witney
Woodgreen
Barnard Gate
Cassington
Oxford Pear Street
Wolvercote
Godstow Nunnery
Wytham
Sunnymead
Marston
Oxford
Elsfield
Stanton St John
Forest Hill
Westwell
Holwell
Shilton
Cotswold Wildlife Park
Curbridge
Brize Norton
Cogges
High Cogges
South Leigh
Ducklington
Eynsham
Toll
Swinford
Park Town
Headington
Barton
Sandhills
Carterton
BRIZE NORTON
Eastleach Martin
Swinford
Alvescot
Lew
Hardwick
Sutton
Stanton Harcourt
Farmoor
Farmoor Reservoir
Ashmolean
Botley
Grandpont
Light Infantry
Shotover
Holton
Wheatley
Cotswold Woollen Weavers
Fyfield
Kencot
Broadwell
Black Bourton
Yelford
Blackditch
Bablock Hythe
Cumnor
Chawley
Conduit House
South Hinksey
Cowley
Horspath
Broughton Poggs
Bampton
Aston
Cote
Brighthampton
Rack End
Northmoor
Eaton
Boars Hill
Kennington
Littlemore
Garsington
Cuddesdon
Denton
Langford
Little Clanfield
Clanfield
OXFORDSHIRE
Standlake
Bessels Leigh
Appleton
R. Thames or Isis
Wootton
Bayworth
Sunningwell
Sandford-on-Thames
Toot Baldon
Little Faringdon
Grafton
Chimney
Duxford
Longworth
Fyfield
Dry Sandford
Cothill
Radley
Nuneham Courtenay
Marsh Baldon
Little Milton
Lechlade on Thames
Kelmscott
Hinton Waldrist
Tubney
Abingdon
Chiselhampton
Father Thames Statue
Manor
Eaton Hastings
Buckland
Kingston Bagpuize
Southmoor
Kingston Bagpuize House
Frilford
Shippon
Northcourt
Harcourt
Stadhampton
Buscot
R. Cole
Buscot Park
Littleworth
Lord Berners Folly
Pusey
Garford
Marcham
Abingdon-on-Thames
Caldecott
County Hall
Clifton Hampden
Berinsfield
Drayton St Leonard
Newington
Badbury Hill
Faringdon
Hatford
Charney Bassett
R. Ock
Lyford
Culham
Burcot
Dorchester on Thames
Abbey
Berrick Salome
Coleshill
Great Coxwell
Barn
Little Coxwell
Shellingford
Stanford in the Vale
East Hanney
Drayton
Manor House
Sutton Courtenay
Appleford
Long Wittenham
Little Wittenham
Warborough
Rokemarsh
Highworth
Longcot
Fernham
VALE OF WHITE HORSE
Goosey
Denchworth
West Hanney
Steventon
Priory Cottages
Milton
Didcot
Railway
Shillingford
Benson
Watchfield
Baulking
Grove
Champs Chapel
Milton Hill
Harwell
Brightwell-cum-Sotwell
Slade End
R. Thames
Castle
Shrivenham
Tom Brown's School
Uffington
West Challow
East Challow
Charlton
Rowstock
Northbourne
East Hagbourne
North Moreton
Wallingford
Crowmarsh Gifford
Roves Farm
Compton Beauchamp
Woolstone
Kingston Lisle
Sparsholt
Childrey
Wantage
Ardington
West Hendred
East Hendred
Coscote
West Hagbourne
South Moreton
Winterbrook
Bourton
Uffington Castle
White Horse
855 Whitehorse Hill
Westcot
Vale & Downland
Letcombe Regis
East Lockinge
West Ginge
East Ginge
Upton
Blewbury
Aston Upthorpe
Aston Tirrold
Cholsey & Wallingford Railway
Cholsey
Ashbury
Wayland's Smithy
Letcombe Bassett
Chilton
North Stoke
Horpit
Hinton Parva
Idstone
Bishopstone
Ridge Way
781
Moulsford
South Stoke
Wanborough
Ashdown House
Liddington
Upper Lambourn
Lambourn Downs
Fawley
Farnborough
West Ilsley
East Ilsley
Compton
Streatley
Cleeve
Goring
Aldworth
Badbury
South Fawley
Catmore
Lambourn
Brightwalton
Brightwalton Green
WEST BERKSHIRE
Stanmore
Beedon
Lower Basildon
Basildon Park
Upper Upham
Baydon
Eastbury
East Garston
Chaddleworth
Peasemore
The Living Rainforest
Hampstead Norreys
Quick's Green
Ashampstead
Pangbourne
Woodsend
Aldbourne
Lambourn Woodlands
R. Lambourn
Leckhampstead Street
Leckhampstead Thicket
Hillgreen
World's End
Bothampstead
Upper Basildon
Membury
Woodlands St Mary
Great Shefford
East Shefford
Downend
Chieveley
Eling
Yattendon
Burnt Hill
Ogbourne St George
Preston
Weston
Oare
Hermitage
Frilsham
Bradfield
Englefield
Whittonditch
Crooked Soley
Shefford Woodlands
Welford Park
Welford
Winterbourne
Chieveley
Wellhouse
Stanford Dingley
Rotten Row
Ramsbury
Straight Soley
Hungerford Newtown
Wickham
Boxford
Snelsmore Common
Curridge
Longlane
Bucklebury
Farm Park
Tutts Clump
South End
Mildenhall
Axford
Knighton
Chilton Foliat
Leverton
Ownham
Ashmore Green
The Slade
Upper Bucklebury
Chapel Row
Stitchcombe
Eddington
Elcot
Wickham Heath
Stockcross
Bagnor
Donnington
Cold Ash
Beenham
St Margaret's
Froxfield
Hungerford
Halfway
Marsh Benham
Speen
Shaw
Thatcham
Midgham
Woolhampton
Kennet & Avon Canal
Savernake Forest
The Priory
Kennet & Avon Canal
Newbury
Nature Discovery Centre
Aldermaston Wharf
Padworth
Chisbury
Little Bedwyn
Kintbury
Templeton
Layland's Green
Enborne
Newbury
Greenham
R. Kennet
Aldermaston
Allesbury Column
Great Bedwyn
Chapel
Bagshot
Hamstead Marshall
Wash Common
Brimpton
Durley
Lower Green
Inkpen
Enborne Row
Crookham
Aldermaston Soke
Ram Alley
Crofton
Beam Engines
Shalbourne
Ham
Upper Green
North End
Ball Hill
Broad Laying
Newtown
Bishop's Green
Stibb Green
Carvers Hill Farm
Combe Gibbet
West Woodhay
Headley
Ashford Hill
Heath End
Burbage
Eastcourt
Wilton
Rivar
Buttermere
Walbury Hill 947
Woolton Hill
Pound Street
Burghclere
Plastow Green
Baughurst
Tadley
Easton Royal
West Grafton
East Grafton
Marten
Combe
East Woodhay
East End
Highclere
Sandham Memorial Chapel
Ecchinswell
Fair Oak
Pamber Heath
Pamber Green
Easton Hill
781
Wexcombe
Oxenwood
Whitway
Old Burghclere
Kingsclere
Wolverton Common
West Heath
Tidcombe
Fosbury
Little Down
Linkenholt
Faccombe
Ashmansworth
Highclere Castle
Towns End
Charter Alley
Haydown Hill 860
Vernham Street
Netherton
Crux Easton
Beacon Hill
Sydmonton
Watership Down
Wolverton
Ramsdell
Monk Sherborne
Aughton
Brunton
Vernham Dean
Hannington
Collingbourne Kingston
Upton
Woodcott
Ibworth
M40
M4
A40
A44
A4095
A361
A4020
B4020
B4047
B4477
B4417
A415
B4449
B4044
B4017
A34
A420
A4142
A4074
B480
B4015
A4183
A417
B4508
B4019
B4000
A338
B4016
A4130
A329
B4001
B4493
A4185
B4016
B4507
B4009
B4494
B4192
A346
A4
A339
A343
B4640
B3051
A340
B3051

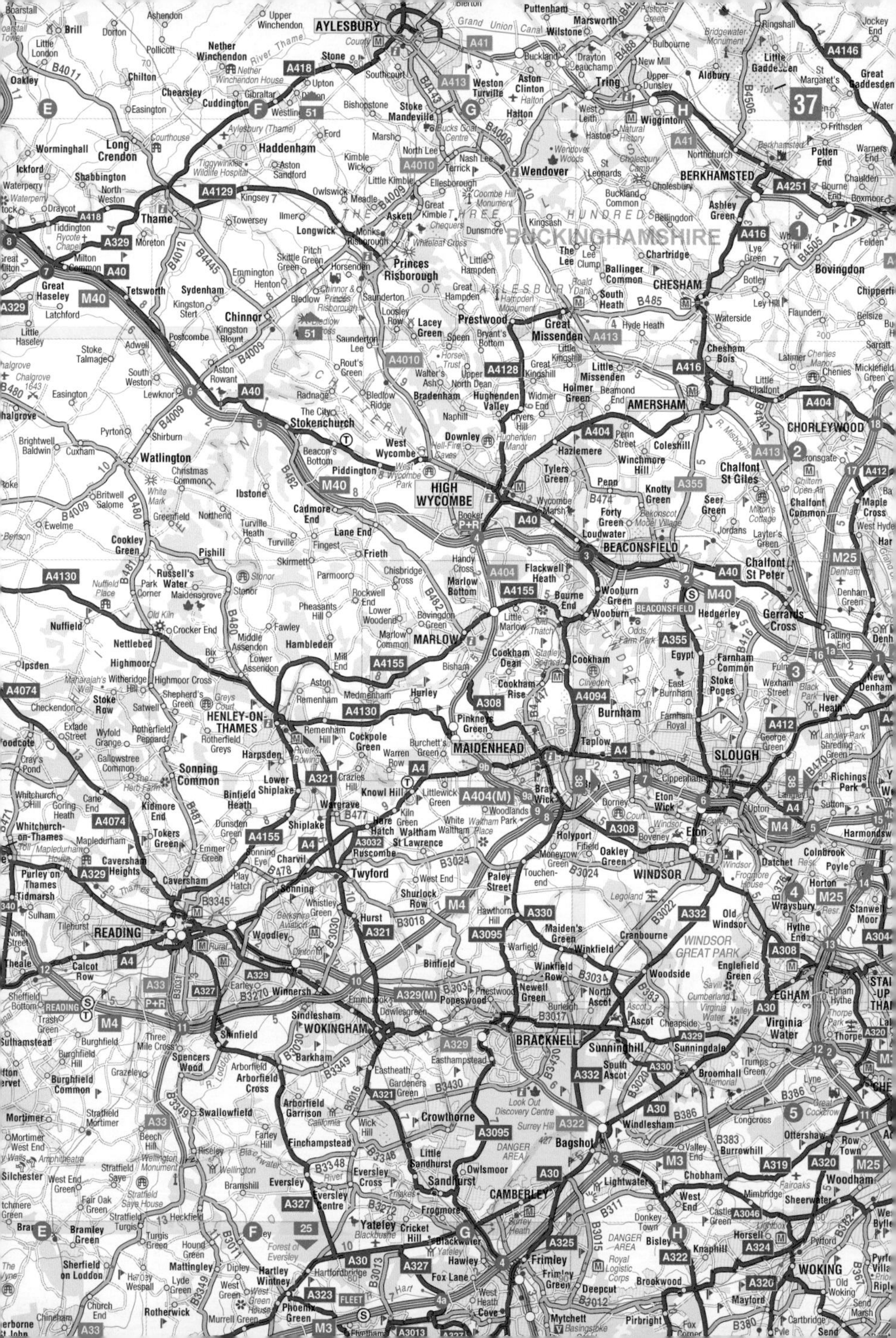

37
Boarstall
Brill
Ashendon
Upper Winchendon
AYLESBURY
Bierton
Puttenham
Marsworth
Pitstone
Ringshall
Jockey End
Grand Union Canal
Wilstone
Bridgewater Monument
Dorton
Nether Winchendon
River Thame
Little London
Pollicott
A418
Stone
A41
Buckland
Drayton Beauchamp
Bulbourne
New Mill
Little Gaddesden
A4146
Oakley
B4011
Chilton
Chearsley
Southcourt
A413
Weston Turville
Aston Clinton
Tring
Upper Dunsley
Aldbury
St Margaret's
Great Gaddesden
Cuddington
Gibraltar
Upton
Halton
Wigginton
Water
E
F
G
H
Easington
Westlington
Bishopstone
Stoke Mandeville
West Leith
Frithsden
Long Crendon
Haddenham
Ford
Bucks Goat Centre
Hastoe
Natural History
Worminghall
Aylesbury (Thame)
Marsh
North Lee
Nash Lee
B4009
Northchurch
Berkhamsted
Potten End
Warners End
Ickford
Shabbington
Tiggywinkles Wildlife Hospital
Aston Sandford
Kimble Wick
A4010
Terrick
Wendover
Wendover Woods
St Leonards
Cholesbury Camp
BERKHAMSTED
Chaulden
Waterperry
North Weston
Little Kimble
Ellesborough
Cholesbury
A4251
Bourne End
Boxmoor
A4129
Kingsey
Owlswick
Meadle
Great Kimble
Coombe Hill Monument
Buckland Common
Ashley Green
Draycot
A418
Thame
Towersey
Ilmer
Askett
Chequers
Kingsash
HUNDREDS
Bellingdon
Tiddington
Moreton
Longwick
Monks Risborough
Whiteleaf Cross
Dunsmore
BUCKINGHAMSHIRE
A416
Felden
Rycote Chapel
A329
B4012
B4445
Pitch Green
Princes Risborough
Little Hampden
The Lee
Lee Clump
Chartridge
Lye Green
Bovingdon
Milton Common
Emmington
Skittle Green
Horsenden
Ballinger Common
CHESHAM
Botley
Great Haseley
A40
Tetsworth
Henton
Chinnor & Princes Risborough
Great Hampden
Roald Dahl
South Heath
B485
Ley Hill
Chipperfield
M40
Sydenham
Bledlow
Saunderton
Hampden Monument
Latchford
Kingston Stert
Chinnor
Loosley Row
Lacey Green
Prestwood
Great Missenden
Hyde Heath
Waterside
Flaunden
Belsize
Little Haseley
Postcombe
Kingston Blount
Bledlow Cross
Speen
Bryant's Bottom
A413
Chesham Bois
Sarratt
Stoke Talmage
Adwell
Saunderton Lee
Latimer
Chenies Manor
Chalgrove
B4009
Rout's Green
A4010
Horse Trust
A4128
Little Kingshill
Great Kingshill
Little Missenden
Chenies
Mickelfield Green
Chalgrove 1643
South Weston
Aston Rowant
Walter's Ash
Upper North Dean
Holmer Green
Beamond End
Little Chalfont
B480
Easington
Lewknor
A40
Radnage
Bledlow Ridge
Bradenham
Hughenden Valley
Widmer End
AMERSHAM
A404
Chalgrove
Pyrton
The City
Stokenchurch
Naphill
Cryers Hill
Hughenden Manor
Penn Street
R. Misbourne
CHORLEYWOOD
Brightwell Baldwin
Cuxham
Shirburn
Watlington
Beacon's Bottom
West Wycombe
Downley
Hell-Fire Caves
Hazlemere
Coleshill
A413
Croxley Green
Christmas Common
Piddington
West Wycombe Park
Tylers Green
Winchmore Hill
Chalfont St Giles
A412
Britwell Salome
White Mark
Ibstone
HIGH WYCOMBE
Penn
Knotty Green
Seer Green
Chiltern Open Air
Maple Cross
B4009
Cadmore End
Wycombe Marsh
B474
A355
Chalfont Common
West Hyde
Ewelme
Greenfield
Northend
Booker
P+R
Lane End
A40
Forty Green
Bekonscot Model Village
Milton's Cottage
Benson
Cookley Green
Turville Heath
Turville
Fingest
Loudwater
Jordans
Layter's Green
Skirmett
Frieth
Handy Cross
Flackwell Heath
BEACONSFIELD
Chalfont St Peter
M25
Pishill
Russell's Water
Stonor
Parmoor
Chisbridge Cross
A404
Denham
A4130
Nuffield Place
Park Corner
Maidensgrove
Marlow Bottom
A4155
Bourne End
Wooburn Green
M40
Denham Green
Nuffield
Rockwell End
Lower Woodend
Pheasant's Hill
Bovingdon Green
Little Marlow
Wooburn
BEACONSFIELD
Hedgerley
Gerrards Cross
Old Kiln
Crocker End
Fawley
Odds Farm Park
Nettlebed
Middle Assendon
Hambleden
MARLOW
Marlow Common
Old Thatch
A355
Tatling End
Bix
Lower Assendon
Cookham Dean
Stanley Spencer
Cookham
Egypt
Farnham Common
Ipsden
Highmoor
Highmoor Cross
Mill End
A4155
Bisham
New Denham
Maharajah's Well
Witheridge Hill
Aston
Medmenham
Cookham Rise
Cliveden
East Burnham
Stoke Poges
Wexham Street
Black Park
A4074
Checkendon
Stoke Row
Satwell
Shepherd's Green
Greys Court
Remenham
Hurley
A308
A4094
Iver Heath
Exlade Street
Wyfold Grange
Rotherfield Peppard
HENLEY-ON-THAMES
A4130
Burnham
Farnham Royal
A412
Langley Park
Woodcote
Rotherfield Greys
Remenham Hill
Cockpole Green
Burchett's Green
Pinkneys Green
MAIDENHEAD
Taplow
A4
George Green
Shredding Green
Cray's Pond
Gallowstree Common
Harpsden
River & Rowing
Warren Row
SLOUGH
Sonning Common
Crazies Hill
A4
Cippenham
Richings Park
Whitchurch Hill
Goring Heath
Cane End
The Herb Farm
Binfield Heath
Lower Shiplake
A321
Knowl Hill
Littlewick Green
A404(M)
Bray Wick
Dorney
Eton Wick
Langley
Kidmore End
Wargrave
B477
Kiln Green
Woodlands Park
Dorney Court
Upton
Sutton
Whitchurch-on-Thames
A4074
Tokers Green
Dunsden Green
Shiplake
Hare Hatch
White Waltham
Waltham Place
Holyport
A308
Windsor
Eton
A4
M4
Harmondsworth
Mapledurham
A4155
A4
A3032
Waltham St Lawrence
Colnbrook
Caversham Heights
Emmer Green
Sonning Eye
Charvil
Ruscombe
Moneyrow Green
Fifield
Oakley Green
Datchet
Poyle
Purley on Thames
A329
Caversham
Play Hatch
Twyford
West End
B3024
Paley Street
Touchen-end
WINDSOR
Frogmore House
Horton
Tidmarsh
B3345
Sonning
Whistley Green
Shurlock Row
Legoland
Wraysbury
M25
Stanwell Moor
Sulham
Tilehurst
READING
Berkshire Aviation
Hurst
M4
Hawthorn Hill
A330
A332
Old Windsor
Hythe End
Woodley
B3030
A321
B3018
A3095
Maiden's Green
Winkfield
Cranbourne
WINDSOR GREAT PARK
A308
Theale
Calcot Row
A4
Dinton
Binfield
Warfield
Englefield Green
A329
Winkfield Row
B3034
Woodside
Savill
EGHAM
STAINES-UPON-THAMES
Sheffield Bottom
READING
A33
A327
Earley
B3270
Winnersh
Emmbrook
A329(M)
Priestwood
Newell Green
North Ascot
B383
Cumberland
Virginia Water
Egham Hythe
Thorpe Park
A30
P+R
Dowlesgreen
Popeswood
Burleigh
Ascot
Cheapside
Trash Green
M4
Sindlesham
WOKINGHAM
B3017
Thorpe
Sulhamstead
Burghfield
Three Mile Cross
Shinfield
A329
BRACKNELL
Sunninghill
A329
Sunningdale
A320
Burghfield Hill
Spencers Wood
Barkham
B3349
Easthampstead
South Ascot
A332
A330
B3020
Broomhall
Trumps Green
Burghfield Common
Grazeley
Arborfield
Arborfield Cross
Eastheath
Gardeners Green
B3430
A321
Memorial
Lyne
Stratfield Mortimer
Swallowfield
Arborfield Garrison
California
B3016
Crowthorne
Look Out Discovery Centre
Surrey Hill
A322
Windlesham
B386
Longcross
Mortimer
A33
Wick Hill
A3095
Bagshot
Great Cockrow
Mortimer West End
Beech Hill
Farley Hill
Finchampstead
DANGER AREA
Ottershaw
Row Town
Amphitheatre
Riseley
Blackwater
B3348
Little Sandhurst
Owlsmoor
M3
B383
Burrowhill
Valley End
A319
A320
Woodham
M25
Wellington Monument
Stratfield Saye
Eversley
River
Eversley Cross
Sandhurst
A30
Lightwater
Chobham
Fairoaks
Silchester
West End Green
Stratfield Saye House
Bramshill
A327
Eversley Centre
Trilakes
CAMBERLEY
B311
West End
Mimbridge
Sheerwater
Fair Oak Green
Stratfield Turgis
Heckfield
B3272
Frogmore
Surrey Heath
Donkey Town
Castle Green
A3046
Bramley
Bramley Green
Turgis Green
Hound Green
Forest of Eversley
25
Yateley
Blackbushe
Cricket Hill
Blackwater
A325
B3015
DANGER AREA
Bisley
Knaphill
Horsell
A324
Pyrford
Sherfield on Loddon
Hartley Wintney
A30
Hartfordbridge
B3013
A327
Yateley
Hawley
Frimley
Royal Logistic Corps
A322
WOKING
Mattingley
Dipley
Fox Lane
Frimley Green
Deepcut
Brookwood
A320
Old Woking
Hazeley
Lyde Green
West Green
West Green House
A323
FLEET
Hart
West Heath
B3012
Mayford
Send Marsh
Church End
Rotherwick
Murrell Green
Phoenix Green
Cove
Mytchett
Basingstoke
Pirbright
Cartbridge
Chineham
A33
M3
Fleet
A3013
Fox Corner
B380
Pyle
Send

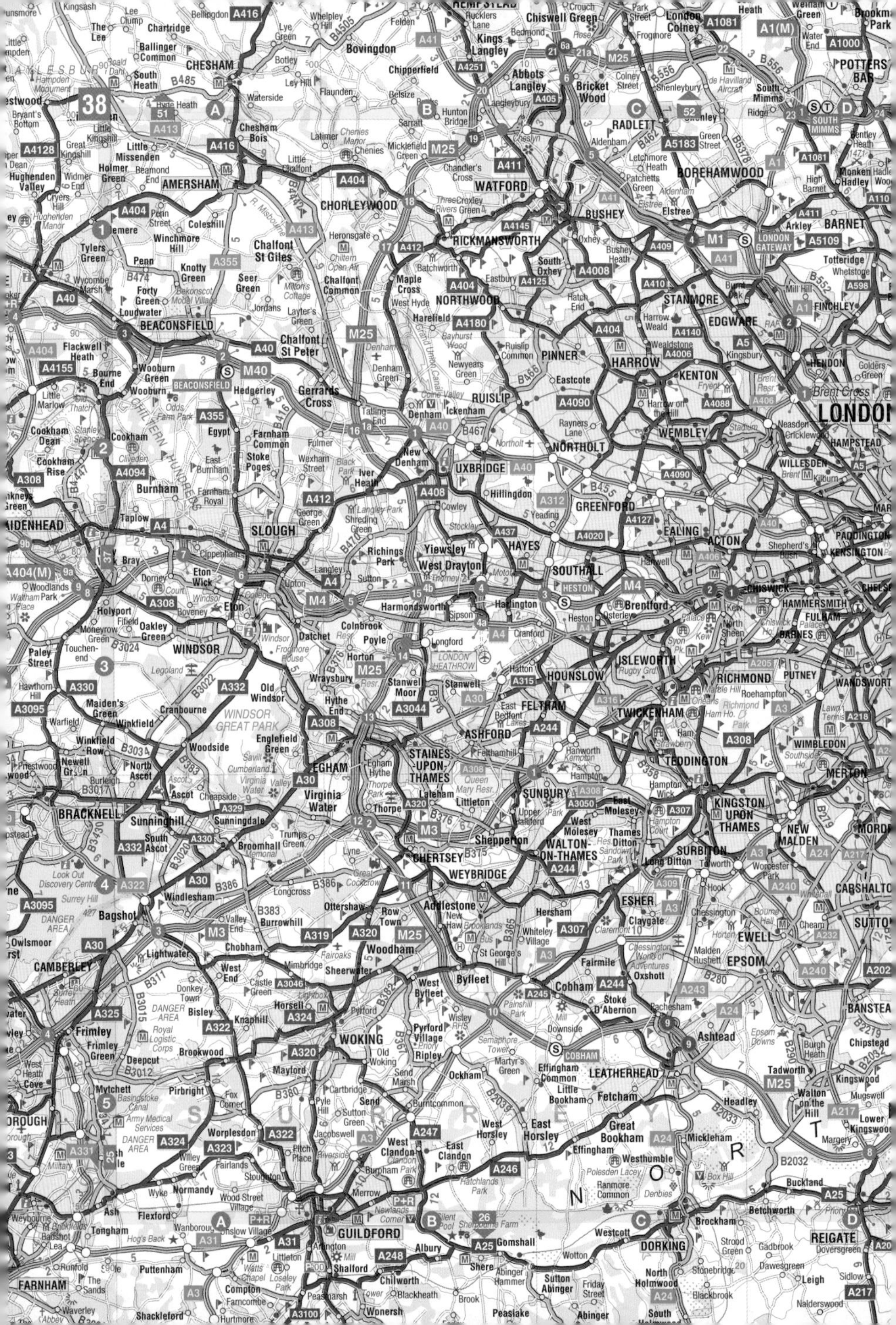
38
HEMPSTEAD
Kingsash
Lee Clump
Chartridge
The Lee
Ballinger Common
CHESHAM
South Heath
Hyde Heath
Bellingdon
Lye Green
Whelpley Hill
Bovingdon
Felden
Rucklers Lane
Kings Langley
Bedmond
Chiswell Green
Park Street
London Colney
Heath
Welham Green
Brookmans Park
Frogmore
Water End
POTTERS BAR
Botley
Ley Hill
Flaunden
Chipperfield
Abbots Langley
Bricket Wood
Colney Street
Shenleybury
de Havilland Aircraft
South Mimms
Waterside
Belsize
Hunton Bridge
Langleybury
RADLETT
Shenley
Ridge
SOUTH MIMMS
Chesham Bois
Sarratt
Latimer
Chenies Manor
Chenies
Micklefield Green
Chandler's Cross
Aldenham
Green Street
Letchmore Heath
Bentley Heath
Little Missenden
Little Kingshill
Great Kingshill
Holmer Green
Beamond End
Little Chalfont
WATFORD
Patchetts Green
BOREHAMWOOD
Monken Hadley
High Barnet
Hughenden Valley
Widmer End
AMERSHAM
CHORLEYWOOD
Three Rivers
Croxley Green
BUSHEY
Elstree
Aldenham
Arkley
BARNET
Hughenden Manor
Penn Street
Coleshill
RICKMANSWORTH
Batchworth
Oxhey
Bushey Heath
LONDON GATEWAY
Totteridge
Whetstone
Tylers Green
Penn
Winchmore Hill
Heronsgate
Chalfont St Giles
Chiltern Open Air
South Oxhey
Knotty Green
Seer Green
Milton's Cottage
Chalfont Common
Maple Cross
Eastbury
Hatch End
STANMORE
Burnt Oak
Mill Hill
FINCHLEY
Wycombe Marsh
Forty Green
Bekonscot Model Village
Jordans
Layter's Green
West Hyde
NORTHWOOD
Harrow Weald
EDGWARE
Loudwater
BEACONSFIELD
Harefield
Bayhurst Wood
Wealdstone
Kingsbury
Flackwell Heath
Chalfont St Peter
Denham
Ruislip Common
PINNER
HARROW
KENTON
HENDON
Golders Green
Bourne End
Wooburn Green
Denham Green
Newyears Green
Eastcote
Fryent
Brent Resr.
Brent Cross
Little Marlow
Wooburn
Hedgerley
Gerrards Cross
Coine Valley
Ickenham
RUISLIP
Harrow on the Hill
LONDON
Odds Farm Park
Tatling End
Rayners Lane
Stadium
Neasden
Cricklewood
HAMPSTEAD
Cookham Dean
Cookham
Stanley Spencer
Egypt
Farnham Common
Fulmer
New Denham
UXBRIDGE
Northolt
NORTHOLT
WEMBLEY
WILLESDEN
Cookham Rise
Cliveden
East Burnham
Stoke Poges
Wexham Street
Black Park
Iver Heath
Hillingdon
Kilburn
Brent
Burnham
Farnham Royal
Langley Park
Cowley
GREENFORD
MAIDENHEAD
Taplow
SLOUGH
George Green
Shreding Green
Stockley
Yeading
EALING
ACTON
PADDINGTON
Richings Park
Yiewsley
HAYES
Shepherd's Bush
KENSINGTON
Bray
Cippenham
West Drayton
Thorney
Hanwell
Dorney
Eton Wick
Langley
Sutton
Motor
SOUTHALL
Woodlands Park
Windsor
Eton College
Upton
Harmondsworth
Sipson
Harlington
HESTON
Brentford
CHISWICK
HAMMERSMITH
Waltham Place
Holyport
Fifield
Boveney
Eton
Heston
Osterley
Kew Palace
FULHAM
Oakley Green
Moneyrow Green
Datchet
Colnbrook
Longford
Cranford
Syon Pk.
Kew
North Sheen
BARNES
Chiswick Ho.
WINDSOR
Touchen-end
Poyle
LONDON HEATHROW
Paley Street
Legoland
Frogmore House
Horton
Hatton
HOUNSLOW
ISLEWORTH
RICHMOND
PUTNEY
WANDSWORTH
Wraysbury
Stanwell
Stanwell Moor
Rugby Grd.
Hawthorn Hill
Old Windsor
Hythe End
East Bedfont
FELTHAM
Orleans
Marble Hill
Roehampton
Maiden's Green
Cranbourne
WINDSOR GREAT PARK
TWICKENHAM
Ham Ho.
Richmond Park
Lawn Tennis
Warfield
Winkfield
Englefield Green
ASHFORD
Ham
Strawberry Hill
Winkfield Row
Woodside
Savill
EGHAM
Egham Hythe
STAINES-UPON-THAMES
Felthamhill
Hanworth
Kempton Park
Hampton
TEDDINGTON
WIMBLEDON
Southside Ho.
Newell Green
North Ascot
Burleigh
Cumberland
Virginia Water
Thorpe Park
Queen Mary Resr.
SUNBURY
MERTON
Prestwood
Ascot
Cheapside
Virginia Water
Laleham
Thorpe
Littleton
Upper Halliford
East Molesey
Hampton Wick
KINGSTON UPON THAMES
BRACKNELL
Sunninghill
Sunningdale
Trumps Green
Shepperton
West Molesey
Hampton Court
Thames Ditton
NEW MALDEN
South Ascot
Broomhall
Memorial
Lyne
CHERTSEY
WALTON-ON-THAMES
Sandown Park
SURBITON
Long Ditton
Tolworth
Worcester Park
CARSHALTON
Look Out Discovery Centre
Windlesham
Longcross
Great Cockcrow
WEYBRIDGE
Hook
Surrey Hill
DANGER AREA
Bagshot
Valley End
Burrowhill
Ottershaw
Row Town
Addlestone
New Haw
Brooklands
Hersham
ESHER
Claygate
Claremont
Chessington
Bourne Hall
Cheam
SUTTON
Owlsmoor
Lightwater
Chobham
Fairoaks
Woodham
Whiteley Village
Chessington World of Adventures
Horton
EWELL
CAMBERLEY
Mimbridge
Sheerwater
St George's Hill
Malden Rushett
EPSOM
West End
Donkey Town
Castle Green
Byfleet
West Byfleet
Fairmile
Cobham
Oxshott
Surrey Heath
Horsell
Painshill Park
Stoke D'Abernon
BANSTEAD
Frimley
Bisley
Knaphill
Pyrford
Wisley
Mill
Rachesham
Epsom Downs
Frimley Green
Royal Logistic Corps
Brookwood
WOKING
Pyrford Village
Priory
Ripley
Semaphore Tower
Downside
COBHAM
Ashtead
Chipstead
Burgh Heath
Deepcut
Old Woking
Martyr's Green
Effingham Common
LEATHERHEAD
Tadworth
Kingswood
West Heath
Cove
Mytchett
Basingstoke Canal
Pirbright
Fox Corner
Mayford
Send Marsh
Cartbridge
Burntcommon
Ockham
Little Bookham
Fetcham
Walton on the Hill
Mugswell
Army Medical Services
Pyle Hill
Send
Sutton Green
West Horsley
East Horsley
Great Bookham
Headley
Lower Kingswood
FARNBOROUGH
Worplesdon
Jacobswell
West Clandon
Clandon Park
East Clandon
Effingham
Mickleham
Westhumble
Box Hill
Margery
Military
Willey Green
Fairlands
Stoughton
Pitch Place
Burpham
Hatchlands Park
Polesden Lacey
Ranmore Common
Denbies
Buckland
Normandy
Wood Street Village
Merrow
Newlands Corner
Silent Pool
Sherbourne Farm
Betchworth
Ash
Wyke
Flexford
Wanborough
Onslow Village
GUILDFORD
Gomshall
Westcott
DORKING
Brockham
REIGATE
Weybourne
Badshot Lea
Tongham
Hog's Back
Albury
Strood Green
Gadbrook
Doversgreen
Lea
Littleton
Artington
Shalford
Shere
Abinger Hammer
Wotton
Dawesgreen
Runfold
Puttenham
Watts Chapel
Loseley Park
Chilworth
Sutton Abinger
Friday Street
North Holmwood
Stonebridge
Leigh
Sidlow
FARNHAM
The Sands
Compton
Farncombe
Peasmarsh
Blackheath
Brook
Blackbrook
Nalderswood
Waverley Abbey
Shackleford
Hurtmore
Wonersh
Peaslake
Abinger
South Holmwood
SURREY
NORTH

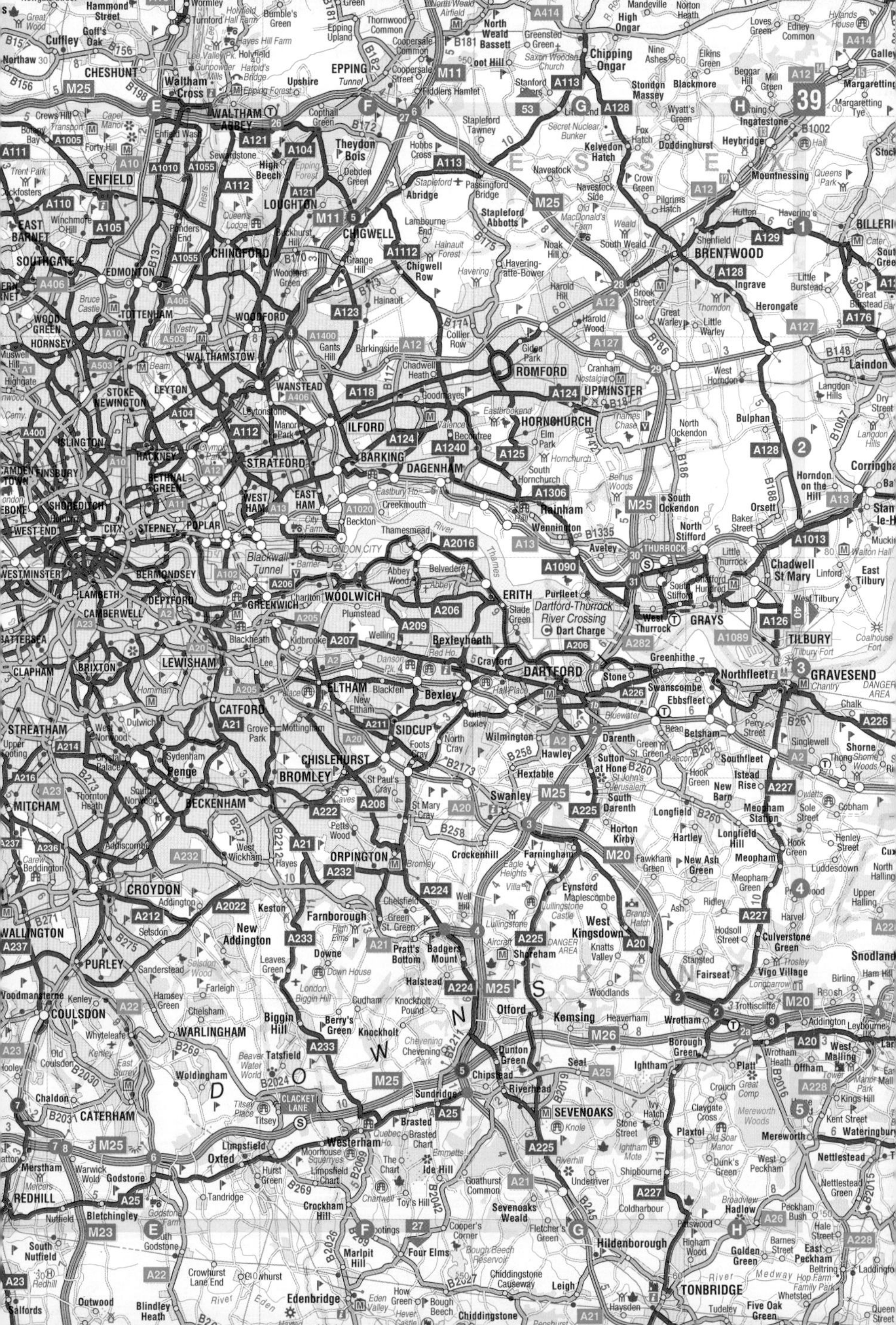
Newgate Street
Hammond Street
Cuffley
Goff's Oak
Northaw
CHESHUNT
Wormley
Turnford
Waltham Cross
WALTHAM ABBEY
Epping Upland
EPPING
Thornwood Common
North Weald Bassett
High Ongar
Chipping Ongar
Norton Mandeville
Loves Green
Edney Common
Blackmore
Stondon Massey
Ingatestone
Margaretting
Mountnessing
Doddinghurst
Kelvedon Hatch
Navestock
Theydon Bois
Upshire
Abridge
Stapleford Tawney
ESSEX
ENFIELD
Forty Hill
Crews Hill
EAST BARNET
SOUTHGATE
EDMONTON
TOTTENHAM
WOOD GREEN
HORNSEY
LOUGHTON
CHIGWELL
CHINGFORD
WOODFORD
WALTHAMSTOW
Chigwell Row
Hainault
Stapleford Abbotts
Havering-atte-Bower
Noak Hill
South Weald
BRENTWOOD
Shenfield
Hutton
BILLERICAY
Ingrave
Herongate
Little Burstead
ROMFORD
Gidea Park
Harold Wood
UPMINSTER
Cranham
HORNCHURCH
Elm Park
Laindon
Langdon Hills
ILFORD
WANSTEAD
LEYTON
STOKE NEWINGTON
ISLINGTON
HACKNEY
STRATFORD
BARKING
DAGENHAM
Becontree
Rainham
Wennington
Aveley
South Ockendon
North Ockendon
Bulphan
Orsett
Horndon on the Hill
Corringham
North Stifford
Little Thurrock
Chadwell St Mary
East Tilbury
Linford
CAMDEN TOWN
FINSBURY
SHOREDITCH
WEST END
CITY
STEPNEY
POPLAR
BETHNAL GREEN
WEST HAM
EAST HAM
Beckton
Thamesmead
LONDON CITY
Blackwall Tunnel
WESTMINSTER
LAMBETH
BERMONDSEY
DEPTFORD
GREENWICH
WOOLWICH
CAMBERWELL
BATTERSEA
Charlton
Plumstead
Abbey Wood
Belvedere
ERITH
Purfleet
Dartford-Thurrock River Crossing
Dart Charge
West Thurrock
GRAYS
TILBURY
CLAPHAM
BRIXTON
LEWISHAM
Blackheath
Kidbrooke
Welling
Bexleyheath
Crayford
DARTFORD
Stone
Greenhithe
Swanscombe
Northfleet
GRAVESEND
Ebbsfleet
STREATHAM
CATFORD
ELTHAM
Bexley
SIDCUP
Wilmington
Hawley
Darenth
Southfleet
Shorne
Chalk
MITCHAM
Penge
BECKENHAM
BROMLEY
CHISLEHURST
Swanley
Hextable
Sutton at Home
South Darenth
Longfield
Meopham
Istead Rise
Cobham
CROYDON
Addiscombe
West Wickham
Hayes
ORPINGTON
Petts Wood
St Mary Cray
Crockenhill
Farningham
Horton Kirby
Hartley
New Ash Green
WALLINGTON
PURLEY
New Addington
Keston
Farnborough
Downe
Eynsford
West Kingsdown
Culverstone Green
Snodland
COULSDON
WARLINGHAM
Biggin Hill
Halstead
Badgers Mount
Shoreham
Otford
Kemsing
Wrotham
Borough Green
Vigo Village
Fairseat
West Malling
Offham
Leybourne
KENT
DOWNS
CATERHAM
Chaldon
Woldingham
Tatsfield
Westerham
Brasted
Sundridge
Chipstead
Riverhead
Dunton Green
SEVENOAKS
Seal
Ightham
Platt
Oxted
Limpsfield
Godstone
Merstham
REDHILL
Bletchingley
Nutfield
South Nutfield
Ide Hill
Sevenoaks Weald
Hildenborough
Shipbourne
Plaxtol
Mereworth
Hadlow
TONBRIDGE
Crockham Hill
Four Elms
Marlpit Hill
Edenbridge
Leigh
Chiddingstone
Golden Green
East Peckham
Five Oak Green
Salfords
Outwood
Blindley Heath
M25
M11
M26
M20
M23
A12
A13
A2
A20
A21
A23
A25
A127
A128
A13
A406
A1306
A282
A226
A227
A225
A228

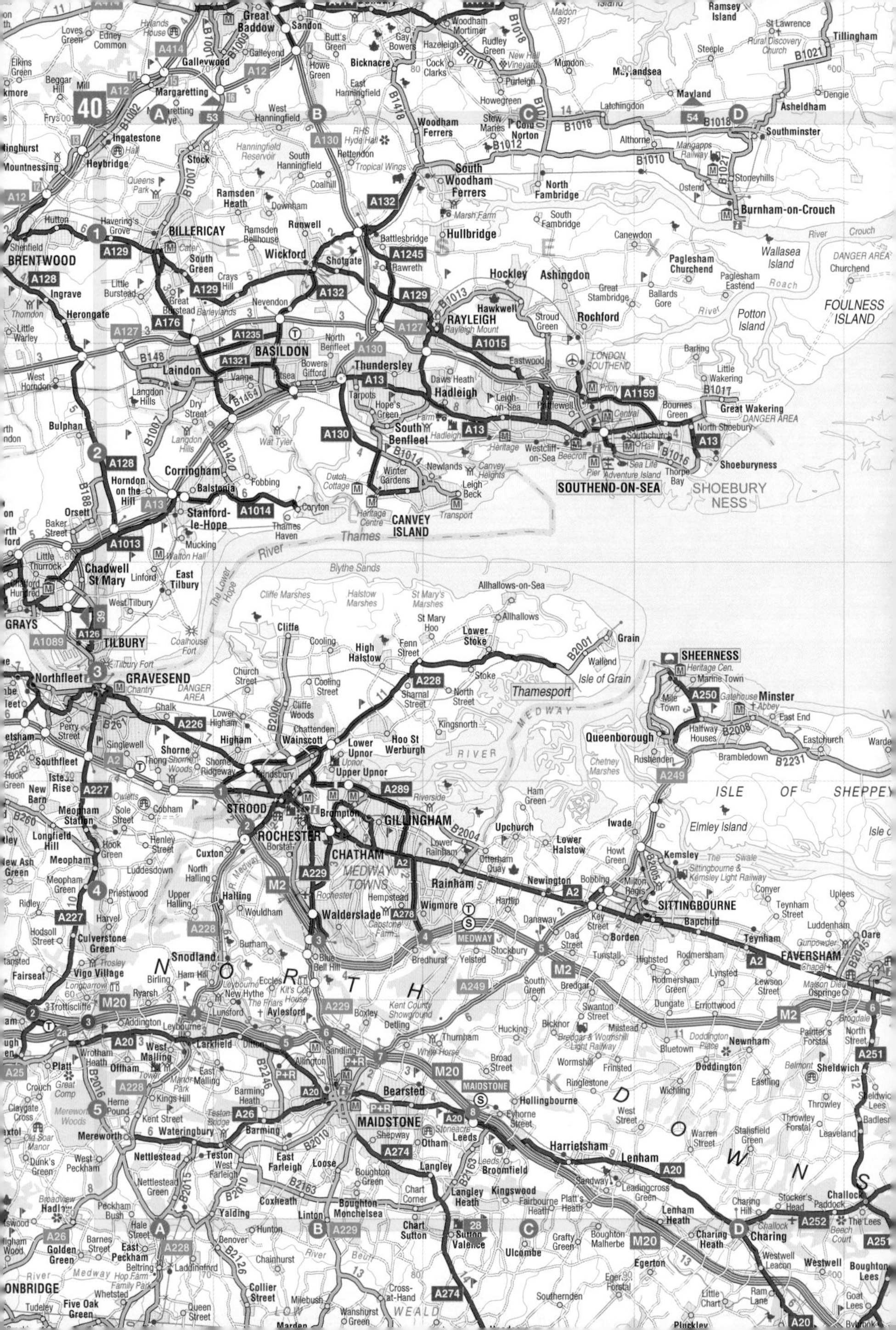

40
53
54
39
28
Great Baddow
Sandon
Loves Green
Edney Common
Hylands House
A414
Galleywood
Galleyend
Elkins Green
Beggar Hill
Mill Green
Margaretting
Margaretting Tye
Frys
Ingatestone
Mountnessing
Heybridge
Stock
Hanningfield Reservoir
West Hanningfield
South Hanningfield
RHS Hyde Hall
Rettendon
Tropical Wings
Butt's Green
Gay Bowers
Howe Green
Bicknacre
East Hanningfield
Woodham Mortimer
Hazeleigh
Cock Clarks
Rudley Green
New Hall Vineyards
Purleigh
Howegreen
Woodham Ferrers
Stow Maries
Cold Norton
Maldon
Mundon
Maylandsea
Mayland
Latchingdon
Althorne
Ramsey Island
St Lawrence
Steeple
Rural Discovery Church
Tillingham
Dengie
Asheldham
Southminster
Mangapps Railway
Stoneyhills
Ostend
Burnham-on-Crouch
River Crouch
South Woodham Ferrers
Marsh Farm
North Fambridge
South Fambridge
Hullbridge
Queens Park
Ramsden Heath
Downham
Coalhill
Runwell
Battlesbridge
Hutton
Havering's Grove
BILLERICAY
Ramsden Bellhouse
Wickford
Shotgate
Rawreth
Shenfield
BRENTWOOD
Ingrave
Little Burstead
South Green
Crays Hill
Great Burstead
Barleylands
Nevendon
Herongate
Thorndon
Little Warley
Laindon
BASILDON
North Benfleet
Bowers Gifford
Pitsea
Vange
Thundersley
RAYLEIGH
Rayleigh Mount
Hawkwell
Hockley
Ashingdon
Canewdon
Wallasea Island
Paglesham Churchend
Paglesham Eastend
Ballards Gore
Great Stambridge
Stroud Green
Rochford
LONDON SOUTHEND
Eastwood
Potton Island
FOULNESS ISLAND
Churchend
DANGER AREA
Barling
Little Wakering
Great Wakering
North Shoebury
Bournes Green
Southchurch
Shoeburyness
SHOEBURY NESS
SOUTHEND-ON-SEA
Prittlewell
Priory
Central
Westcliff-on-Sea
Beecroft
Pier
Sea Life Adventure Island
Thorpe Bay
Leigh-on-Sea
Heritage
Daws Heath
Hadleigh
Tarpots
Hope's Green
South Benfleet
Canvey Heights
Newlands
Leigh Beck
Winter Gardens
Dutch Cottage
Heritage Centre
CANVEY ISLAND
Transport
West Horndon
Langdon Hills
Dry Street
Bulphan
Wat Tyler
Corringham
Fobbing
Balstonia
Horndon on the Hill
Orsett
Stanford-le-Hope
Coryton
Thames Haven
Mucking
Baker Street
Walton Hall
Little Thurrock
Chadwell St Mary
Linford
East Tilbury
West Tilbury
GRAYS
TILBURY
Coalhouse Fort
Tilbury Fort
River Thames
Blythe Sands
The Lower Hope
Cliffe Marshes
Halstow Marshes
St Mary's Marshes
Allhallows-on-Sea
Allhallows
St Mary Hoo
Lower Stoke
Grain
Cliffe
Cooling
High Halstow
Fenn Street
Stoke
Isle of Grain
Thamesport
Wallend
SHEERNESS
Heritage Cen.
Marine Town
Mile Town
Minster
Abbey
East End
Halfway Houses
Eastchurch
Queenborough
Rushenden
Brambledown
Chetney Marshes
ISLE OF SHEPPEY
Elmley Island
Northfleet
GRAVESEND
Chantry
Church Street
Cooling Street
Chalk
Lower Higham
Higham
Cliffe Woods
Chattenden
Sharnal Street
North Street
Kingsnorth
Wainscott
Lower Upnor
Upnor
Hoo St Werburgh
Upper Upnor
Perry Street
Southfleet
Singlewell
Shorne
Shorne Woods
Thong
Shorne Ridgeway
Frindsbury
Istead Rise
New Barn
Owletts
Cobham
Meopham Station
Sole Street
STROOD
ROCHESTER
Borstal
Brompton
GILLINGHAM
Riverside
CHATHAM
MEDWAY TOWNS
Lower Rainham
Rainham
Upchurch
Ham Green
Otterham Quay
Lower Halstow
Iwade
Howt Green
Kemsley
The Swale
Sittingbourne & Kemsley Light Railway
Milton Regis
Bobbing
Newington
SITTINGBOURNE
Conyer
Uplees
Teynham Street
Longfield Hill
Hook Green
Henley Street
Cuxton
Meopham
New Ash Green
Meopham Green
Luddesdown
North Halling
Halling
Upper Halling
Priestwood
Wouldham
Hempstead
Wigmore
Walderslade
Capstone Farm
Hartlip
Danaway
Key Street
Borden
Bapchild
Teynham
Luddenham
Oare
FAVERSHAM
Ridley
Harvel
Hodsoll Street
Culverstone Green
Trosley
Fairseat
Vigo Village
Snodland
Burham
Blue Bell Hill
Bredhurst
Yelsted
Stockbury
Oad Street
Tunstall
Highsted
Rodmersham
Lynsted
Lewson Street
Gunpowder
Chapel
Maison Dieu
Ospringe
Longbarrow
Ham Hill
Birling
Ryarsh
Trottiscliffe
Addington
Leybourne
New Hythe
The Friars
Lunsford
Aylesford
Eccles
Kit's Coty House
Boxley
Kent County Showground
Detling
South Green
Bredgar
Rodmersham Green
Dungate
Erriottwood
Brogdale
Painter's Forstal
North Street
Sheldwich
Wrotham Heath
Platt
Offham
West Malling
Larkfield
Ditton
East Malling
Manor Park
Allington
Sandling
White Horse
Thurnham
Hucking
Bicknor
Bredgar & Wormshill Light Railway
Milstead
Swanton Street
Bluetown
Doddington Place
Newnham
Doddington
Belmont
Eastling
Crouch
Great Comp
Claygate Cross
Herne Pound
Kings Hill
Barming Heath
Teston Bridge
Barming
Bearsted
MAIDSTONE
Stoneacre
Otham
Broad Street
Hollingbourne
Eyhorne Street
Ringlestone
Wormshill
Frinsted
Wichling
Throwley
Throwley Forstal
Leaveland
Mereworth Woods
Old Soar Manor
Mereworth
Kent Street
Wateringbury
Nettlestead
Teston
West Farleigh
East Farleigh
Shepway
Leeds
Leeds Castle
Broomfield
Harrietsham
Lenham
West Street
Warren Street
Stalisfield Green
Dunk's Green
West Peckham
Nettlestead Green
Loose
Boughton Green
Langley
Langley Heath
Kingswood
Fairbourne Heath
Platt's Heath
Sandway
Leadingcross Green
Broadview
Hadlow
Peckham Bush
Yalding
Coxheath
Linton
Chart Corner
Boughton Monchelsea
Chart Sutton
Sutton Valence
Ulcombe
Grafty Green
Boughton Malherbe
Lenham Heath
Charing Hill
Charing Heath
Charing
Stocker's Head
Paddock
Challock
The Lees
Beech Court
Golden Green
Hale Street
Barnes Street
East Peckham
Beltring
Hop Farm Family Park
Laddingford
Benover
Hunton
Chainhurst
River Beult
Egerton
Egerton Forstal
Westwell Leacon
Westwell
Boughton Lees
River Medway
TONBRIDGE
Whetsted
Collier Street
Cross-at-Hand
Southernden
Ram Lane
Little Chart
Goat Lees
Tudeley
Five Oak Green
Queen Street
Milebush
Wanshurst Green
Marden
Pluckley
LOW WEALD
NORTH DOWNS
ESSEX
RIVER MEDWAY
Swale
Roach
A12
A414
A130
A132
A1245
A129
A128
A127
A176
A1235
A1321
A1015
A13
A1159
A1014
A1013
A1089
A126
A226
A2
A227
A228
A289
A229
A278
A249
A250
M2
M20
A20
A25
A26
A274
A251
A252
B1002
B1007
B1009
B1010
B1012
B1018
B1021
B1418
B1013
B1017
B1016
B1014
B1464
B1420
B188
B148
B2001
B2008
B2231
B2000
B2004
B2005
B2045
B260
B262
B261
B2016
B2246
B2010
B2015
B2163
B2126
MEDWAY
MAIDSTONE
P+R

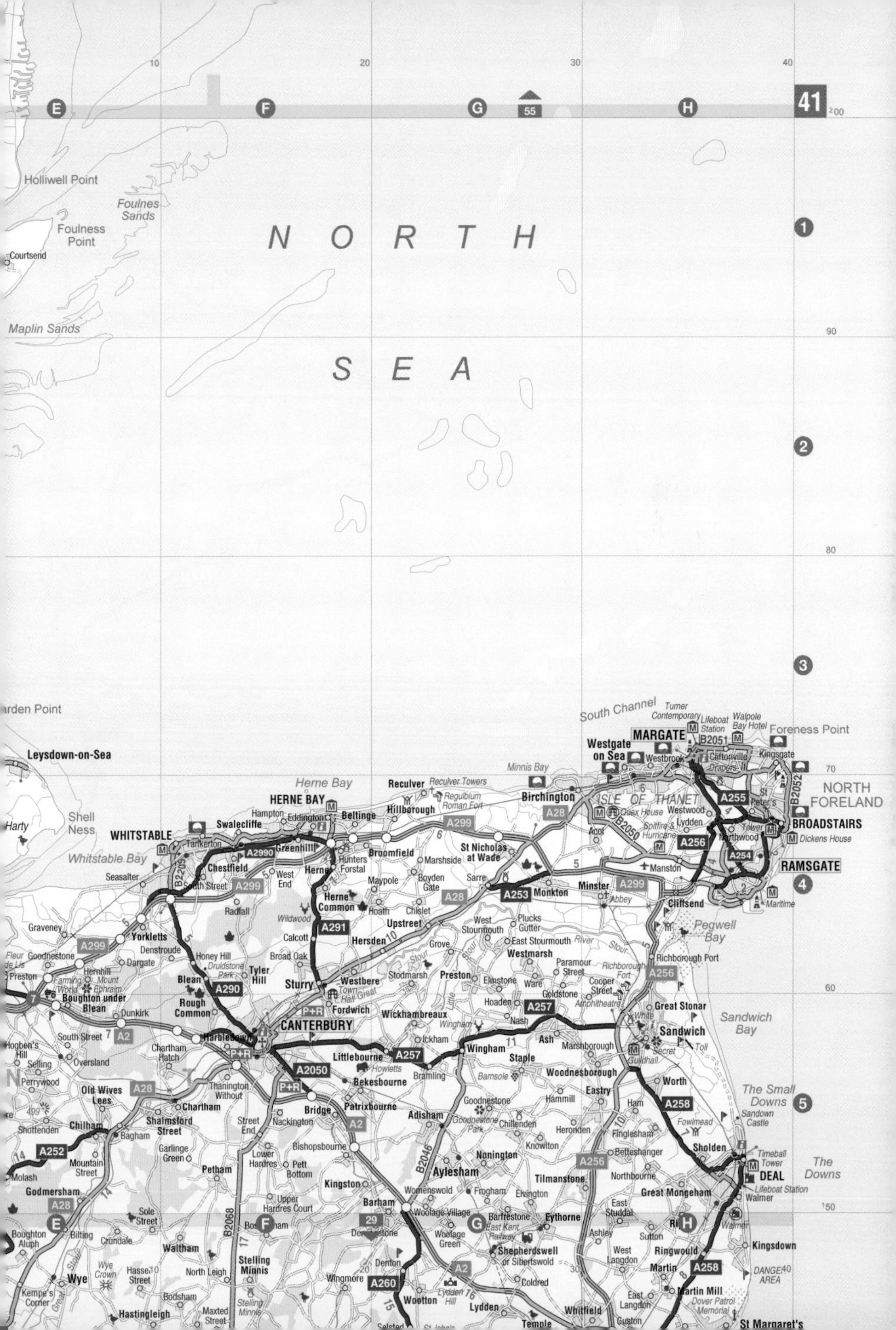

NORTH

SEA

Holliwell Point

Foulness
Sands

Foulness
Point

Courtsend

Maplin Sands

Garden Point

Leysdown-on-Sea

Harty

Shell
Ness

Whitstable Bay

Seasalter

Graveney

Fleur
de Lis

Preston

Goodnestone

Hernhill
Mount
Ephraim

Dargate

Boughton under
Blean

Dunkirk

Hogben's

Selling

Overland

Perrywood

South Street

Molash

Godmersham

Boughton
Aluph

Wye

Kempe's
Corner

Hastingleigh

Bilting

Crundale

Wootton

Bodsham

Maxted
Street

Hassell
Street

North Leigh

Stelling
Minnis

Wormshill

Herne Bay

WHITSTABLE

Swalecliffe

Tankerton

B2205

South Street

Chestfield

West
End

HERNE BAY

Hampton

Eddington

Greenhill

Herne

Maypole

Herne
Common

Broomfield

Hunters
Forstal

Hoath

Reculver

Hillborough

Beltinge

Reculver Towers

Regulbium
Roman Fort

Marshside

St Nicholas
at Wade

Boyden
Gate

Chislet

Sarre

Upstreet

Minnis Bay

Birchington

ISLE OF THANET

Monkton

Minster

**Westgate
on Sea**

Westbrook

MARGATE

Turner
Contemporary

Lifeboat
Station

Walpole
Bay Hotel

Foreness Point

Kingsgate

St
Peter's

**NORTH
FORELAND**

BROADSTAIRS

Dickens House

RAMSGATE

Maritime

Pegwell
Bay

Sandwich
Bay

The Small
Downs

The
Downs

150

DEAL

Walmer

Kingsdown

St Margaret's

Radfall

Wildwood

Honey Hill

Druidstone
Park

Blean

Rough
Common

Tyler
Hill

Broad Oak

Sturry

Calcott

Hersden

Westbere

Fordwich

Harbledown

CANTERBURY

Littlebourne

Bekesbourne

Patrixbourne

Howletts

Bridge

Nackington

Street
End

Lower
Hardres

Pett
Bottom

Kingston

Barham

Womenswold

Woolage
Village

Frogham

Denton

Wingmore

Eythorne

Shepherdswell
or Sibertswold

Coldred

Lydden

Temple

Whitfield

East
Langdon

Martin Mill

Dover Patrol
Memorial

Ringwould

Martin

Sutton

Ripple

Great Mongeham

Sholden

Timeball
Tower

Lifeboat Station

Northbourne

West
Langdon

Ashley

East
Studdal

Guston

Finglesham

Eastry

Worth

Great Stonar

Sandwich

Woodnesborough

Staple

Ash

Marshborough

Hammill

Elvington

Tilmanstone

Knowlton

Chillenden

Nonington

Aylesham

Adisham

Bishopsbourne

Bossingham

Denstroude

Yorkletts

A299

A2990

A290

A291

A28

A253

A299

A256

A255

A254

A256

A257

A2050

A258

A256

A258

A252

A28

A260

A2

B2050

B2052

B2060

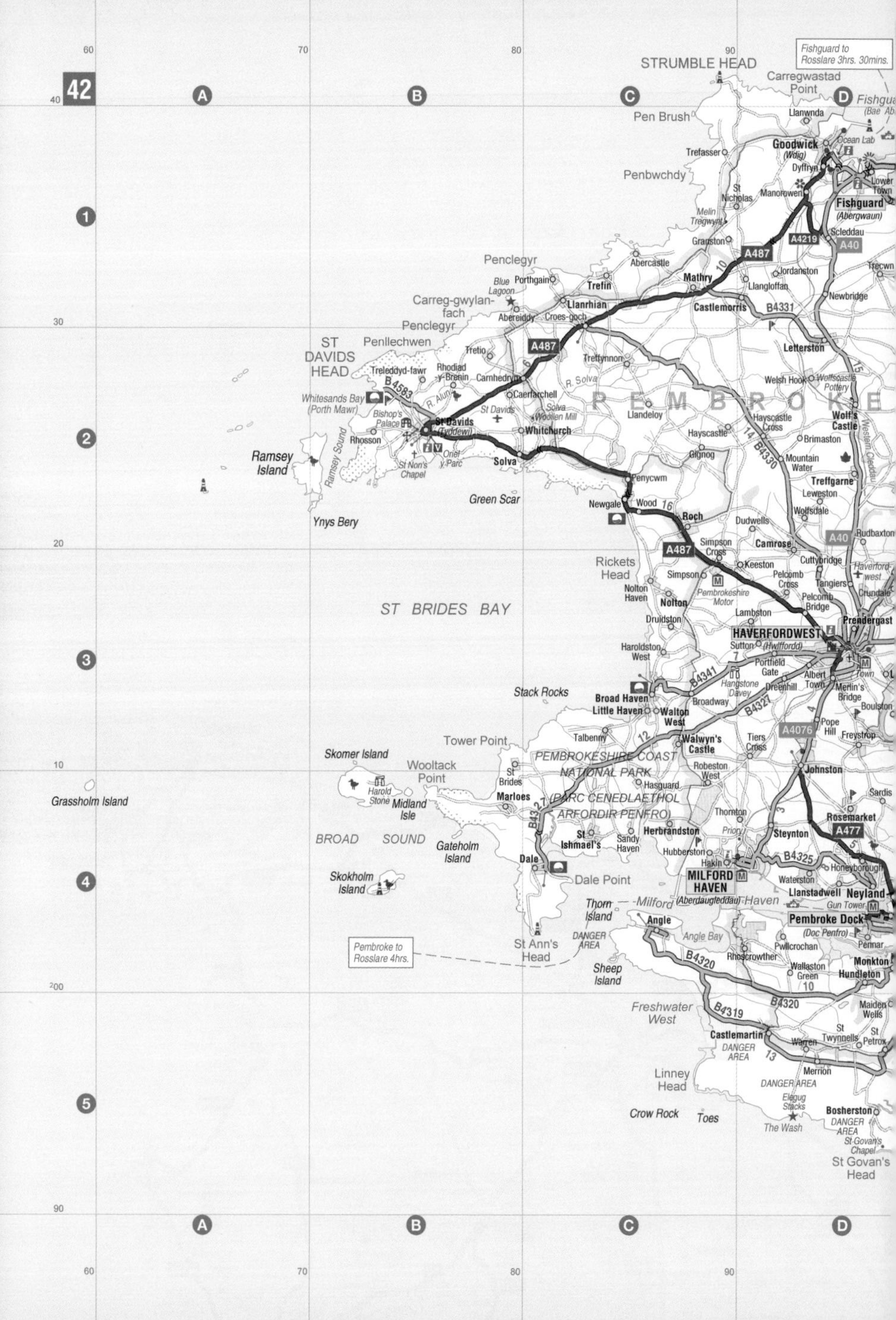

Fishguard to Rosslare 3hrs. 30mins.
STRUMBLE HEAD
Carregwastad Point
Pen Brush
Llanwnda
Goodwick (Wdig)
Ocean Lab
Trefasser
Dyffryn
Lower Town
Penbwchdy
St Nicholas
Manorowen
Fishguard (Abergwaun)
Melin Tregwynt
Scleddau
Granston
A4219
A40
A487
Abercastle
Penclegyr
Jordanston
Trecwn
Blue Lagoon
Porthgain
Trefin
Mathry
Llangloffan
Carreg-gwylan-fach
Llanrhian
Castlemorris
Newbridge
Abereiddy
Croes-goch
B4331
Penclegyr
Letterston
ST DAVIDS HEAD
Penllechwen
Tretio
Treffynnon
Treleddyd-fawr
Rhodiad y-Brenin
Carnhedryn
Welsh Hook
Wolfscastle Pottery
B4583
R. Solva
PEMBROKE
Whitesands Bay (Porth Mawr)
R. Alun
Caerfarchell
Bishop's Palace
St Davids
Solva Woollen Mill
Llandeloy
Hayscastle Cross
Wolf's Castle
St Davids (Tyddewi)
Whitchurch
Hayscastle
Brimaston
Rhosson
Ramsey Sound
Ramsey Island
Oriel y Parc
St Non's Chapel
Solva
Gignog
B4330
Mountain Water
Western Cleddau
Penycwm
Treffgarne
Green Scar
Lewiston
Newgale
Wood
Roch
Wolfsdale
Ynys Bery
Dudwells
Simpson Cross
Camrose
A40
Rudbaxton
Rickets Head
Keeston
Cuttybridge
Haverfordwest
Simpson
Pelcomb Cross
Tangiers
Nolton Haven
Nolton
Pembrokeshire Motor
Pelcomb Bridge
Crundale
ST BRIDES BAY
Lambston
Druidston
Prendergast
HAVERFORDWEST
Haroldston West
Sutton
(Hwlffordd)
Portfield Gate
Albert Town
B4341
Hangstone Davey
Dreenhill
Merlin's Bridge
Stack Rocks
Broad Haven
Broadway
B4327
Boulston
Little Haven
Walton West
Pope Hill
A4076
Freystrop
Talbenny
Tower Point
Walwyn's Castle
Tiers Cross
Skomer Island
PEMBROKESHIRE COAST NATIONAL PARK
Robeston West
Wooltack Point
St Brides
Johnston
Grassholm Island
Hasguard
Harold Stone
(PARC CENEDLAETHOL ARFORDIR PENFRO)
Marloes
Midland Isle
Sardis
B4327
Thornton
Rosemarket
Priory
Herbrandston
A477
BROAD SOUND
St Ishmael's
Sandy Haven
Steynton
Gateholm Island
Hubberston
Hakin
B4325
Honeyborough
Dale
Dale Point
MILFORD HAVEN (Aberdaugleddau)
Waterston
Skokholm Island
Llanstadwell
Neyland
Thorn Island
Milford Haven
Gun Tower
Angle
Pembroke Dock (Doc Penfro)
Angle Bay
Pembroke to Rosslare 4hrs.
St Ann's Head
DANGER AREA
Pwllcrochan
Pennar
Rhoscrowther
Monkton
B4320
Sheep Island
Wallaston Green
Hundleton
B4320
Freshwater West
B4319
Maiden Wells
Castlemartin
St Twynnells
St Petrox
Warren
DANGER AREA
Merrion
Linney Head
DANGER AREA
Elegug Stacks
Crow Rock
Toes
Bosherston
The Wash
DANGER AREA
St Govan's Chapel
St Govan's Head

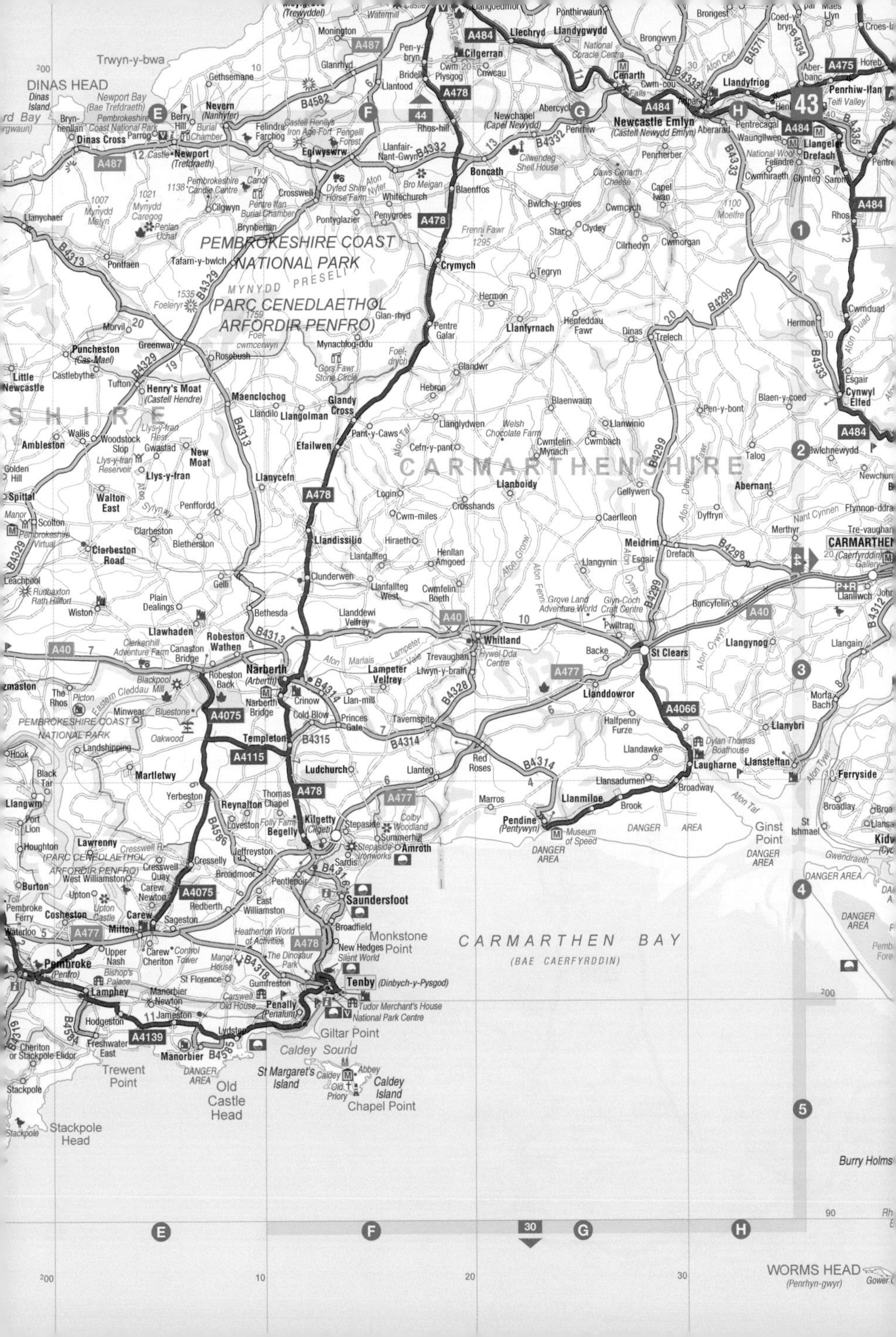

43
DINAS HEAD
Dinas Island
Trwyn-y-bwa
Newport Bay (Bae Trefdraeth)
Pembrokeshire Coast National Park
Dinas Cross
Newport (Trefdraeth)
Nevern (Nanhyfer)
Berry Hill
Parrog
Castle
Gethsemane
Monington
Glanrhyd
Llantood
Felindre Farchog
Castell Henllys Iron Age Fort
Pengelli Forest
Eglwyswrw
Pen-y-bryn
Cwm Plysgog
Bridell
Cilgerran
Llechryd
Llandygwydd
Ponthirwaun
Brongwyn
National Coracle Centre
Cenarth
Cenarth Falls
Cwm-cou
Adpar
Brongest
Coed-y-bryn
Llandyfriog
Aber-banc
Horeb
Croes-lan
Penrhiw-llan
Teifi Valley
Newcastle Emlyn (Castell Newydd Emlyn)
Aberarad
Pentrecagal
Waungilwen
National Wool Museum
Llangeler
Drefach Felindre
Cwmhiraeth
Glynteg
Saron
Penrhiw
Abercych
Newchapel (Capel Newydd)
Cilwendeg Shell House
Rhos-hill
Llanfair-Nant-Gwyn
Boncath
Blaenffos
Bro Meigan
Whitechurch
Dyfed Shire Horse Farm
Crosswell
Pontyglazier
Penygroes
Caws Cenarth Cheese
Capel Iwan
Penrherber
Moelfre
Rhos
Cwmcych
Bwlch-y-groes
Clydey
Star
Cilrhedyn
Cwmorgan
Frenni Fawr
Crymych
Tegryn
Hermon
Llanfyrnach
Henfeddau Fawr
Dinas
Trelech
Cwmduad
Esgair
Cynwyl Elfed
Pembrokeshire Candle Centre
Ty Canol
Pentre Ifan Burial Chamber
Brynberian
Cilgwyn
Mynydd Carregog
Mynydd Melyn
Penlan Uchaf
Llanychaer
Pontfaen
Tafarn-y-bwlch
PEMBROKESHIRE COAST NATIONAL PARK
MYNYDD PRESELI
(PARC CENEDLAETHOL ARFORDIR PENFRO)
Foeleyrn
Foel-cwmcerwyn
Glan-rhyd
Pentre Galar
Mynachlog-ddu
Gors Fawr Stone Circle
Foel-drych
Glandwr
Hebron
Blaenwaun
Blaen-y-coed
Pen-y-bont
Morvil
Puncheston (Cas-Mael)
Greenway
Rosebush
Little Newcastle
Castlebythe
Tufton
Henry's Moat (Castell Hendre)
Maenclochog
Llandilo
Llangolman
Glandy Cross
Pant-y-Caws
Llanglydwen
Welsh Chocolate Farm
Llanwinio
Cwmfelin Mynach
Cwmbach
Bwlchnewydd
Talog
Ambleston
Wallis
Woodstock Slop
Llys-y-fran Resr.
Gwastad
New Moat
Llys-y-fran Reservoir
Llys-y-fran
Efailwen
Cefn-y-pant
CARMARTHENSHIRE
Llanboidy
Gellywen
Abernant
Golden Hill
Spittal
Walton East
Llanycefn
Login
Crosshands
Cwm-miles
Caerlleon
Dyffryn
Nant Cynnen
Ffynnon-ddrain
Merthyr
Tre-vaughan
CARMARTHEN (Caerfyrddin)
Scolton Manor
Pembrokeshire Virtual
Penffordd
Clarbeston
Bletherston
Clarbeston Road
Llandissilio
Hiraeth
Llanfallteg
Henllan Amgoed
Llangynin
Meidrim
Esgair
Drefach
Leachpool
Rudbaxton Rath Hillfort
Gelli
Clunderwen
Llanfallteg West
Cwmfelin Boeth
Grove Land Adventure World
Glyn-Coch Craft Centre
Bancyfelin
Llanllwch
Wiston
Plain Dealings
Bethesda
Llanddewi Velfrey
Pwlltrap
Llawhaden
Robeston Wathen
Whitland
St Clears
Llangynog
Llangain
Clerkenhill Adventure Farm
Canaston Bridge
Hywel Dda Centre
Trevaughan
Llwyn-y-brain
Backe
Lampeter Velfrey
Narberth (Arberth)
Robeston Back
Blackpool Mill
Crinow
Llan-mill
Llanddowror
Rhos
The Rhos
Picton
Eastern Cleddau
Minwear
Bluestone
Narberth Bridge
Cold Blow
Princes Gate
Tavernspite
Halfpenny Furze
Morfa Bach
PEMBROKESHIRE COAST NATIONAL PARK
Oakwood
Templeton
Llanybri
Hook
Landshipping
Red Roses
Llandawke
Dylan Thomas Boathouse
Laugharne
Llansteffan
Ferryside
Black Tar
Martletwy
Ludchurch
Llanteg
Llansadurnen
Broadway
Afon Taf
Afon Tywi
Llangwm
Yerbeston
Reynalton
Thomas Chapel
Marros
Llanmiloe
Brook
Broadlay
Port Lion
Loveston
Folly Farm
Begelly
Kilgetty (Cilgeti)
Stepaside
Colby Woodland
Pendine (Pentywyn)
Museum of Speed
DANGER AREA
Ginst Point
St Ishmael
Houghton
Lawrenny
Cresswell
Summerhill
Jeffreyston
Stepaside Ironworks
Amroth
Gwendraeth
(PARC CENEDLAETHOL ARFORDIR PENFRO)
Cresswell Quay
Cresselly
Sardis
West Williamston
Broadmoor
Pentlepoir
Burton
Upton
Carew Newton
Upton Castle
East Williamston
Saundersfoot
Toll Pembroke Ferry
Cosheston
Redberth
Carew
Milton
Sageston
Broadfield
Monkstone Point
CARMARTHEN BAY
(BAE CAERFYRDDIN)
Waterloo
Heatherton World of Activities
New Hedges
Silent World
Pembroke (Penfro)
Upper Nash
Carew Cheriton
Control Tower
Manor House
The Dinosaur Park
Bishop's Palace
St Florence
Gumfreston
Tenby (Dinbych-y-Pysgod)
Lamphey
Manorbier Newton
Carswell Old House
Tudor Merchant's House
National Park Centre
Hodgeston
Jameston
Penally (Penalun)
Lydstep
Giltar Point
Freshwater East
Manorbier
Caldey Sound
Cheriton or Stackpole Elidor
Trewent Point
DANGER AREA
Old Castle Head
St Margaret's Island
Caldey
Abbey
Old Priory
Caldey Island
Chapel Point
Stackpole
Stackpole Head
Burry Holms
WORMS HEAD (Penrhyn-gwyr)
Gower
A487
A484
A478
A475
A477
A40
A4075
A4115
A4066
A4139
B4582
B4332
B4333
B4571
B4334
B4335
B4313
B4329
B4299
B4298
B4328
B4314
B4315
B4316
B4318
B4586
B4584
B4585
B4312
44
30
E
F
G
H
1
2
3
4
5

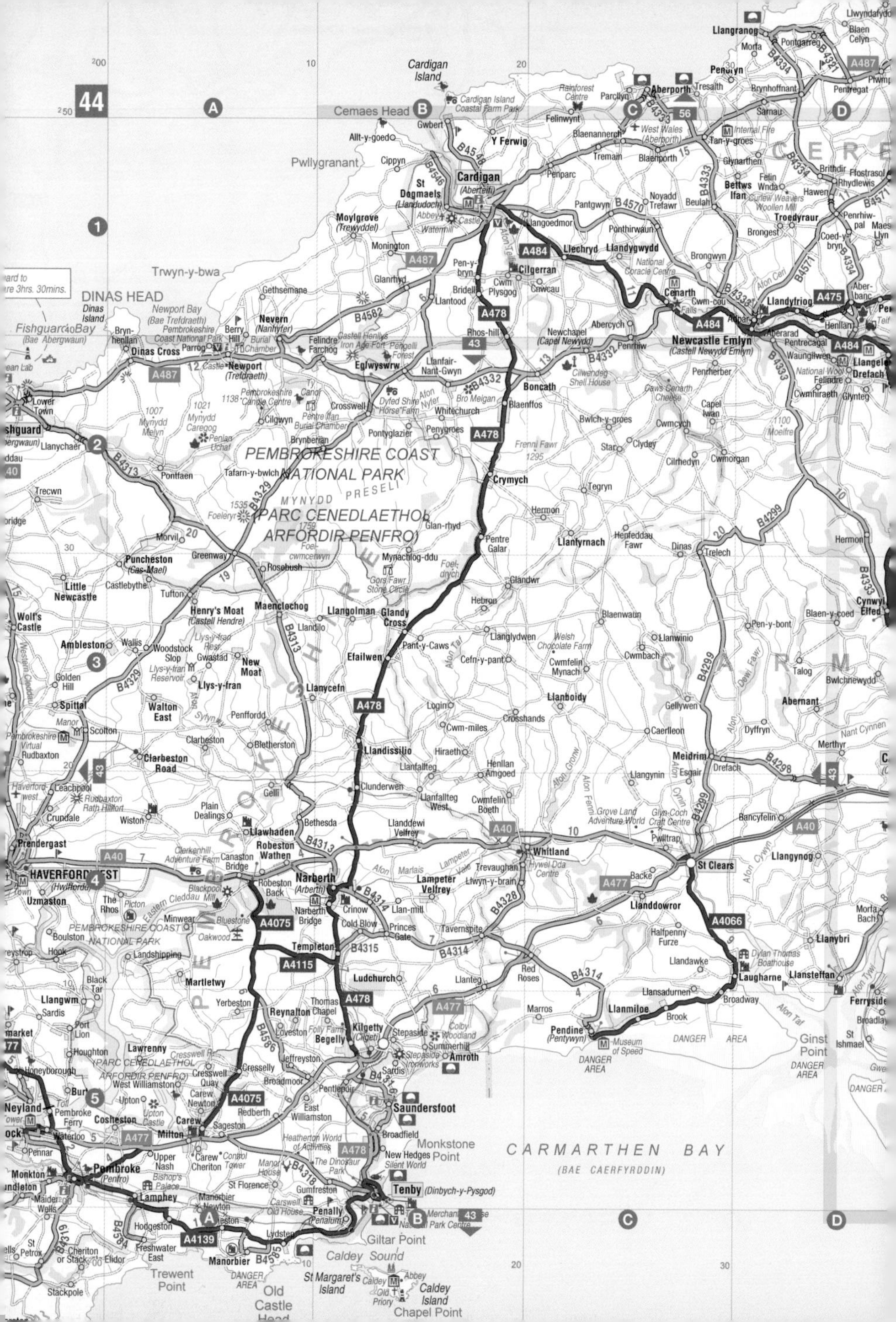
44
Cardigan Island
Cemaes Head
Cardigan Island Coastal Farm Park
Llangranog
Penbryn
Aberporth
Tresaith
Parcllyn
Rainforest Centre
Felinwynt
Gwbert
Y Ferwig
Allt-y-goed
Blaenannerch
West Wales (Aberporth)
Tan-y-groes
Sarnau
Brynhoffnant
Pentregat
Pontgarreg
Morfa
Blaen Celyn
Llwyndafydd
Pwllygranant
Cippyn
Cardigan (Aberteifi)
St Dogmaels (Llandudoch)
Abbey
Castle
Watermill
Moylgrove (Trewyddel)
Monington
Penparc
Tremain
Blaenporth
Glynarthen
Pantgwyn
Noyadd Trefawr
Beulah
Bettws Ifan
Felin Wnda
Curlew Weavers Woollen Mill
Brithdir
Ffostrasol
Rhydlewis
Hawen
Troedyraur
Penrhiw-pal
Maes Llyn
Brongest
Coed-y-bryn
Llangoedmor
Ponthirwaun
Llechryd
Llandygwydd
National Coracle Centre
Brongwyn
Pen-y-bryn
Cilgerran
Cwm Plysgog
Cnwcau
Trwyn-y-bwa
Glanrhyd
Gethsemane
Bridell
Llantood
DINAS HEAD
Dinas Island
Newport Bay (Bae Trefdraeth)
Pembrokeshire Coast National Park
Fishguard Bay (Bae Abergwaun)
Bryn-henllan
Dinas Cross
Parrog
Berry Hill
Burial Chamber
Nevern (Nanhyfer)
Castell Henllys Iron Age Fort
Pengelli Forest
Felindre Farchog
Eglwyswrw
Newport (Trefdraeth)
Rhos-hill
Newchapel (Capel Newydd)
Abercych
Penrhiw
Cenarth
Falls
Cwm-cou
Adpar
Newcastle Emlyn (Castell Newydd Emlyn)
Llandyfriog
Aberarad
Pentrecagal
Henllan
Waunglilwen
Llangeler
Drefach
National Wool Museum
Felindre
Cwmhiraeth
Glynteg
Llanfair-Nant-Gwyn
Boncath
Cilwendeg Shell House
Penrherber
Caws Cenarth Cheese
Lower Town
Fishguard (Abergwaun)
Llanychaer
Pembrokeshire Candle Centre
Ty Canol
Pentre Ifan Burial Chamber
Crosswell
Dyfed Shire Horse Farm
Afon Nyfer
Bro Meigan
Whitechurch
Blaenffos
Capel Iwan
Cwmcych
Mynydd Melyn
Mynydd Caregog
Penlan Uchaf
Cilgwyn
Brynberian
Pontyglazier
Penygroes
Bwlch-y-groes
Moelfre
PEMBROKESHIRE COAST NATIONAL PARK
MYNYDD PRESELI
(PARC CENEDLAETHOL ARFORDIR PENFRO)
Frenni Fawr
Star
Clydey
Cilrhedyn
Cwmorgan
Tafarn-y-bwlch
Pontfaen
Crymych
Tegryn
Trecwn
Foeleryr
Glan-rhyd
Hermon
Llantyrnach
Henfeddau Fawr
Dinas
Trelech
Morvil
Puncheston (Cas-Mael)
Greenway
Foel-cwmcerwyn
Mynachlog-ddu
Foel-drych
Pentre Galar
Rosebush
Gors Fawr Stone Circle
Little Newcastle
Castlebythe
Tufton
Glandwr
Hebron
Wolf's Castle
Henry's Moat (Castell Hendre)
Maenclochog
Llangolman
Glandy Cross
Llandilo
Blaenwaun
Pen-y-bont
Blaen-y-coed
Cynwyl Elfed
Ambleston
Wallis
Woodstock Slop
Llys-y-fran Resr.
Gwastad
New Moat
Llys-y-fran Reservoir
Llys-y-fran
Pant-y-Caws
Efailwen
Llanglydwen
Welsh Chocolate Farm
Llanwinio
Cwmbach
Cwmfelin Mynach
Cefn-y-pant
Talog
Bwlchnewydd
Golden Hill
Spittal
Walton East
Llanycefn
Login
Llanboidy
Gellywen
Abernant
Crosshands
Cwm-miles
Manor
Pembrokeshire Virtual Farm
Scolton
Penffordd
Clarbeston
Bletherston
Caerlleon
Dyffryn
Nant Cynnen
Merthyr
Rudbaxton
Clarbeston Road
Llandissilio
Hiraeth
Meidrim
Drefach
Llanfallteg
Henllan Amgoed
Llangynin
Esgair
Haverfordwest
Leachpool
Rudbaxton Rath Hillfort
Gelli
Clunderwen
Crundale
Wiston
Plain Dealings
Llawhaden
Bethesda
Llanfallteg West
Cwmfelin Boeth
Grove Land Adventure World
Glyn-Coch Craft Centre
Bancyfelin
Prendergast
Robeston Wathen
Llanddewi Velfrey
Whitland
Hywel Dda Centre
Pwlltrap
St Clears
Llangynog
Clerkenhill Adventure Farm
Canaston Bridge
HAVERFORDWEST (Hwlffordd)
Narberth (Arberth)
Robeston Back
Lampeter Velfrey
Trevaughan
Llwyn-y-brain
Backe
Uzmaston
The Rhos
Picton
Blackpool Mill
Eastern Cleddau
Crinow
Llan-mill
Llanddowror
Morfa Bach
Minwear
Bluestone
Narberth Bridge
Cold Blow
Princes Gate
Tavernspite
Halfpenny Furze
Llanybri
PEMBROKESHIRE COAST NATIONAL PARK
Boulston
Oakwood
Templeton
Llandawke
Dylan Thomas Boathouse
Hook
Landshipping
Red Roses
Laugharne
Llansteffan
Ludchurch
Llanteg
Black Tar
Martletwy
Llansadurnen
Llangwm
Yerbeston
Thomas Chapel
Reynalton
Marros
Llanmiloe
Broadway
Brook
Ferryside
Sardis
Port Lion
Loveston
Folly Farm
Kilgetty
Stepaside
Colby Woodland
Begelly
Pendine (Pentywyn)
Museum of Speed
DANGER AREA
Ginst Point
St Ishmael
Houghton
Lawrenny
Cresswell
Jeffreyston
Summerhill
Stepaside Ironworks
Amroth
(PARC CENEDLAETHOL ARFORDIR PENFRO)
Cresswell Quay
Honeyborough
West Williamston
Broadmoor
Sardis
Neyland
Burton
Upton
Carew Newton
Pentlepoir
Pembroke Ferry
Cosheston
Upton Castle
Redberth
East Williamston
Saundersfoot
Pembroke Dock
Waterloo
Milton
Carew
Sageston
Heatherton World of Activities
Broadfield
Pennar
Upper Nash
Carew Cheriton
Control Tower
New Hedges
Monkstone Point
CARMARTHEN BAY
(BAE CAERFYRDDIN)
Monkton
Pembroke (Penfro)
Bishop's Palace
Manor House
St Florence
The Dinosaur Park
Silent World
Gumfreston
Tenby (Dinbych-y-Pysgod)
Maiden Wells
Lamphey
Manorbier Newton
Carswell Old House
Penally (Penalum)
Merchant's House
National Park Centre
Hodgeston
Jameston
Lydstep
Giltar Point
St Petrox
Freshwater East
Manorbier
Caldey Sound
Cheriton or Stackpole Elidor
Trewent Point
DANGER AREA
St Margaret's Island
Caldey Abbey
Old Priory
Caldey Island
Stackpole
Old Castle Head
Chapel Point
A487
A484
A478
A475
A40
A477
A4075
A4115
A4066
A4139
B4548
B4546
B4582
B4332
B4333
B4334
B4321
B4570
B4571
B4313
B4329
B4299
B4298
B4314
B4315
B4328
B4318
B4585
B4584
B4319
B4316
B4586
43
56

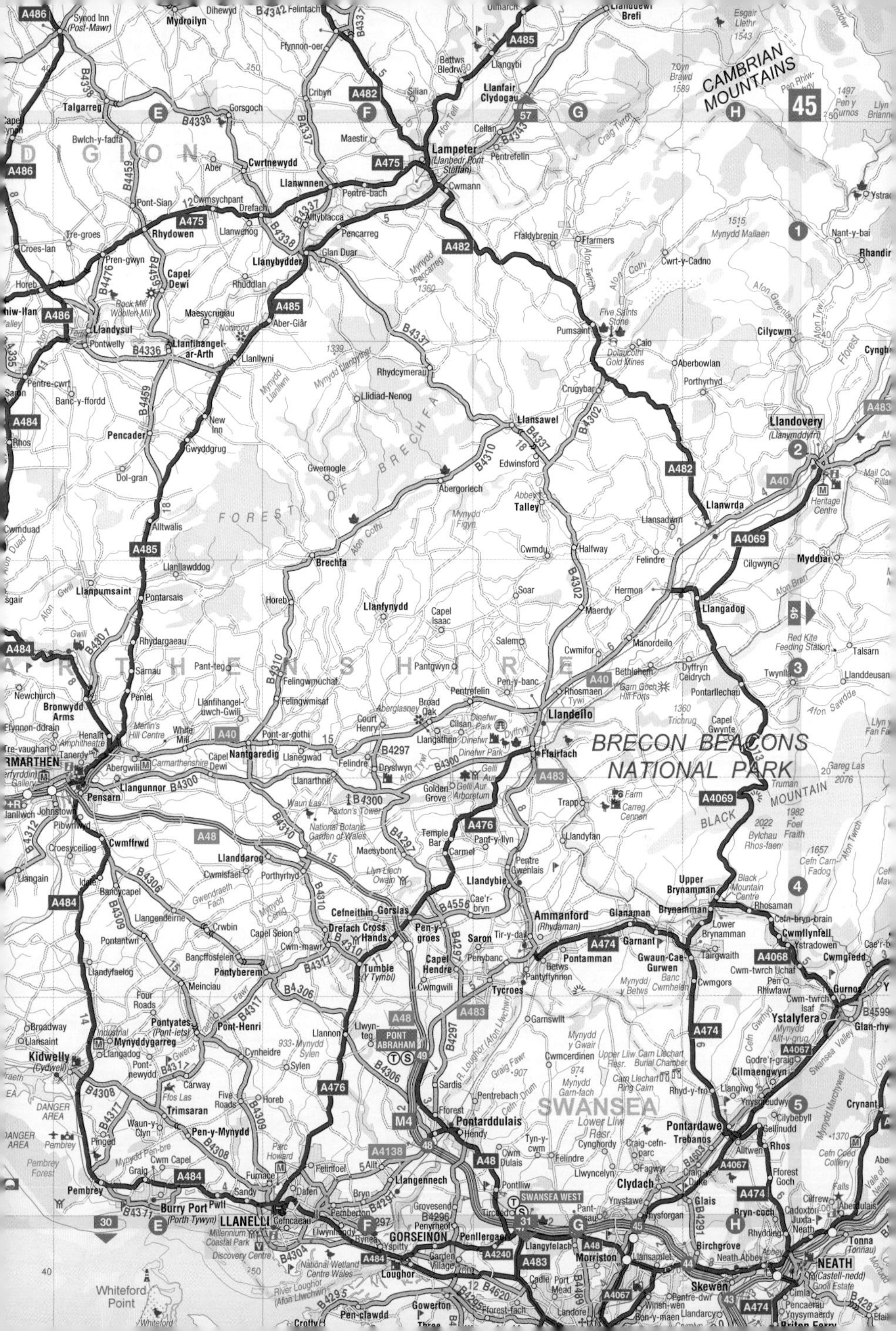
CAMBRIAN MOUNTAINS
BRECON BEACONS NATIONAL PARK
BLACK MOUNTAIN
FOREST OF BRECHFA
SWANSEA
Lampeter
(Llanbedr Pont Steffan)
Llandovery
(Llanymddyfri)
Llandeilo
Ammanford
(Rhydaman)
LLANELLI
GORSEINON
NEATH
(Castell-nedd)
Burry Port
(Porth Tywyn)
Kidwelly
(Cydweli)
Pontardawe
Pontarddulais
Llanybydder
Llandysul
Llanwrda
Llangadog
Llansawel
Talley
Brechfa
Abergorlech
Nantgaredig
Pensarn
Cwmffrwd
Llanddarog
Cefneithin
Gorslas
Drefach
Cross Hands
Tumble
(Y Tymbl)
Pontyberem
Pontyates
(Pont-iets)
Trimsaran
Pembrey
Llangennech
Loughor
Morriston
Clydach
Ystalyfera
Gurnos
Upper Brynamman
Brynamman
Glanaman
Garnant
Gwaun-Cae-Gurwen
Pumsaint
Five Saints Stone
Dolaucothi Gold Mines
Cilycwm
Rhandirmwyn
Talgarreg
Cwrtnewydd
Llanwnnen
Rhydowen
Capel Dewi
Llanfihangel-ar-Arth
Pencader
Gwyddgrug
Alltwalis
Llanpumsaint
Rhydargaeau
Bronwydd Arms
Llanfair Clydogau
Pentre-bach
Cwmann
Llanfynydd
Llangathen
Dinefwr Park
Ffairfach
Trapp
Carreg Cennen
Llandybie
Tycroes
Pontamman
Cwmllynfell
Ystradowen
Pont Abraham
Swansea West
Llyn Llech Owain
National Botanic Garden of Wales
Paxton's Tower
Aberglasney
Red Kite Feeding Station
Gwendraeth Fach
Swansea Valley
Mynydd Mallaen
A40
A48
A474
A476
A482
A483
A484
A485
A486
A4069
A4067
A4068
M4

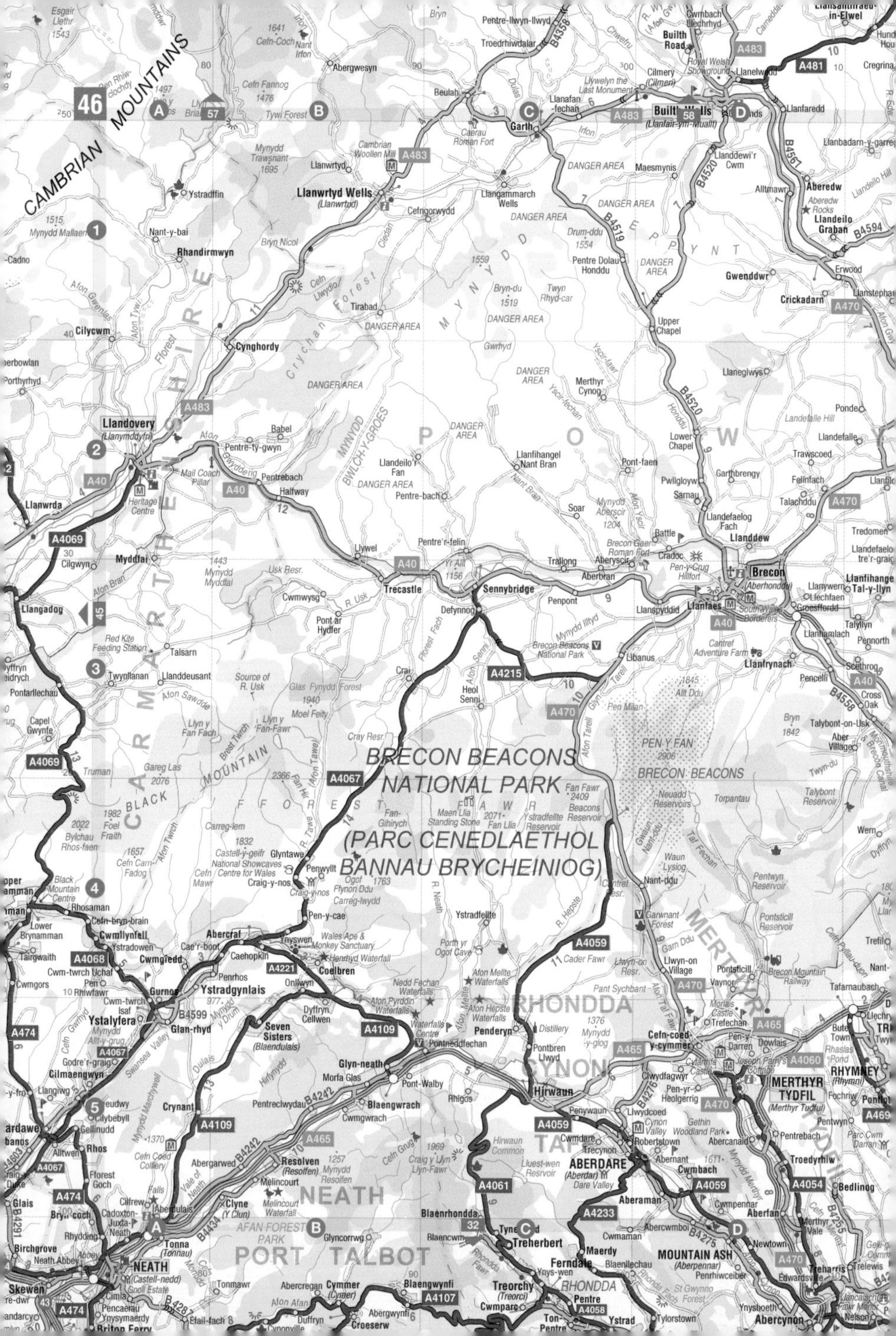
46
CAMBRIAN MOUNTAINS
Esgair Llethr
1543
1641
Cefn-Coch
Nant Irfon
Irfon
Bryn
Pentre-llwyn-llwyd
B4358
Troedrhiwdalar
Cwmbach Llechrhyd
Builth Road
A483
Llansantffraed-in-Elwel
A481
Cregrina
Hundred House
Pen Rhiw-clochdy
1497
Abergwesyn
Cefn Fannog
1476
Tywi Forest
57
Beulah
Dulas
Chwefru
Cilmery (Cilmeri)
Royal Welsh Showground
Llanelwedd
Llywelyn the Last Monument
Llanafan-fechan
Builth Wells
(Llanfair-ym-Muallt)
58
Garth
Caerau Roman Fort
Irfon
Llanfaredd
Llanbadarn-y-garreg
Mynydd Trawsnant
1695
Cambrian Woollen Mill
Llanwrtyd
Llanwrtyd Wells
(Llanwrtud)
Llangammarch Wells
Cefngorwydd
DANGER AREA
Maesmynis
Llanddewi'r Cwm
B4520
B4567
Alltmawr
Aberedw
Aberedw Rocks
Llandeilo Graban
B4594
Ystradffin
1515
Mynydd Mallaen
Nant-y-bai
Rhandirmwyn
Bryn Nicol
Cledan
B4519
Drum-ddu
1554
E P P Y N T
Pentre Dolau Honddu
Cefn Llwydlo
Crychan Forest
1559
Bryn-du
1519
Twyn Rhyd-car
M Y N Y D D
Erwood
Gwenddwr
Crickadarn
Llanstephan
A470
Tirabad
Upper Chapel
Cilycwm
Afon Gwenlas
Afon Tywi
Forest
Cynghordy
Gwrhyd
Yscir-fawr
Llaneglwys
Merthyr Cynog
Yscir-fechan
Porthyrhyd
A483
Llandovery
(Llanymddyfri)
Babel
Pentre-ty-gwyn
MYNYDD BWLCH-Y-GROES
Honddu
Lower Chapel
Landefalle Hill
Ponde
Llandefalle
P O W Y S
Mail Coach Pillar
Heritage Centre
Afon Gwydderig
Pentrebach
Halfway
A40
Llandeilo'r Fan
Pentre-bach
Llanfihangel Nant Bran
Nant Bran
Soar
Mynydd Aberscir
1204
Afon Yscir
Pont-faen
Pwllgloyw
Sarnau
Llandefaelog Fach
Garthbrengy
Trawscoed
Felinfach
Talachddu
Llanfilo
Llanwrda
A4069
Cilgwyn
Myddfai
1443
Mynydd Myddfai
Usk Resr.
Llywel
Pentre'r-felin
Yr Allt
1156
Trallong
Aberyscir
Brecon Gaer Roman Fort
Battle
Cradoc
Pen-y-Crug Hillfort
Llanddew
Brecon
(Aberhonddu)
Tredomen
Llandefaelog tre'r-graig
Llanfihangel Tal-y-llyn
Llangadog
45
Afon Bran
Cwmwysg
R. Usk
Trecastle
Sennybridge
Defynnog
Aberbran
Penpont
Llanspyddid
Llanfaes
South Wales Borderers
Llanywern
Llechfaen
Groesffordd
Talyllyn
Red Kite Feeding Station
Talsarn
Pont ar Hydfer
Forest Fach
Afon Senni
Mynydd Illtyd
Brecon Beacons National Park
Libanus
Cantref Adventure Farm
Llanhamlach
Pennorth
Scethrog
Twynllanan
Llanddeusant
Source of R. Usk
Crai
A4215
Heol Senni
Glyn Tarell
Llanfrynach
Pencelli
A40
Pontarllechau
Afon Sawdde
Glas Fynydd Forest
1940
Moel Feity
10
A470
1845
Allt Ddu
Pen Milan
B4558
Cross Oak
Capel Gwynfe
Llyn y Fan Fach
Brest Twrch
Llyn y Fan-Fawr
Cray Resr.
PEN-Y-FAN
2906
BRECON BEACONS
Bryn
1842
Talybont-on-Usk
Aber Village
Monmouthshire & Brecon Canal
A4069
Truman
Gareg Las
2076
BLACK MOUNTAIN
2366
Fan Hir
Afon Tawe
A4067
BRECON BEACONS
NATIONAL PARK
(PARC CENEDLAETHOL
BANNAU BRYCHEINIOG)
Afon Tarell
Fan Fawr
2409
Beacons Reservoir
Neuadd Reservoirs
Torpantau
Twyn-du
Talybont Reservoir
C A R M A R T H E N S H I R E
F F O R E S T   F A W R
1982
Foel Fraith
2022
Bylchau Rhos-faen
Carreg-lem
R. Tawe
Fan-Gihirych
Maen Llia Standing Stone
2071
Fan Llia
Ystradfellte Reservoir
Gwaun Nant-ddu
Taf Fechan
Wern
Dyffryn
1657
Cefn Carn Fadog
Afon Twrch
1832
Castell-y-geifr
National Showcaves Centre for Wales
Glyntawe
Penwyllt
Cefn Mawr
Craig-y-nos
Ogof Ffynon Ddu
1763
Craig-y-nos
Craig-llwydd
Cantref Resr.
Nant-ddu
Waun Lysiog
Pentwyn Reservoir
Black Mountain Centre
Rhosaman
Lower Brynamman
Cefn-bryn-brain
Cwmllynfell
Ystradowen
Tairgwaith
A4068
Cwmgiedd
Cwm-twrch Uchaf
Cwmgors
Rhiwfawr
Pen-y-cae
Abercraf
Cae'r-bont
Caehopkin
Penrhos
Ystradgynlais
Ynyswen
Wales Ape & Monkey Sanctuary
Henrhyd Waterfall
A4221
Coelbren
R. Neath
Ystradfellte
Porth yr Ogof Cave
R. Hepste
A4059
Cader Fawr
Garwnant Forest
Garn Ddu
Llwyn-on Resr.
Llwyn-on Village
Pontsticill Reservoir
Pontsticill
Brecon Mountain Railway
Vaynor
Trefil
Nant-y-bwch
Tafarnaubach
Gurnos
Cwm-twrch Isaf
977
Ystalyfera
Glan-rhyd
B4599
Mynydd Allt-y-grug
Onllwyn
Dyffryn Cellwen
Seven Sisters
(Blaendulais)
Nedd Fechan Waterfalls
Afon Pyrddin Waterfalls
Afon Mellte Waterfalls
Afon Hepste Waterfalls
Waterfalls Centre
RHONDDA
Distillery
Penderyn
Pant Sychbant
1376
Mynydd y-glog
M E R T H Y R
Morlais Castle
Trefechan
Cefn-coed y-cymmer
Pen-y-Darren
Dowlais
Joseph Parry's Cottage
A465
A4060
Rhasfas Pond
Bute Town
RHYMNEY
(Rhymni)
A474
A4067
A4109
Pontneddfechan
Glyn-neath
Morfa Glas
Pont-Walby
Pontbren Llwyd
CYNON
Hirwaun
Clwydfagwyr
Pen-yr-Heolgerrig
B4276
MERTHYR TYDFIL
(Merthyr Tudful)
Fochriw
Cilmaengwyn
Godre'r-graig
Llangiwg
Swansea Valley
Dulais
Hirfynydd
Crynant
Mynydd Marchywell
Pentreclwydau
B4242
Blaengwrach
Cwmgwrach
Rhigos
Penywaun
A4059
Llwydcoed
Cynon Valley
Gethin Woodland Park
A470
Abercanaid
Pentrebach
Pentwyn
Parc Cwm Darran
Pontlottyn
A469
Pardawe
Ystalyfera
Cilybebyll
Gellinudd
Alltwen
Rhos
A4109
A465
1370
Cefn Coed Colliery
Abergarwed
B4242
Resolven
(Resolfen)
1257
Mynydd Resolfen
Cefn Grug
1969
Craig y Llyn
Llyn-Fawr
Hirwaun Common
Lluest-wen Resrvoir
Cwmdare
Trecynon
Robertstown
TAF
ABERDARE
(Aberdar)
Dare Valley
Abernant
Cwmbach
1671
Mynydd Merthyr
Troedyrhiw
A4054
Bedlinog
A4067
Fforest Goch
A474
Glais
B4291
Bryn-coch
Cadoxton-Juxta-Neath
Rhydding
Birchgrove
Neath Abbey
Skewen
Cilfrew
Aberdulais
Falls
Vale of Neath
Melincourt
Melincourt Waterfall
Clyne
(Y Clun)
B4434
NEATH
A4061
Blaenrhondda
A4233
Aberaman
A4059
Cwmpennar
Aberfan
Merthyr Vale
B4255
AFAN FOREST PARK
Tonna
(Tonnau)
NEATH
(Castell-nedd)
Gnoll Estate
Glyncorrwg
PORT TALBOT
Blaencwm
32
Tynewydd
Treherbert
Maerdy
Cwmaman
Abercwmboi
B4275
MOUNTAIN ASH
(Aberpennar)
Newtown
Treharris
Trelewis
Tonmawr
Cimla
Pencaerau
Ynysymaerdy
Briton Ferry
Rhondda Fawr
Ferndale
Blaenllechau
Ynys-wen
Treorchy
(Treorci)
RHONDDA
Pentre
A4058
Cwmparc
Ton-Pentre
Ystrad
Tylorstown
St Gwynno Forest
Penrhiwceiber
Ynysboeth
Edwardsville
Abercynon
Nelson
Llancaiach Fawr Manor
Abercregan
Cymmer
(Cymer)
Afon Afan
Blaengwynfi
A4107
Abergwynfi
Duffryn
Croeserw
B4287
Efail-fach
A474
Sandarcy
Ffor-dwr
43

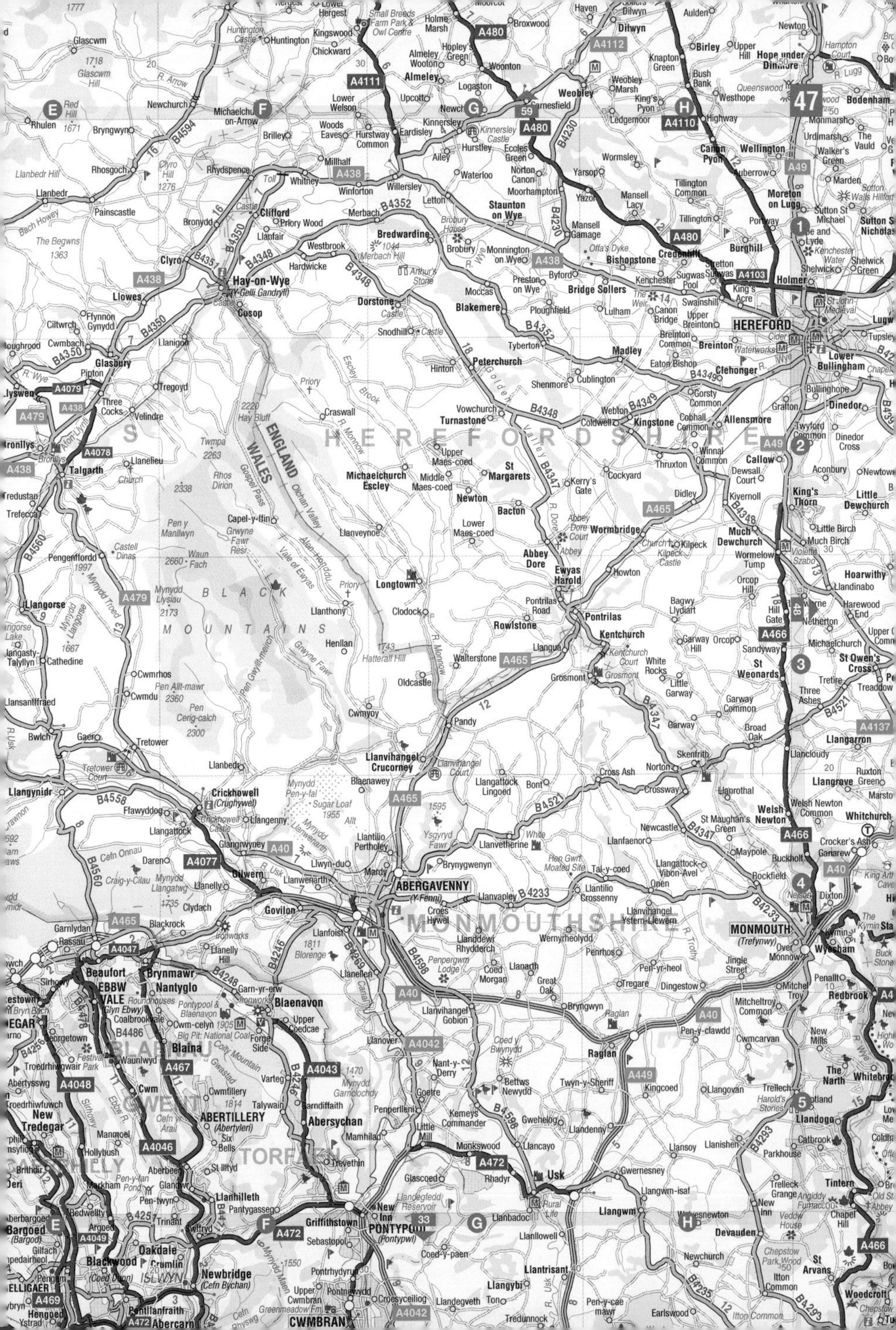
47
HEREFORDSHIRE
MONMOUTHSHIRE
ENGLAND
WALES
BLACK MOUNTAINS
HEREFORD
ABERGAVENNY
(Y Fenni)
MONMOUTH
(Trefynwy)
Hay-on-Wye
(Y Gelli Gandryll)
Crickhowell
(Crughywel)
PONTYPOOL
(Pontypwl)
CWMBRAN
ABERTILLERY
(Abertyleri)
BLAENAU
GWENT
TORFAEN
ISLWYN
EBBW VALE
(Glyn Ebwy)
Huntington
Kingswood
Small Breeds Farm Park & Owl Centre
Holme Marsh
Broxwood
Dilwyn
Weobley
Almeley
Eardisley
Kinnersley
Staunton on Wye
Bredwardine
Dorstone
Peterchurch
Madley
Clehonger
Kingstone
Allensmore
Credenhill
Burghill
Bishopstone
Bridge Sollers
Canon Pyon
Wellington
Moreton on Lugg
Hope under Dinmore
Bodenham
Holmer
Lower Bullingham
Dinedor
Callow
King's Thorn
Much Dewchurch
Little Dewchurch
Hoarwithy
Wormbridge
Kilpeck
Abbey Dore
Ewyas Harold
Pontrilas
Kentchurch
Grosmont
Longtown
Clodock
Michaelchurch Escley
St Margarets
Newton
Bacton
Turnastone
Vowchurch
Rowlstone
Walterstone
Oldcastle
Llanthony
Capel-y-ffin
Craswall
Pandy
Llanvihangel Crucorney
Skenfrith
Garway
St Weonards
Llangarron
Llangrove
Whitchurch
Welsh Newton
Cross Ash
Llanvetherine
Llanvapley
Llantilio Crossenny
Raglan
Usk
Llangwm
Devauden
Trelleck
Tintern
Llandogo
Redbrook
Wyesham
Dingestow
Mitchel Troy
Clifford
Clyro
Llowes
Cusop
Glasbury
Three Cocks
Talgarth
Bronllys
Llangorse
Cathedine
Bwlch
Tretower
Cwmdu
Llangynidr
Gilwern
Govilon
Llanfoist
Blaenavon
Brynmawr
Nantyglo
Beaufort
Blaina
Abersychan
Griffithstown
New Tredegar
Bargoed
Blackwood
Oakdale
Newbridge
(Cefn Bychan)
Abercarn
Llantrisant
Llangybi
St Arvans
Hay Bluff
Black Mountains
Sugar Loaf
Blorenge
Golden Valley
Gospel Pass
Vale of Ewyas
R. Wye
R. Monnow
R. Usk
A465
A466
A49
A40
A4077
A438
A479
A4042
A472
A4043
A4046
A4048
A4047
A480
A4111
A4110
A4103
A449
A467
A469
B4348
B4352
B4350
B4347
B4521
B4233
B4598
B4246
B4248
B4293
B4235
B4560
B4558
B4230

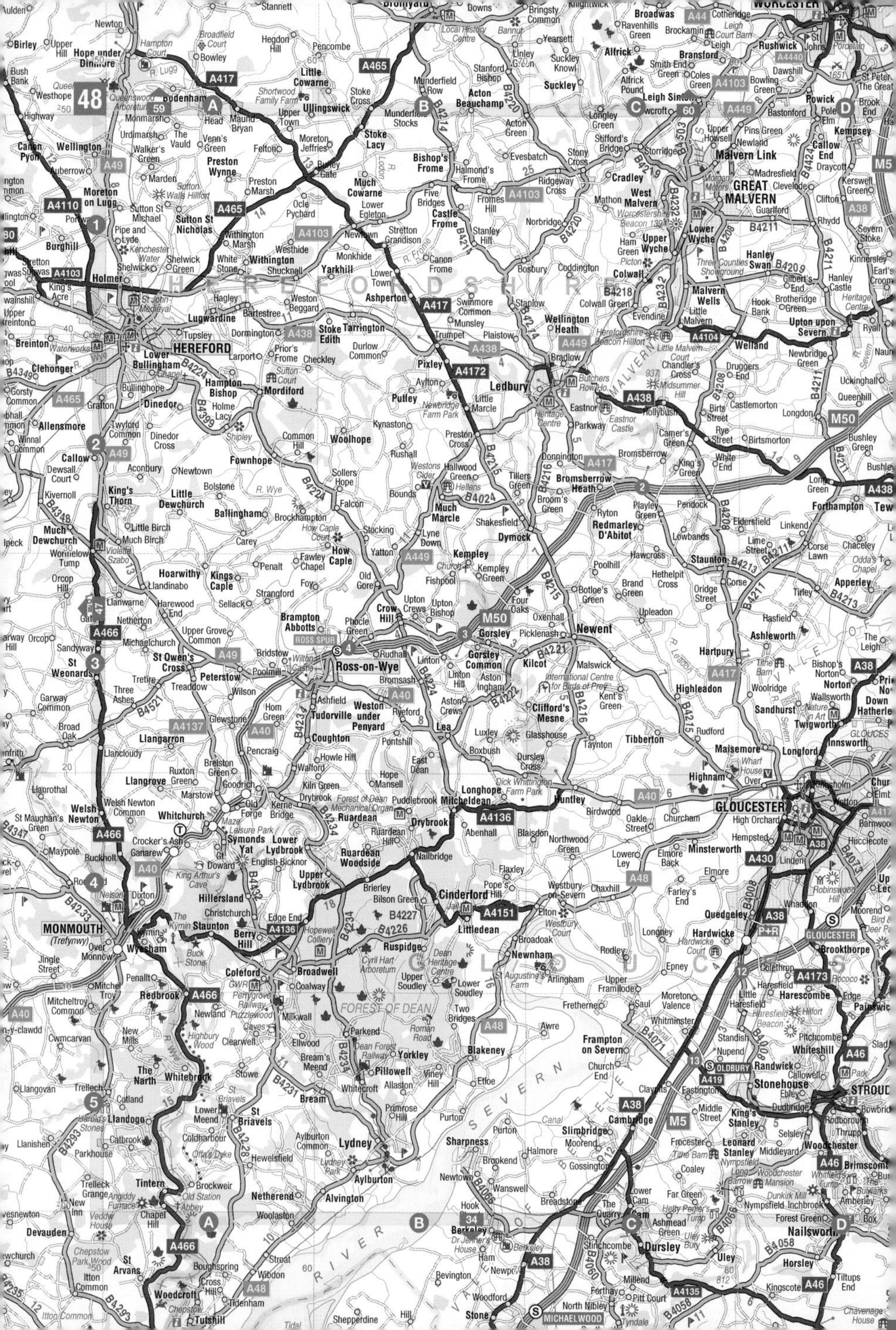

48
HEREFORDSHIRE
GLOUCESTERSHIRE
HEREFORD
Ross-on-Wye
MONMOUTH
(Trefynwy)
GLOUCESTER
GREAT MALVERN
Malvern Link
Ledbury
Newent
Cinderford
Lydney
Coleford
STROUD
Stonehouse
Dursley
Nailsworth
Berkeley
Sharpness
Mitcheldean
Newnham
Blakeney
Chepstow
Tintern
Llandogo
Whitchurch
Symonds Yat
Bromyard
Much Marcle
Dymock
Kempley
Gorsley
Upton upon Severn
Welland
Colwall
Cradley
Hope under Dinmore
Bodenham
Wellington
Moreton on Lugg
Holmer
Fownhope
Mordiford
Much Dewchurch
St Weonards
Welsh Newton
Hoarwithy
How Caple
Woolhope
Ashperton
Yarkhill
Bishop's Frome
Acton Beauchamp
Suckley
Alfrick
Leigh Sinton
Bransford
Rushwick
Powick
Kempsey
Tewkesbury
Staunton
Redmarley D'Abitot
Hartpury
Maisemore
Highnam
Huntley
Longhope
Minsterworth
Quedgeley
Hardwicke
Frampton on Severn
Slimbridge
Cambridge
Uley
Wotton
Painswick
Randwick
Whiteshill
Woodchester
Brimscombe
FOREST OF DEAN
RIVER SEVERN
WORCESTER
A4103
A417
A465
A49
A4110
A438
A4172
A449
A40
A466
A4136
A4151
A48
A38
A419
A46
A4173
A430
A4135
M50
M5
B4224
B4215
B4216
B4221
B4226
B4227
B4234
B4228
B4231
B4293

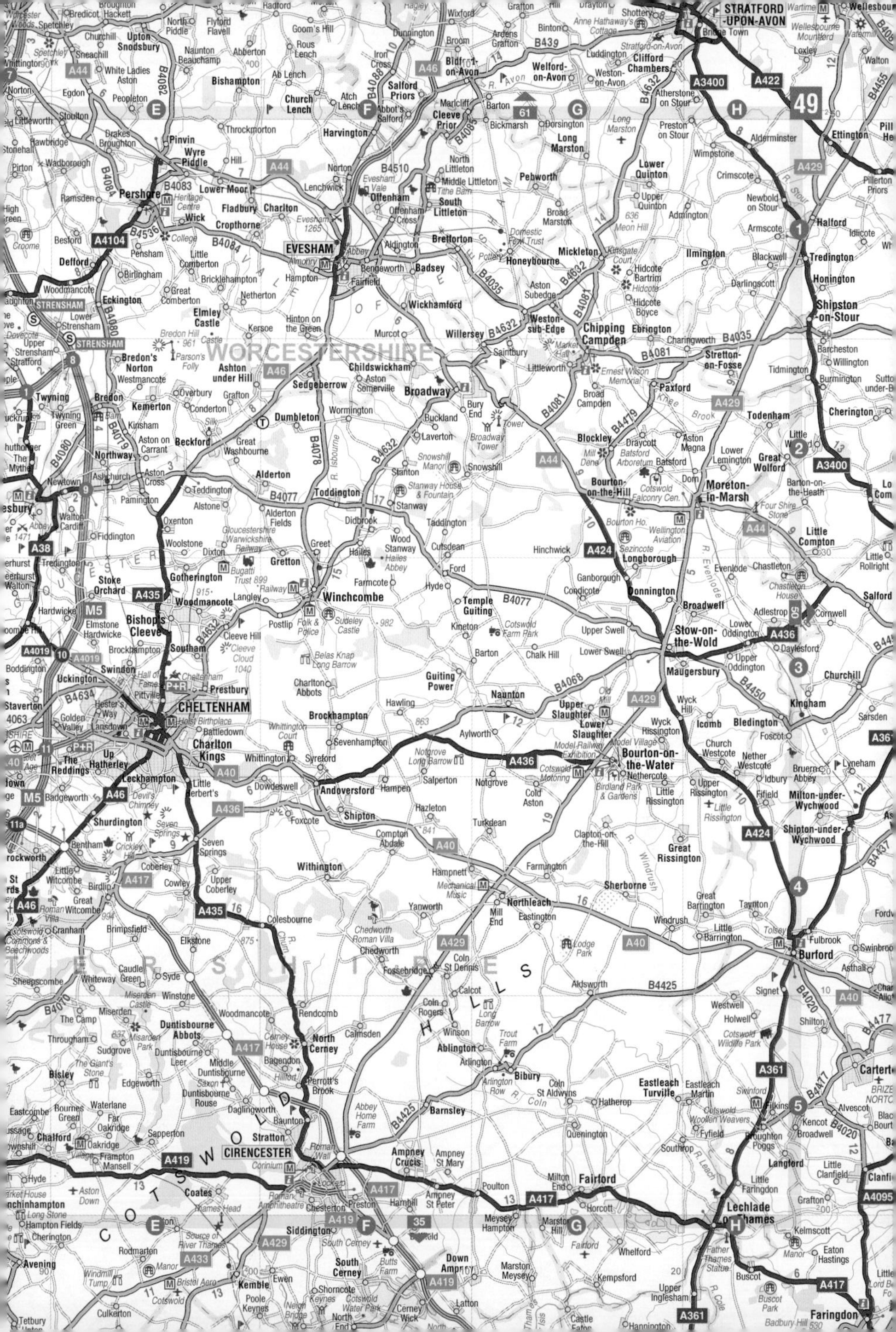

49
STRATFORD -UPON-AVON
Wellesbourne
Wellesbourne Mountford
Spetchley
Churchill
Upton Snodsbury
North Piddle
Flyford Flavell
Radford
Goom's Hill
Rous Lench
Dunnington
Broom
Ardens Grafton
Binton
Anne Hathaway's Cottage
Shottery
Bridge Town
Sneachill
Naunton Beauchamp
Abberton
Ab Lench
Iron Cross
Bidford-on-Avon
Luddington
Clifford Chambers
Stratford-on-Avon
Loxley
Walton
Whittington
White Ladies Aston
Bishampton
Church Lench
Salford Priors
Welford-on-Avon
Weston-on-Avon
Atherstone on Stour
Egdon
Peopleton
Atch Lench
Abbot's Salford
Marlcliff
Barton
Bickmarsh
Dorsington
Long Marston
Preston on Stour
Alderminster
Ettington
Littleworth
Stoulton
Throckmorton
Harvington
Cleeve Prior
Wimpstone
Drakes Broughton
Pinvin
Wyre Piddle
Hill
Norton
North Littleton
Middle Littleton
Lower Quinton
Upper Quinton
Crimscote
Pillerton Priors
Wadborough
Pershore
Heritage Centre
Lower Moor
Fladbury
Charlton
Lenchwick
Evesham Vale
Offenham
Offenham Cross
Tithe Barn
South Littleton
Pebworth
Broad Marston
Meon Hill
Admington
Newbold on Stour
Ramsden
Cropthorne
Wick
College
Pensham
Besford
Defford
Croome
Evesham
Abbey
Almonry
Bengeworth
Hampton
Fairfield
Aldington
Bretforton
Badsey
Domestic Fowl Trust
Honeybourne
Mickleton
Kiftsgate Court
Hidcote Bartrim
Hidcote
Hidcote Boyce
Ilmington
Armscote
Halford
Idlicote
Tredington
Blackwell
Honington
Darlingscott
Little Comberton
Birlingham
Bricklehampton
Great Comberton
Netherton
Woodmancote
Eckington
Strensham
Lower Strensham
Upper Strensham
Elmley Castle
Kersoe
Hinton on the Green
Wickhamford
Murcot
Aston Subedge
Weston-sub-Edge
Willersey
Saintbury
Chipping Campden
Market Hall
Ebrington
Charingworth
Shipston-on-Stour
Barcheston
Willington
Stretton-on-Fosse
Bredon Hill
Parson's Folly
Worcestershire
Bredon's Norton
Westmancote
Ashton under Hill
Childswickham
Aston Somerville
Broadway
Littleworth
Ernest Wilson Memorial
Paxford
Tidmington
Burmington
Twyning
Twyning Green
Bredon
Kemerton
Overbury
Conderton
Grafton
Sedgeberrow
Dumbleton
Wormington
Buckland
Bury End
Broadway Tower
Broad Campden
Knee Brook
Todenham
Cherington
Kinsham
Aston on Carrant
Beckford
Great Washbourne
Laverton
Snowshill Manor
Snowshill
Blockley
Draycott
Aston Magna
Batsford Arboretum
Batsford
Little Wolford
Great Wolford
Lower Lemington
Northway
The Mythe
Ashchurch
Aston Cross
Newtown
Alderton
Stanton
Stanway House & Fountain
Stanway
Bourton-on-the-Hill
Cotswold Falconry Cen.
Moreton-in-Marsh
Dorn
Barton-on-the-Heath
Pamington
Teddington
Toddington
Didbrook
Taddington
Bourton Ho.
Wellington Aviation
Four Shire Stone
Little Compton
Tewkesbury
Abbey
Walton Cardiff
Fiddington
Oxenton
Alstone
Alderton Fields
Gloucestershire Warwickshire Railway
Wood Stanway
Hailes
Hailes Abbey
Cutsdean
Hinchwick
Sezincote
Longborough
Evenlode
Chastleton
Little Rollright
Tredington
Woolstone
Dixton
Gretton
Greet
Ford
Ganborough
Condicote
Chastleton House
Deerhurst
Stoke Orchard
Gotherington
Bugatti Trust
Railway
Farmcote
Hyde
Temple Guiting
Donnington
Broadwell
Salford
Hardwicke
Elmstone Hardwicke
Woodmancote
Langley
Winchcombe
Postlip
Sudeley Castle
Folk & Police
Kineton
Cotswold Farm Park
Upper Swell
Stow-on-the-Wold
Adlestrop
Cornwell
Lower Oddington
Daylesford
Bishop's Cleeve
Cleeve Hill
Cleeve Cloud
Brockhampton
Southam
Belas Knap Long Barrow
Barton
Chalk Hill
Lower Swell
Maugersbury
Upper Oddington
Churchill
Boddington
Uckington
Swindon
Hall of Fame
Cheltenham
Prestbury
Charlton Abbots
Guiting Power
Old Mill
Wyck Hill
Icomb
Bledington
Kingham
Sarsden
Staverton
Golden Valley
Hester's Way
Lansdown
Pittville
Holst Birthplace
Battledown
Hawling
Naunton
Upper Slaughter
Lower Slaughter
Wyck Rissington
Foscot
Brockhampton
Whittington Court
Sevenhampton
Aylworth
Model Railway Exhibition
Model Village
Bourton-on-the-Water
Church Westcote
Nether Westcote
Lyneham
Bruern Abbey
Up Hatherley
The Reddings
Charlton Kings
Whittington
Syreford
Notgrove Long Barrow
Cotswold Motoring
Nethercote
Birdland Park & Gardens
Idbury
Fifield
Milton-under-Wychwood
Leckhampton
Little Herbert's
Dowdeswell
Andoversford
Hampen
Salperton
Notgrove
Cold Aston
Little Rissington
Upper Rissington
Badgeworth
Devil's Chimney
Shipton
Hazleton
Turkdean
Shipton-under-Wychwood
Shurdington
Seven Springs
Foxcote
Compton Abdale
Clapton-on-the-Hill
Windrush
Great Rissington
Brockworth
Bentham
Crickley Hill
Coberley
Withington
Hampnett
Mechanical Music
Farmington
Sherborne
Great Barrington
Taynton
Little Witcombe
Birdlip
Cowley
Upper Coberley
Northleach
Mill End
Eastington
Great Witcombe
Roman Villa
Cranham
Brimpsfield
Elkstone
Colesbourne
Yanworth
Chedworth Roman Villa
Chedworth
Lodge Park
Little Barrington
Tolsey
Burford
Fulbrook
Swinbrook
Cotswold Commons & Beechwoods
Sheepscombe
Caudle Green
Syde
Whiteway
Fossebridge
Coln St Dennis
Calcot
Aldsworth
Signet
Asthall
Miserden Castle
Winstone
Woodmancote
Rendcomb
Coln Rogers
Long Barrow
Winson
Westwell
Holwell
Shilton
The Camp
Miserden
Misarden Park
Duntisbourne Abbots
Cerney House
North Cerney
Calmsden
Trout Farm
Ablington
Arlington
Bibury
Arlington Row
Cotswold Wildlife Park
Throughham
Sudgrove
Duntisbourne Leer
Middle Duntisbourne
Saxon
Duntisbourne Rouse
Bagendon
Perrott's Brook
Coln St Aldwyns
Hatherop
Eastleach Turville
Eastleach Martin
Swinford
Filkins
Carterton
Brize Norton
Bisley
The Giant's Stone
Edgeworth
Daglingworth
Baunton
Abbey Home Farm
Barnsley
Cotswold Woollen Weavers
Kencot
Broadwell
Alvescot
Eastcombe
Bournes Green
Waterlane
Far Oakridge
Sapperton
Stratton
Cirencester
Corinium
Roman Wall
Ampney Crucis
Ampney St Mary
Quenington
Southrop
Fyfield
Broughton Poggs
Langford
Little Clanfield
Clanfield
Chalford
Oakridge
Frampton Mansell
Hyde
Aston Down
Coates
Thames Head
Roman Amphitheatre
Chesterton
Preston
Harnhill
Ampney St Peter
Poulton
Milton End
Fairford
Horcott
Little Faringdon
Grafton
Lechlade on Thames
Kelmscott
Minchinhampton
Long Stone
Hampton Fields
Cherington
Rodmarton
Manor
Source of River Thames
Siddington
South Cerney
Meysey Hampton
Marston Hill
Whelford
Father Thames Statue
Eaton Hastings
Avening
Windmill Tump
Bristol Aero
Kemble
Ewen
Butts Farm
Down Ampney
Marston Meysey
Kempsford
Buscot
Buscot Park
Little Coxwell
Cotswold
Culkerton
Poole Keynes
Shorncote
Neigh Bridge
Somerford Keynes
Cotswold Water Park
Cerney Wick
North End
Latton
Castle Eaton
Hannington
Upper Inglesham
Badbury Hill
Faringdon
Tetbury
R. Avon
R. Stour
R. Isbourne
R. Evenlode
R. Windrush
R. Churn
R. Coln
R. Leach
R. Cole
Thames
Vale of Evesham
Gloucestershire
Cotswold Hills
A44
A46
A422
A3400
A429
A4104
B4082
B4084
B4083
B4088
B4085
B4510
B439
B4632
B4536
B4035
B4081
B4080
B4079
B4078
B4077
B4479
B4068
B4450
B4634
B4425
B4020
B4437
B4477
B4070
A38
A435
A4019
A40
A436
A424
A417
A419
A433
A361
A4095
M5
Strensham

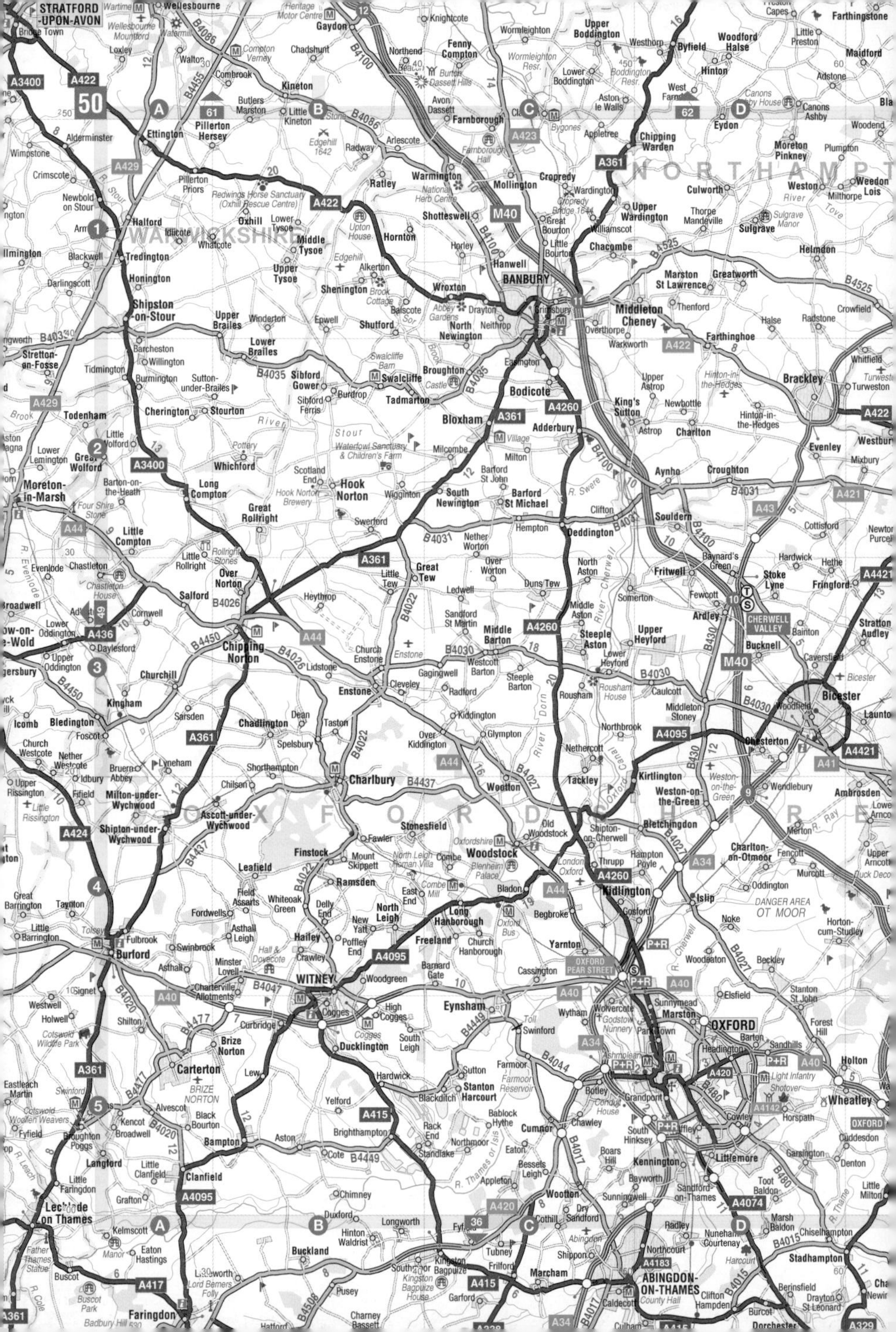
50
STRATFORD-UPON-AVON
Wellesbourne
Gaydon
Knightcote
Farthingstone
Byfield
Upper Boddington
Fenny Compton
Kineton
Ettington
Pillerton Hersey
Butlers Marston
Little Kineton
Edgehill 1642
Avon Dassett
Farnborough
Chipping Warden
Eydon
Canons Ashby
Woodford Halse
Hinton
Maidford
Alderminster
Wimpstone
Crimscote
Newbold on Stour
Pillerton Priors
Redwings Horse Sanctuary (Oxhill Rescue Centre)
Radway
Ratley
Warmington
National Herb Centre
Mollington
Cropredy
Wardington
NORTHAMPT
Culworth
Weston
Weedon Lois
Sulgrave
Sulgrave Manor
Helmdon
Halford
WARWICKSHIRE
Idlicote
Whatcote
Oxhill
Lower Tysoe
Middle Tysoe
Upper Tysoe
Upton House
Hornton
Shotteswell
Hanwell
BANBURY
Great Bourton
Little Bourton
Williamscot
Chacombe
Upper Wardington
Thorpe Mandeville
Marston St Lawrence
Greatworth
Tredington
Honington
Shipston-on-Stour
Blackwell
Darlingscott
Alkerton
Shenington
Wroxton
Abbey Gardens
Drayton
Balscote
Grimsbury
Middleton Cheney
Thenford
Overthorpe
Warkworth
Farthinghoe
Halse
Radstone
Crowfield
Whitfield
Turweston
Brackley
Upper Brailes
Lower Brailes
Winderton
Epwell
Shutford
North Newington
Neithrop
Easington
Barcheston
Willington
Tidmington
Burmington
Sutton-under-Brailes
Stretton-on-Fosse
Sibford Gower
Sibford Ferris
Burdrop
Swalcliffe
Tadmarton
Broughton
Broughton Castle
Bodicote
Upper Astrop
Newbottle
Hinton-in-the-Hedges
Cherington
Stourton
Todenham
Bloxham
Adderbury
King's Sutton
Astrop
Charlton
Evenley
Westbury
Little Wolford
Great Wolford
Lower Lemington
Whichford
Milcombe
Milton
Aynho
Croughton
Mixbury
Moreton-in-Marsh
Barton-on-the-Heath
Long Compton
Scotland End
Hook Norton
Hook Norton Brewery
Wigginton
South Newington
Barford St John
Barford St Michael
Clifton
Souldern
Cottisford
Four Shire Stone
Great Rollright
Swerford
Deddington
Hempton
Nether Worton
Over Worton
Little Compton
Little Rollright
Rollright Stones
Chastleton
Chastleton House
Evenlode
Over Norton
Little Tew
Great Tew
Ledwell
Duns Tew
North Aston
Middle Aston
Fritwell
Somerton
Fewcott
Baynard's Green
Hardwick
Hethe
Stoke Lyne
Fringford
Broadwell
Adlestrop
Lower Oddington
Upper Oddington
Daylesford
Cornwell
Salford
Heythrop
Sandford St Martin
Middle Barton
Steeple Aston
Upper Heyford
Lower Heyford
Ardley
CHERWELL VALLEY
Bainton
Stratton Audley
Stow-on-the-Wold
Chipping Norton
Church Enstone
Enstone
Lidstone
Gagingwell
Westcott Barton
Steeple Barton
Rousham
Rousham House
Caulcott
Bucknell
Caversfield
Bicester
Launton
Churchill
Kingham
Sarsden
Cleveley
Radford
Kiddington
Middleton Stoney
Woodfield
Icomb
Bledington
Foscot
Church Westcote
Nether Westcote
Chadlington
Dean
Taston
Spelsbury
Over Kiddington
Glympton
Northbrook
Nethercott
Chesterton
Idbury
Bruern Abbey
Lyneham
Shorthampton
Charlbury
Wootton
Tackley
Kirtlington
Weston-on-the-Green
Wendlebury
Ambrosden
Upper Rissington
Little Rissington
Fifield
Milton-under-Wychwood
Chilson
Ascott-under-Wychwood
Shipton-under-Wychwood
OXFORDSHIRE
Stonesfield
Old Woodstock
Shipton-on-Cherwell
Bletchingdon
Merton
Lower Arncott
Fawler
Finstock
Mount Skippett
North Leigh Roman Villa
Combe
Woodstock
Blenheim Palace
Oxfordshire Museum
Hampton Poyle
Thrupp
Charlton-on-Otmoor
Fencott
Murcott
Upper Arncott
Leafield
Ramsden
East End
Combe Mill
Bladon
London Oxford
Kidlington
Gosford
Islip
Oddington
DANGER AREA
OT MOOR
Great Barrington
Taynton
Field Assarts
Whiteoak Green
Delly End
New Yatt
North Leigh
Long Hanborough
Oxford Bus
Begbroke
Noke
Horton-cum-Studley
Little Barrington
Fordwells
Asthall Leigh
Hailey
Poffley End
Freeland
Church Hanborough
Yarnton
Woodeaton
Beckley
Burford
Fulbrook
Swinbrook
Minster Lovell
Hall & Dovecote
Crawley
Asthall
Charterville Allotments
WITNEY
Woodgreen
Barnard Gate
Cassington
OXFORD PEAR STREET
Elsfield
Stanton St John
Signet
Westwell
Holwell
Shilton
Cotswold Wildlife Park
Brize Norton
Curbridge
High Cogges
Cogges
South Leigh
Eynsham
Wytham
Wolvercote
Godstow Nunnery
Swinford
Sunnymead
Marston
OXFORD
Barton
Headington
Sandhills
Forest Hill
Holton
Carterton
BRIZE NORTON
Lew
Ducklington
Hardwick
Sutton
Stanton Harcourt
Farmoor
Farmoor Reservoir
Botley
Conduit House
Ashmolean
Grandpont
Light Infantry
Shotover
Wheatley
Eastleach Martin
Swinford
Cotswold Woollen Weavers
Fyfield
Alvescot
Kencot
Broadwell
Black Bourton
Broughton Poggs
Yelford
Blackditch
Bablock Hythe
Rack End
Standlake
Northmoor
Cumnor
Chawley
South Hinksey
Cowley
Horspath
Cuddesdon
Bampton
Aston
Cote
Brighthampton
Eaton
Boars Hill
Kennington
Littlemore
Garsington
Denton
Langford
Little Clanfield
Clanfield
Little Faringdon
Grafton
Chimney
R. Thames or Isis
Appleton
Bessels Leigh
Wootton
Bayworth
Sunningwell
Sandford-on-Thames
Toot Baldon
Little Milton
Lechlade on Thames
Kelmscott
Duxford
Hinton Waldrist
Longworth
Fyfield
Cothill
Dry Sandford
Radley
Nuneham Courtenay
Marsh Baldon
Chiselhampton
Father Thames Statue
Eaton Hastings
Manor
Buckland
Kingston Bagpuize
Kingston Bagpuize House
Southmoor
Tubney
Frilford
Shippon
Abingdon
Northcourt
Harcourt
Stadhampton
Buscot
Buscot Park
Lord Berners Folly
Pusey
Garford
Marcham
ABINGDON-ON-THAMES
County Hall
Clifton Hampden
Berinsfield
Drayton St Leonard
Faringdon
Badbury Hill
Charney Bassett
Hatford
Caldecott
Culham
Burcot
Dorchester
M40
A3400
A422
A429
A361
A4260
A423
A44
A436
A424
A4095
A40
A34
A415
A417
A420
A4074
A4183
A4142
A43
A421
A4421
A41
A329
B4035
B4026
B4450
B4022
B4030
B4031
B4027
B4437
B4047
B4477
B4020
B4449
B4044
B4017
B4015
B4508
B4086
B4100
B4455
B4525

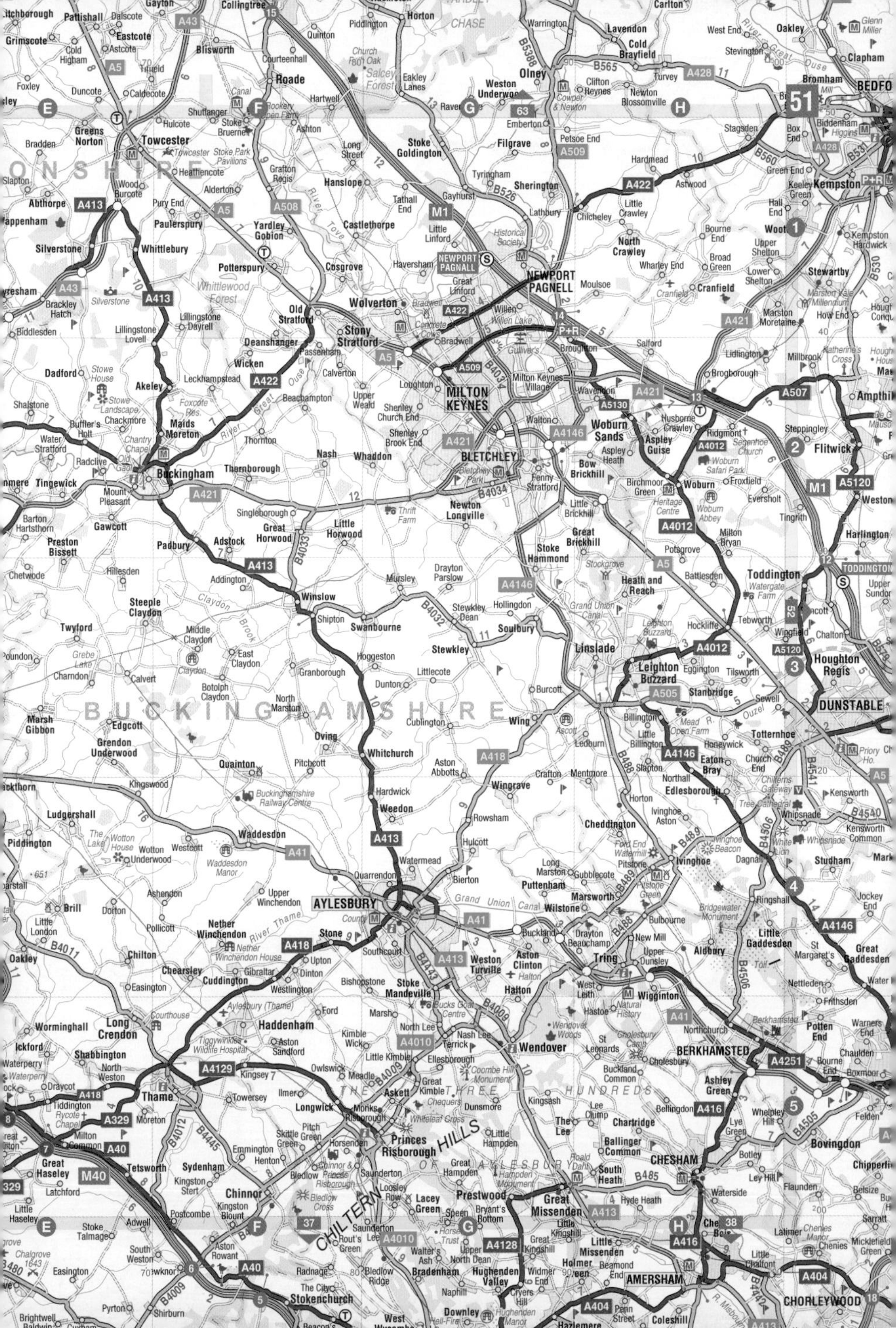

51
Gayton
Collingtree
Piddington
Horton
Chase
Carlton
Warrington
Lavendon
Cold Brayfield
West End
Oakley
Glenn Miller
Clapham
Pattishall
Dalscote
Eastcote
Astcote
Blisworth
Quinton
Courteenhall
Church Oak
Salcey Forest
Eakley Lanes
Olney
Stevington
River Great Ouse
Bromham
Bedford
Grimscote
Cold Higham
Tiffield
Roade
Weston Underwood
Clifton Reynes
Newton Blossomville
Turvey
Foxley
Duncote
Caldecote
Canal
Hartwell
Ravenstone
Cowper & Newton
Shutlanger
Rookery Open Farm
Stoke Bruerne
Emberton
Petsoe End
Stagsden
Box End
Biddenham
Higgins
Bradden
Greens Norton
Towcester
Hulcote
Ashton
Long Street
Stoke Goldington
Filgrave
Towcester
Stoke Park Pavilions
Heathencote
Grafton Regis
Hanslope
Tyringham
Sherington
Hardmead
Astwood
Green End
Kempston
Keeley Green
Slapton
Wood Burcote
Alderton
Tathall End
Gayhurst
Lathbury
Chicheley
Little Crawley
Hall End
Abthorpe
Wappenham
Pury End
Paulerspury
Yardley Gobion
Castlethorpe
Little Linford
Historical Society
Bourne End
Wootton
Kempston Hardwick
Silverstone
Whittlebury
Potterspury
Haversham
Newport Pagnell
North Crawley
Upper Shelton
Broad Green
Lower Shelton
Wharley End
Stewartby
Cosgrove
Great Linford
Moulsoe
Cranfield
Marston Vale Millennium
Whittlewood Forest
Brackley Hatch
Biddlesden
Silverstone
Lillingstone Dayrell
Lillingstone Lovell
Old Stratford
Wolverton
Bradwell
Concrete Cows
Willen
Willen Lake
Marston Moretaine
How End
Deanshanger
Stony Stratford
Bradwell
Gulliver's
Broughton
Salford
Lidlington
Millbrook
Katherine's Cross
Dadford
Stowe House
Stowe Landscape
Wicken
Passenham
Calverton
Leckhampstead
Akeley
Foxcote Res.
River Great Ouse
Beachampton
Upper Weald
Loughton
Milton Keynes
Milton Keynes Village
Wavendon
Brogborough
Ampthill
Shalstone
Chackmore
Maids Moreton
Buffler's Holt
Water Stratford
Chantry Chapel
Old Gaol
Radclive
Thornton
Shenley Church End
Shenley Brook End
Walton
Woburn Sands
Husborne Crawley
Ridgmont
Segenhoe Church
Steppingley
Flitwick
Aspley Guise
Aspley Heath
Bow Brickhill
Woburn Safari Park
Woburn
Froxfield
Buckingham
Thornborough
Nash
Whaddon
Bletchley
Bletchley Park
Fenny Stratford
Birchmoor Green
Heritage Centre
Eversholt
Tingewick
Mount Pleasant
Newton Longville
Little Brickhill
Woburn Abbey
Tingrith
Barton Hartshorn
Gawcott
Singleborough
Great Horwood
Thrift Farm
Little Horwood
Great Brickhill
Milton Bryan
Harlington
Preston Bissett
Padbury
Adstock
Stoke Hammond
Potsgrove
Chetwode
Hillesden
Addington
Drayton Parslow
Stockgrove
Battlesden
Toddington
Watergate Farm
Steeple Claydon
Claydon Brook
Winslow
Mursley
Hollingdon
Heath and Reach
Grand Union Canal
Twyford
Middle Claydon
Shipton
Swanbourne
Stewkley Dean
Soulbury
Leighton Buzzard
Tebworth
Hockliffe
Wingfield
Chalton
Poundon
Grebe Lake
East Claydon
Claydon
Stewkley
Linslade
Charndon
Calvert
Hoggeston
Granborough
Dunton
Littlecote
Leighton Buzzard
Eggington
Tilsworth
Houghton Regis
Botolph Claydon
Burcott
Stanbridge
Sewell
Dunstable
Buckinghamshire
North Marston
Cublington
Wing
Ascott
Billington
Mead Open Farm
Ouzel
Marsh Gibbon
Edgcott
Oving
Little Billington
Ledburn
Totternhoe
Priory Ho.
Grendon Underwood
Pitchcott
Whitchurch
Aston Abbotts
Honeywick
Slapton
Eaton Bray
Church End
Quainton
Crafton
Mentmore
Northall
Edlesborough
Chilterns Gateway
Kingswood
Buckinghamshire Railway Centre
Hardwick
Wingrave
Horton
Tree Cathedral
Whipsnade
Kensworth
Ludgershall
Weedon
Ivinghoe Aston
Cheddington
Rowsham
Whipsnade
Kensworth Common
Piddington
The Lake
Wotton House
Wotton Underwood
Westcott
Waddesdon
Waddesdon Manor
Hulcott
Ford End Watermill
Ivinghoe Beacon
Dagnall
Studham
Watermead
Pitstone
Ivinghoe
Long Marston
Gubblecote
Brill
Dorton
Ashendon
Upper Winchendon
Quarrendon
Aylesbury
County
Bierton
Puttenham
Marsworth
Pitstone Green
Ringshall
Jockey End
Little London
Pollicott
Nether Winchendon
River Thame
Grand Union Canal
Wilstone
Bridgewater Monument
Bulbourne
Little Gaddesden
Great Gaddesden
St Margaret's
Oakley
Chilton
Nether Winchendon House
Stone
Upton
Southcourt
Buckland
Drayton Beauchamp
New Mill
Aldbury
Chearsley
Gibraltar
Dinton
Weston Turville
Aston Clinton
Tring
Upper Dunsley
Toll
Easington
Cuddington
Westlington
Bishopstone
Stoke Mandeville
Halton
West Leith
Wigginton
Nettleden
Aylesbury (Thame)
Courthouse
Ford
Bucks Goat Centre
Natural History
Frithsden
Worminghall
Long Crendon
Haddenham
Marsh
North Lee
Hastoe
Wendover Woods
Northchurch
Berkhamsted
Potten End
Warners End
Tiggywinkles Wildlife Hospital
Aston Sandford
Kimble Wick
Nash Lee
Terrick
Wendover
St Leonards
Cholesbury Camp
Ickford
Shabbington
Little Kimble
Ellesborough
Coombe Hill Monument
Cholesbury
Chaulden
Waterperry
North Weston
Owlswick
Meadle
Buckland Common
Bourne End
Boxmoor
Draycot
Thame
Kingsey
Ilmer
Great Kimble
Askett
The Three Hundreds
Chequers
Kingsash
Ashley Green
Tiddington
Rycote Chapel
Towersey
Longwick
Monks Risborough
Whiteleaf Cross
Dunsmore
Lee Clump
Bellingdon
Whelpley Hill
Felden
Moreton
Milton Common
Skittle Green
Pitch Green
Princes Risborough
Hills
Little Hampden
The Lee
Chartridge
Lye Green
Bovingdon
Great Haseley
Tetsworth
Horsenden
Emmington
Henton
Chinnor & Princes Risborough
Ballinger Common
Chesham
Botley
Chipperfield
Sydenham
Kingston Stert
Bledlow
Saunderton
Great Hampden
Hampden Monument
Of Aylesbury
Roald Dahl
South Heath
Ley Hill
Latchford
Chinnor
Bledlow Cross
Chiltern
Loosley Row
Lacey Green
Prestwood
Bryant's Bottom
Great Missenden
Hyde Heath
Waterside
Flaunden
Belsize
Little Haseley
Postcombe
Kingston Blount
Speen
Little Kingshill
Great Kingshill
Sarratt
Stoke Talmage
Adwell
Saunderton Lee
Horse Trust
Little Missenden
Chenies Manor
Chenies
Micklefield Green
South Weston
Aston Rowant
Rout's Green
Walter's Ash
Upper North Dean
Chalgrove 1643
Latimer
Little Chalfont
Lewknor
Radnage
Bledlow Ridge
Bradenham
Hughenden Valley
Widmer End
Holmer Green
Beamond End
Amersham
Easington
The City
Naphill
Cryers Hill
Chorleywood
Stokenchurch
Pyrton
Downley
Hell-Fire Caves
Hughenden Manor
Penn Street
R. Misbourne
Shirburn
Brightwell Baldwin
Cuxham
Beacon's
West Wycombe
Hazlemere
Coleshill
A43
A5
A413
A508
A422
A421
A428
B565
B5388
A509
B526
M1
B560
B531
B530
A5130
A4146
A4012
A507
A5120
B4034
B4033
B4032
A505
A418
A41
B488
B489
B4506
B4540
A4010
B4443
B4009
A4129
A329
A40
M40
B4012
B4445
A4128
A4251
A416
B4505
B485
A404
B4011
B480
B4442

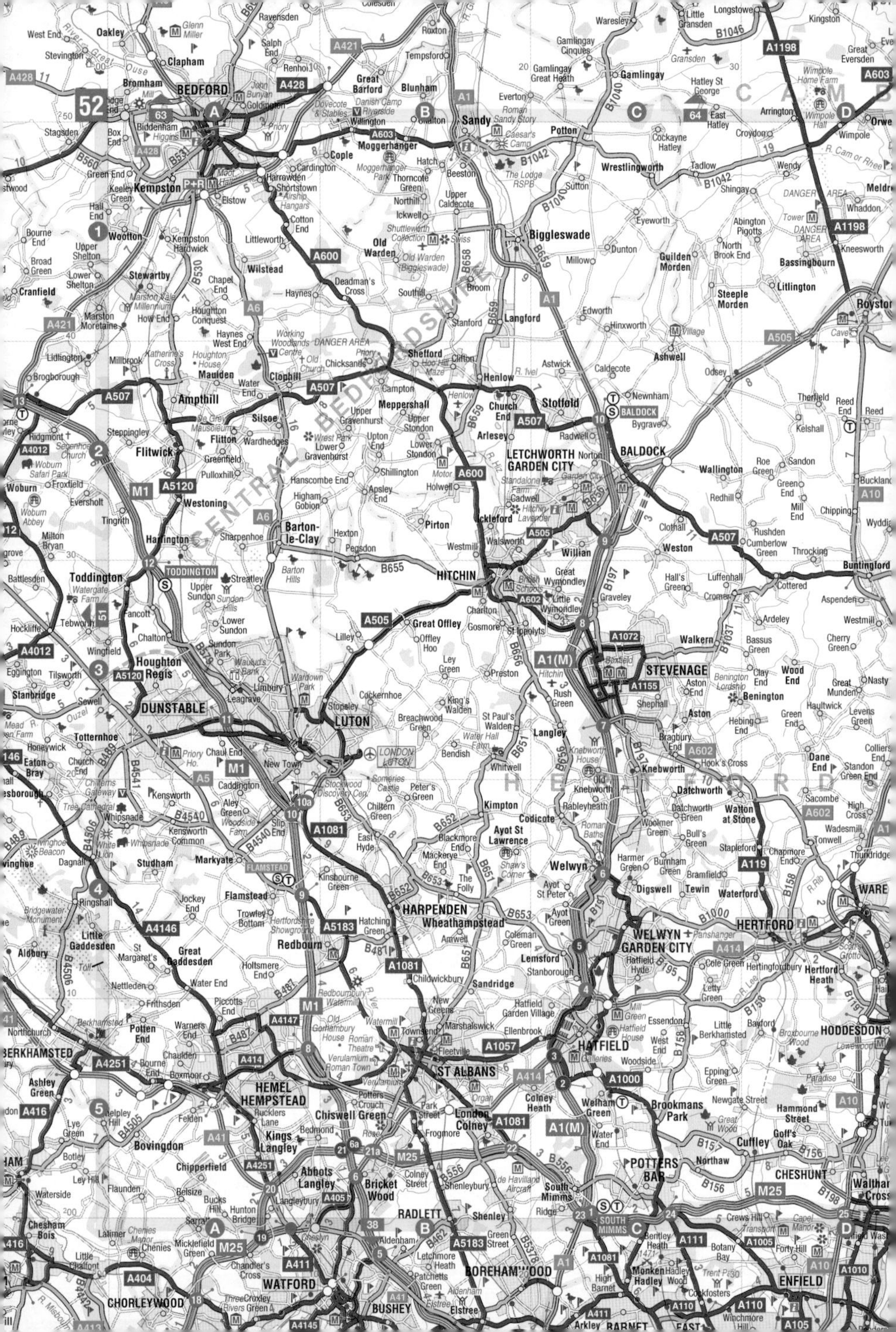

52
Ravensden
Oakley
Glenn Miller
West End
Salph End
Roxton
Stevington
Clapham
Renhold
Tempsford
A421
Little Gransden
Longstowe
Kingston
Waresley
B1046
A1198
Gamlingay Cinques
Great Eversden
Gransden
A428
Bromham
BEDFORD
John Bunyan
Goldington
A428
Great Barford
Blunham
Gamlingay
Gamlingay Great Heath
Everton
Hatley St George
Wimpole Home Farm
A603
CAMB
63
Biddenham
Dovecote & Stables
Danish Camp Riverside
Willington
A1
Sandy
Roman Sandy Story
Potton
B1040
64
East Hatley
Arrington
Wimpole Hall
Orwell
Wimpole
Stagsden
Box End
Higgins
Priory
A603
Moggerhanger
Caesar's Camp
Cockayne Hatley
Croydon
A428
B531
Cople
B1042
R. Cam or Rhee
Green End
Cardington
Moggerhanger Park
Hatch
Beeston
The Lodge RSPB
Wrestlingworth
Tadlow
Wendy
Meldreth
Keeley Green
Kempston
P+R
Moot Hall
Harrowden
Shortstown
Thorncote Green
Sutton
B1042
Shingay
DANGER AREA
Elstow
Airship Hangars
Northill
Upper Caldecote
Whaddon
Hall End
Cotton End
Ickwell
Eyeworth
Abington Pigotts
Tower
A1198
Bourne End
Wootton
Kempston Hardwick
Littleworth
Shuttleworth Collection
Swiss
Biggleswade
B1040
Dunton
Upper Shelton
Old Warden
Old Warden (Biggleswade)
B658
Guilden Morden
North Brook End
Kneesworth
Broad Green
Stewartby
Wilstead
A600
Millow
Bassingbourn
Lower Shelton
B530
Chapel End
Deadman's Cross
Southill
B659
Cranfield
Marston Vale Millennium
Haynes
Broom
Steeple Morden
Litlington
Marston Moretaine
How End
Houghton Conquest
A6
Stanford
Langford
A1
Edworth
Royston
A421
Haynes West End
Working Woodlands Centre
DANGER AREA
Hinxworth
Village
Cave
A505
Lidlington
Millbrook
Katherine's Cross
Houghton House
Old Church
Priory
Chicksands
Shefford
Hoo Hill Maze
Clifton
Astwick
Caldecote
Ashwell
Brogborough
Maulden
Water End
Clophill
Henlow
R. Ivel
Odsey
Therfield
Reed End
Reed
13
A507
Ampthill
A507
Campton
Henlow
Church End
Stotfold
Newnham
BALDOCK
Silsoe
Meppershall
Upper Gravenhurst
Upper Stondon
A507
Bygrave
Ridgmont
Segenhoe Church
Steppingley
De Grey Mausoleum
Flitton
Wardhedges
CENTRAL BEDFORDSHIRE
Wrest Park
Upton End
Lower Stondon
B659
Arlesey
Radwell
Kelshall
A4012
Flitwick
Greenfield
Lower Gravenhurst
Motor
LETCHWORTH GARDEN CITY
Norton
BALDOCK
Woburn Safari Park
Pulloxhill
Shillington
A600
Standalone Farm
Garden City
Wallington
Roe Green
Sandon
Buckland
Woburn
Froxfield
M1
A5120
Hanscombe End
Holwell
Cadwell
Green End
A10
Woburn Abbey
Eversholt
Westoning
Higham Gobion
Apsley End
Hitchin Lavender
B656
Redhill
Mill End
Chipping
Tingrith
A6
Barton-le-Clay
Hexton
Pirton
Ickleford
A505
Clothall
A507
Rushden
Wyddial
Milton Bryan
Harlington
Sharpenhoe
Pegsdon
Westmill
Walsworth
Willian
Weston
Cumberlow Green
Throcking
Buntingford
Toddington
TODDINGTON
Barton Hills
B655
HITCHIN
Great Wymondley
British Schools
Hall's Green
Luffenhall
Cottered
Battlesden
Watergate Farm
Upper Sundon
Streatley
Sundon Hills
A602
Little Wymondley
Graveley
Cromer
Aspenden
Tebworth
Fancott
Lower Sundon
A505
Great Offley
Offley Hoo
Lilley
Charlton
Gosmore
St Ippolyts
B197
B1037
Ardeley
Westmill
Hockliffe
Chalton
Sundon Park
A1072
Walkern
Bassus Green
Cherry Green
A4012
Wingfield
Houghton Regis
B579
Wauluds Bank
Limbury
Wardown Park
Ley Green
B656
A1(M)
Hitchin
Bedfield
STEVENAGE
Clay End
Wood End
Nasty
Eggington
Tilsworth
A5120
Leagrave
Stopsley
Cockernhoe
Preston
A1155
Benington Lordship
Aston End
Great Munden
Stanbridge
Sewell
DUNSTABLE
Luton
Breachwood Green
King's Walden
Rush Green
Shephall
Benington
Haultwick
Ouzel
Chaul End
St Paul's Walden
Langley
Aston
Green End
Levens Green
Mead Farm
Totternhoe
Priory Ho.
M1
New Town
LONDON LUTON
Water Hall Farm
Bendish
B651
Bragbury End
Hebing End
A602
Colliers End
Honeywick
Whitwell
Knebworth House
Hook's Cross
Dane End
Standon
Eaton Bray
Church End
B489
B4541
Chilterns Gateway
A5
Caddington
Stockwood Discovery Cen.
Someries Castle
Peter's Green
HERTFORD
Old Knebworth
Knebworth
Datchworth
Standon Green End
Edlesborough
Kensworth
Aley Green
Woodside Farm
Chiltern Green
Kimpton
Codicote
Rableyheath
Datchworth Green
Watton at Stone
Sacombe
High Cross
Tree Cathedral
Whipsnade
B4540
Kensworth Common
Slip End
A1081
East Hyde
B652
Blackmore End
Ayot St Lawrence
Roman Baths
Woolmer Green
Bull's Green
A602
Wadesmill
Tonwell
Ivinghoe Beacon
White Lion
Whipsnade
B4506
Dagnall
Studham
Markyate
FLAMSTEAD
Mackerye End
The Folly
B651
Shaw's Corner
Welwyn
Harmer Green
Burnham Green
Stapleford
Chapmore End
Thundridge
Ringshall
Kinsbourne Green
B653
Ayot St Peter
Digswell
Tewin
Bramfield
Waterford
B158
R. Rib
WARE
Bridgewater Monument
Jockey End
Flamstead
HARPENDEN
Wheathampstead
B653
Ayot Green
B1000
Little Gaddesden
A4146
Trowley Bottom
Hertfordshire Showground
A5183
Hatching Green
Amwell
Coleman Green
WELWYN GARDEN CITY
Panshanger
HERTFORD
Aldbury
St Margaret's
Great Gaddesden
Redbourn
B481
A1081
Lemsford
Hatfield Hyde
A414
Cole Green
Hertingfordbury
Hertford Heath
Scotts Grotto
Toll
Holtsmere End
Childwickbury
Sandridge
Stanborough
B195
Letty Green
Nettleden
Water End
Redbournbury Watermill
R. Ver
Hatfield Garden Village
Mill Green
Frithsden
Piccotts End
B487
M1
New Greens
Marshalswick
B158
Essendon
Bayford
Little Berkhamsted
Broxbourne Wood
HODDESDON
Berkhamsted
Potten End
Warners End
A4147
Old Gorhambury House
Roman Theatre
Watermill
Townsend
Ellenbrook
Hatfield House
West End
Northchurch
B487
Verulamium Roman Town
Fleetville
A1057
HATFIELD
Galleries
Woodside
BERKHAMSTED
A4251
Bourne End
Chaulden
A414
Verulamium
ST ALBANS
A414
A1000
Epping Green
Ashley Green
Boxmoor
HEMEL HEMPSTEAD
Potters Crouch
Park Street
Organ
Colney Heath
Welham Green
Brookmans Park
Newgate Street
Paradise
A416
Felden
Bucklers Lane
Chiswell Green
London Colney
A1081
A10
Bovingdon
Kings Langley
Bedmond
Frogmore
Rose
A1(M)
Water End
Great Wood
Hammond Street
Goff's Oak
Lye Green
Chipperfield
A41
A4251
Abbots Langley
M25
Colney Street
Shenleybury
de Havilland Aircraft
South Mimms
B556
B157
Northaw
Cuffley
B156
B156
POTTERS BAR
CHESHUNT
Botley
Ley Hill
Flaunden
Belsize
Bricket Wood
Langleybury
A405
M25
Waltham Cross
Waterside
Bucks Hill
Hunton Bridge
RADLETT
Shenley
Ridge
Crews Hill
Capel Manor
Chesham Bois
Latimer
Chenies
Sarratt
Mickleffeld Green
M25
Cheslyn
Aldenham
A5183
Green Street
B5378
SOUTH MIMMS
Bentley Heath
A111
Transport
A1005
Forty Hill
A10
A1010
Little Chalfont
A404
CHORLEYWOOD
Chandler's Cross
A411
WATFORD
Letchmore Heath
Patchetts Green
Aldenham
BOREHAMWOOD
A1
A1081
High Barnet
Monken Hadley
Hadley Wood
Trent Park
Botany Bay
Cockfosters
ENFIELD
Three Rivers
Croxley Green
BUSHEY
A41
Elstree
A411
Arkley
BARNET
A110
A110
Winchmore Hill
A105
A4145
A413

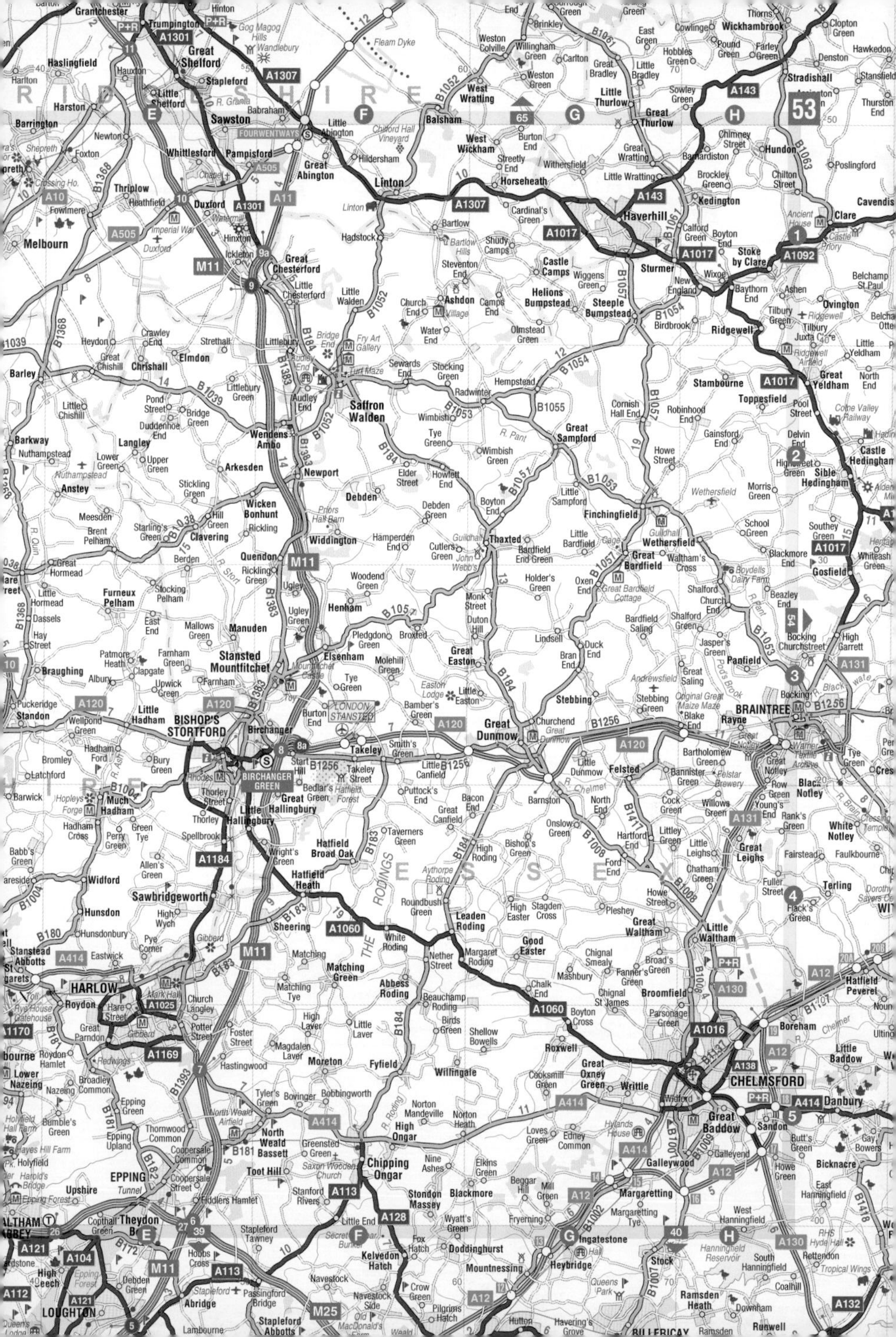

53
Grantchester
Trumpington
Great Shelford
Haslingfield
Harston
Barrington
Sawston
Whittlesford
Pampisford
Thriplow
Duxford
Melbourn
Great Chesterford
Little Chesterford
Balsham
West Wratting
West Wickham
Horseheath
Linton
Haverhill
Great Thurlow
Little Thurlow
Great Bradley
Kedington
Sturmer
Stoke by Clare
Clare
Stradishall
Hundon
Ridgewell
Great Yeldham
Toppesfield
Stambourne
Castle Hedingham
Sible Hedingham
Steeple Bumpstead
Helions Bumpstead
Castle Camps
Ashdon
Saffron Walden
Audley End
Wendens Ambo
Newport
Debden
Widdington
Thaxted
Great Sampford
Little Sampford
Finchingfield
Wethersfield
Great Bardfield
Radwinter
Hempstead
Elmdon
Chrishall
Barley
Barkway
Anstey
Langley
Arkesden
Clavering
Wicken Bonhunt
Quendon
Henham
Manuden
Stansted Mountfitchet
Elsenham
Furneux Pelham
Braughing
Standon
Little Hadham
Much Hadham
Bishop's Stortford
Birchanger
Takeley
Great Dunmow
Great Easton
Stebbing
Felsted
Rayne
Braintree
Gosfield
Black Notley
White Notley
Great Leighs
Terling
Great Waltham
Little Waltham
Broomfield
Chelmsford
Great Baddow
Danbury
Boreham
Hatfield Peverel
Little Baddow
Great Hallingbury
Hatfield Broad Oak
Hatfield Heath
Sheering
Sawbridgeworth
Widford
Hunsdon
Harlow
Roydon
Leaden Roding
Good Easter
Pleshey
Writtle
Roxwell
Fyfield
Moreton
Chipping Ongar
North Weald Bassett
Epping
Theydon Bois
Loughton
Abridge
Stapleford Abbotts
Kelvedon Hatch
Doddinghurst
Mountnessing
Ingatestone
Margaretting
Galleywood
Stock
Billericay
Ramsden Heath
Runwell
Bicknacre
Sandon
London Stansted
Birchanger Green
Fourwentways
E S S E X
R I D G E S H I R E
M11
M25
A1307
A1017
A143
A1092
A120
A1060
A414
A12
A131
A130
A113
A128
A1184
A1016
A138
A1169
A1025
A121
A104
A112
A132
A505
A10
A11
A1301

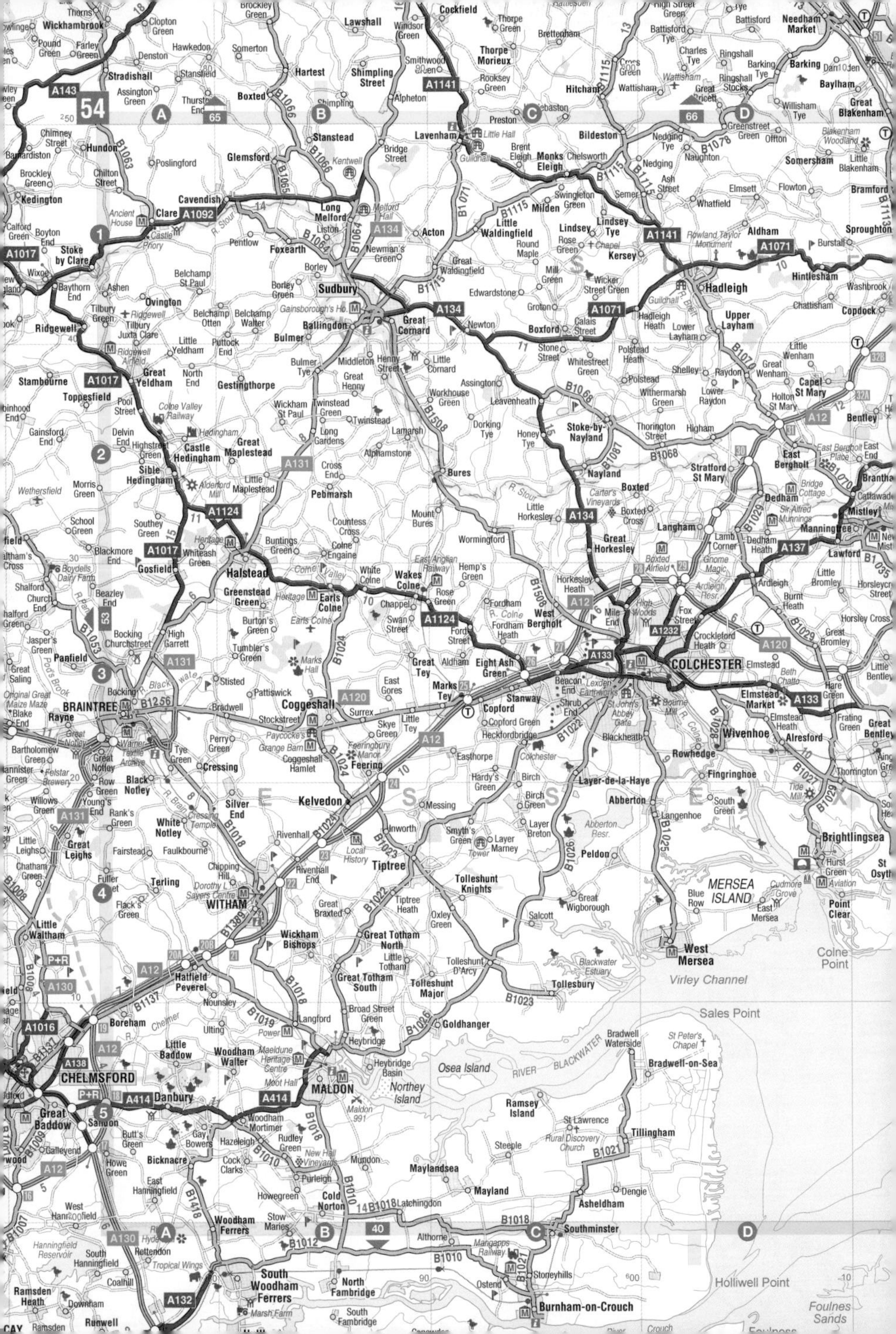

54
Wickhambrook
Clopton Green
Lawshall
Cockfield
Thorpe Green
Needham Market
Battisford
Pound Green
Farley Green
Hawkedon
Somerton
Windsor Green
Brettenham
Battisford Tye
Denston
Stradishall
Stansfield
Hartest
Shimpling Street
Smithwood Green
Thorpe Morieux
Charles Tye
Ringshall
Barking Tye
Barking
Baylham
A143
Assington Green
Thurston End
Boxted
Shimpling
Alpheton
A1141
Rooksey Green
Cross Green
Wattisham
Hitcham
Ringshall Stocks
Great Bricett
Willisham Tye
Great Blakenham
A
B
C
D
65
66
Chimney Street
Hundon
Stanstead
Lavenham
Little Hall
Preston
Kettlebaston
Bildeston
Nedging Tye
Greenstreet Green
Offton
Blakenham Woodland
Little Blakenham
Barnardiston
Poslingford
Glemsford
Bridge Street
Guildhall
Brent Eleigh
Monks Eleigh
Chelsworth
Naughton
Nedging
Somersham
Brockley Green
Chilton Street
Kentwell
Ash Street
Elmsett
Flowton
Bramford
Kedington
Cavendish
Long Melford
Melford Hall
Swingleton Green
Semer
Whatfield
Clare
A1092
Ancient House
Castle
Priory
R. Stour
Liston
Milden
Little Waldingfield
Lindsey Tye
Lindsey
Aldham
Sproughton
Calford Green
Boyton End
Pentlow
Foxearth
A134
Acton
Round Maple
Rose Green
Chapel
Kersey
A1141
Rowland Taylor Monument
A1071
Burstall
A1017
Stoke by Clare
Newman's Green
Great Waldingfield
Mill Green
Wicker Street Green
Hadleigh
Hintlesham
Wixoe
Baythorn End
Ashen
Belchamp St Paul
Borley
Borley Green
Sudbury
Edwardstone
Washbrook
Ovington
Ridgewell
Tilbury Green
Tilbury Juxta Clare
Belchamp Otten
Belchamp Walter
Gainsborough's Ho.
Ballingdon
Great Cornard
Newton
Groton
Boxford
Calais Street
Hadleigh Heath
Lower Layham
Upper Layham
Chattisham
Copdock
Little Yeldham
Puttock End
Bulmer
Stone Street
Polstead Heath
Whitestreet Green
Little Wenham
Stambourne
Great Yeldham
North End
Gestingthorpe
Bulmer Tye
Middleton
Henny Street
Little Cornard
Great Henny
Assington
Polstead
Shelley
Raydon
Great Wenham
Capel St Mary
Toppesfield
Pool Street
Colne Valley Railway
Wickham St Paul
Twinstead Green
Twinstead
Workhouse Green
Leavenheath
Withermarsh Green
Lower Raydon
Holton St Mary
Bentley
Gainsford End
Delvin End
Hedingham
Castle Hedingham
Great Maplestead
Long Gardens
Lamarsh
Dorking Tye
Honey Tye
Stoke-by-Nayland
Thorington Street
Higham
A12
East Bergholt
East End
Highstreet Green
Alphamstone
Bures
Nayland
Stratford St Mary
East Bergholt Place
Wethersfield
Sible Hedingham
Alderford Mill
Little Maplestead
A131
Cross End
Pebmarsh
R. Stour
B1068
Bridge Cottage
Brantham
Morris Green
Carter's Vineyards
Boxted
Dedham
Cattawade
School Green
Southey Green
A1124
Countess Cross
Mount Bures
Little Horkesley
Boxted Cross
Langham
Sir Alfred Munnings
Mistley
Manningtree
Blackmore End
Heritage
Buntings Green
Colne Engaine
Wormingford
Great Horkesley
Lamb Corner
Dedham Heath
A137
Lawford
Gosfield
Whiteash Green
Halstead
Colne Valley
White Colne
Wakes Colne
East Anglian Railway
Hemp's Green
Horkesley Heath
Boxted Airfield
Gnome Magic
Ardleigh
Little Bromley
Shalford
Boydells Dairy Farm
Beazley End
Greenstead Green
Earls Colne
Chappel
Rose Green
Fordham
R. Colne
West Bergholt
Mile End
High Woods
Ardleigh Resr.
Fox Street
Burnt Heath
Horsley Cross
Church End
Swan Street
Fordham Heath
A1232
Crockleford Heath
Great Bromley
Jasper's Green
Bocking Churchstreet
High Garrett
Burton's Green
Tumbler's Green
Marks Hall
Ford Street
Great Tey
Aldham
Eight Ash Green
A133
COLCHESTER
Elmstead
Little Bentley
Panfield
Great Saling
Stisted
Pattiswick
East Gores
Marks Tey
Beacon End
Lexden Earthworks
Beth Chatto
Hare Green
Original Great Maize Maze
Rayne
BRAINTREE
Bocking
Bradwell
Coggeshall
A120
Stanway
Shrub End
St John's Abbey Gate
Bourne Mill
Elmstead Market
Blake End
Stockstreet
Surrex
Skye Green
Little Tey
Copford
Copford Green
Heckfordbridge
Blackheath
Elmstead Heath
Frating Green
Great Bentley
Great Notley
Warner Textile Archive
Perry Green
Tye Green
Paycocke's
Grange Barn
Coggeshall Hamlet
Feeringbury Manor
Feering
Easthorpe
Colchester
Wivenhoe
Alresford
Rowhedge
Bartholomew Green
Felstar Brewery
Cressing
Thorrington
Row Green
Black Notley
Kelvedon
Hardy's Green
Birch
Layer-de-la-Haye
Fingringhoe
Young's End
Rank's Green
Silver End
Messing
Birch Green
Abberton
South Green
Tide Mill
Great Leighs
White Notley
Cressing Temple
Rivenhall
Inworth
Smyth's Green
Layer Marney Tower
Layer Breton
Abberton Resr.
Langenhoe
Brightlingsea
Little Leighs
Fairstead
Faulkbourne
Local History
Tiptree
Tolleshunt Knights
Peldon
Hurst Green
St Osyth
Chatham Green
Terling
Chipping Hill
Dorothy L. Sayers Centre
Rivenhall End
MERSEA ISLAND
Cudmore Grove
Fuller Street
WITHAM
Tiptree Heath
Great Braxted
Oxley Green
Great Wigborough
Blue Row
East Mersea
Aviation
Point Clear
Flack's Green
Salcott
Little Waltham
Wickham Bishops
Great Totham North
Little Totham
West Mersea
P+R
Hatfield Peverel
Great Totham South
Tolleshunt D'Arcy
Blackwater Estuary
Colne Point
A130
Tolleshunt Major
Tollesbury
Virley Channel
Nounsley
Broad Street Green
Sales Point
Boreham
Chelmer
Langford
Goldhanger
Bradwell Waterside
St Peter's Chapel
A1016
Ulting
Power
Heybridge
Little Baddow
Woodham Walter
Maeldune Heritage Centre
Heybridge Basin
Osea Island
RIVER BLACKWATER
Bradwell-on-Sea
A138
CHELMSFORD
Moot Hall
MALDON
Northey Island
Danbury
A414
Maldon 991
Ramsey Island
St Lawrence
Great Baddow
Sandon
Woodham Mortimer
Gay Bowers
Hazeleigh
Rudley Green
New Hall Vineyards
Rural Discovery Church
Tillingham
Galleyend
Butt's Green
Steeple
Bicknacre
Cock Clarks
Mundon
Howe Green
Purleigh
Maylandsea
East Hanningfield
Howegreen
Cold Norton
Mayland
Dengie
West Hanningfield
Latchingdon
Asheldham
Stow Maries
Woodham Ferrers
Rettendon
Hyde Hall
Hanningfield Reservoir
South Hanningfield
Tropical Wings
Althorne
Mangapps Railway Museum
Southminster
40
Coalhill
South Woodham Ferrers
North Fambridge
Ostend
Stoneyhills
Holliwell Point
Ramsden Heath
Downham
Marsh Farm
Burnham-on-Crouch
Runwell
South Fambridge
Foulness Sands

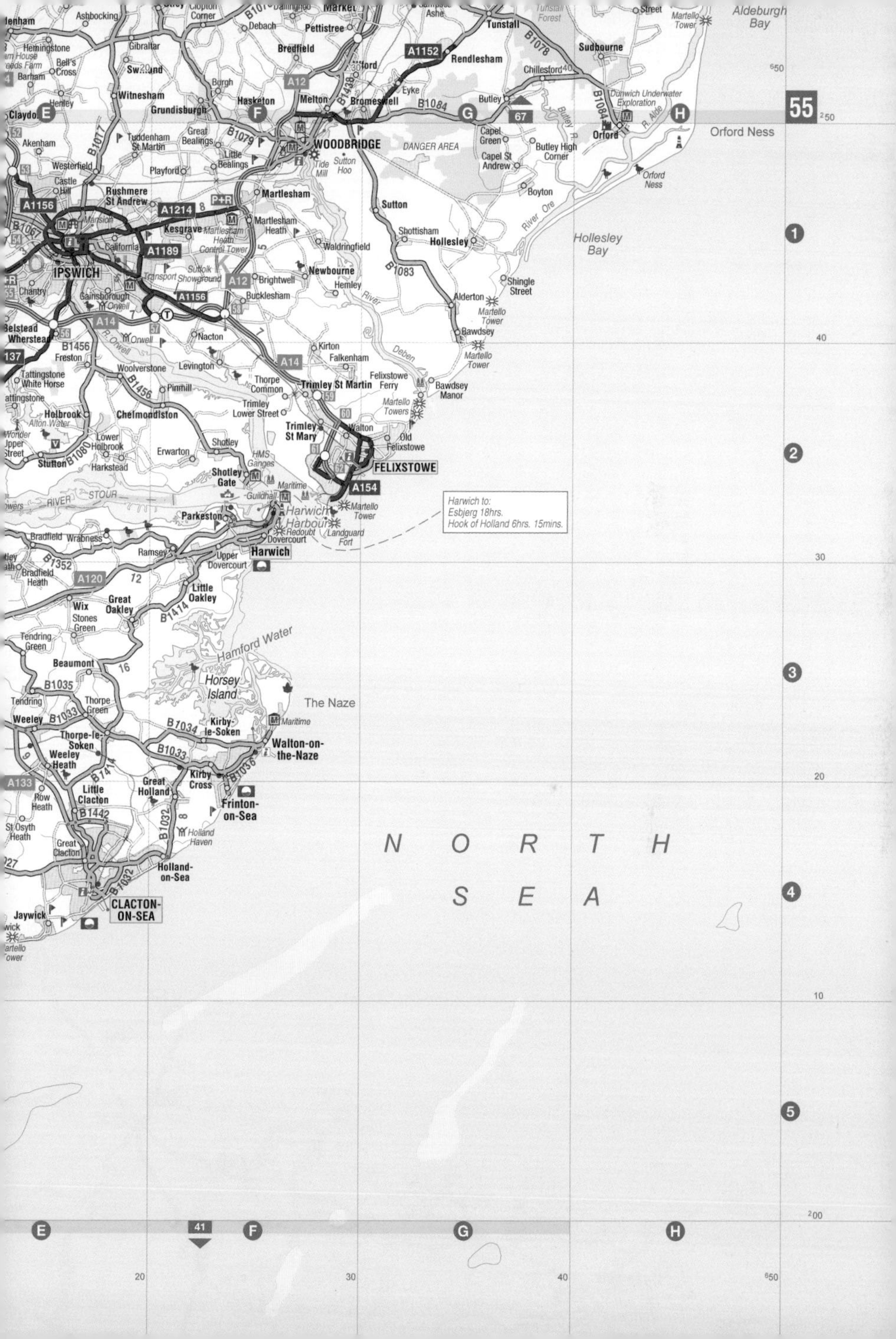
Ashbocking
Clopton Corner
Debach
Pettistree
Bredfield
Tunstall
Tunstall Forest
Street
Martello Tower
Aldeburgh Bay
Hemingstone
Bell's Cross
Barham
Gibraltar
Witnesham
Grundisburgh
Hasketon
Melton
Bromeswell
Eyke
Rendlesham
A1152
Sudbourne
Chillesford
B1078
Butley
B1084
Dunwich Underwater Exploration
Orford
R. Alde
Orford Ness
Henley
Claydon
Akenham
Tuddenham St Martin
Great Bealings
Little Bealings
B1079
WOODBRIDGE
Tide Mill
Sutton Hoo
DANGER AREA
Capel Green
Capel St Andrew
Butley High Corner
Westerfield
Castle Hill
Playford
Rushmere St Andrew
A1156
A1214
P+R
Martlesham
Martlesham Heath
Martlesham Heath Control Tower
Sutton
Boyton
River Ore
Hollesley Bay
Shottisham
Hollesley
Kesgrave
California
A1189
Mansion
IPSWICH
Waldringfield
Newbourne
Hemley
B1083
Shingle Street
Suffolk Showground
Transport
Brightwell
Bucklesham
A12
Chantry
Gainsborough
Orwell
Alderton
Martello Tower
Bawdsey
Belstead
Wherstead
A14
Nacton
Kirton
Falkenham
River Deben
B1456
Freston
Woolverstone
Levington
Felixstowe Ferry
Bawdsey Manor
Tattingstone White Horse
Tattingstone
Pin Mill
Thorpe Common
Trimley St Martin
Martello Towers
Holbrook
Alton Water
Chelmondiston
Trimley Lower Street
Trimley St Mary
Walton
Old Felixstowe
FELIXSTOWE
A154
Lower Holbrook
Upper Street
Stutton
B1080
Harkstead
Erwarton
Shotley
HMS Ganges
Shotley Gate
Maritime
Guildhall
RIVER STOUR
Parkeston
Harwich
Harwich Harbour
Redoubt
Dovercourt
Landguard Fort
Harwich to:
Esbjerg 18hrs.
Hook of Holland 6hrs. 15mins.
Bradfield
Wrabness
Ramsey
Upper Dovercourt
Harwich
B1352
Bradfield Heath
A120
Little Oakley
Wix
Great Oakley
Stones Green
B1414
Hamford Water
Tendring Green
Beaumont
B1035
Horsey Island
The Naze
Tendring
Thorpe Green
Weeley
B1033
B1034
Kirby-le-Soken
Maritime
Thorpe-le-Soken
Weeley Heath
Walton-on-the-Naze
A133
Little Clacton
Great Holland
Kirby Cross
B1036
Frinton-on-Sea
Row Heath
B1442
St Osyth Heath
B1032
Holland Haven
Great Clacton
NORTH SEA
Holland-on-Sea
CLACTON-ON-SEA
Jaywick
Martello Tower
41
E
F
G
H
1
2
3
4
5
20
30
40
650
250
200
10
67

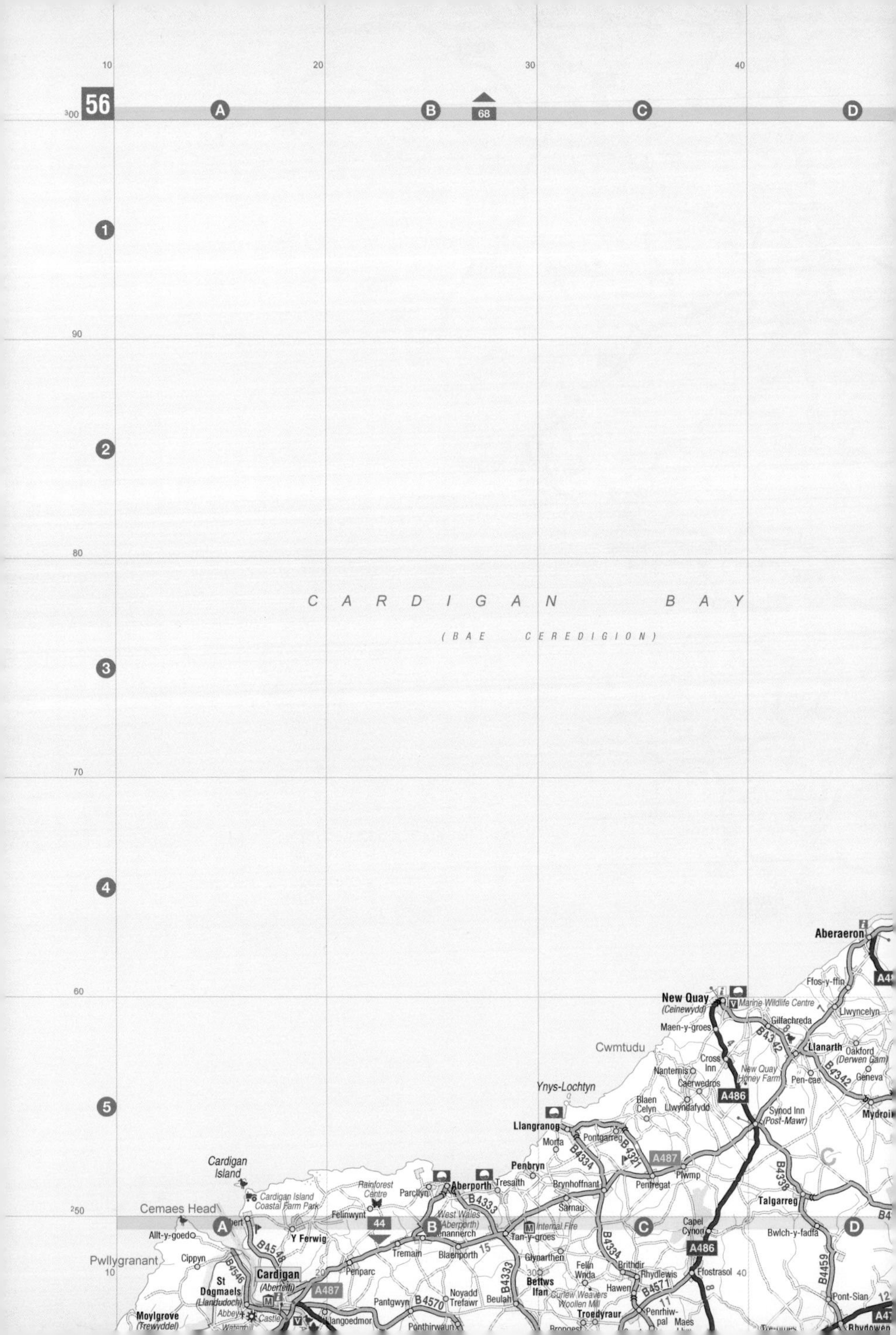

①

90

②

80

C A R D I G A N   B A Y

(B A E   C E R E D I G I O N)

③

70

④

Aberaeron

Ffos-y-ffin A4

60

New Quay
(Ceinewydd) Marine Wildlife Centre

Maen-y-groes Llwyncelyn

Cwmtudu Gilfachreda

Cross Llanarth

Ynys-Lochtyn Nantemis Inn Oakford
Caerwedros New Quay *(Derwen Gam)*
Honey Farm Pen-cae Geneva

⑤ Blaen
Celyn Llwyndafydd A486
Synod Inn
Llangranog A487 *(Post-Mawr)* Mydroil
Morfa Pontgarreg

Penbryn Brynhoffnant Piwmp

Tresaith Pentregat A4

Aberporth Sarnau Talgarreg

250 *Cardigan
Island* Rainforest
Centre Parcllyn Capel
Cynon A486
Cemaes Head Cardigan Island Felinwynt *West Wales Internal Fire* Bwlch-y-fadfa
Coastal Farm Park Aberporth Tan-y-groes
Allt-y-goedo **Ⓐ** **44** **Ⓑ** **Ⓒ** **Ⓓ**

Pwllygranant Cippyn Tremain Blaenporth Glynarthen Brithdir B4459
Glandwr Felin Flostrasol 40
Cardigan Y Ferwig Pantgwyn Wnda Rhydlewis Pont-Sian
St *(Aberteifi)* Noyadd **Bettws** Hawen Maes
Dogmaels A487 Trefawr Beulah **Ifan** Curlew Weavers
(Llandudoch) Woollen Mill **Troedyraur**
Moylgrove Castle Penrhiw- A4
(Trewyddel) Llangoedmor Ponthirwaun B4570 pal

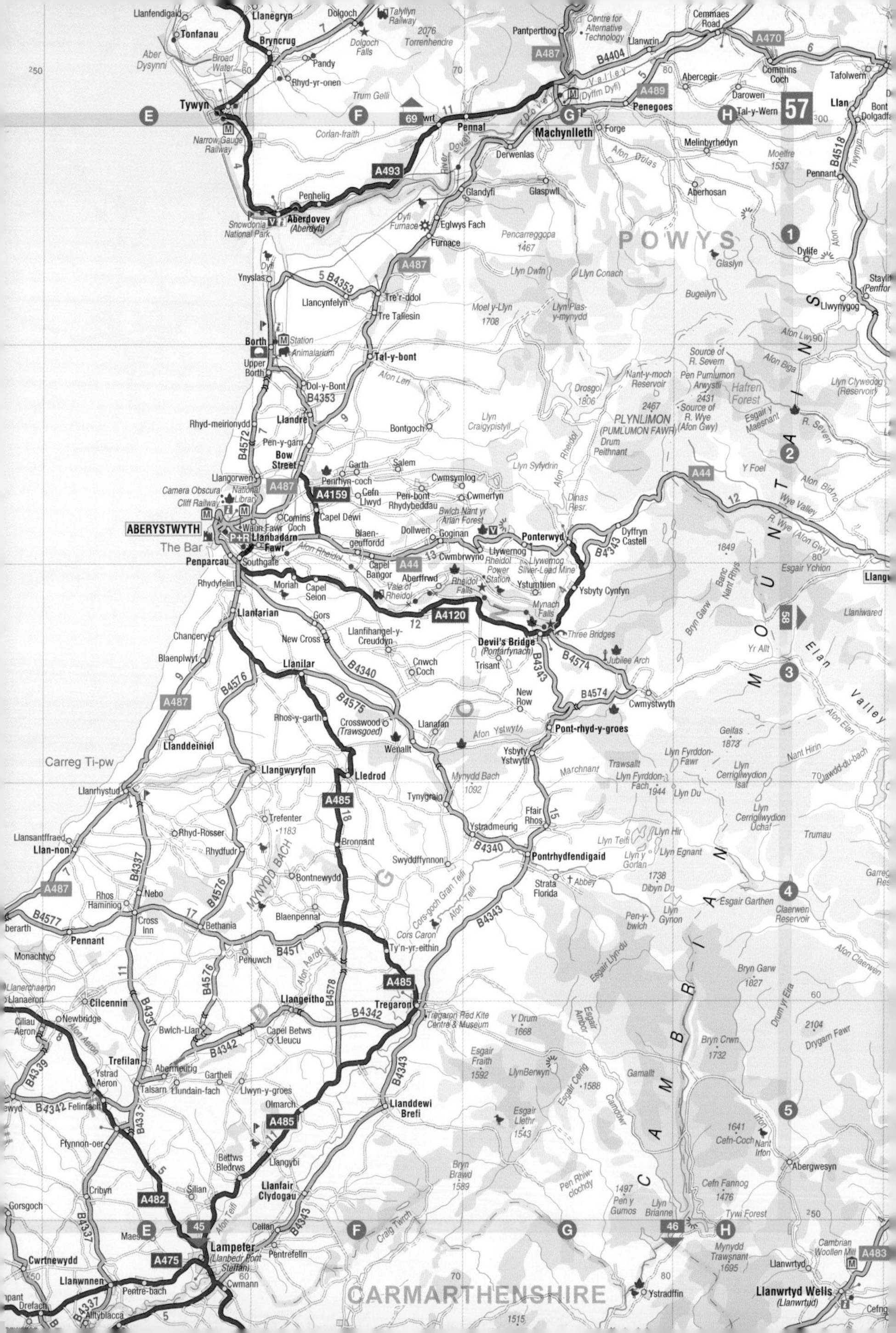

Llanfendigaid
Tonfanau
Llanegryn
Dolgoch
Talyllyn Railway
Dolgoch Falls
2076 Torrenhendre
Bryncrug
Aber Dysynni
Broad Water
Pandy
Rhyd-yr-onen
Trum Gelli
Tywyn
Narrow Gauge Railway
Corlan-fraith
A493
Penhelig
Aberdovey (Aberdyfi)
Snowdonia National Park
Pantperthog
Centre for Alternative Technology
Llanwrin
Cemmaes Road
A470
A487
B4404
Commins Coch
Tafolwern
Abercegir
Darowen
A489
Penegoes
Tal-y-Wern
57
Llan
Bont Dolgadfan
Machynlleth
Forge
Pennal
69
Derwenlas
Afon Dulas
Melinbyrhedyn
Moelfre 1537
Pennant
B4518
Glandyfi
Glaspwll
Aberhosan
Dyfi Furnace
Eglwys Fach
Furnace
Pencarreggopa 1467
POWYS
Dylife
Glaslyn
Dyfi
Ynyslas
B4353
Tre'r-ddol
Llancynfelyn
Tre Taliesin
Llyn Dwfn
Llyn Conach
Moel y-Llyn 1708
Llyn Plas-y-mynydd
Bugeilyn
Llwynygog
Staylittle (Penffordd)
Borth
Station
Animalarium
Upper Borth
Tal-y-bont
Afon Leri
Dol-y-Bont
B4353
Llandre
Bontgoch
Drosgol 1806
Nant-y-moch Reservoir
Source of R. Severn
Pen Pumlumon Arwystli 2431
Source of R. Wye (Afon Gwy)
Hafren Forest
Llyn Clywedog (Reservoir)
2467
PLYNLIMON (PUMLUMON FAWR)
Drum Peithnant
Llyn Craigypistyll
Esgair y Maesnant
R. Severn
Afon Lwyd
Afon Biga
Rhyd-meirionydd
B4572
Pen-y-garn
Bow Street
Garth
Salem
Llyn Syfydrin
Afon Rheidol
Y Foel
Afon Bidno
Llangorwen
Camera Obscura
National Library
Cliff Railway
Penrhyn-coch
Cwmsymlog
A4159
Cefn Llwyd
Pen-bont Rhydybeddau
Cwmerfyn
Dinas Resr.
A44
Wye Valley
ABERYSTWYTH
Comins Coch
Capel Dewi
Bwlch Nant yr Arian Forest
Waun Fawr
Llanbadarn Fawr
P+R
The Bar
Blaen-geuffordd
Dollwen
Goginan
Ponterwyd
Dyffryn Castell
B4343
R. Wye (Afon Gwy)
1849
Penparcau
Southgate
Afon Rheidol
Capel Bangor
Cwmbrwyno
Llywernog
Llywernog Silver-Lead Mine
Rheidol Power Station
Banc Nant Rhys
Esgair Ychion
Rhydyfelin
Moriah
Capel Seion
Aberffrwd
Vale of Rheidol
Rheidol Falls
Ystumtuen
Ysbyty Cynfyn
Mynach Falls
Bryn Garw
58
Llaniwared
Llanfarian
Gors
A4120
Three Bridges
Chancery
New Cross
Llanfihangel-y-Creuddyn
Devil's Bridge (Pontarfynach)
Yr Allt
Elan Valley
Blaenplwyf
Llanilar
Cnwch Coch
Trisant
B4574
Jubilee Arch
B4340
B4576
B4575
New Row
Cwmystwyth
A487
Rhos-y-garth
Crosswood (Trawsgoed)
Llanafan
Pont-rhyd-y-groes
Afon Ystwyth
Wenallt
Afon Elan
Llanddeiniol
Gelfas 1873
Ysbyty Ystwyth
Trawsallt
Llyn Fyrddon-Fawr
Nant Hirin
Carreg Ti-pw
Llangwyryfon
Lledrod
Mynydd Bach 1092
Marchnant
Llyn Fyrddon-Fach 1944
Llyn Du
Llyn Cerrigllwydion Isaf
Llanrhystud
A485
Tynygraig
Ffair Rhos
Llyn Cerrigllwydion Uchaf
Trefenter 1183
Ystradmeurig
Llyn Hir
Trumau
Llansantffraed
Llan-non
Rhyd-Rosser
Rhydfudr
Bronnant
B4340
Llyn Teifi
Llyn Egnant
Llyn y Gorlan
Pontrhydfendigaid
Swyddffynnon
MYNYDD BACH
Bontnewydd
Strata Florida
Abbey
1738
Dibyn Du
B4337
Nebo
Rhos Haminiog
Cors-goch Gran Teifi
Afon Teifi
Llyn Gynon
Esgair Garthen
Claerwen Reservoir
Cross Inn
Bethania
Blaenpennal
Pen-y-bwlch
B4577
Pennant
Cors Caron
B4343
Monachty
Penuwch
Ty'n-yr-eithin
Esgair Llyn-du
Afon Claerwen
Afon Aeron
B4576
Llanerchaeron
Llanaeron
B4578
Bryn Garw 1827
Cilcennin
Llangeitho
Tregaron
Drum yr Eira
Ciliau Aeron
Newbridge
B4342
Tregaron Red Kite Centre & Museum
Y Drum 1668
Esgair Ambor
2104
Drygarn Fawr
Bwlch-Llan
Capel Betws Lleucu
Esgair Fraith 1592
Bryn Crwn 1732
B4339
Trefilan
Ystrad Aeron
Abermeurig
Gartheli
LlynBerwyn
Esgair Cerrig 1588
Gamallt
Talsarn
Llundain-fach
Llwyn-y-groes
Olmarch
Camddwr
Felinfach
Llanddewi Brefi
Esgair Llethr 1543
1641 Cefn-Coch
Nant Irfon
Irfon
Ffynnon-oer
Bettws Bledrws
Llangybi
Abergwesyn
Cribyn
Silian
A482
Llanfair Clydogau
Bryn Brawd 1589
Pen Rhiw-clochdy
1497 Pen y Gumos
Llyn Brianne
Cefn Fannog 1476
Tywi Forest
Gorsgoch
Maes
Cellan
Craig Twrch
45
46
Lampeter (Llanbedr Pont Steffan)
A475
Pentrefelin
Mynydd Trawsnant 1695
Cambrian Woollen Mill
A483
Cwrtnewydd
Llanwnnen
Pentre-bach
Cwmann
Llanwrtyd
Llanwrtyd Wells (Llanwrtyd)
CARMARTHENSHIRE
Ystradffin
Drefach
Alltyblacca
1515
Cefn
CAMBRIAN MOUNTAINS

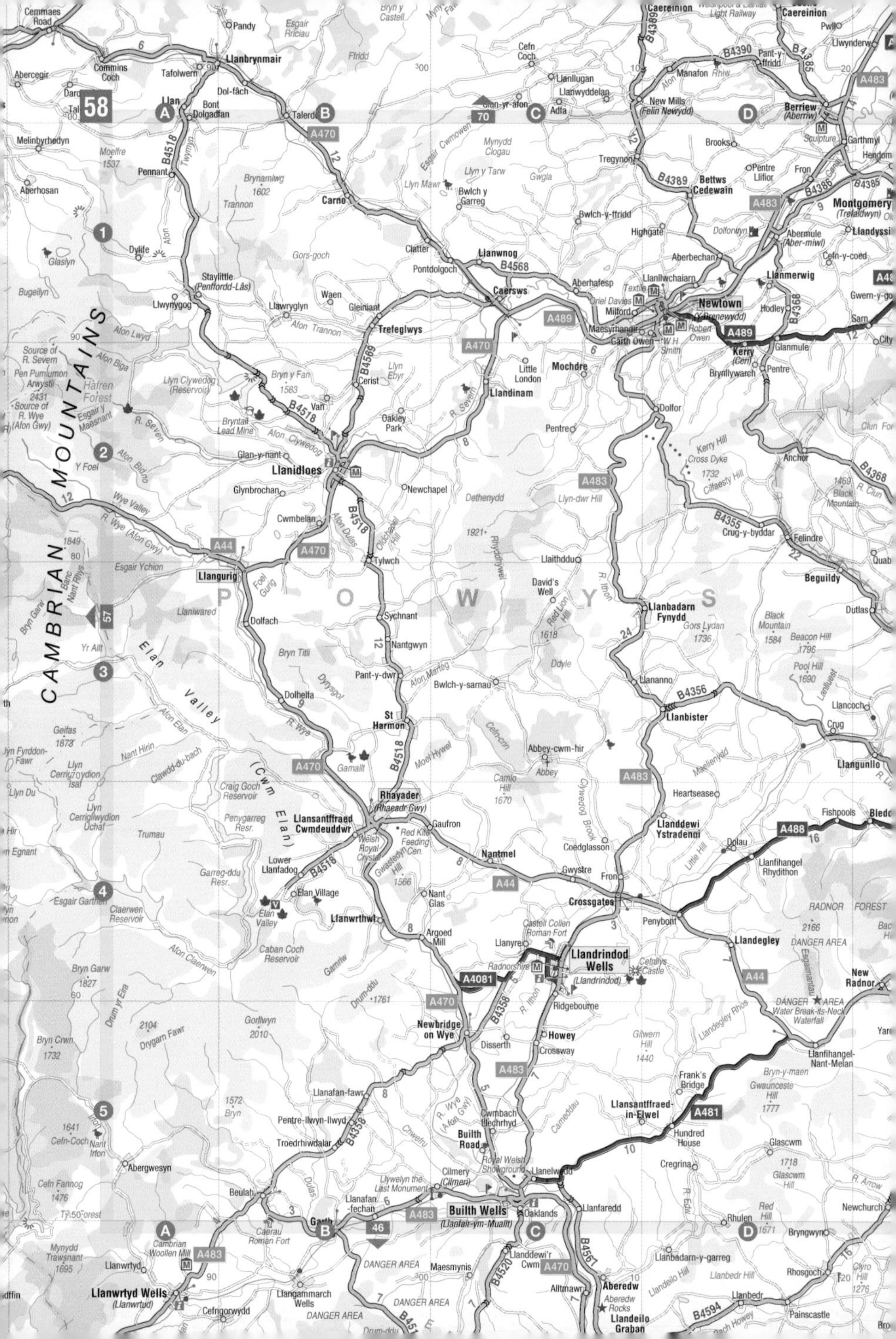

58
Cemmaes Road
Pandy
Llanbrynmair
Commins Coch
Tafolwern
Abercegir
Darowen
Llan
Bont Dolgadfan
Dol-fâch
Talerddig
Melinbyrhedyn
Moelfre 1537
Pennant
Aberhosan
Dylife
Glaslyn
Bugeilyn
Staylittle (Penffordd-Lâs)
Llwynygog
CAMBRIAN MOUNTAINS
Afon Lwyd
Source of R. Severn
Pen Pumlumon Arwystli 2431
Source of R. Wye (Afon Gwy)
Hafren Forest
Afon Biga
Eisgair y Maesnant
R. Severn
Y Foel
Afon Bidno
Wye Valley
R. Wye (Afon Gwy)
Banc Nant Rhys
Esgair Ychion
Bryn Garw
Yr Allt
Elan Valley
Afon Elan
Geifas 1873
Llyn Fyrddon-Fawr
Llyn Cerrigllwydion Isaf
Llyn Du
Llyn Cerrigllwydion Uchaf
Nant Hirin
Clawdd-du-bach
Craig Goch Reservoir
Penygarreg Resr.
Trumau
(Cwm Elan)
Esgair Garthen
Claerwen Reservoir
Garreg-ddu Resr.
Elan Village
Elan Valley
Caban Coch Reservoir
Afon Claerwen
Bryn Garw 1827
Drum yr Eira
Drygarn Fawr 2104
Gorllwyn 2010
Bryn Crwn 1732
Cefn-Coch 1641
Nant Irfon
Abergwesyn
Cefn Fannog 1476
Tywi Forest
Mynydd Trawsnant 1695
Cambrian Woollen Mill
Llanwrtyd
Llanwrtyd Wells (Llanwrtud)
Cefngorwydd
Llangammarch Wells
DANGER AREA
Caerau Roman Fort
Garth
Beulah
Llanafan-fechan
Maesmynis
Llanddewi'r Cwm
Builth Wells (Llanfair-ym-Muallt)
Oaklands
Llanfaredd
Aberedw
Aberedw Rocks
Alltmawr
Llandeilo Graban
Llanelwedd
Royal Welsh Showground
Builth Road
Cwmbach Llechrhyd
Cilmery (Cilmeri)
Llywelyn the Last Monument
Troedrhiwdalar
Pentre-llwyn-llwyd
Llanafan-fawr
Chwefru
Dulas
1572 Bryn
Newbridge on Wye
Disserth
Howey
Crossway
Ridgebourne
Llandrindod Wells (Llandrindod)
Radnorshire
Cefnllys Castle
Llanyre
Castell Collen Roman Fort
Drum-ddu 1761
Gamriw
Argoed Mill
Llanwrthwl
Nant Glas
Gwastedyn Hill 1566
Lower Llanfadog
Llansantffraed Cwmdeuddwr
Welsh Royal Crystal
Red Kite Feeding Cen.
Rhayader (Rhaeadr Gwy)
Gaufron
Nantmel
Gamallt
Moel Hywel
St Harmon
Dolhelfa
Dyrysgol
Pant-y-dwr
Afon Marteg
Bwlch-y-sarnau
Cefn-crin
Bryn Titli
Nantgwyn
Sychnant
Dolfach
Llaniwared
Foel Fadian
Llangurig
Tylwch
Cwmbelan
Afon Dulas
Oldchapel Hill
Glynbrochan
Llanidloes
Glan-y-nant
Newchapel
Dethenydd
1921
Rhydyhywel
Bryntail Lead Mine
Afon Clywedog
Llyn Clywedog (Reservoir)
Bryn y Fan 1583
Van
Cerist
Llyn Ebyr
Oakley Park
Llandinam
Little London
Trefeglwys
Afon Trannon
Llawryglyn
Waen
Gleiniant
Gors-goch
Pontdolgoch
Clatter
Carno
Trannon
Brynamlwg 1602
Twymyn
Afon
Fridd
Esgair Rhiciau
Bryn y Castell
Esgair Cwmowen
Mynydd Clogau
Llyn y Tarw
Llyn Mawr
Bwlch y Garreg
Gwgia
Cefn Coch
Llanllugan
Llanwyddelan
Glan-yr-afon
Adfa
Bwlch-y-ffridd
Llanwnog
Caersws
Aberhafesp
Highgate
Aberbechan
Tregynon
Bettws Cedewain
New Mills (Felin Newydd)
Manafon
Rhiw
Caereinion
Welshpool & Llanfair Light Railway
Pwll
Pant-y-ffridd
Llwynderw
Berriew (Aberriw)
Sculpture
Garthmyl
Brooks
Pentre Llifior
Fron
Hendomen
Montgomery (Trefaldwyn)
Dolforwyn
Abermule (Aber-miwl)
Llandyssil
Cefn-y-coed
Llanmerwig
Llanllwchaiarn
Textile
Oriel Davies
Newtown (Y Drenewydd)
Milford
Maesyrhandir
Garth Owen
W H Smith
Robert Owen
Kerry (Ceri)
Glanmule
Pentre
Bryntlywarch
Hodley
Gwern-y-go
Sarn
Mochdre
Pentre
Dolfor
Kerry Hill
Cross Dyke
1732
Cilfaesty Hill
Clun Forest
Anchor
1469 Black Mountain
R. Clun
Llyn-dwr Hill
Crug-y-byddar
Felindre
Beguildy
Quabbs
Llaithddu
David's Well
Red Lion Hill 1618
R. Ithon
POWYS
Llanbadarn Fynydd
Gors Lydan 1736
Black Mountain 1584
Beacon Hill 1796
Pool Hill 1690
Dutlas
Llanfluest
Llanano
Ddyle
Llanbister
Llancoch
Crug
Llangunllo
Maelienydd
Abbey-cwm-hir
Abbey
Camlo Hill 1670
Clywedog Brook
Heartsease
Llanddewi Ystradenni
Coedglasson
Little Hill
Dolau
Fishpools
Bleddfa
Llanfihangel Rhydithon
Gwystre
Fron
Crossgates
Penybont
RADNOR FOREST
2166
DANGER AREA
Llandegley
Esgairnantau
New Radnor
DANGER AREA
Water Break-its-Neck Waterfall
Llandegley Rhos
Gilwern Hill 1440
Llanfihangel-Nant-Melan
Bryn-y-maen
Gwaunceste Hill 1777
Frank's Bridge
Llansantffraed-in-Elwel
Cameddau
Hundred House
Glascwm
Cregrina
1718 Glascwm Hill
R. Arrow
R. Edw
Newchurch
Rhulen
Red Hill 1671
Bryngwyn
Llanbadarn-y-garreg
Llandeilo Hill
Llanbedr Hill
Clyro Hill 1276
Rhosgoch
Llanbedr
Painscastle
A470
A489
A483
A44
A4081
A488
A481
B4518
B4569
B4568
B4389
B4390
B4385
B4386
B4368
B4355
B4356
B4358
B4520
B4567
B4594
57
70
46

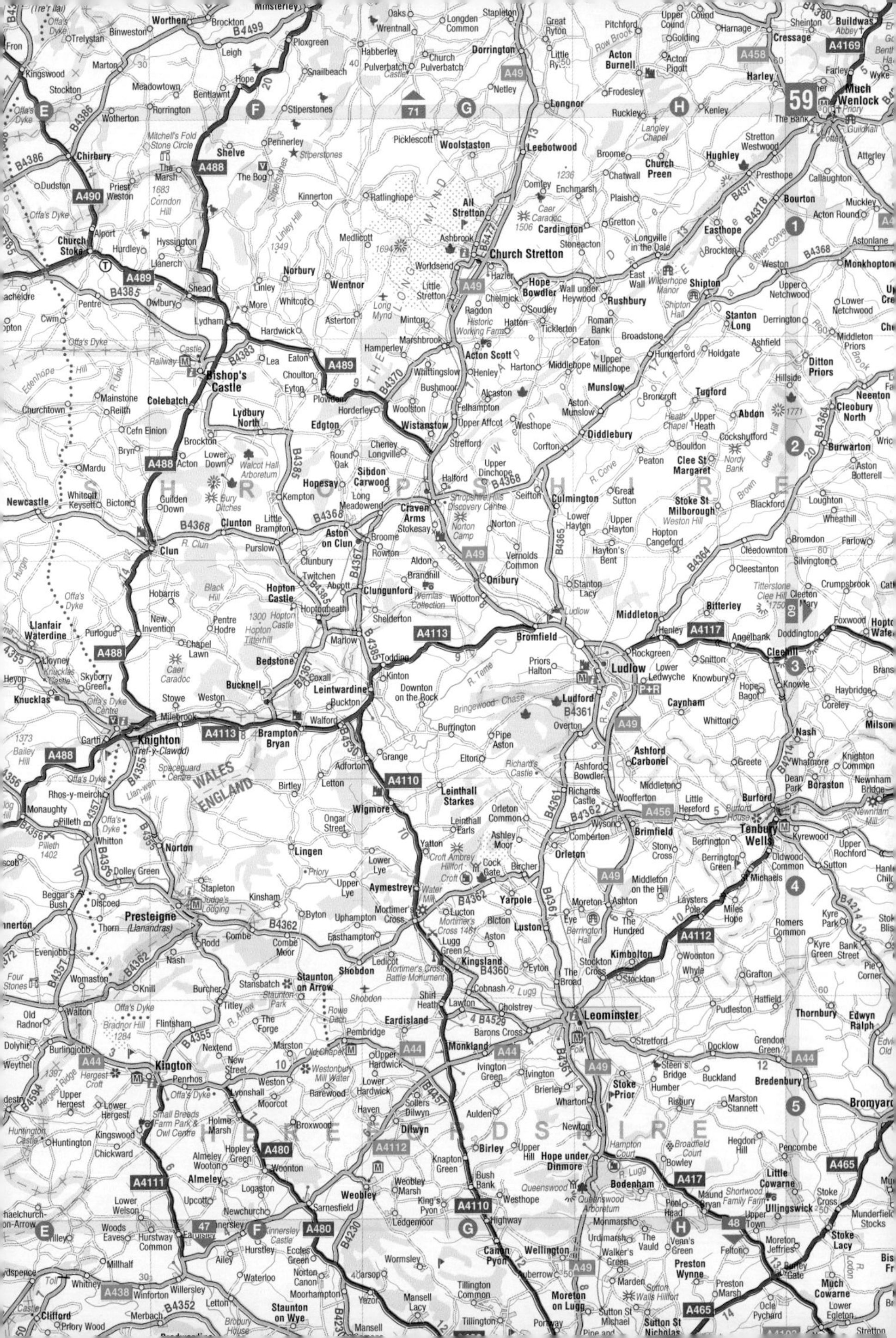
59
Minsterley
Worthen
Brockton
Binweston
Trelystan
Offa's Dyke
Fron
B4499
Ploxgreen
Oaks
Wrentnall
Longden Common
Stapleton
Great Ryton
Pitchford
Upper Cound
Cound
Harnage
Sheinton
Buildwas
Abbey
Cressage
A4169
Leigh
Marton
Habberley
Pulverbatch
Castle
Church Pulverbatch
Dorrington
Little Ryton
Acton Burnell
Golding
Acton Pigott
A458
Harley
Farley
Wyke
Kingswood
Stockton
Meadowtown
Hope
Snailbeach
A49
Netley
Frodesley
Much Wenlock
Priory
Guildhall
Bentlawnt
Rorrington
Wotherton
Stiperstones
71
Longnor
Ruckley
Langley Chapel
Kenley
The Bank
B4386
Mitchell's Fold Stone Circle
Pennerley
Stiperstones
Picklescott
Woolstaston
Leebotwood
Stretton Westwood
Chirbury
Shelve
A488
The Marsh
The Bog
Broome
Church Preen
Hughley
Atterley
Dudston
Priest Weston
1683 Corndon Hill
A490
Kinnerton
Ratlinghope
Chatwall
Presthope
Callaughton
Offa's Dyke
Linley Hill
1236
Comley
Enchmarsh
Plaish
All Stretton
Caer Caradoc
1506
B4371
B4378
Bourton
Muckley
Acton Round
Cardington
Gretton
Church Stoke
Alport
Hurdley
Hyssington
Llanerch
1349
Medlicott
1694
Ashbrook
B5477
Church Stretton
Stoneacton
Longville in the Dale
Easthope
Brockton
Weston
B4368
Astonlane
Monkhopton
A489
Shead
Norbury
Wentnor
Worldsend
Hazler
Hope Bowdler
Wall under Heywood
East Wall
Wilderhope Manor
Shipton
Shipton Hall
Upper Netchwood
Lower Netchwood
Pentre
B4385
Owlbury
Linley
More
Whitcot
Long Mynd
The Long Mynd
Little Stretton
Chelmick
Ragdon
Soudley
Rushbury
Cwm
Lydham
Hardwick
Asterton
Minton
Historic Working Farm
Hatton
Ticklerton
Roman Bank
Broadstone
Stanton Long
Derrington
Offa's Dyke
Marshbrook
Acton Scott
Eaton
Ashfield
Middleton Priors
Castle
Railway
Bishop's Castle
B4383
Lea
Eaton
Hamperley
Whittingslow
Henley
Harton
Middlehope
Upper Millichope
Hungerford
Holdgate
Ditton Priors
Edenhope Hill
Choulton
Eyton
B4370
Bushmoor
Alcaston
Munslow
Aston Munslow
Broncroft
Tugford
Hillside
Neenton
Mainstone
Colebatch
Plowden
Horderley
Woolston
Felhampton
Wistanstow
Upper Affcot
Westhope
Diddlebury
Heath Chapel
Upper Heath
Abdon
1771
Cleobury North
Churchtown
Reilth
Lydbury North
Edgton
Cefn Einion
Bryn
Brockton
Lower Down
Walcot Hall Arboretum
Cheney Longville
Round Oak
Strefford
Corfton
Bouldon
Cockshutford
Nordy Bank
Burwarton
Mardu
A488
Acton
B4385
Sibdon Carwood
Halford
Upper Dinchope
Peaton
Clee St Margaret
Aston Botterell
Newcastle
Whitcot Keysett
Bicton
Bury Ditches
Kempton
Hopesay
Long Meadowend
Craven Arms
Shropshire Hills Discovery Centre
B4368
Seifton
Culmington
Great Sutton
Stoke St Milborough
Weston Hill
Blackford
Loughton
Wheathill
Shropshire
Guilden Down
Clunton
Little Brampton
B4368
Aston on Clun
Broome
Stokesay
Norton Camp
Norton
Lower Hayton
Upper Hayton
Hopton Cangeford
Hayton's Bent
Bromdon
Farlow
Clun
R. Clun
Purslow
Clunbury
Rowton
A49
Vernolds Common
B4365
Cleedownton
Silvington
B4364
Cleestanton
Hobarris
Black Hill
Twitchen
Hopton Castle
Abcott
B4367
Aldon
Brandhill
Clungunford
Wernlas Collection
Onibury
Stanton Lacy
Titterstone Clee Hill
1750
Crumpsbrook
Llanfair Waterdine
New Invention
Pentre Hodre
1300 Hopton Castle
Hopton Titterhill
Hoptonheath
Shelderton
Wootton
Ludlow
Middleton
Bitterley
Cleeton St Mary
Purlogue
Chapel Lawn
Marlow
A4113
Bromfield
Henley
A4117
Angelbank
Foxwood
Doddington
Knuckles Castle
Lloyney
Heyop
Skyborry Green
Caer Caradoc
Bedstone
Todding
Kinton
Priors Halton
Rockgreen
Ludlow
Lower Ledwyche
Snitton
Cleehill
Knowbury
Knowle
Knucklas
Offa's Dyke Centre
Bucknell
Coxall
Leintwardine
Downton on the Rock
R. Teme
Ludford
P+R
Caynham
Hope Bagot
Haybridge
Coreley
Stowe
Weston
Buckton
Bringewood Chase
B4361
Whitton
1373 Bailey Hill
Garth
Knighton
(Tref-y-Clawdd)
Milebrook
A4113
Brampton Bryan
Walford
B4530
Burrington
Pipe Aston
Overton
Nash
Milson
A488
B4355
Spaceguard Centre
Wales
England
Adforton
Grange
Elton
Richard's Castle
Ashford Bowdler
Ashford Carbonel
Greete
Whatmore
Knighton Common
Offa's Dyke
Rhos-y-meirch
Llan-wen Hill
Birtley
Letton
A4110
Leinthall Starkes
Richards Castle
Middleton
Dean Park
Boraston
Newnham Bridge
Monaughty
B4357
Pilleth
Offa's Dyke
Ongar Street
Wigmore
Leinthall Earls
Orleton Common
B4361
B4362
Woofferton
Little Hereford
A456
Burford
Burford House
Tenbury Wells
Kyrewood
Newnham Mill
B4356
Pilleth 1402
Whitton
Norton
B4355
Lingen
Yatton
Ashley Moor
Wyson
Comberton
Brimfield
Stony Cross
Berrington
Berrington Green
Oldwood Common
Upper Rochford
Dolley Green
Priory
Lower Lye
Croft Ambrey Hillfort
Croft
Cock Gate
Bircher
Orleton
Middleton on the Hill
St Michaels
Sutton
Beggar's Bush
Discoed
Stapleton
Judge's Lodging
Kinsham
Upper Lye
Aymestrey
Water Mill
B4362
Yarpole
Moreton
Ashton
Laysters Pole
Miles Hope
Presteigne
(Llanandras)
Thorn
Byton
Uphampton
Mortimer's Cross
Lucton
Mortimer's Cross 1461
Bicton
Luston
Eye
Berrington Hall
The Hundred
A4112
Romers Common
Kyre Park
B4214
Evenjobb
Rodd
Combe
B4362
Combe Moor
Easthampton
Lugg Green
Aston
Kingsland
B4360
Kimbolton
Woonton
Kyre Green
Bank Street
Four Stones
B4357
Nash
Ledicot
Shobdon
Mortimer's Cross Battle Monument
Eyton
The Broad
Stockton Cross
Stockton
Whyle
Grafton
Pie Corner
Womaston
Knill
Burcher
Stansbatch
Staunton on Arrow
Staunton Park
Rowe Ditch
Shobdon
Cobnash
R. Lugg
Hatfield
Titley
Offa's Dyke
Bradnor Hill 1284
Walton
Flintsham
The Forge
Shirl Heath
Lawton
Eardisland
Cholstrey
Leominster
Pudleston
Thornbury
Edwyn Ralph
Old Radnor
B4355
Pembridge
B4529
Barons Cross
Stretford
Grendon Green
Dolyhir
Burlingjobb
Nextend
Marston
Old Chapel
Upper Hardwick
Monkland
A44
Docklow
A44
Weythel
Hergest Croft
Hergest Ridge
1397
Kington
New Street
Weston
Westonbury Mill Water
Ivington Green
Ivington
Brierley
Steen's Bridge
Humber
Buckland
Bredenbury
Bromyard
B4594
Upper Hergest
Lower Hergest
Penrhos
Offa's Dyke
Lyonshall
Moorcot
Barewood
Lower Hardwick
B4457
Sollers Dilwyn
Wharton
Stoke Prior
Risbury
Marston Stannett
Small Breeds Farm Park & Owl Centre
Holme Marsh
Broxwood
Haven
Dilwyn
Aulden
Newton
Huntington Castle
Kingswood
Huntington
Chickward
Herefordshire
A480
A4112
Birley
Upper Hill
Hope under Dinmore
Hampton Court
Broadfield Court
Bowley
Hegdon Hill
Pencombe
Almeley Wooton
Hopley's Green
Woonton
Knapton Green
Bush Bank
Queenswood
Bodenham
A417
Little Cowarne
A465
A4111
Almeley
Logaston
Weobley Marsh
Weobley
King's Pyon
Westhope
Queenswood Arboretum
Maund Bryan
Shortwood Family Farm
Ullingswick
Stone Cross
Lower Welson
Upcott
Newchurch
Sarnesfield
A4110
Poolhead
Upper Town
Munderfield Stocks
Woods Eaves
Hurstway Common
Kinnersley
Kinnersley Castle
A480
B4230
Ledgemoor
Highway
Monmarsh
Urdimarsh
The Vauld
Walker's Green
Venn's Green
Felton
Moreton Jeffries
Stoke Lacy
47
48
Millhalf
Ailey
Hurstley
Eccles Green
Wormsley
Canon Pyon
Wellington
Preston Wynne
Burley Gate
Whitney
Winforton
Willersley
Waterloo
Norton Canon
Garnons
Tillington Common
Auberrow
A49
Marden
Sutton Walls Hillfort
Preston Marsh
Much Cowarne
A438
B4352
Monnington
Mansell Lacy
Moreton on Lugg
Sutton St Michael
Sutton St Nicholas
A465
Ocle Pychard
Lower Egleton
Clifford
Priory Wood
Merbach
Letton
Staunton on Wye
Bredwardine
Brobury House
Yazor
Mansell Gamage
Tillington
Portway
Stretton

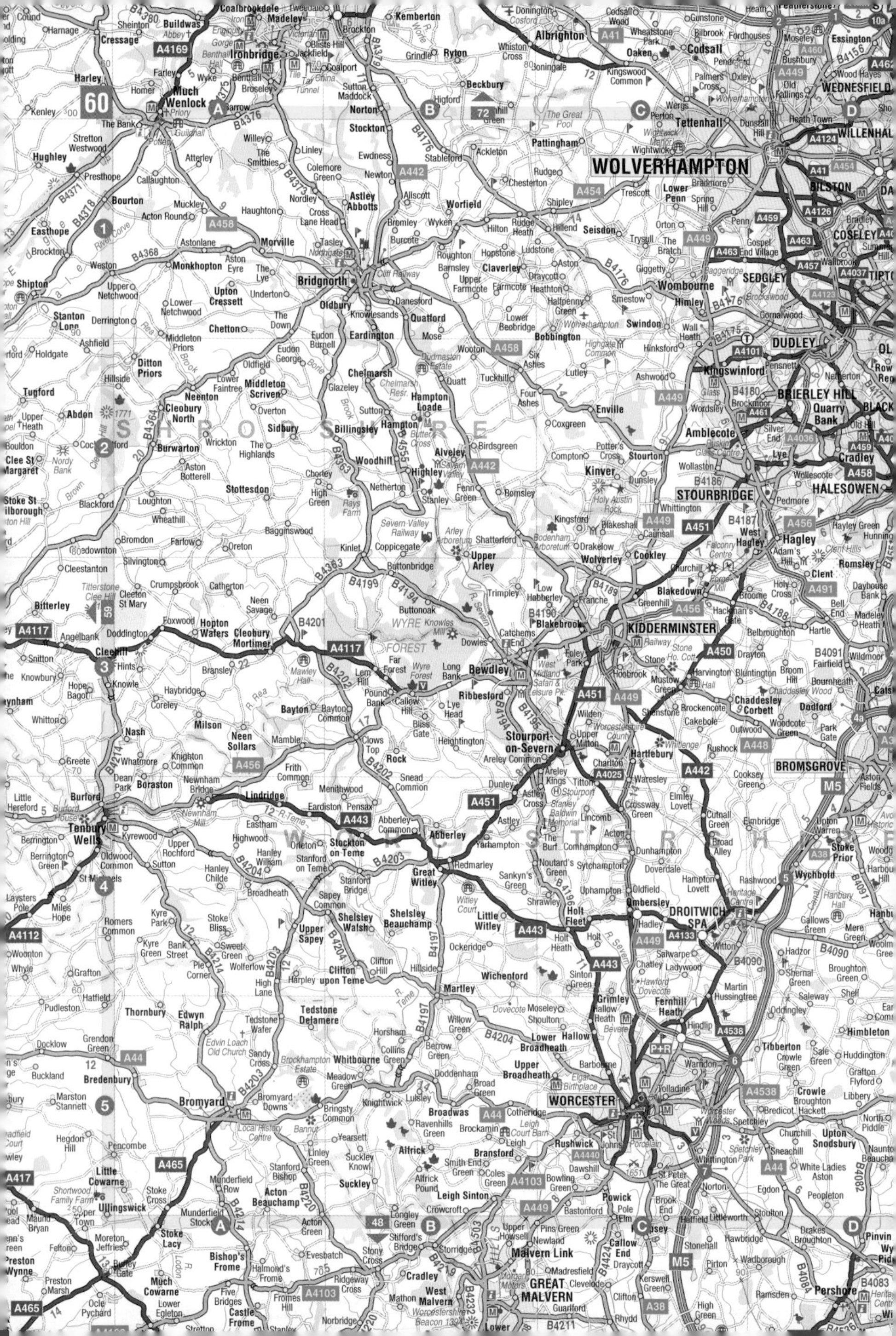

60
59
72
48
A
B
C
D
1
2
3
4
5
SHROPSHIRE
WORCESTERSHIRE
Coalbrookdale
Buildwas
Madeley
Kemberton
Donington
Albrighton
Codsall
Codsall Wood
Bilbrook
Oaken
Cressage
Sheinton
Harnage
Ironbridge
Coalport
Broseley
Much Wenlock
Harley
Kenley
Ryton
Grindle
Beckbury
Sutton Maddock
Norton
Stockton
Higford
Whiston Cross
Kingswood Common
Perton
Tettenhall
WOLVERHAMPTON
Wednesfield
Willenhall
Bilston
Coseley
Sedgley
Tipton
Dudley
Pattingham
Trescott
Lower Penn
Penn
Wombourne
Himley
Gospel End Village
Hughley
Presthope
Bourton
Easthope
Shipton
Brockton
Monkhopton
Morville
Astley Abbotts
Worfield
Bridgnorth
Oldbury
Quatford
Claverley
Seisdon
Trysull
Swindon
Kingswinford
Brierley Hill
Quarry Bank
Amblecote
Stourbridge
Halesowen
Cradley
Lye
Stanton Long
Ditton Priors
Tugford
Abdon
Clee St Margaret
Stoke St Milborough
Cleobury North
Burwarton
Neenton
Middleton Scriven
Chetton
Eardington
Chelmarsh
Hampton Loade
Billingsley
Sidbury
Highley
Alveley
Enville
Kinver
Stourton
Hagley
West Hagley
Clent
Romsley
Stottesdon
Kinlet
Upper Arley
Wolverley
Cookley
Kidderminster
Blakedown
Bewdley
Stourport-on-Severn
Hartlebury
Bromsgrove
Bitterley
Cleehill
Hopton Wafers
Cleobury Mortimer
Wyre Forest
Far Forest
Bayton
Milson
Neen Sollars
Nash
Rock
Boraston
Burford
Tenbury Wells
Lindridge
Abberley
Great Witley
Stockton on Teme
Chaddesley Corbett
Dodford
Droitwich Spa
Ombersley
Holt Fleet
Wychbold
Stoke Prior
Upper Sapey
Shelsley Walsh
Shelsley Beauchamp
Clifton upon Teme
Little Witley
Wichenford
Martley
Tedstone Delamere
Thornbury
Edwyn Ralph
Bredenbury
Bromyard
Whitbourne
Broadwas
Alfrick
Suckley
Bransford
Leigh Sinton
Rushwick
Worcester
Fernhill Heath
Lower Broadheath
Upper Broadheath
Hallow
Grimley
Powick
Malvern Link
Great Malvern
West Malvern
Cradley
Acton Beauchamp
Bishop's Frome
Stoke Lacy
Much Cowarne
Castle Frome
Ullingswick
Little Cowarne
Tibberton
Himbleton
Crowle
Upton Snodsbury
Pershore
Pinvin
M5
A41
A44
A38
A442
A443
A449
A451
A456
A458
A465
A4103
A4117
A4169

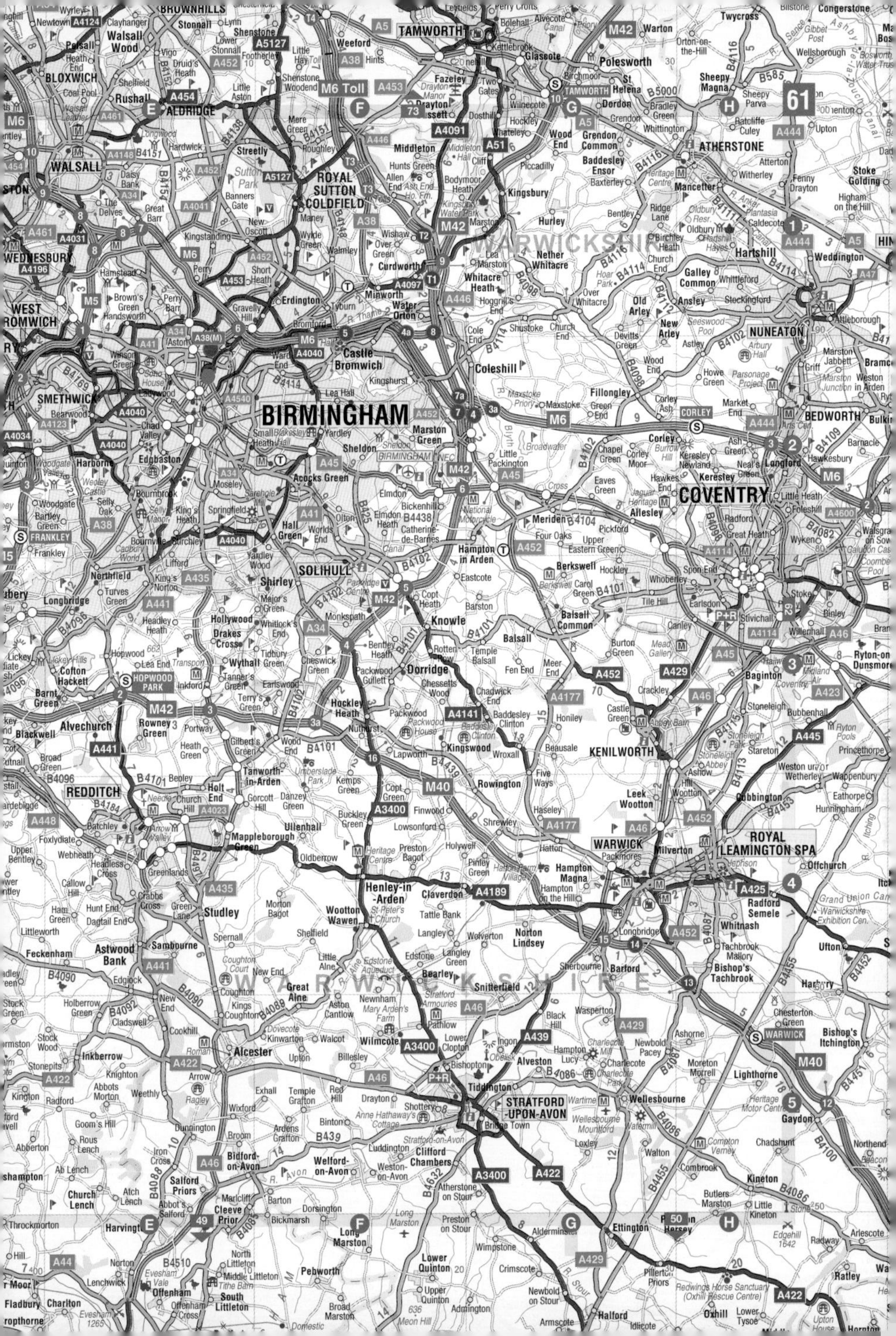
61
BROWNHILLS
TAMWORTH
M42
A5
M6 Toll
BLOXWICH
ALDRIDGE
WALSALL
ATHERSTONE
ROYAL SUTTON COLDFIELD
WARWICKSHIRE
WEDNESBURY
WEST BROMWICH
NUNEATON
SMETHWICK
BIRMINGHAM
BEDWORTH
COVENTRY
SOLIHULL
KENILWORTH
REDDITCH
WARWICK
ROYAL LEAMINGTON SPA
WARWICKSHIRE
STRATFORD -UPON-AVON
M40
A46
A3400
A422
A429

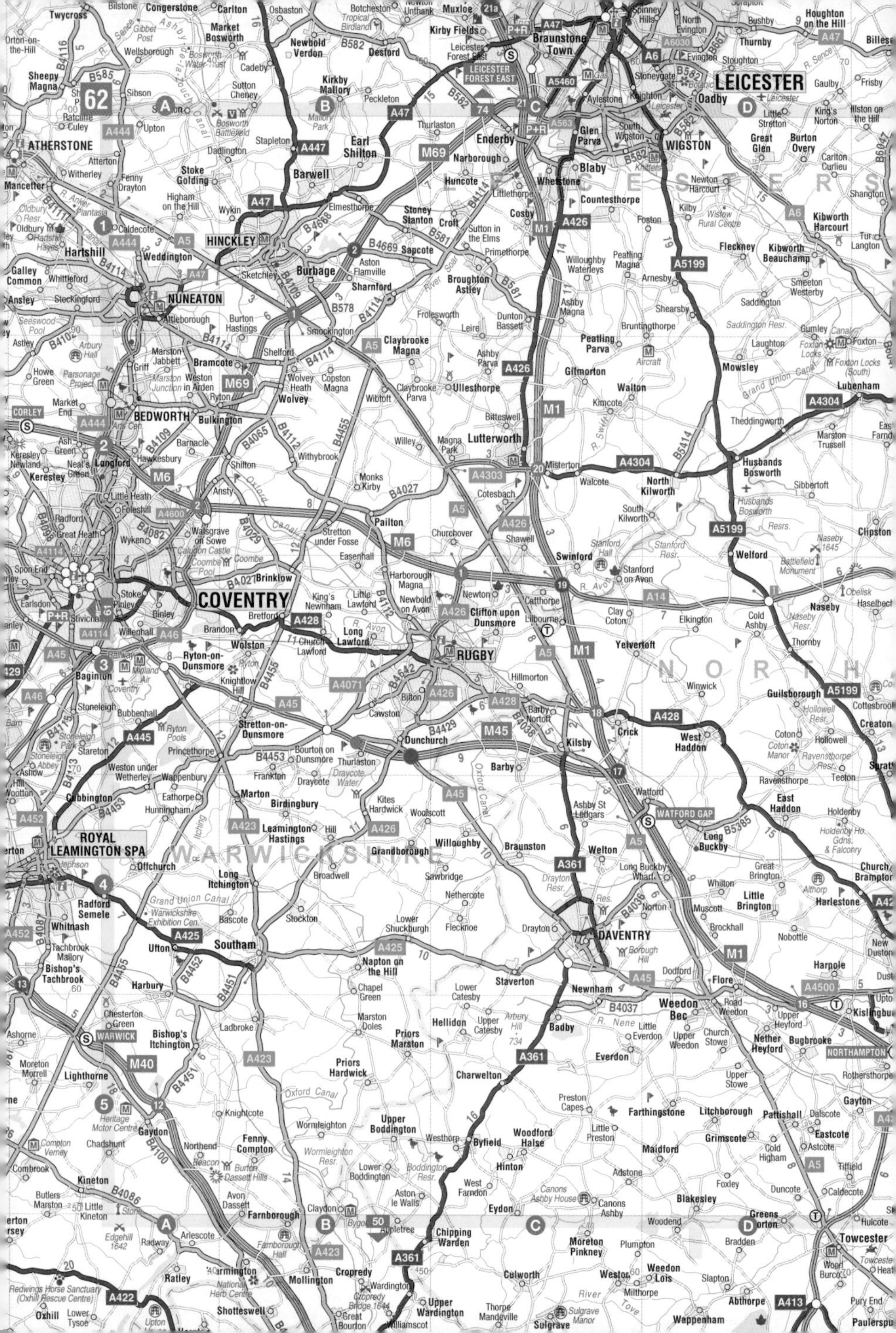
62
Twycross
Bilstone
Congerstone
Carlton
Osbaston
Botcheston
Newton Unthank
Muxloe
Orton-on-the-Hill
Gibbet Post
Market Bosworth
Tropical Birdland
Kirby Fields
Braunstone Town
Leicester Forest East
LEICESTER FOREST EAST
Wellsborough
Newbold Verdon
Desford
Sheepy Magna
Bosworth Water Trust
Cadeby
Kirkby Mallory
Mallory Park
Sibson
Sutton Cheney
Peckleton
Ratcliffe Culey
Upton
Bosworth Battlefield
Thurlaston
Enderby
Glen Parva
Aylestone
Knighton
Stoneygate
Evington
North Evington
Spinney Hills
Houghton on the Hill
Bushby
Thurnby
Stoughton
Billesdon
LEICESTER
Oadby
Gaulby
Frisby
Little Stretton
King's Norton
Illston on the Hill
ATHERSTONE
Atterton
Stapleton
Earl Shilton
South Wigston
WIGSTON
Great Glen
Burton Overy
Carlton Curlieu
Witherley
Dadlington
Barwell
Narborough
Blaby
Whetstone
Mancetter
Fenny Drayton
Stoke Golding
Huncote
Littlethorpe
Countesthorpe
Newton Harcourt
Shangton
Oldbury Resr.
R. Anker
Plantasia
Higham on the Hill
Wykin
Elmesthorpe
Stoney Stanton
Croft
Cosby
Foston
Kilby
Wistow Rural Centre
Kibworth Harcourt
Tur Langton
Oldbury
Hartshill Hayes
Caldecote
HINCKLEY
Sutton in the Elms
Primethorpe
Fleckney
Kibworth Beauchamp
Hartshill
Weddington
Aston Flamville
Sapcote
Willoughby Waterleys
Peatling Magna
Galley Common
Whittleford
Sketchley
Burbage
Sharnford
Broughton Astley
Arnesby
Smeeton Westerby
Ansley
Stockingford
NUNEATON
Saddington
Seeswood Pool
Attleborough
Burton Hastings
Frolesworth
Leire
Dunton Bassett
Ashby Magna
Shearsby
Saddington Resr.
Gumley
Astley
Arbury Hall
Smockington
Bruntingthorpe
Peatling Parva
Laughton
Foxton
Foxton Locks
Marston Jabbett
Shelford
Claybrooke Magna
Ashby Parva
Aircraft
Griff
Bramcote
Howe Green
Parsonage Project
Marston Junction
Weston in Arden
Wolvey Heath
Copston Magna
Claybrooke Parva
Ullesthorpe
Gilmorton
Mowsley
Grand Union Canal
Lubenham
Market End
BEDWORTH
Ryton
Wolvey
Wibtoft
Kimcote
Walton
CORLEY
Bulkington
Bitteswell
Ash Green
Barnacle
Willey
Magna Park
Lutterworth
Theddingworth
Marston Trussell
Keresley Newland
Longford
Hawkesbury
Withybrook
Neal's Green
Keresley
Shilton
Monks Kirby
Misterton
Walcote
North Kilworth
Husbands Bosworth
Sibbertoft
Little Heath
Ansty
Cotesbach
Foleshill
Oxford Canal
Radford
Walsgrave on Sowe
Pailton
South Kilworth
Great Heath
Wyken
Stretton under Fosse
Churchover
Shawell
Clipston
Caludon Castle
Coombe
Coombe Pool
Easenhall
Stanford Hall
Stanford Resr.
Swinford
Welford
Naseby 1645
Spon End
Brinklow
Harborough Magna
Stanford on Avon
Battlefield Monument
Earlsdon
Stoke
Pinley
COVENTRY
King's Newnham
Little Lawford
Newbold on Avon
Newton
R. Avon
Obelisk
Haselbech
Stivichall
Binley
Catthorpe
Clay Coton
Elkington
Cold Ashby
Naseby
Bretford
Clifton upon Dunsmore
Lilbourne
Willenhall
Brandon
Long Lawford
Naseby Resr.
Church Lawford
Thornby
Baginton
Ryton-on-Dunsmore
Wolston
Midland Air
RUGBY
Yelvertoft
Coventry
Knightlow Hill
Hillmorton
NORTH
Stoneleigh
Bilton
Winwick
Bubbenhall
Cawston
Barby Nortoft
Guilsborough
Cottesbrooke
Ryton Pools
Stretton-on-Dunsmore
Dunchurch
Crick
West Haddon
Hollowell Resr.
Stoneleigh Park
Stareton
Kilsby
Coton
Creaton
Stoneleigh Abbey
Princethorpe
Bourton on Dunsmore
Thurlaston
Barby
Coton Manor
Hollowell
Draycote Water
Ravensthorpe Resr.
Ashow
Weston under Wetherley
Wappenbury
Frankton
Draycote
Oxford Canal
Ravensthorpe
Teeton
Hill Wootton
Eathorpe
Marton
Kites Hardwick
Woolscott
Watford
Cubbington
Birdingbury
Ashby St Ledgars
East Haddon
Holdenby
Hunningham
WATFORD GAP
ROYAL LEAMINGTON SPA
Leamington Hastings
Hill
Long Buckby
Holdenby Ho. Gdns. & Falconry
Itchington
WARWICKSHIRE
Grandborough
Willoughby
Braunston
Welton
Long Buckby Wharf
Offchurch
Long Itchington
Broadwell
Sawbridge
Drayton Resr.
Great Brington
Church Brampton
Radford Semele
Grand Union Canal
Nethercote
Whilton
Althorp
Little Brington
Harlestone
Warwickshire Exhibition Cen.
Bascote
Stockton
Lower Shuckburgh
Flecknoe
Norton
Muscott
Whitnash
Brockhall
Nobottle
Tachbrook Mallory
Ufton
Southam
Drayton
DAVENTRY
New Duston
Borough Hill
Bishop's Tachbrook
Napton on the Hill
Staverton
Dodford
Harpole
Harbury
Chapel Green
Lower Catesby
Newnham
Flore
Road Weedon
Weedon Bec
Upper Heyford
Kislingbury
Chesterton Green
Ladbroke
Hellidon
Upper Catesby
Arbury Hill 734
Badby
R. Nene
Little Everdon
Upper Weedon
Church Stowe
Nether Heyford
Bugbrooke
Ashorne
WARWICK
Bishop's Itchington
Marston Doles
Priors Marston
NORTHAMPTON
Moreton Morrell
Lighthorne
Everdon
Priors Hardwick
Charwelton
Upper Stowe
Rothersthorpe
Heritage Motor Centre
Oxford Canal
Preston Capes
Farthingstone
Litchborough
Pattishall
Dalscote
Gayton
Knightcote
Upper Boddington
Eastcote
Compton Verney
Chadshunt
Gaydon
Fenny Compton
Wormleighton
Westhorp
Byfield
Woodford Halse
Little Preston
Grimscote
Astcote
Northend
Wormleighton Resr.
Maidford
Cold Higham
Combrook
Beacon
Burton Dassett Hills
Lower Boddington
Boddington Resr.
Hinton
Adstone
Tiffield
Kineton
West Farndon
Foxley
Duncote
Butlers Marston
Little Kineton
Avon Dassett
Aston le Walls
Canons Ashby House
Canons Ashby
Blakesley
Caldecote
Farnborough
Claydon
Eydon
Greens Norton
Hulcote
Edgehill 1642
Arlescote
Radway
Bygo
Appletree
Chipping Warden
Woodend
Moreton Pinkney
Plumpton
Bradden
Towcester
Farnborough Hall
Ratley
Warmington
National Herb Centre
Mollington
Cropredy
Wardington
Culworth
Weston
Weedon Lois
Slapton
Wood Burcote
Towcester
Redwings Horse Sanctuary (Oxhill Rescue Centre)
Cropredy Bridge 1644
Upper Wardington
Thorpe Mandeville
River Tove
Abthorpe
Pury End
Oxhill
Lower Tysoe
Upton
Shotteswell
Great Bourton
Williamscot
Sulgrave Manor
Sulgrave
Wappenham
Paulerspury
LEICESTER FOREST EAST
WATFORD GAP
CORLEY
WARWICK
NORTHAMPTON

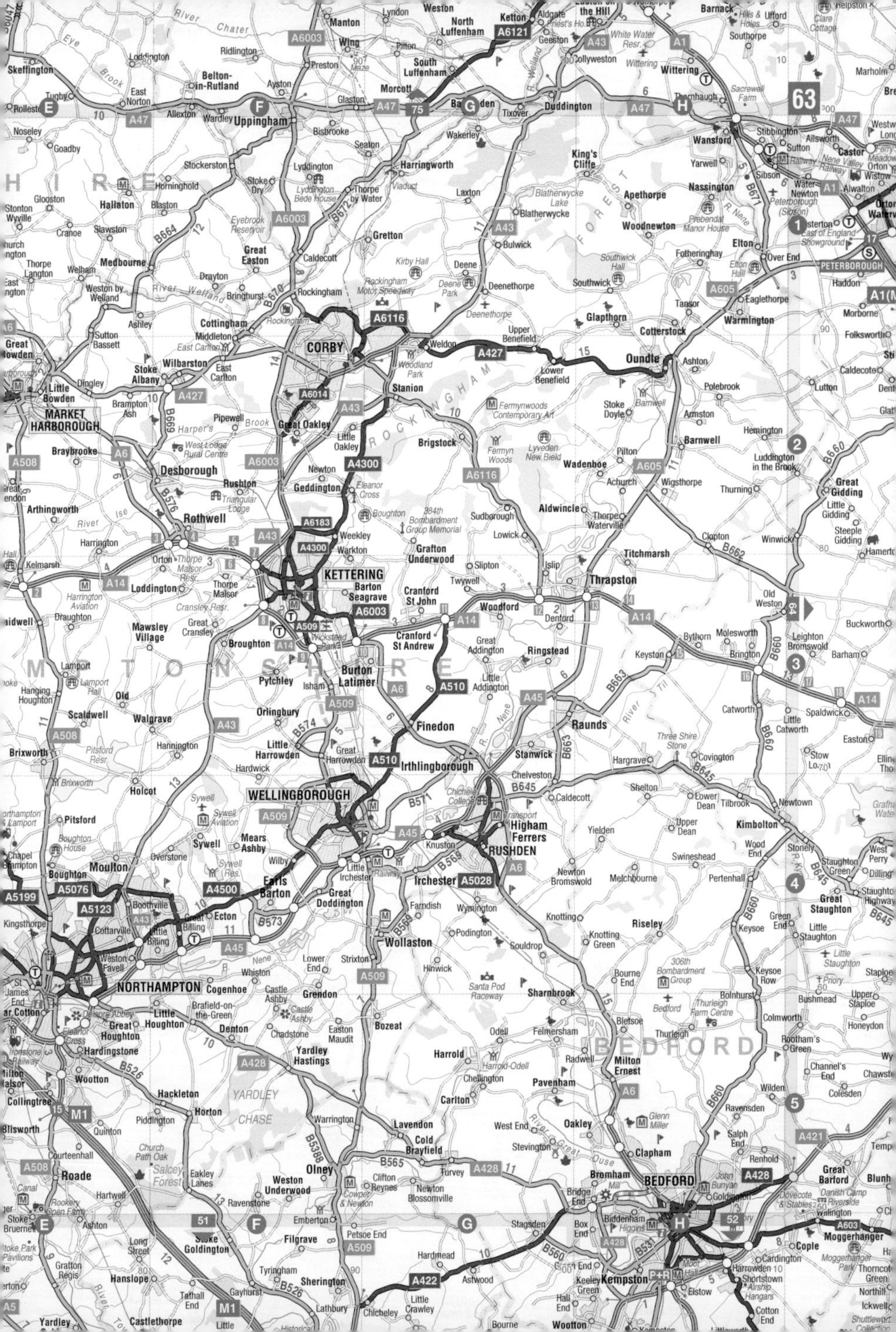

63
64
51
52
Lyndon
Weston
Manton
North Luffenham
Ketton
A6121
Aldgate
Priest's Ho.
Geeston
Collyweston
White Water Resr.
Wittering
Barnack
Hills & Holes
Ufford
Southorpe
Helpston
Clare Cottage
A6003
Wing
Pilton
Ridlington
Loddington
Skeffington
Belton-in-Rutland
East Norton
Preston
Maze
South Luffenham
Morcott
Wittering
Marholm
Tugby
Rolleston
Allexton
Wardley
Uppingham
Ayston
Glaston
A47
75
Barrowden
Tixover
Duddington
Thornhaugh
Sacrewell Farm
A1
E
F
G
H
Noseley
Goadby
Bisbrooke
Seaton
Wakerley
Wansford
Stibbington
Sutton
Ailsworth
Castor
Nene Valley Railway
Orton
Stockerston
Lyddington
Harringworth
King's Cliffe
Yarwell
Nassington
Sibson
Water Newton
Alwalton
Horninghold
Stoke Dry
Lyddington Bede House
Thorpe by Water
Viaduct
Laxton
Blatherwycke Lake
Blatherwycke
Apethorpe
Prebendal Manor House
Peterborough (Sibson)
East of England Showground
Glooston
Hallaton
Blaston
Stonton Wyville
Cranoe
Slawston
Eyebrook Reservoir
A6003
Gretton
A43
Bulwick
Woodnewton
Elton
Over End
Fotheringhay
PETERBOROUGH
Thorpe Langton
Welham
Medbourne
Great Easton
Caldecott
Kirby Hall
Deene
Deene Park
Southwick Hall
Southwick
Elton Hall
A605
Eaglethorpe
Haddon
East Langton
Weston by Welland
Drayton
Bringhurst
River Welland
B670
Rockingham
Rockingham Motor Speedway
Deenethorpe
Tansor
Warmington
Morborne
Glapthorn
Cotterstock
Ashley
Sutton Bassett
Cottingham
Middleton
East Carlton
A6116
CORBY
Weldon
Upper Benefield
A427
Lower Benefield
Oundle
Ashton
Folksworth
Great Bowden
Little Bowden
Dingley
Stoke Albany
Wilbarston
East Carlton
Woodland Park
Stanion
Polebrook
Caldecote
Lutton
MARKET HARBOROUGH
Brampton Ash
Pipewell
B669
Harper's Brook
Great Oakley
A6014
Little Oakley
ROCKINGHAM
Fermynwoods Contemporary Art
Stoke Doyle
Barnwell
Armston
Hemington
Braybrooke
West Lodge Rural Centre
A6003
Brigstock
Fermyn Woods
Lyveden New Bield
Wadenhoe
Pilton
Luddington in the Brook
Desborough
Rushton
Triangular Lodge
Newton
A4300
Geddington
Eleanor Cross
A6116
Achurch
Wigsthorpe
Thurning
Great Gidding
Arthingworth
B576
Rothwell
Boughton
384th Bombardment Group Memorial
Sudborough
Aldwincle
Thorpe Waterville
Little Gidding
Steeple Gidding
Harrington
River Ise
A6183
Weekley
Warkton
Grafton Underwood
Lowick
Titchmarsh
Clopton
Winwick
B662
Hamerton
Kelmarsh
Orton
Thorpe Malsor Resr.
Thorpe Malsor
A43
A4300
KETTERING
Barton Seagrave
Slipton
Islip
Thrapston
Old Weston
A14
Loddington
Harrington Aviation
Cransley Resr.
Cranford St John
Twywell
Woodford
Denford
Draughton
Great Cransley
Mawsley Village
Broughton
A509
Wicksteed Park
A6003
Cranford St Andrew
Great Addington
Ringstead
Bythorn
Molesworth
Keyston
Brington
Leighton Bromswold
B660
Buckworth
Barham
Lamport
Lamport Hall
Pytchley
Isham
Burton Latimer
A6
A510
Little Addington
A45
Raunds
B663
Catworth
Little Catworth
Spaldwick
Hanging Houghton
Old
Walgrave
Orlingbury
Scaldwell
A508
A43
Little Harrowden
B574
Finedon
Stanwick
Three Shire Stone
Covington
Hargrave
Easton
Stow Longa
Brixworth
Pitsford Resr.
Hannington
Great Harrowden
Irthlingborough
Hardwick
Holcot
Brixworth
Sywell
Sywell Aviation
WELLINGBOROUGH
Chichele College
Chelveston
Caldecott
B645
Shelton
Lower Dean
Tilbrook
Newtown
Pitsford
Boughton House
Mears Ashby
B571
Higham Ferrers
Transport
Upper Dean
Yielden
Kimbolton
Northampton & Lamport Railway
Chapel Brampton
Sywell
Overstone
Sywell Res.
Wilby
Knuston
RUSHDEN
Newton Bromswold
Swineshead
Wood End
Stonely
West Perry
Moulton
Boughton
A5199
A5076
A5123
A4500
Earls Barton
Little Irchester
Railway
Irchester
B569
A5028
Melchbourne
Pertenhall
Staughton Green
Dillington
Boothville
Ecton
Great Doddington
Farndish
Wymington
Great Staughton
Staughton Highway
Kingsthorpe
Cottarville
Little Billing
Great Billing
B573
Wollaston
B568
Podington
Knotting
Knotting Green
Riseley
Keysoe
Green End
Little Staughton
Weston Favell
A45
Nene
Lower End
Strixton
Souldrop
Hinwick
A509
Keysoe Row
Priory
St James End
NORTHAMPTON
Cogenhoe
Whiston
Castle Ashby
Grendon
Santa Pod Raceway
Sharnbrook
Bourne End
306th Bombardment Group
Bolnhurst
Staploe
Upper Staploe
Far Cotton
Delapré Abbey
Great Houghton
Little Houghton
Brafield-on-the-Green
Castle Ashby
Easton Maudit
Bozeat
Odell
Felmersham
Bletsoe
Bedford
Thurleigh Farm Centre
Bushmead
Honeydon
Colmworth
Hardingstone
Eleanor Cross
Denton
Chadstone
Yardley Hastings
Harrold
Harrold-Odell
Thurleigh
Radwell
Milton Ernest
BEDFORD
Rootham's Green
Channel's End
Colesden
Chawston
Milton Malsor
Wootton
B526
A428
Chellington
Pavenham
A6
Collingtree
Hackleton
Horton
YARDLEY
CHASE
Carlton
Oakley
Glenn Miller
Wilden
Ravensden
Blisworth
M1
Piddington
Quinton
Warrington
Lavendon
Cold Brayfield
West End
Stevington
River Great Ouse
Clapham
Salph End
Renhold
A421
Courteenhall
Church Path Oak
Salcey Forest
Eakley Lanes
B5388
Olney
B565
Turvey
A428
Bromham
Bromham Mill
John Bunyan
A428
Great Barford
Blunham
Roade
Canal
Hartwell
Weston Underwood
Clifton Reynes
Cowper & Newton
Newton Blossomville
Bridge End
Goldington
Dovecote & Stables
Danish Camp
Riverside
Willington
A603
Moggerhanger
Stoke Bruerne
Rookery Open Farm
Ashton
Ravenstone
Emberton
Stagsden
Box End
Biddenham
Higgins
Cople
Stoke Goldington
Filgrave
Petsoe End
A509
B560
B531
Cardington
Moggerhanger Park
Stoke Park Pavilions
Long Street
Hardmead
Kempston
P+R
Harrowden
Shortstown
Airship Hangars
Thorncote Green
Northill
Grafton Regis
Hanslope
Tyringham
Sherington
A422
Astwood
Keeley Green
Elstow
Ickwell
Tathall End
Gayhurst
B526
Little Crawley
Hall End
Cotton End
Yardley Gobion
Castlethorpe
Lathbury
Chicheley
Bourne End
Wootton
Shuttleworth Collection

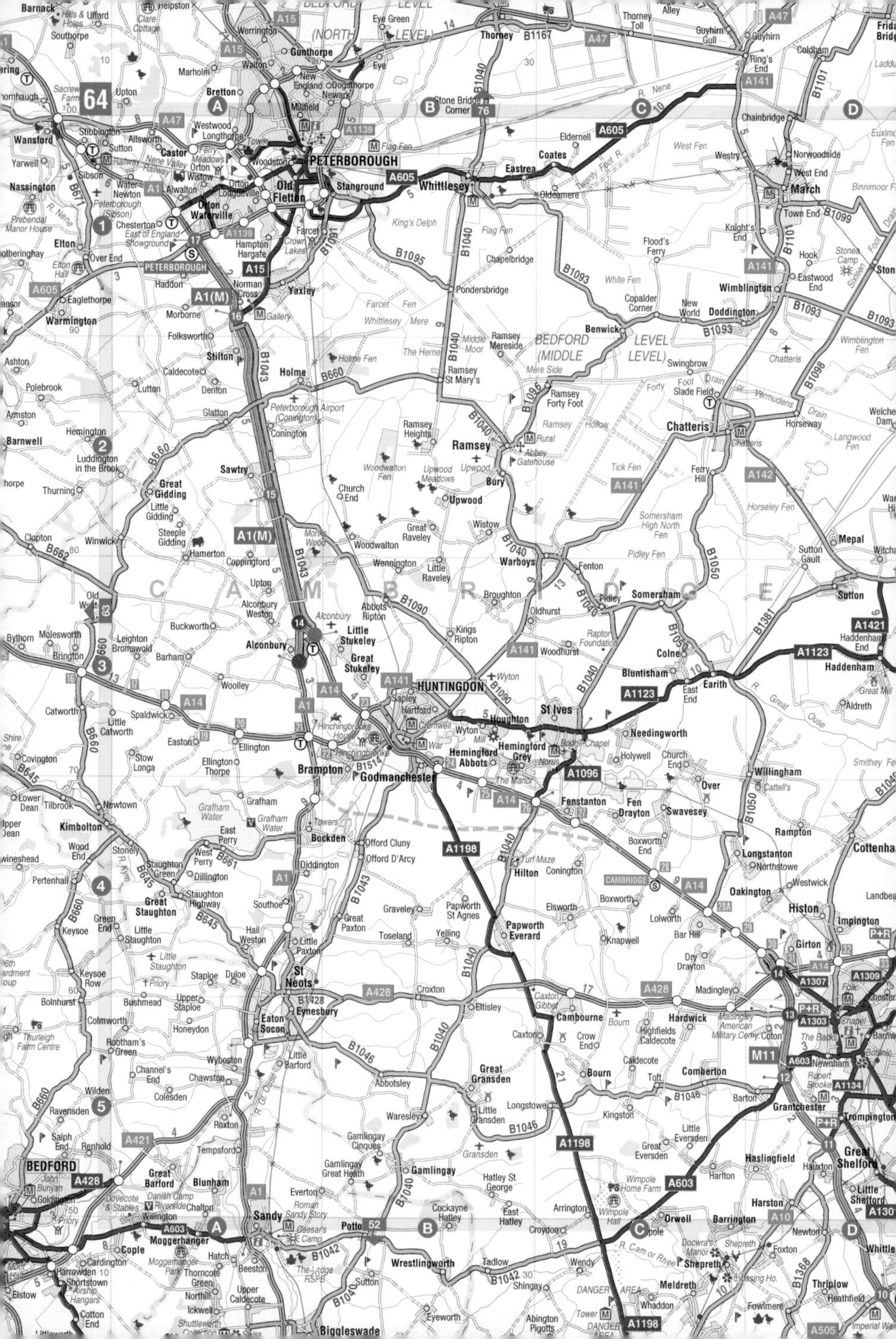

64
Barnack
Helpston
Clare Cottage
Werrington
Eye Green
(NORTH LEVEL)
Thorney
B1167
Thorney Toll
Guyhirn Gull
Guyhirn
Ring's End
Coldham
Southorpe
Gunthorpe
Eye
A47
A15
Marholm
Walton
New England
Dogsthorpe
Newark
Upton
Bretton
Millfield
Stone Bridge Corner
76
R. Nene
A605
A141
Chainbridge
B1101
Wansford
Stibbington
Ailsworth
Westwood
Longthorpe
Sutton
Castor
Ferry Meadows
PETERBOROUGH
Flag Fen
Eldernell
Coates
Eastrea
West Fen
Westry
Norwoodside
West End
March
Yarwell
Sibson
Nene Valley Railway
Orton Wistow
Woodston
Nassington
Water Newton
Alwalton
Orton Longueville
Old Fletton
Stanground
Whittlesey
Oldeamere
Twenty Foot R.
Orton Waterville
Prebendal Manor House
Peterborough (Sibson)
Chesterton
East of England Showground
A1139
King's Delph
Farcet
Crown Lakes
Town End
B1099
Knight's End
Elton
Over End
Hampton Hargate
Flag Fen
Chapelbridge
Flood's Ferry
Hook
Stonea Camp
Elton Hall
PETERBOROUGH
B1091
B1095
B1040
B1093
White Fen
Eastwood End
Wimblington
Haddon
Norman Cross
Yaxley
Pondersbridge
Copalder Corner
New World
Doddington
Eaglethorpe
Warmington
A1(M)
Morborne
Gallery
Farcet Fen
Whittlesey Mere
Benwick
Folksworth
Middle Moor
Ramsey Mereside
BEDFORD (MIDDLE LEVEL)
Chatteris
Wimblington Fen
Ashton
Stilton
B1043
The Herne
Holme Fen
Holme
Caldecote
Ramsey St Mary's
Mere Side
Swingbrow
Polebrook
Lutton
Denton
B660
Forty Foot
Slade Field
Ramsey Forty Foot
Vermudens Drain
B1098
Armston
Glatton
Peterborough Airport (Conington)
Ramsey Heights
Ramsey
Rural
Hollow
Chatteris
Horseway
Welches Dam
Barnwell
Hemington
Conington
Abbey Gatehouse
Langwood Fen
Luddington in the Brook
Woodwalton Fen
Upwood Meadows
Upwood
Tick Fen
Ferry Hill
A142
Sawtry
Bury
Church End
A141
Thurning
Great Gidding
Horseley Fen
Little Gidding
Upwood
Somersham High North Fen
Steeple Gidding
Great Raveley
Wistow
Clopton
Winwick
A1(M)
Monks Wood
Woodwalton
Mepal
Hamerton
Coppingford
B1043
Wennington
Warboys
Fenton
Pidley Fen
B1050
Sutton Gault
B662
Little Raveley
C A M B R I D G E
Upton
Broughton
Pidley
Somersham
Sutton
Old Weston
Alconbury Weston
Abbots Ripton
B1090
Oldhurst
B1381
A1421
Buckworth
Alconbury
Little Stukeley
Kings Ripton
Raptor Foundation
Haddenham End
Bythorn
Molesworth
Leighton Bromswold
Alconbury
A141
Woodhurst
Colne
A1123
Brington
Barham
Great Stukeley
Bluntisham
Earith
Haddenham
Woolley
HUNTINGDON
Wyton
East End
A14
Catworth
Spaldwick
Sapley
Hartford
St Ives
Aldreth
Little Catworth
Hinchingbrooke House
Cromwell
Houghton
Needingworth
Easton
Ellington
Wyton Mill
Hemingford Grey
Bridge Chapel
Holywell
Covington
Stow Longa
Ellington Thorpe
Hinchingbrooke
War
Hemingford Abbots
Norris
Church End
Willingham
B645
Brampton
Godmanchester
B1514
The Manor
A1096
Over
Smithey Fen
Lower Dean
Tilbrook
Newtown
Grafham
Fenstanton
Fen Drayton
Swavesey
Upper Dean
Grafham Water
Towers
A1198
Kimbolton
East Perry
Buckden
Offord Cluny
Boxworth End
Rampton
Wood End
Stonely
West Perry
Offord D'Arcy
B1040
Turf Maze
Longstanton
Cottenham
Swineshead
R. Kym
Staughton Green
B661
Diddington
Hilton
Conington
Northstowe
Pertenhall
Dillington
CAMBRIDGE
Westwick
Great Staughton
Staughton Highway
Southoe
Papworth St Agnes
Elsworth
Boxworth
Oakington
Landbeach
B660
Graveley
Lolworth
Histon
Keysoe
Green End
Little Staughton
B645
Hail Weston
Little Paxton
Great Paxton
Toseland
Yelling
Papworth Everard
Knapwell
Bar Hill
Impington
Girton
Little Staughton
St Neots
Dry Drayton
P+R
Keysoe Row
Staploe
Duloe
Priory
A1307
A1309
Bolnhurst
Bushmead
Upper Staploe
Eatons Socon
B1428
Eynesbury
A428
Croxton
Eltisley
Caxton Gibbet
Cambourne
Madingley
Hardwick
Madingley American Military Cemy.
Coton
A1303
Colmworth
Honeydon
Bourn
Highfields Caldecote
Chesterton
Thurleigh Farm Centre
Rootham's Green
Caxton
Crow End
The Backs
Wyboston
Little Barford
B1046
Caldecote
M11
A603
Newnham
Botanic
Channel's End
Chawston
Abbotsley
Great Gransden
Bourn
Comberton
Toft
Rupert Brooke
A1134
Wilden
Colesden
Little Gransden
Longstowe
Barton
Grantchester
Trumpington
Ravensden
Roxton
Waresley
B1046
Kingston
Little Eversden
R. Gt. Ouse
Salph End
Renhold
A421
Tempsford
Gamlingay Cinques
Gransden
Great Eversden
A1198
Haslingfield
Great Shelford
BEDFORD
John Bunyan
Great Barford
Blunham
A1
Gamlingay Great Heath
Gamlingay
Hatley St George
Wimpole Home Farm
Harlton
Hauxton
A428
Goldington
Danish Camp Riverside
Chalton
Everton
Roman Sandy Story
Cockayne Hatley
East Hatley
Arrington
Wimpole Hall
A603
Little Shelford
Dovecote & Stables
Priory
Willington
Sandy
Caesar's Camp
Potton
52
Orwell
Barrington
Harston
A10
A1301
Moggerhanger
Croydon
Wimpole
Newton
Cople
Moggerhanger Park
Hatch
B1042
Cardington
Thorncote Green
Beeston
The Lodge RSPB
Wrestlingworth
Tadlow
Wendy
R. Cam or Rhee
Docwra's Manor
Shepreth
Foxton
Whittlesford
Harrowden
Shortstown
Airship Hangars
Northill
Upper Caldecote
Sutton
B1042
Shingay
DANGER AREA
Meldreth
Melissing Ho.
B1368
Thriplow
Elstow
Cotton End
Ickwell
Shuttleworth Collection
B1040
Eyeworth
Abington Pigotts
Tower
Whaddon
Fowlmere
Heathfield
Biggleswade
A1198
A505
Imperial War

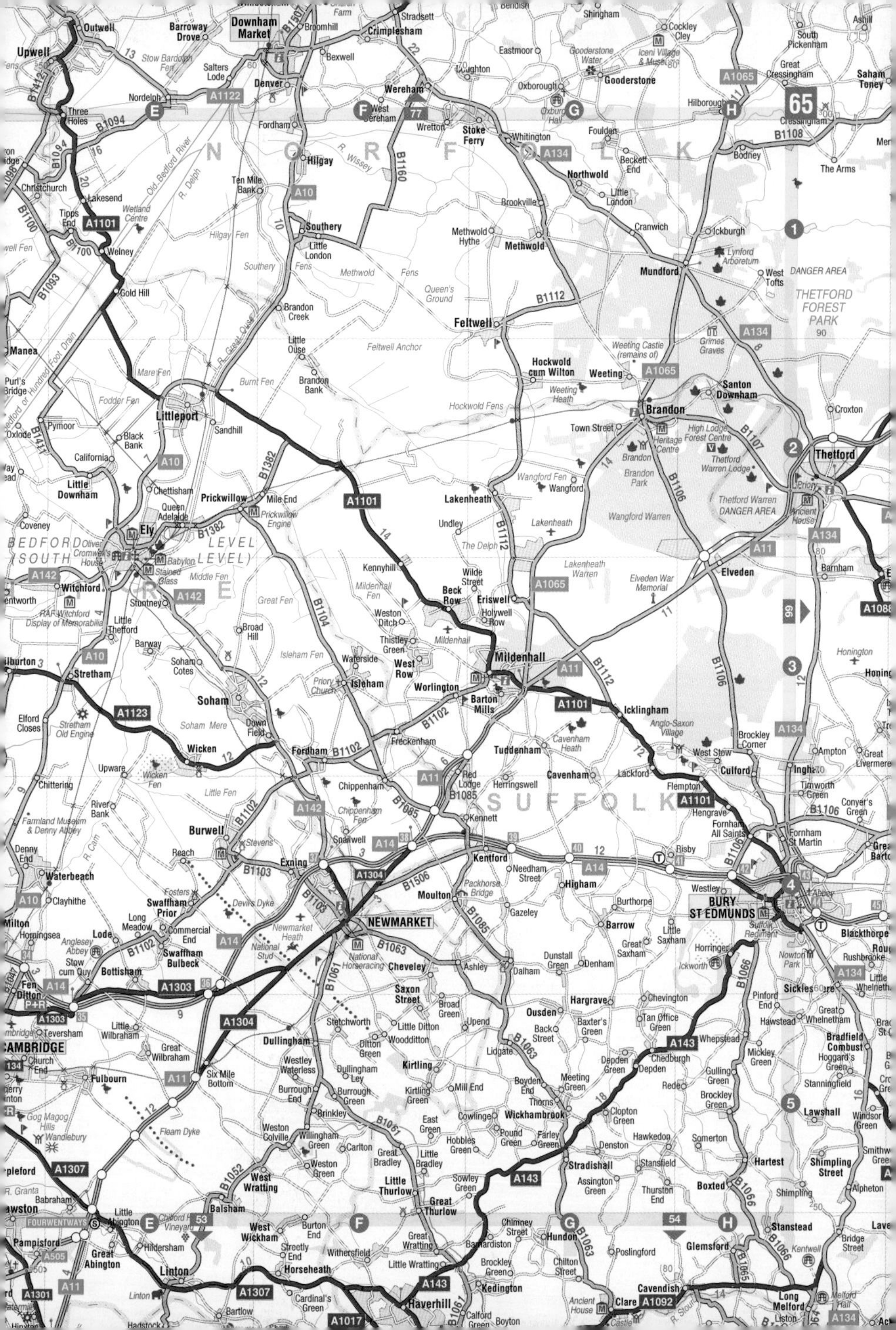

65
Outwell
Upwell
Barroway Drove
Downham Market
B1507
Broomhill
Stradsett
Crimplesham
Bexwell
Shingham
Cockley Cley
South Pickenham
Stow Bardolph Fen
Salters Lode
Denver
Eastmoor
Gooderstone Water
Iceni Village & Museum
Gooderstone
Great Cressingham
Saham Toney
Nordelph
A1122
Boughton
Wereham
Oxborough
Oxburgh Hall
A1065
Hilborough
Three Holes
B1094
West Dereham
77
Wretton
Stoke Ferry
Whitington
Foulden
Cressingham
B1108
Fordham
N O R F O L K
A134
Beckett End
Bodney
The Arms
Hilgay
R. Wissey
B1160
Northwold
Christchurch
Old Bedford River
R. Delph
Ten Mile Bank
A10
Little London
Lakesend
Wetland Centre
A1101
Tipps End
Southery
Brookville
Cranwich
Ickburgh
Welney
Hilgay Fen
Little London
Methwold Hythe
Methwold
Lynford Arboretum
Mundford
West Tofts
DANGER AREA
Southery
Fens
Methwold
Fens
Gold Hill
B1093
Queen's Ground
B1112
THETFORD FOREST PARK
Brandon Creek
Feltwell
Manea
Little Ouse
Feltwell Anchor
Weeting Castle (remains of)
Grimes Graves
Hockwold cum Wilton
Weeting
Santon Downham
Brandon Bank
Burnt Fen
Mare Fen
Purl's Bridge
Fodder Fen
Littleport
Weeting Heath
Hockwold Fens
Brandon
Croxton
Pymoor
Sandhill
Town Street
Heritage Centre
High Lodge Forest Centre
B1107
Black Bank
Oxlode
Brandon
Thetford Warren Lodge
Thetford
California
B1382
Brandon Park
Wangford Fen
Wangford
Little Downham
Chettisham
Prickwillow
Mile End
Prickwillow Engine
Lakenheath
Thetford Warren
DANGER AREA
Priory
Ancient House
Coveney
Queen Adelaide
Undley
Wangford Warren
A1101
Lakenheath
A134
Ely
Oliver Cromwell's House
BEDFORD (SOUTH LEVEL)
Babylon
Stained Glass
The Delph
Elveden
Barnham
A142
Witchford
Middle Fen
Kennyhill
Wilde Street
Lakenheath Warren
Elveden War Memorial
Stuntney
Mildenhall Fen
Beck Row
Eriswell
RAF Witchford Display of Memorabilia
Little Thetford
Great Fen
Weston Ditch
Holywell Row
Broad Hill
B1104
Mildenhall
Honington
Barway
Thistley Green
Soham Cotes
Isleham Fen
Waterside
West Row
Mildenhall
Stretham
Priory Church
Isleham
Worlington
Barton Mills
Icklingham
Soham
Elford Closes
Stretham Old Engine
A1123
Soham Mere
Down Field
B1102
Freckenham
Anglo-Saxon Village
Cavenham Heath
Tuddenham
Brockley Corner
Wicken
Fordham
West Stow
Culford
Ampton
Great Livermere
Upware
Wicken Fen
Chippenham
Red Lodge
Herringswell
Cavenham
Lackford
Flempton
Ingham
Timworth Green
Chittering
Little Fen
SUFFOLK
Hengrave
Chippenham Fen
B1085
Kennett
Fornham All Saints
Fornham St Martin
Conyer's Green
River Bank
Farmland Museum & Denny Abbey
Burwell
Stevens
Snailwell
A14
Kentford
Risby
Denny End
Reach
Exning
A1304
Needham Street
Higham
Waterbeach
B1103
B1506
Westley
BURY ST EDMUNDS
Clayhithe
Fosters
Devil's Dyke
Moulton
Packhorse Bridge
Burthorpe
Abbey
Swaffham Prior
NEWMARKET
Gazeley
Barrow
Little Saxham
Suffolk Regiment
Blackthorpe
Milton
Long Meadow
Commercial End
Newmarket Heath
National Stud
Great Saxham
Horringer
Rushbrooke
Horningsea
Lode
Anglesey Abbey
Swaffham Bulbeck
B1063
National Horseracing
Cheveley
Ashley
Dalham
Dunstall Green
Denham
Ickworth
Nowton Park
Stow cum Quy
Bottisham
B1061
Sicklesmere
Little Whelnetham
Fen Ditton
A1303
Saxon Street
Broad Green
Upend
Hargrave
Chevington
Pinford End
P+R
Ousden
Baxter's Green
Tan Office Green
Hawstead
Great Whelnetham
Teversham
Little Wilbraham
Stetchworth
Little Ditton
Back Street
Whepstead
CAMBRIDGE
Great Wilbraham
Dullingham
Ditton Green
Woodditton
A143
Mickley Green
Bradfield Combust
Church End
Lidgate
Depden Green
Chedburgh
Depden
Hoggard's Green
Fulbourn
Six Mile Bottom
Westley Waterless
Kirtling
Dullingham Ley
Kirtling Green
Mill End
Boyden End
Meeting Green
Rede
Gulling Green
Stanningfield
Burrough End
Burrough Green
Thorns
Brockley Green
Brinkley
East Green
Cowlinge
Wickhambrook
Clopton Green
Lawshall
Windsor Green
Gog Magog Hills
Wandlebury
Fleam Dyke
Weston Colville
Willingham Green
Carlton
Great Bradley
Little Bradley
Pound Green
Hobbles Green
Farley Green
Hawkedon
Somerton
Denston
Weston Green
Stradishall
Stansfield
Hartest
Shimpling Street
A1307
B1052
West Wratting
Little Thurlow
Sowley Green
Assington Green
Thurston End
Boxted
Shimpling
Alpheton
R. Granta
Babraham
Great Thurlow
Balsham
Little Abington
Chilford Hall Vineyard
West Wickham
Burton End
Chimney Street
Hundon
Stanstead
FOURWENTWAYS
Hildersham
Streetly End
Great Wratting
Barnardiston
Poslingford
Glemsford
Kentwell
Bridge Street
Pampisford
Great Abington
Withersfield
B1063
A505
Linton
Horseheath
Little Wratting
Brockley Green
Chilton Street
Kedington
Cavendish
A1092
Clare
Ancient House
Long Melford
Melford Hall
Haverhill
Cardinal's Green
Linton
A1017
Bartlow
Hadstock
Calford Green
Boyton
Castle
R. Stour
Liston

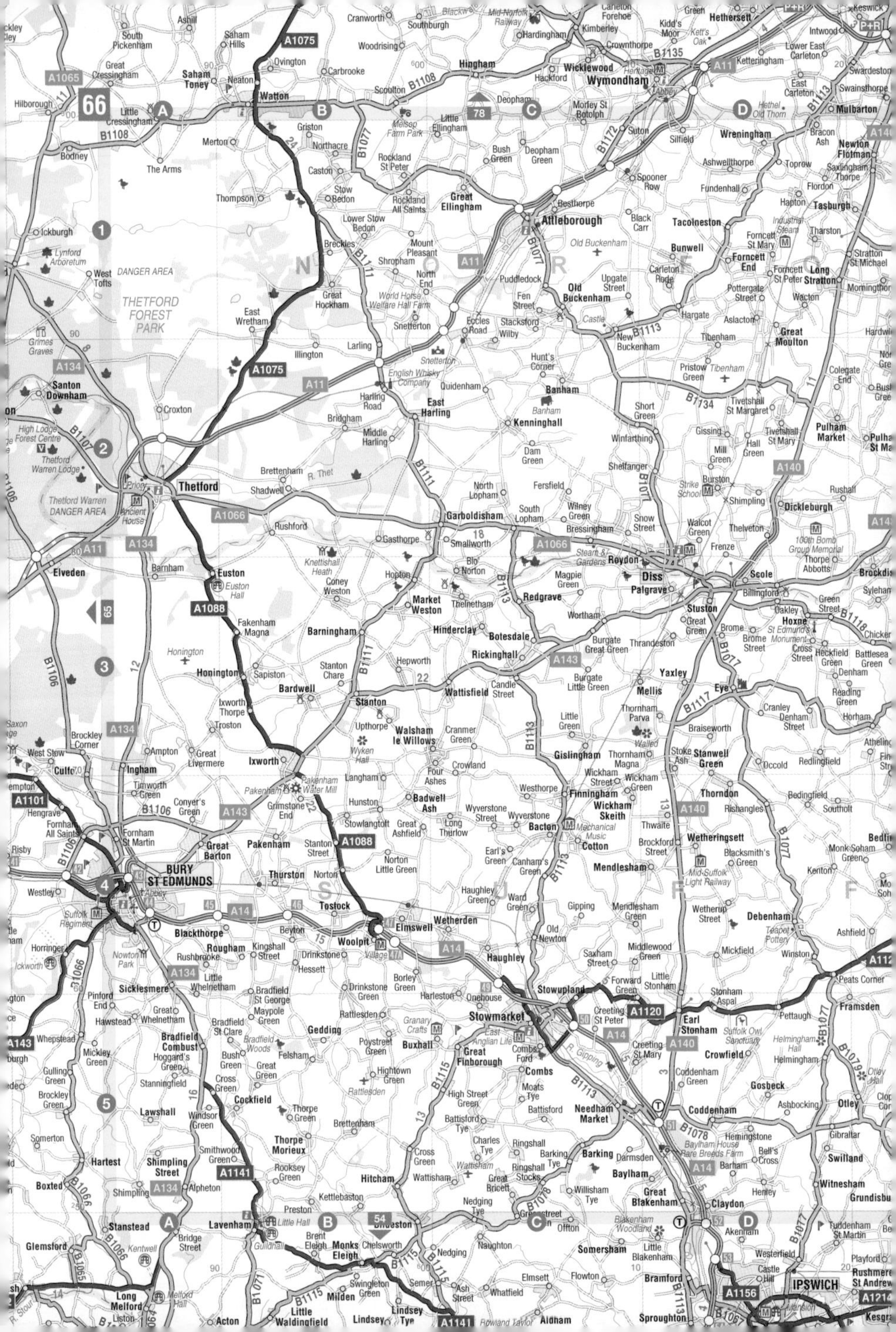

66
A1065
Hilborough
Ashill
South Pickenham
Great Cressingham
Little Cressingham
Saham Hills
Saham Toney
Neaton
Watton
A1075
Ovington
Carbrooke
Cranworth
Southburgh
Woodrising
Scoulton
B1108
Hingham
Mid-Norfolk Railway
Hardingham
Kimberley
Crownthorpe
Wicklewood
Hackford
Deopham
Wymondham
Kidd's Moor
Kett's Oak
B1135
Hethersett
Ketteringham
Intwood
Lower East Carleton
East Carleton
Swardeston
Swainsthorpe
Mulbarton
Keswick
A11
A
B
C
D
78
Merton
Bodney
The Arms
Griston
Northacre
Caston
Thompson
Stow Bedon
B1077
Melsop Farm Park
Little Ellingham
Rockland St Peter
Rockland All Saints
Great Ellingham
Bush Green
Deopham Green
Morley St Botolph
Hethel Old Thorn
B1172
Suton
Silfield
Spooner Row
Besthorpe
Attleborough
Wreningham
Ashwellthorpe
Fundenhall
Bracon Ash
Newton Flotman
Toprow
Saxlingham Thorpe
Flordon
Hapton
Tasburgh
Tharston
Ickburgh
Lynford Arboretum
West Tofts
DANGER AREA
THETFORD FOREST PARK
Grimes Graves
Lower Stow Bedon
Breckles
Shropham
Mount Pleasant
North End
Great Hockham
World Horse Welfare Hall Farm
Snetterton
East Wretham
Illington
Larling
Eccles Road
Stacksford
Wilby
Puddledock
Fen Street
Old Buckenham
Upgate Street
Black Carr
Bunwell
Carleton Rode
Tacolneston
Forncett St Mary
Forncett End
Forncett St Peter
Industrial Steam
Long Stratton
Stratton St Michael
Morningthorpe
Pottergate Street
Wacton
Hargate
Aslacton
Castle
New Buckenham
B1113
Tibenham
Great Moulton
Hardwick
Colegate End
A134
Santon Downham
A1075
A11
English Whisky Company
Harling Road
Quidenham
Hunt's Corner
Banham
Pristow Green
Tivetshall St Margaret
Tivetshall St Mary
B1134
Short Green
Gissing
Pulham Market
Pulham St Mary
Croxton
High Lodge Forest Centre
Thetford Warren Lodge
B1107
Bridgham
East Harling
Middle Harling
Kenninghall
Winfarthing
Dam Green
Mill Green
Hall Green
Shelfanger
Burston
Strike School
A140
Shimpling
Rushall
Dickleburgh
Thetford Warren
DANGER AREA
Priory
Thetford
Ancient House
Brettenham
Shadwell
R. Thet
B1111
North Lopham
Fersfield
South Lopham
Wilney Green
Bressingham
Snow Street
Walcot Green
Thelveton
100th Bomb Group Memorial
Thorpe Abbotts
B1106
A1066
Rushford
Garboldisham
Gasthorpe
Smallworth
Steam & Gardens
Roydon
Diss
Frenze
Scole
Brockdish
Elveden
Barnham
Euston
Euston Hall
Knettishall Heath
Coney Weston
Hopton
Blo Norton
Thelnetham
Magpie Green
Palgrave
Stuston
Billingford
Oakley
Hoxne
St Edmund's Monument
Green Street
Syleham
B1118
A1088
Fakenham Magna
Market Weston
Redgrave
Wortham
Great Green
Brome
Brome Street
Cross Street
Heckfield Green
Chickering
Battlesea Green
Honington
Barningham
Hinderclay
Botesdale
Rickinghall
Burgate Great Green
Thrandeston
Stanton Chare
Hepworth
Sapiston
Bardwell
Stanton
Wattisfield
Candle Street
Burgate Little Green
Mellis
Yaxley
Eye
Denham
Reading Green
Ixworth Thorpe
Troston
Upthorpe
Walsham le Willows
Wyken Hall
Cranmer Green
Little Green
Thornham Parva
Walled
Braiseworth
Cranley
Denham Street
Horham
West Stow
Brockley Corner
Ampton
Great Livermere
Ixworth
Crowland
Gislingham
Thornham Magna
Stoke Ash
Stanwell Green
Occold
Redlingfield
Culford
Ingham
Timworth Green
Conyer's Green
Pakenham Water Mill
Langham
Four Ashes
Wickham Street
Wickham Green
Westhorpe
Finningham
Wickham Skeith
Thorndon
Rishangles
Bedingfield
Southolt
A1101
Hengrave
Fornham All Saints
Fornham St Martin
Risby
B1106
A143
Grimstone End
Hunston
Badwell Ash
Stowlangtoft
Great Ashfield
Long Thurlow
Wyverstone Street
Wyverstone
Bacton
Mechanical Music
Thwaite
Wetheringsett
Blacksmith's Green
Monk Soham Green
Great Barton
Pakenham
Stanton Street
Norton Little Green
Earl's Green
Canham's Green
Cotton
Brockford Street
Mid-Suffolk Light Railway
Kenton
Westley
BURY ST EDMUNDS
Abbey
Thurston
Norton
Mendlesham
Haughley Green
Ward Green
Suffolk Regiment
Blackthorpe
A14
Tostock
Elmswell
Wetherden
Gipping
Mendlesham Green
Wetherup Street
Debenham
Teapot Pottery
Ashfield
Horringer
Ickworth
Rougham
Rushbrooke
Nowton Park
Kingshall Street
Beyton
Drinkstone
Hessett
Woolpit
Village
Old Newton
Saxham Street
Middlewood Green
Mickfield
Winston
Haughley
Little Whelnetham
Sicklesmere
Borley Green
Harleston
Onehouse
Stowupland
Forward Green
Little Stonham
Peats Corner
Pinford End
Hawstead
Great Whelnetham
Bradfield St George
Drinkstone Green
Maypole Green
Rattlesden
Stowmarket
Creeting St Peter
A1120
Earl Stonham
Stonham Aspal
Pettaugh
Framsden
Whepstead
Bradfield St Clare
Bradfield Combust
Bradfield Woods
Gedding
Granary Crafts
East Anglian Life
Poystreet Green
Buxhall
Great Finborough
Combs Ford
Creeting St Mary
Suffolk Owl Sanctuary
Crowfield
Helmingham Hall
Helmingham
Mickley Green
Hoggard's Green
Felsham
Hightown Green
Combs
R. Gipping
Coddenham Green
Gosbeck
Otley Hall
Gulling Green
Stanningfield
Bush Green
Great Green
Cross Green
Cockfield
Moats Tye
High Street Green
Battisford
Battisford Tye
Needham Market
Coddenham
Ashbocking
Otley
Brockley Green
Lawshall
Windsor Green
Thorpe Green
Brettenham
Thorpe Morieux
Charles Tye
Ringshall
Hemingstone
Gibraltar
Bell's Cross
Somerton
Hartest
Shimpling Street
Smithwood Green
Rooksey Green
Cross Green
Wattisham
Hitcham
Great Bricett
Ringshall Stocks
Barking Tye
Barking
Darmsden
Baylham House Rare Breeds Farm
Baylham
Barham
Swilland
Witnesham
Grundisburgh
Boxted
Shimpling
Alpheton
A1141
Kettlebaston
Preston
Nedging Tye
Willisham Tye
Great Blakenham
Claydon
Henley
Stanstead
Bridge Street
Lavenham
Little Hall
Guildhall
Brent Eleigh
Monks Eleigh
Chelsworth
Bildeston
Nedging
Naughton
Greenstreet Green
Offton
Blakenham Woodland
Somersham
Little Blakenham
Akenham
Tuddenham St Martin
Glemsford
Kentwell
Westerfield
Playford
Rushmere St Andrew
Long Melford
Melford Hall
Liston
Swingleton Green
Milden
Little Waldingfield
Semer
Ash Street
Whatfield
Elmsett
Flowton
Bramford
Castle Hill
IPSWICH
A1156
A1214
Acton
Lindsey
Lindsey Tye
Rowland Taylor
Aldham
Sproughton
Kesgrave
54
65

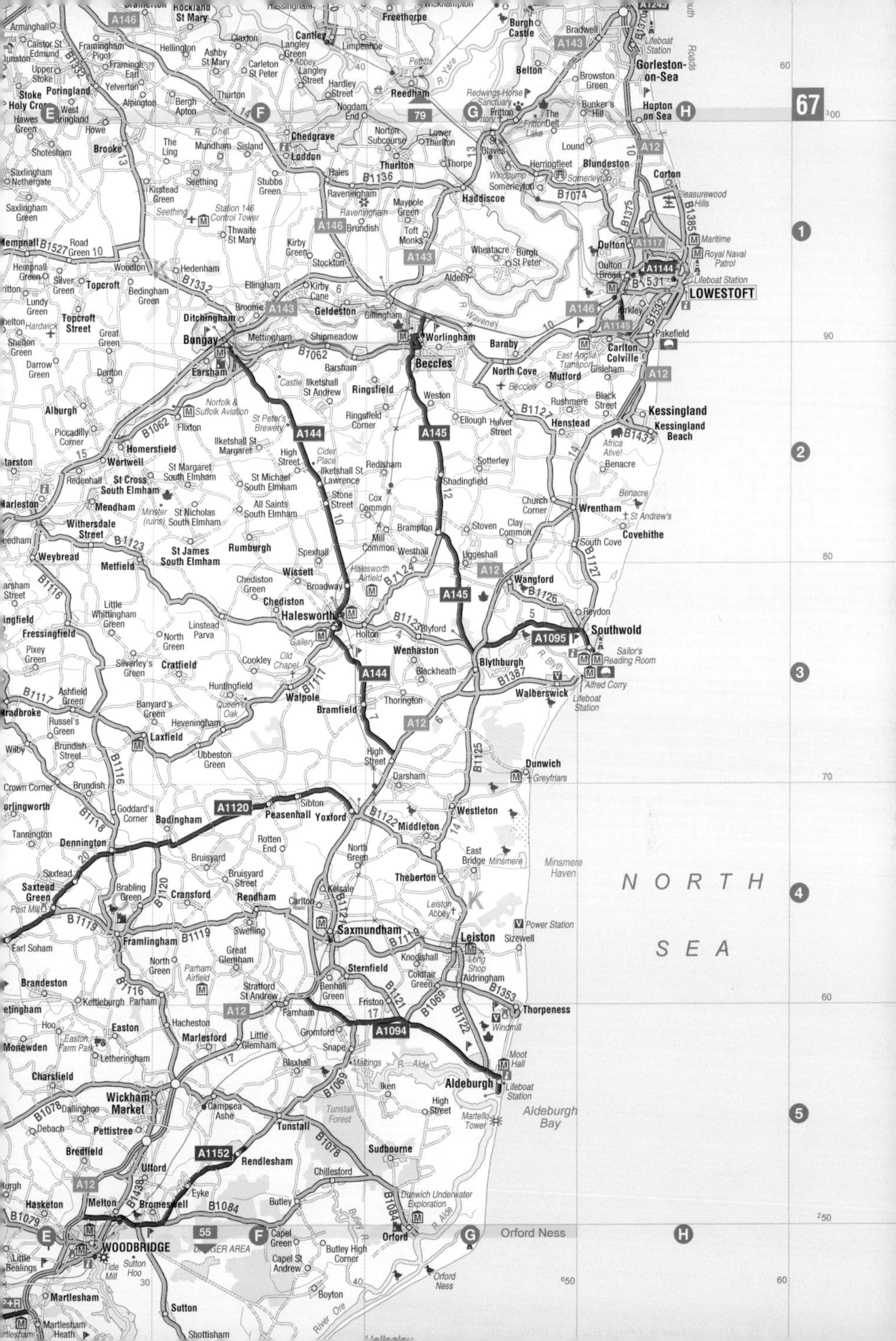

67
NORTH
SEA
LOWESTOFT
Gorleston-on-Sea
Hopton on Sea
Burgh Castle
Belton
Bradwell
Browston Green
Bunker's Hill
Fritton
St Olaves
Herringfleet
Somerleyton
Blundeston
Lound
Corton
Pleasurewood Hills
Oulton
Oulton Broad
Carlton Colville
Pakefield
Kirkley
Barnby
North Cove
Mutford
Gisleham
Kessingland
Kessingland Beach
Africa Alive!
Benacre
Henstead
Rushmere
Black Street
Wrentham
Covehithe
South Cove
Reydon
Southwold
Sailor's Reading Room
Alfred Corry
Walberswick
Lifeboat Station
Wangford
Uggeshall
Stoven
Clay Common
Blythburgh
Wenhaston
Blackheath
Thorington
Blyford
Holton
Halesworth
Halesworth Airfield
Westhall
Brampton
Shadingfield
Sotterley
Ellough
Weston
Beccles
Worlingham
Gillingham
Geldeston
Kirby Cane
Ellingham
Broome
Ditchingham
Bungay
Earsham
Mettingham
Shipmeadow
Barsham
Ringsfield
Ringsfield Corner
Redisham
Ilketshall St Andrew
Ilketshall St Lawrence
Ilketshall St Margaret
St Peter's Brewery
Norfolk & Suffolk Aviation
Flixton
Homersfield
Wortwell
St Cross South Elmham
St Margaret South Elmham
St Michael South Elmham
All Saints South Elmham
St Nicholas South Elmham
St James South Elmham
Rumburgh
Mendham
Metfield
Weybread
Withersdale Street
Fressingfield
Stone Street
Spexhall
Wissett
Chediston
Chediston Green
Linstead Parva
Cookley
Walpole
Bramfield
Huntingfield
Heveningham
Laxfield
Ubbeston Green
Cratfield
Darsham
Dunwich
Greyfriars
Westleton
Middleton
Yoxford
Sibton
Peasenhall
Badingham
Dennington
Saxtead Green
Framlingham
Cransford
Rendham
Carlton
Kelsale
Saxmundham
Theberton
Eastbridge
Minsmere
Minsmere Haven
Leiston
Leiston Abbey
Sizewell
Power Station
Knodishall
Aldringham
Thorpeness
Sternfield
Benhall Green
Friston
Farnham
Snape
Aldeburgh
Moot Hall
Aldeburgh Bay
Martello Tower
Iken
Tunstall
Tunstall Forest
Sudbourne
Chillesford
Butley
Orford
Orford Ness
Dunwich Underwater Exploration
Rendlesham
Wickham Market
Campsea Ashe
Marlesford
Little Glemham
Great Glemham
Parham
Easton
Letheringham
Charsfield
Pettistree
Bredfield
Ufford
Melton
Bromeswell
Eyke
WOODBRIDGE
Sutton Hoo
Tide Mill
Martlesham
Martlesham Heath
Sutton
Shottisham
Boyton
Capel St Andrew
Butley High Corner
DANGER AREA
Reedham
Haddiscoe
Loddon
Chedgrave
Thurlton
Raveningham
Toft Monks
Aldeby
Wheatacre
Burgh St Peter
Brooke
Poringland
Topcroft
Woodton
Hedenham
Denton
Alburgh
Harleston
Seething
Station 146 Control Tower
A12
A143
A144
A145
A146
A1095
A1120
A1094
A1152
A1117
A1144
A1145
B1127
B1126
B1123
B1122
B1121
B1119
B1116
B1069
B1078
B1084
B1353
B1387
B1074
B1062
B1332
B1136

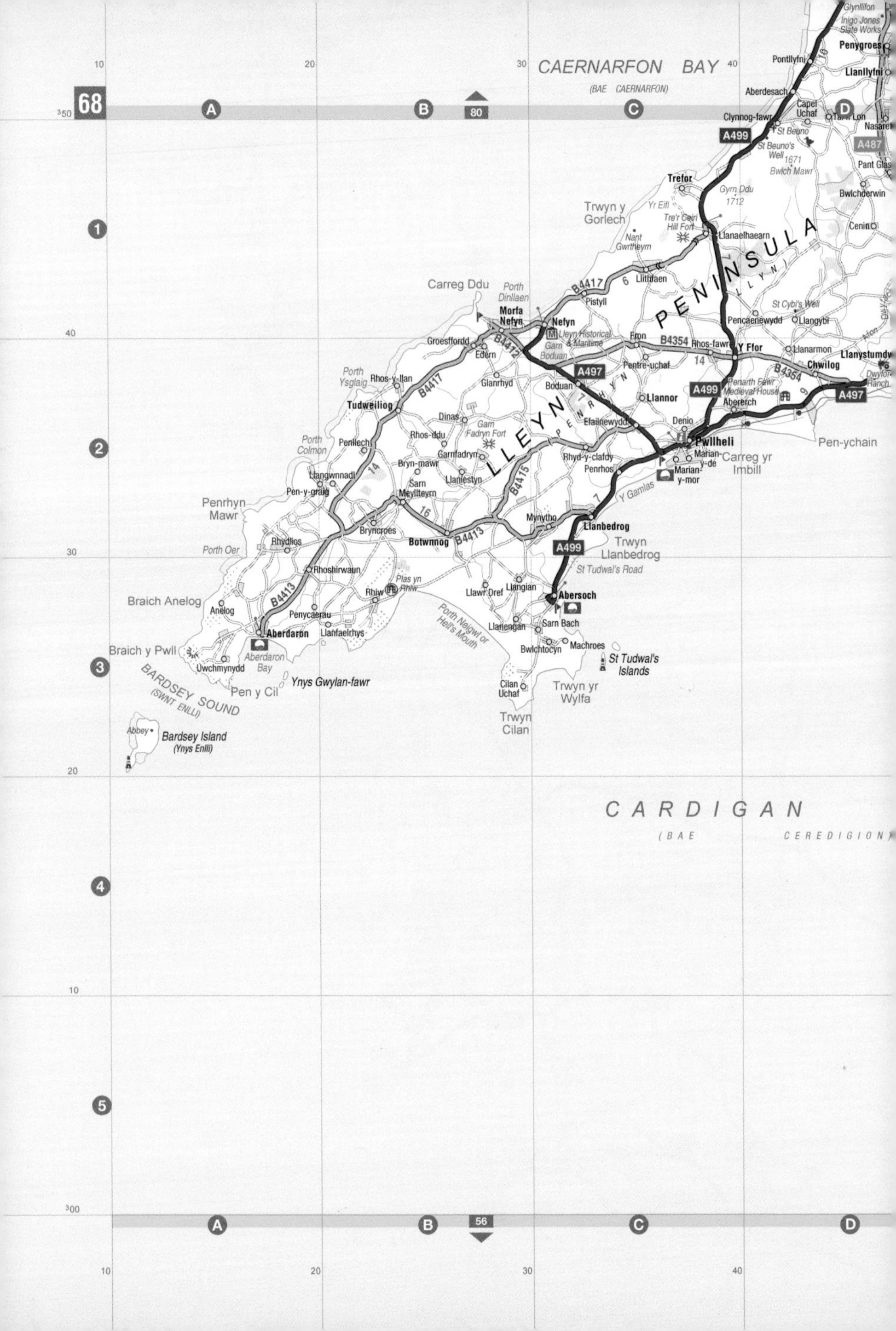
CAERNARFON BAY
(BAE CAERNARFON)
80
56
Glynllifon
Inigo Jones' Slate Works
Penygroes
Pontllyfni
Llanllyfni
Aberdesach
Clynnog-fawr
Capel Uchaf
Tan-y-Lon
Nasareth
St Beuno
St Beuno's Well
1671
Bwlch Mawr
A499
A487
Pant Glas
Trefor
Gyrn Ddu
1712
Bwlchderwin
Trwyn y Gorlech
Yr Eifl
Tre'r Ceiri Hill Fort
Llanaelhaearn
Cenin
Nant Gwrtheyrn
LLEYN PENINSULA
(LLYN)
Llithfaen
Carreg Ddu
Porth Dinllaen
B4417
Pistyll
St Cybi's Well
Morfa Nefyn
Nefyn
Lleyn Historical & Maritime
Pencaenewydd
Llangybi
Fron
Garn Boduan
B4354
Rhos-fawr
Y Ffor
Llanarmon
Llanystumdwy
Groesffordd
Edern
B4412
Pentre-uchaf
Chwilog
Porth Ysgaig
Rhos-y-llan
A497
Glanrhyd
Boduan
Penarth Fawr Medieval House
Dwyfor Ranch
B4417
Llannor
Abererch
Tudweiliog
Dinas
Garn Fadryn Fort
Efailnewydd
Denio
Porth Colmon
Penllech
Rhos-ddu
LLEYN
PENRHYN
Pwllheli
Pen-ychain
Garnfadryn
Rhyd-y-clafdy
Marian-y-de
Carreg yr Imbill
Llangwnnadl
Bryn-mawr
Llaniestyn
Penrhos
Marian-y-mor
Pen-y-graig
Sarn Meyllteyrn
B4415
Y Gamlas
Penrhyn Mawr
16
Mynytho
Bryncroes
Botwnnog
B4413
Llanbedrog
Rhydlios
Trwyn Llanbedrog
Porth Oer
St Tudwal's Road
Rhoshirwaun
Plas yn Rhiw
Rhiw
Llawr Dref
Llangian
Braich Anelog
Abersoch
Anelog
B4413
Penycaerau
Porth Neigwl or Hell's Mouth
Llanengan
Sarn Bach
Aberdaron
Llanfaelrhys
Braich y Pwll
Aberdaron Bay
Bwlchtocyn
Machroes
Uwchmynydd
St Tudwal's Islands
BARDSEY SOUND
(SWNT ENLLI)
Pen y Cil
Ynys Gwylan-fawr
Cilan Uchaf
Trwyn yr Wylfa
Trwyn Cilan
Abbey
Bardsey Island
(Ynys Enlli)
CARDIGAN
(BAE CEREDIGION)
A
B
C
D
1
2
3
4
5
10
20
30
40
350
300

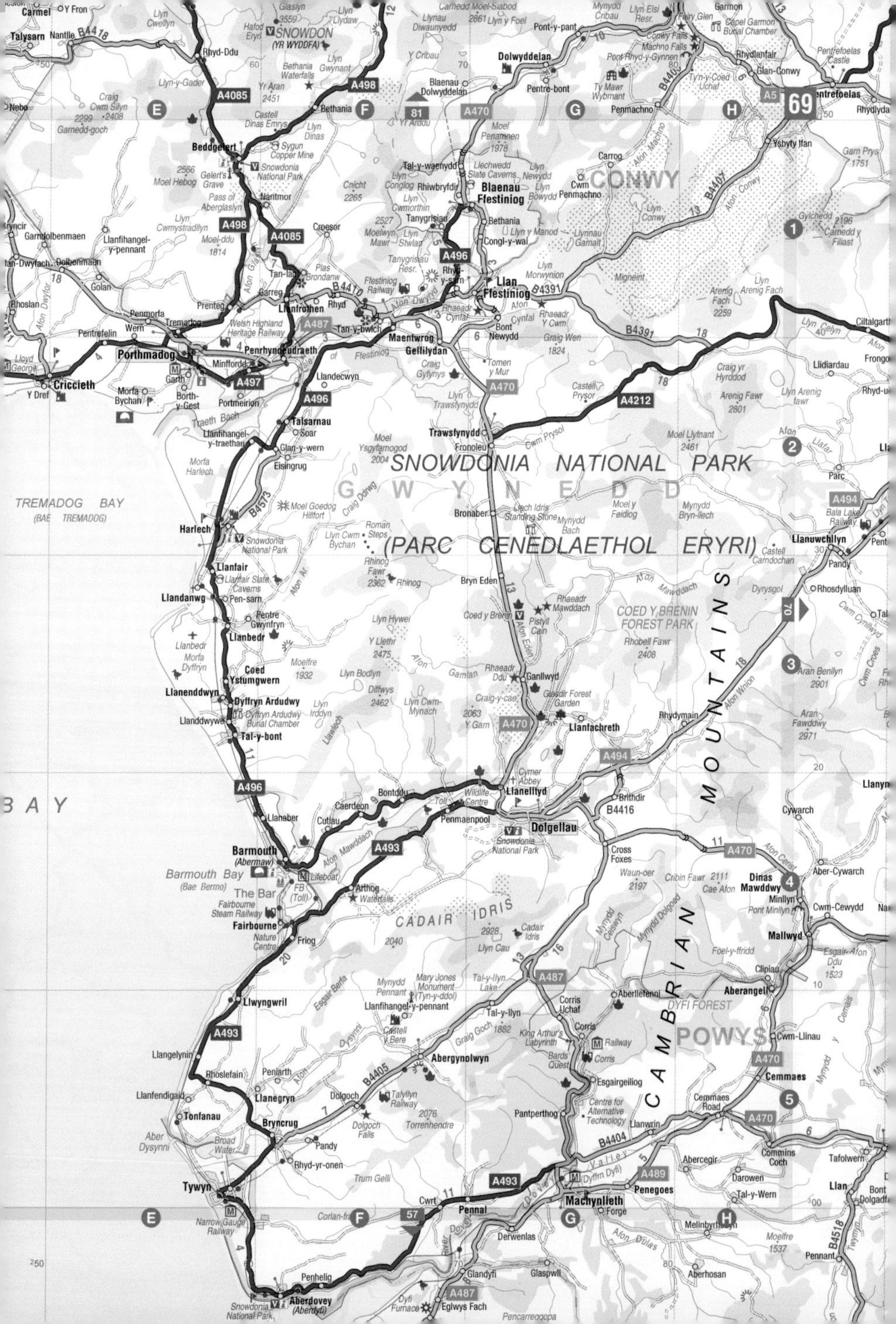

Carmel
Y Fron
Glaslyn
3559
Llyn Llydaw
Carnedd Moel-Siabod
2861
Llyn y Foel
Llynau Diwaunedd
Mynydd Cribau
Llyn Elsi Resr.
Garmon
Fairy Glen
Capel Garmon Burial Chamber
Llyn Cwellyn
Hafod Eryri
SNOWDON
(YR WYDDFA)
Pont-y-pant
Conwy Falls
Machno Falls
Pont Rhyd-y-Gynnen
Talysarn
Nantlle
B4418
Rhyd-Ddu
Y Cribau
Dolwyddelan
Rhydlanfair
Glan-Conwy
Pentrefoelas Castle
Bethania Waterfalls
Llyn Gwynant
Blaenau Dolwyddelan
Pentre-bont
Tŷ Mawr Wybrnant
Tyn-y-Coed Uchaf
B4406
Llyn-y-Gader
Yr Aran
2451
A4085
A498
Craig Cwm Silyn
2408
2299
Garnedd-goch
Nebo
E
Castell Dinas Emrys
Bethania
F
81
Yr Arddu
A470
G
Penmachno
H
A5
69
Pentrefoelas
Rhydlydan
Moel Penamnen
1978
Llyn Dinas
Sygun Copper Mine
Beddgelert
Snowdonia National Park
Tal-y-waenydd
Llechwedd Slate Caverns
Llyn Newydd
Carrog
Ysbyty Ifan
Garn Prys
1751
2566
Moel Hebog
Gelert's Grave
Cnicht
2265
Llyn Conglog
Rhiwbryfdir
Blaenau Ffestiniog
Llyn Bowydd
Cwm Penmachno
CONWY
B4407
Afon Machno
Afon Conwy
Pass of Aberglaslyn
Nantmor
Llyn Cwmorthin
Tanygrisiau
Bethania
Llyn Conwy
Gylchedd
2196
Carnedd y Filiast
Llyn Cwmystradllyn
Moel-ddu
1814
Croesor
2527
Moelwyn Mawr
Llyn Stwlan
Congl-y-wal
Llyn y Manod
Llynnau Gamallt
1
Bryncir
Garndolbenmaen
Llanfihangel-y-pennant
A498
A4085
Tanygrisiau Resr.
A496
Llyn Morwynion
Migneint
Llyn Arenig Fach
Llan-Dwyfach
Dolbenmaen
Plas Brondanw
Rhyd-y-sarn
Llan Ffestiniog
B4391
Arenig Fach
2259
18
Golan
Tan-lan
Ffestiniog Railway
B4410
Afon Dwyryd
Rhoslan
Afon Dwytor
Prenteg
Garreg
Llanfrothen
Rhyd
Rhaeadr Cynfal
Afon Cynfal
Rhaeadr Y Cwm
Penmorfa
Tremadog
Welsh Highland Heritage Railway
A487
Tan-y-bwlch
Bont Newydd
Llyn Celyn
Pentrefelin
Wern
Maentwrog
Gellilydan
Graig Wen
1824
B4391
18
Ciltalgarth
Porthmadog
Penrhyndeudraeth
Vale of Ffestiniog
Minffordd
Craig Gyfynys
Tomen y Mur
Craig yr Hyrddod
Llidiardau
Frongoch
Lloyd George
Criccieth
Y Dref
Garth
Borth-y-Gest
Morfa Bychan
A497
Llandecwyn
Portmeirion
A496
Llyn Trawsfynydd
A470
Castell Prysor
A4212
Arenig Fawr
2801
Llyn Arenig fawr
Rhyd-uchaf
Traeth Bach
Talsarnau
Soar
Trawsfynydd
Llanfihangel-y-traethau
Glan-y-wern
Fronoleu
Cwm Prysol
Moel Ysgyfarnogod
2004
Moel Llyfnant
2461
Afon Llafar
2
Morfa Harlech
Eisingrug
SNOWDONIA NATIONAL PARK
GWYNEDD
Parc
TREMADOG BAY
(BAE TREMADOG)
Craig Ddrwg
Moel y Feidiog
Mynydd Bryn-llech
A494
B4573
Moel Goedog Hillfort
Roman Steps
Bronaber
Llech Idris Standing Stone
Mynydd Bach
Bala Lake Railway
Harlech
Snowdonia National Park
Llyn Cwm Bychan
(PARC CENEDLAETHOL ERYRI)
Llanuwchllyn
Castell Carndochan
Pandy
Llanfair
Llanfair Slate Caverns
Rhinog Fawr
2362
Rhinog
Bryn Eden
Afon Mawddach
Rhosdylluan
Llandanwg
Pen-sarn
Afon Artro
13
Rhaeadr Mawddach
Dyrysgol
70
Pentre Gwynfryn
Llyn Hywel
Coed y Brenin
Pistyll Cain
COED Y BRENIN FOREST PARK
Cwm Cynllwyd
Llanbedr
Afon Eden
Llanbedr Morfa Dyffryn
Y Llethr
2475
Rhobell Fawr
2408
Cwm Croes
3
Aran Benllyn
2901
Coed Ystumgwern
Moelfre
1932
Llyn Bodlyn
Afon Gamlan
Rhaeadr Ddu
Ganllwyd
Llanenddwyn
Dyffryn Ardudwy
Dyffryn Ardudwy Burial Chamber
Diffwys
2462
Llyn Irddyn
Llyn Cwm-Mynach
Craig-y-cae
Glasdir Forest Garden
Afon Wnion
Rhydymain
Aran Fawddwy
2971
Llanddwywe
Tal-y-bont
Llawlech
2063
Y Garn
A470
Llanfachreth
CAMBRIAN MOUNTAINS
A494
20
BAY
A496
Bontddu
Cymer Abbey
Llanelltyd
Brithdir
B4416
Llanymawddwy
Caerdeon
Wildlife Centre
Toll
Llanaber
Cutiau
Penmaenpool
Dolgellau
Cywarch
Snowdonia National Park
Cross Foxes
A470
Afon Mawddach
A493
11
Afon Cerist
Barmouth
(Abermaw)
Lifeboat
Waun-oer
2197
Cribin Fawr
2111
Cae Afon
Dinas Mawddwy
4
Aber-Cywarch
Barmouth Bay
(Bae Bermo)
The Bar
FB (Toll)
Arthog Waterfalls
Minllyn
Pont Minllyn
Cwm-Cewydd
Fairbourne Steam Railway
Fairbourne
CADAIR IDRIS
Mynydd Ceiswyn
Mynydd Dolgoed
Mallwyd
Nature Centre
Friog
2928
Cadair Idris
Llyn Cau
2040
16
Foel-y-ffridd
Esgair-Afon Ddu
1523
20
13
A487
Mary Jones Monument (Tyn-y-ddol)
Tal-y-llyn Lake
Clipiau
Mynydd Pennant
Esgair Berfa
Aberllefenni
Corris Uchaf
DYFI FOREST
Aberangell
10
Llwyngwril
Llanfihangel-y-pennant
Tal-y-llyn
A493
Castell y Bere
Craig Goch
1882
King Arthur's Labyrinth
Corris
Railway
POWYS
Cwm-Llinau
Mynydd y Cemais
Llangelynin
Afon Dysynni
Abergynolwyn
Bards' Quest
Corris
A470
Rhoslefain
Peniarth
B4405
Esgairgeiliog
Cemmaes
Llanfendigaid
Llanegryn
Dolgoch
Talyllyn Railway
2076
Torrenhendre
Centre for Alternative Technology
Pantperthog
Cemmaes Road
5
Tonfanau
Bryncrug
Dolgoch Falls
Llanwrin
A470
Aber Dysynni
Broad Water
Pandy
B4404
Valley
6
Commins Coch
Tafolwern
Rhyd-yr-onen
Abercegir
Darowen
Tywyn
Trum Gelli
A493
Dyffryn Dyfi
A489
Penegoes
Tal-y-Wern
Llan
Bont Dolgadfan
Cwrt
Pennal
Machynlleth
Forge
E
Corlan-fraith
F
57
G
H
Narrow Gauge Railway
River Dovey
Derwenlas
Melinbyrhedyn
Afon Dulas
Moelfre
1537
B4518
Pennant
Afon Twymyn
Penhelig
Glandyfi
Glaspwll
Aberhosan
A487
Snowdonia National Park
Aberdovey
(Aberdyfi)
Dyfi Furnace
Eglwys Fach
Pencarreggopa

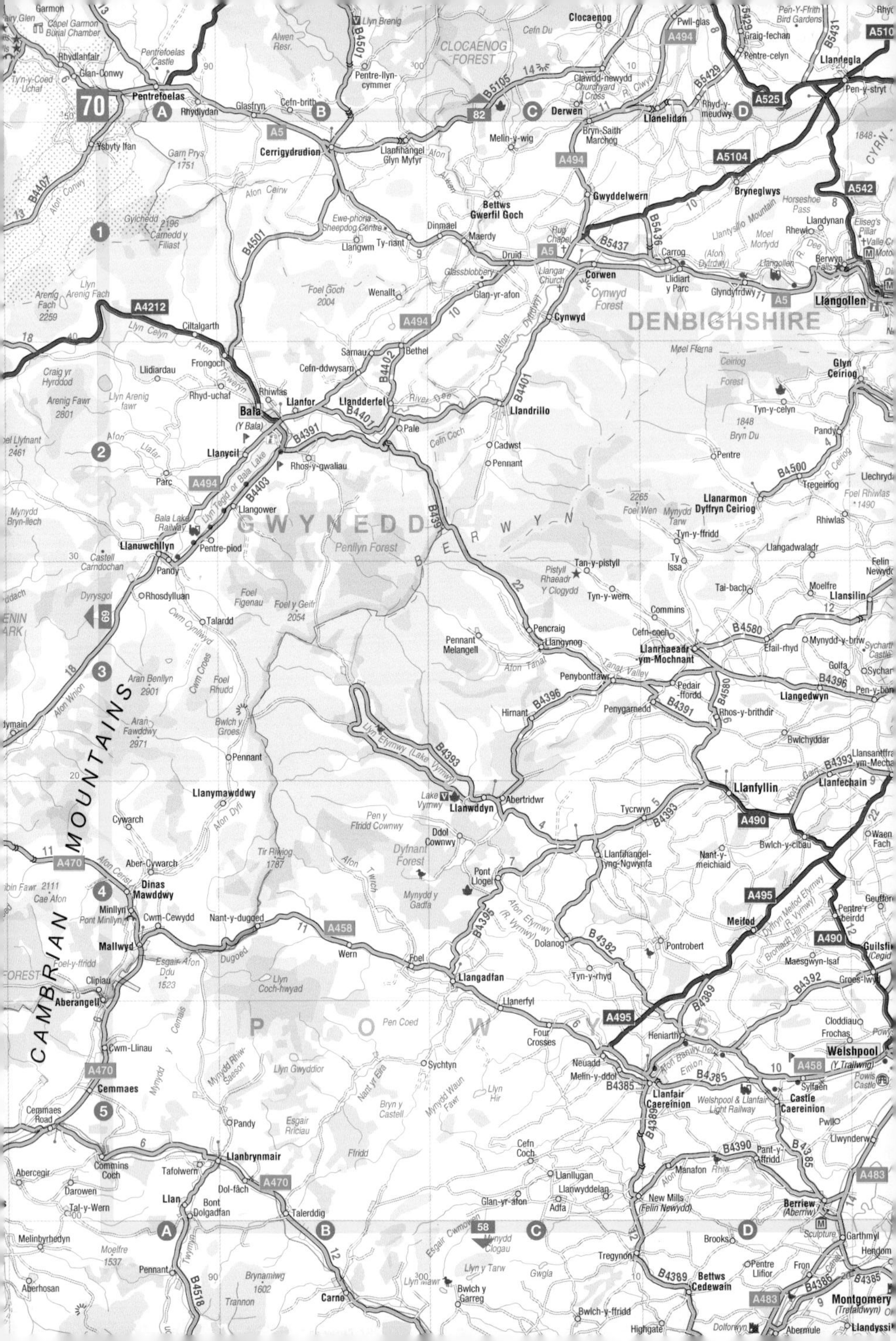

70
82
69
58
A
B
C
D
1
2
3
4
5
DENBIGHSHIRE
GWYNEDD
POWYS
BERWYN
CAMBRIAN MOUNTAINS
CLOCAENOG FOREST
Garmon
Capel Garmon Burial Chamber
Rhydlanfair
Glan-Conwy
Tyn-y-Coed Uchaf
Pentrefoelas
Pentrefoelas Castle
Rhydlydan
Glasfryn
Cefn-brith
Llyn Brenig
Alwen Resr.
Pentre-llyn-cymmer
Cefn Du
Clocaenog
Pwll-glas
Pen-Y-Ffrith Bird Gardens
Graig-fechan
Pentre-celyn
Llandegla
Pen-y-stryt
Clawdd-newydd
Churchyard Cross
R. Clwyd
Derwen
Llanelidan
Rhyd-y-meudwy
Ysbyty Ifan
Cerrigydrudion
Llanfihangel Glyn Myfyr
Melin-y-wig
Bryn-Saith Marchog
Garn Prys 1751
Afon Conwy
Afon Ceirw
Gylchedd 2196
Carnedd y Filiast
Ewe-phoria Sheepdog Centre
Llangwm
Ty-nant
Dinmael
Maerdy
Bettws Gwerfil Goch
Gwyddelwern
Bryneglwys
Horseshoe Pass
Llantysilio Mountain
Moel Morfydd
Llandynan
Rhewl
Eliseg's Pillar
Valle Crucis
Rug Chapel
Druid
Carrog
Llangar Church
Corwen
Glassblobbery
Glan-yr-afon
Foel Goch 2004
Wenallt
Llidiart y Parc
Glyndyfrdwy
Llangollen
Berwyn Falls
Cynwyd Forest
Cynwyd
Llyn Arenig Fach
Arenig Fach 2259
Ciltalgarth
Llyn Celyn
Frongoch
Craig yr Hyrddod
Llidiardau
Arenig Fawr 2801
Llyn Arenig fawr
Rhyd-uchaf
Rhiwlas
Afon Tryweryn
Bala
(Y Bala)
Llanfor
Llandderfel
River Dee
Sarnau
Bethel
Cefn-ddwysarn
Llandrillo
Moel Fferna
Ceiriog Forest
Glyn Ceiriog
Tyn-y-celyn
Pale
Cefn Coch
Cadwst
Pennant
Pandy
Bryn Du 1848
Pentre
Llanycil
Rhos-y-gwaliau
Parc
Llyn Tegid or Bala Lake
Llangower
Bala Lake Railway
Mynydd Bryn-llech
Penllyn Forest
Foel Wen 2265
Mynydd Tarw
Llanarmon Dyffryn Ceiriog
Tregeiriog
Foel Rhiwlas 1490
Rhiwlas
Llechrydau
Llanuwchllyn
Pentre-piod
Castell Carndochan
Tyn-y-ffridd
Llangadwaladr
Tan-y-pistyll
Pistyll Rhaeadr
Y Clogydd
Ty Issa
Tyn-y-wern
Tai-bach
Moelfre
Llansilin
Dyrysgol
Rhosdylluan
Foel Figenau
Foel y Geifr 2054
Talardd
Cwm Cynllwyd
Cwm Croes
Commins
Pencraig
Llangynog
Pennant Melangell
Afon Tanat
Tanat Valley
Cefn-coch
Llanrhaeadr-ym-Mochnant
Efail-rhyd
Mynydd-y-briw
Sycharth Castle
Golfa
Penybontfawr
Pedair-ffordd
Llangedwyn
Pen-y-bont
Aran Benllyn 2901
Foel Rhudd
Aran Fawddwy 2971
Bwlch y Groes
Hirnant
Penygarnedd
Rhos-y-brithdir
Bwlchyddar
Llyn Efyrnwy (Lake Vyrnwy)
Pennant
Llanymawddwy
Lake Vyrnwy
Llanwddyn
Abertridwr
Llansantffraid-ym-Mechain
Llanfyllin
Llanfechain
Afon Dyfi
Cywarch
Aber-Cywarch
Pen y Ffridd Cownwy
Ddol Cownwy
Tycrwyn
Tyn-y-ffridd
Llanfihangel-yng-Ngwynfa
Nant-y-meichiaid
Bwlch-y-cibau
Waen Fach
Tir Rhiwiog 1787
Dyfnant Forest
Afon Twrch
Mynydd y Gadfa
Pont Llogel
Afon Efyrnwy (R. Vyrnwy)
Dinas Mawddwy
Afon Cerist
Cae Afon
Minllyn
Pont Minllyn
Cwm-Cewydd
Nant-y-dugoed
Wern
Foel
Dolanog
Pontrobert
Meifod
Dyffryn Meifod Efyrnwy (R. Vyrnwy)
Geuffordd
Pentre'r beirdd
Guilsfield
Mallwyd
Foel-y-ffridd
Dugoed
Esgair Afon Ddu 1523
Llyn Coch-hwyad
Tyn-y-rhyd
Llangadfan
Broniarth Hill
Maesgwyn-Isaf
Groes-lwyd
Clipiau
Aberangell
Llanerfyl
Pen Coed
Four Crosses
Heniarth
Cloddiau
Frochas
Welshpool
(Y Trallwng)
Powis Castle
Cwm-Llinau
Mynydd Rhiw-Saeson
Llyn Gwyddior
Nant yr Eira
Sychtyn
Neuadd
Melin-y-ddol
Llanfair Caereinion
Afon Banwy
Einion
Sylfaen
Castle Caereinion
Welshpool & Llanfair Light Railway
Cemmaes
Cemmaes Road
Pandy
Esgair Rriciau
Bryn y Castell
Mynydd Waun Fawr
Llyn Hir
Pwll
Llwynderw
Llanbrynmair
Commins Coch
Tafolwern
Abercegir
Darowen
Dol-fâch
Ffridd
Cefn Coch
Llanllugan
Llanwyddelan
Manafon
Rhiw
Pant-y-ffridd
New Mills
(Felin Newydd)
Berriew
(Aberriw)
Sculpture
Garthmyl
Llan
Bont Dolgadfan
Tal-y-Wern
Talerddig
Glan-yr-afon
Adfa
Melinbyrhedyn
Moelfre 1537
Esgair Cwmowen
Mynydd Clogau
Llyn y Tarw
Gwgla
Brooks
Tregynon
Pentre Llifior
Fron
Hendomen
Aberhosan
Pennant
Twymyn
Brynamlwg 1602
Trannon
Carno
Llyn Mawr
Bwlch y Garreg
Bwlch-y-ffridd
Bettws Cedewain
Montgomery
(Trefaldwyn)
Highgate
Dolforwyn
Abermule
Llandyssil
A5
A470
A458
A483
A490
A494
A495
A525
A542
A4212
A5104
B4385
B4386
B4389
B4390
B4391
B4392
B4393
B4395
B4396
B4401
B4402
B4403
B4407
B4500
B4501
B4518
B4580
B5105
B5429
B5430
B5431
B5436
B5437

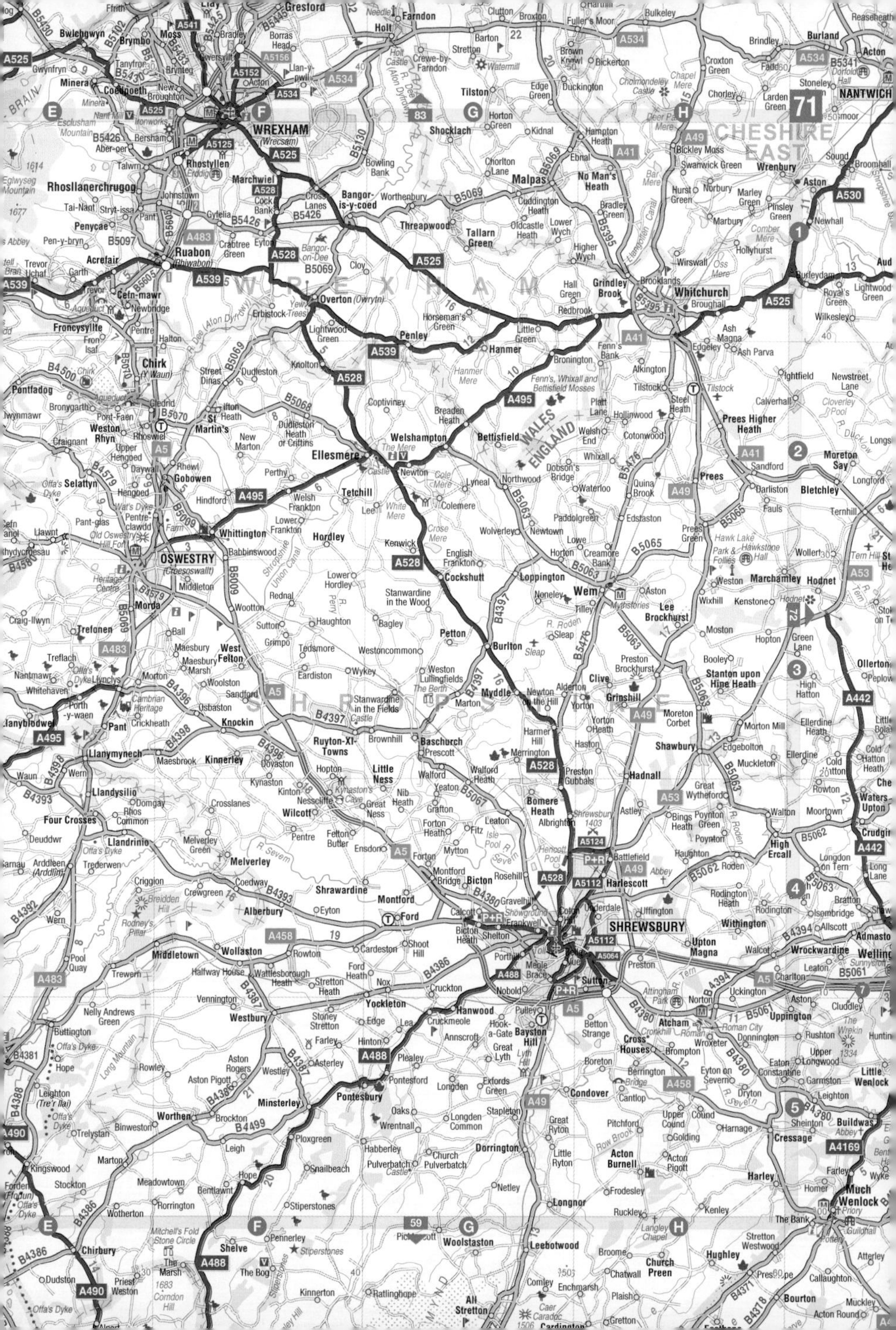
71
CHESHIRE EAST
WREXHAM
SHROPSHIRE
WALES
ENGLAND
WREXHAM
(Wrecsam)
NANTWICH
OSWESTRY
(Croesoswallt)
SHREWSBURY
Whitchurch
Ellesmere
Wem
Malpas
Bangor-is-y-coed
Overton (Owrytn)
Ruabon
(Rhiwabon)
Chirk
(Y Waun)
Gresford
Farndon
Holt
Clutton
Broxton
Fuller's Moor
Bulkeley
Reaseheath
Burland
Acton
Brindley
Bwlchgwyn
Brymbo
Moss
Bradley
Borras Head
Gwersyllt
Tanyfron
Brynteg
Minera
Coedpoeth
New Broughton
Bersham
Rhostyllen
Marchwiel
Johnstown
Rhosllanerchrugog
Tai-Nant
Stryt-issa
Penycae
Pen-y-bryn
Acrefair
Trevor
Garth
Cefn-mawr
Newbridge
Froncysyllte
Pentre
Halton
Pontfadog
Bronygarth
Weston Rhyn
Craignant
Selattyn
Gobowen
St Martin's
Ifton Heath
Street Dinas
Dudleston
Dudleston Heath or Criftins
Hindford
Whittington
Babbinswood
Middleton
Morda
Trefonen
Maesbury
Maesbury Marsh
West Felton
Woolston
Sandford
Knockin
Kinnerley
Dovaston
Kynaston
Llanymynech
Pant
Porth-y-waen
Llanyblodwel
Four Crosses
Llandysilio
Llandrinio
Melverley
Crewgreen
Alberbury
Coedway
Criggion
Middletown
Wollaston
Trewern
Pool Quay
Buttington
Westbury
Vennington
Nelly Andrews Green
Rowley
Aston Rogers
Aston Pigott
Westley
Minsterley
Worthen
Brockton
Binweston
Leigh
Marton
Kingswood
Stockton
Meadowtown
Rorrington
Bentlawnt
Wotherton
Chirbury
Dudston
Priest Weston
The Marsh
The Bog
Shelve
Pennerley
Stiperstones
Snailbeach
Ploxgreen
Hope
Pontesbury
Pontesford
Pulverbatch
Church Pulverbatch
Habberley
Wrentnall
Longden
Longden Common
Exfords Green
Hanwood
Cruckmeole
Annscroft
Plealey
Asterley
Hinton
Yockleton
Edge
Lea
Stoney Stretton
Farley
Nox
Cruckton
Ford Heath
Stretton Heath
Halfway House
Wattlesborough Heath
Rowton
Cardeston
Shoot Hill
Ford
Eyton
Shrawardine
Montford
Montford Bridge
Bicton
Bicton Heath
Shelton
Calcott
Frankwell
Gravelhill
Nobold
Meole Brace
Porthill
Pulley
Bayston Hill
Hook-a-Gate
Great Lyth
Sutton
Condover
Stapleton
Dorrington
Great Ryton
Little Ryton
Netley
Longnor
Leebotwood
Woolstaston
Pickelscott
Ratlinghope
Kinnerton
All Stretton
Comley
Enchmarsh
Chatwall
Plaish
Broome
Church Preen
Cardington
Gretton
Acton Burnell
Acton Pigott
Frodesley
Ruckley
Kenley
Pitchford
Golding
Upper Cound
Cound
Cantlop
Berrington
Boreton
Cross Houses
Brompton
Betton Strange
Atcham
Wroxeter
Eyton on Severn
Dryton
Harnage
Cressage
Sheinton
Leighton
Garmston
Eaton Constantine
Upper Longwood
Rushton
Donnington
Uppington
Aston
Cluddley
Norton
Uckington
Wrockwardine
Charlton
Walcot
Upton Magna
Preston
Withington
Rodington
Rodington Heath
Allscott
Isombridge
Admaston
Wellington
Longdon on Tern
Roden
Uffington
Harlescott
Battlefield
Albrighton
Astley
Bomere Heath
Preston Gubbals
Merrington
Harmer Hill
Hadnall
Shawbury
Edgebolton
Muckleton
Great Wytheford
Bings Heath
Poynton Green
Poynton
Haughton
High Ercall
Walton
Moortown
Rowton
Crudgington
Waters Upton
Ellerdine
Ellerdine Heath
Cold Hatton
Cold Hatton Heath
Ollerton
Peplow
High Hatton
Green Lane
Stanton upon Hine Heath
Booley
Moreton Corbet
Morton Mill
Hopton
Moston
Lee Brockhurst
Preston Brockhurst
Grinshill
Clive
Yorton
Yorton Heath
Haston
Alderton
Newton on the Hill
Myddle
Marton
Burlton
Sleap
Tilley
Noneley
Loppington
Aston
Wem
Horton
Lowe
Creamore Bank
Newtown
Wolverley
Edstaston
Paddolgreen
Waterloo
Dobson's Bridge
Quina Brook
Whixall
Welsh End
Cotonwood
Hollinwood
Platt Lane
Northwood
Lyneal
Bettisfield
Colemere
Newton
Welshampton
Breaden Heath
Coptiviney
Tetchill
Lee
Welsh Frankton
Lower Frankton
Perthy
Hordley
Kenwick
English Frankton
Cockshutt
Lower Hordley
Stanwardine in the Wood
Rednal
Haughton
Bagley
Petton
Sutton
Grimpo
Tedsmore
Weston Lullingfields
Eardiston
Wykey
Stanwardine in the Fields
Ruyton-XI-Towns
Brownhill
Baschurch
Prescott
Walford
Walford Heath
Yeaton
Hopton
Little Ness
Nib Heath
Great Ness
Nesscliffe
Kinton
Wilcott
Grafton
Forton Heath
Fitz
Mytton
Leaton
Forton
Ensdon
Felton Butler
Pentre
Rosehill
Knolton
Lightwood Green
Penley
Hanmer
Horseman's Green
Little Green
Bronington
Fenn's Bank
Redbrook
Alkington
Tilstock
Steel Heath
Prees Higher Heath
Prees
Prees Green
Darliston
Fauls
Sandford
Bletchley
Moreton Say
Longford
Ternhill
Ightfield
Calverhall
Newstreet Lane
Ash Magna
Ash Parva
Edgeley
Broughall
Brooklands
Wirswall
Grindley Brook
Hall Green
Higher Wych
Lower Wych
Oldcastle Heath
Cuddington Heath
Tallarn Green
Threapwood
Worthenbury
Cloy
Erbistock
Bowling Bank
Cross Lanes
Cock Bank
Gyfelia
Eyton
Crabtree Green
Pant
Bradley Green
No Man's Heath
Ebnal
Hampton Heath
Kidnal
Chorlton Lane
Horton Green
Shocklach
Tilston
Edge Green
Duckington
Bickerton
Brown Knowl
Barton
Stretton
Crewe-by-Farndon
Llan-y-pwll
Acton
Croxton Green
Chorley
Larden Green
Stoneley
Bickley Moss
Swanwick Green
Hurst Green
Norbury
Marbury
Marley Green
Pinsley Green
Wrenbury
Sound
Broomhall
Aston
Newhall
Hollyhurst
Burleydam
Royal's Green
Lightwood Green
Wilkesley
Weston
Wixhill
Kenstone
Marchamley
Hodnet
Wollerton
Hawk Lake
Hawkstone Park & Follies
Hawkstone Hall
Harley
Much Wenlock
Homer
Farley
Buildwas
Little Wenlock
The Bank
Stretton Westwood
Hughley
Presthope
Callaughton
Atterley
Bourton
Muckley
Acton Round
A525
A541
A5156
A5152
A534
A528
A539
A483
A5
A495
A41
A49
A442
A53
A458
A488
A490
A4169
A5112
A5124
A5064
A530
B5430
B5102
B5426
B5605
B5070
B5069
B5068
B5009
B4579
B4580
B4396
B4398
B4397
B4393
B4392
B4381
B4386
B4387
B4499
B4380
B4394
B5061
B5062
B5063
B5065
B5067
B5476
B5395
B4371
B4378

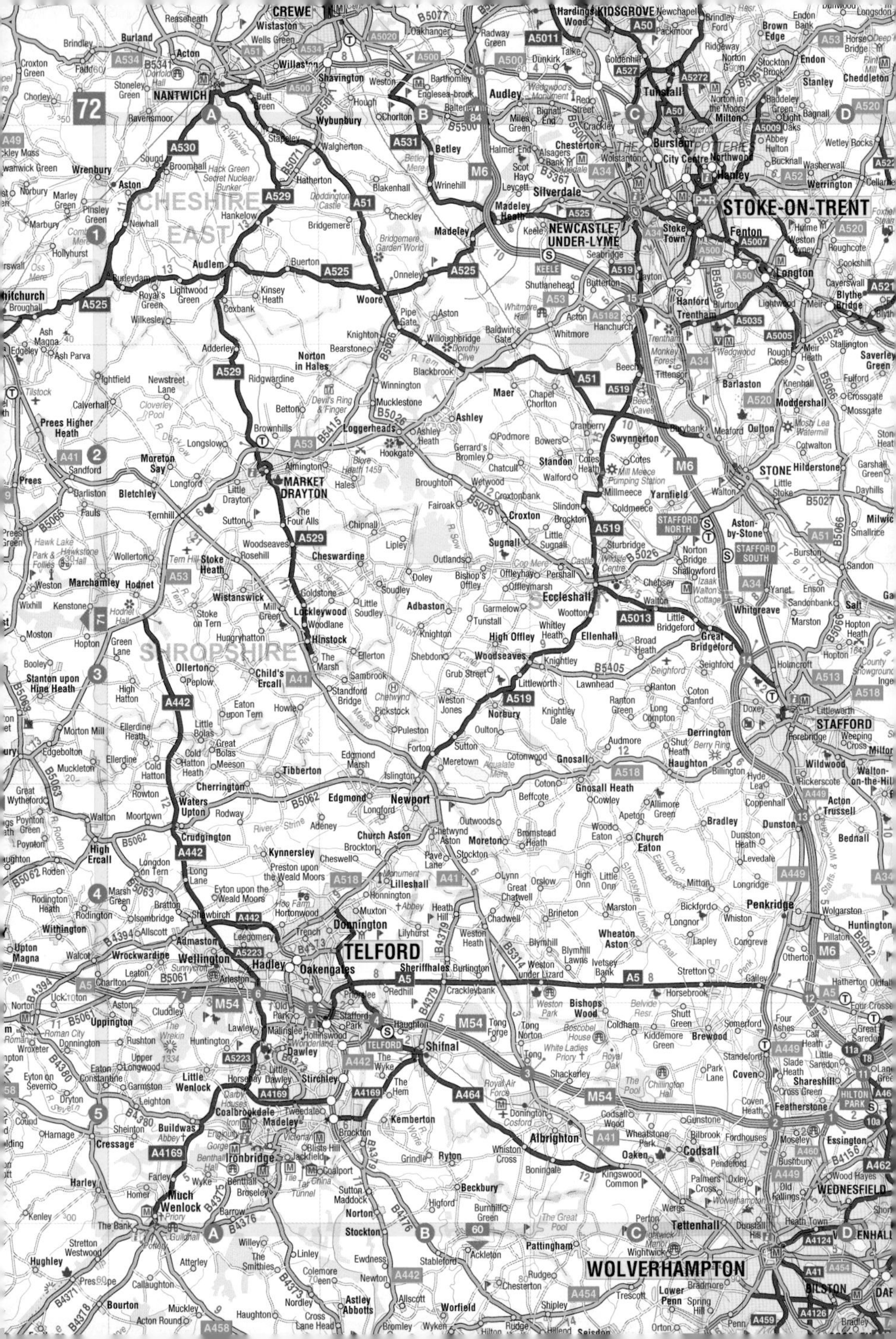

72
CREWE
KIDSGROVE
NANTWICH
CHESHIRE EAST
STOKE-ON-TRENT
NEWCASTLE-UNDER-LYME
THE POTTERIES
Burslem
Hanley
Longton
Fenton
Stoke Town
Tunstall
Audley
Madeley
Betley
Audlem
Woore
Whitchurch
MARKET DRAYTON
Loggerheads
Eccleshall
STONE
STAFFORD
STAFFORD NORTH
STAFFORD SOUTH
Newport
SHROPSHIRE
TELFORD
Wellington
Oakengates
Donnington
Hadley
Dawley
Madeley
Ironbridge
Much Wenlock
Shifnal
Albrighton
Codsall
Penkridge
WOLVERHAMPTON
WEDNESFIELD
BILSTON
Tettenhall
Cannock
Hodnet
Wem
Prees
M6
M54
A5
A41
A442
A529
A519
A51
A53
A525
A34
A449
A500
A50

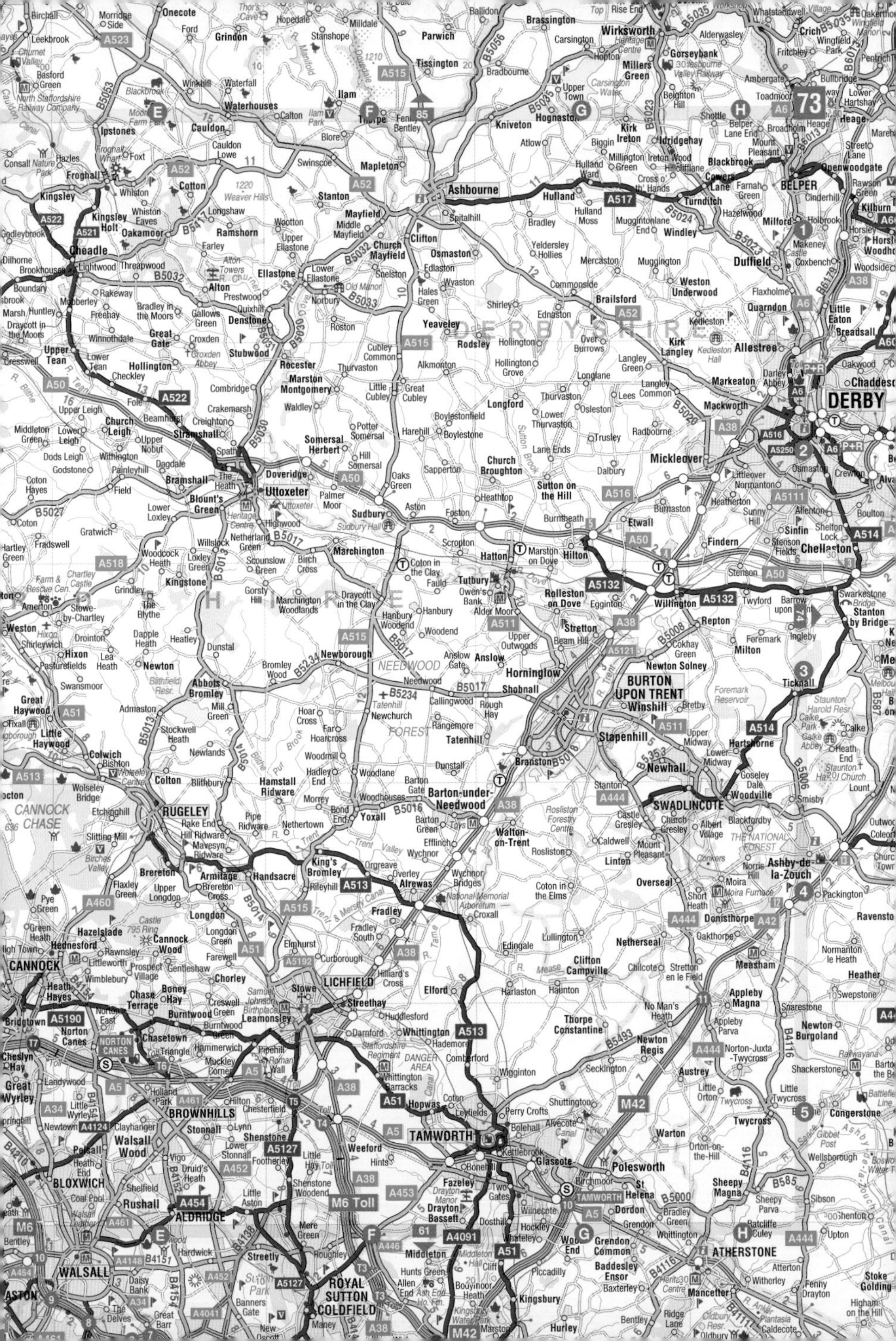

73
85
74
61
DERBYSHIRE
STAFFORDSHIRE
Birchall
Morridge Side
Onecote
Ford
Grindon
Thor's Cave
Hopedale
Milldale
Stanshope
Ballidon
Parwich
Brassington
Wirksworth
Heritage Centre
Carsington
Hopton
Rise End
Alderwasley
Whatstandwell
Crich
Wingfield Manor
Wingfield Park
Fritchley
Leekbrook
A523
Churnet Valley
Basford Green
North Staffordshire Railway Company
Caldon Canal
Blackbrook
Waterfall
Winkhill
Waterhouses
Calton
Ilam
Ilam Park
Thorpe
Fenny Bentley
Tissington
Bradbourne
Millers Green
Gorseybank
Ecclesbourne Valley Railway
Ambergate
Toadmoor
Bullbridge
Lower Hartshay
Heage
Moor Farm Park
Ipstones
Cauldon
Cauldon Lowe
Blore
Swinscoe
Mapleton
Kniveton
Hognaston
Upper Town
Carsington Water
Kirk Ireton
Idridgehay
Biggin
Millington Green
Ireton Wood
Hillcliffiane
Shottle
Belper Lane End
Broadholm
Mount Pleasant
Blackbrook
Cowers Lane
Farnah Green
Openwoodgate
BELPER
Cinderhill
Rawson Green
Kilburn
Froghall Wharf
Consall Nature Park
Consall
Hazles
Froghall
Foxt
A52
Cotton
Weaver Hills
Stanton
Ashbourne
Spitalhill
Hulland Ward
Hulland
Hulland Moss
Cross o' th' Hands
Turnditch
A517
Kingsley
Whiston
Kingsley Holt
Whiston Eaves
Oakamoor
Longshaw
Ramshorn
Wootton
Upper Ellastone
Mayfield
Middle Mayfield
Clifton
Church Mayfield
Osmaston
Bradley
Yeldersley Hollies
Mugginton
Mugginton lane End
Windley
Duffield
Milford
Holbrook
Makeney
Coxbench
Horsley
Woodhouse
Godleybrook
Cheadle
A522
A521
Dilhorne
Brookhouses
Lightwood
Threapwood
Farley
Alton Towers
Alton
Ellastone
Lower Ellastone
Old Manor
Snelston
Edlaston
Wyaston
Mercaston
Weston Underwood
Flaxholme
Woodside
Boundary
Rakeway
Prestwood
Quixhill
Norbury
Hales Green
Commonside
Brailsford
Ednaston
Shirley
Kedleston
Kedleston Hall
Quarndon
Little Eaton
Breadsall
Mobberley
Huntley
Freehay
Bradley in the Moors
Gallows Green
Denstone
B5032
B5033
B5030
B5031
Roston
Yeaveley
Rodsley
Hollington
Over Burrows
Kirk Langley
Allestree
Draycott in the Moors
Winnothdale
Great Gate
Croxden
Croxden Abbey
Stubwood
Cubley Common
Alkmonton
Hollington Grove
Langley Green
Langley Common
Markeaton
Darley Abbey
Oakwood
Chaddesden
Cresswell
Upper Tean
Lower Tean
Checkley
Hollington
Rocester
Thurvaston
Marston Montgomery
Little Cubley
Great Cubley
Longford
Lees
Longlane
Mackworth
DERBY
Upper Leigh
Church Leigh
Combridge
Crakemarsh
Fole
Beamhurst
Creighton
Stramshall
Waldley
Boylestonefield
Boylestone
Harehill
Potter Somersal
Somersal Herbert
Hill Somersal
Lower Thurvaston
Osleston
Radbourne
Trusley
Lane Ends
Mickleover
Middleton Green
Lower Leigh
Withington
Upper Nobut
Dods Leigh
Godstone
Painleyhill
Dagdale
Spath
The Heath
Bramshall
Doveridge
Uttoxeter
Palmer Moor
Sudbury
Sudbury Hall
Oaks Green
Sapperton
Church Broughton
Sutton on the Hill
Dalbury
Littleover
Normanton
Osmaston
Crewton
Alvaston
Coton Hayes
Field
Blount's Green
Heritage Centre
Aston
Heathtop
Foston
Burnaston
Etwall
Heatherton
Sunny Hill
Allenton
Boulton
Sinfin
Shelton Lock
Chellaston
Lower Loxley
Coton
Gratwich
Highwood
Netherland Green
B5017
Marchington
Scropton
Hatton
Marston on Dove
Hilton
Findern
Stenson Fields
Stenson
Hartley Green
Fradswell
Woodcock Heath
Willslock
Loxley Green
Scounslow Green
Birch Cross
Coton in the Clay
Fauld
Tutbury
Owen's Bank
Alder Moor
Rolleston on Dove
Egginton
Willington
Twyford
Barrow upon Trent
Swarkestone
Swarkestone Bridge
Stanton by Bridge
A518
Chartley Castle
Farm & Rescue Cen.
Kingstone
Gorsty Hill
Marchington Woodlands
Draycott in the Clay
A5132
Amerton
Grindley
The Blythe
Stowe-by-Chartley
Hanbury
Hanbury Woodend
Woodend
A511
Upper Outwoods
Stretton
Beam Hill
Repton
Ingleby
Weston
Hixon
Shirleywich
Drointon
Dapple Heath
Heatley
Dunstal
Newborough
Bromley Wood
NEEDWOOD
Anslow Gate
Anslow
Horninglow
Cokhay Green
Newton Solney
Foremark
Milton
Hixon
Pasturefields
Lea Heath
Newton
Blithfield Resr.
Abbots Bromley
Needwood
Shobnall
BURTON UPON TRENT
Winshill
Bretby
Foremark Reservoir
Ticknall
Swansmoor
Great Haywood
Tixall
Admaston
Mill Green
Hoar Cross
Far Hoarcross
Tatenhill
Newchurch
Callingwood
Rough Hay
Rangemore
Tatenhill
Stapenhill
Upper Midway
Hartshorne
Staunton Harold Resr.
Calke Park
Calke Abbey
Calke
Heath End
Little Haywood
Colwich
Bishton
Wolseley Centre
Stockwell Heath
Newlands
FOREST
Woodmill
Hadley End
Woodlane
Dunstall
Branston
Lower Midway
Newhall
Goseley Dale
Staunton Harold Church
Lount
A513
Colton
Blithbury
Hamstall Ridware
Barton Gate
Barton-under-Needwood
Stanton
A444
SWADLINCOTE
Woodville
Smisby
Wolseley Bridge
CANNOCK CHASE
Etchinghill
RUGELEY
Rake End
Hill Ridware
Pipe Ridware
Morrey
Bond End
Yoxall
Woodhouses
Nethertown
Barton Green
Toys
Walton-on-Trent
Rosliston Forestry Centre
Castle Gresley
Church Gresley
Albert Village
Blackfordby
THE NATIONAL FOREST
Outwoods
Coleorton
Slitting Mill
Birches Valley
Mavesyn Ridware
Trent Valley
Efflinch
Wychnor
Caldwell
Rosliston
Linton
Mount Pleasant
Conkers
Norris Hill
Ashby-de-la-Zouch
Brereton
Armitage
Handsacre
King's Bromley
Orgreave
Overley
Wychnor Bridges
Alrewas
Overseal
Moira
Moira Furnace
Packington
Pye Green
Flaxley Green
Upper Longdon
Brereton Cross
Rileyhill
National Memorial Arboretum
Coton in the Elms
Short Heath
Donisthorpe
A460
Longdon
Castle Ring
Fradley
Croxall
Oakthorpe
Ravenstone
Hednesford
Green Heath
Hazelslade
Cannock Wood
Longdon Green
Fradley South
Edingale
Lullington
Netherseal
Measham
Normanton le Heath
Hilton
CANNOCK
Rawnsley
Littleworth
Prospect Village
Gentleshaw
Elmhurst
Curborough
Clifton Campville
Chilcote
Stretton en le Field
Heather
Wimblebury
Chorley
Farewell
Heath Hayes
Chase Terrace
Boney Hay
Creswell Green
Stowe
Samuel Johnson Birthplace
LICHFIELD
Hilliard's Cross
Elford
Harlaston
Haunton
Appleby Magna
Swepstone
Bridgtown
Norton East
Burntwood
Burntwood Green
Streethay
Leamonsley
Huddlesford
No Man's Heath
Thorpe Constantine
Snarestone
A5190
Norton Canes
Chasetown
Hammerwich
Darnford
Whittington
Hademore
Appleby Parva
Newton Burgoland
Cheslyn Hay
NORTON CANES
Triangle
Muckley Corner
Pipehill
Roman Wall
Staffordshire Regiment
DANGER AREA
Comberford
Newton Regis
Norton-Juxta-Twycross
Shackerstone
Great Wyrley
Landywood
Holland Park
Whittington Barracks
Wigginton
Seckington
Austrey
Little Orton
Twycross
Little Twycross
Congerstone
Brownhills
Little Wyrley
Newtown
Stonnall
Lynn
Chesterfield
Shenstone
Hopwas
Coton
Leyfields
Perry Crofts
Bolehall
Shuttington
Alvecote
Twycross
Battlefield Line
Walsall Wood
Clayhanger
Lower Stonnall
Footherley
Weeford
Hints
TAMWORTH
Kettlebrook
Glascote
Polesworth
Warton
Orton-on-the-Hill
Gibbet Post
Wellsborough
Pelsall
Heath End
Vigo
Druid's Heath
Little Hay
Shenstone Woodend
Fazeley
Drayton Manor
Bonehill
Two Gates
Birchmoor
St Helena
Sheepy Magna
Sheepy Parva
Sibson
BLOXWICH
Shelfield
Coal Pool
Little Aston
Drayton Bassett
Dosthill
Wilnecote
Dordon
Bradley Green
Grendon
Shenton
Rushall
ALDRIDGE
M6 Toll
Mere Green
Whateley
Hockley
Wood End
Grendon Common
Whittington
Ratcliffe Culey
Upton
M6
Bentley
Walsall Leather
Hardwick
Streetly
Roughley
Middleton
Middleton Hall
Cliff
ATHERSTONE
WALSALL
Sutton Park
Hunts Green
Allen End
Ash End Ho. Fm.
Bodymoor Heath
Kingsbury
Kingsbury Water Park
Baddesley Ensor
Baxterley
Atterton
Witherley
Mancetter
Fenny Drayton
Stoke Golding
ASTON
Daisy Bank
The Delves
Great Barr
Banners Gate
New Oscott
ROYAL SUTTON COLDFIELD
Maney
Marston
Piccadilly
Hurley
Bentley
Ridge Lane
Oldbury Resr.
Caldecote
Higham on the Hill
Plantasia
A50
A515
A38
A6
A516
A5250
A5111
A514
A5121
B5008
A42
A5192
A51
A5127
A452
A453
A454
A461
A4148
A4124
A34
A4091
A446
A4041
M42
A5
B5493
B4116
B585
B5000
B5006
B587
B5234
B5014
B5013
B5016
B5018
B5353
B5020
B5023
B5024
B5035
B5053
B5417
B5027
B4154
B4151
B4138
B4152
B4210

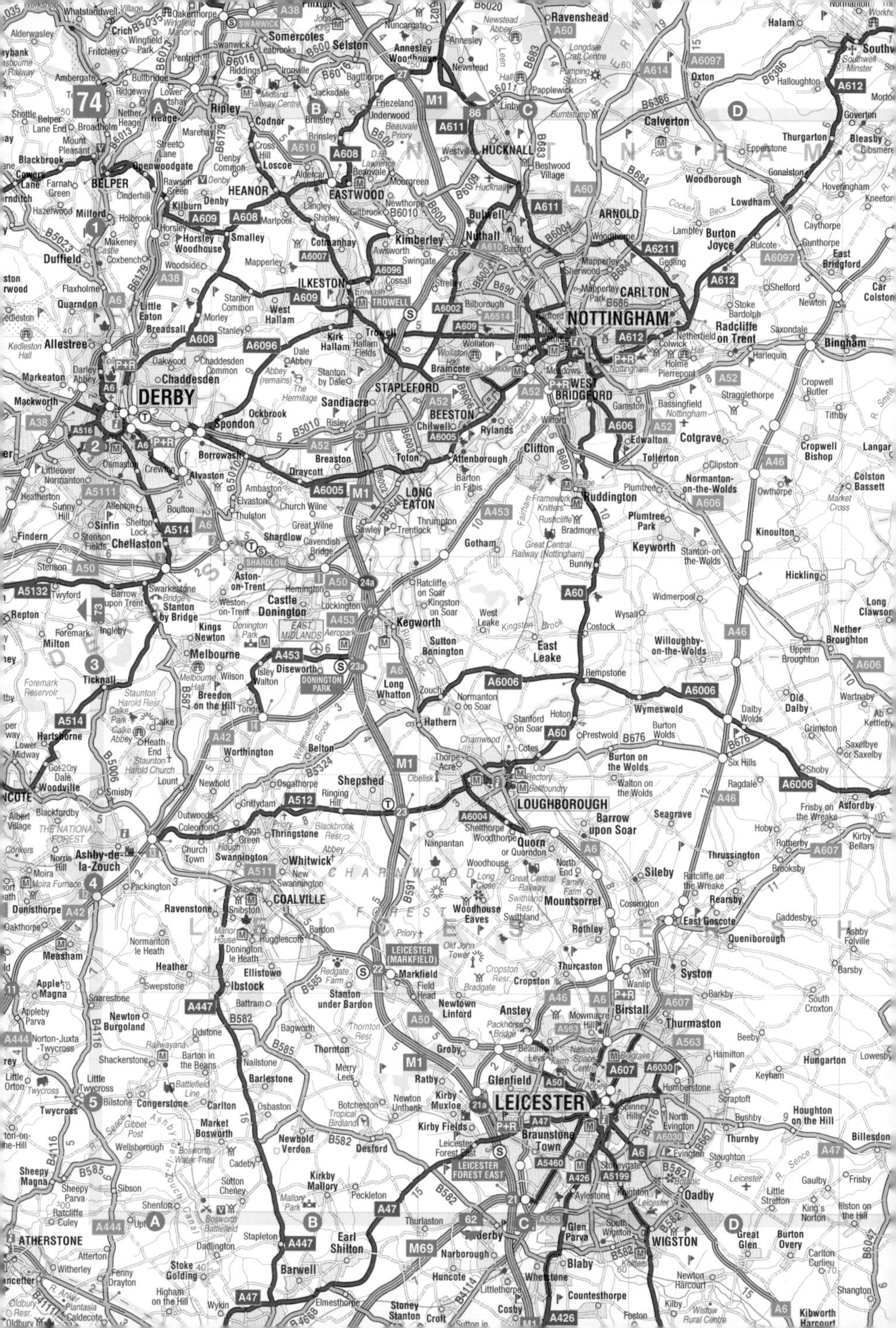

74
73
Whatstandwell
Crich
Oakerthorpe
Wingfield Manor
SWANWICK
A38
Somercotes
Selston
Annesley Woodhouse
Annesley
Newstead Abbey
Newstead
Ravenshead
A60
Longdale Craft Centre
Papplewick Pumping Station
Papplewick
Linby
Halam
Southwell Minster
Oxton
A6097
A614
Halloughton
B6386
A612
Alderwasley
Fritchley
Wingfield Park
Pentrich
Swanwick
Leabrooks
Riddings
Ironville
Jacksdale
Bagthorpe
Nuncargate
Midland Railway Centre
Ambergate
Ridgeway
Bullbridge
Lower Hartshay
Ripley
Heage
Nether Heage
Shottle
Belper Lane End
Broadholm
Codnor
Brinsley
Friezeland
Underwood
Beauvale Priory
M1
A611
HUCKNALL
Bestwood Village
Burntstump
Calverton
Epperstone
Woodborough
Thurgarton
Goverton
Bleasby
Gibsmere
Mount Pleasant
Street Lane
Marehay
Cross Hill
Loscoe
Denby Common
Denby
A610
A608
Aldercar
Beauvale
D.H. Lawrence
Moorgreen
Westville
Blackbrook
Openwoodgate
Cowers Lane
Farnah Green
BELPER
Cinderhill
Rawson Green
HEANOR
EASTWOOD
Newthorpe
Gilbrook
B6010
Langley
Shipley
Marlpool
Kilburn
Hucknall
Bulwell
A611
ARNOLD
Gonalston
Lowdham
Hoveringham
Kneeton
Caythorpe
Gunthorpe
East Bridgford
Milford
Hazelwood
Holbrook
A609
Horsley
Horsley Woodhouse
Smalley
Kimberley
Awsworth
Cotmanhay
Nuthall
Old Basford
Mapperley
Woodthorpe
A6211
Lambley
Burton Joyce
Bulcote
Gedling
Duffield
Makeney
Castle
Coxbench
Woodside
Mapperley
A6007
A6096
Swingate
Sherwood
Mapperley Park
CARLTON
A612
A6097
Shelford
Car Colston
Flaxholme
A38
ILKESTON
Cossall
Strelley
Stoke Bardolph
Newton
Quarndon
A6
Little Eaton
Stanley Common
West Hallam
A609
Erewash
TROWELL
A6002
Bilborough
A6514
B690
B686
NOTTINGHAM
Radcliffe on Trent
Saxondale
Bingham
Kedleston Hall
Allestree
Breadsall
Morley
Stanley
A608
A6096
Kirk Hallam
Trowell
Hallam Fields
A609
Wollaton
Old Lenton
Lenton
Netherfield
Colwick
Harlequin
Darley Abbey
P+R
Oakwood
Chaddesden Common
Chaddesden
Dale Abbey
Abbey (remains)
Stanton by Dale
Wollaton Hall
Bramcote
Lakeside
Meadows
WEST BRIDGFORD
Holme Pierrepont
Cropwell Butler
Markeaton
DERBY
The Hermitage
Sandiacre
STAPLEFORD
A52
BEESTON
A52
Stragglethorpe
Bassingfield
Gamston
Tithby
Mackworth
A38
A516
Ockbrook
Spondon
B5010
Risley
Chilwell
Rylands
Wilford
A606
A52
Edwalton
Cotgrave
Cropwell Bishop
Langar
Littleover
Normanton
Osmaston
Crewton
Alvaston
Borrowash
A6005
Breaston
Draycott
Toton
Attenborough
Barton in Fabis
Clifton
Tollerton
Clipston
A46
Normanton-on-the-Wolds
Colston Bassett
A5111
Heatherton
Sunny Hill
Allenton
Boulton
Ambaston
Elvaston
Thulston
Church Wilne
A6005
M1
LONG EATON
A453
Ruddington
Framework Knitters
Plumtree
Owthorpe
Market Cross
A606
Sinfin
Shelton Lock
Chellaston
A514
A6
Shardlow
Great Wilne
Cavendish Bridge
Sawley
Trentlock
Thrumpton
Rushcliffe
Bradmore
Plumtree Park
Keyworth
Kinoulton
Findern
Stenson Fields
SHARDLOW
Gotham
Great Central Railway (Nottingham)
Bunny
Stanton-on-the-Wolds
Stenson
A50
Swarkestone
Aston-on-Trent
A50
Hickling
A5132
Twyford
Barrow upon Trent
Stanton by Bridge
Weston-on-Trent
Castle Donington
Hemington
Lockington
Ratcliffe on Soar
Kingston on Soar
A60
Widmerpool
Long Clawson
Repton
Ingleby
Kings Newton
Donington Park
EAST MIDLANDS Aeropark
A453
Kegworth
West Leake
Kingston Brook
Costock
Wysall
Nether Broughton
Foremark
Milton
Melbourne
Melbourne Hall
A453
Sutton Bonington
East Leake
A46
Willoughby-on-the-Wolds
Upper Broughton
A606
Foremark Reservoir
Ticknall
Wilson
Isley Walton
Diseworth
DONINGTON PARK
A6
Long Whatton
Zouch
A6006
Rempstone
A6006
Old Dalby
Wartnaby
Ab Kettleby
Staunton Harold Resr.
Calke Park
Calke Abbey
Calke
Breedon on the Hill
Tonge
Hathern
Normanton on Soar
Stanford on Soar
Hoton
Wymeswold
Burton Wolds
Dalby Wolds
Grimston
A514
Hartshorne
Heath End
Staunton Harold Church
A42
Worthington
Belton
Charnwood
Cotes
A60
Prestwold
B676
Burton on the Wolds
Six Hills
Saxelbye or Saxelby
Shoby
A6006
Lower Midway
Lount
Newbold
Osgathorpe
Shepshed
Thorpe Acre
Obelisk
Old Rectory
Bellfoundry
Walton on the Wolds
Ragdale
A46
Woodville
Smisby
Albert Village
Blackfordby
THE NATIONAL FOREST
Conkers
Outwoods
Coleorton
Griffydam
A512
Ringing Hill
Thringstone
LOUGHBOROUGH
A6004
Shelthorpe
Woodthorpe
Barrow upon Soar
Seagrave
Frisby on the Wreake
Asfordby
Kirby Bellars
Hoby
Rotherby
A607
Brooksby
Ashby-de-la-Zouch
Norris Hill
Moira
Moira Furnace
Packington
Church Town
Swannington
Peggs Green
Whitwick
New Swannington
A511
Blackbrook Resr.
CHARNWOOD
Nanpantan
Quorn or Quorndon
Woodhouse
Long Close
Great Central Railway
Swithland Resr.
North End
Mountsorrel
Sileby
Thrussington
Ratcliffe on the Wreake
Rearsby
East Goscote
Gaddesby
Ashby Folville
Cossington
Donisthorpe
A42
Oakthorpe
Ravenstone
Snibston
COALVILLE
FOREST
Woodhouse Eaves
Swithland
Rothley
Queniborough
Measham
Normanton le Heath
Manor House
Hugglescote
Bardon
Donington le Heath
Old John Tower
LEICESTER (MARKFIELD)
Cropston Resr.
Bradgate
Thurcaston
Cropston
Syston
Barsby
Heather
Ellistown
Redgate Farm
Markfield
Field Head
Wanlip
Apple by Magna
Swepstone
Ibstock
Stanton under Bardon
Newtown Linford
A46
A6
P+R
Birstall
A607
Barkby
South Croxton
Snarestone
Appleby Parva
Battram
A447
B582
A50
Anstey
Packhorse Bridge
Mowmacre Hill
A563
Thurmaston
Newton Burgoland
Odstone
Bagworth
Thornton Resr.
Thornton
Groby
Beaumont Leys
National Space Centre
A563
Hamilton
Beeby
Lowesby
A444
Norton-Juxta-Twycross
Railwayana
Shackerstone
Barton in the Beans
Nailstone
B585
Merry Lees
M1
Glenfield
Belgrave
A607
A6030
Hungarton
Little Orton
Twycross
Battlefield Line
Barlestone
Ratby
Kirby Muxloe
Humberstone
Keyham
Twycross
Bilstone
Congerstone
Carlton
Osbaston
Botcheston
Tropical Birdland
Newton Unthank
LEICESTER
A47
Spinney Hills
North Evington
Scraptoft
Bushby
Houghton on the Hill
Gibbet Post
Market Bosworth
Bosworth Water Trust
Newbold Verdon
B582
Desford
Kirby Fields
P+R
Braunstone Town
A6030
Thurnby
Billesdon
Wellsborough
Cadeby
Leicester Forest East
LEICESTER FOREST EAST
A5460
Evington
Stoughton
A47
Sheepy Magna
B585
Sheepy Parva
Sibson
Sutton Cheney
Kirkby Mallory
Mallory Park
Peckleton
A47
B582
A426
A5199
Stoneygate
Knighton
Botanic
Leicester
Gaulby
Frisby
Ratcliffe Culey
Shenton
Bosworth Battlefield
Aylestone
Oadby
Little Stretton
King's Norton
Illston on the Hill
A444
Upton
Ashby-de-la-Zouch Canal
Thurlaston
62
Enderby
A563
Glen Parva
South Wigston
WIGSTON
Great Glen
Burton Overy
ATHERSTONE
Dadlington
Stapleton
A447
Earl Shilton
M69
Narborough
Blaby
Carlton Curlieu
Atterton
Stoke Golding
Barwell
Huncote
Whetstone
Newton Harcourt
Witherley
Fenny Drayton
Higham on the Hill
Littlethorpe
Countesthorpe
Shangton
Mancetter
R. Anker
Plantasia
Oldbury Resr.
Caldecote
Wykin
A47
Elmesthorpe
Stoney Stanton
Croft
Cosby
Sutton in
A426
Kilby
Wistow Rural Centre
Foston
A6
Kibworth Harcourt
B6047

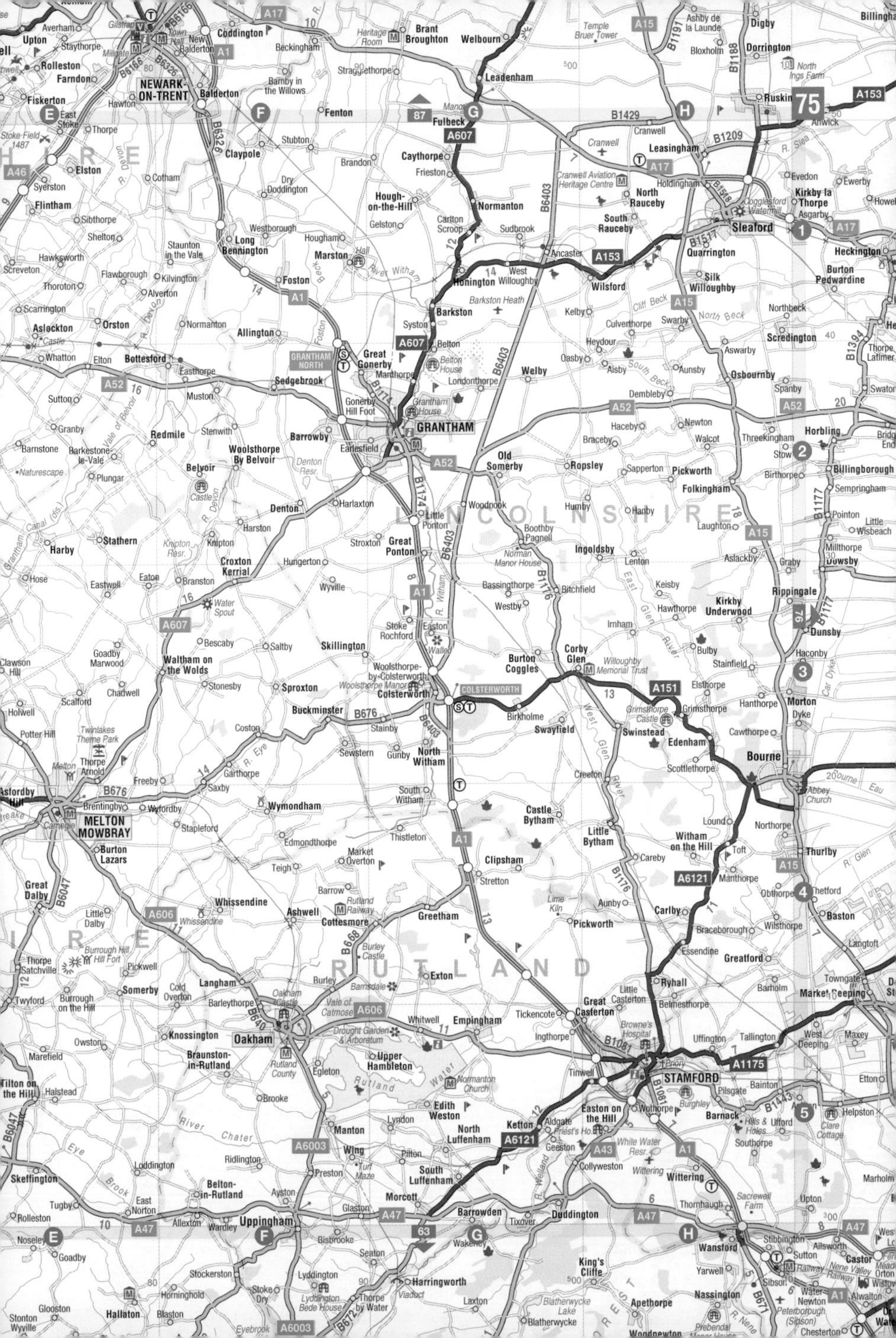

Averham
Upton
Staythorpe
Rolleston
Farndon
Fiskerton
East Stoke
Stoke Field 1487
Thorpe
Elston
Syerston
Flintham
Sibthorpe
Shelton
Hawksworth
Screveton
Thoroton
Scarrington
Aslockton
Orston
Whatton
Elton
Bottesford
Easthorpe
Sutton
Granby
Barnstone
Barkestone-le-Vale
Plungar
Naturescape
Harby
Stathern
Hose
Clawson Hill
Goadby Marwood
Holwell
Scalford
Potter Hill
Chadwell
Stonesby
Waltham on the Wolds
Eastwell
Eaton
Branston
Croxton Kerrial
Water Spout
Bescaby
Knipton
Knipton Resr.
Harston
Denton
Harlaxton
Redmile
Belvoir
Castle
Woolsthorpe By Belvoir
Stenwith
Muston
Sedgebrook
Allington
Normanton
Alverton
Kilvington
Flawborough
Staunton in the Vale
Long Bennington
Westborough
Foston
Dry Doddington
Cotham
Claypole
Stubton
Fenton
Balderton
NEWARK-ON-TRENT
Hawton
Coddington
New Balderton
Beckingham
Barnby in the Willows
Stragglethorpe
Brant Broughton
Heritage Room
Welbourn
Leadenham
Fulbeck
Manor
Caythorpe
Frieston
Brandon
Hough-on-the-Hill
Gelston
Carlton Scroop
Normanton
Hougham
Marston
Honington
Barkston
Syston
Belton
Belton House
Great Gonerby
Manthorpe
Londonthorpe
Gonerby Hill Foot
Grantham House
GRANTHAM
GRANTHAM NORTH
Barrowby
Earlesfield
Denton Resr.
Little Ponton
Stroxton
Great Ponton
Hungerton
Wyville
Stoke Rochford
Easton
Skillington
Saltby
Sproxton
Buckminster
Coston
Woolsthorpe-by-Colsterworth
Woolsthorpe Manor
Colsterworth
COLSTERWORTH
Stainby
Gunby
Sewstern
North Witham
South Witham
Garthorpe
Saxby
Freeby
Wyfordby
Brentingby
Asfordby Hill
Melton
Thorpe Arnold
Twinlakes Theme Park
MELTON MOWBRAY
Burton Lazars
Stapleford
Wymondham
Edmondthorpe
Thistleton
Market Overton
Teigh
Barrow
Whissendine
Ashwell
Cottesmore
Rutland Railway
Greetham
Stretton
Clipsham
Great Dalby
Little Dalby
Burrough Hill Hill Fort
Thorpe Satchville
Pickwell
Somerby
Burrough on the Hill
Twyford
Cold Overton
Langham
Barleythorpe
Oakham Castle
Oakham
Knossington
Owston
Marefield
Braunston-in-Rutland
Rutland County
Vale of Catmose
Burley
Burley Castle
Barnsdale
Exton
Whitwell
Empingham
Drought Garden & Arboretum
Upper Hambleton
Egleton
Rutland Water
Normanton Church
Tilton on the Hill
Halstead
Brooke
Manton
Edith Weston
North Luffenham
Lyndon
River Chater
Wing
Turf Maze
Pilton
South Luffenham
Ridlington
Loddington
Skeffington
Eye Brook
Belton-in-Rutland
East Norton
Tugby
Rolleston
Allexton
Wardley
Uppingham
Ayston
Preston
Glaston
Morcott
Barrowden
Noseley
Goadby
Bisbrooke
Seaton
Wakerley
Stockerston
Lyddington
Lyddington Bede House
Stoke Dry
Horninghold
Harringworth
Viaduct
Thorpe by Water
Glooston
Hallaton
Blaston
Stonton Wyville
Eyebrook
Laxton
Tixover
Duddington
King's Cliffe
Blatherwycke
Blatherwycke Lake
Apethorpe
Woodnewton
Ketton
Aldgate
Priest's Ho.
Geeston
Collyweston
White Water Resr.
Wittering
Easton on the Hill
Wothorpe
Tinwell
STAMFORD
Burghley
Browne's Hospital
Priory
Ingthorpe
Tickencote
Great Casterton
Little Casterton
Ryhall
Belmesthorpe
Uffington
Tallington
Pilsgate
Bainton
Barnack
Hills & Holes
Ufford
Southorpe
Thornhaugh
Sacrewell Farm
Wansford
Stibbington
Yarwell
Nassington
Prebendal Manor House
Sibson
Water Newton
Sutton
Ailsworth
Castor
Nene Valley Railway
Alwalton
Peterborough (Sibson)
Chesterton
Upton
Marholm
Helpston
Clare Cottage
Etton
Maxey
West Deeping
Market Deeping
Towngate
Langtoft
Greatford
Barholm
Essendine
Braceborough
Wilsthorpe
Baston
Thetford
Obthorpe
Manthorpe
Carlby
Pickworth
Aunby
Lime Kiln
Little Bytham
Careby
Witham on the Hill
Toft
Lound
Northorpe
Thurlby
Castle Bytham
Creeton
Swayfield
Swinstead
Grimsthorpe Castle
Grimsthorpe
Edenham
Scottlethorpe
Bourne
Abbey Church
Bourne Eau
Cawthorpe
Morton
Dyke
Hanthorpe
Elsthorpe
Stainfield
Haconby
Car Dyke
Dunsby
Rippingale
Kirkby Underwood
Hawthorpe
Bulby
Irnham
Keisby
Corby Glen
Willoughby Memorial Trust
Burton Coggles
Birkholme
Westby
Bassingthorpe
Bitchfield
Norman Manor House
Boothby Pagnell
Ingoldsby
Lenton
Humby
Hanby
Woodnook
Old Somerby
Ropsley
Sapperton
Braceby
Haceby
Newton
Walcot
Pickworth
Folkingham
Laughton
Aslackby
Graby
Dowsby
Millthorpe
Pointon
Little Wisbeach
Sempringham
Billingborough
Birthorpe
Stow
Horbling
Threekingham
Spanby
Dembleby
Osbournby
Aunsby
Aisby
Oasby
Heydour
South Beck
Welby
Aswarby
Scredington
Northbeck
North Beck
Swarby
Culverthorpe
Kelby
Wilsford
Cliff Beck
Barkston Heath
West Willoughby
Ancaster
Sudbrook
Silk Willoughby
Quarrington
South Rauceby
North Rauceby
Cranwell Aviation Heritage Centre
Cranwell
Leasingham
Holdingham
Sleaford
Cogglesford Watermill
Kirkby la Thorpe
Asgarby
Evedon
Ewerby
Howell
Heckington
Burton Pedwardine
Thorpe Latimer
Swaton
Bridge End
Temple Bruer Tower
Ashby de la Launde
Bloxholm
Digby
Dorrington
North Ings Farm
Ruskington
Anwick
R. Slea
Billinghay
LINCOLNSHIRE
RUTLAND
River Witham
R. Witham
R. Devon
R. Eye
R. Glen
R. Welland
R. Nene
West Glen River
East Glen River
Vale of Belvoir
Grantham Canal (dis.)
A1
A15
A17
A46
A47
A52
A153
A151
A606
A607
A6003
A6121
A1175
A43
B6166
B6326
B1174
B6403
B676
B668
B640
B1176
B1081
B1443
B1191
B1188
B1429
B1209
B1518
B1517
B1394
B1177
B6047
B672
B671
75
87
76
63

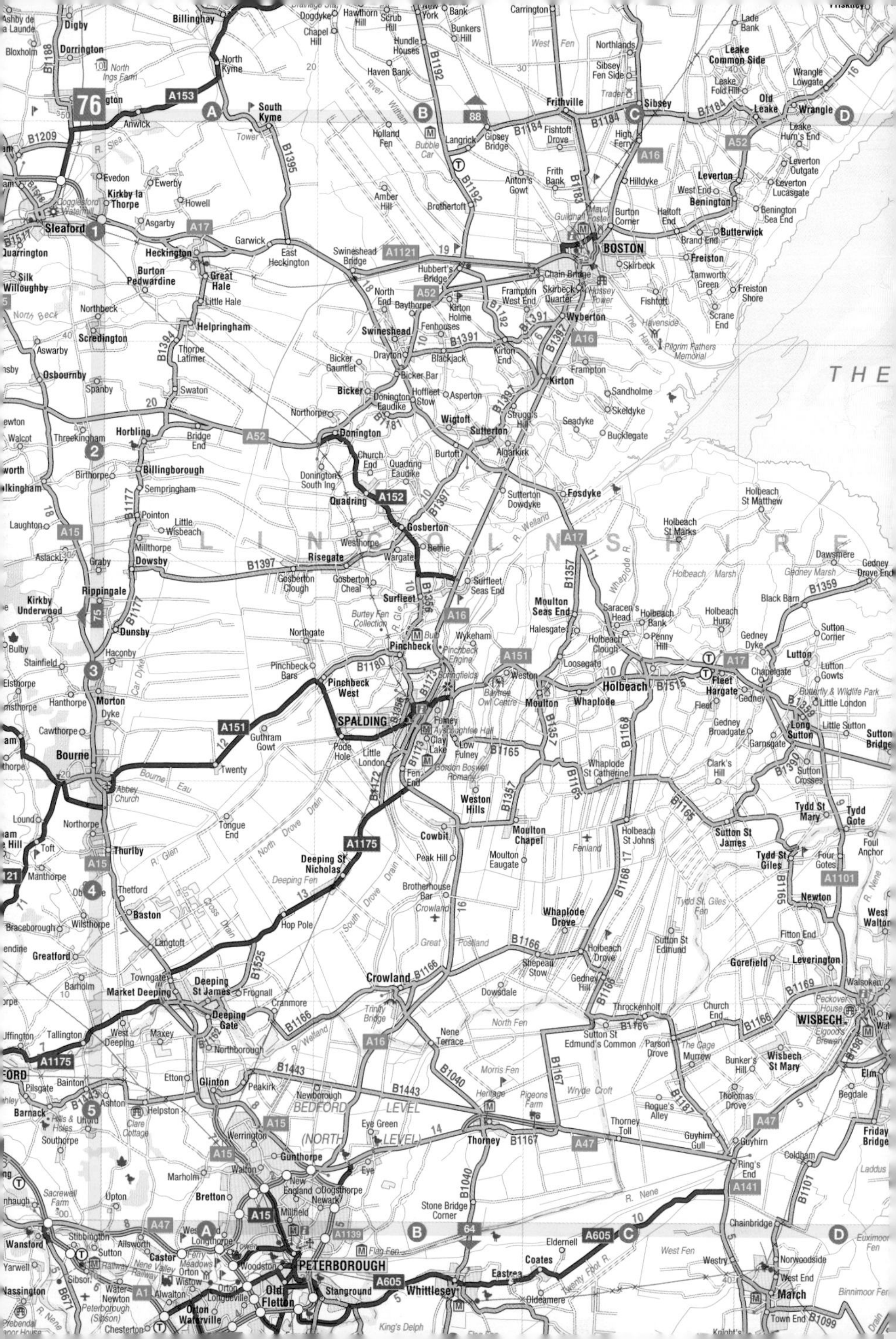
76
88
64
A
B
C
D
Ashby de la Launde
Digby
Billinghay
Dogdyke
Hawthorn Hill
Scrub Hill
New York
Bank
Bunkers Hill
Carrington
Lade Bank
Bloxholm
Dorrington
Chapel Hill
Hundle Houses
West Fen
Northlands
Leake Common Side
North Kyme
North Ings Farm
Haven Bank
Sibsey Fen Side
Leake Fold Hill
Wrangle Lowgate
Old Leake
Wrangle
A153
South Kyme
Frithville
Sibsey
Trader
Anwick
Tower
Holland Fen
Bubble Car
Langrick
Gipsey Bridge
Fishtoft Drove
High Ferry
Leake Hurn's End
B1209
R. Slea
B1395
B1192
B1184
A16
A52
Leverton Outgate
Evedon
Ewerby
Kirkby la Thorpe
Howell
Cogglesford Watermill
Asgarby
Sleaford
Quarrington
A17
Garwick
Heckington
East Heckington
Amber Hill
Brothertoft
Anton's Gowt
Frith Bank
Hilldyke
Leverton
West End
Benington
Leverton Lucasgate
Benington Sea End
Maud Foster
Guildhall
Burton Corner
Haltoft End
Brand End
Butterwick
BOSTON
Skirbeck
Freiston
Tamworth Green
Freiston Shore
Fishtoft
Scrane End
Silk Willoughby
Burton Pedwardine
Great Hale
Little Hale
Swineshead Bridge
A1121
Hubbert's Bridge
Chain Bridge
Frampton West End
Skirbeck Quarter
Hussey Tower
North End
Baythorpe
Kirton Holme
Wyberton
B1391
B1397
Havenside
The Haven
Pilgrim Fathers Memorial
North Beck
Northbeck
Scredington
Helpringham
Swineshead
Fenhouses
Aswarby
B1394
Thorpe Latimer
Drayton
Blackjack
Kirton End
Frampton
Kirton
Bicker Gauntlet
Bicker Bar
THE
Osbournby
Spanby
Swaton
Bicker
Donington Eaudike
Hoffleet Stow
Asperton
Sandholme
Skeldyke
Northorpe
Struggs Hill
Seadyke
Wigtoft
Sutterton
Bucklegate
Walcot
Threekingham
Horbling
Bridge End
Donington
Algarkirk
A52
Burtoft
Church End
Quadring Eaudike
Birthorpe
Billingborough
Donington South Ing
Sempringham
Fosdyke
Sutterton Dowdyke
A152
Quadring
Holbeach St Matthew
Laughton
A15
B1177
Pointon
Little Wisbeach
Gosberton
R. Welland
Holbeach St Marks
Millthorpe
Westhorpe
Belnie
LINCOLNSHIRE
Aslackby
Graby
Dowsby
B1397
Risegate
Wargate
Dawsmere
Gedney Drove End
Holbeach Marsh
Gedney Marsh
Gosberton Clough
Gosberton Cheal
Surfleet Seas End
B1357
Whaplode R.
Rippingale
Surfleet
B1356
Black Barn
B1359
Kirkby Underwood
Moulton Seas End
Saracen's Head
Holbeach Bank
Holbeach Hurn
Burtey Fen Collection
R. Glen
Halesgate
Penny Hill
Sutton Corner
Dunsby
Northgate
Bulb
Wykeham
Holbeach Clough
Gedney Dyke
Lutton
Bulby
Haconby
Pinchbeck
Pinchbeck Engine
A151
Stainfield
Pinchbeck Bars
Springfields
Loosegate
Lutton Gowts
Chapelgate
B1180
Weston
Holbeach
B1515
Fleet Hargate
Butterfly & Wildlife Park
Hanthorpe
Morton
Pinchbeck West
Baytree Owl Centre
Moulton
Whaplode
Fleet
Gedney
Little London
Dyke
Car Dyke
SPALDING
Fulney
Ayscoughfee Hall
Long Sutton
Little Sutton
Sutton Bridge
Cawthorpe
Guthram Gowt
Pode Hole
Clay Lake
Low Fulney
B1165
Gedney Broadgate
Garnsgate
Bourne
Twenty
Little London
Gordon Boswell Romany
Whaplode St Catherine
Clark's Hill
Sutton Crosses
Abbey Church
Bourne Eau
Fen End
Weston Hills
B1168
B1390
Tydd St Mary
Tydd Gote
Lound
Northorpe
Tongue End
North Drove Drain
Moulton Chapel
Holbeach St Johns
Sutton St James
Toft
Thurlby
A1175
Cowbit
Fenland
Foul Anchor
R. Glen
Deeping St Nicholas
Peak Hill
Moulton Eaugate
Tydd St Giles
Four Gotes
Manthorpe
Deeping Fen
A1101
Obthorpe
Thetford
Brotherhouse Bar
Crowland
South Drove Drain
Tydd St. Giles Fen
Newton
R. Nene
Baston
Cross Drain
Whaplode Drove
West Walton
Braceborough
Wilsthorpe
Hop Pole
Fitton End
Langtoft
Great Postland
B1166
Sutton St Edmund
Holbeach Drove
Greatford
Shepeau Stow
Gorefield
Leverington
Towngate
Deeping St James
Crowland
Gedney Hill
Walsoken
Barholm
Market Deeping
Frognall
Cranmore
Dowsdale
Church End
Peckover House
B1169
Deeping Gate
Trinity Bridge
Throckenholt
Tallington
West Deeping
Maxey
Northborough
B1162
R. Welland
North Fen
Sutton St Edmund's Common
Parson Drove
The Cage
Murrow
WISBECH
Elgood's Brewery
Uffington
Nene Terrace
Wisbech St Mary
Bunker's Hill
A1175
Morris Fen
B1040
Elm
FORD
Pilsgate
Bainton
Etton
Glinton
B1443
Peakirk
Newborough
Heritage
Pigeons Farm
Wryde Croft
Begdale
Barnack
Ashton
Hills & Holes
Ufford
Helpston
BEDFORD LEVEL
(NORTH LEVEL)
Rogue's Alley
Tholomas Drove
Clare Cottage
Eye Green
Thorney
B1167
Thorney Toll
A47
Friday Bridge
Southorpe
Werrington
Guyhirn Gull
Guyhirn
Gunthorpe
Walton
Eye
Ring's End
Coldham
Laddus
Marholm
New England
Dogsthorpe
Newark
A141
Sacrewell Farm
Upton
Bretton
Millfield
R. Nene
B1101
Wansford
Stibbington
Sutton
Ailsworth
Castor
Longthorpe
A1139
Stone Bridge Corner
Chainbridge
Ferry Meadows
Nene Valley Railway
Flag Fen
A605
Eldernell
West Fen
Euximoor Fen
Yarwell
Sibson
Woodston
PETERBOROUGH
Coates
Westry
Norwoodside
Nassington
Water Newton
Wistow
Alwalton
Orton Longueville
Old Fletton
Stanground
Whittlesey
Eastrea
Twenty Foot R.
West End
March
Binnimoor Fen
Oldeamere
B671
Peterborough (Sibson)
Orton Waterville
King's Delph
Chesterton
Prebendal Manor House
Town End
B1099

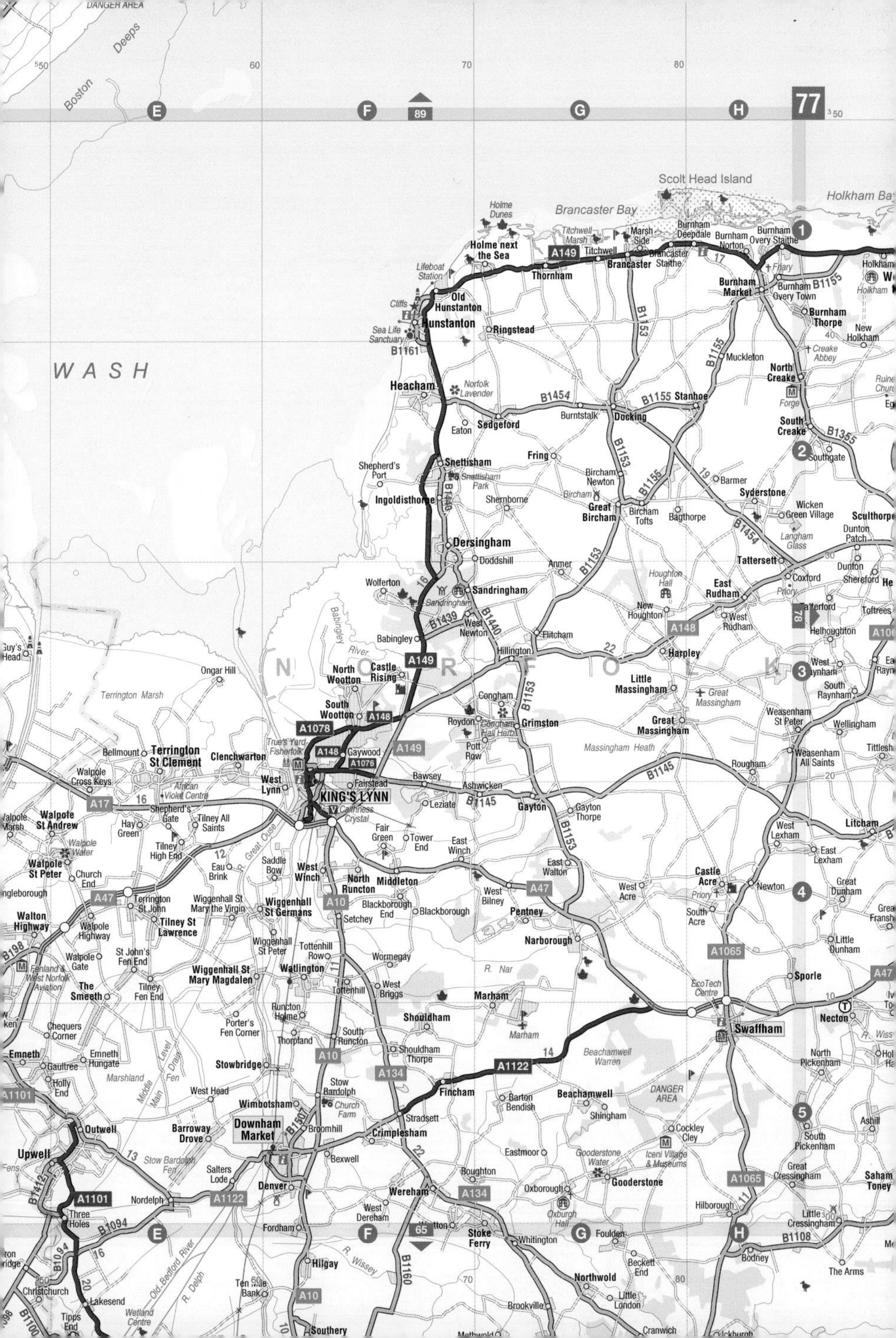
DANGER AREA
Boston
Deeps
WASH
Scolt Head Island
Brancaster Bay
Holkham Bay
Holme Dunes
Holme next the Sea
Titchwell Marsh
Titchwell
Thornham
Brancaster
Brancaster Staithe
Marsh Side
Burnham Deepdale
Burnham Norton
Burnham Overy Staithe
Burnham Market
Burnham Overy Town
Burnham Thorpe
Friary
Holkham
New Holkham
Creake Abbey
North Creake
Forge
South Creake
Southgate
Lifeboat Station
Cliffs
Old Hunstanton
Hunstanton
Sea Life Sanctuary
Ringstead
Heacham
Norfolk Lavender
Eaton
Sedgeford
Burntstalk
Docking
Stanhoe
Muckleton
Fring
Bircham Newton
Bircham
Great Bircham
Bircham Tofts
Bagthorpe
Barmer
Syderstone
Wicken Green Village
Sculthorpe
Langham Glass
Dunton Patch
Dunton
Shereford
Tattersett
Coxford
Priory
Tatterford
Toftrees
Helhoughton
East Rudham
West Rudham
Houghton Hall
New Houghton
Harpley
West Raynham
South Raynham
Little Massingham
Great Massingham
Massingham Heath
Weasenham St Peter
Wellingham
Weasenham All Saints
Tittleshall
Rougham
Litcham
West Lexham
East Lexham
Castle Acre
Newton
Great Dunham
West Acre
South Acre
Little Dunham
Sporle
EcoTech Centre
Swaffham
Necton
North Pickenham
South Pickenham
Ashill
Great Cressingham
Little Cressingham
Saham Toney
The Arms
Bodney
Hilborough
Cockley Cley
Iceni Village & Museums
Gooderstone Water
Gooderstone
Oxborough
Oxburgh Hall
Foulden
Beckett End
Northwold
Little London
Brookville
Methwold
Cranwich
Ickburgh
Beachamwell Warren
Beachamwell
Shingham
Barton Bendish
Eastmoor
Boughton
Stoke Ferry
Whitington
Wereham
West Dereham
Wretton
Fincham
Stradsett
Crimplesham
Bexwell
Denver
Downham Market
Fordham
Hilgay
R. Wissey
Ten Mile Bank
Southery
Snettisham
Snettisham Park
Shepherd's Port
Ingoldisthorpe
Shernborne
Dersingham
Doddshill
Anmer
Wolferton
Sandringham
West Newton
Babingley
Babingley River
Flitcham
Hillington
Congham
Grimston
Roydon
Pott Row
Bawsey
Ashwicken
Gayton
Gayton Thorpe
Leziate
East Walton
Castle Rising
North Wootton
South Wootton
Gaywood
Fairstead
True's Yard Fisherfolk
West Lynn
KING'S LYNN
Caithness Crystal
Fair Green
Tower End
East Winch
West Bilney
Pentney
Narborough
Middleton
North Runcton
West Winch
Saddle Bow
Blackborough End
Blackborough
Setchey
Wormegay
Tottenhill Row
Tottenhill
West Briggs
R. Nar
Marham
Shouldham
Shouldham Thorpe
Runcton Holme
South Runcton
Thorpland
Stow Bardolph
Church Farm
Broomhill
Wimbotsham
Stowbridge
Porter's Fen Corner
Wiggenhall St Mary Magdalen
Watlington
Wiggenhall St Peter
Wiggenhall St Germans
Wiggenhall St Mary the Virgin
Eau Brink
R. Great Ouse
Tilney All Saints
Tilney High End
Hay Green
Shepherd's Gate
African Violet Centre
Terrington St Clement
Bellmount
Clenchwarton
Ongar Hill
Terrington Marsh
Guy's Head
Walpole Cross Keys
Walpole St Andrew
Walpole Marsh
Walpole Water
Walpole St Peter
Church End
Terrington St John
Tilney St Lawrence
Walpole Highway
Walton Highway
Walpole Gate
St John's Fen End
Tilney Fen End
Fenland & West Norfolk Aviation
The Smeeth
Chequers Corner
Emneth
Emneth Hungate
Gaultree
Holly End
Marshland
Middle Level Main Drain
West Head
Barroway Drove
Stow Bardolph Fen
Salters Lode
Nordelph
Outwell
Upwell
Three Holes
Christchurch
Lakesend
Tipps End
Wetland Centre
Old Bedford River
R. Delph
A149
A148
A1078
A1076
A17
A47
A10
A134
A1122
A1101
A1065
B1161
B1153
B1155
B1454
B1355
B1440
B1439
B1145
B1507
B1094
B1108
B1160
B1412
B1100
B1098
N O R F O L K
E
F
G
H
89
65
78
1
2
3
4
5
60
70
80
350
300
30
20
10

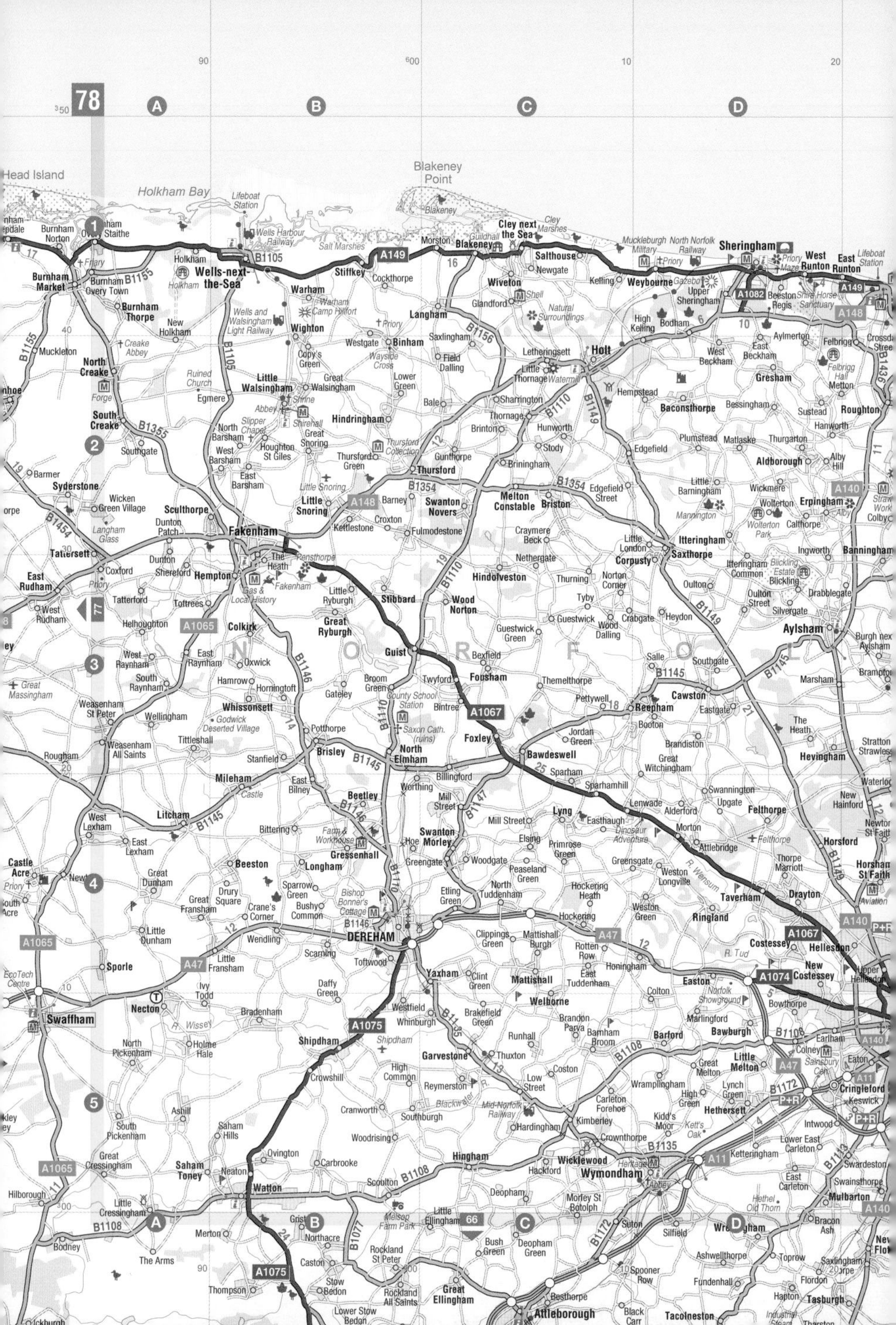

78
A
B
C
D
90
600
10
20
350
Head Island
Holkham Bay
Lifeboat Station
Blakeney Point
Blakeney
Cley next the Sea
Cley Marshes
Salt Marshes
Wells Harbour Railway
Burnham Norton
Burnham Overy Staithe
Burnham Market
Burnham Overy Town
Burnham Thorpe
Holkham
Wells-next-the-Sea
New Holkham
Wells and Walsingham Light Railway
Warham
Warham Camp Hillfort
Stiffkey
Cockthorpe
Morston
Blakeney
Wiveton
Glandford
Salthouse
Newgate
Kelling
Weybourne
Muckleburgh Military
North Norfolk Railway
Priory
Sheringham
Upper Sheringham
Beeston Regis
West Runton
East Runton
Shire Horse Sanctuary
Lifeboat Station
Priory Maze
Gazebo
Natural Surroundings
Shell
A149
A1082
A148
B1105
B1155
B1156
Muckleton
Creake Abbey
North Creake
Forge
Ruined Church
Egmere
Wighton
Copy's Green
Binham
Priory
Westgate
Langham
Saxlingham
Field Dalling
Wayside Cross
Little Walsingham
Great Walsingham
Abbey
Shrine
Shirehall
Lower Green
Hindringham
Bale
Letheringsett
Little Thornage
Watermill
Holt
High Kelling
Bodham
West Beckham
East Beckham
Aylmerton
Felbrigg
Felbrigg Hall
Metton
Gresham
Hempstead
Baconsthorpe
Bessingham
Sustead
Roughton
Hanworth
Sharrington
Thornage
Brinton
Hunworth
Stody
Briningham
Edgefield
Plumstead
Matlaske
Thurgarton
Aldborough
Alby Hill
South Creake
B1355
Southgate
North Barsham
West Barsham
East Barsham
Slipper Chapel
Houghton St Giles
Great Snoring
Thursford Green
Thursford Collection
Thursford
Gunthorpe
Barmer
Syderstone
Wicken Green Village
Sculthorpe
Little Snoring
Little Snoring
Barney
Swanton Novers
Melton Constable
Briston
B1354
Edgefield Street
Little Barningham
Wickmere
Wolterton
Wolterton Park
Mannington
Erpingham
Calthorpe
Alby
A140
Langham Glass
Dunton Patch
Fakenham
Kettlestone
Croxton
Fulmodestone
Craymere Beck
Little London
Saxthorpe
Itteringham
Corpusty
Ingworth
Banningham
Tattersett
Coxford
Dunton
Shereford
Hempton
The Heath
Pensthorpe
Fakenham
Gas & Local History
Nethergate
Hindolveston
Thurning
Norton Corner
Itteringham Common
Blickling Estate
Blickling
Oulton
Oulton Street
Drabblegate
East Rudham
West Rudham
Priory
Tatterford
Toftrees
Little Ryburgh
Stibbard
Wood Norton
Tyby
Guestwick
Wood Dalling
Crabgate
Heydon
Silvergate
Aylsham
Burgh next Aylsham
Helhoughton
A1065
Colkirk
Great Ryburgh
Guist
Guestwick Green
Bexfield
Salle
Southgate
N O R F O L K
West Raynham
East Raynham
Oxwick
B1146
Twyford
Foulsham
Themelthorpe
B1145
Marsham
Brampton
Great Massingham
South Raynham
Hamrow
Horningtoft
Broom Green
Gateley
County School Station
Bintree
A1067
Pettywell
Reepham
Cawston
Eastgate
Booton
Weasenham St Peter
Wellingham
Whissonsett
Godwick Deserted Village
Potthorpe
Saxon Cath. (ruins)
Foxley
Jordan Green
The Heath
Weasenham All Saints
Tittleshall
Brisley
Bawdeswell
Brandiston
Stratton Strawless
Hevingham
Rougham
Stanfield
North Elmham
Sparham
Sparhamhill
Great Witchingham
Mileham
Castle
East Bilney
Billingford
Worthing
Beetley
Mill Street
B1147
Swannington
Upgate
Lenwade
Alderford
Felthorpe
New Hainford
Newton St Faith
West Lexham
Litcham
Bittering
Farm & Workhouse
Gressenhall
Swanton Morley
Hoe
Mill Street
Lyng
Easthaugh
Dinosaur Adventure
Morton
Attlebridge
Horsford
East Lexham
Beeston
Longham
Greengate
Woodgate
Elsing
Primrose Green
Peaseland Green
Greensgate
Weston Longville
R. Wensum
Thorpe Marriott
Horsham St Faith
Aviation
Castle Acre
Priory
South Acre
Newton
Great Dunham
Great Fransham
Drury Square
Crane's Corner
Sparrow Green
Bushy Common
Bishop Bonner's Cottage
Etling Green
North Tuddenham
Hockering Heath
Weston Green
Taverham
Drayton
Ringland
B1149
Little Dunham
Wendling
B1146
Scarning
DEREHAM
Toftwood
Hockering
Clippings Green
Mattishall Burgh
Rotten Row
East Tuddenham
Honingham
A47
Costessey
Hellesdon
R. Tud
Sporle
Little Fransham
Ivy Todd
Daffy Green
Yaxham
Clint Green
Mattishall
Welborne
Easton
Colton
Norfolk Showground
New Costessey
A1074
Upper Hellesdon
EcoTech Centre
Swaffham
Necton
Bradenham
R. Wissey
Westfield
Whinburgh
Brakefield Green
Brandon Parva
Barnham Broom
Marlingford
Bowthorpe
Barford
Bawburgh
Earlham
B1108
A1075
Shipdham
Shipdham
North Pickenham
Holme Hale
Garvestone
Thuxton
Runhall
Colney
Eaton
Sainsbury Centre
Little Melton
Great Melton
Cringleford
Keswick
Crowshill
High Common
Reymerston
Blackwater R.
Low Street
Coston
Wramplingham
Carleton Forehoe
High Green
Lynch Green
Hethersett
B1172
P+R
A11
Cranworth
Southburgh
Mid-Norfolk Railway
Hardingham
Kimberley
Kidd's Moor
Kett's Oak
Intwood
South Pickenham
Ashill
Saham Hills
Woodrising
Crownthorpe
B1135
Lower East Carleton
Great Cressingham
Ovington
Carbrooke
Hingham
Wicklewood
Hackford
Heritage
Wymondham
Abbey
Ketteringham
Swardeston
Saham Toney
Neaton
Watton
Scoulton
B1108
Deopham
Morley St Botolph
East Carleton
Swainsthorpe
Hethel Old Thorn
Mulbarton
Hilborough
Little Cressingham
Merton
Grist
Melsop Farm Park
Little Ellingham
66
Suton
Silfield
Wreningham
Bracon Ash
B1077
B1108
Bodney
Northacre
Rockland St Peter
Bush Green
Deopham Green
Ashwellthorpe
Toprow
Saxlingham Thorpe
The Arms
Caston
Stow Bedon
Rockland All Saints
Great Ellingham
Spooner Row
Fundenhall
Flordon
Thompson
A1075
Lower Stow Bedon
Besthorpe
Attleborough
Black Carr
Tacolneston
Hapton
Tasburgh
Ickburgh
Industrial Steam
Tharston
300

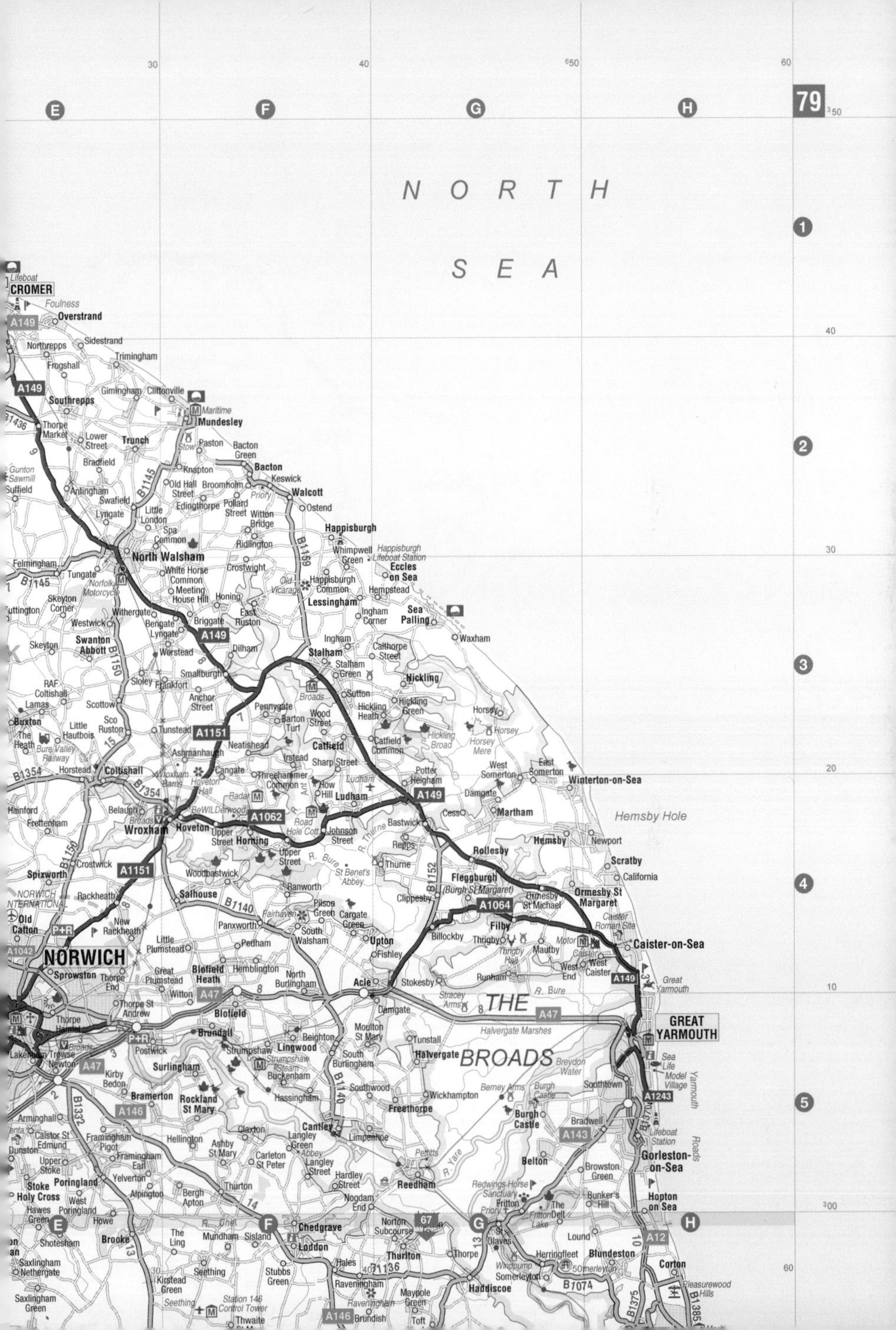
NORTH SEA
CROMER
Lifeboat
Foulness
Overstrand
Northrepps
Sidestrand
Trimingham
Frogshall
Southrepps
Gimingham
Clippesby
Mundesley
Maritime
Thorpe Market
Lower Street
Trunch
Paston
Bacton Green
Bacton
Stow
Bradfield
Knapton
Keswick
Walcott
Gunton Sawmill
Suffield
Antingham
Old Hall Street
Broomholm
Priory
Ostend
Swafield
Edingthorpe
Pollard Street
Witton Bridge
Lyngate
Little London
Happisburgh
Spa Common
Ridlington
Whimpwell Green
Happisburgh Lifeboat Station
North Walsham
Felmingham
Tungate
White Horse Common
Crostwight
Eccles on Sea
Norfolk Motorcycle
Meeting House Hill
Old Vicarage
Happisburgh Common
Hempstead
Skeyton Corner
Honing
Lessingham
Westwick
Withergate
Bengate
East Ruston
Ingham Corner
Sea Palling
Waxham
Swanton Abbott
Lyngate
Briggate
Ingham
Skeyton
Worstead
Dilham
Calthorpe Street
Stalham
Smallburgh
Stalham Green
Hickling
RAF Coltishall
Lamas
Sloley
Frankfort
Broads
Sutton
Scottow
Anchor Street
Pennygate
Wood Street
Hickling Heath
Hickling Green
Horsey
Buxton
Little Hautbois
Sco Ruston
Barton Turf
Hickling Broad
Horsey Mere
The Heath
Bure Valley Railway
Tunstead
Neatishead
Catfield
Catfield Common
Ashmanhaugh
Irstead
Sharp Street
Potter Heigham
West Somerton
East Somerton
Winterton-on-Sea
Horstead
Coltishall
Wroxham Barns
Hoveton Hall
Cangate
Threehammer Common
How Hill
Ludham
Damgate
Martham
Radar
BeWILDerwood
Hemsby Hole
Hainford
Belaugh
Frettenham
Wroxham
Hoveton
Upper Street
Horning
Road Hole Cott
Johnson Street
Bastwick
Cess
Hemsby
Newport
R. Thurne
Repps
Rollesby
Scratby
California
Crostwick
Upper Street
R. Bure
Thurne
Spixworth
Woodbastwick
St Benet's Abbey
Fleggburgh
(Burgh St Margaret)
Ormesby St Michael
Ormesby St Margaret
NORWICH INTERNATIONAL
Rackheath
Salhouse
Ranworth
Clippesby
Old Catton
New Rackheath
Panxworth
Fairhaven
Pilson Green
Cargate Green
South Walsham
Filby
Caister Roman Site
Caister-on-Sea
Upton
Billockby
Thrigby
Thrigby Hall
Mautby
Motor
Caister
NORWICH
Little Plumstead
Pedham
Fishley
Sprowston
Thorpe End
Great Plumstead
Blofield Heath
Hemblington
North Burlingham
Acle
Stokesby
Runham
West End
West Caister
Great Yarmouth
Witton
Thorpe St Andrew
Blofield
Damgate
Stracey Arms
THE BROADS
R. Bure
Thorpe Hamlet
Brundall
Beighton
Moulton St Mary
Tunstall
Halvergate Marshes
GREAT YARMOUTH
Lakenham
Trowse Newton
Postwick
Strumpshaw
Lingwood
South Burlingham
Halvergate
Breydon Water
Sea Life
Model Village
Kirby Bedon
Surlingham
Strumpshaw Steam
Buckenham
Southwood
Berney Arms
Burgh Castle
Southtown
Arminghall
Bramerton
Rockland St Mary
Hassingham
Wickhampton
Freethorpe
Yarmouth Roads
Caistor St Edmund
Dunston
Framingham Pigot
Claxton
Cantley
Langley Green
Limpenhoe
Bradwell
Lifeboat Station
Hellington
Ashby St Mary
Carleton St Peter
Langley Abbey
Pettitts
Belton
Gorleston-on-Sea
Upper Stoke
Framingham Earl
Yelverton
Langley Street
Hardley Street
R. Yare
Browston Green
Stoke Holy Cross
Poringland
Thurton
Reedham
Redwings Horse Sanctuary
West Poringland
Alpington
Bergh Apton
Nogdam End
Bunker's Hill
Hopton on Sea
Hawes Green
Howe
Chedgrave
Norton Subcourse
Fritton
Priory
The Dell
Fritton Lake
Lound
Shotesham
Brooke
The Ling
Mundham
Sisland
Loddon
Thurlton
Thorpe
St Olaves
Windpump
Herringfleet
Blundeston
Saxlingham Nethergate
Hales
Raveningham
Somerleyton
Corton
Kirstead Green
Seething
Stubbs Green
Haddiscoe
Pleasurewood Hills
Saxlingham Green
Station 146 Control Tower
Maypole Green
Thwaite
Brundish
Toft
A149
A1151
A1062
A1064
A47
A146
A143
A1243
A12
A1042
P+R
B1145
B1436
B1150
B1159
B1354
B1152
B1140
B1332
B1136
B1074
B1375
B1385
B1370
67
E
F
G
H
1
2
3
4
5
30
40
650
60
350
300

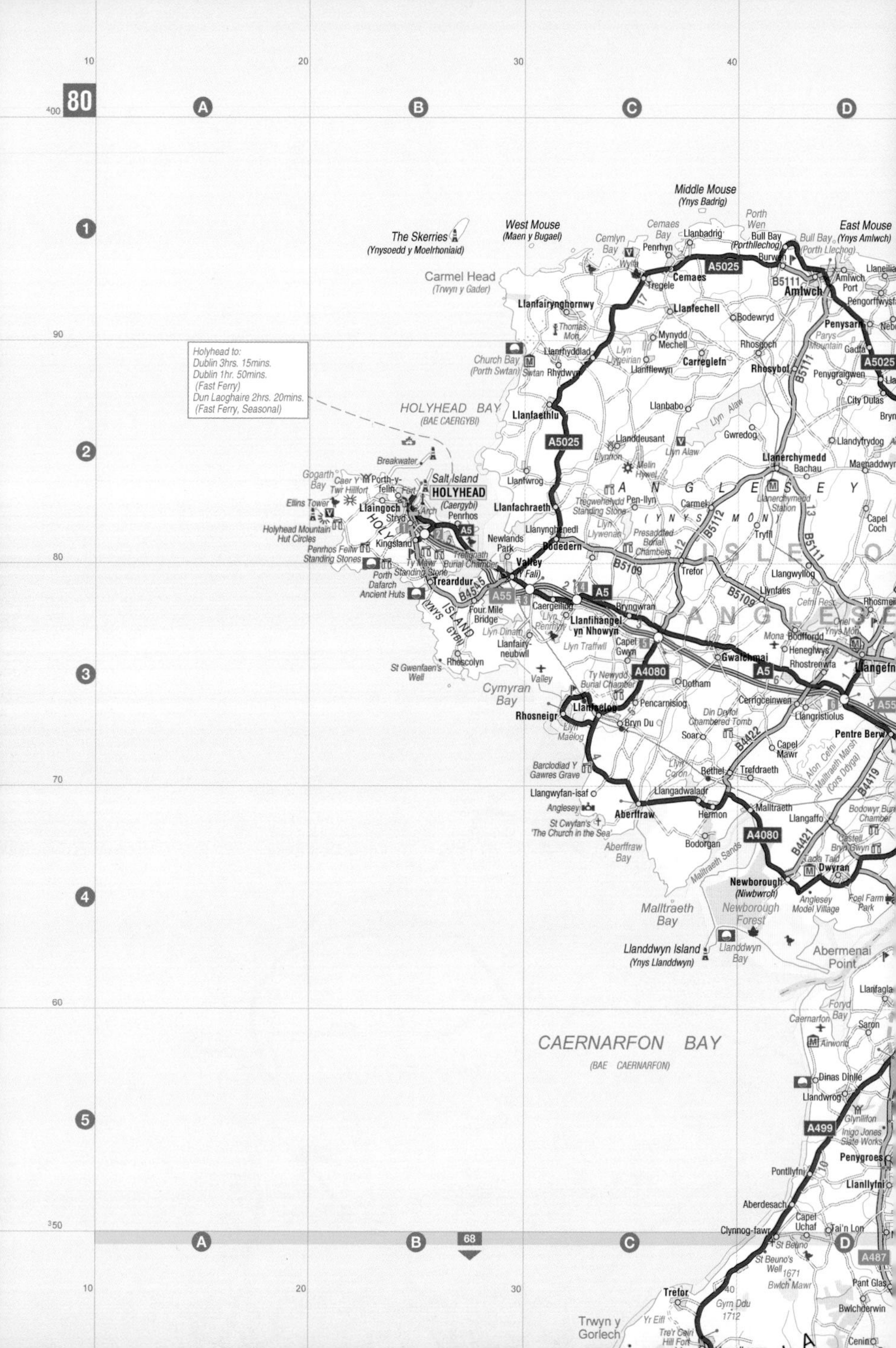
80
A
B
C
D
1
2
3
4
5
10
20
30
40
400
90
80
70
60
350
68
Middle Mouse
(Ynys Badrig)
West Mouse
(Maen y Bugael)
The Skerries
(Ynysoedd y Moelrhoniaid)
East Mouse
(Ynys Amlwch)
Porth Wen
Cemaes Bay
Cemlyn Bay
Llanbadrig
Penrhyn
Bull Bay
(Porthllechog)
Bull Bay
(Porth Llechog)
Burwen
Wylfa
Tregele
Cemaes
A5025
B5111
Amlwch
Amlwch Port
Llaneilian
Pengorffwysfa
Carmel Head
(Trwyn y Gader)
Llanfairynghornwy
Llanfechell
Bodewryd
Penysarn
Nebo
Thomas Mon.
Mynydd Mechell
Parys Mountain
Gadfa
Holyhead to:
Dublin 3hrs. 15mins.
Dublin 1hr. 50mins.
(Fast Ferry)
Dun Laoghaire 2hrs. 20mins.
(Fast Ferry, Seasonal)
Church Bay
(Porth Swtan)
Swtan
Llanrhyddlad
Rhydwyn
Llyn Llygeirian
Llanfflewyn
Carreglefn
Rhosgoch
Rhosybol
Penygraigwen
City Dulas
Brynteg
HOLYHEAD BAY
(BAE CAERGYBI)
Llanfaethlu
Llanbabo
Llyn Alaw
Gwredog
Llandyfrydog
A5025
Llanddeusant
Llynnon
Melin Hywel
Llyn Alaw
Llanerchymedd
Bachau
Maenaddwyn
Breakwater
Gogarth Bay
Caer Y Twr Hillfort
Porth-y-felin
Fort
Salt Island
HOLYHEAD
(Caergybi)
Llanfwrog
ANGLESEY
(YNYS MÔN)
Llanerchymedd Station
Capel Coch
Ellins Tower
Llaingoch
Stryd
Arch
Penrhos
Llanfachraeth
Tregwehelydd Standing Stone
Pen-llyn
Carmel
Tryfil
Holyhead Mountain Hut Circles
HOLY
A5
Kingsland
Llanynghenedl
Llyn Llywenan
Presaddfed Burial Chambers
B5112
Penrhos Feilw Standing Stones
Ty Mawr Standing Stone
Trefignath Burial Chamber
Newlands Park
Bodedern
B5109
Trefor
ISLE OF ANGLESEY
B5111
Porth Dafarch Ancient Huts
Trearddur
Valley
(Y Fali)
Llangwyllog
B4545
A55
A5
Llynfaes
Rhosmeirch
(YNYS GYBI)
ISLAND
Four Mile Bridge
Caergeiliog
Llyn Penrhyn
Llanfihangel yn Nhowyn
Bryngwran
Cefni Res.
Oriel Ynys Môn
Llyn Dinam
Llanfair-yn-neubwll
Llyn Traffwll
Capel Gwyn
Mona
Bodffordd
Heneglwys
Gwalchmai
Rhostrehwfa
Llangefni
St Gwenfaen's Well
Rhoscolyn
Valley
A4080
A5
Cymyran Bay
Ty Newydd Burial Chamber
Dothan
Rhosneigr
Llanfaelog
Pencarnisiog
Cerrigceinwen
Llangristiolus
A55
Llyn Maelog
Bryn Du
Din Dryfol Chambered Tomb
Soar
B4422
Capel Mawr
Pentre Berw
Aton Cefni
Malltraeth Marsh
(Cors Ddyga)
Barclodiad Y Gawres Grave
Llyn Coron
Bethel
Trefdraeth
B4419
Llangwyfan-isaf
Llangadwaladr
Anglesey
Aberffraw
Hermon
Malltraeth
Llangaffo
Bodowyr Burial Chamber
St Cwyfan's 'The Church in the Sea'
A4080
Aberffraw Bay
Bodorgan
Malltraeth Sands
B4421
Castell Bryn Gwyn
Tacla Taid
Dwyran
Newborough
(Niwbwrch)
Anglesey Model Village
Foel Farm Park
Malltraeth Bay
Newborough Forest
Llanddwyn Island
(Ynys Llanddwyn)
Llanddwyn Bay
Abermenai Point
Llanfaglan
Foryd Bay
Caernarfon
Airworld
Saron
CAERNARFON BAY
(BAE CAERNARFON)
Dinas Dinlle
Llandwrog
Glynllifon
A499
Inigo Jones' Slate Works
Penygroes
Pontllyfni
Llanllyfni
Aberdesach
Capel Uchaf
Clynnog-fawr
Tai'n Lon
St Beuno
St Beuno's Well
1671
Bwlch Mawr
A487
Pant Glas
Trefor
Gyrn Ddu
1712
Bwlchderwin
Trwyn y Gorlech
Yr Eifl
Tre'r Ceiri Hill Fort
Cennin

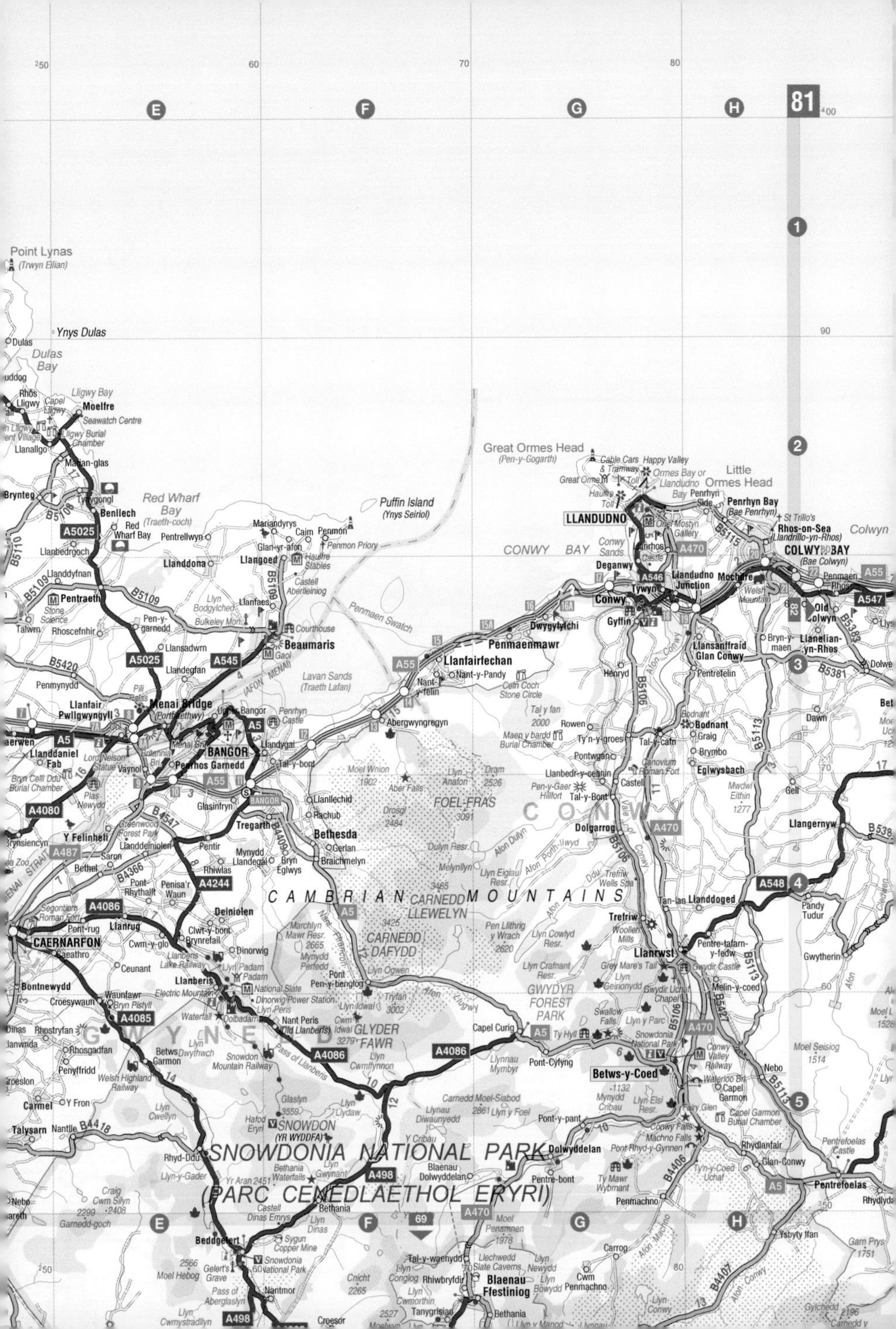
Point Lynas
(Trwyn Eilian)
Ynys Dulas
Dulas Bay
Moelfre
Red Wharf Bay
(Traeth-coch)
Puffin Island
(Ynys Seiriol)
Great Ormes Head
(Pen-y-Gogarth)
Little Ormes Head
LLANDUDNO
CONWY BAY
Penrhyn Bay
(Bae Penrhyn)
Rhos-on-Sea
(Llandrillo-yn-Rhos)
COLWYN BAY
(Bae Colwyn)
Benllech
Pentraeth
Llangoed
Beaumaris
Menai Bridge
(Porthaethwy)
BANGOR
Llanfairfechan
Penmaenmawr
Dwygyfylchi
Conwy
Deganwy
Llandudno Junction
Llanfair Pwllgwyngyll
Y Felinheli
CAERNARFON
Bethesda
Llanberis
Deiniolen
CAMBRIAN MOUNTAINS
CARNEDD LLEWELYN
CARNEDD DAFYDD
FOEL-FRAS
GLYDER FAWR
CONWY
GWYNEDD
Llanrwst
Trefriw
Dolgarrog
Capel Curig
Betws-y-Coed
GWYDYR FOREST PARK
SNOWDON
(YR WYDDFA)
SNOWDONIA NATIONAL PARK
(PARC CENEDLAETHOL ERYRI)
Beddgelert
Dolwyddelan
Blaenau Ffestiniog
Pentrefoelas
Llangernyw
Bodnant
Eglwysbach
A5
A55
A470
A4086
A5025
A545
A4085
A487
A4244
A498
A547
A548

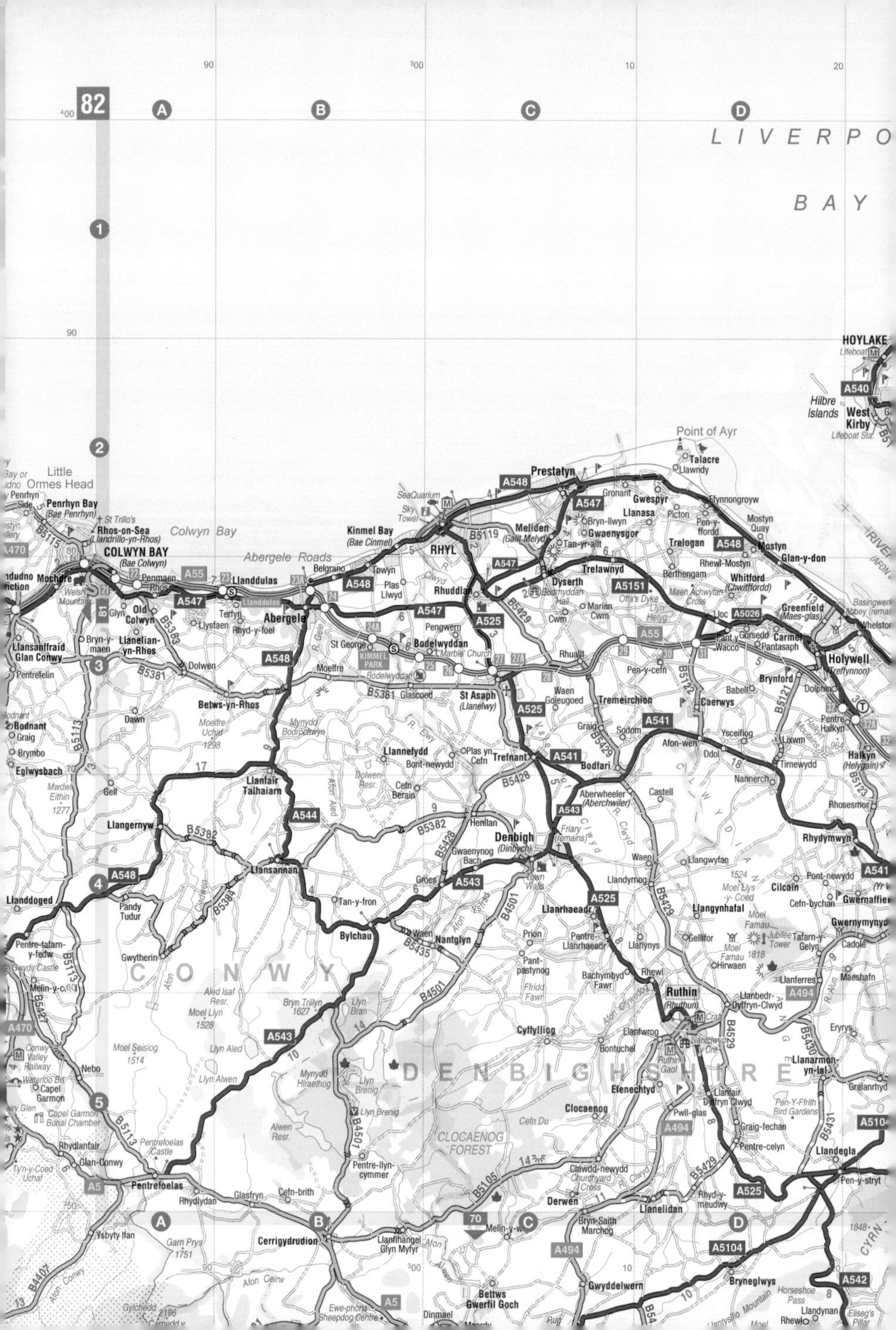

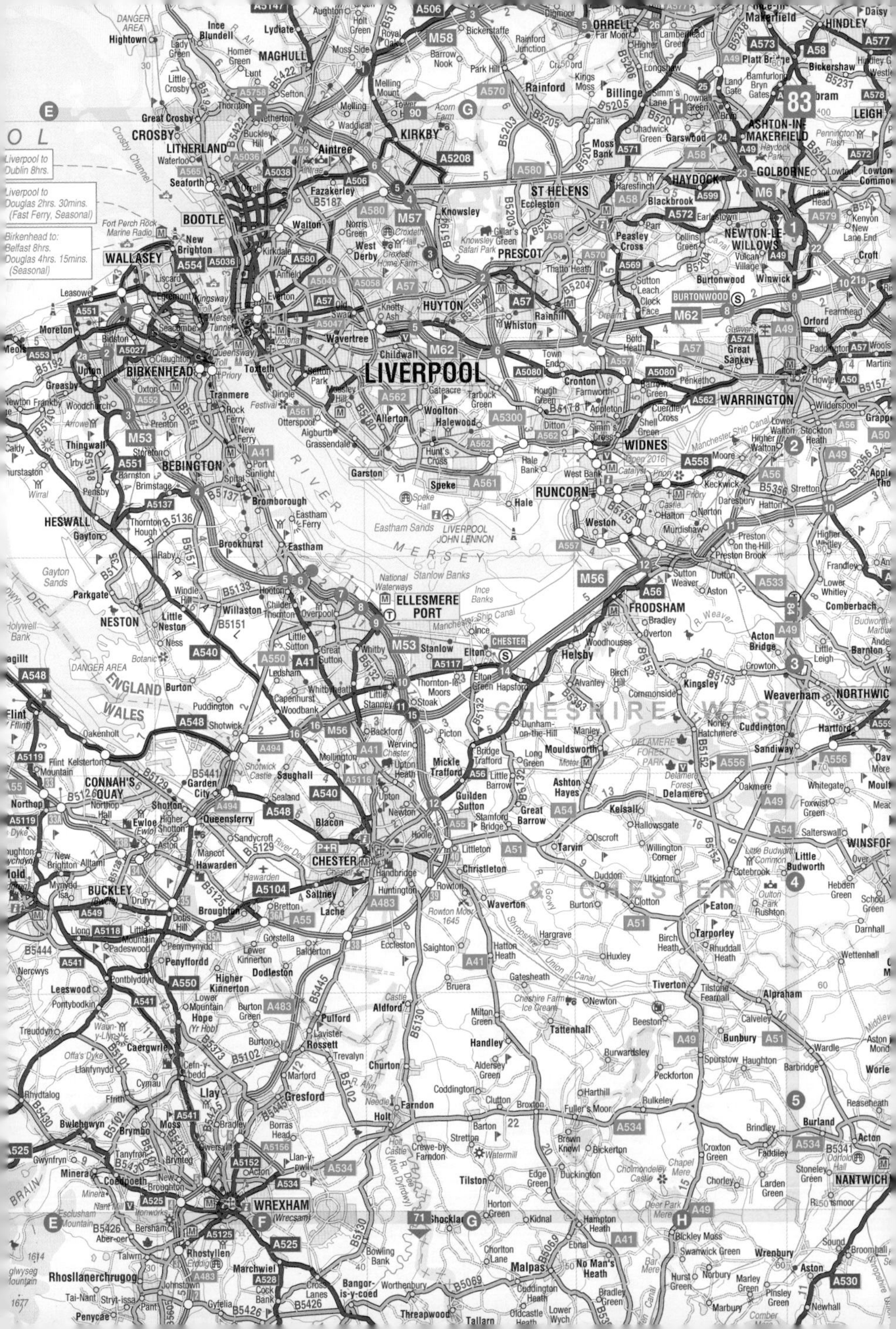
83
LIVERPOOL
Liverpool to Dublin 8hrs.
Liverpool to Douglas 2hrs. 30mins. (Fast Ferry, Seasonal)
Birkenhead to: Belfast 8hrs. Douglas 4hrs. 15mins. (Seasonal)
Fort Perch Rock Marine Radio
Hightown
Ince Blundell
Lydiate
MAGHULL
CROSBY
Great Crosby
LITHERLAND
Seaforth
BOOTLE
WALLASEY
New Brighton
Aintree
Fazakerley
Walton
KIRKBY
Knowsley
Knowsley Safari Park
HUYTON
Wavertree
Childwall
Toxteth
Dingle
Aigburth
Garston
Speke
Hale
Woolton
Halewood
Allerton
Otterspool
Grassendale
LIVERPOOL JOHN LENNON
Eastham Sands
RIVER MERSEY
Stanlow Banks
Ince Banks
National Waterways
ELLESMERE PORT
Manchester Ship Canal
Stanlow
Elton
CHESTER
Helsby
FRODSHAM
RUNCORN
Weston
WIDNES
WARRINGTON
ST HELENS
PRESCOT
Eccleston
Rainford
Rainhill
Whiston
HAYDOCK
GOLBORNE
ASHTON-IN-MAKERFIELD
NEWTON-LE-WILLOWS
Winwick
Burtonwood
BURTONWOOD
Great Sankey
Penketh
Cronton
ORRELL
Billinge
HINDLEY
LEIGH
Moreton
BIRKENHEAD
Tranmere
Rock Ferry
New Ferry
BEBINGTON
Port Sunlight
Bromborough
Eastham
HESWALL
Thingwall
Irby
Pensby
Greasby
Upton
Woodchurch
Prenton
Oxton
Parkgate
NESTON
Little Neston
Willaston
Hooton
Little Sutton
Great Sutton
Whitby
DANGER AREA
ENGLAND
WALES
Burton
Puddington
Shotwick
Saughall
Blacon
Backford
Mollington
Upton
Hoole
Littleton
CHESTER
Handbridge
Huntington
Saltney
Lache
Christleton
Rowton
Waverton
Tarvin
Kelsall
Delamere
Mouldsworth
Ashton Hayes
Manley
Alvanley
Kingsley
Crowton
Weaverham
NORTHWICH
Cuddington
Sandiway
Hartford
WINSFORD
Little Budworth
Tarporley
Eaton
Tiverton
Beeston
Bunbury
Alpraham
Tattenhall
Burwardsley
Peckforton
Bulkeley
Broxton
Harthill
Bickerton
Duckington
Malpas
No Man's Heath
Tilston
Stretton
Farndon
Holt
Churton
Aldford
Pulford
Rossett
Gresford
Marford
Llay
WREXHAM (Wrecsam)
Marchwiel
Rhostyllen
Bersham
Coedpoeth
Minera
Brymbo
Moss
Gwersyllt
Caergwrle
Hope (Yr Hob)
Penyffordd
Higher Kinnerton
Dodleston
Broughton
Buckley (Bwcle)
Hawarden
Queensferry
Shotton
Garden City
CONNAH'S QUAY
Flint (Y Fflint)
Northop
Leeswood
Rhosllanerchrugog
Bangor-is-y-coed
Threapwood
Tallarn
NANTWICH
Acton
Burland
Wrenbury
Aston
CHESHIRE WEST & CHESTER
M53
M56
M57
M58
M6
M62
A41
A49
A51
A55
A483
A534
A540
A548
A550
A5117
A556
A562
A580

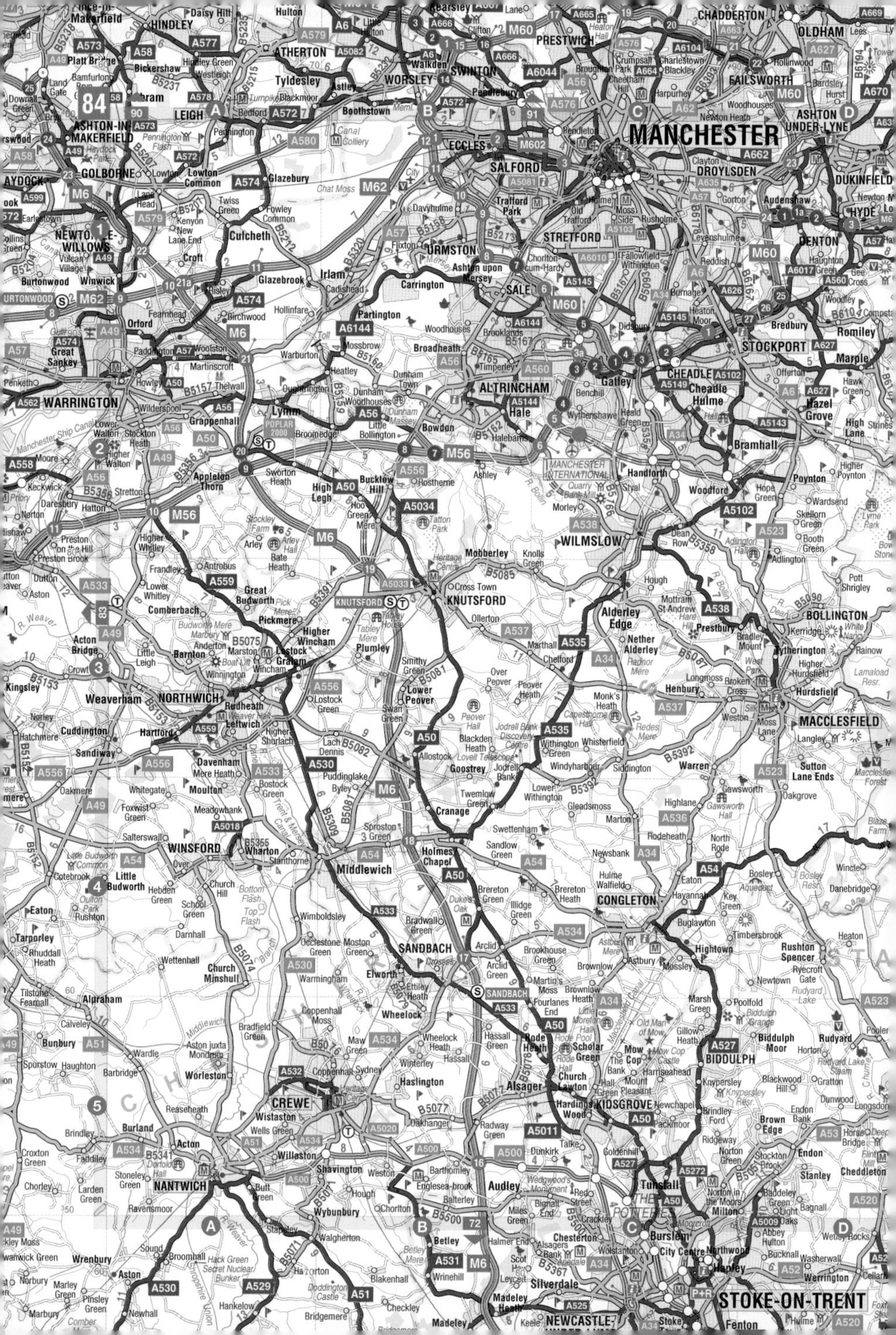

84
MANCHESTER
SALFORD
ECCLES
SWINTON
WORSLEY
ATHERTON
HINDLEY
LEIGH
ASHTON-IN-MAKERFIELD
GOLBORNE
NEWTON-LE-WILLOWS
WARRINGTON
Culcheth
Irlam
Partington
Carrington
URMSTON
STRETFORD
SALE
ALTRINCHAM
Hale
Lymm
PRESTWICH
CHADDERTON
OLDHAM
FAILSWORTH
ASHTON UNDER-LYNE
DROYLSDEN
DUKINFIELD
HYDE
DENTON
STOCKPORT
Romiley
Marple
CHEADLE
Cheadle Hulme
Gatley
Bramhall
Hazel Grove
Poynton
Handforth
WILMSLOW
MANCHESTER INTERNATIONAL
Alderley Edge
Prestbury
BOLLINGTON
MACCLESFIELD
KNUTSFORD
Mobberley
NORTHWICH
Weaverham
Cuddington
Sandiway
Hartford
WINSFORD
Middlewich
Holmes Chapel
Goostrey
CONGLETON
SANDBACH
Elworth
Wheelock
Alsager
KIDSGROVE
BIDDULPH
CREWE
NANTWICH
Wistaston
Willaston
Shavington
Audley
Tunstall
Burslem
Hanley
STOKE-ON-TRENT
NEWCASTLE-
Silverdale
Madeley
Betley
Endon
Stanley
Rudyard
Leek
Tarporley
Bunbury
Wrenbury
Audlem
M6
M60
M62
M56
M602
A6
A34
A50
A56
A49
A556
A530
A533
A54
A523
A527
A500
A51
A529
A534
A537
A538
A535

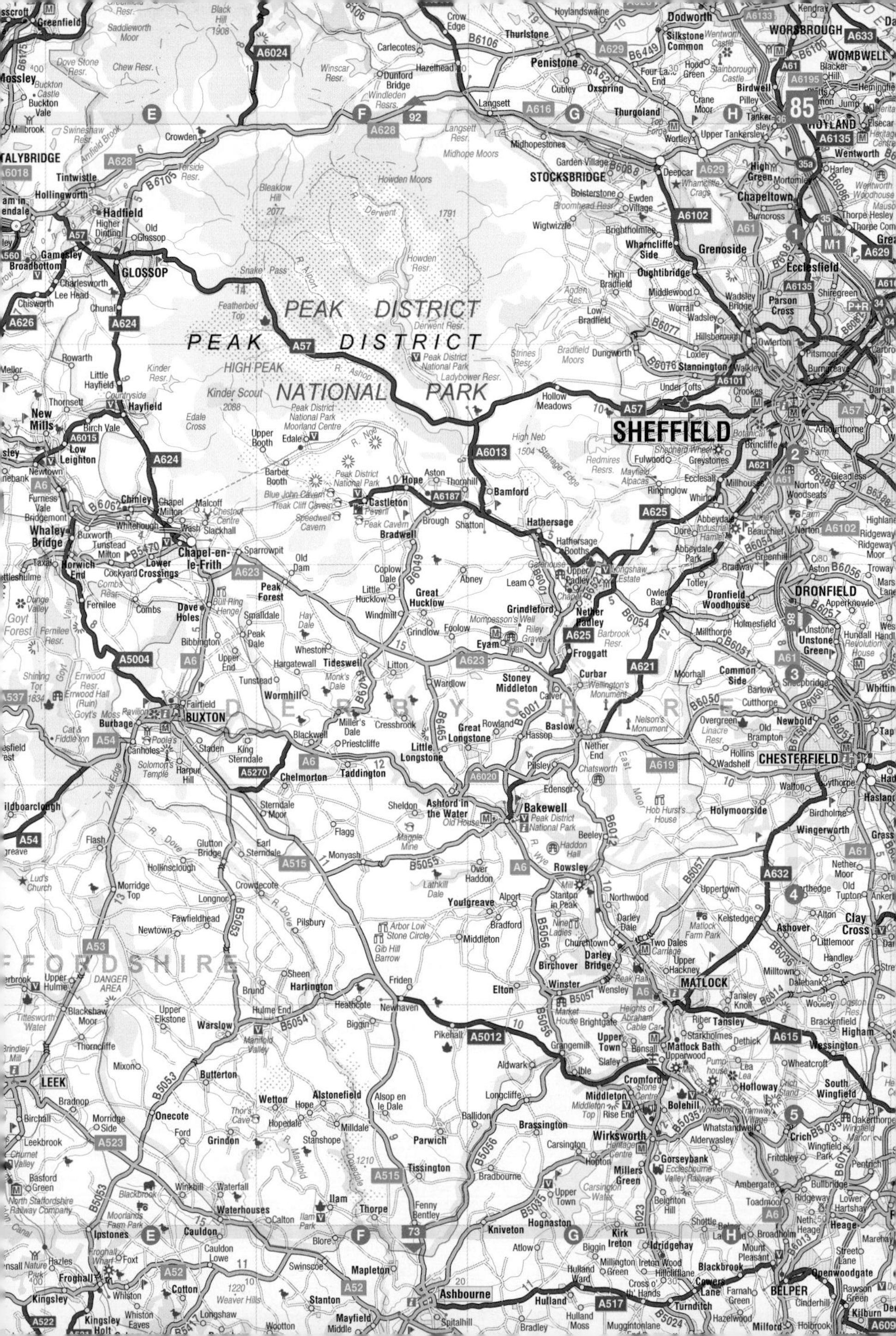
85
Greenfield
Saddleworth Moor
Black Hill 1908
A6024
Crow Edge
Hoylandswaine
Dodworth
Kendray
WORSBROUGH
A633
A6133
Mossley
Dove Stone Resr.
Chew Resr.
Carlecotes
Thurlstone
B6106
Penistone
A629
B6449
Silkstone Common
Wentworth Castle
Buckton Castle
Buckton Vale
Dunford Bridge
Winscar Resr.
Hazelhead
Windleden Resrs.
Cubley
Oxspring
Four Lane End
Hood Green
Stainborough Castle
Birdwell
Pilley
WOMBWELL
Blacker Hill
Hemingfield
Jump
Elsecar
A61
A6195
Millbrook
Swineshaw Resr.
E
F
92
A628
Langsett
A616
G
Thurgoland
Crane Moor
H
Tankersley
36
HOYLAND
A6135
Crowden
Langsett Resr.
Midhope Moors
Midhopestones
Wortley
Upper Tankersley
Wentworth
STALYBRIDGE
A6018
A628
Tintwistle
Torside Resr.
Bleaklow Hill 2077
Howden Moors
Garden Village
STOCKSBRIDGE
Deepcar
A629
High Green
Mortomley
35a
Harley
Hollingworth
B6105
Hadfield
Higher Dinting
Old Glossop
R. Derwent
1791
Bolsterstone
Broomhead Resr.
Ewden Village
Whamcliffe Crags
Chapeltown
Burncross
Thorpe Hesley
A57
Wigtwizzle
Brightholmlee
A6102
35
M1
Wharncliffe Side
Grenoside
Ecclesfield
A629
Gamesley
Broadbottom
GLOSSOP
Snake Pass
R. Alport
Howden Resr.
High Bradfield
Oughtibridge
A6135
Charlesworth
Lee Head
Chisworth
Featherbed Top
PEAK DISTRICT
PEAK DISTRICT
Derwent Resr.
Low Bradfield
Middlewood
Worrall
Wadsley
Wadsley Bridge
Parson Cross
Shiregreen
A626
Chunal
A624
A57
Hillsborough
Owlerton
Pitsmoor
Rowarth
Little Hayfield
Kinder Resr.
HIGH PEAK
Peak District National Park
Ladybower Resr.
Strines Resr.
Bradfield Moors
Dungworth
Loxley
B6076
Stannington
Walkley
Burngreave
Mellor
Thornsett
Countryside
Hayfield
Kinder Scout 2088
NATIONAL PARK
Hollow Meadows
Under Tofts
A6101
Crookes
Darnall
New Mills
Birch Vale
A6015
Low Leighton
Newtown
Edale Cross
Upper Booth
Peak District National Park Moorland Centre
Edale
R. Noe
A57
SHEFFIELD
A57
Arbourthorne
A624
A6013
High Neb 1504
Stanage Edge
Botanical
Shepherd Wheel
Fulwood
Greystones
Brincliffe
Furness Vale
Bridgemont
Barber Booth
Peak District National Park
Hope
Aston
Thornhill
Redmires Resrs.
Mayfield Alpacas
Ringinglow
Ecclesall
Millhouses
A621
Norton Woodseats
Gleadless
Chinley
Chapel Milton
Malcoff
Chestnut Centre
B6062
Blue John Cavern
Treak Cliff Cavern
Speedwell Cavern
Castleton
Peveril
Peak Cavern
A6187
Bamford
Whirlow
Whaley Bridge
Buxworth
Whitehough
Slackhall
Wash
Brough
Shatton
Hathersage
A625
Abbeydale Industrial Hamlet
Beauchief
Norton
A6102
Highlane
Ridgeway
Taxal
Tunstead Milton
B5470
Chapel-en-le-Frith
Sparrowpit
Bradwell
Old Dam
Hathersage Booths
Dore
Abbeydale Park
Greenhill
B6054
Ridgeway Moor
Norwich End
Cockyard
Lower Crossings
A623
Coplow Dale
B6049
Abney
Leam
Upper Padley
Longshaw Estate
Bradway
Totley
Aston
B6056
Troway
Combs Resr.
Peak Forest
Little Hucklow
Great Hucklow
Chapel
Owler Bar
Dronfield Woodhouse
DRONFIELD
Apperknowle
Dunge Valley
Fernilee
Combs
Dove Holes
Bull Ring Henge
Smalldale
Windmill
Grindleford
Mompesson's Well
Nether Padley
B6054
Holmesfield
B6057
Goyt Forest
Fernilee Resr.
Bibbington
Peak Dale
Hay Dale
Grindlow
Foolow
Eyam
Riley Graves
A625
Barbrook Resr.
Millthorpe
Unstone
Unstone Green
Hundall
A5004
Upper End
A6
Wheston
Tideswell
Litton
A623
Eyam Hall
Froggatt
B6051
A61
Errwood Resr.
Errwood Hall (Ruin)
Shining Tor 1834
Goyt
Hargatewall
Tunstead
Wormhill
Monk's Dale
Wardlow
Stoney Middleton
Curbar
A621
Moorhall
Common Side
3
Goyt's Moss
Pavilion
Fairfield
BUXTON
Burbage
DERBYSHIRE
Miller's Dale
Cressbrook
B6465
Great Longstone
Rowland
Calver
Wellington's Monument
Baslow
Nelson's Monument
B6050
Cutthorpe
Barlow
Sheepbridge
Whittington
Cat & Fiddle Inn
A54
Poole's Cavern
Canholes
Solomon's Temple
Staden
King Sterndale
Harpur Hill
A5270
Blackwell
Priestcliffe
A6
Taddington
Chelmorton
Little Longstone
Hassop
Nether End
Pilsley
Chatsworth
Edensor
A619
Overgreen
Linacre Resr.
Old Brampton
Hollins
Wadshelf
Newbold
CHESTERFIELD
Axe Edge
Sterndale Moor
Sheldon
Ashford in the Water
Old House
A6020
Bakewell
Peak District National Park
East Moor
Hob Hurst's House
Holymoorside
Walton
Boythorpe
Hasland
Birdholme
Wildboarclough
Flash
R. Dove
Glutton Bridge
Earl Sterndale
Flagg
Magpie Mine
Haddon Hall
Beeley
B6012
Wingerworth
A54
Hollinsclough
A515
Monyash
B5055
Over Haddon
Lathkill Dale
A6
R. Wye
Rowsley
B5057
A61
A632
Nether Moor
Old Tupton
Lud's Church
Morridge Top
Crowdecote
Longnor
Youlgreave
Alport
Stanton in Peak
Northwood
Uppertown
4
Fawfieldhead
B5053
Pilsbury
Arbor Low Stone Circle
Bradford
Darley Dale
Kelstedge
Ashover
Alton
Clay Cross
Newtown
Middleton
Nine Ladies
Matlock Farm Park
Littlemoor
A53
Gib Hill Barrow
B5056
Churchtown
Two Dales Carriage
B6036
STAFFORDSHIRE
Birchover
Darley Bridge
Upper Hackney
Handley
DANGER AREA
Sheen
Winster
Peak Rail
MATLOCK
Milltown
Dalebank
Upper Hulme
Brund
Hartington
Friden
Elton
Wensley
Tansley Knoll
B6014
Hulme End
Heathcote
Newhaven
B5057
Market House
Heights of Abraham Cable Car
Riber
Tansley
Woolley
Blackshaw Moor
Upper Elkstone
Warslow
B5054
Biggin
Brightgate
Starkholmes
Dethick
Brackenfield
Higham
Tittesworth Water
Manifold Valley
Pikehall
A5012
Grangemill
Upper Town
Bonsall
Matlock Bath
Upperwood
A615
Wessington
Thorncliffe
Aldwark
Ible
Slaley
Pump house
Lea
Wheatcroft
Mixon
LEEK
Butterton
B5053
Cromford
Stone Centre
Holloway
South Wingfield
Bradnop
Onecote
Wetton
Alstonefield
Hope
Alsop en le Dale
Longcliffe
Middleton
Bolehill
Hopedale
Milldale
Ballidon
Brassington
Middleton Top
Rise End
Whatstandwell
5
Crich
Oakerthorpe
Birchall
Morridge Side
Ford
Thor's Cave
Grindon
Stanshope
Parwich
Wirksworth
Heritage Centre
B5035
Alderwasley
Wingfield Manor
Leekbrook
A523
R. Manifold
Dovedale
1210
Carsington
Gorseybank
Fritchley
Wingfield Park
Churnet Valley
Tissington
A515
B5056
Hopton
Ecclesbourne Valley Railway
Pentrich
Basford Green
Winkhill
Waterfall
Bradbourne
Carsington Water
Millers Green
Ambergate
Bullbridge
North Staffordshire Railway Company
Blackbrook
Waterhouses
Calton
Ilam
Ilam Park
Thorpe
Fenny Bentley
B5035
Upper Town
Hognaston
B5023
Beighton Hill
Toadmoor
Ridgeway
Lower Hartshay
Moorlands Farm Park
Ipstones
E
Cauldon
F
73
Kniveton
G
Kirk Ireton
Idridgehay
Shottle
H
Broadholme
Nether Heage
Heage
Cauldon Lowe
Blore
Atlow
Biggin
Mount Pleasant
Marehay
Froghall Wharf
Foxt
Hazles
Nature Park
Froghall
A52
Cotton
11
10
1220
Weaver Hills
Swinscoe
Mapleton
20
Hulland Ward
Millington Green
Ireton Wood
Hillcliffelane
Blackbrook
Openwoodgate
Streetly Lane
Kingsley
Whiston
A52
Stanton
Ashbourne
Hulland
A517
Cross o' th' Hands
Cowers Lane
Farnah Green
BELPER
Rawson Green
Cinderhill
A522
Kingsley Holt
Whiston Eaves
Longshaw
Wootton
Mayfield
Middle
Spitalhill
Bradley
Hulland Moss
Mugginton Lane
B5024
Turnditch
Hazelwood
Milford
Holbrook
Kilburn
A609

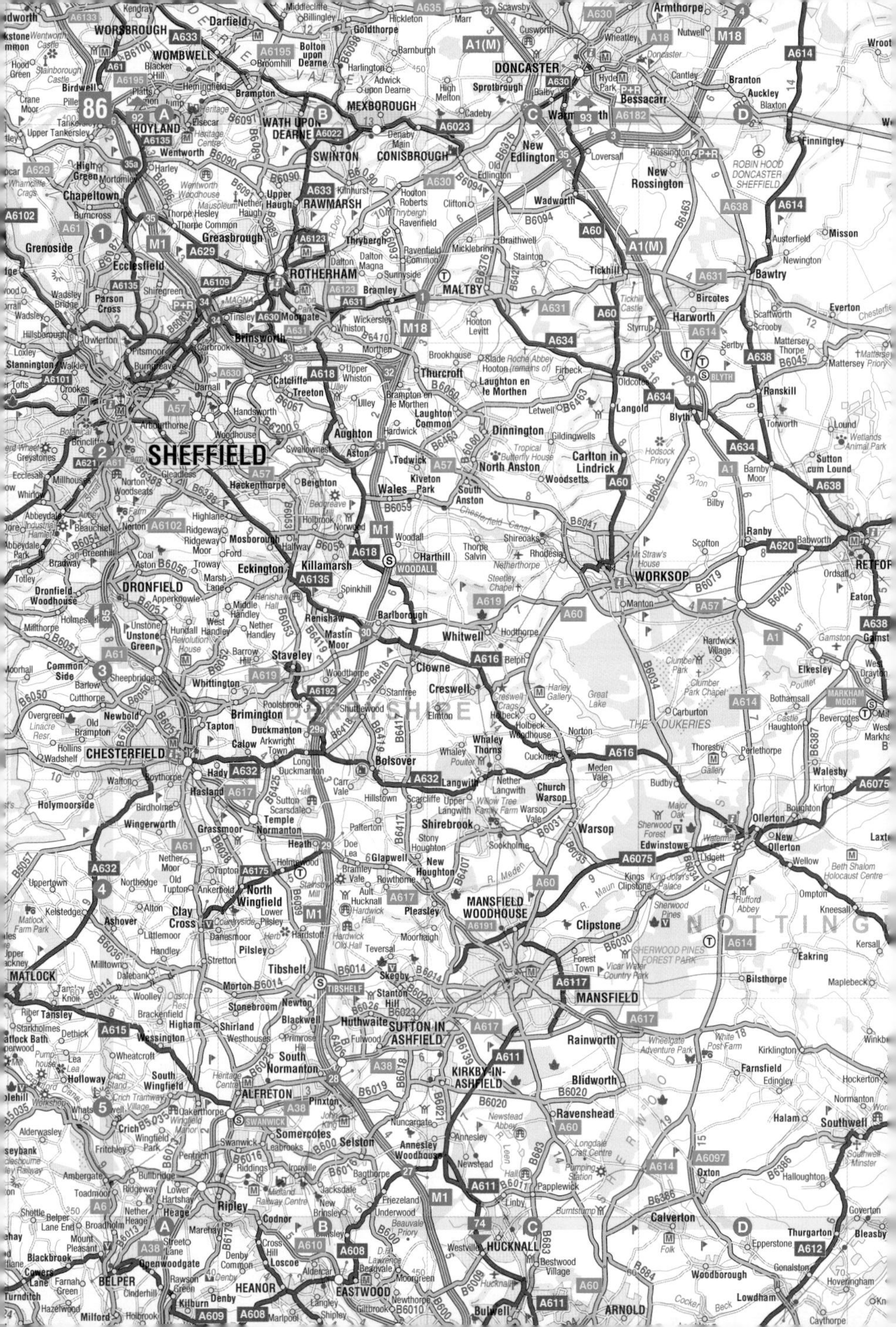
86
WORSBROUGH
Darfield
WOMBWELL
Goldthorpe
Bolton upon Dearne
DEARNE VALLEY
Armthorpe
DONCASTER
Sprotbrough
Bessacarr
Branton
Auckley
HOYLAND
MEXBOROUGH
WATH UPON DEARNE
SWINTON
CONISBROUGH
New Edlington
Rossington
New Rossington
Finningley
ROBIN HOOD DONCASTER SHEFFIELD
Chapeltown
RAWMARSH
Wadworth
Greasbrough
Grenoside
Ecclesfield
ROTHERHAM
Thrybergh
MALTBY
Tickhill
Bawtry
Misson
Parson Cross
Bramley
Bircotes
Harworth
Brinsworth
Catcliffe
Treeton
Thurcroft
Laughton en le Morthen
Langold
Blyth
Ranskill
Aughton
Dinnington
Carlton in Lindrick
SHEFFIELD
North Anston
Woodsetts
Sutton cum Lound
Hackenthorpe
Beighton
Wales
Kiveton Park
South Anston
Mosborough
Eckington
Killamarsh
Harthill
Shireoaks
Rhodesia
WORKSOP
Ranby
Babworth
RETFORD
DRONFIELD
Dronfield Woodhouse
Renishaw
Barlborough
Whitwell
Unstone Green
Staveley
Clowne
Creswell
Elkesley
Brimington
DERBYSHIRE
Whittington
CHESTERFIELD
Duckmanton
Bolsover
Langwith
Whaley Thorns
Cuckney
Church Warsop
Warsop
THE DUKERIES
Ollerton
New Ollerton
Edwinstowe
Holymoorside
Wingerworth
Grassmoor
Temple Normanton
Shirebrook
Clay Cross
North Wingfield
Glapwell
Pleasley
MANSFIELD WOODHOUSE
Clipstone
MATLOCK
Tibshelf
MANSFIELD
SUTTON IN ASHFIELD
KIRKBY-IN-ASHFIELD
Rainworth
Bilsthorpe
Blidworth
Farnsfield
ALFRETON
South Normanton
Somercotes
Selston
Ravenshead
Southwell
Ripley
Heanor
EASTWOOD
HUCKNALL
Calverton
BELPER
ARNOLD
Lowdham
NOTTINGHAMSHIRE
SHERWOOD FOREST
Thurgarton
Bleasby
Woodborough

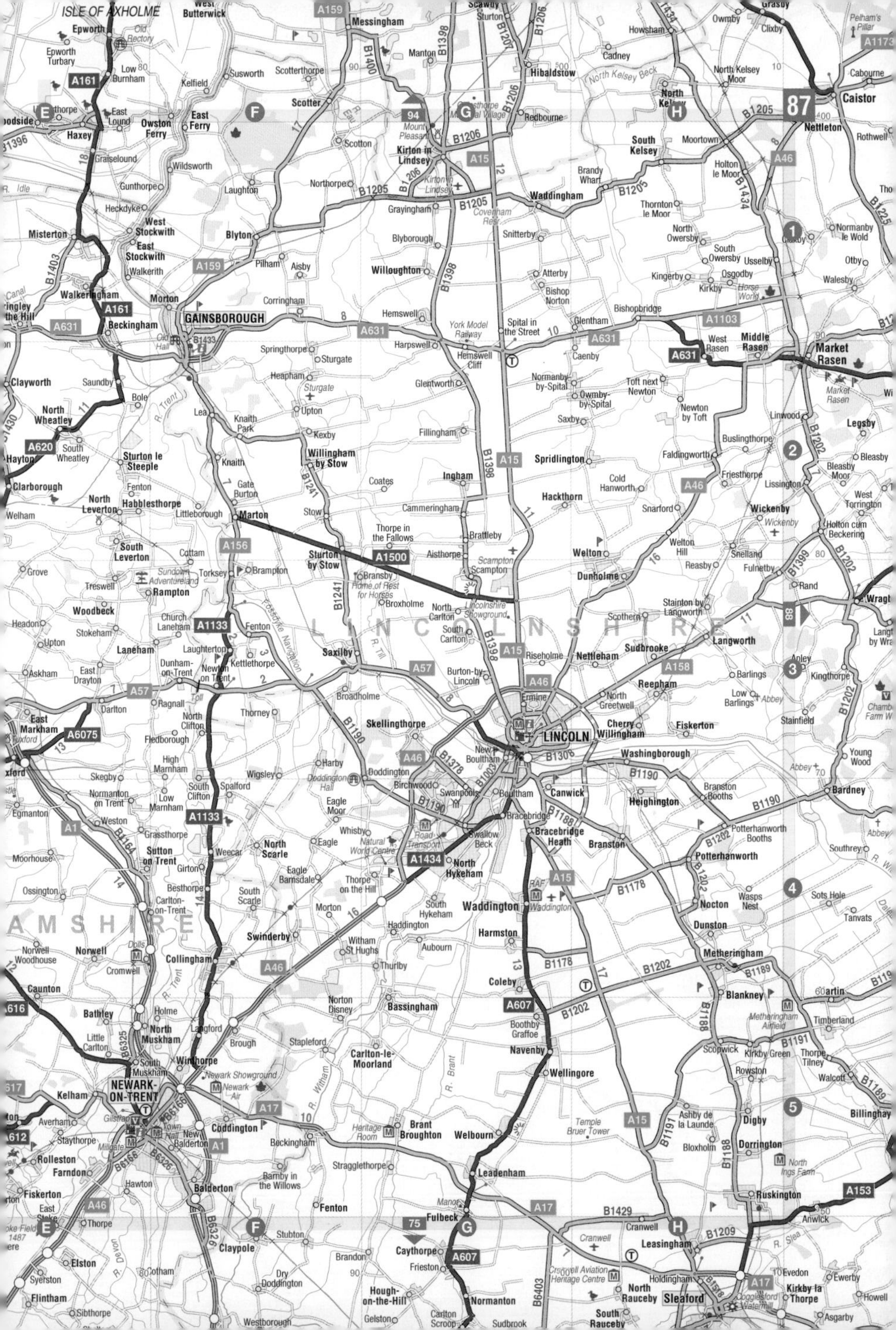

ISLE OF AXHOLME
West Butterwick
A159
Messingham
Scawby
Sturton
B1207
B1206
A15
Grasby
Owmby
Clixby
Pelham's Pillar
A1173
Howsham
Cadney
Epworth
Old Rectory
Epworth Turbary
Low Burnham
A161
Manton
B1398
B1400
Hibaldstow
North Kelsey Beck
North Kelsey Moor
Cabourne
Caistor
87
Susworth
Scotterthorpe
Kelfield
Scotter
R. Eau
94
Mount Pleasant
Gainsthorpe Medieval Village
Redbourne
North Kelsey
Nettleton
Rothwell
E
F
G
H
Haxey
East Lound
Owston Ferry
East Ferry
Woodside
B1396
Graiselound
Scotton
B1206
Kirton in Lindsey
South Kelsey
Moortown
B1205
A46
Wildsworth
Gunthorpe
Laughton
Northorpe
Kirton in Lindsey
Brandy Wharf
Holton le Moor
B1434
R. Idle
Heckdyke
Grayingham
B1205
Waddingham
Cove Resr.
Thornton le Moor
West Stockwith
East Stockwith
Misterton
Blyton
Blyborough
Snitterby
North Owersby
South Owersby
Usselby
Claxby
Normanby le Wold
B1225
B1403
A159
Walkerith
Pilham
Aisby
Willoughton
Atterby
Bishop Norton
Kingerby
Osgodby
Kirkby
Horse World
Otby
Walesby
Walkeringham
A161
Morton
Corringham
Hemswell
Glentham
Bishopbridge
A1103
Gringley on the Hill
Canal
A631
Beckingham
GAINSBOROUGH
Old Hall
B1433
York Model Railway
Spital in the Street
A631
West Rasen
Middle Rasen
Market Rasen
Springthorpe
Sturgate
Harpswell
Hemswell Cliff
Caenby
Clayworth
Saundby
Heapham
Glentworth
Normanby by-Spital
Owmby-by-Spital
Toft next Newton
Market Rasen
Bole
R. Trent
Sturgate
Upton
North Wheatley
South Wheatley
Lea
Knaith Park
Kexby
Fillingham
Saxby
Newton by Toft
Linwood
Legsby
A620
Hayton
Sturton le Steeple
Knaith
Willingham by Stow
B1398
A15
Spridlington
Buslingthorpe
Faldingworth
B1202
Bleasby
Bleasby Moor
Clarborough
Fenton
Gate Burton
B1241
Coates
Ingham
Cold Hanworth
Hackthorn
Friesthorpe
Lissington
West Torrington
Welham
North Leverton
Habblesthorpe
Littleborough
Marton
Stow
Cammeringham
Snarford
Wickenby
Holton cum Beckering
South Leverton
Cottam
A156
Thorpe in the Fallows
Brattleby
A1500
Aisthorpe
Welton Hill
Snelland
Welton
Grove
Sundown Adventureland
Torksey
Brampton
Sturton by Stow
Bransby Home of Rest for Horses
Scampton
Dunholme
Reasby
Fulnetby
Rand
Treswell
Rampton
Woodbeck
Broxholme
North Carlton
Lincolnshire Showground
Stainton by Langworth
Scothern
Wragby
Headon
Church Laneham
A1133
Fossdyke Navigation
LINCOLNSHIRE
Stokeham
Fenton
South Carlton
88
Langworth
Upton
Laneham
Laughterton
Kettlethorpe
Saxilby
R. Till
Riseholme
Nettleham
Sudbrooke
Apley
Kingthorpe
Askham
East Drayton
Dunham-on-Trent
Newton on Trent
A57
Burton-by-Lincoln
A46
A158
Barlings
Reepham
Toll
Broadholme
Ermine
North Greetwell
Low Barlings
Abbey
Ragnall
Darlton
A57
Thorney
Skellingthorpe
LINCOLN
Cherry Willingham
Fiskerton
Stainfield
East Markham
A6075
North Clifton
Tuxford
Fledborough
A46
Harby
B1378
New Boultham
B1308
Washingborough
Young Wood
High Marnham
Wigsley
Doddington
Doddington Hall
Birchwood
Boultham
Canwick
B1190
Branston Booths
Bardney
Skegby
Spalford
Low Marnham
South Clifton
Swanpool
B1003
B1190
Heighington
Normanton on Trent
Weston
Egmanton
Eagle Moor
Bracebridge
B1188
Bracebridge Heath
Branston
Potterhanworth Booths
A1
B1164
Grassthorpe
A1133
Whisby
Road Transport
Swallow Beck
Southrey
Eagle
Natural World Centre
North Scarle
Moorhouse
Sutton on Trent
Weecar
Eagle Barnsdale
A1434
North Hykeham
Potterhanworth
Girton
Thorpe on the Hill
A15
B1178
Ossington
Besthorpe
South Scarle
RAF Waddington
Waddington
Nocton
Wasps Nest
Sots Hole
Tanvats
Carlton-on-Trent
Morton
South Hykeham
Haddington
Dunston
AMSHIRE
Norwell Woodhouse
Norwell
Dolls
Swinderby
Witham St Hughs
Aubourn
Harmston
Metheringham
Cromwell
Collingham
R. Trent
A46
Thurlby
B1178
B1202
B1189
Caunton
Coleby
Blankney
Martin
A616
Holme
Norton Disney
Bassingham
A607
Boothby Graffoe
B1202
Metheringham Airfield
Timberland
Bathley
North Muskham
Langford
Little Carlton
B6325
Brough
Stapleford
Carlton-le-Moorland
R. Brant
Navenby
Scopwick
Kirkby Green
B1191
Thorpe Tilney
Walcott
A617
South Muskham
Winthorpe
Newark Showground
Newark Air
R. Witham
Wellingore
Rowston
B1189
NEWARK-ON-TRENT
Kelham
B6166
A17
Coddington
Temple Bruer Tower
Ashby de la Launde
Digby
Billinghay
Averham
Gilstrap
Town Hall
Millgate
New Balderton
A1
Heritage Room
Brant Broughton
Welbourn
B1191
Bloxholm
Dorrington
A612
Staythorpe
Beckingham
Rolleston
B6326
B6166
Stragglethorpe
Leadenham
North Ings Farm
Farndon
Hawton
Barnby in the Willows
Balderton
Fiskerton
Manor
Ruskington
A153
East Stoke
A46
Thorpe
Fenton
Fulbeck
A17
B1429
Cranwell
B1209
Anwick
Stoke Field 1487
R. Devon
Claypole
Stubton
75
Cranwell
R. Slea
Elston
Caythorpe
A607
Leasingham
Brandon
Frieston
Syerston
Cotham
Dry Doddington
Hough-on-the-Hill
Cranwell Aviation Heritage Centre
Evedon
Ewerby
Flintham
Normanton
B6403
Holdingham
North Rauceby
Sleaford
A17
Cogglesford Watermill
Kirkby la Thorpe
Howell
Sibthorpe
Carlton Scroop
Asgarby
Westborough
Gelston
Sudbrook
South Rauceby

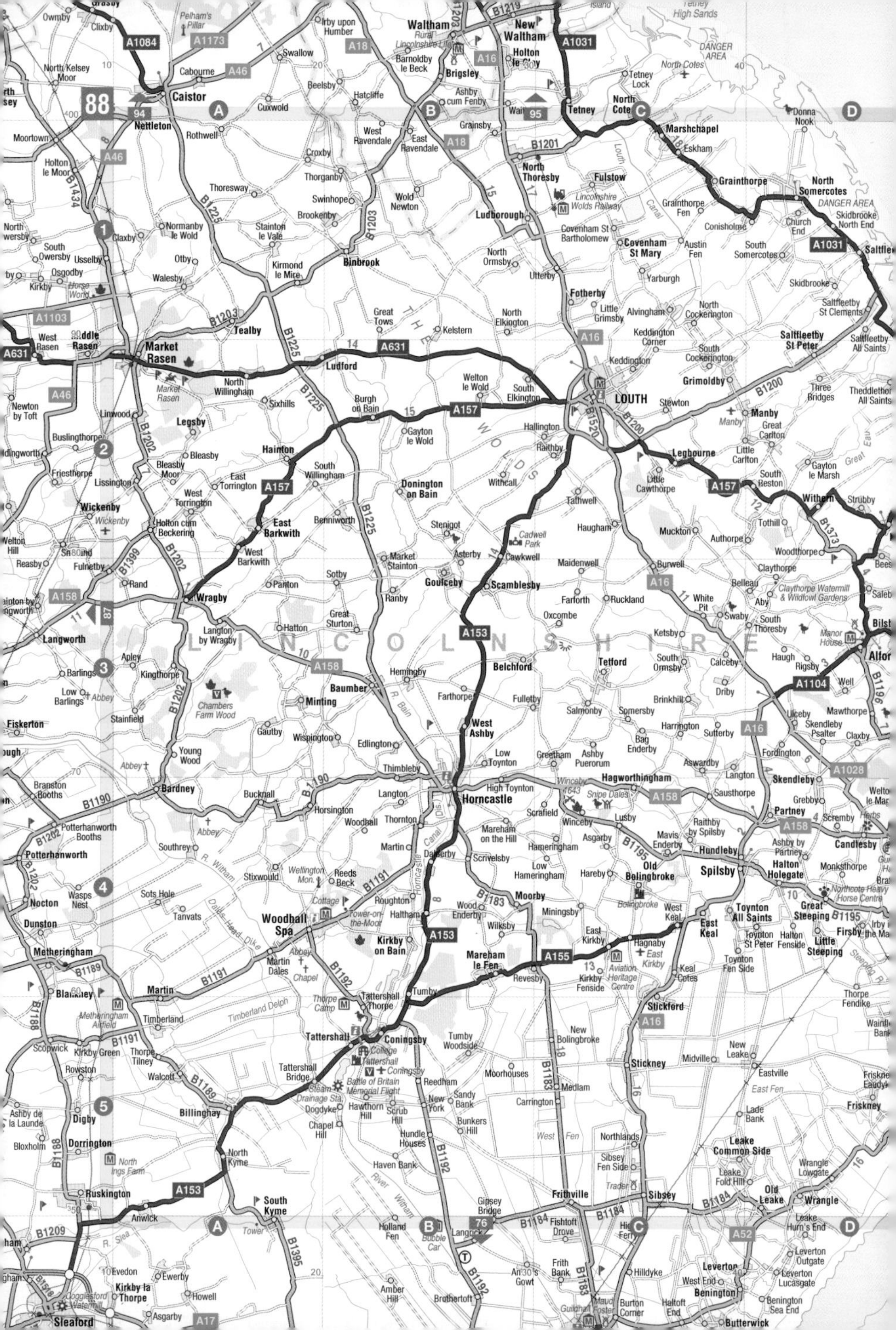
88
94
95
87
76
A
B
C
D
1
2
3
4
5
LINCOLNSHIRE
THE WOLDS
A1084
A1173
A46
A18
A16
B1219
B1203
A1031
B1201
B1225
B1434
A1103
A631
A157
B1202
B1399
A158
A153
B1190
B1191
B1189
B1188
B1202
B1209
B1518
B1395
A17
B1192
B1183
B1184
A155
A52
B1195
A1104
A1028
B1373
B1200
B1520
Grasby
Owmby
Clixby
Pelham's Pillar
Irby upon Humber
Waltham
Rural Lincolnshire Life
New Waltham
Holton le Clay
Tetney High Sands
DANGER AREA
North Cotes
Tetney Lock
Tetney
North Cotes
Swallow
North Kelsey Moor
Cabourne
Caistor
Barnoldby le Beck
Brigsley
Beelsby
Hatcliffe
Ashby cum Fenby
Waithe
Nettleton
Rothwell
Cuxwold
West Ravendale
East Ravendale
Grainsby
Marshchapel
Eskham
Donna Nook
Moortown
Holton le Moor
Croxby
Thorganby
Thoresway
Swinhope
Brookenby
Wold Newton
Binbrook
North Thoresby
Lincolnshire Wolds Railway
Fulstow
Grainthorpe
Grainthorpe Fen
North Somercotes
Conisholme
Church End
Skidbrooke North End
Normanby le Wold
Claxby
Stainton le Vale
Otby
Walesby
Kirmond le Mire
Ludborough
Covenham St Bartholomew
Covenham St Mary
Austin Fen
South Somercotes
Saltfleet
North Owersby
South Owersby
Usselby
Osgodby
Kirkby
Horse World
North Ormsby
Utterby
Yarburgh
Skidbrooke
Saltfleetby St Clements
Fotherby
Little Grimsby
Alvingham
North Cockerington
Tealby
West Rasen
Middle Rasen
Market Rasen
Great Tows
Kelstern
North Elkington
Keddington Corner
South Cockerington
Saltfleetby St Peter
Saltfleetby All Saints
Ludford
Keddington
Grimoldby
Newton by Toft
North Willingham
Sixhills
Burgh on Bain
Welton le Wold
South Elkington
LOUTH
Stewton
Three Bridges
Theddlethorpe All Saints
Linwood
Legsby
Gayton le Wold
Hallington
Manby
Great Carlton
Buslingthorpe
Bleasby
Hainton
Raithby
Legbourne
Little Carlton
Friesthorpe
Lissington
Bleasby Moor
East Torrington
South Willingham
Donington on Bain
Withcall
Little Cawthorpe
South Reston
Gayton le Marsh
Wickenby
West Torrington
Tathwell
Withern
Strubby
Welton Hill
Holton cum Beckering
East Barkwith
Benniworth
Stenigot
Cadwell Park
Haugham
Muckton
Authorpe
Tothill
Snarford
Reasby
Fulnetby
Rand
West Barkwith
Market Stainton
Asterby
Cawkwell
Maidenwell
Burwell
Woodthorpe
Claythorpe
Belleau
Claythorpe Watermill & Wildfowl Gardens
Aby
Wragby
Panton
Sotby
Goulceby
Scamblesby
Farforth
Ruckland
White Pit
Swaby
South Thoresby
Langworth
Ranby
Langton by Wragby
Hatton
Great Sturton
Oxcombe
Ketsby
Manor House
Bilsby
Alford
Apley
Barlings
Low Barlings
Kingthorpe
Hemingby
Belchford
Tetford
South Ormsby
Calceby
Haugh
Rigsby
Well
Chambers Farm Wood
Baumber
Minting
Farthorpe
Fulletby
Brinkhill
Driby
Stainfield
Fiskerton
Gautby
Wispington
Edlington
West Ashby
Salmonby
Somersby
Harrington
Sutterby
Ulceby
Mawthorpe
Skendleby Psalter
Claxby
Young Wood
Low Toynton
Greetham
Ashby Puerorum
Bag Enderby
Fordington
Aswardby
Branston Booths
Thimbleby
Hagworthingham
Langton
Skendleby
Grebby
Bardney
Bucknall
Horsington
Langton
Horncastle
High Toynton
Winceby 1643
Snipe Dales
Sausthorpe
Partney
Scremby
Candlesby
Potterhanworth Booths
Potterhanworth
Southrey
Woodhall
Thornton
Scrafield
Mareham on the Hill
Winceby
Lusby
Mavis Enderby
Raithby by Spilsby
Ashby by Partney
Halton Holegate
Hameringham
Asgarby
Low Hameringham
Hundleby
Spilsby
Monksthorpe
Martin
Dalderby
Scrivelsby
Hareby
Old Bolingbroke
Bolingbroke
Northcote Heavy Horse Centre
Nocton
Wasps Nest
Stixwould
Wellington Mon.
Reeds Beck
Roughton
Moorby
Sots Hole
Tanvats
Dunston
Woodhall Spa
Tower-on-the-Moor
Haltham
Wood Enderby
Wilksby
Miningsby
West Keal
East Keal
Toynton All Saints
Great Steeping
Firsby
Irby in the Marsh
Toynton St Peter
Halton Fenside
Little Steeping
Metheringham
Martin Dales
Abbey
Chapel
Kirkby on Bain
Mareham le Fen
Revesby
East Kirkby
Hagnaby
Aviation Heritage Centre
Kirkby Fenside
Keal Cotes
Toynton Fen Side
Blankney
Martin
Thorpe Camp
Tattershall Thorpe
Tumby
Stickford
Thorpe Fendike
Metheringham Airfield
Timberland
Timberland Delph
Tattershall
Coningsby
Tumby Woodside
New Bolingbroke
Wainfleet Bank
Scopwick
Kirkby Green
Thorpe Tilney
Rowston
Walcott
Tattershall Bridge
College
Tattershall
Battle of Britain Memorial Flight
Reedham
Moorhouses
Medlam
Stickney
Midville
New Leake
Eastville
East Fen
Friskney Eaudyke
Ashby de la Launde
Digby
Billinghay
Steam Drainage Sta.
Dogdyke
Hawthorn Hill
Scrub Hill
New York
Sandy Bank
Bunkers Hill
Carrington
Friskney
Bloxholm
Dorrington
North Kyme
Chapel Hill
Hundle Houses
West Fen
Northlands
Lade Bank
North Ings Farm
Haven Bank
River Witham
Sibsey Fen Side
Leake Common Side
Wrangle Lowgate
Trader
Leake Fold Hill
Ruskington
South Kyme
Gipsey Bridge
Frithville
Sibsey
Old Leake
Wrangle
Anwick
Tower
Holland Fen
Bubble Car
Langrick
Fishtoft Drove
Leake Hurn's End
R. Slea
Evedon
Ewerby
Kirkby la Thorpe
Howell
Asgarby
Doggleford Watermill
Sleaford
Amber Hill
Brothertoft
Anton's Gowt
Frith Bank
Hilldyke
Maud Foster
Burton Corner
Halltoft End
Leverton Outgate
Leverton
West End
Benington
Leverton Lucasgate
Benington Sea End
Butterwick
Guildhall

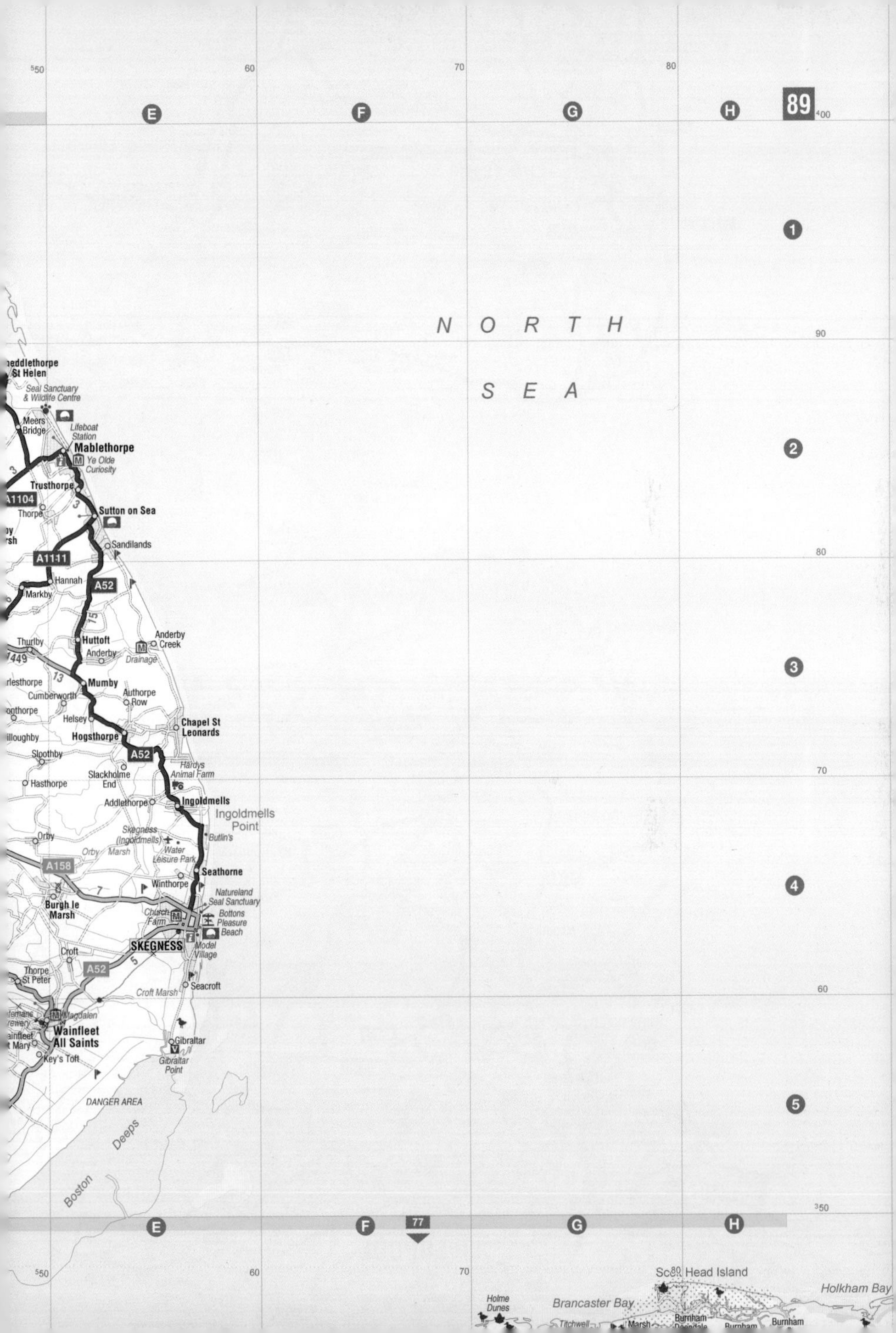

E
F
G
H
NORTH SEA
Saltfleetby St Helen
Seal Sanctuary & Wildlife Centre
Meers Bridge
Lifeboat Station
Mablethorpe
Ye Olde Curiosity
Trusthorpe
A1104
Thorpe
Sutton on Sea
Sandilands
A1111
Hannah
Markby
A52
Thurlby
Huttoft
Anderby
Anderby Creek
Drainage
Mumby
Cumberworth
Authorpe Row
Helsey
Hogsthorpe
Chapel St Leonards
Sloothby
Slackholme End
Hardys Animal Farm
Hasthorpe
Addlethorpe
Ingoldmells
Ingoldmells Point
Butlin's
Orby
Skegness (Ingoldmells)
Orby Marsh
Water Leisure Park
A158
Seathorne
Winthorpe
Burgh le Marsh
Natureland Seal Sanctuary
Church Farm
Bottons Pleasure Beach
SKEGNESS
Model Village
Croft
Thorpe St Peter
Seacroft
Croft Marsh
Magdalen
Wainfleet All Saints
Gibraltar
Gibraltar Point
Key's Toft
DANGER AREA
Boston Deeps
77
Holme Dunes
Brancaster Bay
Titchwell
Scolt Head Island
Burnham Deepdale
Burnham
Holkham Bay

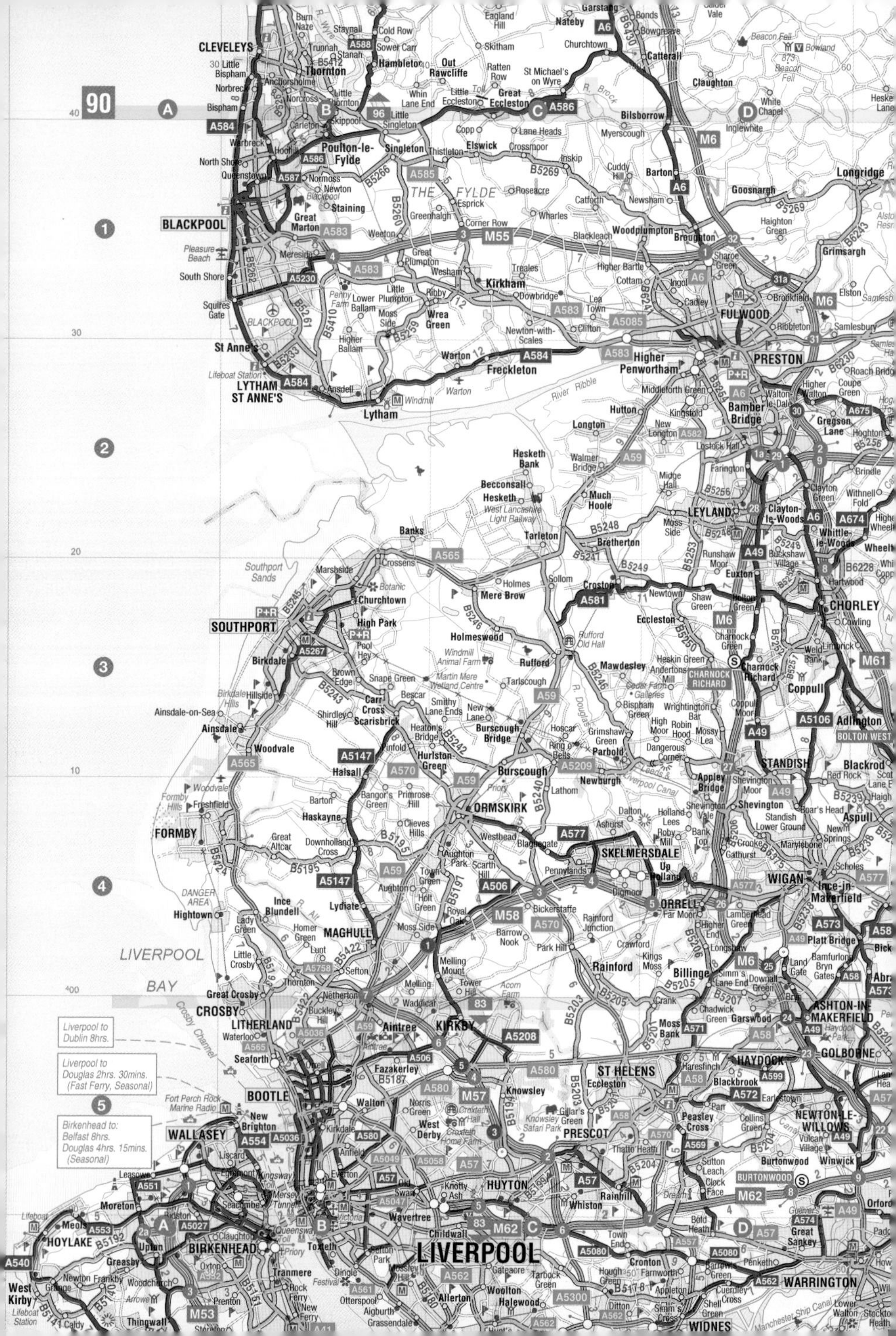
CLEVELEYS
Thornton
Hambleton
Out Rawcliffe
Garstang
Nateby
Churchtown
Catterall
St Michael's on Wyre
Great Eccleston
Little Eccleston
Bilsborrow
Claughton
Beacon Fell
Bowland
White Chapel
Inglewhite
Poulton-le-Fylde
Singleton
Elswick
Inskip
Barton
Goosnargh
Longridge
THE FYLDE
BLACKPOOL
Great Marton
Staining
Weeton
Woodplumpton
Broughton
Grimsargh
Kirkham
Wesham
Treales
Pleasure Beach
South Shore
Squires Gate
St Anne's
LYTHAM ST ANNE'S
Lytham
Warton
Freckleton
FULWOOD
PRESTON
Higher Penwortham
Samlesbury
River Ribble
Hutton
Longton
Bamber Bridge
Hesketh Bank
Becconsall
Hesketh
West Lancashire Light Railway
Much Hoole
LEYLAND
Tarleton
Bretherton
Banks
Southport Sands
Crossens
Marshside
Churchtown
SOUTHPORT
Birkdale
High Park
Mere Brow
Holmeswood
Croston
Eccleston
CHORLEY
Rufford
Rufford Old Hall
Mawdesley
Charnock Richard
CHARNOCK RICHARD
Coppull
Adlington
BOLTON WEST
Windmill Animal Farm
Martin Mere Wetland Centre
Scarisbrick
Ainsdale
Ainsdale-on-Sea
Woodvale
Halsall
Burscough
Burscough Bridge
Parbold
Dangerous Corner
STANDISH
Blackrod
Leeds & Liverpool Canal
Newburgh
Lathom
Appley Bridge
Shevington
ORMSKIRK
FORMBY
Freshfield
Haskayne
Great Altcar
Aughton
SKELMERSDALE
Up Holland
WIGAN
Ince-in-Makerfield
Hightown
Ince Blundell
Lydiate
MAGHULL
ORRELL
Bickerstaffe
Rainford
Billinge
LIVERPOOL BAY
Crosby
Great Crosby
LITHERLAND
Aintree
KIRKBY
ASHTON-IN-MAKERFIELD
HAYDOCK
GOLBORNE
Liverpool to Dublin 8hrs.
Liverpool to Douglas 2hrs. 30mins. (Fast Ferry, Seasonal)
Birkenhead to: Belfast 8hrs. Douglas 4hrs. 15mins. (Seasonal)
BOOTLE
Seaforth
Fazakerley
ST HELENS
Knowsley
Knowsley Safari Park
PRESCOT
NEWTON-LE-WILLOWS
WALLASEY
New Brighton
West Derby
HUYTON
Rainhill
Whiston
Moreton
HOYLAKE
BIRKENHEAD
Wavertree
LIVERPOOL
WARRINGTON
Great Sankey
Burtonwood
West Kirby
Tranmere
Allerton
Woolton
Halewood
Cronton
WIDNES
Manchester Ship Canal
M6
M55
M58
M57
M62
M53
M61

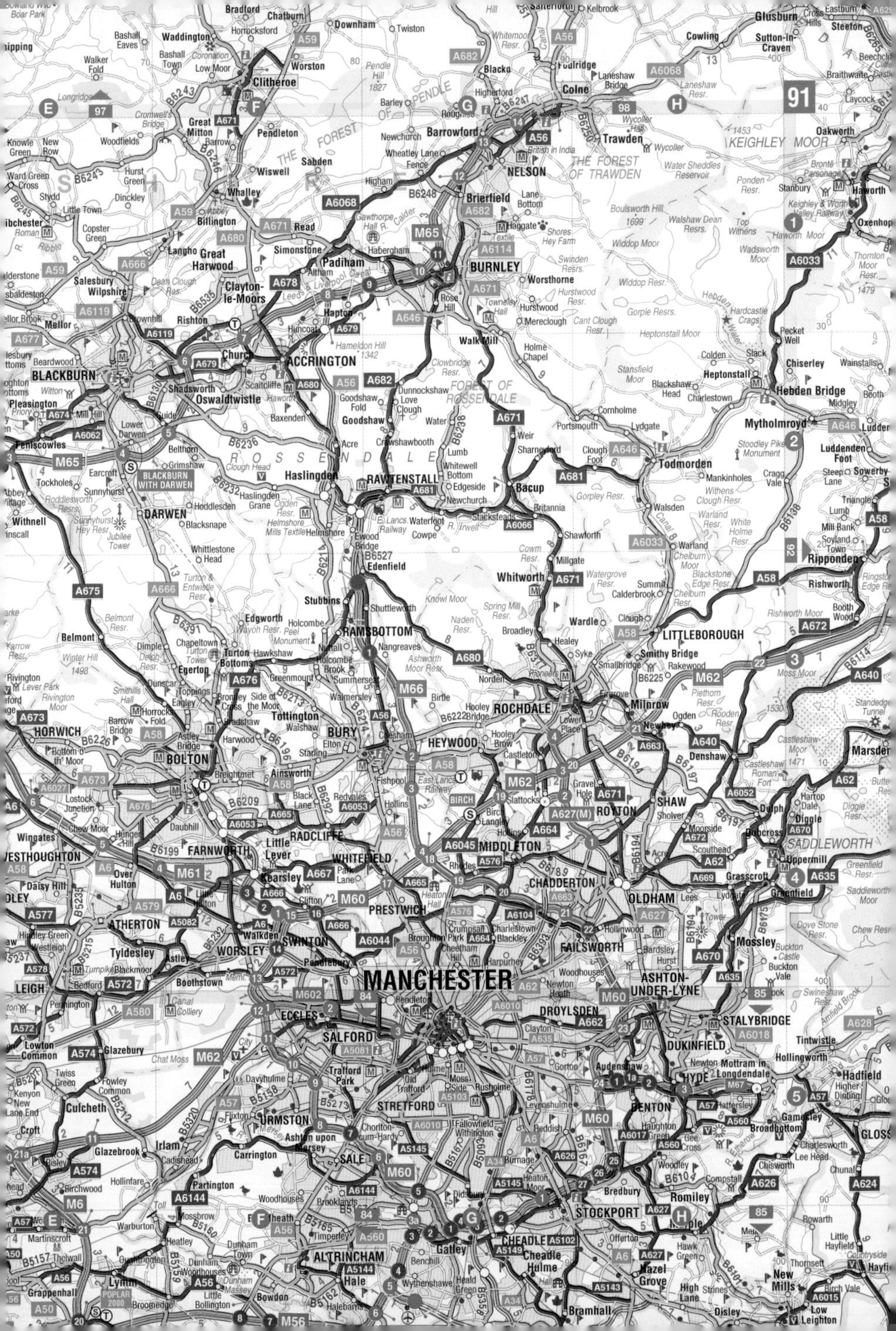

Bradford
Chatburn
Downham
Twiston
Kelbrook
Glusburn
Cross Hills
Eastburn
Steeton
Boar Park
Bashall Eaves
Waddington
Horrocksford
A59
Pendle Hill 1827
Whitemoor Resr.
A56
A682
Cowling
Sutton-in-Craven
Walker Fold
Bashall Town
Low Moor
Worston
Blacko
Foulridge
Laneshaw Bridge
A6068
Beechcliffe
Braithwaite
Clitheroe
Higherford
Colne
Laneshaw Resr.
91
Laycock
Longridge
97
Cromwell's Bridge
B6243
Great Mitton
Barrow
A671
Pendleton
Barley
THE FOREST OF PENDLE
Roughlee
B6247
98
Wycoller Hall
Oakworth
Knowle Green
New Row
Woodfields
Newchurch
Barrowford
A56
B6250
Trawden
Wycoller
1453
KEIGHLEY MOOR
Ward Green Cross
Hurst Green
Wiswell
Sabden
Wheatley Lane
Fence
British in India
NELSON
THE FOREST OF TRAWDEN
Water Sheddles Reservoir
Bronte Parsonage
Stydd
Dinckley
Whalley
Higham
B6248
Brierfield
Lane Bottom
Ponden Resr.
Stanbury
Haworth
Ribchester Roman
Little Town
Billington
A59
A6068
Gawthorpe Hall
A682
Haggate
Boulsworth Hill 1699
Walshaw Dean Resrs.
Top Withens
Keighley & Worth Valley Railway
Oxenhope
Copster Green
A680
A671
Read
M65
Shores Hey Farm
Textile
Haworth Moor
Langho
Great Harwood
Simonstone
Habergham
A6114
Widdop Moor
Wadsworth Moor
Thornton Moor Resr.
Salesbury
Wilpshire
A666
Padiham
Altham
BURNLEY
Swinden Resrs.
A6033
Dean Clough Res.
Clayton-le-Moors
A678
Leeds & Liverpool Canal
Worsthorne
Hurstwood Resr.
Widdop Resr.
1479
B6535
Hapton
Rose Hill
A671
Towneley Hall
Hurstwood
Gorple Resrs.
Hebden Water
Hardcastle Crags
A6119
Brownhill
Rishton
A646
Mereclough
Cant Clough Resr.
Heptonstall Moor
Mellor
A6119
Huncoat
A679
Walk Mill
Pecket Well
A677
Beardwood
Church
Hameldon Hill 1342
Holme Chapel
Colden
Slack
Chiserley
Wainstalls
A679
ACCRINGTON
Clowbridge Resr.
Stansfield Moor
Heptonstall
BLACKBURN
Shadsworth
Oswaldtwistle
Scaitcliffe
Haworth
A680
A56
A682
Dunnockshaw
FOREST OF ROSSENDALE
Blackshaw Head
Charlestown
Hebden Bridge
Booth
Pleasington Priory
Witton
Goodshaw Fold
Love Clough
Cornholme
Midgley
A674
Mill Hill
Guide
Baxenden
Goodshaw
Water
A671
Portsmouth
Lydgate
Mytholmroyd
A646
Luddenden
Feniscowles
A6062
Lower Darwen
Belthorn
B6236
Acre
Crawshawbooth
B6238
Weir
Clough Foot
Todmorden
Stoodley Pike Monument
Luddenden Foot
M65
Grimshaw
ROSSENDALE
Lumb
Sharneyford
A646
Mankinholes
Earcroft
Clough Head
Haslingden
Whitewell Bottom
A681
Cragg Vale
Steep Lane
Sowerby
Tockholes
Sunnyhurst
BLACKBURN WITH DARWEN
RAWTENSTALL
A681
Edgeside
Bacup
Withens Clough Resr.
Roddlesworth Resrs.
B6232
Haslingden Grane
Ogden Resr.
Newchurch
Britannia
Gorpley Resr.
Walsden
Triangle
Abbey Village
Hoddlesden
Helmshore Mills Textile
E. Lancs Railway
Waterfoot
Stacksteads
A6066
Warland Resr.
White Holme Resr.
Lumb
Withnell
DARWEN
Blacksnape
Helmshore
Cowpe
R. Irwell
Shawforth
A6033
Mill Bank
Sunnyhurst Hey Resr.
Jubilee Tower
Ewood Bridge
Cowm Resr.
Warland
Soyland Town
A58
Whittlestone Head
B6527
Edenfield
Millgate
Chelburn Moor
92
Ripponden
A675
A666
Turton & Entwistle Resr.
Whitworth
A671
Watergrove Resr.
Blackstone Edge Resr.
A58
Ringstone Edge Resr.
Stubbins
Shuttleworth
Knowl Moor
Spring Mill Resr.
Summit
Calderbrook
Chelburn Resr.
Rishworth
Belmont Resr.
Edgworth
Wayoh Resr.
Holcombe
Peel Monument
RAMSBOTTOM
Naden Resr.
Rishworth Moor
Booth Wood
Belmont
B6391
Chapeltown
Turton Tower
Nuttall
Broadley
Wardle
Clough
LITTLEBOROUGH
A672
Dimple
Delph Resr.
Turton Bottoms
Hawkshaw
Nangreaves
Ashworth Moor Resr.
Healey
Smithy Bridge
Winter Hill 1498
Egerton
Holcombe Brook
A680
Syke
Smallbridge
Rakewood
22
Moss Moor
Rivington
Lever Park
A676
Greenmount
Summerseat
Norden
Pioneers
B6225
M62
A640
Rivington Moor
Dunscar
Toppings
Smithills Hall
Eagley
B6213
M66
Birtle
Firgrove
Plethorn Resr.
Horrocks Fold
Bromley Cross
Side of the Moor
Walmersley
Milnrow
Ogden
Rooden Resr.
Standedge Tunnel
A673
Barrow Bridge
Bradshaw
Tottington
B6222
Hooley Bridge
ROCHDALE
1530
HORWICH
A58
Astley Bridge
Walshaw
BURY
Chesham
HEYWOOD
Lower Place
Newhey
A663
A640
Castleshaw Moor 1471
Marsden
B6226
Bottom o' th' Moor
Harwood
B6196
Elton
Hooley Brow
Castleton
B6194
B6197
Denshaw
Castleshaw Roman Fort
BOLTON
Starling
A58
A6052
A62
A673
A6027
Breightmet
Ainsworth
Fishpool
East Lancs Railway
M62
Gravel Hole
A671
Harrop Edge
Lostock Junction
A676
Black Lane
B6292
Redvales
A6053
Hollins
BIRCH
Slattocks
A627(M)
ROYTON
SHAW
Delph
Diggle
Diggle Resr.
A6
B6209
A665
Birch
Langley
Hollins
A664
Sholver
B6197
A670
Chew Moor
Hunger Hill
Daubhill
A6053
RADCLIFFE
A56
A6045
MIDDLETON
Moorside
Dobcross
SADDLEWORTH
Wingates
A672
WESTHOUGHTON
B6199
FARNWORTH
Little Lever
WHITEFIELD
Rhodes
A576
Acre
Scouthead
A62
Uppermill
Greenfield Resr.
A58
Over Hulton
M61
Kearsley
A667
Park Lane
A665
Heaton Park
CHADDERTON
A669
Grasscroft
A635
Daisy Hill
A6
Little Hulton
A666
Clifton
M60
PRESTWICH
A576
A663
OLDHAM
Lees
Lydgate
Greenfield
Saddleworth Moor
A577
A579
A5082
A6
A666
A6104
Crumpsall
Charlestown
A627
B6194
B6175
Dove Stone Resr.
Chew Resr.
ATHERTON
B5235
Walkden
SWINTON
A6044
Broughton Park
A664
Blackley
Hollinwood
Tower
Mossley
Hindley Green
Westleigh
Tyldesley
Astley
B5232
WORSLEY
Cheetham Hill
Harpurhey
B6393
FAILSWORTH
Bardsley
Hurst
A670
Buckton Castle
Turnpike
Blackmoor
Pendlebury
A572
Woodhouses
ASHTON-UNDER-LYNE
Buckton Vale
A578
Boothstown
MANCHESTER
A62
Newton Heath
M60
A635
Swineshaw Resr.
LEIGH
Bedford
A572
Canal Colliery
M602
84
Pendleton
A6010
DROYLSDEN
85
STALYBRIDGE
A628
Pennington
A580
ECCLES
SALFORD
A662
A6018
Tintwistle
A572
A5081
Clayton
A635
DUKINFIELD
Hollingworth
Lowton Common
A574
Glazebury
Chat Moss
M62
A57
Gorton
Audenshaw
Newton
Mottram in Longdendale
Twiss Green
Trafford Park
Hulme
Moss Side
Rusholme
B6178
HYDE
Hadfield
Kenyon
Fowley Common
Davyhulme
Old Trafford
A5103
M67
Higher Dinting
B5207
B5212
A57
B5158
STRETFORD
Levenshulme
A57
Hattersley
Gamesley
New Lane End
Culcheth
URMSTON
A6010
M60
DENTON
A560
Broadbottom
Flixton
Ashton upon Mersey
Chorlton-cum-Hardy
Fallowfield
Withington
Reddish
Haughton Green
Croft
B5320
A6017
Gee Cross
Charlesworth
Lee Head
GLOSSOP
Glazebrook
Irlam
Carrington
A5145
B5167
B5093
A6
A626
A560
Cadishead
SALE
A34
Burnage
B6167
River Etherow
Chisworth
Chunal
Woodley
B6104
Compstall
A626
A624
A574
Hollinfare
M60
A5145
Heaton Moor
Bredbury
Romiley
Partington
A6144
Birchwood
A6144
Woodhouses
Brooklands
Didsbury
M6
Toll
Mossbrow
84
STOCKPORT
A627
85
Rowarth
Warburton
B5160
A56
B5165
Timperley
A560
Gatley
CHEADLE
A5102
Marple
Mellor
A57
Martinscroft
Heatley
Dunham Town
Benchill
A5149
Offerton
Cheadle Hulme
A6
A627
Hawk Green
Little Hayfield
A50
B5157
Thelwall
Oughtrington
Dunham Woodhouses
ALTRINCHAM
Wythenshawe
Heald Green
B5358
Hazel Grove
B6101
Thornsett
Countryside
Hayfield
A56
Lymm
B5159
A56
A5144
Hale
A5143
High Lane
Strines
New Mills
Birch Vale
Grappenhall
POPLAR 2000
Dunham Massey
Little Bollington
Bowdon
B5162
Hale Barns
A34
Bramhall
Disley
A6015
A50
Broomedge
M56
Low Leighton

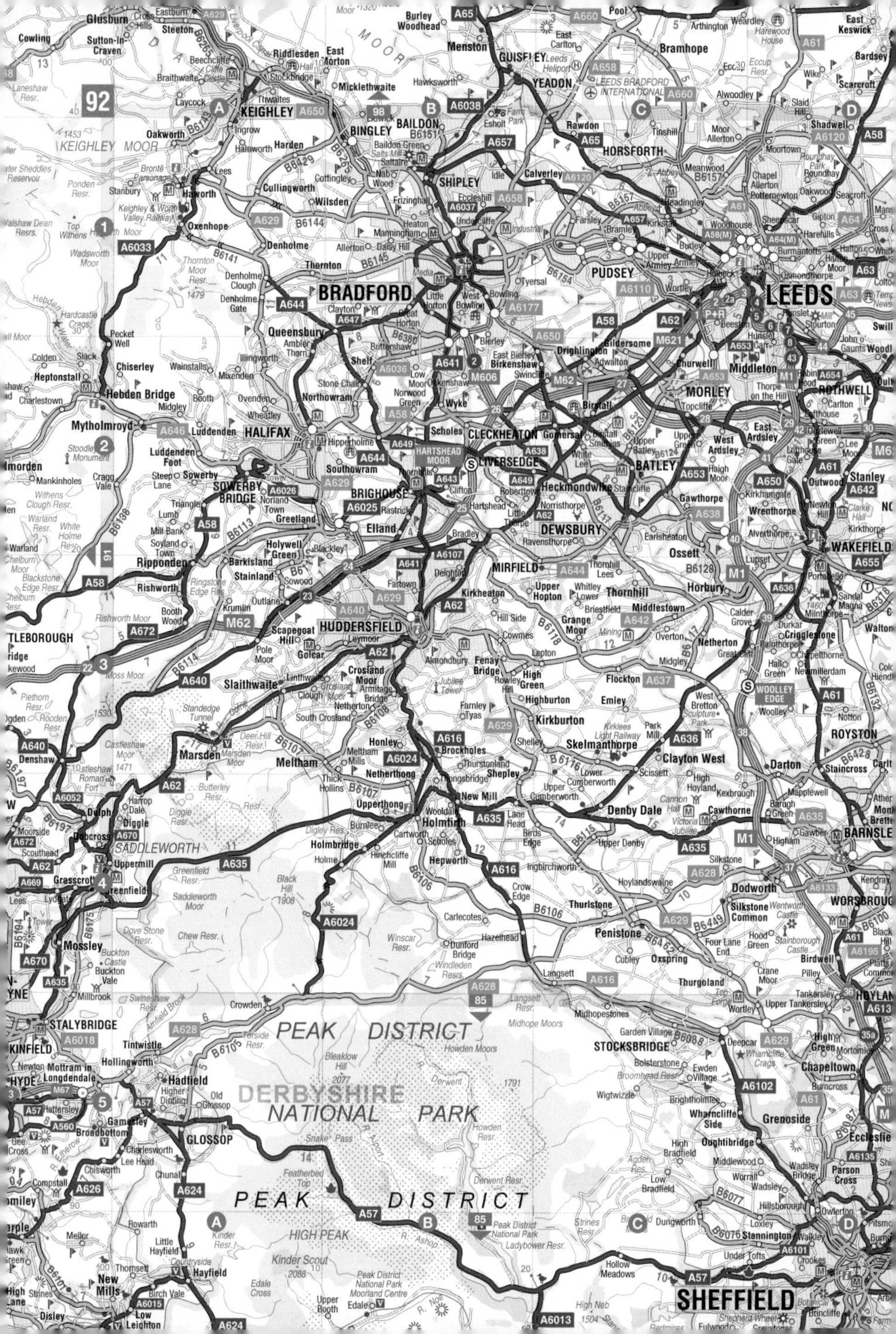

92
Glusburn
Cowling
Sutton-in-Craven
Steeton
Riddlesden
East Morton
Burley Woodhead
Menston
Pool
Arthington
Weardley
East Keswick
Bramhope
GUISELEY
YEADON
KEIGHLEY
BINGLEY
BAILDON
LEEDS BRADFORD INTERNATIONAL
Rawdon
HORSFORTH
Shadwell
Oakworth
KEIGHLEY MOOR
Haworth
Cullingworth
Wilsden
SHIPLEY
Calverley
Oxenhope
Denholme
Thornton
BRADFORD
PUDSEY
LEEDS
Queensbury
Hebden Bridge
Heptonstall
Mytholmroyd
HALIFAX
Northowram
Cleckheaton
LIVERSEDGE
Birstall
MORLEY
ROTHWELL
Middleton
Batley
Heckmondwike
DEWSBURY
BRIGHOUSE
SOWERBY BRIDGE
Elland
Greetland
Ripponden
Rishworth
MIRFIELD
Thornhill
Ossett
Horbury
WAKEFIELD
HUDDERSFIELD
Slaithwaite
Marsden
Meltham
Honley
Holmfirth
Kirkburton
Skelmanthorpe
Clayton West
Denby Dale
Darton
ROYSTON
BARNSLEY
Penistone
Dodworth
Oxspring
Thurgoland
STOCKSBRIDGE
Deepcar
Chapeltown
Grenoside
Ecclesfield
Oughtibridge
SADDLEWORTH
Uppermill
Delph
Diggle
Greenfield
Mossley
STALYBRIDGE
HYDE
Hollingworth
Hadfield
GLOSSOP
PEAK DISTRICT
DERBYSHIRE NATIONAL PARK
PEAK DISTRICT
HIGH PEAK
Kinder Scout
Hayfield
New Mills
Edale
Upper Booth
Stannington
SHEFFIELD

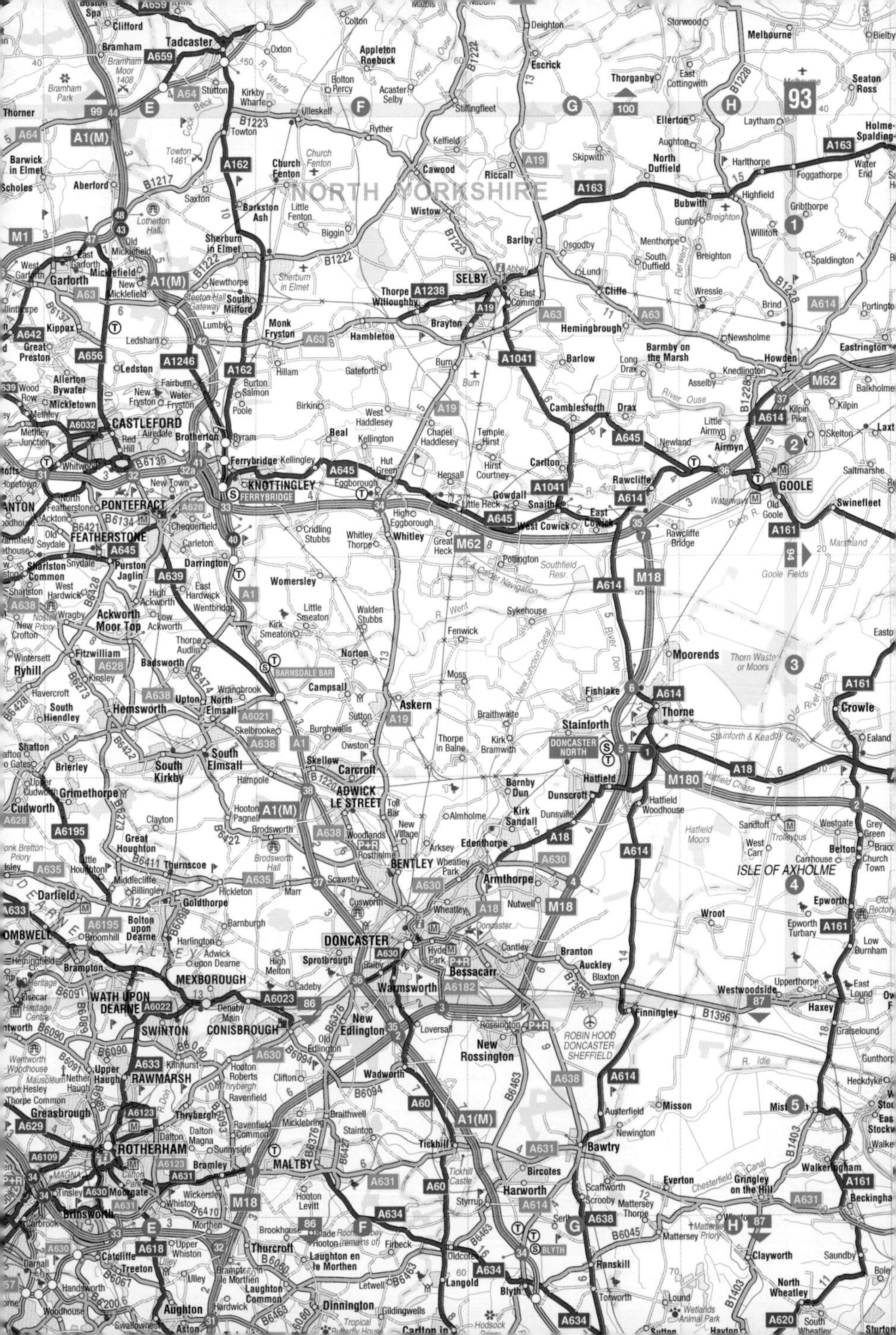

93
NORTH YORKSHIRE
Boston Spa
Clifford
Tadcaster
Bramham
Bramham Moor 1408
Bramham Park
Thorner
Colton
Oxton
Appleton Roebuck
Bolton Percy
Acaster Selby
Ulleskelf
Stutton
Kirkby Wharfe
Towton
Towton 1461
Ryther
Church Fenton
Deighton
Escrick
Stillingfleet
Kelfield
Cawood
Riccall
Storwood
Melbourne
Thorganby
East Cottingwith
Ellerton
Aughton
Skipwith
North Duffield
Bubwith
Seaton Ross
Laytham
Holme-Spalding-Moor
Harlthorpe
Foggathorpe
Highfield
Gribthorpe
Willitoft
Spaldington
Water End
Bielby
Barwick in Elmet
Scholes
Aberford
Saxton
Barkston Ash
Little Fenton
Biggin
Wistow
Barlby
Osgodby
Menthorpe
South Duffield
Breighton
Lund
Lotherton Hall
Old Micklefield
Micklefield
New Micklefield
Sherburn in Elmet
Newthorpe
South Milford
Steeton Hall Gateway
West Garforth
East Garforth
Garforth
Kippax
Great Preston
Ledsham
Lumby
Monk Fryston
Thorpe Willoughby
Selby
Abbey
East Common
Brayton
Hambleton
Cliffe
Hemingbrough
Wressle
Brind
Portington
Newsholme
Howden
Eastrington
Ledston
Fairburn
Burton Salmon
Hillam
Gateforth
Burn
Barlow
Long Drax
Barmby on the Marsh
Asselby
Knedlington
Balkholme
Allerton Bywater
New Fryston
Water Fryston
Poole
Birkin
West Haddlesey
Chapel Haddlesey
Temple Hirst
Camblesforth
Drax
Little Airmyn
Airmyn
Kilpin Pike
Kilpin
Skelton
Laxton
Mickletown
Methley
Methley Junction
Castleford
Airedale
Red Hill
Brotherton
Byram
Beal
Kellington
Hirst Courtney
Carlton
Newland
Whitwood
Ferrybridge
Kellingley
Hut Green
Hensall
Rawcliffe
Goole
Saltmarshe
Knottingley
New Town
Eggborough
Little Heck
Gowdall
Snaith
East Cowick
West Cowick
Old Goole
Swinefleet
Pontefract
North Featherstone
Ackton
Featherstone
Chequerfield
Carleton
Cridling Stubbs
High Eggborough
Whitley Thorpe
Whitley
Great Heck
Pollington
Southfield Resr.
Rawcliffe Bridge
Marshland
Goole Fields
Old Snydale
Snydale
Sharlston Common
Sharlston
West Hardwick
Purston Jaglin
Darrington
East Hardwick
Wentbridge
Womersley
High Ackworth
Low Ackworth
Ackworth Moor Top
Wragby
Nostell Priory
New Crofton
Little Smeaton
Kirk Smeaton
Walden Stubbs
Sykehouse
Fenwick
Thorpe Audlin
Wintersett
Fitzwilliam
Ryhill
Kinsley
Badsworth
Norton
Moss
Moorends
Thorn Waste or Moors
Eastoft
Havercroft
South Hiendley
Hemsworth
Upton
North Elmsall
Wrangbrook
Barnsdale Bar
Campsall
Askern
Fishlake
Thorne
Crowle
Braithwaite
Stainforth
Skelbrooke
Burghwallis
Sutton
Shafton
Brierley
South Kirkby
South Elmsall
Owston
Thorpe in Balne
Kirk Bramwith
Doncaster North
Ealand
Stainforth & Keadby Canal
Upper Cudworth
Grimethorpe
Cudworth
Hampole
Skellow
Carcroft
Adwick le Street
Toll Bar
Barnby Dun
Hatfield
Dunscroft
Hatfield Chase
Hatfield Woodhouse
Sandtoft
Westgate
Grey Green
Hooton Pagnell
Clayton
Brodsworth
Almholme
Kirk Sandall
Dunsville
Hatfield Moors
West Carr
Trolleybus
Carrhouse
Belton
Church Town
Great Houghton
Woodlands
New Village
Arksey
Edenthorpe
Isle of Axholme
Thurnscoe
Brodsworth Hall
Rostholme
Bentley
Wheatley Park
Armthorpe
Little Houghton
Middlecliffe
Billingley
Hickleton
Marr
Scawsby
Cusworth
Nutwell
Epworth
Epworth Turbary
Darfield
Goldthorpe
Bolton upon Dearne
Barnburgh
Wheatley
Wroot
Low Burnham
Wombwell
Broomhill
Dearne Valley
Harlington
Adwick upon Dearne
High Melton
Doncaster
Hyde Park
Balby
Sprotbrough
Bessacarr
Cantley
Branton
Auckley
Blaxton
Hemingfield
Brampton
Elsecar Heritage Centre
Mexborough
Cadeby
Warmsworth
Westwoodside
East Lound
Haxey
Wath upon Dearne
Denaby Main
Conisbrough
Swinton
New Edlington
Old Edlington
Loversall
Rossington
New Rossington
Robin Hood Doncaster Sheffield
Finningley
Graiseslound
Gunthorpe
Wentworth
Wentworth Woodhouse Mausoleum
Kilnhurst
Hooton Roberts
Thrybergh
Clifton
Wadworth
R. Idle
Heckdyke
Upper Haugh
Nether Haugh
Rawmarsh
Ravenfield
Austerfield
Misson
Misterton
Hoyland Common
Thorpe Common
Greasbrough
Micklebring
Stainton
Newington
Dalton
Dalton Magna
Ravenfield Common
Tickhill
Bawtry
Stockwith
Rotherham
Magna
Clifton Park
Sunnyside
Bramley
Maltby
Bircotes
Walkeringham
Tinsley
Moorgate
Wickersley
Whiston
Tickhill Castle
Harworth
Styrrup
Scaftworth
Everton
Chesterfield Canal
Gringley on the Hill
Beckingham
Brinsworth
Hooton Levitt
Scrooby
Mattersey Thorpe
Mattersey
Mattersey Priory
Wiseton
Carbrook
Morthen
Brookhouse
Slade Hooton
Roche Abbey (remains of)
Firbeck
Oldcotes
Serlby
Blyth
Catcliffe
Upper Whiston
Thurcroft
Laughton en le Morthen
Clayworth
Saundby
Darnall
Treeton
Ulley
Brampton en le Morthen
Langold
Ranskill
Handsworth
Laughton Common
Letwell
Woodhouse
Aughton
Hardwick
Dinnington
Gildingwells
Torworth
Lound
Wetlands Animal Park
North Wheatley
South Wheatley
Swallownest
Aston
Tropical Butterfly House
Hodsock Priory
Carlton in Lindrick
Sutton
Hayton
Sturton
River Ouse
River Derwent
R. Aire
R. Went
River Don
Old River Don
Aire & Calder Navigation
New Junction Canal
Dutch R.
A1(M)
A1
M1
M18
M62
M180
A19
A64
A63
A162
A659
A1246
A1238
A1041
A645
A614
A163
A638
A639
A628
A656
A642
A6032
A6021
A630
A6182
A18
A635
A6195
A6023
A6022
A633
A6123
A629
A6109
A631
A618
A634
A60
A161
A620
B1222
B1223
B1217
B1228
B6136
B6134
B6421
B6428
B6474
B6422
B6273
B6411
B6098
B6097
B6089
B6090
B6094
B6376
B6427
B6463
B6410
B6067
B6060
B6200
B6045
B1403
B1396
B1220
B6093
99
100
94
86
87

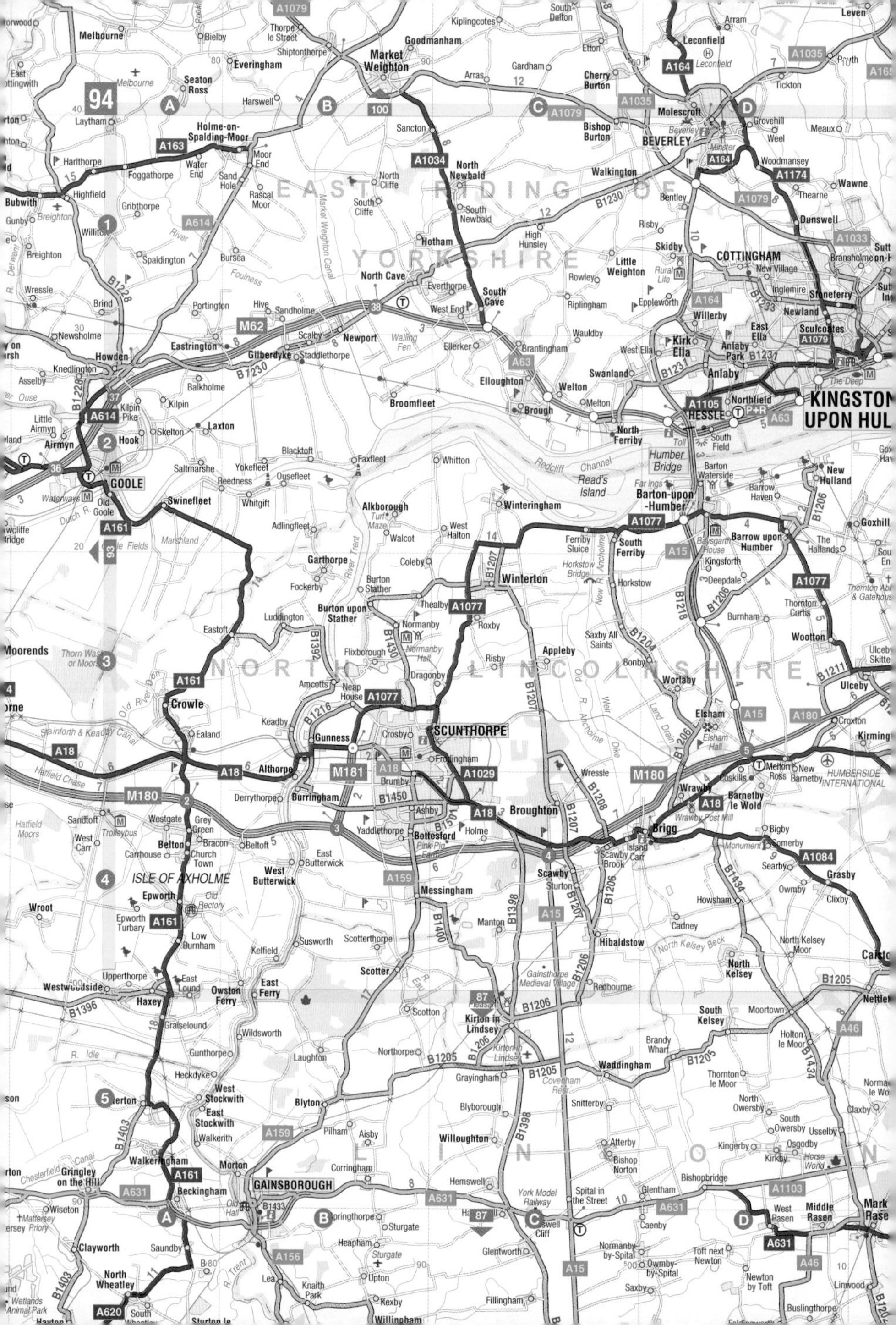

94
A1079
Melbourne
Bielby
Thorpe le Street
South Dalton
Kiplingcotes
Goodmanham
Market Weighton
Shiptonthorpe
Everingham
Seaton Ross
Harswell
Etton
Gardham
Arras
Cherry Burton
Leconfield
Arram
Leven
A1035
A164
Tickton
Laytham
Holme-on-Spalding-Moor
A163
Moor End
Water End
Sand Hole
Harlthorpe
Foggathorpe
Highfield
Bubwith
Gribthorpe
Rascal Moor
Breighton
Willitoft
Spaldington
A614
Bursea
East Cottingwith
100
Sancton
A1034
North Newbald
North Cliffe
South Cliffe
South Newbald
Hotham
EAST RIDING OF YORKSHIRE
Molescroft
Beverley
BEVERLEY
Minster
Bishop Burton
Walkington
Bentley
Risby
Skidby
Rural Life
Little Weighton
Rowley
Riplingham
Eppleworth
COTTINGHAM
New Village
Grovehill
Weel
Meaux
Woodmansey
A1174
Wawne
Thearne
Dunswell
A1033
A1079
B1230
High Hunsley
Wressle
Brind
Portington
Hive
Sandholme
North Cave
Everthorpe
South Cave
West End
M62
Newsholme
Eastrington
Gilberdyke
Staddlethorpe
Scalby
Newport
Walling Fen
Ellerker
Brantingham
Wauldby
West Ella
Kirk Ella
Willerby
Anlaby Park
East Ella
Inglemire
Newland
Sculcoates
Stoneferry
Bransholme
Howden
Knedlington
Asselby
Balkholme
B1230
Swanland
Anlaby
B1231
A63
Elloughton
Welton
Melton
Brough
Broomfleet
Kilpin
Kilpin Pike
Little Airmyn
Airmyn
A614
Hook
Skelton
Laxton
North Ferriby
A1105
HESSLE
Northfield
KINGSTON UPON HULL
The Deep
GOOLE
Old Goole
Waterways
Saltmarshe
Yokefleet
Blacktoft
Faxfleet
Reedness
Ousefleet
Whitgift
Whitton
Redcliff Channel
Read's Island
Humber Bridge
South Field
Barton Waterside
Far Ings
Barton-upon-Humber
Barrow Haven
New Holland
Swinefleet
A161
Marshland
Adlingfleet
Alkborough
Turf Maze
Walcot
West Halton
Winteringham
Ferriby Sluice
South Ferriby
A1077
Barrow upon Humber
Goxhill
The Hallands
Garthorpe
Fockerby
Burton Stather
Burton upon Stather
Coleby
Winterton
Horkstow Bridge
Horkstow
Baysgarth House
Kingsforth
Deepdale
Thornton Abbey & Gatehouse
Thornton Curtis
Burnham
Wootton
Luddington
Eastoft
Moorends
Thorn Waste or Moors
Thealby
Normanby
Normanby Hall
Roxby
Flixborough
Risby
Appleby
Saxby All Saints
Bonby
Worlaby
Ulceby
Ulceby Skitter
NORTH LINCOLNSHIRE
Amcotts
Neap House
Dragonby
Crowle
Eaaland
Keadby
Gunness
Crosby
SCUNTHORPE
Frodingham
Elsham
Elsham Hall
A15
A180
Croxton
Kirmington
Stainforth & Keadby Canal
A18
Hatfield Chase
Althorpe
M181
Brumby
A1029
Wressle
M180
Melton Ross
New Barnetby
HUMBERSIDE INTERNATIONAL
Coskills
Wrawby
Barnetby le Wold
Wrawby Post Mill
Derrythorpe
Burringham
B1450
Ashby
Broughton
Brigg
Island Carr
Bigby
Somerby
Sandtoft
Trolleybus
Westgate
Grey Green
Belton
Bracon
Beltoft
Yaddlethorpe
Bottesford
Holme
Scawby Brook
Scawby
Sturton
Searby
A1084
Grasby
Hatfield Moors
West Carr
Carrhouse
Church Town
East Butterwick
West Butterwick
Pink Pig Farm
Messingham
ISLE OF AXHOLME
Epworth
Old Rectory
Epworth Turbary
Wroot
A159
Manton
Howsham
Cadney
Owmby
Clixby
Low Burnham
Kelfield
Susworth
Scotterthorpe
Hibaldstow
North Kelsey Beck
North Kelsey Moor
North Kelsey
Caistor
Upperthorpe
Westwoodside
East Lound
Haxey
Owston Ferry
East Ferry
Scotter
Gainsthorpe Medieval Village
Redbourne
B1205
Nettleton
B1396
Graiselound
Wildsworth
Scotton
Kirton in Lindsey
B1206
South Kelsey
Moortown
Holton le Moor
A46
R. Idle
Gunthorpe
Laughton
Northorpe
Kirton in Lindsey
Brandy Wharf
Heckdyke
Grayingham
Waddingham
Covenham Resr.
Thornton le Moor
West Stockwith
East Stockwith
Blyton
Blyborough
Snitterby
North Owersby
South Owersby
Usselby
Claxby
Walkerith
Pilham
Aisby
Willoughton
Atterby
Bishop Norton
Kingerby
Osgodby
Kirkby
Horse World
Walkeringham
Chesterfield Canal
Gringley on the Hill
Morton
Corringham
GAINSBOROUGH
Hemswell
Spital in the Street
Glentham
Bishopbridge
A1103
Middle Rasen
West Rasen
Market Rasen
Beckingham
A631
Wiseton
Mattersey Priory
Old Hall
B1433
Springthorpe
Sturgate
York Model Railway
Hemswell Cliff
Caenby
A631
Clayworth
Saundby
Heapham
Glentworth
Normanby-by-Spital
Owmby-by-Spital
Toft next Newton
Newton by Toft
A156
Upton
North Wheatley
A620
South Wheatley
Wetlands Animal Park
Lea
Knaith Park
Kexby
Saxby
Fillingham
Willingham
Linwood
Buslingthorpe
B1403

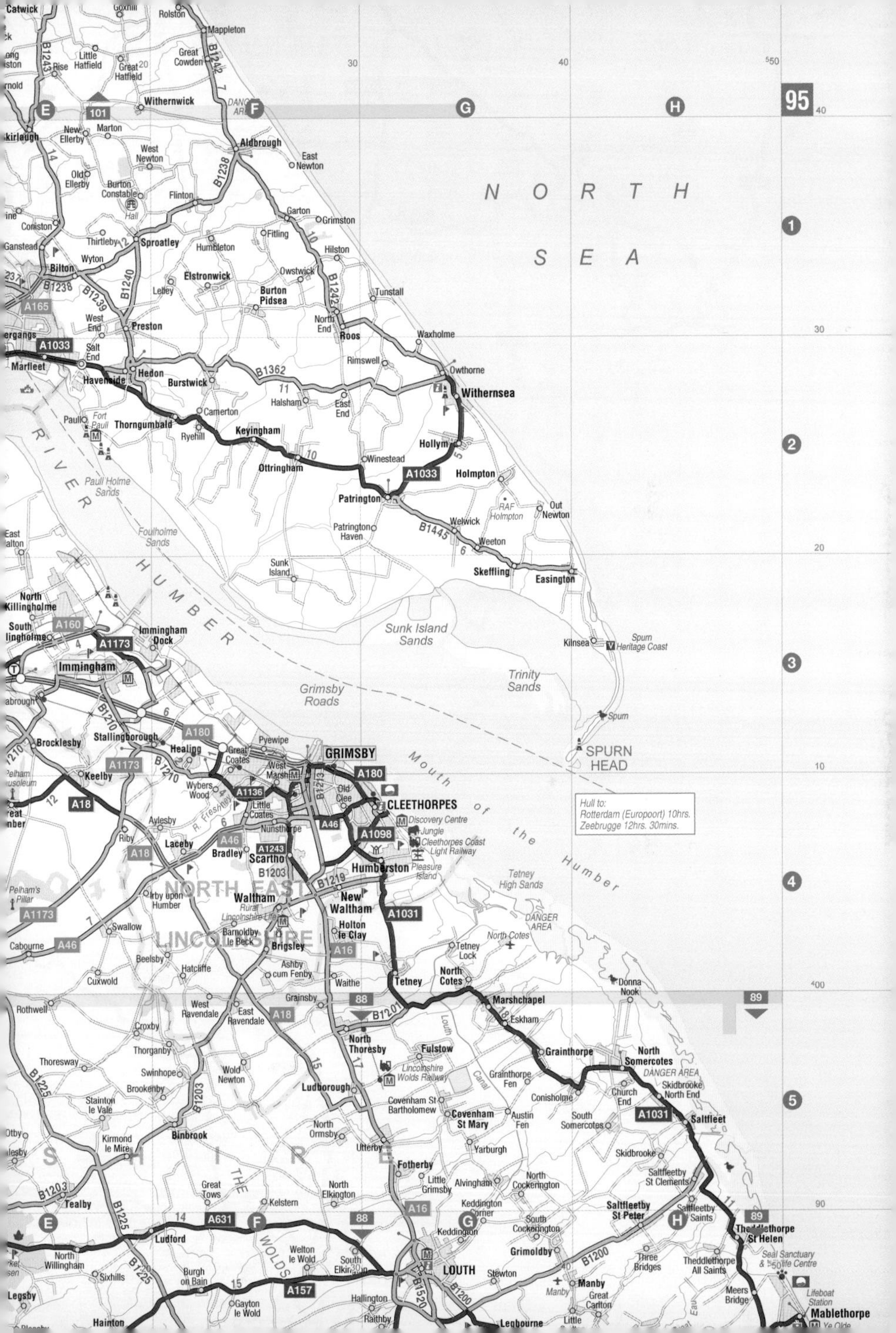
95
NORTH SEA
Catwick
Rolston
Mappleton
Little Hatfield
Great Hatfield
Great Cowden
Rise
Withernwick
Marton
New Ellerby
Skirlaugh
Aldbrough
East Newton
West Newton
Old Ellerby
Burton Constable
Hall
Flinton
Garton
Grimston
Coniston
Thirtleby
Sproatley
Fitling
Hilston
Ganstead
Wyton
Humbleton
Bilton
Elstronwick
Owstwick
Lelley
Burton Pidsea
Tunstall
West End
Preston
North End
Roos
Waxholme
Salt End
Rimswell
Marfleet
Havenside
Hedon
Burstwick
B1362
Owthorne
Withernsea
Halsham
East End
Paull
Fort Paull
Thorngumbald
Camerton
Ryehill
Keyingham
Hollym
Ottringham
Winestead
A1033
Holmpton
Patrington
RAF Holmpton
Out Newton
Paull Holme Sands
Welwick
Patrington Haven
B1445
Weeton
Foulholme Sands
Skeffling
Easington
Sunk Island
East Halton
North Killingholme
South Killingholme
A160
Immingham Dock
A1173
Immingham
Sunk Island Sands
Kilnsea
Spurn Heritage Coast
RIVER HUMBER
Trinity Sands
Grimsby Roads
Spurn
SPURN HEAD
Brocklesby
Stallingborough
A180
Healing
Pyewipe
Great Coates
GRIMSBY
West Marsh
Keelby
Wybers Wood
A1136
Old Clee
CLEETHORPES
Little Coates
A46
Discovery Centre
Jungle
Cleethorpes Coast Light Railway
Mouth of the Humber
Hull to:
Rotterdam (Europoort) 10hrs.
Zeebrugge 12hrs. 30mins.
A18
Aylesby
Nunsthorpe
A1098
Riby
Laceby
Bradley
Scartho
A1243
Humberston
Pleasure Island
B1203
B1219
Tetney High Sands
Irby upon Humber
NORTH EAST LINCOLNSHIRE
Waltham
New Waltham
Rural Lincolnshire Life
A1031
Pelham's Pillar
Swallow
Barnoldby le Beck
Holton le Clay
DANGER AREA
North Cotes
Cabourne
Brigsley
A16
Tetney Lock
Beelsby
Hatcliffe
Ashby cum Fenby
Cuxwold
Waithe
Tetney
North Cotes
Donna Nook
Rothwell
West Ravendale
East Ravendale
Grainsby
88
B1201
Marshchapel
89
Eskham
Croxby
North Thoresby
Fulstow
Thorganby
Thoresway
Grainthorpe
North Somercotes
Swinhope
Wold Newton
Lincolnshire Wolds Railway
Grainthorpe Fen
Skidbrooke North End
Brookenby
Ludborough
Church End
Conisholme
Stainton le Vale
Covenham St Bartholomew
Covenham St Mary
Austin Fen
South Somercotes
Saltfleet
Binbrook
North Ormsby
Kirmond le Mire
Yarburgh
Utterby
Skidbrooke
Fotherby
Little Grimsby
Alvingham
North Cockerington
Saltfleetby St Clements
Great Tows
North Elkington
Kelstern
Keddington Corner
Saltfleetby St Peter
Saltfleetby All Saints
Tealby
Theddlethorpe St Helen
A631
Keddington
South Cockerington
Ludford
North Willingham
Welton le Wold
South Elkington
Grimoldby
Sixhills
B1200
Three Bridges
Theddlethorpe All Saints
Seal Sanctuary & Wildlife Centre
LOUTH
Stewton
Manby
Burgh on Bain
A157
Great Carlton
Meers Bridge
Lifeboat Station
Legsby
Gayton le Wold
Hallington
B1520
Hainton
Raithby
Legbourne
Little
Mablethorpe
THE WOLDS

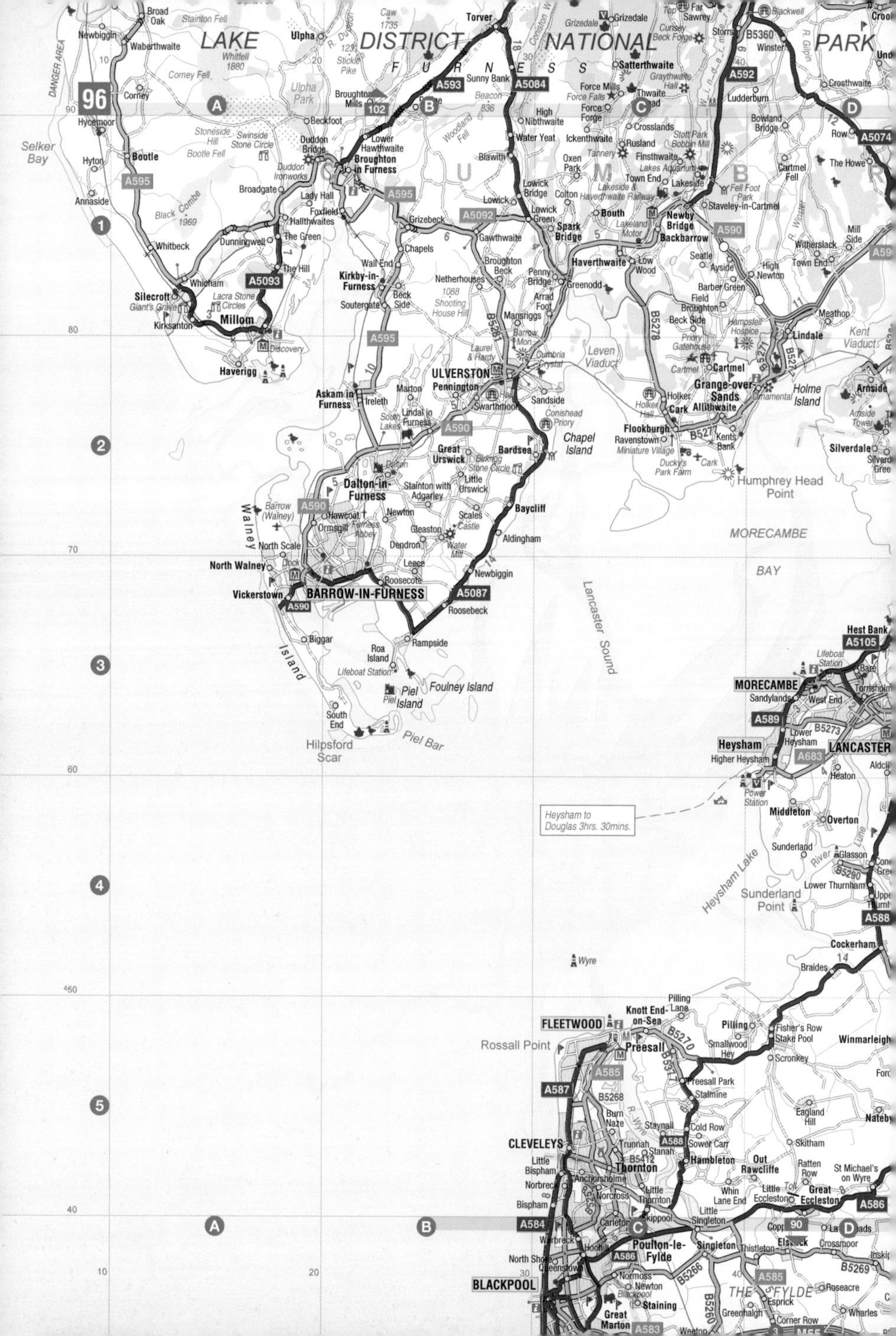

96
LAKE DISTRICT NATIONAL PARK
FURNESS
CUMBRIA
Broad Oak
Stainton Fell
Newbiggin
Waberthwaite
Whitfell 1880
Corney Fell
Corney
Hycemoor
Selker Bay
DANGER AREA
Hyton
Bootle
Bootle Fell
Stoneside Hill
Swinside Stone Circle
Annaside
A595
Black Combe 1969
Whitbeck
Whicham
Silecroft
Giant's Grave
Lacra Stone Circles
Kirksanton
Millom
Discovery
Haverigg
A5093
The Hill
The Green
Dunningwell
Hallthwaites
Foxfield
Lady Hall
Broadgate
Duddon Ironworks
Duddon Bridge
Beckfoot
Ulpha
Ulpha Park
Caw 1735
R. Duddon
Stickle Pike
Broughton Mills
102
Lower Hawthwaite
Broughton in Furness
Torver
A593
Sunny Bank
Beacon 836
Woodland Fell
A5084
Coniston Water
Grizedale
Satterthwaite
Graythwaite Hall
Force Mills
Force Falls
Force Forge
Thwaite Head
High Nibthwaite
Water Yeat
Ickenthwaite
Crosslands
Rusland
Stott Park Bobbin Mill
Tannery
Finsthwaite
Lakes Aquarium
Oxen Park
Colton
Town End
Lakeside
Lakeside & Haverthwaite Railway
Blawith
Lowick Bridge
Lowick
Lowick Green
Spark Bridge
Bouth
A5092
Grizebeck
Gawthwaite
Chapels
Wall End
Kirkby-in-Furness
Beck Side
Soutergate
Netherhouses
1088 Shooting House Hill
Broughton Beck
Penny Bridge
Greenodd
Arrad Foot
Mansriggs
Barrow Mon.
B5281
Laurel & Hardy
Cumbria Crystal
ULVERSTON
Pennington
Swarthmoor
Sandside
Conishead Priory
Chapel Island
Leven Viaduct
Haverthwaite
Low Wood
Lakeland Motor
Newby Bridge
Backbarrow
Cunsey
Beck Forge
Far Sawrey
Storrs
B5360
Winster
Blackwell
A592
Ludderburn
Crosthwaite
Bowland Bridge
Row
A5074
The Howe
Cartmel Fell
Fell Foot Park
Staveley-in-Cartmel
A590
Seatle
Ayside
High Newton
Witherslack
Town End
Mill Side
Barber Green
Field Broughton
Beck Side
Hampsfell Hospice
Priory Gatehouse
Cartmel
B5278
B5271
Meathop
Lindale
Kent Viaduct
Holker
Holker Hall
Cark
Allithwaite
Grange-over-Sands
Ornamental
Holme Island
Arnside
Arnside Tower
Flookburgh
Ravenstown
Miniature Village
B5277
Kents Bank
Ducky's Park Farm
Cark
Humphrey Head Point
Silverdale
MORECAMBE BAY
Askam in Furness
Ireleth
Marton
Lindal in Furness
South Lakes
Great Urswick
Birkrigg Stone Circle
Bardsea
Little Urswick
Stainton with Adgarley
Dalton-in-Furness
Barrow (Walney)
Hawcoat
Ormsgill
Furness Abbey
Newton
Scales
Castle
Gleaston
Water Mill
Baycliff
Aldingham
Dendron
Leece
Roosecote
Newbiggin
A5087
Roosebeck
Walney
North Scale
North Walney
Dock
Vickerstown
BARROW-IN-FURNESS
Biggar
Island
Roa Island
Rampside
Lifeboat Station
Piel Island
Foulney Island
South End
Piel Bar
Hilpsford Scar
Lancaster Sound
Hest Bank
A5105
Lifeboat Station
Bare
Torrisholme
MORECAMBE
Sandylands
West End
A589
B5273
Lower Heysham
Heysham
Higher Heysham
A683
LANCASTER
Aldcliffe
Heaton
Power Station
Heysham to Douglas 3hrs. 30mins.
Middleton
Overton
Sunderland
River Lune
Glasson
B5290
Lower Thurnham
Heysham Lake
Sunderland Point
A588
Cockerham
Braides
Wyre
Pilling Lane
Knott End-on-Sea
FLEETWOOD
Rossall Point
Preesall
B5270
Pilling
Fisher's Row
Stake Pool
Winmarleigh
Smallwood Hey
Scronkey
A585
A587
B5377
Preesall Park
Stalmine
B5268
Burn Naze
R. Wyre
Staynall
Cold Row
Sower Carr
Eagland Hill
CLEVELEYS
Trunnah
Stanah
B5412
Thornton
Hambleton
Skitham
Little Bispham
Anchorsholme
Out Rawcliffe
Ratten Row
St Michael's on Wyre
Norbreck
Norcross
Little Thornton
Whin Lane End
Little Eccleston
Great Eccleston
A586
Bispham
Skippool
Little Singleton
Carleton
A584
Warbreck
Poulton-le-Fylde
Singleton
Thistleton
Elswick
90
Crossmoor
North Shore
Queenstown
B5266
B5269
Inskip
BLACKPOOL
Normoss
Newton
Blackpool
Staining
B5260
A585
THE FYLDE
Roseacre
Great Marton
A583
Greenhalgh
Esprick
Corner Row
Wharles
Weeton
M55
A
B
C
D
1
2
3
4
5

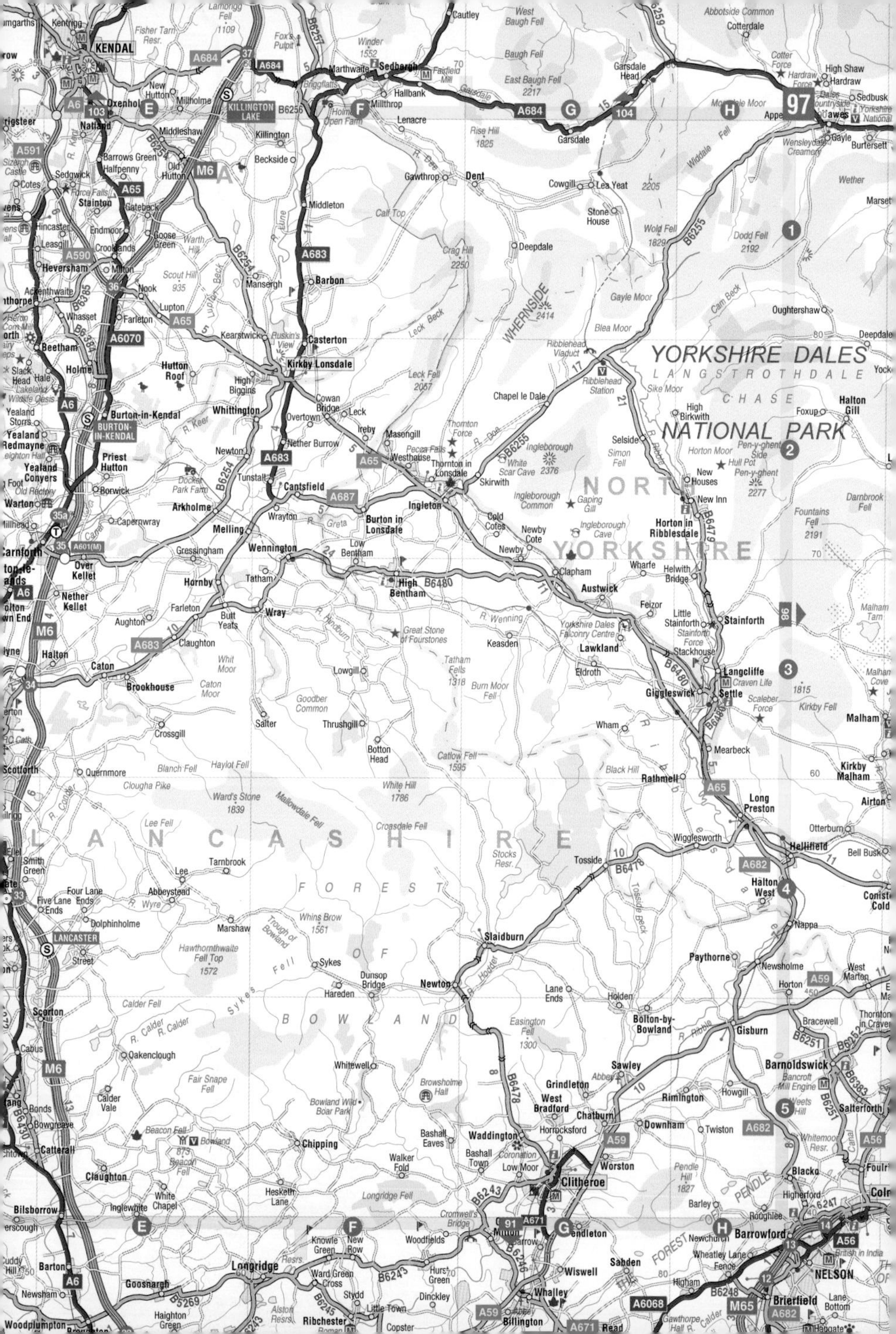

97
KENDAL
Kentrigg
Fisher Tarn Resr.
Lambrigg Fell 1109
A684
37
Fox's Pulpit
B6257
Cautley
West Baugh Fell
Abbotside Common
Cotterdale
B6259
Winder 1552
Sedbergh
Marthwaite
Fairfield Mill
Baugh Fell
East Baugh Fell 2217
Garsdale Head
Cotter Force
Hardraw Force
Hardraw
High Shaw
Sedbusk
Briggflatts
Hallbank
Millthrop
Holme Open Farm
A6
103
Oxenholme
New Hutton
Millholme
KILLINGTON LAKE
B6256
Lenacre
A684
Garsdale
15
104
Mossdale Moor
Dales Countryside Museum
Yorkshire National Park
Hawes
Appersett
Gayle
Burtersett
Wensleydale Creamery
Natland
Middleshaw
Killington
Rise Hill 1825
Brigsteer
A591
Sizergh Castle
Barrows Green
Halfpenny
B6254
Old Hutton
M6
Beckside
Gawthrop
Dent
R. Dee
Cowgill
Lea Yeat
Widdale Fell
2205
Wether Fell
Marsett
Sedgwick
Force Falls
Cotes
Stainton
A65
Gatebeck
Middleton
Call Top
Stone House
Wold Fell 1829
B6255
Dodd Fell 2192
Hincaster
Endmoor
Goose Green
Warth Hill
Leasgill
A590
Crooklands
Milton
Heversham
B6385
A683
Crag Hill 2250
Deepdale
36
Scout Hill 935
B6254
Mansergh
Barbon
Nook
Lupton
WHERNSIDE 2414
Gayle Moor
Cam Beck
Oughtershaw
Ackenthwaite
Farleton
A6070
Whasset
Lupton Beck
A65
Kearstwick
Ruskin's View
Casterton
Leck Beck
Blea Moor
Deepdale
80
Heron Corn Mill
Beetham
Hutton Roof
Kirkby Lonsdale
Ribblehead Viaduct
Ribblehead Station
17
YORKSHIRE DALES
LANGSTROTHDALE CHASE
NATIONAL PARK
Slack Head
Hale
Holme
High Biggins
Lakeland Wildlife Oasis
Cowan Bridge
Leck Fell 2057
Chapel le Dale
Sike Moor
21
High Birkwith
Foxup
Halton Gill
Yealand Storrs
Burton-in-Kendal
BURTON-IN-KENDAL
Whittington
R. Keer
Overtown
Leck
Ireby
Masongill
Thornton Force
Pecca Falls
Selside
Horton Moor
Pen-y-ghent Side
Hull Pot
Pen-y-ghent 2277
Yealand Redmayne
Leighton Hall
Priest Hutton
Newton
Nether Burrow
A683
A65
Westhouse
Thornton in Lonsdale
B6255
White Scar Cave
Ingleborough 2376
Simon Fell
New Houses
New Inn
Yealand Conyers
Borwick
Old Rectory
Docker Park Farm
Tunstall
Cantsfield
A687
Ingleton
Skirwith
Ingleborough Common
Gaping Gill
NORTH
Horton in Ribblesdale
B6479
Darnbrook Fell
Fountains Fell 2191
Warton
Arkholme
Capernwray
Wrayton
R. Greta
Burton in Lonsdale
Cold Cotes
Newby Cote
Ingleborough Cave
YORKSHIRE
70
Millhead
35a
Melling
Carnforth
35
A601(M)
Over Kellet
Gressingham
Wennington
24
Low Bentham
Newby
Clapham
Wharfe
Helwith Bridge
A6
Hornby
Tatham
High Bentham
B6480
Austwick
Nether Kellet
Farleton
Butt Yeats
Wray
R. Wenning
Feizor
Little Stainforth
Stainforth
Stainforth Force
Stackhouse
98
Malham Tarn
M6
Aughton
Claughton
R. Hindburn
Great Stone of Fourstones
Keasden
Yorkshire Dales Falconry Centre
Lawkland
Halton
A683
Tatham Fells 1318
Eldroth
Langcliffe
Craven Lime
3
Caton
Brookhouse
Whit Moor
Caton Moor
Lowgill
Burn Moor Fell
B6480
Giggleswick
Settle
Scaleber Force
1815
Malham Cove
34
Goodber Common
Kirkby Fell
Malham
Crossgill
Salter
Thrushgill
Wham
Botton Head
Catlow Fell 1595
Black Hill
Mearbeck
Scotforth
Quernmore
Blanch Fell
Haylot Fell
Rathmell
Kirkby Malham
60
Clougha Pike
White Hill 1786
A65
Long Preston
Airton
Ward's Stone 1839
Mallowdale Fell
Lee Fell
Croasdale Fell
Otterburn
LANCASHIRE
Wigglesworth
Hellifield
Bell Busk
Smith Green
Tarnbrook
Stocks Resr.
Tosside
10
B6478
A682
11
Lee
FOREST
Tosside Beck
Halton West
4
Coniston Cold
Four Lane Ends
Abbeystead
R. Wyre
33
Five Lane Ends
Dolphinholme
Marshaw
Trough of Bowland
Whins Brow 1561
Nappa
LANCASTER
Slaidburn
Hawthornthwaite Fell Top 1572
OF
Paythorne
Street
Fell
Sykes
Newsholme
West Marton
A59
Dunsop Bridge
Hareden
Newton
R. Hodder
Lane Ends
Holden
Horton
450
Calder Fell
BOWLAND
Bolton-by-Bowland
Gisburn
Scorton
R. Calder
Easington Fell 1300
Bracewell
Thornton in Craven
R. Ribble
B6251
B6252
Cabus
Oakenclough
Whitewell
Barnoldswick
Bancroft Mill Engine
B6383
M6
B6478
Sawley
Fair Snape Fell
Calder Vale
Browsholme Hall
Grindleton
Abbey
Rimington
Howgill
Bonds
Bowgreave
Bowland Wild Boar Park
West Bradford
Chatburn
Weets Hill
5
Salterforth
B6430
Bashall Eaves
Horrocksford
Downham
Twiston
A682
Whitemoor Resr.
A56
Beacon Fell
Bowland
Chipping
Waddington
Coronation
A59
873 Beacon Fell
Catterall
Walker Fold
Bashall Town
Worston
Pendle Hill 1827
Foulridge
Claughton
Low Moor
Clitheroe
Blacko
White Chapel
Inglewhite
Hesketh Lane
Longridge Fell
B6243
Barley
PENDLE
Higherford
Colne
Bilsborrow
E
Cromwell's Bridge
91
A671
G
Roughlee
B6247
Barrowford
Pendleton
Mitton
F
Knowle Green
New Row
Woodfields
Barrow
H
Newchurch
FOREST OF
14
13
A56
British in India
Longridge
Resrs.
Ward Green Cross
B6243
B6246
Wiswell
Sabden
Wheatley Lane
Fence
Barton
A6
Goosnargh
Stydd
Hurst Green
Higham
NELSON
Newsham
B5269
B6245
Dinckley
Whalley
B6248
12
Alston Resrs.
Little Town
A6068
Brierfield
Lane Bottom
Woodplumpton
Haighton Green
Ribchester
Copster
A59
Billington
A671
Read
Gawthorpe Hall
M65
A682
Haggate

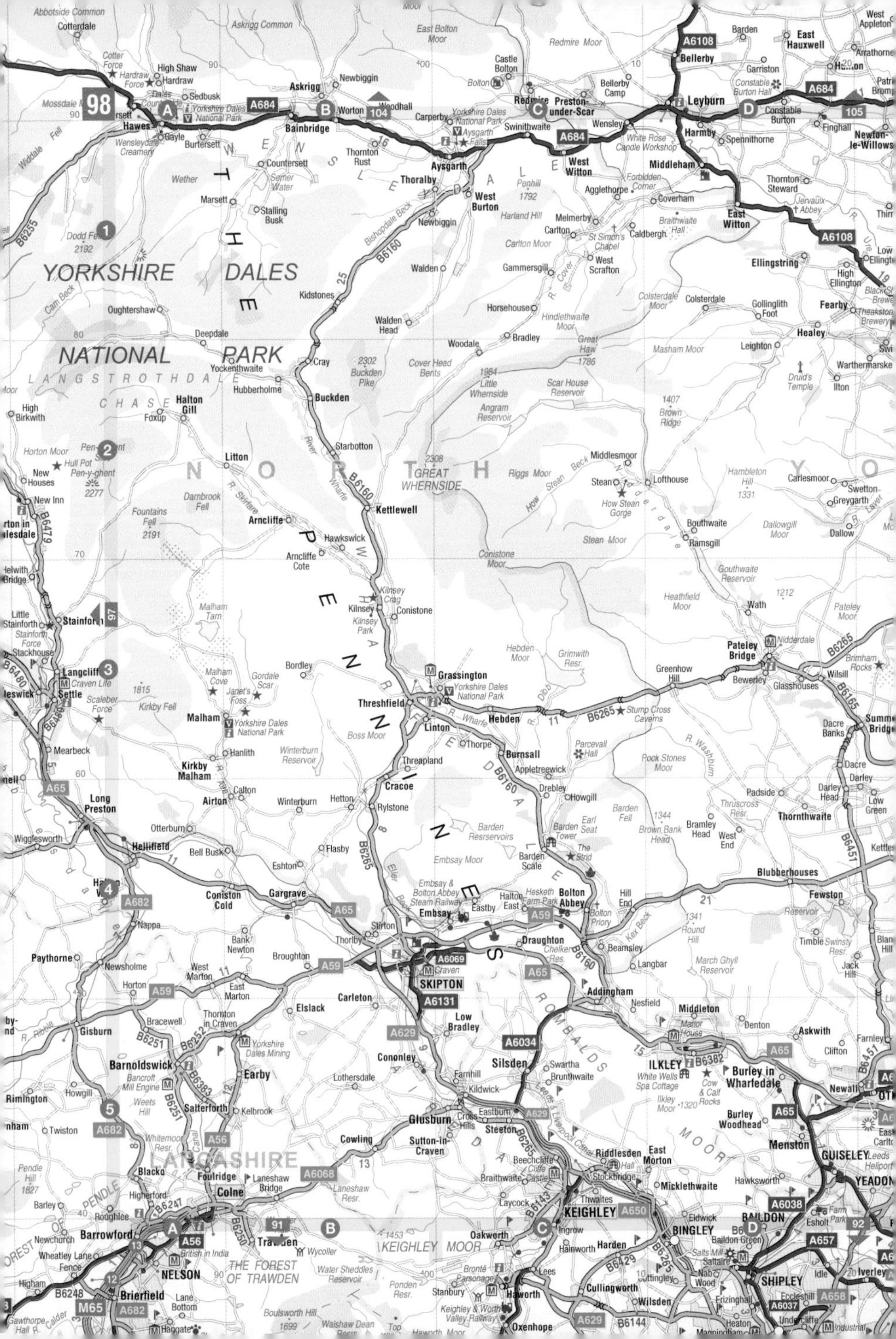
98
Abbotside Common
Cotterdale
Askrigg Common
East Bolton Moor
Redmire Moor
Barden
East Hauxwell
West Appleton
A6108
Bellerby
Garriston
Arrathorne
Cotter Force
High Shaw
Hardraw Force
Hardraw
Dales Countryside
Sedbusk
Yorkshire Dales National Park
Askrigg
Newbiggin
Castle Bolton
Bolton
Redmire
Bellerby Camp
Preston-under-Scar
Leyburn
Constable Burton Hall
A684
Mossdale Moor
Hawes
Gayle
Wensleydale Creamery
Burtersett
Bainbridge
Worton
Woodhall
104
Carperby
Yorkshire Dales National Park
Aysgarth Falls
Swinithwaite
Wensley
White Rose Candle Workshop
Harmby
Spennithorne
Constable Burton
Finghall
105
Newton-le-Willows
Widdale Fell
Countersett
Thornton Rust
Aysgarth
Thoralby
West Witton
Middleham
Wether Fell
Semer Water
Penhill 1792
Forbidden Corner
Agglethorpe
Coverham
Thornton Steward
Jervaulx Abbey
Marsett
Stalling Busk
West Burton
Newbiggin
Harland Hill
Melmerby
Carlton
St Simon's Chapel
Caldbergh
Braithwaite Hall
East Witton
A6108
B6255
Dodd Fell 2192
Bishopdale Beck
B6160
Carlton Moor
Gammersgill
West Scrafton
Ellingstring
High Ellington
Low Ellington
YORKSHIRE DALES
NATIONAL PARK
THE
WENSLEYDALE
Walden
Kidstones
R. Cover
Horsehouse
Colsterdale Moor
Colsterdale
Gollinglith Foot
Fearby
Black Sheep Brewery
Theakston Brewery
Cam Beck
Oughtershaw
Walden Head
Hindlethwaite Moor
Deepdale
Woodale
Bradley
Great Haw 1786
Masham Moor
Leighton
Healey
Cray
2302 Buckden Pike
Cover Head Bents
1984 Little Whernside
Scar House Reservoir
Druid's Temple
Warthermarske
Ilton
Yockenthwaite
Hubberholme
LANGSTROTHDALE
CHASE
Halton Gill
Foxup
Buckden
Angram Reservoir
1407 Brown Ridge
High Birkwith
Horton Moor
Pen-y-ghent
Hull Pot
New Houses
2277
New Inn
Starbotton
2308
GREAT WHERNSIDE
Riggs Moor
How Stean Beck
Middlesmoor
Stean
Lofthouse
How Stean Gorge
Hambleton Hill 1331
Carlesmoor
Swetton
Greygarth
NORTH YORKSHIRE
Litton
R. Skirfare
Darnbrook Fell
Fountains Fell 2191
River Wharfe
Kettlewell
Arncliffe
Hawkswick
Arncliffe Cote
Bouthwaite
Ramsgill
Nidderdale
Dallowgill Moor
Dallow
Stean Moor
Conistone Moor
Gouthwaite Reservoir
Horton in Ribblesdale
B6479
Helwith Bridge
THE PENNINES
WHARFEDALE
Kilnsey Crag
Kilnsey
Kilnsey Park
Conistone
Heathfield Moor
1212
Wath
Pateley Moor
Malham Tarn
Little Stainforth
Stainforth
Stainforth Force
Stackhouse
97
Langcliffe
Craven Life
Settle
Giggleswick
B6480
Scaleber Force
1815
Kirkby Fell
Malham Cove
Janet's Foss
Gordale Scar
Malham
Yorkshire Dales National Park
Bordley
Grassington
Yorkshire Dales National Park
Threshfield
Hebden Moor
Grimwith Resr.
Greenhow Hill
Pateley Bridge
Nidderdale
Brimham Rocks
Bewerley
Wilsill
Glasshouses
B6265
B6165
Linton
Hebden
R. Wharfe
R. Dibb
Stump Cross Caverns
Boss Moor
Winterburn Reservoir
Mearbeck
Hanlith
Kirkby Malham
Threapland
Thorpe
Burnsall
Parcevall Hall
R. Washburn
Rock Stones Moor
Dacre Banks
Summer Bridge
Appletreewick
Dacre
Darley
Cracoe
Drebley
Howgill
Padside
Darley Head
Low Green
A65
Long Preston
Calton
Airton
Winterburn
Hetton
Rylstone
Barden Fell
1344 Brown Bank Head
Thruscross Resr.
Bramley Head
West End
Thornthwaite
Wigglesworth
Otterburn
Barden Resrservoirs
Barden Tower
Earl Seat
The Strid
Hellifield
Bell Busk
Flasby
B6265
Embsay Moor
Barden Scale
B6451
Eshton
Blubberhouses
Hellifield
Halton West
A682
Coniston Cold
Gargrave
Embsay & Bolton Abbey Steam Railway
Embsay
Eastby
Halton East
Hesketh Farm Park
Bolton Abbey
Bolton Priory
Hill End
Fewston
Reservoir
1341 Round Hill
Kex Beck
Nappa
Bank Newton
Stirton
Thorlby
Draughton
Chelker Res.
Beamsley
Timble
Swinsty Resr.
Paythorne
Newsholme
West Marton
Broughton
A59
A6069
Craven
SKIPTON
A6131
Langbar
March Ghyll Reservoir
Jack Hill
Horton
East Marton
Carleton
Addingham
Nesfield
Middleton
Denton
Askwith
Farnley
Gisburn
Bracewell
Thornton in Craven
Elslack
Low Bradley
A6034
ROMBALDS MOOR
Manor House
ILKLEY
B6382
Clifton
R. Ribble
B6251
B6252
Yorkshire Dales Mining
A629
Cononley
Silsden
Swartha
Brunthwaite
White Wells Spa Cottage
Cow & Calf Rocks
Burley in Wharfedale
Newall
Barnoldswick
Bancroft Mill Engine
B6383
Earby
Lothersdale
Farnhill
Kildwick
Ilkley Moor 1320
Rimington
Howgill
Salterforth
Kelbrook
Glusburn
Cross Hills
Eastburn
Steeton
Leeds & Liverpool Canal
Burley Woodhead
Menston
Weets Hill
Twiston
Whitemoor Resr.
A56
Cowling
Sutton-in-Craven
B6265
Riddlesden
East Morton
Guiseley
LANCASHIRE
Pendle Hill 1827
Blacko
Foulridge
Laneshaw Bridge
A6068
13
Beechcliffe
Cliffe Castle
East Riddlesden Hall
Stockbridge
Micklethwaite
Hawksworth
Leeds Heliport
YEADON
Barley
Higherford
Colne
Laneshaw Resr.
Braithwaite
Laycock
Thwaites
A650
A6038
Esholt
FOREST OF PENDLE
Roughlee
B6247
KEIGHLEY
Eldwick
BAILDON
Barrowford
Newchurch
A56
91
Trawden
Wycoller
1453
KEIGHLEY MOOR
Oakworth
Ingrow
BINGLEY
Baildon Green
92
Whealey Lane
Fence
British in India
B6250
Water Sheddles Reservoir
Hainworth
Harden
Saltaire
Salts Mill
A657
Idle
Iverley
Higham
NELSON
THE FOREST OF TRAWDEN
Brontë Parsonage
Lees
B6429
Nab Wood
Cottingley
SHIPLEY
B6248
Brierfield
Lane Bottom
Ponden Resr.
Stanbury
Haworth
Cullingworth
Wilsden
Frizinghall
Eccleshill
A658
M65
A682
Boulsworth Hill 1699
Walshaw Dean Resrs.
Keighley & Worth Valley Railway
Oxenhope
A629
B6144
Heaton
A6037
Undercliffe
Gawthorpe Hall
Calder
Haggate
Haworth Moor
Manningham
Industrial

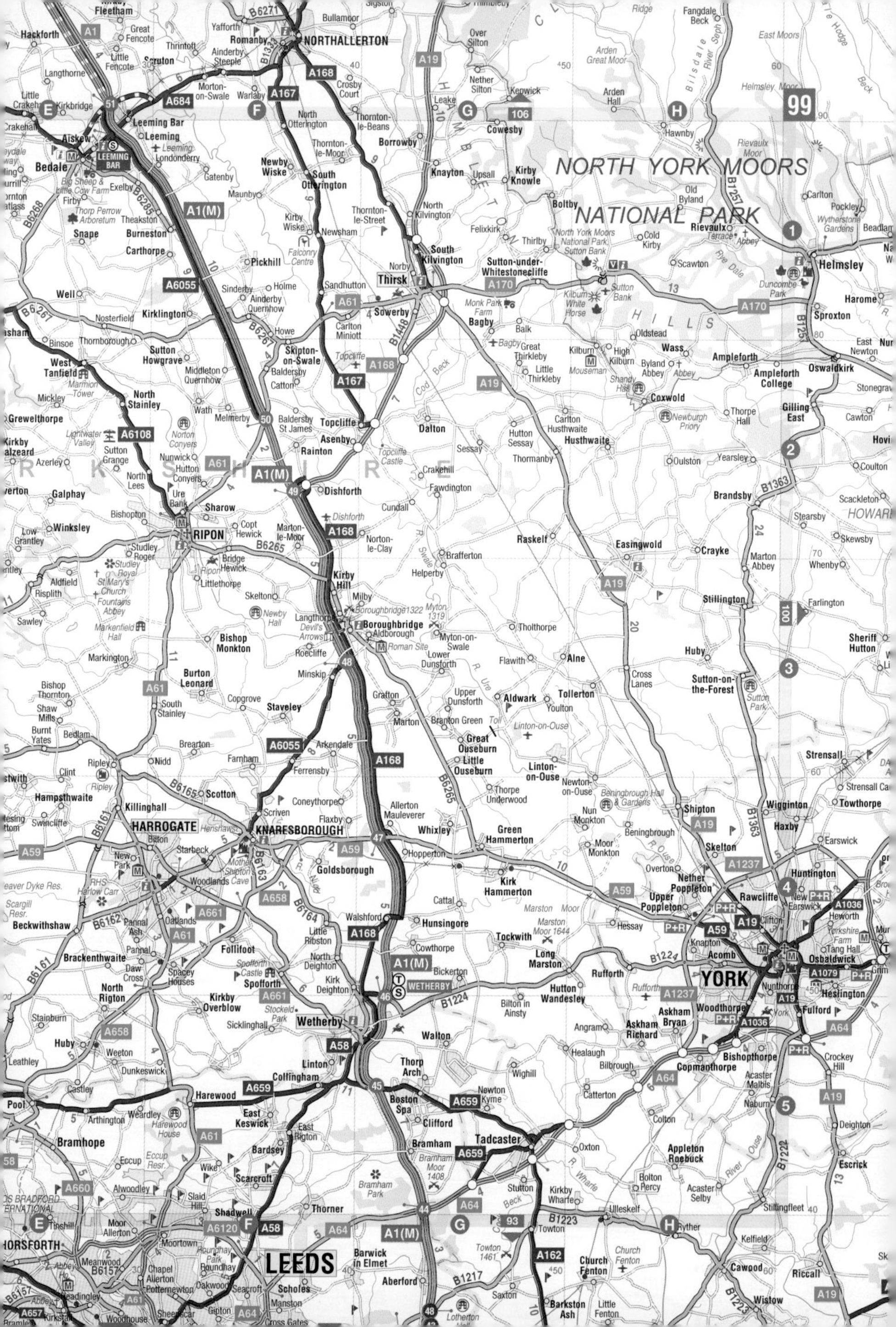

99
NORTH YORK MOORS
NATIONAL PARK
HILLS
NORTHALLERTON
Fleetham
Bullamoor
Hackforth
Great Fencote
Little Fencote
Yafforth
Romanby
Thrintoft
Scruton
Ainderby Steeple
Langthorne
Morton-on-Swale
Warlaby
Little Crakehall
Kirkbridge
Crakehall
Leeming Bar
Leeming
Londonderry
Aiskew
Bedale
LEEMING BAR
Big Sheep & Little Cow Farm
Exelby
Firby
Gatenby
Maunby
Thorp Perrow Arboretum
Theakston
Snape
Burneston
Carthorpe
Pickhill
Well
Sinderby
Holme
Ainderby Quernhow
Kirklington
Nosterfield
Binsoe
Thornborough
West Tanfield
Marmion Tower
Sutton Howgrave
Middleton Quernhow
Mickley
North Stainley
Grewelthorpe
Lightwater Valley
Kirkby Malzeard
Azerley
Sutton Grange
North Lees
Nunwick
Hutton Conyers
Norton Conyers
Wath
Melmerby
Galphay
Ure Bank
Sharow
Bishopton
Winksley
Low Grantley
RIPON
Copt Hewick
Studley Roger
Studley Royal
St Mary's Church
Fountains Abbey
Bridge Hewick
Aldfield
Risplith
Sawley
Littlethorpe
Markenfield Hall
Markington
Bishop Monkton
Bishop Thornton
Shaw Mills
Burnt Yates
Bedlam
Burton Leonard
South Stainley
Copgrove
Staveley
Brearton
Nidd
Ripley
Clint
Hampsthwaite
Killinghall
Swincliffe
Farnham
Scotton
Scriven
HARROGATE
Bilton
Starbeck
KNARESBOROUGH
Henshaws
Mother Shipton's Cave
New Park
RHS Harlow Carr
Beaver Dyke Res.
Scargill Resr.
Beckwithshaw
Woodlands
Oatlands
Pannal Ash
Pannal
Brackenthwaite
Daw Cross
Spacey Houses
Follifoot
Spofforth Castle
Spofforth
North Rigton
Kirkby Overblow
Stockeld Park
Sicklinghall
Stainburn
Huby
Weeton
Dunkeswick
Leathley
Castley
Pool
Arthington
Weardley
Harewood
Harewood House
East Keswick
Bramhope
Eccup
Eccup Resr.
East Rigton
Bardsey
Wike
Scarcroft
Alwoodley
Slaid Hill
Shadwell
Moor Allerton
Tinshill
HORSFORTH
Moortown
Meanwood
Chapel Allerton
Roundhay Park
Roundhay
Potternewton
Oakwood
Seacroft
Headingley
Sheepscar
Gipton
Kirkstall
Bramley
Woodhouse
Cross Gates
Manston
Scholes
LEEDS
Barwick in Elmet
Aberford
Thorner
Collingham
Linton
Wetherby
WETHERBY
Walton
Thorp Arch
Boston Spa
Clifford
Bramham
Bramham Moor 1408
Bramham Park
Tadcaster
Stutton
Newton Kyme
Toulston
Lotherton
Saxton
Barkston Ash
Little Fenton
Church Fenton
Towton
Towton 1461
Ulleskelf
Kirkby Wharfe
Oxton
Grimston
Ryther
Bolton Percy
Acaster Selby
Appleton Roebuck
Cawood
Wistow
Riccall
Kelfield
Stillingfleet
Escrick
Deighton
Naburn
Acaster Malbis
Colton
Bilbrough
Catterton
Copmanthorpe
Bishopthorpe
Askham Richard
Askham Bryan
Healaugh
Wighill
Angram
Bilton in Ainsty
Hutton Wandesley
Long Marston
Marston Moor
Marston Moor 1644
Tockwith
Bickerton
Kirk Deighton
North Deighton
Little Ribston
Walshford
Hunsingore
Cowthorpe
Cattal
Goldsborough
Flaxby
Coneythorpe
Allerton Mauleverer
Hopperton
Whixley
Kirk Hammerton
Green Hammerton
Thorpe Underwood
Little Ouseburn
Great Ouseburn
Branton Green
Marton
Grafton
Ferrensby
Arkendale
Minskip
Roecliffe
Aldborough
Roman Site
Boroughbridge
Boroughbridge 1322
Devil's Arrows
Langthorpe
Milby
Kirby Hill
Myton 1319
Myton-on-Swale
Lower Dunsforth
Upper Dunsforth
Aldwark
Youlton
Tollerton
Linton-on-Ouse
Newton-on-Ouse
Beningbrough Hall & Gardens
Beningbrough
Nun Monkton
Moor Monkton
Rufforth
Hessay
Upper Poppleton
Nether Poppleton
Overton
Skelton
Shipton
Knapton
Acomb
YORK
Rawcliffe
Clifton
Huntington
New Earswick
Heworth
Yorkshire Farm
Tang Hall
Osbaldwick
Heslington
Fulford
Nunthorpe
Woodthorpe
Dringhouses
Crockey Hill
Earswick
Haxby
Wigginton
Towthorpe
Strensall
Strensall Camp
Sutton-on-the-Forest
Sutton Park
Huby
Stillington
Farlington
Sheriff Hutton
Marton Abbey
Whenby
Skewsby
Stearsby
Scackleton
Brandsby
Crayke
Easingwold
Raskelf
Alne
Flawith
Tholthorpe
Cross Lanes
Helperby
Brafferton
Cundall
Norton-le-Clay
Marton-le-Moor
Dishforth
Rainton
Asenby
Topcliffe
Topcliffe Castle
Baldersby St James
Baldersby
Catton
Skipton-on-Swale
Howe
Carlton Miniott
Sowerby
Thirsk
Sandhutton
Newsham
Kirby Wiske
Falconry Centre
Thornton-le-Street
South Otterington
Newby Wiske
Thornton-le-Moor
North Otterington
Thornton-le-Beans
Crosby Court
Borrowby
Knayton
Upsall
Kirby Knowle
Leake
Cowesby
Kepwick
Over Silton
Nether Silton
North Kilvington
South Kilvington
Norby
Felixkirk
Thirlby
Boltby
Sutton-under-Whitestonecliffe
Monk Park Farm
Bagby
Balk
Great Thirkleby
Little Thirkleby
Kilburn
Kilburn White Horse
Sutton Bank
North York Moors National Park, Sutton Bank
Cold Kirby
Scawton
Old Byland
Rievaulx
Rievaulx Terrace
Abbey
Rievaulx Moor
Hawnby
Arden Hall
Arden Great Moor
Fangdale Beck
Bilsdale
East Moors
Helmsley Moor
Carlton
Pockley
Wytherstone Gardens
Beadlam
Helmsley
Duncombe Park
Harome
Sproxton
Oldstead
High Kilburn
Mouseman
Shandy Hall
Coxwold
Byland Abbey
Wass
Ampleforth
Ampleforth College
Oswaldkirk
East Newton
Stonegrave
Gilling East
Thorpe Hall
Newburgh Priory
Cawton
Coulton
Yearsley
Oulston
Husthwaite
Carlton Husthwaite
Hutton Sessay
Sessay
Thormanby
Dalton
Crakehill
Fawdington
HOWARDIAN
Hovingham
A1
A1(M)
A19
A59
A61
A64
A162
A167
A168
A170
A659
A661
A658
A660
A684
A6055
A6108
A6120
A1036
A1079
A1237
A58
A657
B1223
B1222
B1224
B1217
B1363
B1257
B1448
B6157
B6161
B6162
B6163
B6164
B6165
B6265
B6267
B6268
B6271
B6285
R. Ure
R. Swale
R. Nidd
R. Ouse
R. Wharfe
Cod Beck
Rye Dale
100
106
93

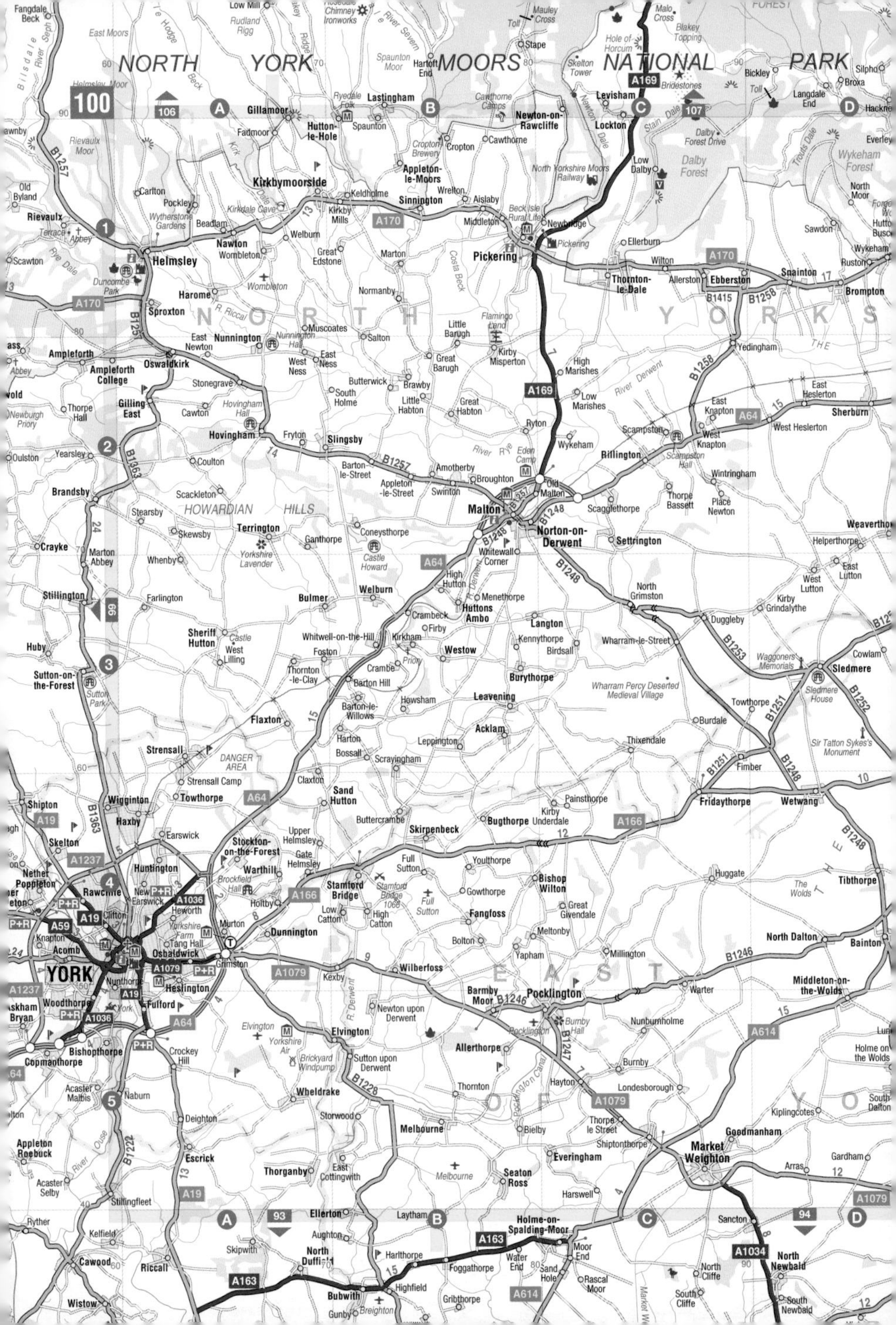
NORTH YORK MOORS NATIONAL PARK
NORTH YORKS
HOWARDIAN HILLS
EAST
OF
THE
The Wolds
Fangdale Beck
Bilsdale
River Seph
East Moors
Low Mill
Rudland Rigg
Rosedale Chimney Ironworks
River Severn
Mauley Cross
Malo Cross
Hole of Horcum
Blakey Topping
Stape
Spaunton Moor
Hartoft End
Skelton Tower
Newton Dale
Bridestones
Bickley
Silpho
Broxa
Langdale End
Hackness
Helmsley Moor
Rievaulx Moor
Gillamoor
Fadmoor
Hutton-le-Hole
Ryedale Folk
Lastingham
Spaunton
Cawthorne Camps
Newton-on-Rawcliffe
Cawthorne
Cropton Brewery
Cropton
Levisham
Lockton
Stain Dale
Dalby Forest Drive
Dalby Forest
Low Dalby
Troutsdale
Wykeham Forest
Everley
Kirkbymoorside
Appleton-le-Moors
Keldholme
Kirkby Mills
Sinnington
Wrelton
Aislaby
Middleton
North Yorkshire Moors Railway
Beck Isle Rural Life
Newbridge
Pickering
Ellerburn
Old Byland
Carlton
Pockley
Wytherstone Gardens
Kirkdale Cave
Beadlam
Rievaulx
Terrace
Abbey
Rye Dale
Scawton
Helmsley
Duncombe Park
Nawton
Wombleton
Welburn
Great Edstone
Marton
Costa Beck
Thornton-le-Dale
Wilton
Allerston
Ebberston
Snainton
Brompton
North Moor
Sawdon
Hutton Buscel
Wykeham
Ruston
Harome
Sproxton
R. Riccal
Normanby
Muscoates
Nunnington
Nunnington Hall
East Newton
Salton
Little Barugh
Flamingo Land
Kirby Misperton
Yedingham
Ampleforth
Ampleforth College
Oswaldkirk
Abbey
West Ness
East Ness
Great Barugh
High Marishes
River Derwent
East Heslerton
Sherburn
Stonegrave
Butterwick
Brawby
South Holme
Low Marishes
East Knapton
West Heslerton
Gilling East
Thorpe Hall
Newburgh Priory
Hovingham Hall
Cawton
Little Habton
Great Habton
Ryton
Scampston
Scampston Hall
West Knapton
Hovingham
Fryton
Slingsby
River Rye
Eden Camp
Wykeham
Rillington
Oulston
Yearsley
Coulton
Barton-le-Street
Amotherby
Wintringham
Appleton-le-Street
Swinton
Broughton
Old Malton
Thorpe Bassett
Place Newton
Brandsby
Scackleton
Malton
Scagglethorpe
Stearsby
Norton-on-Derwent
Settrington
Weaverthorpe
Crayke
Skewsby
Terrington
Ganthorpe
Coneysthorpe
Whitewall Corner
Helperthorpe
Marton Abbey
Yorkshire Lavender
Whenby
Castle Howard
West Lutton
East Lutton
High Hutton
Stillington
Farlington
Bulmer
Welburn
Menethorpe
North Grimston
Kirby Grindalythe
Huttons Ambo
Crambeck
Langton
Duggleby
Huby
Sheriff Hutton
Castle
West Lilling
Firby
Whitwell-on-the-Hill
Kirkham
Priory
Westow
Kennythorpe
Birdsall
Wharram-le-Street
Waggoners' Memorials
Cowlam
Sledmere
Sutton-on-the-Forest
Sutton Park
Foston
Thornton-le-Clay
Crambe
Barton Hill
Burythorpe
Wharram Percy Deserted Medieval Village
Sledmere House
Howsham
Barton-le-Willows
Leavening
Towthorpe
Flaxton
Burdale
Acklam
Harton
Leppington
Thixendale
Sir Tatton Sykes's Monument
Strensall
Danger Area
Bossall
Scrayingham
Fimber
Strensall Camp
Claxton
Towthorpe
Sand Hutton
Painsthorpe
Fridaythorpe
Wetwang
Shipton
Wigginton
Haxby
Kirby Underdale
Buttercrambe
Bugthorpe
Upper Helmsley
Skirpenbeck
Skelton
Earswick
Stockton-on-the-Forest
Gate Helmsley
Youlthorpe
Nether Poppleton
Huntington
Warthill
Full Sutton
Bishop Wilton
Huggate
Tibthorpe
Rawcliffe
Brockfield Hall
New Earswick
Stamford Bridge
Stamford Bridge 1066
Full Sutton
Gowthorpe
Clifton
Heworth
Holtby
Low Catton
High Catton
Fangfoss
Great Givendale
Yorkshire Farm
Murton
Dunnington
Meltonby
Knapton
Acomb
Tang Hall
Osbaldwick
Bolton
Yapham
Millington
North Dalton
Bainton
YORK
Grimston
Wilberfoss
Heslington
Nunthorpe
Kexby
Barmby Moor
Pocklington
Warter
Middleton-on-the-Wolds
Askham Bryan
Woodthorpe
Fulford
R. Derwent
Newton upon Derwent
Burnby Hall
Nunburnholme
Elvington
Yorkshire Air
Elvington
Allerthorpe
Bishopthorpe
Copmanthorpe
Crockey Hill
Brickyard Windpump
Sutton upon Derwent
Burnby
Holme on the Wolds
Pocklington Canal
Hayton
Thornton
Londesborough
Acaster Malbis
Naburn
Wheldrake
South Dalton
Kiplingcotes
Deighton
Storwood
Melbourne
Bielby
Thorpe le Street
Appleton Roebuck
River Ouse
Shiptonthorpe
Goodmanham
Market Weighton
Escrick
Everingham
Gardham
Thorganby
East Cottingwith
Melbourne
Seaton Ross
Arras
Acaster Selby
Stillingfleet
Harswell
Ryther
Ellerton
Laytham
Holme-on-Spalding-Moor
Sancton
Kelfield
Aughton
Moor End
Skipwith
North Duffield
Harlthorpe
Water End
North Newbald
Cawood
Riccall
Foggathorpe
Sand Hole
Rascal Moor
North Cliffe
Highfield
Market Weighton Canal
South Cliffe
Bubwith
Gribthorpe
South Newbald
Wistow
Gunby
Breighton
A170
A169
A64
A19
A1237
A1036
A59
A1079
A166
A163
A614
A1034
B1257
B1363
B1248
B1258
B1415
B1253
B1251
B1252
B1246
B1247
B1228
B1222
P+R
106
107
93
94
99
A B C D
1 2 3 4 5

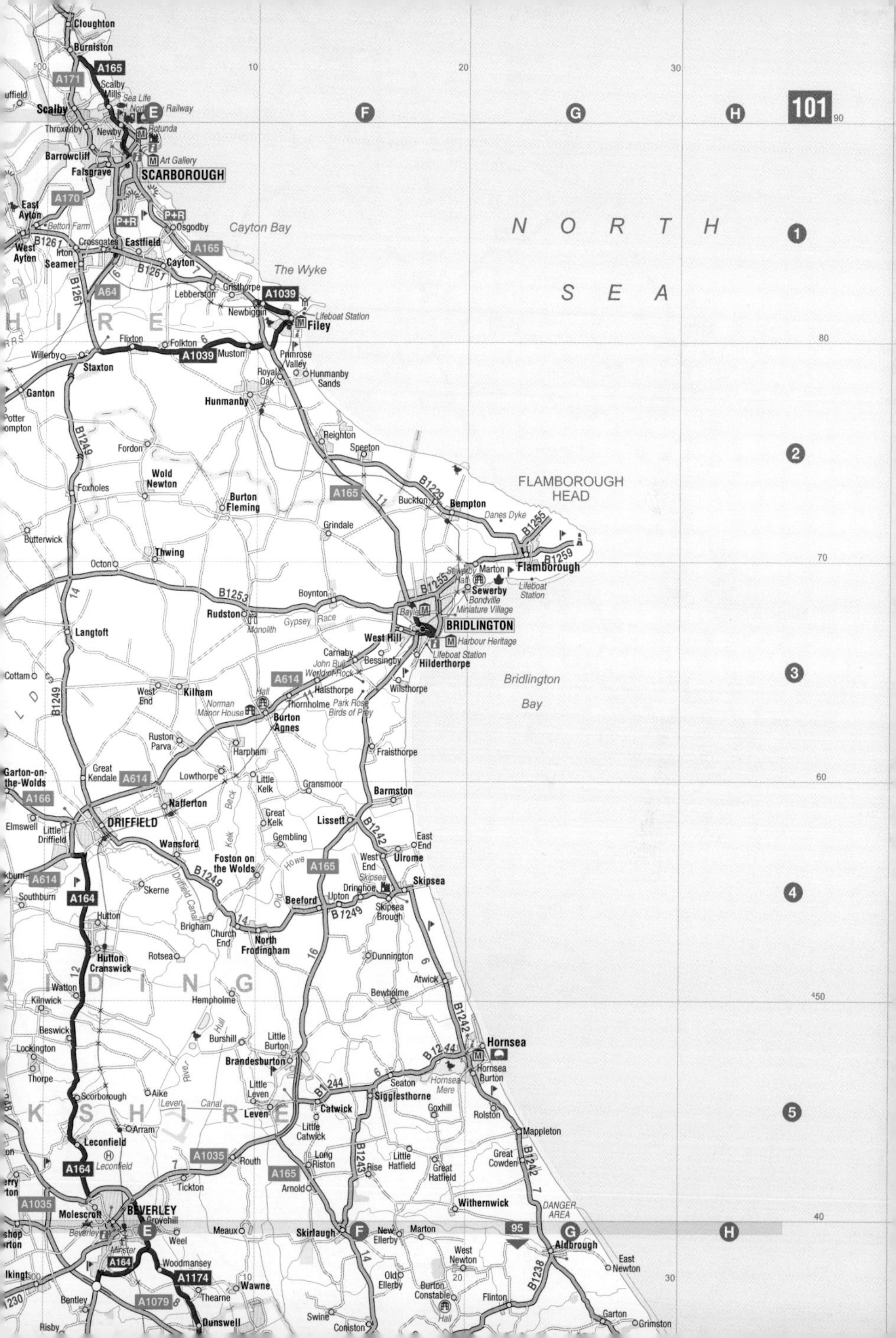

NORTH SEA
SCARBOROUGH
Cayton Bay
The Wyke
Filey
FLAMBOROUGH HEAD
Flamborough
BRIDLINGTON
Bridlington Bay
DRIFFIELD
Hornsea
BEVERLEY
Aldbrough

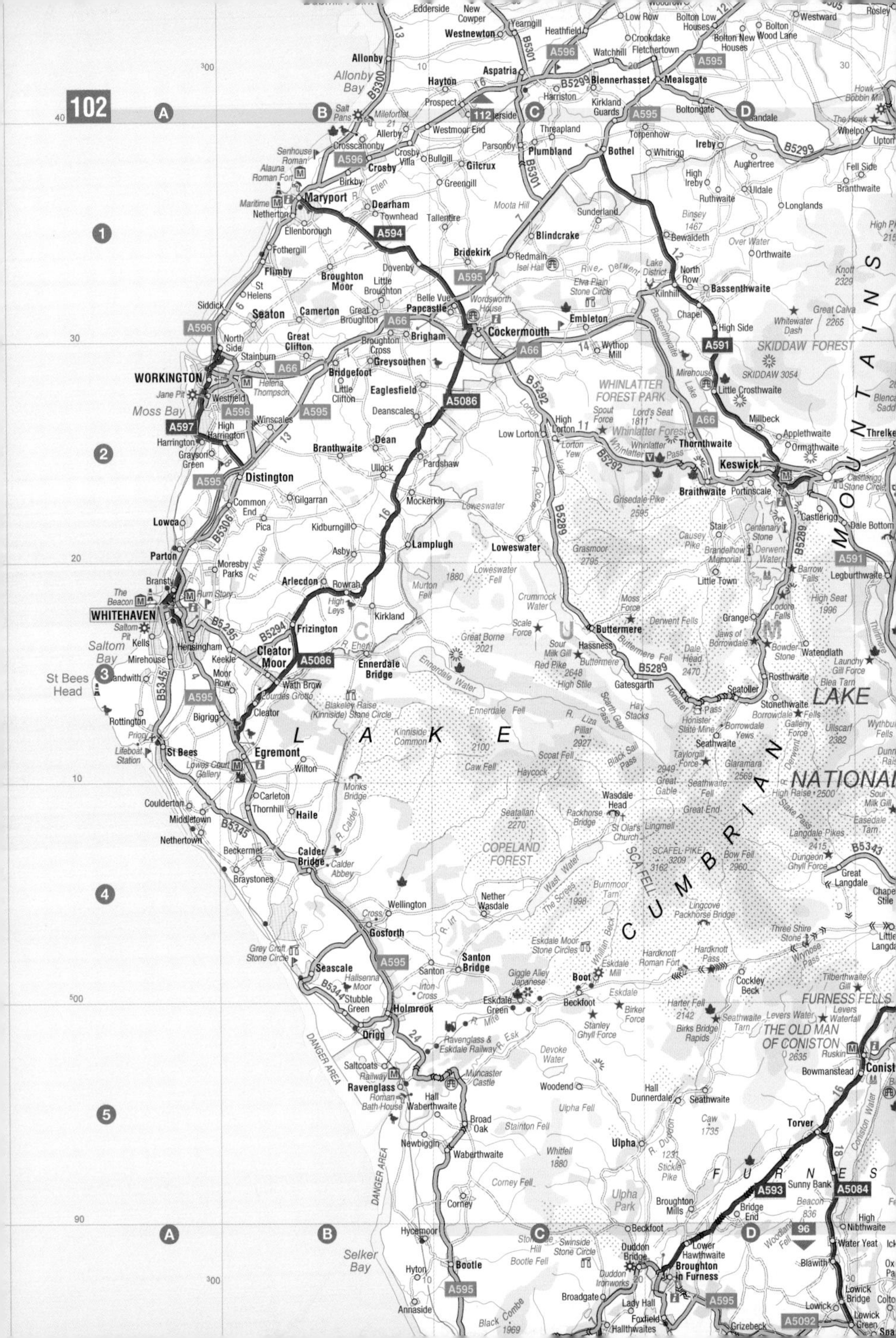
A
B
C
D
1
2
3
4
5
300
40
30
20
10
500
90
Edderside
New Cowper
Yearngill
Heathfield
Low Row
Bolton Low Houses
Westward
Rosley
Westnewton
B5301
Crookdake
Bolton New Houses
Bolton Wood Lane
Allonby
A596
Watchhill
Fletchertown
A595
Allonby Bay
B5300
Hayton
Aspatria
Blennerhasset
Mealsgate
B5299
Harriston
Salt Pans
Milefortlet 21
Prospect
112
Kirkland Guards
Boltongate
Sandale
Howk Bobbin Mill
The Howk
Whelpo
Upton
Allerby
Westmoor End
Threapland
Torpenhow
Crosscanonby
Parsonby
Plumbland
Bothel
Whitrigg
Ireby
B5299
Senhouse Roman
Crosby Villa
Bullgill
Gilcrux
Aughertree
Fell Side
Alauna Roman Fort
Crosby
High Ireby
Uldale
Branthwaite
Birkby
Greengill
Maritime
Maryport
Netherton
Dearham
Townhead
Moota Hill
Tallentire
Sunderland
Ruthwaite
Longlands
Binsey 1467
Ellenborough
A594
Blindcrake
Bewaldeth
Over Water
Orthwaite
Fothergill
Dovenby
Bridekirk
Redmain
Isel Hall
River Derwent
Lake District
Flimby
Broughton Moor
Little Broughton
A595
Elva Plain Stone Circle
North Row
Bassenthwaite
Knott 2329
St Helens
Belle Vue
Kilnhill
Siddick
Seaton
Camerton
Great Broughton
Papcastle
Wordsworth House
Embleton
Chapel
Whitewater Dash
Great Calva 2265
A596
A66
Brigham
Cockermouth
High Side
North Side
Great Clifton
Broughton Cross
A66
Wythop Mill
Bassenthwaite Lake
A591
SKIDDAW FOREST
Stainburn
Greysouthen
SKIDDAW 3054
WORKINGTON
Helena Thompson
A66
Bridgefoot
Eaglesfield
WHINLATTER FOREST PARK
Mirehouse
Little Crosthwaite
Jane Pit
Westfield
Little Clifton
B5292
Moss Bay
A596
A595
A5086
Deanscales
Spout Force
Lord's Seat 1811
Millbeck
Winscales
Whinlatter Forest
A66
Applethwaite
Threlkeld
A597
High Harrington
Harrington
Low Lorton
High Lorton
Lorton Yew
Whinlatter Pass
Thornthwaite
Ormathwaite
Grayson Green
Branthwaite
Dean
Keswick
Castlerigg Stone Circle
Distington
Ullock
Pardshaw
A595
Braithwaite
Portinscale
Common End
Gilgarran
Mockerkin
Loweswater
Grisedale Pike 2595
Castlerigg
Lowca
Pica
Kidburngill
B5306
R. Keekle
B5289
Causey Pike
Stair
Centenary Stone
Dale Bottom
Parton
Asby
Lamplugh
Loweswater
Grasmoor 2795
Brandelhow Memorial
Derwent Water
A591
Moresby Parks
B5289
Barrow Falls
Legburthwaite
Bransty
Arlecdon
Rowrah
1880
Loweswater Fell
Little Town
The Beacon
Rum Story
Murton Fell
Crummock Water
Moss Force
High Seat 1996
WHITEHAVEN
High Leys
Kirkland
Lodore Falls
Grange
Saltom Pit
B5295
Scale Force
Buttermere
Derwent Fells
Jaws of Borrowdale
Kells
B5294
Frizington
Great Borne 2021
Sour Milk Gill
Hassness
Buttermere Fell
Bowder Stone
Watendlath
Saltom Bay
Hensingham
Keekle
Cleator Moor
R. Ehen
Red Pike 2648
Dale Head 2470
Laundry Gill Force
Mirehouse
A5086
Ennerdale Bridge
Buttermere
B5289
Rosthwaite
St Bees Head
Sandwith
Moor Row
Ennerdale Water
High Stile
Gatesgarth
Blea Tarn
B5345
Wath Brow
Lourdes Grotto
Honister Pass
Seatoller
A595
Blakeley Raise (Kinniside) Stone Circle
Hay Stacks
Scarth Gap Pass
Stonethwaite
LAKE
Rottington
Bigrigg
Cleator
Ennerdale Fell
R. Liza
Honister Slate Mine
Borrowdale Yews
Borrowdale Fells
Galleny Force
Ullscarf 2382
Wythburn Fells
Priory
Kinniside Common
Pillar 2927
Lifeboat Station
St Bees
Egremont
2100
Scoat Fell
Black Sail Pass
Seathwaite
Taylorgill Force
Lowes Court Gallery
Wilton
Caw Fell
Haycock
2949 Great Gable
Glaramara 2569
NATIONAL
Monks Bridge
Seathwaite Fell
High Raise 2500
Sour Milk Gill
Couldertoh
Carleton
Wasdale Head
Great End
Stake Pass
Easedale Tarn
Thornhill
Haile
Seatallan 2270
Packhorse Bridge
Langdale Pikes
Middletown
R. Calder
St Olaf's Church
Lingmell
2415
B5343
Nethertown
B5345
COPELAND FOREST
SCAFELL
SCAFELL PIKE 3209
3162
Bow Fell 2960
Dungeon Ghyll Force
Great Langdale
Beckermet
Calder Bridge
Calder Abbey
Wast Water
Burnmoor Tarn
Chapel Stile
Braystones
The Screes 1998
Nether Wasdale
Lingcove Packhorse Bridge
Wellington
Cross
R. Irt
Whillan Beck
Three Shire Stone
Little Langdale
Gosforth
Eskdale Moor Stone Circles
Hardknott Roman Fort
Hardknott Pass
Wrynose Pass
Grey Croft Stone Circle
A595
Seascale
Santon Bridge
Santon
Eskdale Mill
Boot
Cockley Beck
Tilberthwaite Gill
Hallsenna Moor
Giggle Alley Japanese
B5344
Stubble Green
Irton Cross
Eskdale Green
Beckfoot
Eskdale
FURNESS FELLS
Holmrook
R. Mite
Birker Force
Harter Fell 2142
Seathwaite Tarn
Levers Water
Levers Waterfall
DANGER AREA
Drigg
24
Stanley Ghyll Force
Birks Bridge Rapids
THE OLD MAN OF CONISTON 2635
Ravenglass & Eskdale Railway
R. Esk
Devoke Water
Ruskin
Coniston
Saltcoats
Railway
Muncaster Castle
Bowmanstead
Ravenglass
Roman Bath House
Hall Waberthwaite
Woodend
Hall Dunnerdale
Seathwaite
Broad Oak
Ulpha Fell
Stainton Fell
Torver
Coniston Water
Newbiggin
Waberthwaite
Whitfell 1880
Ulpha
R. Duddon
Caw 1735
1231 Stickle Pike
FURNESS
DANGER AREA
Corney Fell
A593
Sunny Bank
A5084
Ulpha Park
Corney
Broughton Mills
Bridge End
Beacon 836
Woodland Fell
High Nibthwaite
Beckfoot
96
Hycemoor
Swinside Stone Circle
Lower Hawthwaite
Water Yeat
Selker Bay
Duddon Bridge
Broughton in Furness
Blawith
Hyton
Bootle
Bootle Fell
Duddon Ironworks
A595
A595
Lowick Bridge
Broadgate
Lady Hall
Lowick
Black Combe 1969
Annaside
Foxfield
Hallthwaites
Grizebeck
A5092
Lowick Green
LAKE
CUMBRIAN
MOUNTAINS

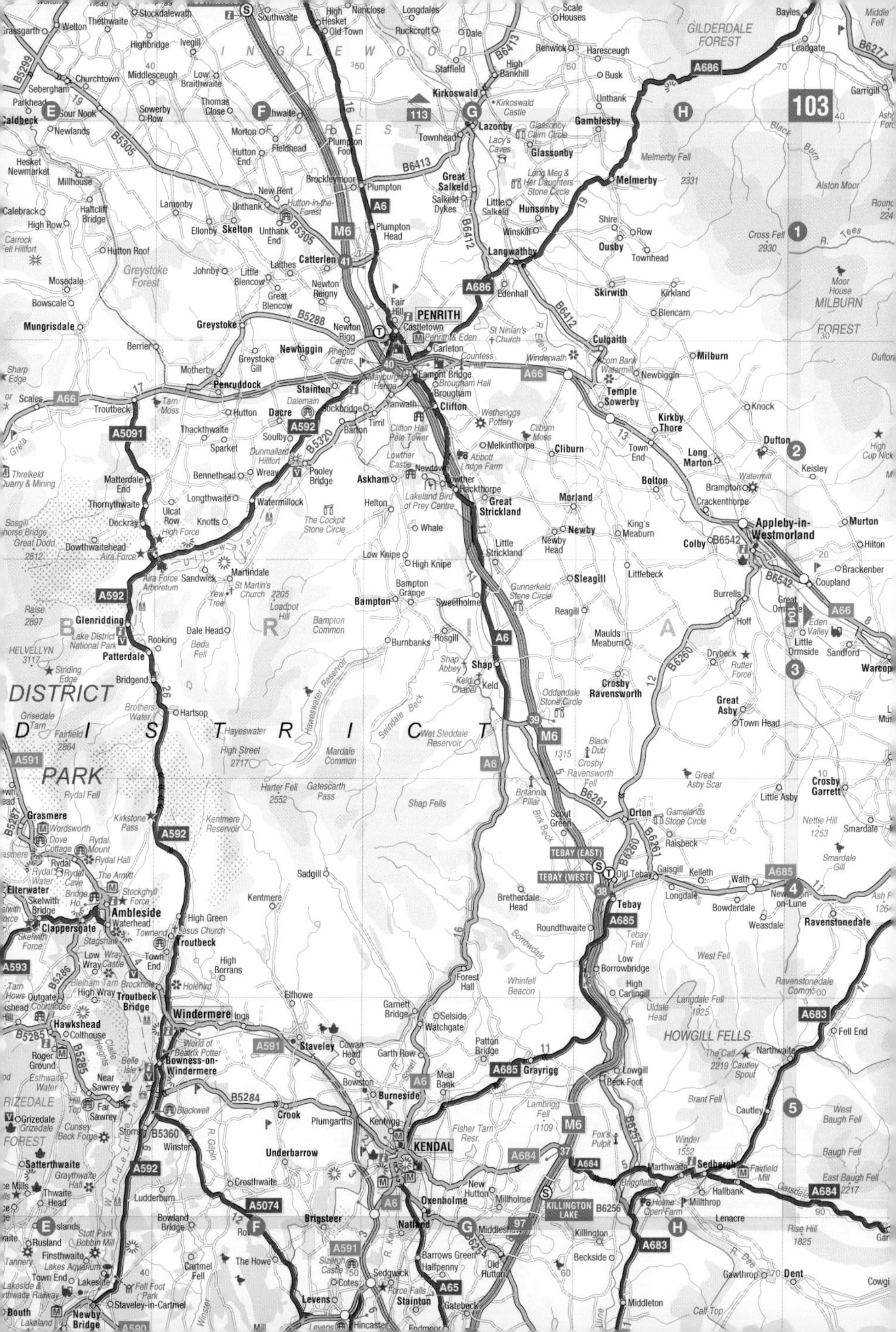
103
Stockdalewath
Southwaite
High Hesket
Nunclose
Longdales
Scale Houses
Bayles
Middle Fell
Grassgarth
Welton
Thethwaite
Old Town
Ruckcroft
Dale
Renwick
Haresceugh
GILDERDALE FOREST
Leadgate
B6277
Highbridge
Ivegill
INGLEWOOD
Staffield
High Bankhill
B6413
Busk
A686
Garrigill
B5299
Churchtown
Middlesceugh
Low Braithwaite
Kirkoswald
Unthank
Sebergham
Thomas Close
Kirkoswald Castle
Gamblesby
Parkhead
Sour Nook
Sowerby Row
113
Lazonby
Caldbeck
FOREST
Glassonby Cairn Circle
Newlands
Morton
Townhead
Lacy's Caves
Glassonby
Hesket Newmarket
Fieldhead
Hutton End
Plumpton Foot
Melmerby Fell
Black Burn
B5305
B6413
Millhouse
Great Salkeld
Long Meg & Her Daughters Stone Circle
Melmerby
2331
Alston Moor
Plumpton
New Rent
Brockleymoor
Lamonby
Unthank
Hutton-in-the-Forest
A6
Salkeld Dykes
Little Salkeld
Hunsonby
Calebrack
Haltcliff Bridge
Skelton
B5305
Shire
Row
High Row
Ellonby
Unthank End
M6
Plumpton Head
B6412
Winskill
Ousby
Cross Fell
2930
R. Tees
Carrock Fell Hillfort
Hutton Roof
Catterlen
41
Langwathby
Townhead
Greystoke Forest
Johnby
Little Blencow
Laithes
Newton Reigny
Moor House
Mosedale
A686
Edenhall
Skirwith
Kirkland
MILBURN FOREST
Bowscale
Great Blencow
Fair Hill
PENRITH
Blencarn
B5288
Castletown
Mungrisdale
Greystoke
Newton Rigg
Penrith & Eden
St Ninian's Church
B6412
R. Eden
Culgaith
Berrier
Carleton
Milburn
Newbiggin
Rheged Centre
Countess Pillar
Winderwath
Acorn Bank Watermill
Newbiggin
Dufton
Sharp Edge
Greystoke Gill
40
A66
Motherby
Penruddock
Mayburgh Henge
Eamont Bridge
Brougham Hall
Temple Sowerby
Scales
A66
Stainton
Brougham
Troutbeck
Tarn Moss
Dalemain
Yanwath
Clifton
Knock
Hutton
Dacre
Kirkby Thore
A5091
Thackthwaite
Sockbridge
A592
Tirril
Barton
Clifton Hall Pele Tower
Wetheriggs Pottery
Soulby
B5320
Cliburn Moss
13
Dufton
High Cup Nick
Greta
Sparket
Dunmallard Hillfort
Melkinthorpe
Cliburn
Town End
Long Marton
Threlkeld Quarry & Mining
Matterdale End
Bennethead
Wreay
Pooley Bridge
Lowther Castle
Abbott Lodge Farm
Bolton
Keisley
Watermill
Askham
Newtown
Lowther
Brampton
Thornythwaite
Longthwaite
Watermillock
Hackthorpe
Lakeland Bird of Prey Centre
Great Strickland
Morland
Crackenthorpe
Helton
Sosgill Horse Bridge
Dockray
Ulcat Row
Knotts
The Cockpit Stone Circle
Whale
Newby
King's Meaburn
Appleby-in-Westmorland
Murton
Great Dodd
2812
Dowthwaitehead
High Force
Newby Head
Colby
B6542
Hilton
Aira Force
Low Knipe
Little Strickland
Martindale
High Knipe
Littlebeck
Brackenber
Sandwick
St Martin's Church
Sleagill
B6542
Coupland
A592
Yew Tree
2205
Loadpot Hill
Bampton Grange
Sweetholme
Gunnerkeld Stone Circle
Burrells
Great Ormside
A66
Raise
2897
Glenridding
Bampton
Reagill
104
Eden Valley
Hoff
Lake District National Park
Bampton Common
Dale Head
Rosgill
A6
Maulds Meaburn
Little Ormside
Sandford
Rooking
Burnbanks
HELVELLYN
3117
Patterdale
Beda Fell
Haweswater Reservoir
Shap Abbey
Shap
Drybeck
Rutter Force
Warcop
Striding Edge
Bridgend
Keld Chapel
Keld
B6260
DISTRICT
Brothers Water
Crosby Ravensworth
Grisedale Tarn
Hartsop
Swindale Beck
Oddendale Stone Circle
Great Asby
Fairfield
2864
Hayeswater
Wet Sleddale Reservoir
39
Town Head
High Street
2717
Mardale Common
M6
A591
A6
Black Dub
1315
Crosby Ravensworth Fell
Great Asby Scar
Crosby Garrett
PARK
Harter Fell
2552
Gatescarth Pass
Rydal Fell
Shap Fells
Britannia Pillar
B6261
Little Asby
Nettle Hill
1253
Grasmere
Kirkstone Pass
Kentmere Reservoir
Scout Green
Orton
Gamelands Stone Circle
Smardale
Wordsworth
Dove Cottage
Birk Beck
B6261
Raisbeck
Rydal Mount
A592
B6260
Smardale Gill
Rydal
Rydal Hall
TEBAY (EAST)
Rydal Cave
The Armitt
Sadgill
TEBAY (WEST)
Old Tebay
Gaisgill
Kelleth
Elterwater
Wath
A685
Stockghyll Force
Kentmere
Bretherdale Head
38
Tebay
Longdale
Newbiggin-on-Lune
Skelwith Bridge
Ambleside
Bowderdale
Ravenstonedale
Clappersgate
Waterhead
High Green
Roundthwaite
A685
Weasdale
Skelwith Force
Stagshaw
Townend
Jesus Church
Troutbeck
Tebay Fell
Borrowdale
A593
Low Wray
Wray Castle
Town End
High Borrans
Low Borrowbridge
West Fell
B5286
Blelham Tarn
Forest Hall
Whinfell Beacon
Tarn Hows
Outgate
High Wray
Brockhole
Holehird
Elfhowe
High Carlingill
Langdale Fell
1925
Ravenstonedale Common
Hawkshead Courthouse
Troutbeck Bridge
Windermere
Ings
Garnett Bridge
Selside
Uldale Head
A683
Hawkshead
Colthouse
Watchgate
Patton Bridge
HOWGILL FELLS
Fell End
B5285
World of Beatrix Potter
A591
Staveley
Cowan Head
Garth Row
11
The Calf
2219
Cautley Spout
Northwaite
Roger Ground
Belle Isle
Bowness-on-Windermere
A685
Grayrigg
Lowgill
Esthwaite Water
Near Sawrey
Bowston
Meal Bank
A6
Beck Foot
B5285
Burneside
Brant Fell
Cautley
West Baugh Fell
GRIZEDALE
Hill Top
B5284
Far Sawrey
Blackwell
Crook
Lambrigg Fell
1109
Grizedale
Plumgarths
Kentrigg
Fisher Tarn Resr.
M6
B6257
Cunsey Beck Forge
Storrs
B5360
R. Gilpin
Fox's Pulpit
Winder
1552
Baugh Fell
FOREST
Winster
KENDAL
Underbarrow
A684
37
Satterthwaite
Graythwaite Hall
A592
A684
Marthwaite
Sedbergh
Fairfield Mill
East Baugh Fell
2217
Force Mills
Crosthwaite
New Hutton
Millholme
Briggflatts
Hallbank
A684
Thwaite Head
Ludderburn
A5074
Oxenholme
KILLINGTON LAKE
B6256
Home Open Farm
Millthrop
Lenacre
Bowland Bridge
A6
Brigsteer
Natland
Middleshaw
Killington
Rise Hill
1825
Eslands
Stott Park Bobbin Mill
97
A683
Rusland
A591
Barrows Green
B6254
Beckside
Tannery
Finsthwaite
The Howe
Halfpenny
R. Kent
Sizergh Castle
R. Dee
Lakes Aquarium
Cartmel Fell
Sedgwick
Old Hutton
Gawthrop
Dent
Cowgill
Town End
Lakeside
Lakeside & Haverthwaite Railway
Fell Foot Park
Cotes
Force Falls
A65
Lune
Staveley-in-Cartmel
Levens
Stainton
Gatebeck
Middleton
Bouth
Newby Bridge
Winster
Hincaster
Calf Top
Lakeland
Mill
Levens
A590
Endmoor

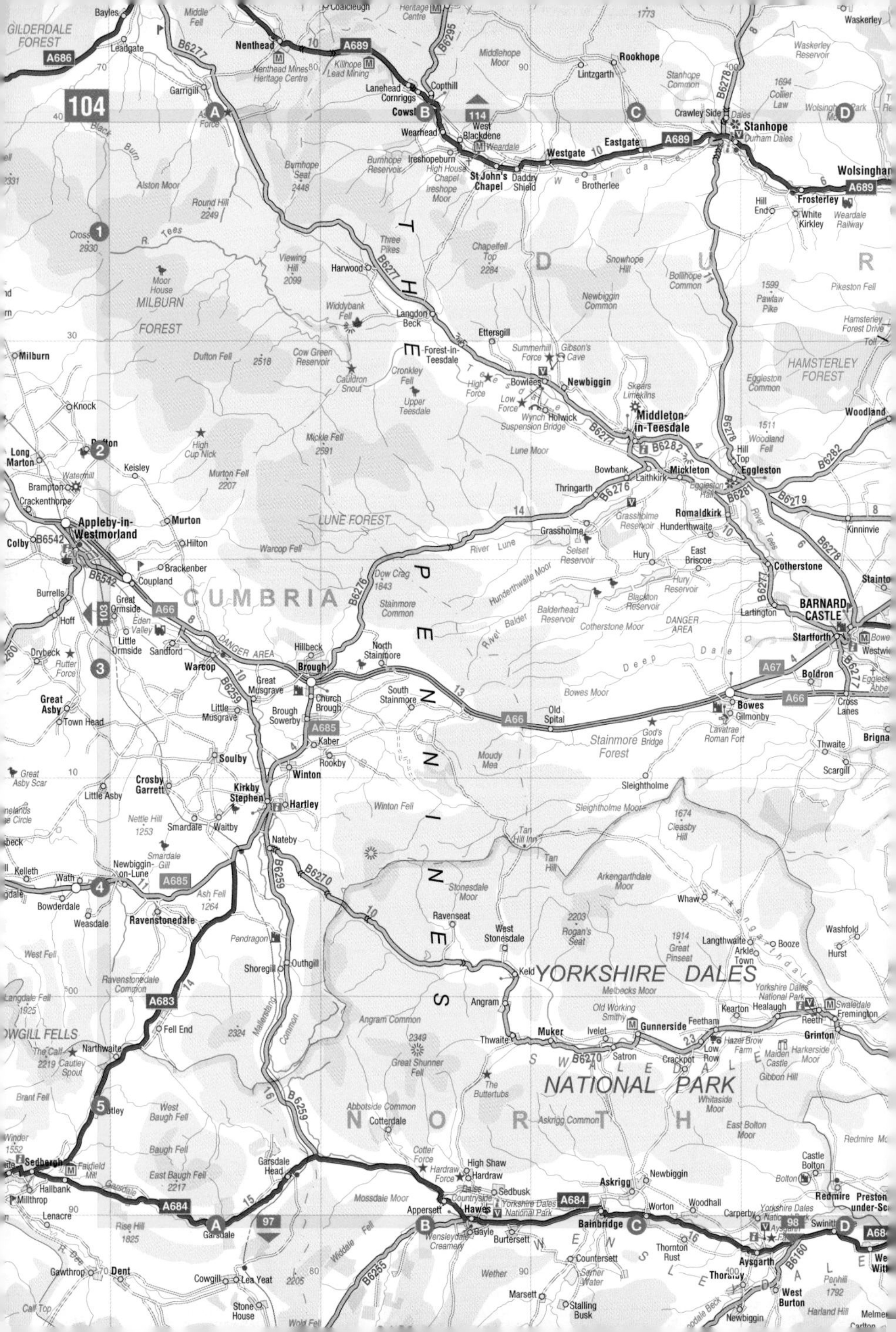
Bayles
GILDERDALE FOREST
A686
Leadgate
Middle Fell
B6277
Nenthead
Nenthead Mines Heritage Centre
A689
Killhope Lead Mining
Coalcleugh
Heritage Centre
B6295
1773
Middlehope Moor
Rookhope
Lintzgarth
Waskerley
Waskerley Reservoir
Stanhope Common
B6278
1694 Collier Law
Garrigill
A
Ashgill Force
Lanehead
Cornriggs
Copthill
Cowshill
B
114
West Blackdene
Weardale
Wearhead
C
Crawley Side
Dales
Stanhope
Durham Dales
Wolsingham Park
D
Eastgate
Westgate
Daddry Shield
St John's Chapel
Brotherlee
Weardale
Ireshopeburn
High House Chapel
Ireshope Moor
Burnhope Reservoir
Burnhope Seat 2448
Black Burn
Alston Moor
2331
Round Hill 2249
Wolsingham
Frosterley
Hill End
White Kirkley
Weardale Railway
Cross Fell 2930
1
R. Tees
Three Pikes
Viewing Hill 2099
Harwood
B6277
Chapelfell Top 2284
D
Snowhope Hill
U
R
Bollihope Common
1599 Pawlaw Pike
Pikeston Fell
Moor House
MILBURN FOREST
Widdybank Fell
Langdon Beck
Newbiggin Common
Hamsterley Forest Drive
Toll
Milburn
Dufton Fell
2518
Cow Green Reservoir
Cauldron Snout
Forest-in-Teesdale
Cronkley Fell
Upper Teesdale
Ettersgill
Summerhill Force
Gibson's Cave
High Force
Bowlees
Newbiggin
Low Force
Wynch Suspension Bridge
Holwick
Skears Limekilns
Middleton-in-Teesdale
HAMSTERLEY FOREST
Eggleston Common
Woodland
Knock
Dufton
2
Long Marton
High Cup Nick
Mickle Fell 2591
Lune Moor
B6277
B6282
1511 Woodland Fell
Hill Top
Eggleston
Eggleston Hall
B6282
Keisley
Watermill
Brampton
Crackenthorpe
Murton Fell 2207
Bowbank
Laithkirk
Mickleton
Thringarth
B6276
B6281
B6279
Appleby-in-Westmorland
Colby
B6542
Murton
Hilton
LUNE FOREST
14
Grassholme
Grassholme Reservoir
Romaldkirk
Hunderthwaite
River Tees
Kinninvie
B6278
Warcop Fell
River Lune
Selset Reservoir
Hury
East Briscoe
Hury Reservoir
Cotherstone
Brackenber
Coupland
CUMBRIA
Burrells
B6542
Great Ormside
Eden Valley
Little Ormside
Hoff
103
A66
Dow Crag 1843
Stainmore Common
Hunderthwaite Moor
Balderhead Reservoir
Blackton Reservoir
Cotherstone Moor
DANGER AREA
Lartington
BARNARD CASTLE
Startforth
Drybeck
Rutter Force
3
Sandford
Warcop
DANGER AREA
Hillbeck
Brough
North Stainmore
Deep Dale
A67
Boldron
B6277
Great Asby
Town Head
Great Musgrave
B6259
Church Brough
Brough Sowerby
South Stainmore
A66
Old Spital
Bowes Moor
Bowes
Gilmonby
A66
Cross Lanes
Little Musgrave
A685
Kaber
Rookby
Moody Mea
God's Bridge
Stainmore Forest
Lavatrae Roman Fort
Thwaite
Scargill
Great Asby Scar
Soulby
Winton
Crosby Garrett
Little Asby
Kirkby Stephen
Hartley
Winton Fell
Sleightholme
Sleightholme Moor
1674 Cleasby Hill
Nettle Hill 1253
Smardale
Waitby
Nateby
Tan Hill Inn
Tan Hill
Kelleth
Newbiggin-on-Lune
Wath
4
A685
Smardale Gill
B6259
B6270
Arkengarthdale Moor
Whaw
Bowderdale
Weasdale
Ravenstonedale
Ash Fell 1264
Stonesdale Moor
Ravenseat
West Stonesdale
2203 Rogan's Seat
1914 Great Pinseat
Langthwaite
Booze
Washfold
Arkle Town
Hurst
West Fell
Pendragon
Shoregill
Outhgill
Ravenstonedale Common
A683
Keld
YORKSHIRE DALES
Melbecks Moor
Yorkshire Dales National Park
Langdale Fell 1925
Mallerstang Common
Angram
Old Working Smithy
Kearton
Healaugh
Swaledale
Fremington
Reeth
HOWGILL FELLS
Fell End
2324
Angram Common
Thwaite
Muker
Ivelet
Gunnerside
Feetham
Hazel Brow Farm
Grinton
The Calf 2219
Cautley Spout
Northwaite
2349 Great Shunner Fell
B6270
Satron
Crackpot
Low Row
Maiden Castle
Harkerside Moor
The Buttertubs
Gibbon Hill
NATIONAL PARK
Brant Fell
5
West Baugh Fell
B6259
Abbotside Common
Whitaside Moor
NORTH
Cotterdale
Askrigg Common
East Bolton Moor
Redmire Moor
Winder 1552
Baugh Fell
Sedbergh
Fairfield Mill
East Baugh Fell 2217
Garsdale Head
Cotter Force
Hardraw Force
High Shaw
Hardraw
Askrigg
Newbiggin
Castle Bolton
Bolton
Hallbank
Millthrop
A684
Mossdale Moor
Sedbusk
Dales Countryside
Yorkshire Dales National Park
A684
Worton
Woodhall
Redmire
Preston-under-Scar
Lenacre
Appersett
Hawes
Bainbridge
Carperby
Yorkshire Dales National Park
Aysgarth Falls
Swinithwaite
A684
Garsdale
A
97
Rise Hill 1825
B
Gayle
Wensleydale Creamery
Burtersett
C
16
Thornton Rust
98
D
Aysgarth
B6160
R. Dee
Gawthrop
Dent
Cowgill
Lea Yeat
2205
Widdale Fell
B6255
Wether
Countersett
Semer Water
Thoralby
Penhill 1792
West Burton
Marsett
Stalling Busk
Stone House
Calf Top
Harland Hill
Newbiggin
Melmerby
Carlton

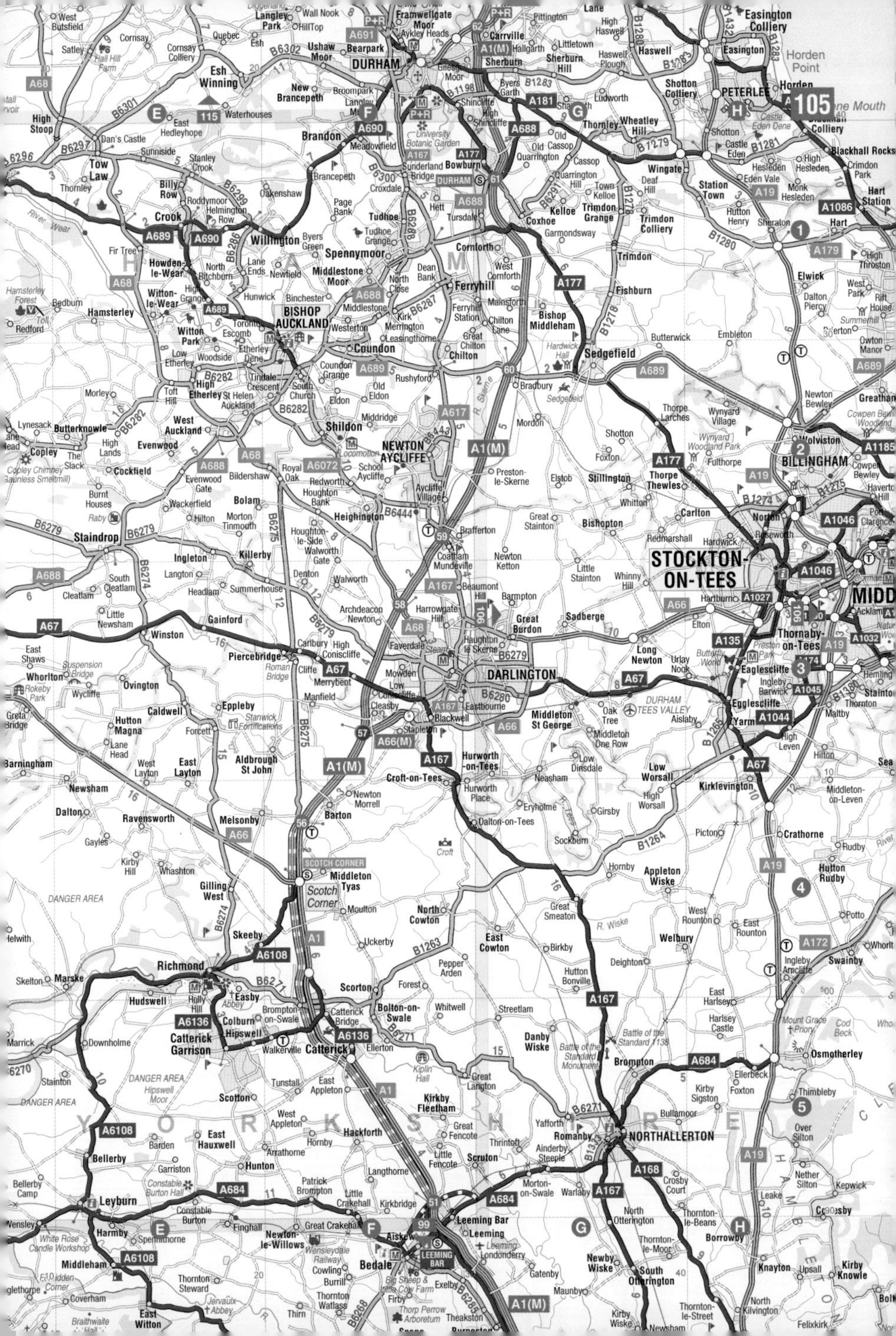
105
West Butsfield
Langley Park
Wall Nook
HillTop
Framwellgate Moor
Aykley Heads
P+R
Carrville
Hallgarth
Pittington
Littletown
High Haswell
Haswell
Haswell Plough
Easington Colliery
Easington
Horden Point
Horden
Satley
Cornsay
Hall Hill Farm
Quebec
Esh
Cornsay Colliery
Ushaw Moor
Bearpark
DURHAM
Gilesgate Moor
Sherburn
Sherburn Hill
Shotton Colliery
PETERLEE
Esh Winning
New Brancepeth
Broompark
Langley Moor
Shincliffe
High Shincliffe
Byers Garth
Shadforth
Ludworth
Thornley
Wheatley Hill
Shotton
Castle Eden Dene
Castle Eden
Blackhall Colliery
Blackhall Rocks
University Botanic Garden
High Stoop
Waterhouses
East Hedleyhope
Dan's Castle
Brandon
Meadowfield
Sunderland Bridge
Bowburn
Old Cassop
Cassop
Quarrington
Quarrington Hill
Wingate
Station Town
Deaf Hill
Hesleden
High Hesleden
Eden Vale
Monk Hesleden
Crimdon Park
Hart Station
Tow Law
Thornley
Sunniside
Stanley Crook
Billy Row
Roddymoor
Helmington Row
Oakenshaw
Brancepeth
Page Bank
Croxdale
Hett
Tursdale
Coxhoe
Kelloe
Town Kelloe
Trimdon Grange
Trimdon Colliery
Hutton Henry
Sheraton
Hart
River Wear
Crook
Willington
Byers Green
Tudhoe
Tudhoe Grange
Spennymoor
Garmondsway
Cornforth
West Cornforth
Trimdon
Fir Tree
Howden-le-Wear
North Bitchburn
Lane Ends
Newfield
Middlestone Moor
Dean Bank
North Close
Ferryhill
High Throston
Elwick
West Park
Rift House
Dalton Piercy
Summerhill
Hamsterley Forest
Bedburn
Redford
Hamsterley
Witton-le-Wear
High Grange
Hunwick
Binchester
BISHOP AUCKLAND
Middlestone
Kirk Merrington
Ferryhill Station
Mainsforth
Chilton Lane
Bishop Middleham
Fishburn
Butterwick
Embleton
Owton Manor
Witton Park
Escomb
Toronto
Westerton
Leasingthorne
Great Chilton
Chilton
Hardwick Hall
Sedgefield
Low Etherley
Etherley Dene
Woodside
Coundon
Coundon Grange
Rushyford
High Etherley
Tindale Crescent
South Church
Old Eldon
Eldon
Bradbury
Sedgefield
Newton Bewley
Greatham
Cowpen Bewley Woodland
Morley
Toft Hill
St Helen Auckland
Middridge
Mordon
Thorpe Larches
Wynyard Village
Wolviston
Lynesack
Butterknowle
West Auckland
Shildon
NEWTON AYCLIFFE
Shotton
Wynyard Woodland Park
BILLINGHAM
Cowpen Bewley
Copley
High Lands
Evenwood
Locomotion
School Aycliffe
Foxton
Fulthorpe
The Slack
Copley Chimney (Gaunless Smeltmill)
Cockfield
Evenwood Gate
Bildershaw
Royal Oak
Redworth
Preston-le-Skerne
Elstob
Stillington
Thorpe Thewles
Haverton Hill
Houghton Bank
Aycliffe Village
Whitton
Carlton
Port Clarence
Burnt Houses
Raby
Wackerfield
Bolam
Morton Tinmouth
Heighington
Bishopton
Norton
Hilton
Great Stainton
Redmarshall
Hardwick
Roseworth
Staindrop
Brafferton
Ingleton
Killerby
Houghton-le-Side
Walworth Gate
Coatham Mundeville
Newton Ketton
Little Stainton
STOCKTON-ON-TEES
Langton
Denton
Whinny Hill
MIDD
South Cleatlam
Headlam
Summerhouse
Walworth
Beaumont Hill
Barmpton
Hartburn
Cleatlam
Little Newsham
Archdeacon Newton
Harrowgate Hill
Great Burdon
Sadberge
Elton
Acklam
Gainford
Thornaby-on-Tees
Winston
Haughton le Skerne
Long Newton
Preston Park
East Shaws
Piercebridge
Carlbury
High Coniscliffe
Faverdale
Urlay Nook
Butterfly World
Eaglescliffe
Whorlton
Suspension Bridge
Roman Bridge
Cliffe
Merrybent
Mowden
Low Coniscliffe
DARLINGTON
Ingleby Barwick
Hemlington
Rokeby Park
Wycliffe
Ovington
Manfield
Cleasby
Eastbourne
Oak Tree
DURHAM TEES VALLEY
Aislaby
Egglescliffe
Maltby
Stainton
Thornton
Greta Bridge
Caldwell
Eppleby
Stanwick Fortifications
Blackwell
Stapleton
Middleton St George
Middleton One Row
Yarm
High Leven
Hutton Magna
Forcett
Hilton
Lane Head
Aldbrough St John
Hurworth-on-Tees
Low Dinsdale
Barningham
West Layton
East Layton
Croft-on-Tees
Neasham
Low Worsall
Kirklevington
Seamer
Newsham
Newton Morrell
Hurworth Place
Eryholme
High Worsall
Middleton-on-Leven
Dalton
Ravensworth
Melsonby
Barton
Girsby
Picton
Crathorne
Gayles
Dalton-on-Tees
Sockburn
Rudby
Kirby Hill
Whashton
Croft
Hornby
Appleton Wiske
Hutton Rudby
DANGER AREA
Gilling West
SCOTCH CORNER
Middleton Tyas
Scotch Corner
Great Smeaton
Potto
Moulton
North Cowton
West Rounton
East Rounton
R. Wiske
Whorlton
Skeeby
Uckerby
East Cowton
Birkby
Welbury
Swainby
Helwith
Deighton
Ingleby Arncliffe
Richmond
Pepper Arden
Hutton Bonville
Skelton
Marske
Easby
Forest
Hudswell
Holly Hill
Abbey
Brompton-on-Swale
Catterick Bridge
Scorton
Bolton-on-Swale
Whitwell
Streetlam
East Harlsey
Harlsey Castle
Mount Grace Priory
Cod Beck
Colburn
Hipswell
Walkerville
Catterick
Ellerton
Danby Wiske
Battle of the Standard 1138
Battle of the Standard Monument
Marrick
Downholme
Catterick Garrison
Kiplin Hall
Brompton
Osmotherley
Ellerbeck
Great Langton
Foxton
Thimbleby
Stainton
DANGER AREA
Hipswell Moor
Tunstall
East Appleton
Kirby Sigston
Scotton
Kirby Fleetham
Bullamoor
DANGER AREA
West Appleton
Great Fencote
Yafforth
Romanby
NORTHALLERTON
Over Silton
YORKSHIRE
Barden
East Hauxwell
Hornby
Hackforth
Thrintoft
Ainderby Steeple
Bellerby
Arrathorne
Hunton
Little Fencote
Scruton
Crosby Court
Nether Silton
Garriston
Langthorne
Morton-on-Swale
Warlaby
Kepwick
Bellerby Camp
Constable Burton Hall
Patrick Brompton
Little Crakehall
Kirkbridge
Leeming Bar
Thornton-le-Beans
Cotcliffe
Leyburn
Constable Burton
Finghall
Great Crakehall
Leeming
Leake
North Otterington
Borrowby
Wensley
Harmby
Spennithorne
Newton-le-Willows
Aiskew
Leeming
Londonderry
Thornton-le-Moor
Knayton
Upsall
Kirby Knowle
White Rose Candle Workshop
Wensleydale Railway
Bedale
LEEMING BAR
Newby Wiske
South Otterington
Middleham
Hidden Corner
Thornton Steward
Cowling
Burrill
Big Sheep & Little Cow Farm
Exelby
Gatenby
Maunby
Coverham
Jervaulx Abbey
Thornton Watlass
Firby
Thornton-le-Street
North Kilvington
Braithwaite Hall
East Witton
Thirn
Thorp Perrow Arboretum
Theakston
Kirby Wiske
Newsham
Felixkirk
A1(M)
A1
A19
A66
A66(M)
A67
A68
A167
A177
A179
A181
A684
A688
A689
A690
A691
A1086
A6108
A6136
A6072
A617
A1185
A1046
A1027
A1032
A1044
A1045
A135
A172
A168
B6302
B6301
B6297
B6296
B6299
B6286
B6300
B6288
B6287
B6291
B1278
B1283
B1280
B1279
B1281
B1432
B1198
B1274
B1275
B6282
B6279
B6275
B6274
B6444
B6443
B6280
B1380
B1264
B1265
B1263
B6271
B6270
B6285
B6268
B1333
E
F
G
H
1
2
3
4
5

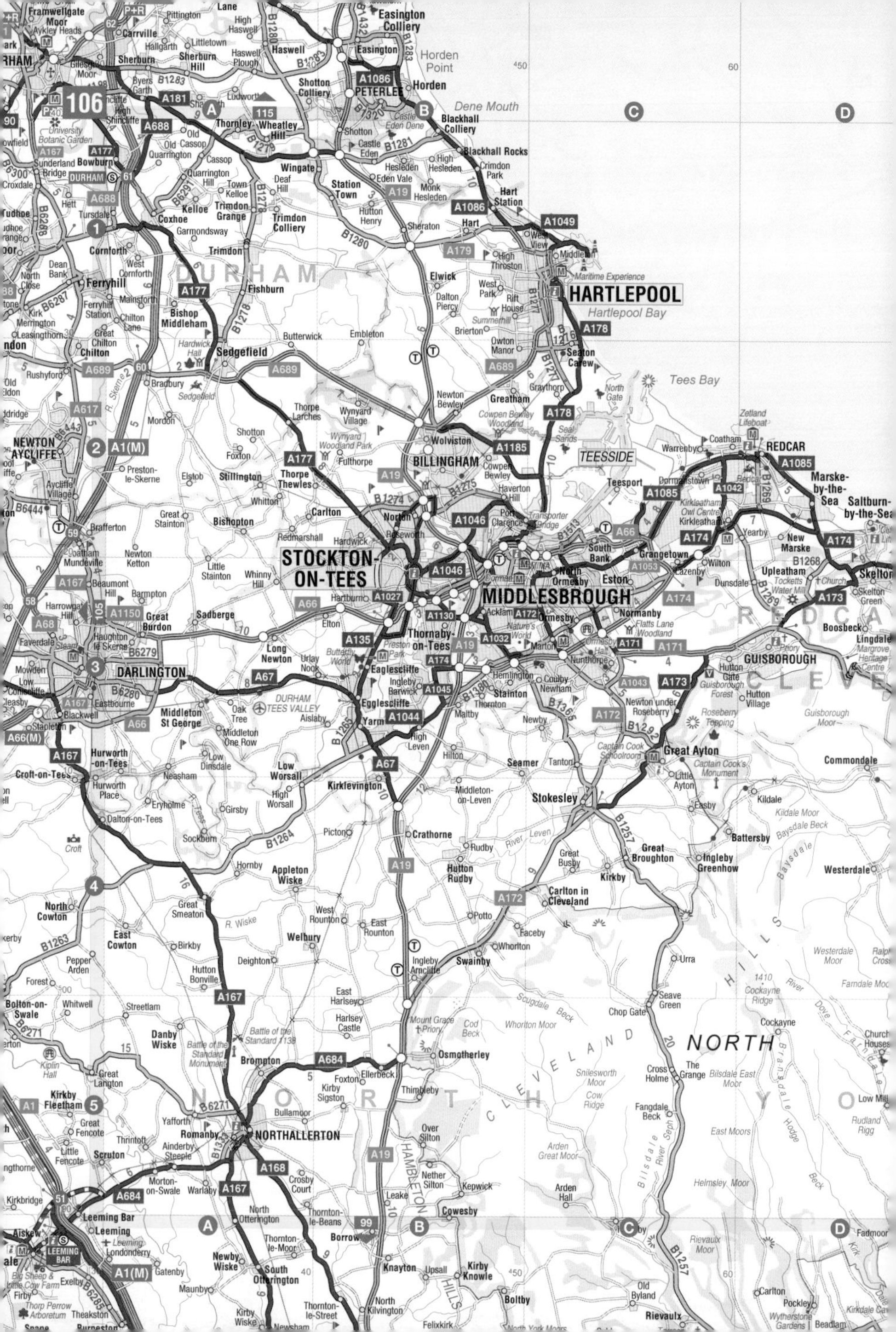

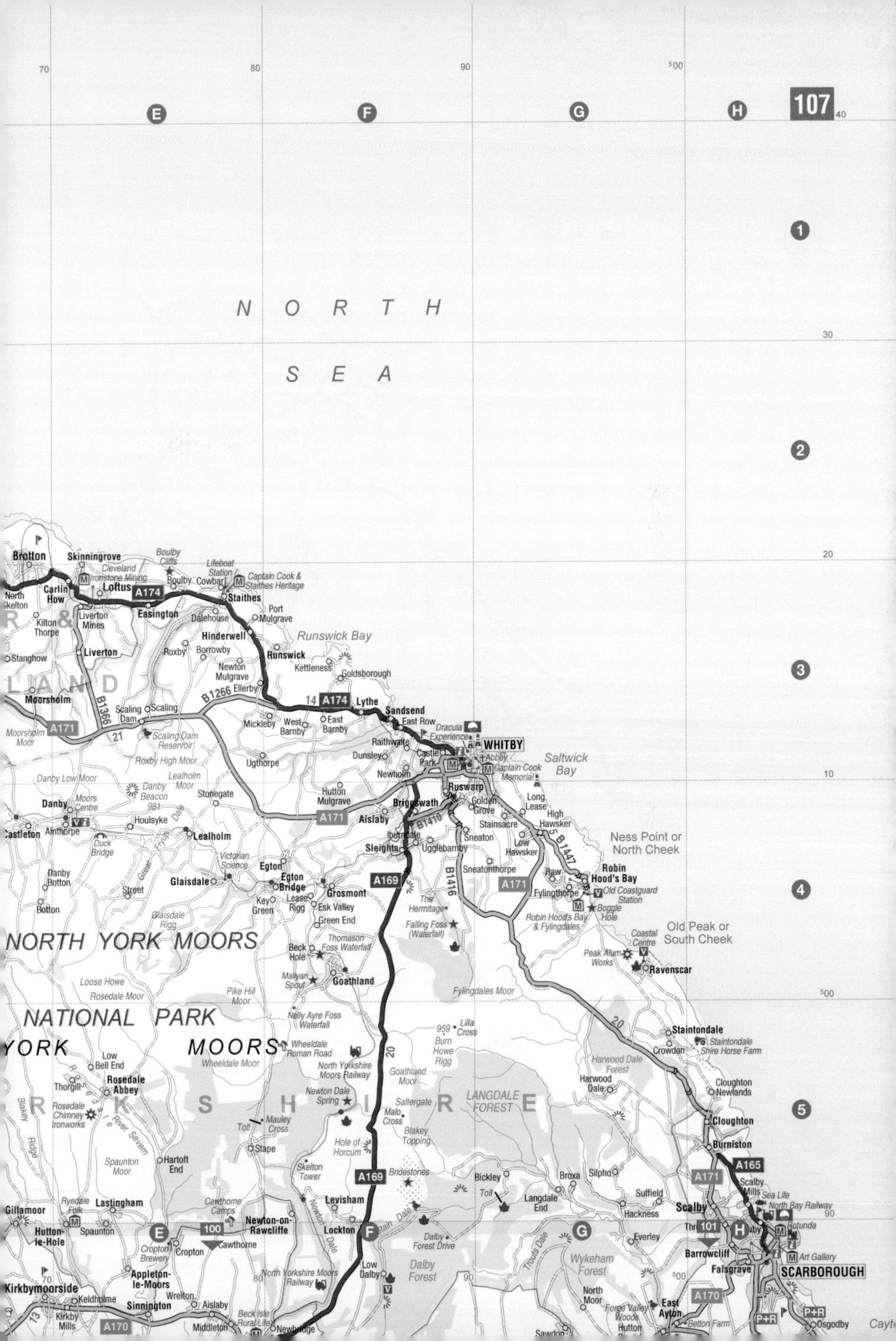
NORTH SEA
WHITBY
SCARBOROUGH
NORTH YORK MOORS
NATIONAL PARK
Brotton
Skinningrove
Loftus
Staithes
Runswick Bay
Runswick
Lythe
Sandsend
Saltwick Bay
Robin Hood's Bay
Ness Point or North Cheek
Old Peak or South Cheek
Ravenscar
Grosmont
Goathland
Sleights
Egton Bridge
Glaisdale
Lealholm
Danby
Castleton
Rosedale Abbey
Hutton-le-Hole
Lastingham
Kirkbymoorside
Levisham
Lockton
Staintondale
Cloughton
Burniston
Scalby
Falsgrave
Langdale Forest
Dalby Forest
Fylingdales Moor
A174
A171
A169
A170
A165
B1266
B1416
B1447

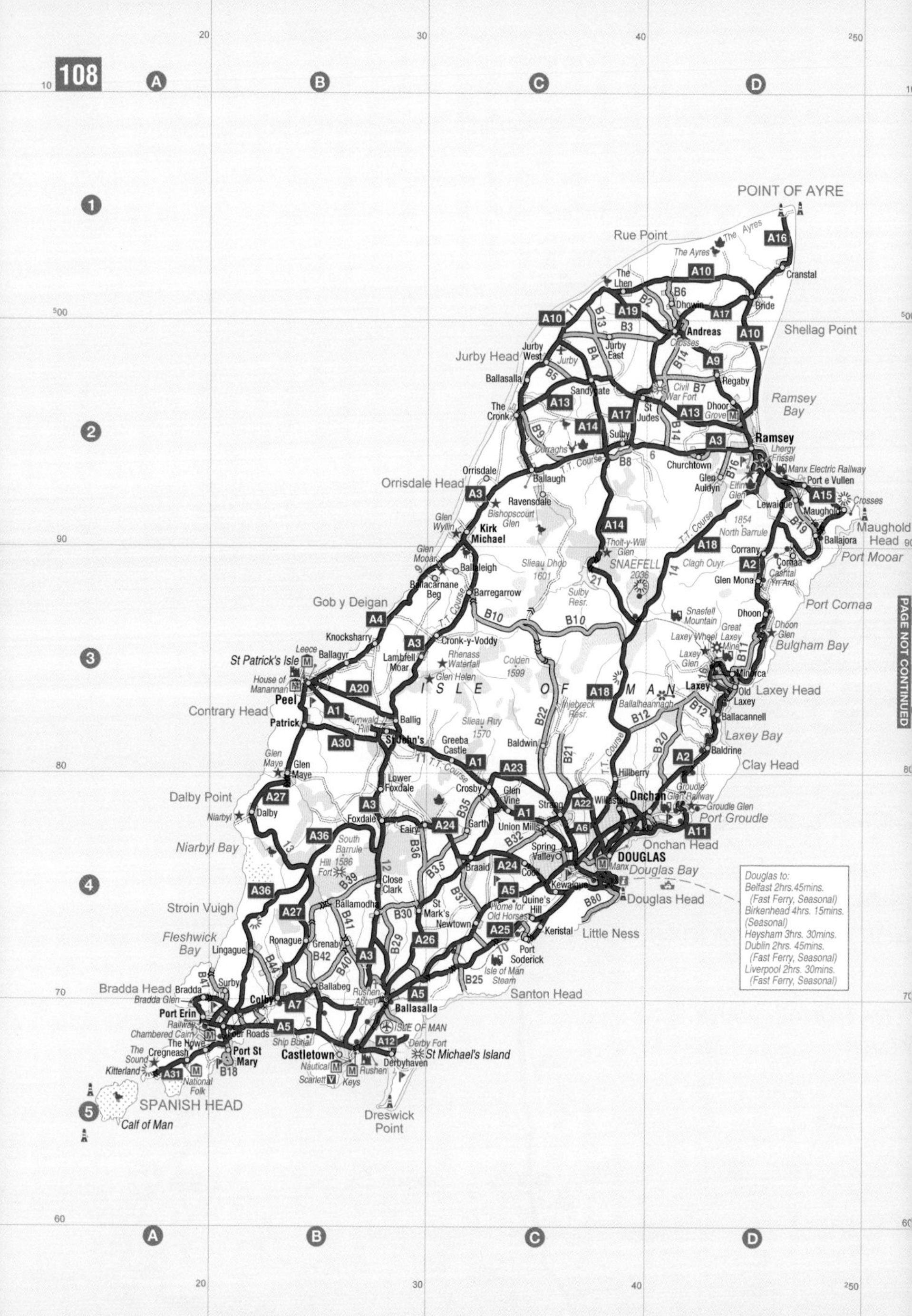

POINT OF AYRE
Rue Point
The Ayres
Cranstal
The Lhen
Dhowin
Bride
Andreas
Shellag Point
Jurby Head
Jurby West
Jurby East
Jurby
Ballasalla
Sandygate
Regaby
Civil War Fort
The Cronk
St Judes
Dhoor
Grove
Ramsey Bay
Ramsey
Lhergy Frissel
Curraghs
Sulby
T.T. Course
Churchtown
Manx Electric Railway
Port e Vullen
Orrisdale
Ballaugh
Glen Auldyn
Elfin Glen
Orrisdale Head
Ravensdale
Bishopscourt Glen
Lewaigue
Crosses
Maughold
Maughold Head
Glen Wyllin
Kirk Michael
Tholt-y-Will Glen
1854
North Barrule
Ballajora
Port Mooar
Glen Mooar
Ballaleigh
Slieau Dhoo 1601
SNAEFELL 2036
Clagh Ouyr
Corrany
Cornaa
Glen Mona
Cashtal Yn Ard
Ballacarnane Beg
Barregarrow
Sulby Resr.
Gob y Deigan
Snaefell Mountain
Dhoon
Port Cornaa
Dhoon Glen
Knocksharry
Cronk-y-Voddy
Laxey Wheel
Great Laxey Mine
Bulgham Bay
St Patrick's Isle
Leece
Ballagyr
Lambfell Moar
Rhenass Waterfall
Colden 1599
Laxey Glen
House of Manannan
Glen Helen
ISLE OF MAN
Minorca
Laxey
Laxey Head
Old Laxey
Peel
Contrary Head
Ballaheannagh
Ballacannell
Patrick
Tynwald Hill
Ballig
Injebreck Resr.
St John's
Slieau Ruy 1570
Greeba Castle
Baldwin
Laxey Bay
Baldrine
Glen Maye
Lower Foxdale
Hillberry
Clay Head
Crosby
Glen Vine
Onchan
Groudle Glen Railway
Groudle Glen
Dalby Point
Strang
Willaston
Port Groudle
Niarbyl
Dalby
Foxdale
Eairy
Garth
Union Mills
Spring Valley
Onchan Head
Niarbyl Bay
South Barrule
Hill Fort 1586
DOUGLAS
Manx
Douglas Bay
Braaid
Cooil
Close Clark
Kewaigue
Douglas Head
Stroin Vuigh
Ballamodha
St Mark's
Quine's Hill
Home for Old Horses
Newtown
Little Ness
Keristal
Fleshwick Bay
Lingague
Ronague
Grenaby
Port Soderick
Isle of Man Steam
Bradda Head
Bradda
Surby
Santon Head
Bradda Glen
Colby
Ballabeg
Rushen Abbey
Port Erin
Railway
Ballasalla
Chambered Cairn
Four Roads
ISLE OF MAN
The Howe
Ship Burial
Derby Fort
The Sound
Cregneash
Port St Mary
Castletown
Derbyhaven
St Michael's Island
Kitterland
National Folk
Nautical
Rushen
Scarlett
Keys
SPANISH HEAD
Calf of Man
Dreswick Point
PAGE NOT CONTINUED
Douglas to:
Belfast 2hrs.45mins. (Fast Ferry, Seasonal)
Birkenhead 4hrs. 15mins. (Seasonal)
Heysham 3hrs. 30mins.
Dublin 2hrs. 45mins. (Fast Ferry, Seasonal)
Liverpool 2hrs. 30mins. (Fast Ferry, Seasonal)

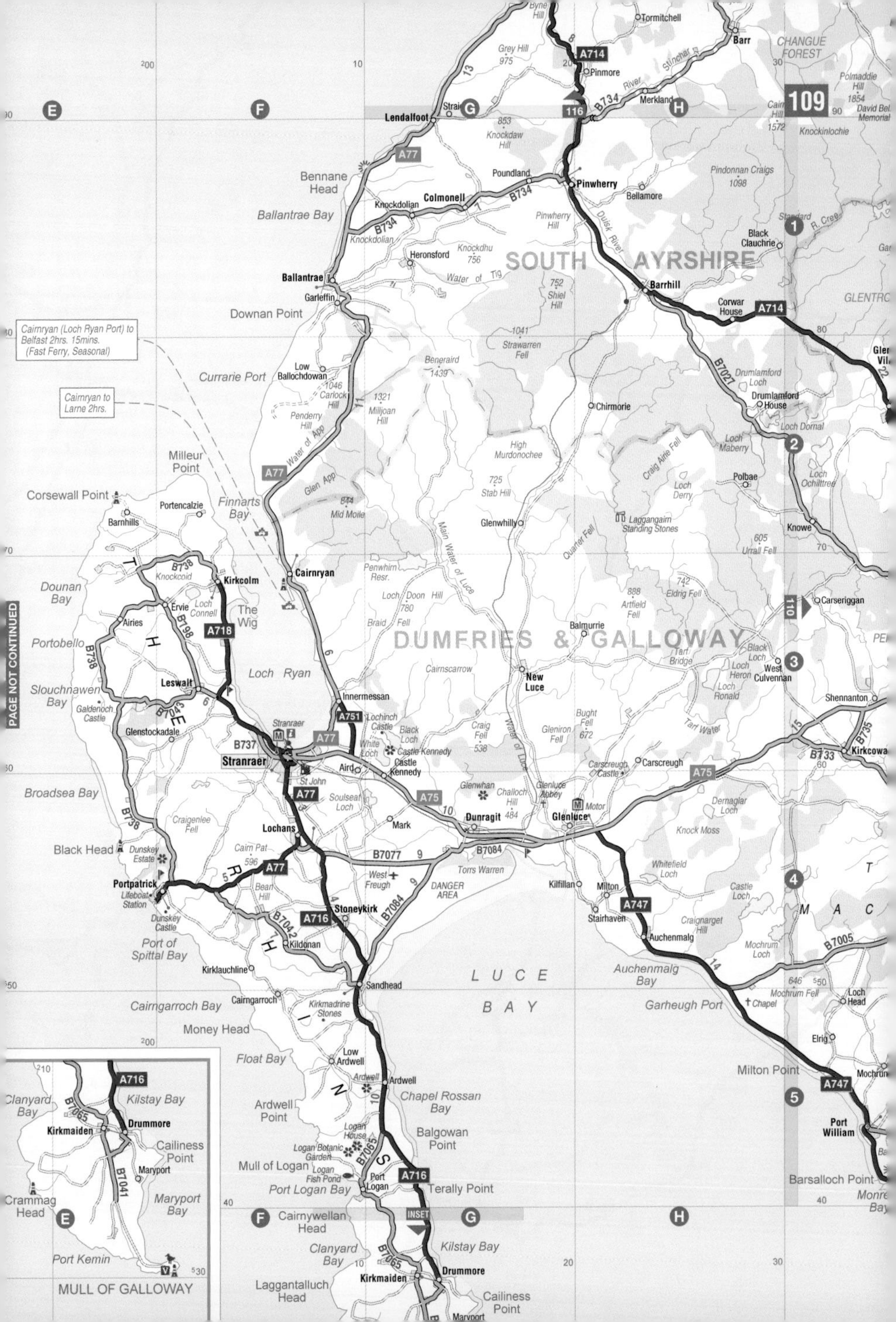

Byne Hill
Tormitchell
Barr
CHANGUE FOREST
Grey Hill 975
A714
Pinmore
Stinchar River
B734
Merkland
Polmaddie Hill 1854
David Bell Memorial
Cairn Hill 1572
109
Knockinlochie
Lendalfoot
Straid
116
853 Knockdaw Hill
A77
Bennane Head
Poundland
Pinwherry
Bellamore
Pindonnan Craigs 1098
Colmonell
Knockdolian
Ballantrae Bay
B734
Knockdolian
Pinwherry Hill
Standard
R. Cree
Black Clauchrie
Heronsford
Knockdhu 756
SOUTH AYRSHIRE
Duisk River
Water of Tig
Ballantrae
Garleffin
752 Shiel Hill
Barrhill
Corwar House
A714
GLENTROOL
Downan Point
Cairnryan (Loch Ryan Port) to Belfast 2hrs. 15mins. (Fast Ferry, Seasonal)
1041 Strawarren Fell
B7027
Glen Village
Currarie Port
Low Ballochdowan
1046 Carlock Hill
Beneraird 1439
Drumlamford Loch
Drumlamford House
Cairnryan to Larne 2hrs.
1321 Milljoan Hill
Penderry Hill
Chirmorie
Loch Dornal
Loch Maberry
Water of App
High Murdonochee
Craig Airie Fell
Milleur Point
A77
Glen App
725 Stab Hill
Polbae
Loch Derry
Loch Ochiltree
Corsewall Point
Portencalzie
Finnarts Bay
844 Mid Moile
Barnhills
Glenwhilly
Laggangairn Standing Stones
Quarter Fell
Knowe
605 Urrall Fell
Main Water of Luce
B738
Knockcoid
Kirkcolm
Cairnryan
Penwhirn Resr.
742 Eldrig Fell
Dounan Bay
Loch Connell
Ervie
Loch Doon Hill 780
888 Artfield Fell
110
Carseriggan
Airies
B798
The Wig
A718
Braid Fell
Balmurrie
Portobello
B738
DUMFRIES & GALLOWAY
PAGE NOT CONTINUED
Loch Ryan
Cairnscarrow
Tarf Bridge
Black Loch
Loch Heron
West Culvennan
Slouchnawen Bay
Galdenoch Castle
Leswalt
New Luce
Loch Ronald
Innermessan
Shennanton
B7043
Glenstockadale
Stranraer
A751
Lochinch Castle
Black Loch
White Loch
Castle Kennedy
Craig Fell 538
Water of Luce
Bught Fell 672
Gleniron Fell
Tarf Water
B735
B737
Stranraer
A77
Airds
Castle Kennedy
Carscreugh Castle
Carscreugh
A75
B733
Kirkcowan
St John
Broadsea Bay
Soulseat Loch
A75
Glenwhan
Challoch Hill 484
Glenluce Abbey
Motor
Dernaglar Loch
Craigenlee Fell
Mark
Dunragit
Glenluce
Lochans
Knock Moss
Black Head
Dunskey Estate
Cairn Pat 596
B7077
B7084
Torrs Warren
Whitefield Loch
A77
West Freugh
DANGER AREA
Kilfillan
Milton
Portpatrick
Lifeboat Station
Bean Hill
Stoneykirk
B7084
Castle Loch
A747
Dunskey Castle
B7042
A716
Stairhaven
Craignarget Hill
Kildonan
Auchenmalg
Port of Spittal Bay
Mochrum Loch
B7005
Kirklauchline
Auchenmalg Bay
LUCE
Sandhead
646
Mochrum Fell
Loch Head
Cairngarroch
Garheugh Port
Cairngarroch Bay
Kirkmadrine Stones
BAY
Chapel
Money Head
Elrig
Float Bay
Low Ardwell
Ardwell
Milton Point
Mochrum
A716
A747
Kilstay Bay
Clanyard Bay
Chapel Rossan Bay
B7065
Ardwell Point
Drummore
Kirkmaiden
Logan House
Balgowan Point
Port William
Cailiness Point
Logan Botanic Garden
B7065
B7041
Maryport
Mull of Logan
Logan Fish Pond
Port Logan
A716
Barsalloch Point
Terally Point
Port Logan Bay
Maryport Bay
Monreith Bay
Crammag Head
Cairnywellan Head
INSET
Clanyard Bay
Kilstay Bay
Port Kemin
B7065
Drummore
Kirkmaiden
MULL OF GALLOWAY
Laggantalluch Head
Cailiness Point
Maryport

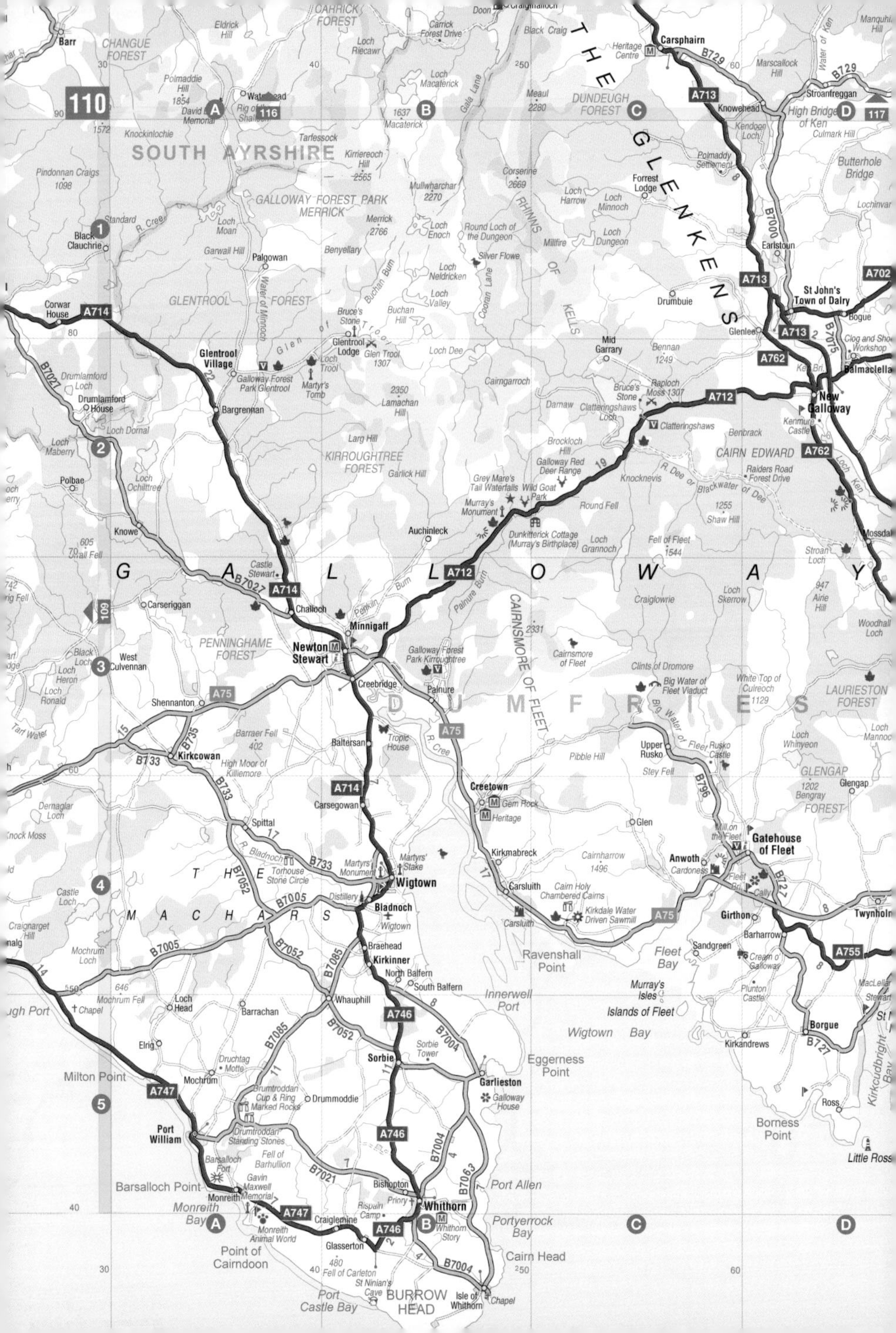
110
Barr
CHANGUE FOREST
Eldrick Hill
CARRICK FOREST
Carrick Forest Drive
Doon
Black Craig
THE GLENKENS
Carsphairn
Heritage Centre
B729
Marscallock Hill
Water of Ken
Manquhill
Polmaddie Hill 1854
Waterhead
Rig of the Shalloch
116
David Bell Memorial
Loch Riecawr
Loch Macaterick
1637 Macaterick
Gala Lane
Meaul 2280
DUNDEUGH FOREST
A713
Knowehead
Stroanfreggan
High Bridge of Ken
117
Kendoon Loch
Culmark Hill
1572
Knockinlochie
Tarfessock
SOUTH AYRSHIRE
Kirriereoch Hill 2565
Corserine 2669
Polmaddy Settlement
Butterhole Bridge
Pindonnan Craigs 1098
GALLOWAY FOREST PARK
MERRICK
Mullwharchar 2270
Forrest Lodge
Loch Harrow
Loch Minnoch
RHINNS OF KELLS
B7000
Lochinvar
Standard
R. Cree
Loch Moan
Merrick 2766
Loch Enoch
Round Loch of the Dungeon
Loch Dungeon
Millfire
Black Clauchrie
Garwall Hill
Palgowan
Benyellary
Silver Flowe
Earlstoun
Loch Neldricken
Buchan Burn
Cooran Lane
A702
GLENTROOL FOREST
Water of Minnoch
Loch Valley
Drumbuie
St John's Town of Dalry
Corwar House
A714
80
Bruce's Stone
Glen of Trool
Buchan Hill
Glenlee
Bogue
Glentrool Lodge
Glen Trool 1307
Loch Dee
Mid Garrary
Bennan 1249
Clog and Shoe Workshop
B7075
A762
Glentrool Village
Loch Trool
Galloway Forest Park Glentrool
Martyr's Tomb
Cairngarroch
Bruce's Stone
Raploch Moss 1307
Ken Bri.
Balmaclellan
B7027
Drumlamford Loch
Drumlamford House
Bargrennan
2350 Lamachan Hill
Darnaw
Clatteringshaws Loch
A712
New Galloway
Loch Dornal
Clatteringshaws
Kenmure Castle
Loch Maberry
Larg Hill
Brockloch Hill
Benbrack
CAIRN EDWARD
KIRROUGHTREE FOREST
Galloway Red Deer Range
Raiders Road Forest Drive
Loch Ken
Polbae
Loch Ochiltree
Garlick Hill
Grey Mare's Tail Waterfalls
Wild Goat Park
Knocknevis
R. Dee or Blackwater of Dee
Murray's Monument
Fell Loch
1255 Shaw Hill
Knowe
Auchinleck
Dunkitterick Cottage (Murray's Birthplace)
Loch Grannoch
Fell of Fleet 1544
Mossdale
605 Urrall Fell
Stroan Loch
G A L L O W A Y
Castle Stewart
A714
Palnure Burn
CAIRNSMORE OF FLEET
Loch Skerrow
947 Airie Hill
Carseriggan
Challoch
Penkiln Burn
Minnigaff
Craiglowrie
109
2331
Woodhall Loch
PENNINGHAME FOREST
Newton Stewart
Galloway Forest Park Kirroughtree
Cairnsmore of Fleet
Black Loch
West Culvennan
Loch Heron
Loch Ronald
Clints of Dromore
Creebridge
Palnure
Big Water of Fleet Viaduct
White Top of Culreoch 1129
LAURIESTON FOREST
Shennanton
A75
D U M F R I E S
Tarf Water
Barraer Fell 402
Baltersan
Tropic House
R. Cree
Upper Rusko
Rusko Castle
Loch Whinyeon
Loch Mannoch
B733
Kirkcowan
High Moor of Killiemore
Pibble Hill
B735
15
Stey Fell
B796
GLENGAP
1202 Bengray
Glengap
FOREST
60
A714
Carsegowan
Creetown
Gem Rock
Heritage
Dernaglar Loch
Spittal
17
Glen
Knock Moss
R. Bladnoch
Torhouse Stone Circle
Martyrs' Monument
Martyrs' Stake
Wigtown
Kirkmabreck
Cairnharrow 1496
Mill on the Fleet
Gatehouse of Fleet
Anwoth
Cardoness
Fleet Bri.
Cally
B727
Castle Loch
T H E
M A C H A R S
B7052
B7005
Distillery
Bladnoch
Wigtown
Carsluith
Cairn Holy Chambered Cairns
Kirkdale Water Driven Sawmill
Girthon
Twynholm
Craignarget Hill
Braehead
Kirkinner
Ravenshall Point
Barharrow
A755
Mochrum Loch
B7052
B7085
North Balfern
South Balfern
Fleet Bay
Sandgreen
Cream o' Galloway
Murray's Isles
Islands of Fleet
646
Mochrum Fell
Loch Head
Whauphill
Innerwell Port
Plunton Castle
MacLellan's
Stewartry
Port
Chapel
Barrachan
A746
Wigtown Bay
Borgue
B727
Elrig
Sorbie Tower
B7004
Kirkandrews
Druchtag Motte
Sorbie
Eggerness Point
Milton Point
Mochrum
Garlieston
Kirkcudbright Bay
A747
Drumtroddan Cup & Ring Marked Rocks
Drummoddie
Galloway House
Port William
Drumtroddan Standing Stones
A746
Fell of Barhullion
B7021
B7004
Borness Point
Ross
Little Ross
Barsalloch Fort
Barsalloch Point
Gavin Maxwell Memorial
Bishopton
Priory
B7063
Port Allen
Monreith
Monreith Bay
A747
Craiglemine
Rispain Camp
Whithorn
Whithorn Story
Portyerrock Bay
Monreith Animal World
Glasserton
Point of Cairndoon
480 Fell of Carleton
B7004
Cairn Head
St Ninian's Cave
Port Castle Bay
BURROW HEAD
Isle of Whithorn
Chapel
A B C D
1 2 3 4 5
30 40 250 60 90 80 70 60 50 40

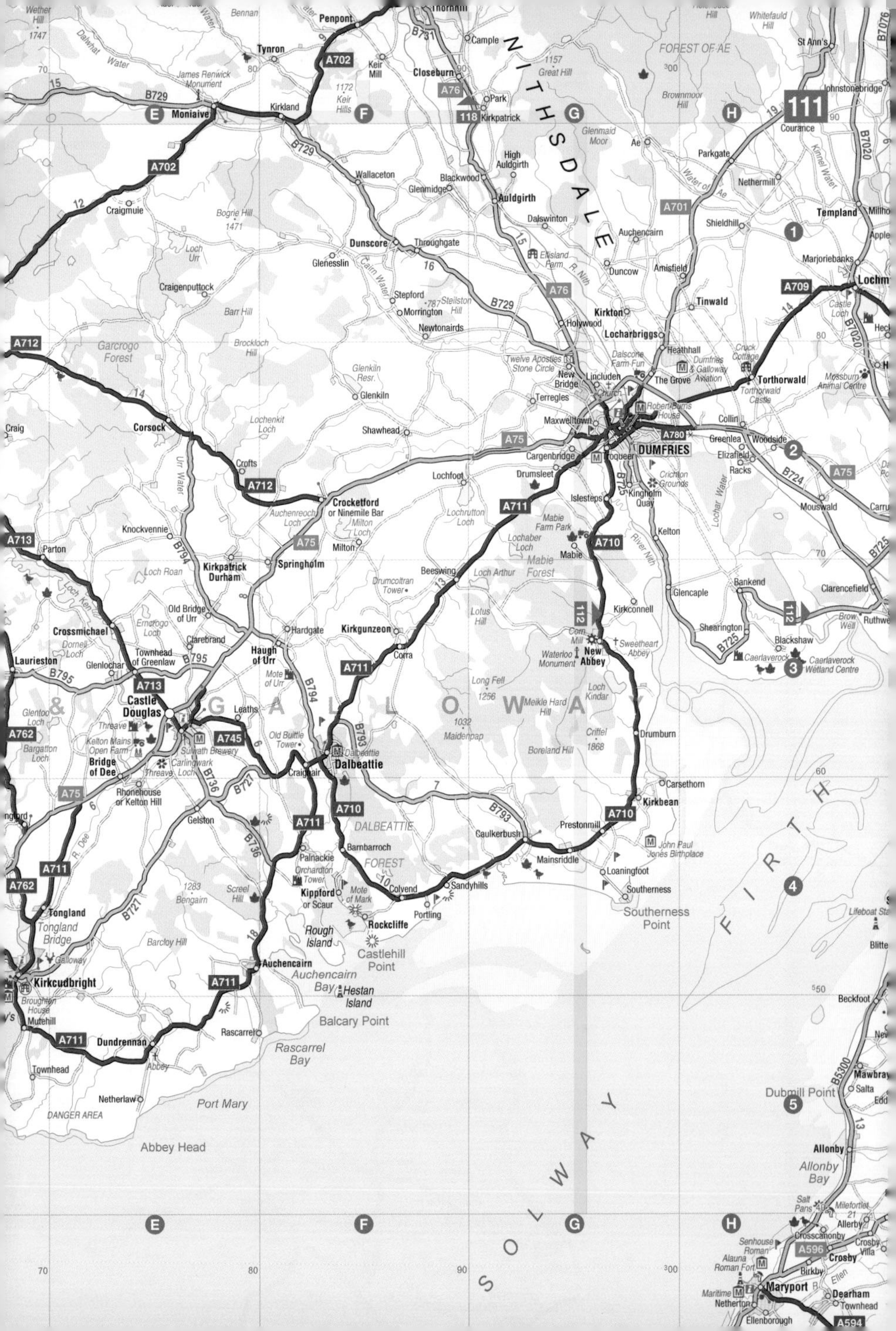
NITHSDALE
GALLOWAY
SOLWAY FIRTH
FOREST OF AE
Penpont
Thornhill
Tynron
Moniaive
Kirkland
Keir Mill
Closeburn
Cample
Park
Kirkpatrick
James Renwick Monument
Keir Hills
Great Hill
Glenmaid Moor
Brownmoor Hill
Whitefauld Hill
St Ann's
Johnstonebridge
Courance
Ae
Parkgate
Nethermill
Kinnel Water
Water of Ae
Templand
Shieldhill
Marjoriebanks
Amisfield
Tinwald
Auchencairn
Duncow
Dalswinton
Auldgirth
High Auldgirth
Blackwood
Glenmidge
Wallaceton
Craigmuie
Bogrie Hill
Loch Urr
Dunscore
Throughgate
Glenesslin
Cairn Water
Stepford
Morrington
Steilston Hill
Newtonairds
Ellisland Farm
R. Nith
Holywood
Kirkton
Locharbriggs
Heathhall
Craigenputtock
Barr Hill
Brockloch Hill
Garcrogo Forest
Glenkiln Resr.
Glenkiln
Twelve Apostles Stone Circle
New Bridge
Lincluden
Dalscone Farm Fun
Dumfries & Galloway Aviation
The Grove
Crook Cottage
Torthorwald
Torthorwald Castle
Mossburn Animal Centre
Castle Loch
Terregles
Robert Burns House
Maxwelltown
DUMFRIES
Collin
Greenlea
Woodside
Elizafield
Racks
Mouswald
Cargenbridge
Troqueer
Drumsleet
Lochfoot
Shawhead
Lochenkit Loch
Corsock
Crofts
Craig
Crocketford or Ninemile Bar
Auchenreoch Loch
Milton Loch
Milton
Lochrutton Loch
Crichton Grounds
Kingholm Quay
Islesteps
Mabie Farm Park
Lochaber Loch
Mabie
Mabie Forest
Kelton
River Nith
Lochar Water
Knockvennie
Urr Water
Parton
Loch Ken
Loch Roan
Kirkpatrick Durham
Springholm
Beeswing
Loch Arthur
Drumcoltran Tower
Lotus Hill
Kirkconnell
Glencaple
Bankend
Clarencefield
Brow Well
Ruthwell
Shearington
Blackshaw
Caerlaverock
Caerlaverock Wetland Centre
Crossmichael
Dornell Loch
Ernespie Loch
Old Bridge of Urr
Clarebrand
Hardgate
Kirkgunzeon
Corra
Corn Mill
New Abbey
Sweetheart Abbey
Waterloo Monument
Laurieston
Glenlochar
Townhead of Greenlaw
Haugh of Urr
Mote of Urr
Long Fell
Meikle Hard Hill
Loch Kindar
Criffel
Glentoo Loch
Castle Douglas
Threave
Leaths
Old Buittle Tower
Dalbeattie
Maidenpap
Boreland Hill
Drumburn
Kelton Mains Open Farm
Sulwath Brewery
Carlingwark Loch
Bargatton Loch
Bridge of Dee
Rhonehouse or Kelton Hill
Craignair
Carsethorn
Kirkbean
Gelston
DALBEATTIE FOREST
Barnbarroch
Caulkerbush
Prestonmill
Mainsriddle
John Paul Jones Birthplace
Loaningfoot
Southerness
Southerness Point
Palnackie
Orchardton Tower
Kippford or Scaur
Mote of Mark
Colvend
Sandyhills
Portling
Rockcliffe
Rough Island
Castlehill Point
Bengairn
Screel Hill
Tongland
Tongland Bridge
R. Dee
Galloway
Kirkcudbright
Barcloy Hill
Auchencairn
Auchencairn Bay
Hestan Island
Balcary Point
Broughton House
Mutehill
Rascarrel
Rascarrel Bay
Dundrennan
Abbey
Townhead
Netherlaw
Port Mary
DANGER AREA
Abbey Head
Lifeboat Station
Blitterlees
Beckfoot
Mawbray
Salta
Dubmill Point
Allonby
Allonby Bay
Salt Pans
Milefortlet 21
Allerby
Crosscanonby
Crosby
Crosby Villa
Senhouse Roman Museum
Alauna Roman Fort
Maritime
Maryport
Birkby
Ellen
Dearham
Townhead
Netherton
Ellenborough
A702
A76
A701
A709
A712
A713
A75
A780
A711
A710
A762
A745
A594
A596
B729
B731
B7020
B7076
B794
B795
B736
B727
B721
B793
B725
B724
B5300
111
112
118
E
F
G
H
1
2
3
4
5

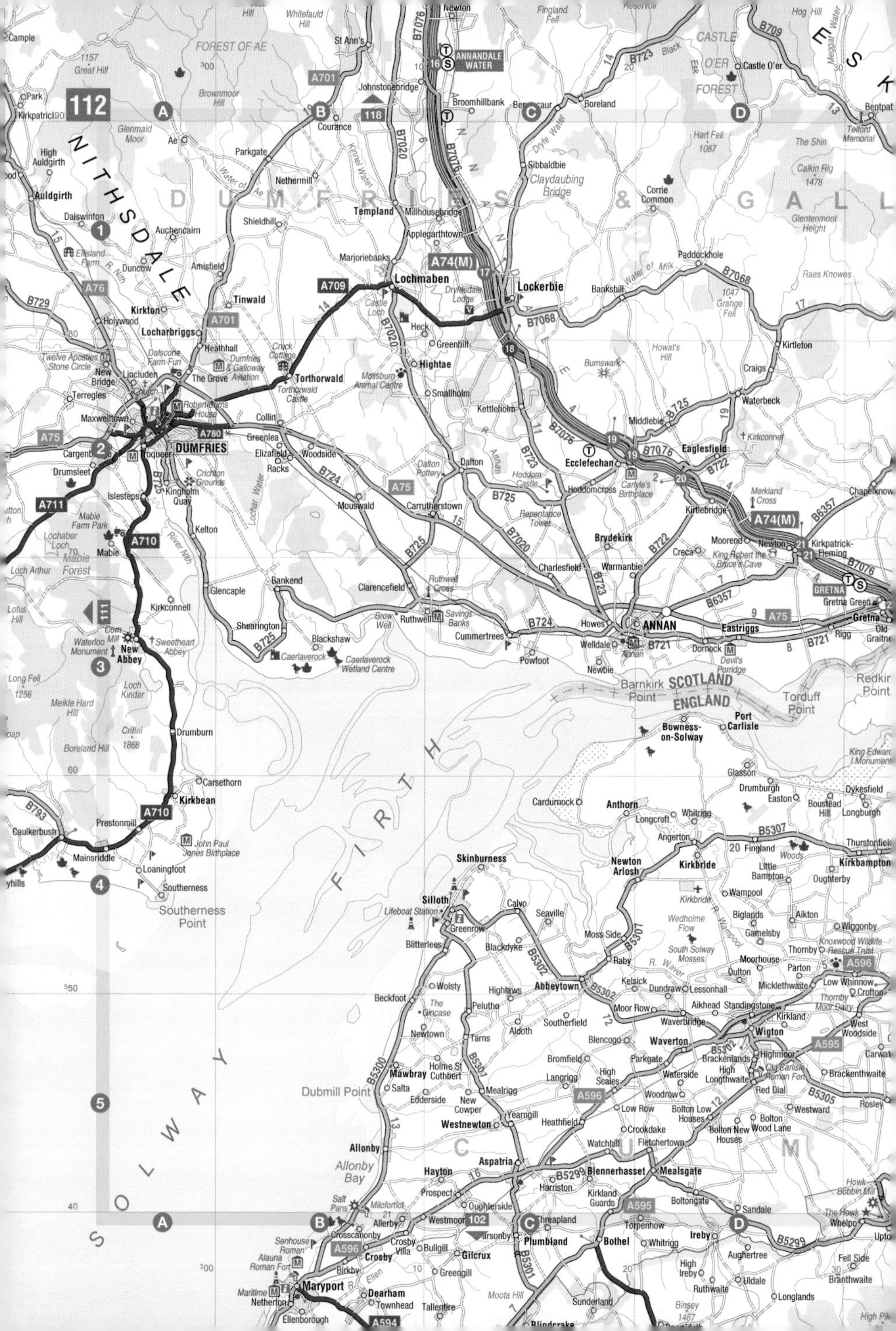
112
A
B
C
D
1
2
3
4
5
118
111
102
NITHSDALE
DUMFRIES & GALL
FOREST OF AE
CASTLE O'ER FOREST
ESK
SOLWAY FIRTH
SCOTLAND
ENGLAND
Cample
1157 Great Hill
Whitefauld Hill
Newton
Fingland Fell
Hog Hill
St Ann's
ANNANDALE WATER
Castle O'er
Park
Kirkpatrick
Brownmoor Hill
Johnstonebridge
Broomhillbank
Boreland
Bentpath
Courance
Hart Fell 1087
Telford Memorial
Glenmaid Moor
Ae
The Shin
High Auldgirth
Parkgate
Sibbaldbie
Calkin Rig 1478
Claydaubing Bridge
Auldgirth
Nethermill
Corrie Common
Templand
Millhousebridge
Dalswinton
Shieldhill
Auchencairn
Applegarthtown
Glentenmont Height
Ellisland Farm
Marjoriebanks
Paddockhole
Duncow
Amisfield
Raes Knowes
Lochmaben
Lockerbie
Bankshill
1047 Grange Fell
Kirkton
Tinwald
Castle Loch
Dryfesdale Lodge
Holywood
Locharbriggs
Heck
Greenhill
Kirtleton
Heathhall
Cruck Cottage
Hightae
Howat's Hill
Twelve Apostles Stone Circle
Dalscone Farm Fun
Dumfries & Galloway Aviation
Burnswark
Craigs
New Bridge
Lincluden
The Grove
Torthorwald
Mossburn Animal Centre
Terregles
Torthorwald Castle
Smallholm
Waterbeck
Robert Burns House
Kettleholm
Maxwelltown
Collin
Middlebie
DUMFRIES
Cargenbridge
Troqueer
Greenlea
Elizafield
Woodside
Ecclefechan
Eaglesfield
Kirkconnel
Drumsleet
Racks
Dalton Pottery
Dalton
Carlyle's Birthplace
Merkland Cross
Chapelknowe
Crichton Grounds
Kingholm Quay
Hoddom Castle
Hoddomcross
Kirtlebridge
Islesteps
Mouswald
Carrutherstown
Repentance Tower
Mabie Farm Park
Moorend
Newton
Kirkpatrick-Fleming
Lochaber Loch
Mabie
Kelton
Brydekirk
Creca
King Robert the Bruce's Cave
Mabie Forest
Loch Arthur
River Nith
Charlesfield
Warmanbie
GRETNA
Bankend
Clarencefield
Ruthwell Cross
Glencaple
Lotus Hill
Kirkconnell
Ruthwell
Savings Banks
Gretna Green
Shearington
Brow Well
ANNAN
Eastriggs
Gretna
Corn Mill
Cummertrees
Howes
Rigg
Old Graitney
Waterloo Monument
Sweetheart Abbey
New Abbey
Blackshaw
Welldale
Dornock
Caerlaverock
Caerlaverock Wetland Centre
Powfoot
Newbie
Devil's Porridge
Long Fell 1256
Loch Kindar
Barnkirk Point
Redkirk Point
Meikle Hard Hill
Torduff Point
Criffel 1868
Drumburn
Bowness-on-Solway
Port Carlisle
Boreland Hill
King Edward I Monument
Glasson
Carsethorn
Drumburgh
Dykesfield
Easton
Cardurnock
Anthorn
Boustead Hill
Longburgh
Kirkbean
Whitrigg
Longcroft
Prestonmill
Caulkerbush
Angerton
Fingland
Thurstonfield
John Paul Jones Birthplace
Woods
Mainsriddle
Skinburness
Newton Arlosh
Kirkbride
Kirkbampton
Loaningfoot
Little Bampton
Oughterby
Southerness
Southerness Point
Wampool
Silloth
Calvo
Seaville
Lifeboat Station
Greenrow
Wedholme Flow
Biglands
Aikton
Gamelsby
Wiggonby
Blitterlees
Moss Side
Blackdyke
South Solway Mosses
Thornby
Knoxwood Wildlife Rescue Trust
Raby
Moorhouse
Parton
R. Waver
Dulton
Kelsick
Dundraw
Lessonhall
Micklethwaite
Low Whinnow
Wolsty
Abbeytown
Crofton
Highlaws
Thornby Moor Dairy
Beckfoot
Moor Row
Aikhead
Standingstone
The Gincase
Pelutho
Kirkland
Southerfield
Waverbridge
West Woodside
Newtown
Aldoth
Wigton
Tarns
Blencogo
Waverton
Highmoor
Carwath
Parkgate
Brackenlands
Bromfield
Old Carlisle Roman Fort
Brackenthwaite
Holme St Cuthbert
High Longthwaite
Mawbray
High Scales
Waterside
Langrigg
Red Dial
Salta
Dubmill Point
Mealrigg
Edderside
Woodrow
Rosley
New Cowper
Low Row
Bolton Low Houses
Westward
Heathfield
Bolton Wood Lane
Westnewton
Yearngill
Bolton New Houses
Crookdake
Allonby
Watchhill
Fletchertown
Allonby Bay
Aspatria
Blennerhasset
Mealsgate
Hayton
Harriston
Howk Bobbin Mill
Kirkland Guards
Boltongate
Prospect
Oughterside
Salt Pans
Milefortlet 21
Sandale
The Howk
Whelpo
Allerby
Westmoor
Threapland
Crosscanonby
Parsonby
Torpenhow
Ireby
Senhouse Roman
Plumbland
Bothel
Whitrigg
Uldale
Crosby Villa
Bullgill
Aughertree
Crosby
Gilcrux
Fell Side
Alauna Roman Fort
Birkby
Greengill
High Ireby
Branthwaite
Ellen
Maryport
Ruthwaite
Maritime
Dearham
Longlands
Netherton
Townhead
Tallentire
Moota Hill
Sunderland
Binsey 1467
High Pike
Ellenborough
Blindcrake
A701
A74(M)
A709
A76
A75
A780
A711
A710
A596
A595
A594
B7076
B7020
B7068
B723
B709
B729
B724
B725
B722
B6357
B721
B793
B5307
B5302
B5301
B5300
B5299
B5305

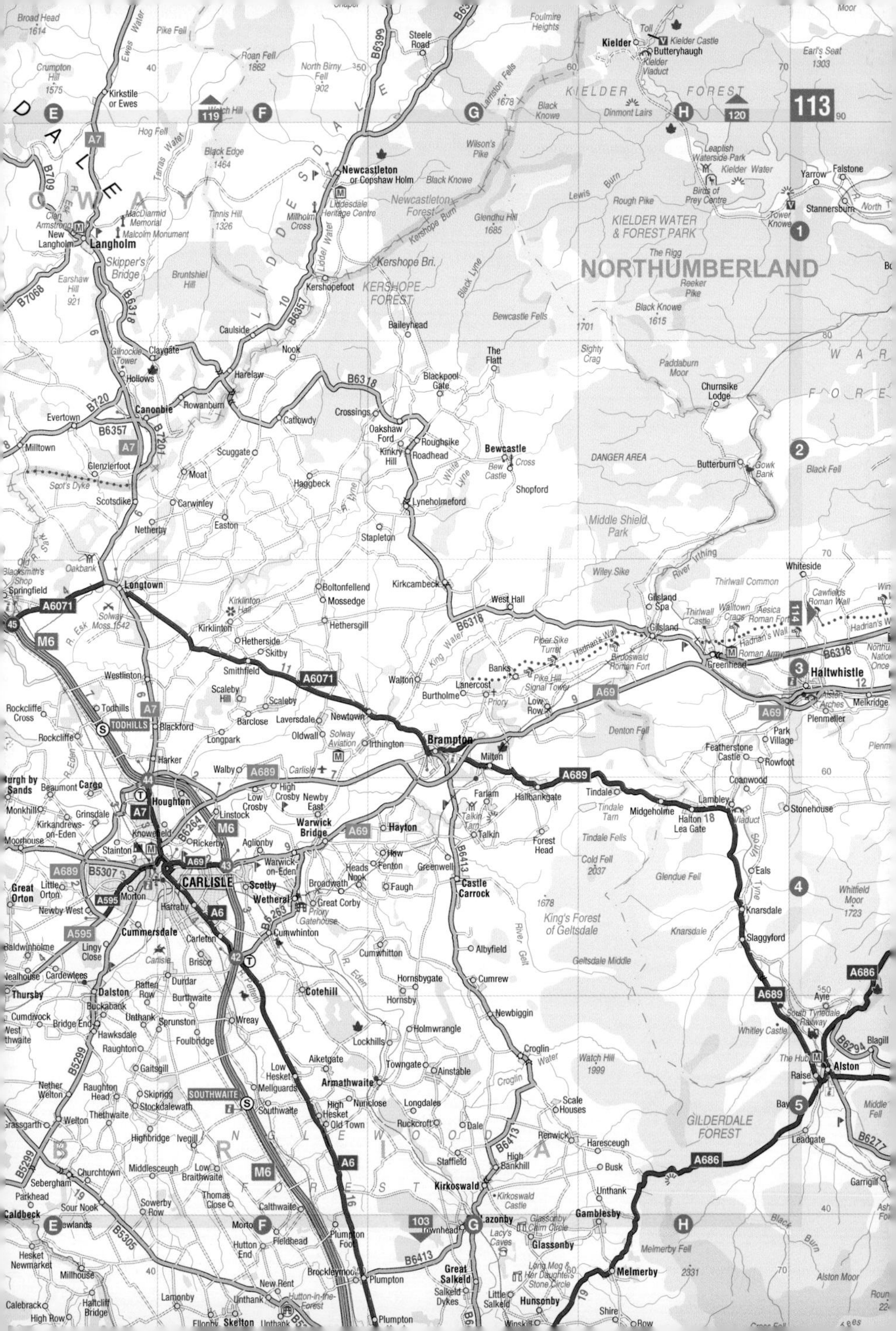
Broad Head
1614
Pike Fell
Ewes Water
Steele Road
B6399
Foulmire Heights
Kielder
Toll
Kielder Castle
Butteryhaugh
Kielder Viaduct
Earl's Seat
1303
Crumpton Hill
1575
Roan Fell
1862
North Birny Fell
902
Larriston Fells
1678
KIELDER FOREST
Black Knowe
Dinmont Lairs
Kirkstile or Ewes
E
119
Watch Hill
F
G
H
120
113
Hog Fell
A7
Tarras Water
Black Edge
1464
Wilson's Pike
Leaplish Waterside Park
Kielder Water
Yarrow
Falstone
B709
Newcastleton or Copshaw Holm
Black Knowe
Lewis Burn
Rough Pike
Birds of Prey Centre
Stannersburn
North Tyne
Tower Knowe
Clan Armstrong
MacDiarmid Memorial
Malcolm Monument
Tinnis Hill
1326
Liddesdale Heritage Centre
Newcastleton Forest
Glendhu Hill
1685
KIELDER WATER & FOREST PARK
1
New Langholm
Langholm
Millholm Cross
Liddel Water
Kershope Burn
Skipper's Bridge
Bruntshiel Hill
Kershope Bri.
The Rigg
NORTHUMBERLAND
Earshaw Hill
921
B7068
B6318
Kershopefoot
KERSHOPE FOREST
Black Lyne
Reeker Pike
Black Knowe
1615
B6357
Baileyhead
Bewcastle Fells
1701
Caulside
Claygate
Gilnockie Tower
Hollows
Nook
The Flatt
Sighty Crag
Paddaburn Moor
Harelaw
Blackpool Gate
B6318
Churnsike Lodge
Canonbie
Rowanburn
Evertown
B720
B6357
B7201
Catlowdy
Crossings
Oakshaw Ford
Roughsike
Kirkby Hill
Roadhead
Bewcastle
Bew Castle
Cross
DANGER AREA
Butterburn
Gowk Bank
2
Black Fell
Milltown
Glenzierfoot
Scuggate
Scot's Dyke
Moat
Haggbeck
White Lyne
Shopford
Scotsdike
Carwinley
Lyneholmeford
Netherby
Easton
Stapleton
Middle Shield Park
Oakbank
Old Blacksmith's Shop
Springfield
Longtown
Boltonfellend
Mossedge
Kirkcambeck
Wiley Sike
River Irthing
Whiteside
Thirlwall Common
A6071
Solway Moss 1542
Kirklinton Hall
Hethersgill
West Hall
Gilsland Spa
Thirlwall Castle
Walltown Crags
Aesica Roman Fort
Cawfields Roman Wall
114
45
M6
R. Esk
Kirklinton
Hetherside
Skitby
B6318
King Water
Piper Sike Turret
Hadrian's Wall
Gilsland
Birdoswald Roman Fort
Roman Army
Hadrian's Wall
B6318
Greenhead
Smithfield
A6071
Banks
Pike Hill Signal Tower
Walton
Lanercost
3
Haltwhistle
Westlinton
Scaleby Hill
Scaleby
Burtholme
Priory
Low Row
A69
Melkridge
Rockcliffe Cross
Todhills
A7
Barclose
Laversdale
Newtown
A69
Plenmeller
Rockcliffe
TODHILLS
Blackford
Oldwall
Solway Aviation
Irthington
Brampton
Denton Fell
Park Village
Longpark
Featherstone Castle
Rowfoot
Harker
Walby
A689
Carlisle
Milton
A689
R. Eden
Burgh by Sands
Beaumont
Cargo
44
High Crosby
Newby East
Farlam
Hallbankgate
Tindale
Coanwood
Houghton
Low Crosby
Tindale Tarn
Midgeholme
Halton Lea Gate
Lambley
Viaduct
Stonehouse
Monkhill
Grinsdale
A7
Linstock
M6
Talkin Tarn
Kirkandrews-on-Eden
B6264
Warwick Bridge
A69
Hayton
Talkin
Forest Head
Tindale Fells
Moorhouse
Knowefield
Rickerby
Aglionby
B6413
Stainton
How
Fenton
Cold Fell
2037
Glendue Fell
A689
B5307
A69
43
Warwick-on-Eden
Heads Nook
Greenwell
Eals
Great Orton
Little Orton
CARLISLE
Scotby
Broadwath
Castle Carrock
South Tyne
4
Whitfield Moor
1723
Morton
Wetheral
Great Corby
Faugh
Newby West
A595
Harraby
A6
Priory Gatehouse
1678
Knarsdale
B6263
King's Forest of Geltsdale
River Gelt
A595
Cummersdale
Carleton
Cumwhinton
Knarsdale
Slaggyford
Baldwinholme
Lingy Close
Carlisle
Brisco
Cumwhitton
Albyfield
Geltsdale Middle
Nealhouse
Cardewlees
42
R. Petteril
A686
Durdar
Hornsbygate
Cumrew
Thursby
Dalston
Ratten Row
Cotehill
A689
Ayle
Burthwaite
Hornsby
Buckabank
Unthank
Newbiggin
South Tynedale Railway
Cumdivock
Bridge End
Sprunston
Wreay
Holmwrangle
Whitley Castle
West Curthwaite
Hawksdale
Foulbridge
Lockhills
B6294
Blagill
Raughton
The Hub
Alston
Gaitsgill
Aiketgate
Croglin Water
Watch Hill
1999
Low Hesket
Towngate
Ainstable
Raise
Nether Welton
Raughton Head
Mellguards
Croglin
B5299
Armathwaite
Skiprigg
SOUTHWAITE
Scale Houses
Stockdalewath
High Hesket
Nunclose
Longdales
Bay
5
Middle Fell
Welton
Thethwaite
Southwaite
Old Town
Grassgarth
GILDERDALE FOREST
Ruckcroft
Dale
Highbridge
Ivegill
Renwick
Hareseugh
Leadgate
INGLEWOOD
B6413
A6
B6277
B5299
Middlesceugh
Low Braithwaite
High Bankhill
Staffield
Busk
A686
Churchtown
M6
Garrigill
Sebergham
Kirkoswald
FOREST
Parkhead
Sowerby Row
Thomas Close
Calthwaite
Kirkoswald Castle
Unthank
Sour Nook
Gamblesby
Caldbeck
Newlands
B5305
Morton
103
Lazonby
Glassonby Cairn Circle
Plumpton Foot
Townhead
Lacy's Caves
H
Glassonby
40
Black Burn
Hesket Newmarket
Hutton End
Fieldhead
B6413
Melmerby Fell
Millhouse
New Rent
Brockleymoor
Plumpton
Great Salkeld
Long Meg & Her Daughters Stone Circle
Melmerby
2331
Alston Moor
Lamonby
Hutton-in-the-Forest
Salkeld Dykes
Little Salkeld
Calebrack
Haltcliff Bridge
Unthank
Hunsonby
High Row
Ellonby
Skelton
Plumpton
Winskill
Shire
Row

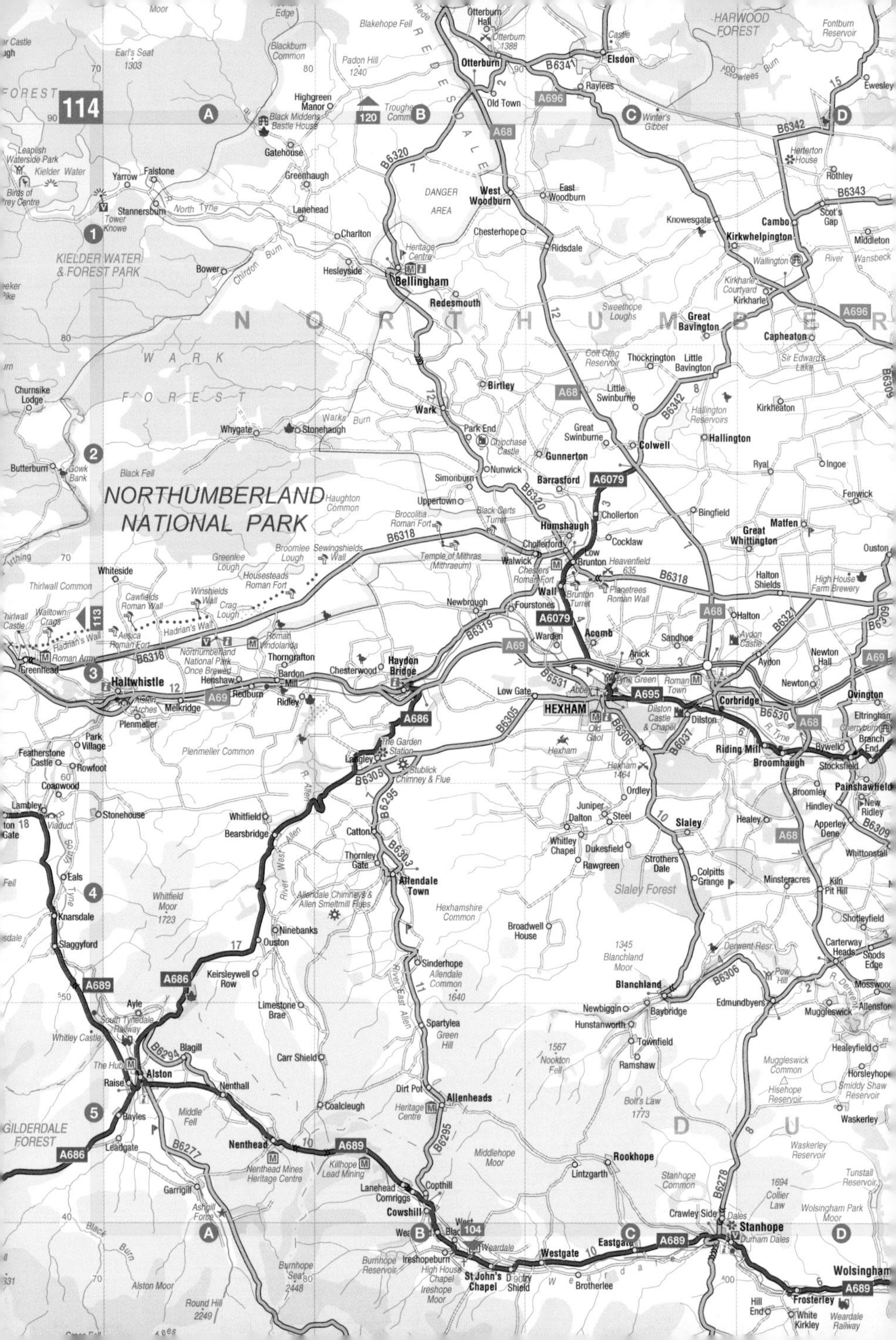

114
120
113
104
A
B
C
D
1
2
3
4
5
Otterburn Hall
Otterburn 1388
Otterburn
Old Town
Elsdon
Castle
HARWOOD FOREST
Fontburn Reservoir
Raylees
Winter's Gibbet
Ewesley
B6341
B6342
B6343
B6320
B6318
B6319
B6305
B6295
B6303
B6531
B6306
B6037
B6530
B6321
B6309
B6278
B6277
B6294
A68
A696
A6079
A69
A695
A686
A689
Blakehope Fell
Blackburn Common
Padon Hill 1240
Earl's Seat 1303
Highgreen Manor
Troughend Common
Black Middens Bastle House
Gatehouse
Greenhaugh
Lanehead
Charlton
Falstone
Yarrow
Stannersburn
North Tyne
Tower Knowe
Leaplish Waterside Park
Kielder Water
Birds of Prey Centre
KIELDER WATER & FOREST PARK
Bower
Chirdon Burn
Hesleyside
Heritage Centre
Bellingham
Redesmouth
DANGER AREA
REDESDALE
West Woodburn
East Woodburn
Chesterhope
Ridsdale
Knowesgate
Kirkwhelpington
Cambo
Scot's Gap
Middleton
Herterton House
Rothley
Wallington
River Wansbeck
Kirkharle Courtyard
Kirkharle
Sweethope Loughs
Great Bavington
Little Bavington
Capheaton
Sir Edward's Lake
Colt Crag Reservoir
Thockrington
Little Swinburne
Hallington Reservoirs
Kirkheaton
NORTHUMBERLAND
WARK FOREST
Churnsike Lodge
Whygate
Stonehaugh
Warks Burn
Birtley
Wark
Park End
Chipchase Castle
Great Swinburne
Colwell
Hallington
Gunnerton
Nunwick
Simonburn
Barrasford
Ryal
Ingoe
Fenwick
Butterburn
Gowk Bank
Black Fell
NORTHUMBERLAND NATIONAL PARK
Haughton Common
Uppertown
Brocolitia Roman Fort
Black Carts Turret
Humshaugh
Chollerton
Bingfield
Great Whittington
Matfen
Cocklaw
Chollerford
Walwick
Temple of Mithras (Mithraeum)
Low Brunton
Heavenfield 635
Chesters Roman Fort
Brunton Turret
Planetrees Roman Wall
Wall
Halton Shields
High House Farm Brewery
Ouston
Broomlee Lough
Sewingshields Wall
Greenlee Lough
Housesteads Roman Fort
Whiteside
Thirlwall Common
Cawfields Roman Wall
Winshields Wall
Crag Lough
Hadrian's Wall
Walltown Crags
Thirlwall Castle
Aesica Roman Fort
Roman Army
Greenhead
Northumberland National Park Once Brewed
Roman Vindolanda
Thorngrafton
Newbrough
Fourstones
Warden
Acomb
Halton
Sandhoe
Aydon Castle
Aydon
Newton Hall
Newton
Haltwhistle
Henshaw
Bardon Mill
Chesterwood
Haydon Bridge
Anick
Tyne Green
Abbey
Roman Town
Corbridge
Ovington
Eltringham
Cherryburn
Branch End
Bywell
Alston Arches
Melkridge
Redburn
Ridley
Low Gate
HEXHAM
Old Gaol
Dilston Castle & Chapel
Dilston
Riding Mill
Broomhaugh
Stocksfield
Painshawfield
New Ridley
Plenmeller
Park Village
Featherstone Castle
Rowfoot
Plenmeller Common
The Garden Station
Langley
Stublick Chimney & Flue
Hexham
Hexham 1464
R. Tyne
Bromley
Hindley
Coanwood
Lambley
Viaduct
Stonehouse
Whitfield
Bearsbridge
R. Allen
Catton
Juniper
Dalton
Steel
Ordley
Slaley
Healey
Apperley Dene
Whittonstall
Whitley Chapel
Dukesfield
Rawgreen
Strothers Dale
Colpitts Grange
Minsteracres
Kiln Pit Hill
Thornley Gate
Allendale Town
Allendale Chimneys & Allen Smeltmill Flues
River West Allen
Eals
South Tyne
Knarsdale
Slaggyford
Whitfield Moor 1723
Hexhamshire Common
Slaley Forest
Shotleyfield
Ninebanks
Ouston
Broadwell House
Sinderhope
Allendale Common 1640
River East Allen
1345 Blanchland Moor
Derwent Resr.
Carterway Heads
Snods Edge
Pow Hill
Keirsleywell Row
Blanchland
Baybridge
Edmundbyers
R. Derwent
Mosswood
Muggleswick
Allensford
Ayle
South Tynedale Railway
Whitley Castle
Limestone Brae
Spartylea
Green Hill
Newbiggin
Hunstanworth
Townfield
Ramshaw
1567 Nookton Fell
Muggleswick Common
Hisehope Reservoir
Healeyfield
Horsleyhope
Smiddy Shaw Reservoir
Blagill
The Hub
Alston
Raise
Carr Shield
Nenthall
Middle Fell
Dirt Pot
Allenheads
Heritage Centre
Coalcleugh
Bolt's Law 1773
Waskerley
Bayles
GILDERDALE FOREST
Leadgate
Nenthead
Nenthead Mines Heritage Centre
Killhope Lead Mining
Middlehope Moor
Rookhope
Lintzgarth
Stanhope Common
Waskerley Reservoir
Tunstall Reservoir
1694 Collier Law
Wolsingham Park Moor
Garrigill
Ashgill Force
Lanehead
Cornriggs
Copthill
Cowshill
Crawley Side
Dales
Stanhope
Durham Dales
Eastgate
Westgate
Weardale
Ireshopeburn
Burnhope Reservoir
High House Chapel
Ireshope Moor
St John's Chapel
Daddry Shield
Brotherlee
Wear
Wolsingham
Frosterley
Hill End
White Kirkley
Weardale Railway
Black Burn
Alston Moor
Burnhope Seat 2448
Round Hill 2249

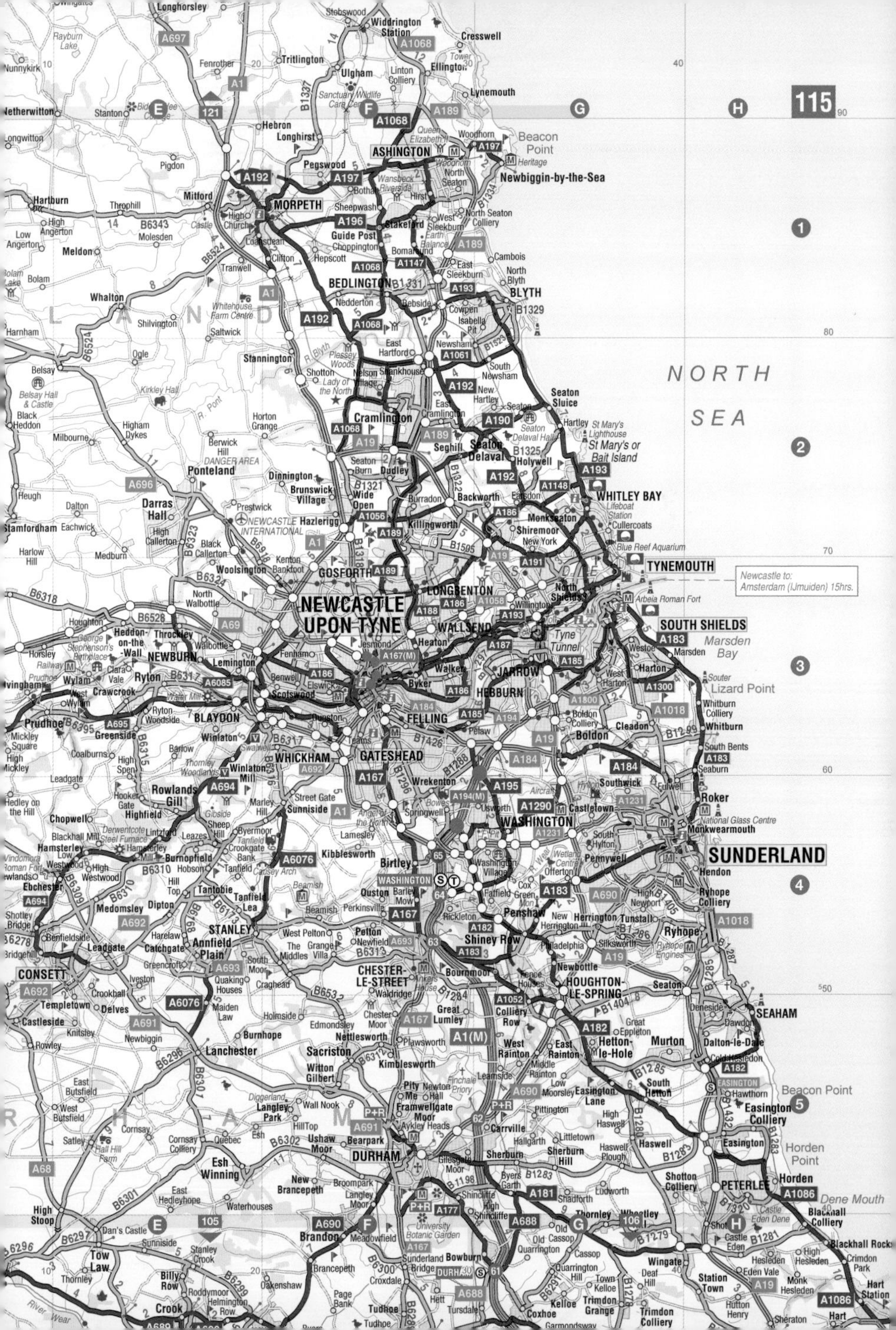
115
NORTH SEA
Newcastle to: Amsterdam (IJmuiden) 15hrs.
Longhorsley
Stobswood
Widdrington Station
Cresswell
Rayburn Lake
Fenrother
Tritlington
Ulgham
Linton Colliery
Ellington
Nunnykirk
Sanctuary Wildlife Care Centre
Lynemouth
Netherwitton
Stanton
Hebron
Longhirst
Woodhorn
Beacon Point
Longwitton
ASHINGTON
Pigdon
Pegswood
Newbiggin-by-the-Sea
Hartburn
Throphill
Mitford
MORPETH
Sheepwash
North Seaton Colliery
High Angerton
Low Angerton
Meldon
Molesden
Guide Post
Choppington
Stakeford
Cambois
North Blyth
BLYTH
Bolam
Tranwell
Hepscott
BEDLINGTON
East Sleekburn
Whalton
Nedderton
Bebside
Cowpen
Isabella Pit
Shilvington
Saltwick
Whitehouse Farm Centre
Harnham
Belsay
Belsay Hall & Castle
Ogle
Stannington
Plessey Woods
East Hartford
Newsham
South Newsham
Shotton
Lady of the North
Nelson Village
Shankhouse
Kirkley Hall
Black Heddon
Higham Dykes
Horton Grange
Cramlington
East Cramlington
New Hartley
Seaton Sluice
Hartley
St Mary's Lighthouse
St Mary's or Bait Island
Seaton Delaval Hall
Seghill
Seaton Delaval
Holywell
Milbourne
Berwick Hill
DANGER AREA
Seaton Burn
Dudley
Ponteland
Dinnington
Brunswick Village
Wide Open
Burradon
Backworth
Earsdon
WHITLEY BAY
Monkseaton
Cullercoats
Heugh
Dalton
Darras Hall
Prestwick
NEWCASTLE INTERNATIONAL
Hazlerigg
Killingworth
Shiremoor
New York
Blue Reef Aquarium
Stamfordham
Eachwick
High Callerton
Black Callerton
Harlow Hill
Medburn
Woolsington
Kenton Bankfoot
GOSFORTH
TYNEMOUTH
North Walbottle
NEWCASTLE UPON TYNE
LONGBENTON
North Shields
Willington
Arbeia Roman Fort
SOUTH SHIELDS
Houghton
Heddon-on-the-Wall
Throckley
Walbottle
WALLSEND
Marsden
Marsden Bay
Horsley
Stephenson's Birthplace
NEWBURN
Lemington
Fenham
Jesmond
Heaton
Tyne Tunnel
Westoe
Harton
Wylam
Clara Vale
Ryton
Benwell
Elswick
Walker
JARROW
West Harton
Souter Lizard Point
Ovingham
Crawcrook
Scotswood
Byker
HEBBURN
Whitburn Colliery
Prudhoe
West Wylam
Ryton Woodside
BLAYDON
Dunston
FELLING
Boldon Colliery
Cleadon
Whitburn
Mickley Square
Greenside
Winlaton
Teams
Pelaw
Boldon
South Bents
High Mickley
Coalburns
High Spen
Barlow
Thornley Woodlands
WHICKHAM
GATESHEAD
Seaburn
Leadgate
Winlaton Mill
Wrekenton
Southwick
Hedley on the Hill
Hooker Gate
Rowlands Gill
Highfield
Street Gate
Sunniside
Marley Hill
Gibside
Springwell
Bowes
Usworth
Castletown
Fulwell
Roker
National Glass Centre
Monkwearmouth
Chopwell
Blackhall Mill
Derwentcote Steel Furnace
Lintzford
Sheep Hill
Byermoor
Tanfield
Angel of the North
WASHINGTON
South Hylton
SUNDERLAND
Hamsterley
Low Westwood
Hamsterley Mill
Leazes
Crookgate Bank
Lamesley
Kibblesworth
Washington Village
Wetland Centre
Pennywell
Vindomora Roman Fort
Newlands
High Westwood
Burnopfield
Hobson
Causey Arch
Birtley
Offerton
Hendon
Ebchester
Hill Top
Tantobie
Tanfield Lea
Beamish
Ouston
Barley Mow
Fatfield
Cox Green
High Newport
Ryhope Colliery
Shotley Bridge
Medomsley
Dipton
Perkinsville
Penshaw
Herrington
Tunstall
Benfieldside
Harelaw
STANLEY
West Pelton
Pelton
Newfield
Rickleton
New Herrington
Ryhope
Bridgehill
Leadgate
Catchgate
Annfield Plain
The Middles
Grange Villa
Shiney Row
Philadelphia
Silksworth
Ryhope Engines
CONSETT
Greencroft
South Moor
Quaking Houses
Craghead
CHESTER-LE-STREET
Waldridge
Bournmoor
Newbottle
Fence Houses
HOUGHTON-LE-SPRING
Seaton
Templetown
Crookhall
Iveston
Delves
Maiden Law
Chester Moor
Great Lumley
Colliery Row
Deneside
Dawdon
SEAHAM
Castleside
Knitsley
Newbiggin
Holmside
Edmondsley
Nettlesworth
Plawsworth
Great Eppleton
Hetton-le-Hole
Murton
Dalton-le-Dale
Rowley
Burnhope
Lanchester
Sacriston
West Rainton
East Rainton
Middle Rainton
Cold Hesledon
Witton Gilbert
Kimblesworth
Leamside
Low Moorsley
South Hetton
East Butsfield
Diggerland
Wall Nook
Pity Me
Newton Hall
Finchale Priory
Easington Lane
EASINGTON
Hawthorn
Beacon Point
West Butsfield
Langley Park
Framwellgate Moor
Pittington
High Haswell
Easington Colliery
Satley
Cornsay
Hall Hill Farm
HillTop
Aykley Heads
Carrville
Littletown
Haswell
Easington
Cornsay Colliery
Quebec
Esh
Ushaw Moor
Bearpark
DURHAM
Gilesgate Moor
Hallgarth
Sherburn
Sherburn Hill
Haswell Plough
Horden Point
Esh Winning
New Brancepeth
Broompark
Byers Garth
Shotton Colliery
Horden
PETERLEE
East Hedleyhope
Waterhouses
Langley Moor
Shincliffe
High Shincliffe
Shadforth
Ludworth
Dene Mouth
Castle Eden Dene
Blackhall Colliery
High Stoop
Dan's Castle
Brandon
Meadowfield
University Botanic Garden
Thornley
Wheatley Hill
Old Cassop
Shotton
Castle Eden
Sunniside
Stanley Crook
Old Quarrington
Cassop
Wingate
Blackhall Rocks
High Hesleden
Hesleden
Crimdon Park
Tow Law
Brancepeth
Sunderland Bridge
Bowburn
Quarrington Hill
Deaf Hill
Station Town
Eden Vale
Monk Hesleden
Thornley
Billy Row
Roddymoor
Helmington Row
Oakenshaw
Croxdale
Page Bank
Hett
Town Kelloe
Hart Station
Crook
Tudhoe
Tursdale
Coxhoe
Kelloe
Trimdon Grange
Trimdon Colliery
Hutton Henry
Sheraton
Hart
Garmondsway
River Wear
A697
A1
A1068
A189
A192
A197
A196
A1147
A193
A1061
B1329
B1523
A190
A19
A1148
A186
A191
A1056
A696
A69
A188
A1058
A187
A167(M)
A183
A185
A184
A194
A1300
A1018
A6085
A695
A1800
A692
A167
A194(M)
A195
A1290
A1231
A694
A6076
A690
A693
A1052
A182
A1(M)
A691
A68
A181
A177
A688
A1086
A689
B6343
B6524
B6318
B6528
B6324
B6323
B6918
B1318
B1321
B1325
B1322
B1505
B6317
B6395
B6315
B6316
B1426
B1288
B1296
B1299
B1404
B1285
B1286
B1405
B1287
B1432
B1283
B1280
B1320
B1281
B1279
B1278
B6310
B6309
B6278
B6173
B6313
B6532
B6312
B6296
B6301
B6302
B6297
B6299
B6300
B1198
B6291
B6288
121
105
106
65
64
63
62
61
40
80
70
60
50
90
1
2
3
4
5
E
F
G
H

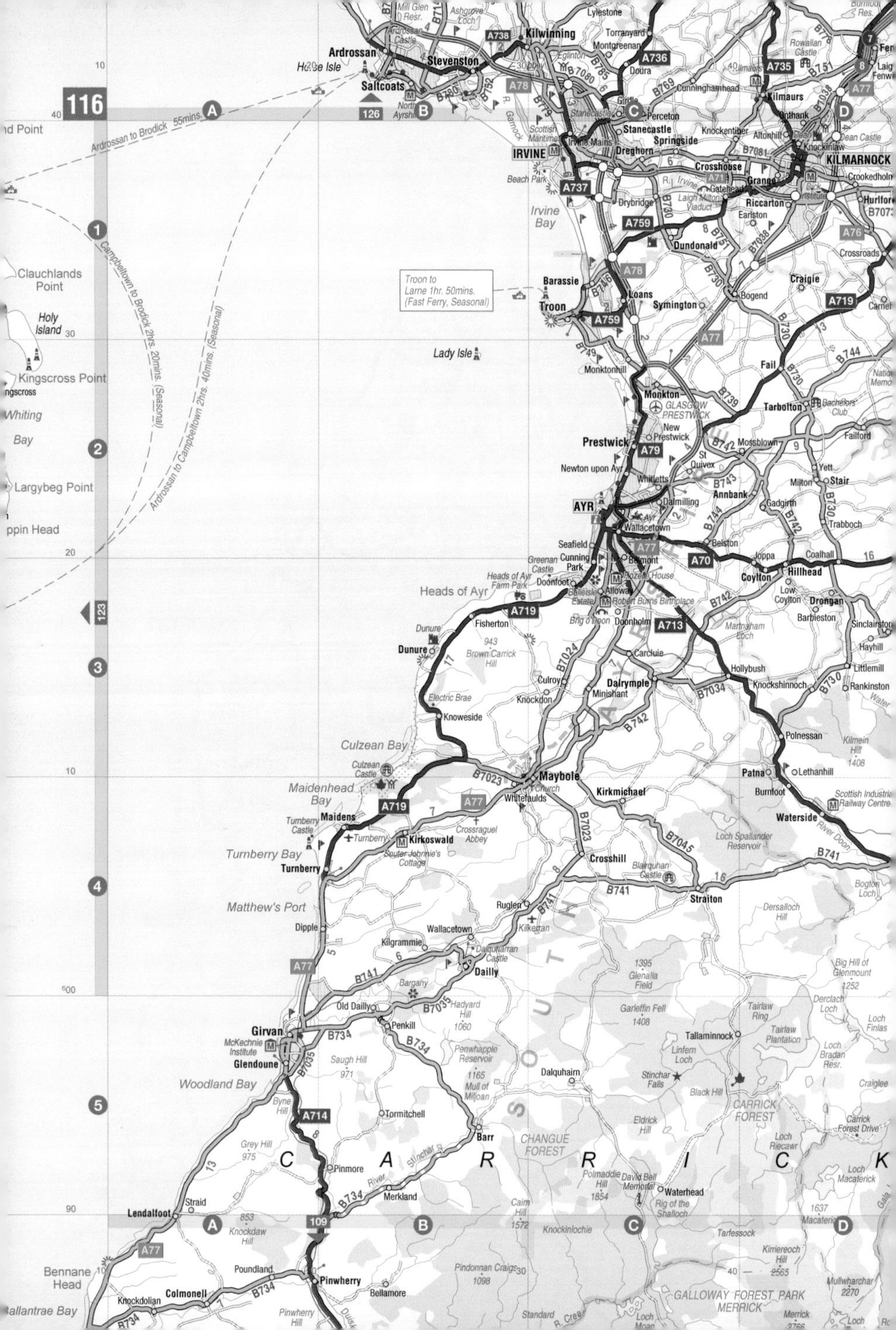
116
126
123
109
A
B
C
D
1
2
3
4
5
Ardrossan to Brodick 55mins.
Campbeltown to Brodick 2hrs. 20mins. (Seasonal)
Ardrossan to Campbeltown 2hrs. 40mins. (Seasonal)
Troon to Larne 1hr. 50mins. (Fast Ferry, Seasonal)
Clauchlands Point
Holy Island
Kingscross Point
Whiting Bay
Largybeg Point
Heads of Ayr
Lady Isle
Horse Isle
Ardrossan
Saltcoats
Stevenston
Kilwinning
Ardrossan Castle
Mill Glen Resr.
Ashgrove Loch
Lylestone
Torranyard
Montgreenan
Eglinton
Doura
Cunninghamhead
Kilmaurs
Rowallan Castle
Perceton
Stanecastle
Springside
Knockentiber
Altonhill
Dean Castle
Knockinlaw
KILMARNOCK
Crookedholm
Hurlford
IRVINE
Scottish Maritime
Irvine Mains
Dreghorn
Crosshouse
Gatehead
Grange
Riccarton
Earlston
Laigh Milton Viaduct
Dick Institute
Beach Park
Drybridge
Irvine Bay
Dundonald
Crossroads
Barassie
Troon
Loans
Symington
Bogend
Craigie
Monktonhill
Fail
Monkton
GLASGOW PRESTWICK
New Prestwick
Tarbolton
Bachelors' Club
Prestwick
Mossblown
Failford
St Quivox
Newton upon Ayr
Whitletts
Annbank
Yett
Milton
Stair
AYR
Dalmilling
Gadgirth
Wallacetown
Trabboch
Seafield
Greenan Castle
Cunning Park
Belston
Belmont
Joppa
Coalhall
Coylton
Hillhead
Heads of Ayr Farm Park
Doonfoot
Rozelle House
Alloway
Robert Burns Birthplace
Belleisle Estate
Low Coylton
Drongan
Barbieston
Brig o'Doon
Doonholm
Martnaham Loch
Sinclairston
Hayhill
Fisherton
Dunure
Brown Carrick Hill
943
Carcluie
Hollybush
Littlemill
Rankinston
Culroy
Dalrymple
Minishant
Knockdon
Knockshinnoch
Electric Brae
Knoweside
Polnessan
Kilmein Hill
1408
Culzean Bay
Culzean Castle
Maidenhead Bay
Maybole
Whitefaulds
Patna
Lethanhill
Burnfoot
Kirkmichael
Scottish Industrial Railway Centre
Waterside
River Doon
Turnberry Castle
Maidens
Turnberry
Kirkoswald
Crossraguel Abbey
Souter Johnnie's Cottage
Loch Spallander Reservoir
Turnberry Bay
Crosshill
Blairquhan Castle
Straiton
Bogton Loch
Matthew's Port
Ruglen
Kilkerran
Dersalloch Hill
Dipple
Wallacetown
Kilgrammie
Dalquharran Castle
Dailly
Bargany
1395
Glenalla Fell
Big Hill of Glenmount
1252
Old Dailly
Penkill
Hadyard Hill
1060
Garleffin Fell
1408
Tairlaw Ring
Tairlaw Plantation
Derclach Loch
Loch Finlas
Girvan
McKechnie Institute
Glendoune
Saugh Hill
971
Penwhapple Reservoir
Tallaminnock
Linfern Loch
Loch Bradan Resr.
Woodland Bay
1165
Mull of Miljoan
Dalquhairn
Stinchar Falls
Black Hill
CARRICK FOREST
Craiglee
Byne Hill
Tormitchell
Eldrick Hill
Carrick Forest Drive
Barr
CHANGUE FOREST
Loch Riecawr
Grey Hill
975
Pinmore
River Stinchar
C A R R I C K
Polmaddie Hill
1854
David Bell Memorial
Loch Macaterick
Straid
Merkland
Waterhead
Cairn Hill
1572
Rig of the Shalloch
1637
Macaterick
Lendalfoot
853
Knockdaw Hill
Knockinlochie
Tarfessock
Kirriereoch Hill
2565
Bennane Head
Poundland
Pinwherry
Bellamore
Pindonnan Craigs
1098
Mullwharchar
2270
GALLOWAY FOREST PARK
MERRICK
Knockdolian
Colmonell
Ballantrae Bay
Pinwherry Hill
Standard
Loch Moan
Merrick
2766
SOUTH AYRSHIRE
A738
A736
A735
A78
A77
A71
A737
A759
A76
A719
A79
A70
A713
A714
B780
B752
B7080
B785
B769
B751
B7038
B7081
B730
B746
B749
B739
B744
B742
B743
B7024
B7034
B7023
B7045
B741
B7035
B734
10
20
30
40
90
600

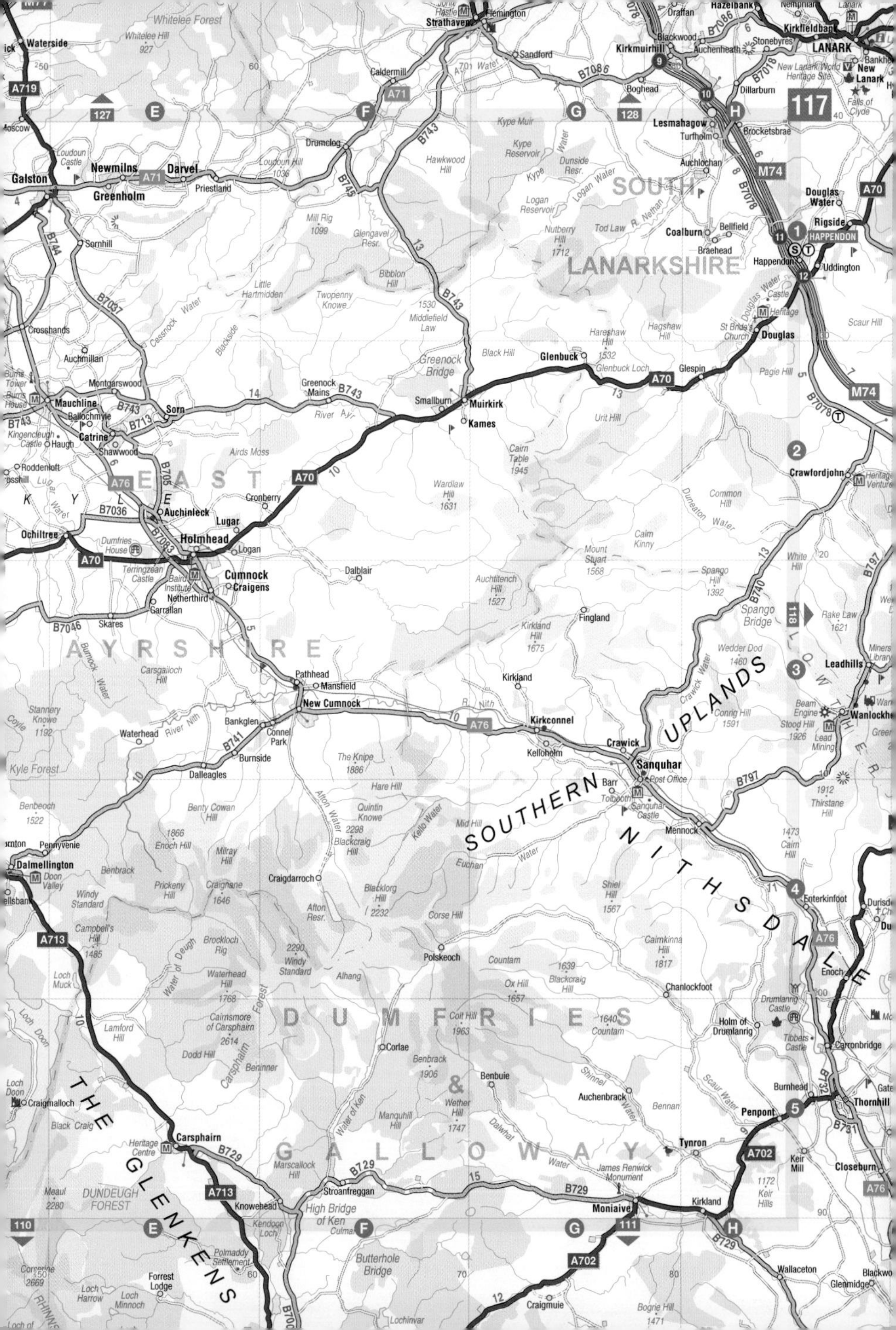

117
Whitelee Forest
Waterside
Whitelee Hill
927
A719
127
E
F
G
128
H
Strathaven
Flemington
Draffan
Hazelbank
Kirkfieldbank
LANARK
Blackwood
Kirkmuirhill
Auchenheath
Stonebyres
New Lanark World Heritage Site
New Lanark
Falls of Clyde
Sandford
Caldermill
A71
B7086
Boghead
Dillarburn
B7018
Lesmahagow
Turfholm
Brocketsbrae
Kype Muir
Kype Reservoir
Kype Water
Dunside Resr.
Logan Water
Logan Reservoir
Auchlochan
M74
Douglas Water
Loudoun Castle
Galston
Newmilns
Greenholm
Darvel
Priestland
Drumclog
Loudoun Hill
1036
B745
B743
Hawkwood Hill
SOUTH
LANARKSHIRE
Mill Rig
1099
Glengavel Resr.
Nutberry Hill
1712
Tod Law
R. Nethan
Coalburn
Bellfield
Braehead
Rigside
HAPPENDON
Happendon
Uddington
B744
Sornhill
Bibblon Hill
Little Hartmidden
Twopenny Knowe
B7037
Cessnock Water
Blackside
1530
Middlefield Law
Crosshands
Auchmillan
Greenock Bridge
Black Hill
Glenbuck
Hareshaw Hill
1532
Glenbuck Loch
Hagshaw Hill
Douglas Water
Castle
Heritage
St Bride's Church
Douglas
Glespin
A70
Pagie Hill
Scaur Hill
Burns Tower
Burns House
Mauchline
Ballochmyle
Montgarswood
Greenock Mains
Smallburn
Muirkirk
Kames
River Ayr
Sorn
B713
Kingencleugh Castle
Haugh
Catrine
Shawwood
Airds Moss
Urit Hill
B7078
Roddenloft
Crosshill
Lugar Water
EAST
KYLE
A76
B705
Cairn Table
1945
Wardlaw Hill
1631
Crawfordjohn
Heritage Venture
Common Hill
Duneaton Water
Cronberry
B7036
Auchinleck
Lugar
Ochiltree
Holmhead
Dumfries House
Logan
Cairn Kinny
Terringzean Castle
Cumnock
Craigens
Baird Institute
Netherthird
Garrallan
Dalblair
Mount Stuart
1568
Spango Hill
1392
White Hill
B797
B740
Auchtitench Hill
1527
B7046
Skares
Fingland
Kirkland Hill
1675
Spango Bridge
118
Rake Law
1621
AYRSHIRE
Burnock Water
Carsgailoch Hill
Wedder Dod
1460
LOWTHER
Leadhills
Miners Library
Pathhead
Mansfield
Kirkland
Crawick Water
UPLANDS
Stannery Knowe
1192
New Cumnock
R. Nith
Coyle
Waterhead
River Nith
Bankglen
Connel Park
Kirkconnel
Crawick
Conrig Hill
1591
Beam Engine
Wanlockhead
Stood Hill
1926
Lead Mining
B741
Burnside
Kelloholm
Kyle Forest
Dalleagles
The Knipe
1886
Sanquhar
Post Office
Barr
Tolbooth
Sanquhar Castle
SOUTHERN
NITHSDALE
Benbeoch
1522
Benty Cowan Hill
Hare Hill
Quintin Knowe
2298
Blackcraig Hill
Afton Water
Kello Water
Mid Hill
1912
Thirstane Hill
Mennock
1866
Enoch Hill
Pennyvenie
Dalmellington
Doon Valley
Milray Hill
Euchan Water
1473
Cairn Hill
Benbrack
Craigdarroch
Shiel Hill
1567
Enterkinfoot
Windy Standard
Prickeny Hill
Craignane
1646
Blacklorg Hill
2232
Afton Resr.
Corse Hill
Campbell's Hill
1485
A713
Brockloch Rig
2290
Windy Standard
Polskeoch
Cairnkinna Hill
1817
Loch Muck
Water of Deugh
Waterhead Hill
1768
Alhang
Countam
1639
Blackcraig Hill
Ox Hill
1657
Chanlockfoot
Enoch
Loch Doon
Lamford Hill
Cairnsmore of Carsphairn
2614
Carsphairn Forest
DUMFRIES
Colt Hill
1963
1640
Countam
Holm of Drumlanrig
Drumlanrig Castle
Tibbers Castle
Carronbridge
Dodd Hill
Beninner
Corlae
Benbrack
1906
&
Benbuie
Shinnel Water
Scaur Water
Burnhead
B732
Thornhill
Craigmalloch
THE GLENKENS
Black Craig
Wether Hill
1747
Manquhill Hill
Water of Ken
Dalwhat Water
Auchenbrack
Bennan
Penpont
Heritage Centre
Carsphairn
B729
GALLOWAY
Tynron
B731
Keir Mill
Closeburn
A702
James Renwick Monument
Meaul
2280
DUNDEUGH FOREST
Marscallock Hill
Stroanfreggan
1172
Keir Hills
Knowehead
High Bridge of Ken
Moniaive
Kirkland
110
111
Kendoon Loch
Culmark
Polmaddy Settlement
Butterhole Bridge
Wallaceton
Corserine
2669
Forrest Lodge
Glenmidge
Loch Harrow
Loch Minnoch
Craigmuie
Bogrie Hill
1471
Lochinvar
B700

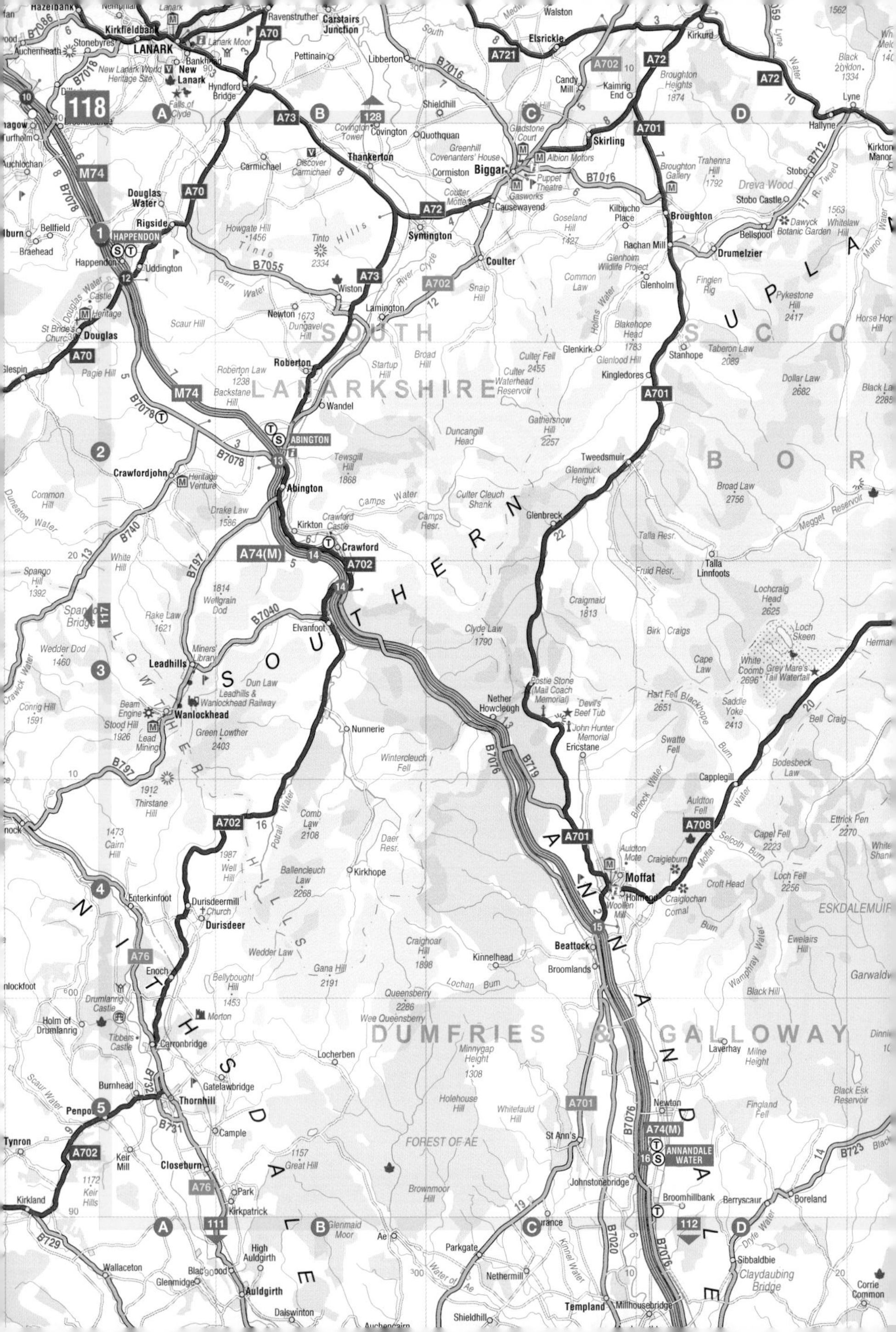

118
Hazelbank
Kirkfieldbank
Ravenstruther
Carstairs Junction
Walston
Elsrickle
Kirkurd
Lyne Water
Stonebyres
LANARK
Lanark Moor
Auchenheath
B7086
B7018
Bankhead
New Lanark World Heritage Site
New Lanark
Falls of Clyde
Hyndford Bridge
Pettinain
Libberton
B7016
A721
A702
A72
A70
A73
Candy Mill
Kaimrig End
Broughton Heights 1874
Black Meldon
Lyne
Hallyne
Shieldhill
Covington Tower
Covington
Quothquan
Thankerton
Gladstone Court
Skirling
Albion Motors
Biggar
Puppet Theatre
Gasworks
B7016
A701
Broughton Gallery
Trahenna Hill 1792
Dreva Wood
Stobo
Stobo Castle
Kirkton Manor
B712
R. Tweed
Turfholm
Auchlochan
M74
B7078
Douglas Water
Carmichael
Discover Carmichael
Greenhill Covenanters' House
Cormiston
Coulter Motte
Causewayend
Rigside
Bellfield
Braehead
HAPPENDON
Happendon
Uddington
Howgate Hill 1456
Tinto Hills
Tinto 2334
Symington
Goseland Hill 1427
Kilbucho Place
Broughton
Dawyck Botanic Garden
Bellspool
Whitelaw Hill
Rachan Mill
Drumelzier
B7055
Wiston
Coulter
Glenholm Wildlife Project
Glenholm
Common Law
Garf Water
Douglas Water
Castle
Heritage
St Bride's Church
Douglas
Scaur Hill
Newton
1673 Dungavel Hill
Lamington
Snaip Hill
Holms Water
Finglen Rig
Pykestone Hill 2417
Horse Hope Hill
SOUTH
LANARKSHIRE
SCOTTISH BORDERS
Glespin
Pagie Hill
Roberton
Broad Hill
Startup Hill
Roberton Law 1238
Backstane Hill
Wandel
Culter Fell 2455
Culter Waterhead Reservoir
Blakehope Head 1783
Glenlood Hill
Glenkirk
Stanhope
Taberon Law 2089
Kingledores
Dollar Law 2682
Black Law 2285
ABINGTON
Abington
Gathersnow Hill 2257
Duncangill Head
Tweedsmuir
Glenmuck Height
Crawfordjohn
Heritage Venture
Tewsgill Hill 1868
Broad Law 2756
Common Hill
Duneaton Water
Drake Law 1586
Camps Water
Culter Cleuch Shank
Megget Reservoir
Glenbreck
B740
Kirkton
Crawford Castle
Crawford
Camps Resr.
Talla Resr.
A74(M)
Talla Linnfoots
White Hill
Spango Hill 1392
Fruid Resr.
Wellgrain Dod 1814
Spango Bridge
117
Rake Law 1621
B7040
Elvanfoot
Clyde Law 1790
Craigmaid 1813
Lochcraig Head 2625
Loch Skeen
Birk Craigs
Hermar
Wedder Dod 1460
Leadhills
Miners' Library
Dun Law
Leadhills & Wanlockhead Railway
Cape Law
White Coomb 2696
Grey Mare's Tail Waterfall
Crawick Water
Conrig Hill 1591
Beam Engine
Wanlockhead
Lead Mining
Stood Hill 1926
Green Lowther 2403
Nether Howcleugh
Postie Stone (Mail Coach Memorial)
Devil's Beef Tub
John Hunter Memorial
Hart Fell 2651
Blackhope Burn
Saddle Yoke 2413
Bell Craig
Nunnerie
Ericstane
Swatte Fell
Wintercleuch Fell
B7076
B719
Bodesbeck Law
Capplegill
B797
1912 Thirstane Hill
LOWTHER HILLS
Potrail Water
Comb Law 2108
Birnock Water
Auldton Fell
Ettrick Pen 2270
A708
Capel Fell 2223
White Shank
1473 Cairn Hill
1987 Well Hill
Daer Resr.
Auldton Mote
Craigieburn
Moffat
Selcoth Burn
Moffat Water
Loch Fell 2256
Ballencleuch Law 2268
Kirkhope
Holmend
Craiglochan
Croft Head
Enterkinfoot
Durisdeermill Church
Durisdeer
Woollen Mill
Corral
ESKDALEMUIR
Beattock
Broomlands
Craighoar Hill 1898
Kinnelhead
Wamphray Water
Ewelairs Hill
Wedder Law
Gana Hill 2191
A76
Enoch
Bellybought Hill 1453
Lochan Burn
Garwald
Black Hill
Drumlanrig Castle
Holm of Drumlanrig
Morton
Queensberry 2286
Wee Queensberry
DUMFRIES & GALLOWAY
Tibbers Castle
Carronbridge
Locherben
Minnygap Height 1308
Laverhay
Milne Height
Dinnie
NITHSDALE
ANNANDALE
Scaur Water
Burnhead
Gatelawbridge
Penpont
Thornhill
B732
B731
Holehouse Hill
Whitefauld Hill
Newton
Fingland Fell
Black Esk Reservoir
Cample
Tynron
A702
Keir Mill
Closeburn
FOREST OF AE
St Ann's
ANNANDALE WATER
B723
1172 Keir Hills
1157 Great Hill
Johnstonebridge
Broomhillbank
Berryscaur
Boreland
Kirkland
Park
Kirkpatrick
Brownmoor Hill
111
112
B729
Glenmaid Moor
Ae
Parkgate
B7020
Dryfe Water
Sibbaldbie
Claydaubing Bridge
High Auldgirth
Wallaceton
Glenmidge
Auldgirth
Nethermill
Kinnel Water
Water of Ae
Templand
Millhousebridge
Corrie Common
Dalswinton
Shieldhill

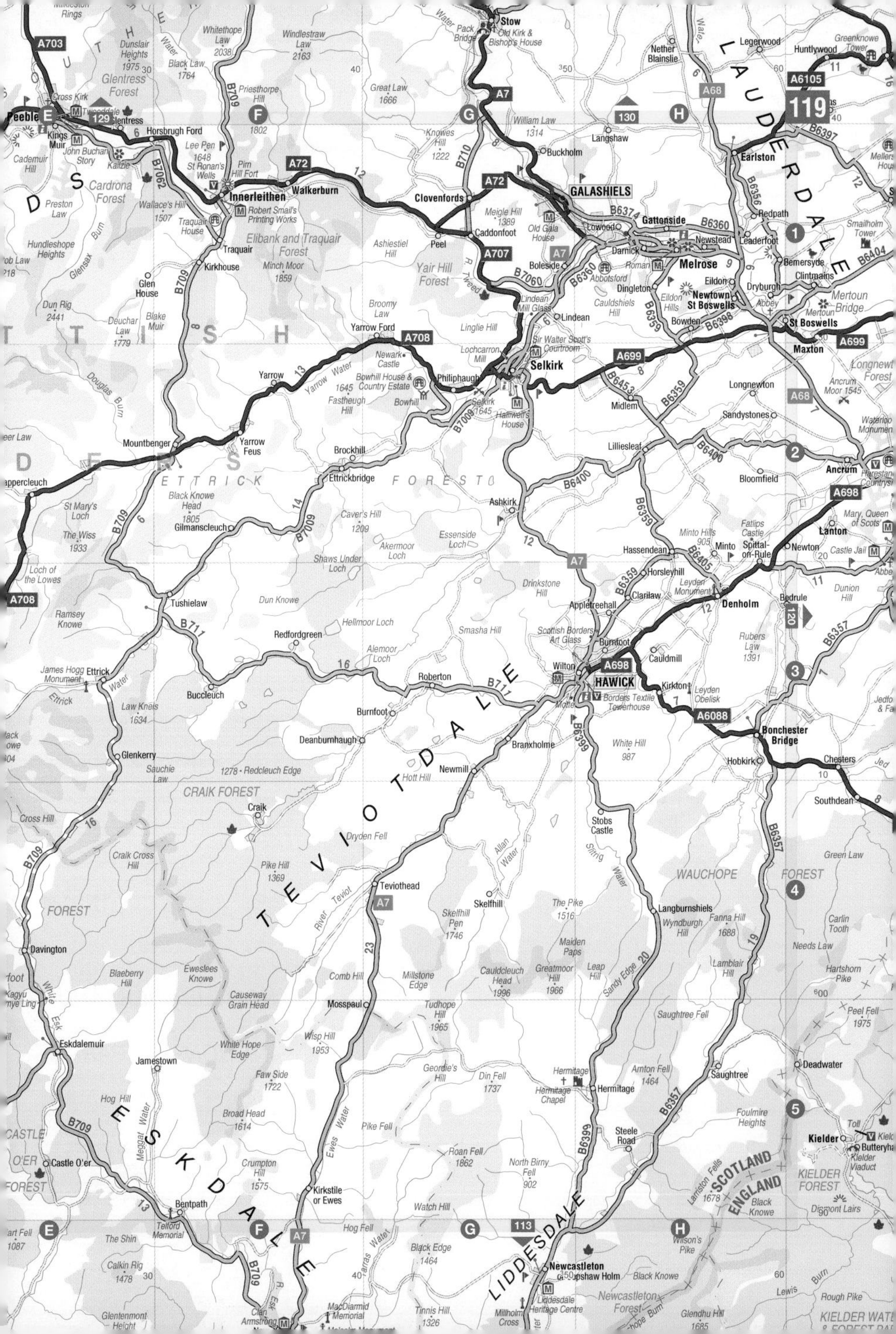
119
A703
Dunslair Heights 1975
Glentress Forest
Whitehope Law 2038
Windlestraw Law 2163
Stow
Water
Pack Bridge
Old Kirk & Bishop's House
Nether Blainslie
Legerwood
Huntlywood
Greenknowe Tower
A6105
Black Law 1764
Priesthorpe Hill
Great Law 1666
A7
A68
LAUDERDALE
Peebles
Cross Kirk
Tweeddale
Glentress
129
F
1802
G
William Law 1314
130
H
B6397
Kings Muir
John Buchan Story
Kailzie
Horsbrugh Ford
Lee Pen 1648
St Ronan's Wells
Pirn Hill Fort
Knowes Hill 1222
B710
Buckholm
Langshaw
Earlston
Cademuir Hill
Cardrona Forest
B7062
A72
Walkerburn
Innerleithen
Robert Smail's Printing Works
Clovenfords
GALASHIELS
B6356
Preston Law
Wallace's Hill 1507
Traquair House
Traquair
Elibank and Traquair Forest
Meigle Hill 1389
Old Gala House
B6374
Gattonside
B6360
Redpath
Leaderfoot
Lowood
Newstead
Ashiestiel Hill
Peel
Caddonfoot
Darnick
Roman
Melrose
Smailholm Tower
Hundleshope Heights
Glensax Burn
Kirkhouse
Minch Moor 1859
A707
Yair Hill Forest
Boleside
Abbotsford
B6360
Bemersyde
Clintmains
B6404
Glen House
B709
B7060
Dingleton
Eildon
Eildon Hills
Newtown St Boswells
Dryburgh Abbey
Mertoun Bridge
Dun Rig 2441
Blake Muir
Broomy Law
Lindean Mill Glass
Lindean
Cauldshiels Hill
B6359
Bowden
B6398
St Boswells
Maxton
A699
Deuchar Law 1779
Yarrow Ford
A708
Linglie Hill
Sir Walter Scott's Courtroom
Newark Castle
Lochcarron Mill
Selkirk
Longnewton Forest
Yarrow
Yarrow Water
Bowhill House & Country Estate
Philiphaugh
B6453
Longnewton
Douglas Burn
Fastheugh Hill 1645
Bowhill
Selkirk 1645
Halliwell's House
Midlem
Ancrum Moor 1545
Sandystones
Waterloo Monument
Mountbenger
Yarrow Feus
B7009
Brockhill
Lilliesleaf
B6400
Ancrum
Harestanes Countryside
Cappercleuch
ETTRICK FOREST
Ettrickbridge
Bloomfield
A698
St Mary's Loch
Black Knowe Head 1805
Ashkirk
Caver's Hill 1209
Mary, Queen of Scots'
Lanton
Gilmanscleuch
Essenside Loch
Minto Hills 905
Fatlips Castle
Minto
Spittal-on-Rule
Newton
Castle Jail
The Wiss 1933
Akermoor Loch
Shaws Under Loch
Hassendean
B6405
Loch of the Lowes
Horsleyhill
Drinkstone Hill
Leyden Monument
Dunion Hill
A708
Tushielaw
Dun Knowe
Appletreehall
Clarilaw
Denholm
Bedrule
120
Ramsey Knowe
B711
Hellmoor Loch
Smasha Hill
Scottish Borders Art Glass
Rubers Law 1391
B6357
Redfordgreen
Burnfoot
Cauldmill
Alemoor Loch
James Hogg Monument
Ettrick
Wilton
A698
HAWICK
Kirkton
Leyden Obelisk
Roberton
Buccleuch
Motte
Borders Textile Towerhouse
A6088
Law Kneis 1634
Burnfoot
Bonchester Bridge
Deanburnhaugh
Branxholme
White Hill 987
B6399
Glenkerry
Hobkirk
Chesters
Sauchie Law
1278 • Redcleuch Edge
Hott Hill
Newmill
Jed
Southdean
CRAIK FOREST
Craik
Stobs Castle
Cross Hill
Dryden Fell
Allan Water
B6357
Green Law
Craik Cross Hill
Pike Hill 1369
Slitrig Water
WAUCHOPE FOREST
TEVIOTDALE
Teviothead
River Teviot
Skelfhill
The Pike 1516
Langburnshiels
FOREST
Skelfhill Pen 1746
Wyndburgh Hill
Fanna Hill 1688
Carlin Tooth
Davington
Maiden Paps
Needs Law
Blaeberry Hill
Eweslees Knowe
Comb Hill
Millstone Edge
Cauldcleuch Head 1996
Greatmoor Hill 1966
Leap Hill
Sandy Edge
Lamblair Hill
Hartshorn Pike
Causeway Grain Head
Mosspaul
Tudhope Hill 1965
Saughtree Fell
Peel Fell 1975
Kagyu Samye Ling
White Esk
Eskdalemuir
White Hope Edge
Wisp Hill 1953
Jamestown
Faw Side 1722
Geordie's Hill
Din Fell 1737
Hermitage
Hermitage Chapel
Arnton Fell 1464
Saughtree
Deadwater
Hog Hill
Meggat Water
Broad Head 1614
Ewes Water
Pike Fell
Steele Road
Foulmire Heights
Kielder
Toll
Butteryhaugh
Kielder Viaduct
CASTLE O'ER FOREST
Castle O'er
ESKDALE
Crumpton Hill 1575
Roan Fell 1862
North Birny Fell 902
Larriston Fells 1678
SCOTLAND
ENGLAND
Black Knowe
KIELDER FOREST
Kirkstile or Ewes
Watch Hill
Bentpath
Telford Memorial
Hart Fell 1087
E
The Shin
Hog Fell
113
LIDDESDALE
Wilson's Pike
Calkin Rig 1478
Black Edge 1464
Tarras Water
Newcastleton
Black Knowe
Lewis Burn
Rough Pike
Newcastleton Forest
Liddesdale Heritage Centre
Glentenmont Height
MacDiarmid Memorial
Tinnis Hill 1326
Millholm Cross
Glendhu Hill 1685
KIELDER WATER & FOREST PARK

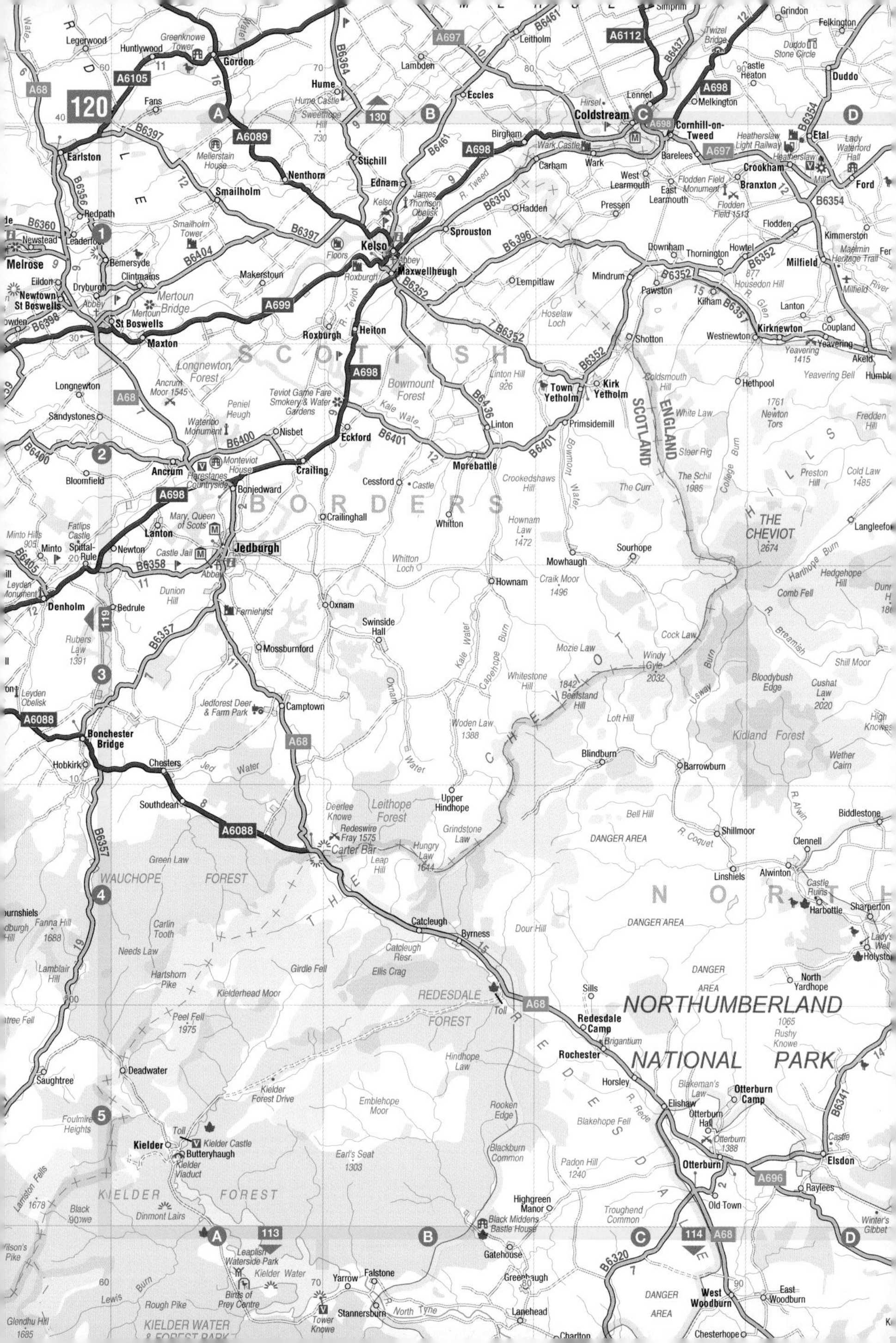
120
Legerwood
Huntlywood
Greenknowe Tower
Gordon
A6105
A68
Hume
Hume Castle
Sweethope Hill
730
130
B6364
Lambden
A697
Leitholm
B6461
A6112
B6437
Twizel Bridge
Grindon
Felkington
Duddo Stone Circle
Castle Heaton
Duddo
Eccles
Lennel
Hirsel
Coldstream
A698
Melkington
Cornhill-on-Tweed
Barelees
A697
Heatherslaw Light Railway
Heatherslaw
Etal
Lady Waterford Hall
B6354
Fans
Earlston
B6397
Mellerstain House
A6089
Nenthorn
Stichill
Ednam
B6461
Birgham
Wark Castle
Wark
Carham
A698
West Learmouth
East Learmouth
Flodden Field Monument
Flodden Field 1513
Branxton
Crookham
Ford
B6354
B6356
Redpath
Smailholm
James Thomson Obelisk
Kelso
R. Tweed
B6350
Hadden
Pressen
Flodden
Kimmerston
Melrose
Newstead
Leaderfoot
B6360
Smailholm Tower
B6404
B6397
Floors
Sprouston
B6396
Downham
Thornington
Howtel
Maelmin Heritage Trail
Milfield
Bemersyde
Clintmains
Makerstoun
Abbey
Maxwellheugh
B6352
Lempitlaw
Mindrum
Pawston
877 Housedon Hill
Kilham
B6351
R. Glen
Milfield
River
Eildon
Newtown St Boswells
Dryburgh
Mertoun Bridge
Roxburgh
A699
Hoselaw Loch
Lanton
B6398
St Boswells
Maxton
Roxburgh
Heiton
R. Teviot
B6352
Shotton
Westnewton
Kirknewton
Coupland
Yeavering
Yeavering 1415
Akeld
Humbleton
SCOTTISH
Longnewton Forest
Linton Hill 926
Town Yetholm
Kirk Yetholm
Coldsmouth Hill
Hethpool
Yeavering Bell
Longnewton
Ancrum Moor 1545
A68
A698
Bowmount Forest
B6436
SCOTLAND
ENGLAND
White Law
1761 Newton Tors
Fredden Hill
Sandystones
Peniel Heugh
Teviot Game Fare Smokery & Water Gardens
Kale Water
Linton
Primsidemill
Steer Rig
Waterloo Monument
Nisbet
B6400
Eckford
B6401
B6401
Bowmont Water
College Burn
The Schil 1985
Preston Hill
Cold Law 1485
B6400
Ancrum
Monteviot House
Harestanes Countryside
Crailing
Morebattle
Bloomfield
Bonjedward
Cessford
Castle
Crookedshaws Hill
The Curr
A698
BORDERS
Fatlips Castle
Mary, Queen of Scots'
Crailinghall
Whitton
Hownam Law 1472
THE CHEVIOT 2674
Langleeford
Minto Hills 905
Minto
Lanton
Spittal-Rule
Newton
Castle Jail
Jedburgh
B6405
B6358
Abbey
Whitton Loch
Mowhaugh
Sourhope
Harthope Burn
Hedgehope Hill
Leyden Monument
Denholm
Dunion Hill
Hownam
Craik Moor 1496
Comb Fell
119
Bedrule
Ferniehirst
Oxnam
Swinside Hall
R. Breamish
Rubers Law 1391
B6357
Mossburnford
Kale Water
Capehope Burn
Mozie Law
Cock Law
Windy Gyle 2032
Shill Moor
Oxnam Water
Whitestone Hill
1842 Beefstand Hill
Usway Burn
Bloodybush Edge
Cushat Law 2020
Leyden Obelisk
Jedforest Deer & Farm Park
Camptown
Loft Hill
High Knowes
A6088
Bonchester Bridge
Woden Law 1388
Kidland Forest
Wether Cairn
A68
Hobkirk
Chesters
Jed Water
Blindburn
Barrowburn
Southdean
Deerlee Knowe
Leithope Forest
Upper Hindhope
R. Alwin
Biddlestone
A6088
Redeswire Fray 1575
Carter Bar
Grindstone Law
Bell Hill
Shillmoor
Clennell
B6357
Hungry Law 1644
DANGER AREA
R. Coquet
Leap Hill
Green Law
Linshiels
Alwinton
WAUCHOPE
FOREST
THE
CHEVIOT
Castle Ruins
Harbottle
Sharperton
NORTH
Fanna Hill 1688
Carlin Tooth
Catcleugh
Byrness
Dour Hill
DANGER AREA
Lady's Well
Holystone
Needs Law
Catcleugh Resr.
Ellis Crag
DANGER
Lamblair Hill
Hartshorn Pike
Girdle Fell
AREA
North Yardhope
Kielderhead Moor
REDESDALE
A68
Sills
NORTHUMBERLAND
Toll
FOREST
Peel Fell 1975
Redesdale Camp
Brigantium
1065 Rushy Knowe
Rochester
NATIONAL
PARK
Hindhope Law
Deadwater
Saughtree
Horsley
Blakeman's Law
Otterburn Camp
B6341
Kielder Forest Drive
Emblehope Moor
REDESDALE
R. Rede
Elishaw
Otterburn Hall
Foulmire Heights
Rooken Edge
Blakehope Fell
Otterburn 1388
Castle
Toll
Kielder Castle
Kielder
Butteryhaugh
Kielder Viaduct
Earl's Seat 1303
Blackburn Common
Padon Hill 1240
Otterburn
Elsdon
A696
Lamston Fells
KIELDER
FOREST
Highgreen Manor
Raylees
1678
Black Knowe
Dinmont Lairs
Black Middens Bastle House
Troughend Common
Old Town
Winter's Gibbet
113
114
A68
Wilson's Pike
Leaplish Waterside Park
Gatehouse
B6320
Kielder Water
Yarrow
Falstone
Greenhaugh
Lewis Burn
Rough Pike
Birds of Prey Centre
Stannersburn
North Tyne
Tower Knowe
Lanehead
DANGER AREA
West Woodburn
East Woodburn
Glendhu Hill 1685
KIELDER WATER & FOREST PARK
Charlton
Chesterhope

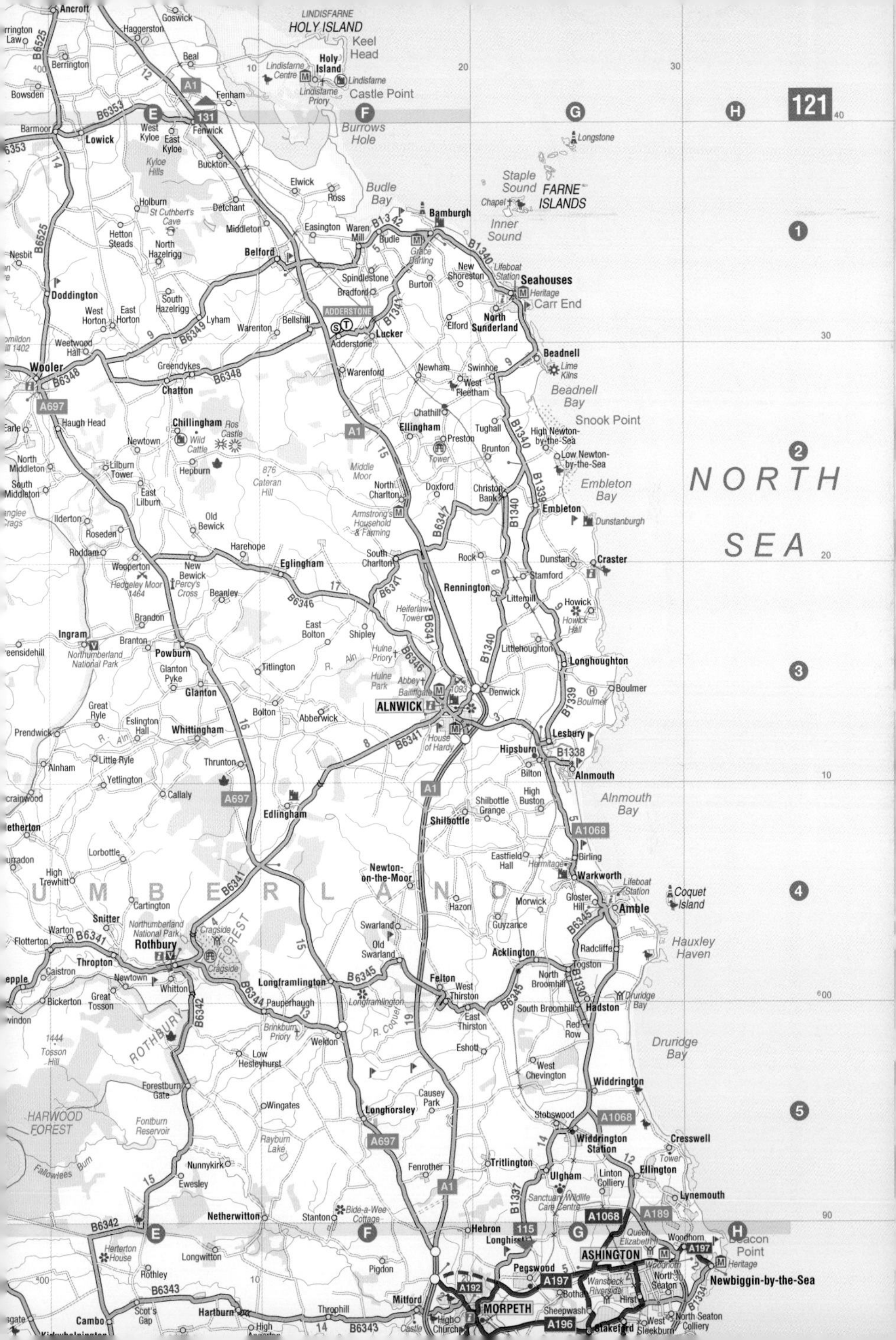
LINDISFARNE
HOLY ISLAND
Keel Head
Holy Island
Lindisfarne Centre
Lindisfarne Priory
Lindisfarne Castle Point
Burrows Hole
Ancroft
Goswick
Haggerston
Berrington Law
Berrington
Bowsden
Beal
Fenham
Barmoor
Lowick
West Kyloe
East Kyloe
Fenwick
Kyloe Hills
Buckton
Elwick
Ross
Budle Bay
Holburn
St Cuthbert's Cave
Detchant
Middleton
Hetton Steads
North Hazelrigg
Belford
Easington
Waren Mill
Budle
Bamburgh
Grace Darling
Spindlestone
Burton
New Shoreston
Lifeboat Station
Seahouses
Heritage
Carr End
Bradford
ADDERSTONE
Adderstone
Lucker
Elford
North Sunderland
Nesbit
Doddington
South Hazelrigg
West Horton
East Horton
Lyham
Warenton
Bellshill
Weetwood Hall
Wooler
Greendykes
Chatton
Warenford
Newham
Swinhoe
West Fleetham
Beadnell
Lime Kilns
Beadnell Bay
Snook Point
Haugh Head
Chillingham
Ros Castle
Wild Cattle
Newtown
Hepburn
Chathill
Ellingham
Preston
Tower
Tughall
Brunton
High Newton-by-the-Sea
Low Newton-by-the-Sea
Embleton Bay
North Middleton
South Middleton
Lilburn Tower
East Lilburn
876 Cateran Hill
Middle Moor
North Charlton
Armstrong's Household & Farming
Doxford
Christon Bank
Embleton
Dunstanburgh
Ilderton
Roseden
Old Bewick
Roddam
Wooperton
Hedgeley Moor 1464
New Bewick
Percy's Cross
Beanley
Harehope
Eglingham
South Charlton
Rock
Dunstan
Craster
Stamford
Rennington
Littlemill
Howick
Howick Hall
Brandon
Ingram
Northumberland National Park
Branton
Powburn
East Bolton
Shipley
Heiferlaw Tower
Hulne Priory
Hulne Park
Littlehoughton
Longhoughton
Boulmer
Glanton Pyke
Glanton
Titlington
Abbey Bailiffgate
ALNWICK
Denwick
Great Ryle
Eslington Hall
Whittingham
Bolton
Abberwick
House of Hardy
Lesbury
Hipsburn
Bilton
Alnmouth
Prendwick
Alnham
Little Ryle
Yetlington
Callaly
Thrunton
Edlingham
Shilbottle
Shilbottle Grange
High Buston
Alnmouth Bay
Lorbottle
High Trewhitt
Newton-on-the-Moor
Eastfield Hall
Hermitage
Birling
Warkworth
Lifeboat Station
Gloster Hill
Amble
Coquet Island
Cartington
Hazon
Morwick
Guyzance
Snitter
Warton
Flotterton
Northumberland National Park
Cragside
FOREST
Rothbury
Thropton
Caistron
Newtown
Whitton
Swarland
Old Swarland
Acklington
Radcliffe
Hauxley Haven
Togston
North Broomhill
Druridge Bay
Longframlington
Felton
West Thirston
Bickerton
Great Tosson
Pauperhaugh
Brinkburn Priory
Weldon
East Thirston
South Broomhill
Hadston
Red Row
ROTHBURY
1444 Tosson Hill
Low Hesleyhurst
Eshott
West Chevington
Druridge Bay
Forestburn Gate
Wingates
Causey Park
Widdrington
HARWOOD FOREST
Fontburn Reservoir
Rayburn Lake
Longhorsley
Stobswood
Widdrington Station
Cresswell
Fallowlees Burn
Nunnykirk
Ewesley
Fenrother
Tritlington
Ulgham
Linton Colliery
Ellington
Lynemouth
Sanctuary Wildlife Care Centre
Netherwitton
Stanton
Bide-a-Wee Cottage
Hebron
Longhirst
Queen Elizabeth II
ASHINGTON
Woodhorn
Beacon Point
Heritage
Herterton House
Longwitton
Rothley
Pigdon
Pegswood
Wansbeck Riverside
North Seaton
Newbiggin-by-the-Sea
Hartburn
Scot's Gap
Cambo
Throphill
Mitford
MORPETH
Bothal
Sheepwash
Hirst
High Church
Castle
Stakeford
West Sleekburn
North Seaton Colliery
Staple Sound
FARNE ISLANDS
Longstone
Chapel
Inner Sound
NORTH SEA
A1
A697
A1068
A189
A197
A192
A196
B6525
B6353
B6349
B6348
B1342
B1341
B1340
B1339
B6347
B6346
B6341
B1338
B6345
B6344
B6342
B6343
B1337
B1330
B1334
131
115
E
F
G
H
1
2
3
4
5

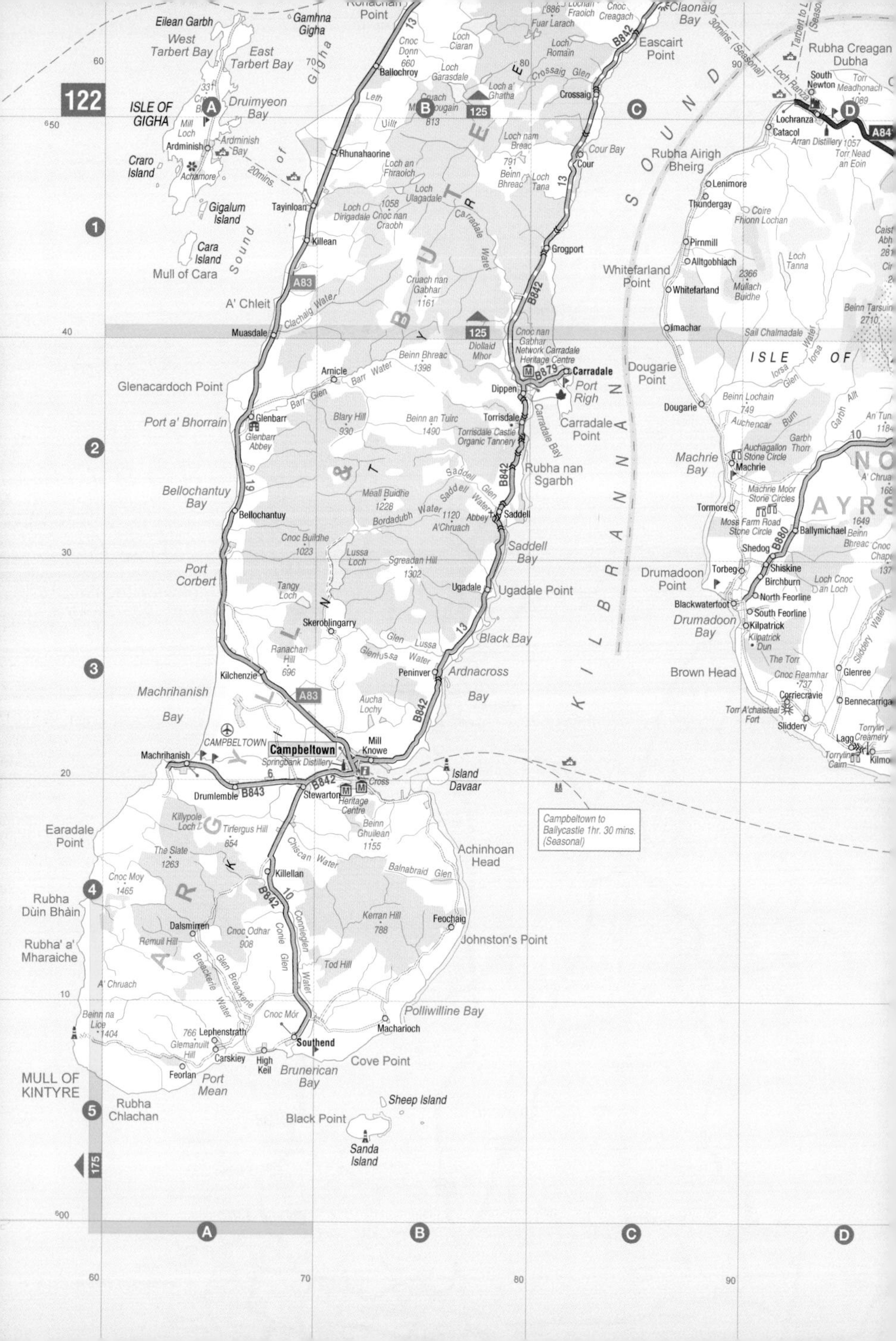

122
Eilean Garbh
West Tarbert Bay
East Tarbert Bay
Gamhna Gigha
Ronachan Point
ISLE OF GIGHA
Druimyeon Bay
Mill Loch
Ardminish
Ardminish Bay
Craro Island
Achamore
20mins.
Gigalum Island
Cara Island
Sound of Gigha
Mull of Cara
A' Chleit
Ballochroy
Rhunahaorine
Tayinloan
Killean
A83
Muasdale
Clachaig Water
Glenacardoch Point
Port a' Bhorrain
Glenbarr
Glenbarr Abbey
Bellochantuy Bay
Bellochantuy
Port Corbert
Machrihanish Bay
Kilchenzie
CAMPBELTOWN
Machrihanish
Campbeltown
Springbank Distillery
Drumlemble
B843
Stewarton
Heritage Centre
Cross
B842
Earadale Point
Rubha Dùin Bhàin
Rubha' a' Mharaiche
Killypole Loch
Tirfergus Hill 854
The Slate 1263
Cnoc Moy 1465
Remuil Hill
Dalsmirren
Cnoc Odhar 908
A' Chruach
Beinn na Lice 1404
Glenmanuilt Hill
Lephenstrath
Carskiey
Feorlan
Port Mean
High Keil
Southend
Brunerican Bay
Cove Point
Machrioch
Polliwilline Bay
Cnoc Mór
Tod Hill
Kerran Hill 788
Feochaig
Johnston's Point
Killellan
Conie Glen
Balnabraid Glen
Achinhoan Head
Beinn Ghuilean 1155
Island Davaar
Mill Knowe
Campbeltown to Ballycastle 1hr. 30 mins. (Seasonal)
MULL OF KINTYRE
Rubha Chlachan
Black Point
Sheep Island
Sanda Island
175
Cnoc Donn 660
Loch Ciaran
Loch Garasdale
Cruach Mhic Gougain 813
Loch a' Ghatha
125
Crossaig Glen
Loch Romain
Fuar Larach
Claonaig Bay
Eascairt Point
Crossaig
Cour Bay
Cour
Loch nam Breac
Beinn Bhreac 791
Loch Tana
Loch an Fhraoich
Loch Ulagadale
Loch Dirigadale
Cnoc nan Craobh 1058
Carradale Water
Cruach nan Gabhar 1161
Grogport
B842
Diollaid Mhor
Cnoc nan Gabhar
Network Carradale Heritage Centre
Carradale
Port Righ
Carradale Point
Dippen
B879
Torrisdale
Torrisdale Castle Organic Tannery
Carradale Bay
Rubha nan Sgarbh
Arnicle
Barr Water
Barr Glen
Beinn Bhreac 1398
Blary Hill 930
Beinn an Tuirc 1490
Saddell Glen
Saddell Water
Saddell
Saddell Abbey
Saddell Bay
Meall Buidhe 1228
Bordadubh Water
A'Chruach 1120
Cnoc Buidhe 1023
Lussa Loch
Sgreadan Hill 1302
Tangy Loch
Ugadale
Ugadale Point
Skeroblingarry
Glen Lussa
Lussa Water
Black Bay
Ranachan Hill 696
Peninver
Ardnacross Bay
Aucha Lochy
ARGYLL & BUTE
KILBRANNAN SOUND
Rubha Creagan Dubha
South Newton
Torr Meadhonach 1089
Loch Ranza
Lochranza
Catacol
Arran Distillery
Torr Nead an Eoin 1057
Rubha Airigh Bheirg
Lenimore
Thundergay
Coire Fhionn Lochan
Pirnmill
Alltgobhlach
Loch Tanna
Mullach Buidhe 2366
Whitefarland Point
Whitefarland
Imachar
Sail Chalmadale
Beinn Tarsuinn 2710
ISLE OF
Dougarie Point
Dougarie
Beinn Lochain 749
Auchencar Burn
Garbh Thorr
Machrie Bay
Auchagallon Stone Circle
Machrie
Machrie Moor Stone Circles
Tormore
Moss Farm Road Stone Circle
Shedog
B880
Ballymichael
Drumadoon Point
Torbeg
Shiskine
Birchburn
North Feorline
Blackwaterfoot
South Feorline
Drumadoon Bay
Kilpatrick
Kilpatrick Dun
The Torr
Brown Head
Cnoc Reamhar 737
Corriecravie
Torr A'chaisteal Fort
Sliddery
Glenree
Bennecarrigan
Lagg
Torrylin Creamery
Torrylin Cairn
Kilmory
A841
AYRS
A B C D
1 2 3 4 5
60 70 80 90
650 40 30 20 10 600

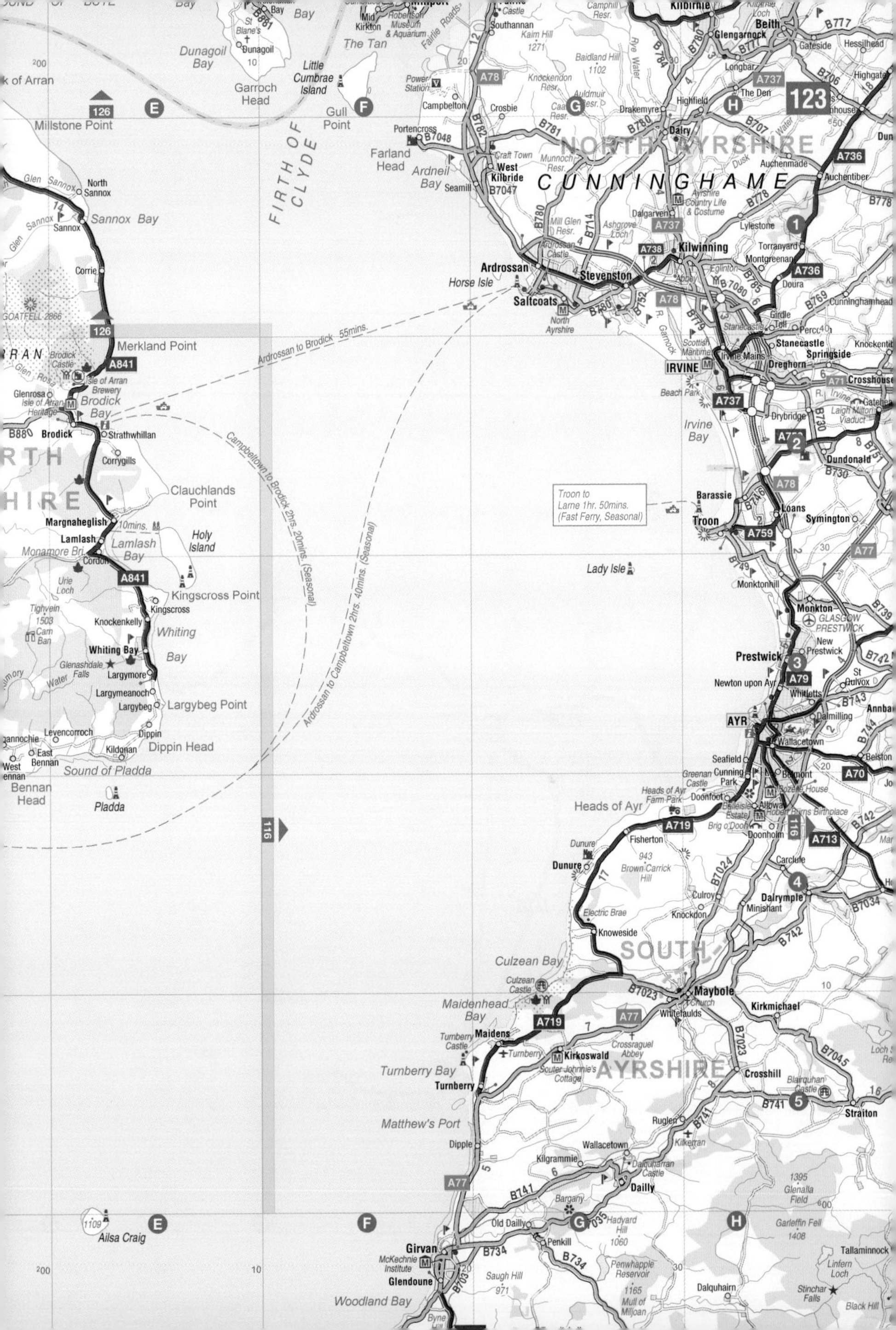

123
Dunagoil Bay
Garroch Head
Little Cumbrae Island
The Tan
Gull Point
Millstone Point
126
E
F
G
H
FIRTH OF CLYDE
Power Station
Campbelton
Portencross
B7048
Farland Head
Ardneil Bay
Seamill
West Kilbride
B7047
Craft Town
Crosbie
Southannan
Kaim Hill
Knockendon Resr.
Baidland Hill
Munnoch Resr.
Beith
Glengarnock
Kilbirnie
Gateside
Hessilhead
Longbar
The Den
Highfield
Drakemyre
Dalry
NORTH AYRSHIRE
CUNNINGHAME
Auchenmade
Auchentiber
Ayrshire Country Life & Costume
Dalgarven
Mill Glen Resr.
Ashgrove Loch
Lylestone
Torranyard
Montgreenan
Kilwinning
Ardrossan
Horse Isle
Stevenston
Saltcoats
North Ayrshire
Doura
Cunninghamhead
Girdle Toll
Stanecastle
Knockentiber
Springside
Dreghorn
Irvine Mains
IRVINE
Crosshouse
Beach Park
Drybridge
Irvine Bay
Laigh Milton Viaduct
Dundonald
Barassie
Troon
Loans
Symington
Troon to Larne 1hr. 50mins. (Fast Ferry, Seasonal)
Lady Isle
Monktonhill
Monkton
GLASGOW PRESTWICK
New Prestwick
Prestwick
Newton upon Ayr
St Quivox
Whitletts
AYR
Dalmilling
Wallacetown
Seafield
Greenan Castle
Cunning Park
Belmont
Heads of Ayr Farm Park
Doonfoot
Alloway
Belleisle Estate
Rozelle House
Robert Burns Birthplace
Brig o'Doon
Doonholm
Heads of Ayr
Dunure
Fisherton
Brown Carrick Hill
Carclue
Dalrymple
Culroy
Minishant
Knockdon
Electric Brae
Knoweside
SOUTH AYRSHIRE
Culzean Bay
Culzean Castle
Maidenhead Bay
Maybole
Whitefaulds
Kirkmichael
Maidens
Turnberry Castle
Turnberry
Kirkoswald
Crossraguel Abbey
Souter Johnnie's Cottage
Turnberry Bay
Crosshill
Straiton
Matthew's Port
Ruglen
Kilkerran
Dipple
Wallacetown
Kilgrammie
Dalquharran Castle
Dailly
Bargany
Glenalla Fell
Old Dailly
Hadyard Hill
Penkill
Garleffin Fell
Girvan
McKechnie Institute
Glendoune
Saugh Hill
Penwhapple Reservoir
Mull of Miljoan
Dalquhairn
Tallaminnock
Linfern Loch
Stinchar Falls
Black Hill
Woodland Bay
Ailsa Craig
Sannox Bay
North Sannox
Sannox
Corrie
GOATFELL
Merkland Point
Brodick Castle
Isle of Arran Brewery
Glenrosa
Isle of Arran Heritage
Brodick Bay
Brodick
Strathwhillan
Corrygills
Clauchlands Point
Margnaheglish
Lamlash
Lamlash Bay
Holy Island
Monamore Bri.
Cordon
Urie Loch
Kingscross Point
Kingscross
Tighvein
Knockenkelly
Whiting Bay
Glenashdale Falls
Largymore
Largymeanoch
Largybeg Point
Largybeg
Levencorroch
Dippin
Dippin Head
Kildonan
East Bennan
West Bennan
Sound of Pladda
Bennan Head
Pladda
Ardrossan to Brodick 55mins.
Campbeltown to Brodick 2hrs. 20mins. (Seasonal)
Ardrossan to Campbeltown 2hrs. 40mins. (Seasonal)
116
A78
A737
A736
A738
A759
A77
A79
A719
A713
A70
A841
B7023
B741
B734

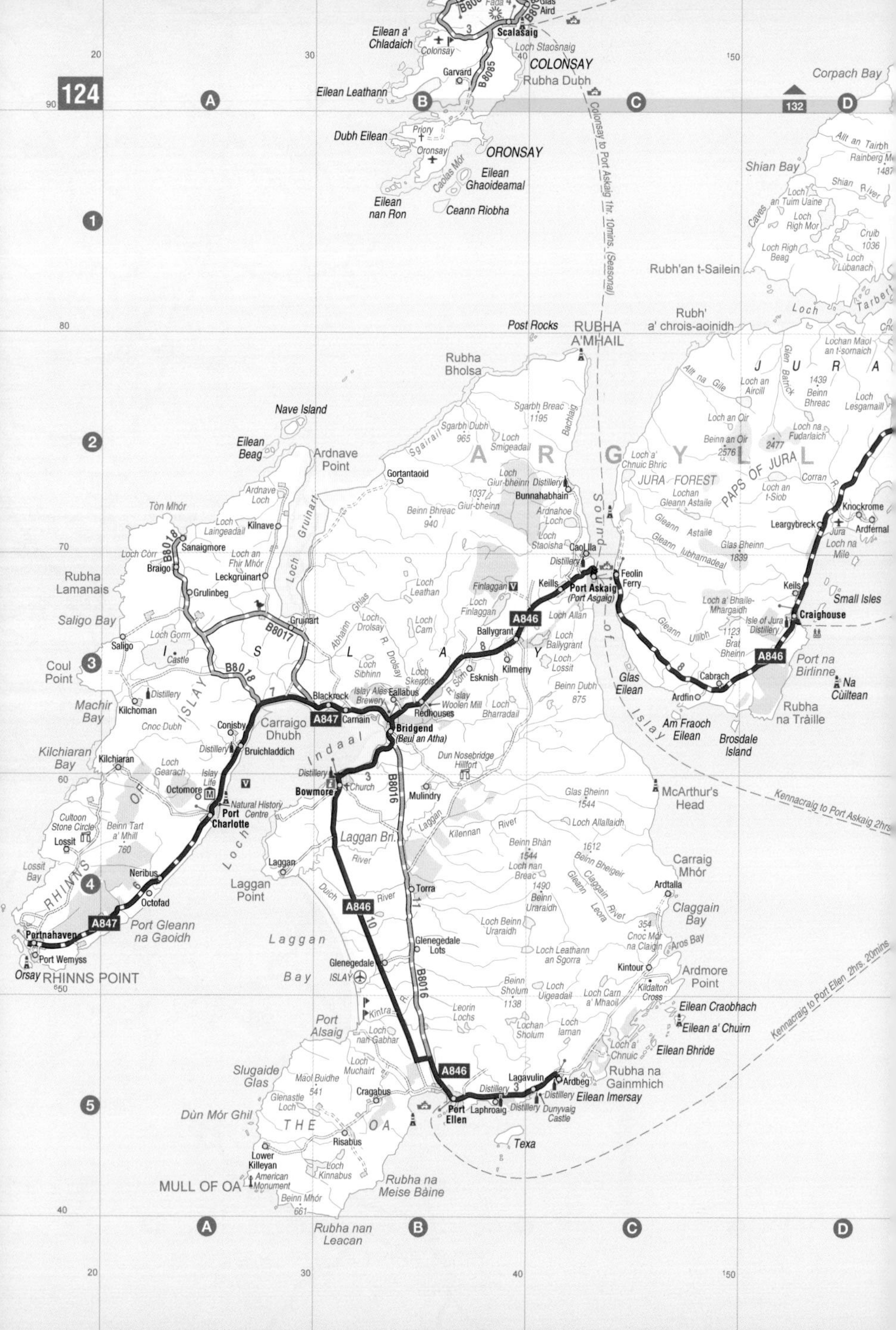

Fada
Glas Aird
Scalasaig
Eilean a' Chladaich
Colonsay
Loch Staosnaig
COLONSAY
Garvard
B8085
Rubha Dubh
Eilean Leathann
Corpach Bay
132
Priory
Dubh Eilean
Oronsay
ORONSAY
Caolas Mór
Eilean Ghaoideamal
Eilean nan Ron
Ceann Riobha
Colonsay to Port Askaig 1hr. 10mins. (Seasonal)
Allt an Tairbh
Rainberg Mòr
Shian Bay
Shian River
Loch an Tuim Uaine
Caves
Loch Righ Mor
Cruib
1036
Loch Righ Beag
Loch Lùbanach
Rubh'an t-Sailein
Loch Tarbert
Rubh' a' chrois-aoinidh
Post Rocks
RUBHA A'MHAIL
Rubha Bholsa
Lochan Maol an t-sornaich
JURA
Allt na Gile
Loch an Aircill
Glen Batrick
1439
Beinn Bhreac
Loch Lesgamaill
Nave Island
Sgarbh Breac
1195
Bachlaig
Sgarbh Dubh
965
Loch Smigeadail
Loch an Oir
Loch na Fudarlaich
Eilean Beag
Ardnave Point
Sgairail
ARGYLL
Beinn an Oir
2576
2477
Loch a' Chnuic Bhric
Gortantaoid
Loch Giur-bheinn
Distillery
Bunnahabhain
Sound of Islay
JURA FOREST
Lochan Gleann Astaile
PAPS OF JURA
Corran
Loch an t-Siob
Ardnave Loch
Tòn Mhór
1037
Giur-bheinn
Beinn Bhreac
940
Ardnahoe Loch
Knockrome
Leargybreck
Jura
Ardfernal
Loch Laingeadail
Kilnave
Loch Gruinart
B8018
Sanaigmore
Loch Staoisha
Gleann Astaile
Gleann Iubhamadeal
Glas Bheinn
1839
Loch na Mile
Loch Còrr
Loch an Fhir Mhór
Braigo
Leckgruinart
Caol Ila
Distillery
Feolin Ferry
Rubha Lamanais
Grulinbeg
Loch Leathan
Finlaggan
Keills
Port Askaig
(Port Asgaig)
Keills
Small Isles
Abhainn Ghlas
Loch Finlaggan
A846
Loch Allan
Loch a' Bhaile-Mhargaidh
Isle of Jura Distillery
Craighouse
Saligo Bay
Gruinart
Loch Drolsay
Loch Cam
Ballygrant
Loch Gorm
B8017
Saligo
ISLAY
Loch Ballygrant
Gleann Ullibh
1123
Brat Bheinn
A846
Port na Birlinne
Coul Point
Castle
B8018
R. Drolsay
Kilmeny
Loch Lossit
Loch Sibhinn
Loch Skerrols
R. Sorn
Esknish
Cabrach
Na Cùiltean
Distillery
Islay Ales Brewery
Eallabus
Blackrock
Islay Woolen Mill
Loch Bharradail
Beinn Dubh
875
Glas Eilean
Ardfin
Rubha na Tràille
Machir Bay
Kilchoman
A847
Carnain
Redhouses
Cnoc Dubh
Carraigo Dhubh
Bridgend
(Beul an Atha)
Am Fraoch Eilean
Brosdale Island
Conisby
Loch Indaal
Distillery
Bruichladdich
Kilchiaran Bay
Kilchiaran
Loch Gearach
Dun Nosebridge Hillfort
Islay Life
Distillery
B8016
Octomore
Bowmore
Church
Mulindry
McArthur's Head
Glas Bheinn
1544
Kennacraig to Port Askaig 2hrs.
Natural History Centre
Port Charlotte
Cultoon Stone Circle
Beinn Tart a' Mhill
760
Lossit
RHINNS OF ISLAY
Loch Gruinart
Laggan Bri.
Laggan River
Kilennan River
Loch Allallaidh
Beinn Bhàn
1544
Loch nan Breac
1612
Beinn Bheigeir
Claggain River
Carraig Mhór
Lossit Bay
Neribus
Laggan
Laggan Point
Gleann Leora
1490
Beinn Uraraidh
Ardtalla
Octofad
Duich River
Torra
A846
Claggain Bay
Portnahaven
A847
Port Gleann na Gaoidh
Loch Beinn Uraraidh
354
Cnoc Mór na Claigin
Aros Bay
Port Wemyss
Laggan Bay
Glenegedale Lots
Loch Leathann an Sgorra
Kintour
Ardmore Point
Orsay
RHINNS POINT
Glenegedale
ISLAY
B8016
Beinn Sholum
1138
Loch Uigeadail
Loch Carn a' Mhaoil
Kildalton Cross
Kennacraig to Port Ellen 2hrs. 20mins.
Kintra
Leorin Lochs
Eilean Craobhach
Eilean a' Chuirn
Port Alsaig
Loch nan Gabhar
Lochan Sholum
Loch Iarnan
Loch a' Chnuic
Eilean Bhride
Loch Muchairt
Rubha na Gainmhich
Slugaide Glas
Maol Buidhe
541
Cragabus
A846
Lagavulin
Ardbeg
Distillery
Glenastle Loch
Port Ellen
Laphroaig
Distillery
Dunyvaig Castle
Eilean Imersay
Dùn Mór Ghil
THE OA
Risabus
Texa
Lower Killeyan
Loch Kinnabus
MULL OF OA
American Monument
Rubha na Meise Bàine
Beinn Mhór
661
Rubha nan Leacan

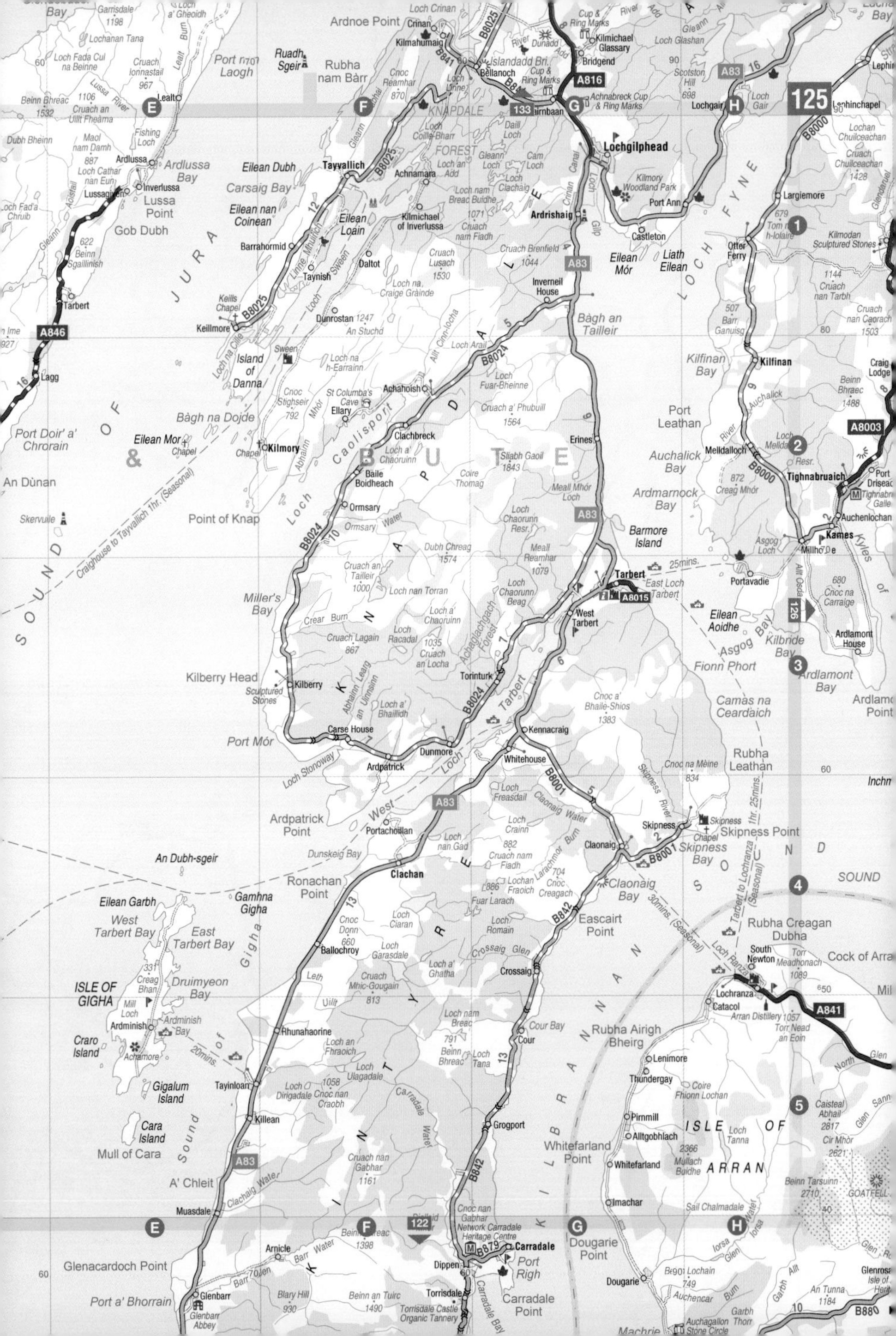

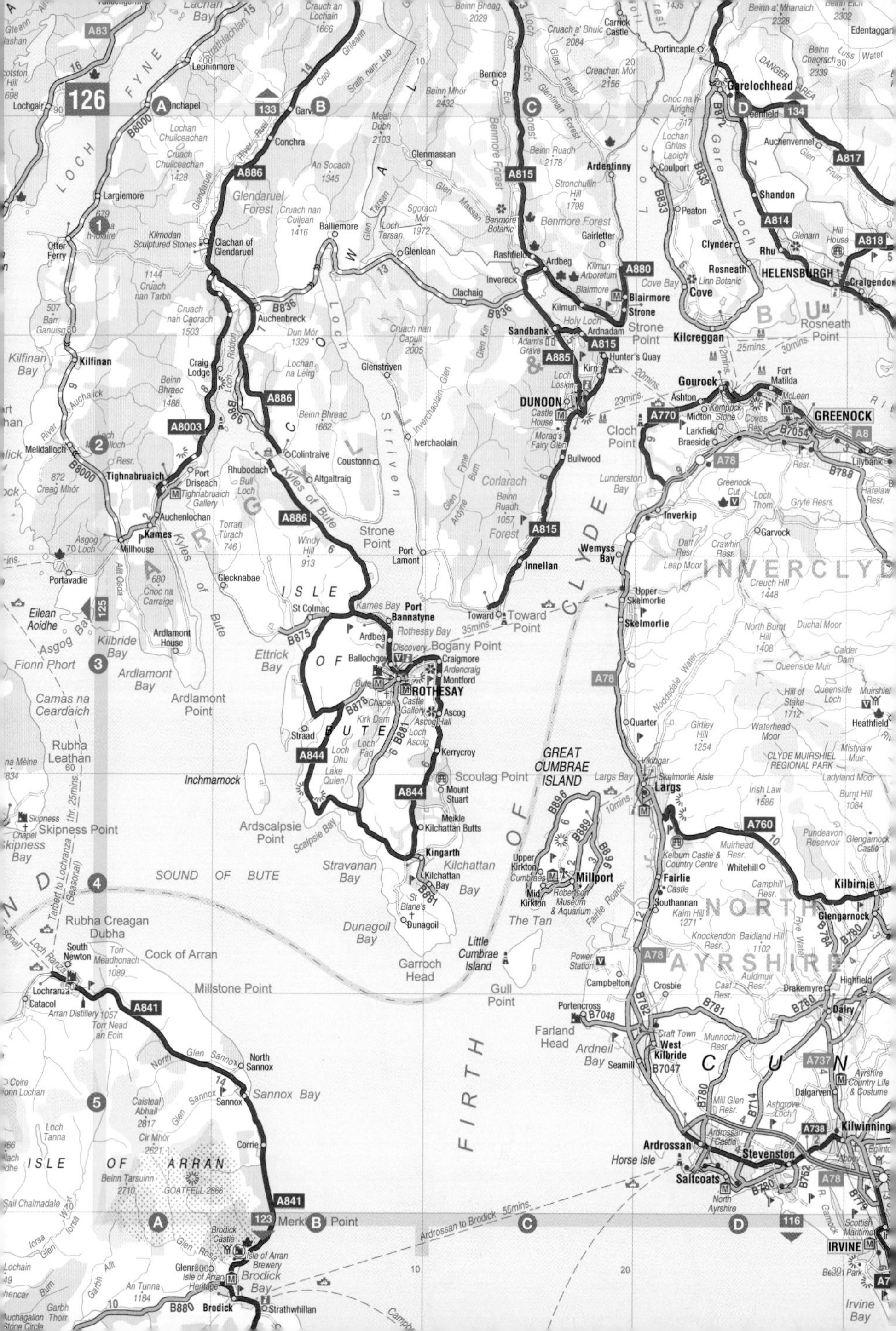

126
A83
LOCH FYNE
Strathlachlan
Lephinmore
Lochgair
Inchapel
B8000
Lochan Chuilceachan
Cruach Chuilceachan 1428
Crauch an Lochain 1666
Caol Ghleann
Strath nan Lub
Garvie
Conchra
133
A886
Glendaruel Forest
Beinn Bheag 2029
Meall Dubh 2103
Beinn Mhòr 2432
Glenmassan
An Socach 1345
Cruach nan Cuilean 1416
Balliemore
Loch Tarsan
Sgorach Mòr 1972
Glen Tarsan
Glenlean
Clachaig
B836
Largiemore
Otter Ferry
Kilmodan Sculptured Stones
Clachan of Glendaruel
Cruach nan Tarbh 1144
Cruach nan Caorach 1503
Auchenbreck
Dun Mòr 1329
Cruach nan Capull 2005
Glenstriven
Lochan na Leirg
Beinn Bhreac 1662
Inverchaolain Glen
Iverchaolain
Loch Striven
Coustonn
Altgaltraig
Colintraive
Rhubodach
Bull Loch
Kyles of Bute
Kilfinan
Kilfinan Bay
Auchalick
Craig Lodge
Beinn Bhraec 1488
A8003
B866
Melldalloch
Creag Mhòr 872
Tighnabruaich
Port Driseach
Tighnabruaich Gallery
Auchenlochan
Kames
Millhouse
Asgog Loch
Portavadie
Torran Tùrach 746
Cnoc na Carraige 680
Glecknabae
Windy Hill 913
Strone Point
Port Lamont
ARGYLL
Eilean Aoidhe
Asgog Bay
Kilbride Bay
Fionn Phort
Ardlamont Bay
Ardlamont House
Ardlamont Point
Camas na Ceardaich
Rubha Leathan
Inchmarnock
ISLE OF BUTE
St Colmac
B875
Ettrick Bay
Kames Bay
Port Bannatyne
Ardbeg
Rothesay Bay
Bogany Point
Ballochgoy
Discovery
Craigmore
Ardencraig
Montford
ROTHESAY
Castle
Gallery
Ascog
Ascog Hall
B878
Chapel
Kirk Dam
Straad
Loch Ascog
Loch Fad
Loch Dhu
Lake Quien
B881
A844
Kerrycroy
Scoulag Point
Mount Stuart
Meikle Kilchattan Butts
Ardscalpsie Point
Scalpsie Bay
Kingarth
Stravanan Bay
Kilchattan Bay
St Blane's
Dunagoil
Dunagoil Bay
Garroch Head
Skipness
Skipness Point
Skipness Bay
SOUND OF BUTE
Tarbert to Lochranza (Seasonal)
1hr. 25mins.
Rubha Creagan Dubha
South Newton
Torr Meadhonach 1089
Cock of Arran
Lochranza
Catacol
Millstone Point
Arran Distillery
Torr Nead an Eoin 1057
A841
North Glen Sannox
North Sannox
Sannox
Sannox Bay
Glen Sannox
Caisteal Abhail 2817
Cìr Mhòr 2621
Loch Tanna
Corrie
ISLE OF ARRAN
Beinn Tarsuinn 2710
GOATFELL 2866
Glen Rosa
Merkland Point
123
Brodick Castle
Isle of Arran Brewery
Isle of Arran Heritage
Brodick Bay
An Tunna 1184
B880
Brodick
Strathwhillan
Ardrossan to Brodick 55mins.
Loch Eck
Cruach a' Bhuic 2084
Carrick Castle
Glen Finart
Creachan Mòr 2156
Bernice
Benmore Forest
Beinn Ruadh 2178
Ardentinny
A815
Stronchullin Hill 1798
Benmore Botanic
Gairletter
Rashfield
Ardbeg
Kilmun Arboretum
Invereck
Blairmore
A880
Kilmun
Strone
Holy Loch
Sandbank
Adam's Grave
Ardnadam
Strone Point
A885
Hunter's Quay
Kirn
Loch Loskin
DUNOON
Castle House
Morag's Fairy Glen
Bullwood
Cloch Point
Corlarach
Beinn Ruadh 1057
Forest
Innellan
Toward
Toward Point
35mins.
Glen Fyne
Ardyne Burn
Portincaple
Beinn a' Mhanaich 2328
Beinn Chaorach 2339
Garelochhead
DANGER AREA
Whistlefield
134
Cnoc na h-Airighe 717
Lochan Ghlas Laoigh
B872
B833
Coulport
Gare Loch
Auchenvennel
A817
Shandon
Peaton
A814
Clynder
Rhu
Glenarn
Hill House
A818
Rosneath
Linn Botanic
HELENSBURGH
Craigendoran
Cove Bay
Cove
Kilcreggan
Rosneath Point
12mins.
25mins.
30mins.
20mins.
23mins.
Gourock
Fort Matilda
Ashton
McLean
Kempock Stone
Midton
Larkfield
Braeside
A770
GREENOCK
B7054
A8
A78
Lilybank
B788
Lunderston Bay
Greenock Cut
Loch Thom
Gryfe Resrs.
Inverkip
Daff Resr.
Garvock
Crawhin Resr.
Leap Moor
Wemyss Bay
INVERCLYDE
Creuch Hill 1448
Upper Skelmorlie
Skelmorlie
FIRTH OF CLYDE
North Burnt Hill 1408
Duchal Moor
Calder Dam
Queenside Muir
Noddsdale Water
Hill of Stake 1712
Queenside Loch
Muirshiel
Heathfield
Quarter
Girtley Hill 1254
Waterhead Moor
GREAT CUMBRAE ISLAND
CLYDE MUIRSHIEL REGIONAL PARK
Mistylaw Muir
Largs Bay
Vikingar
Skelmorlie Aisle
Largs
Irish Law 1586
Ladyland Moor
Burnt Hill 1084
10mins.
B896
B899
Upper Kirkton
Cumbraes
Millport
Mid Kirkton
Robertson Museum & Aquarium
The Tan
Fairlie Roads
A760
Kelburn Castle & Country Centre
Muirhead Resr.
Whitehill
Pundeavon Reservoir
Glengarnock Castle
Kilbirnie
Fairlie
Castle
Southannan
Kaim Hill 1271
Camphill Resr.
NORTH AYRSHIRE
Glengarnock
Knockendon Resr.
Baidland Hill 1102
Rye Water
Little Cumbrae Island
Power Station
Campbelton
Crosbie
Caaf Resr.
Auldmuir Resr.
Drakemyre
Highfield
Gull Point
Portencross
B7048
B782
B781
B780
Dalry
Farland Head
Craft Town
West Kilbride
Munnoch Resr.
Ardneil Bay
Seamill
B7047
CUNNINGHAME
A737
Ayrshire Country Life & Costume
Mill Glen Resr.
B714
Ashgrove Loch
Dalgarven
A738
Kilwinning
Ardrossan
Ardrossan Castle
Stevenston
Horse Isle
Saltcoats
North Ayrshire
B752
Eglinton
A78
116
IRVINE
Scottish Maritime
Irvine Bay
10
20

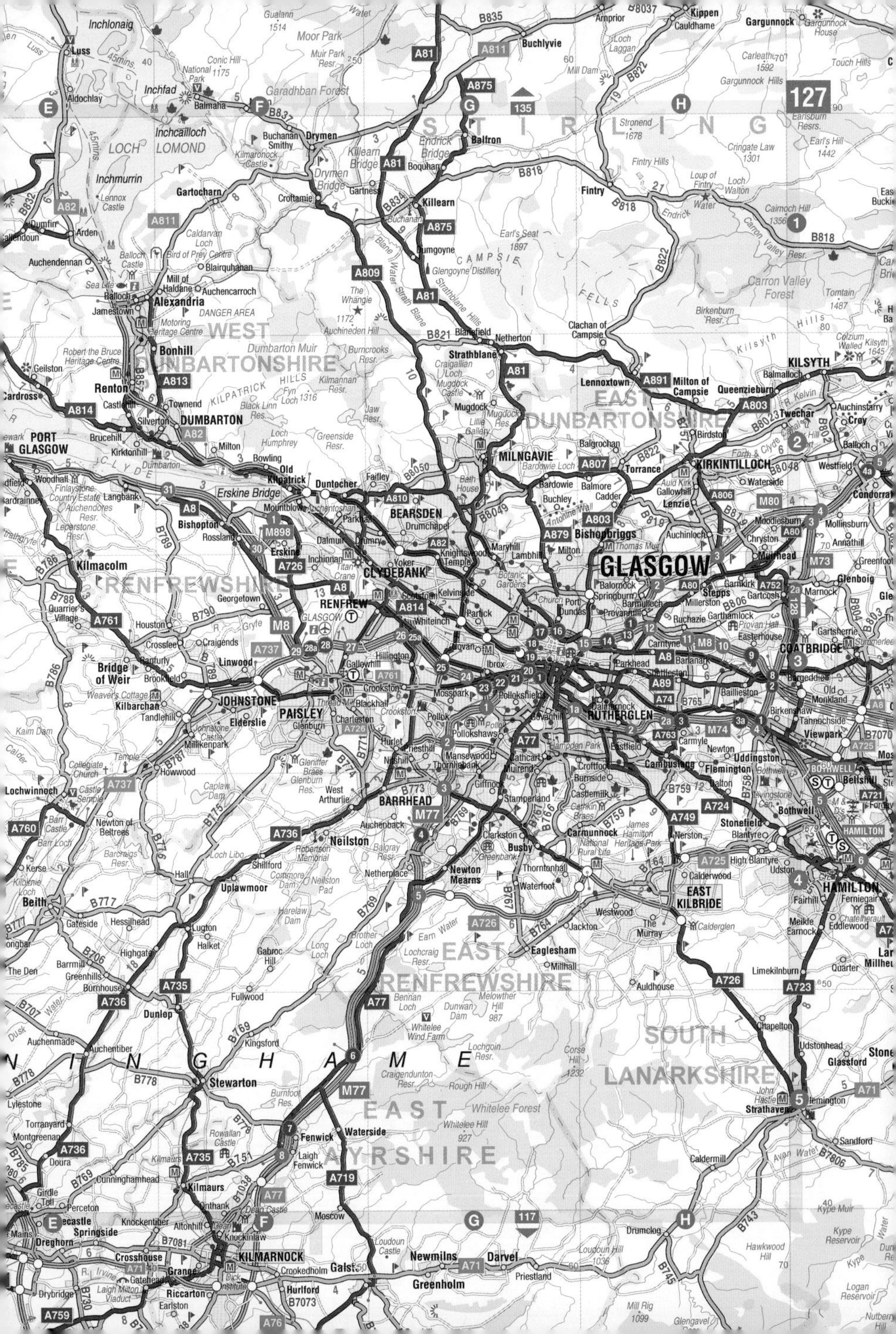
GLASGOW
STIRLING
WEST DUNBARTONSHIRE
EAST DUNBARTONSHIRE
RENFREWSHIRE
EAST RENFREWSHIRE
SOUTH LANARKSHIRE
EAST AYRSHIRE
PAISLEY
CLYDEBANK
KILMARNOCK
HAMILTON
EAST KILBRIDE
DUMBARTON
KILSYTH
COATBRIDGE
RUTHERGLEN
JOHNSTONE
LOCH LOMOND
135
117

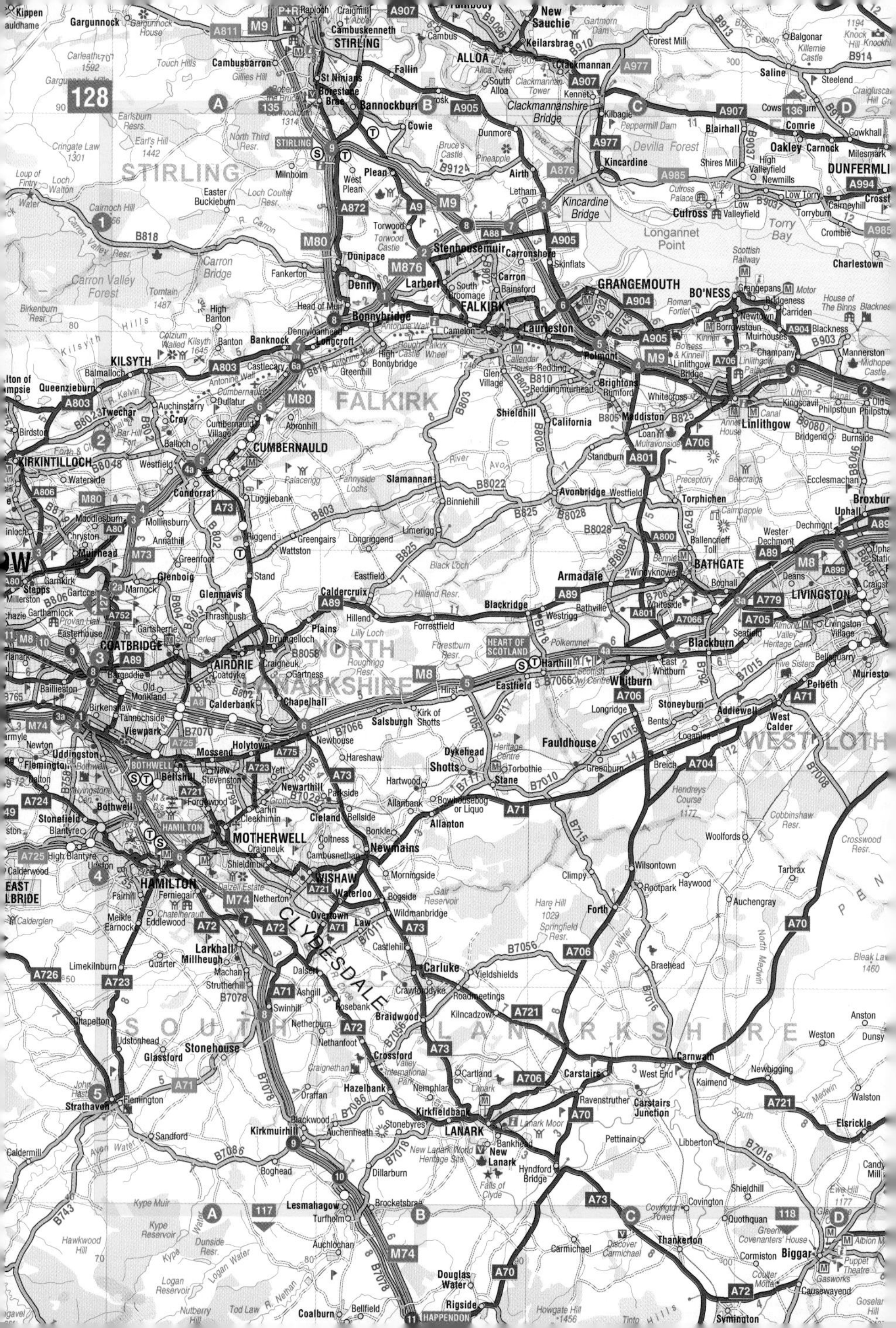

128
STIRLING
FALKIRK
NORTH LANARKSHIRE
SOUTH LANARKSHIRE
CLYDESDALE
WEST LOTHIAN
Kippen
Gargunnock
Raploch
Craigmill
Cambuskenneth
STIRLING
New Sauchie
Keilarsbrae
ALLOA
Clackmannan
Forest Mill
Balgonar
Saline
Steelend
Cambusbarron
St Ninians
Borestone Brae
Bannockburn
Fallin
South Alloa
Kennet
Clackmannanshire Bridge
Kilbagie
Blairhall
Comrie
Oakley
Carnock
Gowkhall
Milesmark
DUNFERMLINE
Cowie
Dunmore
Airth
Kincardine
Shires Mill
High Valleyfield
Newmills
Low Torry
Culross
Torryburn
Crombie
Charlestown
Plean
Milnholm
Easter Buckieburn
Torwood
Letham
Kincardine Bridge
Longannet Point
Dunipace
Stenhousemuir
Carronshore
Skinflats
Fankerton
Denny
Larbert
Carron
Bainsford
GRANGEMOUTH
BO'NESS
Bridgeness
Carriden
Head of Muir
Bonnybridge
FALKIRK
Camelon
Laurieston
Polmont
Newtown
Borrowstoun
Blackness
Banknock
Longcroft
Dennyloanhead
Muirhouses
Champany
Mannerston
KILSYTH
Castlecary
High Bonnybridge
Greenhill
Glen Village
Redding
Reddingmuirhead
Brightons
Rumford
Linlithgow Bridge
Whitecross
Kingscavil
Philpstoun
Balmalloch
Queenzieburn
Twechar
Auchinstarry
Dullatur
Croy
Cumbernauld Village
CUMBERNAULD
Abronhill
Shieldhill
California
Maddiston
Linlithgow
Bridgend
Burnside
KIRKINTILLOCH
Waterside
Westfield
Condorrat
Slamannan
Avonbridge
Standburn
Torphichen
Ecclesmachan
Broxburn
Uphall
Binniehill
Luggiebank
Moodiesburn
Mollinsburn
Chryston
Muirhead
Annathill
Riggend
Greengairs
Wattston
Longriggend
Limerigg
Dechmont
Westfield
Ballencrieff Toll
Greenfoot
Glenboig
Stand
Eastfield
Armadale
Windyknowe
BATHGATE
Boghall
Deans
LIVINGSTON
Stepps
Gartcosh
Marnock
Glenmavis
Caldercruix
Blackridge
Westrigg
Bathville
Whiteside
Millerston
Garthamlock
Thrashbush
Hillend
Forrestfield
Plains
Drumgelloch
Livingston Village
Seafield
Blackburn
Easterhouse
COATBRIDGE
AIRDRIE
Craigneuk
Gartness
Harthill
East Whitburn
Whitburn
Bellsquarry
Murieston
Polbeth
Bargeddie
Coatdyke
Calderbank
Chapelhall
Hirst
Eastfield
Baillieston
Old Monkland
Birkenshaw
Tannochside
Viewpark
Salsburgh
Kirk of Shotts
Longridge
Stoneyburn
Bents
Addiewell
West Calder
Loganlea
Newton
Uddingston
Flemington
Mossend
Holytown
Newhouse
Dykehead
Shotts
Fauldhouse
Greenburn
Breich
BOTHWELL
Bellshill
New Stevenston
Yett
Hareshaw
Torbothie
Stane
Dalton
Bothwell
Newarthill
Carfin
Parkside
Hartwood
Stonefield
Blantyre
Forgewood
Cleekhimin
Cleland
Bellside
Allanbank
Bowhousebog or Liquo
Allanton
Bonkle
MOTHERWELL
HAMILTON
High Blantyre
Coltness
Cambusnethan
Newmains
Woolfords
Craigneuk
Shieldmuir
Calderwood
Udston
WISHAW
Morningside
Wilsontown
Climpy
Tarbrax
EAST KILBRIDE
HAMILTON
Fairhill
Ferniegair
Netherton
Waterloo
Bogside
Rootpark
Haywood
Auchengray
Forth
Overtown
Wildmanbridge
Meikle Earnock
Eddlewood
Law
Calderglen
Larkhall
Millheugh
Castlehill
Quarter
Limekilnburn
Machan
Carluke
Yieldshields
Braehead
Dalserf
Strutherhill
Crawforddyke
Ashgill
Roadmeetings
Swinhill
Rosebank
Kilncadzow
Chapelton
Netherburn
Braidwood
Anston
Udstonhead
Glassford
Stonehouse
Nethanfoot
Crossford
Carnwath
Weston
Dunsyre
Carstairs
West End
Newbigging
Cartland
Kaimend
Hazelbank
Nemphlar
Ravenstruther
Carstairs Junction
Walston
Strathaven
Flemington
Draffan
Kirkfieldbank
LANARK
Elsrickle
Blackwood
Kirkmuirhill
Auchenheath
Stonebyres
Pettinain
Libberton
Sandford
Bankhead
New Lanark
Caldermill
Boghead
Dillarburn
Hyndford Bridge
Shieldhill
Candy Mill
Lesmahagow
Brocketsbrae
Turfholm
Covington
Quothquan
Auchlochan
Carmichael
Thankerton
Cormiston
Biggar
Douglas Water
Causewayend
Coalburn
Bellfield
Rigside
HAPPENDON
Symington
117
118
M9
M80
M876
M73
M8
M74
A811
A907
A977
A905
A876
A985
A994
A872
A9
A88
A904
A706
A803
A801
A800
A806
A80
A89
A899
A779
A7066
A705
A752
A725
A723
A775
A73
A721
A724
A71
A704
A72
A726
A70
HEART OF SCOTLAND
STIRLING
Carron Valley Forest
Devilla Forest
Kincardine Bridge

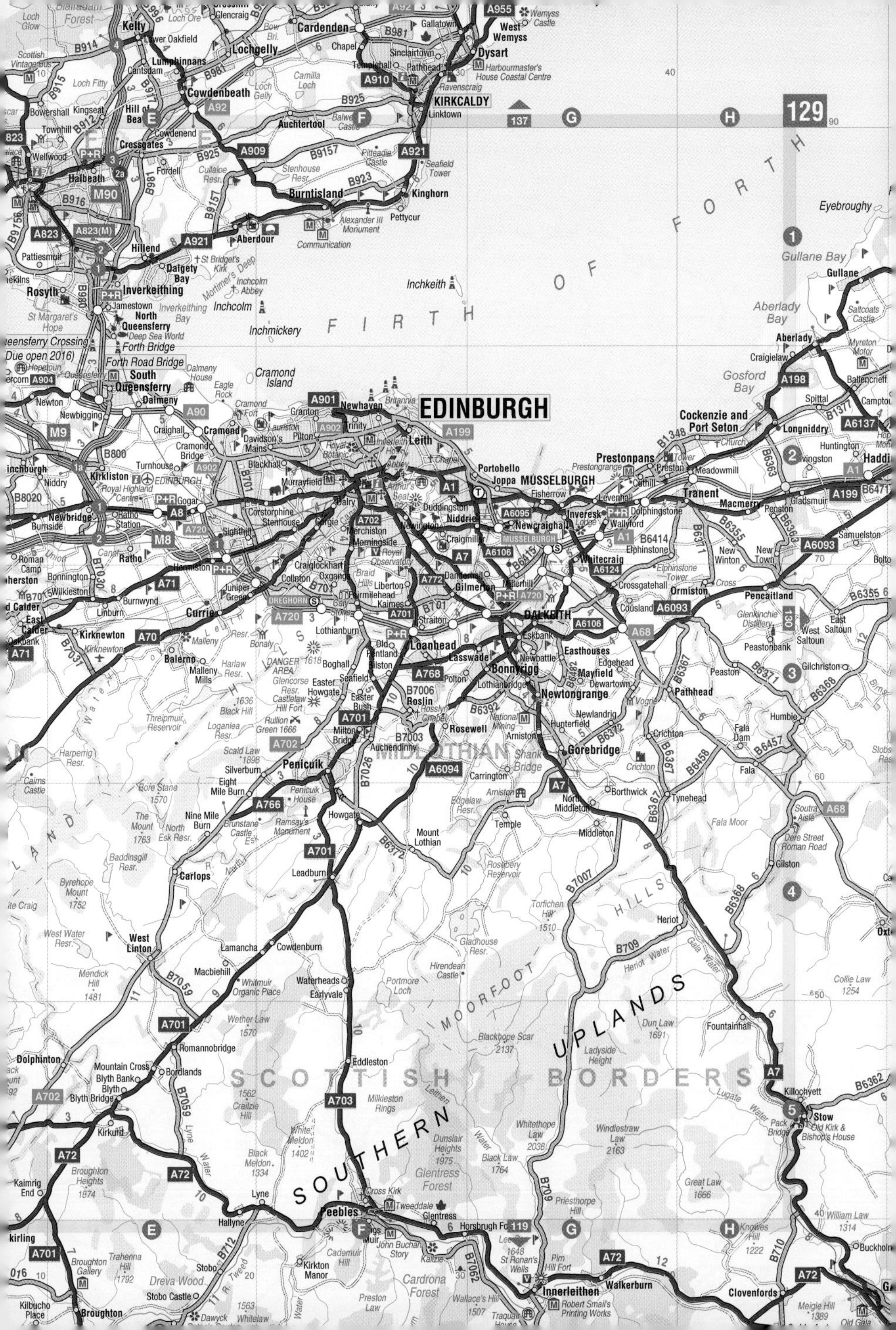

129
137
130
119
EDINBURGH
FIRTH OF FORTH
SCOTTISH BORDERS
SOUTHERN UPLANDS
MOORFOOT HILLS
PENTLAND HILLS
MIDLOTHIAN
FIFE
Kelty
Cardenden
Lochgelly
Lower Oakfield
Lumphinnans
Cowdenbeath
Hill of Beath
Crossgates
Halbeath
Kingseat
Townhill
Wellwood
Loch Fitty
Scottish Vintage Bus
Auchtertool
Kirkcaldy
Dysart
West Wemyss
Wemyss Castle
Gallatown
Sinclairtown
Pathhead
Ravenscraig
Linktown
Harbourmaster's House Coastal Centre
Seafield Tower
Kinghorn
Pettycur
Burntisland
Alexander III Monument
Aberdour
Dalgety Bay
Hillend
Inverkeithing
Rosyth
Pattiesmuir
St Margaret's Hope
North Queensferry
Deep Sea World
Forth Bridge
Forth Road Bridge
Queensferry Crossing (Due open 2016)
Hopetoun
South Queensferry
Dalmeny
Dalmeny House
Inchcolm
Inchcolm Abbey
Inchkeith
Inchmickery
Cramond Island
Eagle Rock
Cramond
Cramond Bridge
Newbigging
Newton
Kirkliston
Turnhouse
Royal Highland Centre
Ratho
Ratho Station
Newbridge
Burnside
Bonnington
Wilkieston
East Calder
Kirknewton
Balerno
Malleny Mills
Currie
Juniper Green
Hermiston
Gogar
Corstorphine
Sighthill
Granton
Newhaven
Trinity
Leith
Portobello
Joppa
Musselburgh
Fisherrow
Inveresk
Wallyford
Newcraighall
Niddrie
Duddingston
Craigmillar
Gilmerton
Danderhall
Millerhill
Dalkeith
Eskbank
Newbattle
Bonnyrigg
Lasswade
Loanhead
Straiton
Bilston
Roslin
Rosewell
Polton
Lothianbridge
Newtongrange
Gorebridge
Arniston
Carrington
Temple
North Middleton
Middleton
Borthwick
Crichton
Pathhead
Edgehead
Mayfield
Easthouses
Dewartown
Newlandrig
Hunterfield
Penicuik
Silverburn
Eight Mile Burn
Nine Mile Burn
Howgate
Auchendinny
Milton Bridge
Mount Lothian
Leadburn
Carlops
West Linton
Lamancha
Cowdenburn
Macbiehill
Whitmuir Organic Place
Waterheads
Earlyvale
Eddleston
Romannobridge
Mountain Cross
Bordlands
Blyth Bank
Blyth
Blyth Bridge
Dolphinton
Kirkurd
Kaimrig End
Broughton
Broughton Gallery
Stobo
Stobo Castle
Dawyck
Lyne
Hallyne
Peebles
Cross Kirk
Tweeddale
Glentress
Glentress Forest
Kings Muir
John Buchan Story
Kailzie
Kirkton Manor
Cardrona Forest
Horsburgh Ford
St Ronan's Wells
Innerleithen
Robert Smail's Printing Works
Walkerburn
Clovenfords
Heriot
Fountainhall
Killochyett
Stow
Old Kirk & Bishop's House
Pack Bridge
Prestonpans
Preston
Cockenzie and Port Seton
Longniddry
Tranent
Macmerry
Gladsmuir
Penston
Meadowmill
Dolphingstone
Elphinstone
Whitecraig
Crossgatehall
Cousland
Ormiston
Pencaitland
New Winton
New Town
Samuelston
East Saltoun
West Saltoun
Peastonbank
Peaston
Gilchriston
Humbie
Fala Dam
Fala
Fala Moor
Soutra Aisle
Dere Street Roman Road
Gilston
Aberlady
Aberlady Bay
Gullane
Gullane Bay
Eyebroughy
Craigielaw
Gosford Bay
Spittal
Ballencrieff
Myreton Motor
Saltcoats Castle
Glenkinchie Distillery
Dun Law 1691
Blackhope Scar 2137
Windlestraw Law 2163
Whitehope Law 2038
Dunslair Heights 1975
Black Law 1764
Great Law 1666
Collie Law 1254
Gladhouse Resr.
Rosebery Reservoir
Portmore Loch
Hirendean Castle
Torfichen Hill 1510
Cairns Castle
Harperrig Resr.
Threipmuir Reservoir
Harlaw Resr.
Loganlea Resr.
Glencorse Resr.
Castlelaw Hill Fort
Rullion Green 1666
Scald Law 1898
Black Hill 1636
West Water Resr.
Mendick Hill 1481
Baddinsgill Resr.
Byrehope Mount 1752
The Mount 1763
North Esk Resr.
Bore Stane 1570
Wether Law 1570
Ramsay's Monument
Penicuik House
Brunstane Castle
Black Meldon 1334
White Meldon 1402
Crailzie Hill 1562
Milkieston Rings
Broughton Heights 1874
Trahenna Hill 1792
Dreva Wood
Cademuir Hill
Preston Law
Wallace's Hill 1507
Priesthorpe Hill
Pirn Hill Fort
Knowes Hill 1222
William Law 1314
Meigle Hill 1389
M90
M9
M8
A90
A8
A71
A70
A720
A702
A701
A703
A766
A6094
A7
A68
A6093
A6106
A6124
A1
A199
A198
A6137
A72
A921
A909
A910
A92
A955
A823
A823(M)
A904
A901
A902
A772
A768
A6095
B709
B710
B7007
B7059
B712
B7062
B6372
B6367
B6458
B6457
B6368
B6371
B6363
B6355
B6414
B6362
B7026
B7003
B7006
B6392
B6482
B701
B800
B8020
B7030
B7031
B7015
B914
B915
B912
B916
B9156
B917
B981
B925
B9157
B923
B980
B1348
B1377
B6471

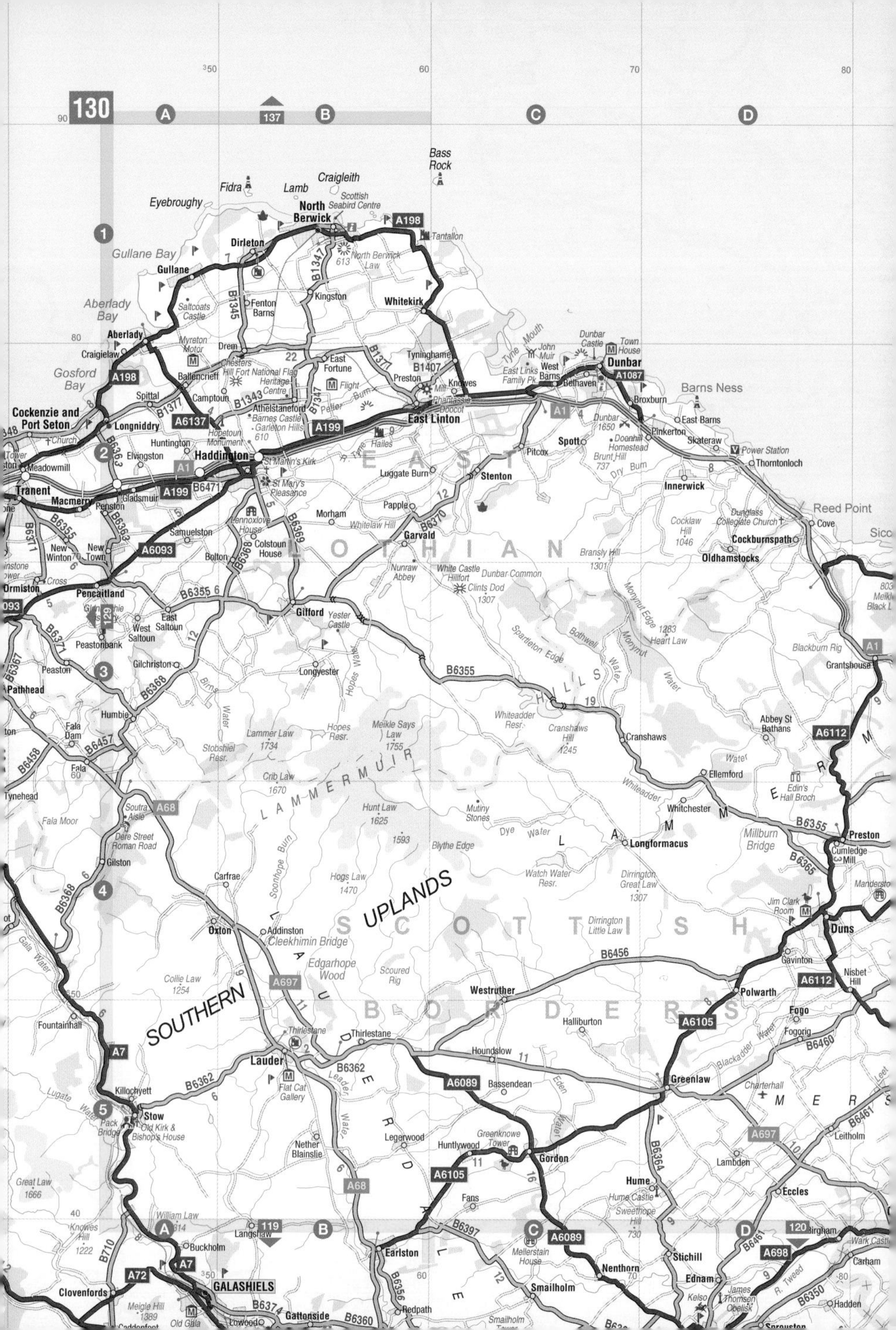

130
137
119
120
129
A
B
C
D
1
2
3
4
5
Bass Rock
Craigleith
Fidra
Lamb
Eyebroughy
North Berwick
Scottish Seabird Centre
A198
Tantallon
Dirleton
Gullane Bay
Gullane
North Berwick Law
613
B1347
Kingston
Whitekirk
Aberlady Bay
Saltcoats Castle
B1345
Fenton Barns
Aberlady
Craigielaw
Myreton Motor
Drem
22
East Fortune
B1377
Tyninghame
B1407
Gosford Bay
Chesters Hill Fort
National Flag Heritage Centre
Flight
Preston
Knowes
Mill
Phantassie Doocot
East Linton
Ballencrieff
Spittal
Camptoun
B1343
Athelstaneford
B1347
Peffer Burn
Cockenzie and Port Seton
Longniddry
B1377
A6137
Barnes Castle
Garleton Hills
610
A199
Hailes
Church
Huntington
Hopetoun Monument
B6363
Elvingston
Haddington
St Martin's Kirk
A1
Meadowmill
Tranent
Macmerry
Gladsmuir
A199
B6471
St Mary's Pleasance
Penston
B6355
B6363
B6371
Samuelston
Lennoxlove House
Colstoun House
B6369
Morham
Whitelaw Hill
Luggate Burn
Stenton
Papple
Pitcox
Garvald
B6370
New Winton
New Town
A6093
Bolton
B6368
Ormiston
Cross
Pencaitland
B6355
West Saltoun
East Saltoun
Gifford
Yester Castle
Peastonbank
B6371
Peaston
Gilchriston
Longyester
Hopes Water
Pathhead
B6368
Humbie
Birns Water
Fala Dam
B6457
Fala
B6458
Tynehead
Soutra Aisle
A68
Fala Moor
Dere Street Roman Road
Gilston
B6368
Stobshiel Resr.
Lammer Law
1734
Hopes Resr.
Meikle Says Law
1755
Crib Law
1670
LAMMERMUIR
Hunt Law
1625
1593
Soonhope Burn
Carfrae
Hogs Law
1470
Oxton
Addinston
Cleekhimin Bridge
Edgarhope Wood
Scoured Rig
Collie Law
1254
A697
SOUTHERN
UPLANDS
Fountainhall
A7
Killochyett
Lauder
Flat Cat Gallery
Thirlestane
B6362
Lugate Water
Stow
Pack Bridge
Old Kirk & Bishop's House
Leader Water
Nether Blainslie
Legerwood
Great Law
1666
William Law
314
Knowes Hill
1222
Buckholm
Langshaw
B710
A72
Clovenfords
GALASHIELS
Meigle Hill
1389
Old Gala
B6374
Gattonside
B6360
Lowood
Earlston
B6356
Redpath
Caddonfoot
Bass Rock
John Muir
Tyne Mouth
East Links Family Pk.
West Barns
Dunbar Castle
Town House
Dunbar
A1087
Belhaven
Barns Ness
Broxburn
Dunbar 1650
Doonhill Homestead
Pinkerton
East Barns
Spott
Skateraw
Power Station
Thorntonloch
Brunt Hill
737
Dry Burn
Innerwick
Reed Point
Dunglass Collegiate Church
Cove
Cocklaw Hill
1046
Cockburnspath
Oldhamstocks
EAST LOTHIAN
Bransly Hill
1301
Nunraw Abbey
White Castle Hillfort
Dunbar Common
Clints Dod
1307
Monynut Edge
1283
Heart Law
Bothwell Water
Monynut Water
Spartleton Edge
HILLS
B6355
Blackburn Rig
Grantshouse
Whiteadder Resr.
Cranshaws Hill
1245
Cranshaws
Abbey St Bathans
A6112
Whiteadder Water
Ellemford
Edin's Hall Broch
Whitchester
Mutiny Stones
Dye Water
LAMMER
Longformacus
B6355
Preston
Millburn Bridge
Cumledge Mill
Blythe Edge
Watch Water Resr.
Dirrington Great Law
1307
B6365
Jim Clark Room
Manderston
SCOTTISH
Dirrington Little Law
Duns
B6456
Gavinton
Westruther
Polwarth
Nisbet Hill
A6112
BORDERS
A6105
Halliburton
Fogo
Fogorig
Houndslow
Blackadder Water
B6460
A6089
Bassendean
Greenlaw
Charterhall
Eden Water
MERSE
B6461
Greenknowe Tower
Huntlywood
Gordon
A697
Leitholm
Lambden
A6105
B6364
Hume
Hume Castle
Eccles
Fans
Sweethope Hill
730
B6397
Mellerstain House
A6089
B6461
Birgham
A698
Wark Castle
Carham
Nenthorn
Stichill
Ednam
R. Tweed
Smailholm
James Thomson Obelisk
Kelso
B6350
Hadden
Smailholm Tower
Sprouston
LAUDERDALE
803
Meikle Black L
Sicc

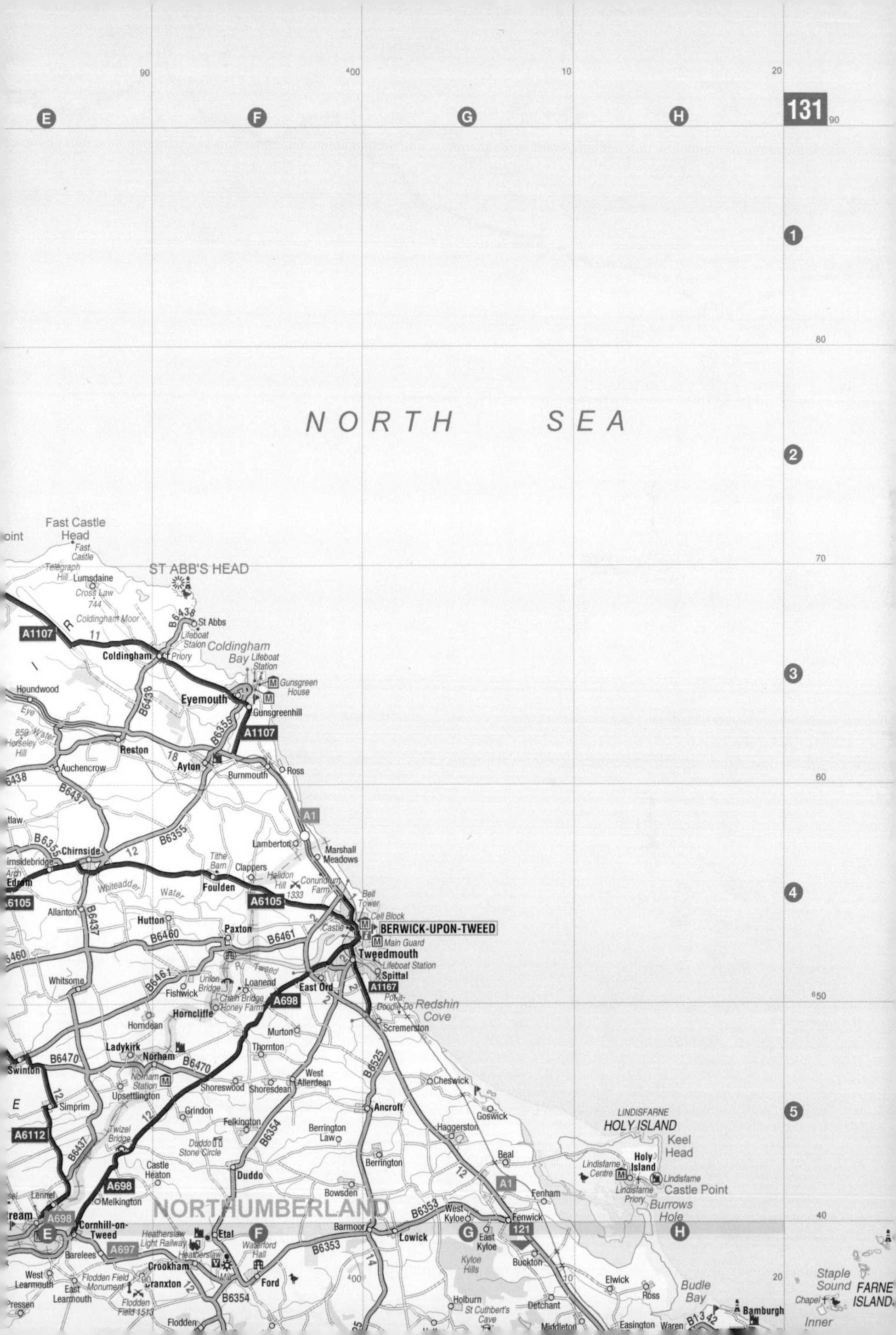

90   400   10   20

NORTH   SEA

Fast Castle
Head
Point   Fast
Castle
Telegraph
Hill Lumsdaine
Cross Law
744   Coldingham Moor
ST ABB'S HEAD

A1107   11   B6438 St Abbs
Lifeboat
Station
Coldingham Priory   Coldingham
Bay Lifeboat
Station
Houndwound   Gunsgreen
House
Eyemouth
859 Water 18   Gunsgreenhill
Horseley
Hill
Reston   A1107
Auchencraw   Ayton   Ross
B6438   B6437   Burnmouth

Chirnside   B6355
imsklebridge   12   Tithe
Barn   Lamberton
Edrom   Clappers Marshall
Meadows
B6355   Halidon
Foulden   Hill
1333 Conundrum
Farm
A6105   A6105   Bell
Tower
Allanton   Cell Block
Hutton   BERWICK-UPON-TWEED
B6437   Castle Main Guard
Whitsome   Paxton B6461 Tweedmouth
B6461   Lifeboat Station
Loanend Spittal
Union Tweed   A1167
Bridge East Ord   Poke
Fishwick Chain Bridge A698   Doodle Do Redshin
Horndean Honey Farm   Cove
Horncliffe   Murton   Scremerston
Ladykirk   Thornton
Norham   West
Norham B6470   Allerdean   Cheswick
Swinton Station   Goswick
Shoreswood Shoresdean
Upsettlington   Ancroft
Simprim Grindon Felkington Haggerston
A6112 Twizel   Berrington LINDISFARNE
Bridge   Duddo   Law   HOLY ISLAND
Stone Circle Berrington   Keel
Castle   Head
Heaton Duddo Beal Lindisfarne
Melkington   Bowsden   Holy Centre Lindisfarne
Island   Castle Point
Lennel   NORTHUMBERLAND Fenham   Lindisfarne Burrows
Cornhill-on-   Priory Hole
Stream Tweed Heatherslaw   Barmoor   West
A698 Bareless Light Railway   Etal   Lowick   Kyloe Fenwick
Crookham Heatherslaw   B6353   East 121
Flodden Field Hall   Waterford   Kyloe
Monument Cranxton Ford   Kyloe Buckton
East Flodden   B6354   Hills   Staple
Learmouth Field 1513   Holburn Sound
Flodden   Elwick   Budle Chapel FARNE
Flodden St Cuthbert's Bay ISLAND
Cave   Ross   Inner
Middleton Easington Waren B1342 Bamburgh

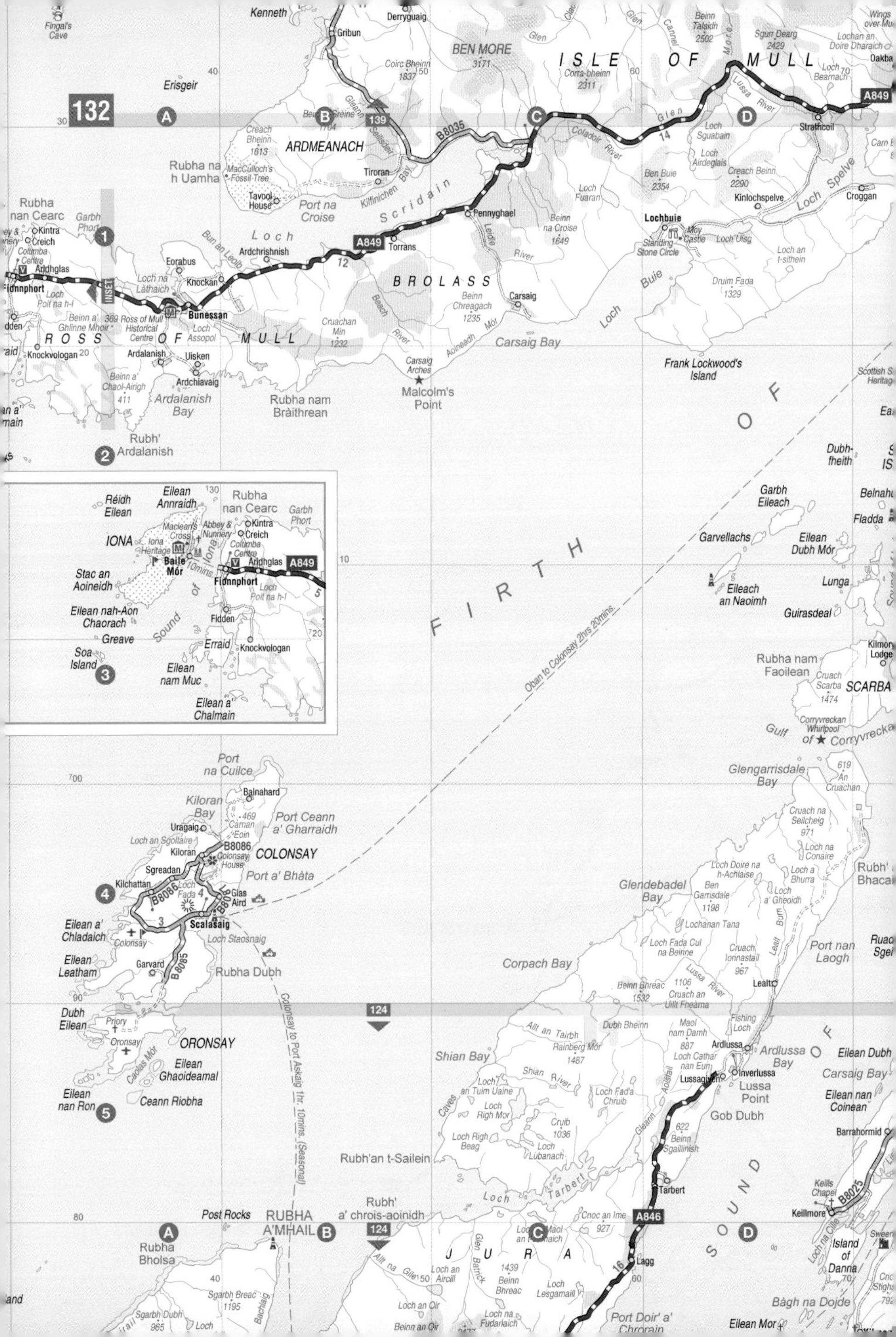
ISLE OF MULL
BEN MORE
ARDMEANACH
BROLASS
ROSS OF MULL
FIRTH OF LORN
IONA
COLONSAY
ORONSAY
SCARBA
JURA
SOUND OF JURA
Fionnphort
Bunessan
Pennyghael
Lochbuie
Strathcoil
Scalasaig
Garvellachs
Frank Lockwood's Island
Corryvreckan Whirlpool
Oban to Colonsay 2hrs 20mins.
Colonsay to Port Askaig 1hr. 10mins. (Seasonal)
Ardlussa
Lussa Point
Tarbert
Lagg
Keillmore
Island of Danna
A849
A846
B8035
B8086
B8085
B8025
INSET
139
124

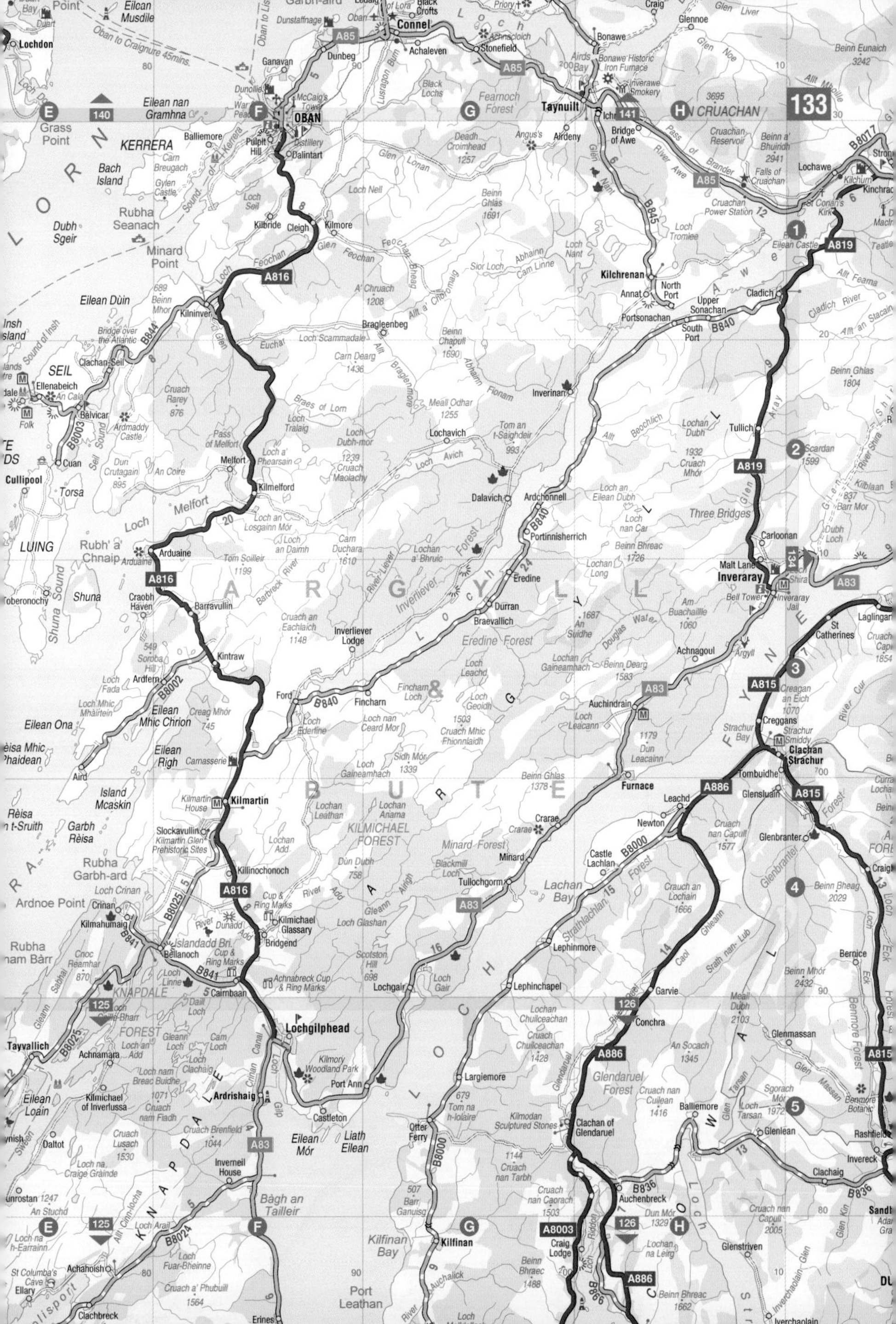

133
OBAN
Connel
Dunbeg
Ganavan
Dunollie
Pulpit Hill
Dalintart
Kilmore
Cleigh
Kilbride
KERRERA
Balliemore
Bach Island
Rubha Seanach
Dubh Sgeir
Minard Point
Eilean Dùin
LORN
Taynuilt
Bonawe
Glennoe
Airdeny
Bridge of Awe
Pass of Brander
Cruachan Reservoir
Falls of Cruachan
Cruachan Power Station
Lochawe
Kilchurn
St Conan's Kirk
Kilchrenan
North Port
Annat
Portsonachan
South Port
Upper Sonachan
Cladich
Fearnoch Forest
Beinn Eunaich 3242
CRUACHAN
Kilninver
Bridge over the Atlantic
Clachan-Seil
SEIL
Ellenabeich
Balvicar
Cuan
Cullipool
Torsa
LUING
Shuna
Toberonochy
Bragleenbeg
Loch Scammadale
Inverinan
Lochavich
Loch Avich
Dalavich
Ardchonnell
Portinnisherrich
Eredine
Durran
Braevallich
Melfort
Kilmelford
Loch Melfort
Arduaine
Craobh Haven
Barravullin
Kintraw
Ardfern
Loch Craignish
Tullich
Scardan
Three Bridges
Carloonan
Malt Land
Inveraray
Bell Tower
Inveraray Jail
Achnagoul
Auchindrain
Furnace
Lochan Dubh
ARGYLL
BUTE
Eredine Forest
Inverliever Lodge
Ford
Fincharn
Carnasserie
Kilmartin
Kilmartin House
Slockavullin
Kilmartin Glen Prehistoric Sites
Killinochonoch
Kilmichael Glassary
Bridgend
Crinan
Kilmahumaig
Bellanoch
Islandadd Bri.
Cairnbaan
Lochgilphead
Ardrishaig
Kilmory Woodland Park
Port Ann
Castleton
Lochgair
KILMICHAEL FOREST
Minard Forest
Minard
Crarae
Tullochgorm
Lachan Bay
Castle Lachlan
Newton
Leachd
Lephinmore
Lephinchapel
Strathlachlan
Largiemore
Otter Ferry
Kilfinan
Kilfinan Bay
Port Leathan
Glendaruel Forest
Clachan of Glendaruel
Kilmodan Sculptured Stones
Auchenbreck
Craig Lodge
Garvie
Conchra
St Catherines
Creggans
Strachur Bay
Clachan Strachur
Tombuidhe
Glensluain
Glenbranter
Laglingarten
Bernice
Glenmassan
Balliemore
Glenlean
Invereck
Clachaig
Glenstriven
Ivercholain
Benmore Forest
Rashfield
KNAPDALE
KNAPDALE FOREST
Tayvallich
Achnamara
Kilmichael of Inverlussa
Daltot
Inverneil House
Achahoish
Clachbreck
Ellary
Erines
Bàgh an Tailleir
Eilean Mór
Liath Eilean
LOCH FYNE
LOCH AWE
Oban to Craignure 45mins.
A85
A816
A819
A83
A815
A886
A8003
B840
B844
B8003
B8002
B8025
B841
B8024
B8000
B836
B845
B8077
140
141
134
125
126

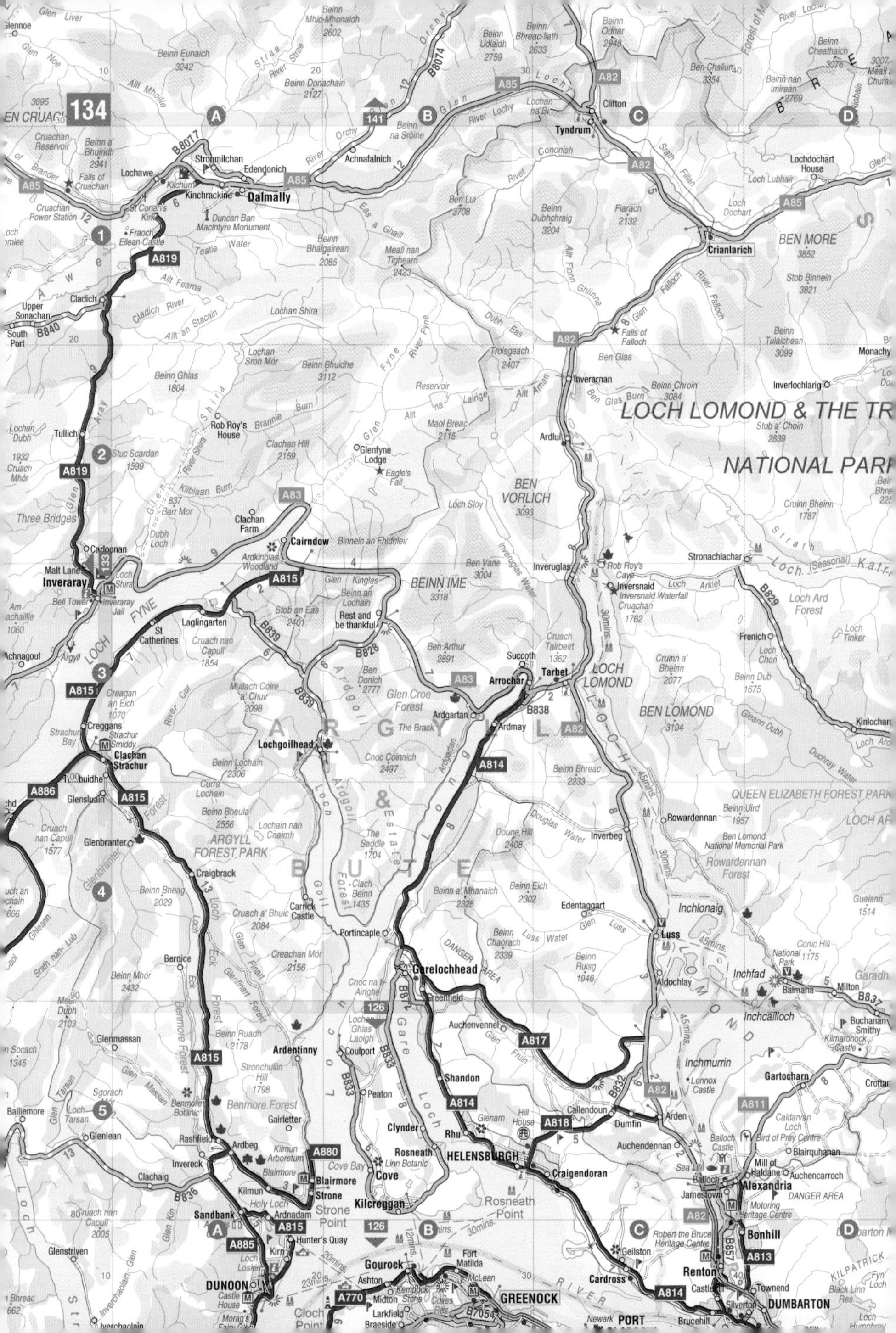

134
Glennoe
Glen Liver
Glen Noe
Beinn Mhic-Mhonaidh
2602
Beinn Eunaich
3242
Strae
River Strae
Orchy
B8074
Beinn Udlaidh
2759
Beinn Bhreac-liath
2633
Beinn Odhar
2948
Forest of Mamore
River Lochay
Beinn Cheathaich
3076
3007
Meall a' Churain
Allt Mhoille
Beinn Donachain
2127
A85
Lochy
A82
Ben Challum
3354
Beinn nan Imirean
2769
BREADALBANE
Allt Riobain
3695
BEN CRUACHAN
141
Glen
River Lochy
Lochan na Bi
Clifton
Tyndrum
Beinn na Sroine
Cruachan Reservoir
Beinn a' Bhuiridh
2941
B8077
Stronmilchan
Edendonich
River Orchy
Achnafalnich
Cononish
River
Strath Fillan
Lochdochart House
Loch Lubhair
Pass of Brander
Falls of Cruachan
Lochawe
Kilchurn
A85
Kinchrackine
Dalmally
Cruachan Power Station
St Conan's Kirk
Duncan Ban MacIntyre Monument
Eas a Ghaill
Ben Lui
3708
Beinn Dubhchraig
3204
Flarach
2132
Loch Dochart
BEN MORE
3852
Fraoch Eilean Castle
Teatle Water
Beinn Bhalgairean
2085
Meall nan Tighearn
2423
Crianlarich
A819
Allt Fearna
Allt Fionn Ghlinne
Stob Binnein
3821
River Falloch
Cladich
Cladich River
Allt an Stacain
Lochan Shira
Dubh Eas
Upper Sonachan
B840
South Port
Glen Falloch
Falls of Falloch
A82
Lochan Sron Mór
Beinn Bhuidhe
3112
Glen Fyne
River Fyne
Troisgeach
2407
Beinn Tulaichean
3099
Monachyle
Beinn Ghlas
1804
Reservoir
Allt na Lairige
Allt Arnan
Inverarnan
Ben Glas
Ben Glas Burn
Beinn Chroin
3084
Inverlochlarig
Glen Shira
Rob Roy's House
Brannie Burn
Maol Breac
2115
LOCH LOMOND & THE TR
Stob a' Choin
2839
Lochan Dubh
Tullich
Glen Aray
Clachan Hill
2159
Glenfyne Lodge
Ardlui
Stuc Scardan
1599
Eagle's Fall
NATIONAL PARK
1932
Cruach Mhór
River Shira
Kilblaan Burn
A83
BEN VORLICH
3093
837
Barr Mor
Loch Sloy
Cruinn Bheinn
1787
Three Bridges
Dubh Loch
Clachan Farm
Strath
Carloonan
Cairndow
Binnein an Fhidhleir
Inveruglas Water
Stronachlachar
Malt Land
133
Loch Shira
Ardkinglas Woodland
Ben Vane
3004
Inveruglas
Rob Roy's Cave
Loch Katrine (Seasonal)
Inveraray
A815
Glen Kinglas
BEINN IME
3318
Inversnaid
Inversnaid Waterfall
Loch Arklet
Bell Tower
Inveraray Jail
Beinn an Lochain
Cruachan
1762
Loch Ard Forest
Am Cnap
Laglingarten
Stob an Eas
2401
Rest and be thankful
B829
1060
St Catherines
LOCH FYNE
Cruach nan Capull
1854
B839
B828
Ben Arthur
2891
Cruach Tairbeirt
1362
30mins.
Frenich
Loch Tinker
Achnagoul
Argyll
Ardgoil
Succoth
Loch Chon
Ben Donich
2777
Arrochar
Tarbet
LOCH LOMOND
Cruinn a' Bheinn
2077
Beinn Dub
1675
Creagan an Eich
1070
Mullach Coire a' Chuir
2098
Glen Croe Forest
B838
Gleann Dubh
River Cur
The Brack
Ardgartan
Ardmay
BEN LOMOND
3194
Kinlochard
Creggans
Strachur Smiddy
ARGYLL
Lochgoilhead
A814
Loch Ard
Strachur Bay
Clachan Strachur
Cnoc Coinnich
2497
Beinn Bhreac
2233
Duchray Water
Beinn Lochain
2306
Ardgoil
Loch Long
Ardgartan
45mins.
A886
Tullochbuidhe
Curra Lochain
QUEEN ELIZABETH FOREST PARK
Glensluain
Loch Goil
Ardgoil Estate
Douglas Water
Rowardennan
Beinn Uird
1957
LOCH ARD
Beinn Bheula
2556
Lochain nan Cnaimh
Doune Hill
2408
Inverbeg
Cruach nan Capull
1577
Glenbranter
ARGYLL FOREST PARK
The Saddle
1704
Ben Lomond National Memorial Park
Rowardennan Forest
BUTE
Craigbrack
Glenbranter
Clach Beinn
1435
Beinn a' Mhanaich
2328
Beinn Eich
2302
Goil Forest
Gualann
1514
Beinn Bheag
2029
Loch Eck
Carrick Castle
Edentaggart
Inchlonaig
Cruach a' Bhuic
2084
Glen Luss
Luss Water
Beinn Chaorach
2339
Luss
Strath nan Lub
Portincaple
DANGER AREA
Conic Hill
1175
Glen Finart
Creachan Mór
2156
Garelochhead
Beinn Ruisg
1946
National Park
Inchfad
Balmaha
Milton
Garadh
Bernice
Glenfinart Forest
Cnoc na h-Airighe
B872
Greenfield
Aldochlay
B837
Beinn Mhór
2432
Eck
126
Lochan Ghlas Laoigh
Gare Loch
Auchenvennel
Glen Fruin
Inchcailloch
Buchanan Smithy
Kilmaronock Castle
Meall Dubh
2103
Benmore Forest
Beinn Ruadh
2178
Ardentinny
Coulport
B833
A817
Glenmassan
Stronchullin Hill
1798
Shandon
Inchmurrin
Lennox Castle
Gartocharn
Croftamie
Glen Massan
A815
Peaton
B832
A82
Glen Tarsan
Sgorach Mór
Benmore Botanic
Benmore Forest
A814
Callendoun
Arden
A811
Caldarvan Loch
Balliemore
Loch Tarsan
Glenlean
Rashfield
Gairletter
Clynder
Glenarn
Hill House
A818
Dumfin
Bird of Prey Centre
Ardbeg
Kilmun Arboretum
A880
Rhu
Rosneath
Linn Botanic
HELENSBURGH
Auchendennan
Balloch Castle
Blairquhanan
Invereck
Cove Bay
Blairmore
Cove
Craigendoran
Sea Life
Mill of Haldane
Auchencarroch
Clachaig
Kilmun
Holy Loch
Strone
Kilcreggan
Balloch
Alexandria
B836
Cruach nan Capull
2005
Sandbank
Ardnadam
Strone Point
Rosneath Point
Jamestown
DANGER AREA
Motoring Heritage Centre
A815
Glen Kin
A885
Hunter's Quay
126
12mins.
30mins.
Robert the Bruce Heritage Centre
A82
Bonhill
Dalmoak Castle
Glenstriven
Kirn
Gourock
Fort Matilda
Geilston
B857
A813
KILPATRICK
Fyn Loch
Loch Loskin
20mins.
Ashton
McLean
Renton
Black Linn Res.
DUNOON
23mins.
Kempock Stone
A770
GREENOCK
Cardross
A814
Castlehill
Townend
Castle House
Midton
Coves Res.
RIVER CLYDE
DUMBARTON
Inverchaolain Glen
Cloch Point
Larkfield
B7054
Silverton
Morag's Fairy Glen
Braeside
Newark
PORT
Brucehill
Loch Humphrey
Inverchaolain
662
Loch Striven

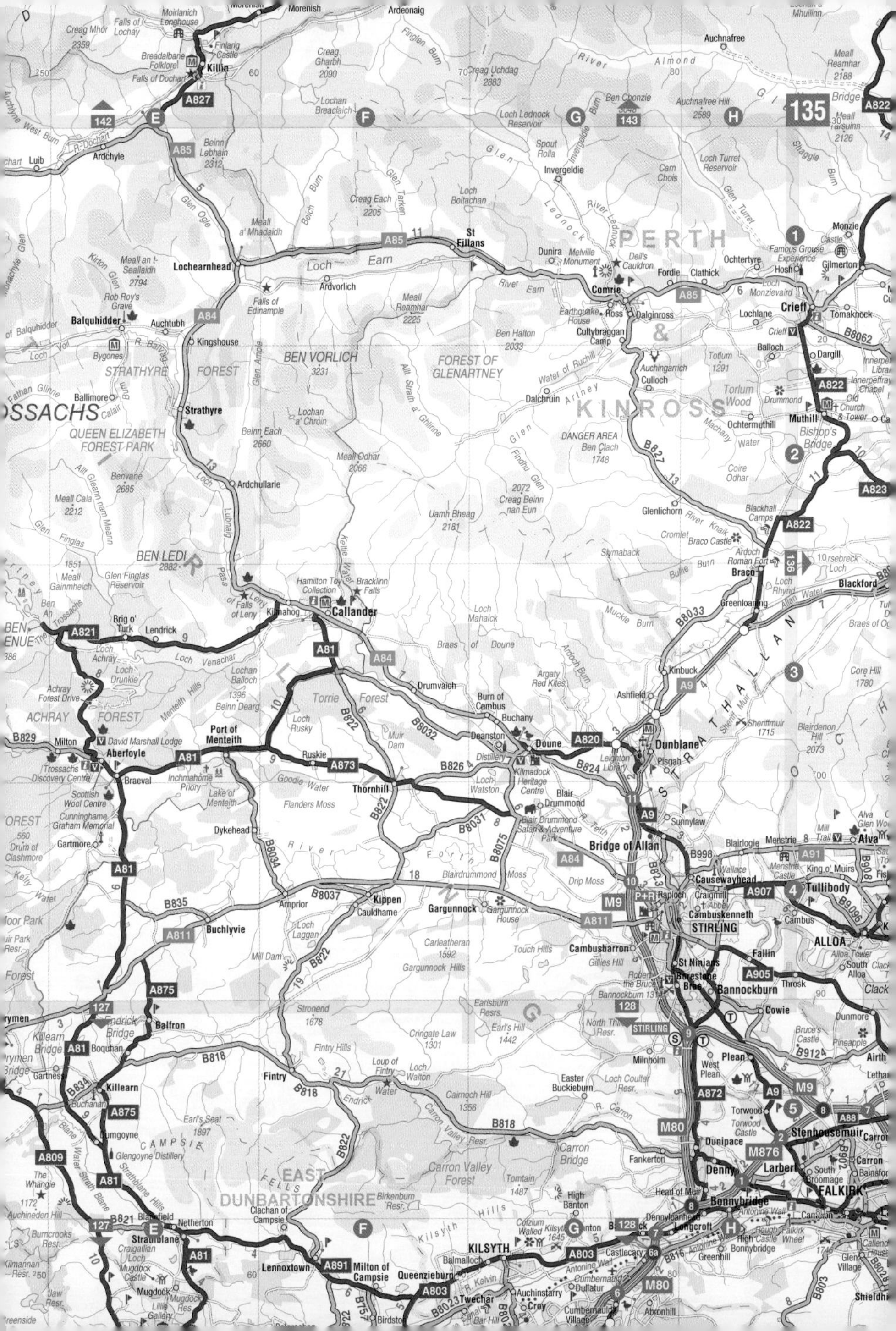

135
142
143
136
127
128
Morenish
Ardeonaig
Moirlanich Longhouse
Falls of Lochay
Creag Mhor 2359
Finlarig Castle
Breadalbane Folklore
Falls of Dochart
Killin
A827
Creag Gharbh 2090
Finglen Burn
Creag Uchdag 2883
River Almond
Auchnafree
Meall Reamhar 2188
Bridge
A822
Lochan Breaclaich
Loch Lednock Reservoir
Ben Chonzie 3048
Auchnafree Hill 2589
Auchtyne West Burn
R. Dochart
Luib
Ardchyle
A85
Beinn Lebhain 2312
Spout Rolla
Invergeldie
Loch Turret Reservoir
Carn Chois
Shaggie Burn
Glen Ogle
Beich Burn
Glen Tarken
Creag Each 2205
Loch Boltachan
Glen Turret
Meall a' Mhadaidh
St Fillans
PERTH
&
KINROSS
Monzie
Famous Grouse Experience
Castle
Gilmerton
Loch Earn
Lochearnhead
Ardvorlich
Meall an t-Seallaidh 2794
Kirkton Glen
Rob Roy's Grave
Falls of Edinample
Meall Reamhar 2225
Dunira
Melville Monument
Deil's Cauldron
River Lednock
Comrie
Earthquake House
Ross
Dalginross
Cultybraggan Camp
Fordie
Clathick
Ochtertyre
Hosh
Loch Monzievaird
Lochlane
Crieff
Tomaknock
B8062
Balquhidder
Auchtubh
A84
Kingshouse
Bygones
Loch Voil
R. Balvag
STRATHYRE
FOREST
Glen Ample
BEN VORLICH 3231
Ben Halton 2033
FOREST OF GLENARTNEY
Water of Ruchill
Auchingarrich
Culloch
Dalchruin
Glen Artney
Totlum 1291
Balloch
Dargill
Torlum Wood
Drummond
Ochtermuthill
Muthill
Bishop's Bridge
Innerpeffray Library
Innerpeffray Chapel
Old Church & Tower
Ballimore
Calair Burn
ROSSACHS
Strathyre
QUEEN ELIZABETH FOREST PARK
Lochan a' Chròin
Allt Strath a' Ghlinne
Beinn Each 2660
Meall Odhar 2066
DANGER AREA
Ben Clach 1748
Glen Findhu Glen
Machany Water
B827
Coire Odhar
A823
Benvane 2685
Allt Gleann nam Meann
Meall Cala 2212
Glen Finglas
Loch Lubnaig
Ardchullarie
2072 Creag Beinn nan Eun
Uamh Bheag 2181
Glenlichorn
River Knaik
Blackhall Camps
Cromlet
Braco Castle
Ardoch Roman Fort
Braco
BEN LEDI 2882
Glen Finglas Reservoir
Meall Gainmheich
Pass of Leny
Falls of Leny
Kilmahog
Hamilton Toy Collection
Bracklinn Falls
Keltie Water
Callander
Loch Mahaick
Muckle Burn
Greenloaning
B8033
Allan Water
Blackford
Ben An
The Trossachs
BEN VENUE
A821
Brig o' Turk
Lendrick
Loch Venachar
Loch Achray
Loch Drunkie
Achray Forest Drive
A81
Lochan Balloch
Menteith Hills
Beinn Dearg
Braes of Doune
Torrie Forest
Drumvaich
B8032
Argaty Red Kites
Ardoch Burn
Burn of Cambus
Buchany
Kinbuck
Ashfield
A9
STRATHALLAN
Sheriff Muir
Sheriffmuir 1715
Core Hill 1780
Blairdenon Hill 2073
ACHRAY FOREST
B829
Milton
David Marshall Lodge
Aberfoyle
Trossachs Discovery Centre
Port of Menteith
Loch Rusky
B822
Ruskie
A873
Muir Dam
Deanston
Distillery
Doune
A820
Dunblane
Leighton Library
Pisgah
B824
Braeval
Scottish Wool Centre
Inchmahome Priory
Lake of Menteith
Goodie Water
Thornhill
B826
Kilmadock Heritage Centre
Loch Watston
Blair Drummond
Blair Drummond Safari & Adventure Park
B8031
B8075
Flanders Moss
Cunninghame Graham Memorial
Drum of Clashmore
Gartmore
Dykehead
B8034
River Forth
Blairdrummond Moss
Drip Moss
A84
Bridge of Allan
Sunnylaw
Blairlogie
Menstrie
Mill Trail
Alva
Alva Glen Woods
A91
Menstrie Castle
King o' Muirs
Wallace Monument
Causewayhead
B998
Craigmill
Abbey
Cambuskenneth
A907
Tullibody
B9096
Cambus
Kelty Water
B835
Arnprior
B8037
Kippen
Cauldhame
Gargunnock
Gargunnock House
M9
P+R
Raploch
STIRLING
A811
ALLOA
Alloa Tower
Buchlyvie
Loch Laggan
Carleatheran 1592
Gargunnock Hills
Touch Hills
Cambusbarron
Gillies Hill
St Ninians
Fallin
A905
South Alloa
Throsk
Clackmannan
Mill Dam
Robert the Bruce
Borestone
Brae
Bannockburn 1314
Bannockburn
Cowie
Dunmore
A875
Stronend 1678
Earlsburn Resrs.
North Third Resr.
Bruce's Castle
Pineapple
Airth
Drymen
Killearn
Endrick Bridge
Balfron
Drymen Bridge
Boquhan
Fintry Hills
Cringate Law 1301
Earl's Hill 1442
Milnholm
Plean
West Plean
B9124
B818
Gartness
Killearn
B834
Buchanan
Fintry
Loup of Fintry
Loch Walton
Endrick Water
Easter Buckieburn
Loch Coulter Resr.
A872
Torwood
Torwood Castle
Stenhousemuir
Carron
A88
Earl's Seat 1897
Dumgoyne
Glengoyne Distillery
CAMPSIE FELLS
Cairnoch Hill 1356
Carron Valley Resr.
R. Carron
M80
Dunipace
M876
Larbert
Carron
Bainsford
Blane Water
Strathblane Hills
A809
The Whangie 1172
Auchineden Hill
EAST DUNBARTONSHIRE
Carron Valley Forest
Tomtain 1487
Carron Bridge
Fankerton
Denny
South Broomage
FALKIRK
Birkenburn Resr.
High Banton
Head of Muir
Bonnybridge
Dennyloanhead
Antonine Wall
Blanefield
B821
Netherton
Clachan of Campsie
Kilsyth Hills
Colzium Walled Garden
Kilsyth 1645
Banton
Longcroft
Rough Castle
Falkirk Wheel
Camelon
Strathblane
Burncrooks Resr.
Craigallian Loch
Mugdock Castle
Kilmannan Resr.
Lennoxtown
A891
Milton of Campsie
KILSYTH
Balmalloch
A803
Queenzieburn
Castlecary
High Bonnybridge
Greenhill
B816
Glen Village
Jaw Resr.
Mugdock
Mugdock Res.
Lillie Gallery
Greenside
B757
Birdston
R. Kelvin
B8023
Twechar
Auchinstarry
Bar Hill
Croy
Dullatur
Cumbernauld
Cumbernauld Village
Abronhill
B803
Shieldhill

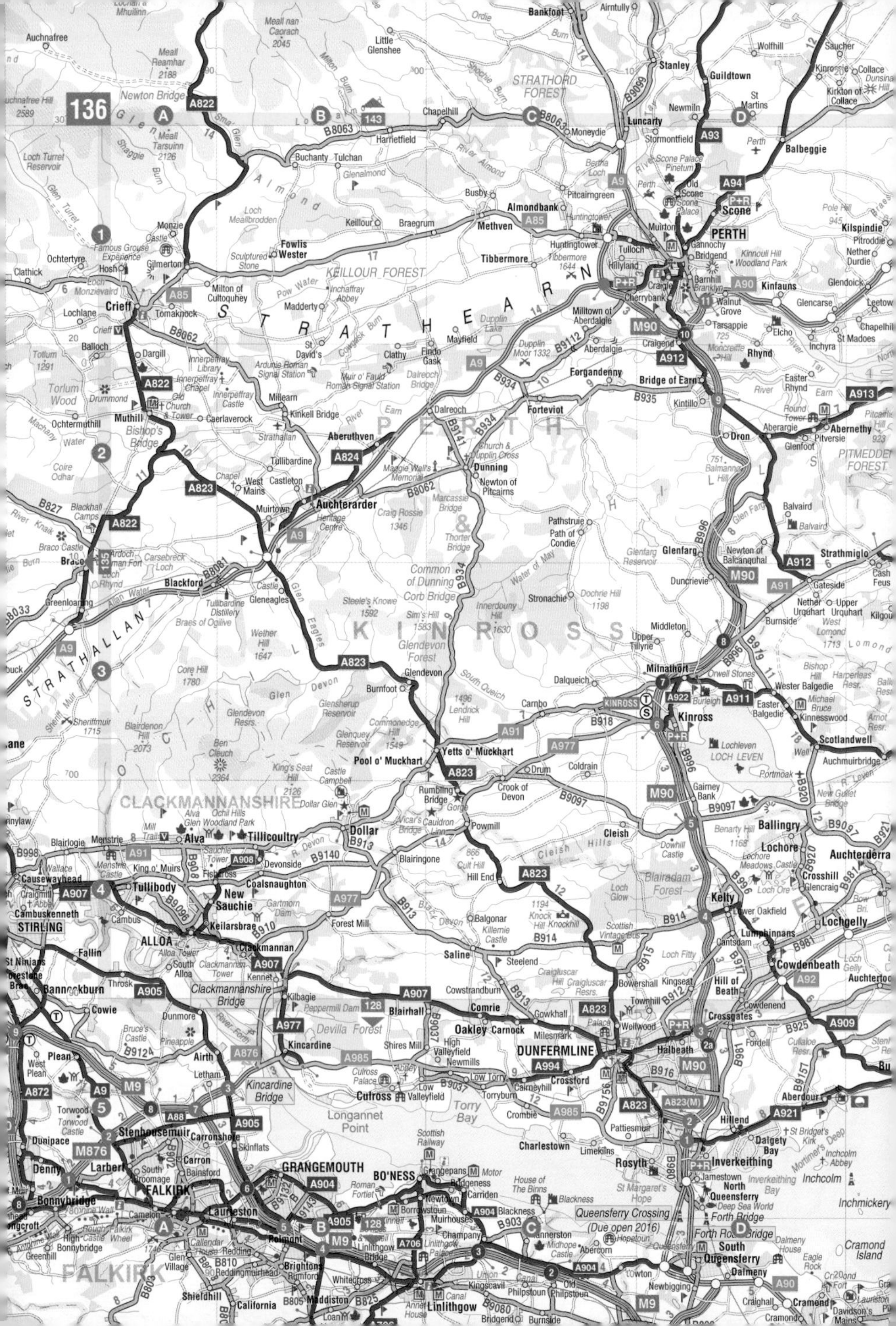

136
143
128
135
A
B
C
D
1
2
3
4
5
Auchnafree
Meall Reamhar 2188
Meall nan Caorach 2045
Little Glenshee
Newton Bridge
Glen Shaggie
Meall Tarsuinn 2126
Loch Turret Reservoir
Glen Turret
Bankfoot
Airntully
Ordie Burn
Shochie Burn
STRATHORD FOREST
Stanley
Guildtown
Wolfhill
Saucher
Kinrossie
Collace
Kirkton of Collace
Dunsinane Hill
Chapelhill
Harrietfield
Moneydie
Luncarty
Newmiln
Stormontfield
St Martins
Perth
Balbeggie
Buchanty
Tulchan
Glenalmond
River Almond
Bertha Loch
Scone Palace Pinetum
Old Scone
Scone Palace
Scone
Pole Hill 945
Kilspindie
Pitroddie
Nether Durdie
Glendoick
Loch Meallbrodden
Keillour
Braegrum
Busby
Almondbank
Pitcairngreen
Huntingtower
Methven
Tibbermore
Tibbermore 1644
Fowlis Wester
Sculptured Stone
KEILLOUR FOREST
Monzie Castle
Famous Grouse Experience
Ochtertyre
Hosh
Gilmerton
Clathick
Loch Monzievaird
Milton of Cultoquhey
Pow Water
Inchaffray Abbey
Madderty
Crieff
Tomaknock
Lochlane
Balloch
Dargill
Torlum 1291
Torlum Wood
Drummond
Muthill
Bishop's Bridge
Ochtermuthill
Machany Water
Coire Odhar
STRATHEARN
St David's
Clathy
Findo Gask
Mayfield
Dupplin Lake
Dupplin Moor 1332
Innerpeffray Library
Innerpeffray Chapel
Innerpeffray Castle
Ardunie Roman Signal Station
Muir o' Fauld Roman Signal Station
Dalreoch Bridge
Old Church & Tower
Caerlaverock
Millearn
Kinkell Bridge
Strathallan
Tullibardine
Aberuthven
River Earn
Dalreoch
Forteviot
Forgandenny
Bridge of Earn
Kintillo
PERTH
Tulloch
Hillyland
Craigie
Cherrybank
Muirton
Gannochy
Bridgend
Kinnoull Hill Woodland Park
Barnhill
Branklyn
Walnut Grove
Kinfauns
Glencarse
Leetown
Chapelhill
St Madoes
Tarsappie 725
Elcho
Inchyra
Milltown of Aberdalgie
Aberdalgie
Craigend
Moncreiffe Hill
Rhynd
River Tay
Easter Rhynd
Round Tower
Abernethy
Pitcairlie Hill
Aberargie
Glenfoot
Pitversie 923
PITMEDDEN FOREST
Dron
Balmanno Hill 751
Church & Dupplin Cross
Maggie Wall's Memorial
Dunning
Newton of Pitcairns
Chapel Hill
West Mains
Castleton
Muirtown
Auchterarder
Heritage Centre
Craig Rossie 1346
Marcassie Bridge
Thorter Bridge
Blackhall Camps
River Knaik
Braco Castle
Braco
Ardoch Roman Fort
Carsebreck Loch
Blackford
Castle
Gleneagles
Glen Eagles
Pathstruie
Path of Condie
Glenfarg Reservoir
Glenfarg
Newton of Balcanquhal
Balvaird
Strathmiglo
Gateside
Cash Feus
Greenloaning
Allan Water
Tullibardine Distillery
Braes of Ogilvie
Common of Dunning
Corb Bridge
Steele's Knowe 1592
Sim's Hill 1583
Water of May
Innerdouny Hill 1630
Stronachie
Dochrie Hill 1198
Duncrievie
Middleton
Upper Tillyrie
Nether Urquhart
Upper Urquhart
Burnside
West Lomond 1713
Kilgour
PERTH & KINROSS
STRATHALLAN
Wether Hill 1647
Glendevon Forest
Core Hill 1780
Glendevon
Burnfoot
Glen Devon
Glensherup Reservoir
Glendevon Resrs.
OCHIL HILLS
South Queich
Lendrick Hill 1496
Dalqueich
Carnbo
Milnathort
Orwell Stones
Burleigh
Bishop Hill
Wester Balgedie
Easter Balgedie
Harperleas Resr.
Michael Bruce
Kinnesswood
Arnot Resr.
Scotlandwell
Kinross
Lochleven
LOCH LEVEN
Portmoak
Auchmuirbridge
River Leven
New Gullet Bridge
Sheriffmuir 1715
Blairdenon Hill 2073
Ben Cleuch 2364
Commonedge Hill 1549
Glenquey Reservoir
Yetts o' Muckhart
Pool o' Muckhart
Drum
Coldrain
Crook of Devon
Gairney Bank
King's Seat Hill 2126
Castle Campbell
CLACKMANNANSHIRE
Alva Glen Woodland Park
Ochil Hills
Dollar Glen
Dollar
Rumbling Bridge
Gorge
Vicar's Bridge
Cauldron Linn
Powmill
Cleish
Cleish Hills
Benarty Hill 1168
Ballingry
Lochore
Lochore Meadows Castle
Auchterderran
Crosshill
Glencraig
Mill Trail
Alva
Tillicoultry
River Devon
Menstrie
Blairlogie
Sauchie Tower
Devonside
Blairingone
Cult Hill 866
Hill End
Dowhill Castle
Blairadam Forest
Loch Glow
Wallace Monument
Causewayhead
Craigmill
Menstrie Castle
King o' Muirs
Fishcross
Coalsnaughton
Tullibody
New Sauchie
Cambuskenneth Abbey
Cambus
Gartmorn Dam
Knock Hill 1194
Knockhill
Balgonar
Killernie Castle
Scottish Vintage Bus
Kelty
Lower Oakfield
Loch Ore
Lochgelly
Bow Bri.
STIRLING
Keilarsbrae
Alloa
Alloa Tower
Clackmannan
Clackmannan Tower
Forest Mill
Saline
Steelend
Loch Fitty
Cantsdam
Lumphinnans
Cowdenbeath
Loch Gelly
Auchtertool
St Ninians
Fallin
South Alloa
Kennet
Craigluscar Hill
Craigluscar Resrs.
Bowershall
Kingseat
Hill of Beath
Cowdenend
Bannockburn
Throsk
Clackmannanshire Bridge
Kilbagie
Peppermill Dam
Cowstrandburn
Townhill
Cowie
Dunmore
River Forth
Devilla Forest
Blairhall
Comrie
Oakley
Carnock
Gowkhall
Milesmark
Palace
Wellwood
Crossgates
Fordell
Cullaloe Resr.
Bruce's Castle
Pineapple
Plean
West Plean
Airth
Kincardine
Shires Mill
High Valleyfield
Newmills
DUNFERMLINE
Halbeath
Letham
Kincardine Bridge
Culross Palace
Culross
Abbey
Low Valleyfield
Low Torry
Cairneyhill
Crossford
Torryburn
Torry Bay
Crombie
Aberdour
Torwood
Torwood Castle
Longannet Point
Pattiesmuir
Hillend
St Bridget's Kirk
Dalgety Bay
Mortimer's Deep
Inchcolm Abbey
Dunipace
Stenhousemuir
Carronshore
Skinflats
Scottish Railway
Charlestown
Limekilns
Rosyth
Inverkeithing
Inchcolm
Denny
Larbert
South Broomage
Carron
Bainsford
GRANGEMOUTH
BO'NESS
Grangepans
Motor Museum
Bridgeness
Carriden
House of The Binns
Blackness
St Margaret's Hope
Jamestown
North Queensferry
Inverkeithing Bay
Deep Sea World
Forth Bridge
Inchmickery
Bonnybridge
FALKIRK
Camelon
Laurieston
Roman Fortlet
Newtown
Borrowstoun
Muirhouses
Blackness
Queensferry Crossing (Due open 2016)
Forth Road Bridge
Dalmeny House
Cramond Island
Antonine Wall
Longcroft
High Bonnybridge
Falkirk Wheel
Callendar House
Polmont
Champany
Linlithgow Bridge
Linlithgow Palace
Hopetoun
Mannerston
Midhope Castle
Abercorn
Queensferry
South Queensferry
Dalmeny
Eagle Rock
Greenhill
Glen Village
Redding
Reddingmuirhead
Brightons
Rumford
Whitecross
Union Canal
Kingscavil
Philpstoun
Old Philpstoun
Duntocher
Newbigging
Craighall
Cramond
Davidson's Mains
Lauriston
Shieldhill
California
Maddiston
Loan
Annet House
Linlithgow
Bridgend
Burnside
Canal
M9
M90
M876
A9
A85
A822
A823
A824
A912
A913
A90
A91
A93
A94
A92
A977
A907
A905
A908
A876
A985
A994
A88
A872
A904
A706
A909
A921
A911
A922
A823(M)
B8063
B8062
B9099
B9112
B934
B935
B9141
B8081
B8033
B827
B996
B919
B918
B9097
B920
B921
B913
B9140
B9096
B9910
B914
B915
B917
B912
B981
B9037
B9156
B916
B925
B980
B9157
B902
B9124
B903
B810
B803
B805
B825
B9080

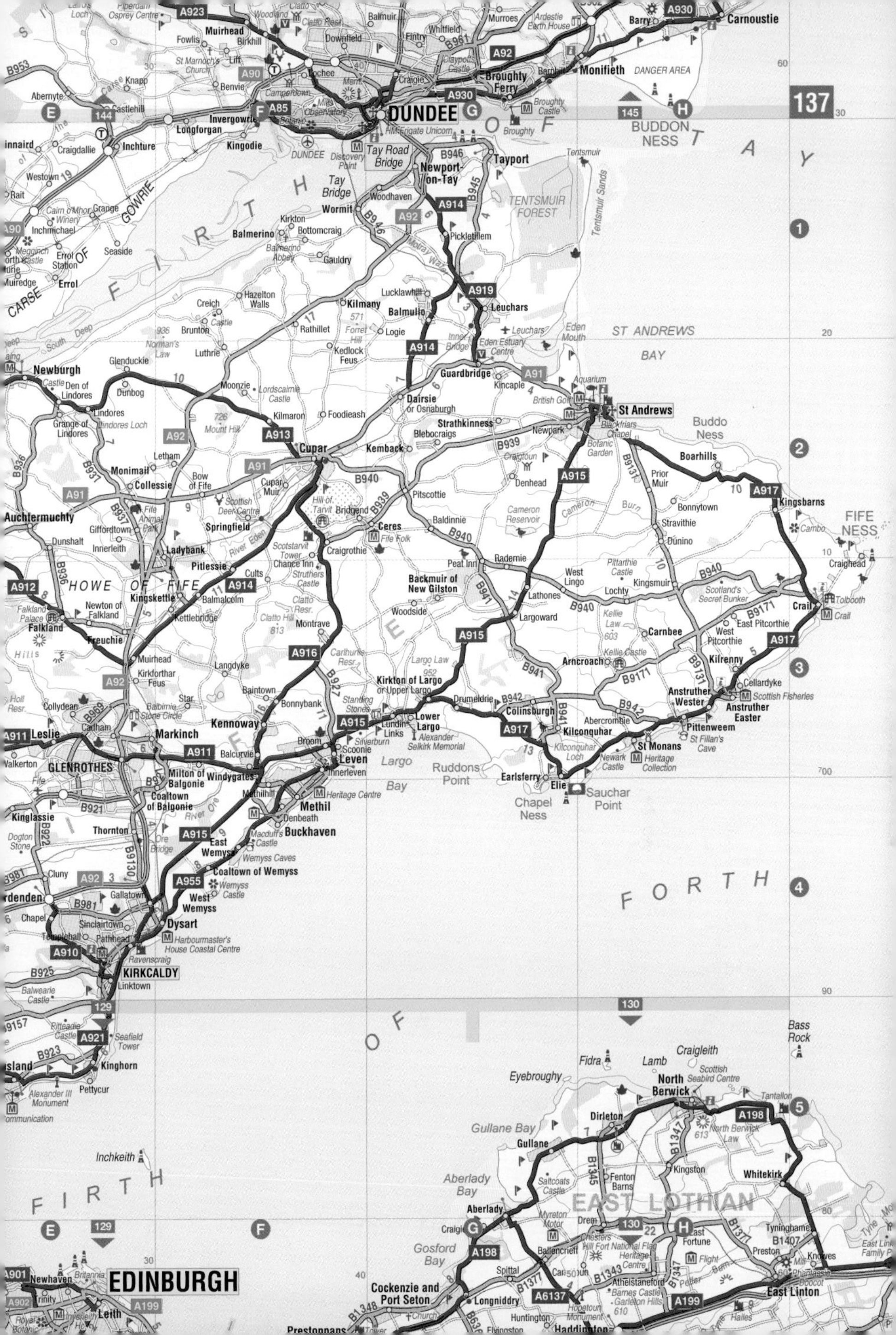
137
A923
Muirhead
Fowlis
Birkhill
Lift
St Marnoch's Church
Benvie
Knapp
Abernyte
Castlehill
Invergowrie
Longforgan
Inchture
Craigdallie
Kingodie
Westown
Rait
Cairn o'Mhor Winery
Grange
Inchmichael
Megginch Castle
Errol Station
Seaside
Errol
Muiredge
CARSE OF GOWRIE
Balmuir
Downfield
Fintry
Whitfield
Murroes
Ardestie Earth House
Barry
Carnoustie
A930
A92
A90
A85
Lochee
Craigie
Claypotts Castle
Broughty Ferry
Monifieth
Barnhill
DANGER AREA
Camperdown
Mills Observatory
DUNDEE
HM Frigate Unicorn
Discovery Point
Tay Road Bridge
Broughty Castle
Broughty
BUDDON NESS
145
144
B946
Tayport
Tentsmuir
Newport-on-Tay
Tay Bridge
Wormit
Woodhaven
A914
B945
TENTSMUIR FOREST
Tentsmuir Sands
Kirkton
Bottomcraig
Balmerino
Balmerino Abbey
Gauldry
B946
Motray Water
Pickletillem
A919
Leuchars
FIRTH OF TAY
Hazelton Walls
Creich
Castle
Brunton
Norman's Law
Luthrie
Kilmany
Lucklawhill
Balmullo
Rathillet
Forret Hill
Logie
Kedlock Feus
Inner Bridge
Eden Estuary Centre
Eden Mouth
ST ANDREWS BAY
Guardbridge
Kincaple
A91
Newburgh
Den of Lindores
Glenduckie
Dunbog
Lindores
Grange of Lindores
Lindores Loch
Moonzie
Lordscairnie Castle
Mount Hill
Kilmaron
Foodieash
Dairsie or Osnaburgh
Aquarium
British Golf Museum
St Andrews
Blackfriars Chapel
Botanic Garden
Buddo Ness
Strathkinness
Blebocraigs
Newpark
Kemback
A913
Cupar
Letham
Monimail
Collessie
Bow of Fife
Cupar Muir
B939
Craigtoun
Denhead
B940
A915
Boarhills
Prior Muir
B9131
A917
Kingsbarns
Bonnytown
Stravithie
Dunino
Cambo
FIFE NESS
Craighead
Pitscottie
Baldinnie
Cameron Reservoir
Cameron Burn
Auchtermuchty
A91
Fife Animal Park
Scottish Deer Centre
Hill of Tarvit
Bridgend
Ceres
Fife Folk Museum
Giffordtown
Springfield
Dunshalt
Innerleith
Ladybank
River Eden
Scotstarvit Tower
Chance Inn
Craigrothie
Struthers Castle
Peat Inn
Radernie
West Lingo
Pittarthie Castle
Kingsmuir
Lathones
Lochty
Scotland's Secret Bunker
Crail
Tolbooth
A912
HOWE OF FIFE
Pitlessie
Cults
Kingskettle
Balmalcolm
Kettlebridge
Falkland Palace
Newton of Falkland
Falkland
Freuchie
Lomond Hills
Clatto Resr.
Clatto Hill
Backmuir of New Gilston
Woodside
Montrave
B941
Largoward
Kellie Law
Carnbee
B9171
East Pitcorthie
West Pitcorthie
Muirhead
Kirkforthar Feus
Langdyke
A916
Carlhurlie Resr.
Largo Law
Kellie Castle
Arncroach
Kilrenny
Cellardyke
Anstruther Wester
Anstruther Easter
Scottish Fisheries Museum
Holl Resr.
Collydean
Cadham
B969
Balbirnie Stone Circle
Star
Baintown
Bonnybank
B927
Kirkton of Largo or Upper Largo
Standing Stones
Drumeldrie
B942
Colinsburgh
Abercrombie
Pittenweem
St Fillan's Cave
St Monans
Heritage Collection
A911
Leslie
Markinch
Kennoway
Balcurvie
Windygates
A915
Lundin Links
Lower Largo
Alexander Selkirk Memorial
Silverburn
Broom
Scoonie
Leven
Innerleven
Kilconquhar
Kilconquhar Loch
Newark Castle
Walkerton
GLENROTHES
Milton of Balgonie
Coaltown of Balgonie
Methilhill
Methil
Heritage Centre
Largo Bay
Ruddons Point
Earlsferry
Elie
Chapel Ness
Sauchar Point
Kinglassie
B921
Thornton
River Ore
Ore Bridge
Denbeath
Buckhaven
Macduff's Castle
East Wemyss
Wemyss Caves
Dogton Stone
B922
B9130
Cluny
A92
A955
Coaltown of Wemyss
Wemyss Castle
West Wemyss
FIRTH OF FORTH
Cardenden
Gallatown
B981
Chapel
Sinclairtown
Dysart
Templehall
Pathhead
Harbourmaster's House Coastal Centre
A910
Ravenscraig
KIRKCALDY
B925
Linktown
Balwearie Castle
129
130
B9157
Pitteadie Castle
A921
Seafield Tower
B923
Burntisland
Kinghorn
Alexander III Monument
Pettycur
Bass Rock
Craigleith
Fidra
Lamb
Scottish Seabird Centre
Eyebroughy
North Berwick
Tantallon Castle
Dirleton
A198
Gullane Bay
North Berwick Law
Gullane
B1347
B1345
Kingston
Fenton Barns
Saltcoats Castle
Whitekirk
Aberlady Bay
EAST LOTHIAN
Aberlady
Myreton Motor Museum
Drem
Chesters Hill Fort
National Flag Heritage Centre
East Fortune
Flight
B1377
Tyninghame
B1407
Preston
Knowes
Phantassie Doocot
East Linton
Craigielaw
Gosford Bay
Ballencrieff
Spittal
Camptoun
B1343
Athelstaneford
Barnes Castle
Garleton Hills
A6137
Hopetoun Monument
A199
Hailes
Cockenzie and Port Seton
Longniddry
Huntington
Haddington
Prestonpans
Tower
EDINBURGH
Newhaven
Britannia
Trinity
Leith
A901
A902
A199

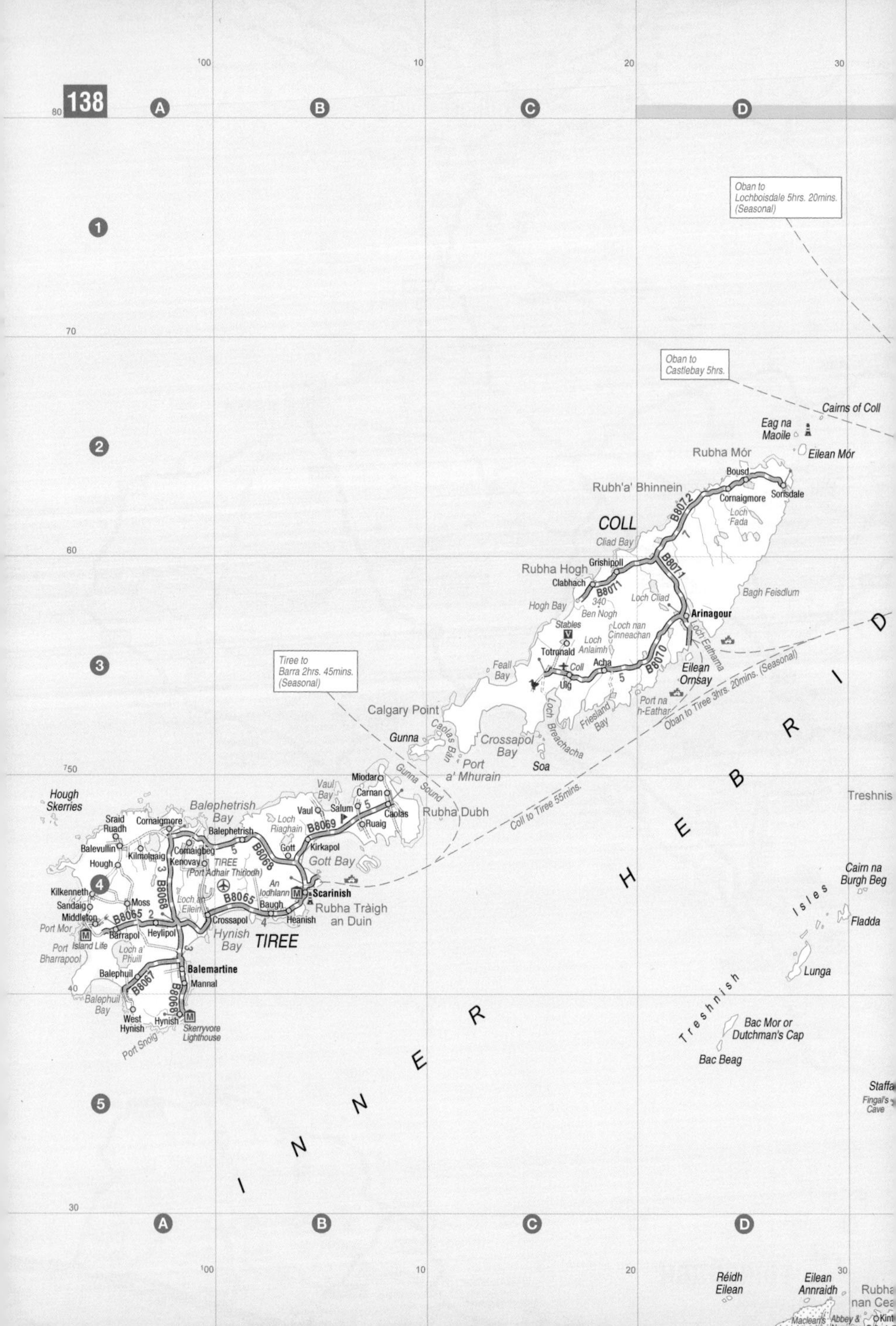
COLL
TIREE
INNER HEBRIDES
Oban to Lochboisdale 5hrs. 20mins. (Seasonal)
Oban to Castlebay 5hrs.
Tiree to Barra 2hrs. 45mins. (Seasonal)
Oban to Tiree 3hrs. 20mins. (Seasonal)
Coll to Tiree 55mins.
Cairns of Coll
Eag na Maoile
Eilean Mór
Rubha Mór
Bousd
Sorisdale
Cornaigmore
Loch Fada
Rubh'a' Bhinnein
Cliad Bay
Grishipoll
Rubha Hogh
Clabhach
Hogh Bay
Ben Nogh
Loch Cliad
Arinagour
Bagh Feisdlum
Loch nan Cinneachan
Stables
Loch Anlaimh
Totronald
Coll
Acha
Uig
Loch Eatharna
Eilean Ornsay
Feall Bay
Calgary Point
Gunna
Caolas Bàn
Port a' Mhurain
Crossapol Bay
Soa
Loch Breachacha
Friesland Bay
Port na h-Eathar
Miodar
Carnan
Caolas
Gunna Sound
Rubha Dubh
Vaul Bay
Vaul
Salum
Ruaig
Loch Riaghain
Kirkapol
Gott
Gott Bay
Scarinish
Rubha Tràigh an Duin
Heanish
Baugh
An Iodhlann
Hough Skerries
Sraid Ruadh
Cornaigmore
Balephetrish Bay
Balephetrish
Balevullin
Kilmoluaig
Cornaigbeg
Kenovay
TIREE (Port Adhair Thiriodh)
Hough
Kilkenneth
Sandaig
Moss
Middleton
Loch an Eilein
Crossapol
Port Mor
Island Life
Barrapol
Heylipol
Hynish Bay
Port Bharrapool
Loch a' Phuill
Balephuil
Balemartine
Mannal
Balephuil Bay
West Hynish
Hynish
Skerryvore Lighthouse
Port Snoig
B8072
B8071
B8070
B8069
B8068
B8065
B8067
340
Treshnish
Cairn na Burgh Beg
Treshnish Isles
Fladda
Lunga
Bac Mor or Dutchman's Cap
Bac Beag
Staffa
Fingal's Cave
Réidh Eilean
Eilean Annraidh
Maclean's Abbey
A
B
C
D
1
2
3
4
5
100
10
20
30
80
70
60
750
40

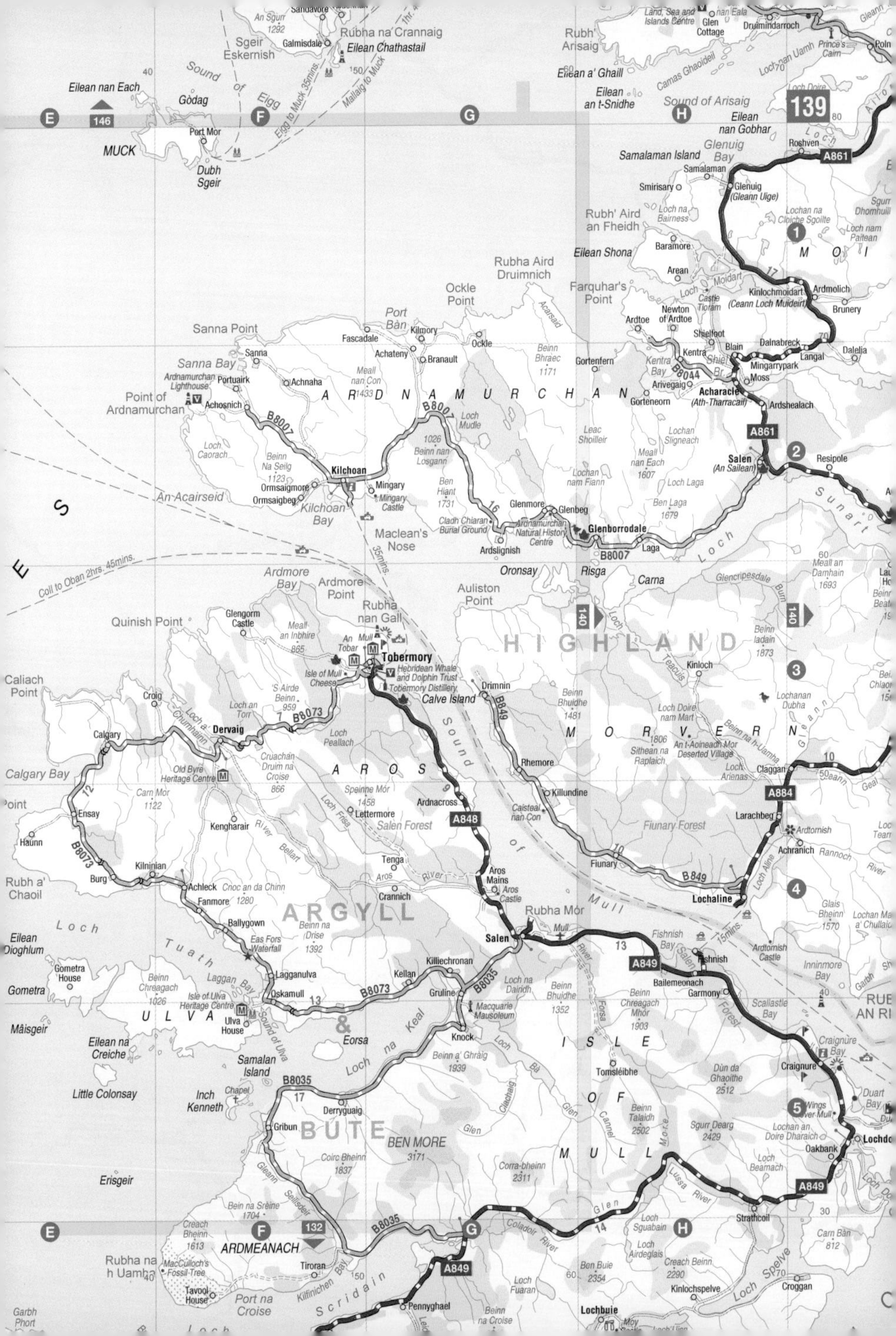

139
Sandavore
An Sgurr
1292
Rubha na' Crannaig
Galmisdale
Eilean Chathastail
Sgeir
Eskernish
Sound
of
Eigg
Eigg to Muck 35mins.
Mallaig to Muck
Eilean nan Each
Gòdag
146
MUCK
Port Mor
Dubh
Sgeir
E
F
G
H
Land, Sea and Islands Centre
Glen Cottage
nan Eala
Druimindarroch
Rubh' Arisaig
Eilean a' Ghaill
Camas Ghaoideil
Loch nan Uamh
Prince's Cairn
Eilean an t-Snidhe
Sound of Arisaig
Loch Doire
Eilean nan Gobhar
Samalaman Island
Glenuig Bay
Roshven
A861
Samalaman
Smirisary
Glenuig
(Gleann Uige)
Loch na Bairness
Lochan na Cloiche Sgoilte
Sgurr Dhomhuill
Loch nam Paitean
Rubh' Aird an Fheidh
Eilean Shona
Baramore
Arean
M O I
Rubha Aird Druimnich
Farquhar's Point
Loch Moidart
Kinlochmoidart
(Ceann Loch Muideirt)
Ardmolich
Brunery
Ockle Point
Castle Tioram
Newton of Ardtoe
Ardtoe
Shielfoot
Blain
Dalnabreck
Dalelia
Port Bàn
Kilmory
Fascadale
Achateny
Branault
Ockle
Acarsaid
Sanna Point
Sanna
Sanna Bay
Ardnamurchan Lighthouse
Portuairk
Achnaha
Meall nan Con
1433
Beinn Bhraec
1171
Gortenfern
Kentra
Kentra Bay
B8044
Arivegaig
Shiel Br.
Mingarrypark
Langal
Moss
Point of Ardnamurchan
Achosnich
A R D N A M U R C H A N
Gorteneorn
Acharacle
(Ath-Tharracail)
Ardshealach
B8007
Loch Mudle
Loch Caorach
Beinn Na Seilg
1123
1026
Beinn nan Losgann
Leac Shoilleir
Lochan Sligneach
Meall nan Each
1607
A861
Salen
(An Sailean)
Resipole
Kilchoan
Ormsaigmore
Ormsaigbeg
Mingary
Mingary Castle
Ben Hiant
1731
Lochan nam Fiann
Loch Laga
Ben Laga
1679
Sunart
An Acairseid
Kilchoan Bay
Glenmore
Glenbeg
Glenborrodale
Cladh Chiaran Burial Ground
Ardnamurchan Natural History Centre
Maclean's Nose
Ardslignish
Laga
Loch
Coll to Oban 2hrs. 45mins.
35mins.
Oronsay
Risga
Carna
Meall an Damhain
1693
Ardmore Bay
Ardmore Point
Auliston Point
Glencripesdale
Burn
Rubha nan Gall
Quinish Point
Glengorm Castle
Meall an Inbhire
865
140
H I G H L A N D
Beinn Iadain
1873
An Tobar
Mull
Tobermory
Kinloch
Loch Teacuis
Caliach Point
Isle of Mull Cheese
Hebridean Whale and Dolphin Trust
Tobermory Distillery
Calve Island
'S Airde Beinn
959
Drimnin
B849
Beinn Bhuidhe
1481
Loch Doire nam Mart
Lochanan Dubha
Croig
Loch an Torr
B8073
Loch a' Chumhainn
Dervaig
Calgary
Loch Peallach
Sound
M O R V E R N
1806
Sithean na Raplaich
An t-Aoineadh Mor Deserted Village
Beinn na h-Uamha
Gleann
Calgary Bay
Old Byre Heritage Centre
Cruachan Druim na Croise
866
A R O S
Rhemore
Loch Arienas
Claggan
Geal
Carn Mor
1122
Speinne Mòr
1458
Loch Frisa
Killundine
A884
Ensay
Kengharair
Lettermore
Ardnacross
Salen Forest
A848
Caisteal nan Con
Larachbeg
Fiunary Forest
Ardtornish
Haunn
River Bellart
Achranich
Rannoch
B8073
Tenga
Aros
River
Fiunary
B849
Burg
Kilninian
Aros Mains
Aros Castle
Loch Aline
Lochaline
Rubh a' Chaoil
Achleck
Cnoc an da Chinn
1280
Crannich
Fanmore
Mull
A R G Y L L
Rubha Mòr
Glais Bheinn
1570
Lochan Mor a' Chullaich
Loch
Ballygown
Beinn na Drise
1392
Salen
Mull
Fishnish Bay
Fishnish
15mins.
Ardtornish Castle
Eilean Dioghlum
Tuath
Eas Fors Waterfall
Forsa
Killiechronan
13
A849
Inninmore Bay
Gometra House
Lagganulva
Laggan Bay
Kellan
Loch na Dainidh
Bailemeonach
Garmony
Gometra
Beinn Chreagach
1026
Isle of Ulva Heritage Centre
Oskamull
B8073
Gruline
B8035
Beinn Bhuidhe
1352
Beinn Chreagach Mhòr
1903
Forest
Scallastle Bay
RUBH AN RI
U L V A
Ulva House
Sound of Ulva
&
Macquarie Mausoleum
Màisgeir
Eorsa
Knock
Craignure Bay
Eilean na Creiche
Loch na Keal
Loch
I S L E
Samalan Island
Beinn a' Ghràig
1939
Bà
Tomsléibhe
Dùn da Ghaoithe
2512
Craignure
Little Colonsay
Inch Kenneth
Chapel
B8035
17
Derryguaig
Clachaig
Glen
O F
Beinn Talaidh
2502
Duart Bay
Wings Over Mull
Gribun
B U T E
Glen
Cannel
Sgurr Dearg
2429
Lochan an Doire Dharaich
Lochdon
Oakbank
BEN MORE
3171
M U L L
More
Loch Beamach
Erisgeir
Coirc Bheinn
1837
Corra-bheinn
2311
Lussa River
A849
Gleann Seilisdeir
Bein na Srèine
1704
Glen
14
Strathcoil
Creach Bheinn
1613
B8035
132
Coladoir River
Loch Sguabain
Carn Bàn
812
ARDMEANACH
Loch Airdeglais
Creach Beinn
2290
Rubha na h Uamha
MacCulloch's Fossil Tree
Tiroran
A849
Ben Buie
2354
Kilfinichen Bay
Loch Fuaran
Loch Spelve
Tavool House
Port na Croise
Scridain
Pennyghael
Kinlochspelve
Croggan
Garbh Phort
Beinn na Croise
Lochbuie
Moy

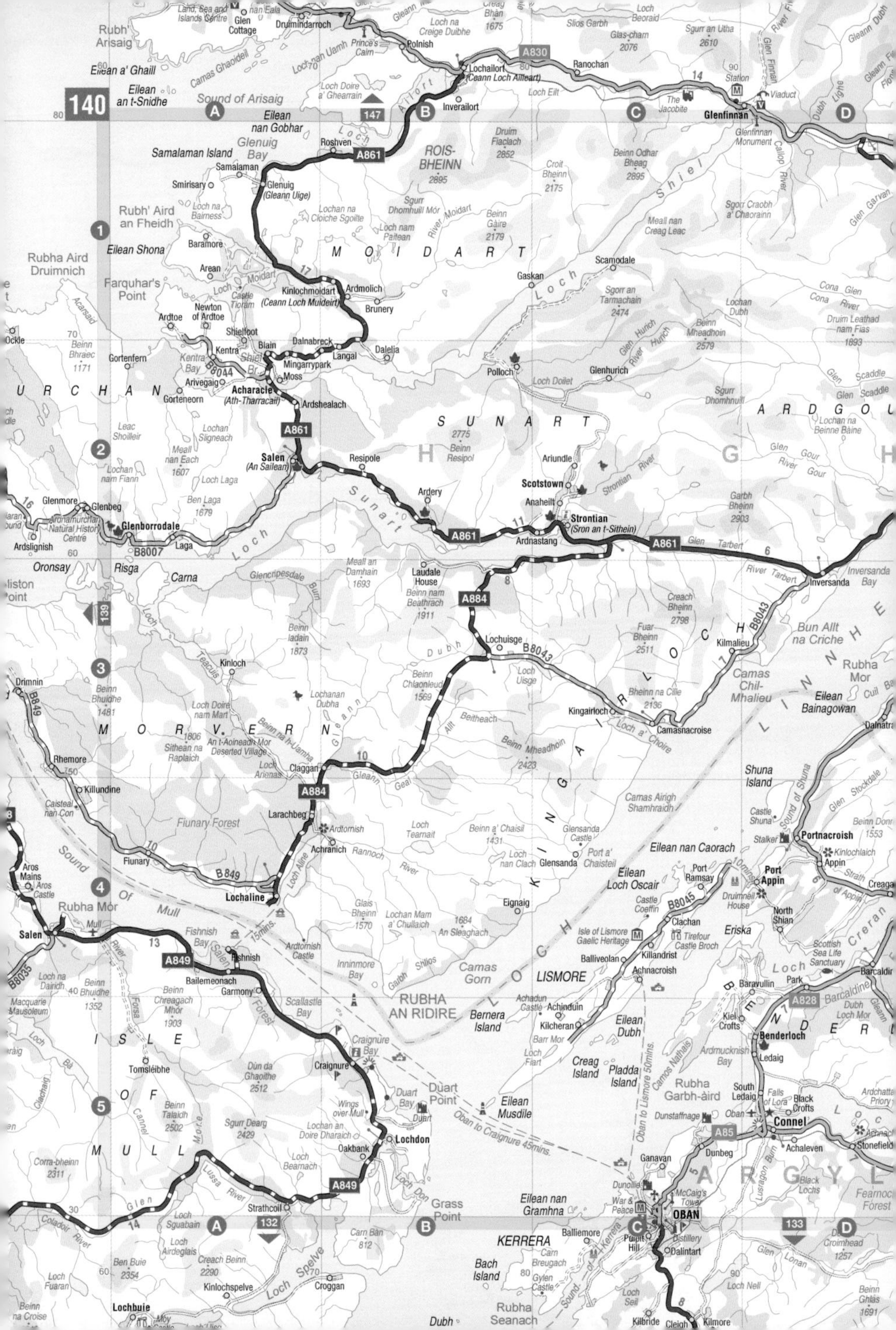

140
Land, Sea and Islands Centre
Glen Cottage
Druimindarroch
Loch na Creige Duibhe
Creag Bhàn 1675
Loch Beoraid
Slios Garbh
Sgurr an Utha 2610
Rubh' Arisaig
Camas Ghaoideil
Loch nan Uamh
Prince's Cairn
Polnish
Glas-cham 2076
A830
Ranochan
Glen Finnan
River Finnan
Gleann Dubh
Eilean a' Ghaill
Lochailort (Ceann Loch Ailleart)
Loch Eilt
Station
Eilean an t-Snidhe
Sound of Arisaig
Loch Doire a' Ghearrain
Inverailort
The Jacobite
Viaduct
Glenfinnan
Glenfinnan Monument
Dubh Lighe
147
Eilean nan Gobhar
Glenuig Bay
Roshven
A861
Druim Fiaclach 2852
ROIS-BHEINN 2895
Samalaman Island
Samalaman
Croit Bheinn 2175
Beinn Odhar Bheag 2895
Callop River
Smirisary
Glenuig (Gleann Uige)
Loch na Bairness
Lochan na Cloiche Sgoilte
Sgurr Dhomhuill Mór
Beinn Gàire 2179
Shiel
Sgorr Craobh a' Chaorainn
Glen Garvan
Rubh' Aird an Fheidh
Loch nam Paitean
River Moidart
Meall nan Creag Leac
Rubha Aird Druimnich
Eilean Shona
Baramore
MOIDART
Arean
Loch Moidart
Scamodale
Gaskan
Farquhar's Point
Castle Tioram
Kinlochmoidart (Ceann Loch Muideirt)
Ardmolich
Brunery
Loch
Sgorr an Tarmachain 2474
Lochan Dubh
Cona Glen
Cona River
Acarsaid
Newton of Ardtoe
Ardtoe
Shielfoot
Druim Leathad nam Fias 1893
Ockle
Beinn Bhraec 1171
Blain
Dalnabreck
Kentra
Dalelia
Glen Hurich
River Hurich
Beinn Mheadhoin 2579
Gortenfern
Kentra Bay
B8044
Shiel Br.
Mingarrypark
Langal
Polloch
Glen Scaddle
Arivegaig
Moss
Loch Doilet
Glenhurich
Gorteneorn
Acharacle (Ath-Tharracail)
Ardshealach
Sgurr Dhomhnuill
URCHAN
SUNART
ARDGOU
Leac Shoilleir
Lochan Sligneach
A861
2775 Beinn Resipol
Lochan na Beinne Bàine
Meall nan Each 1607
Salen (An Sailean)
Resipole
Ariundle
Glen Gour
River Gour
Lochan nam Fiann
Loch Laga
Scotstown
Strontian River
Garbh Bheinn 2903
Glenmore
Glenbeg
Ardnamurchan Natural History Centre
Glenborrodale
Ben Laga 1679
Ardery
Anaheilt
Strontian (Sron an t-Sìthein)
Ardslignish
Laga
B8007
A861
Ardnastang
Glen Tarbert
Oronsay
Risga
Carna
Meall an Damhain 1693
Laudale House
Beinn nam Beathrach 1911
River Tarbert
Inversanda
Inversanda Bay
Glencripesdale Burn
A884
Creach Bheinn 2798
139
Beinn Iadain 1873
Lochuisge
Fuar Bheinn 2511
Kilmalieu
B8043
Bun Allt na Criche
Dubh
B8043
Loch Uisge
Rubha Mor
Kinloch
Loch Teacuis
Beinn Chlaonleud 1569
Camas Chil-Mhalieu
Drimnin
Beinn Bhuidhe 1481
Lochanan Dubha
Bheinn na Cille 2136
Kingairloch
Eilean Bainagowan
B849
Loch Doire nam Mart
Beitheach
Camasnacroise
Loch a' Choire
Dalnatra
MORVERN
Beinn na h-Uamha
Allt
Beinn Mheadhoin 2423
1806 Sìthean na Raplaich
An t-Aoineadh Mor Deserted Village
Rhemore
Loch Arienas
Claggan
Gleann Geal
Shuna Island
Sound of Shuna
Glen Stockdale
Killundine
A884
Camas Airigh Shamhraidh
Caisteal nan Con
Larachbeg
Ardtornish
Loch Tearnait
Beinn a' Chaisil 1431
Glensanda Castle
Castle Shuna
Beinn Churalain 1553
Fiunary Forest
Achranich
Rannoch River
Port a' Chaisteil
Stalker
Portnacroish
Kinlochlaich
Sound of Mull
Fiunary
B849
Loch Aline
Loch nan Clach
Glensanda
Eilean nan Caorach
Aros Mains
Aros Castle
Eilean Loch Oscair
Port Ramsay
Port Appin
Appin
Strath of Appin
Creagan
Rubha Mòr
Lochaline
Glais Bheinn 1570
Lochan Mam a' Chullaich
1684 An Sleaghach
Eignaig
Castle Coeffin
B8045
Druimneil House
North Shian
Salen
Mull
15mins.
Fishnish Bay
Clachan
Eriska
Isle of Lismore Gaelic Heritage
Tirefour Castle Broch
Scottish Sea Life Sanctuary
Fishnish
A849
Ardtornish Castle
Inninmore Bay
Garbh Shlios
Camas Gorn
LISMORE
Balliveolan
Killandrist
Achnacroish
Loch Creran
Barcaldine
Loch na Dairidh
Beinn Bhuidhe 1352
Bailemeonach
Garmony
Baravullin
Park
B8035
Macquarie Mausoleum
Beinn Chreagach Mhòr 1903
Forsa River
Scallastle Bay
RUBHA AN RIDIRE
Bernera Island
Achadun Castle
Achinduin
Kilcheran
Eilean Dubh
A828
Barcaldine
Kiel Crofts
Dubh Loch Mor
LOCH LINNHE
KINGAIRLOCH
ISLE OF MULL
Craignure Bay
Craignure
Barr Mor
Loch Fiart
Creag Island
Pladda Island
Camas Nathais
Ardmucknish Bay
Benderloch
Ledaig
BENDERLOCH
Tomsléibhe
Dùn da Ghaoithe 2512
Duart Point
Duart Bay
Duart
Eilean Musdile
Rubha Garbh-àird
South Ledaig
Falls of Lora
Black Crofts
Ardchattan Priory
Loch Bà
Glen Cannel
Beinn Talaidh 2502
Sgurr Dearg 2429
Wings over Mull
Lochan an Doire Dharaich
Lochdon
Oban to Craignure 45mins.
Oban to Lismore 50mins.
Dunstaffnage
Oban
Connel
A85
Achnacloich
Achaleven
Stonefield
Clachaig
Corra-bheinn 2311
River Moré
Oakbank
Loch Bearnach
Ganavan
Dunbeg
Lusragan Burn
Black Lochs
Fearnoch Forest
ARGYLL
Lussa River
A849
Loch Don
Grass Point
Dunollie
McCaig's Tower
War & Peace
OBAN
Eilean nan Gramhna
Glen
Coladoir River
Loch Sguabain
Strathcoil
132
Carn Bàn 812
Balliemore
KERRERA
Pulpit Hill
Distillery
Dalintart
133
Croimhead 1257
Glen Lonan
Loch Airdeglais
Creach Beinn 2290
Ben Buie 2354
Loch Spelve
Carn Breugach
Bach Island
Gylen Castle
Sound of Kerrera
Loch Nell
Loch Fuaran
Kinlochspelve
Croggan
Rubha Seanach
Loch Seil
Beinn Ghlas 1691
Beinn na Croise
Lochbuie
Moy Castle
Dubh
Kilbride
Cleigh
Kilmore

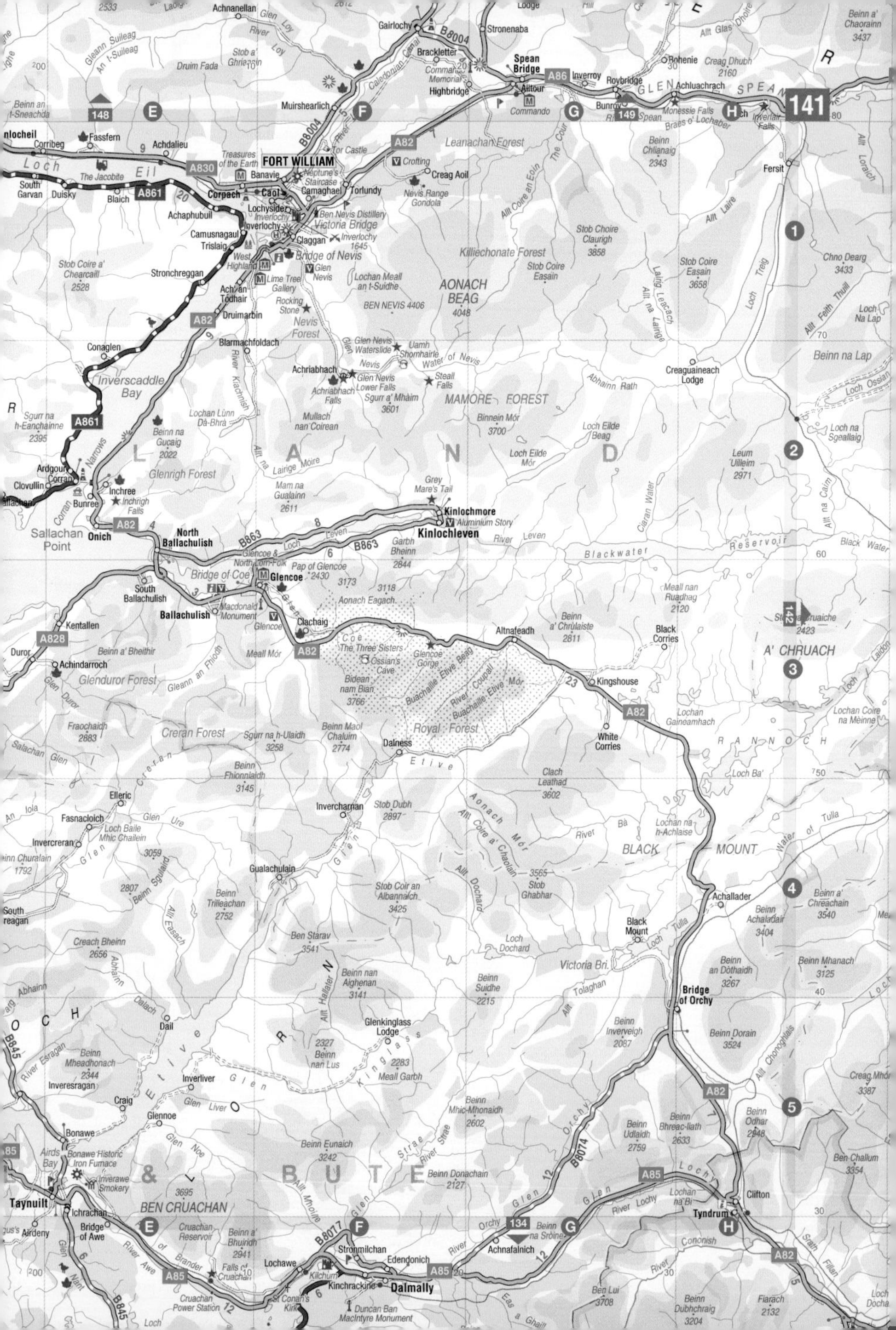
141
148
149
142
134
E
F
G
H
1
2
3
4
5
FORT WILLIAM
Banavie
Caol
Corpach
Lochyside
Inverlochy
Victoria Bridge
Claggan
Bridge of Nevis
Glen Nevis
Lime Tree Gallery
West Highland
Neptune's Staircase
Treasures of the Earth
The Jacobite
Camaghael
Torlundy
Tor Castle
Crofting
Creag Aoil
Nevis Range Gondola
Ben Nevis Distillery
Inverlochy 1645
Achnanellan
Glen Loy
River Loy
Gairlochy
Caledonian Canal
B8004
Brackletter
Commando Memorial
Highbridge
Spean Bridge
Stronenaba
A86
Inverroy
Aultour
Commando
Roybridge
Bohenie
Achluachrach
GLEN SPEAN
Bunroy
Monessie Falls
Braes o' Lochaber
Inverlair Falls
Creag Dhubh 2160
Beinn a' Chaorainn 3437
Allt Glas Dhoire
Muirshearlich
Leanachan Forest
Beinn Chlianaig 2343
Fersit
Allt Loraich
Allt Laire
Loch Treig
Stob Choire Claurigh 3858
Stob Coire Easain 3658
Chno Dearg 3433
Killiechonate Forest
Stob Coire Easain
Allt Coire an Eoin
The Cour
AONACH BEAG 4048
BEN NEVIS 4406
Lochan Meall an t-Suidhe
Rocking Stone
Nevis Forest
Lairig Leacach
Allt na Lairige
Allt Feith Thuill
Loch Na Lap
Beinn na Lap
Loch Ossian
Loch na Sgeallaig
Creaguaineach Lodge
Abhainn Rath
Glen Nevis Waterslide
Uamh Shomhairle
Water of Nevis
Steall Falls
Achriabhach
Achriabhach Falls
Glen Nevis Lower Falls
Sgurr a' Mhàim 3601
Mullach nan Coirean
MAMORE FOREST
Binnein Mór 3700
Loch Eilde Beag
Loch Eilde Mór
Leum Uilleim 2971
Allt na Caim
L A N D
Lochan Lùnn Dà-Bhrà
River Kiachnish
Blarmachfoldach
Druimarbin
Achintore
Stronchreggan
Stob Coire a' Chearcaill 2528
Achaphubuil
Camusnagaul
Trislaig
Conaglen
Inverscaddle Bay
Sgurr na h-Eanchainne 2395
A861
A82
A830
Loch Eil
Fassfern
Corribeg
Achdalieu
South Garvan
Duisky
Blaich
Gleann Suileag
An t-Suileag
Druim Fada
Stob a' Ghrianain
Beinn an t-Sneachda
Beinn na Gucaig 2022
Glenrigh Forest
Allt na Lairige Moire
Mam na Gualainn 2611
Ardgour
Corran
Corran Narrows
Clovullin
Inchree
Inchrigh Falls
Bunree
Sallachan Point
Onich
North Ballachulish
B863
Loch Leven
Grey Mare's Tail
Kinlochmore
Aluminium Story
Kinlochleven
Garbh Bheinn 2644
River Leven
Ciaran Water
Blackwater Reservoir
Black Water
Glencoe & North Lorn Folk
Bridge of Coe
Glencoe
South Ballachulish
Ballachulish
Macdonald Monument
Pap of Glencoe 2430
3173
3118
Aonach Eagach
Clachaig
Glen Coe
The Three Sisters
Ossian's Cave
Glencoe Gorge
Bidean nam Bian 3766
Buachaille Etive Beag
Buachaille Etive Mór
River Coupall
Royal Forest
Altnafeadh
Beinn a' Chrùlaiste 2811
Meall nan Ruadhag 2120
Black Corries
Kingshouse
White Corries
Stob a' Choire Odhair
2423
A' CHRUACH
Lochan Gaineamhach
Lochan Coire na Mèinne
R A N N O C H
Loch Ba'
Kentallen
A828
Duror
Achindarroch
Glen Duror
Glenduror Forest
Beinn a' Bheithir
Meall Mór
Gleann an Fhiodh
Fraochaidh 2683
Creran Forest
Salachan Glen
Sgurr na h-Ulaidh 3258
Beinn Maol Chaluim 2774
Dalness
Glen Etive
Clach Leathad 3602
Aonach Mór
Allt Coire a' Chaolain
River Bà
Lochan na h-Achlaise
BLACK MOUNT
Water of Tulla
Beinn Fhionnlaidh 3145
Elleric
Fasnacloich
Glen Ure
Loch Baile Mhic Chailein
Invercreran
Beinn Churalain 1792
Glen Creran
3059
Beinn Sgulaird
2807
Invercharnan
Stob Dubh 2897
Gualachulain
Stob Coir an Albannaich 3425
Allt Dochard
3565
Stob Ghabhar
Achallader
Beinn a' Chreachain 3540
Beinn Achaladair 3404
Black Mount
Loch Tulla
Loch Dochard
Victoria Bri.
South Creagan
Beinn Trilleachan 2752
Allt Easach
Creach Bheinn 2656
Abhainn
Ben Starav 3541
Beinn nan Aighenan 3141
Allt Hallater
Beinn Suidhe 2215
Allt Tolaghan
Bridge of Orchy
Beinn an Dòthaidh 3267
Beinn Mhanach 3125
Beinn Inverveigh 2087
Beinn Dorain 3524
Allt Chonoghlais
Creag Mhór 3387
Dalach
Dail
Glenkinglass Lodge
Glen Kinglass
2327 Beinn nan Lus
2283 Meall Garbh
B845
River Esragan
Beinn Mheadhonach 2344
Inveresragan
Inverliver
Glen Liver
Craig
Glennoe
Glen Noe
Bonawe
Airds Bay
Bonawe Historic Iron Furnace
Inverawe Smokery
Taynuilt
Ichrachan
Airdeny
Bridge of Awe
Glen Nant
3695
BEN CRUACHAN
Cruachan Reservoir
Beinn Eunaich 3242
Beinn Mhic-Mhonaidh 2602
Glen Strae
River Strae
Beinn Donachain 2127
& BUTE
Beinn Udlaidh 2759
Beinn Bhreac-liath 2633
Beinn Odhar 2948
Ben Challum 3354
Glen Orchy
B8074
A85
Glen Lochy
River Lochy
Lochan na Bi
Clifton
Tyndrum
Allt Mhoine
B8077
Beinn a' Bhuiridh 2941
Stronmilchan
Edendonich
River Orchy
Achnafalnich
Beinn a' Chleibh
Beinn na Sròine
Cononish
River Awe
Pass of Brander
Falls of Cruachan
Cruachan Power Station
Lochawe
Kilchurn
Kinchrackine
Dalmally
St Conan's Kirk
Duncan Ban MacIntyre Monument
Eas a' Ghaill
Ben Lui 3708
Beinn Dubhchraig 3204
Fiarach 2132
Strath Fillan
Loch Dochart
Loch Awe

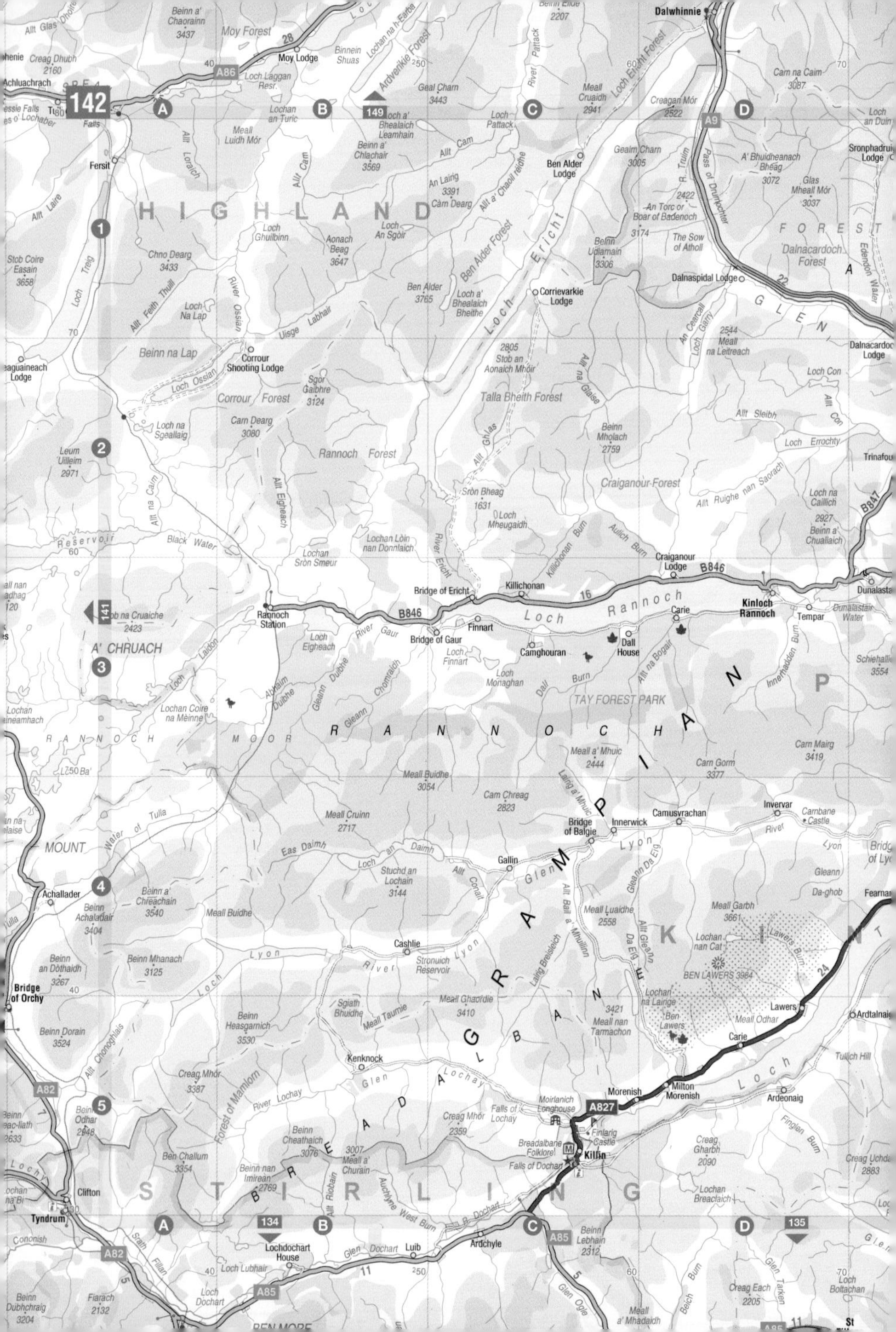

142
Allt Glas Dhoire
Beinn a' Chaorainn
3437
Moy Forest
Creag Dhubh
2160
Achluachrach
Moy Lodge
A86
28
Loch Laggan Resr.
Binnein Shuas
Lochan na h-Earba
Ardverikie Forest
Beinn Eibhinn
2207
Dalwhinnie
River Pattack
Loch Ericht Forest
Geal Charn
3443
Meall Cruaidh
2941
Carn na Caim
3087
Creagan Mòr
2522
149
A
B
C
D
A9
Falls
Lochan an Turic
Loch a' Bhealaich Leamhain
Loch Pattack
Loch an Duin
Meall Luidh Mór
Fersit
Allt Loraich
Allt Cam
Beinn a' Chlachair
3569
An Lairig
3391
Càrn Dearg
Ben Alder Lodge
Geal Charn
3005
R. Truim
Pass of Drumochter
A' Bhuidheanach Bheag
3072
Glas Mheall Mór
3037
Sronphadruig Lodge
Allt Laire
Allt a' Chaoil-reidhe
2422
An Torc or Boar of Badenoch
3174
The Sow of Atholl
HIGHLAND
Loch Ghuilbinn
Aonach Beag
3647
Loch An Sgòir
Ben Alder Forest
Loch Ericht
Beinn Udlamain
3306
FOREST
Dalnacardoch Forest
Edendon Water
Stob Coire Easain
3658
Chno Dearg
3433
Loch Treig
Allt Feith Thuill
River Ossian
Loch Na Lap
Ben Alder
3765
Loch a' Bhealaich Bheithe
Corrievarkie Lodge
Dalnaspidal Lodge
22
GLEN
Uisge Labhair
An Cearcall
Loch Garry
2544
Meall na Leitreach
Dalnacardoch Lodge
70
Beinn na Lap
Corrour Shooting Lodge
Loch Ossian
2805
Stob an Aonaich Mhóir
Allt na Glaise
Loch Con
Corrour Forest
Sgor Gaibhre
3124
Talla Bheith Forest
Allt Con
Loch na Sgeallaig
Carn Dearg
3080
Allt Sleibh
Beinn Mholach
2759
Loch Errochty
Leum Uilleim
2971
Rannoch Forest
Allt Ghlas
Trinafour
Craiganour Forest
Allt na Caim
Allt Eigheach
Sròn Bheag
1631
Loch Mheugaidh
Allt Ruighe nan Saorach
Loch na Caillich
2927
Beinn a' Chuallaich
B847
Reservoir
60
Black Water
Lochan Lòin nan Donnlaich
River Ericht
Killichonan Burn
Aulich Burn
Lochan Sròn Smeur
Craiganour Lodge
B846
Bridge of Ericht
Killichonan
16
Loch Rannoch
Dunalastair
141
2423
Rannoch Station
B846
Carie
Kinloch Rannoch
Tempar
Dunalastair Water
Loch Eigheach
River Gaur
Bridge of Gaur
Finnart
Loch Finnart
Camghouran
Dall House
Allt na Bogair
A' CHRUACH
Loch Laidon
Loch Monaghan
Dall Burn
Innerhadden Burn
Schiehallion
3554
Abhainn Duibhe
Gleann Duibhe
Gleann Chomraidh
TAY FOREST PARK
Lochan Coire na Mèinne
RANNOCH MOOR
RANNOCH
GRAMPIAN
Carn Mairg
3419
Meall a' Mhuic
2444
Carn Gorm
3377
Ba'
Meall Buidhe
3054
Lairig a' Mhuic
Carn Chreag
2823
Meall Cruinn
2717
Bridge of Balgie
Innerwick
Camusvrachan
Invervar
Carnbane Castle
River Lyon
Water of Tulla
MOUNT
Eas Daimh
Loch an Daimh
Allt Conait
Gallin
Glen Lyon
Gleann Da Eig
Bridge of Lyon
Gleann Da-ghob
Achallader
Beinn a' Chreachain
3540
Stuchd an Lochain
3144
Meall Buidhe
Allt Ball a' Mhuilinn
Meall Luaidhe
2558
Meall Garbh
3661
Fearnan
Beinn Achaladair
3404
Cashlie
Lochan nan Cat
Lawers Burn
Beinn an Dòthaidh
3267
Beinn Mhanach
3125
Loch Lyon
Stronuich Reservoir
Allt Gleann Da Eig
BEN LAWERS 3984
Bridge of Orchy
Sgiath Bhuidhe
Meall Taurnie
Meall Ghaordie
3410
Laing Breisleich
3421
Meall nan Tarmachon
Lochan na Lairige
Ben Lawers
Lawers
Meall Odhar
Ardtalnaig
Beinn Dorain
3524
Beinn Heasgarnich
3530
24
Allt Chonoghlais
Kenknock
Carie
Creag Mhór
3387
Glen Lochay
Forest of Mamlorn
BREADALBANE
Morenish
Milton Morenish
Tullich Hill
A82
River Lochay
Moirlanich Longhouse
Falls of Lochay
A827
Loch Tay
Ardeonaig
Beinn Odhar
2948
Beinn Cheathaich
3076
Creag Mhór
2359
Finlarig Castle
Breadalbane Folklore
Killin
Finglen Burn
Ben Challum
3354
3007
Meall a' Churain
Falls of Dochart
Creag Gharbh
2090
Creag Uchdag
2883
Beinn nan Imirean
2769
Allt Riobain
Auchlyne West Burn
STIRLING
Clifton
Tyndrum
R. Dochart
Lochan Breaclaich
A
134
B
C
D
135
Cononish
Lochdochart House
Glen Dochart
Luib
Ardchyle
A85
Beinn Lebhain
2312
Glen Tarken
A82
Strath Fillan
Loch Lubhair
11
250
60
Beich Burn
Loch Boltachan
Beinn Dubhchraig
3204
Fiarach
2132
Loch Dochart
A85
Glen Ogle
Creag Each
2205
Meall a' Mhadaidh
BEN MORE

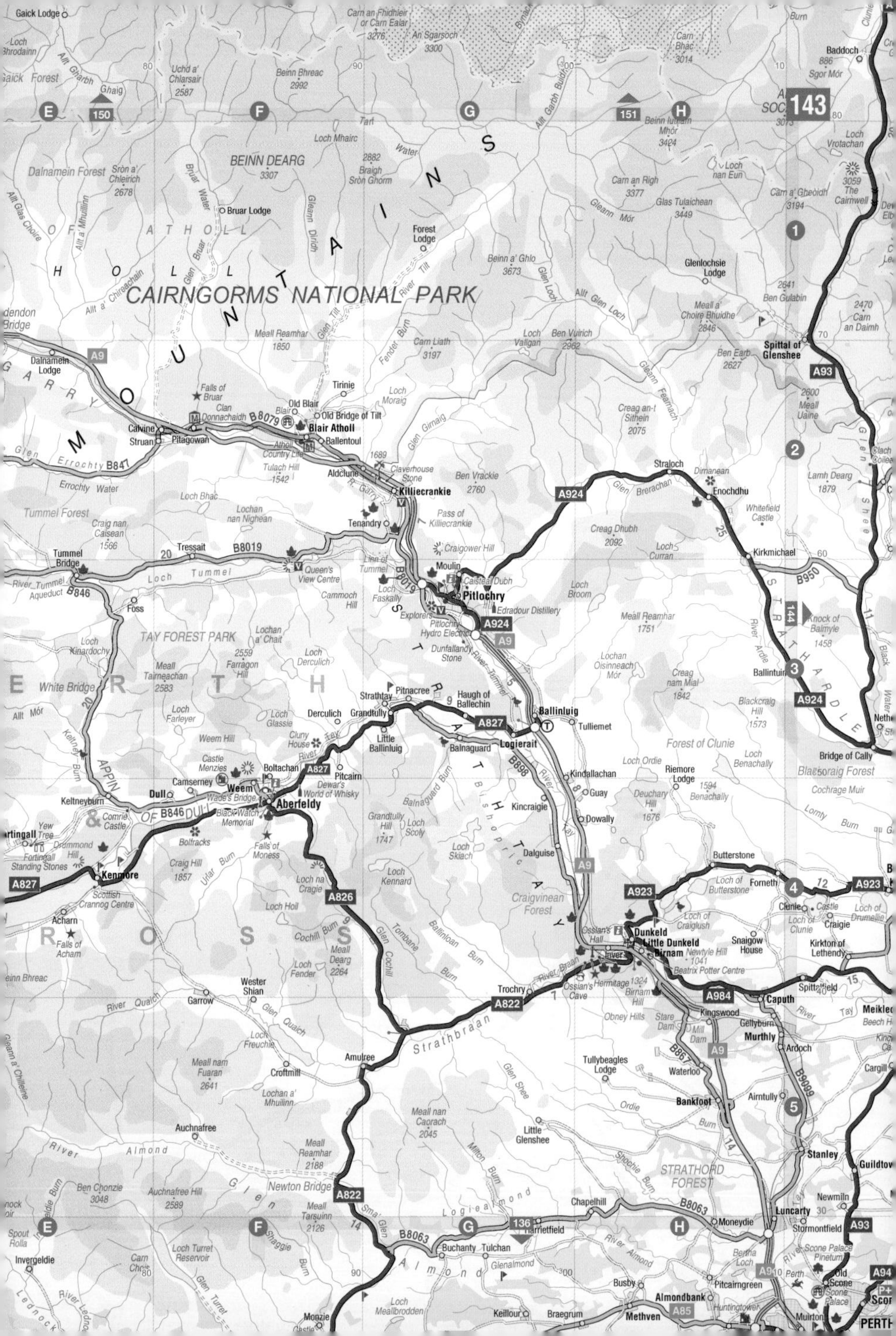

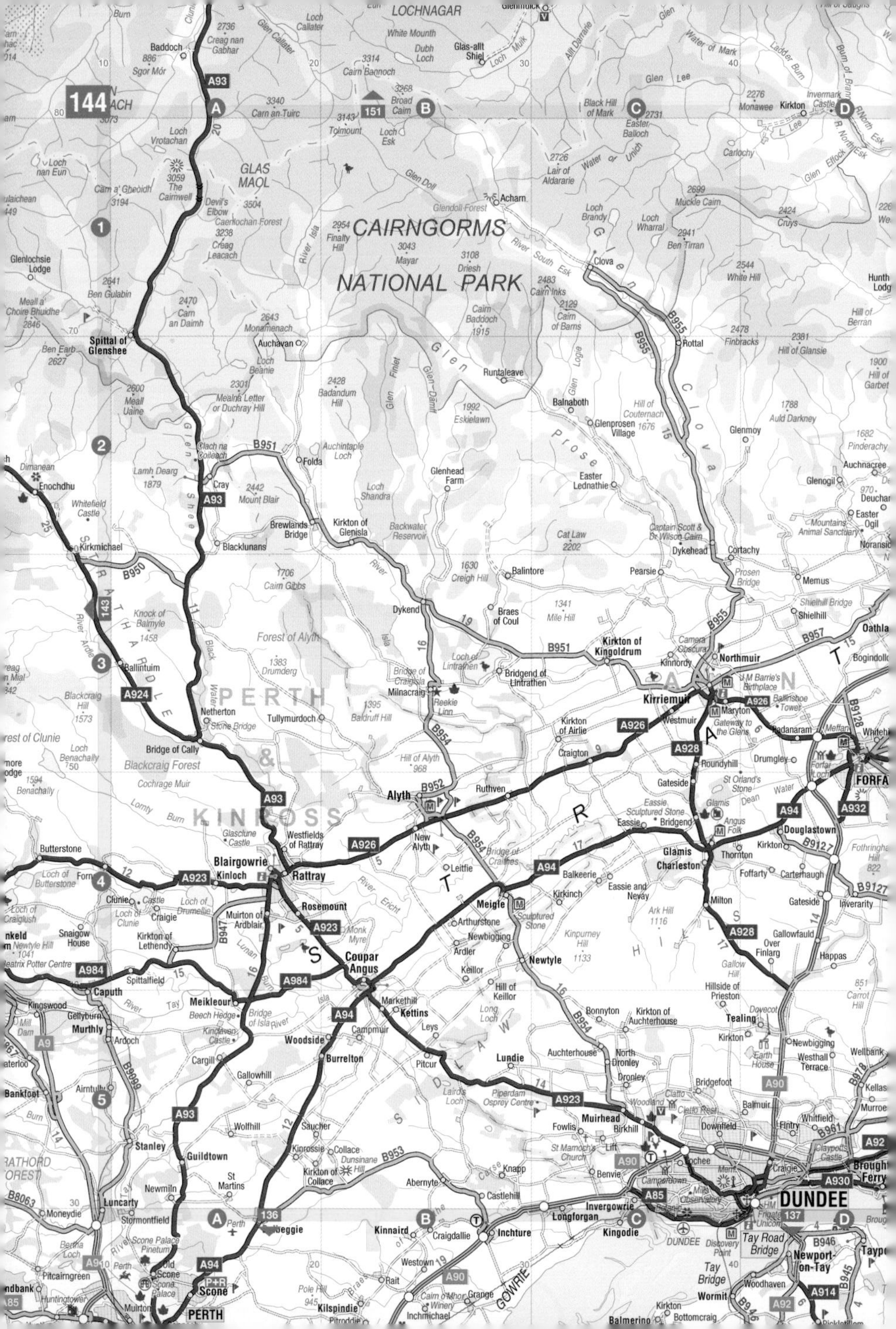
144
LOCHNAGAR
CAIRNGORMS
NATIONAL PARK
PERTH
&
KINROSS
Spittal of Glenshee
Kirkmichael
Ballintuim
Bridge of Cally
Blairgowrie
Rattray
Rosemount
Coupar Angus
Alyth
Meigle
Newtyle
Kirriemuir
Glamis
Forfar
Dundee
Perth
Scone
Stanley
Guildtown
Luncarty
Caputh
Meikleour
Murthly
Burrelton
Woodside
Kettins
Lundie
Muirhead
Invergowrie
Longforgan
Inchture
Kinnaird
Kilspindie
Newport-on-Tay
Wormit
Tay Road Bridge
Tay Bridge
Clova
Glenprosen Village
Kirkton of Glenisla
Kirkton of Kingoldrum
Northmuir
Westmuir
Roundyhill
Douglastown
Charleston
Tealing
Balmerino
Glen Clova
Glen Prosen
Glen Shee
Forest of Alyth
Sidlaw Hills
Strathardle
A93
A924
A923
A926
A94
A984
A928
A932
A90
A85
A9
A92
A914
A930
B951
B955
B954
B952
B950
B947
B953
B957
B9127
B9128
B946
B961
B978
B8063
B9099
B945
143
151
136
137

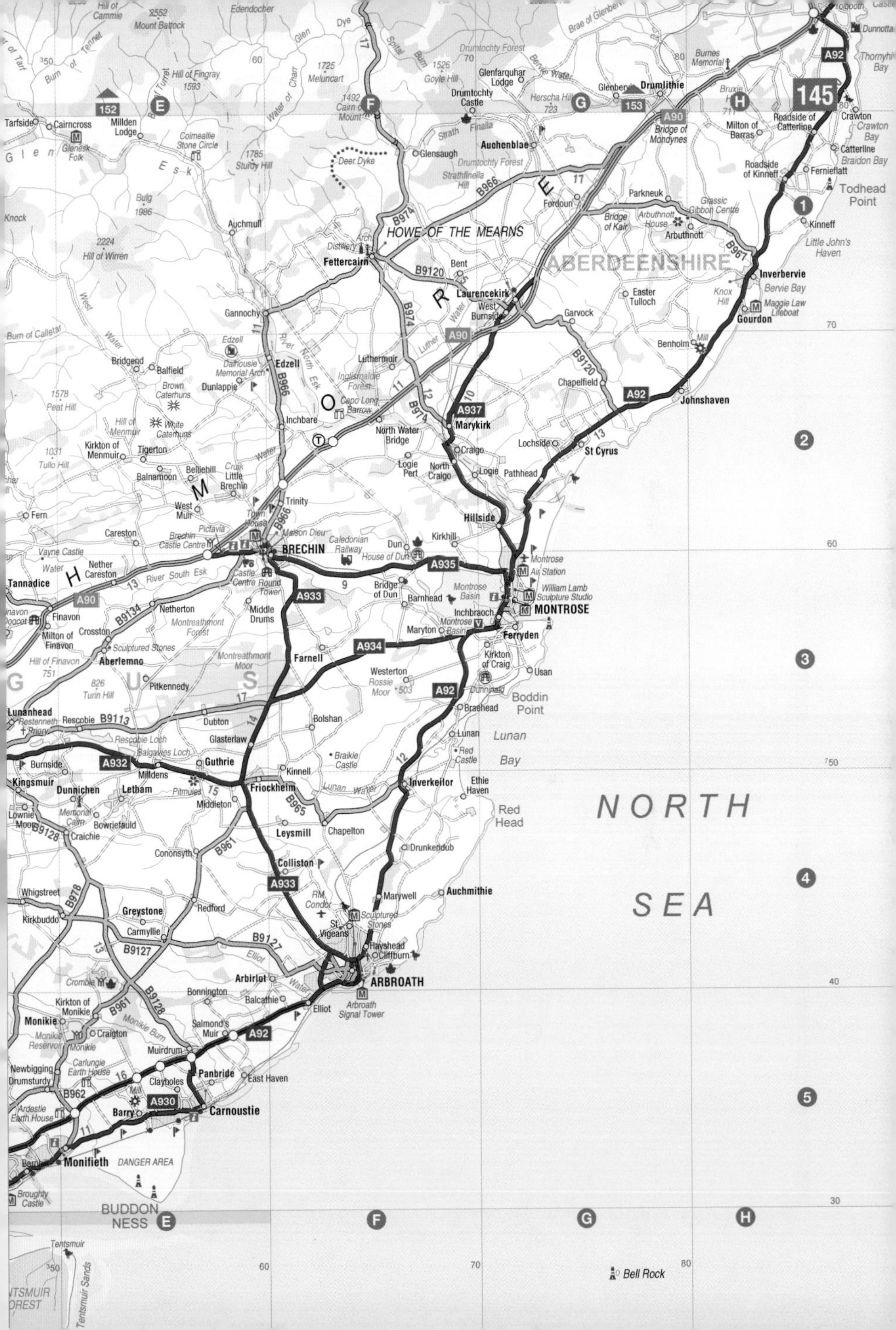
145
NORTH SEA
ABERDEENSHIRE
HOWE OF THE MEARNS
A92
A90
A937
A935
A933
A934
A932
A930
B966
B974
B9120
B967
B9134
B9113
B965
B961
B9128
B978
B9127
B962
Hill of Cammie
2552 Mount Battock
Edendocher
Hill of Fingray 1593
Burn of Tennet
Tarfside
Cairncross
Glenesk Folk
Millden Lodge
Colmeallie Stone Circle
1785 Sturdy Hill
1725 Meluncart
Water of Charr
Glen Dye
1492 Cairn o' Mount
Spital Burn
1526 Goyle Hill
Drumtochty Forest
Drumtochty Castle
Glenfarquhar Lodge
Glensaugh
Deer Dyke
Strath Finella
Auchenblae
Strathfinella Hill
Glenbervie
Drumlithie
Hercha Hill 723
Burnes Memorial
Bridge of Mondynes
Milton of Barras
Roadside of Catterline
Crawton
Crawton Bay
Catterline
Braidon Bay
Roadside of Kinneff
Fernieflatt
Todhead Point
Kinneff
Little John's Haven
Parkneuk
Grassic Gibbon Centre
Arbuthnott House
Arbuthnott
Bridge of Kair
Fordoun
Bulg 1986
Knock
Auchmull
2224 Hill of Wirren
Distillery
Fettercairn
Bent
Laurencekirk
West Burnside
Easter Tulloch
Garvock
Inverbervie
Bervie Bay
Knox Hill
Maggie Law Lifeboat
Gourdon
Benholm
Mill
Gannochy
Burn of Calletar
West Water
Edzell
Dalhousie Memorial Arch
Bridgend
Balfield
Dunlappie
Brown Caterthuns
White Caterthuns
1578 Peat Hill
Hill of Menmuir
River North Esk
Inglismaldie Forest
Luthermuir
Capo Long Barrow
Inchbare
North Water Bridge
Marykirk
Craigo
Logie Pert
North Craigo
Logie
Pathhead
Chapelfield
Johnshaven
Lochside
St Cyrus
Kirkton of Menmuir
Tigerton
1031 Tullo Hill
Balnamoon
Little Brechin
West Muir
Trinity
Fern
Careston
Pictavia
Brechin Castle Centre
Town House
Maison Dieu
BRECHIN
Caledonian Railway
Dun
House of Dun
Kirkhill
Hillside
Montrose Air Station
William Lamb Sculpture Studio
MONTROSE
Montrose Basin
Bridge of Dun
Barnhead
Inchbraoch
Ferryden
Maryton
Vayne Castle
Nether Careston
Tannadice
River South Esk
Castle
Round Tower
Middle Drums
Netherton
Montreathmont Forest
Finavon Doocot
Finavon
Milton of Finavon
Crosston
Sculptured Stones
Aberlemno
Hill of Finavon 751
826 Turin Hill
Pitkennedy
Montreathmont Moor
Farnell
Westerton
Rossie Moor 503
Kirkton of Craig
Usan
Dunninald
Boddin Point
Braehead
Lunan
Lunan Bay
Red Castle
Lunanhead
Restenneth Priory
Rescobie
Rescobie Loch
Balgavies Loch
Dubton
Glasterlaw
Bolshan
Braikie Castle
Burnside
Guthrie
Milldens
Kinnell
Kingsmuir
Dunnichen
Letham
Pitmuies
Friockheim
Middleton
Lunan Water
Inverkeilor
Ethie Haven
Red Head
Lowrie Moor
Memorial Cairn
Bowriefauld
Craichie
Leysmill
Chapelton
Drunkendub
Cononsyth
Colliston
Whigstreet
Auchmithie
Marywell
RM Condor
Sculptured Stones
St Vigeans
Hayshead
Cliffburn
Kirkbuddo
Greystone
Redford
Carmyllie
Elliot Water
Arbirlot
ARBROATH
Arbroath Signal Tower
Crombie
Bonnington
Balcathie
Elliot
Kirkton of Monikie
Monikie
Monikie Reservoir
Craigton
Salmond's Muir
Monikie Burn
Muirdrum
Carlungie Earth House
Newbigging
Drumsturdy
Panbride
East Haven
Clayholes
Ardestie Earth House
Barry
Carnoustie
Barnhill
Monifieth
DANGER AREA
Broughty Castle
BUDDON NESS
Tentsmuir
Tentsmuir Sands
TENTSMUIR FOREST
Bell Rock
Dunnottar

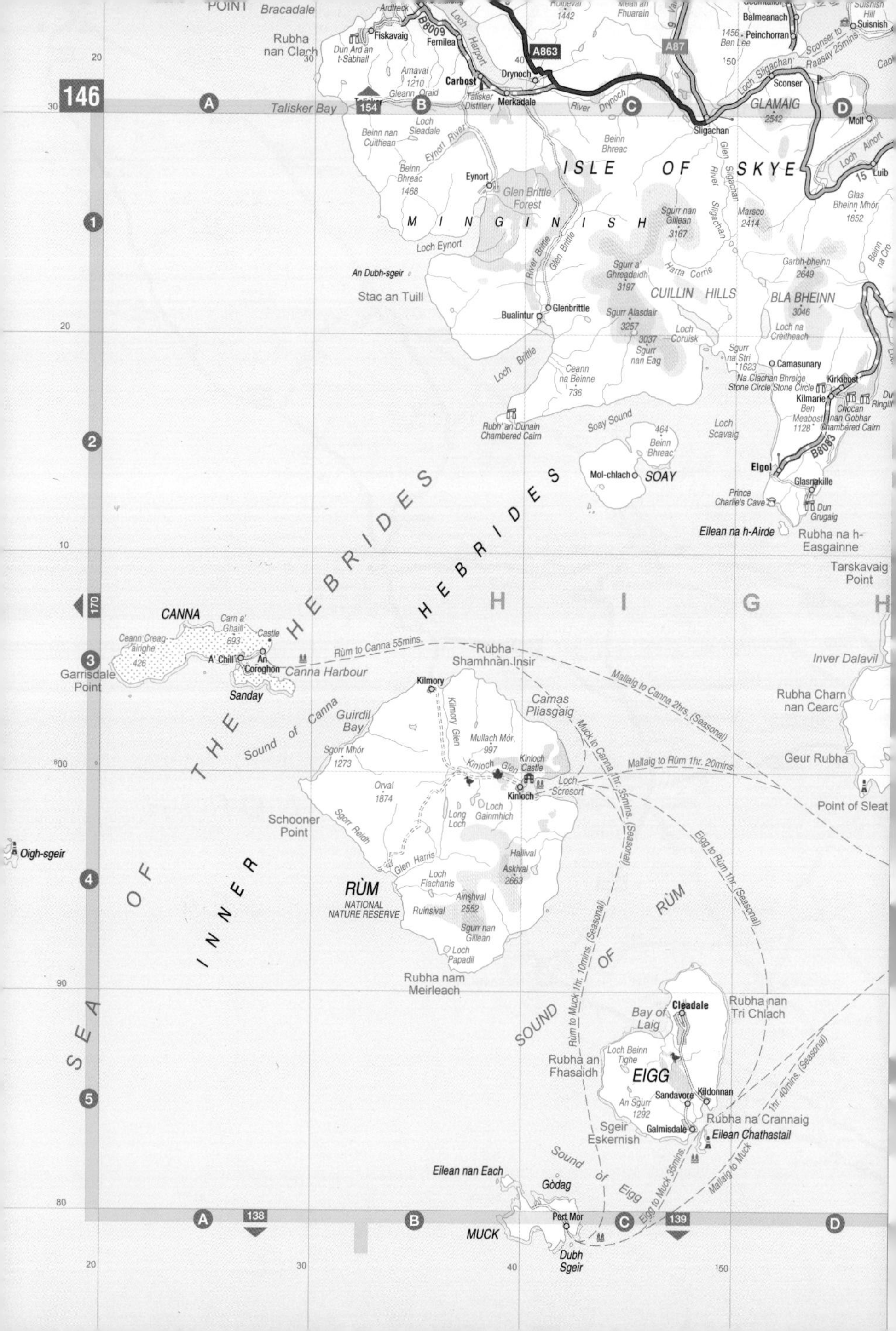

146
Talisker Bay
Bracadale
Rubha nan Clach
Fiskavaig
Fernilea
Carbost
Drynoch
Merkadale
Talisker Distillery
A863
A87
B8009
Loch Harport
Sligachan
Sconser
GLAMAIG 2542
Moll
Luib
ISLE OF SKYE
MINGINISH
Eynort
Glen Brittle Forest
Loch Eynort
An Dubh-sgeir
Stac an Tuill
Glenbrittle
Bualintur
Sgurr Alasdair 3257
Sgurr nan Gillean 3167
Marsco 2414
CUILLIN HILLS
BLA BHEINN 3046
Garbh-bheinn 2649
Loch Coruisk
Loch Brittle
Camasunary
Kirkibost
Kilmarie
Rubh' an Dunain Chambered Cairn
Soay Sound
SOAY
Mol-chlach
Loch Scavaig
Elgol
Glasnakille
Prince Charlie's Cave
Eilean na h-Airde
Rubha na h-Easgainne
Tarskavaig Point
INNER HEBRIDES
SEA OF THE HEBRIDES
HIGH
CANNA
Canna Harbour
A' Chill
An Coroghon
Sanday
Garrisdale Point
Rùm to Canna 55mins.
Rubha Shamhnan Insir
Mallaig to Canna 2hrs. (Seasonal)
Kilmory
Guirdil Bay
Sound of Canna
Camas Pliasgaig
Mullach Mór 997
Kinloch Castle
Kinloch
Loch Scresort
Mallaig to Rùm 1hr. 20mins
Muck to Canna 1hr. 35mins. (Seasonal)
Eigg to Rùm 1hr. (Seasonal)
Schooner Point
Oigh-sgeir
RÙM NATIONAL NATURE RESERVE
Askival 2663
Ainshval 2552
Loch Papadil
Rubha nam Meirleach
Inver Dalavil
Rubha Charn nan Cearc
Geur Rubha
Point of Sleat
SOUND OF RÙM
Rùm to Muck 1hr. 10mins. (Seasonal)
Cleadale
Bay of Laig
Rubha nan Tri Chlach
Rubha an Fhasaidh
EIGG
Kildonnan
Sandavore
An Sgurr 1292
Galmisdale
Rubha na' Crannaig
Eilean Chathastail
Sgeir Eskernish
Sound of Eigg
Eigg to Muck 35mins.
Mallaig to Muck 1hr. 40mins. (Seasonal)
Eilean nan Each
Gòdag
Port Mor
MUCK
Dubh Sgeir
138
139
170

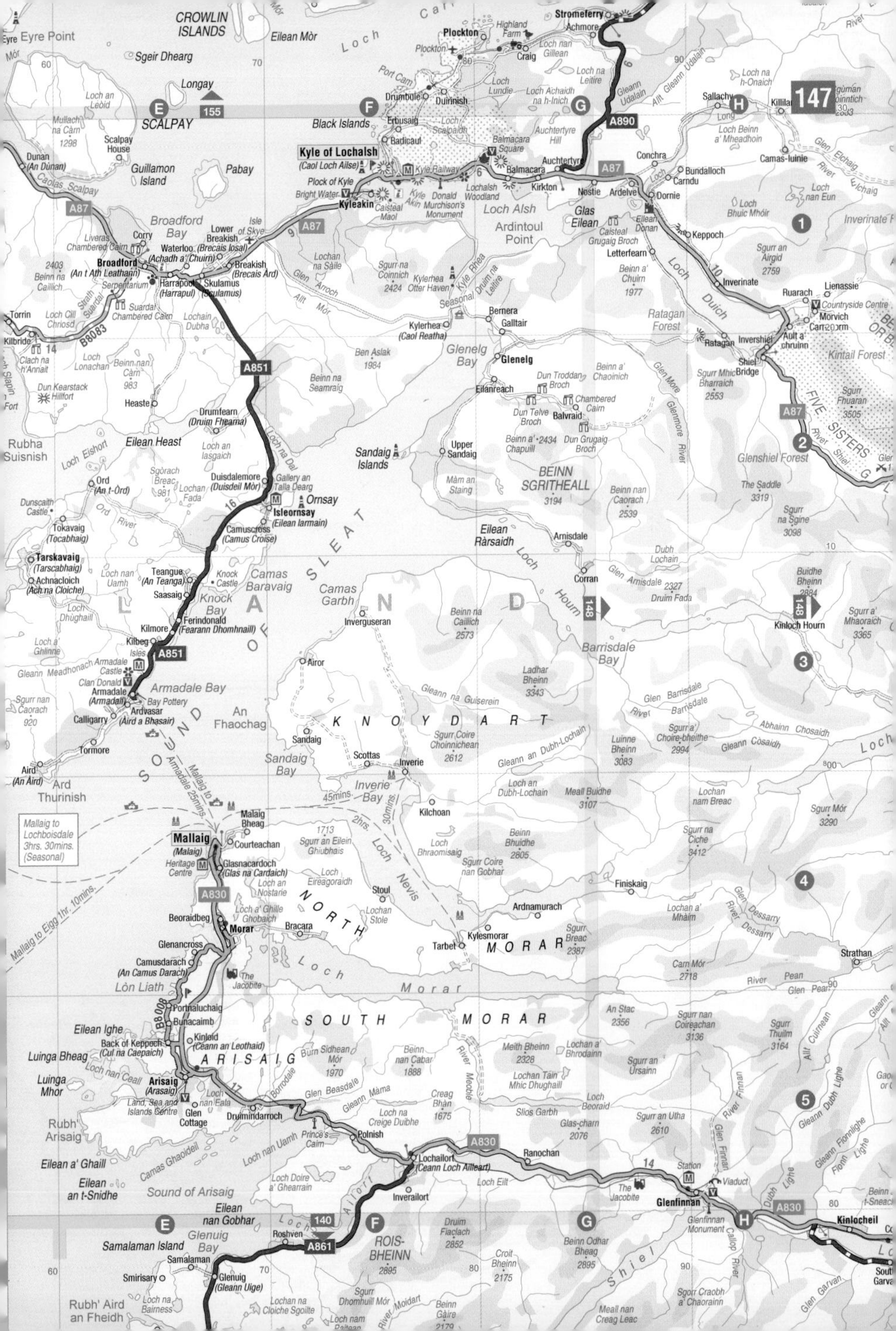

147
Eyre Point
CROWLIN ISLANDS
Eilean Mòr
Sgeir Dhearg
Longay
E
F
G
H
155
SCALPAY
Loch an Leòid
Mullach na Càrn 1298
Scalpay House
Dunan (An Dùnan)
Caolas Scalpay
Guillamon Island
Pabay
Black Islands
Plockton
Highland Farm
Craig
Loch nan Gillean
Stromeferry
Achmore
Port Cam
Drumbuie
Duirinish
Loch Lundie
Loch Achaidh na h-Inich
Loch na Leitire
Gleann Udalain
Allt Gleann Udalain
Erbusaig
Badicaul
Loch Scalpaidh
Balmacara Square
Auchtertyre Hill
A890
Kyle of Lochalsh (Caol Loch Aillse)
Kyle Railway
Balmacara
Auchtertyre
A87
Plock of Kyle
Bright Water
Kyleakin
Kyle Akin
Caisteal Maol
Donald Murchison's Monument
Lochalsh Woodland
Loch Alsh
Kirkton
Nostie
Ardelve
Dornie
Sallachy
Killilan
Loch Beinn a' Mheadhoin
Camas-luinie
Conchra
Bundalloch
Carndu
Loch na h-Onaich
Loch Bhuic Mhóir
Loch nan Eun
Glen Elchaig
Inverinate Forest
A87
Broadford Bay
Lower Breakish
Isle of Skye
Corry
Liveras Chambered Cairn
Waterloo (Achadh a' Chuirn)
Broadford (An t Ath Leathann)
Breakish (Breacais Ìosal)
Breakish (Breacais Àrd)
Harrapool (Harrapul)
Skulamus (Sculamus)
Serpentarium
2403 Beinn na Caillich
Strath Suardal
Suardal Chambered Cairn
Loch Cill Chriosd
Torrin
Kilbride
B8083
Clach na h'Annait
Loch Lonachan
Beinn nan Càrn 983
Dun Kearstack Hillfort
Heaste
Lochain Dubha
Lochan na Sàile
Glen Arroch
Allt Mòr
Sgurr na Coinnich 2424
Kylerhea Otter Haven
Kyle Rhea
Seasonal
Druim na Leitire
Glas Eilean
Ardintoul Point
Caisteal Grugaig Broch
Eilean Donan
Keppoch
Letterfearn
Beinn a' Chuirn 1977
Loch Duich
Inverinate
Sgurr an Airgid 2759
Ruarach
Lienassie
Countryside Centre
Morvich
Ratagan Forest
Ratagan
Invershiel
Ault a' chruinn
Shiel Bridge
Kintail Forest
Kylerhea (Caol Reatha)
Bernera
Galltair
Glenelg Bay
Glenelg
Ben Aslak 1984
Beinn na Seamraig
A851
Eilanreach
Dun Troddan Broch
Beinn a' Chaoinich
Dun Telve Broch
Chambered Cairn
Balvraid
Dun Grugaig Broch
Beinn a' Chapuill 2434
Glen More
Glenmore River
Sgurr Mhic Bharraich 2553
FIVE SISTERS
Sgurr Fhuaran 3505
Glenshiel Forest
River Shiel
Rubha Suisnish
Eilean Heast
Loch Eishort
Drumfearn (Druim Fhearna)
Loch an Iasgaich
Loch na Dal
Sandaig Islands
Upper Sandaig
Sgòrach Breac 981
Lochan Fada
Duisdalemore (Duisdeil Mòr)
Gallery an Talla Dearg
Isleornsay (Eilean Iarmain)
Ornsay
Màm an Staing
BEINN SGRITHEALL 3194
Beinn nan Caorach 2539
The Saddle 3319
Sgurr na Sgine 3098
Ord (An t-Òrd)
Dunscaith Castle
Ord River
Tokavaig (Tocabhaig)
Camuscross (Camus Croise)
Eilean Ràrsaidh
Arnisdale
Loch Hourn
Dubh Lochain
Corran
Glen Arnisdale 2327
Druim Fada
Buidhe Bheinn 2884
Sgurr a' Mhaoraich 3365
Kinloch Hourn
148
Tarskavaig (Tarscabhaig)
Achnacloich (Ach na Cloiche)
Loch nan Uamh
Teangue (An Teanga)
Knock Castle
Saasaig
Camas Baravaig
Camas Garbh
Knock Bay
SLEAT
LAND
Loch Dhùghaill
Kilmore
Ferindonald (Fearann Dhomhnaill)
Inverguseran
Beinn na Caillich 2573
Barrisdale Bay
Loch a' Ghlinne
Kilbeg
Isles
Armadale Castle
Gleann Meadhonach
Clan Donald
Armadale (Armadal)
Armadale Bay
Bay Pottery
Airor
Ladhar Bheinn 3343
Gleann na Guiserein
Glen Barrisdale
River Barrisdale
Sgurr nan Caorach 920
Ardvasar (Àird a Bhasair)
Calligarry
An Fhaochag
SOUND OF SLEAT
KNOYDART
Sandaig
Sgurr Coire Choinnichean 2612
Luinne Bheinn 3083
Sgurr a' Choire-bheithe 2994
Abhainn Chosaidh
Gleann Còsaidh
Tormore
Scottas
Inverie
Sandaig Bay
Gleann an Dubh-Lochain
Aird (An Àird)
Ard Thurinish
Mallaig to Armadale 25mins.
Inverie Bay
45mins.
Loch an Dubh-Lochain
Meall Buidhe 3107
Lochan nam Breac
Sgurr Mòr 3290
Kilchoan
Mallaig to Lochboisdale 3hrs. 30mins. (Seasonal)
Malaig Bheag
2hrs.
30mins.
Mallaig (Malaig)
Courteachan
1713 Sgurr an Eilein Ghiubhais
Loch Nevis
Loch Bhraomisaig
Beinn Bhuidhe 2805
Sgurr na Ciche 3412
Heritage Centre
Glasnacardoch (Glas na Cardaich)
Sgurr Coire nan Gobhar
Loch Eireagoraidh
Loch an Nostarie
A830
Stoul
Finiskaig
Glen Dessarry
River Dessarry
Mallaig to Eigg 1hr. 10mins.
Loch a' Ghille Ghobaich
NORTH
Lochan Stole
Ardnamurach
Lochan a' Mhàim
Beoraidbeg
Morar
Bracara
Kylesmorar
Sgurr Breac 2387
Tarbet
MORAR
Strathan
Glenancross
Camusdarach (An Camus Darach)
The Jacobite
Loch Morar
Carn Mòr 2718
River Pean
Glen Pean
Lòn Liath
B8008
Portnaluchaig
Bunacaimb
SOUTH MORAR
An Stac 2356
Sgurr nan Coireachan 3136
Sgurr Thuilm 3164
Allt Cuirnean
Eilean Ighe
Back of Keppoch (Cul na Caepaich)
Kinloid (Ceann an Leothaid)
Luinga Bheag
Loch nan Ceall
ARISAIG
Burn Sidhean Mòr 1970
Beinn nan Cabar 1888
River Meoble
Meith Bheinn 2328
Lochan a' Bhrodainn
Sgurr an Ursainn
Lochan Tain Mhic Dhughaill
Luinga Mhor
Arisaig (Arasaig)
Loch nan Eala
Borrodale
Glen Beasdale
Gleann Màma
Creag Bhàn 1675
Loch Beoraid
Sgurr an Utha 2610
Glen Finnan
River Finnan
Gleann Dubh Lighe
Gleann Fionnlighe
Land, Sea and Islands Centre
Glen Cottage
Drumindarroch
Loch na Creige Duibhe
Slios Garbh
Glas-charn 2076
Rubh' Arisaig
Prince's Cairn
Polnish
Eilean a' Ghaill
Camas Ghaoideil
Loch nan Uamh
A830
Lochailort (Ceann Loch Ailleart)
Ranochan
Station
Viaduct
Eilean an t-Snidhe
Sound of Arisaig
Loch Doire a' Ghearrain
Loch Ailort
Loch Eilt
The Jacobite
Glenfinnan
Dubh Lighe
Fionn Lighe
Eilean nan Gobhar
Inverailort
Glenfinnan Monument
A830
Kinlocheil
Samalaman Island
Glenuig Bay
140
Roshven
A861
ROIS-BHEINN 2895
Druim Fiaclach 2852
Beinn Odhar Bheag 2895
Callop River
Samalaman
Smirisary
Glenuig (Gleann Uige)
Croit Bheinn 2175
Loch Shiel
Rubh' Aird an Fheidh
Loch na Bairness
Lochan na Cloiche Sgoilte
Sgurr Dhomhnuill Mòr
River Moidart
Beinn Gàire
Meall nan Creag Leac
Sgorr Craobh a' Chaorainn
Glen Garvan
1
2
3
4
5

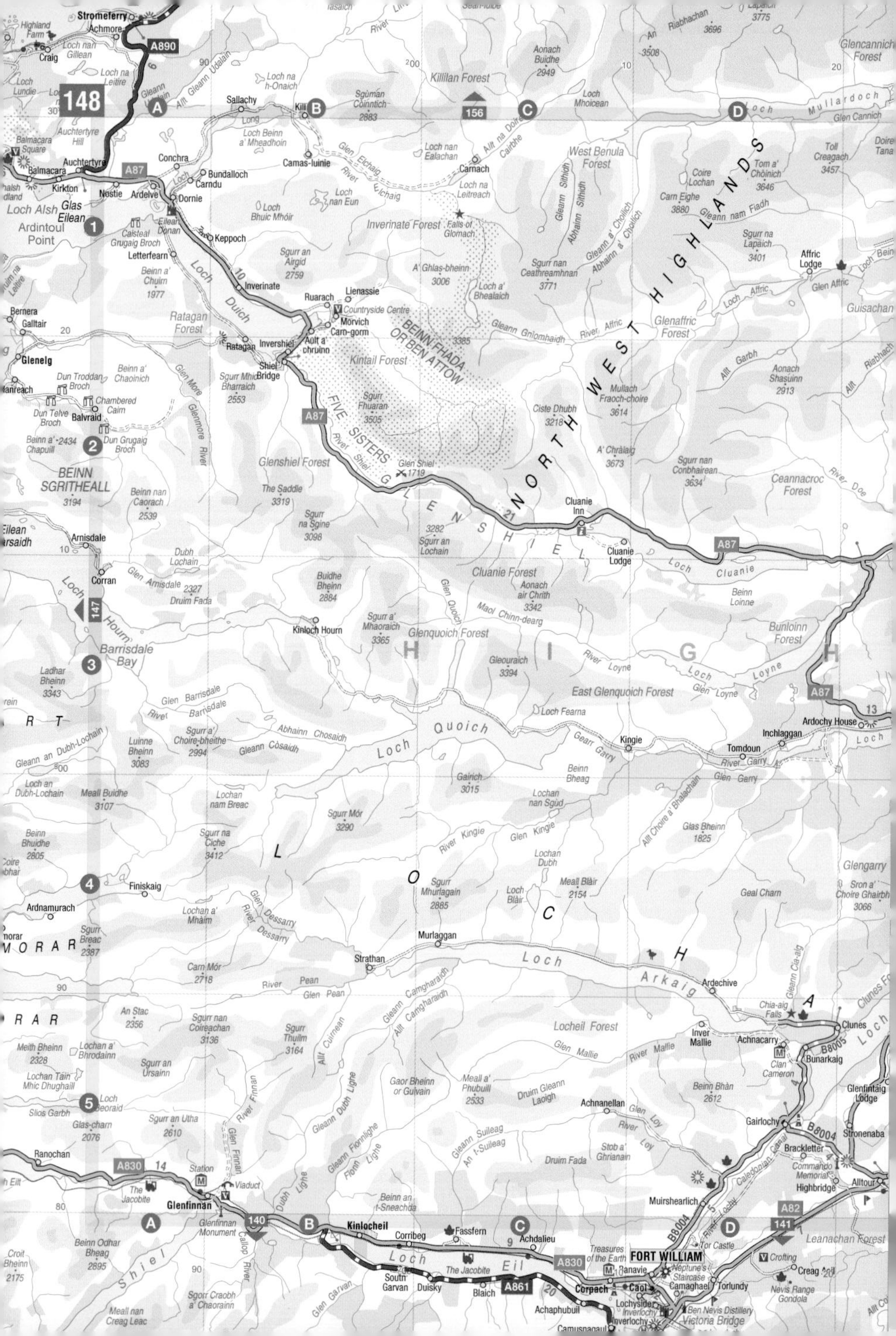

148
Stromeferry
Achmore
A890
Highland Farm
Craig
Loch nan Gillean
Loch na Leitire
Loch Lundie
Gleann Udalain
Allt Gleann Udalain
Loch na h-Onaich
Sallachy
Long
Kill
Loch Beinn a' Mheadhoin
Camas-luinie
Auchtertyre Hill
Balmacara Square
Conchra
Bundalloch
Carndu
Auchtertyre
Balmacara
Kirkton
Nostie
Ardelve
Dornie
A87
Loch Alsh
Glas Eilean
Ardintoul Point
Eilean Donan
Caisteal Grugaig Broch
Keppoch
Letterfearn
Loch nan Eun
Loch Bhuic Mhòir
Beinn a' Chuirn
1977
Loch Duich
Invérinate
Sgurr an Airgid
2759
Ruarach
Lienassie
Countryside Centre
Morvich
Carn-gorm
Aultʼ a' chruinn
Invershiel
Shiel Bridge
Ratagan
Ratagan Forest
Bernera
Galltair
Glenelg
Beinn a' Chaoinich
Dun Troddan Broch
Chambered Cairn
Dun Telve Broch
Balvraid
Dun Grugaig Broch
Beinn a' Chapuill
2434
Glen More
Glenmore River
Sgurr Mhic Bharraich
2553
BEINN SGRITHEALL
3194
Beinn nan Caorach
2539
Glenshiel Forest
The Saddle
3319
Sgurr na Sgine
3098
Arnisdale
Corran
Dubh Lochain
Glen Arnisdale
2327
Druim Fada
Loch Hourn
147
Barrisdale Bay
Ladhar Bheinn
3343
Kinloch Hourn
Buidhe Bheinn
2884
Sgurr a' Mhaoraich
3365
Glen Barrisdale
River Barrisdale
Sgurr a' Choire-bheithe
2994
Gleann Còsaidh
Abhainn Chosaidh
Luinne Bheinn
3083
Gleann an Dubh-Lochain
Loch an Dubh-Lochain
Meall Buidhe
3107
Beinn Bhuidhe
2805
Lochan nam Breac
Sgurr Mòr
3290
Sgurr na Ciche
3412
Finiskaig
Ardnamurach
MORAR
Sgurr Breac
2387
Lochan a' Mhàim
Glen Dessarry
River Dessarry
Carn Mòr
2718
River Pean
Glen Pean
An Stac
2356
Sgurr nan Coireachan
3136
Meith Bheinn
2328
Lochan a' Bhrodainn
Lochan Tain Mhic Dhughaill
Sgurr an Ursainn
Loch Beoraid
Slios Garbh
Glas-charn
2076
Sgurr an Utha
2610
Ranochan
A830
Station
Viaduct
The Jacobite
Glenfinnan
Glenfinnan Monument
140
Callop River
Beinn Odhar Bheag
2895
Croit Bheinn
2175
Loch Shiel
Sgorr Craobh a' Chaorainn
Meall nan Creag Leac
Tasaich
River Ling
Sgurr na Feartaig
Lapaich
3775
An Riabhachan
3696
An Socach
3508
Aonach Buidhe
2949
Killilan Forest
Glencannich Forest
Sgùman Coinntich
2883
156
Loch Mhoicean
Loch Mullardoch
Glen Cannich
Loch nan Ealachan
Allt na Doire Gairbhe
Carnach
Glen Elchaig
River Elchaig
Loch na Leitreach
West Benula Forest
Gleann Sithidh
Abhainn Sithidh
Coire Lochan
Carn Eighe
3880
Tom a' Chòinich
3646
Toll Creagach
3457
Gleann nam Fiadh
Falls of Glomach
Inverinate Forest
Gleann a' Chòilich
Abhainn a' Chòilich
Sgurr nan Ceathreamhnan
3771
Sgurr na Lapaich
3401
Affric Lodge
Glen Affric
Loch Affric
Guisachan
A' Ghlas-bheinn
3006
Loch a' Bhealaich
NORTH WEST HIGHLANDS
BEINN FHADA OR BEN ATTOW
3385
Gleann Gniomhaidh
River Affric
Glenaffric Forest
Kintail Forest
Allt Garbh
Aonach Shasuinn
2913
Allt Riabhach
Sgurr Fhuaran
3505
FIVE SISTERS
Mullach Fraoch-choire
3614
Ciste Dhubh
3218
A' Chràlaig
3673
Sgurr nan Conbhairean
3634
Ceannacroc Forest
River Doe
River Shiel
Glen Shiel
1719
GLEN SHIEL
Cluanie Inn
Cluanie Lodge
Loch Cluanie
3282
Sgurr an Lochain
Cluanie Forest
Aonach air Chrith
3342
Glen Quoich
Maol Chinn-dearg
Beinn Loinne
Bunloinn Forest
Glenquoich Forest
HIGH
Gleouraich
3394
River Loyne
Loch Loyne
Glen Loyne
East Glenquoich Forest
Loch Fearna
Loch Quoich
Gearr Garry
Kingie
Ardochy House
13
Inchlaggan
Tomdoun
River Garry
Glen Garry
Beinn Bheag
Gairich
3015
Lochan nan Sgùd
River Kingie
Glen Kingie
Allt Choire a' Bhalachain
Glas Bheinn
1825
Lochan Dubh
LOCH
Sgurr Mhurlagain
2885
Loch Blàir
Meall Blàir
2154
Geal Charn
Glengarry
Sron a' Choire Ghairbh
3066
Murlaggan
Strathan
Loch Arkaig
Ardechive
Gleann Cia-aig
Chia-aig Falls
LOCHABER
Clunes
Clunes Forest
Gleann Camgharaidh
Allt Camgharaidh
Allt Cuirnean
Sgurr Thuilm
3164
Locheil Forest
Inver Mallie
Achnacarry
Clan Cameron
B8005
Bunarkaig
Glen Mallie
River Mallie
Gaor Bheinn or Gulvain
Meall a' Phubuill
2533
Druim Gleann Laoigh
Beinn Bhàn
2612
Glenfintaig Lodge
River Finnan
Glen Finnan
Gleann Dubh Lighe
Gleann Fionnlighe
Fionn Lighe
Dubh Lighe
Gleann Suileag
An t-Suileag
Achnanellan
Glen Loy
River Loy
Stob a' Ghrianain
Druim Fada
Gairlochy
B8004
Stronenaba
Brackletter
Commando Memorial
Highbridge
Alltour
Caledonian Canal
Beinn an t-Sneachda
Muirshearlich
B8004
River Lochy
A82
141
Leanachan Forest
Kinlochiel
Corribeg
Fassfern
Achdalieu
Treasures of the Earth
FORT WILLIAM
Tor Castle
Loch Eil
The Jacobite
A830
Banavie
Neptune's Staircase
Crofting
Creag Aoil
South Garvan
Duisky
Blaich
A861
Corpach
Caol
Camaghael
Torlundy
Nevis Range Gondola
Glen Garvan
Achaphubuil
Lochyside
Inverlochy
Ben Nevis Distillery
Camusnagaul
Victoria Bridge

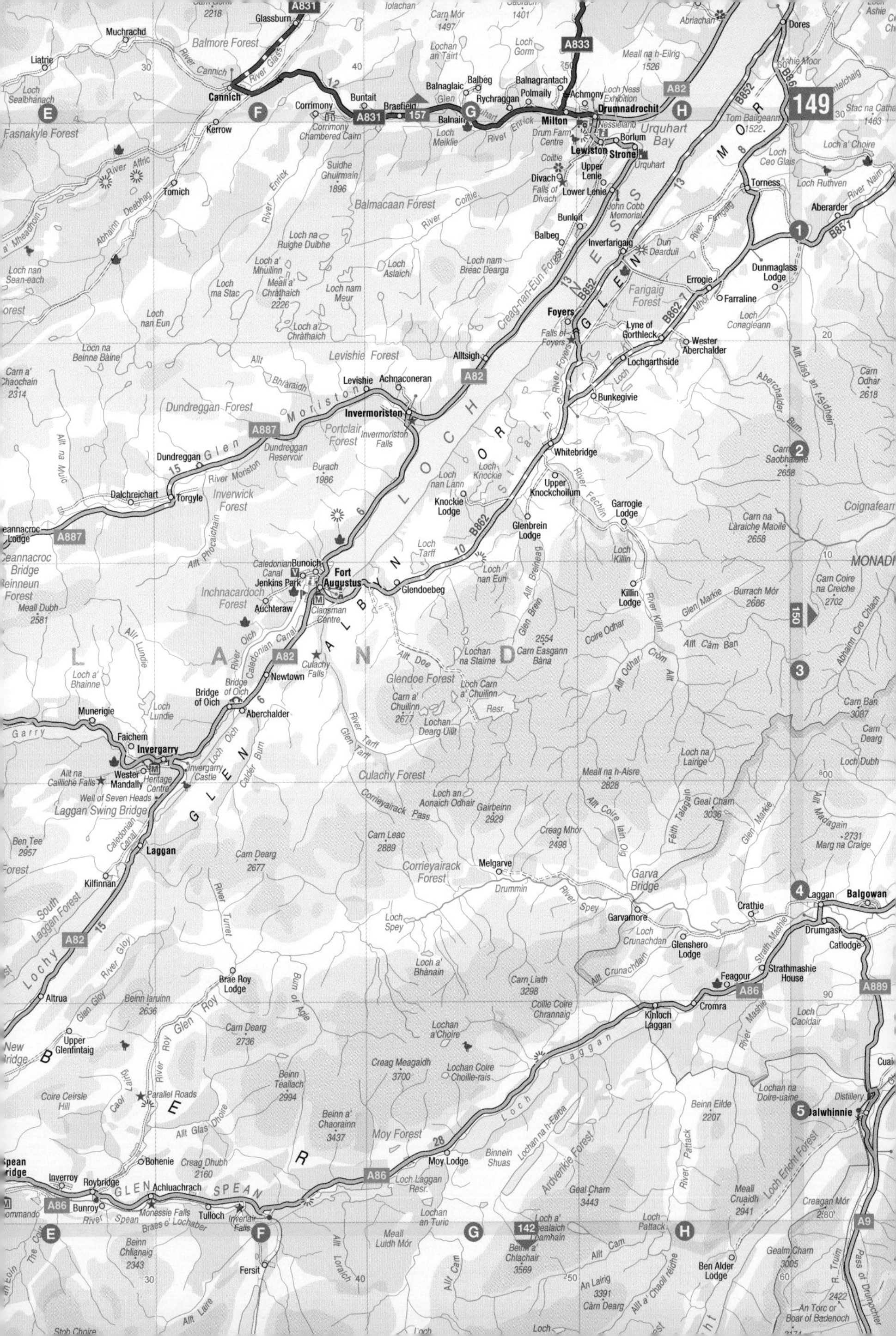
149
150
142
157
A831
A833
A82
A887
A86
A889
A9
B852
B862
B851
B857
Glassburn
Muchrachd
Balmore Forest
Liatrie
River Cannich
River Glass
Cannich
Kerrow
Loch Sealbhanach
Fasnakyle Forest
River Affric
Tomich
Abhainn Deabhag
Loch nan Sean-each
Corrimony
Corrimony Chambered Cairn
Buntait
Braefield
Balnain
Balnaglaic
Balbeg
Glen Urquhart
Loch Meiklie
River Enrick
Balnagrantach
Polmaily
Rychraggan
Achmony
Loch Ness Exhibition
Drumnadrochit
Milton
Nessieland
Drum Farm Centre
Lewiston
Strone
Borlum
Urquhart Bay
Urquhart
Coiltie
Divach
Falls of Divach
Upper Lenie
Lower Lenie
John Cobb Memorial
Bunloit
Balbeg
Inverfarigaig
Dun Deardail
Abriachan
Dores
Ashie Moor
Meall na h-Eilrig 1526
Tom Baileganm 1522
Loch Ceo Glais
Torness
Loch Ruthven
Loch a' Choire
Aberarder
River Nairn
Stac na Cathaig 1483
Dunmaglass Lodge
Errogie
Farraline
Farigaig Forest
Loch Conagleann
Lyne of Gorthleck
Wester Aberchalder
Lochgarthside
Bunkegivie
Foyers
Falls of Foyers
River Foyers
Alltsigh
Creag-nan-Eun Forest
Suidhe Ghuirmain 1896
Balmacaan Forest
River Coiltie
Loch na Ruighe Duibhe
Loch a' Mhuilinn
Meall a' Chràthaich 2226
Loch Aslaich
Loch nam Breac Dearga
Loch nam Meur
Loch ma Stac
Loch nan Eun
Loch a' Chràthaich
Loch na Beinne Bàine
Carn a' Chaochain 2314
Levishie Forest
Levishie
Achnaconeran
Invermoriston
Invermoriston Falls
Glen Moriston
Dundreggan Forest
Dundreggan
Dundreggan Reservoir
River Moriston
Portclair Forest
Burach 1986
Dalchreichart
Torgyle
Inverwick Forest
Allt na Muic
Ceannacroc Lodge
Ceannacroc Bridge
Beinneun Forest
Meall Dubh 2581
Allt Phocaichain
LOCH NESS
GLEN MOR
Whitebridge
Strath Errick
Loch Knockie
Loch nan Lann
Knockie Lodge
Upper Knockchoilum
River Fechlin
Glenbrein Lodge
Garrogie Lodge
Loch Killin
Killin Lodge
River Killin
Loch Tarff
Loch nan Eun
Caledonian Canal
Bunoich
Jenkins Park
Fort Augustus
Glendoebeg
Inchnacardoch Forest
Auchteraw
Clansman Centre
Allt Breineag
Glen Brein
Carn Easgann Bàna 2554
Coire Odhar
Glen Markie
Burrach Mór 2686
Carn Coire na Creiche 2702
Allt Càm Ban
Abhainn Cro Chlach
Carn Saobhaidhe 2658
Carn na Làraiche Maoile 2658
Coignafearn
MONADHLIATH
Carn Odhar 2618
Allt Uisg an t-Sidhein
Aberchalder Burn
Allt Lundie
Loch a' Bhainne
LAND
River Oich
Culachy Falls
Newtown
Bridge of Oich
Aberchalder
Loch Lundie
Munerigie
Faichem
Invergarry
Glen Garry
Allt na Cailliche Falls
Wester Mandally
Heritage Centre
Invergarry Castle
Well of Seven Heads
Laggan Swing Bridge
Loch Oich
Calder Burn
Allt Doe
Glendoe Forest
Lochan na Stairne
Loch Carn a' Chuilinn
Resr.
Carn a' Chuilinn 2677
Lochan Dearg Uillt
River Tarff
Glen Tarff
Culachy Forest
Corrieyairack Pass
Loch an Aonaich Odhair
Gairbeinn 2929
Meall na h-Aisre 2828
Allt Coire Iain Oig
Creag Mhór 2498
Carn Leac 2889
Corrieyairack Forest
Melgarve
Drummin
River Spey
Garva Bridge
Garvamore
Fèith Talagain
Geal Charn 3036
Loch na Lairige
Allt Odhar
Allt Crom
Carn Ban 3087
Carn Dearg
Loch Dubh
Allt Madagain
Marg na Craige 2731
Ben Tee 2957
Laggan
Kilfinnan
South Laggan Forest
Loch Lochy
Carn Dearg 2677
River Turret
Loch Spey
Laggan
Balgowan
Crathie
Drumgask
Catlodge
Loch Crunachdan
Glenshero Lodge
Allt Crunachdain
Strath Mashie
Strathmashie House
Feagour
Cromra
Kinloch Laggan
River Mashie
Loch Caoldair
River Gloy
Brae Roy Lodge
Burn of Agie
Loch a' Bhànain
Carn Liath 3298
Coille Coire Chrannaig
Altrua
Glen Gloy
Beinn Iaruinn 2636
Glen Roy
River Roy
Carn Dearg 2736
Lochan a' Choire
Upper Glenfintaig
New Bridge
BEN NEVIS
Caol Lairig
Coire Ceirsle Hill
Parallel Roads
Allt Glas Dhoire
Beinn Teallach 2994
Creag Meagaidh 3700
Lochan Coire Choille-rais
Beinn a' Chaorainn 3437
Moy Forest
Loch Laggan
Lochan na h-Earba
Ardverikie Forest
Beinn Eilde 2207
Lochan na Doire-uaine
Distillery
Dalwhinnie
Loch Ericht Forest
River Pattack
Bohenie
Creag Dhubh 2160
Moy Lodge
Binnein Shuas
Spean Bridge
Inverroy
Roybridge
Glen Spean
Achluachrach
Bunroy
Monessie Falls
Tulloch
Inverlair Falls
River Spean
Braes o' Lochaber
Commando
Loch Laggan Resr.
Lochan an Turic
Geal Charn 3443
Loch a' Bhealaich Leamhain
Loch Pattack
Meall Cruaidh 2941
Creagan Mór 2780
Beinn Chlianaig 2343
Fersit
Meall Luidh Mór
Allt Loraich
Beinn a' Chlachair 3569
Allt Cam
An Lairig 3391
Càrn Dearg
Allt a' Chaoil-réidhe
Ben Alder Lodge
Gealm Charn 3005
R. Truim
Pass of Drumochter
An Torc or Boar of Badenoch 2422
Stob Choire
Allt Laire

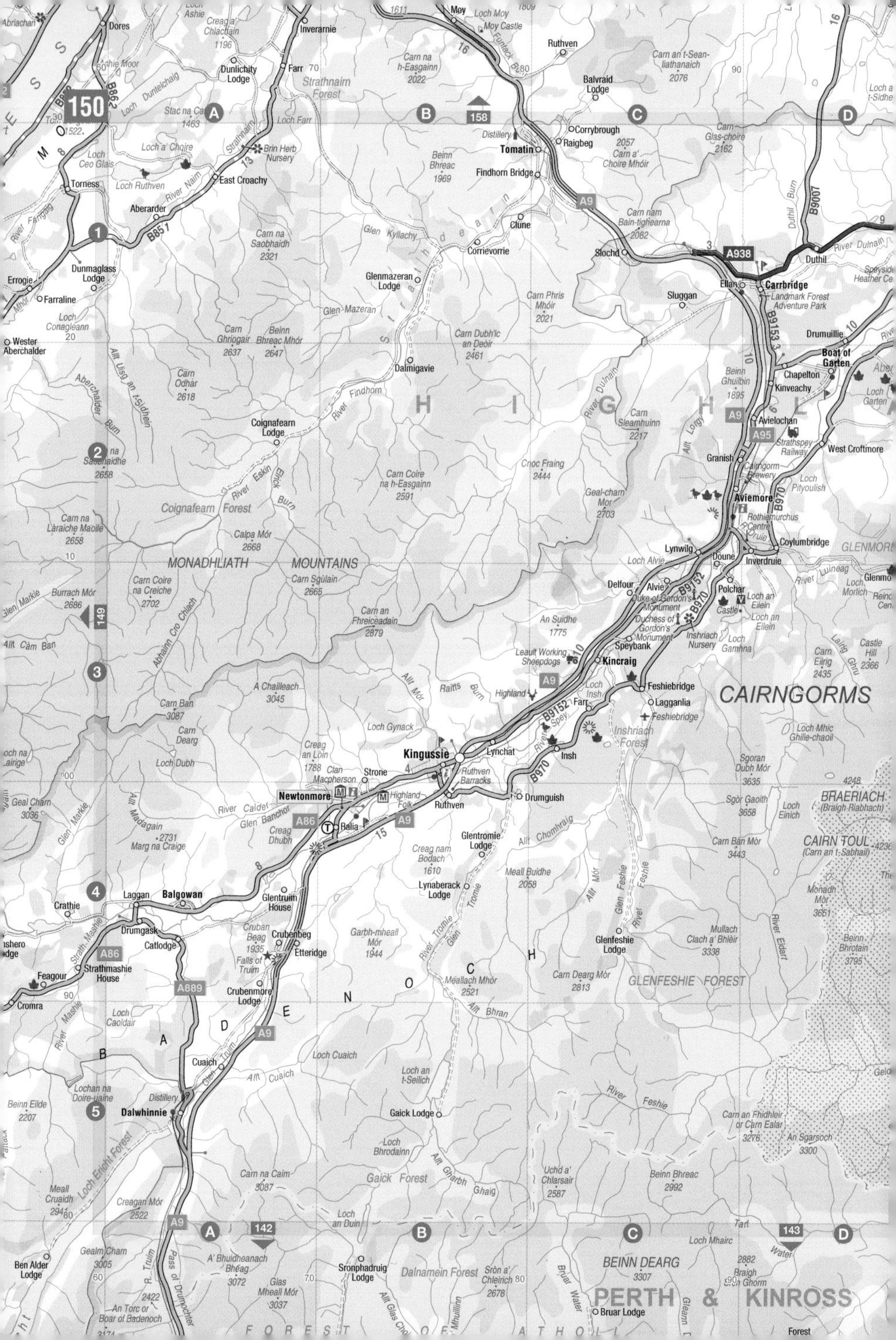
Dores
Inverarnie
Moy
Loch Moy
Moy Castle
Ruthven
Creag a' Chlachain
1196
Dunlichity Lodge
Farr
Carn na h-Easgainn
2022
Strathnairn Forest
Balvraid Lodge
Carn an t-Sean-liathanaich
2076
Ashie Moor
Loch Duntelchaig
Stac na Cailleach
1463
Loch Farr
158
Corrybrough
Raigbeg
Distillery
Tomatin
2057
Carn a' Choire Mhóir
Carn Glas-choire
2162
Loch a' Choire
Brin Herb Nursery
Loch Ceo Glais
Torness
Loch Ruthven
East Croachy
River Nairn
Beinn Bhreac
1969
Findhorn Bridge
Aberarder
B857
B862
Glen Kyllachy
Clune
Carn na Saobhaidh
2321
Corrievorrie
Carn nam Bain-tighearna
2082
Slochd
A938
Duthil
River Dulnain
B9007
Dunmaglass Lodge
Errogie
Farraline
Loch Conagleann
Glenmazeran Lodge
Glen Mazeran
Carn Phris Mhóir
2021
Sluggan
Ellan
Carrbridge
Landmark Forest Adventure Park
B9153
Drumuillie
Boat of Garten
Wester Aberchalder
Carn Ghriogair
2637
Beinn Bhreac Mhór
2647
Carn Dubh'Ic an Deòir
2461
Dalmigavie
River Findhorn
Carn Odhar
2618
Allt Uisg an t-Sìdhein
Aberchalder Burn
Beinn Ghuilbin
1895
Chapelton
Kinveachy
Loch Garten
H I G H L A N D
Coignafearn Lodge
Carn Sleamhuinn
2217
A9
Avielochan
A95
Strathspey Railway
West Croftmore
Carn na Saobhaidhe
2658
River Eskin
Elrick Burn
Carn Coire na h-Easgainn
2591
Cnoc Fraing
2444
Allt Lorgy
Granish
Cairngorm Brewery
Loch Pityoulish
Coignafearn Forest
Geal-charn Mor
2703
Aviemore
Rothiemurchus Centre
B970
Carn na Làraiche Maoile
2658
Calpa Mór
2668
Lynwilg
Coylumbridge
GLENMORE
MONADHLIATH MOUNTAINS
Loch Alvie
Doune
Inverdruie
River Luineag
Carn Sgùlain
2665
Burrach Mór
2686
Carn Coire na Creiche
2702
Delfour
Alvie
Duke of Gordon's Monument
B9152
Polchar
Loch an Eilein
Castle
Loch Morlich
Glen Markie
Abhainn Cro Chlach
Carn an Fhreiceadain
2879
An Suidhe
1775
Duchess of Gordon's Monument
Speybank
Inshriach Nursery
Loch Gamhna
149
Allt Càm Ban
Leault Working Sheepdogs
Kincraig
Carn Eilrig
2435
Castle Hill
2366
Lairig Ghru
A Chailleach
3045
Allt Mór
Raitts Burn
Highland
Loch Insh
Feshiebridge
CAIRNGORMS
Carn Ban
3087
Farr
Lagganlia
Feshiebridge
Carn Dearg
Loch Gynack
River Spey
Insh
Inshriach Forest
Loch Mhic Ghille-chaoil
Creag an Loin
1788
Kingussie
Lynchat
Loch Dubh
Clan Macpherson
Strone
Ruthven Barracks
Sgoran Dubh Mór
3635
Geal Charn
3036
Newtonmore
Highland Folk
Ruthven
Drumguish
4248
BRAERIACH
(Braigh Riabhach)
River Calder
Glen Banchor
Sgòr Gaoith
3658
Loch Einich
A86
Balia
Creag Dhubh
Glentromie Lodge
Allt Chomhraig
Allt Madagain
2731
Marg na Craige
Creag nam Bodach
1610
Carn Bàn Mòr
3443
CAIRN TOUL
(Carn an t-Sabhail)
Meall Buidhe
2058
Monadh Mór
3651
Laggan
Balgowan
Glentruim House
Lynaberack Lodge
Crathie
Drumgask
Catlodge
Cruban Beag
1935
Crubenbeg
Etteridge
Garbh-mheall Mór
1944
River Tromie
Glen Tromie
Glen Feshie
River Feshie
Glenfeshie Lodge
Mullach Clach a' Bhlèir
3338
River Eidart
Beinn Bhrotain
3795
Strath Mashie
Falls of Truim
Feagour
Strathmashie House
A889
Crubenmore Lodge
B A D E N O C H
Meallach Mhór
2521
Carn Dearg Mòr
2813
GLENFESHIE FOREST
Cromra
River Mashie
Loch Caoldair
Allt Bhran
Cuaich
Glen Truim
Loch Cuaich
Allt Cuaich
Loch an t-Seilich
Lochan na Doire-uaine
Beinn Eilde
2207
Distillery
Dalwhinnie
River Feshie
Gaick Lodge
Carn an Fhidhleir or Carn Ealar
3276
An Sgarsoch
3300
Loch Ericht Forest
Loch Bhrodainn
Allt Gharbh Ghaig
Meall Cruaidh
2940
Carn na Caim
3087
Gaick Forest
Uchd a' Chlarsair
2587
Beinn Bhreac
2992
Creagan Mór
2522
Loch an Duin
142
Tarf Water
143
Loch Mhairc
Ben Alder Lodge
Gealm Cham
3005
A' Bhuidheanach Bheag
3072
Sronphadruig Lodge
Dalnamein Forest
Sròn a' Chleirich
2678
BEINN DEARG
3307
2882
Braigh Sron Ghorm
R. Truim
Pass of Drumochter
Glas Mheall Mór
3037
Allt Glas Choire
Bruar Water
PERTH & KINROSS
2422
An Torc or Boar of Badenoch
Bruar Lodge
FOREST OF ATHOLL
Forest

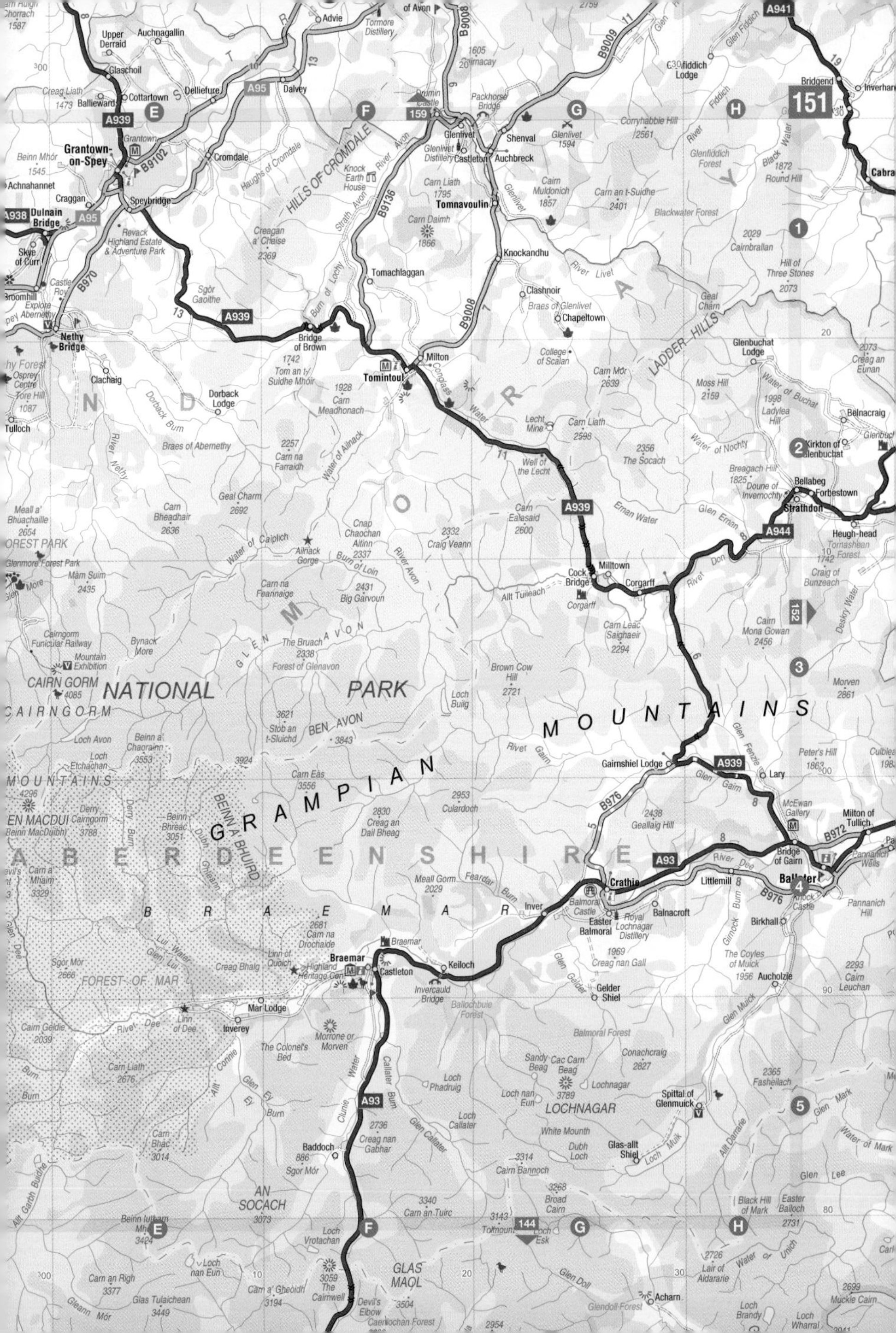

Carn Ruigh Chorrach 1587
Upper Derraid
Auchnagallin
Advie
Tormore Distillery
of Avon
B9008
B9009
A941
Glaschoil
Creag Liath 1473
Balliewards
Cottartown
Dellifure
A95
Dalvey
1605 Carn Ilmacay
Drumin Castle
Packhorse Bridge
Glenfiddich Lodge
Bridgend
151
E
F
G
H
Grantown
Grantown-on-Spey
Beinn Mhór 1545
B9102
Cromdale
HILLS OF CROMDALE
Haughs of Cromdale
159
Glenlivet
Glenlivet Distillery
Castleton
Auchbreck
Shenval
Glenlivet 1594
Corryhabbie Hill 2561
Glenfiddich Forest
River Fiddich
Black Water
1872 Round Hill
Craggan
Speybridge
A938
Dulnain Bridge
A95
Knock Earth House
River Avon
Carn Liath 1795
Tomnavoulin
Cairn Muldonich 1857
Carn an t-Suidhe 2401
Blackwater Forest
B9136
Strath Avon
Carn Daimh 1866
Revack Highland Estate & Adventure Park
Creagan a' Chaise 2369
Knockandhu
River Livet
2029 Cairnbrallan
1
Hill of Three Stones 2073
Skye of Curr
B970
Castle Roy
Tomachlaggan
Clashnoir
Broomhill
Explore Abernethy
Sgòr Gaoithe
Burn of Lochy
B9008
Braes of Glenlivet
Chapeltown
Geal Charn
LADDER HILLS
A939
13
Nethy Bridge
Bridge of Brown
Milton
College of Scalan
Glenbuchat Lodge
2073 Creag an Eunan
Abernethy Forest
Osprey Centre
Tore Hill 1087
Clachaig
1742 Tom an t-Suidhe Mhóir
Tomintoul
Conglass Water
Carn Mòr 2639
Moss Hill 2159
Water of Buchat
1998 Ladylea Hill
Belnacraig
Dorback Lodge
Dorback Burn
1928 Carn Meadhonach
Lecht Mine
Carn Liath 2598
Tulloch
River Nethy
Braes of Abernethy
2257 Carn na Farraidh
Water of Ailnack
Well of the Lecht
11
2356 The Socach
Water of Nochty
Kirkton of Glenbuchat
2
Breagach Hill 1825
Doune of Invernochty
Bellabeg
Forbestown
Strathdon
Meall a' Bhuachaille 2654
Carn Bheadhair 2636
Geal Charm 2692
Carn Ealasaid 2600
Ernan Water
Glen Ernan
A944
Heugh-head
Tornashean Forest
FOREST PARK
Glenmore Forest Park
Water of Caiplich
Ailnack Gorge
Cnap Chaochan Aitinn 2337
Burn of Loin
2332 Craig Veann
River Avon
Milltown
Cock Bridge
Corgarff
River Don
1742 Craig of Bunzeach
Glen More
Màm Suim 2435
Carn na Feannaige
2431 Big Garvoun
Allt Tuileach
Corgarff
Carn Leac Saighaeir 2294
152
Cairn Mona Gowan 2456
Deskry Water
Cairngorm Funicular Railway
Mountain Exhibition
Bynack More
GLEN AVON
The Bruach 2338
Forest of Glenavon
Brown Cow Hill 2721
3
Morven 2861
CAIRN GORM 4085
NATIONAL
PARK
Loch Builg
MOUNTAINS
CAIRNGORM
3621 Stob an t-Sluichd
BEN AVON 3843
Loch Avon
Beinn a' Chaorainn 3553
3924
Rivet Gairn
Gairnshiel Lodge
A939
Glen Fenzie
Glen Gairn
Lary
Peter's Hill 1863
MOUNTAINS 4296
Loch Etchachan
Carn Eàs 3556
GRAMPIAN
BEINN A' BHUIRD
2953 Culardoch
B976
2438 Geallaig Hill
McEwan Gallery
Milton of Tullich
B972
BEN MACDUI (Beinn MacDuibh)
Derry Cairngorm 3788
Beinn Bhreac 3051
Dubh Ghleann
2830 Creag an Dail Bheag
ABERDEENSHIRE
A93
Bridge of Gairn
River Dee
Littlemill
Devil's Point
Cairn a' Mhaim 3329
Meall Gorm 2029
Feardar Burn
Crathie
Balmoral Castle
B976
4
Knock Castle
BRAEMAR
Inver
Easter Balmoral
Royal Lochnagar Distillery
Balnacroft
Birkhall
Pannanich Hill
Glen Dee
2681 Carn na Drochaide
Braemar
Glen Gelder
1969 Creag nan Gall
Girnock Burn
The Coyles of Muick 1956
Aucholzie
Sgor Mòr 2666
Lui Water
Glen Lui
Creag Bhalg
Linn of Quoich
Highland Heritage Centre
Castleton
Keiloch
Invercauld Bridge
Gelder Shiel
2293 Cairn Leuchan
FOREST OF MAR
Mar Lodge
Linn of Dee
Ballochbuie Forest
Cairn Geldie 2039
River Dee
Inverey
Morrone or Morven
Balmoral Forest
Glen Muick
Carn Liath 2676
The Colonel's Bed
Allt Connie
Glen Ey
Callater Burn
Clunie Water
Sandy Beag
Cac Carn Beag
Loch Phadruig
Conachcraig 2827
3789
Lochnagar
2365 Fasheilach
Loch nan Eun
LOCHNAGAR
Spittal of Glenmuick
5
Glen Mark
A93
Loch Callater
Glen Callater
White Mounth
Water of Mark
Carn Bhac 3014
2736 Creag nan Gabhar
Baddoch 886
Sgor Mòr
Dubh Loch
Glas-allt Shiel
Loch Muick
Allt Darrarie
Glen Lee
3314
3268 Broad Cairn
Black Hill of Mark
Easter Balloch 2731
Allt Garbh Buidhe
AN SOCACH 3073
3340 Carn an Tuirc
3143
144
Loch Esk
Beinn Iutharn Mhor 3424
Loch Vrotachan
Loch nan Eun
2726 Lair of Aldararie
Water of Unich
Carn an Righ 3377
3059 The Cairnwell
GLAS MAOL
Glen Doll
Cairn a' Gheoidh 3194
Glas Tulaichean 3449
Gleann Mór
Devil's Elbow
3504
Caenlochan Forest
2954
Acharn
Glendoll Forest
Loch Brandy
Loch Wharral
2699

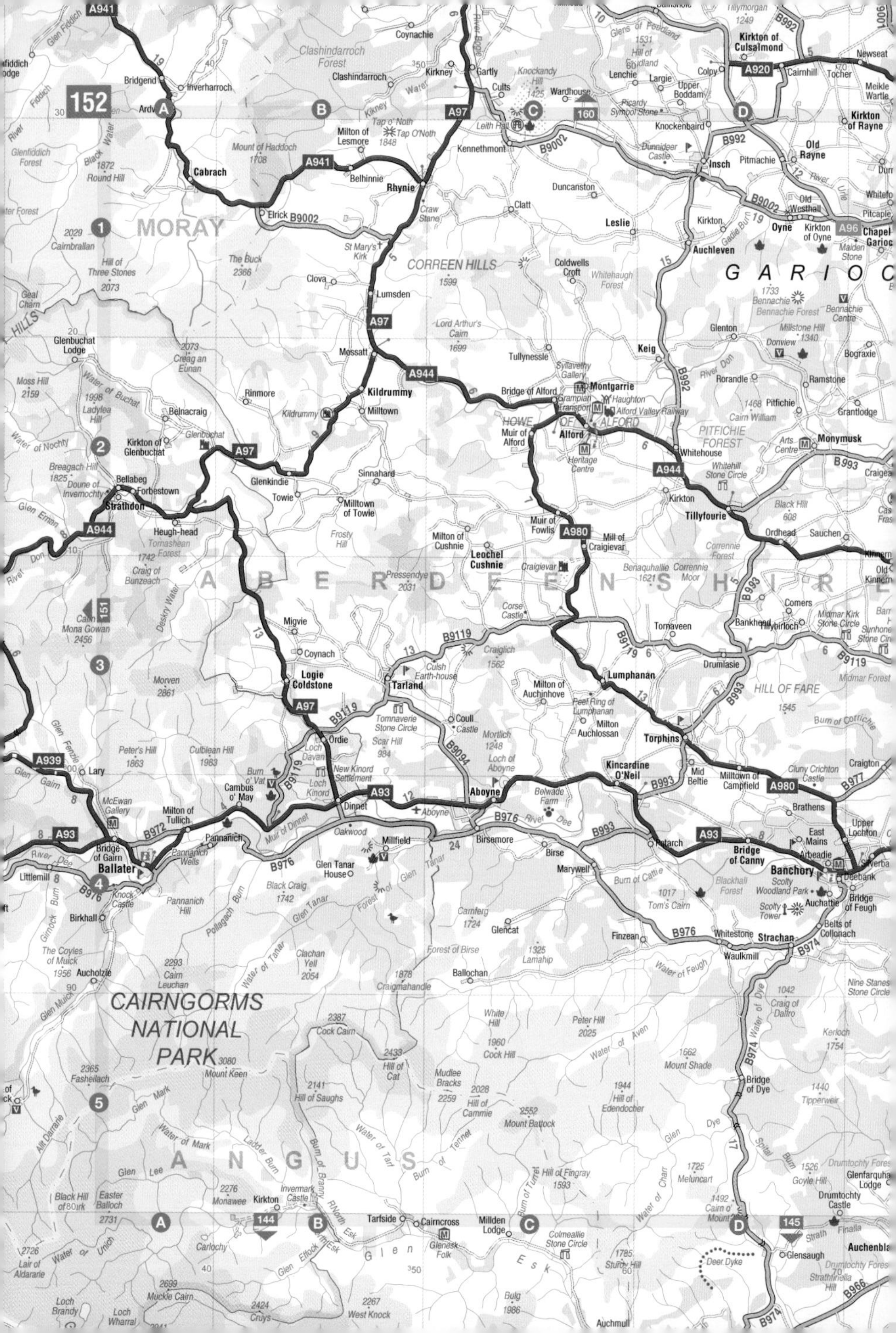
152
A941
Glen Fiddich
Bridgend
Inverharroch
Ardwell
Clashindarroch Forest
Coynachie
Clashindarroch
Kirkney
Gartly
Cults
Knockandy Hill 1425
Wardhouse
Leith Hall
160
Kennethmont
B9002
Milton of Lesmore
Tap o' Noth 1848
Mount of Haddoch 1708
Cabrach
Belhinnie
Rhynie
Craw Stane
Elrick
MORAY
Glenfiddich Forest
Black Water
1872 Round Hill
2029 Cairnbrallan
Hill of Three Stones 2073
The Buck 2366
St Mary's Kirk
CORREEN HILLS
1599
Clova
Lumsden
A97
Mossatt
Lord Arthur's Cairn 1699
Clatt
Leslie
Duncanston
Coldwells Croft
Whitehaugh Forest
Tullynessle
Glenbuchat Lodge
Creag an Eunan 2073
Moss Hill 2159
Water of Buchat
1998 Ladylea Hill
Rinmore
Belnacraig
Glenbuchat
Kildrummy
Milltown
Kirkton of Glenbuchat
Water of Nochty
Breagach Hill 1825
Doune of Invernochty
Bellabeg
Forbestown
Strathdon
Heugh-head
Tornashean Forest
A944
Glen Ernan
River Don
Glenkindie
Towie
Sinnahard
Milltown of Towie
Frosty Hill
1742 Craig of Bunzeach
Deskry Water
151
Cairn Mona Gowan 2456
Bridge of Alford
Montgarrie
Syllavethy Gallery
Grampian Transport
Haughton
Alford Valley Railway
HOWE OF ALFORD
Muir of Alford
Alford
Heritage Centre
Muir of Fowlis
A980
Mill of Craigievar
Milton of Cushnie
Leochel Cushnie
Craigievar
Pressendye 2031
ABERDEENSHIRE
Corse Castle
Benaquhallie 1621
Corrennie Moor
Correnie Forest
Migvie
Coynach
B9119
Craiglich 1562
Culsh Earth-house
Tarland
Logie Coldstone
Morven 2861
Tomnaverie Stone Circle
Coull Castle
Mortlich 1248
Loch of Aboyne
Milton of Auchinhove
Peel Ring of Lumphanan
Milton Auchlossan
Lumphanan
Tornaveen
Drumlasie
Ordie
Loch Davan
Scar Hill 984
New Kinord Settlement
Loch Kinord
Burn o' Vat
Cambus o' May
Culblean Hill 1983
Peter's Hill 1863
Glen Fenzie
A939
Lary
Glen Gairn
McEwan Gallery
Milton of Tullich
B972
Pannanich
Pannanich Wells
Bridge of Gairn
Ballater
A93
Muir of Dinnet
Dinnet
Oakwood
Aboyne
B976
Birsemore
Belwade Farm
River Dee
Kincardine O'Neil
B993
Birse
Marywell
Potarch
B9094
Millfield
Glen Tanar House
Black Craig 1742
Forest of Glen Tanar
Glen Tanar
Littlemill
Knock Castle
Birkhall
Gairnock Burn
Pannanich Hill
Pollagach Burn
The Coyles of Muick 1956
Aucholzie
Glen Muick
2293 Cairn Leuchan
Clachan Yell 2054
Water of Tanar
Carnferg 1724
Glencat
Forest of Birse
1325 Lamahip
Ballochan
1878 Craigmahandle
Burn of Cattie
1017 Tom's Cairn
Blackhall Forest
Finzean
Whitestone
Waulkmill
Strachan
Water of Feugh
CAIRNGORMS NATIONAL PARK
3080 Mount Keen
2387 Cock Cairn
2433 Hill of Cat
White Hill
1960 Cock Hill
Peter Hill 2025
Water of Aven
1662 Mount Shade
Mudlee Bracks 2259
2141 Hill of Saughs
2028 Hill of Cammie
2552 Mount Battock
1944 Hill of Edendocher
2365 Fasheilach
Glen Mark
Water of Mark
Ladder Burn
Burn of Branny
Water of Tarf
Burn of Tennet
ANGUS
Glen Lee
2276 Monawee
Kirkton
Invermark Castle
Hill of Fingray 1593
Burn of Turret
Water of Charr
1725 Meluncart
Glen Dye
Black Hill of Mark
Easter Balloch 2731
144
Tarfside
Cairncross
Glenesk Folk
Millden Lodge
Colmeallie Stone Circle
1785 Sturdy Hill
1492 Cairn o' Mount
145
Carlochy
Glen Effock
North Esk
Glen Esk
Water of Unich
2726 Lair of Aldararie
Allt Darrarie
2699 Muckle Cairn
2424 Cruys
2267 West Knock
Bulg 1986
Auchmull
Loch Brandy
Loch Wharral
Deer Dyke
Glensaugh
B974
B966
Kirkton of Culsalmond
A920
Colpy
Cairnhill
Tocher
Newseat
Meikle Wartle
Glens of Foudland
1531 Hill of Foudland
Lenchie
Largie
Upper Boddam
Picardy Symbol Stone
Knockenbaird
Dunnideer Castle
Insch
B992
Pitmachie
Old Rayne
Kirkton of Rayne
River Urie
B9002
Old Westhall
Kirkton
Oyne
Kirkton of Oyne
A96
Chapel of Garioch
Maiden Stone
Gadie Burn
Auchleven
GARIOCH
1733 Bennachie
Bennachie Forest
Bennachie Centre
Glenton
Millstone Hill 1340
Donview
Keig
Bograxie
River Don
Rorandle
Ramstone
1468 Pitfichie
Cairn William
Grantlodge
PITFICHIE FOREST
Whitehouse
Arts Centre
Monymusk
Whitehill Stone Circle
B993
Craigearn
Kirkton
Tillyfourie
Black Hill 608
Ordhead
Sauchen
Comers
Bankhead
Tillybirloch
Midmar Kirk Stone Circle
Sunhoney Stone Circle
Midmar Forest
HILL OF FARE
1545
Burn of Corrichie
Torphins
Mid Beltie
Milltown of Campfield
Cluny Crichton Castle
Craigton
B977
Brathens
Upper Lochton
East Mains
Bridge of Canny
Arbeadie
Banchory
Deebank
Scolty Woodland Park
Auchattie
Scolty Tower
Bridge of Feugh
Belts of Collonach
Nine Stanes Stone Circle
1042 Craig of Dalfro
Kerloch 1754
Water of Dye
Bridge of Dye
1440 Tipperweir
Spital Burn
1526 Goyle Hill
Drumtochty Forest
Glenfarquhar Lodge
Drumtochty Castle
Strath Finalla
Auchenblae
Strathfinella Hill

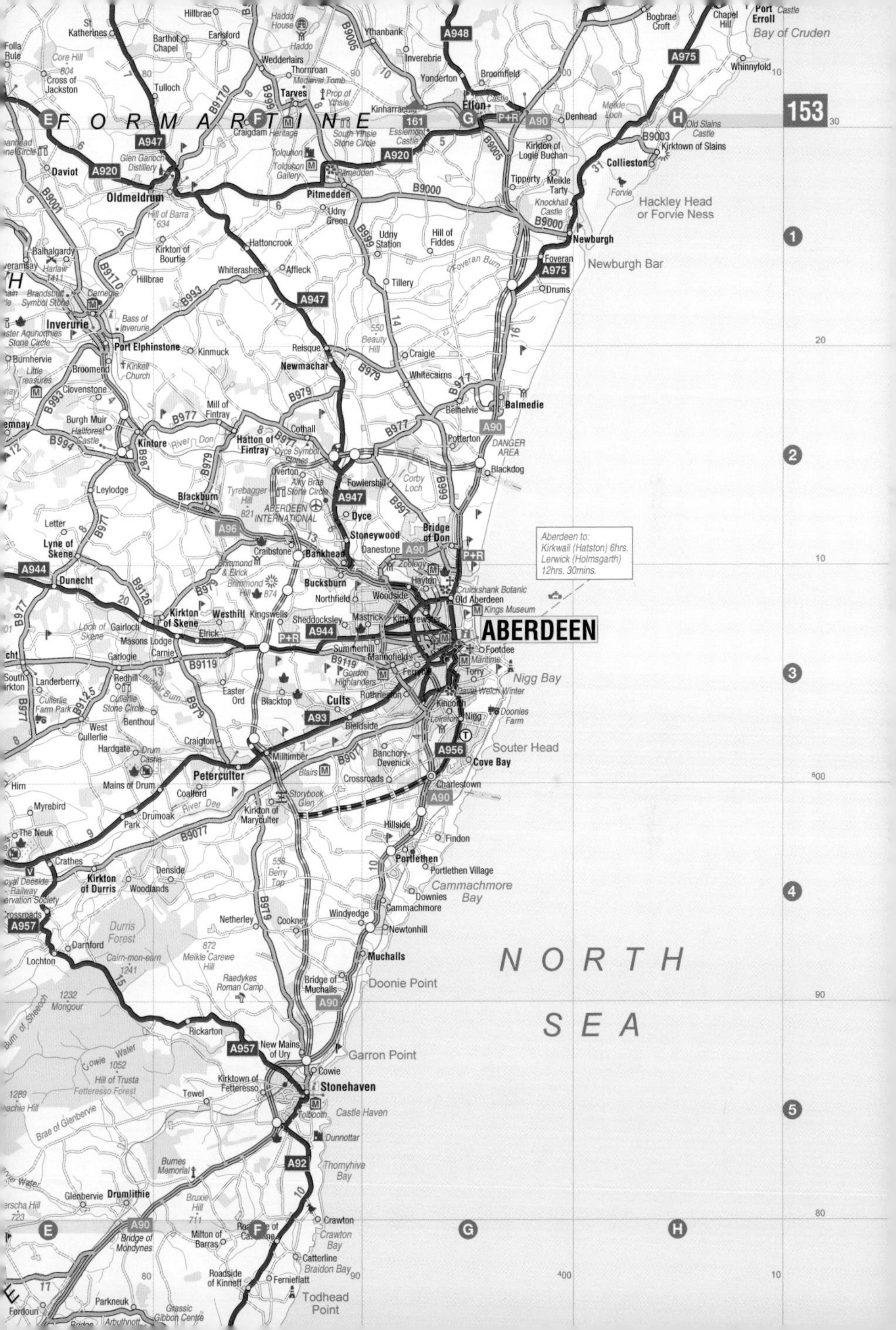

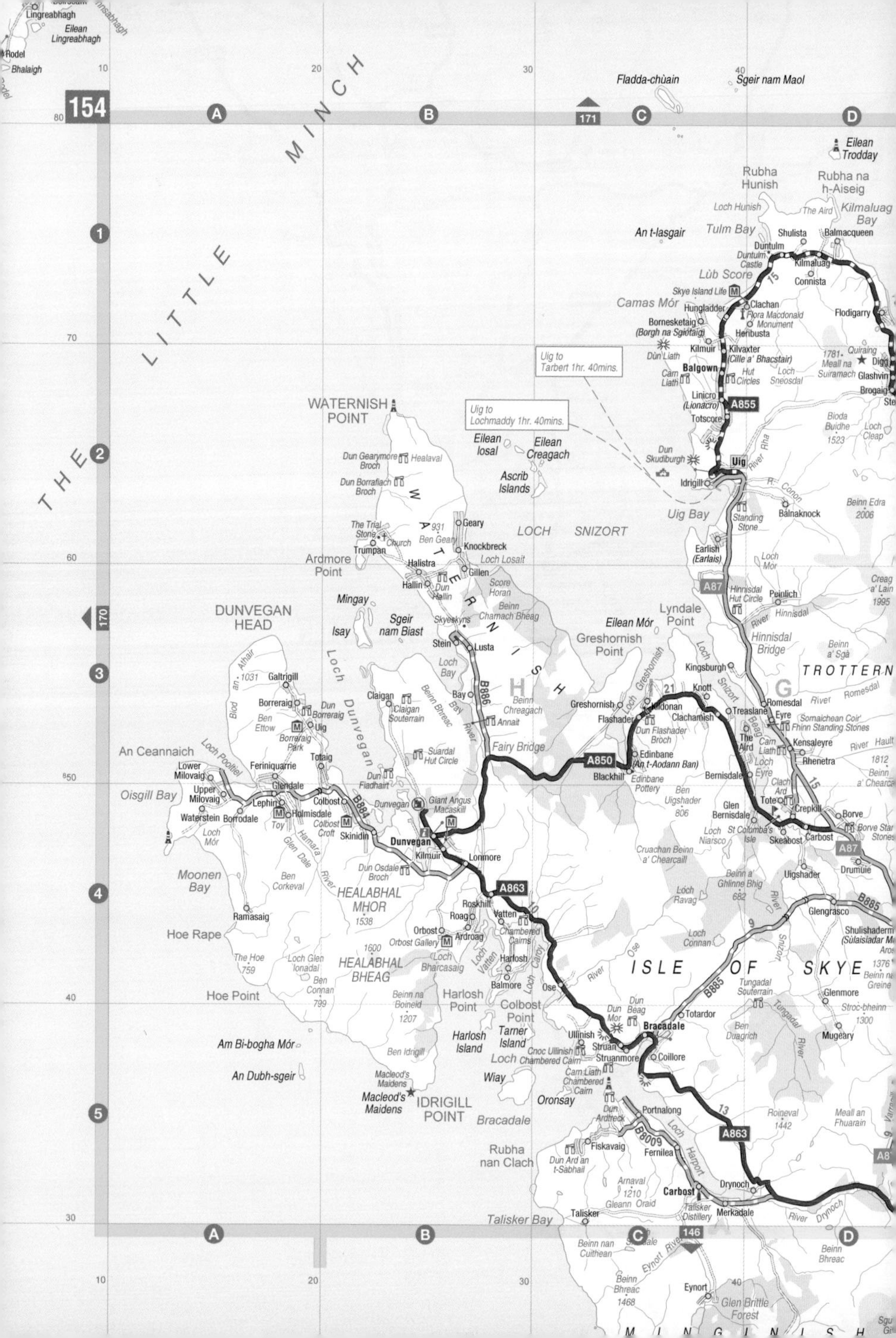

THE LITTLE MINCH

Fladda-chùain

Sgeir nam Maol

171

WATERNISH POINT

Rubha Hunish
Rubha na h-Aiseig

Eilean Trodday

Kilmaluag Bay

An t-Iasgair
Tulm Bay
The Aird
Loch Hunish
Shulista
Balmacqueen

Duntulm
Duntulm Castle
Kilmaluag
Connista

Lùb Score
Skye Island Life
Camas Mór
Hungladder
Bornesketaig
(Borgh na Sgùrtaig)
Flora Macdonald Monument
Clachan
Heribusta
Flodigarry

Kilmuir
Dùn Liath
Carn Liath
Kilvaxter
(Cille a' Bhacstair)
Balgown
Hut Circles
Loch Sneosdal
Quiraing
1781
Meall na Suiramach
Brogaig
Glashvin
Ste

Uig to Tarbert 1hr. 40mins.

Linicro
(Lionacro)
Totscore
A855
Bioda Buidhe 1523
Loch Cleap

Uig to Lochmaddy 1hr. 40mins.

Eilean Iosal
Eilean Creagach

Loch Skudiburgh
Idrigill

Uig

Benn Edra 2006

Ascrib Islands

Balnaknock

LOCH SNIZORT

Uig Bay
Standing Stone

Earlish (Earlais)
Loch Mór

WATERNISH

Dun Gearymore Broch
Healaval
Dun Borrafiach Broch

A87
Hinnisdal Hut Circle
Peinlich

Creag a' Lain 1995

The Trial Stone
Trumpan
Church
Ben Geary
931
Knockbreck
Geary
Score Horan
Benn Charnach Bheag

Lyndale Point
Hinnisdal
Benn a' Sga

Ardmore Point

Halistra
Hallin
Gillen
Loch Losait

Eilean Mór
Greshornish Point

Hinnisdal Bridge

Benn a' Chearcaill

Mingay
Isay
Sgeir nam Biast
Skyeskyns
Lusta

Kingsburgh
Knott

Romesdal
Eyre

TROTTERN

River Romesdal

DUNVEGAN HEAD

170

Stein
Loch Bay
Bay
Hallin

Greshornish
Flashader
Knott
Clachamish
Treaslane
The Aird
Cam Liath

Somaichean Coir'
Fhinn Standing Stones
Kensaleyre
1812

An Ceannaich

Galtrigill
Borreraig
Ben Ettow
Uig
Borreraig Park
Totaig

Dùn Borreraig
Claigan
Claigan Souterrain
B886
Benn Bhreac
Fairy Bridge
Suardal Hut Circle
Dun Flashader Broch
Edinbane
(An t-Aodann Bàn)
Edinbane Pottery
Bernisdale
Glen Eyre
Loch Eyre
Carn Ard
Crepkill

Rhenetra
River Haultin
Benn a' Chearca

Lower Milovaig
Upper Milovaig
Waterstein
Borrodale
Feriniquarrie
Dendale
Lephin
Colbost
Holmisdale
Toy
Skinidin
A850
Blackhill

Dun Fiadhairt

Giant Angus MacAskill

Dunvegan

Glen Bernisdale
Ben Uigshader
806
St Columba's Isle
Skeabost
Loch Snizort Beag
Borve
Borve Star Stones
Carbost
A87

Oisgill Bay
Loch Pooltiel
Colbost Croft
Kilmuir

Dùn Osdale Broch
Lonmore

Cruachan Beinn a' Chearcaill
Loch Ravag

Benn a' Ghlinne Bhig
682

Uligshader
Drumuie

Moonen Bay
Loch Mór

HEALABHAL MHOR
1538

Roskhill
A863
Vatten
Chambered Cairns

Ose
Loch Connan

B885

Ramasaig
Hoe Rape
The Hoe 759

HEALABHAL BHEAG
1600
Loch Glen Tonadal
Ben Connan 799

Orbost
Orbost Gallery
Roag
Harlosh
Ardroag

Loch Vatten
River Ose

ISLE OF SKYE

Glengrasco

Shulishaderin
(Sùlaisiadar Mò
Aro

Hoe Point
Harlosh Point

Balmore

Ose
Dun Beag
Dun Mor
Totardor

Benn Duagrich

Loch Duagrich

Glenmore
Stroc-bheinn
1300
Mugeary

Am Bì-bogha Mór

Ben Idrigill

Harlosh Island

Colbost Point
Tarner Island

Loch Bharcasaig
1207
Ben Idrigill

Ullinish
Struanlish
Struanmore
Bracadale
Coillore

Tungadal Souterrain

An Dubh-sgeir

Macleod's Maidens
Macleod's Maidens
IDRIGILL POINT

Croc Ullinish
Loch Chambered Cairn
Wiay
Oronsay
Dun Chambered Cairn
Dun Ardtreck
Portnalong

Roineval
1442
Meall an Fhuarain

A8

Bracadale

Rubha nan Clach

Fiskavaig
Fernilea
B8009
Carbost

13
A863

Talisker Distillery
Merkadale
River Drynoch

Arnaval
1210
Dun Ard an t-Sàbhal
Gleann Oraid

Drynoch

Rubha Dunan

Carbost

Talisker

Talisker Bay

146

Beinn nan Cuithean

Beinn Bhreac
1468

Eynort

Beinn Breac

A8

MINGINISH

Glen Brittle Forest

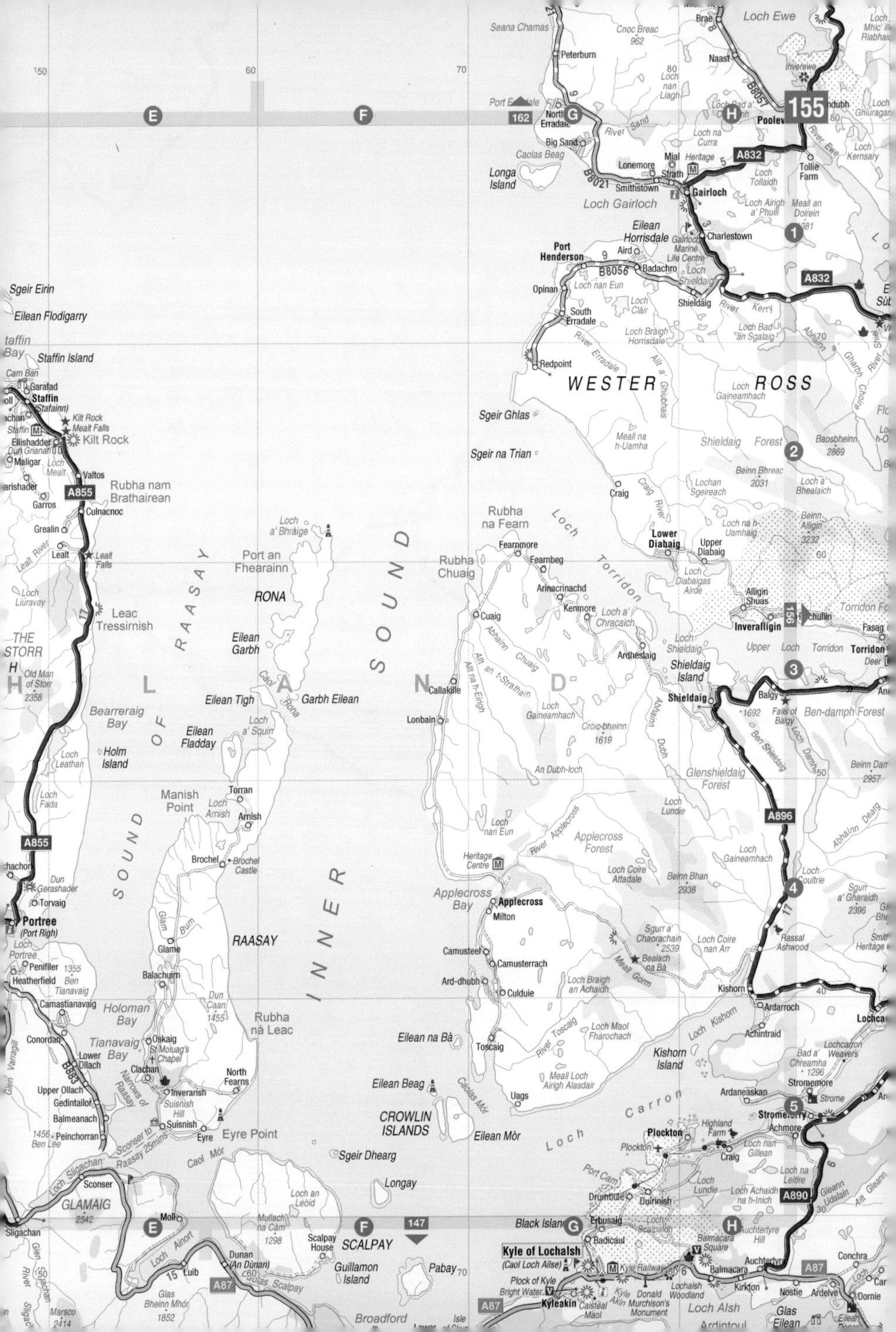

Seana Chamas
Cnoc Breac
962
Brae
Loch Ewe
Peterburn
Naast
Loch nan Liagh
Inverewe
B8057
Port Erradale
North Erradale
162
E
F
G
H
River Sand
Poolew
Big Sand
Caolas Beag
Longa Island
Lonemore
Mial
Heritage
Strath
A832
Smithstown
B8021
Gairloch
Loch Gairloch
Tollie Farm
Loch Tollaidh
Loch Airigh a' Phuill
Meall an Doirein
381
Eilean Horrisdale
Charlestown
Gairloch Marine Life Centre
Port Henderson
Aird
Badachro
B8056
Loch Shieldaig
Opinan
Loch nan Eun
Shieldaig
River Kerry
South Erradale
Loch Clàir
Loch Bràigh Horrisdale
Loch Bad an Sgalaig
River Erradale
Redpoint
WESTER ROSS
Loch Gaineamhach
Allt a' Ghiubhais
Sgeir Ghlas
Sgeir na Trian
Meall na h-Uamha
Shieldaig Forest
Baosbheinn
2869
Craig
Craig River
Lochan Sgeireach
Beinn Bhreac
2031
Loch a' Bhealaich
Rubha na Fearn
Loch Torridon
Lower Diabaig
Upper Diabaig
Loch na h-Uamhaig
Beinn Alligin
3232
Loch Diabaigas Airde
Alligin Shuas
Inveralligin
156
Torridon Forest
Fearnmore
Fearnbeg
Rubha Chuaig
Arinacrinachd
Kenmore
Loch a' Chracaich
Cuaig
Abhainn Chuaig
Ardheslaig
Loch Shieldaig
Upper Loch Torridon
Torridon
Shieldaig Island
Shieldaig
Balgy
Falls of Balgy
Ben-damph Forest
Ben Shieldaig
Loch Damh
Beinn Damh
2957
Allt an t-Srathain
Allt na h-Eirigh
Callakille
Lonbain
Loch Gaineamhach
Cròic-bheinn
1619
An Dubh-loch
Abhainn Dubh
Glenshieldaig Forest
Loch Lundie
A896
Loch nan Eun
River Applecross
Applecross Forest
Abhainn Dearg
Heritage Centre
Loch Coire Attadale
Loch Gaineamhach
Loch Coultrie
Beinn Bhan
2938
Sgurr a' Gharaidh
2396
Applecross Bay
Applecross
Milton
Sgurr a' Chaorachain
2539
Loch Coire nan Arr
Rassal Ashwood
Camusteel
Camusterrach
Bealach na Bà
Meall Gorm
Ard-dhubh
Culduie
Loch Braigh an Achaidh
Kishorn
Ardarroch
Lochcarron
Loch Kishorn
Achintraid
River Toscaig
Loch Maol Fharachach
Toscaig
Eilean na Bà
Kishorn Island
Lochcarron Weavers
Bad a' Chreamha
1296
Eilean Beag
Caolas Mòr
Meall Loch Airigh Alasdair
Uags
Ardaneaskan
Strome
Stromemore
Stromeferry
Achmore
CROWLIN ISLANDS
Eilean Mòr
Loch Carron
Plockton
Highland Farm
Craig
Loch nan Gillean
Sgeir Dhearg
Port Cam
Loch Lundie
Loch na Leitire
Longay
Drumbuie
Duirinish
Loch Achaidh na h-Inich
A890
Gleann Udalain
Black Island
Erbusaig
Badicaul
Loch Scalpaidh
Auchtertyre Hill
Kyle of Lochalsh
(Caol Loch Aillse)
Kyle Railway
Balmacara Square
Auchtertyre
A87
Conchra
Plock of Kyle
Bright Water
Kyleakin
Caisteal Maol
Kyle Akin
Donald Murchison's Monument
Lochalsh Woodland
Balmacara
Kirkton
Nostie
Ardelve
Dornie
Loch Alsh
Glas Eilean
Ardintoul
Sgeir Eirin
Eilean Flodigarry
Staffin Bay
Staffin Island
Carn Ban
Garafad
Staffin
(Stafainn)
Kilt Rock
Mealt Falls
Ellishadder
Dun Grianan
Maligar
Loch Mealt
Valtos
A855
Rubha nam Brathairean
Garros
Culnacnoc
Grealin
Lealt
Lealt Falls
Lealt River
Loch Liuravay
Leac Tressirnish
THE STORR
Old Man of Storr
2358
Bearreraig Bay
Holm Island
Loch Leathan
Loch Fada
Dun Gerashader
Torvaig
Portree
(Port Righ)
Loch Portree
Penifiler
1355
Ben Tianavaig
Heatherfield
Camastianavaig
Conordan
Lower Ollach
B883
Upper Ollach
Gedintailor
Balmeanach
1456
Ben Lee
Peinchorran
Glen Varragill
Loch Sligachan
Sconser
GLAMAIG
2542
Sligachan
Glen Sligachan
River Sligachan
Marsco
2414
Loch Bhràige
Port an Fhearainn
RONA
Eilean Garbh
Caol Rona
Eilean Tigh
Garbh Eilean
Loch a' Squirr
Eilean Fladday
SOUND OF RAASAY
INNER SOUND
Manish Point
Torran
Loch Arnish
Arnish
Brochel
Brochel Castle
Glam Burn
Glame
RAASAY
Balachuirn
Dun Caan
1455
Holoman Bay
Rubha na Leac
Tianavaig Bay
Oskaig
St Moluag's Chapel
Clachan
North Fearns
Inverarish
Narrows of Raasay
Suisnish Hill
Suisnish
Sconser to Raasay 25mins
Eyre
Eyre Point
Caol Mòr
Loch an Leòid
Moll
Mullach na Càrn
1298
147
Scalpay House
SCALPAY
Loch Ainort
Luib
Dunan
(An Dùnan)
Guillamon Island
Pabay
Caolas Scalpay
Glas Bheinn Mhòr
1852
Broadford

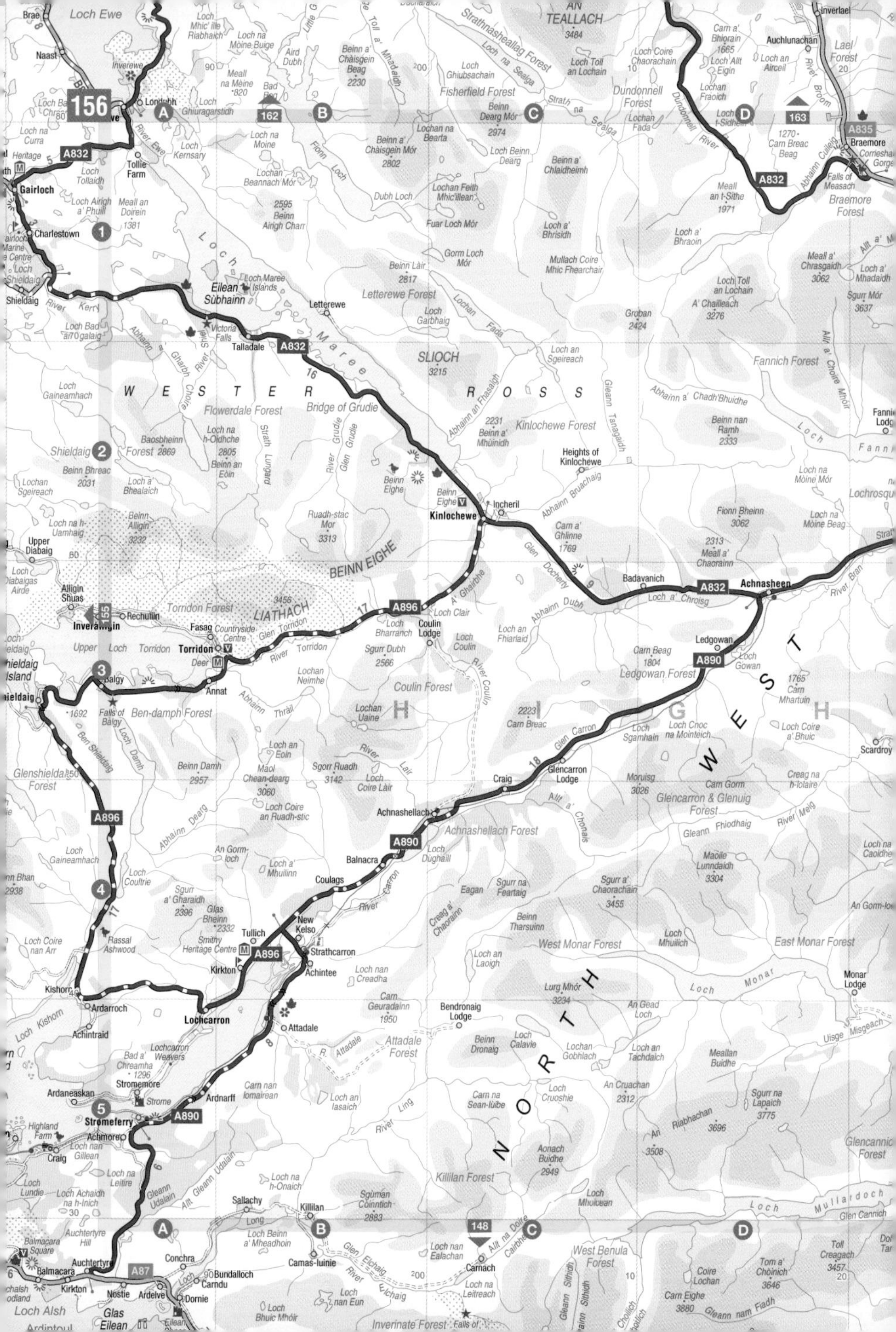

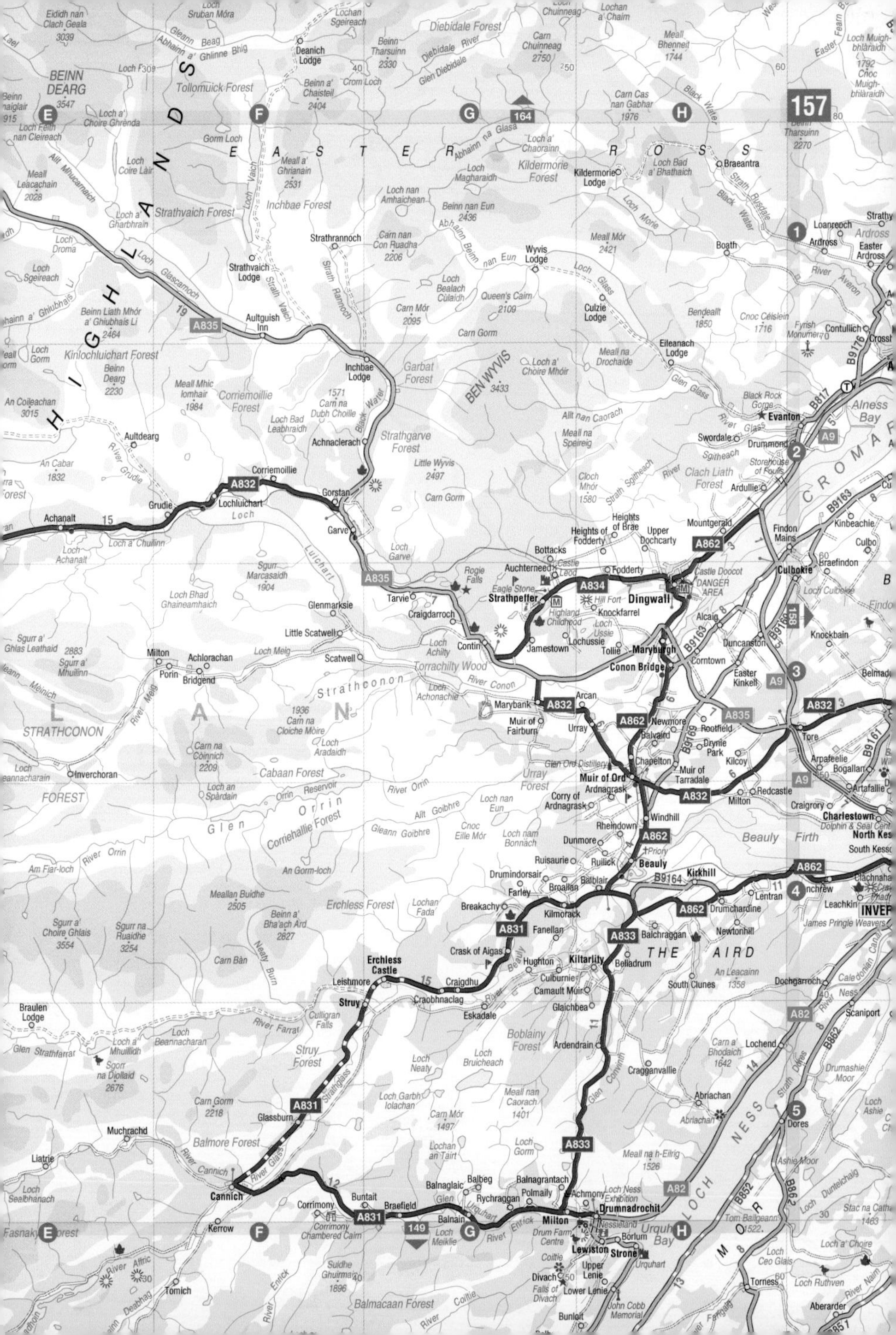
157
164
149
E
F
G
H
1
2
3
4
5
Eididh nan Clach Geala 3039
Loch Sruban Móra
Lochan Sgeireach
Diebidale Forest
Loch Chuinneag
Lochan a' Chairn
Gleann Beag
Abhainn a' Ghlinne Bhig
Deanich Lodge
Beinn Tharsuinn 2330
Carn Chuinneag 2750
Meall Bhenneit 1744
Loch Muigh-bhlàraidh
Diebidale River
Glen Diebidale
BEINN DEARG 3547
Loch F
Tollomuick Forest
Beinn a' Chaisteil 2404
Crom Loch
Cnoc Muigh-bhlàraidh 1792
Carn Cas nan Gabhar 1976
Black Water
Beinn Tharsuinn 2270
Loch a' Choire Ghrànda
Loch Feith nan Cleireach
Gorm Loch
Abhainn na Glasa
Loch a' Chaorainn
E A S T E R R O S S
H I G H L A N D S
Loch Coire Làir
Meall a' Ghrianain 2531
Loch Magharaidh
Kildermorie Forest
Kildermorie Lodge
Loch Bad a' Bhathaich
Braeantra
Strath Rusdale
Allt Mhucarnaich
Meall Leacachain 2028
Loch Vaich
Inchbae Forest
Loch nan Amhaichean
Beinn nan Eun 2436
Loch Morie
Loch a' Gharbhrain
Strathvaich Forest
Loanreoch
Ardross
Strathy
Easter Ardross
Loch Droma
Strathrannoch
Carn nan Con Ruadha 2206
Abhainn Beinn nan Eun
Meall Mór 2421
Boath
River Averon
Loch Sgeireach
Loch Glascarnoch
Strathvaich Lodge
Strath Vaich
Strath Rannoch
Wyvis Lodge
Loch Glass
Loch Bealach Cùlaidh
Queen's Cairn 2109
Culzie Lodge
Bendeallt 1850
Cnoc Céislein 1716
Beinn Liath Mhór a' Ghiubhais Li 2464
A835
Aultguish Inn
Carn Mór 2095
Carn Gorm
Fyrish Monument
Contullich
B9176
Loch Gorm
Kinlochluichart Forest
Inchbae Lodge
Garbat Forest
Eileanach Lodge
Meall na Drochaide
Beinn Dearg 2230
Meall Mhic Iomhair 1984
Corriemoillie Forest
Carn na Dubh Choille 1571
BEN WYVIS 3433
Loch a' Choire Mhóir
Glen Glass
An Coileachan 3015
Loch Bad Leabhraidh
Black Water
Allt nan Caorach
Black Rock Gorge
Evanton
B817
Alness Bay
Aultdearg
Achnaclerach
Strathgarve Forest
Meall na Speireig
River Glass
Swordale
Drummond
A9
An Cabar 1832
River Grudie
Corriemoillie
A832
Little Wyvis 2497
Sgitheach
Clach Liath Forest
Storehouse of Foulis
CROMARTY
Gorstan
Carn Gorm
Cloch Mhór 1580
Strath Sgitheach
Ardullie
B9163
Achanalt
Grudie
Lochluichart
Garve
Loch Luichart
Heights of Brae
Upper Dochcarty
Mountgerald
Findon Mains
Kinbeachie
Culbo
Loch a' Chuilinn
Loch Achanalt
Loch Garve
Heights of Fodderty
A862
Bottacks
Braefindon
Sgurr Marcasaidh 1904
Rogie Falls
Auchterneed
Castle Leod
Fodderty
Castle Doocot
DANGER AREA
Culbokie
A835
Eagle Stone
A834
Loch Bhad Ghaineamhaich
Tarvie
Strathpeffer
Hill Fort
Dingwall
Loch Culbokie
Glenmarksie
Craigdarroch
Highland Childhood
Knockfarrel
Alcaig
B9169
Little Scatwell
Loch Ussie
Lochussie
Knockbain
Loch Achilty
Contin
Jamestown
Tollie
Maryburgh
Duncanston
Sgurr a' Ghlas Leathaid 2883
Sgurr a' Mhuilinn
Loch Meig
Scatwell
Torrachilty Wood
B9163
Corntown
Milton
Porin
Achlorachan
Bridgend
River Conon
Conon Bridge
Easter Kinkell
Belmaduthy
Strathconon
Loch Achonachie
Marybank
Arcan
A832
River Meig
STRATHCONON
1936 Carn na Cloiche Móire
Muir of Fairburn
Urray
A862
Newmore
Rootfield
Tore
Balvaird
Drynie Park
B9161
Loch Aradaidh
Carn na Cóinnich 2209
Chapelton
Kilcoy
Arpafeelie
Bogallan
Loch Beannacharain
Inverchoran
Cabaan Forest
Glen Ord Distillery
Urray Forest
Muir of Ord
Muir of Tarradale
FOREST
Loch an Spàrdain
River Orrin
Orrin Reservoir
Loch nan Eun
Corry of Ardnagrask
Ardnagrask
Redcastle
Milton
Artafallie
Glen Orrin
Allt Goibhre
Windhill
Craigrory
Charlestown
Dolphin & Seal Centre
Corriehallie Forest
Gleann Goibhre
Cnoc Eille Mór
Loch nam Bonnach
Rheindown
Beauly Firth
North Kessock
River Orrin
Dunmore
South Kessock
Am Fiar-loch
An Gorm-loch
Ruisaurie
Ruilick
Priory
Beauly
Drumindorsair
Balblair
B9164
Kirkhill
Lentran
Inchrew
Clachnaharry
Meallan Buidhe 2505
Farley
Broallan
Drumchardine
Leachkin
INVERNESS
Erchless Forest
Lochan Fada
Breakachy
Kilmorack
Newtonhill
James Pringle Weavers
Sgurr a' Choire Ghlais 3554
Sgurr na Ruaidhe 3254
Beinn a' Bha'ach Ard 2827
A831
Fanellan
A833
Balchraggan
THE AIRD
Caledonian Canal
Neaty Burn
Crask of Aigas
Hughton
Kiltarlity
Belladrum
Carn Bàn
Erchless Castle
River Beauly
Culburnie
An Leacainn 1358
Leishmore
Craigdhu
Camault Muir
South Clunes
Dochgarroch
Braulen Lodge
Struy
Craobhnaclag
Eskadale
Glaichbea
River Ness
Culligran Falls
A82
Scaniport
River Farrar
Loch a' Mhuillidh
Loch Beannacharan
Boblainy Forest
Glen Strathfarrar
Struy Forest
Loch Neaty
Ardendrain
Lochend
B862
Sgorr na Diollaid 2676
Loch Bruicheach
Carn a' Bhodaich 1642
Drumashie Moor
Strath Dores
Cragganvallie
Strathglass
Loch Garbh Iolachan
Meall nan Caorach 1401
Abriachan
Loch Ashie
Carn Gorm 2218
A831
Glen Convinth
Glassburn
Carn Mór 1497
LOCH NESS
Dores
Muchrachd
Balmore Forest
Loch Gorm
A833
Meall na h-Eilrig 1526
Liatrie
River Cannich
River Glass
Lochan an Tairt
Ashie Moor
Loch Sealbhanach
Cannich
Balnaglaic
Balbeg
Balnagrantach
Achmony
Loch Ness Exhibition
Loch Duntelchaig
Buntait
Rychraggan
Polmaily
Drumnadrochit
B852
B862
Corrimony
Braefield
Glen Urquhart
Milton
Tom Bailgeann 1522
Stac na Cathaig 1463
Fasnakyle Forest
Kerrow
Corrimony Chambered Cairn
Balnain
Loch Meiklie
River Enrick
Drum Farm Centre
Nessieland
Urquhart Bay
MOR
Lewiston
Borlum
Strone
Urquhart
Loch a' Choire
Loch Ceo Glais
River Affric
Suidhe Ghuirmain 1896
Coiltie
Divach
Upper Lenie
Falls of Divach
Lower Lenie
Torness
Loch Ruthven
River Nairn
Tomich
River Enrick
Glen Deabhag
Balmacaan Forest
River Coiltie
John Cobb Memorial
Bunloit
River Farigaig
Aberarder
B851

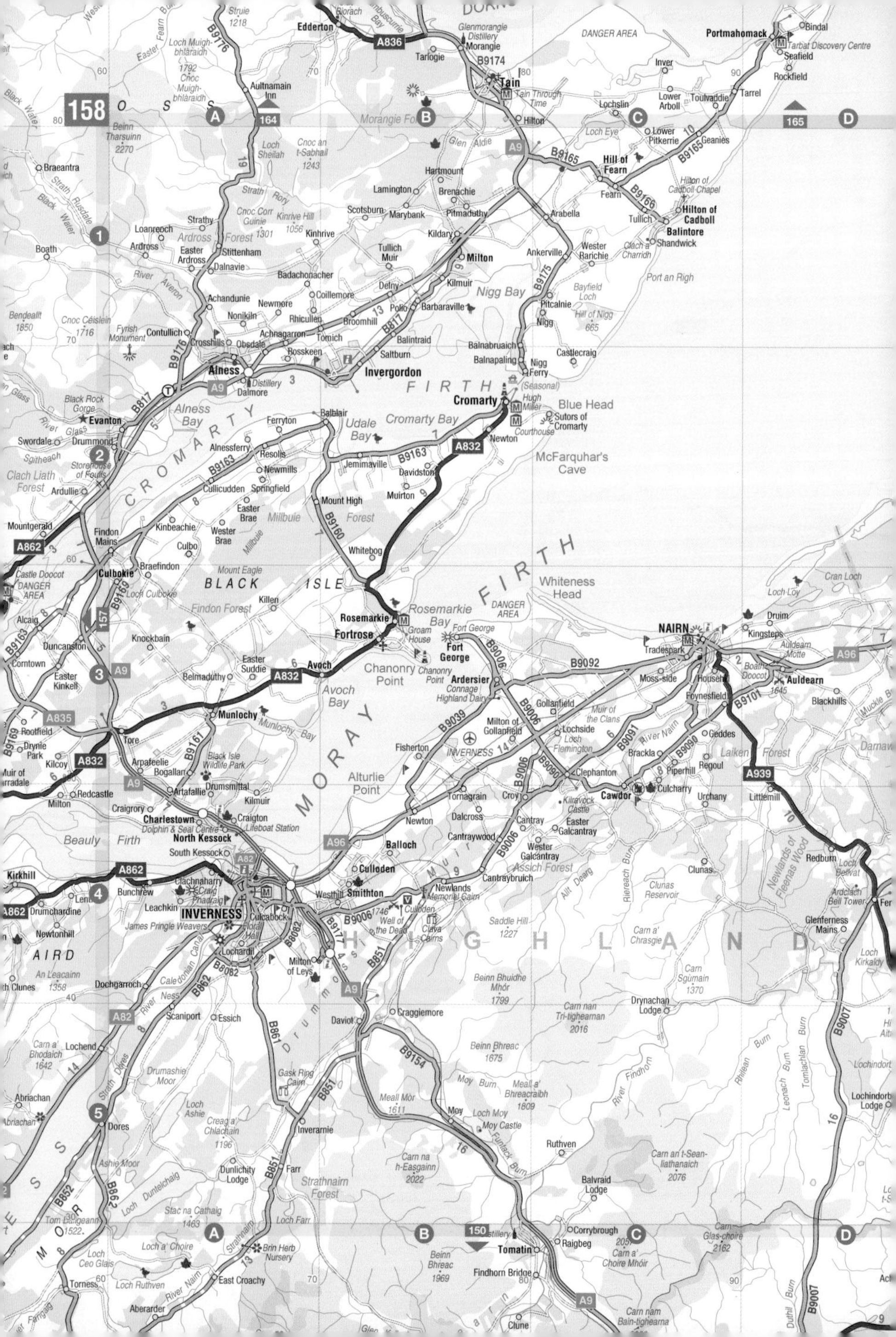
158
Struie 1218
Edderton
Aldie Bay
A836
Glenmorangie Distillery
Morangie
Tarlogie
B9174
Tain
Tain Through Time
DANGER AREA
Portmahomack
Bindal
Tarbat Discovery Centre
Seafield
Rockfield
Inver
Lower Arbol
Toulvaddie
Tarrel
Lochslin
Hilton
Loch Eye
Lower Pitkerrie
Geanies
B9165
Hill of Fearn
Fearn
Hilton of Cadboll Chapel
Hilton of Cadboll
B9166
Tullich
Balintore
Shandwick
Clach a' Charridh
Port an Righ
Loch Muigh-bhlàraidh
Cnoc Muigh-bhlàraidh 1792
B9176
Aultnamain Inn
164
Beinn Tharsuinn 2270
Morangie Forest
Glen Aldie
Loch Sheilah
Cnoc an t-Sabhail 1243
A9
Hartmount
Lamington
Brenachie
Scotsburn
Marybank
Pitmaduthy
Arabella
Kildary
Ankerville
Wester Rarichie
Milton
Tullich Muir
Kinrive Hill 1056
Kinhrive
Cnoc Corr Guinie 1301
Strath Rory
Strathy
Ardross Forest
Loanreoch
Ardross
Easter Ardross
Stittenham
Dalnavie
Boath
Braeantra
Strath Rusdale
Black Water
River Averon
Badachonacher
Kilmuir
Delny
Coillemore
Nigg Bay
Barbaraville
Polio
Bayfield Loch
B9175
Pitcalnie
Hill of Nigg 665
Nigg
Achandunie
Newmore
Nonikiln
Rhicullen
Broomhill
B817
Balintraid
Achnagarron
Tomich
Rosskeen
Saltburn
Invergordon
Balnabruaich
Balnapaling
Nigg Ferry
Castlecraig
Bendeallt 1850
Cnoc Céislein 1716
Fyrish Monument
Contullich
Crosshills
Obsdale
Alness
Distillery
Dalmore
FIRTH
(Seasonal)
Cromarty
Hugh Miller
Blue Head
Sutors of Cromarty
Courthouse
Black Rock Gorge
Evanton
Alness Bay
CROMARTY
Balblair
Ferryton
Udale Bay
Cromarty Bay
Newton
A832
River Glass
Swordale
Drummond
Sgitheach
Storehouse of Foulis
Clach Liath Forest
Ardullie
Alnessferry
Resolis
Newmills
B9163
Jemimaville
Davidston
Cullicudden
Springfield
Muirton
Mount High
Easter Brae
Millbuie Forest
McFarquhar's Cave
Mountgerald
A862
Findon Mains
Kinbeachie
Wester Brae
Culbo
B9160
Whitebog
Braefindon
Culbokie
Castle Doocot
DANGER AREA
Mount Eagle
BLACK ISLE
Loch Culbokie
Findon Forest
Killen
Rosemarkie
Rosemarkie Bay
Whiteness Head
FIRTH
DANGER AREA
Cran Loch
Loch Loy
Druim
Kingsteps
NAIRN
Tradespark
Auldearn Motte
A96
Boath Doocot
Auldearn
Blackhills
Fortrose
Groam House
Fort George
Chanonry Point
Alcaig
Knockbain
157
Duncanston
Corntown
Easter Kinkell
Easter Suddie
Belmaduthy
Avoch
Avoch Bay
Ardersier
Connage Highland Dairy
B9006
B9092
Moss-side
Househill
Foynesfield
B9101
A835
Rootfield
Drynie Park
Kilcoy
Muir of Ord
Tore
Munlochy
Munlochy Bay
B9161
MORAY
B9039
Gollanfield
Milton of Gollanfield
Muir of the Clans
Lochside
Loch Flemington
B9091
River Nairn
Brackla
B9090
Geddes
Laiken Forest
Darnaway
Black Isle Wildlife Park
Arpafeelie
Bogallan
Drumsmittal
Artafallie
Kilmuir
Redcastle
Milton
Craigrory
Charlestown
Craigton
Dolphin & Seal Centre
Lifeboat Station
North Kessock
South Kessock
Beauly Firth
Alturlie Point
Fisherton
INVERNESS
Tornagrain
Croy
Dalcross
Clephanton
Cawdor
Kilravock Castle
Culcharry
Piperhill
Regoul
Urchany
A939
Littlemill
Easter Galcantray
Cantray
Cantraywood
Wester Galcantray
Assich Forest
Cantraybruich
Newton
Balloch
Culloden
Smithton
Westhill
Newlands
Memorial Cairn
Culloden Moor
Allt Dearg
Rireach Burn
Clunas
Clunas Reservoir
Redburn
Loch Belivat
Newlands of Fleenas Wood
Ardclach Bell Tower
Glenferness Mains
Kirkhill
Clachnaharry
Craig Phadraig
Bunchrew
Lentran
Drumchardine
Leachkin
James Pringle Weavers
Floral Hall
Culcabock
B9006
Well of the Dead
Clava Cairns
Saddle Hill 1227
HIGHLAND
Carn a' Chrasgie
Loch Kirkaldy
Newtonhill
AIRD
An Leacainn 1358
Clunes
Lochardil
B8082
Milton of Leys
B9177
B8082
Drummossie
B851
Carn Sgùmain 1370
Dochgarroch
Caledonian Canal
River Ness
B862
A82
Scaniport
Essich
Daviot
Craggiemore
Beinn Bhuidhe Mhòr 1799
Carn nan Tri-tighearnan 2016
Drynachan Lodge
B9007
Carn a' Bhodaich 1642
Lochend
B861
B9154
Beinn Bhreac 1675
Drumashie Moor
Strath Dores
Gask Ring Cairn
Meall Mòr 1611
Moy Burn
Meall a' Bhreacraibh 1809
River Findhorn
Rhilean Burn
Leonach Burn
Tomlachlan Burn
Lochindorb
Lochindorb Lodge
Abriachan
Loch Ashie
Creag a' Chlachain 1196
Moy
Loch Moy
Moy Castle
Funtack Burn
Ruthven
Dores
Inverarnie
Ashie Moor
Dunlichity Lodge
Loch Duntelchaig
Farr
Carn na h-Easgainn 2022
Strathnairn Forest
Carn an t-Sean-liathanaich 2076
Balvraid Lodge
B852
Tom Bailgeann 1522
Stac na Cathaig 1463
Loch Farr
150
Distillery
Tomatin
Corrybrough
Raigbeg
Carn a' Choire Mhòir 2051
Carn Glas-choire 2162
Loch Ceo Glais
Loch a' Choire
Brin Herb Nursery
Strathnairn
Beinn Bhreac 1969
Findhorn Bridge
Torness
Loch Ruthven
River Nairn
East Croachy
Aberarder
River Farigaig
Carn nam Bain-tighearna
Dulnain Burn
Clune
A
B
C
D
165

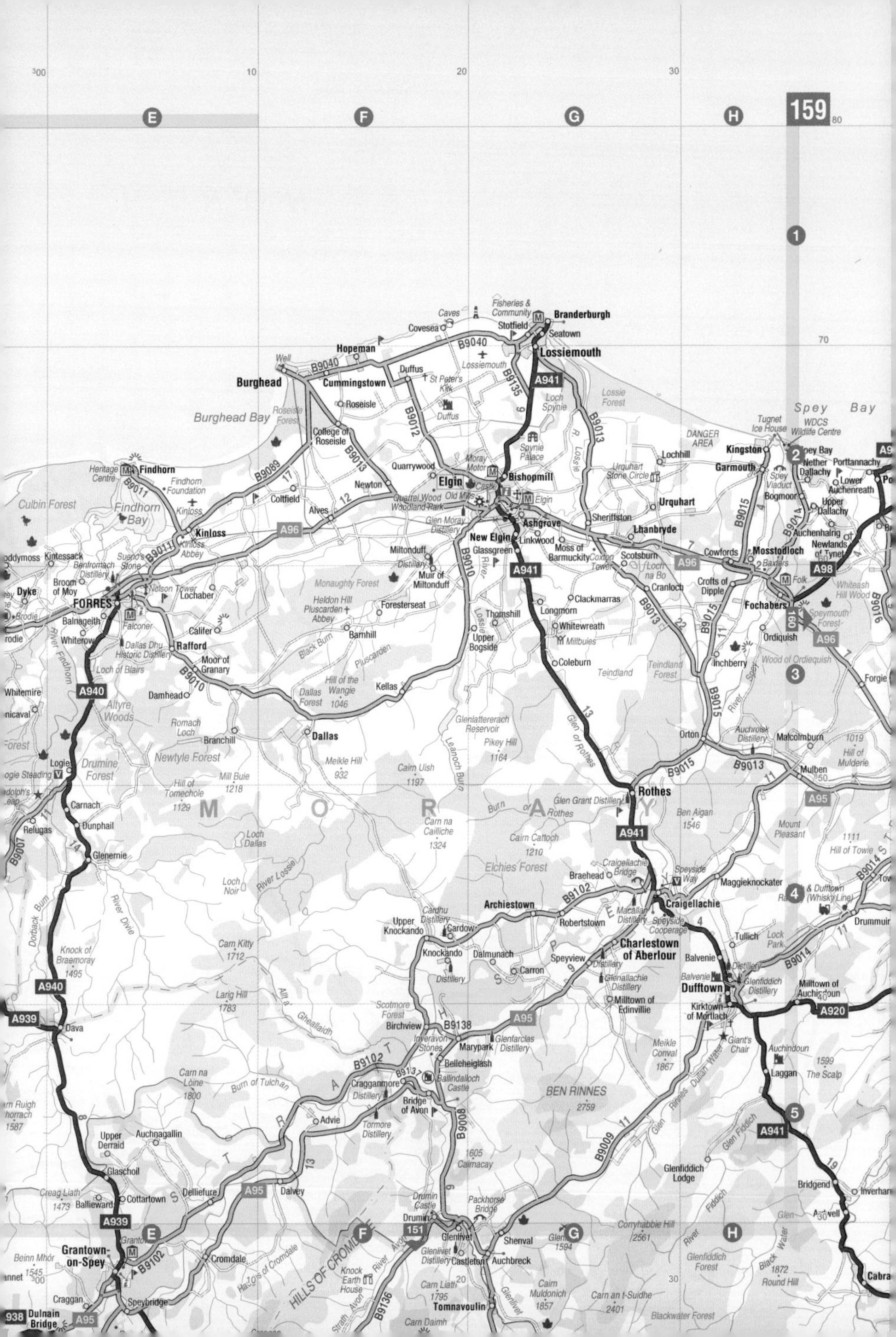
E
F
G
H
Branderburgh
Fisheries & Community
Caves
Covesea
Stotfield
Seatown
Lossiemouth
Hopeman
Burghead
Cummingstown
Duffus
St Peter's Kirk
Roseisle
Burghead Bay
Roseisle Forest
College of Roseisle
Loch Spynie
Lossie Forest
Spey Bay
Tugnet Ice House
WDCS Wildlife Centre
DANGER AREA
Kingston
Garmouth
Spynie Palace
Quarrywood
Moray Motor
Bishopmill
Elgin
Lochhill
Urquhart Stone Circle
Urquhart
Findhorn
Heritage Centre
Findhorn Foundation
Kinloss
Culbin Forest
Findhorn Bay
Coltfield
Newton
Alves
Quarrel Wood Woodland Park
Old Mills
Glen Moray Distillery
Ashgrove
New Elgin
Linkwood
Moss of Barmuckity
Sheriffston
Lhanbryde
Kinloss Abbey
Glassgreen
Miltonduff
Distillery
Muir of Miltonduff
Coxton Tower
Scotsburn
Loch na Bo
Cranloch
Cowfords
Mosstodloch
Baxters
Crofts of Dipple
Fochabers
Folk
Nether Dallachy
Porttannachy
Lower Auchenreath
Bogmoor
Upper Dallachy
Auchenhalrig
Newlands of Tynet
Whiteash Hill Wood
Speymouth Forest
Kintessack
Benromach Distillery
Sueno's Stone
Dyke
Broom of Moy
FORRES
Brodie
Nelson Tower
Lochaber
Monaughty Forest
Heldon Hill
Pluscarden Abbey
Foresterseat
Clackmarras
Longmorn
Thornshill
Whitewreath
Millbuies
Balnageith
Whiterow
Falconer
Dallas Dhu Historic Distillery
Califer
Rafford
Barnhill
Upper Bogside
Coleburn
Teindland
Teindland Forest
Ordiquish
Wood of Ordiequish
Inchberry
Forgie
Loch of Blairs
Moor of Granary
Black Burn
Pluscarden
Hill of the Wangie 1046
Dallas Forest
Kellas
Whitemire
Damhead
Altyre Woods
Romach Loch
Branchill
Dallas
Glenlatterach Reservoir
Pikey Hill 1164
Glen of Rothes
Orton
Auchroisk Distillery
Malcolmburn
1019
Hill of Mulderie
Mulben
Drumine Forest
Logie
Logie Steading
Newtyle Forest
Meikle Hill 932
Cairn Uish 1197
Leanoch Burn
Mill Buie 1218
Hill of Tomechole 1129
Rothes
Glen Grant Distillery
Ben Aigan 1546
M O R A Y
Carnach
Dunphail
Relugas
Carn na Cailliche 1324
Burn of Rothes
Mount Pleasant
1111 Hill of Towie
Loch Dallas
Cairn Cattoch 1210
Elchies Forest
Glenernie
Loch Noir
River Lossie
Craigellachie Bridge
Braehead
Speyside Way
Maggieknockater
Keith & Dufftown (Whisky) Line
Drummuir
Archiestown
Craigellachie
Robertstown
Macallan Distillery
Speyside Cooperage
Tullich
Lock Park
Cardhu Distillery
Upper Knockando
Cardow
Charlestown of Aberlour
Knockando
Dalmunach
Speyview
Carron
Distillery
Glenallachie Distillery
Balvenie
Dufftown
Glenfiddich Distillery
Milltown of Auchindoun
Milltown of Edinvillie
Knock of Braemoray 1495
Carn Kitty 1712
Larig Hill 1783
Scotmore Forest
Birchview
Kirktown of Mortlach
Giant's Chair
Dava
Allt a' Ghealaidh
Inveravon Stones
Marypark
Glenfarclas Distillery
Meikle Conval 1867
Auchindoun
Laggan
1599 The Scalp
Belleheiglash
Ballindalloch Castle
Cragganmore Distillery
Bridge of Avon
Carn na Loine 1800
Burn of Tulchan
BEN RINNES 2759
Advie
Tormore Distillery
Glen Rinnes
Dullan Water
Glen Fiddich
Upper Derraid
Auchnagallin
1605 Cairnacay
Glenfiddich Lodge
Bridgend
Inverharroch
Glaschoil
Delliefure
Dalvey
Creag Liath 1473
Balliewards
Cottartown
Drumin Castle
Packhorse Bridge
Drumin
Corryhabbie Hill 2561
Glen Rinnes 1594
Fiddich
Black Water
Grantown-on-Spey
Cromdale
Hills of Cromdale
Knock Earth House
River Avon
Glenlivet
Glenlivet Distillery
Castleton
Shenval
Auchbreck
Glenfiddich Forest
1872 Round Hill
Carn Liath 1795
Cairn Muldonich 1857
Carn an t-Suidhe 2401
Craggan
Speybridge
Dulnain Bridge
Tomnavoulin
Strath Avon
Carn Daimh
Blackwater Forest
Beinn Mhòr 1545
Carn Ruigh Chorrach 1587
A96
A941
A940
A939
A95
A98
A920
B9040
B9012
B9013
B9135
B9089
B9011
B9010
B9015
B9014
B9016
B9102
B9138
B9008
B9009
B9007
B9136
160
151
10
20
30
70
80
50

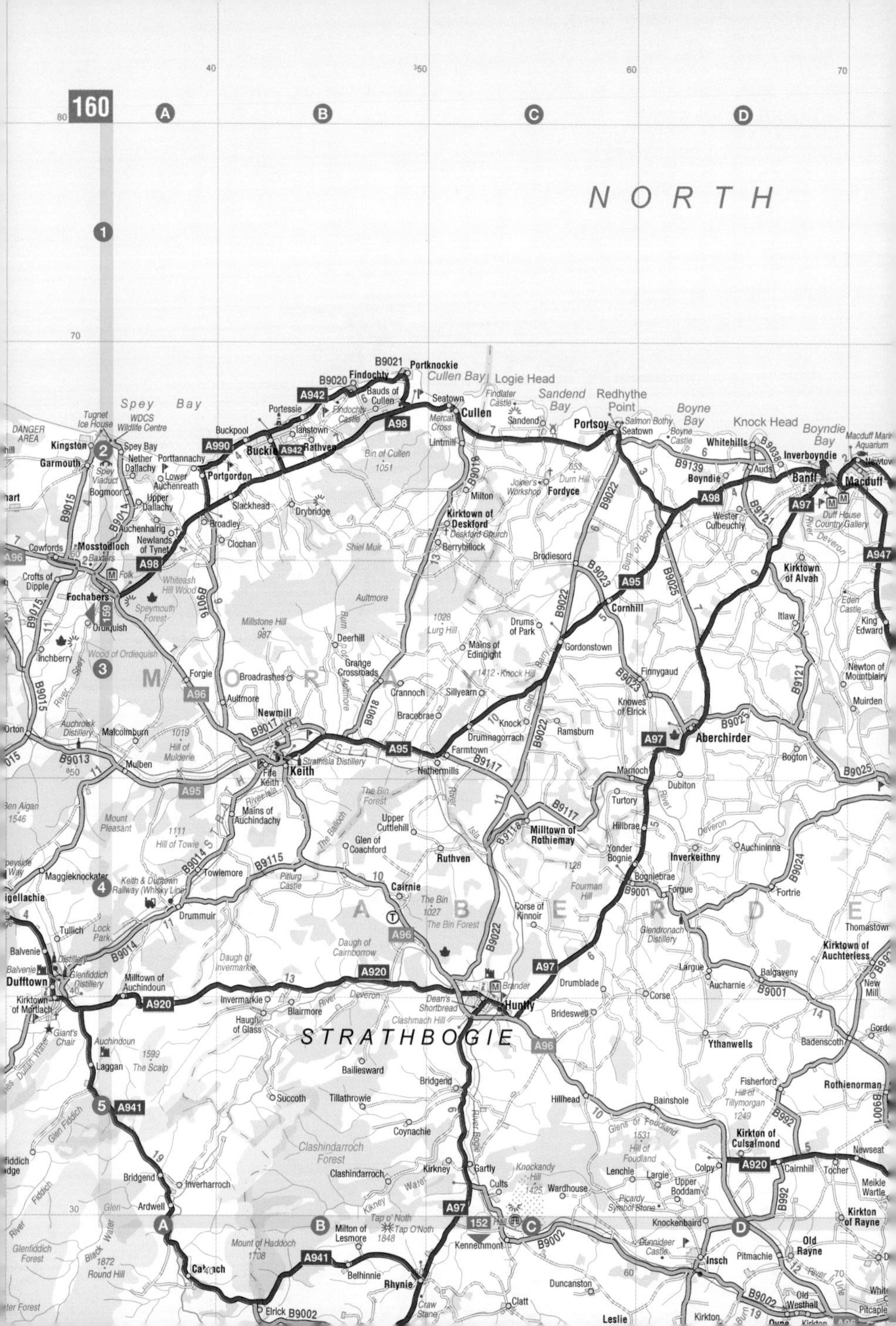

NORTH
Spey Bay
Cullen Bay
Logie Head
Sandend Bay
Redhythe Point
Boyne Bay
Knock Head
Boyndie Bay
Portknockie
Findochty
Buckie
Cullen
Portsoy
Whitehills
Banff
Macduff
Kingston
Garmouth
Mosstodloch
Fochabers
Portgordon
Rathven
Keith
Newmill
Aberchirder
Huntly
Dufftown
Rhynie
Insch
STRATHBOGIE
MORAY
ABERDEEN
Milltown of Rothiemay
Cornhill
Fordyce
Kirktown of Deskford
Inverkeithny
Ythanwells
Rothienorman
Kirkton of Culsalmond
Kennethmont
Cabrach
Clashindarroch Forest
Speymouth Forest
The Bin Forest
Glenfiddich Distillery
Strathisla Distillery
Glendronach Distillery
Duff House Country Gallery
Macduff Marine Aquarium

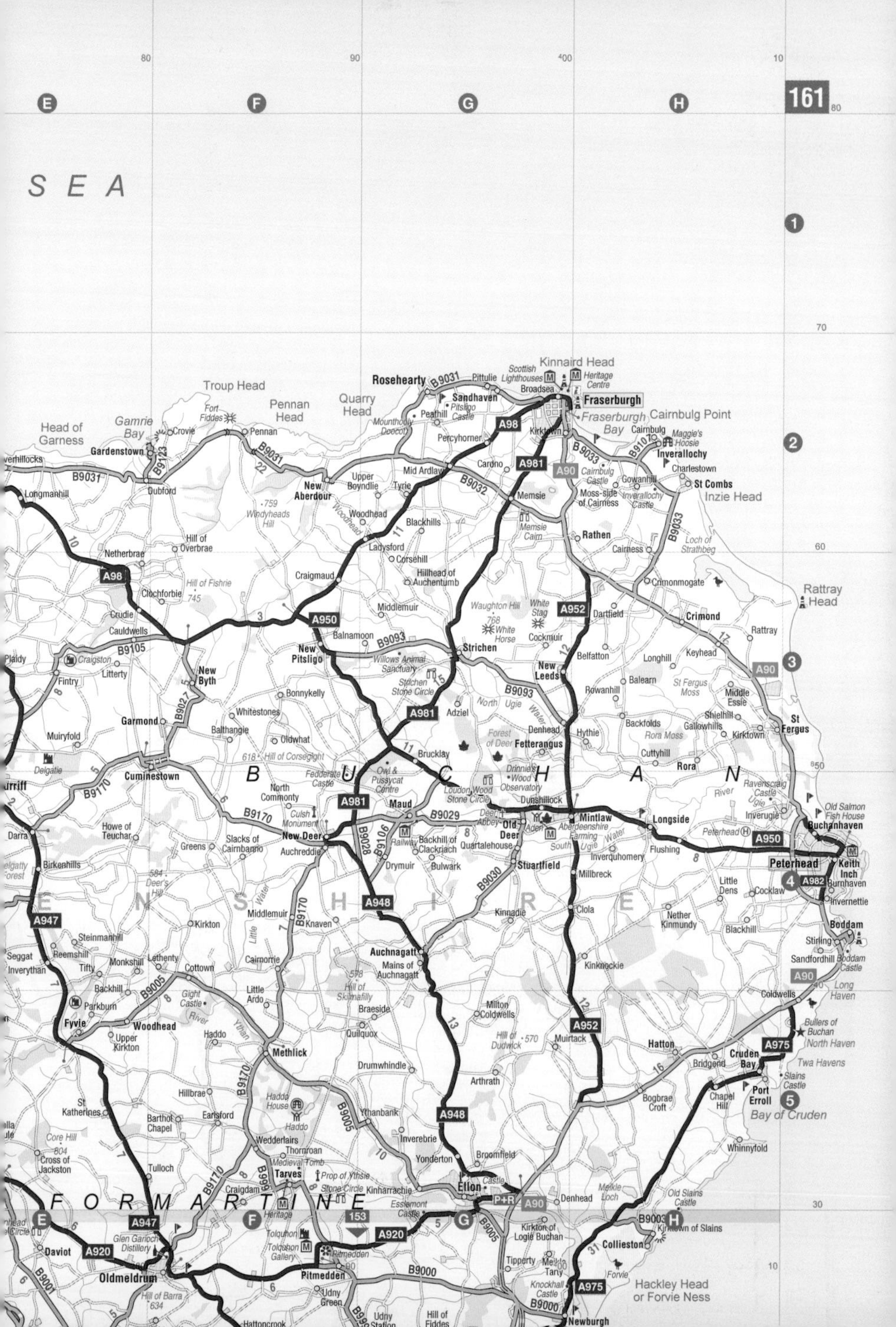
SEA
Troup Head
Head of Garness
Gamrie Bay
Gardenstown
Crovie
Fort Fiddes
Pennan
Pennan Head
Quarry Head
Rosehearty
Pittulie
Sandhaven
Pitsligo Castle
Peathill
Mounthooly Doocot
Scottish Lighthouses
Kinnaird Head
Heritage Centre
Broadsea
Fraserburgh
Fraserburgh Bay
Cairnbulg Point
Cairnbulg
Maggie's Hoosie
Inverallochy
Charlestown
St Combs
Inzie Head
Kirktown
Percyhorner
Cardno
Memsie
Memsie Cairn
Cairnbulg Castle
Gowanhill
Inverallochy Castle
Moss-side of Cairness
Rathen
Cairness
Loch of Strathbeg
Crimonmogate
Rattray Head
Crimond
Rattray
Keyhead
Dubford
Longmanhill
New Aberdour
Upper Boyndlie
Tyrie
Mid Ardlaw
Woodhead
759 Windyheads Hill
Blackhills
Ladysford
Corsehill
Hillhead of Auchentumb
Hill of Overbrae
Netherbrae
Craigmaud
Hill of Fishrie 745
Clochforbie
Crudie
Cauldwells
Middlemuir
Balnamoon
Waughton Hill 768
White Horse
White Stag
Cockmuir
Dartfield
Strichen
New Pitsligo
Willows Animal Sanctuary
Stirchen Stone Circle
Craigston
Plaidy
Fintry
Litterty
New Byth
Bonnykelly
Whitestones
Balthangie
Oldwhat
618 Hill of Corsegight
Garmond
Muiryfold
Delgatie
Cuminestown
Adziel
North Ugie Water
Forest of Deer
Fetterangus
Denhead
New Leeds
Belfatton
Longhill
Balearn
Rowanhill
St Fergus Moss
Middle Essie
Shielhill
Gallowhills
Backfolds
Rora Moss
Hythie
Kirktown
St Fergus
Cuttyhill
Rora
Bruckley
Fedderate Castle
Owl & Pussycat Centre
Drinnies Wood Observatory
Loudon Wood Stone Circle
Dunshillock
B U C H A N
North Commonty
Culsh Monument
Maud
Railway
Deer Abbey
Old Deer
Aden
Mintlaw
Aberdeenshire Farming
South Ugie Water
Longside
River Ugie
Ravenscraig Castle
Inverugie
Old Salmon Fish House
Buchanhaven
Peterhead
Keith Inch
Burnhaven
Invernettie
Howe of Teuchar
Darra
Birkenhills
Greens
Slacks of Cairnbanno
New Deer
Auchreddie
Backhill of Clackriach
Quartalehouse
Drymuir
Bulwark
Stuartfield
Inverquhomery
Flushing
Millbreck
Little Dens
Cocklaw
Nether Kinmundy
Blackhill
584 Deer's Hill
E N S H I R E
Middlemuir
Knaven
Kirkton
Kinnadie
Clola
Boddam
Stirling
Sandfordhill
Boddam Castle
Steinmanhill
Reemshill
Seggat
Inverythan
Tifty
Monkshill
Lethenty
Cottown
Cairnorrie
Little Water
Auchnagatt
Mains of Auchnagatt
578 Hill of Skilmafilly
Kinknockie
Long Haven
Coldwells
Bullers of Buchan
North Haven
Backhill
Parkburn
Gight Castle
Little Ardo
Fyvie
Woodhead
Upper Kirkton
River Ythan
Haddo
Braeside
Quilquox
Milton of Coldwells
Hill of Dudwick 570
Muirtack
Methlick
Hatton
Cruden Bay
Bridgend
Twa Havens
Drumwhindle
Arthrath
Slains Castle
Port Erroll
Chapel Hill
Bogbrae Croft
Bay of Cruden
St Katherines
Hillbrae
Haddo House
Haddo
Barthol Chapel
Earlsford
Ythanbank
Core Hill 804
Cross of Jackston
Wedderlairs
Thornroan
Medieval Tomb
Inverebrie
Whinnyfold
Tulloch
Tarves
Prop of Ythsie
Stone Circle
Yonderton
Broomfield
Ellon
Castle
Meikle Loch
Denhead
Old Slains Castle
F O R M A R T I N E
Craigdam
Heritage
Kinharrachie
Esslemont Castle
153
Glen Garioch Distillery
Daviot
Tolquhon
Tolquhon Gallery
Pitmedden
Kirkton of Logie Buchan
Kirkton of Slains
Collieston
Oldmeldrum
Pitmedden
Udny Green
Udny Station
Hill of Fiddes
Tipperty
Meikle Tarty
Forvie
Knockhall Castle
Hackley Head or Forvie Ness
Hill of Barra 634
Hattoncrook
Newburgh
A98
A981
A90
A950
A952
A948
A947
A920
A975
A982
P+R
B9031
B9123
B9032
B9033
B9107
B9093
B9105
B9027
B9170
B9029
B9028
B9106
B9030
B9005
B9000
B9003
B9001
B9999
80
90
400
10
70
60
50
40
30
E
F
G
H
1
2
3
4
5

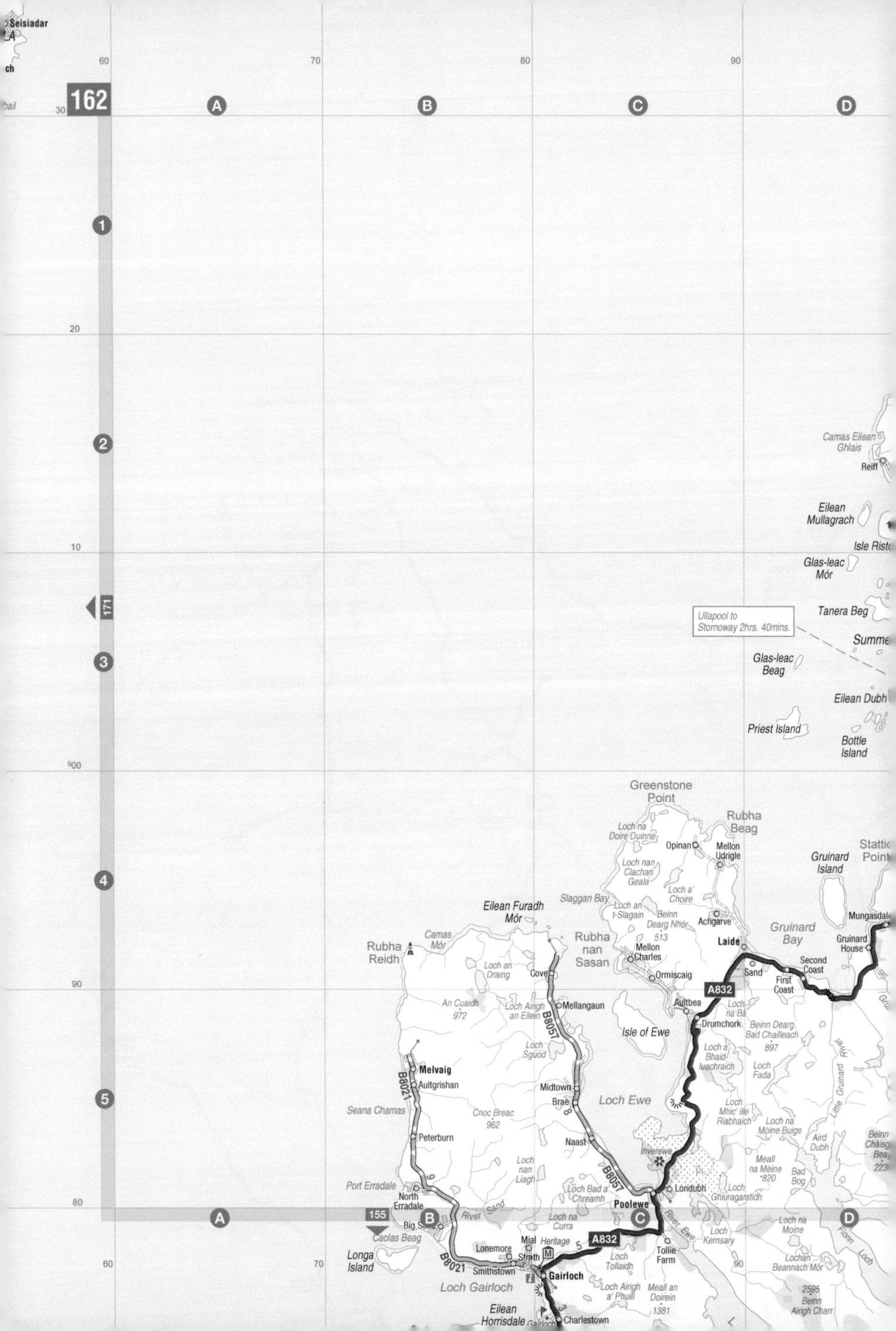

Seisiadar
A
B
C
D
1
2
3
4
5
171
155
Ullapool to Stornoway 2hrs. 40mins.
Camas Eilean Ghlais
Reiff
Eilean Mullagrach
Isle Risto
Glas-leac Mór
Tanera Beg
Summe
Glas-leac Beag
Eilean Dubh
Priest Island
Bottle Island
Greenstone Point
Rubha Beag
Loch na Doire Duinne
Opinan
Mellon Udrigle
Loch nan Clachan Geala
Loch a' Choire
Gruinard Island
Statio Point
Slaggan Bay
Loch an t-Slagain
Beinn Dearg Nhór 513
Achgarve
Eilean Furadh Mór
Rubha nan Sasan
Laide
Gruinard Bay
Mungasdal
Gruinard House
Camas Mór
Rubha Reidh
Mellon Charles
Ormiscaig
Sand
Second Coast
First Coast
Loch an Draing
Cove
A832
Aultbea
An Cuaidh 972
Loch Airigh an Eilein
Mellangaun
Drumchork
Beinn Dearg Bad Chailleach 897
Isle of Ewe
B8057
Loch Sguod
Loch a Bhaid-luachraich
Loch Fada
Little Gruinard River
Melvaig
Aultgrishan
B8021
Midtown
Brae
Loch Ewe
Loch Mhic' ille Riabhaich
Seana Chamas
Cnoc Breac 962
Loch na Moine Buige
Aird Dubh
Peterburn
Naast
Inverewe
Meall na Meine 820
Bad Bog
Loch nan Liagh
Port Erradale
North Erradale
Loch Bad a' Chreamh
Londubh
Loch Ghiuragarstidh
Poolewe
Big Sand
Caolas Beag
Rivet Sand
Loch na Curra
River Ewe
Loch Kernsary
Loch na Moine
Fionn Loch
Longa Island
Lonemore
Mial
Heritage
Strath
Tollie Farm
Loch Tollaidh
Lochan Beannach Mór
Smithstown
Gairloch
Loch Gairloch
Loch Airigh a' Phuill
Meall an Doirein 1381
2595 Beinn Airigh Charr
Eilean Horrisdale
Charlestown

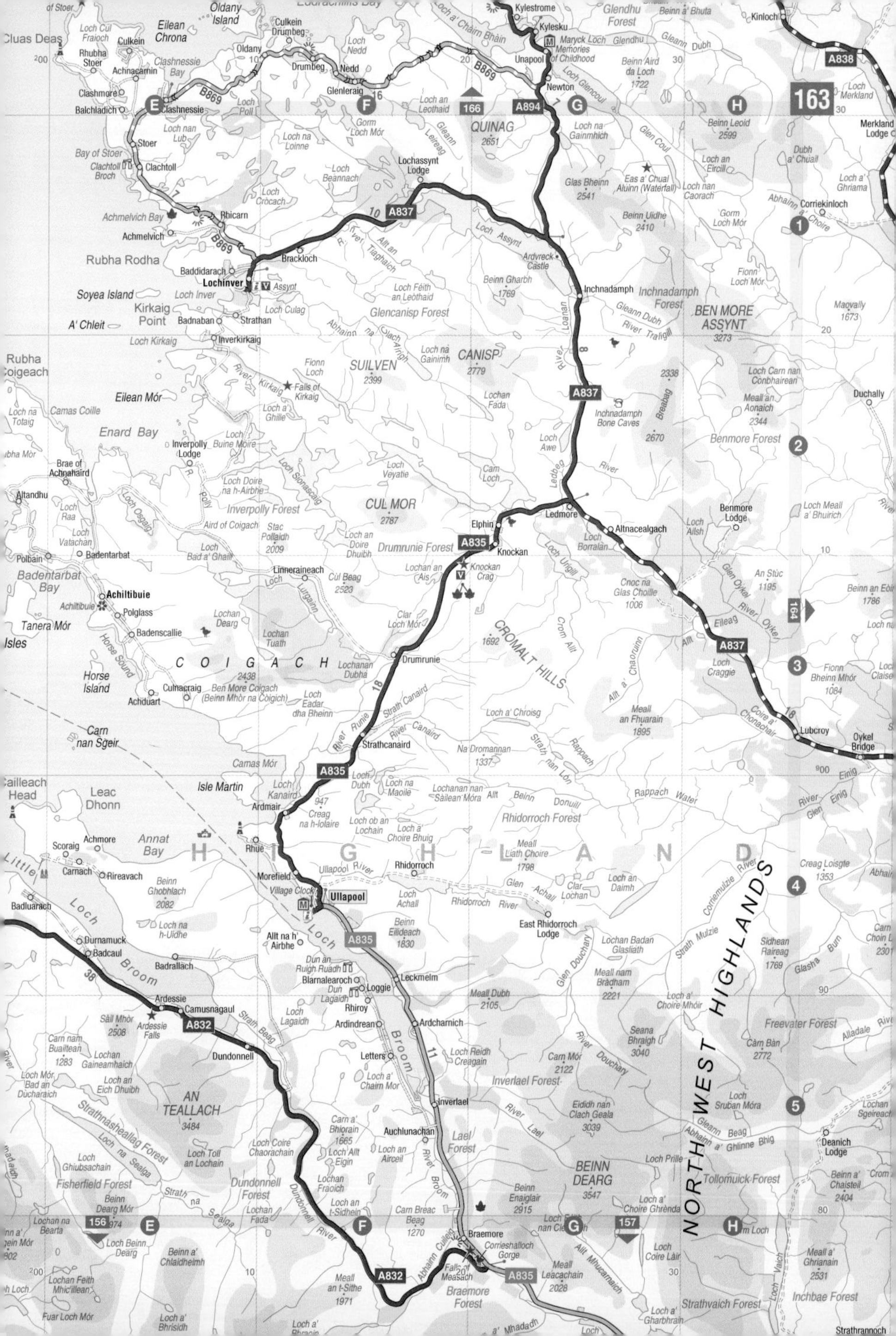

163
of Stoer
Oldany Island
Eilean Chrona
Kylestrome
Kylesku
Glendhu Forest
Beinn a' Bhuta
Kinloch
Cluas Deas
Loch Cùl Fraioch
Culkein
Culkein Drumbeg
Loch Nedd
Loch a' Chàirn Bhàin
Maryck Loch
Memories of Childhood
Glendhu
Gleann Dubh
Rhubha Stoer
Oldany
Drumbeg
Nedd
Unapool
Beinn Aird da Loch
1722
A838
Achnacarnin
Clashnessie Bay
B869
Loch Glencoul
Newton
Loch Merkland
Clashmore
Balchladich
Clashnessie
Glenleraig
Loch Poll
Loch an Leothaid
166
A894
E
F
G
H
Gorm Loch Mór
QUINAG
2651
Loch na Gainmhich
Glen Coul
Beinn Leoid
2599
Merkland Lodge
Loch nan Lub
Stoer
Loch na Loinne
Gleann Leireag
Bay of Stoer
Clachtoll Broch
Clachtoll
Loch Beannach
Lochassynt Lodge
Glas Bheinn
2541
Eas a' Chual Aluinn (Waterfall)
Loch an Eircill
Loch nan Caorach
Dubh a' Chuail
Loch a' Ghriama
Loch Crocach
A837
Beinn Uidhe
2410
Gorm Loch Mór
Corriekinloch
Abhainn a' Choire
Achmelvich Bay
Rhicarn
Loch Assynt
Achmelvich
B869
Allt an Tiaghaich
Ardvreck Castle
Rubha Rodha
Baddidarach
Brackloch
Beinn Gharbh
1769
Inchnadamph
Inchnadamph Forest
Fionn Loch Mór
Lochinver
Assynt
Loch Féith an Leòthaid
Soyea Island
Loch Inver
Kirkaig Point
Badnaban
Strathan
Loch Culag
Glencanisp Forest
Gleann Dubh
River Traligill
BEN MORE ASSYNT
3273
Maovally
1673
A' Chleit
Loch Kirkaig
Inverkirkaig
Loch na Gainimh
CANISP
2779
SUILVEN
2399
Fionn Loch
Rubha Coigeach
River Kirkaig
Falls of Kirkaig
Loch Carn nan Conbhairean
Eilean Mór
Lochan Fada
Inchnadamph Bone Caves
Meall an Aonaich
2344
Duchally
Loch na Totaig
Camas Coille
Loch a' Ghille
Breabag
2670
2338
Enard Bay
Inverpolly Lodge
Loch Buine Moire
Loch Awe
Benmore Forest
Brae of Achnahaird
Loch Sionascaig
Loch Veyatie
Cam Loch
Ledbeg River
Altandhu
Loch Doire na h-Airbhe
Inverpolly Forest
CUL MOR
2787
Loch Raa
Loch Osgaig
Elphin
Ledmore
Benmore Lodge
Loch Meall a' Bhuirich
Loch Vatachan
Aird of Coigach
Stac Pollaidh
2009
Loch an Doire Dhuibh
Drumrunie Forest
A835
Knockan
Altnacealgach
Loch Borralan
Loch Ailsh
Polbain
Badentarbat
Loch Bad a' Ghaill
Loch Urigill
Badentarbat Bay
Linneraineach
Loch Lurgainn
Cùl Beag
2523
Lochan an Ais
Knockan Crag
Cnoc na Glas Choille
1006
An Stùc
1195
Glen Oykel
Beinn an Eoin
1786
164
Achiltibuie
Polglass
Lochan Dearg
Clar Loch Mór
CROMALT HILLS
1692
Crom Allt
River Oykel
Tanera Mór
Isles
Badenscallie
Lochan Tuath
Eileag
A837
Horse Sound
C O I G A C H
Drumrunie
Lochanan Dubha
Allt a' Chaoruinn
Loch Craggie
Fionn Bheinn Mhór
1084
Horse Island
2438
Ben More Coigach (Beinn Mhòr na Coigich)
Culnacraig
Achduart
Loch Eadar dha Bheinn
Strath Canaird
Loch a' Chroisg
Meall an Fhuarain
1895
Coire a' Chonachair
Lubcroy
Oykel Bridge
Carn nan Sgeir
River Runie
River Canaird
Strathcanaird
Na Dromannan
1337
Strath nan Lón
Rappach
Camas Mór
Cailleach Head
Leac Dhonn
Isle Martin
Loch Kanaird
Loch Dubh
Loch na Maoile
Lochanan nan Sailean Móra
Allt Beinn Donuill
Rappach Water
River Einig
Glen Einig
Ardmair
947
Creag na h-Iolaire
Loch ob an Lochain
Loch a' Choire Bhuig
Rhidorroch Forest
Scoraig
Achmore
Annat Bay
Rhue
Meall Liath Choire
1798
H I G H L A N D
Little Loch Broom
Carnach
Rireavach
Morefield
Ullapool River
Rhidorroch
Creag Loisgte
1353
Beinn Ghobhlach
2082
Village Clock
Ullapool
Loch Achall
Glen Achall
Rhidorroch River
Clar Lochan
Loch an Daimh
Cormemulzie River
NORTH WEST HIGHLANDS
Badluarach
Loch na h-Uidhe
Loch Broom
Beinn Eilideach
1830
East Rhidorroch Lodge
Glen Douchary
Lochan Badan Glasliath
Strath Mulzie
Sidhean Raireag
1769
Glasha Burn
Durnamuck
Badcaul
Allt na h' Airbhe
Dun an Ruigh Ruadh
Blarnalearoch
Loggie
Leckmelm
Dun Lagaidh
Rhiroy
Meall nam Bràdham
2221
Badrallach
Ardessie
Camusnagaul
Ardessie Falls
Sàil Mhór
2508
A832
Strath Beag
Loch Lagaidh
Ardindrean
Ardcharnich
Meall Dubh
2105
Loch a' Choire Mhóir
Seana Bhraigh
3040
Freevater Forest
Carn nam Buailtean
1283
Lochan Gaineamhaich
Dundonnell
Letters
Loch a' Chàirn Mor
Loch Reidh Creagain
Cam Mór
2122
River Douchary
Càrn Bàn
2772
Alladale
Loch Mór Bad an Ducharaich
Loch an Eich Dhuibh
AN TEALLACH
3484
Inverlael
Inverlael Forest
Eididh nan Clach Geala
3039
Loch Sruban Móra
Strathnashealag Forest
Carn a' Bhiorain
1665
Auchlunachan
Lael Forest
River Lael
Gleann Beag
Abhainn a' Ghlinne Bhig
Lochan Sgeireach
Loch na Sealga
Loch Coire Chaorachain
Loch Allt Eigin
Loch an Airceil
River Broom
Deanich Lodge
Loch Ghiubsachain
Loch Toll an Lochain
BEINN DEARG
3547
Loch Prille
Tollomuick Forest
Fisherfield Forest
Dundonnell Forest
Lochan Fraoich
Beinn Enaiglair
2915
Beinn a' Chaisteil
2404
Beinn Dearg Mór
2974
Strath na Sealga
Loch an t-Sidhein
Carn Breac Beag
1270
Loch a' Choire Ghrènda
Lochan na Bearta
156
Lochan Fada
Dundonnell River
Braemore
157
Loch Beinn Dearg
Beinn a' Chlaidheimh
Corrieshalloch Gorge
Allt Mhucarnaich
Loch Coire Làir
Meall a' Ghrianain
2531
Lochan Feith Mhic'illean
Meall an t-Sithe
1971
Abhainn Cuileig
Falls of Measach
A835
Meall Leacachain
2028
Braemore Forest
Loch Vaich
Inchbae Forest
Loch a' Bhrisidh
Fuar Loch Mór
Strathvaich Forest
Loch a' Gharbhrain
Strathrannoch

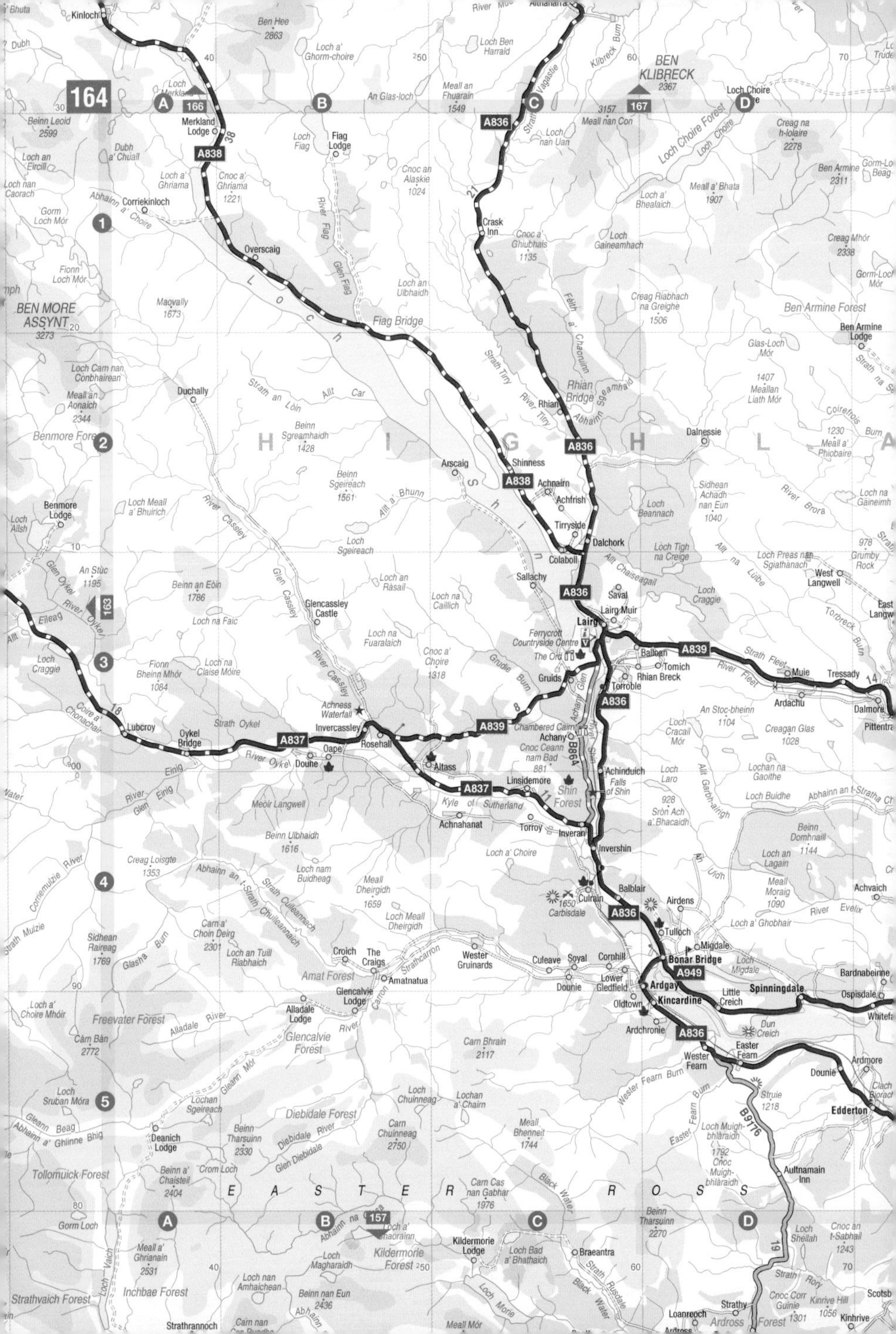

164
A
B
C
D
166
167
163
157
1
2
3
4
5
A838
A836
A837
A839
A949
B864
B9176
Kinloch
Ben Hee
2863
Loch a' Ghorm-choire
Loch Ben Harrald
Klibreck Burn
BEN KLIBRECK
2367
Loch Merkland
Merkland Lodge
Beinn Leoid
2599
An Glas-loch
Meall an Fhuarain
1549
Strath Vagastie
Meall nan Con
3157
Loch nan Uan
Loch Choire
Loch Choire Forest
Creag na h-Iolaire
2278
Loch Fiag
Fiag Lodge
Dubh a' Chuail
Loch an Eircill
Loch a' Ghriama
Cnoc a' Ghriama
1221
Cnoc an Alaskie
1024
Ben Armine
2311
Gorm-Loch Beag
Loch nan Caorach
Abhainn a' Choire
Corriekinloch
Gorm Loch Mór
River Fiag
Crask Inn
Meall a' Bhata
1907
Loch a' Bhealaich
Cnoc a' Ghiubhais
1135
Loch Gaineamhach
Creag Mhór
2338
Overscaig
Glen Fiag
Fionn Loch Mór
Loch an Ulbhaidh
Gorm-Loch Mór
Creag Riabhach na Greighe
1506
Féith a' Chaoruinn
BEN MORE ASSYNT
3273
Maovally
1673
Fiag Bridge
Ben Armine Forest
Ben Armine Lodge
Glas-Loch Mór
Loch Carn nan Conbhairean
Meall an Aonaich
2344
Strath Tirry
Rhian Bridge
Abhainn Sgeamhaidh
1407
Meallan Liath Mór
Duchally
Strath an Lòin
Allt Car
River Tirry
Rhian
Benmore Forest
Beinn Sgreamhaidh
1428
H I G H L A
Dalnessie
Coirefrois
1230
Meall a' Phiobaire
Burn
Arscaig
Shinness
Loch Shin
Beinn Sgeireach
1561
Achnairn
Achfrish
Sidhean Achadh nan Eun
1040
River Brora
Loch na Gaineimh
Benmore Lodge
Loch Meall a' Bhuirich
Allt a' Bhunn
Loch Beannach
Loch Ailsh
River Cassley
Tirryside
Dalchork
Loch Tigh na Creige
Allt na Lùibe
978
Grumby Rock
Loch Sgeireach
Colaboll
Allt Chaiseagail
Loch Preas nan Sgiathanach
West Langwell
An Stùc
1195
Beinn an Eòin
1786
Glen Cassley
Loch an Ràsail
Loch na Caillich
Sallachy
Saval
Loch Craggie
Glen Oykel
River Oykel
Eileag
Allt
Loch na Faic
Glencassley Castle
Lairg
Lairg Muir
East Langwell
Torbreck Burn
Loch na Fuaralaich
Ferrycroft Countryside Centre
The Ord
Balloan
Tomich
Strath Fleet
River Fleet
Loch Craggie
Fionn Bheinn Mhór
1084
Loch na Claise Móire
Cnoc a' Choire
1318
Grudie Burn
Gruids
Torroble
Rhian Breck
Muie
Tressady
Achany Glen
Ardachu
Dalmore
Pittentrail
Coire a' Chonachair
Lubcroy
Strath Oykel
Oykel Bridge
Achness Waterfall
Invercassley
Rosehall
Oape
Doune
Altass
Chambered Cairn
Achany
Cnoc Ceann nam Bad
881
An Stoc-bheinn
1104
Loch Cracail Mór
Creagan Glas
1028
Lochan na Gaoithe
River Einig
Glen Einig
Linsidemore
Shin Forest
Achinduich
Falls of Shin
River Shin
Loch Laro
Allt Garbh-airigh
Loch Buidhe
Abhainn an t-Stratha Ch
Meoir Langwell
Kyle of Sutherland
Achnahanat
Torroy
Inveran
928
Sròn Ach a' Bhacaidh
Beinn Domhnaill
1144
Beinn Ulbhaidh
1616
Invershin
Loch an Lagain
Creag Loisgte
1353
Abhainn an t-Strath Chuileannaich
Strath Cuileannach
Loch a' Choire
Corriemulzie River
Loch nam Buidheag
Meall Dheirgidh
1659
Culrain
1650
Carbisdale
Balblair
Airdens
Meall Moraig
1090
Achvaich
River Evelix
An Ud'h
Loch Meall Dheirgidh
Strath Mulzie
Sidhean Raireag
1769
Glasha Burn
Carn a' Choin Deirg
2301
Loch an Tuill Riabhaich
Croich
The Craigs
Strathcarron
Wester Gruinards
Culeave
Soyal
Cornhill
Tulloch
Migdale
Loch Migdale
Loch a' Ghobhair
Bonar Bridge
Bardnabeinne
Amat Forest
Amatnatua
Glencalvie Lodge
Dounie
Lower Gledfield
Ardgay
Little Creich
Spinningdale
Ospisdale
Whitefa
Loch a' Choire Mhóir
Freevater Forest
Alladale River
Alladale Lodge
Carron
River
Oldtown
Kincardine
Ardchronie
Dun Creich
Càrn Bàn
2772
Glencalvie Forest
Carn Bhrain
2117
Easter Fearn
Wester Fearn
Ardmore
Dounie
Clach Biorach
Loch Sruban Móra
Gleann Mór
Lochan Sgeireach
Loch Chuinneag
Lochan a' Chairn
Wester Fearn Burn
Struie
1218
Edderton
Gleann Beag
Abhainn a' Ghlinne Bhig
Deanich Lodge
Diebidale Forest
Beinn Tharsuinn
2330
Diebidale River
Glen Diebidale
Carn Chuinneag
2750
Meall Bhenneit
1744
Easter Fearn Burn
Loch Muigh-bhlàraidh
1792
Cnoc Muigh-bhlàraidh
Tollomuick Forest
Crom Loch
Beinn a' Chaisteil
2404
Carn Cas nan Gabhar
1976
Black Water
Aultnamain Inn
E A S T E R R O S S
Gorm Loch
Abhainn na Glasa
Loch a' Chaorainn
Beinn Tharsuinn
2270
Loch Sheilah
Cnoc an t-Sabhail
1243
Meall a' Ghrianain
2531
Kildermorie Forest
Kildermorie Lodge
Loch Bad a' Bhathaich
Braeantra
Loch Magharaidh
Strath Rusdale
Loch Vaich
Strathvaich Forest
Inchbae Forest
Loch nan Amhaichean
Beinn nan Eun
2436
Abhainn
Loch Morie
Black Water
Strath Rory
Cnoc Corr Guinie
1301
Kinrive Hill
1056
Scotsb
Kinrive
Strathy
Loanreoch
Ardross Forest
Strathrannoch
Carn nan Gabhar
Meall Mór

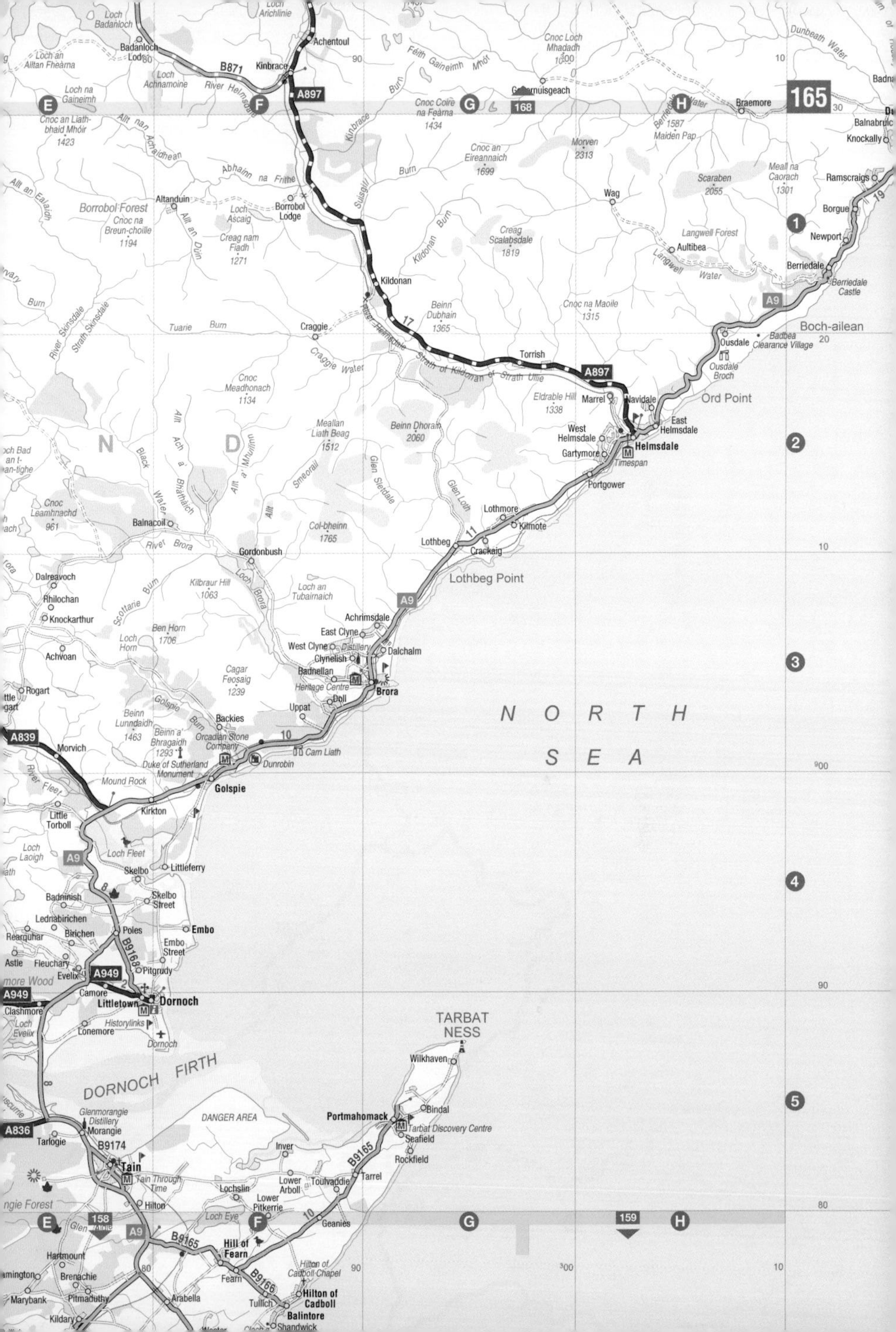
165
NORTH
SEA
Helmsdale
Brora
Golspie
Dornoch
Tain
Portmahomack
TARBAT NESS
DORNOCH FIRTH
Kinbrace
Kildonan
Berriedale
Ord Point
Lothbeg Point
Borrobol Forest
Langwell Forest
Morven 2313
Scaraben 2055
Embo
A9
A897
A839
A949
A836
B871
B9168
B9174
B9165
B9166
168
158
159

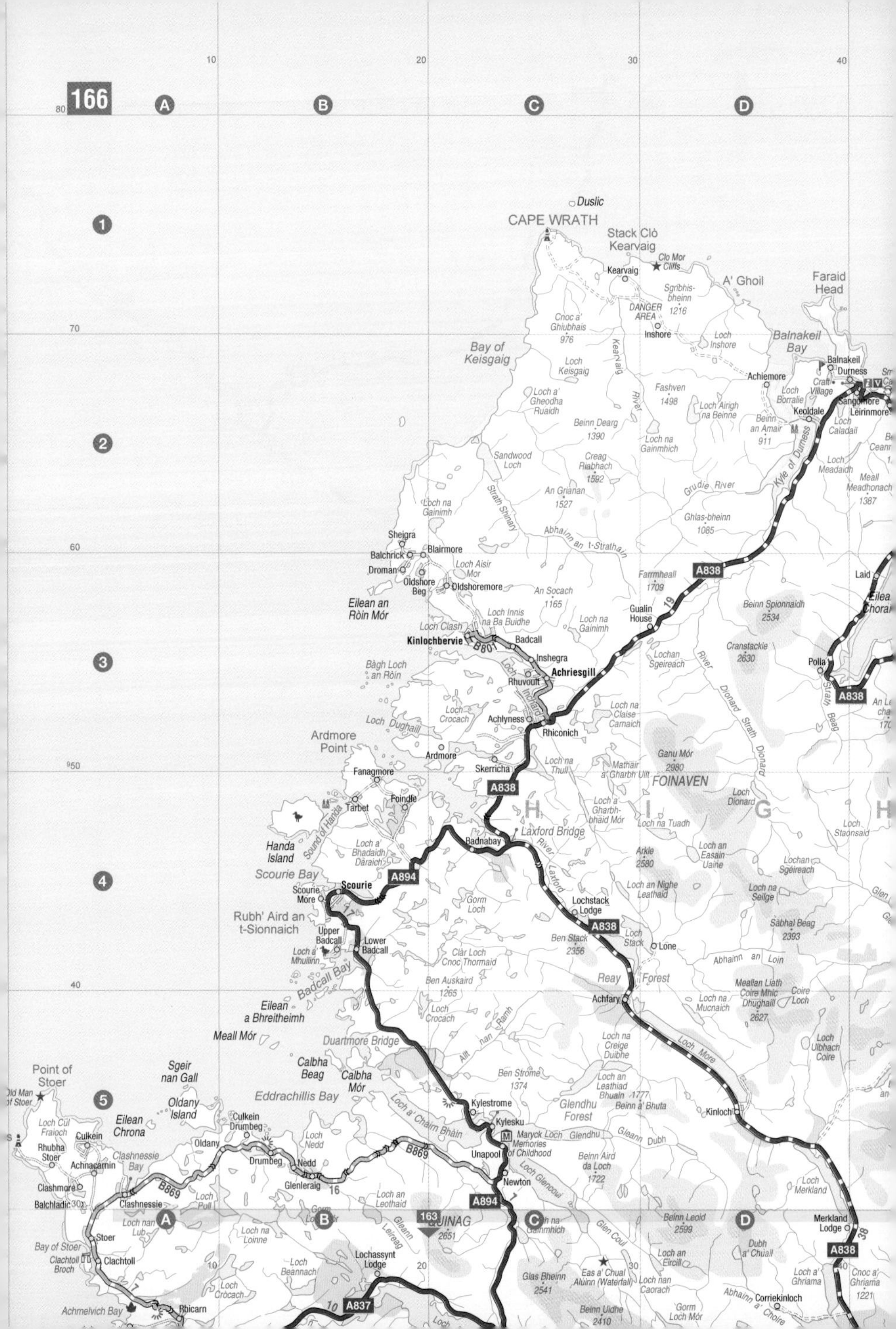

Duslic
CAPE WRATH
Stack Clò Kearvaig
Clo Mor Cliffs
Kearvaig
Sgribhis-bheinn 1216
DANGER AREA
Inshore
A' Ghoil
Faraid Head
Cnoc a' Ghiubhais 976
Bay of Keisgaig
Loch Keisgaig
Loch Inshore
Balnakeil Bay
Balnakeil
Durness
Craft Village
Achiemore
Fashven 1498
Loch a' Gheodha Ruaidh
Loch Airigh na Beinne
Loch Borralie
Sangomore
Leirinmore
Keoldale
Beinn Dearg 1390
Beinn an Amair 911
Loch Caladail
Loch na Gainmhich
Sandwood Loch
Creag Riabhach 1592
Kyle of Durness
Loch Meadaidh
Meall Meadhonach 1387
An Grianan 1527
Grudie River
Strath Shinary
Loch na Gainimh
Ghlas-bheinn 1085
Abhainn an t-Strathain
Sheigra
Balchrick
Blairmore
Droman
Oldshore Beg
Loch Aisir Mor
Oldshoremore
Farrmheall 1709
A838
Laid
An Socach 1165
Eilean an Ròin Mór
Loch Innis na Ba Buidhe
Gualin House
Beinn Spionnaidh 2534
Loch Clash
Loch na Gainimh
Kinlochbervie
B801
Badcall
Inshegra
Achriesgill
Rhuvoult
Loch Inchard
Lochan Sgeireach
Cranstackie 2630
Polla
Bàgh Loch an Ròin
Strath Beag
Loch Crocach
Loch Dughaill
Achlyness
Loch na Claise Carnaich
River Dionard
Strath Dionard
Rhiconich
Ardmore Point
Ardmore
Ganu Mór 2980
Loch na Thull
Skerricha
Mathair a' Gharbh Uilt
FOINAVEN
Fanagmore
Tarbet
Foindle
Loch Dionard
Loch a' Gharbh-bhaid Mór
H I G H
Sound of Handa
Loch Staonsaid
Handa Island
Badnabay
Laxford Bridge
Loch na Tuadh
Loch a' Bhadaidh Daraich
River Laxford
Arkle 2580
Loch an Easain Uaine
Scourie Bay
A894
Lochan Sgéireach
Scourie More
Scourie
Loch an Nighe Leathaid
Gorm Loch
Loch na Seilge
Rubh' Aird an t-Sionnaich
Lochstack Lodge
Upper Badcall
Lower Badcall
Loch a' Mhuilinn
Ben Stack 2356
Loch Stack
Lone
Sàbhal Beag 2393
Clàr Loch Cnoc Thormaid
Abhainn an Loin
Badcall Bay
Ben Auskaird 1265
Reay Forest
Meallan Liath Coire Mhic Dhughaill 2627
Coire Loch
Eilean a Bhreitheimh
Loch Crocach
Achfary
Loch na Mucnaich
Allt nan Ramh
Meall Mór
Duartmore Bridge
Loch na Creige Duibhe
Loch More
Loch Ulbhach Coire
Point of Stoer
Old Man of Stoer
Sgeir nan Gall
Calbha Beag
Calbha Mór
Ben Strome 1374
Oldany Island
Eddrachillis Bay
Loch Leathiad Bhuain 1777
Beinn a' Bhuta
Eilean Chrona
Kylestrome
Loch a' Chàirn Bhàin
Glendhu Forest
Kinloch
Loch Cùl Fraioch
Culkein
Culkein Drumbeg
Loch Nedd
Kylesku
Rhubha Stoer
Oldany
Maryck Loch Glendhu
Memories of Childhood
Gleann Dubh
Clashnessie Bay
Drumbeg
Nedd
B869
Unapool
Achnacarnin
Loch Glencoul
Beinn Aird da Loch 1722
Clashmore
Glenleraig
Newton
Loch Merkland
B869
Loch Poll
Loch an Leothaid
Balchladich
Clashnessie
Loch nan Lub
Gleann Leireag
QUINAG 2651
Loch na Gainmhich
Glen Coul
Beinn Leoid 2599
Merkland Lodge
Stoer
Loch na Loinne
A838
Bay of Stoer
Clachtoll
Clachtoll Broch
Lochassynt Lodge
Loch Beannach
Loch an Eircill
Dubh a' Chuail
Loch a' Ghriama
Cnoc a' Ghriama 1221
Eas a' Chual Aluinn (Waterfall)
Glas Bheinn 2541
Loch nan Caorach
Loch Cròcach
Achmelvich Bay
Rhicarn
A837
Corriekinloch
Abhainn a' Choire
Beinn Uidhe 2410
Gorm Loch Mór
Loch

163

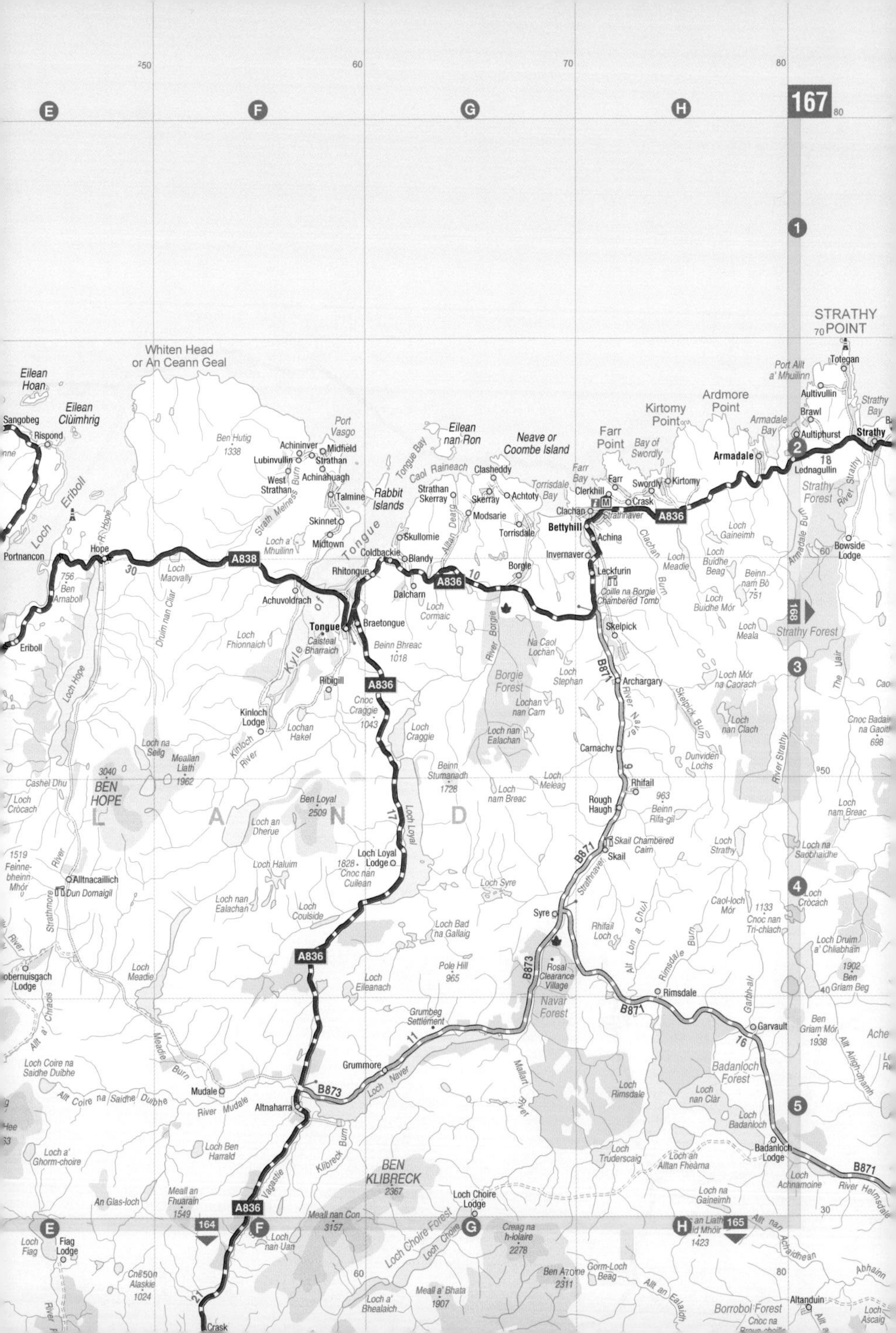
E
F
G
H
1
2
3
4
5
STRATHY POINT
Whiten Head or An Ceann Geal
Eilean Hoan
Eilean Clùimhrig
Sangobeg
Rispond
Loch Eriboll
Portnancon
Hope
Eriboll
Ben Hutig 1338
Port Vasgo
Achininver
Midfield
Lubinvullin
Strathan
West Strathan
Achinahuagh
Talmine
Rabbit Islands
Skinnet
Midtown
Kyle of Tongue
Coldbackie
Rhitongue
Achuvoldrach
Tongue
Braetongue
Caisteal Bharraich
Beinn Bhreac 1018
Ribigill
Tongue Bay
Eilean nan Ron
Caol Raineach
Strathan Skerray
Skullomie
Blandy
Dalcharn
Neave or Coombe Island
Clasheddy
Skerray
Achtoty
Torrisdale Bay
Modsarie
Torrisdale
Borgie
Farr Point
Farr Bay
Farr
Clerkhill
Clachan
Bettyhill
Achina
Invernaver
Leckfurin
Coille na Borgie Chambered Tomb
Skelpick
Bay of Swordly
Swordly
Kirtomy
Kirtomy Point
Crask
Strathnaver
Ardmore Point
Armadale Bay
Armadale
Port Allt a' Mhuilinn
Totegan
Aultivullin
Brawl
Aultiphurst
Strathy Bay
Strathy
Lednagullin
Strathy Forest
River Strathy
Bowside Lodge
168
A836
A838
B871
B873
Loch Maovally
Ben Arnaboll 756
Drium nan Cliar
Loch Fhionnaich
Loch a' Mhuilinn
Strath Melness Burn
Loch Cormaic
River Borgie
Borgie Forest
Na Caol Lochan
Loch Stephan
Lochan nan Carn
Loch nan Ealachan
Archargary
River Naver
Carnachy
Rhifail
Rough Haugh
Beinn Rifa-gil 963
Skail Chambered Cairn
Skail
Skelpick Burn
Dunviden Lochs
Loch nan Clach
Loch Mór na Caorach
Loch Meala
Loch Gaineimh
Loch Meadie
Loch Buidhe Beag
Loch Buidhe Mór
Beinn nam Bò 751
Clachan Burn
Cnoc Craggie 1043
Loch Craggie
Beinn Stumanadh 1728
Loch nam Breac
Loch Meleag
Kinloch Lodge
Kinloch River
Lochan Hakel
Loch na Seilg
Meallan Liath 1962
BEN HOPE 3040
Cashel Dhu
Loch Cròcach
Loch Hope
Ben Loyal 2509
Loch Loyal
Loch Loyal Lodge
Loch an Dherue
Loch Haluim
Cnoc nan Cuilean 1828
Loch nan Ealachan
Loch Coulside
Loch Syre
Syre
Rosal Clearance Village
Navar Forest
Loch Bad na Gallaig
Pole Hill 965
Loch Eileanach
Grumbeg Settlement
Grummore
Loch Naver
Mallart River
Rhifail Loch
Allt Lon a Chuil
Rimsdale Burn
Rimsdale
Garbh-allt
Garvault
Badanloch Forest
Loch nan Clàr
Loch Badanloch
Badanloch Lodge
Loch Rimsdale
Loch Truderscaig
Loch an Alltan Fhearna
Loch Achnamoine
River Helmsdale
Loch na Gaineimh
Loch Strathy
Caol-loch Mór
Cnoc nan Trì-chlach 1133
Loch Druim a' Chliabhain
Ben Griam Beg 1902
Ben Griam Mór 1938
Allt Airigh-dhamh
Loch na Saobhaidhe
Loch Cròcach
Loch nam Breac
Cnoc Badaidh na Gaoith 698
The Uair
1519 Feinne-bheinn Mhór
Strathmore River
Alltnacaillich
Dun Domaigil
Strathmore
Gobernuisgach Lodge
Allt a' Chraois
Loch Meadie
Meadie Burn
Loch Coire na Saidhe Duibhe
Allt Coire na Saidhe Duibhe
Mudale
River Mudale
Altnaharra
Loch a' Ghorm-choire
Loch Ben Harrald
Vagastie
Klibreck Burn
BEN KLIBRECK 2367
Loch Choire Lodge
Meall an Fhuarain 1549
An Glas-loch
Meall nan Con 3157
Loch Choire Forest
Loch Choire
Creag na h-Iolaire 2278
Ben Armine 2311
Gorm-Loch Beag
Allt an Ealaidh
Allt nan Achaidhean
Abhainn
Loch Fiag
Fiag Lodge
164
165
Loch nan Uan
Cnoc Alaskie 1024
Meall a' Bhata 1907
Loch a' Bhealaich
Meall an Liath Mhòir 1423
Borrobol Forest
Altanduin
Crask
L A N D

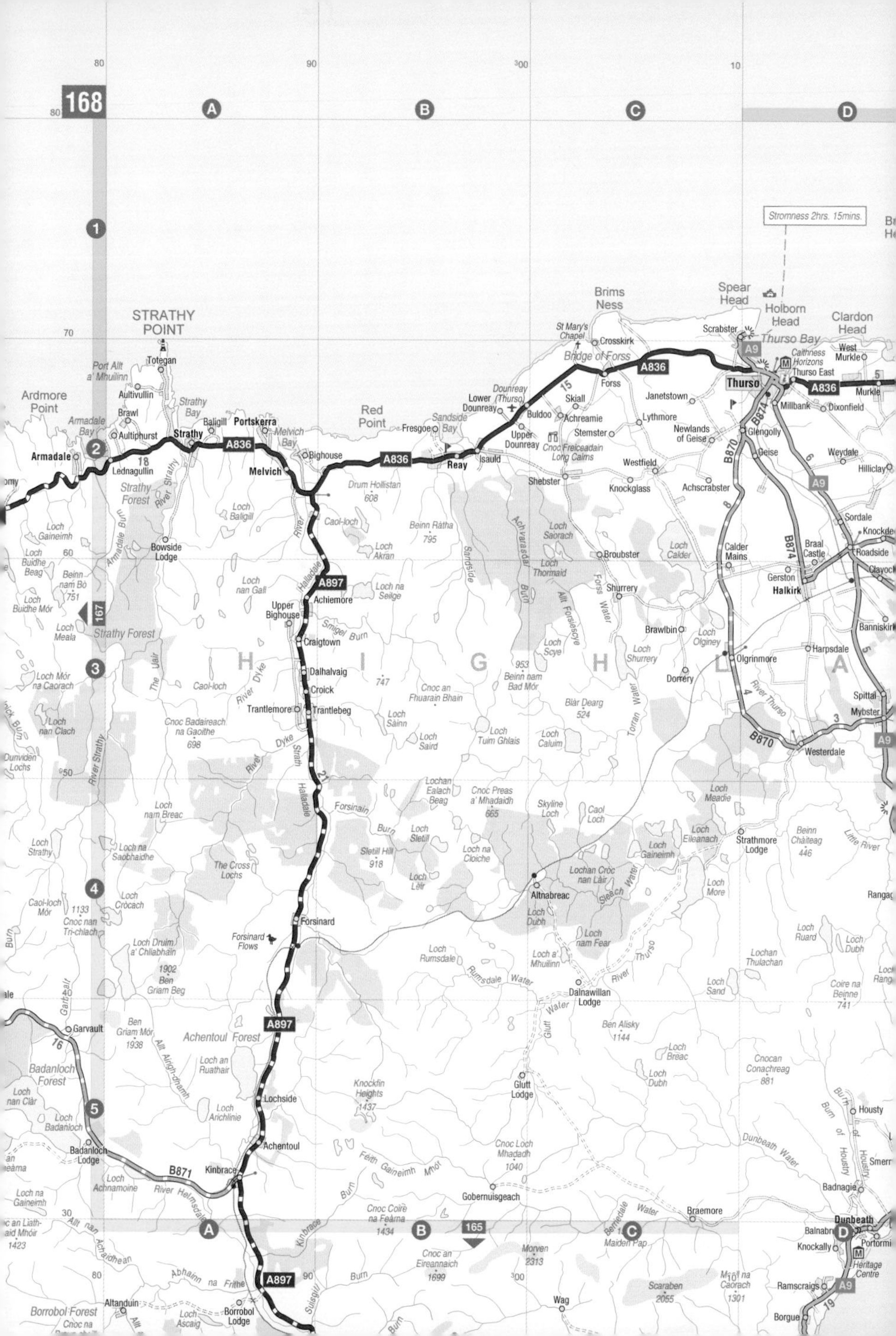

STRATHY POINT
Ardmore Point
Armadale
Strathy
Portskerra
Melvich
Bighouse
Red Point
Fresgoe
Reay
Isauld
Dounreay
Buldoo
Brims Ness
Crosskirk
Bridge of Forss
Forss
Scrabster
Spear Head
Holborn Head
Thurso Bay
Thurso
Thurso East
Clardon Head
Murkle
Stromness 2hrs. 15mins.
Caithness Horizons
Janetstown
Lythmore
Skiall
Achreamie
Stemster
Shebster
Westfield
Knockglass
Achscrabster
Newlands of Geise
Glengolly
Geise
Millbank
Dixonfield
Weydale
Hilliclay
Sordale
Braal Castle
Roadside
Gerston
Halkirk
Calder Mains
Broubster
Shurrery
Brawlbin
Dorrery
Olgrinmore
Harpsdale
Banniskirk
Spittal
Mybster
Westerdale
HIGHLAND
Strathy Forest
Bowside Lodge
Upper Bighouse
Achiemore
Craigtown
Dalhalvaig
Croick
Trantlemore
Trantlebeg
Forsinard
Forsinard Flows
Altnabreac
Strathmore Lodge
Dalnawillan Lodge
Glutt Lodge
Garvault
Badanloch Forest
Badanloch Lodge
Achentoul Forest
Lochside
Achentoul
Kinbrace
Gobernuisgeach
Braemore
Housty
Badnagie
Dunbeath
Balnabruich
Portormin
Knockally
Heritage Centre
Ramscraigs
Borgue
Wag
Altanduin
Borrobol Lodge
Borrobol Forest
Morven 2313
Scaraben 2055
Maiden Pap
Cnoc an Eireannaich 1699
Cnoc Coire na Fearna 1434
Ben Griam Mór 1938
Ben Griam Beg 1902
Knockfin Heights 1437
Ben Alisky 1144
Cnoc Loch Mhadadh 1040
Sletill Hill 918
Beinn Rátha 795
Drum Hollistan 608
Cnocan Conachreag 881
Coire na Beinne 741
A836
A897
A9
B870
B874
B871
165
167

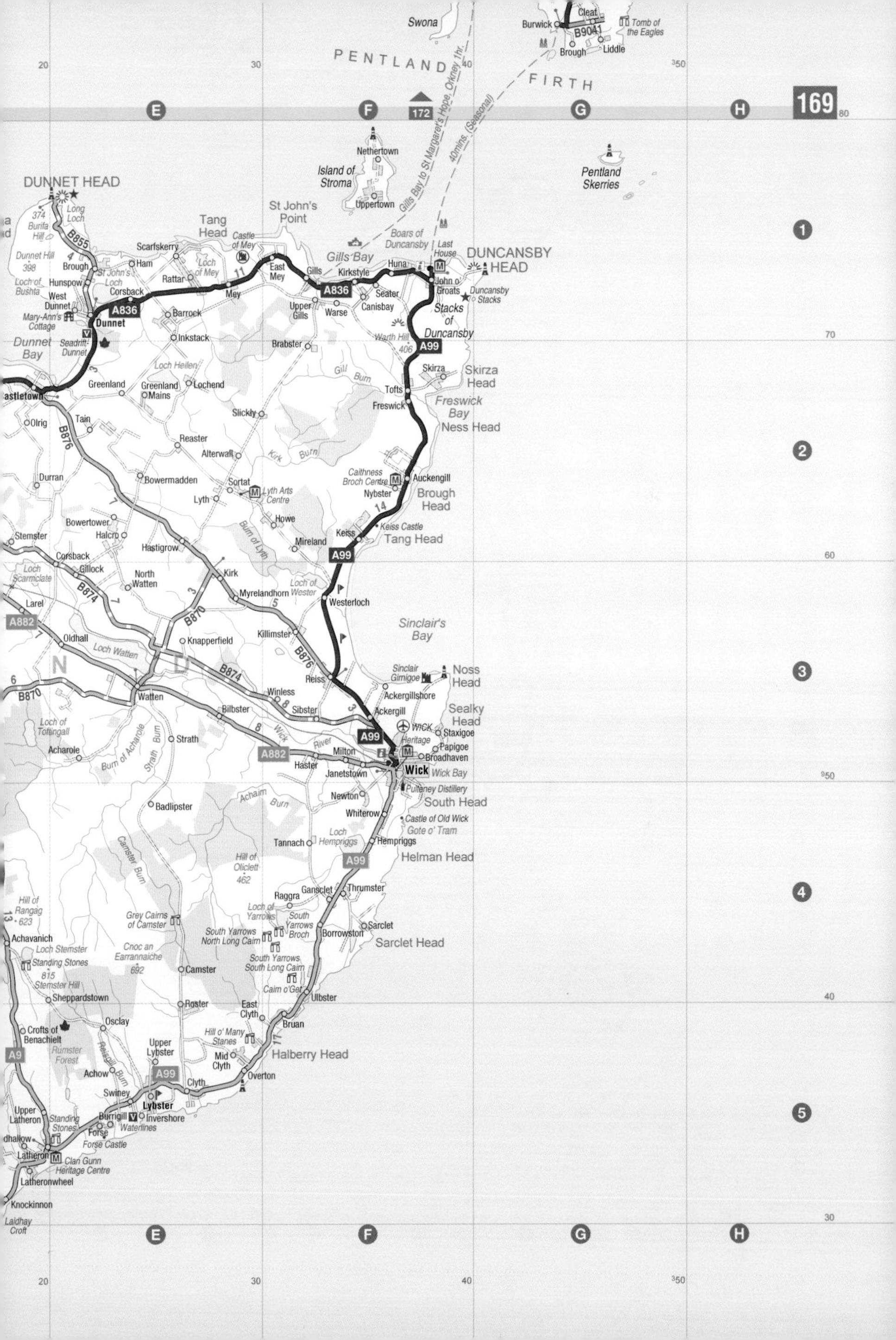
Swona
Cleat
Burwick
B9041
Tomb of the Eagles
Brough
Liddle
PENTLAND FIRTH
172
Gills Bay to St Margaret's Hope, Orkney 1hr.
40mins. (Seasonal)
E
F
G
H
Nethertown
Island of Stroma
Uppertown
Pentland Skerries
DUNNET HEAD
374
Burifa Hill
Long Loch
B855
Dunnet Hill 398
Brough
Loch of Bushta
Hunspow
West Dunnet
Mary-Ann's Cottage
Dunnet
Seadrift-Dunnet
Dunnet Bay
St John's Loch
Ham
Scarfskerry
Tang Head
Castle of Mey
St John's Point
Loch of Mey
Rattar
Corsback
A836
Barrock
Inkstack
Mey
East Mey
Gills
Gills Bay
Boars of Duncansby
Last House
DUNCANSBY HEAD
Kirkstyle
Huna
John o' Groats
Duncansby Stacks
Stacks of Duncansby
Upper Gills
Warse
Seater
Canisbay
Warth Hill 406
A99
Brabster
Skirza
Skirza Head
Loch Heilen
Greenland
Greenland Mains
Lochend
Gill Burn
Tofts
Freswick
Freswick Bay
Ness Head
Castletown
Olrig
Tain
B876
Slickly
Reaster
Alterwall
Kirk Burn
Caithness Broch Centre
Auckengill
Nybster
Brough Head
Durran
Bowermadden
Sortat
Lyth Arts Centre
Lyth
Howe
Keiss Castle
Keiss
Tang Head
Bowertower
Halcro
Stemster
Hastigrow
Burn of Lyth
Mireland
Corsback
Gillock
Loch Scarmclate
North Watten
Kirk
B874
Larel
A882
Myrelandhorn
Loch of Wester
Westerloch
B870
Oldhall
Loch Watten
Knapperfield
Killimster
Sinclair's Bay
B876
Reiss
Sinclair Girnigoe
Noss Head
Watten
Winless
Ackergillshore
Sealky Head
Bilbster
Sibster
Ackergill
Loch of Toftingall
Strath
Wick
WICK
Heritage
Staxigoe
Acharole
Burn of Acharole
Strath Burn
River
Milton
Papigoe
Broadhaven
Haster
Janetstown
Wick Bay
Pulteney Distillery
South Head
Newton
Badlipster
Achairn Burn
Whiterow
Castle of Old Wick
Gote o' Tram
Loch Hempriggs
Tannach
Hempriggs
Helman Head
Camster Burn
Hill of Oliclett 462
Hill of Rangag 623
Raggra
Gansclet
Thrumster
Grey Cairns of Camster
Loch of Yarrows
South Yarrows Broch
Sarclet
South Yarrows North Long Cairn
Borrowston
Sarclet Head
Achavanich
Loch Stemster
Standing Stones
Cnoc an Earrannaiche 692
South Yarrows South Long Cairn
815 Stemster Hill
Camster
Cairn o'Get
Ulbster
Sheppardstown
Roster
East Clyth
Bruan
Crofts of Benachielt
Osclay
Hill o' Many Stanes
Rumster Forest
Upper Lybster
Mid Clyth
Halberry Head
A9
Reisgill Burn
Achow
A99
Overton
Clyth
Swiney
Lybster
Upper Latheron
Standing Stones
Burrigill
Invershore
Waterlines
Forse
Forse Castle
Latheron
Clan Gunn Heritage Centre
Latheronwheel
Knockinnon
Laidhay Croft
20
30
40
350
80
70
60
950
40
30
1
2
3
4
5

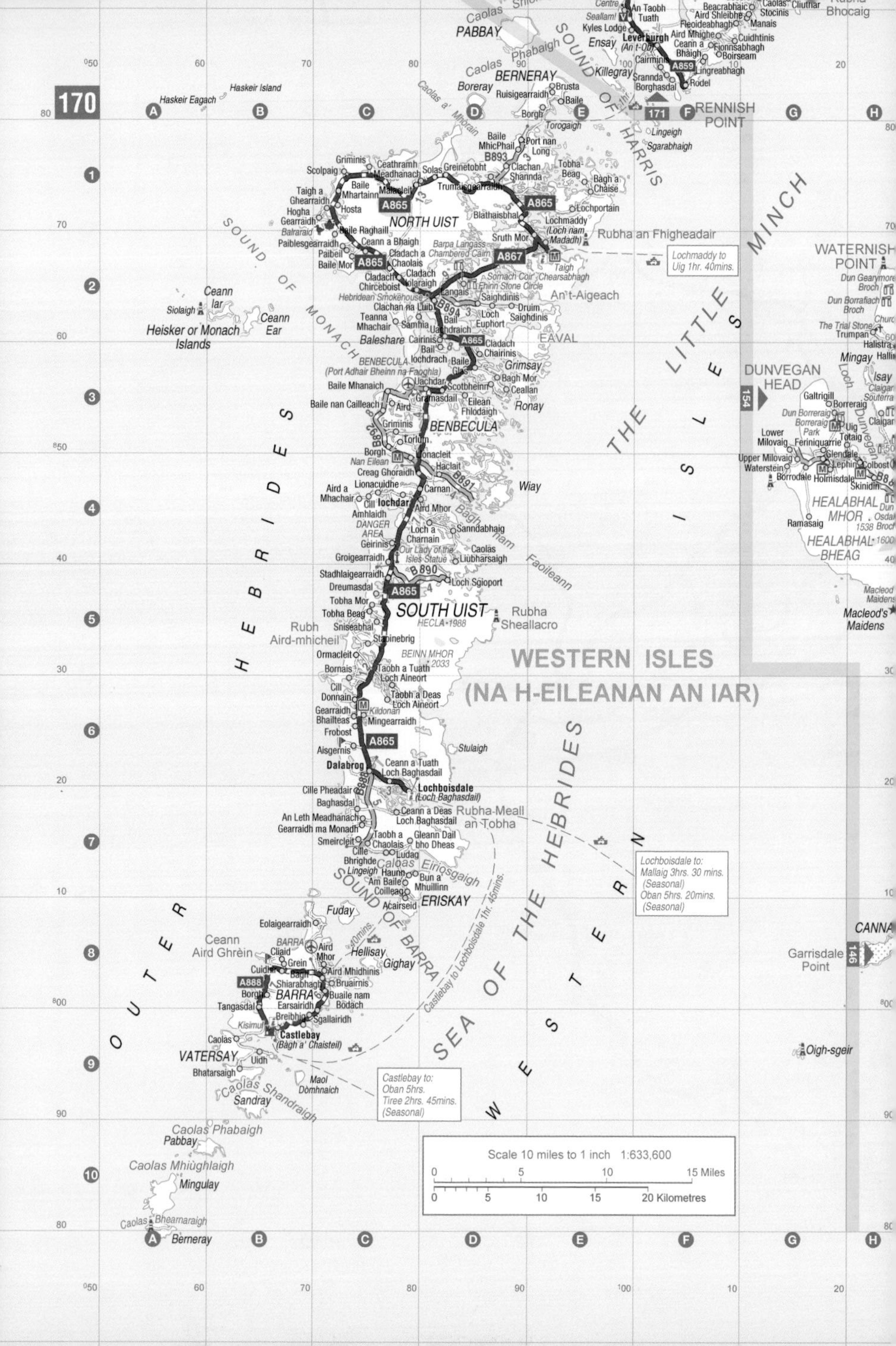
WESTERN ISLES
(NA H-EILEANAN AN IAR)
OUTER HEBRIDES
THE LITTLE MINCH
SEA OF THE HEBRIDES
SOUND OF MONACH
SOUND OF HARRIS
SOUND OF BARRA
NORTH UIST
BENBECULA
SOUTH UIST
BARRA
ERISKAY
VATERSAY
BERNERAY
PABBAY
Heisker or Monach Islands
Lochmaddy
Lochboisdale
Castlebay
Leverburgh
Lochmaddy to Uig 1hr. 40mins.
Lochboisdale to: Mallaig 3hrs. 30 mins. (Seasonal) Oban 5hrs. 20mins. (Seasonal)
Castlebay to: Oban 5hrs. Tiree 2hrs. 45mins. (Seasonal)
Castlebay to Lochboisdale 1hr. 45mins.
Scale 10 miles to 1 inch 1:633,600
0 5 10 15 Miles
0 5 10 15 20 Kilometres
A865
A867
A888
A859
B893
B894
B890
B891
B892
B888
HECLA 1988
BEINN MHOR 2033
EAVAL
DUNVEGAN HEAD
WATERNISH POINT
RENNISH POINT
CANNA
Garrisdale Point
Macleod's Maidens
HEALABHAL MHOR
HEALABHAL BHEAG
Mingulay
Sandray
Pabbay
Berneray
Oigh-sgeir
Wiay
Ronay
Grimsay
Fuday
Hellisay
Gighay
171
154
146

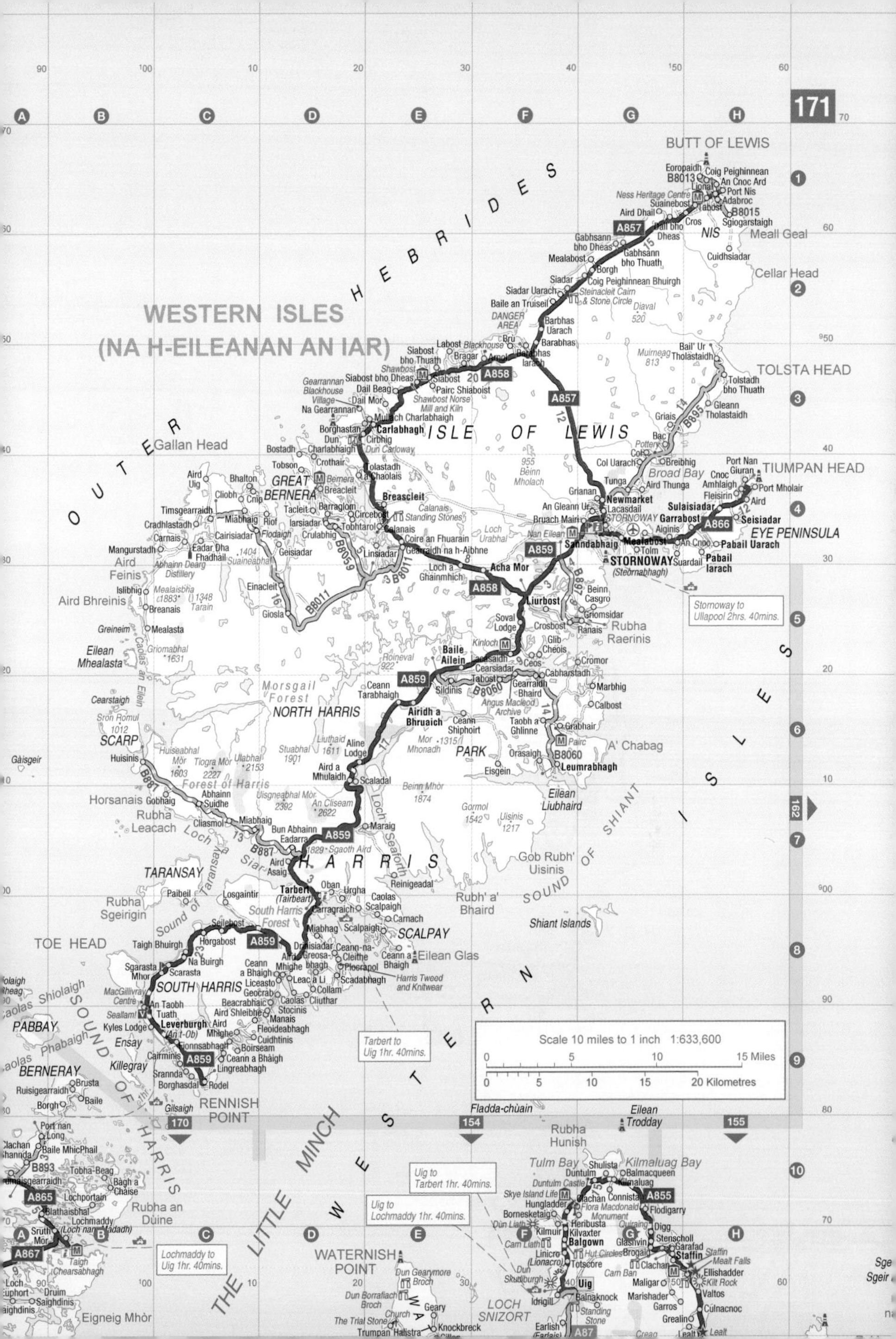
WESTERN ISLES
(NA H-EILEANAN AN IAR)
OUTER HEBRIDES
WESTERN ISLES
THE LITTLE MINCH
SOUND OF HARRIS
SOUND OF SHIANT
BUTT OF LEWIS
Europaidh
Coig Peighinnean
B8013
An Cnoc Ard
Lional
Port Nis
Ness Heritage Centre
Suainebost
Adabroc
Tabost
B8015
Aird Dhail
Sgiogarstaigh
A857
Cros
Dail bho Dheas
NIS
Meall Geal
Gabhsann bho Dheas
Gabhsann bho Thuath
Cuidhsiadar
Mealabost
Borgh
Cellar Head
Siadar
Coig Peighinnean Bhuirgh
Siadar Uarach
Steinacleit Cairn & Stone Circle
Baile an Truiseil
Diaval 520
DANGER AREA
Barbhas Uarach
Brù
Barabhas
Labost
Blackhouse
Bragar
Arnol
Barabhas Iarach
Siabost bho Thuath
Bail' Ur Tholastaidh
Muirneag 813
TOLSTA HEAD
Gearrannan Blackhouse Village
Siabost bho Dheas
Shawbost
Siabost
Pairc Shiaboist
A858
Dail Beag
Dail Mor
Shawbost Norse Mill and Kiln
Tolstadh bho Thuath
Na Gearrannan
Mullach Charlabhaigh
Gleann Tholastaidh
Borghastan
Carlabhagh
ISLE OF LEWIS
Griais
B895
Dun Charlabhaigh
Cirbhig
Dun Carloway
Bac
Pottery
Gallan Head
Bostadh
Col
Tobson
Crothair
955 Beinn Mholach
Col Uarach
Breibhig
Port Nan Giuran
TIUMPAN HEAD
Aird Uig
Bhalton
GREAT BERNERA
Bernera
Tolastadh a' Chaolais
Broad Bay
Cnoc Amhlaigh
Port Mholair
Cliobh
Cnip
Breacleit
Breascleit
Tunga
Aird Thunga
Fleisirin
Aird
Timsgearraidh
Tacleit
Barraglom
Calanais
Griannan
Newmarket
Sulaisiadar
Cradhlastadh
Miabhaig
Riof
Iarsiadar
Circebost
Tobhtarol
Calanais Standing Stones
An Gleann Ur
Lacasdail
STORNOWAY
Garrabost
Seisiadar
Carnais
Cairisiadar
Flodaigh
Crulabhig
Coire an Fhuarain
Loch Urabhal
Bruach Mairi
A866
EYE PENINSULA
Mangurstadh
Eadar Dha Fhadhail
Geisiadar
B8059
Gearraidh na h-Aibhne
Nan Eilean
Sanndabhaig
Mealabost
Aiginis
An Cnoc
Pabail Uarach
Aird Feinis
Abhainn Dearg Distillery
1404 Suaineabhal
Linsiadar
A859
Tolm
Suardail
Pabail Iarach
B8011
Loch a Ghainmhich
Acha Mor
(Steornabhagh)
Islibhig
Mealaisbhal (1883)
1348 Tarain
Einacleit
A858
Liurbost
B897
Beinn Casgro
Stornoway to Ullapool 2hrs. 40mins.
Aird Bhreinis
Breanais
Griomsidar
Giosla
Soval Lodge
Crosbost
Ranais
Rubha Raerinis
Greineim
Mealasta
Kinloch
Glib Cheois
Eilean Mhealasta
Caolas an Eilein
Griomabhal 1631
Roineval 922
Baile Ailein
Lacasaidh
Ceos
Cromor
Cearsiadar
Cabharstadh
Tabost
Gearraidh Bhaird
Marbhig
Morsgail Forest
Ceann Tarabhaigh
Sildinis
B8060
Calbost
Cearstaigh
NORTH HARRIS
Airidh a Bhruaich
Angus Macleod Archive
Sron Romul 1012
Ceann Shiphoirt
Taobh a Ghlinne
Grabhair
SCARP
Liuthaid 1611
Aline Lodge
Mor Mhonadh
PARK
Pairc
A' Chabag
Gàisgeir
Huisinis
Huiseabhal Mòr 1603
Tiogra Mòr 2227
Ulabhal 2153
Stuabhal 1901
Orasaigh
B8060
Aird a Mhulaidh
Eisgein
Leumrabhagh
B887
Forest of Harris
Scaladal
Beinn Mhòr 1874
Horsanais
Gobhaig
Abhainn Suidhe
Uisgneabhal Mòr 2392
An Cliseam 2622
Loch Seaforth
Eilean Liubhaird
Rubha Leacach
Cliasmol
Miabhaig
Gormol 1542
Uisinis 1217
Loch Siar
Bun Abhainn Eadarra
Maraig
1829 Sgaoth Aird
HARRIS
Gob Rubh' Uisinis
TARANSAY
Aird Asaig
Reinigeadal
Sound of Taransay
Tarbert (Tairbeart)
Oban
Urgha
Caolas Scalpaigh
Rubh' a' Bhaird
Paibeil
Losgaintir
South Harris Forest
Carragraich
Carnach
Rubha Sgeirigin
Seilebost
Miabhag
Scalpaigh
SCALPAY
Shiant Islands
TOE HEAD
Taigh Bhuirgh
Horgabost
Drinisiadar
Ceann-na-Cleithe
Eilean Glas
Aird Mhighe
Greosabhagh
Ceann a Bhaigh
Sgarasta Mhor
Na Buirgh
Scarasta
Ceann a Bhaigh
Liceasto
Plocrapol
Leac a Li
Scadabhagh
Harris Tweed and Knitwear
SOUTH HARRIS
Geocrab
Collam
MacGillivray Centre
Caolas Cluithar
Beacrabhaic
An Taobh Tuath
Aird Shleibhe
Stocinis
PABBAY
Seallam!
Manais
Kyles Lodge
Leverburgh (An t-Ob)
Aird Mhighe
Fleoideabhagh
Cuidhtinis
Ensay
Tarbert to Uig 1hr. 40mins.
Fionnsabhagh
Boirseam
Ceann a Bhàigh
BERNERAY
Killegray
Cairminis
A859
Lingreabhagh
Srannda
Borghasdal
Rodel
Ruisigearraidh
Brusta
Baile
Borgh
Gilsaigh
RENNISH POINT
Scale 10 miles to 1 inch 1:633,600
0 5 10 15 Miles
0 5 10 15 20 Kilometres
Fladda-chùain
Eilean Trodday
Rubha Hunish
170
154
155
162
Port nan Long
Baile MhicPhail
B893
Tobha-Beag
Bàgh a Chàise
A865
Lochportain
Rubha an Dùine
Blathaisbhal
Lochmaddy (Loch nam Madadh)
Sruth Mor
A867
Taigh Chearsabhagh
Lochmaddy to Uig 1hr. 40mins.
Uig to Tarbert 1hr. 40mins.
Uig to Lochmaddy 1hr. 40mins.
Tulm Bay
Shulista
Kilmaluag Bay
Duntulm
Balmacqueen
Duntulm Castle
Kilmaluag
Skye Island Life
Hungladder
Flora Macdonald Monument
Connista
A855
Borneskeitaig
Flodigarry
Dùn Liath
Heribusta
Kilvaxter
Quiraing
Digg
Kilmuir
Balgown
Stenscholl
Carn Liath
Glashvin
Brogaig
Garafad
Staffin
Linicro (Lionacro)
Hut Circles
Mealt Falls
Totscore
Clachan
Ellishadder
Dun Skudiburgh
Carn Ban
Kilt Rock
Uig
Maligar
Idrigill
Balnaknock
Marishader
Valtos
Standing Stone
Garros
Culnacnoc
Earlish (Earlais)
A87
Grealin
Lealt
WATERNISH POINT
Dun Gearymore Broch
Dun Borrafiach Broch
The Trial Stone
Church
Geary
Trumpan
Halistra
Knockbreck
LOCH SNIZORT
Eigneig Mhòr
Loch Euphort
Druim
Saighdinis
Pabbay
Caolas Sholaigh
Sge
Sgeir

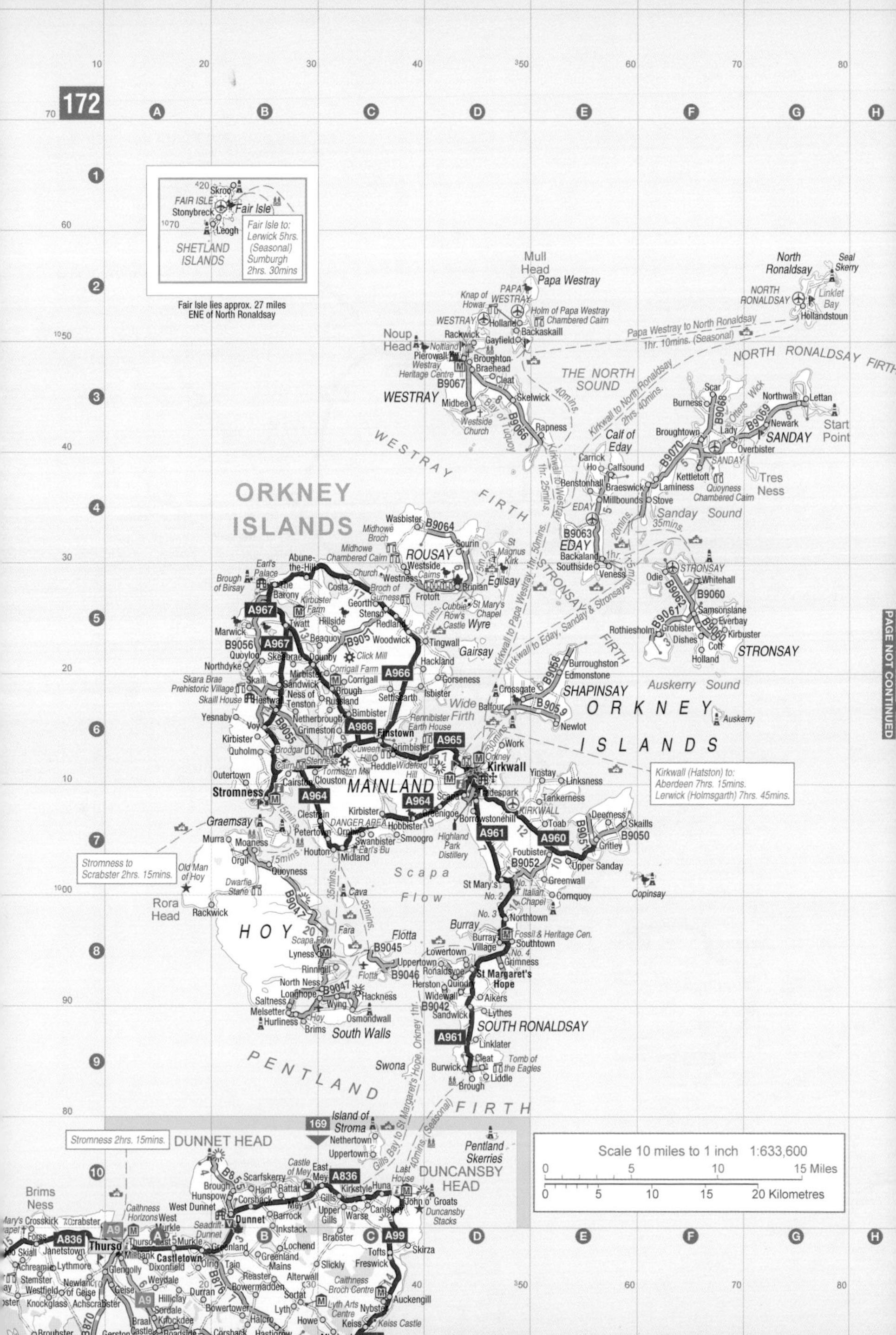

ORKNEY ISLANDS
FAIR ISLE
Skroo
Stonybreck
Fair Isle
Leogh
SHETLAND ISLANDS
Fair Isle to: Lerwick 5hrs. (Seasonal) Sumburgh 2hrs. 30mins
Fair Isle lies approx. 27 miles ENE of North Ronaldsay
Mull Head
Papa Westray
PAPA WESTRAY
Knap of Howar
Holm of Papa Westray Chambered Cairn
WESTRAY
Holland
Backaskaill
Rackwick
Gayfield
Noup Head
Noltland
Pierowall
Westray Heritage Centre
Broughton
Braehead
Cleat
B9067
WESTRAY
Midbea
Bay of Tuquoy
Skelwick
Westside Church
B9066
Rapness
THE NORTH SOUND
North Ronaldsay
Seal Skerry
NORTH RONALDSAY
Linklet Bay
Hollandstoun
Papa Westray to North Ronaldsay 1hr. 10mins. (Seasonal)
NORTH RONALDSAY FIRTH
Kirkwall to North Ronaldsay 2hrs. 40mins.
Kirkwall to Westray 1hr. 25mins.
40mins.
Scar
Burness
B9068
Otters Wick
Northwall
Lettan
B9069
Newark
Start Point
Broughtown
Lady
SANDAY
Overbister
B9070
Calf of Eday
Carrick Ho
Calfsound
Kettletoft
Tres Ness
Quoyness Chambered Cairn
Benstonhall
Braeswick
Laminess
Millbounds
Stove
Sanday Sound
35mins.
EDAY
B9063
EDAY
Backaland
Southside
Veness
20mins.
1hr.
WESTRAY FIRTH
STRONSAY
Odie
B9062
Whitehall
B9060
Samsonslane
Everbay
B9061
Rothiesholm
Grobister
Dishes
Kirbuster
Cott
Holland
STRONSAY
Wasbister
B9064
Midhowe Broch
Midhowe Chambered Cairn
ROUSAY
Sourin
Westside Cairns
Westness
St Magnus Kirk
Egilsay
Brinian
Frotoft
Broch of Gurness
Cubbie Row's Castle
St Mary's Chapel
Wyre
Gairsay
Kirkwall to Papa Westray 1hr. 50mins.
Kirkwall to Eday, Sanday & Stronsay
STRONSAY FIRTH
Abune-the-Hill
Earl's Palace
Brough of Birsay
The Barony
Costa
Church
Georth
Stenso
Kirbuster Farm
Hillside
Redland
A967
Twatt
Marwick
B9056
Quoyloo
Beaquoy
B9057
Woodwick
Tingwall
Skeabrae
Dounby
Click Mill
Northdyke
Skara Brae Prehistoric Village
Skaill House
Mirbister
Corrigall Farm
Corrigall
A966
Hackland
Gorseness
B9058
Burroughston
Edmonstone
SHAPINSAY
Auskerry Sound
Skaill
Sandwick
Brough
Isbister
Crossgate
Ness of Tenston
Russland
Settiscarth
Wide Firth
Balfour
B9059
ORKNEY
Auskerry
Yesnaby
Netherbrough
Bimbister
Rennibister Earth House
Voy
Grimeston
A986
Finstown
A965
Newlot
Kirbister
B9055
Quholm
Brodgar
Cuween Hill
Grimbister
Work
ISLANDS
Stenness
Heddle
Wideford Hill
Orkney
Kirkwall
Outertown
Tormiston Mill
Cairston
Clouston
MAINLAND
Kirkwall (Hatston) to: Aberdeen 7hrs. 15mins. Lerwick (Holmsgarth) 7hrs. 45mins.
Stromness
A964
Yinstay
Linksness
Tankerness
Hatston
Scapa
Kirbister
Greenigoe
Borrowstonehill
KIRKWALL
Graemsay
Clestrain
DANGER AREA
Hobbister
A961
Toab
Deerness
Skaills
B9050
Petertown
Orphir
Highland Park Distillery
A960
Gritley
Murra
Moaness
Swanbister
Earl's Bu
Smoogro
Foubister
B9052
Upper Sanday
Stromness to Scrabster 2hrs. 15mins.
Orgil
Houton
Midland
Old Man of Hoy
Quoyness
Scapa Flow
St Mary's
Greenwall
Dwarfie Stane
Cava
No. 1
No. 2
Italian Chapel
Cornquoy
Copinsay
Rora Head
Rackwick
B9047
35mins.
Northtown
No. 3
HOY
Fara
Burray
Burray Village
Fossil & Heritage Cen.
Southtown
Scapa Flow
Flotta
B9045
Lowertown
No. 4
Lyness
Uppertown
Grimness
Rinnigill
Flotta
B9046
Ronaldsvoe
St Margaret's Hope
North Ness
Herston
Quindry
Longhope
B9047
Hackness
Widewall
Aikers
Saltness
Wyng
B9042
Lythes
Melsetter
Hurliness
Osmondwall
Sandwick
SOUTH RONALDSAY
Brims
South Walls
A961
Linklater
PENTLAND FIRTH
Swona
Orkney 1hr.
Cleat
Tomb of the Eagles
Burwick
Liddle
Brough
Gills Bay to St Margaret's Hope
40mins. (Seasonal)
Island of Stroma
169
Nethertown
Uppertown
Stromness 2hrs. 15mins.
DUNNET HEAD
Pentland Skerries
DUNCANSBY HEAD
Scale 10 miles to 1 inch 1:633,600
0 5 10 15 Miles
0 5 10 15 20 Kilometres
Brims Ness
Brough
Scarfskerry
Castle of Mey
East Mey
A836
Last House
Hunspow
Ham
Rattar
Kirkstyle
Huna
Corsback
Mey
Gills
John o' Groats
Caithness Horizons
West Dunnet
Canisbay
Duncansby Stacks
Crosskirk
Scrabster
Dunnet
Barrock
Upper Gills
Warse
Forss
West Murkle
Seadrift Dunnet
Inkstack
A836
Thurso
Thurso East
Murkle
Brabster
A99
Skaill
Janetstown
Castletown
Greenland
Lochend
Skirza
Millbank
Greenland Mains
Tofts
Achreamie
Lythmore
Glengolly
Dixonfield
Olrig
Tain
Slickly
Freswick
Stemster
Newlands of Geise
Weydale
Reaster
Alterwall
Caithness Broch Centre
Westfield
Geise
Bowermadden
Knockglass
Achscrabster
A9
Hillclay
Durran
Sortat
Lyth Arts Centre
Nybster
Auckengill
Bowertower
Lyth
Braal Castle
Knockdee
Halcro
Howe
Keiss
Keiss Castle
Broubster
B870
Gerston
Roadside
Corsback
Hastigrow
Mireland
PAGE NOT CONTINUED

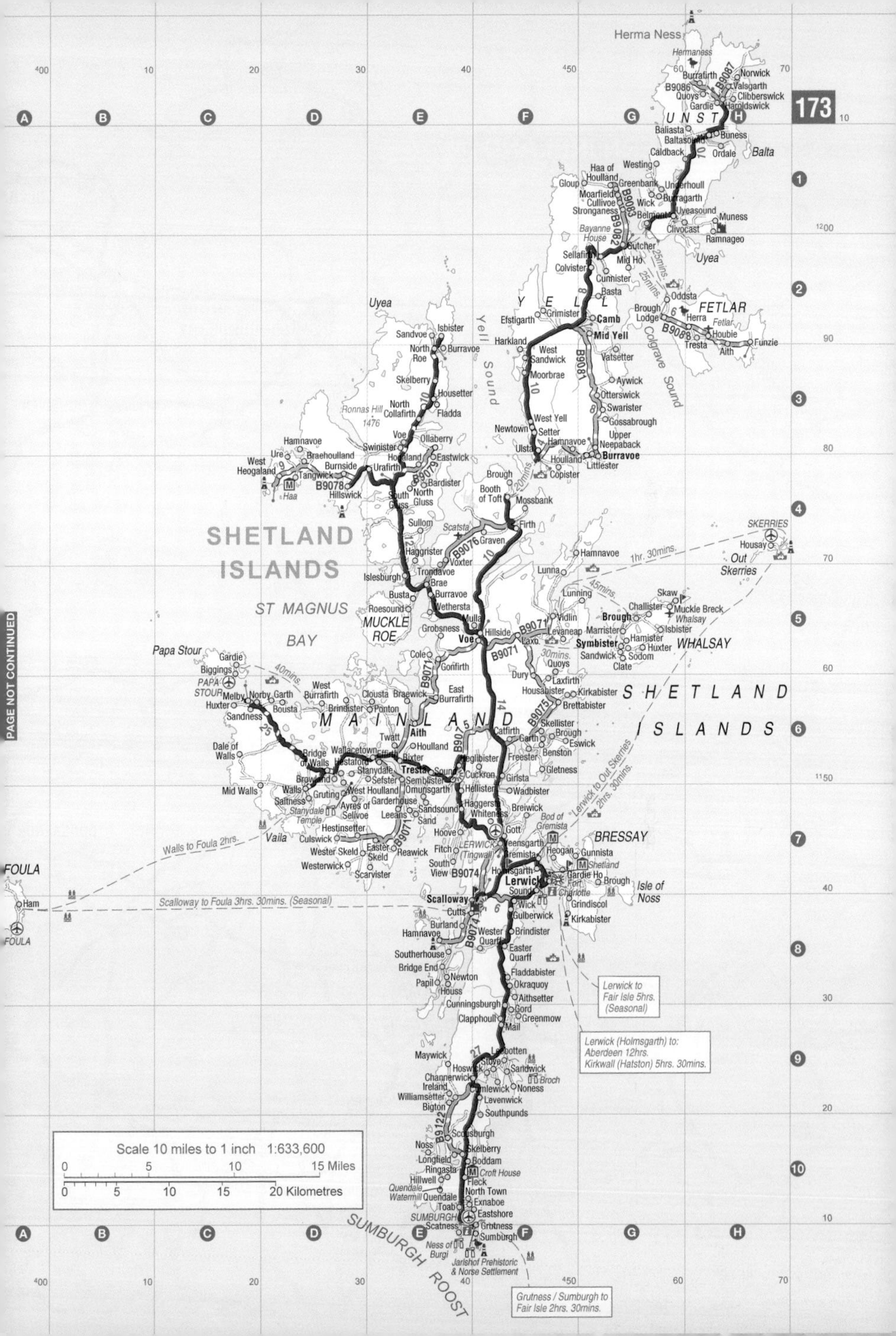

SHETLAND ISLANDS
S H E T L A N D I S L A N D S
Herma Ness
Hermaness
U N S T
Burrafirth
Norwick
Valsgarth
Clibberswick
B9086
Quoys
Gardie
Haroldswick
B9087
Baliasta
Baltasound
Buness
Caldback
Ordale
Balta
Westing
Haa of Houlland
Gloup
Greenbank
Underhoull
Moarfield
Cullivoe
Wick
Gutcher
Buttagarth
Stronganess
B9083
B9082
Belmont
Uyeasound
Muness
Clivocast
Ramnageo
Bayanne House
Sellafirth
Colvister
Mid Ho.
Uyea
Cunnister
Basta
25mins.
Oddsta
FETLAR
Y E L L
Grimister
Efstigarth
Camb
Mid Yell
Brough Lodge
Herra
Fetlar
Houbie
B9088
Tresta
Aith
Funzie
Colgrave Sound
Harkland
West Sandwick
B9081
Vatsetter
Aywick
Otterswick
Swarister
Gossabrough
Moorbrae
West Yell
Newtown
Setter
Hamnavoe
Upper Neepaback
Burravoe
Ulsta
Houlland
Littlester
Copister
20mins.
Yell Sound
Uyea
Isbister
Sandvoe
North Roe
Burravoe
Skelberry
Housetter
Ronnas Hill 1476
North Collafirth
Fladda
Voe
Ollaberry
Swinister
Hamnavoe
Ure
Braehoulland
West Heogaland
Burnside
Hogland
Eastwick
Tangwick
Urafirth
B9079
Bardister
Haa
B9078
Hillswick
North Gluss
South Gluss
Brough
Booth of Toft
Mossbank
Firth
Sullom
Scatsta
Graven
B9076
Haggrister
Voxter
Trondavoe
Brae
Islesburgh
Busta
Burravoe
Wethersta
Roesound
MUCKLE ROE
ST MAGNUS BAY
Mulla
Grobsness
Voe
Hillside
B9071
Cole
Gonfirth
Hamnavoe
Lunna
Lunning
Vidlin
Levaneap
Laxo
Skaw
Challister
Muckle Breck
Brough
Whalsay
Marrister
Isbister
Hamister
Symbister
Huxter
Sandwick
Sodom
Clate
WHALSAY
30mins.
Quoys
Dury
Laxfirth
Housabister
Kirkabister
Brettabister
Skellister
B9075
SKERRIES
Housay
Out Skerries
1hr. 30mins.
45mins.
Papa Stour
Gardie
Biggings
PAPA STOUR
40mins.
Melby
Norby
Garth
Huxter
Sandness
Bousta
West Burrafirth
Brindister
Clousta
Braewick
Ponton
East Burrafirth
M A I N L A N D
Aith
Twatt
Houlland
Catfirth
Garth
Brough
Eswick
Freester
Benston
Gletness
Dale of Walls
Bridge of Walls
Wallacetown
Hestaford
Effirth
Bixter
Tresta
Sound
Stanydale
Sefster
Semblister
Cuckron
Girlsta
Hellister
Wadbister
Omunsgarth
West Houlland
Gruting
Mid Walls
Walls
Brouland
Saltness
Stanydale Temple
Ayres of Selivoe
Garderhouse
Leeans
Sandsound
Sand
Haggersta
Whiteness
Breiwick
Bod of Gremista
Vaila
Hestinsetter
Culswick
Easter Skeld
Wester Skeld
Skeld
Reawick
Westerwick
Scarvister
Hoove
Fitch
Gott
LERWICK (Tingwall)
Veensgarth
Bremista
South View
B9074
Holmsgarth
Lerwick
Sound
Heogan
Gunnista
Shetland
Gardie Ho
Brough
Fort Charlotte
Grindiscol
BRESSAY
Isle of Noss
Kirkabister
Lerwick to Out Skerries 2hrs. 30mins.
FOULA
Ham
FOULA
Walls to Foula 2hrs.
Scalloway to Foula 3hrs. 30mins. (Seasonal)
Scalloway
Cutts
Wick
Gulberwick
Burland
Hamnavoe
Wester Quarff
Brindister
Easter Quarff
Southerhouse
Bridge End
Fladdabister
Papil
Newton
Houss
Okraquoy
Aithsetter
Cunningsburgh
Gord
Clapphoull
Greenmow
Mail
Lerwick to Fair Isle 5hrs. (Seasonal)
Lerwick (Holmsgarth) to: Aberdeen 12hrs. Kirkwall (Hatston) 5hrs. 30mins.
Maywick
Ledbotten
Hoswick
Stove
Sandwick
Channerwick
Broch
Ireland
Sumlewick
Noness
Williamsetter
Levenwick
Bigton
Southpunds
B9122
Scousburgh
Noss
Skelberry
Longfield
Boddam
Ringasta
Croft House
Hillwell
Fleck
Quendale Watermill
Quendale
North Town
Exnaboe
Toab
Eastshore
SUMBURGH
Scatness
Grutness
Sumburgh
Ness of Burgi
Jarlshof Prehistoric & Norse Settlement
SUMBURGH ROOST
Grutness / Sumburgh to Fair Isle 2hrs. 30mins.
Scale 10 miles to 1 inch 1:633,600
0 5 10 15 Miles
0 5 10 15 20 Kilometres
PAGE NOT CONTINUED

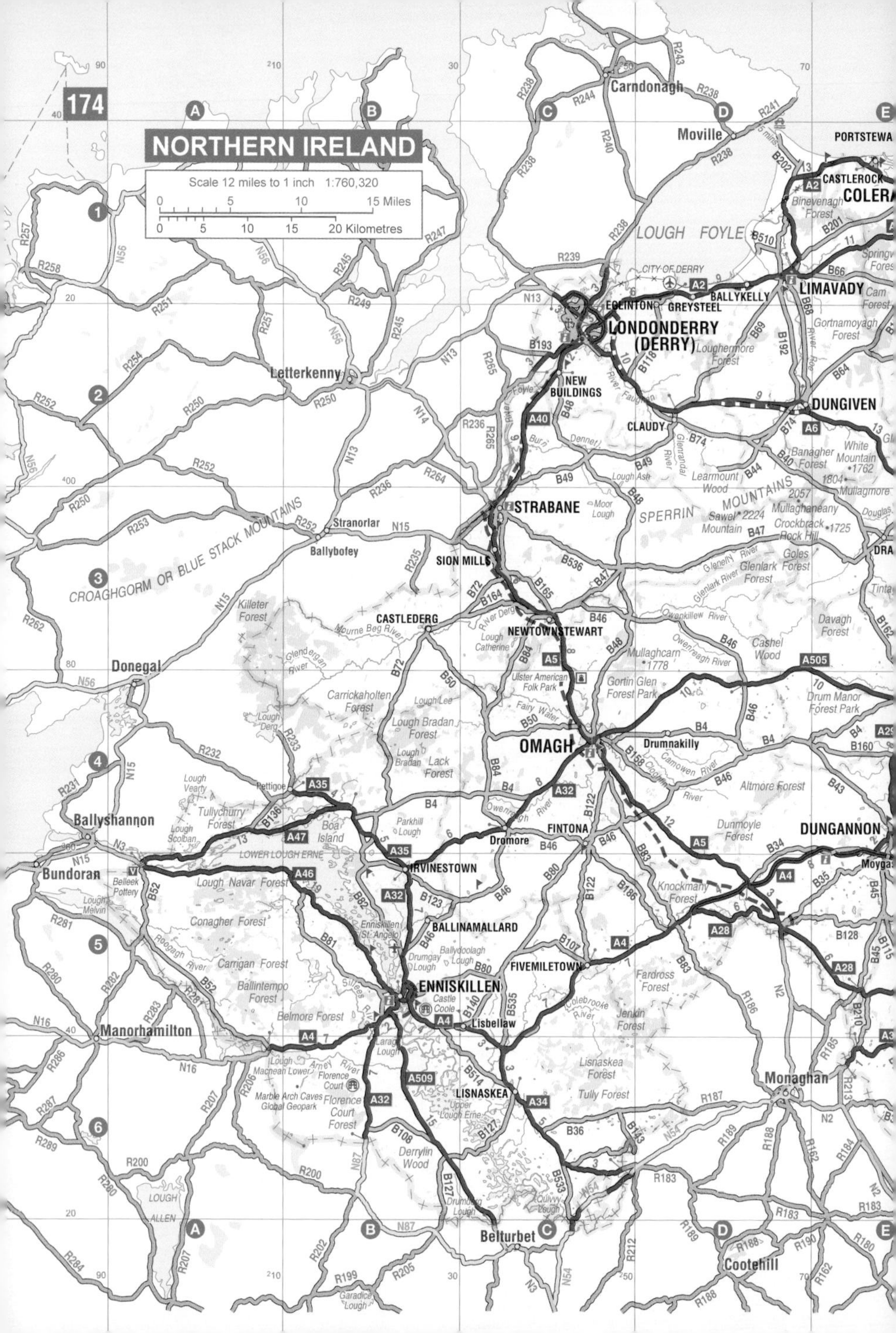

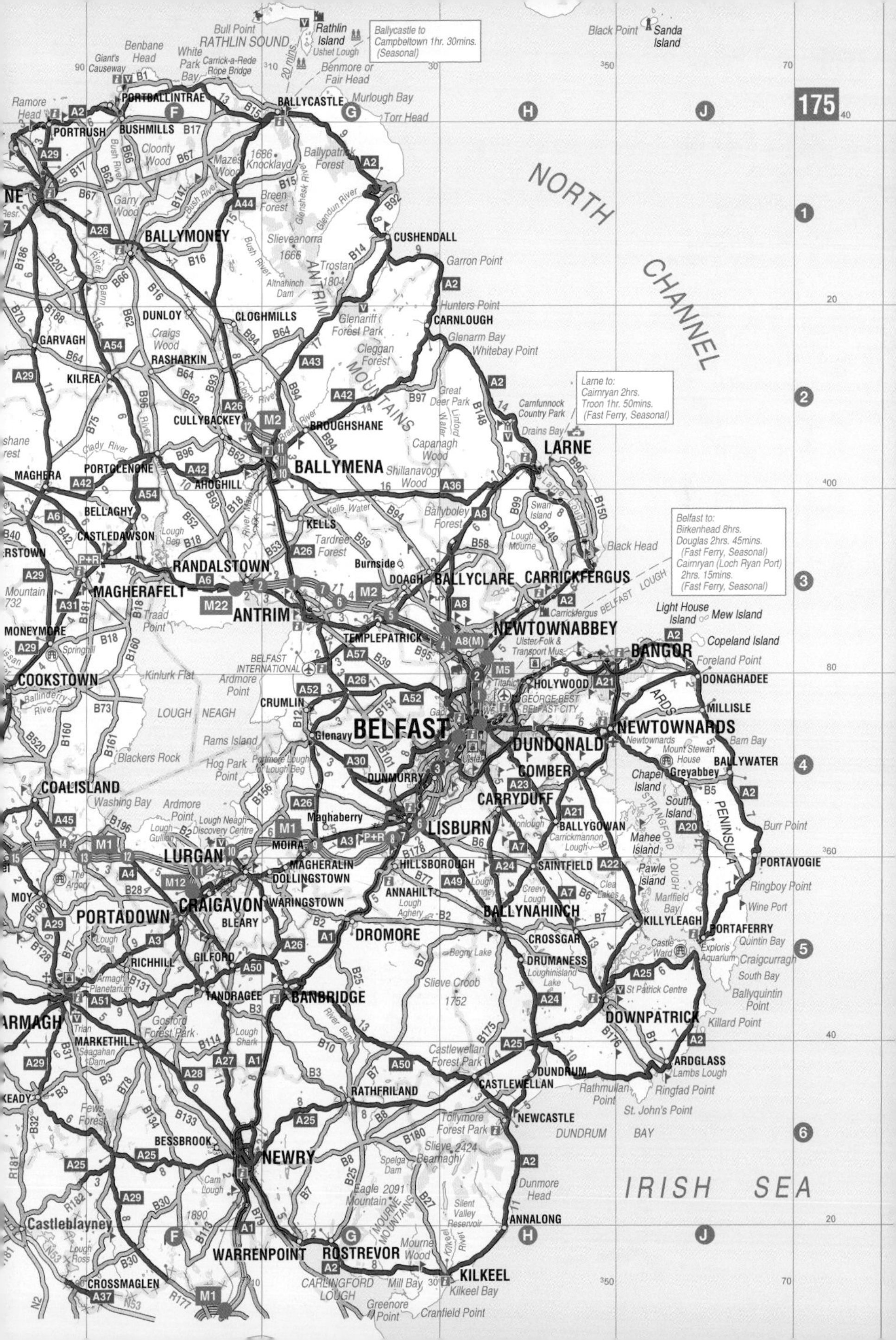
Ballycastle to
Campbeltown 1hr. 30mins.
(Seasonal)
Larne to:
Cairnryan 2hrs.
Troon 1hr. 50mins.
(Fast Ferry, Seasonal)
Belfast to:
Birkenhead 8hrs.
Douglas 2hrs. 45mins.
(Fast Ferry, Seasonal)
Cairnryan (Loch Ryan Port)
2hrs. 15mins.
(Fast Ferry, Seasonal)
NORTH
CHANNEL
IRISH SEA
DUNDRUM BAY
Rathlin Island
RATHLIN SOUND
Bull Point
Ushet Lough
Benmore or Fair Head
Murlough Bay
Torr Head
Black Point
Sanda Island
Benbane Head
Giant's Causeway
White Park Bay
Carrick-a-Rede Rope Bridge
Ramore Head
PORTBALLINTRAE
PORTRUSH
BUSHMILLS
BALLYCASTLE
Ballypatrick Forest
Cloonty Wood
Mazes Wood
Knocklayd
Breen Forest
Garry Wood
Slieveanorra
ANTRIM MOUNTAINS
Trostan
Altnahinch Dam
CUSHENDALL
Garron Point
Hunters Point
BALLYMONEY
DUNLOY
CLOGHMILLS
Craigs Wood
GARVAGH
KILREA
RASHARKIN
Glenariff Forest Park
Cleggan Forest
CARNLOUGH
Glenarm Bay
Whitebay Point
Great Deer Park
Carnfunnock Country Park
Drains Bay
LARNE
CULLYBACKEY
BROUGHSHANE
BALLYMENA
Capanagh Wood
Shillanavogy Wood
PORTGLENONE
AHOGHILL
MAGHERA
BELLAGHY
CASTLEDAWSON
KELLS
Tardree Forest
Ballyboley Forest
Swan Island
Lough Mourne
Black Head
RANDALSTOWN
Burnside
DOAGH
BALLYCLARE
CARRICKFERGUS
BELFAST LOUGH
MAGHERAFELT
ANTRIM
TEMPLEPATRICK
NEWTOWNABBEY
Ulster Folk & Transport Mus.
BANGOR
Light House Island
Mew Island
Copeland Island
Foreland Point
DONAGHADEE
MILLISLE
MONEYMORE
COOKSTOWN
Traad Point
Springhill
BELFAST INTERNATIONAL
Kinlurk Flat
Ardmore Point
CRUMLIN
LOUGH NEAGH
Rams Island
Blackers Rock
Hog Park Point
Glenavy
BELFAST
Titanic
HOLYWOOD
GEORGE BEST BELFAST CITY
DUNDONALD
NEWTOWNARDS
ARDS PENINSULA
Barn Bay
Mount Stewart House
Greyabbey
BALLYWATER
COMBER
DUNMURRY
COALISLAND
Washing Bay
Ardmore Point
Lough Neagh Discovery Centre
CARRYDUFF
Chapel Island
South Island
Mahee Island
STRANGFORD LOUGH
Maghaberry
LISBURN
BALLYGOWAN
Burr Point
LURGAN
MOIRA
MAGHERALIN
DOLLINGSTOWN
HILLSBOROUGH
SAINTFIELD
Pawle Island
PORTAVOGIE
Ringboy Point
MOY
The Argory
PORTADOWN
CRAIGAVON
WARINGSTOWN
ANNAHILT
BALLYNAHINCH
Marlfield Bay
Wine Port
BLEARY
DROMORE
KILLYLEAGH
PORTAFERRY
CROSSGAR
Castle Ward
Exploris Aquarium
Quintin Bay
Craigcurragh
RICHHILL
GILFORD
Begny Lake
DRUMANESS
Loughinisland Lake
South Bay
Ballyquintin Point
Armagh Planetarium
TANDRAGEE
BANBRIDGE
Slieve Croob
St Patrick Centre
DOWNPATRICK
Killard Point
ARMAGH
MARKETHILL
Gosford Forest Park
Lough Shark
Castlewellan Forest Park
ARDGLASS
Lambs Lough
DUNDRUM
CASTLEWELLAN
Rathmullan Point
Ringfad Point
St. John's Point
KEADY
Fews Forest
RATHFRILAND
NEWCASTLE
Tollymore Forest Park
BESSBROOK
NEWRY
Slieve Beanagh
Spelga Dam
Cam Lough
Eagle Mountain
MOURNE MOUNTAINS
Silent Valley Reservoir
Dunmore Head
Castleblayney
ANNALONG
Lough Ross
WARRENPOINT
ROSTREVOR
Mourne Wood
KILKEEL
Kilkeel Bay
CROSSMAGLEN
CARLINGFORD LOUGH
Mill Bay
Greenore Point
Cranfield Point

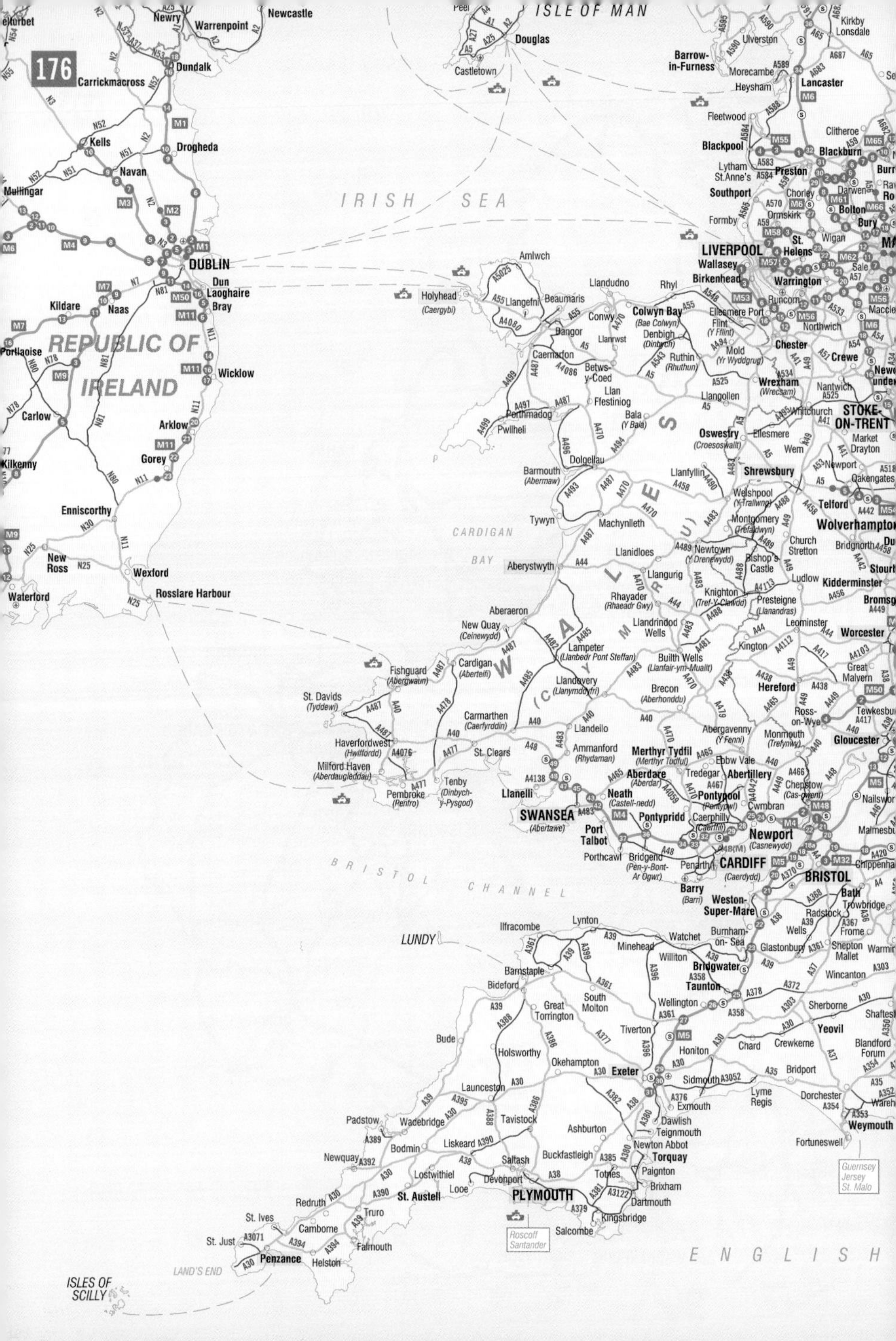
IRISH SEA
ISLE OF MAN
Douglas
Castletown
Peel
REPUBLIC OF IRELAND
DUBLIN
Dun Laoghaire
Bray
Wicklow
Arklow
Gorey
Drogheda
Dundalk
Newry
Warrenpoint
Newcastle
Carrickmacross
Kells
Navan
Mullingar
Kildare
Naas
Portlaoise
Carlow
Kilkenny
Enniscorthy
New Ross
Wexford
Rosslare Harbour
Waterford
WALES (CYMRU)
Holyhead (Caergybi)
Amlwch
Llangefni
Beaumaris
Bangor
Caernarfon
Llandudno
Conwy
Colwyn Bay (Bae Colwyn)
Rhyl
Denbigh (Dinbych)
Ruthin (Rhuthun)
Flint (Y Fflint)
Mold (Yr Wyddgrug)
Betws-y-Coed
Llan Ffestiniog
Porthmadog
Pwllheli
Bala (Y Bala)
Barmouth (Abermaw)
Dolgellau
Tywyn
Machynlleth
CARDIGAN BAY
Aberystwyth
Llanidloes
Llangurig
Rhayader (Rhaeadr Gwy)
Aberaeron
New Quay (Ceinewydd)
Lampeter (Llanbedr Pont Steffan)
Cardigan (Aberteifi)
Fishguard (Abergwaun)
St. Davids (Tyddewi)
Haverfordwest (Hwlffordd)
Milford Haven (Aberdaugleddau)
Pembroke (Penfro)
Tenby (Dinbych-y-Pysgod)
Carmarthen (Caerfyrddin)
St. Clears
Llandovery (Llanymddyfri)
Llandeilo
Ammanford (Rhydaman)
Llanelli
SWANSEA (Abertawe)
Neath (Castell-nedd)
Port Talbot
Porthcawl
Bridgend (Pen-y-Bont-Ar Ogwr)
Aberdare (Aberdar)
Merthyr Tydfil (Merthyr Tudful)
Pontypridd
Caerphilly (Caerffili)
Newport (Casnewydd)
CARDIFF (Caerdydd)
Penarth
Barry (Barri)
Brecon (Aberhonddu)
Builth Wells (Llanfair-ym-Muallt)
Llandrindod Wells
Knighton (Tref-Y-Clawdd)
Presteigne (Llanandras)
Newtown (Y Drenewydd)
Montgomery (Trefaldwyn)
Welshpool (Y Trallwng)
Llanfyllin
Oswestry (Croesoswallt)
Llangollen
Wrexham (Wrecsam)
Abergavenny (Y Fenni)
Monmouth (Trefynwy)
Chepstow (Cas-gwent)
Ebbw Vale
Tredegar
Abertillery
Pontypool (Pontypwl)
Cwmbran
LIVERPOOL
Wallasey
Birkenhead
Southport
Formby
Blackpool
Fleetwood
Lytham St.Anne's
Preston
Barrow-in-Furness
Ulverston
Morecambe
Heysham
Lancaster
Kirkby Lonsdale
Blackburn
Chorley
Ormskirk
St. Helens
Wigan
Bolton
Bury
Warrington
Runcorn
Ellesmere Port
Chester
Northwich
Crewe
Nantwich
Whitchurch
Ellesmere
Wem
STOKE-ON-TRENT
Market Drayton
Newport
Shrewsbury
Telford
Oakengates
Wolverhampton
Bridgnorth
Church Stretton
Bishop's Castle
Ludlow
Kidderminster
Leominster
Kington
Worcester
Great Malvern
Hereford
Ross-on-Wye
Tewkesbury
Gloucester
BRISTOL
Weston-Super-Mare
Bath
Trowbridge
Radstock
Frome
Wells
Glastonbury
Shepton Mallet
Burnham-on-Sea
BRISTOL CHANNEL
LUNDY
Ilfracombe
Lynton
Minehead
Watchet
Williton
Bridgwater
Taunton
Wellington
Barnstaple
Bideford
Great Torrington
South Molton
Tiverton
Bude
Holsworthy
Okehampton
Exeter
Honiton
Sidmouth
Exmouth
Dawlish
Teignmouth
Newton Abbot
Torquay
Paignton
Brixham
Dartmouth
Totnes
Kingsbridge
Salcombe
Ashburton
Buckfastleigh
Tavistock
Launceston
Padstow
Wadebridge
Bodmin
Liskeard
Saltash
Devonport
PLYMOUTH
Newquay
Lostwithiel
Looe
St. Austell
Truro
Redruth
Camborne
Falmouth
Helston
St. Ives
St. Just
Penzance
LAND'S END
ISLES OF SCILLY
Roscoff Santander
Guernsey Jersey St. Malo
Chard
Crewkerne
Yeovil
Sherborne
Wincanton
Bridport
Lyme Regis
Dorchester
Weymouth
Fortuneswell
Blandford Forum
ENGLISH

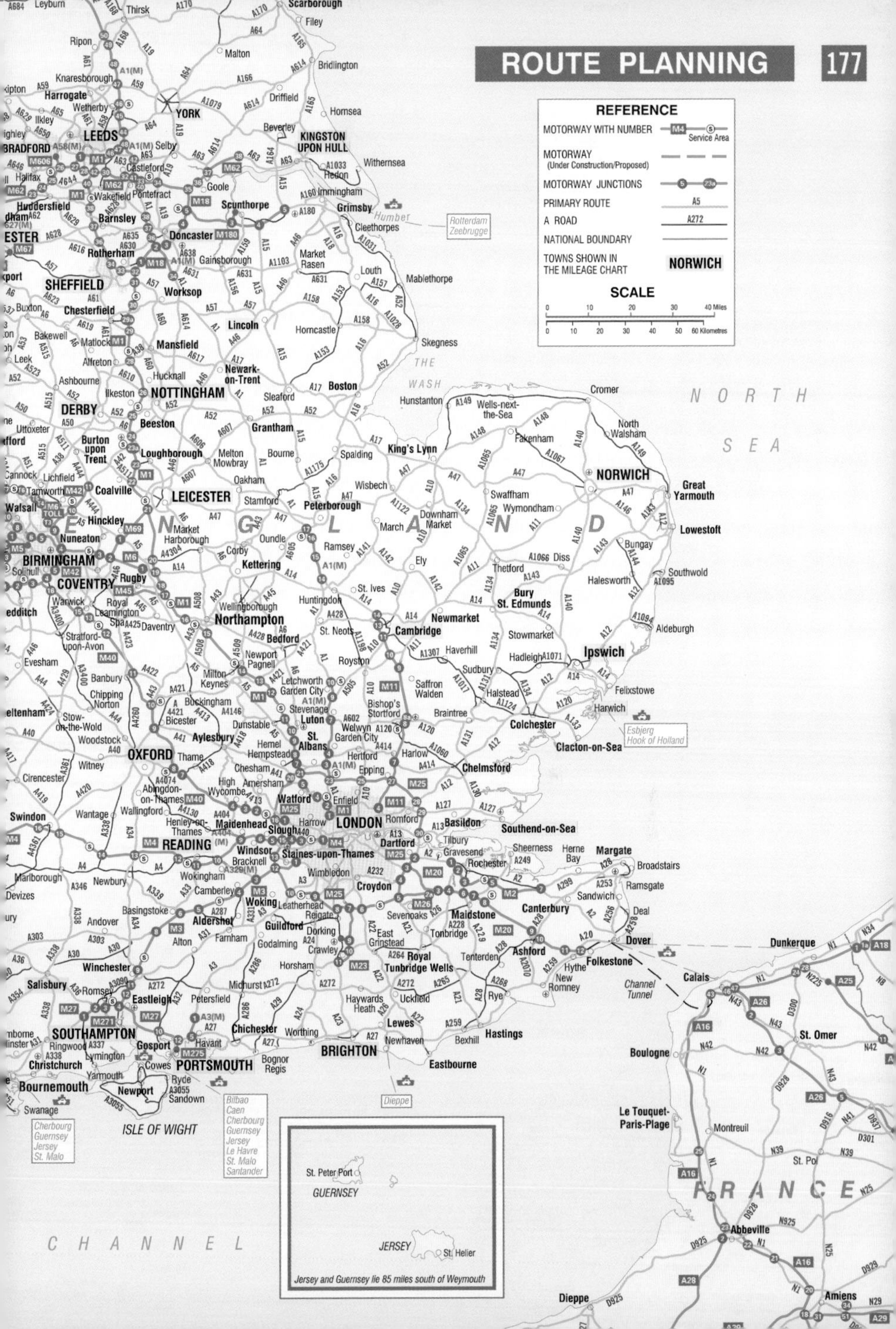

REFERENCE

MOTORWAY WITH NUMBER	M4 / S Service Area
MOTORWAY (Under Construction/Proposed)	
MOTORWAY JUNCTIONS	
PRIMARY ROUTE	A5
A ROAD	A272
NATIONAL BOUNDARY	
TOWNS SHOWN IN THE MILEAGE CHART	**NORWICH**

SCALE

0   10   20   30   40 Miles
0   10   20   30   40   50   60 Kilometres

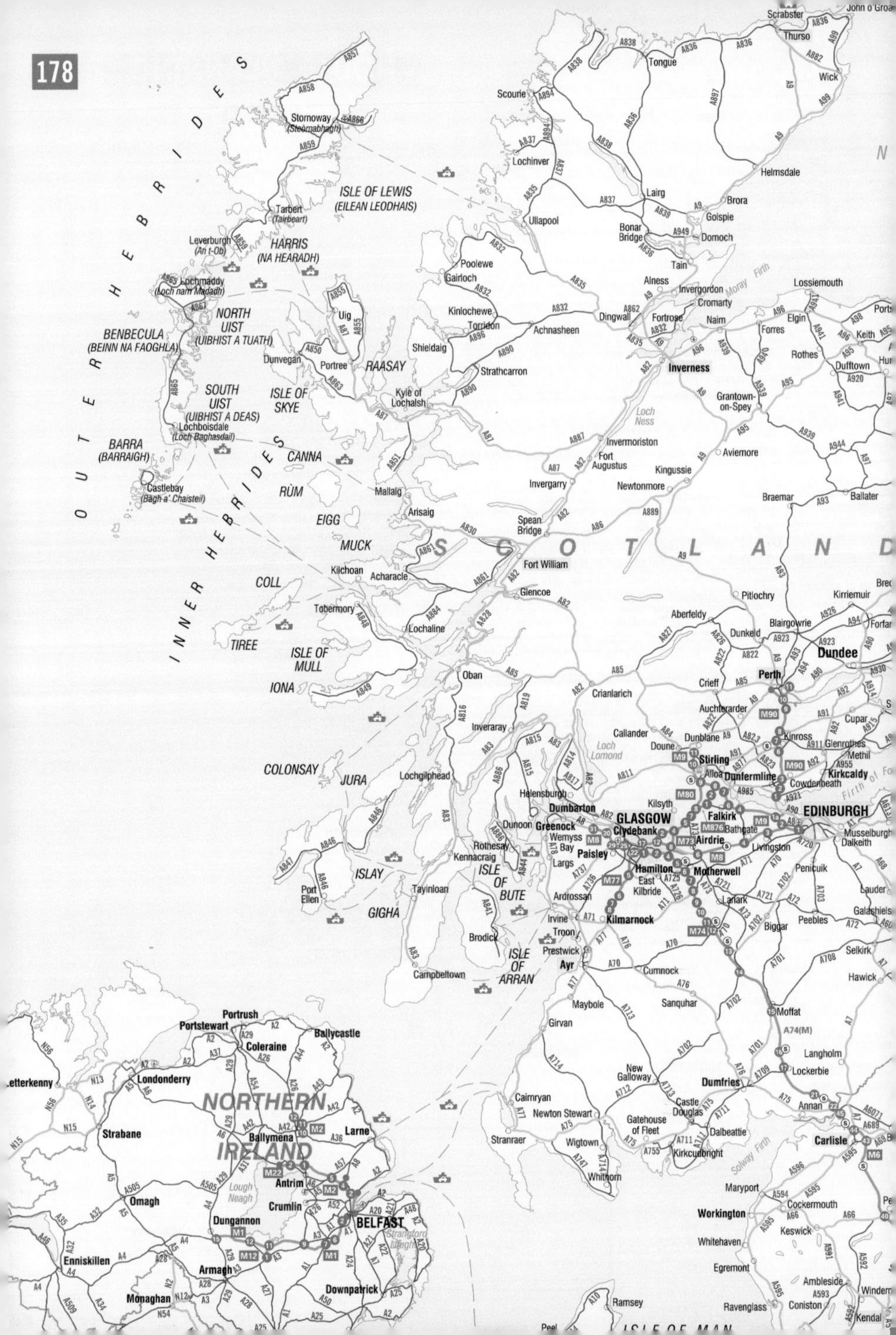

SCOTLAND

NORTHERN IRELAND

OUTER HEBRIDES

INNER HEBRIDES

ISLE OF LEWIS (EILEAN LEODHAIS)

HARRIS (NA HEARADH)

NORTH UIST (UIBHIST A TUATH)

BENBECULA (BEINN NA FAOGHLA)

SOUTH UIST (UIBHIST A DEAS)

BARRA (BARRAIGH)

ISLE OF SKYE

RAASAY

CANNA

RÙM

EIGG

MUCK

COLL

TIREE

ISLE OF MULL

IONA

COLONSAY

JURA

ISLAY

GIGHA

ISLE OF BUTE

ISLE OF ARRAN

ISLE OF MAN

GLASGOW

EDINBURGH

Dundee

Perth

Stirling

Dunfermline

Kirkcaldy

Inverness

Belfast

Stornoway (Steornabhagh)

Tarbert (Tairbeart)

Leverburgh (An t-Ob)

Lochmaddy (Loch nam Madadh)

Lochboisdale (Loch Baghasdail)

Castlebay (Bagh a' Chaisteil)

Scrabster

Thurso

John o'Groats

Wick

Tongue

Scourie

Lochinver

Helmsdale

Brora

Golspie

Dornoch

Lairg

Ullapool

Bonar Bridge

Tain

Alness

Invergordon

Cromarty

Nairn

Lossiemouth

Elgin

Forres

Rothes

Keith

Dufftown

Poolewe

Gairloch

Kinlochewe

Torridon

Achnasheen

Dingwall

Fortrose

Grantown-on-Spey

Aviemore

Braemar

Ballater

Shieldaig

Strathcarron

Kyle of Lochalsh

Dunvegan

Portree

Uig

Invermoriston

Fort Augustus

Kingussie

Newtonmore

Invergarry

Mallaig

Arisaig

Spean Bridge

Fort William

Glencoe

Kilchoan

Acharacle

Lochaline

Tobermory

Oban

Crianlarich

Aberfeldy

Pitlochry

Kirriemuir

Forfar

Dunkeld

Blairgowrie

Crieff

Auchterarder

Callander

Dunblane

Doune

Kinross

Glenrothes

Cupar

Methil

Alloa

Cowdenbeath

Inveraray

Lochgilphead

Helensburgh

Dumbarton

Dunoon

Rothesay

Kennacraig

Wemyss Bay

Greenock

Paisley

Clydebank

Falkirk

Airdrie

Bathgate

Livingston

Musselburgh

Dalkeith

Penicuik

Lauder

Galashiels

Peebles

Selkirk

Hawick

Tayinloan

Port Ellen

Brodick

Largs

Ardrossan

Irvine

Troon

Prestwick

Ayr

Kilmarnock

Hamilton

East Kilbride

Motherwell

Lanark

Biggar

Campbeltown

Maybole

Cumnock

Moffat

Langholm

Lockerbie

Girvan

Sanquhar

New Galloway

Cairnryan

Newton Stewart

Stranraer

Wigtown

Gatehouse of Fleet

Castle Douglas

Dalbeattie

Kirkcudbright

Whithorn

Dumfries

Annan

Carlisle

Maryport

Workington

Cockermouth

Keswick

Whitehaven

Egremont

Ravenglass

Ambleside

Coniston

Kendal

Windermere

Portrush

Portstewart

Ballycastle

Coleraine

Larne

Londonderry

Ballymena

Antrim

Crumlin

Dungannon

Armagh

Monaghan

Downpatrick

Omagh

Enniskillen

Strabane

Letterkenny

Loch Ness

Loch Lomond

Lough Neagh

Moray Firth

Firth of Forth

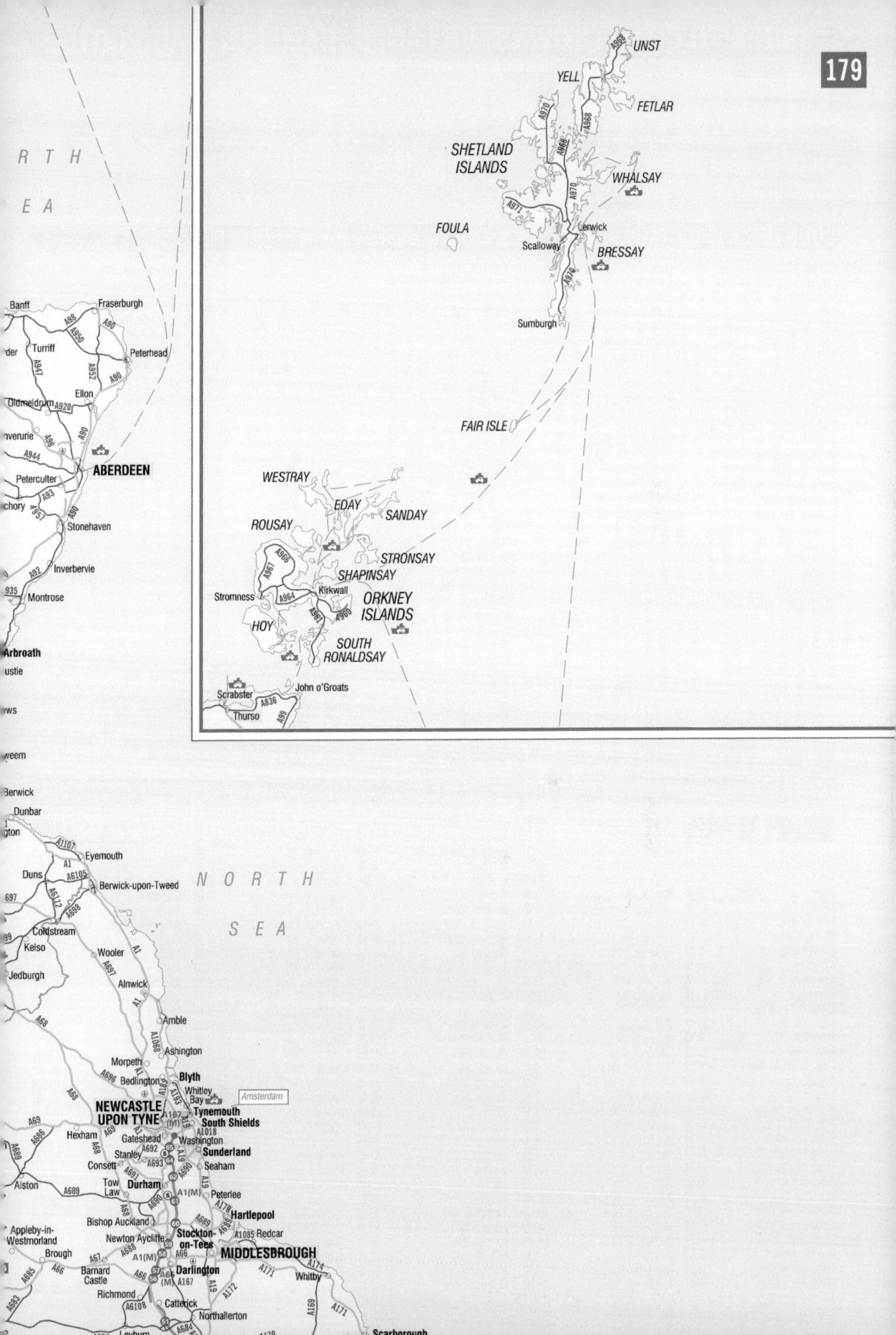
UNST
YELL
FETLAR
SHETLAND ISLANDS
WHALSAY
FOULA
Lerwick
Scalloway
BRESSAY
Sumburgh
FAIR ISLE
WESTRAY
EDAY
SANDAY
ROUSAY
STRONSAY
SHAPINSAY
Kirkwall
Stromness
ORKNEY ISLANDS
HOY
SOUTH RONALDSAY
John o'Groats
Scrabster
Thurso
NORTH SEA
Banff
Fraserburgh
Turriff
Peterhead
Ellon
Oldmeldrum
ABERDEEN
Peterculter
Stonehaven
Inverbervie
Montrose
Arbroath
Dunbar
Eyemouth
Duns
Berwick-upon-Tweed
Coldstream
Kelso
Wooler
Jedburgh
Alnwick
Amble
Ashington
Morpeth
Blyth
Bedlington
Whitley Bay
Amsterdam
NEWCASTLE UPON TYNE
Tynemouth
South Shields
Hexham
Gateshead
Washington
Stanley
Sunderland
Consett
Seaham
Alston
Tow Law
Durham
Peterlee
Hartlepool
Bishop Auckland
Appleby-in-Westmorland
Newton Aycliffe
Stockton-on-Tees
Redcar
Brough
MIDDLESBROUGH
Barnard Castle
Darlington
Whitby
Richmond
Catterick
Northallerton
Scarborough

INDEX TO CITIES, TOWNS, VILLAGES, HAMLETS & AIRPORTS

(1) A strict alphabetical order is used e.g. An Dùnan follows Andreas but precedes Andwell.

(2) The map reference given refers to the actual map square in which the town spot or built-up area is located and not to the place name.

(3) Where two or more places of the same name occur in the same County or Unitary Authority, the nearest large town is also given;
e.g. Achiemore. High . . . .2D 166 (nr. Durness) indicates that Achiemore is located in square 2D on page 166 and is situated near Durness in the Unitary Authority of Highland.

(4) Only one reference is given although due to page overlaps the place may appear on more than one page.

(5) Major towns and destinations are shown in bold, i.e. Aberdeen. Aber 3G 153

COUNTIES and UNITARY AUTHORITIES with the abbreviations used in this index

Aberdeen : Aber
Aberdeenshire : Abers
Angus : Ang
Antrim : Ant
Ards : Ards
Argyll & Bute : Arg
Armagh : Arm
Ballymena : Bmna
Ballymoney : Bmny
Banbridge : Ban
Bath & N E Somerset : Bath
Bedford : Bed
Belfast : Bel
Blackburn with Darwen : Bkbn
Blackpool : Bkpl
Blaenau Gwent : Blae
Bournemouth : Bour
Bracknell Forest : Brac
Bridgend : B'end
Brighton & Hove : Brig
Bristol : Bris
Buckinghamshire : Buck
Caerphilly : Cphy
Cambridgeshire : Cambs
Cardiff : Card
Carmarthenshire : Carm
Carrickfergus : Carr
Castlereagh : Cast
Central Bedfordshire : C Beds
Ceredigion : Cdgn
Cheshire East : Ches E
Cheshire West & Chester : Ches W
Clackmannanshire : Clac
Coleraine : Cole
Conwy : Cnwy

Cookstown : Cook
Cornwall : Corn
Craigavon : Cgvn
Cumbria : Cumb
Darlington : Darl
Denbighshire : Den
Derby : Derb
Derbyshire : Derbs
Derry : Derr
Devon : Devn
Dorset : Dors
Down : Down
Dumfries & Galloway : Dum
Dundee : D'dee
Dungannon : Dngn
Durham : Dur
East Ayrshire : E Ayr
East Dunbartonshire : E Dun
East Lothian : E Lot
East Renfrewshire : E Ren
East Riding of Yorkshire : E Yor
East Sussex : E Sus
Edinburgh : Edin
Essex : Essx
Falkirk : Falk
Fermanagh : Ferm
Fife : Fife
Flintshire : Flin
Glasgow : Glas
Gloucestershire : Glos
Greater London : G Lon
Greater Manchester : G Man
Gwynedd : Gwyn
Halton : Hal
Hampshire : Hants

Hartlepool : Hart
Herefordshire : Here
Hertfordshire : Herts
Highland : High
Inverclyde : Inv
Isle of Anglesey : IOA
Isle of Man : IOM
Isle of Wight : IOW
Isles of Scilly : IOS
Kent : Kent
Kingston upon Hull : Hull
Lancashire : Lanc
Larne : Lar
Leicester : Leic
Leicestershire : Leics
Limavady : Lim
Lincolnshire : Linc
Lisburn : Lis
Luton : Lutn
Magherafelt : Mag
Medway : Medw
Merseyside : Mers
Merthyr Tydfil : Mer T
Middlesbrough : Midd
Midlothian : Midl
Milton Keynes : Mil
Monmouthshire : Mon
Moray : Mor
Moyle : Moy
Neath Port Talbot : Neat
Newport : Newp
Newry & Mourne : New M
Newtownabbey : Newt
Norfolk : Norf
Northamptonshire : Nptn

North Ayrshire : N Ayr
North Down : N Dwn
North East Lincolnshire : NE Lin
North Lanarkshire : N Lan
North Lincolnshire : N Lin
North Somerset : N Som
Northumberland : Nmbd
North Yorkshire : N Yor
Nottingham : Nott
Nottinghamshire : Notts
Omagh : Omag
Orkney : Orkn
Oxfordshire : Oxon
Pembrokeshire : Pemb
Perth & Kinross : Per
Peterborough : Pet
Plymouth : Plym
Poole : Pool
Portsmouth : Port
Powys : Powy
Reading : Read
Redcar & Cleveland : Red C
Renfrewshire : Ren
Rhondda Cynon Taff : Rhon
Rutland : Rut
Scottish Borders : Bord
Shetland : Shet
Shropshire : Shrp
Slough : Slo
Somerset : Som
Southampton : Sotn
South Ayrshire : S Ayr
Southend-on-Sea : S'end
South Gloucestershire : S Glo
South Lanarkshire : S Lan

South Yorkshire : S Yor
Staffordshire : Staf
Stirling : Stir
Stockton-on-Tees : Stoc T
Stoke-on-Trent : Stoke
Strabane : Strab
Suffolk : Suff
Surrey : Surr
Swansea : Swan
Swindon : Swin
Telford & Wrekin : Telf
Thurrock : Thur
Torbay : Torb
Torfaen : Torf
Tyne & Wear : Tyne
Vale of Glamorgan, The : V Glam
Warrington : Warr
Warwickshire : Warw
West Berkshire : W Ber
West Dunbartonshire : W Dun
Western Isles : W Isl
West Lothian : W Lot
West Midlands : W Mid
West Sussex : W Sus
West Yorkshire : W Yor
Wiltshire : Wilts
Windsor & Maidenhead : Wind
Wokingham : Wok
Worcestershire : Worc
Wrexham : Wrex
York : York

INDEX

A

Abbas Combe. Som 4C 22
Abberley. Worc 4B 60
Abberley Common. Worc 4B 60
Abberton. Essx 4D 54
Abberton. Worc 5D 61
Abberwick. Nmbd 3F 121
Abbess Roding. Essx 4F 53
Abbey. Devn 1E 13
Abbey-cwm-hir. Powy 3C 58
Abbeydale. S Yor 2H 85
Abbeydale Park. S Yor 2H 85
Abbey Dore. Here 2G 47
Abbey Gate. Devn 3F 13
Abbey Hulton. Stoke 1D 72
Abbey St Bathans. Bord 3D 130
Abbeystead. Lanc 4E 97
Abbeytown. Cumb 4C 112
Abbey Village. Lanc 2E 91
Abbey Wood. G Lon 3F 39
Abbots Ann. Hants 2B 24
Abbots Bickington. Devn 1D 11
Abbots Bromley. Staf 3E 73
Abbotsbury. Dors 4A 14
Abbotsham. Devn 4E 19
Abbotskerswell. Devn 2E 9
Abbots Langley. Herts 5A 52
Abbots Leigh. N Som 4A 34
Abbotsley. Cambs 5B 64
Abbots Morton. Worc 5E 61
Abbots Ripton. Cambs 3B 64

Abbot's Salford. Warw 5E 61
Abbotstone. Hants 3D 24
Abbots Worthy. Hants 3C 24
Abcott. Shrp 3F 59
Abdon. Shrp 2H 59
Abenhall. Glos 4B 48
Aber. Cdgn 1E 45
Aberaeron. Cdgn 4D 56
Aberafan. Neat 3G 31
Aberaman. Rhon 5D 46
Aberangell. Powy 4H 69
Aberarad. Carm 1H 43
Aberarder. High 1A 150
Aberargie. Per 2D 136
Aberarth. Cdgn 4D 57
Aberavon. Neat 3G 31
Aber-banc. Cdgn 1D 44
Aberbargoed. Cphy 2E 33
Aberbechan. Powy 1D 58
Aberbeeg. Blae 5F 47
Aberbowlan. Carm 2G 45
Aberbran. Powy 3C 46
Abercanaid. Mer T 5D 46
Abercarn. Cphy 2F 33
Abercastle. Pemb 1C 42
Abercegir. Powy 5H 69
Aberchalder. High 3F 149
Aberchirder. Abers 3D 160
Aberchwiler. Den 4C 82
Abercraf. Powy 4B 46
Abercrombie. Fife 3H 137

Abercwmboi. Rhon 2D 32
Abercych. Pemb 1C 44
Abercynon. Rhon 2D 32
Aber-Cywarch. Gwyn 4A 70
Aberdalgie. Per 1C 136
Aberdar. Rhon 5C 46
Aberdare. Rhon 5C 46
Aberdaron. Gwyn 3A 68
Aberdaugleddau. Pemb 4D 42
Aberdeen. Aber 3G 153
Aberdeen International Airport.
 . . . . .2F 153
Aberdesach. Gwyn 5D 80
Aberdour. Fife 1E 129
Aberdovey. Gwyn 1F 57
Aberdulais. Neat 5A 46
Aberdyfi. Gwyn 1F 57
Aberedw. Powy 1D 46
Abereiddy. Pemb 1B 42
Abererch. Gwyn 2C 68
Aberfan. Mer T 5D 46
Aberfeldy. Per 4F 143
Aberffraw. IOA 4C 80
Aberffrwd. Cdgn 3F 57
Aberford. W Yor 1E 93
Aberfoyle. Stir 3E 135
Abergarw. B'end 3C 32
Abergarwed. Neat 5B 46
Abergavenny. Mon 4G 47
Abergele. Cnwy 3B 82
Aber-Giâr. Carm 1F 45
Abergorlech. Carm 2F 45
Abergwaun. Pemb 1D 42

Abergwesyn. Powy 5A 58
Abergwili. Carm 3E 45
Abergwynfi. Neat 2B 32
Abergwyngregyn. Gwyn 3F 81
Abergynolwyn. Gwyn 5F 69
Aberhafesp. Powy 1C 58
Aberhonddu. Powy 3D 46
Aberhosan. Powy 1H 57
Aberkenfig. B'end 3B 32
Aberlady. E Lot 1A 130
Aberlemno. Ang 3E 145
Aberllefenni. Gwyn 5G 69
Abermaw. Gwyn 4F 69
Abermeurig. Cdgn 5E 57
Aber-miwl. Powy 1D 58
Abermule. Powy 1D 58
Abernant. Carm 2H 43
Abernant. Rhon 5D 46
Abernethy. Per 2D 136
Abernyte. Per 5B 144
Aber-oer. Wrex 1E 71
Aberpennar. Rhon 2D 32
Aberporth. Cdgn 5B 56
Aberriw. Powy 5D 70
Abersoch. Gwyn 3C 68
Abersychan. Torf 5F 47
Abertawe. Swan 3F 31
Aberteifi. Cdgn 1B 44
Aberthin. V Glam 4D 32
Abertillery. Blae 5F 47
Abertridwr. Cphy 3E 32
Abertridwr. Powy 4C 70
Abertyleri. Blae 5F 47

Abertysswg. Cphy 5E 47
Aberuthven. Per 2B 136
Aber Village. Powy 3E 46
Aberwheeler. Den 4C 82
Aberyscir. Powy 3C 46
Aberystwyth. Cdgn 2E 57
Abhainn Suidhe. W Isl 7C 171
Abingdon-on-Thames. Oxon . . .2C 36
Abinger Common. Surr 1C 26
Abinger Hammer. Surr 1B 26
Abington. S Lan 2B 118
Abington Pigotts. Cambs 1D 52
Ab Kettleby. Leics 3E 74
Ab Lench. Worc 5E 61
Ablington. Glos 5G 49
Ablington. Wilts 2G 23
Abney. Derbs 3F 85
Aboyne. Abers 4C 152
Abram. G Man 4E 90
Abriachan. High 5H 157
Abridge. Essx 1F 39
Abronhill. N Lan 2A 128
Abson. S Glo 4C 34
Abthorpe. Nptn 1E 51
Abune-the-Hill. Orkn 5B 172
Aby. Linc 3D 88
Acairseid. W Isl 8C 170
Acaster Malbis. York 5H 99
Acaster Selby. N Yor 5H 99
Accott. Devn 3G 19
Accrington. Lanc 2F 91
Acha. Arg 3C 138
Achachork. High 4D 155

Achadh a' Chuirn—Alpraham

Achadh a' Chuirn. *High* 1E **147**
Achahoish. *Arg* 2F **125**
Achaleven. *Arg* 5D **140**
Achallader. *Arg* 4H **141**
Acha Mor. *W Isl* 5F **171**
Achanalt. *High* 2E **157**
Achandunie. *High* 1A **158**
Ach' an Todhair. *High* 1E **141**
Achany. *High* 3C **164**
Achaphubuil. *High* 1E **141**
Acharacle. *High* 2A **140**
Acharn. *Ang* 1B **144**
Acharn. *Per* 4E **143**
Acharole. *High* 3E **169**
Achateny. *High* 2G **139**
Achavanich. *High* 4D **169**
Achdalieu. *High* 1E **141**
Achduart. *High* 3E **163**
Achentoul. *High* 5A **168**
Achfary. *High* 5C **166**
Achfrish. *High* 2C **164**
Achgarve. *High* 4C **162**
Achiemore. *High* 2D **166** (nr. Durness)
Achiemore. *High* 3A **168** (nr. Thurso)
A' Chill. *High* 3A **146**
Achiltibuie. *High* 3E **163**
Achina. *High* 2H **167**
Achinahuagh. *High* 2F **167**
Achindarroch. *High* 3E **141**
Achinduich. *High* 3C **164**
Achinduin. *Arg* 5C **140**
Achininver. *High* 2F **167**
Achintee. *High* 4B **156**
Achintraid. *High* 5H **155**
Achleck. *Arg* 4F **139**
Achlorachan. *High* 3F **157**
Achluachrach. *High* 5E **149**
Achlyness. *High* 3C **166**
Achmelvich. *High* 1E **163**
Achmony. *High* 5H **157**
Achmore. *High* 5A **156** (nr. Stromeferry)
Achmore. *High* 4E **163** (nr. Ullapool)
Achnacarnin. *High* 1E **163**
Achnacarry. *High* 5D **148**
Achnaclerach. *High* 2G **157**
Achnacloich. *High* 3D **147**
Ach na Cloiche. *High* 3D **147**
Achnaconeran. *High* 2G **149**
Achnacroish. *Arg* 4C **140**
Achnafalnich. *Arg* 1B **134**
Achnagarron. *High* 1A **158**
Achnagoul. *Arg* 3H **133**
Achnaha. *High* 2F **139**
Achnahanat. *High* 4C **164**
Achnahannet. *High* 1D **151**
Achnairn. *High* 2C **164**
Achnamara. *Arg* 1F **125**
Achnanellan. *High* 5C **148**
Achnasheen. *High* 3D **156**
Achnashellach. *High* 4C **156**
Achosnich. *High* 2F **139**
Achow. *High* 5E **169**
Achranich. *High* 4B **140**
Achreamie. *High* 2C **168**
Achriabhach. *High* 2F **141**
Achriesgill. *High* 3C **166**
Achrimsdale. *High* 3G **165**
Achscrabster. *High* 2C **168**
Achtoty. *High* 2G **167**
Achurch. *Nptn* 2H **63**
Achuvoldrach. *High* 3F **167**
Achvaich. *High* 4E **164**
Achvoan. *High* 3E **165**
Ackenthwaite. *Cumb* 1E **97**
Ackergill. *High* 3F **169**
Ackergillshore. *High* 3F **169**
Acklam. *Midd* 3B **106**
Acklam. *N Yor* 3B **100**
Ackleton. *Shrp* 1B **60**
Acklington. *Nmbd* 4G **121**
Ackton. *W Yor* 2E **93**
Ackworth Moor Top. *W Yor* 3E **93**
Acle. *Norf* 4G **79**
Acocks Green. *W Mid* 2F **61**
Acol. *Kent* 4H **41**
Acomb. *Nmbd* 3C **114**
Acomb. *York* 4H **99**
Aconbury. *Here* 2A **48**
Acre. *G Man* 4H **91**
Acre. *Lanc* 2F **91**
Acrefair. *Wrex* 1E **71**
Acrise. *Kent* 1F **29**
Acton. *Ches E* 5A **84**
Acton. *Dors* 5E **15**
Acton. *G Lon* 2C **38**
Acton. *Shrp* 2F **59**
Acton. *Staf* 1C **72**
Acton. *Suff* 1B **54**
Acton. *Worc* 4C **60**
Acton. *Wrex* 5F **83**
Acton Beauchamp. *Here* 5A **60**
Acton Bridge. *Ches W* 3H **83**
Acton Burnell. *Shrp* 5H **71**
Acton Green. *Here* 5A **60**
Acton Pigott. *Shrp* 5H **71**
Acton Round. *Shrp* 1A **60**
Acton Scott. *Shrp* 2G **59**
Acton Trussell. *Staf* 4D **72**
Acton Turville. *S Glo* 3D **34**
Adabroc. *W Isl* 1H **171**
Adam's Hill. *Worc* 3D **60**
Adbaston. *Staf* 3B **72**
Adber. *Dors* 4B **22**
Adderbury. *Oxon* 2C **50**
Adderley. *Shrp* 2A **72**
Adderstone. *Nmbd* 1F **121**
Addiewell. *W Lot* 3C **128**
Addingham. *W Yor* 5C **98**
Addington. *Buck* 3F **51**
Addington. *G Lon* 4E **39**
Addington. *Kent* 5A **40**
Addinston. *Bord* 4B **130**
Addiscombe. *G Lon* 4E **39**
Addlestone. *Surr* 4B **38**
Addlethorpe. *Linc* 4E **89**
Adeney. *Telf* 4B **72**
Adfa. *Powy* 5C **70**
Adforton. *Here* 3G **59**
Adgestone. *IOW* 4D **16**
Adisham. *Kent* 5G **41**
Adlestrop. *Glos* 3H **49**
Adlingfleet. *E Yor* 2B **94**
Adlington. *Ches E* 2D **84**
Adlington. *Lanc* 3E **90**
Admaston. *Staf* 3E **73**
Admaston. *Telf* 4A **72**
Admington. *Warw* 1H **49**
Adpar. *Cdgn* 1D **44**
Adsborough. *Som* 4F **21**
Adstock. *Buck* 2F **51**
Adstone. *Nptn* 5C **62**
Adversane. *W Sus* 3B **26**
Advie. *High* 5F **159**
Adwalton. *W Yor* 2C **92**
Adwell. *Oxon* 2E **37**
Adwick le Street. *S Yor* 4F **93**
Adwick upon Dearne. *S Yor* 4E **93**
Adziel. *Abers* 3G **161**
Ae. *Dum* 1A **112**
Affleck. *Abers* 1F **153**
Affpuddle. *Dors* 3D **14**
Affric Lodge. *High* 1D **148**
Afon-wen. *Flin* 3D **82**
Agglethorpe. *N Yor* 1C **98**
Aglionby. *Cumb* 4F **113**
Ahoghill. *Bmna* 2F **175**
Aigburth. *Mers* 2F **83**
Aiginis. *W Isl* 4G **171**
Aike. *E Yor* 5E **101**
Aikers. *Orkn* 8D **172**
Aiketgate. *Cumb* 5F **113**
Aikhead. *Cumb* 5D **112**
Aikton. *Cumb* 4D **112**
Ailey. *Here* 1G **47**
Ailsworth. *Pet* 1A **64**
Ainderby Quernhow. *N Yor* 1F **99**
Ainderby Steeple. *N Yor* 5A **106**
Aingers Green. *Essx* 3E **54**
Ainsdale. *Mers* 3B **90**
Ainsdale-on-Sea. *Mers* 3B **90**
Ainstable. *Cumb* 5G **113**
Ainsworth. *G Man* 3F **91**
Ainthorpe. *N Yor* 4E **107**
Aintree. *Mers* 1F **83**
Aird. *Arg* 3E **133**
Aird. *Dum* 3F **109**
Aird. *High* 1G **155** (nr. Port Henderson)
Aird. *High* 3D **147** (nr. Tarskavaig)
Aird. *W Isl* 3C **170** (on Benbecula)
Aird. *W Isl* 4H **171** (on Isle of Lewis)
Àird a Bhasair. *High* 3E **147**
Aird a Mhachair. *W Isl* 4C **170**
Aird a Mhulaidh. *W Isl* 6D **171**
Aird Asaig. *W Isl* 7D **171**
Aird Dhail. *W Isl* 1G **171**
Airdens. *High* 4D **164**
Airdeny. *Arg* 1G **133**
Aird Mhidhinis. *W Isl* 8C **170**
Aird Mhighe. *W Isl* 8D **171** (nr. Ceann a Bhaigh)
Aird Mhighe. *W Isl* 9C **171** (nr. Fionnsabhagh)
Aird Mhor. *W Isl* 8C **170** (on Barra)
Aird Mhor. *W Isl* 4D **170** (on South Uist)
Airdrie. *N Lan* 3A **128**
Aird Shleibhe. *W Isl* 9D **171**
Aird, The. *High* 3D **154**
Aird Thunga. *W Isl* 4G **171**
Aird Uig. *W Isl* 4C **171**
Airedale. *W Yor* 2E **93**
Airidh a Bhruaich. *W Isl* 6E **171**
Airies. *Dum* 3E **109**
Airmyn. *E Yor* 2H **93**
Airntully. *Per* 5H **143**
Airor. *High* 3F **147**
Airth. *Falk* 1C **128**
Airton. *N Yor* 4B **98**
Aisby. *Linc* 1F **87** (nr. Gainsborough)
Aisby. *Linc* 2H **75** (nr. Grantham)
Aisgernis. *W Isl* 6C **170**
Aish. *Devn* 2C **8** (nr. Buckfastleigh)
Aish. *Devn* 3E **9** (nr. Totnes)
Aisholt. *Som* 3E **21**
Aiskew. *N Yor* 1E **99**
Aislaby. *N Yor* 1B **100** (nr. Pickering)
Aislaby. *N Yor* 4F **107** (nr. Whitby)
Aislaby. *Stoc T* 3B **106**
Aisthorpe. *Linc* 2G **87**
Aith. *Shet* 3H **173** (on Fetlar)
Aith. *Shet* 6E **173** (on Mainland)
Aithsetter. *Shet* 8F **173**
Akeld. *Nmbd* 2D **120**
Akeley. *Buck* 2F **51**
Akenham. *Suff* 1E **55**
Albaston. *Corn* 5E **11**
Alberbury. *Shrp* 4F **71**
Albert Town. *Pemb* 3D **42**
Albert Village. *Leics* 4H **73**
Albourne. *W Sus* 4D **26**
Albrighton. *Shrp* 4G **71** (nr. Shrewsbury)
Albrighton. *Shrp* 5C **72** (nr. Telford)
Alburgh. *Norf* 2E **67**
Albury. *Herts* 3E **53**
Albury. *Surr* 1B **26**
Albyfield. *Cumb* 4G **113**
Alby Hill. *Norf* 2D **78**
Alcaig. *High* 3H **157**
Alcaston. *Shrp* 2G **59**
Alcester. *Warw* 5E **61**
Alciston. *E Sus* 5G **27**
Alcombe. *Som* 2C **20**
Alconbury. *Cambs* 3A **64**
Alconbury Weston. *Cambs* 3A **64**
Aldborough. *Norf* 2D **78**
Aldborough. *N Yor* 3G **99**
Aldbourne. *Wilts* 4A **36**
Aldbrough. *E Yor* 1F **95**
Aldbrough St John. *N Yor* 3F **105**
Aldbury. *Herts* 4H **51**
Aldcliffe. *Lanc* 3D **96**
Aldclune. *Per* 2G **143**
Aldeburgh. *Suff* 5G **67**
Aldeby. *Norf* 1G **67**
Aldenham. *Herts* 1C **38**
Alderbury. *Wilts* 4G **23**
Aldercar. *Derbs* 1B **74**
Alderford. *Norf* 4D **78**
Alderholt. *Dors* 1G **15**
Alderley. *Glos* 2C **34**
Alderley Edge. *Ches E* 3C **84**
Aldermaston. *W Ber* 5D **36**
Aldermaston Soke. *W Ber* 5E **36**
Aldermaston Wharf. *W Ber* 5E **36**
Alderminster. *Warw* 1H **49**
Alder Moor. *Staf* 3G **73**
Aldersey Green. *Ches W* 5G **83**
Aldershot. *Hants* 1G **25**
Alderton. *Glos* 2F **49**
Alderton. *Nptn* 1F **51**
Alderton. *Shrp* 3G **71**
Alderton. *Suff* 1G **55**
Alderton. *Wilts* 3D **34**
Alderton Fields. *Glos* 2F **49**
Alderwasley. *Derbs* 5H **85**
Aldfield. *N Yor* 3E **99**
Aldford. *Ches W* 5G **83**
Aldgate. *Rut* 5G **75**
Aldham. *Essx* 3C **54**
Aldham. *Suff* 1D **54**
Aldingbourne. *W Sus* 5A **26**
Aldingham. *Cumb* 2B **96**
Aldington. *Kent* 2E **29**
Aldington. *Worc* 1F **49**
Aldington Frith. *Kent* 2E **29**
Aldochlay. *Arg* 4C **134**
Aldon. *Shrp* 3G **59**
Aldoth. *Cumb* 5C **112**
Aldreth. *Cambs* 3D **64**
Aldridge. *W Mid* 5E **73**
Aldringham. *Suff* 4G **67**
Aldsworth. *Glos* 4G **49**
Aldsworth. *W Sus* 2F **17**
Aldwark. *Derbs* 5G **85**
Aldwark. *N Yor* 3G **99**
Aldwick. *W Sus* 3H **17**
Aldwincle. *Nptn* 2H **63**
Aldworth. *W Ber* 4D **36**
Alexandria. *W Dun* 1E **127**
Aley. *Som* 3E **21**
Aley Green. *C Beds* 4A **52**
Alfardisworthy. *Devn* 1C **10**
Alfington. *Devn* 3E **12**
Alfold. *Surr* 2B **26**
Alfold Bars. *W Sus* 2B **26**
Alfold Crossways. *Surr* 2B **26**
Alford. *Abers* 2C **152**
Alford. *Linc* 3D **88**
Alford. *Som* 3B **22**
Alfreton. *Derbs* 5B **86**
Alfrick. *Worc* 5B **60**
Alfrick Pound. *Worc* 5B **60**
Alfriston. *E Sus* 5G **27**
Algarkirk. *Linc* 2B **76**
Alhampton. *Som* 3B **22**
Aline Lodge. *W Isl* 6D **171**
Alkborough. *N Lin* 2B **94**
Alkerton. *Oxon* 1B **50**
Alkham. *Kent* 1G **29**
Alkington. *Shrp* 2H **71**
Alkmonton. *Derbs* 2F **73**
Alladale Lodge. *High* 5B **164**
Allaleigh. *Devn* 3E **9**
Allanbank. *N Lan* 4B **128**
Allanton. *N Lan* 4B **128**
Allanton. *Bord* 4E **131**
Allaston. *Glos* 5B **48**
Allbrook. *Hants* 4C **24**
All Cannings. *Wilts* 5F **35**
Allendale Town. *Nmbd* 4B **114**
Allen End. *Warw* 1F **61**
Allenheads. *Nmbd* 5B **114**
Allensford. *Dur* 5D **115**
Allen's Green. *Herts* 4E **53**
Allensmore. *Here* 2H **47**
Allenton. *Derb* 2A **74**
Aller. *Som* 4H **21**
Allerby. *Cumb* 1B **102**
Allercombe. *Devn* 3D **12**
Allerford. *Som* 2C **20**
Allerston. *N Yor* 1C **100**
Allerthorpe. *E Yor* 5B **100**
Allerton. *Mers* 2G **83**
Allerton. *W Yor* 1B **92**
Allerton Bywater. *W Yor* 2E **93**
Allerton Mauleverer. *N Yor* 4G **99**
Allesley. *W Mid* 2G **61**
Allestree. *Derb* 2H **73**
Allet. *Corn* 4B **6**
Allexton. *Leics* 5F **75**
Allgreave. *Ches E* 4D **84**
Allhallows. *Medw* 3C **40**
Allhallows-on-Sea. *Medw* 3C **40**
Alligin Shuas. *High* 3H **155**
Allimore Green. *Staf* 4C **72**
Allington. *Kent* 5B **40**
Allington. *Linc* 1F **75**
Allington. *Wilts* 3H **23** (nr. Amesbury)
Allington. *Wilts* 5F **35** (nr. Devizes)
Allithwaite. *Cumb* 2C **96**
Alloa. *Clac* 4A **136**
Allonby. *Cumb* 5B **112**
Allostock. *Ches W* 3B **84**
Alloway. *S Ayr* 3C **116**
Allowenshay. *Som* 1G **13**
All Saints South Elmham. *Suff* 2F **67**
Allscott. *Shrp* 1B **60**
Allscott. *Telf* 4A **72**
All Stretton. *Shrp* 1G **59**
Allt. *Carm* 5F **45**
Alltami. *Flin* 4E **83**
Alltgobhlach. *N Ayr* 5G **125**
Alltmawr. *Powy* 1D **46**
Alltnacaillich. *High* 4E **167**
Allt na h' Airbhe. *High* 4F **163**
Alltour. *High* 5E **148**
Alltsigh. *High* 2G **149**
Alltwalis. *Carm* 2E **45**
Alltwen. *Neat* 5H **45**
Alltyblacca. *Cdgn* 1F **45**
Allt-y-goed. *Pemb* 1B **44**
Almeley. *Here* 5F **59**
Almeley Wooton. *Here* 5F **59**
Almer. *Dors* 3E **15**
Almholme. *S Yor* 4F **93**
Almington. *Staf* 2B **72**
Alminstone Cross. *Devn* 4D **18**
Almodington. *W Sus* 3G **17**
Almondbank. *Per* 1C **136**
Almondbury. *W Yor* 3B **92**
Almondsbury. *S Glo* 3B **34**
Alne. *N Yor* 3G **99**
Alness. *High* 2A **158**
Alnessferry. *High* 2A **158**
Alnham. *Nmbd* 3D **121**
Alnmouth. *Nmbd* 3G **121**
Alnwick. *Nmbd* 3F **121**
Alphamstone. *Essx* 2B **54**
Alpheton. *Suff* 5A **66**
Alphington. *Devn* 3C **12**
Alpington. *Norf* 5E **79**
Alport. *Derbs* 4G **85**
Alport. *Powy* 1E **59**
Alpraham. *Ches E* 5H **83**

Alresford—Ashbrook

Alresford. Essx 3D 54
Alrewas. Staf 4F 73
Alsager. Ches E 5B 84
Alsagers Bank. Staf 1C 72
Alsop en le Dale. Derbs 5F 85
Alston. Cumb 5A 114
Alston. Devn 2G 13
Alstone. Glos 2E 49
Alstone. Som 2G 21
Alstonefield. Staf 5F 85
Alston Sutton. Som 1H 21
Alswear. Devn 4H 19
Altandhu. High 2D 163
Altanduin. High 1F 165
Altarnun. Corn 4C 10
Altass. High 3B 164
Alterwall. High 2E 169
Altgaltraig. Arg 2B 126
Altham. Lanc 1F 91
Althorne. Essx 1D 40
Althorpe. N Lin 4B 94
Altnabreac. High 4C 168
Altnacealgach. High 2G 163
Altnafeadh. High 3G 141
Altnaharra. High 5F 167
Altofts. W Yor 2D 93
Alton. Derbs 4A 86
Alton. Hants 3F 25
Alton. Staf 1E 73
Alton Barnes. Wilts 5G 35
Altonhill. E Ayr 1D 116
Alton Pancras. Dors 2C 14
Alton Priors. Wilts 5G 35
Altrincham. G Man 2B 84
Altrua. High 4E 149
Alva. Clac 4A 136
Alvanley. Ches W 3G 83
Alvaston. Derb 2A 74
Alvechurch. Worc 3E 61
Alvecote. Warw 5G 73
Alvediston. Wilts 4E 23
Alveley. Shrp 2B 60
Alverdiscott. Devn 4F 19
Alverstoke. Hants 3D 16
Alverstone. IOW 4D 16
Alverthorpe. W Yor 2D 92
Alverton. Notts 1E 75
Alves. Mor 2F 159
Alvescot. Oxon 5A 50
Alveston. S Glo 3B 34
Alveston. Warw 5G 61
Alvie. High 3C 150
Alvingham. Linc 1C 88
Alvington. Glos 5B 48
Alwalton. Cambs 1A 64
Alweston. Dors 1B 14
Alwington. Devn 4E 19
Alwinton. Nmbd 4D 120
Alwoodley. W Yor 5E 99
Alyth. Per 4B 144
Amatnatua. High 4B 164
Am Baile. W Isl 7C 170
Ambaston. Derbs 2B 74
Ambergate. Derbs 5H 85
Amber Hill. Linc 1B 76
Amberley. Glos 5D 48
Amberley. W Sus 4B 26
Amble. Nmbd 4G 121
Amblecote. W Mid 2C 60
Ambler Thorn. W Yor 2A 92
Ambleside. Cumb 4E 103
Ambleston. Pemb 2E 43
Ambrosden. Oxon 4E 50
Amcotts. N Lin 3B 94
Amersham. Buck 1A 38
Amerton. Staf 3D 73
Amesbury. Wilts 2G 23
Amisfield. Dum 1B 112
Amlwch. IOA 1D 80
Amlwch Port. IOA 1D 80
Ammanford. Carm 4G 45
Amotherby. N Yor 2B 100
Ampfield. Hants 4B 24
Ampleforth. N Yor 2H 99
Ampleforth College. N Yor 2H 99
Ampney Crucis. Glos 5F 49
Ampney St Mary. Glos 5F 49
Ampney St Peter. Glos 5F 49
Amport. Hants 2A 24
Ampthill. C Beds 2A 52
Ampton. Suff 3A 66
Amroth. Pemb 4F 43
Amulree. Per 5G 143
Amwell. Herts 4B 52
Anaheilt. High 2C 140
An Àird. High 3D 147
An Camus Darach. High 4E 147
Ancaster. Linc 1G 75
Anchor. Shrp 2D 58
Anchorsholme. Lanc 5C 96
Anchor Street. Norf 3F 79
An Cnoc. W Isl 4G 171
An Cnoc Ard. W Isl 1H 171
An Coroghon. High 3A 146
Ancroft. Nmbd 5G 131
Ancrum. Bord 2A 120
Ancton. W Sus 5A 26
Anderby. Linc 3E 89
Anderby Creek. Linc 3E 89
Anderson. Dors 3D 15
Anderton. Ches W 3A 84
Andertons Mill. Lanc 3D 90
Andover. Hants 2B 24
Andover Down. Hants 2B 24
Andoversford. Glos 4F 49
Andreas. IOM 2D 108
An Dùnan. High 1D 147
Andwell. Hants 1E 25
Anelog. Gwyn 3A 68
Anfield. Mers 1F 83
Angarrack. Corn 3C 4
Angelbank. Shrp 3H 59
Angersleigh. Som 1E 13
Angerton. Cumb 4D 112
Angle. Pemb 4C 42
An Gleann Ur. W Isl 4G 171
Angmering. W Sus 5B 26
Angmering-on-Sea. W Sus 5B 26
Angram. N Yor 5B 104
(nr. Keld)
Angram. N Yor 5H 99
(nr. York)
Anick. Nmbd 3C 114
Ankerbold. Derbs 4A 86
Ankerville. High 1C 158
Anlaby. E Yor 2D 94
Anlaby Park. Hull 2D 94
An Leth Meadhanach. W Isl 7C 170
Anmer. Norf 3G 77
Anmore. Hants 1E 17
Annahilt. Lis 5G 175
Annalong. New M 6H 175
Annan. Dum 3D 112
Annaside. Cumb 1A 96
Annat. Arg 1H 133
Annat. High 3A 156
Annathill. N Lan 2A 128
Anna Valley. Hants 2B 24
Annbank. S Ayr 2D 116
Annesley. Notts 5C 86
Annesley Woodhouse. Notts 5C 86
Annfield Plain. Dur 4E 115
Annscroft. Shrp 5G 71
An Sailean. High 2A 140
Ansdell. Lanc 2B 90
Ansford. Som 3B 22
Ansley. Warw 1G 61
Anslow. Staf 3G 73
Anslow Gate. Staf 3F 73
Ansteadbrook. Surr 2A 26
Anstey. Herts 2E 53
Anstey. Leics 5C 74
Anston. S Lan 5D 128
Anstruther Easter. Fife 3H 137
Anstruther Wester. Fife 3H 137
Ansty. Warw 2A 62
Ansty. W Sus 3D 27
Ansty. Wilts 4E 23
An Taobh Tuath. W Isl 9B 171
An t-Aodann Ban. High 3C 154
An t Ath Leathann. High 1E 147
An Teanga. High 3E 147
Anthill Common. Hants 1E 17
Anthorn. Cumb 4C 112
Antingham. Norf 2E 79
An t-Ob. W Isl 9C 171
Anton's Gowt. Linc 1B 76
Antony. Corn 3A 8
An t-Òrd. High 2E 147
Antrim. Ant 3G 175
Antrobus. Ches W 3A 84
Anvil Corner. Devn 2D 10
Anwick. Linc 5A 88
Anwoth. Dum 4C 110
Apethorpe. Nptn 1H 63
Apeton. Staf 4C 72
Apley. Linc 3A 88
Apperknowle. Derbs 3A 86
Apperley. Glos 3D 48
Apperley Dene. Nmbd 4D 114
Appersett. N Yor 5B 104
Appin. Arg 4D 140
Appleby. N Lin 3C 94
Appleby-in-Westmorland. Cumb 2H 103
Appleby Magna. Leics 5H 73
Appleby Parva. Leics 5H 73
Applecross. High 4G 155
Appledore. Devn 3E 19
(nr. Bideford)
Appledore. Devn 1D 12
(nr. Tiverton)
Appledore. Kent 3D 28
Appledore Heath. Kent 2D 28
Appleford. Oxon 2D 36
Applegarthtown. Dum 1C 112
Applemore. Hants 2B 16
Appleshaw. Hants 2B 24
Applethwaite. Cumb 2D 102
Appleton. Hal 2H 83
Appleton. Oxon 5C 50
Appleton-le-Moors. N Yor 1B 100
Appleton-le-Street. N Yor 2B 100
Appleton Roebuck. N Yor 5H 99
Appleton Thorn. Warr 2A 84
Appleton Wiske. N Yor 4A 106
Appletree. Nptn 1C 50
Appletreehall. Bord 3H 119
Appletreewick. N Yor 3C 98
Appley. Som 4D 20
Appley Bridge. Lanc 3D 90
Apse Heath. IOW 4D 16
Apsley End. C Beds 2B 52
Apuldram. W Sus 2G 17
Arabella. High 1C 158
Arasaig. High 5E 147
Arbeadie. Abers 4D 152
Arberth. Pemb 3F 43
Arbirlot. Ang 4F 145
Arborfield. Wok 5F 37
Arborfield Cross. Wok 5F 37
Arborfield Garrison. Wok 5F 37
Arbourthorne. S Yor 2A 86
Arbroath. Ang 4F 145
Arbuthnott. Abers 1H 145
Arcan. High 3H 157
Archargary. High 3H 167
Archdeacon Newton. Darl 3F 105
Archiestown. Mor 4G 159
Arclid. Ches E 4B 84
Arclid Green. Ches E 4B 84
Ardachu. High 3D 164
Ardalanish. Arg 2A 132
Ardaneaskan. High 5H 155
Ardarroch. High 5H 155
Ardbeg. Arg 1C 126
(nr. Dunoon)
Ardbeg. Arg 5C 124
(on Islay)
Ardbeg. Arg 3B 126
(on Isle of Bute)
Ardcharnich. High 5F 163
Ardchiavaig. Arg 2A 132
Ardchonnell. Arg 2G 133
Ardchrishnish. Arg 1B 132
Ardchronie. High 5D 164
Ardchullarie. Stir 2E 135
Ardchyle. Stir 1E 135
Ard-dhubh. High 4G 155
Arddleen. Powy 4E 71
Arddlîn. Powy 4E 71
Ardechive. High 4D 148
Ardeley. Herts 3D 52
Ardelve. High 1A 148
Arden. Arg 1E 127
Ardendrain. High 5H 157
Arden Hall. N Yor 5C 106
Ardens Grafton. Warw 5F 61
Ardentinny. Arg 1C 126
Ardeonaig. Stir 5D 142
Ardersier. High 3B 158
Ardery. High 2B 140
Ardessie. High 5E 163
Ardfern. Arg 3F 133
Ardfernal. Arg 2D 124
Ardfin. Arg 3C 124
Ardgartan. Arg 3B 134
Ardgay. High 4D 164
Ardglass. Down 6J 175
Ardgour. High 2E 141
Ardheslaig. High 3G 155
Ardindrean. High 5F 163
Ardingly. W Sus 3E 27
Ardington. Oxon 3C 36
Ardlamont House. Arg 3A 126
Ardleigh. Essx 3D 54
Ardler. Per 4B 144
Ardley. Oxon 3D 50
Ardlui. Arg 2C 134
Ardlussa. Arg 1E 125
Ardmair. High 4F 163
Ardmay. Arg 3B 134
Ardminish. Arg 5E 125
Ardmolich. High 1B 140
Ardmore. High 3C 166
(nr. Kinlochbervie)
Ardmore. High 5E 164
(nr. Tain)
Ardnacross. Arg 4G 139
Ardnadam. Arg 1C 126
Ardnagrask. High 4H 157
Ardnamurach. High 4G 147
Ardnarff. High 5A 156
Ardnastang. High 2C 140
Ardoch. Per 5H 143
Ardochy House. High 3E 148
Ardpatrick. Arg 3F 125
Ardrishaig. Arg 1G 125
Ardroag. High 4B 154
Ardross. High 1A 158
Ardrossan. N Ayr 5D 126
Ardshealach. High 2A 140
Ardsley. S Yor 4D 93
Ardslignish. High 2G 139
Ardtalla. Arg 4C 124
Ardtalnaig. Per 5E 142
Ardtoe. High 1A 140
Arduaine. Arg 2E 133
Ardullie. High 2H 157
Ardvasar. High 3E 147
Ardvorlich. Per 1F 135
Ardwell. Dum 5G 109
Ardwell. Mor 5A 160
Arean. High 1A 140
Areley Common. Worc 3C 60
Areley Kings. Worc 3C 60
Arford. Hants 3G 25
Argoed. Cphy 2E 33
Argoed Mill. Powy 4B 58
Aridhglas. Arg 2B 132
Arinacrinachd. High 3G 155
Arinagour. Arg 3D 138
Arisaig. High 5E 147
Ariundle. High 2C 140
Arivegaig. High 2A 140
Arkendale. N Yor 3F 99
Arkesden. Essx 2E 53
Arkholme. Lanc 2E 97
Arkle Town. N Yor 4D 104
Arkley. G Lon 1D 38
Arksey. S Yor 4F 93
Arkwright Town. Derbs 3B 86
Arlecdon. Cumb 3B 102
Arlescote. Warw 1B 50
Arlesey. C Beds 2B 52
Arleston. Telf 4A 72
Arley. Ches E 2A 84
Arlingham. Glos 4C 48
Arlington. Devn 2G 19
Arlington. E Sus 5G 27
Arlington. Glos 5G 49
Arlington Beccott. Devn 2G 19
Armadail. High 3E 147
Armadale. High 3E 147
(nr. Isleornsay)
Armadale. High 2H 167
(nr. Strathy)
Armadale. W Lot 3C 128
Armagh. Arm 5E 175
Armathwaite. Cumb 5G 113
Arminghall. Norf 5E 79
Armitage. Staf 4E 73
Armitage Bridge. W Yor 3B 92
Armley. W Yor 1C 92
Armscote. Warw 1H 49
Arms, The. Norf 1A 66
Armston. Nptn 2H 63
Armthorpe. S Yor 4G 93
Arncliffe. N Yor 2B 98
Arncliffe Cote. N Yor 2B 98
Arncroach. Fife 3H 137
Arne. Dors 4E 15
Arnesby. Leics 1D 62
Arnicle. Arg 2B 122
Arnisdale. High 2G 147
Arnish. High 4E 155
Arniston. Midl 3G 129
Arnol. W Isl 3F 171
Arnold. E Yor 5F 101
Arnold. Notts 1C 74
Arnprior. Stir 4F 135
Arnside. Cumb 2D 96
Aros Mains. Arg 4G 139
Arpafeelie. High 3A 158
Arrad Foot. Cumb 1C 96
Arram. E Yor 5E 101
Arras. E Yor 5D 100
Arrathorne. N Yor 5E 105
Arreton. IOW 4D 16
Arrington. Cambs 5C 64
Arrochar. Arg 3B 134
Arrow. Warw 5E 61
Arscaig. High 2C 164
Artafallie. High 4A 158
Arthington. W Yor 5E 99
Arthingworth. Nptn 2E 63
Arthog. Gwyn 4F 69
Arthrath. Abers 5G 161
Arthurstone. Per 4B 144
Artington. Surr 1A 26
Arundel. W Sus 5B 26
Asby. Cumb 2B 102
Ascog. Arg 3C 126
Ascot. Wind 4A 38
Ascott-under-Wychwood. Oxon 4B 50
Asenby. N Yor 2F 99
Asfordby. Leics 4E 74
Asfordby Hill. Leics 4E 74
Asgarby. Linc 4C 88
(nr. Horncastle)
Asgarby. Linc 1A 76
(nr. Sleaford)
Ash. Devn 4E 9
Ash. Dors 1D 14
Ash. Kent 5G 41
(nr. Sandwich)
Ash. Kent 4H 39
(nr. Swanley)
Ash. Som 4H 21
Ash. Surr 1G 25
Ashampstead. W Ber 4D 36
Ashbocking. Suff 5D 66
Ashbourne. Derbs 1F 73
Ashbrittle. Som 4D 20
Ashbrook. Shrp 1G 59

Badanloch Lodge—Barnham Broom

Badanloch Lodge. *High* 5H **167**
Badavanich. *High* 3D **156**
Badbury. *Swin* 3G **35**
Badby. *Nptn* 5C **62**
Badcall. *High* 3C **166**
Badcaul. *High* 4E **163**
Baddeley Green. *Stoke* 5D **84**
Baddesley Clinton. *W Mid* 3G **61**
Baddesley Ensor. *Warw* 1G **61**
Baddidarach. *High* 1E **163**
Baddoch. *Abers* 5F **151**
Badenscallie. *High* 3E **163**
Badenscoth. *Abers* 5E **160**
Badentarbat. *High* 2E **163**
Badgall. *Corn* 4C **10**
Badgers Mount. *Kent* 4F **39**
Badgeworth. *Glos* 4E **49**
Badgworth. *Som* 1G **21**
Badicaul. *High* 1F **147**
Badingham. *Suff* 4F **67**
Badlesmere. *Kent* 5E **40**
Badlipster. *High* 4E **169**
Badluarach. *High* 4D **163**
Badminton. *S Glo* 3D **34**
Badnaban. *High* 1E **163**
Badnabay. *High* 4C **166**
Badnagie. *High* 5D **168**
Badnellan. *High* 3F **165**
Badninish. *High* 4E **165**
Badrallach. *High* 4E **163**
Badsey. *Worc* 1F **49**
Badshot Lea. *Surr* 2G **25**
Badsworth. *W Yor* 3E **93**
Badwell Ash. *Suff* 4B **66**
Bae Cinmel. *Cnwy* 2B **82**
Bae Colwyn. *Cnwy* 3A **82**
Bae Penrhyn. *Cnwy* 2H **81**
Bagby. *N Yor* 1G **99**
Bag Enderby. *Linc* 3C **88**
Bagendon. *Glos* 5F **49**
Bagginswood. *Shrp* 2A **60**
Bàgh a Chàise. *W Isl* 1E **170**
Bàgh a' Chaisteil. *W Isl* 9B **170**
Bagham. *Kent* 5E **41**
Baghasdal. *W Isl* 7C **170**
Bagh Mor. *W Isl* 3D **170**
Bagh Shiarabhagh. *W Isl* 8C **170**
Bagillt. *Flin* 3E **82**
Baginton. *Warw* 3H **61**
Baglan. *Neat* 2A **32**
Bagley. *Shrp* 3G **71**
Bagley. *Som* 2H **21**
Bagnall. *Staf* 5D **84**
Bagnor. *W Ber* 5C **36**
Bagshot. *Surr* 4A **38**
Bagshot. *Wilts* 5B **36**
Bagstone. *S Glo* 3B **34**
Bagthorpe. *Norf* 2G **77**
Bagthorpe. *Notts* 5B **86**
Bagworth. *Leics* 5B **74**
Bagwy Llydiart. *Here* 3H **47**
Baildon. *W Yor* 1B **92**
Baildon Green. *W Yor* 1B **92**
Baile. *W Isl* 1E **170**
Baile Ailein. *W Isl* 5E **171**
Baile an Truiseil. *W Isl* 2F **171**
Baile Boidheach. *Arg* 2F **125**
Baile Glas. *W Isl* 3D **170**
Bailemeonach. *Arg* 4A **140**
Baile Mhanaich. *W Isl* 3C **170**
Baile Mhartainn. *W Isl* 1C **170**
Baile MhicPhail. *W Isl* 1D **170**
Baile Mór. *Arg* 2A **132**
Baile Mor. *W Isl* 2C **170**
Baile nan Cailleach. *W Isl* 3C **170**
Baile Raghaill. *W Isl* 2C **170**
Bailey Green. *Hants* 4E **25**
Baileyhead. *Cumb* 1G **113**
Bailiesward. *Abers* 5B **160**
Bail' Iochdrach. *W Isl* 3D **170**
Baillieston. *Glas* 3H **127**
Bailrigg. *Lanc* 4D **97**
Bail Uachdraich. *W Isl* 2D **170**
Bail' Ur Tholastaidh. *W Isl* 3H **171**
Bainbridge. *N Yor* 5C **104**
Bainsford. *Falk* 1B **128**
Bainshole. *Abers* 5D **160**
Bainton. *E Yor* 4D **100**
Bainton. *Oxon* 3D **50**
Bainton. *Pet* 5H **75**
Baintown. *Fife* 3F **137**
Baker Street. *Thur* 2H **39**
Bakewell. *Derbs* 4G **85**
Bala. *Gwyn* 2B **70**
Balachuirn. *High* 4E **155**
Balbeg. *High* 5G **157**
(nr. Cannich)
Balbeg. *High* 1G **149**
(nr. Loch Ness)
Balbeggie. *Per* 1D **136**
Balblair. *High* 4C **164**
(nr. Bonar Bridge)
Balblair. *High* 2B **158**
(nr. Invergordon)
Balblair. *High* 4H **157**
(nr. Inverness)
Balby. *S Yor* 4F **93**
Balcathie. *Ang* 5F **145**
Balchladich. *High* 1E **163**
Balchraggan. *High* 4H **157**
Balchrick. *High* 3B **166**
Balcombe. *W Sus* 2E **27**
Balcombe Lane. *W Sus* 2E **27**
Balcurvie. *Fife* 3F **137**
Baldersby. *N Yor* 2F **99**
Baldersby St James. *N Yor* 2F **99**
Balderstone. *Lanc* 1E **91**
Balderton. *Ches W* 4F **83**
Balderton. *Notts* 5F **87**
Baldinnie. *Fife* 2G **137**
Baldock. *Herts* 2C **52**
Baldrine. *IOM* 3D **108**
Baldslow. *E Sus* 4C **28**
Baldwin. *IOM* 3C **108**
Baldwinholme. *Cumb* 4E **113**
Baldwin's Gate. *Staf* 2B **72**
Bale. *Norf* 2C **78**
Balearn. *Abers* 3H **161**
Balemartine. *Arg* 4A **138**
Balephetrish. *Arg* 4B **138**
Balephuil. *Arg* 4A **138**
Balerno. *Edin* 3E **129**
Balevullin. *Arg* 4A **138**
Balfield. *Ang* 2E **145**
Balfour. *Orkn* 6D **172**
Balfron. *Stir* 1G **127**
Balgaveny. *Abers* 4D **160**
Balgonar. *Fife* 4C **136**
Balgowan. *High* 4A **150**
Balgown. *High* 2C **154**
Balgrochan. *E Dun* 2H **127**
Balgy. *High* 3H **155**
Balhalgardy. *Abers* 1E **153**
Baliasta. *Shet* 1H **173**
Baligill. *High* 2A **168**
Balintore. *Ang* 3B **144**
Balintore. *High* 1C **158**
Balintraid. *High* 1B **158**
Balk. *N Yor* 1G **99**
Balkeerie. *Ang* 4C **144**
Balkholme. *E Yor* 2A **94**
Ball. *Shrp* 3F **71**
Ballabeg. *IOM* 4B **108**
Ballacannell. *IOM* 3D **108**
Ballacarnane Beg. *IOM* 3C **108**
Ballachulish. *High* 3E **141**
Ballagyr. *IOM* 3B **108**
Ballajora. *IOM* 2D **108**
Ballaleigh. *IOM* 3C **108**
Ballamodha. *IOM* 4B **108**
Ballantrae. *S Ayr* 1F **109**
Ballards Gore. *Essx* 1D **40**
Ballasalla. *IOM* 4B **108**
(nr. Castletown)
Ballasalla. *IOM* 2C **108**
(nr. Kirk Michael)
Ballater. *Abers* 4A **152**
Ballaugh. *IOM* 2C **108**
Ballencrieff. *E Lot* 2A **130**
Ballencrieff Toll. *W Lot* 2C **128**
Ballentoul. *Per* 2F **143**
Ball Hill. *Hants* 5C **36**
Ballidon. *Derbs* 5G **85**
Balliemore. *Arg* 1B **126**
(nr. Dunoon)
Balliemore. *Arg* 1F **133**
(nr. Oban)
Ballieward. *High* 5E **159**
Ballig. *IOM* 3B **108**
Ballimore. *Stir* 2E **135**
Ballinamallard. *Ferm* 5B **174**
Ballingdon. *Suff* 1B **54**
Ballinger Common. *Buck* 5H **51**
Ballingham. *Here* 2A **48**
Ballingry. *Fife* 4D **136**
Ballinluig. *Per* 3G **143**
Ballintuim. *Per* 3A **144**
Balliveolan. *Arg* 4C **140**
Balloan. *High* 3C **164**
Balloch. *High* 4B **158**
Balloch. *N Lan* 2A **128**
Balloch. *Per* 2H **135**
Balloch. *W Dun* 1E **127**
Ballochan. *Abers* 4C **152**
Ballochgoy. *Arg* 3B **126**
Ballochmyle. *E Ayr* 2E **117**
Ballochroy. *Arg* 4F **125**
Balls Cross. *W Sus* 3A **26**
Ball's Green. *E Sus* 2F **27**
Ballycastle. *Moy* 1G **175**
Ballyclare. *Newt* 3G **175**
Ballygowan. *Ards* 4H **175**
Ballygown. *Arg* 4F **139**
Ballygrant. *Arg* 3B **124**
Ballykelly. *Lim* 1D **174**
Ballymena. *Bmna* 2G **175**
Ballymichael. *N Ayr* 2D **122**
Ballymoney. *Bmny* 1F **175**
Ballynahinch. *Down* 5H **175**
Ballywater. *Ards* 4J **175**
Balmacara. *High* 1G **147**
Balmaclellan. *Dum* 2D **110**
Balmacqueen. *High* 1D **154**
Balmaha. *Stir* 4D **134**
Balmalcolm. *Fife* 3F **137**
Balmalloch. *N Lan* 2A **128**
Balmeanach. *High* 5E **155**
Balmedie. *Abers* 2G **153**
Balmerino. *Fife* 1F **137**
Balmerlawn. *Hants* 2B **16**
Balmore. *E Dun* 2H **127**
Balmore. *High* 4B **154**
Balmuir. *Ang* 5D **144**
Balmullo. *Fife* 1G **137**
Balmurrie. *Dum* 3H **109**
Balnaboth. *Ang* 2C **144**
Balnabruaich. *High* 1B **158**
Balnabruich. *High* 5D **168**
Balnacoil. *High* 2F **165**
Balnacra. *High* 4B **156**
Balnacroft. *Abers* 4G **151**
Balnageith. *Mor* 3E **159**
Balnaglaic. *High* 5G **157**
Balnagrantach. *High* 5G **157**
Balnaguard. *Per* 3G **143**
Balnahard. *Arg* 4B **132**
Balnain. *High* 5G **157**
Balnakeil. *High* 2D **166**
Balnaknock. *High* 2D **154**
Balnamoon. *Abers* 3G **161**
Balnamoon. *Ang* 2E **145**
Balnapaling. *High* 2B **158**
Balornock. *Glas* 3H **127**
Balquhidder. *Stir* 1E **135**
Balsall. *W Mid* 3G **61**
Balsall Common. *W Mid* 3G **61**
Balscote. *Oxon* 1B **50**
Balsham. *Cambs* 5E **65**
Balstonia. *Thur* 2A **40**
Baltasound. *Shet* 1H **173**
Balterley. *Staf* 5B **84**
Baltersan. *Dum* 3B **110**
Balthangie. *Abers* 3F **161**
Baltonsborough. *Som* 3A **22**
Balvaird. *High* 3H **157**
Balvaird. *Per* 2D **136**
Balvenie. *Mor* 4H **159**
Balvicar. *Arg* 2E **133**
Balvraid. *High* 2G **147**
Balvraid Lodge. *High* 5C **158**
Bamber Bridge. *Lanc* 2D **90**
Bamber's Green. *Essx* 3F **53**
Bamburgh. *Nmbd* 1F **121**
Bamford. *Derbs* 2G **85**
Bamfurlong. *G Man* 4D **90**
Bampton. *Cumb* 3G **103**
Bampton. *Devn* 4C **20**
Bampton. *Oxon* 5B **50**
Bampton Grange. *Cumb* 3G **103**
Banavie. *High* 1F **141**
Banbridge. *Ban* 5G **175**
Banbury. *Oxon* 1C **50**
Bancffosfelen. *Carm* 4E **45**
Banchory. *Abers* 4D **152**
Banchory-Devenick. *Abers* 3G **153**
Bancycapel. *Carm* 4E **45**
Bancyfelin. *Carm* 3H **43**
Banc-y-ffordd. *Carm* 2E **45**
Banff. *Abers* 2D **160**
Bangor. *Gwyn* 3E **81**
Bangor. *N Dwn* 3J **175**
Bangor-is-y-coed. *Wrex* 1F **71**
Bangors. *Corn* 3C **10**
Bangor's Green. *Lanc* 4B **90**
Banham. *Norf* 2C **66**
Bank. *Hants* 2A **16**
Bankend. *Dum* 3B **112**
Bankfoot. *Per* 5H **143**
Bankglen. *E Ayr* 3F **117**
Bankhead. *Aber* 2F **153**
Bankhead. *Abers* 3D **152**
Bankhead. *S Lan* 5B **128**
Bankland. *Som* 4G **21**
Bank Newton. *N Yor* 4B **98**
Banknock. *Falk* 2A **128**
Banks. *Cumb* 3G **113**
Banks. *Lanc* 2B **90**
Bankshill. *Dum* 1C **112**
Bank Street. *Worc* 4A **60**
Bank, The. *Ches E* 5C **84**
Bank, The. *Shrp* 1A **60**
Bank Top. *Lanc* 4D **90**
Banners Gate. *W Mid* 1E **61**
Banningham. *Norf* 3E **78**
Banniskirk. *High* 3D **168**
Bannister Green. *Essx* 3G **53**
Bannockburn. *Stir* 4H **135**
Banstead. *Surr* 5D **38**
Bantham. *Devn* 4C **8**
Banton. *N Lan* 2A **128**
Banwell. *N Som* 1G **21**
Banyard's Green. *Suff* 3F **67**
Bapchild. *Kent* 4D **40**
Bapton. *Wilts* 3E **23**
Barabhas. *W Isl* 2F **171**
Barabhas Iarach. *W Isl* 3F **171**
Baramore. *High* 1A **140**
Barassie. *S Ayr* 1C **116**
Baravullin. *Arg* 4D **140**
Barbaraville. *High* 1B **158**
Barber Booth. *Derbs* 2F **85**
Barber Green. *Cumb* 1C **96**
Barbhas Uarach. *W Isl* 2F **171**
Barbieston. *S Ayr* 3D **116**
Barbon. *Cumb* 1F **97**
Barbourne. *Worc* 5C **60**
Barbridge. *Ches E* 5A **84**
Barbrook. *Devn* 2H **19**
Barby. *Nptn* 3C **62**
Barby Nortoft. *Nptn* 3C **62**
Barcaldine. *Arg* 4D **140**
Barcheston. *Warw* 2A **50**
Barclose. *Cumb* 3F **113**
Barcombe. *E Sus* 4F **27**
Barcombe Cross. *E Sus* 4F **27**
Barden. *N Yor* 5E **105**
Barden Scale. *N Yor* 4C **98**
Bardfield End Green. *Essx* 2G **53**
Bardfield Saling. *Essx* 3G **53**
Bardister. *Shet* 4E **173**
Bardnabeinne. *High* 4E **164**
Bardney. *Linc* 4A **88**
Bardon. *Leics* 4B **74**
Bardon Mill. *Nmbd* 3A **114**
Bardowie. *E Dun* 2G **127**
Bardrainney. *Inv* 2E **127**
Bardsea. *Cumb* 2C **96**
Bardsey. *W Yor* 5F **99**
Bardsley. *G Man* 4H **91**
Bardwell. *Suff* 3B **66**
Bare. *Lanc* 3D **96**
Barelees. *Nmbd* 1C **120**
Barewood. *Here* 5F **59**
Barford. *Hants* 3G **25**
Barford. *Norf* 5D **78**
Barford. *Warw* 4G **61**
Barford St John. *Oxon* 2C **50**
Barford St Martin. *Wilts* 3F **23**
Barford St Michael. *Oxon* 2C **50**
Barfrestone. *Kent* 5G **41**
Bargeddie. *N Lan* 3A **128**
Bargod. *Cphy* 2E **33**
Bargoed. *Cphy* 2E **33**
Bargrennan. *Dum* 2A **110**
Barham. *Cambs* 3A **64**
Barham. *Kent* 5G **41**
Barham. *Suff* 5D **66**
Barharrow. *Dum* 4D **110**
Bar Hill. *Cambs* 4C **64**
Barholm. *Linc* 4H **75**
Barkby. *Leics* 5D **74**
Barkestone-le-Vale. *Leics* 2E **75**
Barkham. *Wok* 5F **37**
Barking. *G Lon* 2F **39**
Barking. *Suff* 5C **66**
Barkingside. *G Lon* 2F **39**
Barking Tye. *Suff* 5C **66**
Barkisland. *W Yor* 3A **92**
Barkston. *Linc* 1G **75**
Barkston Ash. *N Yor* 1E **93**
Barkway. *Herts* 2D **53**
Barlanark. *Glas* 3H **127**
Barlaston. *Staf* 2C **72**
Barlavington. *W Sus* 4A **26**
Barlborough. *Derbs* 3B **86**
Barlby. *N Yor* 1G **93**
Barlestone. *Leics* 5B **74**
Barley. *Herts* 2D **53**
Barley. *Lanc* 5H **97**
Barley Mow. *Tyne* 4F **115**
Barleythorpe. *Rut* 5F **75**
Barling. *Essx* 2D **40**
Barlings. *Linc* 3H **87**
Barlow. *Derbs* 3H **85**
Barlow. *N Yor* 2G **93**
Barlow. *Tyne* 3E **115**
Barmby Moor. *E Yor* 5B **100**
Barmby on the Marsh. *E Yor* 2G **93**
Barmer. *Norf* 2H **77**
Barming. *Kent* 5B **40**
Barming Heath. *Kent* 5B **40**
Barmoor. *Nmbd* 1E **121**
Barmouth. *Gwyn* 4F **69**
Barmpton. *Darl* 3A **106**
Barmston. *E Yor* 4F **101**
Barmulloch. *Glas* 3H **127**
Barnack. *Pet* 5H **75**
Barnacle. *Warw* 2A **62**
Barnard Castle. *Dur* 3D **104**
Barnard Gate. *Oxon* 4C **50**
Barnardiston. *Suff* 1H **53**
Barnbarroch. *Dum* 4F **111**
Barnburgh. *S Yor* 4E **93**
Barnby. *Suff* 2G **67**
Barnby Dun. *S Yor* 4G **93**
Barnby in the Willows. *Notts* 5F **87**
Barnby Moor. *Notts* 2D **86**
Barnes. *G Lon* 3D **38**
Barnes Street. *Kent* 1H **27**
Barnet. *G Lon* 1D **38**
Barnetby le Wold. *N Lin* 4D **94**
Barney. *Norf* 2B **78**
Barnham. *Suff* 3A **66**
Barnham. *W Sus* 5A **26**
Barnham Broom. *Norf* 5C **78**

Barnhead—Belper

Barnhead. *Ang* 3F 145
Barnhill. *D'dee* 5D 145
Barnhill. *Mor* 3F 159
Barnhill. *Per* 1D 136
Barnhills. *Dum* 2E 109
Barningham. *Dur* 3D 105
Barningham. *Suff* 3B 66
Barnoldby le Beck. *NE Lin* 4F 95
Barnoldswick. *Lanc* 5A 98
Barns Green. *W Sus* 3C 26
Barnsley. *Glos* 5F 49
Barnsley. *Shrp* 1B 60
Barnsley. *S Yor* 4D 92
Barnstaple. *Devn* 3F 19
Barnston. *Essx* 4G 53
Barnston. *Mers* 2E 83
Barnstone. *Notts* 2E 75
Barnt Green. *Worc* 3E 61
Barnton. *Ches W* 3A 84
Barnwell. *Cambs* 5D 64
Barnwell. *Nptn* 2H 63
Barnwood. *Glos* 4D 48
Barons Cross. *Here* 5G 59
Barony, The. *Orkn* 5B 172
Barr. *Dum* 4G 117
Barr. *S Ayr* 5B 116
Barra Airport. *W Isl* 8B 170
Barrachan. *Dum* 5A 110
Barraglom. *W Isl* 4D 171
Barrahormid. *Arg* 1F 125
Barrapol. *Arg* 4A 138
Barrasford. *Nmbd* 2C 114
Barravullin. *Arg* 3F 133
Barregarrow. *IOM* 3C 108
Barrhead. *E Ren* 4G 127
Barrhill. *S Ayr* 1H 109
Barri. *V Glam* 5E 32
Barrington. *Cambs* 1D 53
Barrington. *Som* 1G 13
Barripper. *Corn* 3D 4
Barrmill. *N Ayr* 4E 127
Barrock. *High* 1E 169
Barrow. *Lanc* 1F 91
Barrow. *Rut* 4F 75
Barrow. *Shrp* 5A 72
Barrow. *Som* 3C 22
Barrow. *Suff* 4G 65
Barroway Drove. *Norf* 5E 77
Barrow Bridge. *G Man* 3E 91
Barrowburn. *Nmbd* 3C 120
Barrowby. *Linc* 2F 75
Barrowcliff. *N Yor* 1E 101
Barrow Common. *N Som* 5A 34
Barrowden. *Rut* 5G 75
Barrowford. *Lanc* 1G 91
Barrow Gurney. *N Som* 5A 34
Barrow Haven. *N Lin* 2D 94
Barrow Hill. *Derbs* 3B 86
Barrow-in-Furness. *Cumb* 3B 96
Barrow Nook. *Lanc* 4C 90
Barrows Green. *Cumb* 1E 97
Barrow's Green. *Hal* 2H 83
Barrow Street. *Wilts* 3D 22
Barrow upon Humber. *N Lin* 2D 94
Barrow upon Soar. *Leics* 4C 74
Barrow upon Trent. *Derbs* 3A 74
Barry. *Ang* 5E 145
Barry. *V Glam* 5E 32
Barry Island. *V Glam* 5E 32
Barsby. *Leics* 4D 74
Barsham. *Suff* 2F 67
Barston. *W Mid* 3G 61
Bartestree. *Here* 1A 48
Barthol Chapel. *Abers* 5F 161
Bartholomew Green. *Essx* 3H 53
Barthomley. *Ches E* 5B 84
Bartley. *Hants* 1B 16
Bartley Green. *W Mid* 2E 61
Bartlow. *Cambs* 1F 53
Barton. *Cambs* 5D 64
Barton. *Ches W* 5G 83
Barton. *Cumb* 2F 103
Barton. *Glos* 3G 49
Barton. *IOW* 4D 16
Barton. *Lanc* 4B 90 (nr. Ormskirk)
Barton. *Lanc* 1D 90 (nr. Preston)
Barton. *N Som* 1G 21
Barton. *N Yor* 4F 105
Barton. *Oxon* 5D 50
Barton. *Torb* 2F 9
Barton. *Warw* 5F 61
Barton Bendish. *Norf* 5G 77
Barton Gate. *Staf* 4F 73
Barton Green. *Staf* 4F 73
Barton Hartshorn. *Buck* 2E 51
Barton Hill. *N Yor* 3B 100
Barton in Fabis. *Notts* 2C 74
Barton in the Beans. *Leics* 5A 74
Barton-le-Clay. *C Beds* 2A 52
Barton-le-Street. *N Yor* 2B 100
Barton-le-Willows. *N Yor* 3B 100
Barton Mills. *Suff* 3G 65
Barton on Sea. *Hants* 3H 15
Barton-on-the-Heath. *Warw* 2A 50
Barton St David. *Som* 3A 22
Barton Seagrave. *Nptn* 3F 63
Barton Stacey. *Hants* 2C 24
Barton Town. *Devn* 2G 19
Barton Turf. *Norf* 3F 79
Barton-under-Needwood. *Staf* 4F 73
Barton-upon-Humber. *N Lin* 2D 94
Barton Waterside. *N Lin* 2D 94
Barugh Green. *S Yor* 4D 92
Barway. *Cambs* 3E 65
Barwell. *Leics* 1B 62
Barwick. *Herts* 4D 53
Barwick. *Som* 1A 14
Barwick in Elmet. *W Yor* 1D 93
Baschurch. *Shrp* 3G 71
Bascote. *Warw* 4B 62
Basford Green. *Staf* 5D 85
Bashall Eaves. *Lanc* 5F 97
Bashall Town. *Lanc* 5G 97
Bashley. *Hants* 3H 15
Basildon. *Essx* 2B 40
Basingstoke. *Hants* 1E 25
Baslow. *Derbs* 3G 85
Bason Bridge. *Som* 2G 21
Bassaleg. *Newp* 3F 33
Bassendean. *Bord* 5C 130
Bassenthwaite. *Cumb* 1D 102
Bassett. *Sotn* 1C 16
Bassingbourn. *Cambs* 1D 52
Bassingfield. *Notts* 2D 74
Bassingham. *Linc* 4G 87
Bassingthorpe. *Linc* 3G 75
Bassus Green. *Herts* 3D 52
Basta. *Shet* 2G 173
Baston. *Linc* 4A 76
Bastonford. *Worc* 5C 60
Bastwick. *Norf* 4G 79
Batchley. *Worc* 4E 61
Batchworth. *Herts* 1B 38
Batcombe. *Dors* 2B 14
Batcombe. *Som* 3B 22
Bate Heath. *Ches E* 3A 84
Bath. *Bath* 5C 34
Bathampton. *Bath* 5C 34
Bathealton. *Som* 4D 20
Batheaston. *Bath* 5C 34
Bathford. *Bath* 5C 34
Bathgate. *W Lot* 3C 128
Bathley. *Notts* 5E 87
Bathpool. *Corn* 5C 10
Bathpool. *Som* 4F 21
Bathville. *W Lot* 3C 128
Bathway. *Som* 1A 22
Batley. *W Yor* 2C 92
Batsford. *Glos* 2G 49
Batson. *Devn* 5D 8
Battersby. *N Yor* 4C 106
Battersea. *G Lon* 3D 39
Battisborough Cross. *Devn* 4C 8
Battisford. *Suff* 5C 66
Battisford Tye. *Suff* 5C 66
Battle. *E Sus* 4B 28
Battle. *Powy* 2D 46
Battleborough. *Som* 1G 21
Battledown. *Glos* 3E 49
Battlefield. *Shrp* 4H 71
Battlesbridge. *Essx* 1B 40
Battlesden. *C Beds* 3H 51
Battlesea Green. *Suff* 3E 66
Battleton. *Som* 4C 20
Battram. *Leics* 5B 74
Battramsley. *Hants* 3B 16
Batt's Corner. *Surr* 2G 25
Bauds of Cullen. *Mor* 2B 160
Baugh. *Arg* 4B 138
Baughton. *Worc* 1D 49
Baughurst. *Hants* 5D 36
Baulking. *Oxon* 2B 36
Baumber. *Linc* 3B 88
Baunton. *Glos* 5F 49
Baverstock. *Wilts* 3F 23
Bawburgh. *Norf* 5D 78
Bawdeswell. *Norf* 3C 78
Bawdrip. *Som* 3G 21
Bawdsey. *Suff* 1G 55
Bawdsey Manor. *Suff* 2G 55
Bawsey. *Norf* 4F 77
Bawtry. *S Yor* 1D 86
Baxenden. *Lanc* 2F 91
Baxterley. *Warw* 1G 61
Baxter's Green. *Suff* 5G 65
Bay. *High* 3B 154
Baybridge. *Hants* 4D 24
Baybridge. *Nmbd* 4C 114
Baycliff. *Cumb* 2B 96
Baydon. *Wilts* 4A 36
Bayford. *Herts* 5D 52
Bayford. *Som* 4C 22
Bayles. *Cumb* 5A 114
Baylham. *Suff* 5D 66
Baynard's Green. *Oxon* 3D 50
Bayston Hill. *Shrp* 5G 71
Baythorn End. *Essx* 1H 53
Baythorpe. *Linc* 1B 76
Bayton. *Worc* 3A 60
Bayton Common. *Worc* 3B 60
Bayworth. *Oxon* 5D 50
Beach. *S Glo* 4C 34
Beachampton. *Buck* 2F 51
Beachamwell. *Norf* 5G 77
Beachley. *Glos* 2A 34
Beacon. *Devn* 2E 13
Beacon End. *Essx* 3C 54
Beacon Hill. *Surr* 3G 25
Beacon's Bottom. *Buck* 2F 37
Beaconsfield. *Buck* 1A 38
Beacrabhaic. *W Isl* 8D 171
Beadlam. *N Yor* 1A 100
Beadnell. *Nmbd* 2G 121
Beaford. *Devn* 1F 11
Beal. *Nmbd* 5G 131
Beal. *N Yor* 2F 93
Bealsmill. *Corn* 5D 10
Beam Hill. *Staf* 3G 73
Beamhurst. *Staf* 2E 73
Beaminster. *Dors* 2H 13
Beamish. *Dur* 4F 115
Beamond End. *Buck* 1A 38
Beamsley. *N Yor* 4C 98
Bean. *Kent* 3G 39
Beanacre. *Wilts* 5E 35
Beanley. *Nmbd* 3E 121
Beaquoy. *Orkn* 5C 172
Beardwood. *Bkbn* 2E 91
Beare Green. *Surr* 1C 26
Bearley. *Warw* 4F 61
Bearpark. *Dur* 5F 115
Bearsbridge. *Nmbd* 4A 114
Bearsden. *E Dun* 2G 127
Bearsted. *Kent* 5B 40
Bearstone. *Shrp* 2B 72
Bearwood. *Pool* 3F 15
Bearwood. *W Mid* 2E 61
Beattock. *Dum* 4C 118
Beauchamp Roding. *Essx* 4F 53
Beauchief. *S Yor* 2H 85
Beaufort. *Blae* 4E 47
Beaulieu. *Hants* 2B 16
Beauly. *High* 4H 157
Beaumaris. *IOA* 3F 81
Beaumont. *Cumb* 4E 113
Beaumont. *Essx* 3E 55
Beaumont Hill. *Darl* 3F 105
Beaumont Leys. *Leic* 5C 74
Beausale. *Warw* 3G 61
Beauvale. *Notts* 1B 74
Beauworth. *Hants* 4D 24
Beaworthy. *Devn* 3E 11
Beazley End. *Essx* 3H 53
Bebington. *Mers* 2F 83
Bebside. *Nmbd* 1F 115
Beccles. *Suff* 2G 67
Becconsall. *Lanc* 2C 90
Beckbury. *Shrp* 5B 72
Beckenham. *G Lon* 4E 39
Beckermet. *Cumb* 4B 102
Beckett End. *Norf* 1G 65
Beckfoot. *Cumb* 1A 96 (nr. Broughton in Furness)
Beck Foot. *Cumb* 5H 103 (nr. Kendal)
Beckfoot. *Cumb* 4C 102 (nr. Seascale)
Beckfoot. *Cumb* 5B 112 (nr. Silloth)
Beckford. *Worc* 2E 49
Beckhampton. *Wilts* 5F 35
Beck Hole. *N Yor* 4F 107
Beckingham. *Linc* 5F 87
Beckingham. *Notts* 1E 87
Beckington. *Som* 1D 22
Beckley. *E Sus* 3C 28
Beckley. *Hants* 3H 15
Beckley. *Oxon* 4D 50
Beck Row. *Suff* 3F 65
Beck Side. *Cumb* 1C 96 (nr. Cartmel)
Beckside. *Cumb* 1F 97 (nr. Sedbergh)
Beck Side. *Cumb* 1B 96 (nr. Ulverston)
Beckton. *G Lon* 2F 39
Beckwithshaw. *N Yor* 4E 99
Becontree. *G Lon* 2F 39
Bedale. *N Yor* 1E 99
Bedburn. *Dur* 1E 105
Bedchester. *Dors* 1D 14
Beddau. *Rhon* 3D 32
Beddgelert. *Gwyn* 1E 69
Beddingham. *E Sus* 5F 27
Beddington. *G Lon* 4E 39
Bedfield. *Suff* 4E 66
Bedford. *Bed* 1A 52
Bedford. *G Man* 1A 84
Bedham. *W Sus* 3B 26
Bedhampton. *Hants* 2F 17
Bedingfield. *Suff* 4D 66
Bedingham Green. *Norf* 1E 67
Bedlam. *N Yor* 3E 99
Bedlar's Green. *Essx* 3F 53
Bedlington. *Nmbd* 1F 115
Bedlinog. *Mer T* 5D 46
Bedminster. *Bris* 4A 34
Bedmond. *Herts* 5A 52
Bednall. *Staf* 4D 72
Bedrule. *Bord* 3A 120
Bedstone. *Shrp* 3F 59
Bedwas. *Cphy* 3E 33
Bedwellty. *Cphy* 5E 47
Bedworth. *Warw* 2A 62
Beeby. *Leics* 5D 74
Beech. *Hants* 3E 25
Beech. *Staf* 2C 72
Beechcliffe. *W Yor* 5C 98
Beech Hill. *W Ber* 5E 37
Beechingstoke. *Wilts* 1F 23
Beedon. *W Ber* 4C 36
Beeford. *E Yor* 4F 101
Beeley. *Derbs* 4G 85
Beelsby. *NE Lin* 4F 95
Beenham. *W Ber* 5D 36
Beeny. *Corn* 3B 10
Beer. *Devn* 4F 13
Beer. *Som* 3H 21
Beercrocombe. *Som* 4G 21
Beer Hackett. *Dors* 1B 14
Beesands. *Devn* 4E 9
Beesby. *Linc* 2D 88
Beeson. *Devn* 4E 9
Beeston. *C Beds* 1B 52
Beeston. *Ches W* 5H 83
Beeston. *Norf* 4B 78
Beeston. *Notts* 2C 74
Beeston. *W Yor* 1C 92
Beeston Regis. *Norf* 1D 78
Beeswing. *Dum* 3F 111
Beetham. *Cumb* 2D 97
Beetham. *Som* 1F 13
Beetley. *Norf* 4B 78
Beffcote. *Staf* 4C 72
Began. *Card* 3F 33
Begbroke. *Oxon* 4C 50
Begdale. *Cambs* 5D 76
Begelly. *Pemb* 4F 43
Beggar Hill. *Essx* 5G 53
Beggar's Bush. *Powy* 4E 59
Beggearn Huish. *Som* 3D 20
Beguildy. *Powy* 3D 58
Beighton. *Norf* 5F 79
Beighton. *S Yor* 2B 86
Beighton Hill. *Derbs* 5G 85
Beinn Casgro. *W Isl* 5G 171
Beith. *N Ayr* 4E 127
Bekesbourne. *Kent* 5F 41
Belaugh. *Norf* 4E 79
Belbroughton. *Worc* 3D 60
Belchalwell. *Dors* 2C 14
Belchalwell Street. *Dors* 2C 14
Belchamp Otten. *Essx* 1B 54
Belchamp St Paul. *Essx* 1A 54
Belchamp Walter. *Essx* 1B 54
Belchford. *Linc* 3B 88
Belfast. *Bel* 4H 175
Belfast International Airport. *Ant* 3G 175
Belfatton. *Abers* 3H 161
Belford. *Nmbd* 1F 121
Belgrano. *Cnwy* 3B 82
Belhaven. *E Lot* 2C 130
Belhelvie. *Abers* 2G 153
Belhinnie. *Abers* 1B 152
Bellabeg. *Abers* 2A 152
Belladrum. *High* 4H 157
Bellaghy. *Mag* 3F 175
Bellamore. *S Ayr* 1H 109
Bellanoch. *Arg* 4F 133
Bell Busk. *N Yor* 4B 98
Belleau. *Linc* 3D 88
Belleheiglash. *Mor* 5F 159
Bell End. *Worc* 3D 60
Bellerby. *N Yor* 5E 105
Bellerby Camp. *N Yor* 5D 105
Bellever. *Devn* 5G 11
Belle Vue. *Cumb* 1C 102
Belle Vue. *Shrp* 4G 71
Bellfield. *S Lan* 1H 117
Belliehill. *Ang* 2E 145
Bellingdon. *Buck* 5H 51
Bellingham. *Nmbd* 1B 114
Bellmount. *Norf* 3E 77
Bellochantuy. *Arg* 2A 122
Bellsbank. *E Ayr* 4D 117
Bell's Cross. *Suff* 5D 66
Bellshill. *N Lan* 4A 128
Bellshill. *Nmbd* 1F 121
Bellside. *N Lan* 4B 128
Bellspool. *Bord* 1D 118
Bellsquarry. *W Lot* 3D 128
Bells Yew Green. *E Sus* 2H 27
Belmaduthy. *High* 3A 158
Belmesthorpe. *Rut* 4H 75
Belmont. *Bkbn* 3E 91
Belmont. *Shet* 1G 173
Belmont. *S Ayr* 2C 116
Belnacraig. *Abers* 2A 152
Belnie. *Linc* 2B 76
Belowda. *Corn* 2D 6
Belper. *Derbs* 1A 74

Belper Lane End—Bishopsbourne

Belper Lane End. *Derbs* 1H **73**
Belph. *Derbs* 3C **86**
Belsay. *Nmbd* 2E **115**
Belsford. *Devn* 3D **8**
Belsize. *Herts* 5A **52**
Belstead. *Suff* 1E **55**
Belston. *S Ayr* 2C **116**
Belstone. *Devn* 3G **11**
Belstone Corner. *Devn* 3G **11**
Belthorn. *Lanc* 2F **91**
Beltinge. *Kent* 4F **41**
Beltoft. *N Lin* 4B **94**
Belton. *Leics* 3B **74**
Belton. *Linc* 2G **75**
Belton. *Norf* 5G **79**
Belton. *N Lin* 4A **94**
Belton-in-Rutland. *Rut* 5F **75**
Beltring. *Kent* 1A **28**
Belts of Collonach. *Abers* 4D **152**
Belvedere. *G Lon* 3F **39**
Belvoir. *Leics* 2F **75**
Bembridge. *IOW* 4E **17**
Bemersyde. *Bord* 1H **119**
Bemerton. *Wilts* 3G **23**
Bempton. *E Yor* 2F **101**
Benacre. *Suff* 2H **67**
Ben Alder Lodge. *High* 1C **142**
Ben Armine Lodge. *High* 2E **164**
Benbecula Airport. *W Isl* 3C **170**
Benbuie. *Dum* 5G **117**
Benchill. *G Man* 2C **84**
Benderloch. *Arg* 5D **140**
Bendish. *Herts* 3B **52**
Bendronaig Lodge. *High* 5C **156**
Benenden. *Kent* 2C **28**
Benfieldside. *Dur* 4D **115**
Bengate. *Norf* 3F **79**
Bengeworth. *Worc* 1F **49**
Benhall Green. *Suff* 4F **67**
Benholm. *Abers* 2H **145**
Beningbrough. *N Yor* 4H **99**
Benington. *Herts* 3C **52**
Benington. *Linc* 1C **76**
Benington Sea End. *Linc* 1D **76**
Benllech. *IOA* 2E **81**
Benmore Lodge. *High* 2H **163**
Bennacott. *Corn* 3C **10**
Bennah. *Devn* 4B **12**
Bennecarrigan. *N Ayr* 3D **122**
Bennethead. *Cumb* 2F **103**
Benniworth. *Linc* 2B **88**
Benover. *Kent* 1B **28**
Benson. *Oxon* 2E **36**
Benston. *Shet* 6F **173**
Benstonhall. *Orkn* 4E **172**
Bent. *Abers* 1F **145**
Benthall. *Shrp* 5A **72**
Bentham. *Glos* 4E **49**
Benthoul. *Aber* 3F **153**
Bentlawnt. *Shrp* 5F **71**
Bentley. *E Yor* 1D **94**
Bentley. *Hants* 2F **25**
Bentley. *S Yor* 4F **93**
Bentley. *Suff* 2E **54**
Bentley. *Warw* 1G **61**
Bentley. *W Mid* 1D **61**
Bentley Heath. *Herts* 1D **38**
Bentley Heath. *W Mid* 3F **61**
Bentpath. *Dum* 5F **119**
Bents. *W Lot* 3C **128**
Bentworth. *Hants* 2E **25**
Benvie. *D'dee* 5C **144**
Benville. *Dors* 2A **14**
Benwell. *Tyne* 3F **115**
Benwick. *Cambs* 1C **64**
Beoley. *Worc* 4E **61**
Beoraidbeg. *High* 4E **147**
Bepton. *W Sus* 1G **17**
Berden. *Essx* 3E **53**
Bere Alston. *Devn* 2A **8**
Bere Ferrers. *Devn* 2A **8**
Berepper. *Corn* 4D **4**
Bere Regis. *Dors* 3D **14**
Bergh Apton. *Norf* 5F **79**
Berinsfield. *Oxon* 2D **36**
Berkeley. *Glos* 2B **34**
Berkhamsted. *Herts* 5H **51**
Berkley. *Som* 2D **22**
Berkswell. *W Mid* 3G **61**
Bermondsey. *G Lon* 3E **39**
Bernera. *High* 1G **147**
Bernice. *Arg* 4A **134**
Bernisdale. *High* 3D **154**
Berrick Salome. *Oxon* 2E **36**
Berriedale. *High* 1H **165**
Berrier. *Cumb* 2E **103**
Berriew. *Powy* 5D **70**
Berrington. *Nmbd* 5G **131**
Berrington. *Shrp* 5H **71**
Berrington. *Worc* 4H **59**
Berrington Green. *Worc* 4H **59**
Berrington Law. *Nmbd* 5F **131**
Berrow. *Som* 1G **21**
Berrow Green. *Worc* 5B **60**
Berry Cross. *Devn* 1E **11**
Berry Down Cross. *Devn* 2F **19**
Berry Hill. *Glos* 4A **48**
Berry Hill. *Pemb* 1A **44**
Berryhillock. *Mor* 2C **160**
Berrynarbor. *Devn* 2F **19**
Berry Pomeroy. *Devn* 2E **9**
Berryscaur. *Dum* 5D **118**
Berry's Green. *G Lon* 5F **39**
Bersham. *Wrex* 1F **71**
Berthengam. *Flin* 3D **82**
Berwick. *E Sus* 5G **27**
Berwick Bassett. *Wilts* 4G **35**
Berwick Hill. *Nmbd* 2E **115**
Berwick St James. *Wilts* 3F **23**
Berwick St John. *Wilts* 4E **23**
Berwick St Leonard. *Wilts* 3E **23**
Berwick-upon-Tweed. *Nmbd* 4F **131**
Berwyn. *Den* 1D **70**
Bescaby. *Leics* 3F **75**
Bescar. *Lanc* 3B **90**
Besford. *Worc* 1E **49**
Bessacarr. *S Yor* 4G **93**
Bessbrook. *New M* 6F **175**
Bessels Leigh. *Oxon* 5C **50**
Bessingby. *E Yor* 3F **101**
Bessingham. *Norf* 2D **78**
Best Beech Hill. *E Sus* 2H **27**
Besthorpe. *Norf* 1C **66**
Besthorpe. *Notts* 4F **87**
Bestwood Village. *Notts* 1C **74**
Beswick. *E Yor* 5E **101**
Betchworth. *Surr* 5D **38**
Bethania. *Cdgn* 4E **57**
Bethania. *Gwyn* 1G **69**
(nr. Blaenau Ffestiniog)
Bethania. *Gwyn* 5F **81**
(nr. Caernarfon)
Bethel. *Gwyn* 2B **70**
(nr. Bala)
Bethel. *Gwyn* 4E **81**
(nr. Caernarfon)
Bethel. *IOA* 3C **80**
Bethersden. *Kent* 1D **28**
Bethesda. *Gwyn* 4F **81**
Bethesda. *Pemb* 3E **43**
Bethlehem. *Carm* 3G **45**
Bethnal Green. *G Lon* 2E **39**
Betley. *Staf* 1B **72**
Betsham. *Kent* 3H **39**
Betteshanger. *Kent* 5H **41**
Bettiscombe. *Dors* 3H **13**
Bettisfield. *Wrex* 2G **71**
Betton. *Shrp* 2A **72**
Betton Strange. *Shrp* 5H **71**
Bettws. *B'end* 3C **32**
Bettws. *Newp* 2F **33**
Bettws Bledrws. *Cdgn* 5E **57**
Bettws Cedewain. *Powy* 1D **58**
Bettws Gwerfil Goch. *Den* 1C **70**
Bettws Ifan. *Cdgn* 1D **44**
Bettws Newydd. *Mon* 5G **47**
Bettyhill. *High* 2H **167**
Betws. *Carm* 4G **45**
Betws Garmon. *Gwyn* 5E **81**
Betws-y-Coed. *Cnwy* 5G **81**
Betws-yn-Rhos. *Cnwy* 3B **82**
Beulah. *Cdgn* 1C **44**
Beulah. *Powy* 5B **58**
Beul an Atha. *Arg* 3B **124**
Bevendean. *Brig* 5E **27**
Bevercotes. *Notts* 3E **86**
Beverley. *E Yor* 1D **94**
Beverston. *Glos* 2D **34**
Bevington. *Glos* 2B **34**
Bewaldeth. *Cumb* 1D **102**
Bewcastle. *Cumb* 2G **113**
Bewdley. *Worc* 3B **60**
Bewerley. *N Yor* 3D **98**
Bewholme. *E Yor* 4F **101**
Bexfield. *Norf* 3C **78**
Bexhill. *E Sus* 5B **28**
Bexley. *G Lon* 3F **39**
Bexleyheath. *G Lon* 3F **39**
Bexleyhill. *W Sus* 3A **26**
Bexwell. *Norf* 5F **77**
Beyton. *Suff* 4B **66**
Bhalton. *W Isl* 4C **171**
Bhatarsaigh. *W Isl* 9B **170**
Bibbington. *Derbs* 3E **85**
Bibury. *Glos* 5G **49**
Bicester. *Oxon* 3D **50**
Bickenhall. *Som* 1F **13**
Bickenhill. *W Mid* 2F **61**
Bicker. *Linc* 2B **76**
Bicker Bar. *Linc* 2B **76**
Bicker Gauntlet. *Linc* 2B **76**
Bickershaw. *G Man* 4E **91**
Bickerstaffe. *Lanc* 4C **90**
Bickerton. *Ches E* 5H **83**
Bickerton. *Nmbd* 4D **121**
Bickerton. *N Yor* 4G **99**
Bickford. *Staf* 4C **72**
Bickington. *Devn* 3F **19**
(nr. Barnstaple)
Bickington. *Devn* 5A **12**
(nr. Newton Abbot)
Bickleigh. *Devn* 2B **8**
(nr. Plymouth)
Bickleigh. *Devn* 2C **12**
(nr. Tiverton)
Bickleton. *Devn* 3F **19**
Bickley. *N Yor* 5G **107**
Bickley Moss. *Ches W* 1H **71**
Bickmarsh. *Warw* 1G **49**
Bicknacre. *Essx* 5A **54**
Bicknoller. *Som* 3E **20**
Bicknor. *Kent* 5C **40**
Bickton. *Hants* 1G **15**
Bicton. *Here* 4G **59**
Bicton. *Shrp* 2E **59**
(nr. Bishop's Castle)
Bicton. *Shrp* 4G **71**
(nr. Shrewsbury)
Bicton Heath. *Shrp* 4G **71**
Bidborough. *Kent* 1G **27**
Biddenden. *Kent* 2C **28**
Biddenden Green. *Kent* 1C **28**
Biddenham. *Bed* 5H **63**
Biddestone. *Wilts* 4D **34**
Biddisham. *Som* 1G **21**
Biddlesden. *Buck* 1E **51**
Biddlestone. *Nmbd* 4D **120**
Biddulph. *Staf* 5C **84**
Biddulph Moor. *Staf* 5D **84**
Bideford. *Devn* 4E **19**
Bidford-on-Avon. *Warw* 5E **61**
Bidlake. *Devn* 4F **11**
Bidston. *Mers* 1E **83**
Bielby. *E Yor* 5B **100**
Bieldside. *Aber* 3F **153**
Bierley. *IOW* 5D **16**
Bierley. *W Yor* 1B **92**
Bierton. *Buck* 4G **51**
Bigbury. *Devn* 4C **8**
Bigbury-on-Sea. *Devn* 4C **8**
Bigby. *Linc* 4D **94**
Biggar. *Cumb* 3A **96**
Biggar. *S Lan* 1C **118**
Biggin. *Derbs* 5F **85**
(nr. Hartington)
Biggin. *Derbs* 1G **73**
(nr. Hulland)
Biggin. *N Yor* 1F **93**
Biggings. *Shet* 5C **173**
Biggin Hill. *G Lon* 5F **39**
Biggleswade. *C Beds* 1B **52**
Bighouse. *High* 2A **168**
Bighton. *Hants* 3E **24**
Biglands. *Cumb* 4D **112**
Bignall End. *Staf* 5C **84**
Bignor. *W Sus* 4A **26**
Bigrigg. *Cumb* 3B **102**
Big Sand. *High* 1G **155**
Bigton. *Shet* 9E **173**
Bilberry. *Corn* 3E **6**
Bilborough. *Nott* 1C **74**
Bilbrook. *Som* 2D **20**
Bilbrook. *Staf* 5C **72**
Bilbrough. *N Yor* 5H **99**
Bilbster. *High* 3E **169**
Bilby. *Notts* 2D **86**
Bildershaw. *Dur* 2F **105**
Bildeston. *Suff* 1C **54**
Billericay. *Essx* 1A **40**
Billesdon. *Leics* 5E **74**
Billesley. *Warw* 5F **61**
Billingborough. *Linc* 2A **76**
Billinge. *Mers* 4D **90**
Billingford. *Norf* 3C **78**
(nr. Dereham)
Billingford. *Norf* 3D **66**
(nr. Diss)
Billingham. *Stoc T* 2B **106**
Billinghay. *Linc* 5A **88**
Billingley. *S Yor* 4E **93**
Billingshurst. *W Sus* 3B **26**
Billingsley. *Shrp* 2B **60**
Billington. *C Beds* 3H **51**
Billington. *Lanc* 1F **91**
Billington. *Staf* 3C **72**
Billockby. *Norf* 4G **79**
Billy Row. *Dur* 1E **105**
Bilsborrow. *Lanc* 5E **97**
Bilsby. *Linc* 3D **88**
Bilsham. *W Sus* 5A **26**
Bilsington. *Kent* 2E **29**
Bilson Green. *Glos* 4B **48**
Bilsthorpe. *Notts* 4D **86**
Bilston. *Midl* 3F **129**
Bilston. *W Mid* 1D **60**
Bilstone. *Leics* 5A **74**
Bilting. *Kent* 1E **29**
Bilton. *E Yor* 1E **95**
Bilton. *Nmbd* 3G **121**
Bilton. *N Yor* 4F **99**
Bilton. *Warw* 3B **62**
Bilton in Ainsty. *N Yor* 5G **99**
Bimbister. *Orkn* 6C **172**
Binbrook. *Linc* 1B **88**
Binchester. *Dur* 1F **105**
Bincombe. *Dors* 4B **14**
Bindal. *High* 5G **165**
Binegar. *Som* 2B **22**
Bines Green. *W Sus* 4C **26**
Binfield. *Brac* 4G **37**
Binfield Heath. *Oxon* 4F **37**
Bingfield. *Nmbd* 2C **114**
Bingham. *Notts* 2E **74**
Bingham's Melcombe. *Dors* 2C **14**
Bingley. *W Yor* 1B **92**
Bings Heath. *Shrp* 4H **71**
Binham. *Norf* 2B **78**
Binley. *Hants* 1C **24**
Binley. *W Mid* 3A **62**
Binnegar. *Dors* 4D **15**
Binniehill. *Falk* 2B **128**
Binsoe. *N Yor* 2E **99**
Binstead. *IOW* 3D **16**
Binstead. *W Sus* 5A **26**
Binsted. *Hants* 2F **25**
Binton. *Warw* 5F **61**
Bintree. *Norf* 3C **78**
Binweston. *Shrp* 5F **71**
Birch. *Essx* 4C **54**
Birchall. *Staf* 5D **85**
Bircham Newton. *Norf* 2G **77**
Bircham Tofts. *Norf* 2G **77**
Birchanger. *Essx* 3F **53**
Birchburn. *N Ayr* 3D **122**
Birch Cross. *Staf* 2F **73**
Bircher. *Here* 4G **59**
Birch Green. *Essx* 4C **54**
Birchgrove. *Card* 3E **33**
Birchgrove. *Swan* 3G **31**
Birch Heath. *Ches W* 4H **83**
Birch Hill. *Ches W* 3H **83**
Birchill. *Devn* 2G **13**
Birchington. *Kent* 4G **41**
Birch Langley. *G Man* 4G **91**
Birchley Heath. *Warw* 1G **61**
Birchmoor. *Warw* 5G **73**
Birchmoor Green. *C Beds* 2H **51**
Birchover. *Derbs* 4G **85**
Birch Vale. *Derbs* 2E **85**
Birchview. *Mor* 5F **159**
Birchwood. *Linc* 4G **87**
Birchwood. *Som* 1F **13**
Birchwood. *Warr* 1A **84**
Bircotes. *Notts* 1D **86**
Birdbrook. *Essx* 1H **53**
Birdham. *W Sus* 2G **17**
Birdholme. *Derbs* 4A **86**
Birdingbury. *Warw* 4B **62**
Birdlip. *Glos* 4E **49**
Birdsall. *N Yor* 3C **100**
Birds Edge. *W Yor* 4C **92**
Birds Green. *Essx* 5F **53**
Birdsgreen. *Shrp* 2B **60**
Birdsmoorgate. *Dors* 2G **13**
Birdston. *E Dun* 2H **127**
Birdwell. *S Yor* 4D **92**
Birdwood. *Glos* 4C **48**
Birgham. *Bord* 1B **120**
Birichen. *High* 4E **165**
Birkby. *Cumb* 1B **102**
Birkby. *N Yor* 4A **106**
Birkdale. *Mers* 3B **90**
Birkenhead. *Mers* 2F **83**
Birkenhills. *Abers* 4E **161**
Birkenshaw. *N Lan* 3H **127**
Birkenshaw. *W Yor* 2C **92**
Birkhall. *Abers* 4H **151**
Birkhill. *Ang* 5C **144**
Birkholme. *Linc* 3G **75**
Birkin. *N Yor* 2F **93**
Birley. *Here* 5G **59**
Birling. *Kent* 4A **40**
Birling. *Nmbd* 4G **121**
Birling Gap. *E Sus* 5G **27**
Birlingham. *Worc* 1E **49**
Birmingham. *W Mid* 2E **61**
Birmingham Airport. *W Mid* 2F **61**
Birnam. *Per* 4H **143**
Birse. *Abers* 4C **152**
Birsemore. *Abers* 4C **152**
Birstall. *Leics* 5C **74**
Birstall. *W Yor* 2C **92**
Birstall Smithies. *W Yor* 2C **92**
Birstwith. *N Yor* 4E **99**
Birthorpe. *Linc* 2A **76**
Birtle. *Lanc* 3G **91**
Birtley. *Here* 4F **59**
Birtley. *Nmbd* 2B **114**
Birtley. *Tyne* 4F **115**
Birtsmorton. *Worc* 2D **48**
Birts Street. *Worc* 2C **48**
Bisbrooke. *Rut* 1F **63**
Bisham. *Wind* 3G **37**
Bishampton. *Worc* 5D **61**
Bish Mill. *Devn* 4H **19**
Bishop Auckland. *Dur* 2F **105**
Bishopbridge. *Linc* 1H **87**
Bishopbriggs. *E Dun* 2H **127**
Bishop Burton. *E Yor* 1C **94**
Bishopdown. *Wilts* 3G **23**
Bishop Middleham. *Dur* 1A **106**
Bishopmill. *Mor* 2G **159**
Bishop Monkton. *N Yor* 3F **99**
Bishop Norton. *Linc* 1G **87**
Bishopsbourne. *Kent* 5F **41**

Bishops Cannings—Bolton upon Dearne

Bishops Cannings. *Wilts* 5F 35
Bishop's Castle. *Shrp* 2F 59
Bishop's Caundle. *Dors* 1B 14
Bishop's Cleeve. *Glos* 3E 49
Bishop's Down. *Dors* 1B 14
Bishop's Frome. *Here* 1B 48
Bishop's Green. *Essx* 4G 53
Bishop's Green. *Hants* 5D 36
Bishop's Hull. *Som* 4F 21
Bishop's Itchington. *Warw* 5A 62
Bishops Lydeard. *Som* 4E 21
Bishop's Norton. *Glos* 3D 48
Bishop's Nympton. *Devn* 4A 20
Bishop's Offley. *Staf* 3B 72
Bishop's Stortford. *Herts* 3E 53
Bishops Sutton. *Hants* 3E 24
Bishop's Tachbrook. *Warw* 4H 61
Bishop's Tawton. *Devn* 3F 19
Bishopsteignton. *Devn* 5C 12
Bishopstoke. *Hants* 1C 16
Bishopston. *Swan* 4E 31
Bishopstone. *Buck* 4G 51
Bishopstone. *E Sus* 5F 27
Bishopstone. *Here* 1H 47
Bishopstone. *Swin* 3H 35
Bishopstone. *Wilts* 4F 23
Bishopstrow. *Wilts* 2D 23
Bishop Sutton. *Bath* 1A 22
Bishop's Waltham. *Hants* 1D 16
Bishopswood. *Som* 1F 13
Bishops Wood. *Staf* 5C 72
Bishopsworth. *Bris* 5A 34
Bishop Thornton. *N Yor* 3E 99
Bishopthorpe. *York* 5H 99
Bishopton. *Darl* 2A 106
Bishopton. *Dum* 5B 110
Bishopton. *N Yor* 2E 99
Bishopton. *Ren* 2F 127
Bishopton. *Warw* 5F 61
Bishop Wilton. *E Yor* 4B 100
Bishton. *Newp* 3G 33
Bishton. *Staf* 3E 73
Bisley. *Glos* 5E 49
Bisley. *Surr* 5A 38
Bispham. *Bkpl* 5C 96
Bispham Green. *Lanc* 3C 90
Bissoe. *Corn* 4B 6
Bisterne. *Hants* 2G 15
Bisterne Close. *Hants* 2H 15
Bitchfield. *Linc* 3G 75
Bittadon. *Devn* 2F 19
Bittaford. *Devn* 3C 8
Bittering. *Norf* 4B 78
Bitterley. *Shrp* 3H 59
Bitterne. *Sotn* 1C 16
Bitteswell. *Leics* 2C 62
Bitton. *S Glo* 5B 34
Bix. *Oxon* 3F 37
Bixter. *Shet* 6E 173
Blaby. *Leics* 1C 62
Blackawton. *Devn* 3E 9
Black Bank. *Cambs* 2E 65
Black Barn. *Linc* 3D 76
Blackborough. *Devn* 2D 12
Blackborough. *Norf* 4F 77
Blackborough End. *Norf* 4F 77
Black Bourton. *Oxon* 5A 50
Blackboys. *E Sus* 3G 27
Blackbrook. *Derbs* 1H 73
Blackbrook. *Mers* 1H 83
Blackbrook. *Staf* 2B 72
Blackbrook. *Surr* 1C 26
Blackburn. *Abers* 2F 153
Blackburn. *Bkbn* 2E 91
Blackburn. *W Lot* 3C 128
Black Callerton. *Tyne* 3E 115
Black Carr. *Norf* 1C 66
Black Clauchrie. *S Ayr* 1H 109
Black Corries. *High* 3G 141
Black Crofts. *Arg* 5D 140
Black Cross. *Corn* 2D 6
Blackden Heath. *Ches E* 3B 84
Blackditch. *Oxon* 5C 50
Blackdog. *Abers* 2G 153
Black Dog. *Devn* 2B 12
Blackdown. *Dors* 2G 13
Blackdyke. *Cumb* 4C 112
Blacker Hill. *S Yor* 4D 92
Blackfen. *G Lon* 3F 39
Blackfield. *Hants* 2C 16
Blackford. *Cumb* 3E 113
Blackford. *Per* 3A 136
Blackford. *Shrp* 2H 59
Blackford. *Som* 2H 21
(nr. Burnham-on-Sea)
Blackford. *Som* 4B 22
(nr. Wincanton)
Blackfordby. *Leics* 4H 73
Blackgang. *IOW* 5C 16
Blackhall. *Edin* 2F 129
Blackhall. *Ren* 3F 127
Blackhall Colliery. *Dur* 1B 106
Blackhall Mill. *Tyne* 4E 115
Blackhall Rocks. *Dur* 1B 106
Blackham. *E Sus* 2F 27
Blackheath. *Essx* 3D 54
Blackheath. *G Lon* 3E 39
Blackheath. *Suff* 3G 67
Blackheath. *Surr* 1B 26
Blackheath. *W Mid* 2D 61
Black Heddon. *Nmbd* 2D 115
Blackhill. *Abers* 4H 161
Blackhill. *High* 3C 154
Black Hill. *Warw* 5G 61
Blackhills. *Abers* 2G 161
Blackhills. *High* 3D 158
Blackjack. *Linc* 2B 76
Blackland. *Wilts* 5F 35
Black Lane. *G Man* 4F 91
Blackleach. *Lanc* 1C 90
Blackley. *G Man* 4G 91
Blackley. *W Yor* 3B 92
Blacklunans. *Per* 2A 144
Blackmill. *B'end* 3C 32
Blackmoor. *G Man* 4E 91
Blackmoor. *Hants* 3F 25
Blackmoor Gate. *Devn* 2G 19
Blackmore. *Essx* 5G 53
Blackmore End. *Essx* 2H 53
Blackmore End. *Herts* 4B 52
Black Mount. *Arg* 4G 141
Blackness. *Falk* 2D 128
Blacknest. *Hants* 2F 25
Blackney. *Dors* 3H 13
Blacknoll. *Dors* 4D 14
Black Notley. *Essx* 3A 54
Blacko. *Lanc* 5A 98
Black Pill. *Swan* 3F 31
Blackpool. *Bkpl* 1B 90
Blackpool. *Devn* 4E 9
Blackpool Airport. *Lanc* 1B 90
Blackpool Corner. *Devn* 3G 13
Blackpool Gate. *Cumb* 2G 113
Blackridge. *W Lot* 3B 128
Blackrock. *Arg* 3B 124
Blackrock. *Mon* 4F 47
Blackrod. *G Man* 3E 90
Blackshaw. *Dum* 3B 112
Blackshaw Head. *W Yor* 2H 91
Blackshaw Moor. *Staf* 5E 85
Blacksmith's Green. *Suff* 4D 66
Blacksnape. *Bkbn* 2F 91
Blackstone. *W Sus* 4D 26
Black Street. *Suff* 2H 67
Black Tar. *Pemb* 4D 43
Blackthorn. *Oxon* 4E 50
Blackthorpe. *Suff* 4B 66
Blacktoft. *E Yor* 2B 94
Blacktop. *Aber* 3F 153
Black Torrington. *Devn* 2E 11
Blacktown. *Newp* 3F 33
Blackwall Tunnel. *G Lon* 2E 39
Blackwater. *Corn* 4B 6
Blackwater. *Hants* 1G 25
Blackwater. *IOW* 4D 16
Blackwater. *Som* 1F 13
Blackwaterfoot. *N Ayr* 3C 122
Blackwell. *Darl* 3F 105
Blackwell. *Derbs* 5B 86
(nr. Alfreton)
Blackwell. *Derbs* 3F 85
(nr. Buxton)
Blackwell. *Som* 4D 20
Blackwell. *Warw* 1H 49
Blackwell. *Worc* 3D 61
Blackwood. *Cphy* 2E 33
Blackwood. *Dum* 1G 111
Blackwood. *S Lan* 5A 128
Blackwood Hill. *Staf* 5D 84
Blacon. *Ches W* 4F 83
Bladnoch. *Dum* 4B 110
Bladon. *Oxon* 4C 50
Blaenannerch. *Cdgn* 1C 44
Blaenau Dolwyddelan. *Cnwy* 5F 81
Blaenau Ffestiniog. *Gwyn* 1G 69
Blaenavon. *Torf* 5F 47
Blaenawey. *Mon* 4F 47
Blaen Celyn. *Cdgn* 5C 56
Blaen Clydach. *Rhon* 2C 32
Blaencwm. *Rhon* 2C 32
Blaendulais. *Neat* 5B 46
Blaenffos. *Pemb* 1F 43
Blaengarw. *B'end* 2C 32
Blaen-geuffordd. *Cdgn* 2F 57
Blaengwrach. *Neat* 5B 46
Blaengwynfi. *Neat* 2B 32
Blaenllechau. *Rhon* 2D 32
Blaenpennal. *Cdgn* 4F 57
Blaenplwyf. *Cdgn* 3E 57
Blaenporth. *Cdgn* 1C 44
Blaenrhondda. *Rhon* 5C 46
Blaenwaun. *Carm* 2G 43
Blaen-y-coed. *Carm* 2H 43
Blagdon. *N Som* 1A 22
Blagdon. *Torb* 2E 9
Blagdon Hill. *Som* 1F 13
Blagill. *Cumb* 5A 114
Blaguegate. *Lanc* 4C 90
Blaich. *High* 1E 141
Blain. *High* 2A 140
Blaina. *Blae* 5F 47
Blair Atholl. *Per* 2F 143
Blair Drummond. *Stir* 4G 135
Blairgowrie. *Per* 4A 144
Blairhall. *Fife* 1D 128
Blairingone. *Per* 4B 136
Blairlogie. *Stir* 4H 135
Blairmore. *Abers* 5B 160
Blairmore. *Arg* 1C 126
Blairmore. *High* 3B 166
Blairquhanan. *W Dun* 1F 127
Blaisdon. *Glos* 4C 48
Blakebrook. *Worc* 3C 60
Blakedown. *Worc* 3C 60
Blake End. *Essx* 3H 53
Blakemere. *Here* 1G 47
Blakeney. *Glos* 5B 48
Blakeney. *Norf* 1C 78
Blakenhall. *Ches E* 1B 72
Blakeshall. *Worc* 2C 60
Blakesley. *Nptn* 5D 62
Blanchland. *Nmbd* 4C 114
Blandford Camp. *Dors* 2E 15
Blandford Forum. *Dors* 2D 15
Blandford St Mary. *Dors* 2D 15
Bland Hill. *N Yor* 4E 98
Blandy. *High* 2G 167
Blanefield. *Stir* 2G 127
Blankney. *Linc* 4H 87
Blantyre. *S Lan* 4H 127
Blarmachfoldach. *High* 2E 141
Blarnalearoch. *High* 4F 163
Blashford. *Hants* 2G 15
Blaston. *Leics* 1F 63
Blatchbridge. *Som* 2C 22
Blathaisbhal. *W Isl* 1D 170
Blatherwycke. *Nptn* 1G 63
Blawith. *Cumb* 1B 96
Blaxhall. *Suff* 5F 67
Blaxton. *S Yor* 4G 93
Blaydon. *Tyne* 3E 115
Bleadney. *Som* 2H 21
Bleadon. *N Som* 1G 21
Blean. *Kent* 4F 41
Bleary. *Cgvn* 5F 175
Bleasby. *Linc* 2A 88
Bleasby. *Notts* 1E 74
Bleasby Moor. *Linc* 2A 88
Blebocraigs. *Fife* 2G 137
Bleddfa. *Powy* 4E 58
Bledington. *Glos* 3H 49
Bledlow. *Buck* 5F 51
Bledlow Ridge. *Buck* 2F 37
Blencarn. *Cumb* 1H 103
Blencogo. *Cumb* 5C 112
Blendworth. *Hants* 1F 17
Blennerhasset. *Cumb* 5C 112
Bletchingdon. *Oxon* 4D 50
Bletchingley. *Surr* 5E 39
Bletchley. *Mil* 2G 51
Bletchley. *Shrp* 2A 72
Bletherston. *Pemb* 2E 43
Bletsoe. *Bed* 5H 63
Blewbury. *Oxon* 3D 36
Blickling. *Norf* 3D 78
Blidworth. *Notts* 5C 86
Blindburn. *Nmbd* 3C 120
Blindcrake. *Cumb* 1C 102
Blindley Heath. *Surr* 1E 27
Blindmoor. *Som* 1F 13
Blisland. *Corn* 5B 10
Blissford. *Hants* 1G 15
Bliss Gate. *Worc* 3B 60
Blists Hill. *Telf* 5A 72
Blisworth. *Nptn* 5E 63
Blithbury. *Staf* 3E 73
Blitterlees. *Cumb* 4C 112
Blockley. *Glos* 2G 49
Blofield. *Norf* 5F 79
Blofield Heath. *Norf* 4F 79
Blo' Norton. *Norf* 3C 66
Bloomfield. *Bord* 2H 119
Blore. *Staf* 1F 73
Blount's Green. *Staf* 2E 73
Bloxham. *Oxon* 2C 50
Bloxholm. *Linc* 5H 87
Bloxwich. *W Mid* 5D 73
Bloxworth. *Dors* 3D 15
Blubberhouses. *N Yor* 4D 98
Blue Anchor. *Som* 2D 20
Blue Anchor. *Swan* 3E 31
Blue Bell Hill. *Kent* 4B 40
Blue Row. *Essx* 4D 54
Bluetown. *Kent* 5D 40
Blundeston. *Suff* 1H 67
Blunham. *C Beds* 5A 64
Blunsdon St Andrew. *Swin* 3G 35
Bluntington. *Worc* 3C 60
Bluntisham. *Cambs* 3C 64
Blunts. *Corn* 2H 7
Blurton. *Stoke* 1C 72
Blyborough. *Linc* 1G 87
Blyford. *Suff* 3G 67
Blymhill. *Staf* 4C 72
Blymhill Lawns. *Staf* 4C 72
Blyth. *Nmbd* 1G 115
Blyth. *Notts* 2D 86
Blyth. *Bord* 5E 129
Blyth Bank. *Bord* 5E 129
Blyth Bridge. *Bord* 5E 129
Blythburgh. *Suff* 3G 67
Blythe Bridge. *Staf* 1D 72
Blythe Marsh. *Staf* 1D 72
Blythe, The. *Staf* 3E 73
Blyton. *Linc* 1F 87
Boarhills. *Fife* 2H 137
Boarhunt. *Hants* 2E 16
Boarshead. *E Sus* 2G 27
Boar's Head. *G Man* 4D 90
Boars Hill. *Oxon* 5C 50
Boarstall. *Buck* 4E 51
Boasley Cross. *Devn* 3F 11
Boath. *High* 1H 157
Boat of Garten. *High* 2D 150
Bobbing. *Kent* 4C 40
Bobbington. *Staf* 1C 60
Bobbingworth. *Essx* 5F 53
Bocaddon. *Corn* 3F 7
Bocking. *Essx* 3A 54
Bocking Churchstreet. *Essx* 3A 54
Boddam. *Abers* 4H 161
Boddam. *Shet* 10E 173
Boddington. *Glos* 3D 49
Bodedern. *IOA* 2C 80
Bodelwyddan. *Den* 3C 82
Bodenham. *Here* 5H 59
Bodenham. *Wilts* 4G 23
Bodewryd. *IOA* 1C 80
Bodfari. *Den* 3C 82
Bodffordd. *IOA* 3D 80
Bodham. *Norf* 1D 78
Bodiam. *E Sus* 3B 28
Bodicote. *Oxon* 2C 50
Bodieve. *Corn* 1D 6
Bodinnick. *Corn* 3F 7
Bodle Street Green. *E Sus* 4A 28
Bodmin. *Corn* 2E 7
Bodnant. *Cnwy* 3H 81
Bodney. *Norf* 1H 65
Bodorgan. *IOA* 4C 80
Bodrane. *Corn* 2G 7
Bodsham. *Kent* 1F 29
Boduan. *Gwyn* 2C 68
Bodymoor Heath. *Warw* 1F 61
Bogallan. *High* 3A 158
Bogbrae Croft. *Abers* 5H 161
Bogend. *S Ayr* 1C 116
Boghall. *Midl* 3F 129
Boghall. *W Lot* 3C 128
Boghead. *S Lan* 5A 128
Bogindollo. *Ang* 3D 144
Bogmoor. *Mor* 2A 160
Bogniebrae. *Abers* 4C 160
Bognor Regis. *W Sus* 3H 17
Bograxie. *Abers* 2E 152
Bogside. *N Lan* 4B 128
Bog, The. *Shrp* 1F 59
Bogton. *Abers* 3D 160
Bogue. *Dum* 1D 110
Bohenie. *High* 5E 149
Bohortha. *Corn* 5C 6
Boirseam. *W Isl* 9C 171
Bokiddick. *Corn* 2E 7
Bolam. *Dur* 2E 105
Bolam. *Nmbd* 1D 115
Bolberry. *Devn* 5C 8
Bold Heath. *Mers* 2H 83
Boldon. *Tyne* 3G 115
Boldon Colliery. *Tyne* 3G 115
Boldre. *Hants* 3B 16
Boldron. *Dur* 3D 104
Bole. *Notts* 2E 87
Bolehall. *Staf* 5G 73
Bolehill. *Derbs* 5G 85
Bolenowe. *Corn* 5A 6
Boleside. *Bord* 1G 119
Bolham. *Devn* 1C 12
Bolham Water. *Devn* 1E 13
Bolingey. *Corn* 3B 6
Bollington. *Ches E* 3D 84
Bolney. *W Sus* 3D 26
Bolnhurst. *Bed* 5H 63
Bolshan. *Ang* 3F 145
Bolsover. *Derbs* 3B 86
Bolsterstone. *S Yor* 1G 85
Bolstone. *Here* 2A 48
Boltachan. *Per* 3F 143
Boltby. *N Yor* 1G 99
Bolton. *Cumb* 2H 103
Bolton. *E Lot* 2B 130
Bolton. *E Yor* 4B 100
Bolton. *G Man* 4F 91
Bolton. *Nmbd* 3F 121
Bolton Abbey. *N Yor* 4C 98
Bolton-by-Bowland. *Lanc* 5G 97
Boltonfellend. *Cumb* 3F 113
Boltongate. *Cumb* 5D 112
Bolton Green. *Lanc* 3D 90
Bolton-le-Sands. *Lanc* 3D 97
Bolton Low Houses. *Cumb* 5D 112
Bolton New Houses. *Cumb* 5D 112
Bolton-on-Swale. *N Yor* 5F 105
Bolton Percy. *N Yor* 5H 99
Bolton Town End. *Lanc* 3D 97
Bolton upon Dearne. *S Yor* 4E 93

Bolton Wood Lane—Brafferton

Bolton Wood Lane. *Cumb* 5D 112
Bolventor. *Corn* 5B 10
Bomarsund. *Nmbd* 1F 115
Bomere Heath. *Shrp* 4G 71
Bonar Bridge. *High* 4D 164
Bonawe. *Arg* 5E 141
Bonby. *N Lin* 3D 94
Boncath. *Pemb* 1G 43
Bonchester Bridge. *Bord* 3H 119
Bonchurch. *IOW* 5D 16
Bond End. *Staf* 4F 73
Bondleigh. *Devn* 2G 11
Bonds. *Lanc* 5D 97
Bonehill. *Devn* 5H 11
Bonehill. *Staf* 5F 73
Bo'ness. *Falk* 1C 128
Boney Hay. *Staf* 4E 73
Bonham. *Wilts* 3C 22
Bonhill. *W Dun* 2E 127
Boningale. *Shrp* 5C 72
Bonjedward. *Bord* 2A 120
Bonkle. *N Lan* 4B 128
Bonnington. *Ang* 5E 145
Bonnington. *Edin* 3E 129
Bonnington. *Kent* 2E 29
Bonnybank. *Fife* 3F 137
Bonnybridge. *Falk* 1B 128
Bonnykelly. *Abers* 3F 161
Bonnyrigg. *Midl* 3G 129
Bonnyton. *Ang* 5C 144
Bonnytown. *Fife* 2H 137
Bonsall. *Derbs* 5G 85
Bont. *Mon* 4G 47
Bontddu. *Gwyn* 4F 69
Bont Dolgadfan. *Powy* 5A 70
Bontgoch. *Cdgn* 2F 57
Bonthorpe. *Linc* 3D 89
Bontnewydd. *Cdgn* 4F 57
Bont-newydd. *Cnwy* 3C 82
Bontnewydd. *Gwyn* 4D 81 (nr. Caernarfon)
Bont Newydd. *Gwyn* 1G 69 (nr. Llan Ffestiniog)
Bontuchel. *Den* 5C 82
Bonvilston. *V Glam* 4D 32
Bon-y-maen. *Swan* 3F 31
Booker. *Buck* 2G 37
Booley. *Shrp* 3H 71
Boorley Green. *Hants* 1D 16
Boosbeck. *Red C* 3D 106
Boot. *Cumb* 4C 102
Booth. *W Yor* 2A 92
Boothby Graffoe. *Linc* 5G 87
Boothby Pagnell. *Linc* 2G 75
Booth Green. *Ches E* 2D 84
Booth of Toft. *Shet* 4F 173
Boothstown. *G Man* 4F 91
Boothville. *Nptn* 4E 63
Booth Wood. *W Yor* 3A 92
Bootle. *Cumb* 1A 96
Bootle. *Mers* 1F 83
Booton. *Norf* 3D 78
Booze. *N Yor* 4D 104
Boquhan. *Stir* 1G 127
Boraston. *Shrp* 3A 60
Borden. *Kent* 4C 40
Borden. *W Sus* 4G 25
Bordlands. *Bord* 5E 129
Bordley. *N Yor* 3B 98
Bordon. *Hants* 3F 25
Boreham. *Essx* 5A 54
Boreham. *Wilts* 2D 23
Boreham Street. *E Sus* 4A 28
Borehamwood. *Herts* 1C 38
Boreland. *Dum* 5D 118
Boreston. *Devn* 3D 8
Borestone Brae. *Stir* 4G 135
Boreton. *Shrp* 5H 71
Borgh. *W Isl* 8B 170 (on Barra)
Borgh. *W Isl* 3C 170 (on Benbecula)
Borgh. *W Isl* 1E 170 (on Berneray)
Borgh. *W Isl* 2G 171 (on Isle of Lewis)
Borghasdal. *W Isl* 9C 171
Borghastan. *W Isl* 3D 171
Borgh na Sgiotaig. *High* 1C 154
Borgie. *High* 3G 167
Borgue. *Dum* 5D 110
Borgue. *High* 1H 165
Borley. *Essx* 1B 54
Borley Green. *Essx* 1B 54
Borley Green. *Suff* 4B 66
Borlum. *High* 1H 149
Bornais. *W Isl* 6C 170
Bornesketaig. *High* 1C 154
Boroughbridge. *N Yor* 3F 99
Borough Green. *Kent* 5H 39
Borras Head. *Wrex* 5F 83
Borreraig. *High* 3A 154
Borrobol Lodge. *High* 1F 165
Borrodale. *High* 4A 154
Borrowash. *Derbs* 2B 74
Borrowby. *N Yor* 1G 99 (nr. Northallerton)
Borrowby. *N Yor* 3E 107 (nr. Whitby)
Borrowston. *High* 4F 169
Borrowstonehill. *Orkn* 7D 172
Borrowstoun. *Falk* 1C 128
Borstal. *Medw* 4B 40
Borth. *Cdgn* 2F 57
Borthwick. *Midl* 4G 129
Borth-y-Gest. *Gwyn* 2E 69
Borve. *High* 4D 154
Borwick. *Lanc* 2E 97
Bosbury. *Here* 1B 48
Boscastle. *Corn* 3A 10
Boscombe. *Bour* 3G 15
Boscombe. *Wilts* 3H 23
Boscoppa. *Corn* 3E 7
Bosham. *W Sus* 2G 17
Bosherston. *Pemb* 5D 42
Bosley. *Ches E* 4D 84
Bossall. *N Yor* 3B 100
Bossiney. *Corn* 4A 10
Bossingham. *Kent* 1F 29
Bossington. *Som* 2B 20
Bostadh. *W Isl* 3D 171
Bostock Green. *Ches W* 4A 84
Boston. *Linc* 1C 76
Boston Spa. *W Yor* 5G 99
Boswarthen. *Corn* 3B 4
Boswinger. *Corn* 4D 6
Botallack. *Corn* 3A 4
Botany Bay. *G Lon* 1D 39
Botcheston. *Leics* 5B 74
Botesdale. *Suff* 3C 66
Bothal. *Nmbd* 1F 115
Bothampstead. *W Ber* 4D 36
Bothamsall. *Notts* 3D 86
Bothel. *Cumb* 1C 102
Bothenhampton. *Dors* 3H 13
Bothwell. *S Lan* 4A 128
Botley. *Buck* 5H 51
Botley. *Hants* 1D 16
Botley. *Oxon* 5C 50
Botloe's Green. *Glos* 3C 48
Botolph Claydon. *Buck* 3F 51
Botolphs. *W Sus* 5C 26
Bottacks. *High* 2G 157
Bottesford. *Leics* 2F 75
Bottesford. *N Lin* 4B 94
Bottisham. *Cambs* 4E 65
Bottlesford. *Wilts* 1G 23
Bottomcraig. *Fife* 1F 137
Bottom o' th' Moor. *G Man* 3E 91
Botton. *N Yor* 4D 107
Botton Head. *Lanc* 3F 97
Bottreaux Mill. *Devn* 4B 20
Botus Fleming. *Corn* 2A 8
Botwnnog. *Gwyn* 2B 68
Bough Beech. *Kent* 1F 27
Boughrood. *Powy* 2E 47
Boughspring. *Glos* 2A 34
Boughton. *Norf* 5F 77
Boughton. *Nptn* 4E 63
Boughton. *Notts* 4D 86
Boughton Aluph. *Kent* 1E 29
Boughton Green. *Kent* 5B 40
Boughton Lees. *Kent* 1E 28
Boughton Malherbe. *Kent* 1C 28
Boughton Monchelsea. *Kent* 5B 40
Boughton under Blean. *Kent* 5E 41
Boulby. *Red C* 3E 107
Bouldnor. *IOW* 4B 16
Bouldon. *Shrp* 2H 59
Boulmer. *Nmbd* 3G 121
Boulston. *Pemb* 3D 42
Boultham. *Linc* 4G 87
Boulton. *Derb* 2A 74
Boundary. *Staf* 1D 73
Bounds. *Here* 2B 48
Bourn. *Cambs* 5C 64
Bournbrook. *W Mid* 2E 61
Bourne. *Linc* 3H 75
Bourne End. *Bed* 4H 63
Bourne End. *Buck* 3G 37
Bourne End. *C Beds* 1H 51
Bourne End. *Herts* 5A 52
Bournemouth. *Bour* 3F 15
Bournemouth Airport. *Dors* 3G 15
Bournes Green. *Glos* 5E 49
Bournes Green. *S'end* 2D 40
Bourne, The. *Surr* 2G 25
Bournheath. *Worc* 3D 60
Bournmoor. *Dur* 4G 115
Bournville. *W Mid* 2E 61
Bourton. *Dors* 3C 22
Bourton. *N Som* 5G 33
Bourton. *Oxon* 3H 35
Bourton. *Shrp* 1H 59
Bourton. *Wilts* 5F 35
Bourton on Dunsmore. *Warw* 3B 62
Bourton-on-the-Hill. *Glos* 2G 49
Bourton-on-the-Water. *Glos* 3G 49
Bousd. *Arg* 2D 138
Bousta. *Shet* 6D 173
Boustead Hill. *Cumb* 4D 112
Bouth. *Cumb* 1C 96
Bouthwaite. *N Yor* 2D 98
Boveney. *Buck* 3A 38
Boveridge. *Dors* 1F 15
Boverton. *V Glam* 5C 32
Bovey Tracey. *Devn* 5B 12
Bovingdon. *Herts* 5A 52
Bovingdon Green. *Buck* 3G 37
Bovinger. *Essx* 5F 53
Bovington Camp. *Dors* 4D 14
Bow. *Devn* 2H 11
Bowbank. *Dur* 2C 104
Bow Brickhill. *Mil* 2H 51
Bowbridge. *Glos* 5D 48
Bowburn. *Dur* 1A 106
Bowcombe. *IOW* 4C 16
Bowd. *Devn* 4E 12
Bowden. *Devn* 4E 9
Bowden. *Bord* 1H 119
Bowden Hill. *Wilts* 5E 35
Bowdens. *Som* 4H 21
Bowderdale. *Cumb* 4H 103
Bowdon. *G Man* 2B 84
Bower. *Nmbd* 1A 114
Bowerchalke. *Wilts* 4F 23
Bowerhill. *Wilts* 5E 35
Bower Hinton. *Som* 1H 13
Bowermadden. *High* 2E 169
Bowers. *Staf* 2C 72
Bowers Gifford. *Essx* 2B 40
Bowershall. *Fife* 4C 136
Bowertower. *High* 2E 169
Bowes. *Dur* 3C 104
Bowgreave. *Lanc* 5D 97
Bowhousebog. *N Lan* 4B 128
Bowithick. *Corn* 4B 10
Bowland Bridge. *Cumb* 1D 96
Bowlees. *Dur* 2C 104
Bowley. *Here* 5H 59
Bowlhead Green. *Surr* 2A 26
Bowling. *W Dun* 2F 127
Bowling. *W Yor* 1B 92
Bowling Bank. *Wrex* 1F 71
Bowling Green. *Worc* 5C 60
Bowlish. *Som* 2B 22
Bowmanstead. *Cumb* 5E 102
Bowmore. *Arg* 4B 124
Bowness-on-Solway. *Cumb* 3D 112
Bowness-on-Windermere. *Cumb* 5F 103
Bow of Fife. *Fife* 2F 137
Bowriefauld. *Ang* 4E 145
Bowscale. *Cumb* 1E 103
Bowsden. *Nmbd* 5F 131
Bowside Lodge. *High* 2A 168
Bowston. *Cumb* 5F 103
Bow Street. *Cdgn* 2F 57
Bowthorpe. *Norf* 5D 78
Box. *Glos* 5D 48
Box. *Wilts* 5D 34
Boxbush. *Glos* 3B 48
Box End. *Bed* 1A 52
Boxford. *Suff* 1C 54
Boxford. *W Ber* 4C 36
Boxgrove. *W Sus* 5A 26
Box Hill. *Wilts* 5D 34
Boxley. *Kent* 5B 40
Boxmoor. *Herts* 5A 52
Box's Shop. *Corn* 2C 10
Boxted. *Essx* 2C 54
Boxted. *Suff* 5H 65
Boxted Cross. *Essx* 2D 54
Boxworth. *Cambs* 4C 64
Boxworth End. *Cambs* 4C 64
Boyden End. *Suff* 5G 65
Boyden Gate. *Kent* 4G 41
Boylestone. *Derbs* 2F 73
Boylestonfield. *Derbs* 2F 73
Boyndie. *Abers* 2D 160
Boynton. *E Yor* 3F 101
Boys Hill. *Dors* 1B 14
Boythorpe. *Derbs* 4A 86
Boyton. *Corn* 3D 10
Boyton. *Suff* 1G 55
Boyton. *Wilts* 3E 23
Boyton Cross. *Essx* 5G 53
Boyton End. *Essx* 2G 53
Boyton End. *Suff* 1H 53
Bozeat. *Nptn* 5G 63
Braaid. *IOM* 4C 108
Braal Castle. *High* 3D 168
Brabling Green. *Suff* 4E 67
Brabourne. *Kent* 1F 29
Brabourne Lees. *Kent* 1E 29
Brabster. *High* 2F 169
Bracadale. *High* 5C 154
Bracara. *High* 4F 147
Braceborough. *Linc* 4H 75
Bracebridge. *Linc* 4G 87
Bracebridge Heath. *Linc* 4G 87
Braceby. *Linc* 2H 75
Bracewell. *Lanc* 5A 98
Brackenber. *Cumb* 3A 104
Brackenfield. *Derbs* 5A 86
Brackenlands. *Cumb* 5D 112
Brackenthwaite. *Cumb* 5D 112
Brackenthwaite. *N Yor* 4E 99
Brackla. *B'end* 4C 32
Brackla. *High* 3C 158
Bracklesham. *W Sus* 3G 17
Brackletter. *High* 5D 148
Brackley. *Nptn* 2D 50
Brackley Hatch. *Nptn* 1E 51
Brackloch. *High* 1F 163
Bracknell. *Brac* 5G 37
Braco. *Per* 3H 135
Bracobrae. *Mor* 3C 160
Bracon. *N Lin* 4A 94
Bracon Ash. *Norf* 1D 66
Bradbourne. *Derbs* 5G 85
Bradbury. *Dur* 2A 106
Bradda. *IOM* 4A 108
Bradden. *Nptn* 1E 51
Bradenham. *Buck* 2G 37
Bradenham. *Norf* 5B 78
Bradenstoke. *Wilts* 4F 35
Bradfield. *Essx* 2E 55
Bradfield. *Norf* 2E 79
Bradfield. *W Ber* 4E 36
Bradfield Combust. *Suff* 5A 66
Bradfield Green. *Ches E* 5A 84
Bradfield Heath. *Essx* 3E 55
Bradfield St Clare. *Suff* 5B 66
Bradfield St George. *Suff* 4B 66
Bradford. *Derbs* 4G 85
Bradford. *Devn* 2E 11
Bradford. *Nmbd* 1F 121
Bradford. *W Yor* 1B 92
Bradford Abbas. *Dors* 1A 14
Bradford Barton. *Devn* 1B 12
Bradford Leigh. *Wilts* 5D 34
Bradford-on-Avon. *Wilts* 5D 34
Bradford-on-Tone. *Som* 4E 21
Bradford Peverell. *Dors* 3B 14
Bradiford. *Devn* 3F 19
Brading. *IOW* 4E 16
Bradley. *Ches W* 3H 83
Bradley. *Derbs* 1G 73
Bradley. *Glos* 2C 34
Bradley. *Hants* 2E 25
Bradley. *NE Lin* 4F 95
Bradley. *N Yor* 1C 98
Bradley. *Staf* 4C 72
Bradley. *W Mid* 1D 60
Bradley. *W Yor* 2B 92
Bradley. *Wrex* 5F 83
Bradley Cross. *Som* 1H 21
Bradley Green. *Ches W* 1H 71
Bradley Green. *Som* 3F 21
Bradley Green. *Warw* 5G 73
Bradley Green. *Worc* 4D 61
Bradley in the Moors. *Staf* 1E 73
Bradley Mount. *Ches E* 3D 84
Bradley Stoke. *S Glo* 3B 34
Bradlow. *Here* 2C 48
Bradmore. *Notts* 2C 74
Bradmore. *W Mid* 1C 60
Bradninch. *Devn* 2D 12
Bradnop. *Staf* 5E 85
Bradpole. *Dors* 3H 13
Bradshaw. *G Man* 3F 91
Bradstone. *Devn* 4D 11
Bradwall Green. *Ches E* 4B 84
Bradway. *S Yor* 2H 85
Bradwell. *Derbs* 2F 85
Bradwell. *Essx* 3B 54
Bradwell. *Mil* 2G 51
Bradwell. *Norf* 5H 79
Bradwell-on-Sea. *Essx* 5D 54
Bradwell Waterside. *Essx* 5C 54
Bradworthy. *Devn* 1D 10
Brae. *High* 5C 162
Brae. *Shet* 5E 173
Braeantra. *High* 1H 157
Braefield. *High* 5G 157
Braefindon. *High* 3A 158
Braegrum. *Per* 1C 136
Braehead. *Ang* 3F 145
Braehead. *Dum* 4B 110
Braehead. *Mor* 4G 159
Braehead. *Orkn* 3D 172
Braehead. *S Lan* 1H 117 (nr. Coalburn)
Braehead. *S Lan* 4C 128 (nr. Forth)
Braehoulland. *Shet* 4D 173
Braemar. *Abers* 4F 151
Braemore. *High* 5C 168 (nr. Dunbeath)
Braemore. *High* 1D 156 (nr. Ullapool)
Brae of Achnahaird. *High* 2E 163
Brae Roy Lodge. *High* 4F 149
Braeside. *Abers* 5G 161
Braeside. *Inv* 2D 126
Braes of Coul. *Ang* 3B 144
Braeswick. *Orkn* 4F 172
Braetongue. *High* 3F 167
Braeval. *Stir* 3E 135
Braevallich. *Arg* 3G 133
Braewick. *Shet* 6E 173
Brafferton. *Darl* 2F 105
Brafferton. *N Yor* 2G 99

Brafield-on-the-Green—Broadholm

Brafield-on-the-Green. *Nptn* 5F **63**
Bragar. *W Isl* 3E **171**
Bragbury End. *Herts* 3C **52**
Bragleenbeg. *Arg* 1G **133**
Braichmelyn. *Gwyn* 4F **81**
Braides. *Lanc* 4D **96**
Braidwood. *S Lan* 5B **128**
Braigo. *Arg* 3A **124**
Brailsford. *Derbs* 1G **73**
Braintree. *Essx* 3A **54**
Braiseworth. *Suff* 3D **66**
Braishfield. *Hants* 4B **24**
Braithwaite. *Cumb* 2D **102**
Braithwaite. *S Yor* 3G **93**
Braithwaite. *W Yor* 5C **98**
Braithwell. *S Yor* 1C **86**
Brakefield Green. *Norf* 5C **78**
Bramber. *W Sus* 4C **26**
Brambledown. *Kent* 3D **40**
Brambridge. *Hants* 4C **24**
Bramcote. *Notts* 2C **74**
Bramcote. *Warw* 2B **62**
Bramdean. *Hants* 4E **24**
Bramerton. *Norf* 5E **79**
Bramfield. *Herts* 4C **52**
Bramfield. *Suff* 3F **67**
Bramford. *Suff* 1E **54**
Bramhall. *G Man* 2C **84**
Bramham. *W Yor* 5G **99**
Bramhope. *W Yor* 5E **99**
Bramley. *Hants* 1E **25**
Bramley. *S Yor* 1B **86**
Bramley. *Surr* 1B **26**
Bramley. *W Yor* 1C **92**
Bramley Green. *Hants* 1E **25**
Bramley Head. *N Yor* 4D **98**
Bramley Vale. *Derbs* 4B **86**
Bramling. *Kent* 5G **41**
Brampford Speke. *Devn* 3C **12**
Brampton. *Cambs* 3B **64**
Brampton. *Cumb* 2H **103**
(nr. Appleby-in-Westmorland)
Brampton. *Cumb* 3G **113**
(nr. Carlisle)
Brampton. *Linc* 3F **87**
Brampton. *Norf* 3E **78**
Brampton. *S Yor* 4E **93**
Brampton. *Suff* 2G **67**
Brampton Abbotts. *Here* 3B **48**
Brampton Ash. *Nptn* 2E **63**
Brampton Bryan. *Here* 3F **59**
Brampton en le Morthen. *S Yor* 2B **86**
Bramshall. *Staf* 2E **73**
Bramshaw. *Hants* 1A **16**
Bramshill. *Hants* 5F **37**
Bramshott. *Hants* 3G **25**
Branault. *High* 2G **139**
Brancaster. *Norf* 1G **77**
Brancaster Staithe. *Norf* 1G **77**
Brancepeth. *Dur* 1F **105**
Branch End. *Nmbd* 3D **114**
Branchill. *Mor* 3E **159**
Brand End. *Linc* 1C **76**
Branderburgh. *Mor* 1G **159**
Brandesburton. *E Yor* 5F **101**
Brandeston. *Suff* 4E **67**
Brand Green. *Glos* 3C **48**
Brandhill. *Shrp* 3G **59**
Brandis Corner. *Devn* 2E **11**
Brandish Street. *Som* 2C **20**
Brandiston. *Norf* 3D **78**
Brandon. *Dur* 1F **105**
Brandon. *Linc* 1G **75**
Brandon. *Nmbd* 3E **121**
Brandon. *Suff* 2G **65**
Brandon. *Warw* 3B **62**
Brandon Bank. *Cambs* 2F **65**
Brandon Creek. *Norf* 1F **65**
Brandon Parva. *Norf* 5C **78**
Brandsby. *N Yor* 2H **99**
Brandy Wharf. *Linc* 1H **87**
Brane. *Corn* 4B **4**
Bran End. *Essx* 3G **53**
Branksome. *Pool* 3F **15**
Bransbury. *Hants* 2C **24**
Bransby. *Linc* 3F **87**
Branscombe. *Devn* 4E **13**
Bransford. *Worc* 5B **60**
Bransgore. *Hants* 3G **15**
Bransholme. *Hull* 1E **94**
Bransley. *Shrp* 3A **60**
Branston. *Leics* 3F **75**
Branston. *Linc* 4H **87**
Branston. *Staf* 3G **73**
Branston Booths. *Linc* 4H **87**
Branstone. *IOW* 4D **16**
Bransty. *Cumb* 3A **102**
Brant Broughton. *Linc* 5G **87**
Brantham. *Suff* 2E **54**
Branthwaite. *Cumb* 1D **102**
(nr. Caldbeck)
Branthwaite. *Cumb* 2B **102**
(nr. Workington)
Brantingham. *E Yor* 2C **94**
Branton. *Nmbd* 3E **121**
Branton. *S Yor* 4G **93**
Branton Green. *N Yor* 3G **99**
Branxholme. *Bord* 3G **119**
Branxton. *Nmbd* 1C **120**
Brassington. *Derbs* 5G **85**
Brasted. *Kent* 5F **39**
Brasted Chart. *Kent* 5F **39**
Bratch, The. *Staf* 1C **60**
Brathens. *Abers* 4D **152**
Bratoft. *Linc* 4D **88**
Brattleby. *Linc* 2G **87**
Bratton. *Som* 2C **20**
Bratton. *Telf* 4A **72**
Bratton. *Wilts* 1E **23**
Bratton Clovelly. *Devn* 3E **11**
Bratton Fleming. *Devn* 3G **19**
Bratton Seymour. *Som* 4B **22**
Braughing. *Herts* 3D **53**
Braulen Lodge. *High* 5E **157**
Braunston. *Nptn* 4C **62**
Braunstone Town. *Leics* 5C **74**
Braunston-in-Rutland. *Rut* 5F **75**
Braunton. *Devn* 3E **19**
Brawby. *N Yor* 2B **100**
Brawl. *High* 2A **168**
Brawlbin. *High* 3C **168**
Bray. *Wind* 3A **38**
Braybrooke. *Nptn* 2E **63**
Brayford. *Devn* 3G **19**
Bray Shop. *Corn* 5D **10**
Braystones. *Cumb* 4B **102**
Brayton. *N Yor* 1G **93**
Bray Wick. *Wind* 4G **37**
Brazacott. *Corn* 3C **10**
Brea. *Corn* 4A **6**
Breach. *W Sus* 2F **17**
Breachwood Green. *Herts* 3B **52**
Breacleit. *W Isl* 4D **171**
Breaden Heath. *Shrp* 2G **71**
Breadsall. *Derbs* 1A **74**
Breadstone. *Glos* 5C **48**
Breage. *Corn* 4D **4**
Breakachy. *High* 4G **157**
Breakish. *High* 1E **147**
Bream. *Glos* 5B **48**
Breamore. *Hants* 1G **15**
Bream's Meend. *Glos* 5B **48**
Brean. *Som* 1F **21**
Breanais. *W Isl* 5B **171**
Brearton. *N Yor* 3F **99**
Breascleit. *W Isl* 4E **171**
Breaston. *Derbs* 2B **74**
Brecais Àrd. *High* 1E **147**
Brecais Iosal. *High* 1E **147**
Brechfa. *Carm* 2F **45**
Brechin. *Ang* 3F **145**
Breckles. *Norf* 1B **66**
Brecon. *Powy* 3D **46**
Brecon Beacons. *Powy* 3C **46**
Bredbury. *G Man* 1D **84**
Brede. *E Sus* 4C **28**
Bredenbury. *Here* 5A **60**
Bredfield. *Suff* 5E **67**
Bredgar. *Kent* 4C **40**
Bredhurst. *Kent* 4B **40**
Bredicot. *Worc* 5D **60**
Bredon. *Worc* 2E **49**
Bredon's Norton. *Worc* 2E **49**
Bredwardine. *Here* 1G **47**
Breedon on the Hill. *Leics* 3B **74**
Breibhig. *W Isl* 9B **170**
(on Barra)
Breibhig. *W Isl* 4G **171**
(on Isle of Lewis)
Breich. *W Lot* 3C **128**
Breightmet. *G Man* 4F **91**
Breighton. *E Yor* 1H **93**
Breinton. *Here* 2H **47**
Breinton Common. *Here* 2H **47**
Breiwick. *Shet* 7F **173**
Brelston Green. *Here* 3A **48**
Bremhill. *Wilts* 4E **35**
Brenachie. *High* 1B **158**
Brenchley. *Kent* 1A **28**
Brendon. *Devn* 2A **20**
Brent Cross. *G Lon* 2D **38**
Brent Eleigh. *Suff* 1C **54**
Brentford. *G Lon* 3C **38**
Brentingby. *Leics* 4E **75**
Brent Knoll. *Som* 1G **21**
Brent Pelham. *Herts* 2E **53**
Brentwood. *Essx* 1G **39**
Brenzett. *Kent* 3E **28**
Brereton. *Staf* 4E **73**
Brereton Cross. *Staf* 4E **73**
Brereton Green. *Ches E* 4B **84**
Brereton Heath. *Ches E* 4C **84**
Bressingham. *Norf* 2C **66**
Bretby. *Derbs* 3G **73**
Bretford. *Warw* 3B **62**
Bretforton. *Worc* 1F **49**
Bretherdale Head. *Cumb* 4G **103**
Bretherton. *Lanc* 2C **90**
Brettabister. *Shet* 6F **173**
Brettenham. *Norf* 2B **66**
Brettenham. *Suff* 5B **66**
Bretton. *Flin* 4F **83**
Bretton. *Pet* 5A **76**
Brewlands Bridge. *Ang* 2A **144**
Brewood. *Staf* 5C **72**
Briantspuddle. *Dors* 3D **14**
Bricket Wood. *Herts* 5B **52**
Bricklehampton. *Worc* 1E **49**
Bride. *IOM* 1D **108**
Bridekirk. *Cumb* 1C **102**
Bridell. *Pemb* 1B **44**
Bridestowe. *Devn* 4F **11**
Brideswell. *Abers* 5C **160**
Bridford. *Devn* 4B **12**
Bridge. *Corn* 4A **6**
Bridge. *Kent* 5F **41**
Bridge. *Som* 2G **13**
Bridge End. *Bed* 5H **63**
Bridge End. *Cumb* 5D **102**
(nr. Broughton in Furness)
Bridge End. *Cumb* 5E **113**
(nr. Dalston)
Bridge End. *Linc* 2A **76**
Bridge End. *Shet* 8E **173**
Bridgefoot. *Ang* 5C **144**
Bridgefoot. *Cumb* 2B **102**
Bridge Green. *Essx* 2E **53**
Bridgehampton. *Som* 4A **22**
Bridge Hewick. *N Yor* 2F **99**
Bridgehill. *Dur* 4D **115**
Bridgemary. *Hants* 2D **16**
Bridgemere. *Ches E* 1B **72**
Bridgemont. *Derbs* 2E **85**
Bridgend. *Abers* 5C **160**
(nr. Huntly)
Bridgend. *Abers* 5H **161**
(nr. Peterhead)
Bridgend. *Ang* 2E **145**
(nr. Brechin)
Bridgend. *Ang* 4C **144**
(nr. Kirriemuir)
Bridgend. *Arg* 4F **133**
(nr. Lochgilphead)
Bridgend. *Arg* 3B **124**
(on Islay)
Bridgend. *B'end* 3C **32**
Bridgend. *Cumb* 3E **103**
Bridgend. *Devn* 4B **8**
Bridgend. *Fife* 2F **137**
Bridgend. *High* 3F **157**
Bridgend. *Mor* 5A **160**
Bridgend. *Per* 1D **136**
Bridgend. *W Lot* 2D **128**
Bridgend of Lintrathen. *Ang* 3B **144**
Bridgeness. *Falk* 1D **128**
Bridge of Alford. *Abers* 2C **152**
Bridge of Allan. *Stir* 4G **135**
Bridge of Avon. *Mor* 5F **159**
Bridge of Awe. *Arg* 1H **133**
Bridge of Balgie. *Per* 4C **142**
Bridge of Brown. *High* 1F **151**
Bridge of Cally. *Per* 3A **144**
Bridge of Canny. *Abers* 4D **152**
Bridge of Dee. *Dum* 3E **111**
Bridge of Don. *Aber* 2G **153**
Bridge of Dun. *Ang* 3F **145**
Bridge of Dye. *Abers* 5D **152**
Bridge of Earn. *Per* 2D **136**
Bridge of Ericht. *Per* 3C **142**
Bridge of Feugh. *Abers* 4E **152**
Bridge of Gairn. *Abers* 4A **152**
Bridge of Gaur. *Per* 3C **142**
Bridge of Muchalls. *Abers* 4F **153**
Bridge of Oich. *High* 3F **149**
Bridge of Orchy. *Arg* 5H **141**
Bridge of Walls. *Shet* 6D **173**
Bridge of Weir. *Ren* 3E **127**
Bridge Reeve. *Devn* 1G **11**
Bridgerule. *Devn* 2C **10**
Bridge Sollers. *Here* 1H **47**
Bridge Street. *Suff* 1B **54**
Bridgetown. *Devn* 2E **9**
Bridgetown. *Som* 3C **20**
Bridge Town. *Warw* 5G **61**
Bridge Trafford. *Ches W* 3G **83**
Bridgeyate. *S Glo* 4B **34**
Bridgham. *Norf* 2B **66**
Bridgnorth. *Shrp* 1B **60**
Bridgtown. *Staf* 5D **73**
Bridgwater. *Som* 3G **21**
Bridlington. *E Yor* 3F **101**
Bridport. *Dors* 3H **13**
Bridstow. *Here* 3A **48**
Brierfield. *Lanc* 1G **91**
Brierley. *Glos* 4B **48**
Brierley. *Here* 5G **59**
Brierley. *S Yor* 3E **93**
Brierley Hill. *W Mid* 2D **60**
Brierton. *Hart* 1B **106**
Briestfield. *W Yor* 3C **92**
Brigg. *N Lin* 4D **94**
Briggate. *Norf* 3F **79**
Briggswath. *N Yor* 4F **107**
Brigham. *Cumb* 1B **102**
Brigham. *E Yor* 4E **101**
Brighouse. *W Yor* 2B **92**
Brighstone. *IOW* 4C **16**
Brightgate. *Derbs* 5G **85**
Brighthampton. *Oxon* 5B **50**
Brightholmlee. *S Yor* 1G **85**
Brightley. *Devn* 3G **11**
Brightling. *E Sus* 3A **28**
Brightlingsea. *Essx* 4D **54**
Brighton. *Brig* 5E **27**
Brighton. *Corn* 3D **6**
Brighton Hill. *Hants* 2E **24**
Brightons. *Falk* 2C **128**
Brightwalton. *W Ber* 4C **36**
Brightwalton Green. *W Ber* 4C **36**
Brightwell. *Suff* 1F **55**
Brightwell Baldwin. *Oxon* 2E **37**
Brightwell-cum-Sotwell. *Oxon* 2D **36**
Brigmerston. *Wilts* 2G **23**
Brignall. *Dur* 3D **104**
Brig o' Turk. *Stir* 3E **135**
Brigsley. *NE Lin* 4F **95**
Brigsteer. *Cumb* 1D **97**
Brigstock. *Nptn* 2G **63**
Brill. *Buck* 4E **51**
Brill. *Corn* 4E **5**
Brilley. *Here* 1F **47**
Brimaston. *Pemb* 2D **42**
Brimfield. *Here* 4H **59**
Brimington. *Derbs* 3B **86**
Brimley. *Devn* 5B **12**
Brimpsfield. *Glos* 4E **49**
Brimpton. *W Ber* 5D **36**
Brims. *Orkn* 9B **172**
Brimscombe. *Glos* 5D **48**
Brimstage. *Mers* 2F **83**
Brincliffe. *S Yor* 2H **85**
Brind. *E Yor* 1H **93**
Brindister. *Shet* 6D **173**
(nr. West Burrafirth)
Brindister. *Shet* 8F **173**
(nr. West Lerwick)
Brindle. *Lanc* 2D **90**
Brindley. *Ches E* 5H **83**
Brindley Ford. *Stoke* 5C **84**
Brineton. *Staf* 4C **72**
Bringhurst. *Leics* 1F **63**
Bringsty Common. *Here* 5A **60**
Brington. *Cambs* 3H **63**
Brinian. *Orkn* 5D **172**
Briningham. *Norf* 2C **78**
Brinkhill. *Linc* 3C **88**
Brinkley. *Cambs* 5F **65**
Brinklow. *Warw* 3B **62**
Brinkworth. *Wilts* 3F **35**
Brinscall. *Lanc* 2E **91**
Brinscombe. *Som* 1H **21**
Brinsley. *Notts* 1B **74**
Brinsworth. *S Yor* 2B **86**
Brinton. *Norf* 2C **78**
Brisco. *Cumb* 4F **113**
Brisley. *Norf* 3B **78**
Brislington. *Bris* 4B **34**
Brissenden Green. *Kent* 2D **28**
Bristol. *Bris* 4A **34**
Bristol International Airport.
N Som 5A **34**
Briston. *Norf* 2C **78**
Britannia. *Lanc* 2G **91**
Britford. *Wilts* 4G **23**
Brithdir. *Cphy* 5E **47**
Brithdir. *Cdgn* 1D **44**
Brithdir. *Gwyn* 4G **69**
Briton Ferry. *Neat* 3G **31**
Britwell Salome. *Oxon* 2E **37**
Brixham. *Torb* 3F **9**
Brixton. *Devn* 3B **8**
Brixton. *G Lon* 3E **39**
Brixton Deverill. *Wilts* 3D **22**
Brixworth. *Nptn* 3E **63**
Brize Norton. *Oxon* 5B **50**
Broad Alley. *Worc* 4C **60**
Broad Blunsdon. *Swin* 2G **35**
Broadbottom. *G Man* 1D **85**
Broadbridge. *W Sus* 2G **17**
Broadbridge Heath. *W Sus* 2C **26**
Broad Campden. *Glos* 2G **49**
Broad Chalke. *Wilts* 4F **23**
Broadclyst. *Devn* 3C **12**
Broadfield. *Inv* 2E **127**
Broadfield. *Pemb* 4F **43**
Broadfield. *W Sus* 2D **26**
Broadford. *High* 1E **147**
Broadford Bridge. *W Sus* 3B **26**
Broadgate. *Cumb* 1A **96**
Broad Green. *Cambs* 5F **65**
Broad Green. *C Beds* 1H **51**
Broad Green. *Worc* 3D **61**
(nr. Bromsgrove)
Broad Green. *Worc* 5B **60**
(nr. Worcester)
Broadhaven. *High* 3F **169**
Broad Haven. *Pemb* 3C **42**
Broadheath. *G Man* 2B **84**
Broad Heath. *Staf* 3C **72**
Broadheath. *Worc* 4A **60**
Broadhembury. *Devn* 2E **12**
Broadhempston. *Devn* 2E **9**
Broad Hill. *Cambs* 3E **65**
Broad Hinton. *Wilts* 4G **35**
Broadholm. *Derbs* 1A **74**

Broadholme—Buckland Common

Broadholme. *Linc* 3F 87
Broadlay. *Carm* 5D 44
Broad Laying. *Hants* 5C 36
Broadley. *Lanc* 3G 91
Broadley. *Mor* 2A 160
Broadley Common. *Essx* 5E 53
Broad Marston. *Worc* 1G 49
Broadmayne. *Dors* 4C 14
Broadmere. *Hants* 2E 24
Broadmoor. *Pemb* 4E 43
Broad Oak. *Carm* 3F 45
Broad Oak. *Cumb* 5C 102
Broad Oak. *Devn* 3D 12
Broadoak. *Dors* 3H 13
(nr. Bridport)
Broad Oak. *Dors* 1C 14
(nr. Sturminster Newton)
Broad Oak. *E Sus* 4C 28
(nr. Hastings)
Broad Oak. *E Sus* 3H 27
(nr. Heathfield)
Broadoak. *Glos* 4B 48
Broadoak. *Hants* 1C 16
Broad Oak. *Here* 3H 47
Broad Oak. *Kent* 4F 41
Broadrashes. *Mor* 3B 160
Broads. *Norf* 5G 79
Broadsea. *Abers* 2G 161
Broad's Green. *Essx* 4G 53
Broadshard. *Som* 1H 13
Broadstairs. *Kent* 4H 41
Broadstone. *Pool* 3F 15
Broadstone. *Shrp* 2H 59
Broad Street. *E Sus* 4C 28
Broad Street. *Kent* 1F 29
(nr. Ashford)
Broad Street. *Kent* 5C 40
(nr. Maidstone)
Broad Street Green. *Essx* 5B 54
Broad, The. *Here* 4G 59
Broad Town. *Wilts* 4F 35
Broadwas. *Worc* 5B 60
Broadwath. *Cumb* 4F 113
Broadway. *Carm* 5D 45
(nr. Kidwelly)
Broadway. *Carm* 4G 43
(nr. Laugharne)
Broadway. *Pemb* 3C 42
Broadway. *Som* 1G 13
Broadway. *Suff* 3F 67
Broadway. *Worc* 2F 49
Broadwell. *Glos* 4A 48
(nr. Cinderford)
Broadwell. *Glos* 3H 49
(nr. Stow-on-the-Wold)
Broadwell. *Oxon* 5A 50
Broadwell. *Warw* 4B 62
Broadwell House. *Nmbd* 4C 114
Broadwey. *Dors* 4B 14
Broadwindsor. *Dors* 2H 13
Broadwoodkelly. *Devn* 2G 11
Broadwoodwidger. *Devn* 4E 11
Broallan. *High* 4G 157
Brobury. *Here* 1G 47
Brochel. *High* 4E 155
Brockamin. *Worc* 5B 60
Brockbridge. *Hants* 1E 16
Brockdish. *Norf* 3E 66
Brockencote. *Worc* 3C 60
Brockenhurst. *Hants* 2A 16
Brocketsbrae. *S Lan* 1H 117
Brockford Street. *Suff* 4D 66
Brockhall. *Nptn* 4D 62
Brockham. *Surr* 1C 26
Brockhampton. *Glos* 3E 49
(nr. Bishop's Cleeve)
Brockhampton. *Glos* 3F 49
(nr. Sevenhampton)
Brockhampton. *Here* 2A 48
Brockhill. *Bord* 2F 119
Brockholes. *W Yor* 3B 92
Brockhurst. *Hants* 2D 16
Brocklesby. *Linc* 3E 95
Brockley. *N Som* 5H 33
Brockley Corner. *Suff* 3H 65
Brockley Green. *Suff* 1H 53
(nr. Bury St Edmunds)
Brockley Green. *Suff* 5H 65
(nr. Haverhill)
Brockleymoor. *Cumb* 1F 103
Brockmoor. *W Mid* 2D 60
Brockton. *Shrp* 2F 59
(nr. Bishop's Castle)
Brockton. *Shrp* 5B 72
(nr. Madeley)
Brockton. *Shrp* 1H 59
(nr. Much Wenlock)
Brockton. *Shrp* 5F 71
(nr. Pontesbury)
Brockton. *Staf* 2C 72
Brockton. *Telf* 4B 72
Brockweir. *Glos* 5A 48
Brockworth. *Glos* 4D 49
Brocton. *Staf* 4D 72
Brodick. *N Ayr* 2E 123
Brodie. *Mor* 3D 159
Brodiesord. *Abers* 3C 160
Brodsworth. *S Yor* 4F 93
Brogaig. *High* 2D 154
Brogborough. *C Beds* 2H 51
Brokenborough. *Wilts* 3E 35
Broken Cross. *Ches E* 3C 84
Bromborough. *Mers* 2F 83
Bromdon. *Shrp* 2A 60
Brome. *Suff* 3D 66
Brome Street. *Suff* 3D 66
Bromeswell. *Suff* 5F 67
Bromfield. *Cumb* 5C 112
Bromfield. *Shrp* 3G 59
Bromford. *W Mid* 1F 61
Bromham. *Bed* 5H 63
Bromham. *Wilts* 5E 35
Bromley. *G Lon* 4F 39
Bromley. *Herts* 3E 53
Bromley. *Shrp* 1B 60
Bromley Cross. *G Man* 3F 91
Bromley Green. *Kent* 2D 28
Bromley Wood. *Staf* 3F 73
Brompton. *Medw* 4B 40
Brompton. *N Yor* 5A 106
(nr. Northallerton)
Brompton. *N Yor* 1D 100
(nr. Scarborough)
Brompton. *Shrp* 5H 71
Brompton-on-Swale. *N Yor* 5F 105
Brompton Ralph. *Som* 3D 20
Brompton Regis. *Som* 3C 20
Bromsash. *Here* 3B 48
Bromsberrow. *Glos* 2C 48
Bromsberrow Heath. *Glos* 2C 48
Bromsgrove. *Worc* 3D 60
Bromstead Heath. *Staf* 4B 72
Bromyard. *Here* 5A 60
Bromyard Downs. *Here* 5A 60
Bronaber. *Gwyn* 2G 69
Broncroft. *Shrp* 2H 59
Brongest. *Cdgn* 1D 44
Brongwyn. *Cdgn* 1C 44
Bronington. *Wrex* 2G 71
Bronllys. *Powy* 2E 47
Bronnant. *Cdgn* 4F 57
Bronwydd Arms. *Carm* 3E 45
Bronydd. *Powy* 1F 47
Bronygarth. *Shrp* 2E 71
Brook. *Carm* 4G 43
Brook. *Hants* 1A 16
(nr. Cadnam)
Brook. *Hants* 4B 24
(nr. Romsey)
Brook. *IOW* 4B 16
Brook. *Kent* 1E 29
Brook. *Surr* 1B 26
(nr. Guildford)
Brook. *Surr* 2A 26
(nr. Haslemere)
Brooke. *Norf* 1E 67
Brooke. *Rut* 5F 75
Brookenby. *Linc* 1B 88
Brookend. *Glos* 5B 48
Brook End. *Worc* 1D 48
Brookfield. *Lanc* 1D 90
Brookfield. *Ren* 3F 127
Brookhouse. *Lanc* 3E 97
Brookhouse. *S Yor* 2C 86
Brookhouse Green. *Ches E* 4C 84
Brookhouses. *Staf* 1D 73
Brookhurst. *Mers* 2F 83
Brookland. *Kent* 3D 28
Brooklands. *G Man* 1B 84
Brooklands. *Shrp* 1H 71
Brookmans Park. *Herts* 5C 52
Brooks. *Powy* 1D 58
Brooksby. *Leics* 4D 74
Brooks Green. *W Sus* 3C 26
Brook Street. *Essx* 1G 39
Brook Street. *Kent* 2D 28
Brook Street. *W Sus* 3E 27
Brookthorpe. *Glos* 4D 48
Brookville. *Norf* 1G 65
Brookwood. *Surr* 5A 38
Broom. *C Beds* 1B 52
Broom. *Fife* 3F 137
Broom. *Warw* 5E 61
Broome. *Norf* 1F 67
Broome. *Shrp* 1H 59
(nr. Cardington)
Broome. *Shrp* 2G 59
(nr. Craven Arms)
Broome. *Worc* 3D 60
Broomedge. *Warr* 2B 84
Broomend. *Abers* 2E 153
Broomer's Corner. *W Sus* 3C 26
Broomfield. *Abers* 5G 161
Broomfield. *Essx* 4H 53
Broomfield. *Kent* 4F 41
(nr. Herne Bay)
Broomfield. *Kent* 5C 40
(nr. Maidstone)
Broomfield. *Som* 3F 21
Broomfleet. *E Yor* 2B 94
Broom Green. *Norf* 3B 78
Broomhall. *Ches E* 1A 72
Broomhall. *Wind* 4A 38
Broomhaugh. *Nmbd* 3D 114
Broom Hill. *Dors* 2F 15
Broomhill. *High* 1D 151
(nr. Grantown-on-Spey)
Broomhill. *High* 1B 158
(nr. Invergordon)
Broomhill. *Norf* 5F 77
Broomhill. *S Yor* 4E 93
Broom Hill. *Worc* 3D 60
Broomhillbank. *Dum* 5D 118
Broomholm. *Norf* 2F 79
Broomlands. *Dum* 4C 118
Broomley. *Nmbd* 3D 114
Broom of Moy. *Mor* 3E 159
Broompark. *Dur* 5F 115
Broom's Green. *Glos* 2C 48
Brora. *High* 3G 165
Broseley. *Shrp* 5A 72
Brotherhouse Bar. *Linc* 4B 76
Brotheridge Green. *Worc* 1D 48
Brotherlee. *Dur* 1C 104
Brothertoft. *Linc* 1B 76
Brotherton. *N Yor* 2E 93
Brotton. *Red C* 3D 107
Broubster. *High* 2C 168
Brough. *Cumb* 3A 104
Brough. *Derbs* 2F 85
Brough. *E Yor* 2C 94
Brough. *High* 1E 169
Brough. *Notts* 5F 87
Brough. *Orkn* 6C 172
(nr. Finstown)
Brough. *Orkn* 9D 172
(nr. St Margaret's Hope)
Brough. *Shet* 6F 173
(nr. Benston)
Brough. *Shet* 4F 173
(nr. Booth of Toft)
Brough. *Shet* 7G 173
(on Bressay)
Brough. *Shet* 5G 173
(on Whalsay)
Broughall. *Shrp* 1H 71
Brougham. *Cumb* 2G 103
Brough Lodge. *Shet* 2G 173
Broughshane. *Bmna* 2G 175
Brough Sowerby. *Cumb* 3A 104
Broughton. *Cambs* 3B 64
Broughton. *Flin* 4F 83
Broughton. *Hants* 3B 24
Broughton. *Lanc* 1D 90
Broughton. *Mil* 2G 51
Broughton. *Nptn* 3F 63
Broughton. *N Lin* 4C 94
Broughton. *N Yor* 2B 100
(nr. Malton)
Broughton. *N Yor* 4B 98
(nr. Skipton)
Broughton. *Orkn* 3D 172
Broughton. *Oxon* 2C 50
Broughton. *Bord* 1D 118
Broughton. *Staf* 2B 72
Broughton. *V Glam* 4C 32
Broughton Astley. *Leics* 1C 62
Broughton Beck. *Cumb* 1B 96
Broughton Cross. *Cumb* 1B 102
Broughton Gifford. *Wilts* 5D 35
Broughton Green. *Worc* 4D 60
Broughton Hackett. *Worc* 5D 60
Broughton in Furness. *Cumb* 1B 96
Broughton Mills. *Cumb* 5D 102
Broughton Moor. *Cumb* 1B 102
Broughton Park. *G Man* 4G 91
Broughton Poggs. *Oxon* 5H 49
Broughtown. *Orkn* 3F 172
Broughty Ferry. *D'dee* 5D 144
Browland. *Shet* 6D 173
Brownbread Street. *E Sus* 4A 28
Brown Candover. *Hants* 3D 24
Brown Edge. *Lanc* 3B 90
Brown Edge. *Staf* 5D 84
Brownhill. *Bkbn* 1E 91
Brownhill. *Shrp* 3G 71
Brownhills. *Shrp* 2A 72
Brownhills. *W Mid* 5E 73
Brown Knowl. *Ches W* 5G 83
Brownlow. *Ches E* 4C 84
Brownlow Heath. *Ches E* 4C 84
Brown's Green. *W Mid* 1E 61
Brownshill. *Glos* 5D 49
Brownston. *Devn* 3C 8
Brownstone. *Devn* 2A 12
Browston Green. *Norf* 5G 79
Broxa. *N Yor* 5G 107
Broxbourne. *Herts* 5D 52
Broxburn. *E Lot* 2C 130
Broxburn. *W Lot* 2D 128
Broxholme. *Linc* 3G 87
Broxted. *Essx* 3F 53
Broxton. *Ches W* 5G 83
Broxwood. *Here* 5F 59
Broyle Side. *E Sus* 4F 27
Brù. *W Isl* 3F 171
Bruach Mairi. *W Isl* 4G 171
Bruairnis. *W Isl* 8C 170
Bruan. *High* 5F 169
Bruar Lodge. *Per* 1F 143
Brucehill. *W Dun* 2E 127
Brucklay. *Abers* 3G 161
Bruera. *Ches W* 4G 83
Bruern Abbey. *Oxon* 3A 50
Bruichladdich. *Arg* 3A 124
Bruisyard. *Suff* 4F 67
Bruisyard Street. *Suff* 4F 67
Brumby. *N Lin* 4B 94
Brund. *Staf* 4F 85
Brundall. *Norf* 5F 79
Brundish. *Norf* 1F 67
Brundish. *Suff* 4E 67
Brundish Street. *Suff* 3E 67
Brunery. *High* 1B 140
Brunswick Village. *Tyne* 2F 115
Brunthwaite. *W Yor* 5C 98
Bruntingthorpe. *Leics* 1D 62
Brunton. *Fife* 1F 137
Brunton. *Nmbd* 2G 121
Brunton. *Wilts* 1H 23
Brushford. *Devn* 2G 11
Brushford. *Som* 4C 20
Brusta. *W Isl* 1E 170
Bruton. *Som* 3B 22
Bryanston. *Dors* 2D 14
Bryant's Bottom. *Buck* 2G 37
Brydekirk. *Dum* 2C 112
Brymbo. *Cnwy* 3H 81
Brymbo. *Wrex* 5E 83
Brympton D'Evercy. *Som* 1A 14
Bryn. *Carm* 5F 45
Bryn. *G Man* 4D 90
Bryn. *Neat* 2B 32
Bryn. *Shrp* 2E 59
Brynamman. *Carm* 4H 45
Brynberian. *Pemb* 1F 43
Brynbryddan. *Neat* 2A 32
Bryncae. *Rhon* 3C 32
Bryncethin. *B'end* 3C 32
Bryncir. *Gwyn* 1D 69
Bryn-coch. *Neat* 3G 31
Bryncroes. *Gwyn* 2B 68
Bryncrug. *Gwyn* 5F 69
Bryn Du. *IOA* 3C 80
Bryn Eden. *Gwyn* 3G 69
Brynegiwys. *Den* 1D 70
Bryn Eglwys. *Gwyn* 4F 81
Brynford. *Flin* 3D 82
Bryn Gates. *G Man* 4D 90
Bryn Golau. *Rhon* 3D 32
Bryngwran. *IOA* 3C 80
Bryngwyn. *Mon* 5G 47
Bryngwyn. *Powy* 1E 47
Bryn-henllan. *Pemb* 1E 43
Brynhoffnant. *Cdgn* 5C 56
Bryn-llwyn. *Flin* 2C 82
Brynllywarch. *Powy* 2D 58
Brynmawr. *Blae* 4E 47
Bryn-mawr. *Gwyn* 2B 68
Brynmenyn. *B'end* 3C 32
Brynmill. *Swan* 3F 31
Brynna. *Rhon* 3C 32
Brynrefail. *Gwyn* 4E 81
Brynrefail. *IOA* 2D 81
Brynsadler. *Rhon* 3D 32
Bryn-Saith Marchog. *Den* 5C 82
Brynsiencyn. *IOA* 4D 81
Brynteg. *IOA* 2D 81
Brynteg. *Wrex* 5F 83
Brynygwenyn. *Mon* 4G 47
Bryn-y-maen. *Cnwy* 3H 81
Buaile nam Bodach. *W Isl* 8C 170
Bualintur. *High* 1C 146
Bubbenhall. *Warw* 3A 62
Bubwith. *E Yor* 1H 93
Buccleuch. *Bord* 3F 119
Buchanan Smithy. *Stir* 1F 127
Buchanhaven. *Abers* 4H 161
Buchanty. *Per* 1B 136
Buchany. *Stir* 3G 135
Buchley. *E Dun* 2G 127
Buchlyvie. *Stir* 4E 135
Buckabank. *Cumb* 5E 113
Buckden. *Cambs* 4A 64
Buckden. *N Yor* 2B 98
Buckenham. *Norf* 5F 79
Buckerell. *Devn* 2E 12
Buckfast. *Devn* 2D 8
Buckfastleigh. *Devn* 2D 8
Buckhaven. *Fife* 4F 137
Buckholm. *Bord* 1G 119
Buckholt. *Here* 4A 48
Buckhorn Weston. *Dors* 4C 22
Buckhurst Hill. *Essx* 1F 39
Buckie. *Mor* 2B 160
Buckingham. *Buck* 2E 51
Buckland. *Buck* 4G 51
Buckland. *Glos* 2F 49
Buckland. *Here* 5H 59
Buckland. *Herts* 2D 52
Buckland. *Kent* 1H 29
Buckland. *Oxon* 2B 36
Buckland. *Surr* 5D 38
Buckland Brewer. *Devn* 4E 19
Buckland Common. *Buck* 5H 51

Buckland Dinham—Bwlch-y-fadfa

Buckland Dinham. *Som* 1C **22**
Buckland Filleigh. *Devn* 2E **11**
Buckland in the Moor. *Devn* 5H **11**
Buckland Monachorum. *Devn* 2A **8**
Buckland Newton. *Dors* 2B **14**
Buckland Ripers. *Dors* 4B **14**
Buckland St Mary. *Som* 1F **13**
Buckland-tout-Saints. *Devn* 4D **8**
Bucklebury. *W Ber* 4D **36**
Bucklegate. *Linc* 2C **76**
Buckleigh. *Devn* 4E **19**
Buckler's Hard. *Hants* 3C **16**
Bucklesham. *Suff* 1F **55**
Buckley. *Flin* 4E **83**
Buckley Green. *Warw* 4F **61**
Buckley Hill. *Mers* 1F **83**
Bucklow Hill. *Ches E* 2B **84**
Buckminster. *Leics* 3F **75**
Bucknall. *Linc* 4A **88**
Bucknall. *Stoke* 1D **72**
Bucknell. *Oxon* 3D **50**
Bucknell. *Shrp* 3F **59**
Buckpool. *Mor* 2B **160**
Bucksburn. *Aber* 3F **153**
Buck's Cross. *Devn* 4D **18**
Bucks Green. *W Sus* 2B **26**
Buckshaw Village. *Lanc* 2D **90**
Bucks Hill. *Herts* 5A **52**
Bucks Horn Oak. *Hants* 2G **25**
Buck's Mills. *Devn* 4D **18**
Buckton. *E Yor* 2F **101**
Buckton. *Here* 3F **59**
Buckton. *Nmbd* 1E **121**
Buckton Vale. *G Man* 4H **91**
Buckworth. *Cambs* 3A **64**
Budby. *Notts* 4D **86**
Bude. *Corn* 2C **10**
Budge's Shop. *Corn* 3H **7**
Budlake. *Devn* 2C **12**
Budle. *Nmbd* 1F **121**
Budleigh Salterton. *Devn* 4D **12**
Budock Water. *Corn* 5B **6**
Buerton. *Ches E* 1A **72**
Buffler's Holt. *Buck* 2E **51**
Bugbrooke. *Nptn* 5D **62**
Buglawton. *Ches E* 4C **84**
Bugle. *Corn* 3E **6**
Bugthorpe. *E Yor* 4B **100**
Buildwas. *Shrp* 5A **72**
Builth Road. *Powy* 5C **58**
Builth Wells. *Powy* 5C **58**
Bulbourne. *Buck* 4H **51**
Bulby. *Linc* 3H **75**
Bulcote. *Notts* 1D **74**
Buldoo. *High* 2B **168**
Bulford. *Wilts* 2G **23**
Bulford Camp. *Wilts* 2G **23**
Bulkeley. *Ches E* 5H **83**
Bulkington. *Warw* 2A **62**
Bulkington. *Wilts* 1E **23**
Bulkworthy. *Devn* 1D **11**
Bullamoor. *N Yor* 5A **106**
Bull Bay. *IOA* 1D **80**
Bullbridge. *Derbs* 5A **86**
Bullgill. *Cumb* 1B **102**
Bull Hill. *Hants* 3B **16**
Bullinghope. *Here* 2A **48**
Bull's Green. *Herts* 4C **52**
Bullwood. *Arg* 2C **126**
Bulmer. *Essx* 1B **54**
Bulmer. *N Yor* 3A **100**
Bulmer Tye. *Essx* 2B **54**
Bulphan. *Thur* 2H **39**
Bulverhythe. *E Sus* 5B **28**
Bulwark. *Abers* 4G **161**
Bulwell. *Nott* 1C **74**
Bulwick. *Nptn* 1G **63**
Bumble's Green. *Essx* 5E **53**
Bun Abhainn Eadarra. *W Isl* 7D **171**
Bunacaimb. *High* 5E **147**
Bun a' Mhuillinn. *W Isl* 7C **170**
Bunarkaig. *High* 5D **148**
Bunbury. *Ches E* 5H **83**
Bunchrew. *High* 4A **158**
Bundalloch. *High* 1A **148**
Buness. *Shet* 1H **173**
Bunessan. *Arg* 1A **132**
Bungay. *Suff* 2F **67**
Bunkegivie. *High* 2H **149**
Bunker's Hill. *Cambs* 5D **76**
Bunkers Hill. *Linc* 5B **88**
Bunker's Hill. *Suff* 5H **79**
Bunloit. *High* 1H **149**
Bunnahabhain. *Arg* 2C **124**
Bunny. *Notts* 3C **74**
Bunoich. *High* 3F **149**
Bunree. *High* 2E **141**
Bunroy. *High* 5E **149**
Buntait. *High* 5G **157**
Buntingford. *Herts* 3D **52**
Buntings Green. *Essx* 2B **54**
Bunwell. *Norf* 1D **66**
Burbage. *Derbs* 3E **85**
Burbage. *Leics* 1B **62**
Burbage. *Wilts* 5H **35**
Burcher. *Here* 4F **59**
Burchett's Green. *Wind* 3G **37**
Burcombe. *Wilts* 3F **23**
Burcot. *Oxon* 2D **36**
Burcot. *Worc* 3D **61**
Burcote. *Shrp* 1B **60**
Burcott. *Buck* 3G **51**
Burcott. *Som* 2A **22**
Burdale. *N Yor* 3C **100**
Burdrop. *Oxon* 2B **50**
Bures. *Suff* 2C **54**
Burford. *Oxon* 4A **50**
Burford. *Shrp* 4H **59**
Burf, The. *Worc* 4C **60**
Burg. *Arg* 4E **139**
Burgate Great Green. *Suff* 3C **66**
Burgate Little Green. *Suff* 3C **66**
Burgess Hill. *W Sus* 4E **27**
Burgh. *Suff* 5E **67**
Burgh by Sands. *Cumb* 4E **113**
Burgh Castle. *Norf* 5G **79**
Burghclere. *Hants* 5C **36**
Burghead. *Mor* 2F **159**
Burghfield. *W Ber* 5E **37**
Burghfield Common. *W Ber* 5E **37**
Burghfield Hill. *W Ber* 5E **37**
Burgh Heath. *Surr* 5D **38**
Burghill. *Here* 1H **47**
Burgh le Marsh. *Linc* 4E **89**
Burgh Muir. *Abers* 2E **153**
Burgh next Aylsham. *Norf* 3E **78**
Burgh on Bain. *Linc* 2B **88**
Burgh St Margaret. *Norf* 4G **79**
Burgh St Peter. *Norf* 1G **67**
Burghwallis. *S Yor* 3F **93**
Burham. *Kent* 4B **40**
Buriton. *Hants* 4F **25**
Burland. *Ches E* 5A **84**
Burland. *Shet* 8E **173**
Burlawn. *Corn* 2D **6**
Burleigh. *Brac* 4G **37**
Burleigh. *Glos* 5D **48**
Burlescombe. *Devn* 1D **12**
Burleston. *Dors* 3C **14**
Burlestone. *Devn* 4E **9**
Burley. *Hants* 2H **15**
Burley. *Rut* 4F **75**
Burley. *W Yor* 1C **92**
Burleydam. *Ches E* 1A **72**
Burley Gate. *Here* 1A **48**
Burley in Wharfedale. *W Yor* 5D **98**
Burley Street. *Hants* 2H **15**
Burley Woodhead. *W Yor* 5D **98**
Burlingjobb. *Powy* 5E **59**
Burlington. *Shrp* 4B **72**
Burlton. *Shrp* 3G **71**
Burmantofts. *W Yor* 1D **92**
Burmarsh. *Kent* 2F **29**
Burmington. *Warw* 2A **50**
Burn. *N Yor* 2F **93**
Burnage. *G Man* 1C **84**
Burnaston. *Derbs* 2G **73**
Burnbanks. *Cumb* 3G **103**
Burnby. *E Yor* 5C **100**
Burncross. *S Yor* 1H **85**
Burneside. *Cumb* 5G **103**
Burness. *Orkn* 3F **172**
Burneston. *N Yor* 1F **99**
Burnett. *Bath* 5B **34**
Burnfoot. *E Ayr* 4D **116**
Burnfoot. *Per* 3B **136**
Burnfoot. *Bord* 3H **119** (nr. Hawick)
Burnfoot. *Bord* 3G **119** (nr. Roberton)
Burngreave. *S Yor* 2A **86**
Burnham. *Buck* 2A **38**
Burnham. *N Lin* 3D **94**
Burnham Deepdale. *Norf* 1H **77**
Burnham Green. *Herts* 4C **52**
Burnham Market. *Norf* 1H **77**
Burnham Norton. *Norf* 1H **77**
Burnham-on-Crouch. *Essx* 1D **40**
Burnham-on-Sea. *Som* 2G **21**
Burnham Overy Staithe. *Norf* 1H **77**
Burnham Overy Town. *Norf* 1H **77**
Burnham Thorpe. *Norf* 1A **78**
Burnhaven. *Abers* 4H **161**
Burnhead. *Dum* 5A **118**
Burnhervie. *Abers* 2E **153**
Burnhill Green. *Staf* 5B **72**
Burnhope. *Dur* 5E **115**
Burnhouse. *N Ayr* 4E **127**
Burniston. *N Yor* 5H **107**
Burnlee. *W Yor* 4B **92**
Burnley. *Lanc* 1G **91**
Burnmouth. *Bord* 3F **131**
Burn Naze. *Lanc* 5C **96**
Burn of Cambus. *Stir* 3G **135**
Burnopfield. *Dur* 4E **115**
Burnsall. *N Yor* 3C **98**
Burnside. *Ang* 3E **145**
Burnside. *E Ayr* 3E **117**
Burnside. *Newt* 3G **175**
Burnside. *Per* 3D **136**
Burnside. *Shet* 4D **173**
Burnside. *S Lan* 4H **127**
Burnside. *W Lot* 2D **129** (nr. Broxburn)
Burnside. *W Lot* 2D **128** (nr. Winchburgh)
Burntcommon. *Surr* 5B **38**
Burntheath. *Derbs* 2G **73**
Burnt Heath. *Essx* 3D **54**
Burnt Hill. *W Ber* 4D **36**
Burnt Houses. *Dur* 2E **105**
Burntisland. *Fife* 1F **129**
Burnt Oak. *G Lon* 1D **38**
Burnton. *E Ayr* 4D **117**
Burntstalk. *Norf* 2G **77**
Burntwood. *Staf* 5E **73**
Burntwood Green. *Staf* 5E **73**
Burnt Yates. *N Yor* 3E **99**
Burnwynd. *Edin* 3E **129**
Burpham. *Surr* 5B **38**
Burpham. *W Sus* 5B **26**
Burradon. *Nmbd* 4D **121**
Burradon. *Tyne* 2F **115**
Burrafirth. *Shet* 1H **173**
Burragarth. *Shet* 1G **173**
Burras. *Corn* 5A **6**
Burraton. *Corn* 3A **8**
Burravoe. *Shet* 3E **173** (nr. North Roe)
Burravoe. *Shet* 5E **173** (on Mainland)
Burravoe. *Shet* 4G **173** (on Yell)
Burray Village. *Orkn* 8D **172**
Burrells. *Cumb* 3H **103**
Burrelton. *Per* 5A **144**
Burridge. *Devn* 2G **13**
Burridge. *Hants* 1D **16**
Burrigill. *High* 5E **169**
Burrill. *N Yor* 1E **99**
Burringham. *N Lin* 4B **94**
Burrington. *Devn* 1G **11**
Burrington. *Here* 3G **59**
Burrington. *N Som* 1H **21**
Burrough End. *Cambs* 5F **65**
Burrough Green. *Cambs* 5F **65**
Burrough on the Hill. *Leics* 4E **75**
Burroughston. *Orkn* 5E **172**
Burrow. *Devn* 4D **12**
Burrow. *Som* 2C **20**
Burrowbridge. *Som* 4G **21**
Burrowhill. *Surr* 4A **38**
Burry. *Swan* 3D **30**
Burry Green. *Swan* 3D **30**
Burry Port. *Carm* 5E **45**
Burscough. *Lanc* 3C **90**
Burscough Bridge. *Lanc* 3C **90**
Bursea. *E Yor* 1B **94**
Burshill. *E Yor* 5E **101**
Bursledon. *Hants* 2C **16**
Burslem. *Stoke* 1C **72**
Burstall. *Suff* 1D **54**
Burstock. *Dors* 2H **13**
Burston. *Devn* 2H **11**
Burston. *Norf* 2D **66**
Burston. *Staf* 2D **72**
Burstow. *Surr* 1E **27**
Burstwick. *E Yor* 2F **95**
Burtersett. *N Yor* 1A **98**
Burtholme. *Cumb* 3G **113**
Burthorpe. *Suff* 4G **65**
Burthwaite. *Cumb* 5F **113**
Burtle. *Som* 2H **21**
Burtoft. *Linc* 2B **76**
Burton. *Ches W* 4H **83** (nr. Kelsall)
Burton. *Ches W* 3F **83** (nr. Neston)
Burton. *Dors* 3G **15** (nr. Christchurch)
Burton. *Dors* 3B **14** (nr. Dorchester)
Burton. *Nmbd* 1F **121**
Burton. *Pemb* 4D **43**
Burton. *Som* 2E **21**
Burton. *Wilts* 4D **34** (nr. Chippenham)
Burton. *Wilts* 3D **22** (nr. Warminster)
Burton. *Wrex* 5F **83**
Burton Agnes. *E Yor* 3F **101**
Burton Bradstock. *Dors* 4H **13**
Burton-by-Lincoln. *Linc* 3G **87**
Burton Coggles. *Linc* 3G **75**
Burton Constable. *E Yor* 1E **95**
Burton Corner. *Linc* 1C **76**
Burton End. *Cambs* 1G **53**
Burton End. *Essx* 3F **53**
Burton Fleming. *E Yor* 2E **101**
Burton Green. *W Mid* 3G **61**
Burton Green. *Wrex* 5F **83**
Burton Hastings. *Warw* 2B **62**
Burton-in-Kendal. *Cumb* 2E **97**
Burton in Lonsdale. *N Yor* 2F **97**
Burton Joyce. *Notts* 1D **74**
Burton Latimer. *Nptn* 3G **63**
Burton Lazars. *Leics* 4E **75**
Burton Leonard. *N Yor* 3F **99**
Burton on the Wolds. *Leics* 3C **74**
Burton Overy. *Leics* 1D **62**
Burton Pedwardine. *Linc* 1A **76**
Burton Pidsea. *E Yor* 1F **95**
Burton Salmon. *N Yor* 2E **93**
Burton's Green. *Essx* 3B **54**
Burton Stather. *N Lin* 3B **94**
Burton upon Stather. *N Lin* 3B **94**
Burton upon Trent. *Staf* 3G **73**
Burton Wolds. *Leics* 3D **74**
Burtonwood. *Warr* 1H **83**
Burwardsley. *Ches W* 5H **83**
Burwarton. *Shrp* 2A **60**
Burwash. *E Sus* 3A **28**
Burwash Common. *E Sus* 3H **27**
Burwash Weald. *E Sus* 3A **28**
Burwell. *Cambs* 4E **65**
Burwell. *Linc* 3C **88**
Burwen. *IOA* 1D **80**
Burwick. *Orkn* 9D **172**
Bury. *Cambs* 2B **64**
Bury. *G Man* 3G **91**
Bury. *Som* 4C **20**
Bury. *W Sus* 4B **26**
Burybank. *Staf* 2C **72**
Bury End. *Worc* 2F **49**
Bury Green. *Herts* 3E **53**
Bury St Edmunds. *Suff* 4H **65**
Burythorpe. *N Yor* 3B **100**
Busbridge. *Surr* 1A **26**
Busby. *Per* 1C **136**
Busby. *S Lan* 4G **127**
Buscot. *Oxon* 2H **35**
Bush. *Corn* 2C **10**
Bush Bank. *Here* 5G **59**
Bushbury. *W Mid* 5D **72**
Bushby. *Leics* 5D **74**
Bushey. *Dors* 4E **15**
Bushey. *Herts* 1C **38**
Bushey Heath. *Herts* 1C **38**
Bush Green. *Norf* 1C **66** (nr. Attleborough)
Bush Green. *Norf* 2E **66** (nr. Harleston)
Bush Green. *Suff* 5B **66**
Bushley. *Worc* 2D **49**
Bushley Green. *Worc* 2D **48**
Bushmead. *Bed* 4A **64**
Bushmills. *Moy* 1F **175**
Bushmoor. *Shrp* 2G **59**
Bushton. *Wilts* 4F **35**
Bushy Common. *Norf* 4B **78**
Busk. *Cumb* 5H **113**
Buslingthorpe. *Linc* 2H **87**
Bussage. *Glos* 5D **49**
Bussex. *Som* 3G **21**
Busta. *Shet* 5E **173**
Butcher's Cross. *E Sus* 3G **27**
Butcombe. *N Som* 5A **34**
Bute Town. *Cphy* 5E **46**
Butleigh. *Som* 3A **22**
Butleigh Wootton. *Som* 3A **22**
Butlers Marston. *Warw* 1B **50**
Butley. *Suff* 5F **67**
Butley High Corner. *Suff* 1G **55**
Butlocks Heath. *Hants* 2C **16**
Butterburn. *Cumb* 2H **113**
Buttercrambe. *N Yor* 4B **100**
Butterknowle. *Dur* 2E **105**
Butterleigh. *Devn* 2C **12**
Buttermere. *Cumb* 3C **102**
Buttermere. *Wilts* 5B **36**
Buttershaw. *W Yor* 2B **92**
Butterstone. *Per* 4H **143**
Butterton. *Staf* 5E **85** (nr. Leek)
Butterton. *Staf* 1C **72** (nr. Stoke-on-Trent)
Butterwick. *Dur* 2A **106**
Butterwick. *Linc* 1C **76**
Butterwick. *N Yor* 2B **100** (nr. Malton)
Butterwick. *N Yor* 2D **101** (nr. Weaverthorpe)
Butteryhaugh. *Nmbd* 5A **120**
Butt Green. *Ches E* 5A **84**
Buttington. *Powy* 5E **71**
Buttonbridge. *Shrp* 3B **60**
Buttonoak. *Shrp* 3B **60**
Buttsash. *Hants* 2C **16**
Butt's Green. *Essx* 5A **54**
Butt Yeats. *Lanc* 3E **97**
Buxhall. *Suff* 5C **66**
Buxted. *E Sus* 3F **27**
Buxton. *Derbs* 3E **85**
Buxton. *Norf* 3E **79**
Buxworth. *Derbs* 2E **85**
Bwcle. *Flin* 4E **83**
Bwlch. *Powy* 3E **47**
Bwlchderwin. *Gwyn* 1D **68**
Bwlchgwyn. *Wrex* 5E **83**
Bwlch-Llan. *Cdgn* 5E **57**
Bwlchnewydd. *Carm* 3D **44**
Bwlchtocyn. *Gwyn* 3C **68**
Bwlch-y-cibau. *Powy* 4D **70**
Bwlchyddar. *Powy* 3D **70**
Bwlch-y-fadfa. *Cdgn* 1E **45**

Bwlch-y-ffridd—Carlton

Bwlch-y-ffridd. *Powy* 1C **58**
Bwlch y Garreg. *Powy* 1C **58**
Bwlch-y-groes. *Pemb* 1G **43**
Bwlch-y-sarnau. *Powy* 3C **58**
Bybrook. *Kent* 1E **28**
Byermoor. *Tyne* 4E **115**
Byers Garth. *Dur* 5G **115**
Byers Green. *Dur* 1F **105**
Byfield. *Nptn* 5C **62**
Byfleet. *Surr* 4B **38**
Byford. *Here* 1G **47**
Bygrave. *Herts* 2C **52**
Byker. *Tyne* 3F **115**
Byland Abbey. *N Yor* 2H **99**
Bylchau. *Cnwy* 4B **82**
Byley. *Ches W* 4B **84**
Bynea. *Carm* 3E **31**
Byram. *N Yor* 2E **93**
Byrness. *Nmbd* 4B **120**
Bystock. *Devn* 4D **12**
Bythorn. *Cambs* 3H **63**
Byton. *Here* 4F **59**
Bywell. *Nmbd* 3D **114**
Byworth. *W Sus* 3A **26**

C

Cabharstadh. *W Isl* 6F **171**
Cabourne. *Linc* 4E **95**
Cabrach. *Arg* 3C **124**
Cabrach. *Mor* 1A **152**
Cabus. *Lanc* 5D **97**
Cadbury. *Devn* 2C **12**
Cadder. *E Dun* 2H **127**
Caddington. *C Beds* 4A **52**
Caddonfoot. *Bord* 1G **119**
Cadeby. *Leics* 5B **74**
Cadeby. *S Yor* 4F **93**
Cadeleigh. *Devn* 2C **12**
Cade Street. *E Sus* 3H **27**
Cadgwith. *Corn* 5E **5**
Cadham. *Fife* 3E **137**
Cadishead. *G Man* 1B **84**
Cadle. *Swan* 3F **31**
Cadley. *Lanc* 1D **90**
Cadley. *Wilts* 1H **23**
(nr. Ludgershall)
Cadley. *Wilts* 5H **35**
(nr. Marlborough)
Cadmore End. *Buck* 2F **37**
Cadnam. *Hants* 1A **16**
Cadney. *N Lin* 4D **94**
Cadole. *Flin* 4E **82**
Cadoxton-Juxta-Neath. *Neat* 2A **32**
Cadwell. *Herts* 2B **52**
Cadwst. *Den* 2C **70**
Caeathro. *Gwyn* 4E **81**
Caehopkin. *Powy* 4B **46**
Caenby. *Linc* 2H **87**
Caerau. *B'end* 2B **32**
Caerau. *Card* 4E **33**
Cae'r-bont. *Powy* 4B **46**
Cae'r-bryn. *Carm* 4F **45**
Caerdeon. *Gwyn* 4F **69**
Caerdydd. *Card* 4E **33**
Caerfarchell. *Pemb* 2B **42**
Caerffili. *Cphy* 3E **33**
Caerfyrddin. *Carm* 4E **45**
Caergeiliog. *IOA* 3C **80**
Caergwrle. *Flin* 5F **83**
Caergybi. *IOA* 2B **80**
Caerlaverock. *Per* 2A **136**
Caerleon. *Newp* 2G **33**
Caerlleon. *Carm* 2G **43**
Caerllion. *Newp* 2G **33**
Caernarfon. *Gwyn* 4D **81**
Caerphilly. *Cphy* 3E **33**
Caersws. *Powy* 1C **58**
Caerwedros. *Cdgn* 5C **56**
Caerwent. *Mon* 2H **33**
Caerwys. *Flin* 3D **82**
Caim. *IOA* 2F **81**
Caio. *Carm* 2G **45**
Cairinis. *W Isl* 2D **170**
Cairisiadar. *W Isl* 4C **171**
Cairminis. *W Isl* 9C **171**
Cairnbaan. *Arg* 4F **133**
Cairnbulg. *Abers* 2H **161**
Cairncross. *Ang* 1D **145**
Cairndow. *Arg* 2A **134**
Cairness. *Abers* 2H **161**
Cairneyhill. *Fife* 1D **128**
Cairngarroch. *Dum* 5F **109**
Cairngorms. *High* 3D **151**
Cairnhill. *Abers* 5D **160**
Cairnie. *Abers* 4B **160**
Cairnorrie. *Abers* 4F **161**
Cairnryan. *Dum* 3F **109**
Cairston. *Orkn* 6B **172**
Caister-on-Sea. *Norf* 4H **79**
Caistor. *Linc* 4E **94**
Caistor St Edmund. *Norf* 5E **79**
Caistron. *Nmbd* 4D **121**
Cakebole. *Worc* 3C **60**
Calais Street. *Suff* 1C **54**
Calanais. *W Isl* 4E **171**
Calbost. *W Isl* 6G **171**
Calbourne. *IOW* 4C **16**
Calceby. *Linc* 3C **88**
Calcot. *Glos* 4F **49**
Calcot Row. *W Ber* 4E **37**
Calcott. *Kent* 4F **41**
Calcott. *Shrp* 4G **71**
Caldback. *Shet* 1H **173**
Caldbeck. *Cumb* 1E **102**
Caldbergh. *N Yor* 1C **98**
Caldecote. *Cambs* 5C **64**
(nr. Cambridge)
Caldecote. *Cambs* 2A **64**
(nr. Peterborough)
Caldecote. *Herts* 2C **52**
Caldecote. *Nptn* 5D **62**
Caldecote. *Warw* 1A **62**
Caldecott. *Nptn* 4G **63**
Caldecott. *Oxon* 2C **36**
Caldecott. *Rut* 1F **63**
Calderbank. *N Lan* 3A **128**
Calder Bridge. *Cumb* 4B **102**
Calderbrook. *G Man* 3H **91**
Caldercruix. *N Lan* 3B **128**
Calder Grove. *W Yor* 3D **92**
Calder Mains. *High* 3C **168**
Caldermill. *S Lan* 5H **127**
Calder Vale. *Lanc* 5E **97**
Calderwood. *S Lan* 4H **127**
Caldicot. *Mon* 3H **33**
Caldwell. *Derbs* 4G **73**
Caldwell. *N Yor* 3E **105**
Caldy. *Mers* 2E **83**
Calebrack. *Cumb* 1E **103**
Calf Heath. *Staf* 5D **72**
Calford Green. *Suff* 1G **53**
Calfsound. *Orkn* 4E **172**
Calgary. *Arg* 3E **139**
Califer. *Mor* 3E **159**
California. *Cambs* 2E **65**
California. *Falk* 2C **128**
California. *Norf* 4H **79**
California. *Suff* 1E **55**
Calke. *Derbs* 3A **74**
Callakille. *High* 3F **155**
Callaly. *Nmbd* 4E **121**
Callander. *Stir* 3F **135**
Callaughton. *Shrp* 1A **60**
Callendoun. *Arg* 1E **127**
Callestick. *Corn* 3B **6**
Calligarry. *High* 3E **147**
Callington. *Corn* 2H **7**
Callingwood. *Staf* 3F **73**
Callow. *Here* 2H **47**
Callowell. *Glos* 5D **48**
Callow End. *Worc* 1D **48**
Callow Hill. *Wilts* 3F **35**
Callow Hill. *Worc* 3B **60**
(nr. Bewdley)
Callow Hill. *Worc* 4E **61**
(nr. Redditch)
Calmore. *Hants* 1B **16**
Calmsden. *Glos* 5F **49**
Calne. *Wilts* 4E **35**
Calow. *Derbs* 3B **86**
Calshot. *Hants* 2C **16**
Calstock. *Corn* 2A **8**
Calstone Wellington. *Wilts* 5F **35**
Calthorpe. *Norf* 2D **78**
Calthorpe Street. *Norf* 3G **79**
Calthwaite. *Cumb* 5F **113**
Calton. *N Yor* 4B **98**
Calton. *Staf* 5F **85**
Calveley. *Ches E* 5H **83**
Calver. *Derbs* 3G **85**
Calverhall. *Shrp* 2A **72**
Calverleigh. *Devn* 1C **12**
Calverley. *W Yor* 1C **92**
Calvert. *Buck* 3E **51**
Calverton. *Mil* 2F **51**
Calverton. *Notts* 1D **74**
Calvine. *Per* 2F **143**
Calvo. *Cumb* 4C **112**
Cam. *Glos* 2C **34**
Camaghael. *High* 1F **141**
Camas-luinie. *High* 1B **148**
Camasnacroise. *High* 3C **140**
Camastianavaig. *High* 5E **155**
Camasunary. *High* 2D **146**
Camault Muir. *High* 4H **157**
Camb. *Shet* 2G **173**
Camber. *E Sus* 4D **28**
Camberley. *Surr* 5G **37**
Camberwell. *G Lon* 3E **39**
Camblesforth. *N Yor* 2G **93**
Cambo. *Nmbd* 1D **114**
Cambois. *Nmbd* 1G **115**
Camborne. *Corn* 5A **6**
Cambourne. *Cambs* 5C **64**
Cambridge. *Cambs* 5D **64**
Cambridge. *Glos* 5C **48**
Cambrose. *Corn* 4A **6**
Cambus. *Clac* 4A **136**
Cambusbarron. *Stir* 4G **135**
Cambuskenneth. *Stir* 4H **135**
Cambuslang. *S Lan* 3H **127**
Cambusnethan. *N Lan* 4B **128**
Cambus o' May. *Abers* 4B **152**
Camden Town. *G Lon* 2D **39**
Cameley. *Bath* 1B **22**
Camelford. *Corn* 4B **10**
Camelon. *Falk* 1B **128**
Camelsdale. *Surr* 3G **25**
Camer's Green. *Worc* 2C **48**
Camerton. *Bath* 1B **22**
Camerton. *Cumb* 1B **102**
Camerton. *E Yor* 2F **95**
Camghouran. *Per* 3C **142**
Camlough. *New M* 6F **175**
Cammachmore. *Abers* 4G **153**
Cammeringham. *Linc* 2G **87**
Camore. *High* 4E **165**
Campbelton. *N Ayr* 4C **126**
Campbeltown. *Arg* 3B **122**
Campbeltown Airport. *Arg* 3A **122**
Cample. *Dum* 5A **118**
Campmuir. *Per* 5B **144**
Campsall. *S Yor* 3F **93**
Campsea Ashe. *Suff* 5F **67**
Camps End. *Cambs* 1G **53**
Camp, The. *Glos* 5E **49**
Campton. *C Beds* 2B **52**
Camptoun. *E Lot* 2B **130**
Camptown. *Bord* 3A **120**
Camrose. *Pemb* 2D **42**
Camserney. *Per* 4F **143**
Camster. *High* 4E **169**
Camus Croise. *High* 2E **147**
Camuscross. *High* 2E **147**
Camusdarach. *High* 4E **147**
Camusnagaul. *High* 1E **141**
(nr. Fort William)
Camusnagaul. *High* 5E **163**
(nr. Little Loch Broom)
Camusteel. *High* 4G **155**
Camusterrach. *High* 4G **155**
Camusvrachan. *Per* 4D **142**
Canada. *Hants* 1A **16**
Canadia. *E Sus* 4B **28**
Canaston Bridge. *Pemb* 3E **43**
Candlesby. *Linc* 4D **88**
Candle Street. *Suff* 3C **66**
Candy Mill. *S Lan* 5D **128**
Cane End. *Oxon* 4E **37**
Canewdon. *Essx* 1D **40**
Canford Cliffs. *Pool* 4F **15**
Canford Heath. *Pool* 3F **15**
Canford Magna. *Pool* 3F **15**
Cangate. *Norf* 4F **79**
Canham's Green. *Suff* 4C **66**
Canholes. *Derbs* 3E **85**
Canisbay. *High* 1F **169**
Canley. *W Mid* 3H **61**
Cann. *Dors* 4D **22**
Cann Common. *Dors* 4D **23**
Cannich. *High* 5F **157**
Cannington. *Som* 3F **21**
Cannock. *Staf* 4D **73**
Cannock Wood. *Staf* 4E **73**
Canonbie. *Dum* 2E **113**
Canon Bridge. *Here* 1H **47**
Canon Frome. *Here* 1B **48**
Canon Pyon. *Here* 1H **47**
Canons Ashby. *Nptn* 5C **62**
Canonstown. *Corn* 3C **4**
Canterbury. *Kent* 5F **41**
Cantley. *Norf* 5F **79**
Cantley. *S Yor* 4G **93**
Cantlop. *Shrp* 5H **71**
Canton. *Card* 4E **33**
Cantray. *High* 4B **158**
Cantraybruich. *High* 4B **158**
Cantraywood. *High* 4B **158**
Cantsdam. *Fife* 4D **136**
Cantsfield. *Lanc* 2F **97**
Canvey Island. *Essx* 2B **40**
Canwick. *Linc* 4G **87**
Canworthy Water. *Corn* 3C **10**
Caol. *High* 1F **141**
Caolas. *Arg* 4B **138**
Caolas. *W Isl* 9B **170**
Caolas Liubharsaigh. *W Isl* 4D **170**
Caolas Scalpaigh. *W Isl* 8E **171**
Caolas Stocinis. *W Isl* 8D **171**
Caol Ila. *Arg* 2C **124**
Caol Loch Ailse. *High* 1F **147**
Caol Reatha. *High* 1F **147**
Capel. *Kent* 1H **27**
Capel. *Surr* 1C **26**
Capel Bangor. *Cdgn* 2F **57**
Capel Betws Lleucu. *Cdgn* 5F **57**
Capel Coch. *IOA* 2D **80**
Capel Curig. *Cnwy* 5G **81**
Capel Cynon. *Cdgn* 1D **45**
Capel Dewi. *Carm* 3E **45**
Capel Dewi. *Cdgn* 2F **57**
(nr. Aberystwyth)
Capel Dewi. *Cdgn* 1E **45**
(nr. Llandysul)
Capel Garmon. *Cnwy* 5H **81**
Capel Green. *Suff* 1G **55**
Capel Gwyn. *IOA* 3C **80**
Capel Gwynfe. *Carm* 3H **45**
Capel Hendre. *Carm* 4F **45**
Capel Isaac. *Carm* 3F **45**
Capel Iwan. *Carm* 1G **43**
Capel-le-Ferne. *Kent* 2G **29**
Capel Llanilterne. *Card* 3D **32**
Capel Mawr. *IOA* 3D **80**
Capel Newydd. *Pemb* 1G **43**
Capel St Andrew. *Suff* 1G **55**
Capel St Mary. *Suff* 2D **54**
Capel Seion. *Carm* 4F **45**
Capel Seion. *Cdgn* 3F **57**
Capel Uchaf. *Gwyn* 1D **68**
Capel-y-ffin. *Powy* 2F **47**
Capenhurst. *Ches W* 3F **83**
Capernwray. *Lanc* 2E **97**
Capheaton. *Nmbd* 1D **114**
Cappercleuch. *Bord* 2E **119**
Capplegill. *Dum* 4D **118**
Capton. *Devn* 3E **9**
Capton. *Som* 3D **20**
Caputh. *Per* 5H **143**
Caradon Town. *Corn* 5C **10**
Carbis Bay. *Corn* 3C **4**
Carbost. *High* 5C **154**
(nr. Loch Harport)
Carbost. *High* 4D **154**
(nr. Portree)
Carbrook. *S Yor* 2A **86**
Carbrooke. *Norf* 5B **78**
Carburton. *Notts* 3D **86**
Carcluie. *S Ayr* 3C **116**
Car Colston. *Notts* 1E **74**
Carcroft. *S Yor* 4F **93**
Cardenden. *Fife* 4E **136**
Cardeston. *Shrp* 4F **71**
Cardewlees. *Cumb* 4E **113**
Cardiff. *Card* 4E **33**
Cardiff International Airport.
V Glam 5D **32**
Cardigan. *Cdgn* 1B **44**
Cardinal's Green. *Cambs* 1G **53**
Cardington. *Bed* 1A **52**
Cardington. *Shrp* 1H **59**
Cardinham. *Corn* 2F **7**
Cardno. *Abers* 2G **161**
Cardow. *Mor* 4F **159**
Cardross. *Arg* 2E **127**
Cardurnock. *Cumb* 4C **112**
Careby. *Linc* 4H **75**
Careston. *Ang* 2E **145**
Carew. *Pemb* 4E **43**
Carew Cheriton. *Pemb* 4E **43**
Carew Newton. *Pemb* 4E **43**
Carey. *Here* 2A **48**
Carfin. *N Lan* 4A **128**
Carfrae. *Bord* 4B **130**
Cargate Green. *Norf* 4F **79**
Cargenbridge. *Dum* 2G **111**
Cargill. *Per* 5A **144**
Cargo. *Cumb* 4E **113**
Cargreen. *Corn* 2A **8**
Carham. *Nmbd* 1C **120**
Carhampton. *Som* 2D **20**
Carharrack. *Corn* 4B **6**
Carie. *Per* 3D **142**
(nr. Loch Rannah)
Carie. *Per* 5D **142**
(nr. Loch Tay)
Carisbrooke. *IOW* 4C **16**
Cark. *Cumb* 2C **96**
Carkeel. *Corn* 2A **8**
Carlabhagh. *W Isl* 3E **171**
Carland Cross. *Corn* 3C **6**
Carlbury. *Darl* 3F **105**
Carlby. *Linc* 4H **75**
Carlecotes. *S Yor* 4B **92**
Carleen. *Corn* 4D **4**
Carlesmoor. *N Yor* 2D **98**
Carleton. *Cumb* 4F **113**
(nr. Carlisle)
Carleton. *Cumb* 4B **102**
(nr. Egremont)
Carleton. *Cumb* 2G **103**
(nr. Penrith)
Carleton. *Lanc* 5C **96**
Carleton. *N Yor* 5B **98**
Carleton. *W Yor* 2E **93**
Carleton Forehoe. *Norf* 5C **78**
Carleton Rode. *Norf* 1D **66**
Carleton St Peter. *Norf* 5F **79**
Carlidnack. *Corn* 4E **5**
Carlingcott. *Bath* 1B **22**
Carlin How. *Red C* 3E **107**
Carlisle. *Cumb* 4F **113**
Carloonan. *Arg* 2H **133**
Carlops. *Bord* 4E **129**
Carlton. *Bed* 5G **63**
Carlton. *Cambs* 5F **65**
Carlton. *Leics* 5A **74**
Carlton. *N Yor* 1A **100**
(nr. Helmsley)
Carlton. *N Yor* 1C **98**
(nr. Middleham)
Carlton. *N Yor* 2G **93**
(nr. Selby)

Carlton—Chapelgate

Carlton. *Notts* 1D **74**
Carlton. *S Yor* 3D **92**
Carlton. *Stoc T* 2A **106**
Carlton. *Suff* 4F **67**
Carlton. *W Yor* 2D **92**
Carlton Colville. *Suff* 1H **67**
Carlton Curlieu. *Leics* 1D **62**
Carlton Husthwaite. *N Yor* 2G **99**
Carlton in Cleveland. *N Yor* 4C **106**
Carlton in Lindrick. *Notts* 2C **86**
Carlton-le-Moorland. *Linc* 5G **87**
Carlton Miniott. *N Yor* 1F **99**
Carlton-on-Trent. *Notts* 4F **87**
Carlton Scroop. *Linc* 1G **75**
Carluke. *S Lan* 4B **128**
Carlyon Bay. *Corn* 3E **7**
Carmarthen. *Carm* 4E **45**
Carmel. *Carm* 4F **45**
Carmel. *Flin* 3D **82**
Carmel. *Gwyn* 5D **81**
Carmel. *IOA* 2C **80**
Carmichael. *S Lan* 1B **118**
Carmunnock. *Glas* 4H **127**
Carmyle. *Glas* 3H **127**
Carmyllie. *Ang* 4E **145**
Carnaby. *E Yor* 3F **101**
Carnach. *High* 1C **148**
(nr. Lochcarron)
Carnach. *High* 4E **163**
(nr. Ullapool)
Carnach. *Mor* 4E **159**
Carnach. *W Isl* 8E **171**
Carnachy. *High* 3H **167**
Carnain. *Arg* 3B **124**
Carnais. *W Isl* 4C **171**
Carnan. *Arg* 4B **138**
Carnan. *W Isl* 4C **170**
Carnbee. *Fife* 3H **137**
Carnbo. *Per* 3C **136**
Carn Brea Village. *Corn* 4A **6**
Carndu. *High* 1A **148**
Carne. *Corn* 5D **6**
Carnell. *S Ayr* 1D **116**
Carnforth. *Lanc* 2E **97**
Carn-gorm. *High* 1B **148**
Carnhedryn. *Pemb* 2C **42**
Carnhell Green. *Corn* 3D **4**
Carnie. *Abers* 3F **153**
Carnkie. *Corn* 5B **6**
(nr. Falmouth)
Carnkie. *Corn* 5A **6**
(nr. Redruth)
Carnkief. *Corn* 3B **6**
Carno. *Powy* 1B **58**
Carnock. *Fife* 1D **128**
Carnon Downs. *Corn* 4B **6**
Carnoustie. *Ang* 5E **145**
Carntyne. *Glas* 3H **127**
Carnwath. *S Lan* 5C **128**
Carnyorth. *Corn* 3A **4**
Carol Green. *W Mid* 3G **61**
Carpalla. *Corn* 3D **6**
Carperby. *N Yor* 1C **98**
Carradale. *Arg* 2C **122**
Carragraich. *W Isl* 8D **171**
Carrbridge. *High* 1D **150**
Carr Cross. *Lanc* 3B **90**
Carreglefn. *IOA* 2C **80**
Carrhouse. *N Lin* 4A **94**
Carrick Castle. *Arg* 4A **134**
Carrickfergus. *Carr* 3H **175**
Carrick Ho. *Orkn* 4E **172**
Carriden. *Falk* 1D **128**
Carrington. *G Man* 1B **84**
Carrington. *Linc* 5C **88**
Carrington. *Midl* 3G **129**
Carrog. *Cnwy* 1G **69**
Carrog. *Den* 1D **70**
Carron. *Falk* 1B **128**
Carron. *Mor* 4G **159**
Carronbridge. *Dum* 5A **118**
Carronshore. *Falk* 1B **128**
Carrow Hill. *Mon* 2H **33**
Carr Shield. *Nmbd* 5B **114**
Carrutherstown. *Dum* 2C **112**
Carr Vale. *Derbs* 4B **86**
Carrville. *Dur* 5G **115**
Carryduff. *Cast* 4H **175**
Carsaig. *Arg* 1C **132**
Carscreugh. *Dum* 3H **109**
Carsegowan. *Dum* 4B **110**
Carse House. *Arg* 3F **125**
Carseriggan. *Dum* 3A **110**
Carsethorn. *Dum* 4A **112**
Carshalton. *G Lon* 4D **39**
Carsington. *Derbs* 5G **85**
Carskiey. *Arg* 5A **122**
Carsluith. *Dum* 4B **110**
Carsphairn. *Dum* 5E **117**
Carstairs. *S Lan* 5C **128**
Carstairs Junction. *S Lan* 5C **128**
Cartbridge. *Surr* 5B **38**
Carterhaugh. *Ang* 4D **144**
Carter's Clay. *Hants* 4B **24**
Carterton. *Oxon* 5A **50**
Carterway Heads. *Nmbd* 4D **114**
Carthew. *Corn* 3E **6**
Carthorpe. *N Yor* 1F **99**
Cartington. *Nmbd* 4E **121**
Cartland. *S Lan* 5B **128**
Cartmel. *Cumb* 2C **96**
Cartmel Fell. *Cumb* 1D **96**
Cartworth. *W Yor* 4B **92**
Carwath. *Cumb* 5E **112**
Carway. *Carm* 5E **45**
Carwinley. *Cumb* 2F **113**
Cascob. *Powy* 4E **59**
Cas-gwent. *Mon* 2A **34**
Cash Feus. *Fife* 3E **136**
Cashlie. *Per* 4B **142**
Cashmoor. *Dors* 1E **15**
Cas-Mael. *Pemb* 2E **43**
Casnewydd. *Newp* 3G **33**
Cassington. *Oxon* 4C **50**
Cassop. *Dur* 1A **106**
Castell. *Cnwy* 4G **81**
Castell. *Den* 4D **82**
Castell Hendre. *Pemb* 2E **43**
Castell-nedd. *Neat* 2A **32**
Castell Newydd Emlyn.
Carm 1D **44**
Castell-y-bwch. *Torf* 2F **33**
Casterton. *Cumb* 2F **97**
Castle. *Som* 2A **22**
Castle Acre. *Norf* 4H **77**
Castle Ashby. *Nptn* 5F **63**
Castlebay. *W Isl* 9B **170**
Castle Bolton. *N Yor* 5D **104**
Castle Bromwich. *W Mid* 2F **61**
Castle Bytham. *Linc* 4G **75**
Castlebythe. *Pemb* 2E **43**
Castle Caereinion. *Powy* 5D **70**
Castle Camps. *Cambs* 1G **53**
Castle Carrock. *Cumb* 4G **113**
Castlecary. *N Lan* 2A **128**
Castle Cary. *Som* 3B **22**
Castle Combe. *Wilts* 4D **34**
Castlecraig. *High* 2C **158**
Castledawson. *Mag* 3F **175**
Castlederg. *Strab* 3B **174**
Castle Donington. *Leics* 3B **74**
Castle Douglas. *Dum* 3E **111**
Castle Eaton. *Swin* 2G **35**
Castle Eden. *Dur* 1B **106**
Castleford. *W Yor* 2E **93**
Castle Frome. *Here* 1B **48**
Castle Green. *Surr* 4A **38**
Castle Green. *Warw* 3G **61**
Castle Gresley. *Derbs* 4G **73**
Castle Heaton. *Nmbd* 5F **131**
Castle Hedingham. *Essx* 2A **54**
Castle Hill. *Kent* 1A **28**
Castlehill. *Per* 5B **144**
Castlehill. *S Lan* 4B **128**
Castle Hill. *Suff* 1E **55**
Castlehill. *W Dun* 2E **127**
Castle Kennedy. *Dum* 4G **109**
Castle Lachlan. *Arg* 4H **133**
Castlemartin. *Pemb* 5D **42**
Castlemilk. *Glas* 4H **127**
Castlemorris. *Pemb* 1D **42**
Castlemorton. *Worc* 2C **48**
Castle O'er. *Dum* 5E **119**
Castle Park. *N Yor* 3F **107**
Castlerigg. *Cumb* 2D **102**
Castle Rising. *Norf* 3F **77**
Castlerock. *Cole* 1E **174**
Castleside. *Dur* 5D **115**
Castlethorpe. *Mil* 1F **51**
Castleton. *Abers* 4F **151**
Castleton. *Arg* 1G **125**
Castleton. *Derbs* 2F **85**
Castleton. *G Man* 3G **91**
Castleton. *Mor* 1F **151**
Castleton. *Newp* 3F **33**
Castleton. *N Yor* 4D **107**
Castleton. *Per* 2B **136**
Castletown. *Cumb* 1G **103**
Castletown. *Dors* 5B **14**
Castletown. *High* 2D **169**
Castletown. *IOM* 5B **108**
Castletown. *Tyne* 4G **115**
Castlewellan. *Down* 6H **175**
Castley. *N Yor* 5E **99**
Caston. *Norf* 1B **66**
Castor. *Pet* 1A **64**
Caswell. *Swan* 4E **31**
Catacol. *N Ayr* 5H **125**
Catbrook. *Mon* 5A **48**
Catchems End. *Worc* 3B **60**
Catchgate. *Dur* 4E **115**
Catcleugh. *Nmbd* 4B **120**
Catcliffe. *S Yor* 2B **86**
Catcott. *Som* 3G **21**
Caterham. *Surr* 5E **39**
Catfield. *Norf* 3F **79**
Catfield Common. *Norf* 3F **79**
Catfirth. *Shet* 6F **173**
Catford. *G Lon* 3E **39**
Catforth. *Lanc* 1C **90**
Cathcart. *Glas* 3G **127**
Cathedine. *Powy* 3E **47**
Catherine-de-Barnes. *W Mid* 2F **61**
Catherington. *Hants* 1E **17**
Catherston Leweston. *Dors* 3G **13**
Catherton. *Shrp* 3A **60**
Catisfield. *Hants* 2D **16**
Catlodge. *High* 4A **150**
Catlowdy. *Cumb* 2F **113**
Catmore. *W Ber* 3C **36**
Caton. *Devn* 5A **12**
Caton. *Lanc* 3E **97**
Catrine. *E Ayr* 2E **117**
Cat's Ash. *Newp* 2G **33**
Catsfield. *E Sus* 4B **28**
Catsgore. *Som* 4A **22**
Catshill. *Worc* 3D **60**
Cattal. *N Yor* 4G **99**
Cattawade. *Suff* 2E **54**
Catterall. *Lanc* 5E **97**
Catterick. *N Yor* 5F **105**
Catterick Bridge. *N Yor* 5F **105**
Catterick Garrison. *N Yor* 5E **105**
Catterlen. *Cumb* 1F **103**
Catterline. *Abers* 1H **145**
Catterton. *N Yor* 5H **99**
Catteshall. *Surr* 1A **26**
Catthorpe. *Leics* 3C **62**
Cattistock. *Dors* 3A **14**
Catton. *Nmbd* 4B **114**
Catton. *N Yor* 2F **99**
Catwick. *E Yor* 5F **101**
Catworth. *Cambs* 3H **63**
Caudle Green. *Glos* 4E **49**
Caulcott. *Oxon* 3D **50**
Cauldhame. *Stir* 4F **135**
Cauldmill. *Bord* 3H **119**
Cauldon. *Staf* 1E **73**
Cauldon Lowe. *Staf* 1E **73**
Cauldwells. *Abers* 3E **161**
Caulkerbush. *Dum* 4G **111**
Caulside. *Dum* 1F **113**
Caunsall. *Worc* 2C **60**
Caunton. *Notts* 4E **87**
Causewayend. *S Lan* 1C **118**
Causewayhead. *Stir* 4H **135**
Causey Park. *Nmbd* 5F **121**
Caute. *Devn* 1E **11**
Cautley. *Cumb* 5H **103**
Cavendish. *Suff* 1B **54**
Cavendish Bridge. *Leic* 3B **74**
Cavenham. *Suff* 3G **65**
Caversfield. *Oxon* 3D **50**
Caversham. *Read* 4F **37**
Caversham Heights. *Read* 4F **37**
Caverswall. *Staf* 1D **72**
Cawdor. *High* 4C **158**
Cawkwell. *Linc* 2B **88**
Cawood. *N Yor* 1F **93**
Cawsand. *Corn* 3A **8**
Cawston. *Norf* 3D **78**
Cawston. *Warw* 3B **62**
Cawthorne. *N Yor* 1B **100**
Cawthorne. *S Yor* 4C **92**
Cawthorpe. *Linc* 3H **75**
Cawton. *N Yor* 2A **100**
Caxton. *Cambs* 5C **64**
Caynham. *Shrp* 3H **59**
Caythorpe. *Linc* 1G **75**
Caythorpe. *Notts* 1D **74**
Cayton. *N Yor* 1E **101**
Ceallan. *W Isl* 3D **170**
Ceann a Bhàigh. *W Isl* 9C **171**
(on Harris)
Ceann a Bhaigh. *W Isl* 2C **170**
(on North Uist)
Ceann a Bhaigh. *W Isl* 8E **171**
(on Scalpay)
Ceann a Bhaigh. *W Isl* 8D **171**
(on South Harris)
Ceannacroc Lodge. *High* 2E **149**
Ceann a Deas Loch Baghasdail.
W Isl 7C **170**
Ceann an Leothaid. *High* 5E **147**
Ceann a Tuath Loch Baghasdail.
W Isl 6C **170**
Ceann Loch Ailleart. *High* 5F **147**
Ceann Loch Muideirt. *High* 1B **140**
Ceann-na-Cleithe. *W Isl* 8D **171**
Ceann Shiphoirt. *W Isl* 6E **171**
Ceann Tarabhaigh. *W Isl* 6E **171**
Cearsiadar. *W Isl* 5F **171**
Ceathramh Meadhanach.
W Isl 1D **170**
Cefn Berain. *Cnwy* 4B **82**
Cefn-brith. *Cnwy* 5B **82**
Cefn-bryn-brain. *Carm* 4H **45**
Cefn Bychan. *Cphy* 2F **33**
Cefn-bychan. *Flin* 4D **82**
Cefncaeau. *Carm* 3E **31**
Cefn Canol. *Powy* 2E **71**
Cefn Coch. *Powy* 5C **70**
(nr. Llanfair Caereinion)
Cefn-coch. *Powy* 3D **70**
(nr. Llanrhaeadr-ym-Mochnant)
Cefn-coed-y-cymmer. *Mer T* 5D **46**
Cefn Cribwr. *B'end* 3B **32**
Cefn-ddwysarn. *Gwyn* 2B **70**
Cefn Einion. *Shrp* 2E **59**
Cefneithin. *Carm* 4F **45**
Cefn Glas. *B'end* 3B **32**
Cefngorwydd. *Powy* 1C **46**
Cefn Llwyd. *Cdgn* 2F **57**
Cefn-mawr. *Wrex* 1E **71**
Cefn-y-bedd. *Flin* 5F **83**
Cefn-y-coed. *Powy* 1D **58**
Cefn-y-pant. *Carm* 2F **43**
Cegidfa. *Powy* 4E **70**
Ceinewydd. *Cdgn* 5C **56**
Cellan. *Cdgn* 1G **45**
Cellardyke. *Fife* 3H **137**
Cellarhead. *Staf* 1D **72**
Cemaes. *IOA* 1C **80**
Cemmaes. *Powy* 5H **69**
Cemmaes Road. *Powy* 5H **69**
Cenarth. *Cdgn* 1C **44**
Cenin. *Gwyn* 1D **68**
Ceos. *W Isl* 5F **171**
Ceres. *Fife* 2G **137**
Ceri. *Powy* 2D **58**
Cerist. *Powy* 2B **58**
Cerne Abbas. *Dors* 2B **14**
Cerney Wick. *Glos* 2F **35**
Cerrigceinwen. *IOA* 3D **80**
Cerrigydrudion. *Cnwy* 1B **70**
Cess. *Norf* 4G **79**
Cessford. *Bord* 2B **120**
Ceunant. *Gwyn* 4E **81**
Chaceley. *Glos* 2D **48**
Chacewater. *Corn* 4B **6**
Chackmore. *Buck* 2E **51**
Chacombe. *Nptn* 1C **50**
Chadderton. *G Man* 4H **91**
Chaddesden. *Derb* 2A **74**
Chaddesden Common. *Derb* 2A **74**
Chaddesley Corbett. *Worc* 3C **60**
Chaddlehanger. *Devn* 5E **11**
Chaddleworth. *W Ber* 4C **36**
Chadlington. *Oxon* 3B **50**
Chadshunt. *Warw* 5H **61**
Chadstone. *Nptn* 5F **63**
Chad Valley. *W Mid* 2E **61**
Chadwell. *Leics* 3E **75**
Chadwell. *Shrp* 4B **72**
Chadwell Heath. *G Lon* 2F **39**
Chadwell St Mary. *Thur* 3H **39**
Chadwick End. *W Mid* 3G **61**
Chadwick Green. *Mers* 1H **83**
Chaffcombe. *Som* 1G **13**
Chafford Hundred. *Thur* 3H **39**
Chagford. *Devn* 4H **11**
Chailey. *E Sus* 4E **27**
Chainbridge. *Cambs* 5D **76**
Chain Bridge. *Linc* 1C **76**
Chainhurst. *Kent* 1B **28**
Chalbury. *Dors* 2F **15**
Chalbury Common. *Dors* 2F **15**
Chaldon. *Surr* 5E **39**
Chaldon Herring. *Dors* 4C **14**
Chale. *IOW* 5C **16**
Chale Green. *IOW* 5C **16**
Chalfont Common. *Buck* 1B **38**
Chalfont St Giles. *Buck* 1A **38**
Chalfont St Peter. *Buck* 2B **38**
Chalford. *Glos* 5D **49**
Chalgrove. *Oxon* 2E **37**
Chalk. *Kent* 3A **40**
Chalk End. *Essx* 4G **53**
Chalk Hill. *Glos* 3G **49**
Challaborough. *Devn* 4C **8**
Challacombe. *Devn* 2G **19**
Challister. *Shet* 5G **173**
Challoch. *Dum* 3A **110**
Challock. *Kent* 5E **40**
Chalton. *C Beds* 5A **64**
(nr. Bedford)
Chalton. *C Beds* 3A **52**
(nr. Luton)
Chalton. *Hants* 1F **17**
Chalvington. *E Sus* 5G **27**
Champany. *Falk* 2D **128**
Chance Inn. *Fife* 2F **137**
Chancery. *Cdgn* 3E **57**
Chandler's Cross. *Herts* 1B **38**
Chandler's Cross. *Worc* 2C **48**
Chandler's Ford. *Hants* 4C **24**
Chanlockfoot. *Dum* 4G **117**
Channel's End. *Bed* 5A **64**
Channel Tunnel. *Kent* 2F **29**
Channerwick. *Shet* 9F **173**
Chantry. *Som* 2C **22**
Chantry. *Suff* 1E **55**
Chapel. *Cumb* 1D **102**
Chapel. *Fife* 4E **137**
Chapel Allerton. *Som* 1H **21**
Chapel Allerton. *W Yor* 1C **92**
Chapel Amble. *Corn* 1D **6**
Chapel Brampton. *Nptn* 4E **63**
Chapelbridge. *Cambs* 1B **64**
Chapel Chorlton. *Staf* 2C **72**
Chapel Cleeve. *Som* 2D **20**
Chapel End. *C Beds* 1A **52**
Chapel-en-le-Frith. *Derbs* 2E **85**
Chapelfield. *Abers* 2G **145**
Chapelgate. *Linc* 3D **76**

Church Brampton—Clough Foot

Church Brampton. *Nptn* 4E **62**
Church Brough. *Cumb* 3A **104**
Church Broughton. *Derbs* 2G **73**
Church Corner. *Suff* 2G **67**
Church Crookham. *Hants* 1G **25**
Churchdown. *Glos* 3D **49**
Church Eaton. *Staf* 4C **72**
Church End. *Cambs* 5D **65** (nr. Cambridge)
Church End. *Cambs* 2B **64** (nr. Sawtry)
Church End. *Cambs* 3C **64** (nr. Willingham)
Church End. *Cambs* 5C **76** (nr. Wisbech)
Church End. *C Beds* 3H **51** (nr. Dunstable)
Church End. *C Beds* 2B **52** (nr. Stotfold)
Church End. *E Yor* 4E **101**
Church End. *Essx* 3H **53** (nr. Braintree)
Churchend. *Essx* 3G **53** (nr. Great Dunmow)
Church End. *Essx* 1F **53** (nr. Saffron Walden)
Churchend. *Essx* 1E **40** (nr. Southend-on-Sea)
Church End. *Glos* 5C **48**
Church End. *Hants* 1E **25**
Church End. *Linc* 2B **76** (nr. Donington)
Church End. *Linc* 1D **88** (nr. North Somercotes)
Church End. *Norf* 4E **77**
Church End. *Warw* 1G **61** (nr. Coleshill)
Church End. *Warw* 1G **61** (nr. Nuneaton)
Church End. *Wilts* 4F **35**
Church Enstone. *Oxon* 3B **50**
Church Fenton. *N Yor* 1F **93**
Church Green. *Devn* 3E **13**
Church Gresley. *Derbs* 4G **73**
Church Hanborough. *Oxon* 4C **50**
Church Hill. *Ches W* 4A **84**
Church Hill. *Worc* 4E **61**
Church Hougham. *Kent* 1G **29**
Church Houses. *N Yor* 5D **106**
Churchill. *Devn* 2G **13** (nr. Axminster)
Churchill. *Devn* 2F **19** (nr. Barnstaple)
Churchill. *N Som* 1H **21**
Churchill. *Oxon* 3A **50**
Churchill. *Worc* 3C **60** (nr. Kidderminster)
Churchill. *Worc* 5D **60** (nr. Worcester)
Churchinford. *Som* 1F **13**
Church Knowle. *Dors* 4E **15**
Church Laneham. *Notts* 3F **87**
Church Langley. *Essx* 5E **53**
Church Langton. *Leics* 1E **62**
Church Lawford. *Warw* 3B **62**
Church Lawton. *Ches E* 5C **84**
Church Leigh. *Staf* 2E **73**
Church Lench. *Worc* 5E **61**
Church Mayfield. *Staf* 1F **73**
Church Minshull. *Ches E* 4A **84**
Church Norton. *W Sus* 3G **17**
Churchover. *Warw* 2C **62**
Church Preen. *Shrp* 1H **59**
Church Pulverbatch. *Shrp* 5G **71**
Churchstanton. *Som* 1E **13**
Church Stoke. *Powy* 1E **59**
Churchstow. *Devn* 4D **8**
Church Stowe. *Nptn* 5D **62**
Church Street. *Kent* 3B **40**
Church Stretton. *Shrp* 1G **59**
Churchtown. *Cumb* 5E **113**
Churchtown. *Derbs* 4G **85**
Churchtown. *Devn* 2G **19**
Churchtown. *IOM* 2D **108**
Churchtown. *Lanc* 5D **97**
Church Town. *Leics* 4A **74**
Churchtown. *Mers* 3B **90**
Church Town. *N Lin* 4A **94**
Churchtown. *Shrp* 2E **59**
Church Village. *Rhon* 3D **32**
Church Warsop. *Notts* 4C **86**
Church Westcote. *Glos* 3H **49**
Church Wilne. *Derbs* 2B **74**
Churnsike Lodge. *Nmbd* 2H **113**
Churston Ferrers. *Torb* 3F **9**
Churt. *Surr* 3G **25**
Churton. *Ches W* 5G **83**
Churwell. *W Yor* 2C **92**
Chute Standen. *Wilts* 1B **24**
Chwilog. *Gwyn* 2D **68**
Chwittfordd. *Flin* 3D **82**
Chyandour. *Corn* 3B **4**
Cilan Uchaf. *Gwyn* 3B **68**
Cilcain. *Flin* 4D **82**
Cilcennin. *Cdgn* 4E **57**
Cilfrew. *Neat* 5A **46**
Cilfynydd. *Rhon* 2D **32**
Cilgerran. *Pemb* 1B **44**
Cilgeti. *Pemb* 4F **43**
Cilgwyn. *Carm* 3H **45**
Cilgwyn. *Pemb* 1E **43**
Ciliau Aeron. *Cdgn* 5D **57**
Cill Amhlaidh. *W Isl* 4C **170**
Cill Donnain. *W Isl* 6C **170**
Cille a' Bhacstair. *High* 2C **154**
Cille Bhrighde. *W Isl* 7C **170**
Cille Pheadair. *W Isl* 7C **170**
Cilmaengwyn. *Neat* 5H **45**
Cilmeri. *Powy* 5C **58**
Cilmery. *Powy* 5C **58**
Cilrhedyn. *Pemb* 1G **43**
Cilsan. *Carm* 3F **45**
Ciltalgarth. *Gwyn* 1A **70**
Ciltwrch. *Powy* 1E **47**
Cilybebyll. *Neat* 5H **45**
Cilycwm. *Carm* 1A **46**
Cimla. *Neat* 2A **32**
Cinderford. *Glos* 4B **48**
Cinderhill. *Derbs* 1A **74**
Cippenham. *Slo* 2A **38**
Cippyn. *Pemb* 1B **44**
Cirbhig. *W Isl* 3D **171**
Circebost. *W Isl* 4D **171**
Cirencester. *Glos* 5F **49**
City. *Powy* 1E **58**
City. *V Glam* 4C **32**
City Centre. *Stoke* 1C **72**
City Dulas. *IOA* 2D **80**
City (London) Airport. *G Lon* 2F **39**
City of Derry Airport. *Derr* 1D **174**
City of London. *G Lon* 2E **39**
City, The. *Buck* 2F **37**
Clabhach. *Arg* 3C **138**
Clachaig. *Arg* 1C **126**
Clachaig. *High* 3F **141** (nr. Kinlochleven)
Clachaig. *High* 2E **151** (nr. Nethy Bridge)
Clachamish. *High* 3C **154**
Clachan. *Arg* 4F **125** (on Kintyre)
Clachan. *Arg* 4C **140** (on Lismore)
Clachan. *High* 2H **167** (nr. Bettyhill)
Clachan. *High* 2D **155** (nr. Staffin)
Clachan. *High* 1D **154** (nr. Uig)
Clachan. *High* 5E **155** (on Raasay)
Clachan Farm. *Arg* 2A **134**
Clachan na Luib. *W Isl* 2D **170**
Clachan of Campsie. *E Dun* 2H **127**
Clachan of Glendaruel. *Arg* 1A **126**
Clachan-Seil. *Arg* 2E **133**
Clachan Shannda. *W Isl* 1D **170**
Clachan Strachur. *Arg* 3H **133**
Clachbreck. *Arg* 2F **125**
Clachnaharry. *High* 4A **158**
Clachtoll. *High* 1E **163**
Clackmannan. *Clac* 4B **136**
Clackmannanshire Bridge. *Falk* 1C **128**
Clackmarras. *Mor* 3G **159**
Clacton-on-Sea. *Essx* 4E **55**
Cladach a Chaolais. *W Isl* 2C **170**
Cladach Chairinis. *W Isl* 3D **170**
Cladach Chireboist. *W Isl* 2C **170**
Cladach Iolaraigh. *W Isl* 2C **170**
Cladich. *Arg* 1H **133**
Cladswell. *Worc* 5E **61**
Claggan. *High* 1F **141** (nr. Fort William)
Claggan. *High* 3B **140** (nr. Lochaline)
Claigan. *High* 3B **154**
Clandown. *Bath* 1B **22**
Clanfield. *Hants* 1E **17**
Clanfield. *Oxon* 5A **50**
Clanville. *Hants* 2B **24**
Clanville. *Som* 3B **22**
Claonaig. *Arg* 4G **125**
Clapgate. *Dors* 2F **15**
Clapgate. *Herts* 3E **53**
Clapham. *Bed* 5H **63**
Clapham. *Devn* 4B **12**
Clapham. *G Lon* 3D **39**
Clapham. *N Yor* 3G **97**
Clapham. *W Sus* 5B **26**
Clap Hill. *Kent* 2E **29**
Clappers. *Bord* 4F **131**
Clappersgate. *Cumb* 4E **103**
Clapphoull. *Shet* 9F **173**
Clapton. *Som* 2H **13** (nr. Crewkerne)
Clapton. *Som* 1B **22** (nr. Radstock)
Clapton-in-Gordano. *N Som* 4H **33**
Clapton-on-the-Hill. *Glos* 4G **49**
Clapworthy. *Devn* 4G **19**
Clara Vale. *Tyne* 3E **115**
Clarbeston. *Pemb* 2E **43**
Clarbeston Road. *Pemb* 2E **43**
Clarborough. *Notts* 2E **87**
Clare. *Suff* 1A **54**
Clarebrand. *Dum* 3E **111**
Clarencefield. *Dum* 3B **112**
Clarilaw. *Bord* 3H **119**
Clark's Green. *Surr* 2C **26**
Clark's Hill. *Linc* 3C **76**
Clarkston. *E Ren* 4G **127**
Clasheddy. *High* 2G **167**
Clashindarroch. *Abers* 5B **160**
Clashmore. *High* 5E **165** (nr. Dornoch)
Clashmore. *High* 1E **163** (nr. Stoer)
Clashnessie. *High* 5A **166**
Clashnoir. *Mor* 1G **151**
Clate. *Shet* 5G **173**
Clathick. *Per* 1H **135**
Clathy. *Per* 2B **136**
Clatt. *Abers* 1C **152**
Clatter. *Powy* 1B **58**
Clatterford. *IOW* 4C **16**
Clatworthy. *Som* 3D **20**
Claudy. *Derr* 2D **174**
Claughton. *Lanc* 3E **97** (nr. Caton)
Claughton. *Lanc* 5E **97** (nr. Garstang)
Claughton. *Mers* 2E **83**
Claverdon. *Warw* 4F **61**
Claverham. *N Som* 5H **33**
Clavering. *Essx* 2E **53**
Claverley. *Shrp* 1B **60**
Claverton. *Bath* 5C **34**
Clawdd-coch. *V Glam* 4D **32**
Clawdd-newydd. *Den* 5C **82**
Clawson Hill. *Leics* 3E **75**
Clawton. *Devn* 3D **10**
Claxby. *Linc* 3D **88** (nr. Alford)
Claxby. *Linc* 1A **88** (nr. Market Rasen)
Claxton. *Norf* 5F **79**
Claxton. *N Yor* 3A **100**
Claybrooke Magna. *Leics* 2B **62**
Claybrooke Parva. *Leics* 2B **62**
Clay Common. *Suff* 2G **67**
Clay Coton. *Nptn* 3C **62**
Clay Cross. *Derbs* 4A **86**
Claydon. *Oxon* 5B **62**
Claydon. *Suff* 5D **66**
Clay End. *Herts* 3D **52**
Claygate. *Dum* 2E **113**
Claygate. *Kent* 1B **28**
Claygate. *Surr* 4C **38**
Claygate Cross. *Kent* 5H **39**
Clayhall. *Hants* 3E **16**
Clayhanger. *Devn* 4D **20**
Clayhanger. *W Mid* 5E **73**
Clayhidon. *Devn* 1E **13**
Clay Hill. *Bris* 4B **34**
Clayhill. *E Sus* 3C **28**
Clayhill. *Hants* 2B **16**
Clayhithe. *Cambs* 4E **65**
Clayholes. *Ang* 5E **145**
Clay Lake. *Linc* 3B **76**
Clayock. *High* 3D **168**
Claypits. *Glos* 5C **48**
Claypole. *Linc* 1F **75**
Claythorpe. *Linc* 3D **88**
Clayton. *G Man* 1C **84**
Clayton. *S Yor* 4E **93**
Clayton. *Staf* 1C **72**
Clayton. *W Sus* 4E **27**
Clayton. *W Yor* 1B **92**
Clayton Green. *Lanc* 2D **90**
Clayton-le-Moors. *Lanc* 1F **91**
Clayton-le-Woods. *Lanc* 2D **90**
Clayton West. *W Yor* 3C **92**
Clayworth. *Notts* 2E **87**
Cleadale. *High* 5C **146**
Cleadon. *Tyne* 3G **115**
Clearbrook. *Devn* 2B **8**
Clearwell. *Glos* 5A **48**
Cleasby. *N Yor* 3F **105**
Cleat. *Orkn* 3D **172** (nr. Braehead)
Cleat. *Orkn* 9D **172** (nr. St Margaret's Hope)
Cleatlam. *Dur* 3E **105**
Cleator. *Cumb* 3B **102**
Cleator Moor. *Cumb* 3B **102**
Cleckheaton. *W Yor* 2B **92**
Cleedownton. *Shrp* 2H **59**
Cleehill. *Shrp* 3H **59**
Cleekhimin. *N Lan* 4A **128**
Clee St Margaret. *Shrp* 2H **59**
Cleestanton. *Shrp* 3H **59**
Cleethorpes. *NE Lin* 4G **95**
Cleeton St Mary. *Shrp* 3A **60**
Cleeve. *N Som* 5H **33**
Cleeve. *Oxon* 3E **36**
Cleeve Hill. *Glos* 3E **49**
Cleeve Prior. *Worc* 1F **49**
Clehonger. *Here* 2H **47**
Cleigh. *Arg* 1F **133**
Cleish. *Per* 4C **136**
Cleland. *N Lan* 4B **128**
Clench Common. *Wilts* 5G **35**
Clenchwarton. *Norf* 3E **77**
Clennell. *Nmbd* 4D **120**
Clent. *Worc* 3D **60**
Cleobury Mortimer. *Shrp* 3A **60**
Cleobury North. *Shrp* 2A **60**
Clephanton. *High* 3C **158**
Clerkhill. *High* 2H **167**
Clestrain. *Orkn* 7C **172**
Clevancy. *Wilts* 4F **35**
Clevedon. *N Som* 4H **33**
Cleveley. *Oxon* 3B **50**
Cleveleys. *Lanc* 5C **96**
Clevelode. *Worc* 1D **48**
Cleverton. *Wilts* 3E **35**
Clewer. *Som* 1H **21**
Cley next the Sea. *Norf* 1C **78**
Cliaid. *W Isl* 8B **170**
Cliasmol. *W Isl* 7C **171**
Clibberswick. *Shet* 1H **173**
Cliburn. *Cumb* 2G **103**
Cliddesden. *Hants* 2E **25**
Clieves Hills. *Lanc* 4B **90**
Cliff. *Warw* 1G **61**
Cliffburn. *Ang* 4F **145**
Cliffe. *Medw* 3B **40**
Cliffe. *N Yor* 3F **105** (nr. Darlington)
Cliffe. *N Yor* 1G **93** (nr. Selby)
Cliff End. *E Sus* 4C **28**
Cliffe Woods. *Medw* 3B **40**
Clifford. *Here* 1F **47**
Clifford. *W Yor* 5G **99**
Clifford Chambers. *Warw* 5F **61**
Clifford's Mesne. *Glos* 3C **48**
Cliffsend. *Kent* 4H **41**
Clifton. *Bris* 4A **34**
Clifton. *C Beds* 2B **52**
Clifton. *Cumb* 2G **103**
Clifton. *Derbs* 1F **73**
Clifton. *Devn* 2G **19**
Clifton. *G Man* 4F **91**
Clifton. *Lanc* 1C **90**
Clifton. *Nmbd* 1F **115**
Clifton. *N Yor* 5D **98**
Clifton. *Nott* 2C **74**
Clifton. *Oxon* 2C **50**
Clifton. *S Yor* 1C **86**
Clifton. *Stir* 5H **141**
Clifton. *W Yor* 2B **92**
Clifton. *Worc* 1D **48**
Clifton. *York* 4H **99**
Clifton Campville. *Staf* 4G **73**
Clifton Hampden. *Oxon* 2D **36**
Clifton Hill. *Worc* 4B **60**
Clifton Reynes. *Mil* 5G **63**
Clifton upon Dunsmore. *Warw* 3C **62**
Clifton upon Teme. *Worc* 4B **60**
Cliftonville. *Kent* 3H **41**
Cliftonville. *Norf* 2F **79**
Climping. *W Sus* 5A **26**
Climpy. *S Lan* 4C **128**
Clink. *Som* 2C **22**
Clint. *N Yor* 4E **99**
Clint Green. *Norf* 4C **78**
Clintmains. *Bord* 1A **120**
Cliobh. *W Isl* 4C **171**
Clipiau. *Gwyn* 4H **69**
Clippesby. *Norf* 4G **79**
Clippings Green. *Norf* 4C **78**
Clipsham. *Rut* 4G **75**
Clipston. *Nptn* 2E **62**
Clipston. *Notts* 2D **74**
Clipstone. *Notts* 4C **86**
Clitheroe. *Lanc* 5G **97**
Cliuthar. *W Isl* 8D **171**
Clive. *Shrp* 3H **71**
Clivocast. *Shet* 1G **173**
Clixby. *Linc* 4D **94**
Clocaenog. *Den* 5C **82**
Clochan. *Mor* 2B **160**
Clochforbie. *Abers* 3F **161**
Clock Face. *Mers* 1H **83**
Cloddiau. *Powy* 5E **70**
Cloddymoss. *Mor* 2D **159**
Clodock. *Here* 3G **47**
Cloford. *Som* 2C **22**
Cloghmills. *Bmny* 2F **175**
Clola. *Abers* 4H **161**
Clophill. *C Beds* 2A **52**
Clopton. *Nptn* 2H **63**
Clopton Corner. *Suff* 5E **66**
Clopton Green. *Suff* 5G **65**
Closeburn. *Dum* 5A **118**
Close Clark. *IOM* 4B **108**
Closworth. *Som* 1A **14**
Clothall. *Herts* 2C **52**
Clotton. *Ches W* 4H **83**
Clough. *G Man* 3H **91**
Clough. *W Yor* 3A **92**
Clough Foot. *W Yor* 2H **91**

Cloughton—Connista

Cloughton. *N Yor* 5H 107
Cloughton Newlands. *N Yor* 5H 107
Clousta. *Shet* 6E 173
Clouston. *Orkn* 6B 172
Clova. *Abers* 1B 152
Clova. *Ang* 1C 144
Clovelly. *Devn* 4D 18
Clovenfords. *Bord* 1G 119
Clovenstone. *Abers* 2E 153
Clovullin. *High* 2E 141
Clowne. *Derbs* 3B 86
Clows Top. *Worc* 3B 60
Cloy. *Wrex* 1F 71
Cluanie Inn. *High* 2C 148
Cluanie Lodge. *High* 2C 148
Cluddley. *Telf* 5A 72
Clun. *Shrp* 2F 59
Clunas. *High* 4C 158
Clunbury. *Shrp* 2F 59
Clunderwen. *Pemb* 3F 43
Clune. *High* 1B 150
Clunes. *High* 5E 148
Clungunford. *Shrp* 3F 59
Clunie. *Per* 4A 144
Clunton. *Shrp* 2F 59
Cluny. *Fife* 4E 137
Clutton. *Bath* 1B 22
Clutton. *Ches W* 5G 83
Clwt-y-bont. *Gwyn* 4E 81
Clwydfagwyr. *Mer T* 5D 46
Clydach. *Mon* 4F 47
Clydach. *Swan* 5G 45
Clydach Vale. *Rhon* 2C 32
Clydebank. *W Dun* 3G 127
Clydey. *Pemb* 1G 43
Clyffe Pypard. *Wilts* 4F 35
Clynder. *Arg* 1D 126
Clyne. *Neat* 5B 46
Clynelish. *High* 3F 165
Clynnog-fawr. *Gwyn* 1D 68
Clyro. *Powy* 1F 47
Clyst Honiton. *Devn* 3C 12
Clyst Hydon. *Devn* 2D 12
Clyst St George. *Devn* 4C 12
Clyst St Lawrence. *Devn* 2D 12
Clyst St Mary. *Devn* 3C 12
Clyth. *High* 5E 169
Cnip. *W Isl* 4C 171
Cnoc Amhlaigh. *W Isl* 4H 171
Cnwcau. *Pemb* 1C 44
Cnwch Coch. *Cdgn* 3F 57
Coad's Green. *Corn* 5C 10
Coal Aston. *Derbs* 3A 86
Coalbrookdale. *Telf* 5A 72
Coalbrookvale. *Blae* 5E 47
Coalburn. *S Lan* 1H 117
Coalburns. *Tyne* 3E 115
Coalcleugh. *Nmbd* 5B 114
Coaley. *Glos* 5C 48
Coalford. *Abers* 4F 153
Coalhall. *E Ayr* 3D 116
Coalhill. *Essx* 1B 40
Coalisland. *Dngn* 4E 175
Coalpit Heath. *S Glo* 3B 34
Coal Pool. *W Mid* 5E 73
Coalport. *Telf* 5B 72
Coalsnaughton. *Clac* 4B 136
Coaltown of Balgonie. *Fife* 4F 137
Coaltown of Wemyss. *Fife* 4F 137
Coalville. *Leics* 4B 74
Coalway. *Glos* 4A 48
Coanwood. *Nmbd* 4H 113
Coat. *Som* 4H 21
Coatbridge. *N Lan* 3A 128
Coatdyke. *N Lan* 3A 128
Coate. *Swin* 3G 35
Coate. *Wilts* 5F 35
Coates. *Cambs* 1C 64
Coates. *Glos* 5E 49
Coates. *Linc* 2G 87
Coates. *W Sus* 4A 26
Coatham. *Red C* 2C 106
Coatham Mundeville. *Darl* 2F 105
Cobbaton. *Devn* 4G 19
Coberley. *Glos* 4E 49
Cobhall Common. *Here* 2H 47
Cobham. *Kent* 4A 40
Cobham. *Surr* 5C 38
Cobnash. *Here* 4G 59
Coburg. *Devn* 5B 12
Cockayne. *N Yor* 5D 106
Cockayne Hatley. *C Beds* 1C 52
Cock Bank. *Wrex* 1F 71
Cock Bridge. *Abers* 3G 151
Cockburnspath. *Bord* 2D 130
Cock Clarks. *Essx* 5B 54
Cockenzie and Port Seton. *E Lot* 2H 129
Cockerham. *Lanc* 4D 96
Cockermouth. *Cumb* 1C 102
Cockernhoe. *Herts* 3B 52
Cockfield. *Dur* 2E 105
Cockfield. *Suff* 5B 66
Cockfosters. *G Lon* 1D 39
Cock Gate. *Here* 4G 59
Cock Green. *Essx* 4G 53
Cocking. *W Sus* 1G 17
Cocking Causeway. *W Sus* 1G 17
Cockington. *Torb* 2E 9
Cocklake. *Som* 2H 21
Cocklaw. *Abers* 4H 161
Cocklaw. *Nmbd* 2C 114
Cockley Beck. *Cumb* 4D 102
Cockley Cley. *Norf* 5G 77
Cockmuir. *Abers* 3G 161
Cockpole Green. *Wok* 3F 37
Cockshutford. *Shrp* 2H 59
Cockshutt. *Shrp* 3G 71
Cockthorpe. *Norf* 1B 78
Cockwood. *Devn* 4C 12
Cockyard. *Derbs* 3E 85
Cockyard. *Here* 2H 47
Codda. *Corn* 5B 10
Coddenham. *Suff* 5D 66
Coddenham Green. *Suff* 5D 66
Coddington. *Ches W* 5G 83
Coddington. *Here* 1C 48
Coddington. *Notts* 5F 87
Codford. *Wilts* 3E 23
Codicote. *Herts* 4C 52
Codmore Hill. *W Sus* 3B 26
Codnor. *Derbs* 1B 74
Codrington. *S Glo* 4C 34
Codsall. *Staf* 5C 72
Codsall Wood. *Staf* 5C 72
Coed Duon. *Cphy* 2E 33
Coedely. *Rhon* 3D 32
Coedglasson. *Powy* 4C 58
Coedkernew. *Newp* 3F 33
Coed Morgan. *Mon* 4G 47
Coedpoeth. *Wrex* 5E 83
Coedway. *Powy* 4F 71
Coed-y-bryn. *Cdgn* 1D 44
Coed-y-paen. *Mon* 2G 33
Coed Ystumgwern. *Gwyn* 3E 69
Coelbren. *Powy* 4B 46
Coffinswell. *Devn* 2E 9
Cofton Hackett. *Worc* 3E 61
Cogan. *V Glam* 4E 33
Cogenhoe. *Nptn* 4F 63
Cogges. *Oxon* 5B 50
Coggeshall. *Essx* 3B 54
Coggeshall Hamlet. *Essx* 3B 54
Coggins Mill. *E Sus* 3G 27
Coignafearn Lodge. *High* 2A 150
Coig Peighinnean. *W Isl* 1H 171
Coig Peighinnean Bhuirgh. *W Isl* 2G 171
Coilleag. *W Isl* 7C 170
Coillemore. *High* 1A 158
Coillore. *High* 5C 154
Coire an Fhuarain. *W Isl* 4E 171
Coity. *B'end* 3C 32
Cokhay Green. *Derbs* 3G 73
Col. *W Isl* 3G 171
Colaboll. *High* 2C 164
Colan. *Corn* 2C 6
Colaton Raleigh. *Devn* 4D 12
Colbost. *High* 4B 154
Colburn. *N Yor* 5E 105
Colby. *Cumb* 2H 103
Colby. *IOM* 4B 108
Colby. *Norf* 2E 78
Colchester. *Essx* 3D 54
Cold Ash. *W Ber* 5D 36
Cold Ashby. *Nptn* 3D 62
Cold Ashton. *S Glo* 4C 34
Cold Aston. *Glos* 4G 49
Coldbackie. *High* 3G 167
Cold Blow. *Pemb* 3F 43
Cold Brayfield. *Mil* 5G 63
Cold Cotes. *N Yor* 2G 97
Coldean. *Brig* 5E 27
Coldeast. *Devn* 5B 12
Colden. *W Yor* 2H 91
Colden Common. *Hants* 4C 24
Coldfair Green. *Suff* 4G 67
Coldham. *Cambs* 5D 76
Coldham. *Staf* 5C 72
Cold Hanworth. *Linc* 2H 87
Coldharbour. *Corn* 4B 6
Cold Harbour. *Dors* 3E 15
Coldharbour. *Glos* 5A 48
Coldharbour. *Kent* 5G 39
Coldharbour. *Surr* 1C 26
Cold Hatton. *Telf* 3A 72
Cold Hatton Heath. *Telf* 3A 72
Cold Hesledon. *Dur* 5H 115
Cold Hiendley. *W Yor* 3D 92
Cold Higham. *Nptn* 5D 62
Coldingham. *Bord* 3F 131
Cold Kirby. *N Yor* 1H 99
Coldmeece. *Staf* 2C 72
Cold Northcott. *Corn* 4C 10
Cold Norton. *Essx* 5B 54
Cold Overton. *Leics* 4F 75
Coldrain. *Per* 3C 136
Coldred. *Kent* 1G 29
Coldridge. *Devn* 2G 11
Cold Row. *Lanc* 5C 96
Coldstream. *Bord* 5E 131
Coldwaltham. *W Sus* 4B 26
Coldwell. *Here* 2H 47
Coldwells. *Abers* 5H 161
Coldwells Croft. *Abers* 1C 152
Cole. *Shet* 5E 173
Cole. *Som* 3B 22
Colebatch. *Shrp* 2F 59
Colebrook. *Devn* 2D 12
Colebrooke. *Devn* 3A 12
Coleburn. *Mor* 3G 159
Coleby. *Linc* 4G 87
Coleby. *N Lin* 3B 94
Cole End. *Warw* 2G 61
Coleford. *Devn* 2A 12
Coleford. *Glos* 4A 48
Coleford. *Som* 2B 22
Colegate End. *Norf* 2D 66
Cole Green. *Herts* 4C 52
Cole Henley. *Hants* 1C 24
Colehill. *Dors* 2F 15
Coleman Green. *Herts* 4B 52
Coleman's Hatch. *E Sus* 2F 27
Colemere. *Shrp* 2G 71
Colemore. *Hants* 3F 25
Colemore Green. *Shrp* 1B 60
Coleorton. *Leics* 4B 74
Coleraine. *Cole* 1E 175
Colerne. *Wilts* 4D 34
Colesbourne. *Glos* 4F 49
Colesden. *Bed* 5A 64
Coles Green. *Worc* 5B 60
Coleshill. *Buck* 1A 38
Coleshill. *Oxon* 2H 35
Coleshill. *Warw* 2G 61
Colestocks. *Devn* 2D 12
Colethrop. *Glos* 4D 48
Coley. *Bath* 1A 22
Colgate. *W Sus* 2D 26
Colinsburgh. *Fife* 3G 137
Colinton. *Edin* 3F 129
Colintraive. *Arg* 2B 126
Colkirk. *Norf* 3B 78
Collace. *Per* 5B 144
Collam. *W Isl* 8D 171
Collaton. *Devn* 5D 8
Collaton St Mary. *Torb* 2E 9
College of Roseisle. *Mor* 2F 159
Collessie. *Fife* 2E 137
Collier Row. *G Lon* 1F 39
Colliers End. *Herts* 3D 52
Collier Street. *Kent* 1B 28
Colliery Row. *Tyne* 5G 115
Collieston. *Abers* 1H 153
Collin. *Dum* 2B 112
Collingbourne Ducis. *Wilts* 1H 23
Collingbourne Kingston. *Wilts* 1H 23
Collingham. *Notts* 4F 87
Collingham. *W Yor* 5F 99
Collingtree. *Nptn* 5E 63
Collins Green. *Warr* 1H 83
Collins Green. *Worc* 5B 60
Colliston. *Ang* 4F 145
Colliton. *Devn* 2D 12
Collydean. *Fife* 3E 137
Collyweston. *Nptn* 5G 75
Colmonell. *S Ayr* 1G 109
Colmworth. *Bed* 5A 64
Colnbrook. *Slo* 3B 38
Colne. *Cambs* 3C 64
Colne. *Lanc* 5A 98
Colne Engaine. *Essx* 2B 54
Colney. *Norf* 5D 78
Colney Heath. *Herts* 5C 52
Colney Street. *Herts* 5B 52
Coln Rogers. *Glos* 5F 49
Coln St Aldwyns. *Glos* 5G 49
Coln St Dennis. *Glos* 4F 49
Colpitts Grange. *Nmbd* 4C 114
Colpy. *Abers* 5D 160
Colscott. *Devn* 1D 10
Colsterdale. *N Yor* 1D 98
Colsterworth. *Linc* 3G 75
Colston Bassett. *Notts* 2E 74
Colstoun House. *E Lot* 2B 130
Coltfield. *Mor* 2F 159
Colthouse. *Cumb* 5E 103
Coltishall. *Norf* 4E 79
Coltness. *N Lan* 4B 128
Colton. *Cumb* 1C 96
Colton. *Norf* 5D 78
Colton. *N Yor* 5H 99
Colton. *Staf* 3E 73
Colton. *W Yor* 1D 92
Colt's Hill. *Kent* 1H 27
Col Uarach. *W Isl* 4G 171
Colvend. *Dum* 4F 111
Colvister. *Shet* 2G 173
Colwall. *Here* 1C 48
Colwall Green. *Here* 1C 48
Colwell. *Nmbd* 2C 114
Colwich. *Staf* 3E 73
Colwick. *Notts* 1D 74
Colwinston. *V Glam* 4C 32
Colworth. *W Sus* 5A 26
Colwyn Bay. *Cnwy* 3A 82
Colyford. *Devn* 3F 13
Colyton. *Devn* 3F 13
Combe. *Devn* 2D 8
Combe. *Here* 4F 59
Combe. *Oxon* 4C 50
Combe. *W Ber* 5B 36
Combe Almer. *Dors* 3E 15
Combebow. *Devn* 4E 11
Combe Down. *Bath* 5C 34
Combe Fishacre. *Devn* 2E 9
Combe Florey. *Som* 3E 21
Combe Hay. *Bath* 5C 34
Combeinteignhead. *Devn* 5C 12
Combe Martin. *Devn* 2F 19
Combe Moor. *Here* 4F 59
Comber. *Ards* 4H 175
Combe Raleigh. *Devn* 2E 13
Comberbach. *Ches W* 3A 84
Comberford. *Staf* 5F 73
Comberton. *Cambs* 5C 64
Comberton. *Here* 4G 59
Combe St Nicholas. *Som* 1G 13
Combpyne. *Devn* 3F 13
Combridge. *Staf* 2E 73
Combrook. *Warw* 5H 61
Combs. *Derbs* 3E 85
Combs. *Suff* 5C 66
Combs Ford. *Suff* 5C 66
Combwich. *Som* 2F 21
Comers. *Abers* 3D 152
Comhampton. *Worc* 4C 60
Comins Coch. *Cdgn* 2F 57
Comley. *Shrp* 1G 59
Commercial End. *Cambs* 4E 65
Commins. *Powy* 3D 70
Commins Coch. *Powy* 5H 69
Commondale. *N Yor* 3D 106
Common End. *Cumb* 2B 102
Common Hill. *Here* 2A 48
Common Moor. *Corn* 2G 7
Commonside. *Ches W* 3H 83
Common Side. *Derbs* 3H 85 (nr. Chesterfield)
Commonside. *Derbs* 1G 73 (nr. Derby)
Common, The. *Wilts* 3H 23 (nr. Salisbury)
Common, The. *Wilts* 3F 35 (nr. Swindon)
Compstall. *G Man* 1D 84
Compton. *Devn* 2E 9
Compton. *Hants* 4C 24
Compton. *Staf* 2C 60
Compton. *Surr* 1A 26
Compton. *W Ber* 4D 36
Compton. *W Sus* 1F 17
Compton. *Wilts* 1G 23
Compton Abbas. *Dors* 1D 15
Compton Abdale. *Glos* 4F 49
Compton Bassett. *Wilts* 4F 35
Compton Beauchamp. *Oxon* 3A 36
Compton Bishop. *Som* 1G 21
Compton Chamberlayne. *Wilts* 4F 23
Compton Dando. *Bath* 5B 34
Compton Dundon. *Som* 3H 21
Compton Greenfield. *S Glo* 3A 34
Compton Martin. *Bath* 1A 22
Compton Pauncefoot. *Som* 4B 22
Compton Valence. *Dors* 3A 14
Comrie. *Fife* 1D 128
Comrie. *Per* 1G 135
Conaglen. *High* 2E 141
Conchra. *Arg* 1B 126
Conchra. *High* 1A 148
Conder Green. *Lanc* 4D 96
Conderton. *Worc* 2E 49
Condicote. *Glos* 3G 49
Condorrat. *N Lan* 2A 128
Condover. *Shrp* 5G 71
Coneyhurst Common. *W Sus* 3C 26
Coneysthorpe. *N Yor* 2B 100
Coneythorpe. *N Yor* 4F 99
Coney Weston. *Suff* 3B 66
Conford. *Hants* 3G 25
Congdon's Shop. *Corn* 5C 10
Congerstone. *Leics* 5A 74
Congham. *Norf* 3G 77
Congleton. *Ches E* 4C 84
Congl-y-wal. *Gwyn* 1G 69
Congresbury. *N Som* 5H 33
Congreve. *Staf* 4D 72
Conham. *S Glo* 4B 34
Conicaval. *Mor* 3D 159
Coningsby. *Linc* 5B 88
Conington. *Cambs* 4C 64 (nr. Fenstanton)
Conington. *Cambs* 2A 64 (nr. Sawtry)
Conisbrough. *S Yor* 1C 86
Conisby. *Arg* 3A 124
Conisholme. *Linc* 1D 88
Coniston. *Cumb* 5E 102
Coniston. *E Yor* 1E 95
Coniston Cold. *N Yor* 4B 98
Conistone. *N Yor* 3B 98
Connah's Quay. *Flin* 3E 83
Connel. *Arg* 5D 140
Connel Park. *E Ayr* 3F 117
Connista. *High* 1D 154

Connor Downs—Craigdhu

Connor Downs. Corn 3C 4
Conock. Wilts 1F 23
Conon Bridge. High 3H 157
Cononley. N Yor 5B 98
Cononsyth. Ang 4E 145
Conordan. High 5E 155
Consall. Staf 1D 73
Consett. Dur 4E 115
Constable Burton. N Yor 5E 105
Constantine. Corn 4E 5
Constantine Bay. Corn 1C 6
Contin. High 3G 157
Contullich. High 1A 158
Conwy. Cnwy 3G 81
Conyer. Kent 4D 40
Conyer's Green. Suff 4A 66
Cooden. E Sus 5B 28
Cooil. IOM 4C 108
Cookbury. Devn 2E 11
Cookbury Wick. Devn 2D 11
Cookham. Wind 3G 37
Cookham Dean. Wind 3G 37
Cookham Rise. Wind 3G 37
Cookhill. Worc 5E 61
Cookley. Suff 3F 67
Cookley. Worc 2C 60
Cookley Green. Oxon 2E 37
Cookney. Abers 4F 153
Cooksbridge. E Sus 4F 27
Cooksey Green. Worc 4D 60
Cookshill. Staf 1D 72
Cooksmill Green. Essx 5G 53
Cookstown. Cook 4E 175
Coolham. W Sus 3C 26
Cooling. Medw 3B 40
Cooling Street. Medw 3B 40
Coombe. Corn 1C 10
(nr. Bude)
Coombe. Corn 3D 6
(nr. St Austell)
Coombe. Corn 4C 6
(nr. Truro)
Coombe. Devn 3E 12
(nr. Sidmouth)
Coombe. Devn 5C 12
(nr. Teignmouth)
Coombe. Glos 2C 34
Coombe. Hants 4E 25
Coombe. Wilts 1G 23
Coombe Bissett. Wilts 4G 23
Coombe Hill. Glos 3D 49
Coombe Keynes. Dors 4D 14
Coombes. W Sus 5C 26
Coopersale Common. Essx 5E 53
Coopersale Street. Essx 5E 53
Cooper's Corner. Kent 1F 27
Cooper Street. Kent 5H 41
Cootham. W Sus 4B 26
Copalder Corner. Cambs 1C 64
Copdock. Suff 1E 54
Copford. Essx 3C 54
Copford Green. Essx 3C 54
Copgrove. N Yor 3F 99
Copister. Shet 4F 173
Cople. Bed 1B 52
Copley. Dur 2D 105
Coplow Dale. Derbs 3F 85
Copmanthorpe. York 5H 99
Copp. Lanc 1C 90
Coppathorne. Corn 2C 10
Coppenhall. Ches E 5B 84
Coppenhall. Staf 4D 72
Coppenhall Moss. Ches E 5B 84
Copperhouse. Corn 3C 4
Coppicegate. Shrp 2B 60
Coppingford. Cambs 2A 64
Copplestone. Devn 2A 12
Coppull. Lanc 3D 90
Coppull Moor. Lanc 3D 90
Copsale. W Sus 3C 26
Copshaw Holm. Bord 1F 113
Copster Green. Lanc 1E 91
Copston Magna. Warw 2B 62
Copt Green. Warw 4F 61
Copthall Green. Essx 5E 53
Copt Heath. W Mid 3F 61
Copt Hewick. N Yor 2F 99
Copthill. Dur 5B 114
Copthorne. W Sus 2E 27
Coptiviney. Shrp 2G 71
Copy's Green. Norf 2B 78
Copythorne. Hants 1B 16
Corbridge. Nmbd 3C 114
Corby. Nptn 2F 63
Corby Glen. Linc 3G 75
Cordon. N Ayr 2E 123
Coreley. Shrp 3A 60
Corfe. Som 1F 13
Corfe Castle. Dors 4E 15
Corfe Mullen. Dors 3E 15
Corfton. Shrp 2G 59
Corgarff. Abers 3G 151
Corhampton. Hants 4E 24
Corlae. Dum 5F 117
Corlannau. Neat 2A 32
Corley. Warw 2H 61
Corley Ash. Warw 2G 61
Corley Moor. Warw 2G 61
Cormiston. S Lan 1C 118
Cornaa. IOM 3D 108
Cornaigbeg. Arg 4A 138
Cornaigmore. Arg 2D 138
(on Coll)
Cornaigmore. Arg 4A 138
(on Tiree)
Corner Row. Lanc 1C 90
Corney. Cumb 5C 102
Cornforth. Dur 1A 106
Cornhill. Abers 3C 160
Cornhill. High 4C 164
Cornhill-on-Tweed. Nmbd 1C 120
Cornholme. W Yor 2H 91
Cornish Hall End. Essx 2G 53
Cornquoy. Orkn 7E 172
Cornriggs. Dur 5B 114
Cornsay. Dur 5E 115
Cornsay Colliery. Dur 5E 115
Corntown. High 3H 157
Corntown. V Glam 4C 32
Cornwell. Oxon 3A 50
Cornwood. Devn 3C 8
Cornworthy. Devn 3E 9
Corpach. High 1E 141
Corpusty. Norf 3D 78
Corra. Dum 3F 111
Corran. High 2E 141
(nr. Arnisdale)
Corran. High 3A 148
(nr. Fort William)
Corrany. IOM 3D 108
Corribeg. High 1D 141
Corrie. N Ayr 5B 126
Corrie Common. Dum 1D 112
Corriecravie. N Ayr 3D 122
Corriekinloch. High 1A 164
Corriemoillie. High 2F 157
Corrievarkie Lodge. Per 1C 142
Corrievorrie. High 1B 150
Corrigall. Orkn 6C 172
Corrimony. High 5F 157
Corringham. Linc 1F 87
Corringham. Thur 2B 40
Corris. Gwyn 5G 69
Corris Uchaf. Gwyn 5G 69
Corrour Shooting Lodge. High 2B 142
Corry. High 1E 147
Corrybrough. High 1C 150
Corrygills. N Ayr 2E 123
Corry of Ardnagrask. High 4H 157
Corsback. High 1E 169
(nr. Dunnet)
Corsback. High 3E 169
(nr. Halkirk)
Corscombe. Dors 2A 14
Corse. Abers 4D 160
Corse. Glos 3C 48
Corsehill. Abers 3G 161
Corse Lawn. Worc 2D 48
Corse of Kinnoir. Abers 4C 160
Corsham. Wilts 4D 34
Corsley. Wilts 2D 22
Corsley Heath. Wilts 2D 22
Corsock. Dum 2E 111
Corston. Bath 5B 34
Corston. Wilts 3E 35
Corstorphine. Edin 2F 129
Cortachy. Ang 3C 144
Corton. Suff 1H 67
Corton. Wilts 2E 23
Corton Denham. Som 4B 22
Corwar House. S Ayr 1H 109
Corwen. Den 1C 70
Coryates. Dors 4B 14
Coryton. Devn 4E 11
Coryton. Thur 2B 40
Cosby. Leics 1C 62
Coscote. Oxon 3D 36
Coseley. W Mid 1D 60
Cosgrove. Nptn 1F 51
Cosham. Port 2E 17
Cosheston. Pemb 4E 43
Coskills. N Lin 3D 94
Cosmeston. V Glam 5E 33
Cossall. Notts 1B 74
Cossington. Leics 4D 74
Cossington. Som 2G 21
Costa. Orkn 5C 172
Costessey. Norf 4D 78
Costock. Notts 3C 74
Coston. Leics 3F 75
Coston. Norf 5C 78
Cote. Oxon 5B 50
Cotebrook. Ches W 4H 83
Cotehill. Cumb 4F 113
Cotes. Cumb 1D 97
Cotes. Leics 3C 74
Cotes. Staf 2C 72
Cotesbach. Leics 2C 62
Cotes Heath. Staf 2C 72
Cotford St Luke. Som 4E 21
Cotgrave. Notts 2D 74
Cothall. Abers 2F 153
Cotham. Notts 1E 75
Cothelstone. Som 3E 21
Cotheridge. Worc 5B 60
Cotherstone. Dur 3D 104
Cothill. Oxon 2C 36
Cotland. Mon 5A 48
Cotleigh. Devn 2F 13
Cotmanhay. Derbs 1B 74
Coton. Cambs 5D 64
Coton. Nptn 3D 62
Coton. Staf 3C 72
(nr. Gnosall)
Coton. Staf 2D 73
(nr. Stone)
Coton. Staf 5F 73
(nr. Tamworth)
Coton Clanford. Staf 3C 72
Coton Hayes. Staf 2D 73
Coton Hill. Shrp 4G 71
Coton in the Clay. Staf 3F 73
Coton in the Elms. Derbs 4G 73
Cotonwood. Shrp 2H 71
Cotonwood. Staf 3C 72
Cott. Devn 2D 9
Cott. Orkn 5F 172
Cottam. E Yor 3D 101
Cottam. Lanc 1D 90
Cottam. Notts 3F 87
Cottartown. High 5E 159
Cottarville. Nptn 4E 63
Cottenham. Cambs 4D 64
Cotterdale. N Yor 5B 104
Cottered. Herts 3D 52
Cotterstock. Nptn 1H 63
Cottesbrooke. Nptn 3E 62
Cottesmore. Rut 4G 75
Cotteylands. Devn 1C 12
Cottingham. E Yor 1D 94
Cottingham. Nptn 1F 63
Cottingley. W Yor 1B 92
Cottisford. Oxon 2D 50
Cotton. Staf 1E 73
Cotton. Suff 4C 66
Cotton End. Bed 1A 52
Cottown. Abers 4F 161
Cotts. Devn 2A 8
Cotwalton. Staf 2D 72
Couch's Mill. Corn 3F 7
Coughton. Here 3A 48
Coughton. Warw 4E 61
Coulags. High 4B 156
Coulby Newham. Midd 3C 106
Coulderton. Cumb 4A 102
Coulin Lodge. High 3C 156
Coull. Abers 3C 152
Coulport. Arg 1D 126
Coulsdon. G Lon 5D 39
Coulston. Wilts 1E 23
Coulter. S Lan 1C 118
Coultershaw Bridge. W Sus 4A 26
Coultings. Som 2F 21
Coulton. N Yor 2A 100
Cound. Shrp 5H 71
Coundon. Dur 2F 105
Coundon Grange. Dur 2F 105
Countersett. N Yor 1B 98
Countess. Wilts 2G 23
Countess Cross. Essx 2B 54
Countesthorpe. Leics 1C 62
Countisbury. Devn 2H 19
Coupar Angus. Per 4B 144
Coupe Green. Lanc 2D 90
Coupland. Cumb 3A 104
Coupland. Nmbd 1D 120
Cour. Arg 5G 125
Courance. Dum 5C 118
Court-at-Street. Kent 2E 29
Courteachan. High 4E 147
Courteenhall. Nptn 5E 63
Court Henry. Carm 3F 45
Courtsend. Essx 1E 41
Courtway. Som 3F 21
Cousland. Midl 3G 129
Cousley Wood. E Sus 2A 28
Coustonn. Arg 2B 126
Cove. Arg 1D 126
Cove. Devn 1C 12
Cove. Hants 1G 25
Cove. High 4C 162
Cove. Bord 2D 130
Cove Bay. Aber 3G 153
Covehithe. Suff 2H 67
Coven. Staf 5D 72
Coveney. Cambs 2D 65
Covenham St Bartholomew. Linc 1C 88
Covenham St Mary. Linc 1C 88
Coven Heath. Staf 5D 72
Coventry. W Mid 3H 61
Coverack. Corn 5E 5
Coverham. N Yor 1D 98
Covesea. Mor 1F 159
Covingham. Swin 3G 35
Covington. Cambs 3H 63
Covington. S Lan 1B 118
Cowan Bridge. Lanc 2F 97
Cowan Head. Cumb 5F 103
Cowbar. Red C 3E 107
Cowbeech. E Sus 4H 27
Cowbit. Linc 4B 76
Cowbridge. V Glam 4C 32
Cowden. Kent 1F 27
Cowdenbeath. Fife 4D 136
Cowdenburn. Bord 4F 129
Cowdenend. Fife 4D 136
Cowers Lane. Derbs 1H 73
Cowes. IOW 3C 16
Cowesby. N Yor 1G 99
Cowfold. W Sus 3D 26
Cowfords. Mor 2H 159
Cowgill. Cumb 1G 97
Cowie. Abers 5F 153
Cowie. Stir 1B 128
Cowlam. E Yor 3D 100
Cowley. Devn 3C 12
Cowley. Glos 4E 49
Cowley. G Lon 2B 38
Cowley. Oxon 5D 50
Cowley. Staf 4C 72
Cowleymoor. Devn 1C 12
Cowling. Lanc 3D 90
Cowling. N Yor 1E 99
(nr. Bedale)
Cowling. N Yor 5B 98
(nr. Glusburn)
Cowlinge. Suff 5G 65
Cowmes. W Yor 3B 92
Cowpe. Lanc 2G 91
Cowpen. Nmbd 1F 115
Cowpen Bewley. Stoc T 2B 106
Cowplain. Hants 1E 17
Cowshill. Dur 5B 114
Cowslip Green. N Som 5H 33
Cowstrandburn. Fife 4C 136
Cowthorpe. N Yor 4G 99
Coxall. Here 3F 59
Coxbank. Ches E 1A 72
Coxbench. Derbs 1A 74
Cox Common. Suff 2G 67
Coxford. Norf 3H 77
Coxgreen. Staf 2C 60
Cox Green. Surr 2B 26
Cox Green. Tyne 4G 115
Coxheath. Kent 5B 40
Coxhoe. Dur 1A 106
Coxley. Som 2A 22
Coxwold. N Yor 2H 99
Coychurch. B'end 3C 32
Coylton. S Ayr 3D 116
Coylumbridge. High 2D 150
Coynach. Abers 3B 152
Coynachie. Abers 5B 160
Coytrahen. B'end 3B 32
Crabbs Cross. Worc 4E 61
Crabgate. Norf 3C 78
Crab Orchard. Dors 2F 15
Crabtree. W Sus 3D 26
Crabtree Green. Wrex 1F 71
Crackaig. High 2G 165
Crackenthorpe. Cumb 2H 103
Crackington Haven. Corn 3B 10
Crackley. Staf 5C 84
Crackley. Warw 3G 61
Crackleybank. Shrp 4B 72
Crackpot. N Yor 5C 104
Cracoe. N Yor 3B 98
Craddock. Devn 1D 12
Cradhlastadh. W Isl 4C 171
Cradley. Here 1C 48
Cradley. W Mid 2D 60
Cradoc. Powy 2D 46
Crafthole. Corn 3H 7
Crafton. Buck 4G 51
Cragabus. Arg 5B 124
Crag Foot. Lanc 2D 97
Craggan. High 1E 151
Cragganmore. Mor 5F 159
Cragganvallie. High 5H 157
Craggie. High 2F 165
Craggiemore. High 5B 158
Cragg Vale. W Yor 2A 92
Craghead. Dur 4F 115
Crai. Powy 3B 46
Craibstone. Aber 2F 153
Craichie. Ang 4E 145
Craig. Arg 5E 141
Craig. Dum 2D 111
Craig. High 4C 156
(nr. Achnashellach)
Craig. High 2G 155
(nr. Lower Diabaig)
Craig. High 5H 155
(nr. Stromeferry)
Craiganour Lodge. Per 3D 142
Craigavon. Cgvn 5F 175
Craigbrack. Arg 4A 134
Craig-cefn-parc. Swan 5G 45
Craigdallie. Per 1E 137
Craigdam. Abers 5F 161
Craigdarroch. E Ayr 4F 117
Craigdarroch. High 3G 157
Craigdhu. High 4G 157

Darnhall. *Ches W* 4A **84**
Darnick. *Bord* 1H **119**
Darowen. *Powy* 5H **69**
Darra. *Abers* 4E **161**
Darracott. *Devn* 3E **19**
Darras Hall. *Nmbd* 2E **115**
Darrington. *W Yor* 2E **93**
Darrow Green. *Norf* 2E **67**
Darsham. *Suff* 4G **67**
Dartfield. *Abers* 3H **161**
Dartford. *Kent* 3G **39**
Dartford-Thurrock River Crossing. *Kent* 3G **39**
Dartington. *Devn* 2D **9**
Dartmeet. *Devn* 5G **11**
Dartmoor. *Devn* 4F **11**
Dartmouth. *Devn* 3E **9**
Darton. *S Yor* 3D **92**
Darvel. *E Ayr* 1E **117**
Darwen. *Bkbn* 2E **91**
Dassels. *Herts* 3D **53**
Datchet. *Wind* 3A **38**
Datchworth. *Herts* 4C **52**
Datchworth Green. *Herts* 4C **52**
Daubhill. *G Man* 4F **91**
Dauntsey. *Wilts* 3E **35**
Dauntsey Green. *Wilts* 3E **35**
Dauntsey Lock. *Wilts* 3E **35**
Dava. *Mor* 5E **159**
Davenham. *Ches W* 3A **84**
Daventry. *Nptn* 4C **62**
Davidson's Mains. *Edin* 2F **129**
Davidston. *High* 2B **158**
Davidstow. *Corn* 4B **10**
David's Well. *Powy* 3C **58**
Davington. *Dum* 4E **119**
Daviot. *Abers* 1E **153**
Daviot. *High* 5B **158**
Davyhulme. *G Man* 1B **84**
Daw Cross. *N Yor* 4E **99**
Dawdon. *Dur* 5H **115**
Dawesgreen. *Surr* 1D **26**
Dawley. *Telf* 5A **72**
Dawlish. *Devn* 5C **12**
Dawlish Warren. *Devn* 5C **12**
Dawn. *Cnwy* 3A **82**
Daws Heath. *Essx* 2C **40**
Dawshill. *Worc* 5C **60**
Daw's House. *Corn* 4D **10**
Dawsmere. *Linc* 2D **76**
Dayhills. *Staf* 2D **72**
Dayhouse Bank. *Worc* 3D **60**
Daylesford. *Glos* 3H **49**
Daywall. *Shrp* 2E **71**
Ddol. *Flin* 3D **82**
Ddol Cownwy. *Powy* 4C **70**
Deadman's Cross. *C Beds* 1B **52**
Deadwater. *Nmbd* 5A **120**
Deaf Hill. *Dur* 1A **106**
Deal. *Kent* 5H **41**
Dean. *Cumb* 2B **102**
Dean. *Devn* 2G **19** (nr. Combe Martin)
Dean. *Devn* 2H **19** (nr. Lynton)
Dean. *Dors* 1E **15**
Dean. *Hants* 1D **16** (nr. Bishop's Waltham)
Dean. *Hants* 3C **24** (nr. Winchester)
Dean. *Oxon* 3B **50**
Dean. *Som* 2B **22**
Dean Bank. *Dur* 1F **105**
Deanburnhaugh. *Bord* 3F **119**
Dean Cross. *Devn* 2F **19**
Deane. *Hants* 1D **24**
Deanich Lodge. *High* 5A **164**
Deanland. *Dors* 1E **15**
Deanlane End. *W Sus* 1F **17**
Dean Park. *Shrp* 4A **60**
Dean Prior. *Devn* 2D **8**
Dean Row. *Ches E* 2C **84**
Deans. *W Lot* 3D **128**
Deanscales. *Cumb* 2B **102**
Deanshanger. *Nptn* 1F **51**
Deanston. *Stir* 3G **135**
Dearham. *Cumb* 1B **102**
Dearne Valley. *S Yor* 4D **93**
Debach. *Suff* 5E **67**
Debden. *Essx* 2F **53**
Debden Green. *Essx* 1F **39** (nr. Loughton)
Debden Green. *Essx* 2F **53** (nr. Saffron Walden)
Debenham. *Suff* 4D **66**
Dechmont. *W Lot* 2D **128**
Deddington. *Oxon* 2C **50**
Dedham. *Essx* 2D **54**
Dedham Heath. *Essx* 2D **54**
Deebank. *Abers* 4D **152**
Deene. *Nptn* 1G **63**
Deenethorpe. *Nptn* 1G **63**
Deepcar. *S Yor* 1G **85**
Deepcut. *Surr* 5A **38**
Deepdale. *Cumb* 1G **97**
Deepdale. *N Lin* 3D **94**
Deepdale. *N Yor* 2A **98**
Deeping Gate. *Pet* 5A **76**
Deeping St James. *Linc* 4A **76**
Deeping St Nicholas. *Linc* 4B **76**
Deerhill. *Mor* 3B **160**
Deerhurst. *Glos* 3D **48**
Deerhurst Walton. *Glos* 3D **49**
Deerness. *Orkn* 7E **172**
Defford. *Worc* 1E **49**
Defynnog. *Powy* 3C **46**
Deganwy. *Cnwy* 3G **81**
Deighton. *N Yor* 4A **106**
Deighton. *W Yor* 3B **92**
Deighton. *York* 5A **100**
Deiniolen. *Gwyn* 4E **81**
Delabole. *Corn* 4A **10**
Delamere. *Ches W* 4H **83**
Delfour. *High* 3C **150**
Delliefure. *High* 5E **159**
Dell, The. *Suff* 1G **67**
Delly End. *Oxon* 4B **50**
Delny. *High* 1B **158**
Delph. *G Man* 4H **91**
Delves. *Dur* 5E **115**
Delves, The. *W Mid* 1E **61**
Delvin End. *Essx* 2A **54**
Dembleby. *Linc* 2H **75**
Demelza. *Corn* 2D **6**
Denaby Main. *S Yor* 1B **86**
Denbeath. *Fife* 4F **137**
Denbigh. *Den* 4C **82**
Denbury. *Devn* 2E **9**
Denby. *Derbs* 1A **74**
Denby Common. *Derbs* 1B **74**
Denby Dale. *W Yor* 4C **92**
Denchworth. *Oxon* 2B **36**
Dendron. *Cumb* 2B **96**
Deneside. *Dur* 5H **115**
Denford. *Nptn* 3G **63**
Dengie. *Essx* 5C **54**
Denham. *Buck* 2B **38**
Denham. *Suff* 4G **65** (nr. Bury St Edmunds)
Denham. *Suff* 3D **66** (nr. Eye)
Denham Green. *Buck* 2B **38**
Denham Street. *Suff* 3D **66**
Denhead. *Abers* 5G **161** (nr. Ellon)
Denhead. *Abers* 3G **161** (nr. Strichen)
Denhead. *Fife* 2G **137**
Denholm. *Bord* 3H **119**
Denholme. *W Yor* 1A **92**
Denholme Clough. *W Yor* 1A **92**
Denholme Gate. *W Yor* 1A **92**
Denio. *Gwyn* 2C **68**
Denmead. *Hants* 1E **17**
Dennington. *Suff* 4E **67**
Denny. *Falk* 1B **128**
Denny End. *Cambs* 4D **65**
Dennyloanhead. *Falk* 1B **128**
Den of Lindores. *Fife* 2E **137**
Denshaw. *G Man* 3H **91**
Denside. *Abers* 4F **153**
Densole. *Kent* 1G **29**
Denston. *Suff* 5G **65**
Denstone. *Staf* 1F **73**
Denstroude. *Kent* 4F **41**
Dent. *Cumb* 1G **97**
Den, The. *N Ayr* 4E **127**
Denton. *Cambs* 2A **64**
Denton. *Darl* 3F **105**
Denton. *E Sus* 5F **27**
Denton. *G Man* 1D **84**
Denton. *Kent* 1G **29**
Denton. *Linc* 2F **75**
Denton. *Norf* 2E **67**
Denton. *Nptn* 5F **63**
Denton. *N Yor* 5D **98**
Denton. *Oxon* 5D **50**
Denver. *Norf* 5F **77**
Denwick. *Nmbd* 3G **121**
Deopham. *Norf* 5C **78**
Deopham Green. *Norf* 1C **66**
Depden. *Suff* 5G **65**
Depden Green. *Suff* 5G **65**
Deptford. *G Lon* 3E **39**
Deptford. *Wilts* 3F **23**
Derby. *Derb* 2A **74**
Derbyhaven. *IOM* 5B **108**
Derculich. *Per* 3F **143**
Dereham. *Norf* 4B **78**
Deri. *Cphy* 5E **47**
Derril. *Devn* 2D **10**
Derringstone. *Kent* 1G **29**
Derrington. *Shrp* 1A **60**
Derrington. *Staf* 3C **72**
Derriton. *Devn* 2D **10**
Derry. *Derr* 2C **174**
Derryguaig. *Arg* 5F **139**
Derry Hill. *Wilts* 4E **35**
Derrythorpe. *N Lin* 4B **94**
Dersingham. *Norf* 2F **77**
Dervaig. *Arg* 3F **139**
Derwen. *Den* 5C **82**
Derwen Gam. *Cdgn* 5D **56**
Derwenlas. *Powy* 1G **57**
Desborough. *Nptn* 2F **63**
Desford. *Leics* 5B **74**
Detchant. *Nmbd* 1E **121**
Dethick. *Derbs* 5H **85**
Detling. *Kent* 5B **40**
Deuchar. *Ang* 2D **144**
Deuddwr. *Powy* 4E **71**
Devauden. *Mon* 2H **33**
Devil's Bridge. *Cdgn* 3G **57**
Devitts Green. *Warw* 1G **61**
Devizes. *Wilts* 5F **35**
Devonport. *Plym* 3A **8**
Devonside. *Clac* 4B **136**
Devoran. *Corn* 5B **6**
Dewartown. *Midl* 3G **129**
Dewlish. *Dors* 3C **14**
Dewsall Court. *Here* 2H **47**
Dewsbury. *W Yor* 2C **92**
Dexbeer. *Devn* 2C **10**
Dhoon. *IOM* 3D **108**
Dhoor. *IOM* 2D **108**
Dhowin. *IOM* 1D **108**
Dial Green. *W Sus* 3A **26**
Dial Post. *W Sus* 4C **26**
Dibberford. *Dors* 2H **13**
Dibden. *Hants* 2C **16**
Dibden Purlieu. *Hants* 2C **16**
Dickleburgh. *Norf* 2D **66**
Didbrook. *Glos* 2F **49**
Didcot. *Oxon* 2D **36**
Diddington. *Cambs* 4A **64**
Diddlebury. *Shrp* 2H **59**
Didley. *Here* 2H **47**
Didling. *W Sus* 1G **17**
Didmarton. *Glos* 3D **34**
Didsbury. *G Man* 1C **84**
Didworthy. *Devn* 2C **8**
Digby. *Linc* 5H **87**
Digg. *High* 2D **154**
Diggle. *G Man* 4A **92**
Digmoor. *Lanc* 4C **90**
Digswell. *Herts* 4C **52**
Dihewyd. *Cdgn* 5D **57**
Dilham. *Norf* 3F **79**
Dilhorne. *Staf* 1D **72**
Dillarburn. *S Lan* 5B **128**
Dillington. *Cambs* 4A **64**
Dilston. *Nmbd* 3C **114**
Dilton Marsh. *Wilts* 2D **22**
Dilwyn. *Here* 5G **59**
Dimmer. *Som* 3B **22**
Dimple. *G Man* 3F **91**
Dinas. *Carm* 1G **43**
Dinas. *Gwyn* 5D **81** (nr. Caernarfon)
Dinas. *Gwyn* 2B **68** (nr. Tudweiliog)
Dinas Cross. *Pemb* 1E **43**
Dinas Dinlle. *Gwyn* 5D **80**
Dinas Mawddwy. *Gwyn* 4A **70**
Dinas Powys. *V Glam* 4E **33**
Dinbych. *Den* 4C **82**
Dinbych-y-Pysgod. *Pemb* 4F **43**
Dinckley. *Lanc* 1E **91**
Dinder. *Som* 2A **22**
Dinedor. *Here* 2A **48**
Dinedor Cross. *Here* 2A **48**
Dingestow. *Mon* 4H **47**
Dingle. *Mers* 2F **83**
Dingleden. *Kent* 2C **28**
Dingleton. *Bord* 1H **119**
Dingley. *Nptn* 2E **63**
Dingwall. *High* 3H **157**
Dinmael. *Cnwy* 1C **70**
Dinnet. *Abers* 4B **152**
Dinnington. *Som* 1H **13**
Dinnington. *S Yor* 2C **86**
Dinnington. *Tyne* 2F **115**
Dinorwig. *Gwyn* 4E **81**
Dinton. *Buck* 4F **51**
Dinton. *Wilts* 3F **23**
Dinworthy. *Devn* 1D **10**
Dipley. *Hants* 1F **25**
Dippen. *Arg* 2B **122**
Dippenhall. *Surr* 2G **25**
Dippertown. *Devn* 4E **11**
Dippin. *N Ayr* 3E **123**
Dipple. *S Ayr* 4B **116**
Diptford. *Devn* 3D **8**
Dipton. *Dur* 4E **115**
Dirleton. *E Lot* 1B **130**
Dirt Pot. *Nmbd* 5B **114**
Discoed. *Powy* 4E **59**
Diseworth. *Leics* 3B **74**
Dishes. *Orkn* 5F **172**
Dishforth. *N Yor* 2F **99**
Disley. *Ches E* 2D **85**
Diss. *Norf* 3D **66**
Disserth. *Powy* 5C **58**
Distington. *Cumb* 2B **102**
Ditchampton. *Wilts* 3F **23**
Ditcheat. *Som* 3B **22**
Ditchingham. *Norf* 1F **67**
Ditchling. *E Sus* 4E **27**
Ditteridge. *Wilts* 5D **34**
Dittisham. *Devn* 3E **9**
Ditton. *Hal* 2G **83**
Ditton. *Kent* 5B **40**
Ditton Green. *Cambs* 5F **65**
Ditton Priors. *Shrp* 2A **60**
Divach. *High* 1G **149**
Dixonfield. *High* 2D **168**
Dixton. *Glos* 2E **49**
Dixton. *Mon* 4A **48**
Dizzard. *Corn* 3B **10**
Doagh. *Newt* 3G **175**
Dobcross. *G Man* 4H **91**
Dobs Hill. *Flin* 4F **83**
Dobson's Bridge. *Shrp* 2G **71**
Dobwalls. *Corn* 2G **7**
Doccombe. *Devn* 4A **12**
Dochgarroch. *High* 4A **158**
Docking. *Norf* 2G **77**
Docklow. *Here* 5H **59**
Dockray. *Cumb* 2E **103**
Doc Penfro. *Pemb* 4D **42**
Dodbrooke. *Devn* 4D **8**
Doddenham. *Worc* 5B **60**
Doddinghurst. *Essx* 1G **39**
Doddington. *Cambs* 1C **64**
Doddington. *Kent* 5D **40**
Doddington. *Linc* 3G **87**
Doddington. *Nmbd* 1D **121**
Doddington. *Shrp* 3A **60**
Doddiscombsleigh. *Devn* 4B **12**
Doddshill. *Norf* 2G **77**
Dodford. *Nptn* 4D **62**
Dodford. *Worc* 3D **60**
Dodington. *Som* 2E **21**
Dodington. *S Glo* 4C **34**
Dodleston. *Ches W* 4F **83**
Dods Leigh. *Staf* 2E **73**
Dodworth. *S Yor* 4D **92**
Doe Lea. *Derbs* 4B **86**
Dogdyke. *Linc* 5B **88**
Dogmersfield. *Hants* 1F **25**
Dogsthorpe. *Pet* 5B **76**
Dog Village. *Devn* 3C **12**
Dolanog. *Powy* 4C **70**
Dolau. *Powy* 4D **58**
Dolau. *Rhon* 3D **32**
Dolbenmaen. *Gwyn* 1E **69**
Doley. *Staf* 3B **72**
Dol-fâch. *Powy* 5B **70** (nr. Llanbrynmair)
Dolfach. *Powy* 3B **58** (nr. Llanidloes)
Dolfor. *Powy* 2D **58**
Dolgarrog. *Cnwy* 4G **81**
Dolgellau. *Gwyn* 4G **69**
Dolgoch. *Gwyn* 5F **69**
Dol-gran. *Carm* 2E **45**
Dolhelfa. *Powy* 3B **58**
Doll. *High* 3F **165**
Dollar. *Clac* 4B **136**
Dolley Green. *Powy* 4E **59**
Dollingstown. *Cgvn* 5G **175**
Dollwen. *Cdgn* 2F **57**
Dolphin. *Flin* 3D **82**
Dolphingstone. *E Lot* 2G **129**
Dolphinholme. *Lanc* 4E **97**
Dolphinton. *S Lan* 5E **129**
Dolton. *Devn* 1F **11**
Dolwen. *Cnwy* 3A **82**
Dolwyddelan. *Cnwy* 5G **81**
Dol-y-Bont. *Cdgn* 2F **57**
Dolyhir. *Powy* 5E **59**
Domgay. *Powy* 4E **71**
Donaghadee. *Ards* 4J **175**
Doncaster. *S Yor* 4F **93**
Donhead St Andrew. *Wilts* 4E **23**
Donhead St Mary. *Wilts* 4E **23**
Doniford. *Som* 2D **20**
Donington. *Linc* 2B **76**
Donington. *Shrp* 5C **72**
Donington Eaudike. *Linc* 2B **76**
Donington le Heath. *Leics* 4B **74**
Donington on Bain. *Linc* 2B **88**
Donington South Ing. *Linc* 2B **76**
Donisthorpe. *Leics* 4H **73**
Donkey Street. *Kent* 2F **29**
Donkey Town. *Surr* 4A **38**
Donna Nook. *Linc* 1D **88**
Donnington. *Glos* 3G **49**
Donnington. *Here* 2C **48**
Donnington. *Shrp* 5H **71**
Donnington. *Telf* 4B **72**
Donnington. *W Ber* 5C **36**
Donnington. *W Sus* 2G **17**
Donyatt. *Som* 1G **13**
Doomsday Green. *W Sus* 3C **26**
Doonfoot. *S Ayr* 3C **116**
Doonholm. *S Ayr* 3C **116**
Dorback Lodge. *High* 2E **151**
Dorchester. *Dors* 3B **14**
Dorchester on Thames. *Oxon* 2D **36**
Dordon. *Warw* 5G **73**
Dore. *S Yor* 2H **85**
Dores. *High* 5H **157**
Dorking. *Surr* 1C **26**
Dorking Tye. *Suff* 2C **54**

Dormansland—Dunston

Dormansland. *Surr* 1F **27**
Dormans Park. *Surr* 1E **27**
Dormanstown. *Red C* 2C **106**
Dormington. *Here* 1A **48**
Dormston. *Worc* 5D **61**
Dorn. *Glos* 2H **49**
Dorney. *Buck* 3A **38**
Dornie. *High* 1A **148**
Dornoch. *High* 5E **165**
Dornock. *Dum* 3D **112**
Dorrery. *High* 3C **168**
Dorridge. *W Mid* 3F **61**
Dorrington. *Linc* 5H **87**
Dorrington. *Shrp* 5G **71**
Dorsington. *Warw* 1G **49**
Dorstone. *Here* 1G **47**
Dorton. *Buck* 4E **51**
Dosthill. *Staf* 5G **73**
Dotham. *IOA* 3C **80**
Dottery. *Dors* 3H **13**
Doublebois. *Corn* 2F **7**
Dougarie. *N Ayr* 2C **122**
Doughton. *Glos* 2D **35**
Douglas. *IOM* 4C **108**
Douglas. *S Lan* 1H **117**
Douglastown. *Ang* 4D **144**
Douglas Water. *S Lan* 1A **118**
Doulting. *Som* 2B **22**
Dounby. *Orkn* 5B **172**
Doune. *High* 2C **150**
(nr. Kingussie)
Doune. *High* 3B **164**
(nr. Lairg)
Doune. *Stir* 3G **135**
Dounie. *High* 4C **164**
(nr. Bonar Bridge)
Dounie. *High* 5D **164**
(nr. Tain)
Dounreay. *High* 2B **168**
Doura. *N Ayr* 5E **127**
Dousland. *Devn* 2B **8**
Dovaston. *Shrp* 3F **71**
Dove Holes. *Derbs* 3E **85**
Dovenby. *Cumb* 1B **102**
Dover. *Kent* 1H **29**
Dovercourt. *Essx* 2F **55**
Doverdale. *Worc* 4C **60**
Doveridge. *Derbs* 2F **73**
Doversgreen. *Surr* 1D **26**
Dowally. *Per* 4H **143**
Dowbridge. *Lanc* 1C **90**
Dowdeswell. *Glos* 4F **49**
Dowlais. *Mer T* 5D **46**
Dowland. *Devn* 1F **11**
Dowlands. *Devn* 3F **13**
Dowles. *Worc* 3B **60**
Dowlesgreen. *Wok* 5G **37**
Dowlish Wake. *Som* 1G **13**
Downall Green. *Mers* 4D **90**
Down Ampney. *Glos* 2G **35**
Downderry. *Corn* 3H **7**
(nr. Looe)
Downderry. *Corn* 3D **6**
(nr. St Austell)
Downe. *G Lon* 4F **39**
Downend. *IOW* 4D **16**
Downend. *S Glo* 4B **34**
Downend. *W Ber* 4C **36**
Down Field. *Cambs* 3F **65**
Downfield. *D'dee* 5C **144**
Downgate. *Corn* 5D **10**
(nr. Kelly Bray)
Downgate. *Corn* 5C **10**
(nr. Upton Cross)
Downham. *Essx* 1B **40**
Downham. *Lanc* 5G **97**
Downham. *Nmbd* 1C **120**
Downham Market. *Norf* 5F **77**
Down Hatherley. *Glos* 3D **48**
Downhead. *Som* 2B **22**
(nr. Frome)
Downhead. *Som* 4A **22**
(nr. Yeovil)
Downholland Cross. *Lanc* 4B **90**
Downholme. *N Yor* 5E **105**
Downies. *Abers* 4G **153**
Downley. *Buck* 2G **37**
Downpatrick. *Down* 5H **175**
Down St Mary. *Devn* 2H **11**
Downside. *Som* 1B **22**
(nr. Chilcompton)
Downside. *Som* 2B **22**
(nr. Shepton Mallet)
Downside. *Surr* 5C **38**
Down, The. *Shrp* 1A **60**
Down Thomas. *Devn* 3B **8**
Downton. *Hants* 3A **16**
Downton. *Wilts* 4G **23**
Downton on the Rock. *Here* 3G **59**
Dowsby. *Linc* 3A **76**
Dowsdale. *Linc* 4B **76**
Dowthwaitehead. *Cumb* 2E **103**
Doxey. *Staf* 3D **72**
Doxford. *Nmbd* 2F **121**
Doynton. *S Glo* 4C **34**
Drabblegate. *Norf* 3E **78**
Draethen. *Cphy* 3F **33**
Draffan. *S Lan* 5A **128**
Dragonby. *N Lin* 3C **94**
Dragons Green. *W Sus* 3C **26**
Drakelow. *Worc* 2C **60**
Drakemyre. *N Ayr* 4D **126**
Drakes Broughton. *Worc* 1E **49**
Drakes Cross. *Worc* 3E **61**
Drakewalls. *Corn* 5E **11**
Draperstown. *Mag* 3E **174**
Draughton. *Nptn* 3E **63**
Draughton. *N Yor* 4C **98**
Drax. *N Yor* 2G **93**
Draycot. *Oxon* 5E **51**
Draycote. *Warw* 3B **62**
Draycot Foliat. *Swin* 4G **35**
Draycott. *Derbs* 2B **74**
Draycott. *Glos* 2G **49**
Draycott. *Shrp* 1C **60**
Draycott. *Som* 1H **21**
(nr. Cheddar)
Draycott. *Som* 4A **22**
(nr. Yeovil)
Draycott. *Worc* 1D **48**
Draycott in the Clay. *Staf* 3F **73**
Draycott in the Moors. *Staf* 1D **73**
Drayford. *Devn* 1A **12**
Drayton. *Leics* 1F **63**
Drayton. *Linc* 2B **76**
Drayton. *Norf* 4D **78**
Drayton. *Nptn* 4C **62**
Drayton. *Oxon* 2C **36**
(nr. Abingdon)
Drayton. *Oxon* 1C **50**
(nr. Banbury)
Drayton. *Port* 2E **17**
Drayton. *Som* 4H **21**
Drayton. *Warw* 5F **61**
Drayton. *Worc* 3D **60**
Drayton Bassett. *Staf* 5F **73**
Drayton Beauchamp. *Buck* 4H **51**
Drayton Parslow. *Buck* 3G **51**
Drayton St Leonard. *Oxon* 2D **36**
Drebley. *N Yor* 4C **98**
Dreenhill. *Pemb* 3D **42**
Drefach. *Carm* 4F **45**
(nr. Meidrim)
Drefach. *Carm* 2D **44**
(nr. Newcastle Emlyn)
Drefach. *Carm* 2G **43**
(nr. Tumble)
Drefach. *Cdgn* 1E **45**
Dreghorn. *N Ayr* 1C **116**
Drellingore. *Kent* 1G **29**
Drem. *E Lot* 2B **130**
Dreumasdal. *W Isl* 5C **170**
Drewsteignton. *Devn* 3H **11**
Driby. *Linc* 3C **88**
Driffield. *E Yor* 4E **101**
Driffield. *Glos* 2F **35**
Drift. *Corn* 4B **4**
Drigg. *Cumb* 5B **102**
Drighlington. *W Yor* 2C **92**
Drimnin. *High* 3G **139**
Drimpton. *Dors* 2H **13**
Dringhoe. *E Yor* 4F **101**
Drinisiadar. *W Isl* 8D **171**
Drinkstone. *Suff* 4B **66**
Drinkstone Green. *Suff* 4B **66**
Drointon. *Staf* 3E **73**
Droitwich Spa. *Worc* 4C **60**
Droman. *High* 3B **166**
Dromore. *Ban* 5G **175**
Dromore. *Omag* 4C **174**
Dron. *Per* 2D **136**
Dronfield. *Derbs* 3A **86**
Dronfield Woodhouse. *Derbs* 3H **85**
Drongan. *E Ayr* 3D **116**
Dronley. *Ang* 5C **144**
Droop. *Dors* 2C **14**
Drope. *V Glam* 4E **32**
Droxford. *Hants* 1E **16**
Droylsden. *G Man* 1C **84**
Druggers End. *Worc* 2C **48**
Druid. *Den* 1C **70**
Druid's Heath. *W Mid* 5E **73**
Druidston. *Pemb* 3C **42**
Druim. *High* 3D **158**
Druimarbin. *High* 1E **141**
Druim Fhearna. *High* 2E **147**
Druimindarroch. *High* 5E **147**
Druim Saighdinis. *W Isl* 2D **170**
Drum. *Per* 3C **136**
Drumaness. *Down* 5H **175**
Drumbeg. *High* 5B **166**
Drumblade. *Abers* 4C **160**
Drumbuie. *Dum* 1C **110**
Drumbuie. *High* 5G **155**
Drumburgh. *Cumb* 4D **112**
Drumburn. *Dum* 3A **112**
Drumchapel. *Glas* 2G **127**
Drumchardine. *High* 4H **157**
Drumchork. *High* 5C **162**
Drumclog. *S Lan* 1F **117**
Drumeldrie. *Fife* 3G **137**
Drumelzier. *Bord* 1D **118**
Drumfearn. *High* 2E **147**
Drumgask. *High* 4A **150**
Drumgelloch. *N Lan* 3A **128**
Drumgley. *Ang* 3D **144**
Drumguish. *High* 4B **150**
Drumin. *Mor* 5F **159**
Drumindorsair. *High* 4G **157**
Drumlamford House. *S Ayr* 2H **109**
Drumlasie. *Abers* 3D **152**
Drumlemble. *Arg* 4A **122**
Drumlithie. *Abers* 5E **153**
Drummoddie. *Dum* 5A **110**
Drummond. *High* 2A **158**
Drummore. *Dum* 5E **109**
Drummuir. *Mor* 4A **160**
Drumnadrochit. *High* 5H **157**
Drumnagorrach. *Mor* 3C **160**
Drumnakilly. *Omag* 4D **174**
Drumoak. *Abers* 4E **153**
Drumrunie. *High* 3F **163**
Drumry. *W Dun* 2G **127**
Drums. *Abers* 1G **153**
Drumsleet. *Dum* 2G **111**
Drumsmittal. *High* 4A **158**
Drums of Park. *Abers* 3C **160**
Drumsturdy. *Ang* 5D **145**
Drumtochty Castle. *Abers* 5D **152**
Drumuie. *High* 4D **154**
Drumuillie. *High* 1D **150**
Drumvaich. *Stir* 3F **135**
Drumwhindle. *Abers* 5G **161**
Drunkendub. *Ang* 4F **145**
Drury. *Flin* 4E **83**
Drury Square. *Norf* 4B **78**
Drybeck. *Cumb* 3H **103**
Drybridge. *Mor* 2B **160**
Drybridge. *N Ayr* 1C **116**
Drybrook. *Glos* 4B **48**
Drybrook. *Here* 4A **48**
Dryburgh. *Bord* 1H **119**
Dry Doddington. *Linc* 1F **75**
Dry Drayton. *Cambs* 4C **64**
Drym. *Corn* 3D **4**
Drymen. *Stir* 1F **127**
Drymuir. *Abers* 4G **161**
Drynachan Lodge. *High* 5C **158**
Drynie Park. *High* 3H **157**
Drynoch. *High* 5D **154**
Dry Sandford. *Oxon* 5C **50**
Dryslwyn. *Carm* 3F **45**
Dry Street. *Essx* 2A **40**
Dryton. *Shrp* 5H **71**
Dubford. *Abers* 2E **161**
Dubiton. *Abers* 3D **160**
Dubton. *Ang* 3E **145**
Duchally. *High* 2A **164**
Duck End. *Essx* 3G **53**
Duckington. *Ches W* 5G **83**
Ducklington. *Oxon* 5B **50**
Duckmanton. *Derbs* 3B **86**
Duck Street. *Hants* 2B **24**
Dudbridge. *Glos* 5D **48**
Duddenhoe End. *Essx* 2E **53**
Duddingston. *Edin* 2F **129**
Duddington. *Nptn* 5G **75**
Duddleswell. *E Sus* 3F **27**
Duddo. *Nmbd* 5F **131**
Duddon. *Ches W* 4H **83**
Duddon Bridge. *Cumb* 1A **96**
Dudleston. *Shrp* 2F **71**
Dudleston Heath. *Shrp* 2F **71**
Dudley. *Tyne* 2F **115**
Dudley. *W Mid* 2D **60**
Dudston. *Shrp* 1E **59**
Dudwells. *Pemb* 2D **42**
Duffield. *Derbs* 1H **73**
Duffryn. *Neat* 2B **32**
Dufftown. *Mor* 4H **159**
Duffus. *Mor* 2F **159**
Dufton. *Cumb* 2H **103**
Duggleby. *N Yor* 3C **100**
Duirinish. *High* 5G **155**
Duisdalemore. *High* 2E **147**
Duisdeil Mòr. *High* 2E **147**
Duisky. *High* 1E **141**
Dukesfield. *Nmbd* 4C **114**
Dukestown. *Blae* 5E **47**
Dukinfield. *G Man* 1D **84**
Dulas. *IOA* 2D **81**
Dulcote. *Som* 2A **22**
Dulford. *Devn* 2D **12**
Dull. *Per* 4F **143**
Dullatur. *N Lan* 2A **128**
Dullingham. *Cambs* 5F **65**
Dullingham Ley. *Cambs* 5F **65**
Dulnain Bridge. *High* 1D **151**
Duloe. *Bed* 4A **64**
Duloe. *Corn* 3G **7**
Dulverton. *Som* 4C **20**
Dulwich. *G Lon* 3E **39**
Dumbarton. *W Dun* 2F **127**
Dumbleton. *Glos* 2F **49**
Dumfin. *Arg* 1E **127**
Dumfries. *Dum* 2A **112**
Dumgoyne. *Stir* 1G **127**
Dummer. *Hants* 2D **24**
Dumpford. *W Sus* 4G **25**
Dun. *Ang* 2F **145**
Dunagoil. *Arg* 4B **126**
Dunalastair. *Per* 3E **142**
Dunan. *High* 1D **147**
Dunball. *Som* 2G **21**
Dunbar. *E Lot* 2C **130**
Dunbeath. *High* 5D **168**
Dunbeg. *Arg* 5C **140**
Dunblane. *Stir* 3G **135**
Dunbog. *Fife* 2E **137**
Dunbridge. *Hants* 4B **24**
Duncanston. *Abers* 1C **152**
Duncanston. *High* 3H **157**
Dun Charlabhaigh. *W Isl* 3D **171**
Dunchideock. *Devn* 4B **12**
Dunchurch. *Warw* 3B **62**
Duncote. *Nptn* 5D **62**
Duncow. *Dum* 1A **112**
Duncrievie. *Per* 3D **136**
Duncton. *W Sus* 4A **26**
Dundee. *D'dee* 5D **144**
Dundee Airport. *D'dee* 1F **137**
Dundon. *Som* 3H **21**
Dundonald. *Cast* 4H **175**
Dundonald. *S Ayr* 1C **116**
Dundonnell. *High* 5E **163**
Dundraw. *Cumb* 5D **112**
Dundreggan. *High* 2F **149**
Dundrennan. *Dum* 5E **111**
Dundridge. *Hants* 1D **16**
Dundrum. *Down* 6H **175**
Dundry. *N Som* 5A **34**
Dunecht. *Abers* 3E **153**
Dunfermline. *Fife* 1D **129**
Dunford Bridge. *S Yor* 4B **92**
Dungannon. *Dngn* 4E **174**
Dungate. *Kent* 5D **40**
Dunge. *Wilts* 1D **23**
Dungeness. *Kent* 4E **29**
Dungiven. *Lim* 2D **174**
Dungworth. *S Yor* 2G **85**
Dunham-on-the-Hill. *Ches W* 3G **83**
Dunham-on-Trent. *Notts* 3F **87**
Dunhampton. *Worc* 4C **60**
Dunham Town. *G Man* 2B **84**
Dunham Woodhouses. *G Man* 2B **84**
Dunholme. *Linc* 3H **87**
Dunino. *Fife* 2H **137**
Dunipace. *Falk* 1B **128**
Dunira. *Per* 1G **135**
Dunkeld. *Per* 4H **143**
Dunkerton. *Bath* 1C **22**
Dunkeswell. *Devn* 2E **13**
Dunkeswick. *N Yor* 5F **99**
Dunkirk. *Kent* 5E **41**
Dunkirk. *S Glo* 3C **34**
Dunkirk. *Staf* 5C **84**
Dunkirk. *Wilts* 5E **35**
Dunk's Green. *Kent* 5H **39**
Dunlappie. *Ang* 2E **145**
Dunley. *Hants* 1C **24**
Dunley. *Worc* 4B **60**
Dunlichity Lodge. *High* 5A **158**
Dunlop. *E Ayr* 5F **127**
Dunloy. *Bmny* 2F **175**
Dunmaglass Lodge. *High* 1H **149**
Dunmore. *Arg* 3F **125**
Dunmore. *Falk* 1B **128**
Dunmore. *High* 4H **157**
Dunmurry. *Lis* 4G **175**
Dunnet. *High* 1E **169**
Dunnichen. *Ang* 4E **145**
Dunning. *Per* 2C **136**
Dunnington. *E Yor* 4F **101**
Dunnington. *Warw* 5E **61**
Dunnington. *York* 4A **100**
Dunningwell. *Cumb* 1A **96**
Dunnockshaw. *Lanc* 2G **91**
Dunoon. *Arg* 2C **126**
Dunphail. *Mor* 4E **159**
Dunragit. *Dum* 4G **109**
Dunrostan. *Arg* 1F **125**
Duns. *Bord* 4D **130**
Dunsby. *Linc* 3A **76**
Dunscar. *G Man* 3F **91**
Dunscore. *Dum* 1F **111**
Dunscroft. *S Yor* 4G **93**
Dunsdale. *Red C* 3D **106**
Dunsden Green. *Oxon* 4F **37**
Dunsfold. *Surr* 2B **26**
Dunsford. *Devn* 4B **12**
Dunshalt. *Fife* 2E **137**
Dunshillock. *Abers* 4G **161**
Dunsley. *N Yor* 3F **107**
Dunsley. *Staf* 2C **60**
Dunsmore. *Buck* 5G **51**
Dunsop Bridge. *Lanc* 4F **97**
Dunstable. *C Beds* 3A **52**
Dunstal. *Staf* 3E **73**
Dunstall. *Staf* 3F **73**
Dunstall Green. *Suff* 4G **65**
Dunstall Hill. *W Mid* 5D **72**
Dunstan. *Nmbd* 3G **121**
Dunster. *Som* 2C **20**
Duns Tew. *Oxon* 3C **50**
Dunston. *Linc* 4H **87**

Dunston—East Lulworth

Dunston. *Norf* 5E 79
Dunston. *Staf* 4D 72
Dunston. *Tyne* 3F 115
Dunstone. *Devn* 3B 8
Dunston Heath. *Staf* 4D 72
Dunsville. *S Yor* 4G 93
Dunswell. *E Yor* 1D 94
Dunsyre. *S Lan* 5D 128
Dunterton. *Devn* 5D 11
Duntisbourne Abbots. *Glos* 5E 49
Duntisbourne Leer. *Glos* 5E 49
Duntisbourne Rouse. *Glos* 5E 49
Duntish. *Dors* 2B 14
Duntocher. *W Dun* 2F 127
Dunton. *Buck* 3G 51
Dunton. *C Beds* 1C 52
Dunton. *Norf* 2A 78
Dunton Bassett. *Leics* 1C 62
Dunton Green. *Kent* 5G 39
Dunton Patch. *Norf* 2A 78
Duntulm. *High* 1D 154
Dunure. *S Ayr* 3B 116
Dunvant. *Swan* 3E 31
Dunvegan. *High* 4B 154
Dunwich. *Suff* 3G 67
Dunwood. *Staf* 5D 84
Durdar. *Cumb* 4F 113
Durgates. *E Sus* 2H 27
Durham. *Dur* 5F 115
Durham Tees Valley Airport. *Darl* 3A 106
Durisdeer. *Dum* 4A 118
Durisdeermill. *Dum* 4A 118
Durkar. *W Yor* 3D 92
Durleigh. *Som* 3F 21
Durley. *Hants* 1D 16
Durley. *Wilts* 5H 35
Durley Street. *Hants* 1D 16
Durlow Common. *Here* 2B 48
Durnamuck. *High* 4E 163
Durness. *High* 2E 166
Durno. *Abers* 1E 152
Durns Town. *Hants* 3A 16
Duror. *High* 3D 141
Durran. *Arg* 3G 133
Durran. *High* 2D 169
Durrant Green. *Kent* 2C 28
Durrants. *Hants* 1F 17
Durrington. *W Sus* 5C 26
Durrington. *Wilts* 2G 23
Dursley. *Glos* 2C 34
Dursley Cross. *Glos* 4B 48
Durston. *Som* 4F 21
Durweston. *Dors* 2D 14
Dury. *Shet* 6F 173
Duston. *Nptn* 4E 63
Duthil. *High* 1D 150
Dutlas. *Powy* 3E 58
Duton Hill. *Essx* 3G 53
Dutson. *Corn* 4D 10
Dutton. *Ches W* 3H 83
Duxford. *Cambs* 1E 53
Duxford. *Oxon* 2B 36
Dwygyfylchi. *Cnwy* 3G 81
Dwyran. *IOA* 4D 80
Dyce. *Aber* 2F 153
Dyffryn. *B'end* 2B 32
Dyffryn. *Carm* 2H 43
Dyffryn. *Pemb* 1D 42
Dyffryn. *V Glam* 4D 32
Dyffryn Ardudwy. *Gwyn* 3E 69
Dyffryn Castell. *Cdgn* 2G 57
Dyffryn Ceidrych. *Carm* 3H 45
Dyffryn Cellwen. *Neat* 5B 46
Dyke. *Linc* 3A 76
Dyke. *Mor* 3D 159
Dykehead. *Ang* 2C 144
Dykehead. *N Lan* 3B 128
Dykehead. *Stir* 4E 135
Dykend. *Ang* 3B 144
Dykesfield. *Cumb* 4E 112
Dylife. *Powy* 1A 58
Dymchurch. *Kent* 3F 29
Dymock. *Glos* 2C 48
Dyrham. *S Glo* 4C 34
Dysart. *Fife* 4F 137
Dyserth. *Den* 3C 82

E

Eachwick. *Nmbd* 2E 115
Eadar Dha Fhadhail. *W Isl* 4C 171
Eagland Hill. *Lanc* 5D 96
Eagle. *Linc* 4F 87
Eagle Barnsdale. *Linc* 4F 87
Eagle Moor. *Linc* 4F 87
Eaglescliffe. *Stoc T* 3B 106
Eaglesfield. *Cumb* 2B 102
Eaglesfield. *Dum* 2D 112
Eaglesham. *E Ren* 4G 127
Eaglethorpe. *Nptn* 1H 63
Eagley. *G Man* 3F 91
Eairy. *IOM* 4B 108
Eakley Lanes. *Mil* 5F 63
Eakring. *Notts* 4D 86
Ealand. *N Lin* 3A 94
Ealing. *G Lon* 2C 38
Eallabus. *Arg* 3B 124
Eals. *Nmbd* 4H 113
Eamont Bridge. *Cumb* 2G 103
Earby. *Lanc* 5B 98
Earcroft. *Bkbn* 2E 91
Eardington. *Shrp* 1B 60
Eardisland. *Here* 5G 59
Eardisley. *Here* 1G 47
Eardiston. *Shrp* 3F 71
Eardiston. *Worc* 4A 60
Earith. *Cambs* 3C 64
Earlais. *High* 2C 154
Earle. *Nmbd* 2D 121
Earlesfield. *Linc* 2G 75
Earlestown. *Mers* 1H 83
Earley. *Wok* 4F 37
Earlham. *Norf* 5D 78
Earlish. *High* 2C 154
Earls Barton. *Nptn* 4F 63
Earls Colne. *Essx* 3B 54
Earls Common. *Worc* 5D 60
Earl's Croome. *Worc* 1D 48
Earlsdon. *W Mid* 3H 61
Earlsferry. *Fife* 3G 137
Earlsford. *Abers* 5F 161
Earl's Green. *Suff* 4C 66
Earlsheaton. *W Yor* 2C 92
Earl Shilton. *Leics* 1B 62
Earl Soham. *Suff* 4E 67
Earl Sterndale. *Derbs* 4E 85
Earlston. *E Ayr* 1D 116
Earlston. *Bord* 1H 119
Earl Stonham. *Suff* 5D 66
Earlstoun. *Dum* 1D 110
Earlswood. *Mon* 2H 33
Earlswood. *Warw* 3F 61
Earlyvale. *Bord* 4F 129
Earnley. *W Sus* 3G 17
Earsairidh. *W Isl* 9C 170
Earsdon. *Tyne* 2G 115
Earsham. *Norf* 2F 67
Earsham Street. *Suff* 3E 67
Earswick. *York* 4A 100
Eartham. *W Sus* 5A 26
Earthcott Green. *S Glo* 3B 34
Easby. *N Yor* 4C 106 (nr. Great Ayton)
Easby. *N Yor* 4E 105 (nr. Richmond)
Easdale. *Arg* 2E 133
Easebourne. *W Sus* 4G 25
Easenhall. *Warw* 3B 62
Eashing. *Surr* 1A 26
Easington. *Buck* 4E 51
Easington. *Dur* 5H 115
Easington. *E Yor* 3G 95
Easington. *Nmbd* 1F 121
Easington. *Oxon* 2C 50 (nr. Banbury)
Easington. *Oxon* 2E 37 (nr. Watlington)
Easington. *Red C* 3E 107
Easington Colliery. *Dur* 5H 115
Easington Lane. *Tyne* 5G 115
Easingwold. *N Yor* 2H 99
Eassie. *Ang* 4C 144
Eassie and Nevay. *Ang* 4C 144
East Aberthaw. *V Glam* 5D 32
Eastacombe. *Devn* 4F 19
Eastacott. *Devn* 4G 19
East Allington. *Devn* 4D 8
East Anstey. *Devn* 4B 20
East Anton. *Hants* 2B 24
East Appleton. *N Yor* 5F 105
East Ardsley. *W Yor* 2D 92
East Ashley. *Devn* 1G 11
East Ashling. *W Sus* 2G 17
East Aston. *Hants* 2C 24
East Ayton. *N Yor* 1D 101
East Barkwith. *Linc* 2A 88
East Barnby. *N Yor* 3F 107
East Barnet. *G Lon* 1D 39
East Barns. *E Lot* 2D 130
East Barsham. *Norf* 2B 78
East Beach. *W Sus* 3G 17
East Beckham. *Norf* 2D 78
East Bedfont. *G Lon* 3B 38
East Bennan. *N Ayr* 3D 123
East Bergholt. *Suff* 2D 54
East Bierley. *W Yor* 2C 92
East Bilney. *Norf* 4B 78
East Blatchington. *E Sus* 5F 27
East Bloxworth. *Dors* 3D 15
East Boldre. *Hants* 2B 16
East Bolton. *Nmbd* 3F 121
Eastbourne. *Darl* 3F 105
Eastbourne. *E Sus* 5H 27
East Brent. *Som* 1G 21
East Bridge. *Suff* 4G 67
East Bridgford. *Notts* 1D 74
East Briscoe. *Dur* 3C 104
East Buckland. *Devn* 3G 19 (nr. Barnstaple)
East Buckland. *Devn* 4C 8 (nr. Thurlestone)
East Budleigh. *Devn* 4D 12
Eastburn. *W Yor* 5C 98
East Burnham. *Buck* 2A 38
East Burrafirth. *Shet* 6E 173
East Burton. *Dors* 4D 14
Eastbury. *Herts* 1B 38
Eastbury. *W Ber* 4B 36
East Butsfield. *Dur* 5E 115
East Butterleigh. *Devn* 2C 12
East Butterwick. *N Lin* 4B 94
Eastby. *N Yor* 4C 98
East Calder. *W Lot* 3D 129
East Carleton. *Norf* 5D 78
East Carlton. *Nptn* 2F 63
East Carlton. *W Yor* 5E 98
East Chaldon. *Dors* 4C 14
East Challow. *Oxon* 3B 36
East Charleton. *Devn* 4D 8
East Chelborough. *Dors* 2A 14
East Chiltington. *E Sus* 4E 27
East Chinnock. *Som* 1H 13
East Chisenbury. *Wilts* 1G 23
Eastchurch. *Kent* 3D 40
East Clandon. *Surr* 5B 38
East Claydon. *Buck* 3F 51
East Clevedon. *N Som* 4H 33
East Clyne. *High* 3F 165
East Clyth. *High* 5E 169
East Coker. *Som* 1A 14
Eastcombe. *Glos* 5D 49
East Combe. *Som* 3E 21
East Common. *N Yor* 1G 93
East Compton. *Som* 2B 22
East Cornworthy. *Devn* 3E 9
Eastcote. *G Lon* 2C 38
Eastcote. *Nptn* 5D 62
Eastcote. *W Mid* 3F 61
Eastcott. *Corn* 1C 10
Eastcott. *Wilts* 1F 23
East Cottingwith. *E Yor* 5B 100
Eastcourt. *Wilts* 5H 35 (nr. Pewsey)
Eastcourt. *Wilts* 2E 35 (nr. Tetbury)
East Cowes. *IOW* 3D 16
East Cowick. *E Yor* 2G 93
East Cowton. *N Yor* 4A 106
East Cramlington. *Nmbd* 2F 115
East Cranmore. *Som* 2B 22
East Creech. *Dors* 4E 15
East Croachy. *High* 1A 150
East Dean. *E Sus* 5G 27
East Dean. *Glos* 3B 48
East Dean. *Hants* 4A 24
East Dean. *W Sus* 4A 26
East Down. *Devn* 2G 19
East Drayton. *Notts* 3E 87
East Dundry. *N Som* 5A 34
East Ella. *Hull* 2D 94
East End. *Cambs* 3C 64
East End. *Dors* 3E 15
East End. *E Yor* 4F 101 (nr. Ulrome)
East End. *E Yor* 2F 95 (nr. Withernsea)
East End. *Hants* 3B 16 (nr. Lymington)
East End. *Hants* 5C 36 (nr. Newbury)
East End. *Herts* 3E 53
East End. *Kent* 3D 40 (nr. Minster)
East End. *Kent* 2C 28 (nr. Tenterden)
East End. *N Som* 4H 33
East End. *Oxon* 4B 50
East End. *Som* 1A 22
East End. *Suff* 2E 54
Easter Ardross. *High* 1A 158
Easter Balgedie. *Per* 3D 136
Easter Balmoral. *Abers* 4G 151
Easter Brae. *High* 2A 158
Easter Buckieburn. *Stir* 1A 128
Easter Bush. *Midl* 3F 129
Easter Compton. *S Glo* 3A 34
Easter Fearn. *High* 5D 164
Easter Galcantray. *High* 4C 158
Eastergate. *W Sus* 5A 26
Easterhouse. *Glas* 3H 127
Easter Howgate. *Midl* 3F 129
Easter Kinkell. *High* 3H 157
Easter Lednathie. *Ang* 2C 144
Easter Ogil. *Ang* 2D 144
Easter Ord. *Abers* 3F 153
Easter Quarff. *Shet* 8F 173
Easter Rhynd. *Per* 2D 136
Easter Skeld. *Shet* 7E 173
Easter Suddie. *High* 3A 158
Easterton. *Wilts* 1F 23
Eastertown. *Som* 1G 21
Easter Tulloch. *Abers* 1G 145
East Everleigh. *Wilts* 1H 23
East Farleigh. *Kent* 5B 40
East Farndon. *Nptn* 2E 62
East Ferry. *Linc* 1F 87
Eastfield. *N Lan* 3B 128 (nr. Caldercruix)
Eastfield. *N Lan* 3B 128 (nr. Harthill)
Eastfield. *N Yor* 1E 101
Eastfield. *S Lan* 3H 127
Eastfield Hall. *Nmbd* 4G 121
East Fortune. *E Lot* 2B 130
East Garforth. *W Yor* 1E 93
East Garston. *W Ber* 4B 36
Eastgate. *Dur* 1C 104
Eastgate. *Norf* 3D 78
East Ginge. *Oxon* 3C 36
East Gores. *Essx* 3B 54
East Goscote. *Leics* 4D 74
East Grafton. *Wilts* 5A 36
East Green. *Suff* 5F 65
East Grimstead. *Wilts* 4H 23
East Grinstead. *W Sus* 2E 27
East Guldeford. *E Sus* 3D 28
East Haddon. *Nptn* 4D 62
East Hagbourne. *Oxon* 3D 36
East Halton. *N Lin* 2E 95
East Ham. *G Lon* 2F 39
Eastham. *Mers* 2F 83
Eastham. *Worc* 4A 60
Eastham Ferry. *Mers* 2F 83
Easthampstead. *Brac* 5G 37
Easthampton. *Here* 4G 59
East Hanney. *Oxon* 2C 36
East Hanningfield. *Essx* 5A 54
East Hardwick. *W Yor* 3E 93
East Harling. *Norf* 2B 66
East Harlsey. *N Yor* 5B 106
East Harnham. *Wilts* 4G 23
East Harptree. *Bath* 1A 22
East Hartford. *Nmbd* 2F 115
East Harting. *W Sus* 1G 17
East Hatch. *Wilts* 4E 23
East Hatley. *Cambs* 5B 64
Easthaugh. *Norf* 4C 78
East Hauxwell. *N Yor* 5E 105
East Haven. *Ang* 5E 145
Eastheath. *Wok* 5G 37
East Heckington. *Linc* 1A 76
East Hedleyhope. *Dur* 5E 115
East Helmsdale. *High* 2H 165
East Hendred. *Oxon* 3C 36
East Heslerton. *N Yor* 2D 100
East Hoathly. *E Sus* 4G 27
East Holme. *Dors* 4D 15
Easthope. *Shrp* 1H 59
Easthorpe. *Essx* 3C 54
Easthorpe. *Leics* 2F 75
East Horrington. *Som* 2A 22
East Horsley. *Surr* 5B 38
East Horton. *Nmbd* 1E 121
Easthouses. *Midl* 3G 129
East Howe. *Bour* 3F 15
East Huntspill. *Som* 2G 21
East Hyde. *C Beds* 4B 52
East Ilsley. *W Ber* 3C 36
Eastington. *Devn* 2H 11
Eastington. *Glos* 4G 49 (nr. Northleach)
Eastington. *Glos* 5C 48 (nr. Stonehouse)
East Keal. *Linc* 4C 88
East Kennett. *Wilts* 5G 35
East Keswick. *W Yor* 5F 99
East Kilbride. *S Lan* 4H 127
East Kirkby. *Linc* 4C 88
East Knapton. *N Yor* 2C 100
East Knighton. *Dors* 4D 14
East Knowstone. *Devn* 4B 20
East Knoyle. *Wilts* 3D 23
East Kyloe. *Nmbd* 1E 121
East Lambrook. *Som* 1H 13
East Langdon. *Kent* 1H 29
East Langton. *Leics* 1E 63
East Langwell. *High* 3E 164
East Lavant. *W Sus* 2G 17
East Lavington. *W Sus* 4A 26
East Layton. *N Yor* 4E 105
Eastleach Martin. *Glos* 5H 49
Eastleach Turville. *Glos* 5G 49
East Leake. *Notts* 3C 74
East Learmouth. *Nmbd* 1C 120
Eastleigh. *Devn* 4E 19 (nr. Bideford)
East Leigh. *Devn* 2G 11 (nr. Crediton)
East Leigh. *Devn* 3C 8 (nr. Modbury)
Eastleigh. *Hants* 1C 16
East Lexham. *Norf* 4A 78
East Lilburn. *Nmbd* 2E 121
Eastling. *Kent* 5D 40
East Linton. *E Lot* 2B 130
East Liss. *Hants* 4F 25
East Lockinge. *Oxon* 3C 36
East Looe. *Corn* 3G 7
East Lound. *N Lin* 1E 87
East Lulworth. *Dors* 4D 14

Elston. *Notts* 1E 75
Elston. *Wilts* 2F 23
Elstone. *Devn* 1G 11
Elstow. *Bed* 1A 52
Elstree. *Herts* 1C 38
Elstronwick. *E Yor* 1F 95
Elswick. *Lanc* 1C 90
Elswick. *Tyne* 3F 115
Elsworth. *Cambs* 4C 64
Elterwater. *Cumb* 4E 103
Eltham. *G Lon* 3F 39
Eltisley. *Cambs* 5B 64
Elton. *Cambs* 1H 63
Elton. *Ches W* 3G 83
Elton. *Derbs* 4G 85
Elton. *Glos* 4C 48
Elton. *G Man* 3F 91
Elton. *Here* 3G 59
Elton. *Notts* 2E 75
Elton. *Stoc T* 3B 106
Elton Green. *Ches W* 3G 83
Eltringham. *Nmbd* 3D 115
Elvanfoot. *S Lan* 3B 118
Elvaston. *Derbs* 2B 74
Elveden. *Suff* 3H 65
Elvetham Heath. *Hants* 1F 25
Elvingston. *E Lot* 2A 130
Elvington. *Kent* 5G 41
Elvington. *York* 5B 100
Elwick. *Hart* 1B 106
Elwick. *Nmbd* 1F 121
Elworth. *Ches E* 4B 84
Elworth. *Dors* 4A 14
Elworthy. *Som* 3D 20
Ely. *Cambs* 2E 65
Ely. *Card* 4E 33
Emberton. *Mil* 1G 51
Embleton. *Cumb* 1C 102
Embleton. *Dur* 2B 106
Embleton. *Nmbd* 2G 121
Embo. *High* 4F 165
Emborough. *Som* 1B 22
Embo Street. *High* 4F 165
Embsay. *N Yor* 4C 98
Emery Down. *Hants* 2A 16
Emley. *W Yor* 3C 92
Emmbrook. *Wok* 5F 37
Emmer Green. *Read* 4F 37
Emmington. *Oxon* 5F 51
Emneth. *Norf* 5D 77
Emneth Hungate. *Norf* 5E 77
Empingham. *Rut* 5G 75
Empshott. *Hants* 3F 25
Emsworth. *Hants* 2F 17
Enborne. *W Ber* 5C 36
Enborne Row. *W Ber* 5C 36
Enchmarsh. *Shrp* 1H 59
Enderby. *Leics* 1C 62
Endmoor. *Cumb* 1E 97
Endon. *Staf* 5D 84
Endon Bank. *Staf* 5D 84
Enfield. *G Lon* 1E 39
Enfield Wash. *G Lon* 1E 39
Enford. *Wilts* 1G 23
Engine Common. *S Glo* 3B 34
Englefield. *W Ber* 4E 37
Englefield Green. *Surr* 3A 38
Englesea-brook. *Ches E* 5B 84
English Bicknor. *Glos* 4A 48
Englishcombe. *Bath* 5C 34
English Frankton. *Shrp* 3G 71
Enham Alamein. *Hants* 2B 24
Enmore. *Som* 3F 21
Ennerdale Bridge. *Cumb* 3B 102
Enniscaven. *Corn* 3D 6
Enniskillen. *Ferm* 5B 174
Enoch. *Dum* 4A 118
Enochdhu. *Per* 2H 143
Ensay. *Arg* 4E 139
Ensbury. *Bour* 3F 15
Ensdon. *Shrp* 4G 71
Ensis. *Devn* 4F 19
Enson. *Staf* 3D 72
Enstone. *Oxon* 3B 50
Enterkinfoot. *Dum* 4A 118
Enville. *Staf* 2C 60
Eolaigearraidh. *W Isl* 8C 170
Eorabus. *Arg* 1A 132
Eoropaidh. *W Isl* 1H 171
Epney. *Glos* 4C 48
Epperstone. *Notts* 1D 74
Epping. *Essx* 5E 53
Epping Green. *Essx* 5E 53
Epping Green. *Herts* 5C 52
Epping Upland. *Essx* 5E 53
Eppleby. *N Yor* 3E 105
Eppleworth. *E Yor* 1D 94
Epsom. *Surr* 4D 38
Epwell. *Oxon* 1B 50
Epworth. *N Lin* 4A 94
Epworth Turbary. *N Lin* 4A 94
Erbistock. *Wrex* 1F 71
Erbusaig. *High* 1F 147
Erchless Castle. *High* 4G 157
Erdington. *W Mid* 1F 61
Eredine. *Arg* 3G 133
Eriboll. *High* 3E 167
Ericstane. *Dum* 3C 118
Eridge Green. *E Sus* 2G 27
Erines. *Arg* 2G 125
Eriswell. *Suff* 3G 65
Erith. *G Lon* 3G 39
Erlestoke. *Wilts* 1E 23
Ermine. *Linc* 3G 87
Ermington. *Devn* 3C 8
Ernesettle. *Plym* 3A 8
Erpingham. *Norf* 2D 78
Erriottwood. *Kent* 5D 40
Errogie. *High* 1H 149
Errol. *Per* 1E 137
Errol Station. *Per* 1E 137
Erskine. *Ren* 2F 127
Erskine Bridge. *Ren* 2F 127
Ervie. *Dum* 3F 109
Erwarton. *Suff* 2F 55
Erwood. *Powy* 1D 46
Eryholme. *N Yor* 4A 106
Eryrys. *Den* 5E 82
Escalls. *Corn* 4A 4
Escomb. *Dur* 1E 105
Escrick. *N Yor* 5A 100
Esgair. *Carm* 3D 45
(nr. Carmarthen)
Esgair. *Carm* 3G 43
(nr. St Clears)
Esgairgeiliog. *Powy* 5G 69
Esh. *Dur* 5E 115
Esher. *Surr* 4C 38
Esholt. *W Yor* 5D 98
Eshott. *Nmbd* 5G 121
Eshton. *N Yor* 4B 98
Esh Winning. *Dur* 5E 115
Eskadale. *High* 5G 157
Eskbank. *Midl* 3G 129
Eskdale Green. *Cumb* 4C 102
Eskdalemuir. *Dum* 5E 119
Eskham. *Linc* 1C 88
Esknish. *Arg* 3B 124
Esk Valley. *N Yor* 4F 107
Eslington Hall. *Nmbd* 3E 121
Esprick. *Lanc* 1C 90
Essendine. *Rut* 4H 75
Essendon. *Herts* 5C 52
Essich. *High* 5A 158
Essington. *Staf* 5D 72
Eston. *Red C* 3C 106
Estover. *Plym* 3B 8
Eswick. *Shet* 6F 173
Etal. *Nmbd* 1D 120
Etchilhampton. *Wilts* 5F 35
Etchingham. *E Sus* 3B 28
Etchinghill. *Kent* 2F 29
Etchinghill. *Staf* 4E 73
Etherley Dene. *Dur* 2E 105
Ethie Haven. *Ang* 4F 145
Etling Green. *Norf* 4C 78
Etloe. *Glos* 5B 48
Eton. *Wind* 3A 38
Eton Wick. *Wind* 3A 38
Etteridge. *High* 4A 150
Ettersgill. *Dur* 2B 104
Ettiley Heath. *Ches E* 4B 84
Ettington. *Warw* 1A 50
Etton. *E Yor* 5D 101
Etton. *Pet* 5A 76
Ettrick. *Bord* 3E 119
Ettrickbridge. *Bord* 2F 119
Etwall. *Derbs* 2G 73
Eudon Burnell. *Shrp* 2B 60
Eudon George. *Shrp* 2A 60
Euston. *Suff* 3A 66
Euxton. *Lanc* 3D 90
Evanstown. *B'end* 3C 32
Evanton. *High* 2A 158
Evedon. *Linc* 1H 75
Evelix. *High* 4E 165
Evendine. *Here* 1C 48
Evenjobb. *Powy* 4E 59
Evenley. *Nptn* 2D 50
Evenlode. *Glos* 3H 49
Even Swindon. *Swin* 3G 35
Evenwood. *Dur* 2E 105
Evenwood Gate. *Dur* 2E 105
Everbay. *Orkn* 5F 172
Evercreech. *Som* 3B 22
Everdon. *Nptn* 5C 62
Everingham. *E Yor* 5C 100
Everleigh. *Wilts* 1H 23
Everley. *N Yor* 1D 100
Eversholt. *C Beds* 2H 51
Evershot. *Dors* 2A 14
Eversley. *Hants* 5F 37
Eversley Centre. *Hants* 5F 37
Eversley Cross. *Hants* 5F 37
Everthorpe. *E Yor* 1C 94
Everton. *C Beds* 5B 64
Everton. *Hants* 3A 16
Everton. *Mers* 1F 83
Everton. *Notts* 1D 86
Evertown. *Dum* 2E 113
Evesbatch. *Here* 1B 48
Evesham. *Worc* 1F 49
Evington. *Leic* 5D 74
Ewden Village. *S Yor* 1G 85
Ewdness. *Shrp* 1B 60
Ewell. *Surr* 4D 38
Ewell Minnis. *Kent* 1G 29
Ewelme. *Oxon* 2E 37
Ewen. *Glos* 2F 35
Ewenny. *V Glam* 4C 32
Ewerby. *Linc* 1A 76
Ewes. *Dum* 5F 119
Ewesley. *Nmbd* 5E 121
Ewhurst. *Surr* 1B 26
Ewhurst Green. *E Sus* 3B 28
Ewhurst Green. *Surr* 2B 26
Ewlo. *Flin* 4E 83
Ewloe. *Flin* 4E 83
Ewood Bridge. *Lanc* 2F 91
Eworthy. *Devn* 3E 11
Ewshot. *Hants* 1G 25
Ewyas Harold. *Here* 3G 47
Exbourne. *Devn* 2G 11
Exbury. *Hants* 2C 16
Exceat. *E Sus* 5G 27
Exebridge. *Som* 4C 20
Exelby. *N Yor* 1E 99
Exeter. *Devn* 3C 12
Exeter International Airport. *Devn* 3D 12
Exford. *Som* 3B 20
Exfords Green. *Shrp* 5G 71
Exhall. *Warw* 5F 61
Exlade Street. *Oxon* 3E 37
Exminster. *Devn* 4C 12
Exmoor. *Som* 3B 20
Exmouth. *Devn* 4D 12
Exnaboe. *Shet* 10E 173
Exning. *Suff* 4F 65
Exton. *Devn* 4C 12
Exton. *Hants* 4E 24
Exton. *Rut* 4G 75
Exton. *Som* 3C 20
Exwick. *Devn* 3C 12
Eyam. *Derbs* 3G 85
Eydon. *Nptn* 5C 62
Eye. *Here* 4G 59
Eye. *Pet* 5B 76
Eye. *Suff* 3D 66
Eye Green. *Pet* 5B 76
Eyemouth. *Bord* 3F 131
Eyeworth. *C Beds* 1C 52
Eyhorne Street. *Kent* 5C 40
Eyke. *Suff* 5F 67
Eynesbury. *Cambs* 5A 64
Eynort. *High* 1B 146
Eynsford. *Kent* 4G 39
Eynsham. *Oxon* 5C 50
Eyre. *High* 3D 154
(on Isle of Skye)
Eyre. *High* 5E 155
(on Raasay)
Eythorne. *Kent* 1G 29
Eyton. *Here* 4G 59
Eyton. *Shrp* 2F 59
(nr. Bishop's Castle)
Eyton. *Shrp* 4F 71
(nr. Shrewsbury)
Eyton. *Wrex* 1F 71
Eyton on Severn. *Shrp* 5H 71
Eyton upon the Weald Moors. *Telf* 4A 72

F

Faccombe. *Hants* 1B 24
Faceby. *N Yor* 4B 106
Faddiley. *Ches E* 5H 83
Fadmoor. *N Yor* 1A 100
Fagwyr. *Swan* 5G 45
Faichem. *High* 3E 149
Faifley. *W Dun* 2G 127
Fail. *S Ayr* 2D 116
Failand. *N Som* 4A 34
Failford. *S Ayr* 2D 116
Failsworth. *G Man* 4H 91
Fairbourne. *Gwyn* 4F 69
Fairbourne Heath. *Kent* 5C 40
Fairburn. *N Yor* 2E 93
Fairfield. *Derbs* 3E 85
Fairfield. *Kent* 3D 28
Fairfield. *Worc* 3D 60
(nr. Bromsgrove)
Fairfield. *Worc* 1F 49
(nr. Evesham)
Fairford. *Glos* 5G 49
Fair Green. *Norf* 4F 77
Fair Hill. *Cumb* 1G 103
Fairhill. *S Lan* 4A 128
Fair Isle Airport. *Shet* 1B 172
Fairlands. *Surr* 5A 38
Fairlie. *N Ayr* 4D 126
Fairlight. *E Sus* 4C 28
Fairlight Cove. *E Sus* 4C 28
Fairmile. *Devn* 3D 12
Fairmile. *Surr* 4C 38
Fairmilehead. *Edin* 3F 129
Fair Oak. *Devn* 1D 12
Fair Oak. *Hants* 1C 16
(nr. Eastleigh)
Fair Oak. *Hants* 5D 36
(nr. Kingsclere)
Fairoak. *Staf* 2B 72
Fair Oak Green. *Hants* 5E 37
Fairseat. *Kent* 4H 39
Fairstead. *Essx* 4A 54
Fairstead. *Norf* 4F 77
Fairwarp. *E Sus* 3F 27
Fairwater. *Card* 4E 33
Fairy Cross. *Devn* 4E 19
Fakenham. *Norf* 3B 78
Fakenham Magna. *Suff* 3B 66
Fala. *Midl* 3H 129
Fala Dam. *Midl* 3H 129
Falcon. *Here* 2B 48
Faldingworth. *Linc* 2H 87
Falfield. *S Glo* 2B 34
Falkenham. *Suff* 2F 55
Falkirk. *Falk* 1B 128
Falkland. *Fife* 3E 137
Fallin. *Stir* 4H 135
Fallowfield. *G Man* 1C 84
Falmer. *E Sus* 5E 27
Falmouth. *Corn* 5C 6
Falsgrave. *N Yor* 1E 101
Falstone. *Nmbd* 1A 114
Fanagmore. *High* 4B 166
Fancott. *C Beds* 3A 52
Fanellan. *High* 4G 157
Fangdale Beck. *N Yor* 5C 106
Fangfoss. *E Yor* 4B 100
Fankerton. *Falk* 1A 128
Fanmore. *Arg* 4F 139
Fanner's Green. *Essx* 4G 53
Fannich Lodge. *High* 2E 156
Fans. *Bord* 5C 130
Farcet. *Cambs* 1B 64
Far Cotton. *Nptn* 5E 63
Fareham. *Hants* 2D 16
Farewell. *Staf* 4E 73
Far Forest. *Worc* 3B 60
Farforth. *Linc* 3C 88
Far Green. *Glos* 5C 48
Far Hoarcross. *Staf* 3F 73
Faringdon. *Oxon* 2A 36
Farington. *Lanc* 2D 90
Farlam. *Cumb* 4G 113
Farleigh. *N Som* 5H 33
Farleigh. *Surr* 4E 39
Farleigh Hungerford. *Som* 1D 22
Farleigh Wallop. *Hants* 2E 24
Farleigh Wick. *Wilts* 5D 34
Farlesthorpe. *Linc* 3D 88
Farleton. *Cumb* 1E 97
Farleton. *Lanc* 3E 97
Farley. *High* 4G 157
Farley. *N Som* 4H 33
Farley. *Shrp* 5F 71
(nr. Shrewsbury)
Farley. *Shrp* 5A 72
(nr. Telford)
Farley. *Staf* 1E 73
Farley. *Wilts* 4H 23
Farley Green. *Suff* 5G 65
Farley Green. *Surr* 1B 26
Farley Hill. *Wok* 5F 37
Farley's End. *Glos* 4C 48
Farlington. *N Yor* 3A 100
Farlington. *Port* 2E 17
Farlow. *Shrp* 2A 60
Farmborough. *Bath* 5B 34
Farmcote. *Glos* 3F 49
Farmcote. *Shrp* 1B 60
Farmington. *Glos* 4G 49
Far Moor. *G Man* 4D 90
Farmoor. *Oxon* 5C 50
Farmtown. *Mor* 3C 160
Farnah Green. *Derbs* 1H 73
Farnborough. *G Lon* 4F 39
Farnborough. *Hants* 1G 25
Farnborough. *Warw* 1C 50
Farnborough. *W Ber* 3C 36
Farncombe. *Surr* 1A 26
Farndish. *Bed* 4G 63
Farndon. *Ches W* 5G 83
Farndon. *Notts* 5E 87
Farnell. *Ang* 3F 145
Farnham. *Dors* 1E 15
Farnham. *Essx* 3E 53
Farnham. *N Yor* 3F 99
Farnham. *Suff* 4F 67
Farnham. *Surr* 2G 25
Farnham Common. *Buck* 2A 38
Farnham Green. *Essx* 3E 53
Farnham Royal. *Buck* 2A 38
Farnhill. *N Yor* 5C 98
Farningham. *Kent* 4G 39
Farnley. *N Yor* 5E 98
Farnley Tyas. *W Yor* 3B 92
Farnsfield. *Notts* 5D 86
Farnworth. *G Man* 4F 91
Farnworth. *Hal* 2H 83
Far Oakridge. *Glos* 5E 49

Farr. *High* 2H 167
(nr. Bettyhill)
Farr. *High* 5A 158
(nr. Inverness)
Farr. *High* 3C 150
(nr. Kingussie)
Farraline. *High* 1H 149
Farringdon. *Devn* 3D 12
Farrington. *Dors* 1D 14
Farrington Gurney. *Bath* 1B 22
Far Sawrey. *Cumb* 5E 103
Farsley. *W Yor* 1C 92
Farthinghoe. *Nptn* 2D 50
Farthingstone. *Nptn* 5D 62
Farthorpe. *Linc* 3B 88
Fartown. *W Yor* 3B 92
Farway. *Devn* 3E 13
Fasag. *High* 3A 156
Fascadale. *High* 1G 139
Fasnacloich. *Arg* 4E 141
Fassfern. *High* 1E 141
Fatfield. *Tyne* 4G 115
Faugh. *Cumb* 4G 113
Fauld. *Staf* 3F 73
Fauldhouse. *W Lot* 3C 128
Faulkbourne. *Essx* 4A 54
Faulkland. *Som* 1C 22
Fauls. *Shrp* 2H 71
Faverdale. *Darl* 3F 105
Faversham. *Kent* 4E 40
Fawdington. *N Yor* 2G 99
Fawfieldhead. *Staf* 4E 85
Fawkham Green. *Kent* 4G 39
Fawler. *Oxon* 4B 50
Fawley. *Buck* 3F 37
Fawley. *Hants* 2C 16
Fawley. *W Ber* 3B 36
Fawley Chapel. *Here* 3A 48
Fawton. *Corn* 2F 7
Faxfleet. *E Yor* 2B 94
Faygate. *W Sus* 2D 26
Fazakerley. *Mers* 1F 83
Fazeley. *Staf* 5F 73
Feagour. *High* 4H 149
Fearann Dhomhnaill. *High* 3E 147
Fearby. *N Yor* 1D 98
Fearn. *High* 1C 158
Fearnan. *Per* 4E 142
Fearnbeg. *High* 3G 155
Fearnhead. *Warr* 1A 84
Fearnmore. *High* 2G 155
Featherstone. *Staf* 5D 72
Featherstone. *W Yor* 2E 93
Featherstone Castle. *Nmbd* 3H 113
Feckenham. *Worc* 4E 61
Feering. *Essx* 3B 54
Feetham. *N Yor* 5C 104
Feizor. *N Yor* 3G 97
Felbridge. *Surr* 2E 27
Felbrigg. *Norf* 2E 78
Felcourt. *Surr* 1E 27
Felden. *Herts* 5A 52
Felhampton. *Shrp* 2G 59
Felindre. *Carm* 3F 45
(nr. Llandeilo)
Felindre. *Carm* 2G 45
(nr. Llandovery)
Felindre. *Carm* 2D 44
(nr. Newcastle Emlyn)
Felindre. *Powy* 2D 58
Felindre. *Swan* 5G 45
Felindre Farchog. *Pemb* 1F 43
Felinfach. *Cdgn* 5E 57
Felinfach. *Powy* 2D 46
Felinfoel. *Carm* 5F 45
Felingwmisaf. *Carm* 3F 45
Felingwmuchaf. *Carm* 3F 45
Felin Newydd. *Powy* 5C 70
(nr. Newtown)
Felin Newydd. *Powy* 3E 70
(nr. Oswestry)
Felin Wnda. *Cdgn* 1D 44
Felinwynt. *Cdgn* 5B 56
Felixkirk. *N Yor* 1G 99
Felixstowe. *Suff* 2F 55
Felixstowe Ferry. *Suff* 2G 55
Felkington. *Nmbd* 5F 131
Fell End. *Cumb* 5A 104
Felling. *Tyne* 3F 115
Fell Side. *Cumb* 1E 102
Felmersham. *Bed* 5G 63
Felmingham. *Norf* 3E 79
Felpham. *W Sus* 3H 17
Felsham. *Suff* 5B 66
Felsted. *Essx* 3G 53
Feltham. *G Lon* 3C 38
Felthamhill. *Surr* 3B 38
Felthorpe. *Norf* 4D 78
Felton. *Here* 1A 48
Felton. *N Som* 5A 34
Felton. *Nmbd* 4F 121
Felton Butler. *Shrp* 4F 71
Feltwell. *Norf* 1G 65
Fenay Bridge. *W Yor* 3B 92
Fence. *Lanc* 1G 91
Fence Houses. *Tyne* 4G 115
Fencott. *Oxon* 4D 50
Fen Ditton. *Cambs* 4D 65
Fen Drayton. *Cambs* 4C 64
Fen End. *Linc* 3B 76
Fen End. *W Mid* 3G 61
Fenham. *Nmbd* 5G 131
Fenham. *Tyne* 3F 115
Fenhouses. *Linc* 1B 76
Feniscowles. *Bkbn* 2E 91
Feniton. *Devn* 3D 12
Fenn Green. *Shrp* 2B 60
Fenn's Bank. *Wrex* 2H 71
Fenn Street. *Medw* 3B 40
Fenny Bentley. *Derbs* 5F 85
Fenny Bridges. *Devn* 3E 12
Fenny Compton. *Warw* 5B 62
Fenny Drayton. *Leics* 1H 61
Fenny Stratford. *Mil* 2G 51
Fenrother. *Nmbd* 5F 121
Fenstanton. *Cambs* 4C 64
Fen Street. *Norf* 1C 66
Fenton. *Cambs* 3C 64
Fenton. *Cumb* 4G 113
Fenton. *Linc* 5F 87
(nr. Caythorpe)
Fenton. *Linc* 3F 87
(nr. Saxilby)
Fenton. *Nmbd* 1D 120
Fenton. *Notts* 2E 87
Fenton. *Stoke* 1C 72
Fentonadle. *Corn* 5A 10
Fenton Barns. *E Lot* 1B 130
Fenwick. *E Ayr* 5F 127
Fenwick. *Nmbd* 5G 131
(nr. Berwick-upon-Tweed)
Fenwick. *Nmbd* 2D 114
(nr. Hexham)
Fenwick. *S Yor* 3F 93
Feochaig. *Arg* 4B 122
Feock. *Corn* 5C 6
Feolin Ferry. *Arg* 3C 124
Feorlan. *Arg* 5A 122
Ferindonald. *High* 3E 147
Feriniquarrie. *High* 3A 154
Fern. *Ang* 2D 145
Ferndale. *Rhon* 2C 32
Ferndown. *Dors* 2F 15
Ferness. *High* 4D 158
Fernham. *Oxon* 2A 36
Fernhill. *W Sus* 1E 27
Fernhill Heath. *Worc* 5C 60
Fernhurst. *W Sus* 4G 25
Fernieflatt. *Abers* 1H 145
Ferniegair. *S Lan* 4A 128
Fernilea. *High* 5C 154
Fernilee. *Derbs* 3E 85
Ferrensby. *N Yor* 3F 99
Ferriby Sluice. *N Lin* 2C 94
Ferring. *W Sus* 5B 26
Ferrybridge. *W Yor* 2E 93
Ferryden. *Ang* 3G 145
Ferryhill. *Aber* 3G 153
Ferry Hill. *Cambs* 2C 64
Ferryhill. *Dur* 1F 105
Ferryhill Station. *Dur* 1A 106
Ferryside. *Carm* 4D 44
Ferryton. *High* 2A 158
Fersfield. *Norf* 2C 66
Fersit. *High* 1A 142
Feshiebridge. *High* 3C 150
Fetcham. *Surr* 5C 38
Fetterangus. *Abers* 3G 161
Fettercairn. *Abers* 1F 145
Fewcott. *Oxon* 3D 50
Fewston. *N Yor* 4D 98
Ffairfach. *Carm* 3G 45
Ffair Rhos. *Cdgn* 4G 57
Ffaldybrenin. *Carm* 1G 45
Ffarmers. *Carm* 1G 45
Ffawyddog. *Powy* 4F 47
Ffodun. *Powy* 5E 71
Ffont-y-gari. *V Glam* 5D 32
Fforest. *Carm* 5F 45
Fforest-fach. *Swan* 3F 31
Fforest Goch. *Neat* 5H 45
Ffostrasol. *Cdgn* 1D 44
Ffos-y-ffin. *Cdgn* 4D 56
Ffrith. *Flin* 5E 83
Ffwl-y-mwn. *V Glam* 5D 32
Ffynnon-ddrain. *Carm* 3E 45
Ffynnongroyw. *Flin* 2D 82
Ffynnon Gynydd. *Powy* 1E 47
Ffynnon-oer. *Cdgn* 5E 57
Fiag Lodge. *High* 1B 164
Fidden. *Arg* 2B 132
Fiddington. *Glos* 2E 49
Fiddington. *Som* 2F 21
Fiddleford. *Dors* 1D 14
Fiddlers Hamlet. *Essx* 5E 53
Field. *Staf* 2E 73
Field Assarts. *Oxon* 4B 50
Field Broughton. *Cumb* 1C 96
Field Dalling. *Norf* 2C 78
Fieldhead. *Cumb* 1F 103
Field Head. *Leics* 5B 74
Fifehead Magdalen. *Dors* 4C 22
Fifehead Neville. *Dors* 1C 14
Fifehead St Quintin. *Dors* 1C 14
Fife Keith. *Mor* 3B 160
Fifield. *Oxon* 4H 49
Fifield. *Wilts* 1G 23
Fifield. *Wind* 3A 38
Fifield Bavant. *Wilts* 4F 23
Figheldean. *Wilts* 2G 23
Filby. *Norf* 4G 79
Filey. *N Yor* 1F 101
Filford. *Dors* 3H 13
Filgrave. *Mil* 1G 51
Filkins. *Oxon* 5H 49
Filleigh. *Devn* 1H 11
(nr. Crediton)
Filleigh. *Devn* 4G 19
(nr. South Molton)
Fillingham. *Linc* 2G 87
Fillongley. *Warw* 2G 61
Filton. *S Glo* 4B 34
Fimber. *E Yor* 3C 100
Finavon. *Ang* 3D 145
Fincham. *Norf* 5F 77
Finchampstead. *Wok* 5F 37
Fincharn. *Arg* 3G 133
Finchdean. *Hants* 1F 17
Finchingfield. *Essx* 2G 53
Finchley. *G Lon* 1D 38
Findern. *Derbs* 2H 73
Findhorn. *Mor* 2E 159
Findhorn Bridge. *High* 1C 150
Findochty. *Mor* 2B 160
Findo Gask. *Per* 1C 136
Findon. *Abers* 4G 153
Findon. *W Sus* 5C 26
Findon Mains. *High* 2A 158
Findon Valley. *W Sus* 5C 26
Finedon. *Nptn* 3G 63
Fingal Street. *Suff* 3E 66
Fingest. *Buck* 2F 37
Finghall. *N Yor* 1D 98
Fingland. *Cumb* 4D 112
Fingland. *Dum* 3G 117
Finglesham. *Kent* 5H 41
Fingringhoe. *Essx* 3D 54
Finiskaig. *High* 4A 148
Finmere. *Oxon* 2E 51
Finnart. *Per* 3C 142
Finningham. *Suff* 4C 66
Finningley. *S Yor* 1D 86
Finnygaud. *Abers* 3D 160
Finsbury. *G Lon* 2E 39
Finstall. *Worc* 4D 61
Finsthwaite. *Cumb* 1C 96
Finstock. *Oxon* 4B 50
Finstown. *Orkn* 6C 172
Fintona. *Omag* 4C 174
Fintry. *Abers* 3E 161
Fintry. *D'dee* 5D 144
Fintry. *Stir* 1H 127
Finwood. *Warw* 4F 61
Finzean. *Abers* 4D 152
Fionnphort. *Arg* 2B 132
Fionnsabhagh. *W Isl* 9C 171
Firbeck. *S Yor* 2C 86
Firby. *N Yor* 1E 99
(nr. Bedale)
Firby. *N Yor* 3B 100
(nr. Malton)
Firgrove. *G Man* 3H 91
Firle. *E Sus* 5F 27
Firsby. *Linc* 4D 88
Firsdown. *Wilts* 3H 23
First Coast. *High* 4D 162
Firth. *Shet* 4F 173
Fir Tree. *Dur* 1E 105
Fishbourne. *IOW* 3D 16
Fishbourne. *W Sus* 2G 17
Fishburn. *Dur* 1A 106
Fishcross. *Clac* 4A 136
Fisherford. *Abers* 5D 160
Fisherrow. *E Lot* 2G 129
Fisher's Pond. *Hants* 4C 24
Fisher's Row. *Lanc* 5D 96
Fisherstreet. *W Sus* 2A 26
Fisherton. *High* 3B 158
Fisherton. *S Ayr* 3B 116
Fisherton de la Mere. *Wilts* 3E 23
Fishguard. *Pemb* 1D 42
Fishlake. *S Yor* 3G 93
Fishley. *Norf* 4G 79
Fishnish. *Arg* 4A 140
Fishpond Bottom. *Dors* 3G 13
Fishponds. *Bris* 4B 34
Fishpool. *Glos* 3B 48
Fishpool. *G Man* 3G 91
Fishpools. *Powy* 4D 58
Fishtoft. *Linc* 1C 76
Fishtoft Drove. *Linc* 1C 76
Fishwick. *Bord* 4F 131
Fiskavaig. *High* 5C 154
Fiskerton. *Linc* 3H 87
Fiskerton. *Notts* 5E 87
Fitch. *Shet* 7E 173
Fitling. *E Yor* 1F 95
Fittleton. *Wilts* 2G 23
Fittleworth. *W Sus* 4B 26
Fitton End. *Cambs* 4D 76
Fitz. *Shrp* 4G 71
Fitzhead. *Som* 4E 20
Fitzwilliam. *W Yor* 3E 93
Fiunary. *High* 4A 140
Five Ash Down. *E Sus* 3F 27
Five Ashes. *E Sus* 3G 27
Five Bells. *Som* 2D 20
Five Bridges. *Here* 1B 48
Fivehead. *Som* 4G 21
Five Lane Ends. *Lanc* 4E 97
Fivelanes. *Corn* 4C 10
Fivemiletown. *Dngn* 5C 174
Five Oak Green. *Kent* 1H 27
Five Oaks. *W Sus* 3B 26
Five Roads. *Carm* 5E 45
Five Ways. *Warw* 3G 61
Flack's Green. *Essx* 4A 54
Flackwell Heath. *Buck* 3G 37
Fladbury. *Worc* 1E 49
Fladda. *Shet* 3E 173
Fladdabister. *Shet* 8F 173
Flagg. *Derbs* 4F 85
Flamborough. *E Yor* 2G 101
Flamstead. *Herts* 4A 52
Flansham. *W Sus* 5A 26
Flasby. *N Yor* 4B 98
Flash. *Staf* 4E 85
Flashader. *High* 3C 154
Flatt, The. *Cumb* 2G 113
Flaunden. *Herts* 5A 52
Flawborough. *Notts* 1E 75
Flawith. *N Yor* 3G 99
Flax Bourton. *N Som* 5A 34
Flaxby. *N Yor* 4F 99
Flaxholme. *Derbs* 1H 73
Flaxley. *Glos* 4B 48
Flaxley Green. *Staf* 4E 73
Flaxpool. *Som* 3E 21
Flaxton. *N Yor* 3A 100
Fleck. *Shet* 10E 173
Fleckney. *Leics* 1D 62
Flecknoe. *Warw* 4C 62
Fledborough. *Notts* 3F 87
Fleet. *Dors* 4B 14
Fleet. *Hants* 1G 25
(nr. Farnborough)
Fleet. *Hants* 2F 17
(nr. South Hayling)
Fleet. *Linc* 3C 76
Fleet Hargate. *Linc* 3C 76
Fleetville. *Herts* 5B 52
Fleetwood. *Lanc* 5C 96
Fleggburgh. *Norf* 4G 79
Fleisirin. *W Isl* 4H 171
Flemingston. *V Glam* 5D 32
Flemington. *S Lan* 3H 127
(nr. Glasgow)
Flemington. *S Lan* 5A 128
(nr. Strathaven)
Flempton. *Suff* 4H 65
Fleoideabhagh. *W Isl* 9C 171
Fletcher's Green. *Kent* 1G 27
Fletchertown. *Cumb* 5D 112
Fletching. *E Sus* 3F 27
Fleuchary. *High* 4E 165
Flexbury. *Corn* 2C 10
Flexford. *Surr* 1A 26
Flimby. *Cumb* 1B 102
Flimwell. *E Sus* 2B 28
Flint. *Flin* 3E 83
Flintham. *Notts* 1E 75
Flint Mountain. *Flin* 3E 83
Flinton. *E Yor* 1F 95
Flintsham. *Here* 5F 59
Flishinghurst. *Kent* 2B 28
Flitcham. *Norf* 3G 77
Flitton. *C Beds* 2A 52
Flitwick. *C Beds* 2A 52
Flixborough. *N Lin* 3B 94
Flixton. *G Man* 1B 84
Flixton. *N Yor* 2E 101
Flixton. *Suff* 2F 67
Flockton. *W Yor* 3C 92
Flodden. *Nmbd* 1D 120
Flodigarry. *High* 1D 154
Flood's Ferry. *Cambs* 1C 64
Flookburgh. *Cumb* 2C 96
Flordon. *Norf* 1D 66
Flore. *Nptn* 4D 62
Flotterton. *Nmbd* 4E 121
Flowton. *Suff* 1D 54
Flushing. *Abers* 4H 161
Flushing. *Corn* 5C 6
Fluxton. *Devn* 3D 12
Flyford Flavell. *Worc* 5D 61
Fobbing. *Thur* 2B 40
Fochabers. *Mor* 3H 159
Fochriw. *Cphy* 5E 46
Fockerby. *N Lin* 3B 94
Fodderty. *High* 3H 157
Foddington. *Som* 4A 22
Foel. *Powy* 4B 70
Foffarty. *Ang* 4D 144
Foggathorpe. *E Yor* 1A 94
Fogo. *Bord* 5D 130

Fogorig. *Bord* 5D **130**
Foindle. *High* 4B **166**
Folda. *Ang* 2A **144**
Fole. *Staf* 2E **73**
Foleshill. *W Mid* 2A **62**
Foley Park. *Worc* 3C **60**
Folke. *Dors* 1B **14**
Folkestone. *Kent* 2G **29**
Folkingham. *Linc* 2H **75**
Folkington. *E Sus* 5G **27**
Folksworth. *Cambs* 1A **64**
Folkton. *N Yor* 2E **101**
Folla Rule. *Abers* 5E **161**
Follifoot. *N Yor* 4F **99**
Folly Cross. *Devn* 2E **11**
Folly Gate. *Devn* 3F **11**
Folly, The. *Herts* 4B **52**
Fonmon. *V Glam* 5D **32**
Fonthill Bishop. *Wilts* 3E **23**
Fonthill Gifford. *Wilts* 3E **23**
Fontmell Magna. *Dors* 1D **14**
Fontwell. *W Sus* 5A **26**
Font-y-gary. *V Glam* 5D **32**
Foodieash. *Fife* 2F **137**
Foolow. *Derbs* 3F **85**
Footdee. *Aber* 3G **153**
Footherley. *Staf* 5F **73**
Foots Cray. *G Lon* 3F **39**
Forbestown. *Abers* 2A **152**
Force Forge. *Cumb* 5E **103**
Force Mills. *Cumb* 5E **103**
Forcett. *N Yor* 3E **105**
Ford. *Arg* 3F **133**
Ford. *Buck* 5F **51**
Ford. *Derbs* 2B **86**
Ford. *Devn* 4E **19**
(nr. Bideford)
Ford. *Devn* 3C **8**
(nr. Holbeton)
Ford. *Devn* 4D **9**
(nr. Salcombe)
Ford. *Glos* 3F **49**
Ford. *Nmbd* 1D **120**
Ford. *Plym* 3A **8**
Ford. *Shrp* 4G **71**
Ford. *Som* 1A **22**
(nr. Wells)
Ford. *Som* 4D **20**
(nr. Wiveliscombe)
Ford. *Staf* 5E **85**
Ford. *W Sus* 5B **26**
Ford. *Wilts* 4D **34**
(nr. Chippenham)
Ford. *Wilts* 3G **23**
(nr. Salisbury)
Forda. *Devn* 3E **19**
Ford Barton. *Devn* 1C **12**
Fordcombe. *Kent* 1G **27**
Fordell. *Fife* 1E **129**
Forden. *Powy* 5E **71**
Ford End. *Essx* 4G **53**
Forder Green. *Devn* 2D **9**
Ford Green. *Lanc* 5D **97**
Fordham. *Cambs* 3F **65**
Fordham. *Essx* 3C **54**
Fordham. *Norf* 1F **65**
Fordham Heath. *Essx* 3C **54**
Ford Heath. *Shrp* 4G **71**
Fordhouses. *W Mid* 5D **72**
Fordie. *Per* 1G **135**
Fordingbridge. *Hants* 1G **15**
Fordington. *Linc* 3D **88**
Fordon. *E Yor* 2E **101**
Fordoun. *Abers* 1G **145**
Ford Street. *Essx* 3C **54**
Ford Street. *Som* 1E **13**
Fordton. *Devn* 3B **12**
Fordwells. *Oxon* 4B **50**
Fordwich. *Kent* 5F **41**
Fordyce. *Abers* 2C **160**
Forebridge. *Staf* 3D **72**
Foremark. *Derbs* 3H **73**
Forest. *N Yor* 4F **105**
Forestburn Gate. *Nmbd* 5E **121**
Foresterseat. *Mor* 3F **159**
Forest Green. *Glos* 2D **34**
Forest Green. *Surr* 1C **26**
Forest Hall. *Cumb* 4G **103**
Forest Head. *Cumb* 4G **113**
Forest Hill. *Oxon* 5D **50**
Forest-in-Teesdale. *Dur* 2B **104**
Forest Lodge. *Per* 1G **143**
Forest Mill. *Clac* 4B **136**
Forest Row. *E Sus* 2F **27**
Forestside. *W Sus* 1F **17**
Forest Town. *Notts* 4C **86**
Forfar. *Ang* 3D **144**
Forgandenny. *Per* 2C **136**
Forge. *Powy* 1G **57**
Forge Side. *Torf* 5F **47**
Forge, The. *Here* 5F **59**
Forgewood. *N Lan* 4A **128**
Forgie. *Mor* 3A **160**
Forgue. *Abers* 4D **160**
Formby. *Mers* 4B **90**
Forncett End. *Norf* 1D **66**
Forncett St Mary. *Norf* 1D **66**
Forncett St Peter. *Norf* 1D **66**
Forneth. *Per* 4H **143**
Fornham All Saints. *Suff* 4H **65**
Fornham St Martin. *Suff* 4A **66**
Forres. *Mor* 3E **159**
Forrestfield. *N Lan* 3B **128**
Forrest Lodge. *Dum* 1C **110**
Forsbrook. *Staf* 1D **72**
Forse. *High* 5E **169**
Forsinard. *High* 4A **168**
Forss. *High* 2C **168**
Forstal, The. *Kent* 2E **29**
Forston. *Dors* 3B **14**
Fort Augustus. *High* 3F **149**
Forteviot. *Per* 2C **136**
Fort George. *High* 3B **158**
Forth. *S Lan* 4C **128**
Forthampton. *Glos* 2D **48**
Forthay. *Glos* 2C **34**
Forth Road Bridge. *Fife* 2E **129**
Fortingall. *Per* 4E **143**
Fort Matilda. *Inv* 2D **126**
Forton. *Hants* 2C **24**
Forton. *Lanc* 4D **97**
Forton. *Shrp* 4G **71**
Forton. *Som* 2G **13**
Forton. *Staf* 3B **72**
Forton Heath. *Shrp* 4G **71**
Fortrie. *Abers* 4D **160**
Fortrose. *High* 3B **158**
Fortuneswell. *Dors* 5B **14**
Fort William. *High* 1F **141**
Forty Green. *Buck* 1A **38**
Forty Hill. *G Lon* 1E **39**
Forward Green. *Suff* 5C **66**
Fosbury. *Wilts* 1B **24**
Foscot. *Oxon* 3H **49**
Fosdyke. *Linc* 2C **76**
Foss. *Per* 3E **143**
Fossebridge. *Glos* 4F **49**
Foster Street. *Essx* 5E **53**
Foston. *Derbs* 2F **73**
Foston. *Leics* 1D **62**
Foston. *Linc* 1F **75**
Foston. *N Yor* 3A **100**
Foston on the Wolds. *E Yor* 4F **101**
Fotherby. *Linc* 1C **88**
Fothergill. *Cumb* 1B **102**
Fotheringhay. *Nptn* 1H **63**
Foubister. *Orkn* 7E **172**
Foula Airport. *Shet* 8A **173**
Foul Anchor. *Cambs* 4D **76**
Foulbridge. *Cumb* 5F **113**
Foulden. *Norf* 1G **65**
Foulden. *Bord* 4F **131**
Foul Mile. *E Sus* 4H **27**
Foulridge. *Lanc* 5A **98**
Foulsham. *Norf* 3C **78**
Fountainhall. *Bord* 5H **129**
Four Alls, The. *Shrp* 2A **72**
Four Ashes. *Staf* 5D **72**
(nr. Cannock)
Four Ashes. *Staf* 2C **60**
(nr. Kinver)
Four Ashes. *Suff* 3C **66**
Four Crosses. *Powy* 5C **70**
(nr. Llanerfyl)
Four Crosses. *Powy* 4E **71**
(nr. Llanymynech)
Four Crosses. *Staf* 5D **72**
Four Elms. *Kent* 1F **27**
Four Forks. *Som* 3F **21**
Four Gotes. *Cambs* 4D **76**
Four Lane End. *S Yor* 4C **92**
Four Lane Ends. *Lanc* 4E **97**
Four Lanes. *Corn* 5A **6**
Fourlanes End. *Ches E* 5C **84**
Four Marks. *Hants* 3E **25**
Four Mile Bridge. *IOA* 3B **80**
Four Oaks. *E Sus* 3C **28**
Four Oaks. *Glos* 3B **48**
Four Oaks. *W Mid* 2G **61**
Four Roads. *Carm* 5E **45**
Four Roads. *IOM* 5B **108**
Fourstones. *Nmbd* 3B **114**
Four Throws. *Kent* 3B **28**
Fovant. *Wilts* 4F **23**
Foveran. *Abers* 1G **153**
Fowey. *Corn* 3F **7**
Fowlershill. *Abers* 2G **153**
Fowley Common. *Warr* 1A **84**
Fowlis. *Ang* 5C **144**
Fowlis Wester. *Per* 1B **136**
Fowlmere. *Cambs* 1E **53**
Fownhope. *Here* 2A **48**
Fox Corner. *Surr* 5A **38**
Foxcote. *Glos* 4F **49**
Foxcote. *Som* 1C **22**
Foxdale. *IOM* 4B **108**
Foxearth. *Essx* 1B **54**
Foxfield. *Cumb* 1B **96**
Foxham. *Wilts* 4E **35**
Fox Hatch. *Essx* 1G **39**
Foxhole. *Corn* 3D **6**
Foxholes. *N Yor* 2E **101**
Foxhunt Green. *E Sus* 4G **27**
Fox Lane. *Hants* 1G **25**
Foxley. *Norf* 3C **78**
Foxley. *Nptn* 5D **62**
Foxley. *Wilts* 3D **35**
Foxlydiate. *Worc* 4E **61**
Fox Street. *Essx* 3D **54**
Foxt. *Staf* 1E **73**
Foxton. *Cambs* 1E **53**
Foxton. *Dur* 2A **106**
Foxton. *Leics* 2D **62**
Foxton. *N Yor* 5B **106**
Foxup. *N Yor* 2A **98**
Foxwist Green. *Ches W* 4A **84**
Foxwood. *Shrp* 3A **60**
Foy. *Here* 3A **48**
Foyers. *High* 1G **149**
Foynesfield. *High* 3C **158**
Fraddam. *Corn* 3C **4**
Fraddon. *Corn* 3D **6**
Fradley. *Staf* 4F **73**
Fradley South. *Staf* 4F **73**
Fradswell. *Staf* 2D **73**
Fraisthorpe. *E Yor* 3F **101**
Framfield. *E Sus* 3F **27**
Framingham Earl. *Norf* 5E **79**
Framingham Pigot. *Norf* 5E **79**
Framlingham. *Suff* 4E **67**
Frampton. *Dors* 3B **14**
Frampton. *Linc* 2C **76**
Frampton Cotterell. *S Glo* 3B **34**
Frampton Mansell. *Glos* 5E **49**
Frampton on Severn. *Glos* 5C **48**
Frampton West End. *Linc* 1B **76**
Framsden. *Suff* 5D **66**
Framwellgate Moor. *Dur* 5F **115**
Franche. *Worc* 3C **60**
Frandley. *Ches W* 3A **84**
Frankby. *Mers* 2E **83**
Frankfort. *Norf* 3F **79**
Frankley. *Worc* 2D **61**
Frank's Bridge. *Powy* 5D **58**
Frankton. *Warw* 3B **62**
Frankwell. *Shrp* 4G **71**
Frant. *E Sus* 2G **27**
Fraserburgh. *Abers* 2G **161**
Frating Green. *Essx* 3D **54**
Fratton. *Port* 2E **17**
Freathy. *Corn* 3A **8**
Freckenham. *Suff* 3F **65**
Freckleton. *Lanc* 2C **90**
Freeby. *Leics* 3F **75**
Freefolk Priors. *Hants* 2C **24**
Freehay. *Staf* 1E **73**
Freeland. *Oxon* 4C **50**
Freester. *Shet* 6F **173**
Freethorpe. *Norf* 5G **79**
Freiston. *Linc* 1C **76**
Freiston Shore. *Linc* 1C **76**
Fremington. *Devn* 3F **19**
Fremington. *N Yor* 5D **104**
Frenchay. *S Glo* 4B **34**
Frenchbeer. *Devn* 4G **11**
Frenich. *Stir* 3D **134**
Frensham. *Surr* 2G **25**
Frenze. *Norf* 2D **66**
Fresgoe. *High* 2B **168**
Freshfield. *Mers* 4A **90**
Freshford. *Bath* 5C **34**
Freshwater. *IOW* 4B **16**
Freshwater Bay. *IOW* 4B **16**
Freshwater East. *Pemb* 5E **43**
Fressingfield. *Suff* 3E **67**
Freston. *Suff* 2E **55**
Freswick. *High* 2F **169**
Fretherne. *Glos* 5C **48**
Frettenham. *Norf* 4E **79**
Freuchie. *Fife* 3E **137**
Freystrop. *Pemb* 3D **42**
Friar's Gate. *E Sus* 2F **27**
Friar Waddon. *Dors* 4B **14**
Friday Bridge. *Cambs* 5D **76**
Friday Street. *E Sus* 5H **27**
Friday Street. *Surr* 1C **26**
Fridaythorpe. *E Yor* 4C **100**
Friden. *Derbs* 4F **85**
Friern Barnet. *G Lon* 1D **39**
Friesthorpe. *Linc* 2H **87**
Frieston. *Linc* 1G **75**
Frieth. *Buck* 2F **37**
Friezeland. *Notts* 5B **86**
Frilford. *Oxon* 2C **36**
Frilsham. *W Ber* 4D **36**
Frimley. *Surr* 1G **25**
Frimley Green. *Surr* 1G **25**
Frindsbury. *Medw* 4B **40**
Fring. *Norf* 2G **77**
Fringford. *Oxon* 3E **50**
Frinsted. *Kent* 5C **40**
Frinton-on-Sea. *Essx* 4F **55**
Friockheim. *Ang* 4E **145**
Friog. *Gwyn* 4F **69**
Frisby. *Leics* 5E **74**
Frisby on the Wreake. *Leics* 4D **74**
Friskney. *Linc* 5D **88**
Friskney Eaudyke. *Linc* 5D **88**
Friston. *E Sus* 5G **27**
Friston. *Suff* 4G **67**
Fritchley. *Derbs* 5A **86**
Fritham. *Hants* 1H **15**
Frith Bank. *Linc* 1C **76**
Frith Common. *Worc* 4A **60**
Frithelstock. *Devn* 1E **11**
Frithelstock Stone. *Devn* 1E **11**
Frithsden. *Herts* 5A **52**
Frithville. *Linc* 5C **88**
Frittenden. *Kent* 1C **28**
Frittiscombe. *Devn* 4E **9**
Fritton. *Norf* 5G **79**
(nr. Great Yarmouth)
Fritton. *Norf* 1E **67**
(nr. Long Stratton)
Fritwell. *Oxon* 3D **50**
Frizinghall. *W Yor* 1B **92**
Frizington. *Cumb* 3B **102**
Frobost. *W Isl* 6C **170**
Frocester. *Glos* 5C **48**
Frochas. *Powy* 5D **70**
Frodesley. *Shrp* 5H **71**
Frodingham. *N Lin* 3C **94**
Frodsham. *Ches W* 3H **83**
Froggatt. *Derbs* 3G **85**
Froghall. *Staf* 1E **73**
Frogham. *Hants* 1G **15**
Frogham. *Kent* 5G **41**
Frogmore. *Devn* 4D **8**
Frogmore. *Hants* 5G **37**
Frogmore. *Herts* 5B **52**
Frognall. *Linc* 4A **76**
Frogshall. *Norf* 2E **79**
Frogwell. *Corn* 2H **7**
Frolesworth. *Leics* 1C **62**
Frome. *Som* 2C **22**
Fromefield. *Som* 2C **22**
Frome St Quintin. *Dors* 2A **14**
Fromes Hill. *Here* 1B **48**
Fron. *Gwyn* 2C **68**
Fron. *Powy* 4C **58**
(nr. Llandrindod Wells)
Fron. *Powy* 1D **58**
(nr. Newtown)
Fron. *Powy* 5E **71**
(nr. Welshpool)
Froncysyllte. *Wrex* 1E **71**
Frongoch. *Gwyn* 2B **70**
Fron Isaf. *Wrex* 1E **71**
Fronoleu. *Gwyn* 2G **69**
Frosterley. *Dur* 1D **104**
Frotoft. *Orkn* 5D **172**
Froxfield. *C Beds* 2H **51**
Froxfield. *Wilts* 5A **36**
Froxfield Green. *Hants* 4F **25**
Fryern Hill. *Hants* 4C **24**
Fryerning. *Essx* 5G **53**
Fryton. *N Yor* 2A **100**
Fugglestone St Peter. *Wilts* 3G **23**
Fulbeck. *Linc* 5G **87**
Fulbourn. *Cambs* 5E **65**
Fulbrook. *Oxon* 4A **50**
Fulflood. *Hants* 3C **24**
Fulford. *Som* 4F **21**
Fulford. *Staf* 2D **72**
Fulford. *York* 5A **100**
Fulham. *G Lon* 3D **38**
Fulking. *W Sus* 4D **26**
Fuller's Moor. *Ches W* 5G **83**
Fuller Street. *Essx* 4H **53**
Fullerton. *Hants* 3B **24**
Fulletby. *Linc* 3B **88**
Full Sutton. *E Yor* 4B **100**
Fullwood. *E Ayr* 4F **127**
Fulmer. *Buck* 2A **38**
Fulmodestone. *Norf* 2B **78**
Fulnetby. *Linc* 3H **87**
Fulney. *Linc* 3B **76**
Fulstow. *Linc* 1C **88**
Fulthorpe. *Stoc T* 2B **106**
Fulwell. *Tyne* 4G **115**
Fulwood. *Lanc* 1D **90**
Fulwood. *Notts* 5B **86**
Fulwood. *Som* 1F **13**
Fulwood. *S Yor* 2G **85**
Fundenhall. *Norf* 1D **66**
Funtington. *W Sus* 2G **17**
Funtley. *Hants* 2D **16**
Funzie. *Shet* 2H **173**
Furley. *Devn* 2F **13**
Furnace. *Arg* 3H **133**
Furnace. *Carm* 5F **45**
Furnace. *Cdgn* 1F **57**
Furner's Green. *E Sus* 3F **27**
Furness Vale. *Derbs* 2E **85**
Furneux Pelham. *Herts* 3E **53**
Furzebrook. *Dors* 4E **15**
Furzehill. *Devn* 2H **19**
Furzehill. *Dors* 2F **15**
Furzeley Corner. *Hants* 1E **17**
Furzey Lodge. *Hants* 2B **16**
Furzley. *Hants* 1A **16**
Fyfield. *Essx* 5F **53**
Fyfield. *Glos* 5H **49**
Fyfield. *Hants* 2A **24**

Grindon—Hamstreet

Grindon. *Staf* 5E **85**
Gringley on the Hill. *Notts* 1E **87**
Grinsdale. *Cumb* 4E **113**
Grinshill. *Shrp* 3H **71**
Grinton. *N Yor* 5D **104**
Griomsidar. *W Isl* 5G **171**
Grishipoll. *Arg* 3C **138**
Grisling Common. *E Sus* 3F **27**
Gristhorpe. *N Yor* 1E **101**
Griston. *Norf* 1B **66**
Gritley. *Orkn* 7E **172**
Grittenham. *Wilts* 3F **35**
Grittleton. *Wilts* 3D **34**
Grizebeck. *Cumb* 1B **96**
Grizedale. *Cumb* 5E **103**
Grobister. *Orkn* 5F **172**
Grobsness. *Shet* 5E **173**
Groby. *Leics* 5C **74**
Groes. *Cnwy* 4C **82**
Groes. *Neat* 3A **32**
Groes-faen. *Rhon* 3D **32**
Groesffordd. *Gwyn* 2B **68**
Groesffordd. *Powy* 3D **46**
Groeslon. *Gwyn* 5D **81**
Groes-lwyd. *Powy* 4E **70**
Groes-wen. *Cphy* 3E **33**
Grogport. *Arg* 5G **125**
Groigearraidh. *W Isl* 4C **170**
Gromford. *Suff* 5F **67**
Gronant. *Flin* 2C **82**
Groombridge. *E Sus* 2G **27**
Grosmont. *Mon* 3H **47**
Grosmont. *N Yor* 4F **107**
Groton. *Suff* 1C **54**
Grove. *Dors* 5B **14**
Grove. *Kent* 4G **41**
Grove. *Notts* 3E **87**
Grove. *Oxon* 2B **36**
Grovehill. *E Yor* 1D **94**
Grove Park. *G Lon* 3F **39**
Grovesend. *Swan* 5F **45**
Grove, The. *Dum* 2A **112**
Grove, The. *Worc* 1D **48**
Grub Street. *Staf* 3B **72**
Grudie. *High* 2F **157**
Gruids. *High* 3C **164**
Gruinard House. *High* 4D **162**
Gruinart. *Arg* 3A **124**
Grulinbeg. *Arg* 3A **124**
Gruline. *Arg* 4G **139**
Grummore. *High* 5G **167**
Grundisburgh. *Suff* 5E **66**
Gruting. *Shet* 7D **173**
Grutness. *Shet* 10F **173**
Gualachulain. *High* 4F **141**
Gualin House. *High* 3D **166**
Guardbridge. *Fife* 2G **137**
Guarlford. *Worc* 1D **48**
Guay. *Per* 4H **143**
Gubblecote. *Herts* 4H **51**
Guestling Green. *E Sus* 4C **28**
Guestling Thorn. *E Sus* 4C **28**
Guestwick. *Norf* 3C **78**
Guestwick Green. *Norf* 3C **78**
Guide. *Bkbn* 2F **91**
Guide Post. *Nmbd* 1F **115**
Guilden Down. *Shrp* 2F **59**
Guilden Morden. *Cambs* 1C **52**
Guilden Sutton. *Ches W* 4G **83**
Guildford. *Surr* 1A **26**
Guildtown. *Per* 5A **144**
Guilsborough. *Nptn* 3D **62**
Guilsfield. *Powy* 4E **70**
Guineaford. *Devn* 3F **19**
Guisborough. *Red C* 3D **106**
Guiseley. *W Yor* 5D **98**
Guist. *Norf* 3B **78**
Guiting Power. *Glos* 3F **49**
Gulberwick. *Shet* 8F **173**
Gullane. *E Lot* 1A **130**
Gulling Green. *Suff* 5H **65**
Gulval. *Corn* 3B **4**
Gulworthy. *Devn* 5E **11**
Gumfreston. *Pemb* 4F **43**
Gumley. *Leics* 1D **62**
Gunby. *E Yor* 1H **93**
Gunby. *Linc* 3G **75**
Gundleton. *Hants* 3E **24**
Gun Green. *Kent* 2B **28**
Gun Hill. *E Sus* 4G **27**
Gunn. *Devn* 3G **19**
Gunnerside. *N Yor* 5C **104**
Gunnerton. *Nmbd* 2C **114**
Gunness. *N Lin* 3B **94**
Gunnislake. *Corn* 5E **11**
Gunnista. *Shet* 7F **173**
Gunsgreenhill. *Bord* 3F **131**
Gunstone. *Staf* 5C **72**
Gunthorpe. *Norf* 2C **78**
Gunthorpe. *N Lin* 1F **87**
Gunthorpe. *Notts* 1D **74**
Gunthorpe. *Pet* 5A **76**
Gunville. *IOW* 4C **16**
Gupworthy. *Som* 3C **20**
Gurnard. *IOW* 3C **16**
Gurney Slade. *Som* 2B **22**
Gurnos. *Powy* 5A **46**
Gussage All Saints. *Dors* 1F **15**
Gussage St Andrew. *Dors* 1E **15**
Gussage St Michael. *Dors* 1E **15**
Guston. *Kent* 1H **29**
Gutcher. *Shet* 2G **173**
Guthram Gowt. *Linc* 3A **76**
Guthrie. *Ang* 3E **145**
Guyhirn. *Cambs* 5D **76**
Guyhirn Gull. *Cambs* 5C **76**
Guy's Head. *Linc* 3D **77**
Guy's Marsh. *Dors* 4D **22**
Guyzance. *Nmbd* 4G **121**
Gwaelod-y-garth. *Card* 3E **32**
Gwaenynog Bach. *Den* 4C **82**
Gwaenysgor. *Flin* 2C **82**
Gwalchmai. *IOA* 3C **80**
Gwastad. *Pemb* 2E **43**
Gwaun-Cae-Gurwen. *Neat* 4H **45**
Gwaun-y-bara. *Cphy* 3E **33**
Gwbert. *Cdgn* 1B **44**
Gweek. *Corn* 4E **5**
Gwehelog. *Mon* 5G **47**
Gwenddwr. *Powy* 1D **46**
Gwennap. *Corn* 4B **6**
Gwenter. *Corn* 5E **5**
Gwernaffield. *Flin* 4E **82**
Gwernesney. *Mon* 5H **47**
Gwernogle. *Carm* 2F **45**
Gwern-y-go. *Powy* 1E **58**
Gwernymynydd. *Flin* 4E **82**
Gwersyllt. *Wrex* 5F **83**
Gwespyr. *Flin* 2D **82**
Gwinear. *Corn* 3C **4**
Gwithian. *Corn* 2C **4**
Gwredog. *IOA* 2D **80**
Gwyddelwern. *Den* 1C **70**
Gwyddgrug. *Carm* 2E **45**
Gwynfryn. *Wrex* 5E **83**
Gwystre. *Powy* 4C **58**
Gwytherin. *Cnwy* 4A **82**
Gyfelia. *Wrex* 1F **71**
Gyffin. *Cnwy* 3G **81**

H

Haa of Houlland. *Shet* 1G **173**
Habberley. *Shrp* 5G **71**
Habblesthorpe. *Notts* 2E **87**
Habergham. *Lanc* 1G **91**
Habin. *W Sus* 4G **25**
Habrough. *NE Lin* 3E **95**
Haceby. *Linc* 2H **75**
Hacheston. *Suff* 5F **67**
Hackenthorpe. *S Yor* 2B **86**
Hackford. *Norf* 5C **78**
Hackforth. *N Yor* 5F **105**
Hackland. *Orkn* 5C **172**
Hackleton. *Nptn* 5F **63**
Hackman's Gate. *Worc* 3C **60**
Hackness. *N Yor* 5G **107**
Hackness. *Orkn* 8C **172**
Hackney. *G Lon* 2E **39**
Hackthorn. *Linc* 2G **87**
Hackthorpe. *Cumb* 2G **103**
Haclait. *W Isl* 4D **170**
Haconby. *Linc* 3A **76**
Hadden. *Bord* 1B **120**
Haddenham. *Buck* 5F **51**
Haddenham. *Cambs* 3D **64**
Haddenham End. *Cambs* 3D **64**
Haddington. *E Lot* 2B **130**
Haddington. *Linc* 4G **87**
Haddiscoe. *Norf* 1G **67**
Haddo. *Abers* 5F **161**
Haddon. *Cambs* 1A **64**
Hademore. *Staf* 5F **73**
Hadfield. *Derbs* 1E **85**
Hadham Cross. *Herts* 4E **53**
Hadham Ford. *Herts* 3E **53**
Hadleigh. *Essx* 2C **40**
Hadleigh. *Suff* 1D **54**
Hadleigh Heath. *Suff* 1C **54**
Hadley. *Telf* 4A **72**
Hadley. *Worc* 4C **60**
Hadley End. *Staf* 3F **73**
Hadley Wood. *G Lon* 1D **38**
Hadlow. *Kent* 1H **27**
Hadlow Down. *E Sus* 3G **27**
Hadnall. *Shrp* 3H **71**
Hadstock. *Essx* 1F **53**
Hadston. *Nmbd* 4G **121**
Hady. *Derbs* 3A **86**
Hadzor. *Worc* 4D **60**
Haffenden Quarter. *Kent* 1C **28**
Haggate. *Lanc* 1G **91**
Haggbeck. *Cumb* 2F **113**
Haggersta. *Shet* 7E **173**
Haggerston. *Nmbd* 5G **131**
Haggrister. *Shet* 4E **173**
Hagley. *Here* 1A **48**
Hagley. *Worc* 2D **60**
Hagnaby. *Linc* 4C **88**
Hagworthingham. *Linc* 4C **88**
Haigh. *G Man* 4E **90**
Haigh Moor. *W Yor* 2C **92**
Haighton Green. *Lanc* 1D **90**
Haile. *Cumb* 4B **102**
Hailes. *Glos* 2F **49**
Hailey. *Herts* 4D **52**
Hailey. *Oxon* 4B **50**
Hailsham. *E Sus* 5G **27**
Hail Weston. *Cambs* 4A **64**
Hainault. *G Lon* 1F **39**
Hainford. *Norf* 4E **78**
Hainton. *Linc* 2A **88**
Hainworth. *W Yor* 1A **92**
Haisthorpe. *E Yor* 3F **101**
Hakin. *Pemb* 4C **42**
Halam. *Notts* 5D **86**
Halbeath. *Fife* 1E **129**
Halberton. *Devn* 1D **12**
Halcro. *High* 2E **169**
Hale. *Cumb* 2E **97**
Hale. *G Man* 2B **84**
Hale. *Hal* 2G **83**
Hale. *Hants* 1G **15**
Hale. *Surr* 2G **25**
Hale Bank. *Hal* 2G **83**
Halebarns. *G Man* 2B **84**
Hales. *Norf* 1F **67**
Hales. *Staf* 2B **72**
Halesgate. *Linc* 3C **76**
Hales Green. *Derbs* 1F **73**
Halesowen. *W Mid* 2D **60**
Hale Street. *Kent* 1A **28**
Halesworth. *Suff* 3F **67**
Halewood. *Mers* 2G **83**
Halford. *Shrp* 2G **59**
Halford. *Warw* 1A **50**
Halfpenny. *Cumb* 1E **97**
Halfpenny Furze. *Carm* 3G **43**
Halfpenny Green. *Staf* 1C **60**
Halfway. *Carm* 2G **45**
Halfway. *Powy* 2B **46**
Halfway. *S Yor* 2B **86**
Halfway. *W Ber* 5C **36**
Halfway House. *Shrp* 4F **71**
Halfway Houses. *Kent* 3D **40**
Halgabron. *Corn* 4A **10**
Halifax. *W Yor* 2A **92**
Halistra. *High* 3B **154**
Halket. *E Ayr* 4F **127**
Halkirk. *High* 3D **168**
Halkyn. *Flin* 3E **82**
Hall. *E Ren* 4F **127**
Hallam Fields. *Derbs* 1B **74**
Halland. *E Sus* 4G **27**
Hallands, The. *N Lin* 2D **94**
Hallaton. *Leics* 1E **63**
Hallatrow. *Bath* 1B **22**
Hallbank. *Cumb* 5H **103**
Hallbankgate. *Cumb* 4G **113**
Hall Dunnerdale. *Cumb* 5D **102**
Hallen. *S Glo* 3A **34**
Hall End. *Bed* 1A **52**
Hallgarth. *Dur* 5G **115**
Hall Green. *Ches E* 5C **84**
Hall Green. *Norf* 2D **66**
Hall Green. *W Mid* 2F **61**
Hall Green. *W Yor* 3D **92**
Hall Green. *Wrex* 1G **71**
Halliburton. *Bord* 5C **130**
Hallin. *High* 3B **154**
Halling. *Medw* 4B **40**
Hallington. *Linc* 2C **88**
Hallington. *Nmbd* 2C **114**
Halloughton. *Notts* 5D **86**
Hallow. *Worc* 5C **60**
Hallow Heath. *Worc* 5C **60**
Hallowsgate. *Ches W* 4H **83**
Hallsands. *Devn* 5E **9**
Hall's Green. *Herts* 3C **52**
Hallspill. *Devn* 4E **19**
Hallthwaites. *Cumb* 1A **96**
Hall Waberthwaite. *Cumb* 5C **102**
Hallwood Green. *Glos* 2B **48**
Hallworthy. *Corn* 4B **10**
Hallyne. *Bord* 5E **129**
Halmer End. *Staf* 1C **72**
Halmond's Frome. *Here* 1B **48**
Halmore. *Glos* 5B **48**
Halnaker. *W Sus* 5A **26**
Halsall. *Lanc* 3B **90**
Halse. *Nptn* 1D **50**
Halse. *Som* 4E **21**
Halsetown. *Corn* 3C **4**
Halsham. *E Yor* 2F **95**
Halsinger. *Devn* 3F **19**
Halstead. *Essx* 2B **54**
Halstead. *Kent* 4F **39**
Halstead. *Leics* 5E **75**
Halstock. *Dors* 2A **14**
Halsway. *Som* 3E **21**
Haltcliff Bridge. *Cumb* 1E **103**
Haltham. *Linc* 4B **88**
Haltoft End. *Linc* 1C **76**
Halton. *Buck* 5G **51**
Halton. *Hal* 2H **83**
Halton. *Lanc* 3E **97**
Halton. *Nmbd* 3C **114**
Halton. *W Yor* 1D **92**
Halton. *Wrex* 2F **71**
Halton East. *N Yor* 4C **98**
Halton Fenside. *Linc* 4D **88**
Halton Gill. *N Yor* 2A **98**
Halton Holegate. *Linc* 4D **88**
Halton Lea Gate. *Nmbd* 4H **113**
Halton Moor. *W Yor* 1D **92**
Halton Shields. *Nmbd* 3D **114**
Halton West. *N Yor* 4H **97**
Haltwhistle. *Nmbd* 3A **114**
Halvergate. *Norf* 5G **79**
Halwell. *Devn* 3D **9**
Halwill. *Devn* 3E **11**
Halwill Junction. *Devn* 3E **11**
Ham. *Devn* 2F **13**
Ham. *Glos* 2B **34**
Ham. *G Lon* 3C **38**
Ham. *High* 1E **169**
Ham. *Kent* 5H **41**
Ham. *Plym* 3A **8**
Ham. *Shet* 8A **173**
Ham. *Som* 1F **13** (nr. Ilminster)
Ham. *Som* 4F **21** (nr. Taunton)
Ham. *Som* 4E **21** (nr. Wellington)
Ham. *Wilts* 5B **36**
Hambleden. *Buck* 3F **37**
Hambledon. *Hants* 1E **17**
Hambledon. *Surr* 2A **26**
Hamble-le-Rice. *Hants* 2C **16**
Hambleton. *Lanc* 5C **96**
Hambleton. *N Yor* 1F **93**
Hambridge. *Som* 4G **21**
Hambrook. *S Glo* 4B **34**
Hambrook. *W Sus* 2F **17**
Ham Common. *Dors* 4D **22**
Hameringham. *Linc* 4C **88**
Hamerton. *Cambs* 3A **64**
Ham Green. *Here* 1C **48**
Ham Green. *Kent* 4C **40**
Ham Green. *N Som* 4A **34**
Ham Green. *Worc* 4E **61**
Ham Hill. *Kent* 4A **40**
Hamilton. *Leics* 5D **74**
Hamilton. *S Lan* 4A **128**
Hamister. *Shet* 5G **173**
Hammer. *W Sus* 3G **25**
Hammersmith. *G Lon* 3D **38**
Hammerwich. *Staf* 5E **73**
Hammerwood. *E Sus* 2F **27**
Hammill. *Kent* 5G **41**
Hammond Street. *Herts* 5D **52**
Hammoon. *Dors* 1D **14**
Hamnavoe. *Shet* 3D **173** (nr. Braehoulland)
Hamnavoe. *Shet* 8E **173** (nr. Burland)
Hamnavoe. *Shet* 4F **173** (nr. Lunna)
Hamnavoe. *Shet* 3F **173** (on Yell)
Hamp. *Som* 3G **21**
Hampden Park. *E Sus* 5G **27**
Hampen. *Glos* 4F **49**
Hamperden End. *Essx* 2F **53**
Hamperley. *Shrp* 2G **59**
Hampnett. *Glos* 4F **49**
Hampole. *S Yor* 3F **93**
Hampreston. *Dors* 3F **15**
Hampstead. *G Lon* 2D **38**
Hampstead Norreys. *W Ber* 4D **36**
Hampsthwaite. *N Yor* 4E **99**
Hampton. *Devn* 3F **13**
Hampton. *G Lon* 3C **38**
Hampton. *Kent* 4F **41**
Hampton. *Shrp* 2B **60**
Hampton. *Swin* 2G **35**
Hampton. *Worc* 1F **49**
Hampton Bishop. *Here* 2A **48**
Hampton Fields. *Glos* 2D **35**
Hampton Hargate. *Pet* 1A **64**
Hampton Heath. *Ches W* 1H **71**
Hampton in Arden. *W Mid* 2G **61**
Hampton Loade. *Shrp* 2B **60**
Hampton Lovett. *Worc* 4C **60**
Hampton Lucy. *Warw* 5G **61**
Hampton Magna. *Warw* 4G **61**
Hampton on the Hill. *Warw* 4G **61**
Hampton Poyle. *Oxon* 4D **50**
Hampton Wick. *G Lon* 4C **38**
Hamptworth. *Wilts* 1H **15**
Hamrow. *Norf* 3B **78**
Hamsey. *E Sus* 4F **27**
Hamsey Green. *Surr* 5E **39**
Hamstall Ridware. *Staf* 4F **73**
Hamstead. *IOW* 3C **16**
Hamstead. *W Mid* 1E **61**
Hamstead Marshall. *W Ber* 5C **36**
Hamsterley. *Dur* 4E **115** (nr. Consett)
Hamsterley. *Dur* 1E **105** (nr. Wolsingham)
Hamsterley Mill. *Dur* 4E **115**
Hamstreet. *Kent* 2E **28**

Hawthorn Hill—Heywood

Hawthorn Hill. *Linc* 5B 88
Hawthorpe. *Linc* 3H 75
Hawton. *Notts* 5E 87
Haxby. *York* 4A 100
Haxey. *N Lin* 1E 87
Haybridge. *Shrp* 3A 60
Haybridge. *Som* 2A 22
Haydock. *Mers* 1H 83
Haydon. *Bath* 1B 22
Haydon. *Dors* 1B 14
Haydon. *Som* 4F 21
Haydon Bridge. *Nmbd* 3B 114
Haydon Wick. *Swin* 3G 35
Haye. *Corn* 2H 7
Hayes. *G Lon* 4F 39
(nr. Bromley)
Hayes. *G Lon* 2B 38
(nr. Uxbridge)
Hayfield. *Derbs* 2E 85
Hay Green. *Norf* 4E 77
Hayhill. *E Ayr* 3D 116
Haylands. *IOW* 3D 16
Hayle. *Corn* 3C 4
Hayley Green. *W Mid* 2D 60
Hayling Island. *Hants* 3F 17
Hayne. *Devn* 2B 12
Haynes. *C Beds* 1A 52
Haynes West End. *C Beds* 1A 52
Hay-on-Wye. *Powy* 1F 47
Hayscastle. *Pemb* 2C 42
Hayscastle Cross. *Pemb* 2D 42
Haysden. *Kent* 1G 27
Hayshead. *Ang* 4F 145
Hay Street. *Herts* 3D 53
Hayton. *Aber* 3G 153
Hayton. *Cumb* 5C 112
(nr. Aspatria)
Hayton. *Cumb* 4G 113
(nr. Brampton)
Hayton. *E Yor* 5C 100
Hayton. *Notts* 2E 87
Hayton's Bent. *Shrp* 2H 59
Haytor Vale. *Devn* 5A 12
Haytown. *Devn* 1D 11
Haywards Heath. *W Sus* 3E 27
Haywood. *S Lan* 4C 128
Hazelbank. *S Lan* 5B 128
Hazelbury Bryan. *Dors* 2C 14
Hazeleigh. *Essx* 5B 54
Hazeley. *Hants* 1F 25
Hazel Grove. *G Man* 2D 84
Hazelhead. *S Yor* 4B 92
Hazelslade. *Staf* 4E 73
Hazel Street. *Kent* 2A 28
Hazelton Walls. *Fife* 1F 137
Hazelwood. *Derbs* 1H 73
Hazlemere. *Buck* 2G 37
Hazler. *Shrp* 1G 59
Hazlerigg. *Tyne* 2F 115
Hazles. *Staf* 1E 73
Hazleton. *Glos* 4F 49
Hazon. *Nmbd* 4F 121
Heacham. *Norf* 2F 77
Headbourne Worthy. *Hants* 3C 24
Headcorn. *Kent* 1C 28
Headingley. *W Yor* 1C 92
Headington. *Oxon* 5D 50
Headlam. *Dur* 3E 105
Headless Cross. *Worc* 4E 61
Headley. *Hants* 3G 25
(nr. Haslemere)
Headley. *Hants* 5D 36
(nr. Kingsclere)
Headley. *Surr* 5D 38
Headley Down. *Hants* 3G 25
Headley Heath. *Worc* 3E 61
Headley Park. *Bris* 5A 34
Head of Muir. *Falk* 1B 128
Headon. *Notts* 3E 87
Heads Nook. *Cumb* 4F 113
Heage. *Derbs* 5A 86
Healaugh. *N Yor* 5D 104
(nr. Grinton)
Healaugh. *N Yor* 5H 99
(nr. York)
Heald Green. *G Man* 2C 84
Heale. *Devn* 2G 19
Healey. *G Man* 3G 91
Healey. *Nmbd* 4D 114
Healey. *N Yor* 1D 98
Healeyfield. *Dur* 5D 114
Healing. *NE Lin* 3F 95
Heamoor. *Corn* 3B 4
Heanish. *Arg* 4B 138
Heanor. *Derbs* 1B 74
Heanton Punchardon. *Devn* 3F 19
Heapham. *Linc* 2F 87
Heartsease. *Powy* 4D 58
Heasley Mill. *Devn* 3H 19
Heaste. *High* 2E 147
Heath. *Derbs* 4B 86
Heath and Reach. *C Beds* 3H 51
Heath Common. *W Sus* 4C 26
Heathcote. *Derbs* 4F 85
Heath Cross. *Devn* 3H 11
Heathencote. *Nptn* 1F 51
Heath End. *Derbs* 3A 74
Heath End. *Hants* 5D 36
Heath End. *W Mid* 5E 73
Heather. *Leics* 4A 74
Heatherfield. *High* 4D 155
Heatherton. *Derb* 2H 73
Heathfield. *Cambs* 1E 53
Heathfield. *Cumb* 5C 112
Heathfield. *Devn* 5B 12
Heathfield. *E Sus* 3G 27
Heathfield. *Ren* 3E 126
Heathfield. *Som* 3E 21
(nr. Lydeard St Lawrence)
Heathfield. *Som* 4E 21
(nr. Norton Fitzwarren)
Heath Green. *Worc* 3E 61
Heathhall. *Dum* 2A 112
Heath Hayes. *Staf* 4E 73
Heath Hill. *Shrp* 4B 72
Heath House. *Som* 2H 21
Heathrow (London) Airport.
G Lon 3B 38
Heathstock. *Devn* 2F 13
Heath, The. *Norf* 3E 79
(nr. Buxton)
Heath, The. *Norf* 3B 78
(nr. Fakenham)
Heath, The. *Norf* 3D 78
(nr. Hevingham)
Heath, The. *Staf* 2E 73
Heath, The. *Suff* 2E 55
Heathton. *Shrp* 1C 60
Heathtop. *Derbs* 2G 73
Heath Town. *W Mid* 1D 60
Heatley. *Staf* 3E 73
Heatley. *Warr* 2B 84
Heaton. *Lanc* 3D 96
Heaton. *Staf* 4D 84
Heaton. *Tyne* 3F 115
Heaton. *W Yor* 1B 92
Heaton Moor. *G Man* 1C 84
Heaton's Bridge. *Lanc* 3C 90
Heaverham. *Kent* 5G 39
Heavitree. *Devn* 3C 12
Hebburn. *Tyne* 3G 115
Hebden. *N Yor* 3C 98
Hebden Bridge. *W Yor* 2H 91
Hebden Green. *Ches W* 4A 84
Hebing End. *Herts* 3D 52
Hebron. *Carm* 2F 43
Hebron. *Nmbd* 1E 115
Heck. *Dum* 1B 112
Heckdyke. *N Lin* 1E 87
Heckfield. *Hants* 5F 37
Heckfield Green. *Suff* 3D 66
Heckfordbridge. *Essx* 3C 54
Heckington. *Linc* 1A 76
Heckmondwike. *W Yor* 2C 92
Heddington. *Wilts* 5E 35
Heddle. *Orkn* 6C 172
Heddon. *Devn* 4G 19
Heddon-on-the-Wall. *Nmbd* 3E 115
Hedenham. *Norf* 1F 67
Hedge End. *Hants* 1C 16
Hedgerley. *Buck* 2A 38
Hedging. *Som* 4G 21
Hedley on the Hill. *Nmbd* 4D 115
Hednesford. *Staf* 4E 73
Hedon. *E Yor* 2E 95
Hegdon Hill. *Here* 5H 59
Heglibister. *Shet* 6E 173
Heighington. *Darl* 2F 105
Heighington. *Linc* 4H 87
Heightington. *Worc* 3B 60
Heights of Brae. *High* 2H 157
Heights of Fodderty. *High* 2H 157
Heights of Kinlochewe. *High* 2C 156
Heiton. *Bord* 1B 120
Hele. *Devn* 2C 12
(nr. Exeter)
Hele. *Devn* 3D 10
(nr. Holsworthy)
Hele. *Devn* 2F 19
(nr. Ilfracombe)
Hele. *Torb* 2F 9
Helensburgh. *Arg* 1D 126
Helford. *Corn* 4E 5
Helhoughton. *Norf* 3A 78
Helions Bumpstead. *Essx* 1G 53
Helland. *Corn* 5A 10
Helland. *Som* 4G 21
Hellandbridge. *Corn* 5A 10
Hellesdon. *Norf* 4E 78
Hellesveor. *Corn* 2C 4
Hellidon. *Nptn* 5C 62
Hellifield. *N Yor* 4A 98
Hellingly. *E Sus* 4G 27
Hellington. *Norf* 5F 79
Hellister. *Shet* 7E 173
Helmdon. *Nptn* 1D 50
Helmingham. *Suff* 5D 66
Helmington Row. *Dur* 1E 105
Helmsdale. *High* 2H 165
Helmshore. *Lanc* 2F 91
Helmsley. *N Yor* 1A 100
Helperby. *N Yor* 3G 99
Helperthorpe. *N Yor* 2D 100
Helpringham. *Linc* 1A 76
Helpston. *Pet* 5A 76
Helsby. *Ches W* 3G 83
Helsey. *Linc* 3E 89
Helston. *Corn* 4D 4
Helstone. *Corn* 4A 10
Helton. *Cumb* 2G 103
Helwith. *N Yor* 4D 105
Helwith Bridge. *N Yor* 3H 97
Helygain. *Flin* 3E 82
Hemblington. *Norf* 4F 79
Hemel Hempstead. *Herts* 5A 52
Hemerdon. *Devn* 3B 8
Hemingbrough. *N Yor* 1G 93
Hemingby. *Linc* 3B 88
Hemingfield. *S Yor* 4D 93
Hemingford Abbots. *Cambs* 3B 64
Hemingford Grey. *Cambs* 3B 64
Hemingstone. *Suff* 5D 66
Hemington. *Leics* 3B 74
Hemington. *Nptn* 2H 63
Hemington. *Som* 1C 22
Hemley. *Suff* 1F 55
Hemlington. *Midd* 3B 106
Hempholme. *E Yor* 4E 101
Hempnall. *Norf* 1E 67
Hempnall Green. *Norf* 1E 67
Hempriggs. *High* 4F 169
Hemp's Green. *Essx* 3C 54
Hempstead. *Essx* 2G 53
Hempstead. *Medw* 4B 40
Hempstead. *Norf* 2D 78
(nr. Holt)
Hempstead. *Norf* 3G 79
(nr. Stalham)
Hempsted. *Glos* 4D 48
Hempton. *Norf* 3B 78
Hempton. *Oxon* 2C 50
Hemsby. *Norf* 4G 79
Hemswell. *Linc* 1G 87
Hemswell Cliff. *Linc* 2G 87
Hemsworth. *Dors* 2E 15
Hemsworth. *W Yor* 3E 93
Hem, The. *Shrp* 5B 72
Hemyock. *Devn* 1E 13
Henallt. *Carm* 3E 45
Henbury. *Bris* 4A 34
Henbury. *Ches E* 3C 84
Hendomen. *Powy* 1E 58
Hendon. *G Lon* 2D 38
Hendon. *Tyne* 4H 115
Hendra. *Corn* 3D 6
Hendre. *B'end* 3C 32
Hendreforgan. *Rhon* 3C 32
Hendy. *Carm* 5F 45
Heneglwys. *IOA* 3D 80
Henfeddau Fawr. *Pemb* 1G 43
Henfield. *S Glo* 4B 34
Henfield. *W Sus* 4D 26
Henford. *Devn* 3D 10
Hengoed. *Cphy* 2E 33
Hengoed. *Shrp* 2E 71
Hengrave. *Suff* 4H 65
Henham. *Essx* 3F 53
Heniarth. *Powy* 5D 70
Henlade. *Som* 4F 21
Henley. *Dors* 2B 14
Henley. *Shrp* 2G 59
(nr. Church Stretton)
Henley. *Shrp* 3H 59
(nr. Ludlow)
Henley. *Som* 3H 21
Henley. *Suff* 5D 66
Henley. *W Sus* 4G 25
Henley-in-Arden. *Warw* 4F 61
Henley-on-Thames. *Oxon* 3F 37
Henley's Down. *E Sus* 4B 28
Henley Street. *Kent* 4A 40
Henllan. *Cdgn* 1D 44
Henllan. *Den* 4C 82
Henllan. *Mon* 3F 47
Henllan Amgoed. *Carm* 3F 43
Henllys. *Torf* 2F 33
Henlow. *C Beds* 2B 52
Hennock. *Devn* 4B 12
Henny Street. *Essx* 2B 54
Henryd. *Cnwy* 3G 81
Henry's Moat. *Pemb* 2E 43
Hensall. *N Yor* 2F 93
Henshaw. *Nmbd* 3A 114
Hensingham. *Cumb* 3A 102
Henstead. *Suff* 2G 67
Hensting. *Hants* 4C 24
Henstridge. *Som* 1C 14
Henstridge Ash. *Som* 4C 22
Henstridge Bowden. *Som* 4B 22
Henstridge Marsh. *Som* 4C 22
Henton. *Oxon* 5F 51
Henton. *Som* 2H 21
Henwood. *Corn* 5C 10
Heogan. *Shet* 7F 173
Heol Senni. *Powy* 3C 46
Heol-y-Cyw. *B'end* 3C 32
Hepburn. *Nmbd* 2E 121
Hepple. *Nmbd* 4D 121
Hepscott. *Nmbd* 1F 115
Heptonstall. *W Yor* 2H 91
Hepworth. *Suff* 3B 66
Hepworth. *W Yor* 4B 92
Herbrandston. *Pemb* 4C 42
Hereford. *Here* 2A 48
Heribusta. *High* 1D 154
Heriot. *Bord* 4H 129
Hermiston. *Edin* 2E 129
Hermitage. *Dors* 2B 14
Hermitage. *Bord* 5H 119
Hermitage. *W Ber* 4D 36
Hermitage. *W Sus* 2F 17
Hermon. *Carm* 3G 45
(nr. Llandeilo)
Hermon. *Carm* 2D 44
(nr. Newcastle Emlyn)
Hermon. *IOA* 4C 80
Hermon. *Pemb* 1G 43
Herne. *Kent* 4F 41
Herne Bay. *Kent* 4F 41
Herne Common. *Kent* 4F 41
Herne Pound. *Kent* 5A 40
Herner. *Devn* 4F 19
Hernhill. *Kent* 4E 41
Herodsfoot. *Corn* 2G 7
Heronden. *Kent* 5G 41
Herongate. *Essx* 1H 39
Heronsford. *S Ayr* 1G 109
Heronsgate. *Herts* 1B 38
Heron's Ghyll. *E Sus* 3F 27
Herra. *Shet* 2H 173
Herriard. *Hants* 2E 25
Herringfleet. *Suff* 1G 67
Herringswell. *Suff* 4G 65
Herrington. *Tyne* 4G 115
Hersden. *Kent* 4G 41
Hersham. *Corn* 2C 10
Hersham. *Surr* 4C 38
Herstmonceux. *E Sus* 4H 27
Herston. *Dors* 5F 15
Herston. *Orkn* 8D 172
Hertford. *Herts* 4D 52
Hertford Heath. *Herts* 4D 52
Hertingfordbury. *Herts* 4D 52
Hesketh. *Lanc* 2C 90
Hesketh Bank. *Lanc* 2C 90
Hesketh Lane. *Lanc* 5F 97
Hesket Newmarket. *Cumb* 1E 103
Heskin Green. *Lanc* 3D 90
Hesleden. *Dur* 1B 106
Hesleyside. *Nmbd* 1B 114
Heslington. *York* 4A 100
Hessay. *York* 4H 99
Hessenford. *Corn* 3H 7
Hessett. *Suff* 4B 66
Hessilhead. *N Ayr* 4E 127
Hessle. *E Yor* 2D 94
Hestaford. *Shet* 6D 173
Hest Bank. *Lanc* 3D 96
Hester's Way. *Glos* 3E 49
Hestinsetter. *Shet* 7D 173
Heston. *G Lon* 3C 38
Hestwall. *Orkn* 6B 172
Heswall. *Mers* 2E 83
Hethe. *Oxon* 3D 50
Hethelpit Cross. *Glos* 3C 48
Hethersett. *Norf* 5D 78
Hethersgill. *Cumb* 3F 113
Hetherside. *Cumb* 3F 113
Hethpool. *Nmbd* 2C 120
Hett. *Dur* 1F 105
Hetton. *N Yor* 4B 98
Hetton-le-Hole. *Tyne* 5G 115
Hetton Steads. *Nmbd* 1E 121
Heugh. *Nmbd* 2D 115
Heugh-head. *Abers* 2A 152
Heveningham. *Suff* 3F 67
Hever. *Kent* 1F 27
Heversham. *Cumb* 1D 97
Hevingham. *Norf* 3D 78
Hewas Water. *Corn* 4D 6
Hewelsfield. *Glos* 5A 48
Hewish. *N Som* 5H 33
Hewish. *Som* 2H 13
Hewood. *Dors* 2G 13
Heworth. *York* 4A 100
Hexham. *Nmbd* 3C 114
Hextable. *Kent* 3G 39
Hexton. *Herts* 2B 52
Hexworthy. *Devn* 5G 11
Heybridge. *Essx* 1H 39
(nr. Brentwood)
Heybridge. *Essx* 5B 54
(nr. Maldon)
Heybridge Basin. *Essx* 5B 54
Heybrook Bay. *Devn* 4A 8
Heydon. *Cambs* 1E 53
Heydon. *Norf* 3D 78
Heydour. *Linc* 2H 75
Heylipol. *Arg* 4A 138
Heyop. *Powy* 3E 59
Heysham. *Lanc* 3D 96
Heyshott. *W Sus* 1G 17
Heytesbury. *Wilts* 2E 23
Heythrop. *Oxon* 3B 50
Heywood. *G Man* 3G 91

Heywood—Hogben's Hill

Heywood. *Wilts* 1D 22
Hibaldstow. *N Lin* 4C 94
Hickleton. *S Yor* 4E 93
Hickling. *Norf* 3G 79
Hickling. *Notts* 3D 74
Hickling Green. *Norf* 3G 79
Hickling Heath. *Norf* 3G 79
Hickstead. *W Sus* 3D 26
Hidcote Bartrim. *Glos* 1G 49
Hidcote Boyce. *Glos* 1G 49
Higford. *Shrp* 5B 72
High Ackworth. *W Yor* 3E 93
Higham. *Derbs* 5A 86
Higham. *Kent* 3B 40
Higham. *Lanc* 1G 91
Higham. *S Yor* 4D 92
Higham. *Suff* 2D 54
(nr. Ipswich)
Higham. *Suff* 4G 65
(nr. Newmarket)
Higham Dykes. *Nmbd* 2E 115
Higham Ferrers. *Nptn* 4G 63
Higham Gobion. *C Beds* 2B 52
Higham on the Hill. *Leics* 1A 62
Highampton. *Devn* 2E 11
Higham Wood. *Kent* 1H 27
High Angerton. *Nmbd* 1D 115
High Auldgirth. *Dum* 1G 111
High Bankhill. *Cumb* 5G 113
High Banton. *N Lan* 1A 128
High Barnet. *G Lon* 1D 38
High Beech. *Essx* 1F 39
High Bentham. *N Yor* 3F 97
High Bickington. *Devn* 4G 19
High Biggins. *Cumb* 2E 97
High Birkwith. *N Yor* 2H 97
High Blantyre. *S Lan* 4H 127
High Bonnybridge. *Falk* 2B 128
High Borrans. *Cumb* 4F 103
High Bradfield. *S Yor* 1G 85
High Bray. *Devn* 3G 19
Highbridge. *Cumb* 5E 113
Highbridge. *High* 5E 148
Highbridge. *Som* 2G 21
Highbrook. *W Sus* 2E 27
High Brooms. *Kent* 1G 27
High Bullen. *Devn* 4F 19
Highburton. *W Yor* 3B 92
Highbury. *Som* 2B 22
High Buston. *Nmbd* 4G 121
High Callerton. *Nmbd* 2E 115
High Carlingill. *Cumb* 4H 103
High Catton. *E Yor* 4B 100
High Church. *Nmbd* 1E 115
Highclere. *Hants* 5C 36
Highcliffe. *Dors* 3H 15
High Cogges. *Oxon* 5B 50
High Common. *Norf* 5B 78
High Coniscliffe. *Darl* 3F 105
High Crosby. *Cumb* 4F 113
High Cross. *Hants* 4F 25
High Cross. *Herts* 4D 52
High Easter. *Essx* 4G 53
High Eggborough. *N Yor* 2F 93
High Ellington. *N Yor* 1D 98
Higher Alham. *Som* 2B 22
Higher Ansty. *Dors* 2C 14
Higher Ashton. *Devn* 4B 12
Higher Ballam. *Lanc* 1B 90
Higher Bartle. *Lanc* 1D 90
Higher Bockhampton. *Dors* 3C 14
Higher Bojewyan. *Corn* 3A 4
High Ercall. *Telf* 4H 71
Higher Cheriton. *Devn* 2E 12
Higher Clovelly. *Devn* 4D 18
Higher Compton. *Plym* 3A 8
Higher Dean. *Devn* 2D 8
Higher Dinting. *Derbs* 1E 85
Higher Dunstone. *Devn* 5H 11
Higher End. *G Man* 4D 90
Higherford. *Lanc* 5A 98
Higher Gabwell. *Devn* 2F 9
Higher Halstock Leigh. *Dors* 2A 14
Higher Heysham. *Lanc* 3D 96
Higher Hurdsfield. *Ches E* 3D 84
Higher Kingcombe. *Dors* 3A 14
Higher Kinnerton. *Flin* 4F 83
Higher Melcombe. *Dors* 2C 14
Higher Penwortham. *Lanc* 2D 90
Higher Porthpean. *Corn* 3E 7
Higher Poynton. *Ches E* 2D 84
Higher Shotton. *Flin* 4F 83
Higher Shurlach. *Ches W* 3A 84
Higher Slade. *Devn* 2F 19
Higher Tale. *Devn* 2D 12
Highertown. *Corn* 4C 6
Higher Town. *IOS* 1B 4
Higher Town. *Som* 2C 20
Higher Vexford. *Som* 3E 20
Higher Walton. *Lanc* 2D 90
Higher Walton. *Warr* 2H 83
Higher Whatcombe. *Dors* 2D 14
Higher Wheelton. *Lanc* 2E 90
Higher Whiteleigh. *Corn* 3C 10
Higher Whitley. *Ches W* 2A 84
Higher Wincham. *Ches W* 3A 84
Higher Wraxall. *Dors* 2A 14
Higher Wych. *Wrex* 1G 71
Higher Yalberton. *Torb* 3E 9
High Etherley. *Dur* 2E 105
High Ferry. *Linc* 1C 76
Highfield. *E Yor* 1H 93
Highfield. *N Ayr* 4E 126
Highfield. *Tyne* 4E 115
Highfields Caldecote. *Cambs* 5C 64
High Garrett. *Essx* 3A 54
Highgate. *G Lon* 2D 39
Highgate. *N Ayr* 4E 127
Highgate. *Powy* 1D 58
High Grange. *Dur* 1E 105
High Green. *Cumb* 4F 103
High Green. *Norf* 5D 78
High Green. *Shrp* 2B 60
High Green. *S Yor* 1H 85
High Green. *W Yor* 3B 92
High Green. *Worc* 1D 49
Highgreen Manor. *Nmbd* 5C 120
High Halden. *Kent* 2C 28
High Halstow. *Medw* 3B 40
High Ham. *Som* 3H 21
High Harrington. *Cumb* 2B 102
High Haswell. *Dur* 5G 115
High Hatton. *Shrp* 3A 72
High Hawsker. *N Yor* 4G 107
High Hesket. *Cumb* 5F 113
High Hesleden. *Dur* 1B 106
High Hoyland. *S Yor* 3C 92
High Hunsley. *E Yor* 1C 94
High Hurstwood. *E Sus* 3F 27
High Hutton. *N Yor* 3B 100
High Ireby. *Cumb* 1D 102
High Keil. *Arg* 5A 122
High Kelling. *Norf* 2D 78
High Kilburn. *N Yor* 2H 99
High Knipe. *Cumb* 3G 103
High Lands. *Dur* 2E 105
Highlands, The. *Shrp* 2A 60
Highlane. *Ches E* 4C 84
Highlane. *Derbs* 2B 86
High Lane. *G Man* 2D 84
High Lane. *Here* 4A 60
High Laver. *Essx* 5F 53
Highlaws. *Cumb* 5C 112
Highleadon. *Glos* 3C 48
High Legh. *Ches E* 2B 84
Highleigh. *W Sus* 3G 17
High Leven. *Stoc T* 3B 106
Highley. *Shrp* 2B 60
High Littleton. *Bath* 1B 22
High Longthwaite. *Cumb* 5D 112
High Lorton. *Cumb* 2C 102
High Marishes. *N Yor* 2C 100
High Marnham. *Notts* 3F 87
High Melton. *S Yor* 4F 93
High Mickley. *Nmbd* 3D 115
Highmoor. *Cumb* 5D 112
High Moor. *Lanc* 3D 90
Highmoor. *Oxon* 3F 37
Highmoor Cross. *Oxon* 3F 37
Highmoor Hill. *Mon* 3H 33
Highnam. *Glos* 4C 48
High Newport. *Tyne* 4G 115
High Newton. *Cumb* 1D 96
High Newton-by-the-Sea. *Nmbd* 2G 121
High Nibthwaite. *Cumb* 1B 96
High Offley. *Staf* 3B 72
High Ongar. *Essx* 5F 53
High Onn. *Staf* 4C 72
High Orchard. *Glos* 4D 48
High Park. *Mers* 3B 90
High Roding. *Essx* 4G 53
High Row. *Cumb* 1E 103
High Salvington. *W Sus* 5C 26
High Scales. *Cumb* 5C 112
High Shaw. *N Yor* 5B 104
High Shincliffe. *Dur* 5F 115
High Side. *Cumb* 1D 102
High Spen. *Tyne* 3E 115
Highsted. *Kent* 4D 40
High Stoop. *Dur* 5E 115
High Street. *Corn* 3D 6
High Street. *Suff* 5G 67
(nr. Aldeburgh)
High Street. *Suff* 2F 67
(nr. Bungay)
High Street. *Suff* 3G 67
(nr. Yoxford)
Highstreet Green. *Essx* 2A 54
High Street Green. *Suff* 5C 66
Highstreet Green. *Surr* 2A 26
Hightae. *Dum* 2B 112
High Throston. *Hart* 1B 106
Hightown. *Ches E* 4C 84
Hightown. *Mers* 4A 90
High Town. *Staf* 4D 73
Hightown Green. *Suff* 5B 66
High Toynton. *Linc* 4B 88
High Trewhitt. *Nmbd* 4E 121
High Valleyfield. *Fife* 1D 128
Highway. *Here* 1H 47
Highweek. *Devn* 5B 12
High Westwood. *Dur* 4E 115
Highwood. *Staf* 2E 73
Highwood. *Worc* 4A 60
High Worsall. *N Yor* 4A 106
Highworth. *Swin* 2H 35
High Wray. *Cumb* 5E 103
High Wych. *Herts* 4E 53
High Wycombe. *Buck* 2G 37
Hilborough. *Norf* 5H 77
Hilcott. *Wilts* 1G 23
Hildenborough. *Kent* 1G 27
Hildersham. *Cambs* 1F 53
Hilderstone. *Staf* 2D 72
Hilderthorpe. *E Yor* 3F 101
Hilfield. *Dors* 2B 14
Hilgay. *Norf* 1F 65
Hill. *S Glo* 2B 34
Hill. *Warw* 4B 62
Hill. *Worc* 1E 49
Hillam. *N Yor* 2F 93
Hillbeck. *Cumb* 3A 104
Hillberry. *IOM* 4C 108
Hillborough. *Kent* 4G 41
Hillbourne. *Pool* 3F 15
Hillbrae. *Abers* 4D 160
(nr. Aberchirder)
Hillbrae. *Abers* 1E 153
(nr. Inverurie)
Hillbrae. *Abers* 5F 161
(nr. Methlick)
Hill Brow. *Hants* 4F 25
Hillbutts. *Dors* 2E 15
Hillclifflane. *Derbs* 1G 73
Hillcommon. *Som* 4E 21
Hill Deverill. *Wilts* 2D 22
Hilldyke. *Linc* 1C 76
Hill End. *Dur* 1D 104
Hillend. *Fife* 1E 129
(nr. Inverkeithing)
Hill End. *Fife* 4C 136
(nr. Saline)
Hillend. *N Lan* 3B 128
Hill End. *N Yor* 4C 98
Hillend. *Shrp* 1C 60
Hillend. *Swan* 3D 30
Hillersland. *Glos* 4A 48
Hillerton. *Devn* 3H 11
Hillesden. *Buck* 3E 51
Hillesley. *Glos* 3C 34
Hillfarrance. *Som* 4E 21
Hill Gate. *Here* 3H 47
Hill Green. *Essx* 2E 53
Hillgreen. *W Ber* 4C 36
Hillhead. *Abers* 5C 160
Hill Head. *Hants* 2D 16
Hillhead. *S Ayr* 3D 116
Hillhead. *Torb* 3F 9
Hillhead of Auchentumb. *Abers* 3G 161
Hilliard's Cross. *Staf* 4F 73
Hilliclay. *High* 2D 168
Hillingdon. *G Lon* 2B 38
Hillington. *Glas* 3G 127
Hillington. *Norf* 3G 77
Hillmorton. *Warw* 3C 62
Hill of Beath. *Fife* 4D 136
Hill of Fearn. *High* 1C 158
Hill of Fiddes. *Abers* 1G 153
Hill of Keillor. *Ang* 4B 144
Hill of Overbrae. *Abers* 2F 161
Hill Ridware. *Staf* 4E 73
Hillsborough. *Lis* 5G 175
Hillsborough. *S Yor* 1H 85
Hillside. *Abers* 4G 153
Hillside. *Ang* 2G 145
Hillside. *Devn* 2D 8
Hillside. *Mers* 3B 90
Hillside. *Orkn* 5C 172
Hillside. *Shet* 5F 173
Hillside. *Shrp* 2A 60
Hill Side. *W Yor* 3B 92
Hillside. *Worc* 4B 60
Hillside of Prieston. *Ang* 5C 144
Hill Somersal. *Derbs* 2F 73
Hillstown. *Derbs* 4B 86
Hillstreet. *Hants* 1B 16
Hillswick. *Shet* 4D 173
Hill, The. *Cumb* 1A 96
Hill Top. *Dur* 2C 104
(nr. Barnard Castle)
Hill Top. *Dur* 5F 115
(nr. Durham)
Hill Top. *Dur* 4E 115
(nr. Stanley)
Hill View. *Dors* 3E 15
Hillwell. *Shet* 10E 173
Hill Wootton. *Warw* 4H 61
Hillyland. *Per* 1C 136
Hilmarton. *Wilts* 4F 35
Hilperton. *Wilts* 1D 22
Hilperton Marsh. *Wilts* 1D 22
Hilsea. *Port* 2E 17
Hilston. *E Yor* 1F 95
Hiltingbury. *Hants* 4C 24
Hilton. *Cambs* 4B 64
Hilton. *Cumb* 2A 104
Hilton. *Derbs* 2G 73
Hilton. *Dors* 2C 14
Hilton. *Dur* 2E 105
Hilton. *High* 5E 165
Hilton. *Shrp* 1B 60
Hilton. *Staf* 5E 73
Hilton. *Stoc T* 3B 106
Hilton of Cadboll. *High* 1C 158
Himbleton. *Worc* 5D 60
Himley. *Staf* 1C 60
Hincaster. *Cumb* 1E 97
Hinchcliffe Mill. *W Yor* 4B 92
Hinchwick. *Glos* 3G 49
Hinckley. *Leics* 1B 62
Hinderclay. *Suff* 3C 66
Hinderwell. *N Yor* 3E 107
Hindford. *Shrp* 2F 71
Hindhead. *Surr* 3G 25
Hindley. *G Man* 4E 90
Hindley. *Nmbd* 4D 114
Hindley Green. *G Man* 4E 91
Hindlip. *Worc* 5C 60
Hindolveston. *Norf* 3C 78
Hindon. *Wilts* 3E 23
Hindringham. *Norf* 2B 78
Hingham. *Norf* 5C 78
Hinksford. *Staf* 2C 60
Hinstock. *Shrp* 3A 72
Hintlesham. *Suff* 1D 54
Hinton. *Hants* 3H 15
Hinton. *Here* 2G 47
Hinton. *Nptn* 5C 62
Hinton. *Shrp* 5G 71
Hinton. *S Glo* 4C 34
Hinton Ampner. *Hants* 4D 24
Hinton Blewett. *Bath* 1A 22
Hinton Charterhouse. *Bath* 1C 22
Hinton-in-the-Hedges. *Nptn* 2D 50
Hinton Martell. *Dors* 2F 15
Hinton on the Green. *Worc* 1F 49
Hinton Parva. *Swin* 3H 35
Hinton St George. *Som* 1H 13
Hinton St Mary. *Dors* 1C 14
Hinton Waldrist. *Oxon* 2B 36
Hints. *Shrp* 3A 60
Hints. *Staf* 5F 73
Hinwick. *Bed* 4G 63
Hinxhill. *Kent* 1E 29
Hinxton. *Cambs* 1E 53
Hinxworth. *Herts* 1C 52
Hipley. *Hants* 1E 16
Hipperholme. *W Yor* 2B 92
Hipsburn. *Nmbd* 3G 121
Hipswell. *N Yor* 5E 105
Hiraeth. *Carm* 2F 43
Hirn. *Abers* 3E 153
Hirnant. *Powy* 3C 70
Hirst. *N Lan* 3B 128
Hirst. *Nmbd* 1F 115
Hirst Courtney. *N Yor* 2G 93
Hirwaen. *Den* 4D 82
Hirwaun. *Rhon* 5C 46
Hiscott. *Devn* 4F 19
Histon. *Cambs* 4D 64
Hitcham. *Suff* 5B 66
Hitchin. *Herts* 3B 52
Hittisleigh. *Devn* 3H 11
Hittisleigh Barton. *Devn* 3H 11
Hive. *E Yor* 1B 94
Hixon. *Staf* 3E 73
Hoaden. *Kent* 5G 41
Hoar Cross. *Staf* 3F 73
Hoarwithy. *Here* 3A 48
Hoath. *Kent* 4G 41
Hobarris. *Shrp* 3F 59
Hobbister. *Orkn* 7C 172
Hobbles Green. *Suff* 5G 65
Hobbs Cross. *Essx* 1F 39
Hobkirk. *Bord* 3H 119
Hobson. *Dur* 4E 115
Hoby. *Leics* 4D 74
Hockering. *Norf* 4C 78
Hockering Heath. *Norf* 4C 78
Hockerton. *Notts* 5E 86
Hockley. *Essx* 1C 40
Hockley. *Staf* 5G 73
Hockley. *W Mid* 3G 61
Hockley Heath. *W Mid* 3F 61
Hockliffe. *C Beds* 3H 51
Hockwold cum Wilton. *Norf* 2G 65
Hockworthy. *Devn* 1D 12
Hoddesdon. *Herts* 5D 52
Hoddlesden. *Bkbn* 2F 91
Hoddomcross. *Dum* 2C 112
Hodgeston. *Pemb* 5E 43
Hodley. *Powy* 1D 58
Hodnet. *Shrp* 3A 72
Hodsoll Street. *Kent* 4H 39
Hodson. *Swin* 3G 35
Hodthorpe. *Derbs* 3C 86
Hoe. *Norf* 4B 78
Hoe Gate. *Hants* 1E 17
Hoe, The. *Plym* 3A 8
Hoff. *Cumb* 3H 103
Hoffleet Stow. *Linc* 2B 76
Hogaland. *Shet* 4E 173
Hogben's Hill. *Kent* 5E 41

Little Coates—Llanelwedd

Little Coates. NE Lin 4F 95
Little Comberton. Worc 1E 49
Little Common. E Sus 5B 28
Little Compton. Warw 2A 50
Little Cornard. Suff 2B 54
Littlecote. Buck 3G 51
Littlecott. Wilts 1G 23
Little Cowarne. Here 5A 60
Little Coxwell. Oxon 2A 36
Little Crakehall. N Yor 5F 105
Little Crawley. Mil 1H 51
Little Creich. High 5D 164
Little Cressingham. Norf 5A 78
Little Crosby. Mers 4B 90
Little Crosthwaite. Cumb 2D 102
Little Cubley. Derbs 2F 73
Little Dalby. Leics 4E 75
Little Dawley. Telf 5A 72
Littledean. Glos 4B 48
Little Dens. Abers 4H 161
Little Dewchurch. Here 2A 48
Little Ditton. Cambs 5F 65
Little Down. Hants 1B 24
Little Downham. Cambs 2E 65
Little Drayton. Shrp 2A 72
Little Driffield. E Yor 4E 101
Little Dunham. Norf 4A 78
Little Dunkeld. Per 4H 143
Little Dunmow. Essx 3G 53
Little Easton. Essx 3G 53
Little Eaton. Derbs 1A 74
Little Eccleston. Lanc 5D 96
Little Ellingham. Norf 1C 66
Little Elm. Som 2C 22
Little End. Essx 5F 53
Little Everdon. Nptn 5C 62
Little Eversden. Cambs 5C 64
Little Faringdon. Oxon 5H 49
Little Fencote. N Yor 5F 105
Little Fenton. N Yor 1F 93
Littleferry. High 4F 165
Little Fransham. Norf 4B 78
Little Gaddesden. Herts 4H 51
Little Garway. Here 3H 47
Little Gidding. Cambs 2A 64
Little Glemham. Suff 5F 67
Little Glenshee. Per 5G 143
Little Gransden. Cambs 5B 64
Little Green. Suff 3C 66
Little Green. Wrex 1G 71
Little Grimsby. Linc 1C 88
Little Habton. N Yor 2B 100
Little Hadham. Herts 3E 53
Little Hale. Linc 1A 76
Little Hallingbury. Essx 4E 53
Littleham. Devn 4E 19
(nr. Bideford)
Littleham. Devn 4D 12
(nr. Exmouth)
Little Hampden. Buck 5G 51
Littlehampton. W Sus 5B 26
Little Haresfield. Glos 5D 48
Little Harrowden. Nptn 3F 63
Little Haseley. Oxon 5E 51
Little Hatfield. E Yor 5F 101
Little Hautbois. Norf 3E 79
Little Haven. Pemb 3C 42
Little Hay. Staf 5F 73
Little Hayfield. Derbs 2E 85
Little Haywood. Staf 3E 73
Little Heath. W Mid 2H 61
Little Heck. N Yor 2F 93
Littlehempston. Devn 2E 9
Little Herbert's. Glos 4E 49
Little Hereford. Here 4H 59
Little Horkesley. Essx 2C 54
Little Hormead. Herts 3D 53
Little Horsted. E Sus 4F 27
Little Horton. W Yor 1B 92
Little Horwood. Buck 2F 51
Little Houghton. Nptn 5F 63
Littlehoughton. Nmbd 3G 121
Little Houghton. S Yor 4E 93
Little Hucklow. Derbs 3F 85
Little Hulton. G Man 4F 91
Little Irchester. Nptn 4G 63
Little Kelk. E Yor 3E 101
Little Kimble. Buck 5G 51
Little Kineton. Warw 5H 61
Little Kingshill. Buck 2G 37
Little Langdale. Cumb 4E 102
Little Langford. Wilts 3F 23
Little Laver. Essx 5F 53
Little Lawford. Warw 3B 62
Little Leigh. Ches W 3A 84
Little Leighs. Essx 4H 53
Little Leven. E Yor 5E 101
Little Lever. G Man 4F 91
Little Linford. Mil 1G 51
Little London. Buck 4E 51
Little London. E Sus 4G 27
Little London. Hants 2B 24
(nr. Andover)
Little London. Hants 1E 24
(nr. Basingstoke)
Little London. Linc 3D 76
(nr. Long Sutton)
Little London. Linc 3B 76
(nr. Spalding)
Little London. Norf 2E 79
(nr. North Walsham)
Little London. Norf 1G 65
(nr. Northwold)
Little London. Norf 2D 78
(nr. Saxthorpe)
Little London. Norf 1F 65
(nr. Southery)
Little London. Powy 2C 58
Little Longstone. Derbs 3F 85
Little Malvern. Worc 1C 48
Little Maplestead. Essx 2B 54
Little Marcle. Here 2B 48
Little Marlow. Buck 3G 37
Little Massingham. Norf 3G 77
Little Melton. Norf 5D 78
Littlemill. Abers 4H 151
Littlemill. E Ayr 3D 116
Littlemill. High 4D 158
Little Mill. Mon 5G 47
Little Milton. Oxon 5E 50
Little Missenden. Buck 1A 38
Littlemoor. Derbs 4A 86
Littlemoor. Dors 4B 14
Littlemore. Oxon 5D 50
Little Mountain. Flin 4E 83
Little Musgrave. Cumb 3A 104
Little Ness. Shrp 4G 71
Little Neston. Ches W 3E 83
Little Newcastle. Pemb 2D 43
Little Newsham. Dur 3E 105
Little Oakley. Essx 3F 55
Little Oakley. Nptn 2F 63
Little Onn. Staf 4C 72
Little Ormside. Cumb 3A 104
Little Orton. Cumb 4E 113
Little Orton. Leics 5H 73
Little Ouse. Norf 2F 65
Little Ouseburn. N Yor 3G 99
Littleover. Derb 2H 73
Little Packington. Warw 2G 61
Little Paxton. Cambs 4A 64
Little Petherick. Corn 1D 6
Little Plumpton. Lanc 1B 90
Little Plumstead. Norf 4F 79
Little Ponton. Linc 2G 75
Littleport. Cambs 2E 65
Little Posbrook. Hants 2D 16
Little Potheridge. Devn 1F 11
Little Preston. Nptn 5C 62
Little Raveley. Cambs 3B 64
Little Reynoldston. Swan 4D 31
Little Ribston. N Yor 4F 99
Little Rissington. Glos 4G 49
Little Rogart. High 3E 165
Little Rollright. Oxon 2A 50
Little Ryburgh. Norf 3B 78
Little Ryle. Nmbd 3E 121
Little Ryton. Shrp 5G 71
Little Salkeld. Cumb 1G 103
Little Sampford. Essx 2G 53
Little Sandhurst. Brac 5G 37
Little Saredon. Staf 5D 72
Little Saxham. Suff 4G 65
Little Scatwell. High 3F 157
Little Shelford. Cambs 5D 64
Little Shoddesden. Hants 2A 24
Little Singleton. Lanc 1B 90
Little Smeaton. N Yor 3F 93
Little Snoring. Norf 2B 78
Little Sodbury. S Glo 3C 34
Little Somborne. Hants 3B 24
Little Somerford. Wilts 3E 35
Little Soudley. Shrp 3B 72
Little Stainforth. N Yor 3H 97
Little Stainton. Darl 3A 106
Little Stanney. Ches W 3G 83
Little Staughton. Bed 4A 64
Little Steeping. Linc 4D 88
Littlester. Shet 3G 173
Little Stoke. Staf 2D 72
Littlestone-on-Sea. Kent 3E 29
Little Stonham. Suff 4D 66
Little Stretton. Leics 5D 74
Little Stretton. Shrp 1G 59
Little Strickland. Cumb 3G 103
Little Stukeley. Cambs 3B 64
Little Sugnall. Staf 2C 72
Little Sutton. Ches W 3F 83
Little Sutton. Linc 3D 76
Little Swinburne. Nmbd 2C 114
Little Tew. Oxon 3B 50
Little Tey. Essx 3B 54
Little Thetford. Cambs 3E 65
Little Thirkleby. N Yor 2G 99
Little Thornage. Norf 2C 78
Little Thornton. Lanc 5C 96
Littlethorpe. Leics 1C 62
Littlethorpe. N Yor 3F 99
Little Thorpe. W Yor 2B 92
Little Thurlow. Suff 5F 65
Little Thurrock. Thur 3H 39
Littleton. Ches W 4G 83
Littleton. Hants 3C 24
Littleton. Som 3H 21
Littleton. Surr 1A 26
(nr. Guildford)
Littleton. Surr 4B 38
(nr. Staines)
Littleton Drew. Wilts 3D 34
Littleton Pannell. Wilts 1F 23
Littleton-upon-Severn. S Glo 3A 34
Little Torboll. High 4E 165
Little Torrington. Devn 1E 11
Little Totham. Essx 4B 54
Little Town. Cumb 3D 102
Littletown. Dur 5G 115
Littletown. High 5E 165
Little Town. Lanc 1E 91
Little Twycross. Leics 5H 73
Little Urswick. Cumb 2B 96
Little Wakering. Essx 2D 40
Little Walden. Essx 1F 53
Little Waldingfield. Suff 1C 54
Little Walsingham. Norf 2B 78
Little Waltham. Essx 4H 53
Little Warley. Essx 1H 39
Little Weighton. E Yor 1C 94
Little Wenham. Suff 2D 54
Little Wenlock. Telf 5A 72
Little Whelnetham. Suff 4A 66
Little Whittingham Green. Suff 3E 67
Littlewick Green. Wind 4G 37
Little Wilbraham. Cambs 5E 65
Littlewindsor. Dors 2H 13
Little Wisbeach. Linc 2A 76
Little Witcombe. Glos 4E 49
Little Witley. Worc 4B 60
Little Wittenham. Oxon 2D 36
Little Wolford. Warw 2A 50
Littleworth. Bed 1A 52
Littleworth. Glos 2G 49
Littleworth. Oxon 2B 36
Littleworth. Staf 4E 73
(nr. Cannock)
Littleworth. Staf 3B 72
(nr. Eccleshall)
Littleworth. Staf 3D 72
(nr. Stafford)
Littleworth. W Sus 3C 26
Littleworth. Worc 4D 61
(nr. Redditch)
Littleworth. Worc 5C 60
(nr. Worcester)
Little Wratting. Suff 1G 53
Little Wymondley. Herts 3C 52
Little Wyrley. Staf 5E 73
Little Yeldham. Essx 2A 54
Littley Green. Essx 4G 53
Litton. Derbs 3F 85
Litton. N Yor 2B 98
Litton. Som 1A 22
Litton Cheney. Dors 3A 14
Liurbost. W Isl 5F 171
Liverpool. Mers 1F 83
Liverpool John Lennon Airport. Mers 2G 83
Liversedge. W Yor 2B 92
Liverton. Devn 5B 12
Liverton. Red C 3E 107
Liverton Mines. Red C 3E 107
Livingston. W Lot 3D 128
Livingston Village. W Lot 3D 128
Lixwm. Flin 3D 82
Lizard. Corn 5E 5
Llaingoch. IOA 2B 80
Llaithddu. Powy 2C 58
Llampha. V Glam 4C 32
Llan. Powy 5A 70
Llanaber. Gwyn 4F 69
Llanaelhaearn. Gwyn 1C 68
Llanaeron. Cdgn 4D 57
Llanafan. Cdgn 3F 57
Llanafan-fawr. Powy 5B 58
Llanafan-fechan. Powy 5B 58
Llanallgo. IOA 2D 81
Llanandras. Powy 4F 59
Llananno. Powy 3C 58
Llanarmon. Gwyn 2D 68
Llanarmon Dyffryn Ceiriog. Wrex 2D 70
Llanarmon-yn-Ial. Den 5D 82
Llanarth. Cdgn 5D 56
Llanarth. Mon 4G 47
Llanarthne. Carm 3F 45
Llanasa. Flin 2D 82
Llanbabo. IOA 2C 80
Llanbadarn Fawr. Cdgn 2F 57
Llanbadarn Fynydd. Powy 3D 58
Llanbadarn-y-garreg. Powy 1E 46
Llanbadoc. Mon 5G 47
Llanbadrig. IOA 1C 80
Llanbeder. Newp 2G 33
Llanbedr. Gwyn 3E 69
Llanbedr. Powy 3F 47
(nr. Crickhowell)
Llanbedr. Powy 1E 47
(nr. Hay-on-Wye)
Llanbedr-Dyffryn-Clwyd. Den 5D 82
Llanbedrgoch. IOA 2E 81
Llanbedrog. Gwyn 2C 68
Llanbedr Pont Steffan. Cdgn 1F 45
Llanbedr-y-cennin. Cnwy 4G 81
Llanberis. Gwyn 4E 81
Llanbethery. V Glam 5D 32
Llanbister. Powy 3D 58
Llanblethian. V Glam 4C 32
Llanboidy. Carm 2G 43
Llanbradach. Cphy 2E 33
Llanbrynmair. Powy 5A 70
Llanbydderi. V Glam 5D 32
Llancadle. V Glam 5D 32
Llancarfan. V Glam 4D 32
Llancatal. V Glam 5D 32
Llancayo. Mon 5G 47
Llancloudy. Here 3H 47
Llancoch. Powy 3E 58
Llancynfelyn. Cdgn 1F 57
Llandaff. Card 4E 33
Llandanwg. Gwyn 3E 69
Llandarcy. Neat 3G 31
Llandawke. Carm 3G 43
Llanddaniel Fab. IOA 3D 81
Llanddarog. Carm 4F 45
Llanddeiniol. Cdgn 3E 57
Llanddeiniolen. Gwyn 4E 81
Llandderfel. Gwyn 2B 70
Llanddeusant. Carm 3A 46
Llanddeusant. IOA 2C 80
Llanddew. Powy 2D 46
Llanddewi. Swan 4D 30
Llanddewi Brefi. Cdgn 5F 57
Llanddewi'r Cwm. Powy 1D 46
Llanddewi Rhydderch. Mon 4G 47
Llanddewi Velfrey. Pemb 3F 43
Llanddewi Ystradenni. Powy 4D 58
Llanddoged. Cnwy 4H 81
Llanddona. IOA 3E 81
Llanddowror. Carm 3G 43
Llanddulas. Cnwy 3B 82
Llanddwywe. Gwyn 3E 69
Llanddyfnan. IOA 3E 81
Llandecwyn. Gwyn 2F 69
Llandefaelog Fach. Powy 2D 46
Llandefaelog-tre'r-graig. Powy 2E 47
Llandefalle. Powy 2E 46
Llandegfan. IOA 3E 81
Llandegla. Den 5D 82
Llandegley. Powy 4D 58
Llandegveth. Mon 2G 33
Llandeilo. Carm 3G 45
Llandeilo Graban. Powy 1D 46
Llandeilo'r Fan. Powy 2B 46
Llandeloy. Pemb 2C 42
Llandenny. Mon 5H 47
Llandevaud. Newp 2H 33
Llandevenny. Mon 3H 33
Llandilo. Pemb 2F 43
Llandinabo. Here 3A 48
Llandinam. Powy 2C 58
Llandissilio. Pemb 2F 43
Llandogo. Mon 5A 48
Llandough. V Glam 4C 32
(nr. Cowbridge)
Llandough. V Glam 4E 33
(nr. Penarth)
Llandovery. Carm 2A 46
Llandow. V Glam 4C 32
Llandre. Cdgn 2F 57
Llandrillo. Den 2C 70
Llandrillo-yn-Rhos. Cnwy 2H 81
Llandrindod. Powy 4C 58
Llandrindod Wells. Powy 4C 58
Llandrinio. Powy 4E 71
Llandudno. Cnwy 2G 81
Llandudno Junction. Cnwy 3G 81
Llandudoch. Pemb 1B 44
Llandw. V Glam 4C 32
Llandwrog. Gwyn 5D 80
Llandybie. Carm 4G 45
Llandyfaelog. Carm 4E 45
Llandyfan. Carm 4G 45
Llandyfriog. Cdgn 1D 44
Llandyfrydog. IOA 2D 80
Llandygai. Gwyn 3F 81
Llandygwydd. Cdgn 1C 44
Llandynan. Den 1D 70
Llandyrnog. Den 4D 82
Llandysilio. Powy 4E 71
Llandyssil. Powy 1D 58
Llandysul. Cdgn 1E 45
Llanedeyrn. Card 3F 33
Llaneglwys. Powy 2D 46
Llanegryn. Gwyn 5F 69
Llanegwad. Carm 3F 45
Llaneilian. IOA 1D 80
Llanelian-yn-Rhos. Cnwy 3A 82
Llanelidan. Den 5D 82
Llanelieu. Powy 2E 47
Llanellen. Mon 4G 47
Llanelli. Carm 3E 31
Llanelltyd. Gwyn 4G 69
Llanelly. Mon 4F 47
Llanelly Hill. Mon 4F 47
Llanelwedd. Powy 5C 58

Low Whinnow. *Cumb* 4E **112**
Low Wood. *Cumb* 1C **96**
Low Worsall. *N Yor* 4A **106**
Low Wray. *Cumb* 4E **103**
Loxbeare. *Devn* 1C **12**
Loxhill. *Surr* 2B **26**
Loxhore. *Devn* 3G **19**
Loxley. *S Yor* 2H **85**
Loxley. *Warw* 5G **61**
Loxley Green. *Staf* 2E **73**
Loxton. *N Som* 1G **21**
Loxwood. *W Sus* 2B **26**
Lubcroy. *High* 3A **164**
Lubenham. *Leics* 2E **62**
Lubinvullin. *High* 2F **167**
Luccombe. *Som* 2C **20**
Luccombe Village. *IOW* 4D **16**
Lucker. *Nmbd* 1F **121**
Luckett. *Corn* 5D **11**
Luckington. *Wilts* 3D **34**
Lucklawhill. *Fife* 1G **137**
Luckwell Bridge. *Som* 3C **20**
Lucton. *Here* 4G **59**
Ludag. *W Isl* 7C **170**
Ludborough. *Linc* 1B **88**
Ludchurch. *Pemb* 3F **43**
Luddenden. *W Yor* 2A **92**
Luddenden Foot. *W Yor* 2A **92**
Luddenham. *Kent* 4D **40**
Ludderburn. *Cumb* 5F **103**
Luddesdown. *Kent* 4A **40**
Luddington. *N Lin* 3B **94**
Luddington. *Warw* 5F **61**
Luddington in the Brook. *Nptn* 2A **64**
Ludford. *Linc* 2A **88**
Ludford. *Shrp* 3H **59**
Ludgershall. *Buck* 4E **51**
Ludgershall. *Wilts* 1A **24**
Ludgvan. *Corn* 3C **4**
Ludham. *Norf* 4F **79**
Ludlow. *Shrp* 3H **59**
Ludstone. *Shrp* 1C **60**
Ludwell. *Wilts* 4E **23**
Ludworth. *Dur* 5G **115**
Luffenhall. *Herts* 3C **52**
Luffincott. *Devn* 3D **10**
Lugar. *E Ayr* 2E **117**
Luggate Burn. *E Lot* 2C **130**
Lugg Green. *Here* 4G **59**
Luggiebank. *N Lan* 2A **128**
Lugton. *E Ayr* 4F **127**
Lugwardine. *Here* 1A **48**
Luib. *High* 1D **146**
Luib. *Stir* 1D **135**
Lulham. *Here* 1H **47**
Lullington. *Derbs* 4G **73**
Lullington. *E Sus* 5G **27**
Lullington. *Som* 1C **22**
Lulsgate Bottom. *N Som* 5A **34**
Lulsley. *Worc* 5B **60**
Lulworth Camp. *Dors* 4D **14**
Lumb. *Lanc* 2G **91**
Lumb. *W Yor* 2A **92**
Lumby. *N Yor* 1E **93**
Lumphanan. *Abers* 3C **152**
Lumphinnans. *Fife* 4D **136**
Lumsdaine. *Bord* 3E **131**
Lumsden. *Abers* 1B **152**
Lunan. *Ang* 3F **145**
Lunanhead. *Ang* 3D **145**
Luncarty. *Per* 1C **136**
Lund. *E Yor* 5D **100**
Lund. *N Yor* 1G **93**
Lundie. *Ang* 5B **144**
Lundin Links. *Fife* 3G **137**
Lundy Green. *Norf* 1E **67**
Lunna. *Shet* 5F **173**
Lunning. *Shet* 5G **173**
Lunnon. *Swan* 4E **31**
Lunsford. *Kent* 5A **40**
Lunsford's Cross. *E Sus* 4B **28**
Lunt. *Mers* 4B **90**
Luppitt. *Devn* 2E **13**
Lupridge. *Devn* 3D **8**
Lupset. *W Yor* 3D **92**
Lupton. *Cumb* 1E **97**
Lurgan. *Cgvn* 5F **175**
Lurgashall. *W Sus* 3A **26**
Lurley. *Devn* 1C **12**
Lusby. *Linc* 4C **88**
Luscombe. *Devn* 3D **9**
Luson. *Devn* 4C **8**
Luss. *Arg* 4C **134**
Lussagiven. *Arg* 1E **125**
Lusta. *High* 3B **154**
Lustleigh. *Devn* 4A **12**
Luston. *Here* 4G **59**
Luthermuir. *Abers* 2F **145**
Luthrie. *Fife* 2F **137**
Lutley. *Staf* 2C **60**
Luton. *Devn* 2D **12**
(nr. Honiton)
Luton. *Devn* 5C **12**
(nr. Teignmouth)
Luton. *Lutn* 3A **52**
Luton (London) Airport. *Lutn* 3B **52**
Lutterworth. *Leics* 2C **62**
Lutton. *Devn* 3B **8**
(nr. Ivybridge)
Lutton. *Devn* 2C **8**
(nr. South Brent)
Lutton. *Linc* 3D **76**
Lutton. *Nptn* 2A **64**
Lutton Gowts. *Linc* 3D **76**
Lutworthy. *Devn* 1A **12**
Luxborough. *Som* 3C **20**
Luxley. *Glos* 3B **48**
Luxulyan. *Corn* 3E **7**
Lybster. *High* 5E **169**
Lydbury North. *Shrp* 2F **59**
Lydcott. *Devn* 3G **19**
Lydd. *Kent* 3E **29**
Lydden. *Kent* 1G **29**
(nr. Dover)
Lydden. *Kent* 4H **41**
(nr. Margate)
Lyddington. *Rut* 1F **63**
Lydd (London Ashford) Airport. *Kent* 3E **29**
Lydd-on-Sea. *Kent* 3E **29**
Lydeard St Lawrence. *Som* 3E **21**
Lyde Green. *Hants* 1F **25**
Lydford. *Devn* 4F **11**
Lydford Fair Place. *Som* 3A **22**
Lydgate. *G Man* 4H **91**
Lydgate. *W Yor* 2H **91**
Lydham. *Shrp* 1F **59**
Lydiard Millicent. *Wilts* 3F **35**
Lydiate. *Mers* 4B **90**
Lydiate Ash. *Worc* 3D **60**
Lydlinch. *Dors* 1C **14**
Lydmarsh. *Som* 2G **13**
Lydney. *Glos* 5B **48**
Lydstep. *Pemb* 5E **43**
Lye. *W Mid* 2D **60**
Lye Green. *Buck* 5H **51**
Lye Green. *E Sus* 2G **27**
Lye Head. *Worc* 3B **60**
Lye, The. *Shrp* 1A **60**
Lyford. *Oxon* 2B **36**
Lyham. *Nmbd* 1E **121**
Lylestone. *N Ayr* 5E **127**
Lymbridge Green. *Kent* 1F **29**
Lyme Regis. *Dors* 3G **13**
Lyminge. *Kent* 1F **29**
Lymington. *Hants* 3B **16**
Lyminster. *W Sus* 5B **26**
Lymm. *Warr* 2A **84**
Lymore. *Hants* 3A **16**
Lympne. *Kent* 2F **29**
Lympsham. *Som* 1G **21**
Lympstone. *Devn* 4C **12**
Lynaberack Lodge. *High* 4B **150**
Lynbridge. *Devn* 2H **19**
Lynch. *Som* 2C **20**
Lynchat. *High* 3B **150**
Lynch Green. *Norf* 5D **78**
Lyndhurst. *Hants* 2B **16**
Lyndon. *Rut* 5G **75**
Lyne. *Bord* 5F **129**
Lyne. *Surr* 4B **38**
Lyneal. *Shrp* 2G **71**
Lyne Down. *Here* 2B **48**
Lyneham. *Oxon* 3A **50**
Lyneham. *Wilts* 4F **35**
Lyneholmeford. *Cumb* 2G **113**
Lynemouth. *Nmbd* 5G **121**
Lyne of Gorthleck. *High* 1H **149**
Lyne of Skene. *Abers* 2E **153**
Lynesack. *Dur* 2D **105**
Lyness. *Orkn* 8C **172**
Lyng. *Norf* 4C **78**
Lyngate. *Norf* 2E **79**
(nr. North Walsham)
Lyngate. *Norf* 3F **79**
(nr. Worstead)
Lynmouth. *Devn* 2H **19**
Lynn. *Staf* 5E **73**
Lynn. *Telf* 4B **72**
Lynsted. *Kent* 4D **40**
Lynstone. *Corn* 2C **10**
Lynton. *Devn* 2H **19**
Lynwilg. *High* 2C **150**
Lyon's Gate. *Dors* 2B **14**
Lyonshall. *Here* 5F **59**
Lytchett Matravers. *Dors* 3E **15**
Lytchett Minster. *Dors* 3E **15**
Lyth. *High* 2E **169**
Lytham. *Lanc* 2B **90**
Lytham St Anne's. *Lanc* 2B **90**
Lythe. *N Yor* 3F **107**
Lythes. *Orkn* 9D **172**
Lythmore. *High* 2C **168**

M

Mabe Burnthouse. *Corn* 5B **6**
Mabie. *Dum* 2A **112**
Mablethorpe. *Linc* 2E **89**
Macbiehill. *Bord* 4E **129**
Macclesfield. *Ches E* 3D **84**
Macclesfield Forest. *Ches E* 3D **84**
Macduff. *Abers* 2E **160**
Machan. *S Lan* 4A **128**
Macharioch. *Arg* 5B **122**
Machen. *Cphy* 3F **33**
Machrie. *N Ayr* 2C **122**
Machrihanish. *Arg* 3A **122**
Machroes. *Gwyn* 3C **68**
Machynlleth. *Powy* 5G **69**
Mackerye End. *Herts* 4B **52**
Mackworth. *Derb* 2H **73**
Macmerry. *E Lot* 2H **129**
Madderty. *Per* 1B **136**
Maddington. *Wilts* 2F **23**
Maddiston. *Falk* 2C **128**
Madehurst. *W Sus* 4A **26**
Madeley. *Staf* 1B **72**
Madeley. *Telf* 5A **72**
Madeley Heath. *Staf* 1B **72**
Madeley Heath. *Worc* 3D **60**
Madford. *Devn* 1E **13**
Madingley. *Cambs* 4C **64**
Madley. *Here* 2H **47**
Madresfield. *Worc* 1D **48**
Madron. *Corn* 3B **4**
Maenaddwyn. *IOA* 2D **80**
Maenclochog. *Pemb* 2E **43**
Maendy. *V Glam* 4D **32**
Maenporth. *Corn* 4E **5**
Maentwrog. *Gwyn* 1F **69**
Maen-y-groes. *Cdgn* 5C **56**
Maer. *Staf* 2B **72**
Maerdy. *Carm* 3G **45**
Maerdy. *Cnwy* 1C **70**
Maerdy. *Rhon* 2C **32**
Maesbrook. *Shrp* 3F **71**
Maesbury. *Shrp* 3F **71**
Maesbury Marsh. *Shrp* 3F **71**
Maes-glas. *Flin* 3D **82**
Maesgwyn-Isaf. *Powy* 4D **70**
Maeshafn. *Den* 4E **82**
Maes Llyn. *Cdgn* 1D **44**
Maesmynis. *Powy* 1D **46**
Maesteg. *B'end* 2B **32**
Maestir. *Cdgn* 1F **45**
Maesybont. *Carm* 4F **45**
Maesycrugiau. *Carm* 1E **45**
Maesycwmmer. *Cphy* 2E **33**
Maesyrhandir. *Powy* 1C **58**
Magdalen Laver. *Essx* 5F **53**
Maggieknockater. *Mor* 4H **159**
Maghaberry. *Lis* 4G **175**
Magham Down. *E Sus* 4H **27**
Maghera. *Mag* 2E **175**
Magherafelt. *Mag* 3E **175**
Magheralin. *Cgvn* 5G **175**
Maghull. *Mers* 4B **90**
Magna Park. *Leics* 2C **62**
Magor. *Mon* 3H **33**
Magpie Green. *Suff* 3C **66**
Magwyr. *Mon* 3H **33**
Maidenbower. *W Sus* 2D **27**
Maiden Bradley. *Wilts* 3D **22**
Maidencombe. *Torb* 2F **9**
Maidenhayne. *Devn* 3F **13**
Maidenhead. *Wind* 3G **37**
Maiden Law. *Dur* 5E **115**
Maiden Newton. *Dors* 3A **14**
Maidens. *S Ayr* 4B **116**
Maiden's Green. *Brac* 4G **37**
Maidensgrove. *Oxon* 3F **37**
Maidenwell. *Corn* 5B **10**
Maidenwell. *Linc* 3C **88**
Maiden Wells. *Pemb* 5D **42**
Maidford. *Nptn* 5D **62**
Maids Moreton. *Buck* 2F **51**
Maidstone. *Kent* 5B **40**
Maidwell. *Nptn* 3E **63**
Mail. *Shet* 9F **173**
Maindee. *Newp* 3G **33**
Mainsforth. *Dur* 1A **106**
Mains of Auchindachy. *Mor* 4B **160**
Mains of Auchnagatt. *Abers* 4G **161**
Mains of Drum. *Abers* 4F **153**
Mains of Edingight. *Mor* 3C **160**
Mainsriddle. *Dum* 4G **111**
Mainstone. *Shrp* 2E **59**
Maisemore. *Glos* 3D **48**
Major's Green. *Worc* 3F **61**
Makeney. *Derbs* 1A **74**
Makerstoun. *Bord* 1A **120**
Malacleit. *W Isl* 1C **170**
Malaig. *High* 4E **147**
Malaig Bheag. *High* 4E **147**
Malborough. *Devn* 5D **8**
Malcoff. *Derbs* 2E **85**
Malcolmburn. *Mor* 3A **160**
Malden Rushett. *G Lon* 4C **38**
Maldon. *Essx* 5B **54**
Malham. *N Yor* 3B **98**
Maligar. *High* 2D **155**
Malinslee. *Telf* 5A **72**
Mallaig. *High* 4E **147**
Malleny Mills. *Edin* 3E **129**
Mallows Green. *Essx* 3E **53**
Malltraeth. *IOA* 4D **80**
Mallwyd. *Gwyn* 4A **70**
Malmesbury. *Wilts* 3E **35**
Malmsmead. *Devn* 2A **20**
Malpas. *Ches W* 1G **71**
Malpas. *Corn* 4C **6**
Malpas. *Newp* 2G **33**
Malswick. *Glos* 3C **48**
Maltby. *S Yor* 1C **86**
Maltby. *Stoc T* 3B **106**
Maltby le Marsh. *Linc* 2D **88**
Malt Lane. *Arg* 3H **133**
Maltman's Hill. *Kent* 1D **28**
Malton. *N Yor* 2B **100**
Malvern Link. *Worc* 1C **48**
Malvern Wells. *Worc* 1C **48**
Mamble. *Worc* 3A **60**
Mamhilad. *Mon* 5G **47**
Manaccan. *Corn* 4E **5**
Manafon. *Powy* 5D **70**
Manais. *W Isl* 9D **171**
Manaton. *Devn* 4A **12**
Manby. *Linc* 2C **88**
Mancetter. *Warw* 1H **61**
Manchester. *G Man* 1C **84**
Manchester International Airport. *G Man* 2C **84**
Mancot. *Flin* 4F **83**
Manea. *Cambs* 2D **65**
Maney. *W Mid* 1F **61**
Manfield. *N Yor* 3F **105**
Mangotsfield. *S Glo* 4B **34**
Mangurstadh. *W Isl* 4C **171**
Mankinholes. *W Yor* 2H **91**
Manley. *Ches W* 3H **83**
Manmoel. *Cphy* 5E **47**
Mannal. *Arg* 4A **138**
Mannerston. *Falk* 2D **128**
Manningford Bohune. *Wilts* 1G **23**
Manningford Bruce. *Wilts* 1G **23**
Manningham. *W Yor* 1B **92**
Mannings Heath. *W Sus* 3D **26**
Mannington. *Dors* 2F **15**
Manningtree. *Essx* 2E **54**
Mannofield. *Aber* 3G **153**
Manorbier. *Pemb* 5E **43**
Manorbier Newton. *Pemb* 5E **43**
Manordeilo. *Carm* 3G **45**
Manorowen. *Pemb* 1D **42**
Manor Park. *G Lon* 2F **39**
Mansell Gamage. *Here* 1G **47**
Mansell Lacy. *Here* 1H **47**
Mansergh. *Cumb* 1F **97**
Mansewood. *Glas* 3G **127**
Mansfield. *E Ayr* 3F **117**
Mansfield. *Notts* 4C **86**
Mansfield Woodhouse. *Notts* 4C **86**
Mansriggs. *Cumb* 1B **96**
Manston. *Dors* 1D **14**
Manston. *Kent* 4H **41**
Manston. *W Yor* 1D **92**
Manswood. *Dors* 2E **15**
Manthorpe. *Linc* 4H **75**
(nr. Bourne)
Manthorpe. *Linc* 2G **75**
(nr. Grantham)
Manton. *N Lin* 4C **94**
Manton. *Notts* 3C **86**
Manton. *Rut* 5F **75**
Manton. *Wilts* 5G **35**
Manuden. *Essx* 3E **53**
Maperton. *Som* 4B **22**
Maplebeck. *Notts* 4E **86**
Maple Cross. *Herts* 1B **38**
Mapledurham. *Oxon* 4E **37**
Mapledurwell. *Hants* 1E **25**
Maplehurst. *W Sus* 3C **26**
Maplescombe. *Kent* 4G **39**
Mapleton. *Derbs* 1F **73**
Mapperley. *Derbs* 1B **74**
Mapperley. *Notts* 1C **74**
Mapperley Park. *Nott* 1C **74**
Mapperton. *Dors* 3A **14**
(nr. Beaminster)
Mapperton. *Dors* 3E **15**
(nr. Poole)
Mappleborough Green. *Warw* 4E **61**
Mappleton. *E Yor* 5G **101**
Mapplewell. *S Yor* 4D **92**
Mappowder. *Dors* 2C **14**
Maraig. *W Isl* 7E **171**
Marazion. *Corn* 3C **4**
Marbhig. *W Isl* 6G **171**
Marbury. *Ches E* 1H **71**
March. *Cambs* 1D **64**
Marcham. *Oxon* 2C **36**
Marchamley. *Shrp* 3H **71**
Marchington. *Staf* 2F **73**
Marchington Woodlands. *Staf* 3F **73**
Marchwiel. *Wrex* 1F **71**
Marchwood. *Hants* 1B **16**
Marcross. *V Glam* 5C **32**
Marden. *Here* 1A **48**
Marden. *Kent* 1B **28**
Marden. *Wilts* 1F **23**
Marden Beech. *Kent* 1B **28**
Marden Thorn. *Kent* 1B **28**

Meon. *Hants* 2D **16**
Meonstoke. *Hants* 4E **24**
Meopham. *Kent* 4H **39**
Meopham Green. *Kent* 4H **39**
Meopham Station. *Kent* 4H **39**
Mepal. *Cambs* 2D **64**
Meppershall. *C Beds* 2B **52**
Merbach. *Here* 1G **47**
Mercaston. *Derbs* 1G **73**
Merchiston. *Edin* 2F **129**
Mere. *Ches E* 2B **84**
Mere. *Wilts* 3D **22**
Mere Brow. *Lanc* 3C **90**
Mereclough. *Lanc* 1G **91**
Mere Green. *W Mid* 1F **61**
Mere Green. *Worc* 4D **60**
Mere Heath. *Ches W* 3A **84**
Mereside. *Bkpl* 1B **90**
Meretown. *Staf* 3B **72**
Mereworth. *Kent* 5A **40**
Meriden. *W Mid* 2G **61**
Merkadale. *High* 5C **154**
Merkland. *S Ayr* 5B **116**
Merkland Lodge. *High* 1A **164**
Merley. *Pool* 3F **15**
Merlin's Bridge. *Pemb* 3D **42**
Merridge. *Som* 3F **21**
Merrington. *Shrp* 3G **71**
Merrion. *Pemb* 5D **42**
Merriott. *Som* 1H **13**
Merrivale. *Devn* 5F **11**
Merrow. *Surr* 5B **38**
Merrybent. *Darl* 3F **105**
Merry Lees. *Leics* 5B **74**
Merrymeet. *Corn* 2G **7**
Mersham. *Kent* 2E **29**
Merstham. *Surr* 5D **39**
Merston. *W Sus* 2G **17**
Merstone. *IOW* 4D **16**
Merther. *Corn* 4C **6**
Merthyr. *Carm* 3D **44**
Merthyr Cynog. *Powy* 2C **46**
Merthyr Dyfan. *V Glam* 4E **32**
Merthyr Mawr. *B'end* 4B **32**
Merthyr Tudful. *Mer T* 5D **46**
Merthyr Tydfil. *Mer T* 5D **46**
Merthyr Vale. *Mer T* 5D **46**
Merton. *Devn* 1F **11**
Merton. *G Lon* 4D **38**
Merton. *Norf* 1B **66**
Merton. *Oxon* 4D **50**
Meshaw. *Devn* 1A **12**
Messing. *Essx* 4B **54**
Messingham. *N Lin* 4B **94**
Metcombe. *Devn* 3D **12**
Metfield. *Suff* 2E **67**
Metherell. *Corn* 2A **8**
Metheringham. *Linc* 4H **87**
Methil. *Fife* 4F **137**
Methilhill. *Fife* 4F **137**
Methley. *W Yor* 2D **93**
Methley Junction. *W Yor* 2D **93**
Methlick. *Abers* 5F **161**
Methven. *Per* 1C **136**
Methwold. *Norf* 1G **65**
Methwold Hythe. *Norf* 1G **65**
Mettingham. *Suff* 2F **67**
Metton. *Norf* 2D **78**
Mevagissey. *Corn* 4E **6**
Mexborough. *S Yor* 4E **93**
Mey. *High* 1E **169**
Meysey Hampton. *Glos* 2G **35**
Miabhag. *W Isl* 8D **171**
Miabhag. *W Isl* 7C **171** (nr. Cliasmol)
Miabhaig. *W Isl* 4C **171** (nr. Timsgearraidh)
Mial. *High* 1G **155**
Michaelchurch. *Here* 3A **48**
Michaelchurch Escley. *Here* 2G **47**
Michaelchurch-on-Arrow. *Powy* 5E **59**
Michaelston-le-Pit. *V Glam* 4E **33**
Michaelston-y-Fedw. *Newp* 3F **33**
Michaelstow. *Corn* 5A **10**
Michelcombe. *Devn* 2C **8**
Micheldever. *Hants* 3D **24**
Micheldever Station. *Hants* 2D **24**
Michelmersh. *Hants* 4B **24**
Mickfield. *Suff* 4D **66**
Micklebring. *S Yor* 1C **86**
Mickleby. *N Yor* 3F **107**
Micklefield. *W Yor* 1E **93**
Micklefield Green. *Herts* 1B **38**
Mickleham. *Surr* 5C **38**
Mickleover. *Derb* 2H **73**
Micklethwaite. *Cumb* 4D **112**
Micklethwaite. *W Yor* 5D **98**
Mickleton. *Dur* 2C **104**
Mickleton. *Glos* 1G **49**
Mickletown. *W Yor* 2D **93**
Mickle Trafford. *Ches W* 4G **83**
Mickley. *N Yor* 2E **99**
Mickley Green. *Suff* 5H **65**
Mickley Square. *Nmbd* 3D **115**
Mid Ardlaw. *Abers* 2G **161**
Midbea. *Orkn* 3D **172**
Mid Beltie. *Abers* 3D **152**
Mid Calder. *W Lot* 3D **129**
Mid Clyth. *High* 5E **169**
Middle Assendon. *Oxon* 3F **37**
Middle Aston. *Oxon* 3C **50**
Middle Barton. *Oxon* 3C **50**
Middlebie. *Dum* 2D **112**
Middle Chinnock. *Som* 1H **13**
Middle Claydon. *Buck* 3F **51**
Middlecliffe. *S Yor* 4E **93**
Middlecott. *Devn* 4H **11**
Middle Drums. *Ang* 3E **145**
Middle Duntisbourne. *Glos* 5E **49**
Middle Essie. *Abers* 3H **161**
Middleforth Green. *Lanc* 2D **90**
Middleham. *N Yor* 1D **98**
Middle Handley. *Derbs* 3B **86**
Middle Harling. *Norf* 2B **66**
Middlehope. *Shrp* 2G **59**
Middle Littleton. *Worc* 1F **49**
Middle Maes-coed. *Here* 2G **47**
Middlemarsh. *Dors* 2B **14**
Middle Marwood. *Devn* 3F **19**
Middle Mayfield. *Staf* 1F **73**
Middlemoor. *Devn* 5E **11**
Middlemuir. *Abers* 4F **161** (nr. New Deer)
Middlemuir. *Abers* 3G **161** (nr. Strichen)
Middle Rainton. *Tyne* 5G **115**
Middle Rasen. *Linc* 2H **87**
Middlesbrough. *Midd* 3B **106**
Middlesceugh. *Cumb* 5E **113**
Middleshaw. *Cumb* 1E **97**
Middlesmoor. *N Yor* 2C **98**
Middles, The. *Dur* 4F **115**
Middlestone. *Dur* 1F **105**
Middlestone Moor. *Dur* 1F **105**
Middle Stoughton. *Som* 2H **21**
Middlestown. *W Yor* 3C **92**
Middle Street. *Glos* 5C **48**
Middle Taphouse. *Corn* 2F **7**
Middleton. *Ang* 4E **145**
Middleton. *Arg* 4A **138**
Middleton. *Cumb* 1F **97**
Middleton. *Derbs* 4F **85** (nr. Bakewell)
Middleton. *Derbs* 5G **85** (nr. Wirksworth)
Middleton. *Essx* 2B **54**
Middleton. *G Man* 4G **91**
Middleton. *Hants* 2C **24**
Middleton. *Hart* 1C **106**
Middleton. *Here* 4H **59**
Middleton. *IOW* 4B **16**
Middleton. *Lanc* 4D **96**
Middleton. *Midl* 4G **129**
Middleton. *Norf* 4F **77**
Middleton. *Nptn* 2F **63**
Middleton. *Nmbd* 1F **121** (nr. Belford)
Middleton. *Nmbd* 1D **114** (nr. Morpeth)
Middleton. *N Yor* 5D **98** (nr. Ilkley)
Middleton. *N Yor* 1B **100** (nr. Pickering)
Middleton. *Per* 3D **136**
Middleton. *Shrp* 3H **59** (nr. Ludlow)
Middleton. *Shrp* 3F **71** (nr. Oswestry)
Middleton. *Suff* 4G **67**
Middleton. *Swan* 4D **30**
Middleton. *Warw* 1F **61**
Middleton. *W Yor* 2C **92**
Middleton Cheney. *Nptn* 1D **50**
Middleton Green. *Staf* 2D **73**
Middleton-in-Teesdale. *Dur* 2C **104**
Middleton One Row. *Darl* 3A **106**
Middleton-on-Leven. *N Yor* 4B **106**
Middleton-on-Sea. *W Sus* 5A **26**
Middleton on the Hill. *Here* 4H **59**
Middleton-on-the-Wolds. *E Yor* 5D **100**
Middleton Priors. *Shrp* 1A **60**
Middleton Quernhow. *N Yor* 2F **99**
Middleton St George. *Darl* 3A **106**
Middleton Scriven. *Shrp* 2A **60**
Middleton Stoney. *Oxon* 3D **50**
Middleton Tyas. *N Yor* 4F **105**
Middletown. *Cumb* 4A **102**
Middle Town. *IOS* 1B **4**
Middletown. *Powy* 4F **71**
Middle Tysoe. *Warw* 1B **50**
Middle Wallop. *Hants* 3A **24**
Middlewich. *Ches E* 4B **84**
Middle Winterslow. *Wilts* 3H **23**
Middlewood. *Corn* 5C **10**
Middlewood. *S Yor* 1H **85**
Middle Woodford. *Wilts* 3G **23**
Middlewood Green. *Suff* 4C **66**
Middleyard. *Glos* 5D **48**
Middlezoy. *Som* 3G **21**
Middridge. *Dur* 2F **105**
Midelney. *Som* 4H **21**
Midfield. *High* 2F **167**
Midford. *Bath* 5C **34**
Mid Garrary. *Dum* 2C **110**
Midge Hall. *Lanc* 2D **90**
Midgeholme. *Cumb* 4H **113**
Midgham. *W Ber* 5D **36**
Midgley. *W Yor* 2A **92** (nr. Halifax)
Midgley. *W Yor* 3C **92** (nr. Horbury)
Mid Ho. *Shet* 2G **173**
Midhopestones. *S Yor* 1G **85**
Midhurst. *W Sus* 4G **25**
Mid Kirkton. *N Ayr* 4C **126**
Mid Lambrook. *Som* 1H **13**
Midland. *Orkn* 7C **172**
Mid Lavant. *W Sus* 2G **17**
Midlem. *Bord* 2H **119**
Midney. *Som* 4A **22**
Midsomer Norton. *Bath* 1B **22**
Midton. *Inv* 2D **126**
Midtown. *High* 5C **162** (nr. Poolewe)
Midtown. *High* 2F **167** (nr. Tongue)
Midville. *Linc* 5C **88**
Mid Walls. *Shet* 7C **173**
Mid Yell. *Shet* 2G **173**
Migdale. *High* 4D **164**
Migvie. *Abers* 3B **152**
Milborne Port. *Som* 1B **14**
Milborne St Andrew. *Dors* 3D **14**
Milborne Wick. *Som* 4B **22**
Milbourne. *Nmbd* 2E **115**
Milbourne. *Wilts* 3E **35**
Milburn. *Cumb* 2H **103**
Milbury Heath. *S Glo* 2B **34**
Milby. *N Yor* 3G **99**
Milcombe. *Oxon* 2C **50**
Milden. *Suff* 1C **54**
Mildenhall. *Suff* 3G **65**
Mildenhall. *Wilts* 5H **35**
Milebrook. *Powy* 3F **59**
Milebush. *Kent* 1B **28**
Mile End. *Cambs* 2F **65**
Mile End. *Essx* 3C **54**
Mileham. *Norf* 4B **78**
Mile Oak. *Brig* 5D **26**
Miles Green. *Staf* 5C **84**
Miles Hope. *Here* 4H **59**
Milesmark. *Fife* 1D **128**
Mile Town. *Kent* 3D **40**
Milfield. *Nmbd* 1D **120**
Milford. *Derbs* 1A **74**
Milford. *Devn* 4C **18**
Milford. *Powy* 1C **58**
Milford. *Staf* 3D **72**
Milford. *Surr* 1A **26**
Milford Haven. *Pemb* 4D **42**
Milford on Sea. *Hants* 3A **16**
Milkwall. *Glos* 5A **48**
Milkwell. *Wilts* 4E **23**
Milland. *W Sus* 4G **25**
Millbank. *High* 2D **168**
Mill Bank. *W Yor* 2A **92**
Millbeck. *Cumb* 2D **102**
Millbounds. *Orkn* 4E **172**
Millbreck. *Abers* 4H **161**
Millbridge. *Surr* 2G **25**
Millbrook. *C Beds* 2A **52**
Millbrook. *Corn* 3A **8**
Millbrook. *G Man* 1D **85**
Millbrook. *Sotn* 1B **16**
Mill Common. *Suff* 2G **67**
Mill Corner. *E Sus* 3C **28**
Milldale. *Staf* 5F **85**
Millden Lodge. *Ang* 1E **145**
Milldens. *Ang* 3E **145**
Millearn. *Per* 2B **136**
Mill End. *Buck* 3F **37**
Mill End. *Cambs* 5F **65**
Millend. *Glos* 2C **34** (nr. Dursley)
Mill End. *Glos* 4G **49** (nr. Northleach)
Mill End. *Herts* 2D **52**
Millerhill. *Midl* 3G **129**
Miller's Dale. *Derbs* 3F **85**
Millers Green. *Derbs* 5G **85**
Millerston. *N Lan* 3H **127**
Millfield. *Abers* 4B **152**
Millfield. *Pet* 5A **76**
Millgate. *Lanc* 3G **91**
Mill Green. *Essx* 5G **53**
Mill Green. *Norf* 2D **66**
Mill Green. *Shrp* 3A **72**
Mill Green. *Staf* 3E **73**
Mill Green. *Suff* 1C **54**
Millhalf. *Here* 1F **47**
Millhall. *E Ren* 4G **127**
Millhayes. *Devn* 2F **13** (nr. Honiton)
Millhayes. *Devn* 1E **13** (nr. Wellington)
Millhead. *Lanc* 2D **97**
Millheugh. *S Lan* 4A **128**
Mill Hill. *Bkbn* 2E **91**
Mill Hill. *G Lon* 1D **38**
Millholme. *Cumb* 5G **103**
Millhouse. *Arg* 2A **126**
Millhouse. *Cumb* 1E **103**
Millhousebridge. *Dum* 1C **112**
Millhouses. *S Yor* 2H **85**
Millikenpark. *Ren* 3F **127**
Millington. *E Yor* 4C **100**
Millington Green. *Derbs* 1G **73**
Millisle. *Ards* 4J **175**
Mill Knowe. *Arg* 3B **122**
Mill Lane. *Hants* 1F **25**
Millmeece. *Staf* 2C **72**
Mill of Craigievar. *Abers* 2C **152**
Mill of Fintray. *Abers* 2F **153**
Mill of Haldane. *W Dun* 1F **127**
Millom. *Cumb* 1A **96**
Millow. *C Beds* 1C **52**
Millpool. *Corn* 5B **10**
Millport. *N Ayr* 4C **126**
Mill Side. *Cumb* 1D **96**
Mill Street. *Norf* 4C **78** (nr. Lyng)
Mill Street. *Norf* 4C **78** (nr. Swanton Morley)
Millthorpe. *Derbs* 3H **85**
Millthorpe. *Linc* 2A **76**
Millthrop. *Cumb* 5H **103**
Milltimber. *Aber* 3F **153**
Milltown. *Abers* 3G **151** (nr. Corgarff)
Milltown. *Abers* 2B **152** (nr. Lumsden)
Milltown. *Corn* 3F **7**
Milltown. *Derbs* 4A **86**
Milltown. *Devn* 3F **19**
Milltown. *Dum* 2E **113**
Milltown of Aberdalgie. *Per* 1C **136**
Milltown of Auchindoun. *Mor* 4A **160**
Milltown of Campfield. *Abers* 3D **152**
Milltown of Edinvillie. *Mor* 4G **159**
Milltown of Rothiemay. *Mor* 4C **160**
Milltown of Towie. *Abers* 2B **152**
Milnacraig. *Ang* 3B **144**
Milnathort. *Per* 3D **136**
Milngavie. *E Dun* 2G **127**
Milnholm. *Stir* 1A **128**
Milnrow. *G Man* 3H **91**
Milnthorpe. *Cumb* 1D **97**
Milnthorpe. *W Yor* 3D **92**
Milson. *Shrp* 3A **60**
Milstead. *Kent* 5D **40**
Milston. *Wilts* 2G **23**
Milthorpe. *Nptn* 1D **50**
Milton. *Ang* 4C **144**
Milton. *Cambs* 4D **65**
Milton. *Cumb* 3G **113** (nr. Brampton)
Milton. *Cumb* 1E **97** (nr. Crooklands)
Milton. *Derbs* 3H **73**
Milton. *Dum* 2F **111** (nr. Crocketford)
Milton. *Dum* 4H **109** (nr. Glenluce)
Milton. *Glas* 3G **127**
Milton. *High* 3F **157** (nr. Achnasheen)
Milton. *High* 4G **155** (nr. Applecross)
Milton. *High* 5G **157** (nr. Drumnadrochit)
Milton. *High* 1B **158** (nr. Invergordon)
Milton. *High* 4H **157** (nr. Inverness)
Milton. *High* 3F **169** (nr. Wick)
Milton. *Mor* 2C **160** (nr. Cullen)
Milton. *Mor* 2F **151** (nr. Tomintoul)
Milton. *N Som* 5G **33**
Milton. *Notts* 3E **86**
Milton. *Oxon* 2C **50** (nr. Bloxham)
Milton. *Oxon* 2C **36** (nr. Didcot)
Milton. *Pemb* 4E **43**
Milton. *Port* 3E **17**
Milton. *Som* 4H **21**
Milton. *S Ayr* 2D **116**
Milton. *Stir* 3E **135** (nr. Aberfoyle)
Milton. *Stir* 4D **134** (nr. Drymen)
Milton. *Stoke* 5D **84**
Milton. *W Dun* 2F **127**
Milton Abbas. *Dors* 2D **14**
Milton Abbot. *Devn* 5E **11**
Milton Auchlossan. *Abers* 3C **152**
Milton Bridge. *Midl* 3F **129**
Milton Bryan. *C Beds* 2H **51**
Milton Clevedon. *Som* 3B **22**
Milton Coldwells. *Abers* 5G **161**

Newton Regis—North Street

Newton Regis. *Warw* 5G **73**
Newton Reigny. *Cumb* 1F **103**
Newton Rigg. *Cumb* 1F **103**
Newton St Cyres. *Devn* 3B **12**
Newton St Faith. *Norf* 4E **78**
Newton St Loe. *Bath* 5C **34**
Newton St Petrock. *Devn* 1E **11**
Newton Solney. *Derbs* 3G **73**
Newton Stacey. *Hants* 2C **24**
Newton Stewart. *Dum* 3B **110**
Newton Toney. *Wilts* 2H **23**
Newton Tony. *Wilts* 2H **23**
Newton Tracey. *Devn* 4F **19**
Newton under Roseberry. *Red C* 3C **106**
Newton Unthank. *Leics* 5B **74**
Newton upon Ayr. *S Ayr* 2C **116**
Newton upon Derwent. *E Yor* 5B **100**
Newton Valence. *Hants* 3F **25**
Newton-with-Scales. *Lanc* 1C **90**
Newtown. *Abers* 2E **160**
Newtown. *Cambs* 4H **63**
Newtown. *Corn* 5C **10**
Newtown. *Cumb* 5B **112** (nr. Aspatria)
Newtown. *Cumb* 3G **113** (nr. Brampton)
Newtown. *Cumb* 2G **103** (nr. Penrith)
Newtown. *Derbs* 2D **85**
Newtown. *Devn* 4A **20**
Newtown. *Dors* 2H **13** (nr. Beaminster)
New Town. *Dors* 1E **15** (nr. Sixpenny Handley)
New Town. *E Lot* 2H **129**
Newtown. *Falk* 1C **128**
Newtown. *Glos* 5B **48** (nr. Lydney)
Newtown. *Glos* 2E **49** (nr. Tewkesbury)
Newtown. *Hants* 1D **16** (nr. Bishop's Waltham)
Newtown. *Hants* 3G **25** (nr. Liphook)
Newtown. *Hants* 1A **16** (nr. Lyndhurst)
Newtown. *Hants* 5C **36** (nr. Newbury)
Newtown. *Hants* 4B **24** (nr. Romsey)
Newtown. *Hants* 2C **16** (nr. Warsash)
Newtown. *Hants* 1E **16** (nr. Wickham)
Newtown. *Here* 2A **48** (nr. Little Dewchurch)
Newtown. *Here* 1B **48** (nr. Stretton Grandison)
Newtown. *High* 3F **149**
Newtown. *IOM* 4C **108**
Newtown. *IOW* 3C **16**
Newtown. *Lanc* 3D **90**
New Town. *Lutn* 3A **52**
Newtown. *Nmbd* 4E **121** (nr. Rothbury)
Newtown. *Nmbd* 2E **121** (nr. Wooler)
Newtown. *Pool* 3F **15**
Newtown. *Powy* 1D **58**
Newtown. *Rhon* 2D **32**
Newtown. *Shet* 3F **173**
Newtown. *Shrp* 2G **71**
Newtown. *Som* 1F **13**
Newtown. *Staf* 4D **84** (nr. Biddulph)
Newtown. *Staf* 5D **73** (nr. Cannock)
Newtown. *Staf* 4E **85** (nr. Longnor)
New Town. *W Yor* 2E **93**
Newtown. *Wilts* 4E **23**
Newtownabbey. *Newt* 3H **175**
Newtownards. *Ards* 4H **175**
Newtown-in-St Martin. *Corn* 4E **5**
Newtown Linford. *Leics* 5C **74**
Newtown St Boswells. *Bord* 1H **119**
Newtownstewart. *Strab* 3C **174**
New Tredegar. *Cphy* 5E **47**
Newtyle. *Ang* 4B **144**
New Village. *E Yor* 1D **94**
New Village. *S Yor* 4F **93**
New Walsoken. *Cambs* 5D **76**
New Waltham. *NE Lin* 4F **95**
New Winton. *E Lot* 2H **129**
New World. *Cambs* 1C **64**
New Yatt. *Oxon* 4B **50**
Newyears Green. *G Lon* 2B **38**
New York. *Linc* 5B **88**
New York. *Tyne* 2G **115**
Nextend. *Here* 5F **59**
Neyland. *Pemb* 4D **42**
Nib Heath. *Shrp* 4G **71**
Nicholashayne. *Devn* 1E **12**
Nicholaston. *Swan* 4E **31**
Nidd. *N Yor* 3F **99**
Niddrie. *Edin* 2G **129**
Niddry. *Edin* 2D **129**
Nigg. *Aber* 3G **153**
Nigg. *High* 1C **158**
Nigg Ferry. *High* 2B **158**
Nightcott. *Som* 4B **20**
Nimmer. *Som* 1G **13**
Nine Ashes. *Essx* 5F **53**
Ninebanks. *Nmbd* 4A **114**
Nine Elms. *Swin* 3G **35**
Ninemile Bar. *Dum* 2F **111**
Nine Mile Burn. *Midl* 4E **129**
Ninfield. *E Sus* 4B **28**
Ningwood. *IOW* 4C **16**
Nisbet. *Bord* 2A **120**
Nisbet Hill. *Bord* 4D **130**
Niton. *IOW* 5D **16**
Nitshill. *Glas* 3G **127**
Niwbwrch. *IOA* 4D **80**
Noak Hill. *G Lon* 1G **39**
Nobold. *Shrp* 4G **71**
Nobottle. *Nptn* 4D **62**
Nocton. *Linc* 4H **87**
Nogdam End. *Norf* 5F **79**
Noke. *Oxon* 4D **50**
Nolton. *Pemb* 3C **42**
Nolton Haven. *Pemb* 3C **42**
No Man's Heath. *Ches W* 1H **71**
No Man's Heath. *Warw* 5G **73**
Nomansland. *Devn* 1B **12**
Nomansland. *Wilts* 1A **16**
Noneley. *Shrp* 3G **71**
Noness. *Shet* 9F **173**
Nonikiln. *High* 1A **158**
Nonington. *Kent* 5G **41**
Nook. *Cumb* 2F **113** (nr. Longtown)
Nook. *Cumb* 1E **97** (nr. Milnthorpe)
Noranside. *Ang* 2D **144**
Norbreck. *Bkpl* 5C **96**
Norbridge. *Here* 1C **48**
Norbury. *Ches E* 1H **71**
Norbury. *Derbs* 1F **73**
Norbury. *Shrp* 1F **59**
Norbury. *Staf* 3B **72**
Norby. *N Yor* 1G **99**
Norby. *Shet* 6C **173**
Norcross. *Lanc* 5C **96**
Nordelph. *Norf* 5E **77**
Norden. *G Man* 3G **91**
Nordley. *Shrp* 1A **60**
Norfolk Broads. *Norf* 5G **79**
Norham. *Nmbd* 5F **131**
Norland Town. *W Yor* 2A **92**
Norley. *Ches W* 3H **83**
Norleywood. *Hants* 3B **16**
Normanby. *N Lin* 3B **94**
Normanby. *N Yor* 1B **100**
Normanby. *Red C* 3C **106**
Normanby-by-Spital. *Linc* 2H **87**
Normanby le Wold. *Linc* 1A **88**
Norman Cross. *Cambs* 1A **64**
Normandy. *Surr* 5A **38**
Norman's Bay. *E Sus* 5A **28**
Norman's Green. *Devn* 2D **12**
Normanton. *Derb* 2H **73**
Normanton. *Leics* 1F **75**
Normanton. *Linc* 1G **75**
Normanton. *Notts* 5E **86**
Normanton. *W Yor* 2D **93**
Normanton le Heath. *Leics* 4A **74**
Normanton on Soar. *Notts* 3C **74**
Normanton-on-the-Wolds. *Notts* 2D **74**
Normanton on Trent. *Notts* 4E **87**
Normoss. *Lanc* 1B **90**
Norrington Common. *Wilts* 5D **35**
Norris Green. *Mers* 1F **83**
Norris Hill. *Leics* 4H **73**
Norristhorpe. *W Yor* 2C **92**
Northacre. *Norf* 1B **66**
Northall. *Buck* 3H **51**
Northallerton. *N Yor* 5A **106**
Northam. *Devn* 4E **19**
Northam. *Sotn* 1C **16**
Northampton. *Nptn* 4E **63**
North Anston. *S Yor* 2C **86**
North Ascot. *Brac* 4A **38**
North Aston. *Oxon* 3C **50**
Northaw. *Herts* 5C **52**
Northay. *Som* 1F **13**
North Baddesley. *Hants* 4B **24**
North Balfern. *Dum* 4B **110**
North Ballachulish. *High* 2E **141**
North Barrow. *Som* 4B **22**
North Barsham. *Norf* 2B **78**
Northbeck. *Linc* 1H **75**
North Benfleet. *Essx* 2B **40**
North Bersted. *W Sus* 5A **26**
North Berwick. *E Lot* 1B **130**
North Bitchburn. *Dur* 1E **105**
North Blyth. *Nmbd* 1G **115**
North Boarhunt. *Hants* 1E **16**
North Bockhampton. *Dors* 3G **15**
Northborough. *Pet* 5A **76**
Northbourne. *Kent* 5H **41**
Northbourne. *Oxon* 3D **36**
North Bovey. *Devn* 4H **11**
North Bowood. *Dors* 3H **13**
North Bradley. *Wilts* 1D **22**
North Brentor. *Devn* 4E **11**
North Brewham. *Som* 3C **22**
Northbrook. *Oxon* 3C **50**
North Brook End. *Cambs* 1C **52**
North Broomhill. *Nmbd* 4G **121**
North Buckland. *Devn* 2E **19**
North Burlingham. *Norf* 4F **79**
North Cadbury. *Som* 4B **22**
North Carlton. *Linc* 3G **87**
North Cave. *E Yor* 1B **94**
North Cerney. *Glos* 5F **49**
North Chailey. *E Sus* 3E **27**
Northchapel. *W Sus* 3A **26**
North Charford. *Hants* 1G **15**
North Charlton. *Nmbd* 2F **121**
North Cheriton. *Som* 4B **22**
North Chideock. *Dors* 3H **13**
Northchurch. *Herts* 5H **51**
North Cliffe. *E Yor* 1B **94**
North Clifton. *Notts* 3F **87**
North Close. *Dur* 1F **105**
North Cockerington. *Linc* 1C **88**
North Coker. *Som* 1A **14**
North Collafirth. *Shet* 3E **173**
North Common. *E Sus* 3E **27**
North Commonty. *Abers* 4F **161**
North Coombe. *Devn* 1B **12**
North Cornelly. *B'end* 3B **32**
North Cotes. *Linc* 4G **95**
Northcott. *Devn* 3D **10** (nr. Boyton)
Northcott. *Devn* 1D **12** (nr. Culmstock)
Northcourt. *Oxon* 2D **36**
North Cove. *Suff* 2G **67**
North Cowton. *N Yor* 4F **105**
North Craigo. *Ang* 2F **145**
North Crawley. *Mil* 1H **51**
North Cray. *G Lon* 3F **39**
North Creake. *Norf* 2A **78**
North Curry. *Som* 4G **21**
North Dalton. *E Yor* 4D **100**
North Deighton. *N Yor* 4F **99**
North Dronley. *Ang* 5C **144**
North Duffield. *N Yor* 1G **93**
Northdyke. *Orkn* 5B **172**
Northedge. *Derbs* 4A **86**
North Elkington. *Linc* 1B **88**
North Elmham. *Norf* 3B **78**
North Elmsall. *W Yor* 3E **93**
Northend. *Buck* 2F **37**
North End. *E Yor* 1F **95**
North End. *Essx* 4G **53** (nr. Great Dunmow)
North End. *Essx* 2A **54** (nr. Great Yeldham)
North End. *Hants* 5C **36**
North End. *Leics* 4C **74**
North End. *Linc* 1B **76**
North End. *Norf* 1B **66**
North End. *N Som* 5H **33**
North End. *Port* 2E **17**
Northend. *Warw* 5A **62**
North End. *W Sus* 5C **26**
North End. *Wilts* 2F **35**
North Erradale. *High* 5B **162**
North Evington. *Leic* 5D **74**
North Fambridge. *Essx* 1C **40**
North Fearns. *High* 5E **155**
North Featherstone. *W Yor* 2E **93**
North Feorline. *N Ayr* 3D **122**
North Ferriby. *E Yor* 2C **94**
Northfield. *Aber* 3F **153**
Northfield. *E Yor* 2D **94**
Northfield. *Som* 3F **21**
Northfield. *W Mid* 3E **61**
Northfleet. *Kent* 3H **39**
North Frodingham. *E Yor* 4F **101**
Northgate. *Linc* 3A **76**
North Gluss. *Shet* 4E **173**
North Gorley. *Hants* 1G **15**
North Green. *Norf* 2E **66**
North Green. *Suff* 4F **67** (nr. Framlingham)
North Green. *Suff* 3F **67** (nr. Halesworth)
North Green. *Suff* 4F **67** (nr. Saxmundham)
North Greetwell. *Linc* 3H **87**
North Grimston. *N Yor* 3C **100**
North Halling. *Medw* 4B **40**
North Hayling. *Hants* 2F **17**
North Hazelrigg. *Nmbd* 1E **121**
North Heasley. *Devn* 3H **19**
North Heath. *W Sus* 3B **26**
North Hill. *Corn* 5C **10**
North Holmwood. *Surr* 1C **26**
North Huish. *Devn* 3D **8**
North Hykeham. *Linc* 4G **87**
Northiam. *E Sus* 3C **28**
Northill. *C Beds* 1B **52**
Northington. *Hants* 3D **24**
North Kelsey. *Linc* 4D **94**
North Kelsey Moor. *Linc* 4D **94**
North Kessock. *High* 4A **158**
North Killingholme. *N Lin* 3E **95**
North Kilvington. *N Yor* 1G **99**
North Kilworth. *Leics* 2D **62**
North Kyme. *Linc* 5A **88**
North Lancing. *W Sus* 5C **26**
Northlands. *Linc* 5C **88**
Northleach. *Glos* 4G **49**
North Lee. *Buck* 5G **51**
North Lees. *N Yor* 2E **99**
Northleigh. *Devn* 3G **19** (nr. Barnstaple)
Northleigh. *Devn* 3E **13** (nr. Honiton)
North Leigh. *Kent* 1F **29**
North Leigh. *Oxon* 4B **50**
North Leverton. *Notts* 2E **87**
Northlew. *Devn* 3F **11**
North Littleton. *Worc* 1F **49**
North Lopham. *Norf* 2C **66**
North Luffenham. *Rut* 5G **75**
North Marden. *W Sus* 1G **17**
North Marston. *Buck* 3F **51**
North Middleton. *Midl* 4G **129**
North Middleton. *Nmbd* 2E **121**
North Molton. *Devn* 4H **19**
North Moor. *N Yor* 1D **100**
Northmoor. *Oxon* 5C **50**
Northmoor Green. *Som* 3G **21**
North Moreton. *Oxon* 3D **36**
Northmuir. *Ang* 3C **144**
North Mundham. *W Sus* 2G **17**
North Murie. *Per* 1E **137**
North Muskham. *Notts* 5E **87**
North Ness. *Orkn* 8C **172**
North Newbald. *E Yor* 1C **94**
North Newington. *Oxon* 2C **50**
North Newnton. *Wilts* 1G **23**
North Newton. *Som* 3F **21**
Northney. *Hants* 2F **17**
North Nibley. *Glos* 2C **34**
North Oakley. *Hants* 1D **24**
North Ockendon. *G Lon* 2G **39**
Northolt. *G Lon* 2C **38**
Northop. *Flin* 4E **83**
Northop Hall. *Flin* 4E **83**
North Ormesby. *Midd* 3C **106**
North Ormsby. *Linc* 1B **88**
Northorpe. *Linc* 4H **75** (nr. Bourne)
Northorpe. *Linc* 2B **76** (nr. Donington)
Northorpe. *Linc* 1F **87** (nr. Gainsborough)
North Otterington. *N Yor* 1F **99**
Northover. *Som* 3H **21** (nr. Glastonbury)
Northover. *Som* 4A **22** (nr. Yeovil)
North Owersby. *Linc* 1H **87**
Northowram. *W Yor* 2B **92**
North Perrott. *Som* 2H **13**
North Petherton. *Som* 3F **21**
North Petherwin. *Corn* 4C **10**
North Pickenham. *Norf* 5A **78**
North Piddle. *Worc* 5D **60**
North Poorton. *Dors* 3A **14**
North Port. *Arg* 1H **133**
Northport. *Dors* 4E **15**
North Queensferry. *Fife* 1E **129**
North Radworthy. *Devn* 3A **20**
North Rauceby. *Linc* 1H **75**
Northrepps. *Norf* 2E **79**
North Rigton. *N Yor* 5E **99**
North Rode. *Ches E* 4C **84**
North Roe. *Shet* 3E **173**
North Ronaldsay Airport. *Orkn* 2G **172**
North Row. *Cumb* 1D **102**
North Runcton. *Norf* 4F **77**
North Sannox. *N Ayr* 5B **126**
North Scale. *Cumb* 2A **96**
North Scarle. *Linc* 4F **87**
North Seaton. *Nmbd* 1F **115**
North Seaton Colliery. *Nmbd* 1F **115**
North Sheen. *G Lon* 3C **38**
North Shian. *Arg* 4D **140**
North Shields. *Tyne* 3G **115**
North Shoebury. *S'end* 2D **40**
North Shore. *Bkpl* 1B **90**
North Side. *Cumb* 2B **102**
North Skelton. *Red C* 3D **106**
North Somercotes. *Linc* 1D **88**
North Stainley. *N Yor* 2E **99**
North Stainmore. *Cumb* 3B **104**
North Stifford. *Thur* 2H **39**
North Stoke. *Bath* 5C **34**
North Stoke. *Oxon* 3E **36**
North Stoke. *W Sus* 4B **26**
Northstowe. *Cambs* 4D **64**
North Street. *Hants* 3E **25**
North Street. *Kent* 5E **40**
North Street. *Medw* 3C **40**

North Street. W Ber 4E 37
North Sunderland. Nmbd 1G 121
North Tamerton. Corn 3D 10
North Tawton. Devn 2G 11
North Thoresby. Linc 1B 88
North Tidworth. Wilts 2H 23
North Town. Devn 2F 11
Northtown. Orkn 8D 172
North Town. Shet 10E 173
North Tuddenham. Norf 4C 78
North Walbottle. Tyne 3E 115
Northwall. Orkn 3G 172
North Walney. Cumb 3A 96
North Walsham. Norf 2E 79
North Waltham. Hants 2D 24
North Warnborough. Hants 1F 25
North Water Bridge. Ang 2F 145
North Watten. High 3E 169
Northway. Glos 2E 49
Northway. Swan 4E 31
North Weald Bassett. Essx 5F 53
North Weston. N Som 4H 33
North Weston. Oxon 5E 51
North Wheatley. Notts 2E 87
North Whilborough. Devn 2E 9
Northwich. Ches W 3A 84
North Wick. Bath 5A 34
Northwick. Som 2G 21
Northwick. S Glo 3A 34
North Widcombe. Bath 1A 22
North Willingham. Linc 2A 88
North Wingfield. Derbs 4B 86
North Witham. Linc 3G 75
Northwold. Norf 1G 65
Northwood. Derbs 4G 85
Northwood. G Lon 1B 38
Northwood. IOW 3C 16
Northwood. Kent 4H 41
Northwood. Shrp 2G 71
Northwood. Stoke 1C 72
Northwood Green. Glos 4C 48
North Wootton. Dors 1B 14
North Wootton. Norf 3F 77
North Wootton. Som 2A 22
North Wraxall. Wilts 4D 34
North Wroughton. Swin 3G 35
North Yardhope. Nmbd 4D 120
North York Moors. N Yor 5D 107
Norton. Devn 3E 9
Norton. Glos 3D 48
Norton. Hal 2H 83
Norton. Herts 2C 52
Norton. IOW 4B 16
Norton. Mon 3H 47
Norton. Nptn 4D 62
Norton. Notts 3C 86
Norton. Powy 4F 59
Norton. Shrp 2G 59
(nr. Ludlow)
Norton. Shrp 5B 72
(nr. Madeley)
Norton. Shrp 5H 71
(nr. Shrewsbury)
Norton. S Yor 3F 93
(nr. Askern)
Norton. S Yor 2A 86
(nr. Sheffield)
Norton. Stoc T 2B 106
Norton. Suff 4B 66
Norton. Swan 4F 31
Norton. W Sus 5A 26
(nr. Arundel)
Norton. W Sus 3G 17
(nr. Selsey)
Norton. Wilts 3D 35
Norton. Worc 1F 49
(nr. Evesham)
Norton. Worc 5C 60
(nr. Worcester)
Norton Bavant. Wilts 2E 23
Norton Bridge. Staf 2C 72
Norton Canes. Staf 5E 73
Norton Canon. Here 1G 47
Norton Corner. Norf 3C 78
Norton Disney. Linc 5F 87
Norton East. Staf 5E 73
Norton Ferris. Wilts 3C 22
Norton Fitzwarren. Som 4F 21
Norton Green. IOW 4B 16
Norton Green. Stoke 5D 84
Norton Hawkfield. Bath 5A 34
Norton Heath. Essx 5F 53
Norton in Hales. Shrp 2B 72
Norton in the Moors. Stoke 5C 84
Norton-Juxta-Twycross. Leics 5H 73
Norton-le-Clay. N Yor 2G 99
Norton Lindsey. Warw 4G 61
Norton Little Green. Suff 4B 66
Norton Malreward. Bath 5B 34
Norton Mandeville. Essx 5F 53
Norton-on-Derwent. N Yor 2B 100
Norton St Philip. Som 1C 22
Norton Subcourse. Norf 1G 67
Norton sub Hamdon. Som 1H 13
Norton Woodseats. S Yor 2A 86
Norwell. Notts 4E 87
Norwell Woodhouse. Notts 4E 87
Norwich. Norf 5E 79
Norwich International Airport. Norf 4E 79
Norwick. Shet 1H 173
Norwood. Derbs 2B 86
Norwood Green. W Yor 2B 92
Norwood Hill. Surr 1D 26
Norwood Park. Som 3A 22
Norwoodside. Cambs 1D 64
Noseley. Leics 1E 63
Noss. Shet 10E 173
Noss Mayo. Devn 4B 8
Nosterfield. N Yor 1E 99
Nostie. High 1A 148
Notgrove. Glos 3G 49
Nottage. B'end 4B 32
Nottingham. Nott 1C 74
Nottington. Dors 4B 14
Notton. Dors 3B 14
Notton. W Yor 3D 92
Notton. Wilts 5E 35
Nounsley. Essx 4A 54
Noutard's Green. Worc 4B 60
Nox. Shrp 4G 71
Noyadd Trefawr. Cdgn 1C 44
Nuffield. Oxon 3E 37
Nunburnholme. E Yor 5C 100
Nuncargate. Notts 5C 86
Nunclose. Cumb 5F 113
Nuneaton. Warw 1A 62
Nuneham Courtenay. Oxon 2D 36
Nun Monkton. N Yor 4H 99
Nunnerie. S Lan 3B 118
Nunney. Som 2C 22
Nunnington. N Yor 2A 100
Nunnykirk. Nmbd 5E 121
Nunsthorpe. NE Lin 4F 95
Nunthorpe. Red C 3C 106
Nunthorpe. York 4H 99
Nunton. Wilts 4G 23
Nunwick. Nmbd 2B 114
Nunwick. N Yor 2F 99
Nupend. Glos 5C 48
Nursling. Hants 1B 16
Nursted. Hants 4F 25
Nursteed. Wilts 5F 35
Nurston. V Glam 5D 32
Nutbourne. W Sus 2F 17
(nr. Chichester)
Nutbourne. W Sus 4B 26
(nr. Pulborough)
Nutfield. Surr 5E 39
Nuthall. Notts 1C 74
Nuthampstead. Herts 2E 53
Nuthurst. Warw 3F 61
Nuthurst. W Sus 3C 26
Nutley. E Sus 3F 27
Nuttall. G Man 3F 91
Nutwell. S Yor 4G 93
Nybster. High 2F 169
Nyetimber. W Sus 3G 17
Nyewood. W Sus 4G 25
Nymet Rowland. Devn 2H 11
Nymet Tracey. Devn 2H 11
Nympsfield. Glos 5D 48
Nynehead. Som 4E 21
Nyton. W Sus 5A 26

O

Oadby. Leics 5D 74
Oad Street. Kent 4C 40
Oakamoor. Staf 1E 73
Oakbank. Arg 5B 140
Oakbank. W Lot 3D 129
Oakdale. Cphy 2E 33
Oakdale. Pool 3F 15
Oake. Som 4E 21
Oaken. Staf 5C 72
Oakenclough. Lanc 5E 97
Oakengates. Telf 4A 72
Oakenholt. Flin 3E 83
Oakenshaw. Dur 1F 105
Oakenshaw. W Yor 2B 92
Oakerthorpe. Derbs 5A 86
Oakford. Cdgn 5D 56
Oakford. Devn 4C 20
Oakfordbridge. Devn 4C 20
Oakgrove. Ches E 4D 84
Oakham. Rut 5F 75
Oakhanger. Ches E 5B 84
Oakhanger. Hants 3F 25
Oakhill. Som 2B 22
Oakington. Cambs 4D 64
Oaklands. Powy 5C 58
Oakle Street. Glos 4C 48
Oakley. Bed 5H 63
Oakley. Buck 4E 51
Oakley. Fife 1D 128
Oakley. Hants 1D 24
Oakley. Suff 3D 66
Oakley Green. Wind 3A 38
Oakley Park. Powy 2B 58
Oakmere. Ches W 4H 83
Oakridge. Glos 5E 49
Oaks. Shrp 5G 71
Oaksey. Wilts 2E 35
Oaks Green. Derbs 2F 73
Oakshaw Ford. Cumb 2G 113
Oakshott. Hants 4F 25
Oakthorpe. Leics 4H 73
Oak Tree. Darl 3A 106
Oakwood. Derb 2A 74
Oakwood. W Yor 1D 92
Oakwoodhill. Surr 2C 26
Oakworth. W Yor 1A 92
Oape. High 3B 164
Oare. Kent 4E 40
Oare. Som 2B 20
Oare. W Ber 4D 36
Oare. Wilts 5G 35
Oareford. Som 2B 20
Oasby. Linc 2H 75
Oath. Som 4G 21
Oathlaw. Ang 3D 145
Oatlands. N Yor 4F 99
Oban. Arg 1F 133
Oban. W Isl 7D 171
Oborne. Dors 1B 14
Obsdale. High 2A 158
Obthorpe. Linc 4H 75
Occlestone Green. Ches W 4A 84
Occold. Suff 3D 66
Ochiltree. E Ayr 2E 117
Ochtermuthill. Per 2H 135
Ochtertyre. Per 1H 135
Ockbrook. Derbs 2B 74
Ockeridge. Worc 4B 60
Ockham. Surr 5B 38
Ockle. High 1G 139
Ockley. Surr 1C 26
Ocle Pychard. Here 1A 48
Octofad. Arg 4A 124
Octomore. Arg 4A 124
Octon. E Yor 3E 101
Odcombe. Som 1A 14
Odd Down. Bath 5C 34
Oddingley. Worc 5D 60
Oddington. Oxon 4D 50
Oddsta. Shet 2G 173
Odell. Bed 5G 63
Odie. Orkn 5F 172
Odiham. Hants 1F 25
Odsey. Cambs 2C 52
Odstock. Wilts 4G 23
Odstone. Leics 5A 74
Offchurch. Warw 4A 62
Offenham. Worc 1F 49
Offenham Cross. Worc 1F 49
Offerton. G Man 2D 84
Offerton. Tyne 4G 115
Offham. E Sus 4E 27
Offham. Kent 5A 40
Offham. W Sus 5B 26
Offleyhay. Staf 3C 72
Offley Hoo. Herts 3B 52
Offleymarsh. Staf 3B 72
Offord Cluny. Cambs 4B 64
Offord D'Arcy. Cambs 4B 64
Offton. Suff 1D 54
Offwell. Devn 3E 13
Ogbourne Maizey. Wilts 4G 35
Ogbourne St Andrew. Wilts 4G 35
Ogbourne St George. Wilts 4H 35
Ogden. G Man 3H 91
Ogle. Nmbd 2E 115
Ogmore. V Glam 4B 32
Ogmore-by-Sea. V Glam 4B 32
Ogmore Vale. B'end 2C 32
Okeford Fitzpaine. Dors 1D 14
Okehampton. Devn 3F 11
Okehampton Camp. Devn 3F 11
Okraquoy. Shet 8F 173
Okus. Swin 3G 35
Old. Nptn 3E 63
Old Aberdeen. Aber 3G 153
Old Alresford. Hants 3D 24
Oldany. High 5B 166
Old Arley. Warw 1G 61
Old Basford. Nott 1C 74
Old Basing. Hants 1E 25
Oldberrow. Warw 4F 61
Old Bewick. Nmbd 2E 121
Old Bexley. G Lon 3F 39
Old Blair. Per 2F 143
Old Bolingbroke. Linc 4C 88
Oldborough. Devn 2A 12
Old Brampton. Derbs 3H 85
Old Bridge of Tilt. Per 2F 143
Old Bridge of Urr. Dum 3E 111
Old Buckenham. Norf 1C 66
Old Burghclere. Hants 1C 24
Oldbury. Shrp 1B 60
Oldbury. Warw 1H 61
Oldbury. W Mid 2D 61
Oldbury-on-Severn. S Glo 2B 34
Oldbury on the Hill. Glos 3D 34
Old Byland. N Yor 1H 99
Old Cassop. Dur 1A 106
Oldcastle. Mon 3G 47
Oldcastle Heath. Ches W 1G 71
Old Catton. Norf 4E 79
Old Clee. NE Lin 4F 95
Old Cleeve. Som 2D 20
Old Colwyn. Cnwy 3A 82
Oldcotes. Notts 2C 86
Old Coulsdon. G Lon 5E 39
Old Dailly. S Ayr 5B 116
Old Dalby. Leics 3D 74
Old Dam. Derbs 3F 85
Old Deer. Abers 4G 161
Old Dilton. Wilts 2D 22
Old Down. S Glo 3B 34
Oldeamere. Cambs 1C 64
Old Edlington. S Yor 1C 86
Old Eldon. Dur 2F 105
Old Ellerby. E Yor 1E 95
Old Fallings. W Mid 5D 72
Oldfallow. Staf 4D 73
Old Felixstowe. Suff 2G 55
Oldfield. Shrp 2A 60
Oldfield. Worc 4C 60
Old Fletton. Pet 1A 64
Oldford. Som 1C 22
Old Forge. Here 4A 48
Old Glossop. Derbs 1E 85
Old Goole. E Yor 2H 93
Old Gore. Here 3B 48
Old Graitney. Dum 3E 112
Old Grimsby. IOS 1A 4
Oldhall. High 3E 169
Old Hall Street. Norf 2F 79
Oldham. G Man 4H 91
Oldhamstocks. E Lot 2D 130
Old Heathfield. E Sus 3G 27
Old Hill. W Mid 2D 60
Old Hunstanton. Norf 1F 77
Oldhurst. Cambs 3B 64
Old Hutton. Cumb 1E 97
Old Kea. Corn 4C 6
Old Kilpatrick. W Dun 2F 127
Old Kinnernie. Abers 3E 152
Old Knebworth. Herts 3C 52
Oldland. S Glo 4B 34
Old Laxey. IOM 3D 108
Old Leake. Linc 5D 88
Old Lenton. Nott 2C 74
Old Llanberis. Gwyn 5F 81
Old Malton. N Yor 2B 100
Oldmeldrum. Abers 1F 153
Old Micklefield. W Yor 1E 93
Old Mill. Corn 5D 10
Oldmixon. N Som 1G 21
Old Monkland. N Lan 3A 128
Old Newton. Suff 4C 66
Old Park. Telf 5A 72
Old Pentland. Midl 3F 129
Old Philpstoun. W Lot 2D 128
Old Quarrington. Dur 1A 106
Old Radnor. Powy 5E 59
Old Rayne. Abers 1D 152
Oldridge. Devn 3B 12
Old Romney. Kent 3E 29
Old Scone. Per 1D 136
Oldshore Beg. High 3B 166
Oldshoremore. High 3C 166
Old Snydale. W Yor 2E 93
Old Sodbury. S Glo 3C 34
Old Somerby. Linc 2G 75
Old Spital. Dur 3C 104
Oldstead. N Yor 1H 99
Old Stratford. Nptn 1F 51
Old Swan. Mers 1F 83
Old Swarland. Nmbd 4F 121
Old Tebay. Cumb 4H 103
Old Town. Cumb 5F 113
Old Town. E Sus 5G 27
Oldtown. High 5C 164
Old Town. IOS 1B 4
Old Town. Nmbd 5C 120
Old Trafford. G Man 1C 84
Old Tupton. Derbs 4A 86
Oldwall. Cumb 3F 113
Oldwalls. Swan 3D 31
Old Warden. C Beds 1B 52
Oldways End. Som 4B 20
Old Westhall. Abers 1D 152
Old Weston. Cambs 3H 63
Oldwhat. Abers 3F 161
Old Windsor. Wind 3A 38
Old Wives Lees. Kent 5E 41
Old Woking. Surr 5B 38
Oldwood Common. Worc 4H 59
Old Woodstock. Oxon 4C 50
Olgrinmore. High 3C 168
Oliver's Battery. Hants 4C 24
Ollaberry. Shet 3E 173
Ollerton. Ches E 3B 84
Ollerton. Notts 4D 86
Ollerton. Shrp 3A 72
Olmarch. Cdgn 5F 57
Olmstead Green. Cambs 1G 53
Olney. Mil 5F 63
Olrig. High 2D 169
Olton. W Mid 2F 61
Olveston. S Glo 3B 34
Omagh. Omag 4C 174

Ombersley. Worc 4C 60
Ompton. Notts 4D 86
Omunsgarth. Shet 7E 173
Onchan. IOM 4D 108
Onecote. Staf 5E 85
Onehouse. Suff 5C 66
Onen. Mon 4H 47
Ongar Hill. Norf 3E 77
Ongar Street. Here 4F 59
Onibury. Shrp 3G 59
Onich. High 2E 141
Onllwyn. Neat 4B 46
Onneley. Staf 1B 72
Onslow Green. Essx 4G 53
Onslow Village. Surr 1A 26
Onthank. E Ayr 1D 116
Openwoodgate. Derbs 1A 74
Opinan. High 1G 155
(nr. Gairloch)
Opinan. High 4C 162
(nr. Laide)
Orasaigh. W Isl 6F 171
Orbost. High 4B 154
Orby. Linc 4D 89
Orchard Hill. Devn 4E 19
Orchard Portman. Som 4F 21
Orcheston. Wilts 2F 23
Orcop. Here 3H 47
Orcop Hill. Here 3H 47
Ord. High 2E 147
Ordale. Shet 1H 173
Ordhead. Abers 2D 152
Ordie. Abers 3B 152
Ordiquish. Mor 3H 159
Ordley. Nmbd 4C 114
Ordsall. Notts 3E 86
Ore. E Sus 4C 28
Oreham Common. W Sus 4D 26
Oreton. Shrp 2A 60
Orford. Suff 1H 55
Orford. Warr 1A 84
Organford. Dors 3E 15
Orgil. Orkn 7B 172
Orgreave. Staf 4F 73
Oridge Street. Glos 3C 48
Orlestone. Kent 2D 28
Orleton. Here 4G 59
Orleton. Worc 4A 60
Orleton Common. Here 4G 59
Orlingbury. Nptn 3F 63
Ormacleit. W Isl 5C 170
Ormathwaite. Cumb 2D 102
Ormesby. Midd 3C 106
Ormesby St Margaret. Norf 4G 79
Ormesby St Michael. Norf 4G 79
Ormiscaig. High 4C 162
Ormiston. E Lot 3H 129
Ormsaigbeg. High 2F 139
Ormsaigmore. High 2F 139
Ormsary. Arg 2F 125
Ormsgill. Cumb 2A 96
Ormskirk. Lanc 4C 90
Orphir. Orkn 7C 172
Orpington. G Lon 4F 39
Orrell. G Man 4D 90
Orrell. Mers 1F 83
Orrisdale. IOM 2C 108
Orsett. Thur 2H 39
Orslow. Staf 4C 72
Orston. Notts 1E 75
Orthwaite. Cumb 1D 102
Orton. Cumb 4H 103
Orton. Mor 3H 159
Orton. Nptn 3F 63
Orton. Staf 1C 60
Orton Longueville. Pet 1A 64
Orton-on-the-Hill. Leics 5H 73
Orton Waterville. Pet 1A 64
Orton Wistow. Pet 1A 64
Orwell. Cambs 5C 64
Osbaldeston. Lanc 1E 91
Osbaldwick. York 4A 100
Osbaston. Leics 5B 74
Osbaston. Shrp 3F 71
Osbournby. Linc 2H 75
Osclay. High 5E 169
Oscroft. Ches W 4H 83
Ose. High 4C 154
Osgathorpe. Leics 4B 74
Osgodby. Linc 1H 87
Osgodby. N Yor 1E 101
(nr. Scarborough)
Osgodby. N Yor 1G 93
(nr. Selby)
Oskaig. High 5E 155
Oskamull. Arg 5F 139
Osleston. Derbs 2G 73
Osmaston. Derb 2A 74
Osmaston. Derbs 1G 73
Osmington. Dors 4C 14
Osmington Mills. Dors 4C 14
Osmondthorpe. W Yor 1D 92
Osmondwall. Orkn 9C 172
Osmotherley. N Yor 5B 106
Osnaburgh. Fife 2G 137
Ospisdale. High 5E 164
Ospringe. Kent 4E 40
Ossett. W Yor 2C 92
Ossington. Notts 4E 87
Ostend. Essx 1D 40
Ostend. Norf 2F 79
Osterley. G Lon 3C 38
Oswaldkirk. N Yor 2A 100
Oswaldtwistle. Lanc 2F 91
Oswestry. Shrp 3E 71
Otby. Linc 1A 88
Otford. Kent 5G 39
Otham. Kent 5B 40
Otherton. Staf 4D 72
Othery. Som 3G 21
Otley. Suff 5E 66
Otley. W Yor 5E 98
Otterbourne. Hants 4C 24
Otterburn. Nmbd 5C 120
Otterburn. N Yor 4A 98
Otterburn Camp. Nmbd 5C 120
Otterburn Hall. Nmbd 5C 120
Otter Ferry. Arg 1H 125
Otterford. Som 1F 13
Otterham. Corn 3B 10
Otterhampton. Som 2F 21
Otterham Quay. Kent 4C 40
Ottershaw. Surr 4B 38
Otterspool. Mers 2F 83
Otterswick. Shet 3G 173
Otterton. Devn 4D 12
Otterwood. Hants 2C 16
Ottery St Mary. Devn 3D 12
Ottinge. Kent 1F 29
Ottringham. E Yor 2F 95
Oughterby. Cumb 4D 112
Oughtershaw. N Yor 1A 98
Oughterside. Cumb 5C 112
Oughtibridge. S Yor 1H 85
Oughtrington. Warr 2A 84
Oulston. N Yor 2H 99
Oulton. Cumb 4D 112
Oulton. Norf 3D 78
Oulton. Staf 3B 72
(nr. Gnosall Heath)
Oulton. Staf 2D 72
(nr. Stone)
Oulton. Suff 1H 67
Oulton. W Yor 2D 92
Oulton Broad. Suff 1H 67
Oulton Street. Norf 3D 78
Oundle. Nptn 2H 63
Ousby. Cumb 1H 103
Ousdale. High 2H 165
Ousden. Suff 5G 65
Ousefleet. E Yor 2B 94
Ouston. Dur 4F 115
Ouston. Nmbd 4A 114
(nr. Bearsbridge)
Ouston. Nmbd 2D 114
(nr. Stamfordham)
Outer Hope. Devn 4C 8
Outertown. Orkn 6B 172
Outgate. Cumb 5E 103
Outhgill. Cumb 4A 104
Outlands. Staf 2B 72
Outlane. W Yor 3A 92
Out Newton. E Yor 2G 95
Out Rawcliffe. Lanc 5D 96
Outwell. Norf 5E 77
Outwick. Hants 1G 15
Outwood. Surr 1E 27
Outwood. W Yor 2D 92
Outwood. Worc 3D 60
Outwoods. Leics 4B 74
Outwoods. Staf 4B 72
Ouzlewell Green. W Yor 2D 92
Ovenden. W Yor 2A 92
Over. Cambs 3C 64
Over. Ches W 4A 84
Over. Glos 4D 48
Over. S Glo 3A 34
Overbister. Orkn 3F 172
Over Burrows. Derbs 2G 73
Overbury. Worc 2E 49
Overcombe. Dors 4B 14
Over Compton. Dors 1A 14
Over End. Cambs 1H 63
Over Finlarg. Ang 4D 144
Overgreen. Derbs 3H 85
Over Green. W Mid 1F 61
Over Haddon. Derbs 4G 85
Over Hulton. G Man 4E 91
Over Kellet. Lanc 2E 97
Over Kiddington. Oxon 3C 50
Overleigh. Som 3H 21
Overley. Staf 4F 73
Over Monnow. Mon 4A 48
Over Norton. Oxon 3B 50
Over Peover. Ches E 3B 84
Overpool. Ches W 3F 83
Overscaig. High 1B 164
Overseal. Derbs 4G 73
Over Silton. N Yor 5B 106
Oversland. Kent 5E 41
Overstone. Nptn 4F 63
Over Stowey. Som 3E 21
Overstrand. Norf 1E 79
Over Stratton. Som 1H 13
Over Street. Wilts 3F 23
Overthorpe. Nptn 1C 50
Overton. Aber 2F 153
Overton. Ches W 3H 83
Overton. Hants 2D 24
Overton. High 5E 169
Overton. Lanc 4D 96
Overton. N Yor 4H 99
Overton. Shrp 2A 60
(nr. Bridgnorth)
Overton. Shrp 3H 59
(nr. Ludlow)
Overton. Swan 4D 30
Overton. W Yor 3C 92
Overton. Wrex 1F 71
Overtown. Lanc 2F 97
Overtown. N Lan 4B 128
Overtown. Swin 4G 35
Over Wallop. Hants 3A 24
Over Whitacre. Warw 1G 61
Over Worton. Oxon 3C 50
Oving. Buck 3F 51
Oving. W Sus 5A 26
Ovingdean. Brig 5E 27
Ovingham. Nmbd 3D 115
Ovington. Dur 3E 105
Ovington. Essx 1A 54
Ovington. Hants 3D 24
Ovington. Norf 5B 78
Ovington. Nmbd 3D 114
Owen's Bank. Staf 3G 73
Ower. Hants 2C 16
(nr. Holbury)
Ower. Hants 1B 16
(nr. Totton)
Owermoigne. Dors 4C 14
Owlbury. Shrp 1F 59
Owler Bar. Derbs 3G 85
Owlerton. S Yor 1H 85
Owlsmoor. Brac 5G 37
Owlswick. Buck 5F 51
Owmby. Linc 4D 94
Owmby-by-Spital. Linc 2H 87
Ownham. W Ber 4C 36
Owrytn. Wrex 1F 71
Owslebury. Hants 4D 24
Owston. Leics 5E 75
Owston. S Yor 3F 93
Owston Ferry. N Lin 4B 94
Owstwick. E Yor 1F 95
Owthorne. E Yor 2G 95
Owthorpe. Notts 2D 74
Owton Manor. Hart 2B 106
Oxborough. Norf 5G 77
Oxbridge. Dors 3H 13
Oxcombe. Linc 3C 88
Oxen End. Essx 3G 53
Oxenhall. Glos 3C 48
Oxenholme. Cumb 5G 103
Oxenhope. W Yor 1A 92
Oxen Park. Cumb 1C 96
Oxenpill. Som 2H 21
Oxenton. Glos 2E 49
Oxenwood. Wilts 1B 24
Oxford. Oxon 5D 50
Oxgangs. Edin 3F 129
Oxhey. Herts 1C 38
Oxhill. Warw 1B 50
Oxley. W Mid 5D 72
Oxley Green. Essx 4C 54
Oxley's Green. E Sus 3A 28
Oxlode. Cambs 2D 65
Oxnam. Bord 3B 120
Oxshott. Surr 4C 38
Oxspring. S Yor 4C 92
Oxted. Surr 5E 39
Oxton. Mers 2F 83
Oxton. N Yor 5H 99
Oxton. Notts 5D 86
Oxton. Bord 4A 130
Oxwich. Swan 4D 31
Oxwich Green. Swan 4D 31
Oxwick. Norf 3B 78
Oykel Bridge. High 3A 164
Oyne. Abers 1D 152
Oystermouth. Swan 4F 31
Ozleworth. Glos 2C 34

P

Pabail Iarach. W Isl 4H 171
Pabail Uarach. W Isl 4H 171
Pachesham. Surr 5C 38
Packers Hill. Dors 1C 14
Packington. Leics 4A 74
Packmoor. Stoke 5C 84
Packmores. Warw 4G 61
Packwood. W Mid 3F 61
Packwood Gullett. W Mid 3F 61
Padanaram. Ang 3D 144
Padbury. Buck 2F 51
Paddington. G Lon 2D 38
Paddington. Warr 2A 84
Paddlesworth. Kent 2F 29
Paddock. Kent 5D 40
Paddockhole. Dum 1D 112
Paddock Wood. Kent 1A 28
Paddolgreen. Shrp 2H 71
Padeswood. Flin 4E 83
Padiham. Lanc 1F 91
Padside. N Yor 4D 98
Padson. Devn 3F 11
Padstow. Corn 1D 6
Padworth. W Ber 5E 36
Page Bank. Dur 1F 105
Pagham. W Sus 3G 17
Paglesham Churchend. Essx 1D 40
Paglesham Eastend. Essx 1D 40
Paibeil. W Isl 2C 170
(on North Uist)
Paibeil. W Isl 8C 171
(on Taransay)
Paiblesgearraidh. W Isl 2C 170
Paignton. Torb 2E 9
Pailton. Warw 2B 62
Paine's Corner. E Sus 3H 27
Painleyhill. Staf 2E 73
Painscastle. Powy 1E 47
Painshawfield. Nmbd 3D 114
Painsthorpe. E Yor 4C 100
Painswick. Glos 5D 48
Painter's Forstal. Kent 5D 40
Painthorpe. W Yor 3D 92
Pairc Shiaboist. W Isl 3E 171
Paisley. Ren 3F 127
Pakefield. Suff 1H 67
Pakenham. Suff 4B 66
Pale. Gwyn 2B 70
Palehouse Common. E Sus 4F 27
Palestine. Hants 2A 24
Paley Street. Wind 4G 37
Palgowan. Dum 1A 110
Palgrave. Suff 3D 66
Pallington. Dors 3C 14
Palmarsh. Kent 2F 29
Palmer Moor. Derbs 2F 73
Palmers Cross. W Mid 5C 72
Palmerstown. V Glam 5E 33
Palnackie. Dum 4F 111
Palnure. Dum 3B 110
Palterton. Derbs 4B 86
Pamber End. Hants 1E 24
Pamber Green. Hants 1E 24
Pamber Heath. Hants 5E 36
Pamington. Glos 2E 49
Pamphill. Dors 2E 15
Pampisford. Cambs 1E 53
Panborough. Som 2H 21
Panbride. Ang 5E 145
Pancrasweek. Devn 2C 10
Pandy. Gwyn 2A 70
(nr. Bala)
Pandy. Gwyn 5F 69
(nr. Tywyn)
Pandy. Mon 3G 47
Pandy. Powy 5B 70
Pandy. Wrex 2D 70
Pandy Tudur. Cnwy 4A 82
Panfield. Essx 3H 53
Pangbourne. W Ber 4E 37
Pannal. N Yor 4F 99
Pannal Ash. N Yor 4E 99
Pannanich. Abers 4A 152
Pant. Shrp 3E 71
Pant. Wrex 1E 71
Pantasaph. Flin 3D 82
Pant Glas. Gwyn 1D 68
Pant-glas. Shrp 2E 71
Pantgwyn. Carm 3F 45
Pantgwyn. Cdgn 1C 44
Pant-lasau. Swan 3F 31
Panton. Linc 3A 88
Pant-pastynog. Den 4C 82
Pantperthog. Gwyn 5G 69
Pant-teg. Carm 3E 45
Pant-y-Caws. Carm 2F 43
Pant-y-dwr. Powy 3B 58
Pant-y-ffridd. Powy 5D 70
Pantyffynnon. Carm 4G 45
Pantygasseg. Torf 5F 47
Pant-y-llyn. Carm 4G 45
Pant-yr-awel. B'end 3C 32
Pant y Wacco. Flin 3D 82
Panxworth. Norf 4F 79
Papa Stour Airport. Shet 6C 173
Papa Westray Airport. Orkn 2D 172
Papcastle. Cumb 1C 102
Papigoe. High 3F 169
Papil. Shet 8E 173
Papple. E Lot 2B 130
Papplewick. Notts 5C 86
Papworth Everard. Cambs 4B 64
Papworth St Agnes. Cambs 4B 64
Par. Corn 3E 7
Paramour Street. Kent 4G 41
Parbold. Lanc 3C 90
Parbrook. Som 3A 22
Parbrook. W Sus 3B 26
Parc. Gwyn 2A 70
Parcllyn. Cdgn 5B 56

Pen-y-Darren—Pontrilas

Pen-y-Darren. *Mer T* 5D **46**
Pen-y-fai. *B'end* 3B **32**
Penyffordd. *Flin* 4F **83**
(nr. Mold)
Pen-y-ffordd. *Flin* 2D **82**
(nr. Prestatyn)
Penyffridd. *Gwyn* 5E **81**
Pen-y-garn. *Cdgn* 2F **57**
Pen-y-garnedd. *IOA* 3E **81**
Penygarnedd. *Powy* 3D **70**
Pen-y-graig. *Gwyn* 2B **68**
Penygraig. *Rhon* 2C **32**
Penygraigwen. *IOA* 2D **80**
Pen-y-groes. *Carm* 4F **45**
Penygroes. *Gwyn* 5D **80**
Penygroes. *Pemb* 1F **43**
Pen-y-Mynydd. *Carm* 5E **45**
Penymynydd. *Flin* 4F **83**
Penyrheol. *Cphy* 3E **33**
Pen-yr-heol. *Mon* 4H **47**
Penyrheol. *Swan* 3E **31**
Pen-yr-Heolgerrig. *Mer T* 5D **46**
Penysarn. *IOA* 1D **80**
Pen-y-stryt. *Den* 5D **82**
Penywaun. *Rhon* 5C **46**
Penzance. *Corn* 3B **4**
Peopleton. *Worc* 5D **60**
Peover Heath. *Ches E* 3B **84**
Peper Harow. *Surr* 1A **26**
Peplow. *Shrp* 3A **72**
Pepper Arden. *N Yor* 4F **105**
Perceton. *N Ayr* 5E **127**
Percyhorner. *Abers* 2G **161**
Perham Down. *Wilts* 2A **24**
Periton. *Som* 2C **20**
Perkinsville. *Dur* 4F **115**
Perlethorpe. *Notts* 3D **86**
Perranarworthal. *Corn* 5B **6**
Perranporth. *Corn* 3B **6**
Perranuthnoe. *Corn* 4C **4**
Perranwell. *Corn* 5B **6**
Perranzabuloe. *Corn* 3B **6**
Perrott's Brook. *Glos* 5F **49**
Perry. *W Mid* 1E **61**
Perry Barr. *W Mid* 1E **61**
Perry Crofts. *Staf* 5G **73**
Perry Green. *Essx* 3B **54**
Perry Green. *Herts* 4E **53**
Perry Green. *Wilts* 3E **35**
Perry Street. *Kent* 3H **39**
Perry Street. *Som* 2G **13**
Perrywood. *Kent* 5E **41**
Pershall. *Staf* 3C **72**
Pershore. *Worc* 1E **49**
Pertenhall. *Bed* 4H **63**
Perth. *Per* 1D **136**
Perthy. *Shrp* 2F **71**
Perton. *Staf* 1C **60**
Pertwood. *Wilts* 3D **23**
Peterborough. *Pet* 1A **64**
Peterburn. *High* 5B **162**
Peterchurch. *Here* 2G **47**
Peterculter. *Aber* 3F **153**
Peterhead. *Abers* 4H **161**
Peterlee. *Dur* 5H **115**
Petersfield. *Hants* 4F **25**
Petersfinger. *Wilts* 4G **23**
Peter's Green. *Herts* 4B **52**
Peters Marland. *Devn* 1E **11**
Peterstone Wentlooge. *Newp* 3F **33**
Peterston-super-Ely. *V Glam* 4D **32**
Peterstow. *Here* 3A **48**
Peter Tavy. *Devn* 5F **11**
Petertown. *Orkn* 7C **172**
Petham. *Kent* 5F **41**
Petherwin Gate. *Corn* 4C **10**
Petrockstowe. *Devn* 2F **11**
Petsoe End. *Mil* 1G **51**
Pett. *E Sus* 4C **28**
Pettaugh. *Suff* 5D **66**
Pett Bottom. *Kent* 5F **41**
Petteridge. *Kent* 1A **28**
Pettinain. *S Lan* 5C **128**
Pettistree. *Suff* 5E **67**
Petton. *Devn* 4D **20**
Petton. *Shrp* 3G **71**
Petts Wood. *G Lon* 4F **39**
Pettycur. *Fife* 1F **129**
Pettywell. *Norf* 3C **78**
Petworth. *W Sus* 3A **26**
Pevensey. *E Sus* 5H **27**
Pevensey Bay. *E Sus* 5A **28**
Pewsey. *Wilts* 5G **35**
Pheasants Hill. *Buck* 3F **37**
Philadelphia. *Tyne* 4G **115**
Philham. *Devn* 4C **18**
Philiphaugh. *Bord* 2G **119**
Phillack. *Corn* 3C **4**
Philleigh. *Corn* 5C **6**
Philpstoun. *W Lot* 2D **128**
Phocle Green. *Here* 3B **48**
Phoenix Green. *Hants* 1F **25**
Pibsbury. *Som* 4H **21**
Pibwrlwyd. *Carm* 4E **45**
Pica. *Cumb* 2B **102**
Piccadilly. *Warw* 1G **61**
Piccadilly Corner. *Norf* 2E **67**
Piccotts End. *Herts* 5A **52**
Pickering. *N Yor* 1B **100**
Picket Piece. *Hants* 2B **24**
Picket Post. *Hants* 2G **15**
Pickford. *W Mid* 2G **61**
Pickhill. *N Yor* 1F **99**
Picklenash. *Glos* 3C **48**
Picklescott. *Shrp* 1G **59**
Pickletillem. *Fife* 1G **137**
Pickmere. *Ches E* 3A **84**
Pickstock. *Telf* 3B **72**
Pickwell. *Devn* 2E **19**
Pickwell. *Leics* 4E **75**
Pickworth. *Linc* 2H **75**
Pickworth. *Rut* 4G **75**
Picton. *Ches W* 3G **83**
Picton. *Flin* 2D **82**
Picton. *N Yor* 4B **106**
Pict's Hill. *Som* 4H **21**
Piddinghoe. *E Sus* 5F **27**
Piddington. *Buck* 2G **37**
Piddington. *Nptn* 5F **63**
Piddington. *Oxon* 4E **51**
Piddlehinton. *Dors* 3C **14**
Piddletrenthide. *Dors* 2C **14**
Pidley. *Cambs* 3C **64**
Pidney. *Dors* 2C **14**
Pie Corner. *Here* 4A **60**
Piercebridge. *Darl* 3F **105**
Pierowall. *Orkn* 3D **172**
Pigdon. *Nmbd* 1E **115**
Pightley. *Som* 3F **21**
Pikehall. *Derbs* 5F **85**
Pikeshill. *Hants* 2A **16**
Pilford. *Dors* 2F **15**
Pilgrims Hatch. *Essx* 1G **39**
Pilham. *Linc* 1F **87**
Pill. *N Som* 4A **34**
Pillaton. *Corn* 2H **7**
Pillaton. *Staf* 4D **72**
Pillerton Hersey. *Warw* 1B **50**
Pillerton Priors. *Warw* 1A **50**
Pilleth. *Powy* 4E **59**
Pilley. *Hants* 3B **16**
Pilley. *S Yor* 4D **92**
Pillgwenlly. *Newp* 3G **33**
Pilling. *Lanc* 5D **96**
Pilling Lane. *Lanc* 5C **96**
Pillowell. *Glos* 5B **48**
Pill, The. *Mon* 3H **33**
Pillwell. *Dors* 1C **14**
Pilning. *S Glo* 3A **34**
Pilsbury. *Derbs* 4F **85**
Pilsdon. *Dors* 3H **13**
Pilsgate. *Pet* 5H **75**
Pilsley. *Derbs* 3G **85**
(nr. Bakewell)
Pilsley. *Derbs* 4B **86**
(nr. Clay Cross)
Pilson Green. *Norf* 4F **79**
Piltdown. *E Sus* 3F **27**
Pilton. *Edin* 2F **129**
Pilton. *Nptn* 2H **63**
Pilton. *Rut* 5G **75**
Pilton. *Som* 2A **22**
Pilton Green. *Swan* 4D **30**
Pimperne. *Dors* 2E **15**
Pinchbeck. *Linc* 3B **76**
Pinchbeck Bars. *Linc* 3A **76**
Pinchbeck West. *Linc* 3B **76**
Pinfold. *Lanc* 3B **90**
Pinford End. *Suff* 5H **65**
Pinged. *Carm* 5E **45**
Pinhoe. *Devn* 3C **12**
Pinkerton. *E Lot* 2D **130**
Pinkneys Green. *Wind* 3G **37**
Pinley. *W Mid* 3A **62**
Pinley Green. *Warw* 4G **61**
Pinmill. *Suff* 2F **55**
Pinmore. *S Ayr* 5B **116**
Pinner. *G Lon* 2C **38**
Pins Green. *Worc* 1C **48**
Pinsley Green. *Ches E* 1H **71**
Pinvin. *Worc* 1E **49**
Pinwherry. *S Ayr* 1G **109**
Pinxton. *Derbs* 5B **86**
Pipe and Lyde. *Here* 1A **48**
Pipe Aston. *Here* 3G **59**
Pipe Gate. *Shrp* 1B **72**
Pipehill. *Staf* 5E **73**
Piperhill. *High* 3C **158**
Pipe Ridware. *Staf* 4E **73**
Pipers Pool. *Corn* 4C **10**
Pipewell. *Nptn* 2F **63**
Pippacott. *Devn* 3F **19**
Pipton. *Powy* 2E **47**
Pirbright. *Surr* 5A **38**
Pirnmill. *N Ayr* 5G **125**
Pirton. *Herts* 2B **52**
Pirton. *Worc* 1D **49**
Pisgah. *Stir* 3G **135**
Pishill. *Oxon* 3F **37**
Pistyll. *Gwyn* 1C **68**
Pitagowan. *Per* 2F **143**
Pitcairn. *Per* 3F **143**
Pitcairngreen. *Per* 1C **136**
Pitcalnie. *High* 1C **158**
Pitcaple. *Abers* 1E **152**
Pitchcombe. *Glos* 5D **48**
Pitchcott. *Buck* 3F **51**
Pitchford. *Shrp* 5H **71**
Pitch Green. *Buck* 5F **51**
Pitch Place. *Surr* 5A **38**
Pitcombe. *Som* 3B **22**
Pitcox. *E Lot* 2C **130**
Pitcur. *Per* 5B **144**
Pitfichie. *Abers* 2D **152**
Pitgrudy. *High* 4E **165**
Pitkennedy. *Ang* 3E **145**
Pitlessie. *Fife* 3F **137**
Pitlochry. *Per* 3G **143**
Pitmachie. *Abers* 1D **152**
Pitmaduthy. *High* 1B **158**
Pitmedden. *Abers* 1F **153**
Pitminster. *Som* 1F **13**
Pitnacree. *Per* 3G **143**
Pitney. *Som* 4H **21**
Pitroddie. *Per* 1E **136**
Pitscottie. *Fife* 2G **137**
Pitsea. *Essx* 2B **40**
Pitsford. *Nptn* 4E **63**
Pitsford Hill. *Som* 3E **20**
Pitsmoor. *S Yor* 2A **86**
Pitstone. *Buck* 4H **51**
Pitt. *Hants* 4C **24**
Pitt Court. *Glos* 2C **34**
Pittentrail. *High* 3E **164**
Pittenweem. *Fife* 3H **137**
Pittington. *Dur* 5G **115**
Pitton. *Swan* 4D **30**
Pitton. *Wilts* 3H **23**
Pittswood. *Kent* 1H **27**
Pittulie. *Abers* 2G **161**
Pittville. *Glos* 3E **49**
Pitversie. *Per* 2D **136**
Pityme. *Corn* 1D **6**
Pity Me. *Dur* 5F **115**
Pixey Green. *Suff* 3E **67**
Pixley. *Here* 2B **48**
Place Newton. *N Yor* 2C **100**
Plaidy. *Abers* 3E **161**
Plaidy. *Corn* 3G **7**
Plain Dealings. *Pemb* 3E **43**
Plains. *N Lan* 3A **128**
Plainsfield. *Som* 3E **21**
Plaish. *Shrp* 1H **59**
Plaistow. *Here* 2B **48**
Plaistow. *W Sus* 2B **26**
Plaitford. *Wilts* 1A **16**
Plas Llwyd. *Cnwy* 3B **82**
Plastow Green. *Hants* 5D **36**
Plas yn Cefn. *Den* 3C **82**
Platt. *Kent* 5H **39**
Platt Bridge. *G Man* 4E **90**
Platt Lane. *Shrp* 2H **71**
Platts Common. *S Yor* 4D **92**
Platt's Heath. *Kent* 5C **40**
Platt, The. *E Sus* 2G **27**
Plawsworth. *Dur* 5F **115**
Plaxtol. *Kent* 5H **39**
Playden. *E Sus* 3D **28**
Playford. *Suff* 1F **55**
Play Hatch. *Oxon* 4F **37**
Playing Place. *Corn* 4C **6**
Playley Green. *Glos* 2C **48**
Plealey. *Shrp* 5G **71**
Plean. *Stir* 1B **128**
Pleasington. *Bkbn* 2E **91**
Pleasley. *Derbs* 4C **86**
Pledgdon Green. *Essx* 3F **53**
Plenmeller. *Nmbd* 3A **114**
Pleshey. *Essx* 4G **53**
Plockton. *High* 5H **155**
Plocrapol. *W Isl* 8D **171**
Ploughfield. *Here* 1G **47**
Plowden. *Shrp* 2F **59**
Ploxgreen. *Shrp* 5F **71**
Pluckley. *Kent* 1D **28**
Plucks Gutter. *Kent* 4G **41**
Plumbland. *Cumb* 1C **102**
Plumgarths. *Cumb* 5F **103**
Plumley. *Ches E* 3B **84**
Plummers Plain. *W Sus* 3D **26**
Plumpton. *Cumb* 1F **103**
Plumpton. *E Sus* 4E **27**
Plumpton. *Nptn* 1D **50**
Plumpton Foot. *Cumb* 1F **103**
Plumpton Green. *E Sus* 4E **27**
Plumpton Head. *Cumb* 1G **103**
Plumstead. *G Lon* 3F **39**
Plumstead. *Norf* 2D **78**
Plumtree. *Notts* 2D **74**
Plumtree Park. *Notts* 2D **74**
Plungar. *Leics* 2E **75**
Plush. *Dors* 2C **14**
Plushabridge. *Corn* 5D **10**
Plwmp. *Cdgn* 5C **56**
Plymouth. *Plym* 3A **8**
Plympton. *Plym* 3B **8**
Plymstock. *Plym* 3B **8**
Plymtree. *Devn* 2D **12**
Pockley. *N Yor* 1A **100**
Pocklington. *E Yor* 5C **100**
Pode Hole. *Linc* 3B **76**
Podimore. *Som* 4A **22**
Podington. *Bed* 4G **63**
Podmore. *Staf* 2B **72**
Poffley End. *Oxon* 4B **50**
Point Clear. *Essx* 4D **54**
Pointon. *Linc* 2A **76**
Pokesdown. *Bour* 3G **15**
Polbae. *Dum* 2H **109**
Polbain. *High* 3E **163**
Polbathic. *Corn* 3H **7**
Polbeth. *W Lot* 3D **128**
Polbrock. *Corn* 2E **6**
Polchar. *High* 3C **150**
Polebrook. *Nptn* 2H **63**
Pole Elm. *Worc* 1D **48**
Polegate. *E Sus* 5G **27**
Pole Moor. *W Yor* 3A **92**
Poles. *High* 4E **165**
Polesworth. *Warw* 5G **73**
Polglass. *High* 3E **163**
Polgooth. *Corn* 3D **6**
Poling. *W Sus* 5B **26**
Poling Corner. *W Sus* 5B **26**
Polio. *High* 1B **158**
Polkerris. *Corn* 3E **7**
Polla. *High* 3D **166**
Pollard Street. *Norf* 2F **79**
Pollicott. *Buck* 4F **51**
Pollington. *E Yor* 3G **93**
Polloch. *High* 2B **140**
Pollok. *Glas* 3G **127**
Pollokshaws. *Glas* 3G **127**
Pollokshields. *Glas* 3G **127**
Polmaily. *High* 5G **157**
Polmassick. *Corn* 4D **6**
Polmont. *Falk* 2C **128**
Polnessan. *E Ayr* 3D **116**
Polnish. *High* 5F **147**
Polperro. *Corn* 3G **7**
Polruan. *Corn* 3F **7**
Polscoe. *Corn* 2F **7**
Polsham. *Som* 2A **22**
Polskeoch. *Dum* 4F **117**
Polstead. *Suff* 2C **54**
Polstead Heath. *Suff* 1C **54**
Poltesco. *Corn* 5E **5**
Poltimore. *Devn* 3C **12**
Polton. *Midl* 3F **129**
Polwarth. *Bord* 4D **130**
Polyphant. *Corn* 4C **10**
Polzeath. *Corn* 1D **6**
Ponde. *Powy* 2E **46**
Pondersbridge. *Cambs* 1B **64**
Ponders End. *G Lon* 1E **39**
Pond Street. *Essx* 2E **53**
Pondtail. *Hants* 1G **25**
Ponsanooth. *Corn* 5B **6**
Ponsongath. *Corn* 5E **5**
Ponsworthy. *Devn* 5H **11**
Pontamman. *Carm* 4G **45**
Pontantwn. *Carm* 4E **45**
Pontardawe. *Neat* 5H **45**
Pontarddulais. *Swan* 5F **45**
Pontarfynach. *Cdgn* 3G **57**
Pont-ar-gothi. *Carm* 3F **45**
Pont ar Hydfer. *Powy* 3B **46**
Pontarllechau. *Carm* 3H **45**
Pontarsais. *Carm* 3E **45**
Pontblyddyn. *Flin* 4E **83**
Pontbren Llwyd. *Rhon* 5C **46**
Pont-Cyfyng. *Cnwy* 5G **81**
Pontdolgoch. *Powy* 1C **58**
Pontefract. *W Yor* 2E **93**
Ponteland. *Nmbd* 2E **115**
Ponterwyd. *Cdgn* 2G **57**
Pontesbury. *Shrp* 5G **71**
Pontesford. *Shrp* 5G **71**
Pontfadog. *Wrex* 2E **71**
Pontfaen. *Pemb* 1E **43**
Pont-faen. *Powy* 2C **46**
Pont-Faen. *Shrp* 2E **71**
Pontgarreg. *Cdgn* 5C **56**
Pont-Henri. *Carm* 5E **45**
Ponthir. *Torf* 2G **33**
Ponthirwaun. *Cdgn* 1C **44**
Pont-iets. *Carm* 5E **45**
Pontllanfraith. *Cphy* 2E **33**
Pontlliw. *Swan* 5G **45**
Pont Llogel. *Powy* 4C **70**
Pontllyfni. *Gwyn* 5D **80**
Pontlottyn. *Cphy* 5E **46**
Pontneddfechan. *Neat* 5C **46**
Pont-newydd. *Carm* 5E **45**
Pont-newydd. *Flin* 4D **82**
Pontnewydd. *Torf* 2F **33**
Ponton. *Shet* 6E **173**
Pont Pen-y-benglog. *Gwyn* 4F **81**
Pontrhydfendigaid. *Cdgn* 4G **57**
Pont Rhyd-y-cyff. *B'end* 3B **32**
Pontrhydyfen. *Neat* 2A **32**
Pont-rhyd-y-groes. *Cdgn* 3G **57**
Pontrhydyrun. *Torf* 2F **33**
Pont-Rhythallt. *Gwyn* 4E **81**
Pontrilas. *Here* 3G **47**

Purton Stoke—Rescorla

Purton Stoke. *Wilts* 2F 35
Pury End. *Nptn* 1F 51
Pusey. *Oxon* 2B 36
Putley. *Here* 2B 48
Putney. *G Lon* 3D 38
Putsborough. *Devn* 2E 19
Puttenham. *Herts* 4G 51
Puttenham. *Surr* 1A 26
Puttock End. *Essx* 1B 54
Puttock's End. *Essx* 4F 53
Puxey. *Dors* 1C 14
Puxton. *N Som* 5H 33
Pwll. *Carm* 5E 45
Pwll. *Powy* 5D 70
Pwllcrochan. *Pemb* 4D 42
Pwll-glas. *Den* 5D 82
Pwllgloyw. *Powy* 2D 46
Pwllheli. *Gwyn* 2C 68
Pwllmeyric. *Mon* 2A 34
Pwlltrap. *Carm* 3G 43
Pwll-y-glaw. *Neat* 2A 32
Pyecombe. *W Sus* 4D 27
Pye Corner. *Herts* 4E 53
Pye Corner. *Newp* 3G 33
Pye Green. *Staf* 4D 73
Pyewipe. *NE Lin* 3F 95
Pyle. *B'end* 3B 32
Pyle. *IOW* 5C 16
Pyle Hill. *Surr* 5A 38
Pylle. *Som* 3B 22
Pymoor. *Cambs* 2D 65
Pymoor. *Dors* 3H 13
Pyrford. *Surr* 5B 38
Pyrford Village. *Surr* 5B 38
Pyrton. *Oxon* 2E 37
Pytchley. *Nptn* 3F 63
Pyworthy. *Devn* 2D 10

Q

Quabbs. *Shrp* 2E 58
Quadring. *Linc* 2B 76
Quadring Eaudike. *Linc* 2B 76
Quainton. *Buck* 3F 51
Quaking Houses. *Dur* 4E 115
Quarley. *Hants* 2A 24
Quarndon. *Derbs* 1H 73
Quarrendon. *Buck* 4G 51
Quarrier's Village. *Inv* 3E 127
Quarrington. *Linc* 1H 75
Quarrington Hill. *Dur* 1A 106
Quarry Bank. *W Mid* 2D 60
Quarry, The. *Glos* 2C 34
Quarrywood. *Mor* 2F 159
Quartalehouse. *Abers* 4G 161
Quarter. *N Ayr* 3C 126
Quarter. *S Lan* 4A 128
Quatford. *Shrp* 1B 60
Quatt. *Shrp* 2B 60
Quebec. *Dur* 5E 115
Quedgeley. *Glos* 4D 48
Queen Adelaide. *Cambs* 2E 65
Queenborough. *Kent* 3D 40
Queen Camel. *Som* 4A 22
Queen Charlton. *Bath* 5B 34
Queen Dart. *Devn* 1B 12
Queenhill. *Worc* 2D 48
Queen Oak. *Dors* 3C 22
Queensbury. *W Yor* 1B 92
Queensferry. *Flin* 4F 83
Queenstown. *Bkpl* 1B 90
Queen Street. *Kent* 1A 28
Queenzieburn. *N Lan* 2H 127
Quemerford. *Wilts* 5F 35
Quendale. *Shet* 10E 173
Quendon. *Essx* 2F 53
Queniborough. *Leics* 4D 74
Quenington. *Glos* 5G 49
Quernmore. *Lanc* 3E 97
Quethiock. *Corn* 2H 7
Quholm. *Orkn* 6B 172
Quick's Green. *W Ber* 4D 36
Quidenham. *Norf* 2C 66
Quidhampton. *Hants* 1D 24
Quidhampton. *Wilts* 3G 23
Quilquox. *Abers* 5G 161
Quina Brook. *Shrp* 2H 71
Quindry. *Orkn* 8D 172
Quine's Hill. *IOM* 4C 108
Quinton. *Nptn* 5E 63
Quinton. *W Mid* 2D 61
Quintrell Downs. *Corn* 2C 6
Quixhill. *Staf* 1F 73
Quoditch. *Devn* 3E 11
Quorn. *Leics* 4C 74
Quorndon. *Leics* 4C 74
Quothquan. *S Lan* 1B 118
Quoyloo. *Orkn* 5B 172
Quoyness. *Orkn* 7B 172
Quoys. *Shet* 5F 173 (on Mainland)
Quoys. *Shet* 1H 173 (on Unst)

R

Rableyheath. *Herts* 4C 52
Raby. *Cumb* 4C 112
Raby. *Mers* 3F 83
Rachan Mill. *Bord* 1D 118
Rachub. *Gwyn* 4F 81
Rack End. *Oxon* 5C 50
Rackenford. *Devn* 1B 12
Rackham. *W Sus* 4B 26
Rackheath. *Norf* 4E 79
Racks. *Dum* 2B 112
Rackwick. *Orkn* 8B 172 (on Hoy)
Rackwick. *Orkn* 3D 172 (on Westray)
Radbourne. *Derbs* 2G 73
Radcliffe. *G Man* 4F 91
Radcliffe. *Nmbd* 4G 121
Radcliffe on Trent. *Notts* 2D 74
Radclive. *Buck* 2E 51
Radernie. *Fife* 3G 137
Radfall. *Kent* 4F 41
Radford. *Bath* 1B 22
Radford. *Nott* 1C 74
Radford. *Oxon* 3C 50
Radford. *W Mid* 2H 61
Radford. *Worc* 5E 61
Radford Semele. *Warw* 4H 61
Radipole. *Dors* 4B 14
Radlett. *Herts* 1C 38
Radley. *Oxon* 2D 36
Radnage. *Buck* 2F 37
Radstock. *Bath* 1B 22
Radstone. *Nptn* 1D 50
Radway. *Warw* 1B 50
Radway Green. *Ches E* 5B 84
Radwell. *Bed* 5H 63
Radwell. *Herts* 2C 52
Radwinter. *Essx* 2G 53
Radyr. *Card* 3E 33
RAF Coltishall. *Norf* 3E 79
Rafford. *Mor* 3E 159
Ragdale. *Leics* 4D 74
Ragdon. *Shrp* 1G 59
Ragged Appleshaw. *Hants* 2B 24
Raggra. *High* 4F 169
Raglan. *Mon* 5H 47
Ragnall. *Notts* 3F 87
Raigbeg. *High* 1C 150
Rainford. *Mers* 4C 90
Rainford Junction. *Mers* 4C 90
Rainham. *G Lon* 2G 39
Rainham. *Medw* 4C 40
Rainhill. *Mers* 1G 83
Rainow. *Ches E* 3D 84
Rainton. *N Yor* 2F 99
Rainworth. *Notts* 5C 86
Raisbeck. *Cumb* 4H 103
Raise. *Cumb* 5A 114
Rait. *Per* 1E 137
Raithby. *Linc* 2C 88
Raithby by Spilsby. *Linc* 4C 88
Raithwaite. *N Yor* 3F 107
Rake. *W Sus* 4G 25
Rake End. *Staf* 4E 73
Rakeway. *Staf* 1E 73
Rakewood. *G Man* 3H 91
Ralia. *High* 4B 150
Ram Alley. *Wilts* 5H 35
Ramasaig. *High* 4A 154
Rame. *Corn* 4A 8 (nr. Millbrook)
Rame. *Corn* 5B 6 (nr. Penryn)
Ram Lane. *Kent* 1D 28
Ramnageo. *Shet* 1H 173
Rampisham. *Dors* 2A 14
Rampside. *Cumb* 3B 96
Rampton. *Cambs* 4D 64
Rampton. *Notts* 3E 87
Ramsbottom. *G Man* 3F 91
Ramsburn. *Mor* 3C 160
Ramsbury. *Wilts* 4A 36
Ramscraigs. *High* 1H 165
Ramsdean. *Hants* 4F 25
Ramsdell. *Hants* 1D 24
Ramsden. *Oxon* 4B 50
Ramsden. *Worc* 1E 49
Ramsden Bellhouse. *Essx* 1B 40
Ramsden Heath. *Essx* 1B 40
Ramsey. *Cambs* 2B 64
Ramsey. *Essx* 2F 55
Ramsey. *IOM* 2D 108
Ramsey Forty Foot. *Cambs* 2C 64
Ramsey Heights. *Cambs* 2B 64
Ramsey Island. *Essx* 5C 54
Ramsey Mereside. *Cambs* 2B 64
Ramsey St Mary's. *Cambs* 2B 64
Ramsgate. *Kent* 4H 41
Ramsgill. *N Yor* 2D 98
Ramshaw. *Dur* 5C 114
Ramshorn. *Staf* 1E 73
Ramsley. *Devn* 3G 11
Ramsnest Common. *Surr* 2A 26
Ramstone. *Abers* 2D 152
Ranais. *W Isl* 5G 171
Ranby. *Linc* 3B 88
Ranby. *Notts* 2D 86
Rand. *Linc* 3A 88
Randalstown. *Ant* 3F 175
Randwick. *Glos* 5D 48
Ranfurly. *Ren* 3E 127
Rangag. *High* 4D 169
Rangemore. *Staf* 3F 73
Rangeworthy. *S Glo* 3B 34
Rankinston. *E Ayr* 3D 116
Rank's Green. *Essx* 4H 53
Ranmore Common. *Surr* 5C 38
Rannoch Station. *Per* 3B 142
Ranochan. *High* 5G 147
Ranskill. *Notts* 2D 86
Ranton. *Staf* 3C 72
Ranton Green. *Staf* 3C 72
Ranworth. *Norf* 4F 79
Raploch. *Stir* 4G 135
Rapness. *Orkn* 3E 172
Rapps. *Som* 1G 13
Rascal Moor. *E Yor* 1B 94
Rascarrel. *Dum* 5E 111
Rasharkin. *Bmny* 2F 175
Rashfield. *Arg* 1C 126
Rashwood. *Worc* 4D 60
Raskelf. *N Yor* 2G 99
Rassau. *Blae* 4E 47
Rastrick. *W Yor* 2B 92
Ratagan. *High* 2B 148
Ratby. *Leics* 5C 74
Ratcliffe Culey. *Leics* 1H 61
Ratcliffe on Soar. *Notts* 3B 74
Ratcliffe on the Wreake. *Leics* 4D 74
Rathen. *Abers* 2H 161
Rathfriland. *Ban* 6G 175
Rathillet. *Fife* 1F 137
Rathmell. *N Yor* 3H 97
Ratho. *Edin* 2E 129
Ratho Station. *Edin* 2E 129
Rathven. *Mor* 2B 160
Ratley. *Hants* 4B 24
Ratley. *Warw* 1B 50
Ratlinghope. *Shrp* 1G 59
Rattar. *High* 1E 169
Ratten Row. *Cumb* 5E 113
Ratten Row. *Lanc* 5D 96
Rattery. *Devn* 2D 8
Rattlesden. *Suff* 5B 66
Ratton Village. *E Sus* 5G 27
Rattray. *Abers* 3H 161
Rattray. *Per* 4A 144
Raughton. *Cumb* 5E 113
Raughton Head. *Cumb* 5E 113
Raunds. *Nptn* 3G 63
Ravenfield. *S Yor* 1B 86
Ravenfield Common. *S Yor* 1B 86
Ravenglass. *Cumb* 5B 102
Ravenhills Green. *Worc* 5B 60
Raveningham. *Norf* 1F 67
Ravenscar. *N Yor* 4G 107
Ravensdale. *IOM* 2C 108
Ravensden. *Bed* 5H 63
Ravenseat. *N Yor* 4B 104
Ravenshead. *Notts* 5C 86
Ravensmoor. *Ches E* 5A 84
Ravensthorpe. *Nptn* 3D 62
Ravensthorpe. *W Yor* 2C 92
Ravenstone. *Leics* 4B 74
Ravenstone. *Mil* 5F 63
Ravenstonedale. *Cumb* 4A 104
Ravenstown. *Cumb* 2C 96
Ravenstruther. *S Lan* 5C 128
Ravensworth. *N Yor* 4E 105
Raw. *N Yor* 4G 107
Rawcliffe. *E Yor* 2G 93
Rawcliffe. *York* 4H 99
Rawcliffe Bridge. *E Yor* 2G 93
Rawdon. *W Yor* 1C 92
Rawgreen. *Nmbd* 4C 114
Rawmarsh. *S Yor* 1B 86
Rawnsley. *Staf* 4E 73
Rawreth. *Essx* 1B 40
Rawridge. *Devn* 2F 13
Rawson Green. *Derbs* 1A 74
Rawtenstall. *Lanc* 2G 91
Raydon. *Suff* 2D 54
Raylees. *Nmbd* 5D 120
Rayleigh. *Essx* 1C 40
Raymond's Hill. *Devn* 3G 13
Rayne. *Essx* 3H 53
Rayners Lane. *G Lon* 2C 38
Reach. *Cambs* 4E 65
Read. *Lanc* 1F 91
Reading. *Read* 4F 37
Reading Green. *Suff* 3D 66
Reading Street. *Kent* 2D 28
Readymoney. *Corn* 3F 7
Reagill. *Cumb* 3H 103
Rearquhar. *High* 4E 165
Rearsby. *Leics* 4D 74
Reasby. *Linc* 3H 87
Reaseheath. *Ches E* 5A 84
Reaster. *High* 2E 169
Reawick. *Shet* 7E 173
Reay. *High* 2B 168
Rechullin. *High* 3A 156
Reculver. *Kent* 4G 41
Redberth. *Pemb* 4E 43
Redbourn. *Herts* 4B 52
Redbourne. *N Lin* 4C 94
Redbrook. *Glos* 5A 48
Redbrook. *Wrex* 1H 71
Redburn. *High* 4D 158
Redburn. *Nmbd* 3A 114
Redcar. *Red C* 2D 106
Redcastle. *High* 4H 157
Redcliff Bay. *N Som* 4H 33
Red Dial. *Cumb* 5D 112
Redding. *Falk* 2C 128
Reddingmuirhead. *Falk* 2C 128
Reddings, The. *Glos* 3E 49
Reddish. *G Man* 1C 84
Redditch. *Worc* 4E 61
Rede. *Suff* 5H 65
Redenhall. *Norf* 2E 67
Redesdale Camp. *Nmbd* 5C 120
Redesmouth. *Nmbd* 1B 114
Redford. *Ang* 4E 145
Redford. *Dur* 1D 105
Redford. *W Sus* 4G 25
Redfordgreen. *Bord* 3F 119
Redgate. *Corn* 2G 7
Redgrave. *Suff* 3C 66
Redhill. *Abers* 3E 153
Redhill. *Herts* 2C 52
Redhill. *N Som* 5A 34
Redhill. *Shrp* 4B 72
Redhill. *Surr* 5D 39
Red Hill. *Warw* 5F 61
Red Hill. *W Yor* 2E 93
Redhouses. *Arg* 3B 124
Redisham. *Suff* 2G 67
Redland. *Bris* 4A 34
Redland. *Orkn* 5C 172
Redlingfield. *Suff* 3D 66
Red Lodge. *Suff* 3F 65
Redlynch. *Som* 3C 22
Redlynch. *Wilts* 4H 23
Redmain. *Cumb* 1C 102
Redmarley. *Worc* 4B 60
Redmarley D'Abitot. *Glos* 2C 48
Redmarshall. *Stoc T* 2A 106
Redmile. *Leics* 2E 75
Redmire. *N Yor* 5D 104
Rednal. *Shrp* 3F 71
Redpath. *Bord* 1H 119
Redpoint. *High* 2G 155
Red Post. *Corn* 2C 10
Red Rock. *G Man* 4D 90
Red Roses. *Carm* 3G 43
Red Row. *Nmbd* 5G 121
Redruth. *Corn* 4B 6
Red Street. *Staf* 5C 84
Redvales. *G Man* 4G 91
Red Wharf Bay. *IOA* 2E 81
Redwick. *Newp* 3H 33
Redwick. *S Glo* 3A 34
Redworth. *Darl* 2F 105
Reed. *Herts* 2D 52
Reed End. *Herts* 2D 52
Reedham. *Linc* 5B 88
Reedham. *Norf* 5G 79
Reedness. *E Yor* 2B 94
Reeds Beck. *Linc* 4B 88
Reemshill. *Abers* 4E 161
Reepham. *Linc* 3H 87
Reepham. *Norf* 3C 78
Reeth. *N Yor* 5D 104
Regaby. *IOM* 2D 108
Regil. *N Som* 5A 34
Regoul. *High* 3C 158
Reiff. *High* 2D 162
Reigate. *Surr* 5D 38
Reighton. *N Yor* 2F 101
Reilth. *Shrp* 2E 59
Reinigeadal. *W Isl* 7E 171
Reisque. *Abers* 2F 153
Reiss. *High* 3F 169
Rejerrah. *Corn* 3B 6
Releath. *Corn* 5A 6
Relubbus. *Corn* 3C 4
Relugas. *Mor* 4D 159
Remenham. *Wok* 3F 37
Remenham Hill. *Wok* 3F 37
Rempstone. *Notts* 3C 74
Rendcomb. *Glos* 5F 49
Rendham. *Suff* 4F 67
Rendlesham. *Suff* 5F 67
Renfrew. *Ren* 3G 127
Renhold. *Bed* 5H 63
Renishaw. *Derbs* 3B 86
Rennington. *Nmbd* 3G 121
Renton. *W Dun* 2E 127
Renwick. *Cumb* 5G 113
Repps. *Norf* 4G 79
Repton. *Derbs* 3H 73
Rescassa. *Corn* 4D 6
Rescobie. *Ang* 3E 145
Rescorla. *Corn* 3E 7 (nr. Rosevean)

Rescorla. *Corn* 4D 6
(nr. St Ewe)
Resipole. *High* 2B 140
Resolfen. *Neat* 5B 46
Resolis. *High* 2A 158
Resolven. *Neat* 5B 46
Rest and be thankful. *Arg* 3B 134
Reston. *Bord* 3E 131
Restrop. *Wilts* 3F 35
Retford. *Notts* 2E 86
Retire. *Corn* 2E 6
Rettendon. *Essx* 1B 40
Revesby. *Linc* 4B 88
Rew. *Devn* 5D 8
Rewe. *Devn* 3C 12
Rew Street. *IOW* 3C 16
Rexon. *Devn* 4E 11
Reybridge. *Wilts* 5E 35
Reydon. *Suff* 3H 67
Reymerston. *Norf* 5C 78
Reynalton. *Pemb* 4E 43
Reynoldston. *Swan* 4D 31
Rezare. *Corn* 5D 10
Rhadyr. *Mon* 5G 47
Rhaeadr Gwy. *Powy* 4B 58
Rhandirmwyn. *Carm* 1A 46
Rhayader. *Powy* 4B 58
Rheindown. *High* 4H 157
Rhemore. *High* 3G 139
Rhenetra. *High* 3D 154
Rhewl. *Den* 1D 70
(nr. Llangollen)
Rhewl. *Den* 4D 82
(nr. Ruthin)
Rhewl. *Shrp* 2F 71
Rhewl-Mostyn. *Flin* 2D 82
Rhian. *High* 2C 164
Rhian Breck. *High* 3C 164
Rhicarn. *High* 1E 163
Rhiconich. *High* 3C 166
Rhicullen. *High* 1A 158
Rhidorroch. *High* 4F 163
Rhifail. *High* 4H 167
Rhigos. *Rhon* 5C 46
Rhilochan. *High* 3E 165
Rhiroy. *High* 5F 163
Rhitongue. *High* 3G 167
Rhiw. *Gwyn* 3B 68
Rhiwabon. *Wrex* 1F 71
Rhiwbina. *Card* 3E 33
Rhiwbryfdir. *Gwyn* 1F 69
Rhiwderin. *Newp* 3F 33
Rhiwlas. *Gwyn* 2B 70
(nr. Bala)
Rhiwlas. *Gwyn* 4E 81
(nr. Bangor)
Rhiwlas. *Powy* 2D 70
Rhodes. *G Man* 4G 91
Rhodesia. *Notts* 2C 86
Rhodes Minnis. *Kent* 1F 29
Rhodiad-y-Brenin. *Pemb* 2B 42
Rhondda. *Rhon* 2C 32
Rhonehouse. *Dum* 4E 111
Rhoose. *V Glam* 5D 32
Rhos. *Carm* 2D 45
Rhos. *Neat* 5H 45
Rhosaman. *Carm* 4H 45
Rhoscefnhir. *IOA* 3E 81
Rhoscolyn. *IOA* 3B 80
Rhos Common. *Powy* 4E 71
Rhoscrowther. *Pemb* 4D 42
Rhos-ddu. *Gwyn* 2B 68
Rhosdylluan. *Gwyn* 3A 70
Rhosesmor. *Flin* 4E 82
Rhos-fawr. *Gwyn* 2C 68
Rhosgadfan. *Gwyn* 5E 81
Rhosgoch. *IOA* 2D 80
Rhosgoch. *Powy* 1E 47
Rhos Haminiog. *Cdgn* 4E 57
Rhos-hill. *Pemb* 1B 44
Rhoshirwaun. *Gwyn* 3A 68
Rhoslan. *Gwyn* 1D 69
Rhoslefain. *Gwyn* 5E 69
Rhosllanerchrugog. *Wrex* 1E 71
Rhôs Lligwy. *IOA* 2D 81
Rhosmaen. *Carm* 3G 45
Rhosmeirch. *IOA* 3D 80
Rhosneigr. *IOA* 3C 80
Rhos-on-Sea. *Cnwy* 2H 81
Rhossili. *Swan* 4D 30
Rhosson. *Pemb* 2B 42
Rhos, The. *Pemb* 3E 43
Rhostrenwfa. *IOA* 3D 80
Rhostryfan. *Gwyn* 5D 81
Rhostyllen. *Wrex* 1F 71
Rhoswiel. *Shrp* 2E 71
Rhosybol. *IOA* 2D 80
Rhos-y-brithdir. *Powy* 3D 70
Rhos-y-garth. *Cdgn* 3F 57
Rhos-y-gwaliau. *Gwyn* 2B 70
Rhos-y-llan. *Gwyn* 2B 68
Rhos-y-meirch. *Powy* 4E 59
Rhu. *Arg* 1D 126
Rhuallt. *Den* 3C 82
Rhubha Stoer. *High* 1E 163
Rhubodach. *Arg* 2B 126
Rhuddall Heath. *Ches W* 4H 83
Rhuddlan. *Cdgn* 1E 45
Rhuddlan. *Den* 3C 82
Rhue. *High* 4E 163
Rhulen. *Powy* 1E 47
Rhunahaorine. *Arg* 5F 125
Rhuthun. *Den* 5D 82
Rhuvoult. *High* 3C 166
Rhyd. *Gwyn* 1F 69
Rhydaman. *Carm* 4G 45
Rhydargaeau. *Carm* 3E 45
Rhydcymerau. *Carm* 2F 45
Rhydd. *Worc* 1D 48
Rhyd-Ddu. *Gwyn* 5E 81
Rhydding. *Neat* 3G 31
Rhydfudr. *Cdgn* 4E 57
Rhydlanfair. *Cnwy* 5H 81
Rhydlewis. *Cdgn* 1D 44
Rhydlios. *Gwyn* 2A 68
Rhydlydan. *Cnwy* 5A 82
Rhyd-meirionydd. *Cdgn* 2F 57
Rhydowen. *Cdgn* 1E 45
Rhyd-Rosser. *Cdgn* 4E 57
Rhydspence. *Powy* 1F 47
Rhydtalog. *Flin* 5E 83
Rhyd-uchaf. *Gwyn* 2B 70
Rhydwyn. *IOA* 2C 80
Rhyd-y-clafdy. *Gwyn* 2C 68
Rhydycroesau. *Shrp* 2E 71
Rhydyfelin. *Cdgn* 3E 57
Rhydyfelin. *Rhon* 3E 32
Rhyd-y-foel. *Cnwy* 3B 82
Rhyd-y-fro. *Neat* 5H 45
Rhydymain. *Gwyn* 3H 69
Rhyd-y-meudwy. *Den* 5D 82
Rhydymwyn. *Flin* 4E 82
Rhyd-yr-onen. *Gwyn* 5F 69
Rhyd-y-sarn. *Gwyn* 1F 69
Rhyl. *Den* 2C 82
Rhymney. *Cphy* 5E 46
Rhymni. *Cphy* 5E 46
Rhynd. *Per* 1D 136
Rhynie. *Abers* 1B 152
Ribbesford. *Worc* 3B 60
Ribbleton. *Lanc* 1D 90
Ribby. *Lanc* 1C 90
Ribchester. *Lanc* 1E 91
Riber. *Derbs* 5H 85
Ribigill. *High* 3F 167
Riby. *Linc* 4E 95
Riccall. *N Yor* 1G 93
Riccarton. *E Ayr* 1D 116
Richards Castle. *Here* 4G 59
Richborough Port. *Kent* 4H 41
Richhill. *Arm* 5F 175
Richings Park. *Buck* 3B 38
Richmond. *G Lon* 3C 38
Richmond. *N Yor* 4E 105
Rickarton. *Abers* 5F 153
Rickerby. *Cumb* 4F 113
Rickerscote. *Staf* 3D 72
Rickford. *N Som* 1H 21
Rickham. *Devn* 5D 8
Rickinghall. *Suff* 3C 66
Rickleton. *Tyne* 4F 115
Rickling. *Essx* 2E 53
Rickling Green. *Essx* 3F 53
Rickmansworth. *Herts* 1B 38
Riddings. *Derbs* 5B 86
Riddlecombe. *Devn* 1G 11
Riddlesden. *W Yor* 5C 98
Ridge. *Dors* 4E 15
Ridge. *Herts* 5C 52
Ridge. *Wilts* 3E 23
Ridgebourne. *Powy* 4C 58
Ridge Lane. *Warw* 1G 61
Ridgeway. *Derbs* 5A 86
(nr. Alfreton)
Ridgeway. *Derbs* 2B 86
(nr. Sheffield)
Ridgeway. *Stoke* 5C 84
Ridgeway Cross. *Here* 1C 48
Ridgeway Moor. *Derbs* 2B 86
Ridgewell. *Essx* 1H 53
Ridgewood. *E Sus* 3F 27
Ridgmont. *C Beds* 2H 51
Ridgwardine. *Shrp* 2A 72
Riding Mill. *Nmbd* 3D 114
Ridley. *Kent* 4H 39
Ridley. *Nmbd* 3A 114
Ridlington. *Norf* 2F 79
Ridlington. *Rut* 5F 75
Ridsdale. *Nmbd* 1C 114
Riemore Lodge. *Per* 4H 143
Rievaulx. *N Yor* 1H 99
Rift House. *Hart* 1B 106
Rigg. *Dum* 3D 112
Riggend. *N Lan* 2A 128
Rigsby. *Linc* 3D 88
Rigside. *S Lan* 1A 118
Riley Green. *Lanc* 2E 90
Rileyhill. *Staf* 4F 73
Rilla Mill. *Corn* 5C 10
Rillington. *N Yor* 2C 100
Rimington. *Lanc* 5H 97
Rimpton. *Som* 4B 22
Rimsdale. *High* 4H 167
Rimswell. *E Yor* 2G 95
Ringasta. *Shet* 10E 173
Ringford. *Dum* 4D 111
Ringing Hill. *Leics* 4B 74
Ringinglow. *S Yor* 2G 85
Ringland. *Norf* 4D 78
Ringlestone. *Kent* 5C 40
Ringmer. *E Sus* 4F 27
Ringmore. *Devn* 4C 8
(nr. Kingsbridge)
Ringmore. *Devn* 5C 12
(nr. Teignmouth)
Ring o' Bells. *Lanc* 3C 90
Ring's End. *Cambs* 5C 76
Ringsfield. *Suff* 2G 67
Ringsfield Corner. *Suff* 2G 67
Ringshall. *Buck* 4H 51
Ringshall. *Suff* 5C 66
Ringshall Stocks. *Suff* 5C 66
Ringstead. *Norf* 1G 77
Ringstead. *Nptn* 3G 63
Ringwood. *Hants* 2G 15
Ringwould. *Kent* 1H 29
Rinmore. *Abers* 2B 152
Rinnigill. *Orkn* 8C 172
Rinsey. *Corn* 4C 4
Riof. *W Isl* 4D 171
Ripe. *E Sus* 4G 27
Ripley. *Derbs* 5B 86
Ripley. *Hants* 3G 15
Ripley. *N Yor* 3E 99
Ripley. *Surr* 5B 38
Riplingham. *E Yor* 1C 94
Riplington. *Hants* 4E 25
Ripon. *N Yor* 2F 99
Rippingale. *Linc* 3H 75
Ripple. *Kent* 1H 29
Ripple. *Worc* 2D 48
Ripponden. *W Yor* 3A 92
Rireavach. *High* 4E 163
Risabus. *Arg* 5B 124
Risbury. *Here* 5H 59
Risby. *E Yor* 1D 94
Risby. *N Lin* 3C 94
Risby. *Suff* 4G 65
Risca. *Cphy* 2F 33
Rise. *E Yor* 5F 101
Riseden. *E Sus* 2H 27
Riseden. *Kent* 2B 28
Rise End. *Derbs* 5G 85
Risegate. *Linc* 3B 76
Riseholme. *Linc* 3G 87
Riseley. *Bed* 4H 63
Riseley. *Wok* 5F 37
Rishangles. *Suff* 4D 66
Rishton. *Lanc* 1F 91
Rishworth. *W Yor* 3A 92
Risley. *Derbs* 2B 74
Risley. *Warr* 1A 84
Risplith. *N Yor* 3E 99
Rispond. *High* 2E 167
Rivar. *Wilts* 5B 36
Rivenhall. *Essx* 4B 54
Rivenhall End. *Essx* 4B 54
River. *Kent* 1G 29
River. *W Sus* 3A 26
River Bank. *Cambs* 4E 65
Riverhead. *Kent* 5G 39
Rivington. *Lanc* 3E 91
Roach Bridge. *Lanc* 2D 90
Roachill. *Devn* 4B 20
Roade. *Nptn* 5E 63
Road Green. *Norf* 1E 67
Roadhead. *Cumb* 2G 113
Roadmeetings. *S Lan* 5B 128
Roadside. *High* 2D 168
Roadside of Catterline. *Abers* 1H 145
Roadside of Kinneff. *Abers* 1H 145
Roadwater. *Som* 3D 20
Road Weedon. *Nptn* 5D 62
Roag. *High* 4B 154
Roa Island. *Cumb* 3B 96
Roath. *Card* 4E 33
Roberton. *Bord* 3G 119
Roberton. *S Lan* 2B 118
Robertsbridge. *E Sus* 3B 28
Robertstown. *Mor* 4G 159
Robertstown. *Rhon* 5C 46
Roberttown. *W Yor* 2B 92
Robeston Back. *Pemb* 3E 43
Robeston Wathen. *Pemb* 3E 43
Robeston West. *Pemb* 4C 42
Robin Hood. *Lanc* 3D 90
Robin Hood. *W Yor* 2D 92
Robin Hood Airport Doncaster Sheffield. *S Yor* 1D 86
Robinhood End. *Essx* 2H 53
Robin Hood's Bay. *N Yor* 4G 107
Roborough. *Devn* 1F 11
(nr. Great Torrington)
Roborough. *Devn* 2B 8
(nr. Plymouth)
Rob Roy's House. *Arg* 2A 134
Roby Mill. *Lanc* 4D 90
Rocester. *Staf* 2F 73
Roch. *Pemb* 2C 42
Rochdale. *G Man* 3G 91
Roche. *Corn* 2D 6
Rochester. *Medw* 4B 40
Rochester. *Nmbd* 5C 120
Rochford. *Essx* 1C 40
Rock. *Corn* 1D 6
Rock. *Nmbd* 2G 121
Rock. *W Sus* 4C 26
Rock. *Worc* 3B 60
Rockbeare. *Devn* 3D 12
Rockbourne. *Hants* 1G 15
Rockcliffe. *Cumb* 3E 113
Rockcliffe. *Dum* 4F 111
Rockcliffe Cross. *Cumb* 3E 113
Rock Ferry. *Mers* 2F 83
Rockfield. *High* 5G 165
Rockfield. *Mon* 4H 47
Rockford. *Hants* 2G 15
Rockgreen. *Shrp* 3H 59
Rockhampton. *S Glo* 2B 34
Rockhead. *Corn* 4A 10
Rockingham. *Nptn* 1F 63
Rockland All Saints. *Norf* 1B 66
Rockland St Mary. *Norf* 5F 79
Rockland St Peter. *Norf* 1B 66
Rockley. *Wilts* 4G 35
Rockwell End. *Buck* 3F 37
Rockwell Green. *Som* 1E 13
Rodborough. *Glos* 5D 48
Rodbourne. *Wilts* 3E 35
Rodd. *Here* 4F 59
Roddam. *Nmbd* 2E 121
Rodden. *Dors* 4B 14
Roddenloft. *E Ayr* 2D 117
Roddymoor. *Dur* 1E 105
Rode. *Som* 1D 22
Rodeheath. *Ches E* 4C 84
(nr. Congleton)
Rode Heath. *Ches E* 5C 84
(nr. Kidsgrove)
Rodel. *W Isl* 9C 171
Roden. *Telf* 4H 71
Rodhuish. *Som* 3D 20
Rodington. *Telf* 4H 71
Rodington Heath. *Telf* 4H 71
Rodley. *Glos* 4C 48
Rodmarton. *Glos* 2E 35
Rodmell. *E Sus* 5F 27
Rodmersham. *Kent* 4D 40
Rodmersham Green. *Kent* 4D 40
Rodney Stoke. *Som* 2H 21
Rodsley. *Derbs* 1G 73
Rodway. *Som* 3F 21
Rodway. *Telf* 4A 72
Rodwell. *Dors* 5B 14
Roecliffe. *N Yor* 3F 99
Roe Green. *Herts* 2D 52
Roehampton. *G Lon* 3D 38
Roesound. *Shet* 5E 173
Roffey. *W Sus* 2C 26
Rogart. *High* 3E 165
Rogate. *W Sus* 4G 25
Roger Ground. *Cumb* 5E 103
Rogerstone. *Newp* 3F 33
Rogiet. *Mon* 3H 33
Rogue's Alley. *Cambs* 5C 76
Roke. *Oxon* 2E 37
Rokemarsh. *Oxon* 2E 36
Roker. *Tyne* 4H 115
Rollesby. *Norf* 4G 79
Rolleston. *Leics* 5E 75
Rolleston. *Notts* 5E 87
Rolleston on Dove. *Staf* 3G 73
Rolston. *E Yor* 5G 101
Rolvenden. *Kent* 2C 28
Rolvenden Layne. *Kent* 2C 28
Romaldkirk. *Dur* 2C 104
Roman Bank. *Shrp* 1H 59
Romanby. *N Yor* 5A 106
Roman Camp. *W Lot* 2D 129
Romannobridge. *Bord* 5E 129
Romansleigh. *Devn* 4H 19
Romers Common. *Worc* 4H 59
Romesdal. *High* 3D 154
Romford. *Dors* 2F 15
Romford. *G Lon* 2G 39
Romiley. *G Man* 1D 84
Romsey. *Hants* 4B 24
Romsley. *Shrp* 2B 60
Romsley. *Worc* 3D 60
Ronague. *IOM* 4B 108
Ronaldsvoe. *Orkn* 8D 172
Rookby. *Cumb* 3B 104
Rookhope. *Dur* 5C 114
Rooking. *Cumb* 3F 103
Rookley. *IOW* 4D 16
Rooks Bridge. *Som* 1G 21
Rooksey Green. *Suff* 5B 66
Rook's Nest. *Som* 3D 20
Rookwood. *W Sus* 3F 17
Roos. *E Yor* 1F 95
Roosebeck. *Cumb* 3B 96
Roosecote. *Cumb* 3B 96
Rootfield. *High* 3H 157
Rootham's Green. *Bed* 5A 64

S

Staunton—Strathaven

Staunton. *Glos* 3C **48** (nr. Cheltenham)
Staunton. *Glos* 4A **48** (nr. Monmouth)
Staunton in the Vale. *Notts* 1F **75**
Staunton on Arrow. *Here* 4F **59**
Staunton on Wye. *Here* 1G **47**
Staveley. *Cumb* 5F **103**
Staveley. *Derbs* 3B **86**
Staveley. *N Yor* 3F **99**
Staveley-in-Cartmel. *Cumb* 1C **96**
Staverton. *Devn* 2D **9**
Staverton. *Glos* 3D **49**
Staverton. *Nptn* 4C **62**
Staverton. *Wilts* 5D **34**
Stawell. *Som* 3G **21**
Stawley. *Som* 4D **20**
Staxigoe. *High* 3F **169**
Staxton. *N Yor* 2E **101**
Staylittle. *Powy* 1A **58**
Staynall. *Lanc* 5C **96**
Staythorpe. *Notts* 5E **87**
Stean. *N Yor* 2C **98**
Stearsby. *N Yor* 2A **100**
Steart. *Som* 2F **21**
Stebbing. *Essx* 3G **53**
Stebbing Green. *Essx* 3G **53**
Stedham. *W Sus* 4G **25**
Steel. *Nmbd* 4C **114**
Steel Cross. *E Sus* 2G **27**
Steelend. *Fife* 4C **136**
Steele Road. *Bord* 5H **119**
Steel Heath. *Shrp* 2H **71**
Steen's Bridge. *Here* 5H **59**
Steep. *Hants* 4F **25**
Steep Lane. *W Yor* 2A **92**
Steeple. *Dors* 4E **15**
Steeple. *Essx* 5C **54**
Steeple Ashton. *Wilts* 1E **23**
Steeple Aston. *Oxon* 3C **50**
Steeple Barton. *Oxon* 3C **50**
Steeple Bumpstead. *Essx* 1G **53**
Steeple Claydon. *Buck* 3E **51**
Steeple Gidding. *Cambs* 2A **64**
Steeple Langford. *Wilts* 3F **23**
Steeple Morden. *Cambs* 1C **52**
Steeton. *W Yor* 5C **98**
Stein. *High* 3B **154**
Steinmanhill. *Abers* 4E **161**
Stelling Minnis. *Kent* 1F **29**
Stembridge. *Som* 4H **21**
Stemster. *High* 2D **169** (nr. Halkirk)
Stemster. *High* 2C **168** (nr. Westfield)
Stenalees. *Corn* 3E **6**
Stenhill. *Devn* 1D **12**
Stenhouse. *Edin* 2F **129**
Stenhousemuir. *Falk* 1B **128**
Stenigot. *Linc* 2B **88**
Stenscholl. *High* 2D **155**
Stenso. *Orkn* 5C **172**
Stenson. *Derbs* 3H **73**
Stenson Fields. *Derbs* 2H **73**
Stenton. *E Lot* 2C **130**
Stenwith. *Linc* 2F **75**
Steòrnabhagh. *W Isl* 4G **171**
Stepaside. *Pemb* 4F **43**
Stepford. *Dum* 1F **111**
Stepney. *G Lon* 2E **39**
Steppingley. *C Beds* 2A **52**
Stepps. *N Lan* 3H **127**
Sterndale Moor. *Derbs* 4F **85**
Sternfield. *Suff* 4F **67**
Stert. *Wilts* 1F **23**
Stetchworth. *Cambs* 5F **65**
Stevenage. *Herts* 3C **52**
Stevenston. *N Ayr* 5D **126**
Stevenstone. *Devn* 1F **11**
Steventon. *Hants* 2D **24**
Steventon. *Oxon* 2C **36**
Steventon End. *Essx* 1F **53**
Stevington. *Bed* 5G **63**
Stewartby. *Bed* 1A **52**
Stewarton. *Arg* 4A **122**
Stewarton. *E Ayr* 5F **127**
Stewkley. *Buck* 3G **51**
Stewkley Dean. *Buck* 3G **51**
Stewley. *Som* 1G **13**
Stewton. *Linc* 2C **88**
Steyning. *W Sus* 4C **26**
Steynton. *Pemb* 4D **42**
Stibb. *Corn* 1C **10**
Stibbard. *Norf* 3B **78**
Stibb Cross. *Devn* 1E **11**
Stibb Green. *Wilts* 5H **35**
Stibbington. *Cambs* 1H **63**
Stichill. *Bord* 1B **120**
Sticker. *Corn* 3D **6**
Stickford. *Linc* 4C **88**
Sticklepath. *Devn* 3G **11**
Sticklinch. *Som* 3A **22**
Stickling Green. *Essx* 2E **53**
Stickney. *Linc* 5C **88**
Stiffkey. *Norf* 1B **78**
Stifford's Bridge. *Here* 1C **48**
Stileway. *Som* 2H **21**
Stillingfleet. *N Yor* 5H **99**
Stillington. *N Yor* 3H **99**
Stillington. *Stoc T* 2A **106**
Stilton. *Cambs* 2A **64**
Stinchcombe. *Glos* 2C **34**
Stinsford. *Dors* 3C **14**
Stiperstones. *Shrp* 5F **71**
Stirchley. *Telf* 5B **72**
Stirchley. *W Mid* 2E **61**
Stirling. *Abers* 4H **161**
Stirling. *Stir* 4G **135**
Stirton. *N Yor* 4B **98**
Stisted. *Essx* 3A **54**
Stitchcombe. *Wilts* 5H **35**
Stithians. *Corn* 5B **6**
Stittenham. *High* 1A **158**
Stivichall. *W Mid* 3H **61**
Stixwould. *Linc* 4A **88**
Stoak. *Ches W* 3G **83**
Stobo. *Bord* 1D **118**
Stobo Castle. *Bord* 1D **118**
Stoborough. *Dors* 4E **15**
Stoborough Green. *Dors* 4E **15**
Stobs Castle. *Bord* 4H **119**
Stobswood. *Nmbd* 5G **121**
Stock. *Essx* 1A **40**
Stockbridge. *Hants* 3B **24**
Stockbridge. *W Yor* 5C **98**
Stockbury. *Kent* 4C **40**
Stockcross. *W Ber* 5C **36**
Stockdalewath. *Cumb* 5E **113**
Stocker's Head. *Kent* 5D **40**
Stockerston. *Leics* 1F **63**
Stock Green. *Worc* 5D **61**
Stocking. *Here* 2B **48**
Stockingford. *Warw* 1H **61**
Stocking Green. *Essx* 2F **53**
Stocking Pelham. *Herts* 3E **53**
Stockland. *Devn* 2F **13**
Stockland Bristol. *Som* 2F **21**
Stockleigh English. *Devn* 2B **12**
Stockleigh Pomeroy. *Devn* 2B **12**
Stockley. *Wilts* 5F **35**
Stocklinch. *Som* 1G **13**
Stockport. *G Man* 2C **84**
Stocksbridge. *S Yor* 1G **85**
Stocksfield. *Nmbd* 3D **114**
Stocks, The. *Kent* 3D **28**
Stockstreet. *Essx* 3B **54**
Stockton. *Here* 4H **59**
Stockton. *Norf* 1F **67**
Stockton. *Shrp* 1B **60** (nr. Bridgnorth)
Stockton. *Shrp* 5E **71** (nr. Chirbury)
Stockton. *Telf* 4B **72**
Stockton. *Warw* 4B **62**
Stockton. *Wilts* 3E **23**
Stockton Brook. *Staf* 5D **84**
Stockton Cross. *Here* 4H **59**
Stockton Heath. *Warr* 2A **84**
Stockton-on-Tees. *Stoc T* 3B **106**
Stockton on Teme. *Worc* 4B **60**
Stockton-on-the-Forest. *York* 4A **100**
Stockwell Heath. *Staf* 3E **73**
Stockwood. *Bris* 5B **34**
Stock Wood. *Worc* 5E **61**
Stodmarsh. *Kent* 4G **41**
Stody. *Norf* 2C **78**
Stoer. *High* 1E **163**
Stoford. *Som* 1A **14**
Stoford. *Wilts* 3F **23**
Stogumber. *Som* 3D **20**
Stogursey. *Som* 2F **21**
Stoke. *Devn* 4C **18**
Stoke. *Hants* 1C **24** (nr. Andover)
Stoke. *Hants* 2F **17** (nr. South Hayling)
Stoke. *Medw* 3C **40**
Stoke. *W Mid* 3A **62**
Stoke Abbott. *Dors* 2H **13**
Stoke Albany. *Nptn* 2F **63**
Stoke Ash. *Suff* 3D **66**
Stoke Bardolph. *Notts* 1D **74**
Stoke Bliss. *Worc* 4A **60**
Stoke Bruerne. *Nptn* 1F **51**
Stoke by Clare. *Suff* 1H **53**
Stoke-by-Nayland. *Suff* 2C **54**
Stoke Canon. *Devn* 3C **12**
Stoke Charity. *Hants* 3C **24**
Stoke Climsland. *Corn* 5D **10**
Stoke Cross. *Here* 5A **60**
Stoke D'Abernon. *Surr* 5C **38**
Stoke Doyle. *Nptn* 2H **63**
Stoke Dry. *Rut* 1F **63**
Stoke Edith. *Here* 1B **48**
Stoke Farthing. *Wilts* 4F **23**
Stoke Ferry. *Norf* 5G **77**
Stoke Fleming. *Devn* 4E **9**
Stokeford. *Dors* 4D **14**
Stoke Gabriel. *Devn* 3E **9**
Stoke Gifford. *S Glo* 4B **34**
Stoke Golding. *Leics* 1A **62**
Stoke Goldington. *Mil* 1G **51**
Stokeham. *Notts* 3E **87**
Stoke Hammond. *Buck* 3G **51**
Stoke Heath. *Shrp* 3A **72**
Stoke Holy Cross. *Norf* 5E **79**
Stokeinteignhead. *Devn* 5C **12**
Stoke Lacy. *Here* 1B **48**
Stoke Lyne. *Oxon* 3D **50**
Stoke Mandeville. *Buck* 4G **51**
Stokenchurch. *Buck* 2F **37**
Stoke Newington. *G Lon* 2E **39**
Stokenham. *Devn* 4E **9**
Stoke on Tern. *Shrp* 3A **72**
Stoke-on-Trent. *Stoke* 1C **72**
Stoke Orchard. *Glos* 3E **49**
Stoke Pero. *Som* 2B **20**
Stoke Poges. *Buck* 2A **38**
Stoke Prior. *Here* 5H **59**
Stoke Prior. *Worc* 4D **60**
Stoke Rivers. *Devn* 3G **19**
Stoke Rochford. *Linc* 3G **75**
Stoke Row. *Oxon* 3E **37**
Stoke St Gregory. *Som* 4G **21**
Stoke St Mary. *Som* 4F **21**
Stoke St Michael. *Som* 2B **22**
Stoke St Milborough. *Shrp* 2H **59**
Stokesay. *Shrp* 2G **59**
Stokesby. *Norf* 4G **79**
Stokesley. *N Yor* 4C **106**
Stoke sub Hamdon. *Som* 1H **13**
Stoke Talmage. *Oxon* 2E **37**
Stoke Town. *Stoke* 1C **72**
Stoke Trister. *Som* 4C **22**
Stoke Wake. *Dors* 2C **14**
Stolford. *Som* 2F **21**
Stondon Massey. *Essx* 5F **53**
Stone. *Buck* 4F **51**
Stone. *Glos* 2D **34**
Stone. *Kent* 3G **39**
Stone. *Som* 3A **22**
Stone. *Staf* 2D **72**
Stone. *Worc* 3C **60**
Stonea. *Cambs* 1D **64**
Stoneacton. *Shrp* 1H **59**
Stone Allerton. *Som* 1H **21**
Ston Easton. *Som* 1B **22**
Stonebridge. *N Som* 1G **21**
Stonebridge. *Surr* 1C **26**
Stone Bridge Corner. *Pet* 5B **76**
Stonebroom. *Derbs* 5B **86**
Stonebyres. *S Lan* 5B **128**
Stone Chair. *W Yor* 2B **92**
Stone Cross. *E Sus* 5H **27**
Stone Cross. *Kent* 2G **27**
Stone-edge-Batch. *N Som* 4H **33**
Stoneferry. *Hull* 1D **94**
Stonefield. *Arg* 5D **140**
Stonefield. *S Lan* 4H **127**
Stonegate. *E Sus* 3A **28**
Stonegate. *N Yor* 4E **107**
Stonegrave. *N Yor* 2A **100**
Stonehall. *Worc* 1D **49**
Stonehaugh. *Nmbd* 2A **114**
Stonehaven. *Abers* 5F **153**
Stone Heath. *Staf* 2D **72**
Stone Hill. *Kent* 2E **29**
Stone House. *Cumb* 1G **97**
Stonehouse. *Glos* 5D **48**
Stonehouse. *Nmbd* 4H **113**
Stonehouse. *S Lan* 5A **128**
Stone in Oxney. *Kent* 3D **28**
Stoneleigh. *Warw* 3H **61**
Stoneley Green. *Ches E* 5A **84**
Stonely. *Cambs* 4A **64**
Stonepits. *Worc* 5E **61**
Stoner Hill. *Hants* 4F **25**
Stonesby. *Leics* 3F **75**
Stonesfield. *Oxon* 4B **50**
Stones Green. *Essx* 3E **55**
Stone Street. *Kent* 5G **39**
Stone Street. *Suff* 2C **54** (nr. Boxford)
Stone Street. *Suff* 2F **67** (nr. Halesworth)
Stonethwaite. *Cumb* 3D **102**
Stoneyburn. *W Lot* 3C **128**
Stoney Cross. *Hants* 1A **16**
Stoneyford. *Devn* 2D **12**
Stoneygate. *Leic* 5D **74**
Stoneyhills. *Essx* 1D **40**
Stoneykirk. *Dum* 4F **109**
Stoney Middleton. *Derbs* 3G **85**
Stoney Stanton. *Leics* 1B **62**
Stoney Stoke. *Som* 3C **22**
Stoney Stratton. *Som* 3B **22**
Stoney Stretton. *Shrp* 5F **71**
Stoneywood. *Aber* 2F **153**
Stonham Aspal. *Suff* 5D **66**
Stonnall. *Staf* 5E **73**
Stonor. *Oxon* 3F **37**
Stonton Wyville. *Leics* 1E **63**
Stonybreck. *Shet* 1B **172**
Stony Cross. *Devn* 4F **19**
Stony Cross. *Here* 1C **48** (nr. Great Malvern)
Stony Cross. *Here* 4H **59** (nr. Leominster)
Stony Houghton. *Derbs* 4B **86**
Stony Stratford. *Mil* 1F **51**
Stoodleigh. *Devn* 3G **19** (nr. Barnstaple)
Stoodleigh. *Devn* 1C **12** (nr. Tiverton)
Stopham. *W Sus* 4B **26**
Stopsley. *Lutn* 3B **52**
Stoptide. *Corn* 1D **6**
Storeton. *Mers* 2F **83**
Stormontfield. *Per* 1D **136**
Stornoway. *W Isl* 4G **171**
Stornoway Airport. *W Isl* 4G **171**
Storridge. *Here* 1C **48**
Storrington. *W Sus* 4B **26**
Storrs. *Cumb* 5E **103**
Storth. *Cumb* 1D **97**
Storwood. *E Yor* 5B **100**
Stotfield. *Mor* 1G **159**
Stotfold. *C Beds* 2C **52**
Stottesdon. *Shrp* 2A **60**
Stoughton. *Leics* 5D **74**
Stoughton. *Surr* 5A **38**
Stoughton. *W Sus* 1G **17**
Stoul. *High* 4F **147**
Stoulton. *Worc* 1E **49**
Stourbridge. *W Mid* 2C **60**
Stourpaine. *Dors* 2D **14**
Stourport-on-Severn. *Worc* 3C **60**
Stour Provost. *Dors* 4C **22**
Stour Row. *Dors* 4D **22**
Stourton. *Staf* 2C **60**
Stourton. *Warw* 2A **50**
Stourton. *W Yor* 1D **92**
Stourton. *Wilts* 3C **22**
Stourton Caundle. *Dors* 1C **14**
Stove. *Orkn* 4F **172**
Stove. *Shet* 9F **173**
Stoven. *Suff* 2G **67**
Stow. *Linc* 2H **75** (nr. Billingborough)
Stow. *Linc* 2F **87** (nr. Gainsborough)
Stow. *Bord* 5A **130**
Stow Bardolph. *Norf* 5F **77**
Stow Bedon. *Norf* 1B **66**
Stowbridge. *Norf* 5F **77**
Stow cum Quy. *Cambs* 4E **65**
Stowe. *Glos* 5A **48**
Stowe. *Shrp* 3F **59**
Stowe. *Staf* 4F **73**
Stowe-by-Chartley. *Staf* 3E **73**
Stowell. *Som* 4B **22**
Stowey. *Bath* 1A **22**
Stowford. *Devn* 2G **19** (nr. Combe Martin)
Stowford. *Devn* 4D **12** (nr. Exmouth)
Stowford. *Devn* 4E **11** (nr. Tavistock)
Stowlangtoft. *Suff* 4B **66**
Stow Longa. *Cambs* 3A **64**
Stow Maries. *Essx* 1C **40**
Stowmarket. *Suff* 5C **66**
Stow-on-the-Wold. *Glos* 3G **49**
Stowting. *Kent* 1F **29**
Stowupland. *Suff* 5C **66**
Straad. *Arg* 3B **126**
Strabane. *Strab* 3C **174**
Strachan. *Abers* 4D **152**
Stradbroke. *Suff* 3E **67**
Stradishall. *Suff* 5G **65**
Stradsett. *Norf* 5F **77**
Stragglethorpe. *Linc* 5G **87**
Stragglethorpe. *Notts* 2D **74**
Straid. *S Ayr* 5A **116**
Straight Soley. *Wilts* 4B **36**
Straiton. *Edin* 3F **129**
Straiton. *S Ayr* 4C **116**
Straloch. *Per* 2H **143**
Stramshall. *Staf* 2E **73**
Strang. *IOM* 4C **108**
Strangford. *Here* 3A **48**
Stranraer. *Dum* 3F **109**
Strata Florida. *Cdgn* 4G **57**
Stratfield Mortimer. *W Ber* 5E **37**
Stratfield Saye. *Hants* 5E **37**
Stratfield Turgis. *Hants* 1E **25**
Stratford. *Glos* 2D **49**
Stratford. *G Lon* 2E **39**
Stratford St Andrew. *Suff* 4F **67**
Stratford St Mary. *Suff* 2D **54**
Stratford sub Castle. *Wilts* 3G **23**
Stratford Tony. *Wilts* 4F **23**
Stratford-upon-Avon. *Warw* 5G **61**
Strath. *High* 1G **155** (nr. Gairloch)
Strath. *High* 3E **169** (nr. Wick)
Strathan. *High* 4B **148** (nr. Fort William)
Strathan. *High* 1E **163** (nr. Lochinver)
Strathan. *High* 2F **167** (nr. Tongue)
Strathan Skerray. *High* 2G **167**
Strathaven. *S Lan* 5A **128**

Thorngrove—Tomich

Thorngrove. *Som* 3G 21
Thorngumbald. *E Yor* 2F 95
Thornham. *Norf* 1G 77
Thornham Magna. *Suff* 3D 66
Thornham Parva. *Suff* 3D 66
Thornhaugh. *Pet* 5H 75
Thornhill. *Cphy* 3E 33
Thornhill. *Cumb* 4B 102
Thornhill. *Derbs* 2F 85
Thornhill. *Dum* 5A 118
Thornhill. *Sotn* 1C 16
Thornhill. *Stir* 4F 135
Thornhill. *W Yor* 3C 92
Thornhill Lees. *W Yor* 3C 92
Thornhills. *W Yor* 2B 92
Thornholme. *E Yor* 3F 101
Thornicombe. *Dors* 2D 14
Thornington. *Nmbd* 1C 120
Thornley. *Dur* 1A 106 (nr. Durham)
Thornley. *Dur* 1E 105 (nr. Tow Law)
Thornley Gate. *Nmbd* 4B 114
Thornliebank. *E Ren* 3G 127
Thornroan. *Abers* 5F 161
Thorns. *Suff* 5G 65
Thornsett. *Derbs* 2E 85
Thornthwaite. *Cumb* 2D 102
Thornthwaite. *N Yor* 4D 98
Thornton. *Ang* 4C 144
Thornton. *Buck* 2F 51
Thornton. *E Yor* 5B 100
Thornton. *Fife* 4E 137
Thornton. *Lanc* 5C 96
Thornton. *Leics* 5B 74
Thornton. *Linc* 4B 88
Thornton. *Mers* 4B 90
Thornton. *Midd* 3B 106
Thornton. *Nmbd* 5F 131
Thornton. *Pemb* 4D 42
Thornton. *W Yor* 1A 92
Thornton Curtis. *N Lin* 3D 94
Thorntonhall. *S Lan* 4G 127
Thornton Heath. *G Lon* 4E 39
Thornton Hough. *Mers* 2F 83
Thornton in Craven. *N Yor* 5B 98
Thornton in Lonsdale. *N Yor* 2F 97
Thornton-le-Beans. *N Yor* 5A 106
Thornton-le-Clay. *N Yor* 3A 100
Thornton-le-Dale. *N Yor* 1C 100
Thornton le Moor. *Linc* 1H 87
Thornton-le-Moor. *N Yor* 1F 99
Thornton-le-Moors. *Ches W* 3G 83
Thornton-le-Street. *N Yor* 1G 99
Thorntonloch. *E Lot* 2D 130
Thornton Rust. *N Yor* 1B 98
Thornton Steward. *N Yor* 1D 98
Thornton Watlass. *N Yor* 1E 99
Thornwood Common. *Essx* 5E 53
Thornythwaite. *Cumb* 2E 103
Thoroton. *Notts* 1E 75
Thorp Arch. *W Yor* 5G 99
Thorpe. *Derbs* 5F 85
Thorpe. *E Yor* 5D 101
Thorpe. *Linc* 2D 89
Thorpe. *Norf* 1G 67
Thorpe. *N Yor* 3C 98
Thorpe. *Notts* 1E 75
Thorpe. *Surr* 4B 38
Thorpe Abbotts. *Norf* 3D 66
Thorpe Acre. *Leics* 3C 74
Thorpe Arnold. *Leics* 3E 75
Thorpe Audlin. *W Yor* 3E 93
Thorpe Bassett. *N Yor* 2C 100
Thorpe Bay. *S'end* 2D 40
Thorpe by Water. *Rut* 1F 63
Thorpe Common. *S Yor* 1A 86
Thorpe Common. *Suff* 2F 55
Thorpe Constantine. *Staf* 5G 73
Thorpe End. *Norf* 4E 79
Thorpe Fendike. *Linc* 4D 88
Thorpe Green. *Essx* 3E 55
Thorpe Green. *Suff* 5B 66
Thorpe Hall. *N Yor* 2H 99
Thorpe Hamlet. *Norf* 5E 79
Thorpe Hesley. *S Yor* 1A 86
Thorpe in Balne. *S Yor* 3F 93
Thorpe in the Fallows. *Linc* 2G 87
Thorpe Langton. *Leics* 1E 63
Thorpe Larches. *Dur* 2A 106
Thorpe Latimer. *Linc* 1A 76
Thorpe-le-Soken. *Essx* 3E 55
Thorpe le Street. *E Yor* 5C 100
Thorpe Malsor. *Nptn* 3F 63
Thorpe Mandeville. *Nptn* 1D 50
Thorpe Market. *Norf* 2E 79
Thorpe Marriott. *Norf* 4D 78
Thorpe Morieux. *Suff* 5B 66
Thorpeness. *Suff* 5G 67
Thorpe on the Hill. *Linc* 4G 87
Thorpe on the Hill. *W Yor* 2D 92
Thorpe St Andrew. *Norf* 5E 79
Thorpe St Peter. *Linc* 4D 89
Thorpe Salvin. *S Yor* 2C 86
Thorpe Satchville. *Leics* 4E 75
Thorpe Thewles. *Stoc T* 2A 106
Thorpe Tilney. *Linc* 5A 88
Thorpe Underwood. *N Yor* 4G 99
Thorpe Waterville. *Nptn* 2H 63
Thorpe Willoughby. *N Yor* 1F 93
Thorpland. *Norf* 5F 77
Thorrington. *Essx* 3D 54
Thorverton. *Devn* 2C 12
Thrandeston. *Suff* 3D 66
Thrapston. *Nptn* 3G 63
Thrashbush. *N Lan* 3A 128
Threapland. *Cumb* 1C 102
Threapland. *N Yor* 3B 98
Threapwood. *Ches W* 1G 71
Threapwood. *Staf* 1E 73
Three Ashes. *Here* 3A 48
Three Bridges. *Linc* 2D 88
Three Bridges. *W Sus* 2D 27
Three Burrows. *Corn* 4B 6
Three Chimneys. *Kent* 2C 28
Three Cocks. *Powy* 2E 47
Three Crosses. *Swan* 3E 31
Three Cups Corner. *E Sus* 3H 27
Threehammer Common. *Norf* 3F 79
Three Holes. *Norf* 5E 77
Threekingham. *Linc* 2H 75
Three Leg Cross. *E Sus* 2A 28
Three Legged Cross. *Dors* 2F 15
Three Mile Cross. *Wok* 5F 37
Threemilestone. *Corn* 4B 6
Three Oaks. *E Sus* 4C 28
Threlkeld. *Cumb* 2E 102
Threshfield. *N Yor* 3B 98
Thrigby. *Norf* 4G 79
Thringarth. *Dur* 2C 104
Thringstone. *Leics* 4B 74
Thrintoft. *N Yor* 5A 106
Thriplow. *Cambs* 1E 53
Throckenholt. *Linc* 5C 76
Throcking. *Herts* 2D 52
Throckley. *Tyne* 3E 115
Throckmorton. *Worc* 1E 49
Throop. *Bour* 3G 15
Throphill. *Nmbd* 1E 115
Thropton. *Nmbd* 4E 121
Throsk. *Stir* 4A 136
Througham. *Glos* 5E 49
Throughgate. *Dum* 1F 111
Throwleigh. *Devn* 3G 11
Throwley. *Kent* 5D 40
Throwley Forstal. *Kent* 5D 40
Throxenby. *N Yor* 1E 101
Thrumpton. *Notts* 2C 74
Thrumster. *High* 4F 169
Thrunton. *Nmbd* 3E 121
Thrupp. *Glos* 5D 48
Thrupp. *Oxon* 4C 50
Thrushelton. *Devn* 4E 11
Thrushgill. *Lanc* 3F 97
Thrussington. *Leics* 4D 74
Thruxton. *Hants* 2A 24
Thruxton. *Here* 2H 47
Thrybergh. *S Yor* 1B 86
Thulston. *Derbs* 2B 74
Thundergay. *N Ayr* 5G 125
Thundersley. *Essx* 2B 40
Thundridge. *Herts* 4D 52
Thurcaston. *Leics* 4C 74
Thurcroft. *S Yor* 2B 86
Thurdon. *Corn* 1C 10
Thurgarton. *Norf* 2D 78
Thurgarton. *Notts* 1D 74
Thurgoland. *S Yor* 4C 92
Thurlaston. *Leics* 1C 62
Thurlaston. *Warw* 3B 62
Thurlbear. *Som* 4F 21
Thurlby. *Linc* 3D 89 (nr. Alford)
Thurlby. *Linc* 4A 76 (nr. Baston)
Thurlby. *Linc* 4G 87 (nr. Lincoln)
Thurleigh. *Bed* 5H 63
Thurlestone. *Devn* 4C 8
Thurloxton. *Som* 3F 21
Thurlstone. *S Yor* 4C 92
Thurlton. *Norf* 1G 67
Thurmaston. *Leics* 5D 74
Thurnby. *Leics* 5D 74
Thurne. *Norf* 4G 79
Thurnham. *Kent* 5C 40
Thurning. *Norf* 3C 78
Thurning. *Nptn* 2H 63
Thurnscoe. *S Yor* 4E 93
Thursby. *Cumb* 4E 113
Thursford. *Norf* 2B 78
Thursford Green. *Norf* 2B 78
Thursley. *Surr* 2A 26
Thurso. *High* 2D 168
Thurso East. *High* 2D 168
Thurstaston. *Mers* 2E 83
Thurston. *Suff* 4B 66
Thurston End. *Suff* 5G 65
Thurstonfield. *Cumb* 4E 112
Thurstonland. *W Yor* 3B 92
Thurton. *Norf* 5F 79
Thurvaston. *Derbs* 2F 73 (nr. Ashbourne)
Thurvaston. *Derbs* 2G 73 (nr. Derby)
Thuxton. *Norf* 5C 78
Thwaite. *Dur* 3D 104
Thwaite. *N Yor* 5B 104
Thwaite. *Suff* 4D 66
Thwaite Head. *Cumb* 5E 103
Thwaites. *W Yor* 5C 98
Thwaite St Mary. *Norf* 1F 67
Thwing. *E Yor* 2E 101
Tibbermore. *Per* 1C 136
Tibberton. *Glos* 3C 48
Tibberton. *Telf* 3A 72
Tibberton. *Worc* 5D 60
Tibenham. *Norf* 2D 66
Tibshelf. *Derbs* 4B 86
Tibthorpe. *E Yor* 4D 100
Ticehurst. *E Sus* 2A 28
Tichborne. *Hants* 3D 24
Tickencote. *Rut* 5G 75
Tickenham. *N Som* 4H 33
Tickhill. *S Yor* 1C 86
Ticklerton. *Shrp* 1G 59
Ticknall. *Derbs* 3A 74
Tickton. *E Yor* 5E 101
Tidbury Green. *W Mid* 3F 61
Tidcombe. *Wilts* 1A 24
Tiddington. *Oxon* 5E 51
Tiddington. *Warw* 5G 61
Tiddleywink. *Wilts* 4D 34
Tidebrook. *E Sus* 3H 27
Tideford. *Corn* 3H 7
Tideford Cross. *Corn* 2H 7
Tidenham. *Glos* 2A 34
Tideswell. *Derbs* 3F 85
Tidmarsh. *W Ber* 4E 37
Tidmington. *Warw* 2A 50
Tidpit. *Hants* 1F 15
Tidworth. *Wilts* 2H 23
Tidworth Camp. *Wilts* 2H 23
Tiers Cross. *Pemb* 3D 42
Tiffield. *Nptn* 5D 62
Tifty. *Abers* 4E 161
Tigerton. *Ang* 2E 145
Tighnabruaich. *Arg* 2A 126
Tigley. *Devn* 2D 8
Tilbrook. *Cambs* 4H 63
Tilbury. *Thur* 3H 39
Tilbury Green. *Essx* 1H 53
Tilbury Juxta Clare. *Essx* 1A 54
Tile Hill. *W Mid* 3G 61
Tilehurst. *Read* 4E 37
Tilford. *Surr* 2G 25
Tilgate Forest Row. *W Sus* 2D 26
Tillathrowie. *Abers* 5B 160
Tillers Green. *Glos* 2B 48
Tillery. *Abers* 1G 153
Tilley. *Shrp* 3H 71
Tillicoultry. *Clac* 4B 136
Tillingham. *Essx* 5C 54
Tillington. *Here* 1H 47
Tillington. *W Sus* 3A 26
Tillington Common. *Here* 1H 47
Tillybirloch. *Abers* 3D 152
Tillyfourie. *Abers* 2D 152
Tilmanstone. *Kent* 5H 41
Tilney All Saints. *Norf* 4E 77
Tilney Fen End. *Norf* 4E 77
Tilney High End. *Norf* 4E 77
Tilney St Lawrence. *Norf* 4E 77
Tilshead. *Wilts* 2F 23
Tilstock. *Shrp* 2H 71
Tilston. *Ches W* 5G 83
Tilstone Fearnall. *Ches W* 4H 83
Tilsworth. *C Beds* 3H 51
Tilton on the Hill. *Leics* 5E 75
Tiltups End. *Glos* 2D 34
Timberland. *Linc* 5A 88
Timbersbrook. *Ches E* 4C 84
Timberscombe. *Som* 2C 20
Timble. *N Yor* 4D 98
Timperley. *G Man* 2B 84
Timsbury. *Bath* 1B 22
Timsbury. *Hants* 4B 24
Timsgearraidh. *W Isl* 4C 171
Timworth Green. *Suff* 4A 66
Tincleton. *Dors* 3C 14
Tindale. *Cumb* 4H 113
Tindale Crescent. *Dur* 2F 105
Tingewick. *Buck* 2E 51
Tingrith. *C Beds* 2A 52
Tingwall. *Orkn* 5D 172
Tinhay. *Devn* 4D 11
Tinshill. *W Yor* 1C 92
Tinsley. *S Yor* 1B 86
Tinsley Green. *W Sus* 2D 27
Tintagel. *Corn* 4A 10
Tintern. *Mon* 5A 48
Tintinhull. *Som* 1H 13
Tintwistle. *Derbs* 1E 85
Tinwald. *Dum* 1B 112
Tinwell. *Rut* 5H 75
Tippacott. *Devn* 2A 20
Tipperty. *Abers* 1G 153
Tipps End. *Cambs* 1E 65
Tiptoe. *Hants* 3A 16
Tipton. *W Mid* 1D 60
Tipton St John. *Devn* 3D 12
Tiptree. *Essx* 4B 54
Tiptree Heath. *Essx* 4B 54
Tirabad. *Powy* 1B 46
Tircoed. *Swan* 5G 45
Tiree Airport. *Arg* 4B 138
Tirinie. *Per* 2F 143
Tirley. *Glos* 3D 48
Tirnewydd. *Flin* 3D 82
Tiroran. *Arg* 1B 132
Tirphil. *Cphy* 5E 47
Tirril. *Cumb* 2G 103
Tirryside. *High* 2C 164
Tir-y-dail. *Carm* 4G 45
Tisbury. *Wilts* 4E 23
Tisman's Common. *W Sus* 2B 26
Tissington. *Derbs* 5F 85
Titchberry. *Devn* 4C 18
Titchfield. *Hants* 2D 16
Titchmarsh. *Nptn* 3H 63
Titchwell. *Norf* 1G 77
Tithby. *Notts* 2D 74
Titley. *Here* 5F 59
Titlington. *Nmbd* 3E 121
Titsey. *Surr* 5F 39
Titson. *Corn* 2C 10
Tittensor. *Staf* 2C 72
Tittleshall. *Norf* 3A 78
Titton. *Worc* 4C 60
Tiverton. *Ches W* 4H 83
Tiverton. *Devn* 1C 12
Tivetshall St Margaret. *Norf* 2D 66
Tivetshall St Mary. *Norf* 2D 66
Tivington. *Som* 2C 20
Tixall. *Staf* 3D 73
Tixover. *Rut* 5G 75
Toab. *Orkn* 7E 172
Toab. *Shet* 10E 173
Toadmoor. *Derbs* 5A 86
Tobermory. *Arg* 3G 139
Toberonochy. *Arg* 3E 133
Tobha-Beag. *W Isl* 1E 170 (on North Uist)
Tobha Beag. *W Isl* 5C 170 (on South Uist)
Tobha Mor. *W Isl* 5C 170
Tobhtarol. *W Isl* 4D 171
Tobson. *W Isl* 4D 171
Tocabhaig. *High* 2E 147
Tocher. *Abers* 5D 160
Tockenham. *Wilts* 4F 35
Tockenham Wick. *Wilts* 3F 35
Tockholes. *Bkbn* 2E 91
Tockington. *S Glo* 3B 34
Tockwith. *N Yor* 4G 99
Todber. *Dors* 4D 22
Todding. *Here* 3G 59
Toddington. *C Beds* 3A 52
Toddington. *Glos* 2F 49
Todenham. *Glos* 2H 49
Todhills. *Cumb* 3E 113
Todmorden. *W Yor* 2H 91
Todwick. *S Yor* 2B 86
Toft. *Cambs* 5C 64
Toft. *Linc* 4H 75
Toft Hill. *Dur* 2E 105
Toft Monks. *Norf* 1G 67
Toft next Newton. *Linc* 2H 87
Toftrees. *Norf* 3A 78
Tofts. *High* 2F 169
Toftwood. *Norf* 4B 78
Togston. *Nmbd* 4G 121
Tokavaig. *High* 2E 147
Tokers Green. *Oxon* 4F 37
Tolastadh a Chaolais. *W Isl* 4D 171
Tolladine. *Worc* 5C 60
Tolland. *Som* 3E 20
Tollard Farnham. *Dors* 1E 15
Tollard Royal. *Wilts* 1E 15
Toll Bar. *S Yor* 4F 93
Toller Fratrum. *Dors* 3A 14
Toller Porcorum. *Dors* 3A 14
Tollerton. *N Yor* 3H 99
Tollerton. *Notts* 2D 74
Toller Whelme. *Dors* 2A 14
Tollesbury. *Essx* 4C 54
Tolleshunt D'Arcy. *Essx* 4C 54
Tolleshunt Knights. *Essx* 4C 54
Tolleshunt Major. *Essx* 4C 54
Tollie. *High* 3H 157
Tollie Farm. *High* 1A 156
Tolm. *W Isl* 4G 171
Tolpuddle. *Dors* 3C 14
Tolstadh bho Thuath. *W Isl* 3H 171
Tolworth. *G Lon* 4C 38
Tomachlaggan. *Mor* 1F 151
Tomaknock. *Per* 1A 136
Tomatin. *High* 1C 150
Tombuidhe. *Arg* 3H 133
Tomdoun. *High* 3D 148
Tomich. *High* 1F 149 (nr. Cannich)
Tomich. *High* 1B 158 (nr. Invergordon)

Upper Cwmbran—Wallacetown

Upper Cwmbran. *Torf* 2F **33**
Upper Dallachy. *Mor* 2A **160**
Upper Dean. *Bed* 4H **63**
Upper Denby. *W Yor* 4C **92**
Upper Derraid. *High* 5E **159**
Upper Diabaig. *High* 2H **155**
Upper Dicker. *E Sus* 5G **27**
Upper Dinchope. *Shrp* 2G **59**
Upper Dochcarty. *High* 2H **157**
Upper Dounreay. *High* 2B **168**
Upper Dovercourt. *Essx* 2F **55**
Upper Dunsforth. *N Yor* 3G **99**
Upper Dunsley. *Herts* 4H **51**
Upper Eastern Green. *W Mid* 2G **61**
Upper Elkstone. *Staf* 5E **85**
Upper Ellastone. *Staf* 1F **73**
Upper End. *Derbs* 3E **85**
Upper Enham. *Hants* 2B **24**
Upper Farmcote. *Shrp* 1B **60**
Upper Farringdon. *Hants* 3F **25**
Upper Framilode. *Glos* 4C **48**
Upper Froyle. *Hants* 2F **25**
Upper Gills. *High* 1F **169**
Upper Glenfintaig. *High* 5E **149**
Upper Godney. *Som* 2H **21**
Upper Gravenhurst. *C Beds* 2B **52**
Upper Green. *Essx* 2E **53**
Upper Green. *W Ber* 5B **36**
Upper Green. *W Yor* 2C **92**
Upper Grove Common. *Here* 3A **48**
Upper Hackney. *Derbs* 4G **85**
Upper Hale. *Surr* 2G **25**
Upper Halliford. *Surr* 4B **38**
Upper Halling. *Medw* 4A **40**
Upper Hambleton. *Rut* 5G **75**
Upper Hardres Court. *Kent* 5F **41**
Upper Hardwick. *Here* 5G **59**
Upper Hartfield. *E Sus* 2F **27**
Upper Haugh. *S Yor* 1B **86**
Upper Hayton. *Shrp* 2H **59**
Upper Heath. *Shrp* 2H **59**
Upper Hellesdon. *Norf* 4E **78**
Upper Helmsley. *N Yor* 4A **100**
Upper Hengoed. *Shrp* 2E **71**
Upper Hergest. *Here* 5E **59**
Upper Heyford. *Nptn* 5D **62**
Upper Heyford. *Oxon* 3C **50**
Upper Hill. *Here* 5G **59**
Upper Hindhope. *Bord* 4B **120**
Upper Hopton. *W Yor* 3B **92**
Upper Howsell. *Worc* 1C **48**
Upper Hulme. *Staf* 4E **85**
Upper Inglesham. *Swin* 2H **35**
Upper Kilcott. *Glos* 3C **34**
Upper Killay. *Swan* 3E **31**
Upper Kirkton. *Abers* 5E **161**
Upper Kirkton. *N Ayr* 4C **126**
Upper Knockando. *Mor* 4F **159**
Upper Knockchoilum. *High* 2G **149**
Upper Lambourn. *W Ber* 3B **36**
Upper Langford. *N Som* 1H **21**
Upper Langwith. *Derbs* 4C **86**
Upper Largo. *Fife* 3G **137**
Upper Latheron. *High* 5D **169**
Upper Layham. *Suff* 1D **54**
Upper Leigh. *Staf* 2E **73**
Upper Lenie. *High* 1H **149**
Upper Lochton. *Abers* 4D **152**
Upper Longdon. *Staf* 4E **73**
Upper Longwood. *Shrp* 5A **72**
Upper Lybster. *High* 5E **169**
Upper Lydbrook. *Glos* 4B **48**
Upper Lye. *Here* 4F **59**
Upper Maes-coed. *Here* 2G **47**
Upper Midway. *Derbs* 3G **73**
Uppermill. *G Man* 4H **91**
Upper Millichope. *Shrp* 2H **59**
Upper Milovaig. *High* 4A **154**
Upper Minety. *Wilts* 2F **35**
Upper Mitton. *Worc* 3C **60**
Upper Nash. *Pemb* 4E **43**
Upper Neepaback. *Shet* 3G **173**
Upper Netchwood. *Shrp* 1A **60**
Upper Nobut. *Staf* 2E **73**
Upper North Dean. *Buck* 2G **37**
Upper Norwood. *W Sus* 4A **26**
Upper Nyland. *Dors* 4C **22**
Upper Oddington. *Glos* 3H **49**
Upper Ollach. *High* 5E **155**
Upper Outwoods. *Staf* 3G **73**
Upper Padley. *Derbs* 3G **85**
Upper Pennington. *Hants* 3B **16**
Upper Poppleton. *York* 4H **99**
Upper Quinton. *Warw* 1G **49**
Upper Rissington. *Glos* 4H **49**
Upper Rochford. *Worc* 4A **60**
Upper Rusko. *Dum* 3C **110**
Upper Sandaig. *High* 2F **147**
Upper Sanday. *Orkn* 7E **172**
Upper Sapey. *Here* 4A **60**
Upper Seagry. *Wilts* 3E **35**
Upper Shelton. *C Beds* 1H **51**
Upper Sheringham. *Norf* 1D **78**
Upper Skelmorlie. *N Ayr* 3C **126**
Upper Slaughter. *Glos* 3G **49**
Upper Sonachan. *Arg* 1H **133**
Upper Soudley. *Glos* 4B **48**
Upper Staploe. *Bed* 5A **64**
Upper Stoke. *Norf* 5E **79**
Upper Stondon. *C Beds* 2B **52**
Upper Stowe. *Nptn* 5D **62**
Upper Street. *Hants* 1G **15**
Upper Street. *Norf* 4F **79** (nr. Horning)
Upper Street. *Norf* 4F **79** (nr. Hoveton)
Upper Street. *Suff* 2E **55**
Upper Strensham. *Worc* 2E **49**
Upper Studley. *Wilts* 1D **22**
Upper Sundon. *C Beds* 3A **52**
Upper Swell. *Glos* 3G **49**
Upper Tankersley. *S Yor* 1H **85**
Upper Tean. *Staf* 2E **73**
Upperthong. *W Yor* 4B **92**
Upperthorpe. *N Lin* 4A **94**
Upper Thurnham. *Lanc* 4D **96**
Upper Tillyrie. *Per* 3D **136**
Upperton. *W Sus* 3A **26**
Upper Tooting. *G Lon* 3D **39**
Uppertown. *Derbs* 4H **85** (nr. Ashover)
Upper Town. *Derbs* 5G **85** (nr. Bonsall)
Upper Town. *Derbs* 5G **85** (nr. Hognaston)
Upper Town. *Here* 1A **48**
Uppertown. *High* 1F **169**
Upper Town. *N Som* 5A **34**
Uppertown. *Nmbd* 2B **114**
Uppertown. *Orkn* 8D **172**
Upper Tysoe. *Warw* 1B **50**
Upper Upham. *Wilts* 4H **35**
Upper Upnor. *Medw* 3B **40**
Upper Urquhart. *Fife* 3D **136**
Upper Wardington. *Oxon* 1C **50**
Upper Weald. *Mil* 2F **51**
Upper Weedon. *Nptn* 5D **62**
Upper Wellingham. *E Sus* 4F **27**
Upper Whiston. *S Yor* 2B **86**
Upper Wield. *Hants* 3E **25**
Upper Winchendon. *Buck* 4F **51**
Upperwood. *Derbs* 5G **85**
Upper Woodford. *Wilts* 3G **23**
Upper Wootton. *Hants* 1D **24**
Upper Wraxall. *Wilts* 4D **34**
Upper Wyche. *Here* 1C **48**
Uppincott. *Devn* 2B **12**
Uppingham. *Rut* 1F **63**
Uppington. *Shrp* 5A **72**
Upsall. *N Yor* 1G **99**
Upsettlington. *Bord* 5E **131**
Upshire. *Essx* 5E **53**
Up Somborne. *Hants* 3B **24**
Upstreet. *Kent* 4G **41**
Up Sydling. *Dors* 2B **14**
Upthorpe. *Suff* 3B **66**
Upton. *Buck* 4F **51**
Upton. *Cambs* 3A **64**
Upton. *Ches W* 4G **83**
Upton. *Corn* 2C **10** (nr. Bude)
Upton. *Corn* 5C **10** (nr. Liskeard)
Upton. *Cumb* 1E **102**
Upton. *Devn* 2D **12** (nr. Honiton)
Upton. *Devn* 4D **8** (nr. Kingsbridge)
Upton. *Dors* 3E **15** (nr. Poole)
Upton. *Dors* 4C **14** (nr. Weymouth)
Upton. *E Yor* 4F **101**
Upton. *Hants* 1B **24** (nr. Andover)
Upton. *Hants* 1B **16** (nr. Southampton)
Upton. *IOW* 3D **16**
Upton. *Leics* 1A **62**
Upton. *Linc* 2F **87**
Upton. *Mers* 2E **83**
Upton. *Norf* 4F **79**
Upton. *Nptn* 4E **62**
Upton. *Notts* 3E **87** (nr. Retford)
Upton. *Notts* 5E **87** (nr. Southwell)
Upton. *Oxon* 3D **36**
Upton. *Pemb* 4E **43**
Upton. *Pet* 5A **76**
Upton. *Slo* 3A **38**
Upton. *Som* 4H **21** (nr. Somerton)
Upton. *Som* 4C **20** (nr. Wiveliscombe)
Upton. *Warw* 5F **61**
Upton. *W Yor* 3E **93**
Upton. *Wilts* 3D **22**
Upton Bishop. *Here* 3B **48**
Upton Cheyney. *S Glo* 5B **34**
Upton Cressett. *Shrp* 1A **60**
Upton Crews. *Here* 3B **48**
Upton Cross. *Corn* 5C **10**
Upton End. *C Beds* 2B **52**
Upton Grey. *Hants* 2E **25**
Upton Heath. *Ches W* 4G **83**
Upton Hellions. *Devn* 2B **12**
Upton Lovell. *Wilts* 2E **23**
Upton Magna. *Shrp* 4H **71**
Upton Noble. *Som* 3C **22**
Upton Pyne. *Devn* 3C **12**
Upton St Leonards. *Glos* 4D **48**
Upton Scudamore. *Wilts* 2D **22**
Upton Snodsbury. *Worc* 5D **60**
Upton upon Severn. *Worc* 1D **48**
Upton Warren. *Worc* 4D **60**
Upwaltham. *W Sus* 4A **26**
Upware. *Cambs* 3E **65**
Upwell. *Norf* 5E **77**
Upwey. *Dors* 4B **14**
Upwick Green. *Herts* 3E **53**
Upwood. *Cambs* 2B **64**
Urafirth. *Shet* 4E **173**
Uragaig. *Arg* 4A **132**
Urchany. *High* 4C **158**
Urchfont. *Wilts* 1F **23**
Urdimarsh. *Here* 1A **48**
Ure. *Shet* 4D **173**
Ure Bank. *N Yor* 2F **99**
Urgha. *W Isl* 8D **171**
Urlay Nook. *Stoc T* 3B **106**
Urmston. *G Man* 1B **84**
Urquhart. *Mor* 2G **159**
Urra. *N Yor* 4C **106**
Urray. *High* 3H **157**
Usan. *Ang* 3G **145**
Ushaw Moor. *Dur* 5F **115**
Usk. *Mon* 5G **47**
Usselby. *Linc* 1H **87**
Usworth. *Tyne* 4G **115**
Utkinton. *Ches W* 4H **83**
Uton. *Devn* 3B **12**
Utterby. *Linc* 1C **88**
Uttoxeter. *Staf* 2E **73**
Uwchmynydd. *Gwyn* 3A **68**
Uxbridge. *G Lon* 2B **38**
Uyeasound. *Shet* 1G **173**
Uzmaston. *Pemb* 3D **42**

V

Valley. *IOA* 3B **80**
Valley End. *Surr* 4A **38**
Valley Truckle. *Corn* 4B **10**
Valsgarth. *Shet* 1H **173**
Valtos. *High* 2E **155**
Van. *Powy* 2B **58**
Vange. *Essx* 2B **40**
Varteg. *Torf* 5F **47**
Vatsetter. *Shet* 3G **173**
Vatten. *High* 4B **154**
Vaul. *Arg* 4B **138**
Vauld, The. *Here* 1A **48**
Vaynol. *Gwyn* 3E **81**
Vaynor. *Mer T* 4D **46**
Veensgarth. *Shet* 7F **173**
Velindre. *Powy* 2E **47**
Vellow. *Som* 3D **20**
Velly. *Devn* 4C **18**
Veness. *Orkn* 5E **172**
Venhay. *Devn* 1A **12**
Venn. *Devn* 4D **8**
Venngreen. *Devn* 1D **11**
Vennington. *Shrp* 5F **71**
Venn Ottery. *Devn* 3D **12**
Venn's Green. *Here* 1A **48**
Venny Tedburn. *Devn* 3B **12**
Venterdon. *Corn* 5D **10**
Ventnor. *IOW* 5D **16**
Vernham Dean. *Hants* 1B **24**
Vernham Street. *Hants* 1B **24**
Vernolds Common. *Shrp* 2G **59**
Verwood. *Dors* 2F **15**
Veryan. *Corn* 5D **6**
Veryan Green. *Corn* 5D **6**
Vicarage. *Devn* 4F **13**
Vickerstown. *Cumb* 3A **96**
Victoria. *Corn* 2D **6**
Vidlin. *Shet* 5F **173**
Viewpark. *N Lan* 3A **128**
Vigo. *W Mid* 5E **73**
Vigo Village. *Kent* 4H **39**
Vinehall Street. *E Sus* 3B **28**
Vine's Cross. *E Sus* 4G **27**
Viney Hill. *Glos* 5B **48**
Virginia Water. *Surr* 4A **38**
Virginstow. *Devn* 3D **11**
Vobster. *Som* 2C **22**
Voe. *Shet* 5F **173** (nr. Hillside)
Voe. *Shet* 3E **173** (nr. Swinister)
Vole. *Som* 2G **21**
Vowchurch. *Here* 2G **47**
Voxter. *Shet* 4E **173**
Voy. *Orkn* 6B **172**
Vulcan Village. *Mers* 1H **83**

W

Waberthwaite. *Cumb* 5C **102**
Wackerfield. *Dur* 2E **105**
Wacton. *Norf* 1D **66**
Wadbister. *Shet* 7F **173**
Wadborough. *Worc* 1E **49**
Wadbrook. *Devn* 2G **13**
Waddesdon. *Buck* 4F **51**
Waddeton. *Devn* 3E **9**
Waddicar. *Mers* 1F **83**
Waddingham. *Linc* 1G **87**
Waddington. *Lanc* 5G **97**
Waddington. *Linc* 4G **87**
Waddon. *Devn* 5B **12**
Wadebridge. *Corn* 1D **6**
Wadeford. *Som* 1G **13**
Wadenhoe. *Nptn* 2H **63**
Wadesmill. *Herts* 4D **52**
Wadhurst. *E Sus* 2H **27**
Wadshelf. *Derbs* 3H **85**
Wadsley. *S Yor* 1H **85**
Wadsley Bridge. *S Yor* 1H **85**
Wadswick. *Wilts* 5D **34**
Wadwick. *Hants* 1C **24**
Wadworth. *S Yor* 1C **86**
Waen. *Den* 4D **82** (nr. Llandymog)
Waen. *Den* 4B **82** (nr. Nantglyn)
Waen. *Powy* 1B **58**
Waen Fach. *Powy* 4E **70**
Waen Goleugoed. *Den* 3C **82**
Wag. *High* 1H **165**
Wainfleet All Saints. *Linc* 5D **89**
Wainfleet Bank. *Linc* 5D **88**
Wainfleet St Mary. *Linc* 5D **89**
Wainhouse Corner. *Corn* 3B **10**
Wainscott. *Medw* 3B **40**
Wainstalls. *W Yor* 2A **92**
Waitby. *Cumb* 4A **104**
Waithe. *Linc* 4F **95**
Wakefield. *W Yor* 2D **92**
Wakerley. *Nptn* 1G **63**
Wakes Colne. *Essx* 3B **54**
Walberswick. *Suff* 3G **67**
Walberton. *W Sus* 5A **26**
Walbottle. *Tyne* 3E **115**
Walby. *Cumb* 3F **113**
Walcombe. *Som* 2A **22**
Walcot. *Linc* 2H **75**
Walcot. *N Lin* 2B **94**
Walcot. *Swin* 3G **35**
Walcot. *Telf* 4H **71**
Walcot. *Warw* 5F **61**
Walcote. *Leics* 2C **62**
Walcot Green. *Norf* 2D **66**
Walcott. *Linc* 5A **88**
Walcott. *Norf* 2F **79**
Walden. *N Yor* 1C **98**
Walden Head. *N Yor* 1B **98**
Walden Stubbs. *N Yor* 3F **93**
Walderslade. *Medw* 4B **40**
Walderton. *W Sus* 1F **17**
Walditch. *Dors* 3H **13**
Waldley. *Derbs* 2F **73**
Waldridge. *Dur* 4F **115**
Waldringfield. *Suff* 1F **55**
Waldron. *E Sus* 4G **27**
Wales. *S Yor* 2B **86**
Walesby. *Linc* 1A **88**
Walesby. *Notts* 3D **86**
Walford. *Here* 3F **59** (nr. Leintwardine)
Walford. *Here* 3A **48** (nr. Ross-on-Wye)
Walford. *Shrp* 3G **71**
Walford. *Staf* 2C **72**
Walford Heath. *Shrp* 4G **71**
Walgherton. *Ches E* 1A **72**
Walgrave. *Nptn* 3F **63**
Walhampton. *Hants* 3B **16**
Walkden. *G Man* 4F **91**
Walker. *Tyne* 3F **115**
Walkerburn. *Bord* 1F **119**
Walker Fold. *Lanc* 5F **97**
Walkeringham. *Notts* 1E **87**
Walkerith. *Linc* 1E **87**
Walkern. *Herts* 3C **52**
Walker's Green. *Here* 1A **48**
Walkerton. *Fife* 3E **137**
Walkerville. *N Yor* 5F **105**
Walkford. *Dors* 3H **15**
Walkhampton. *Devn* 2B **8**
Walkington. *E Yor* 1C **94**
Walkley. *S Yor* 2H **85**
Walk Mill. *Lanc* 1G **91**
Wall. *Corn* 3D **4**
Wall. *Nmbd* 3C **114**
Wall. *Staf* 5F **73**
Wallaceton. *Dum* 1F **111**
Wallacetown. *Shet* 6E **173**
Wallacetown. *S Ayr* 2C **116** (nr. Ayr)

Wallacetown—Well Hill

Wallacetown. *S Ayr* 4B 116 (nr. Dailly)
Wallands Park. *E Sus* 4F 27
Wallasey. *Mers* 1E 83
Wallaston Green. *Pemb* 4D 42
Wallbrook. *W Mid* 1D 60
Wallcrouch. *E Sus* 2A 28
Wall End. *Cumb* 1B 96
Wallend. *Medw* 3C 40
Wall Heath. *W Mid* 2C 60
Wallingford. *Oxon* 3E 36
Wallington. *G Lon* 4D 39
Wallington. *Hants* 2D 16
Wallington. *Herts* 2C 52
Wallis. *Pemb* 2E 43
Wallisdown. *Pool* 3F 15
Walliswood. *Surr* 2C 26
Wall Nook. *Dur* 5F 115
Walls. *Shet* 7D 173
Wallsend. *Tyne* 3G 115
Wallsworth. *Glos* 3D 48
Wall under Heywood. *Shrp* 1H 59
Wallyford. *E Lot* 2G 129
Walmer. *Kent* 5H 41
Walmer Bridge. *Lanc* 2C 90
Walmersley. *G Man* 3G 91
Walmley. *W Mid* 1F 61
Walnut Grove. *Per* 1D 136
Walpole. *Suff* 3F 67
Walpole Cross Keys. *Norf* 4E 77
Walpole Gate. *Norf* 4E 77
Walpole Highway. *Norf* 4E 77
Walpole Marsh. *Norf* 4D 77
Walpole St Andrew. *Norf* 4E 77
Walpole St Peter. *Norf* 4E 77
Walsall. *W Mid* 1E 61
Walsall Wood. *W Mid* 5E 73
Walsden. *W Yor* 2H 91
Walsgrave on Sowe. *W Mid* 2A 62
Walsham le Willows. *Suff* 3C 66
Walshaw. *G Man* 3F 91
Walshford. *N Yor* 4G 99
Walsoken. *Cambs* 4D 76
Walston. *S Lan* 5D 128
Walsworth. *Herts* 2B 52
Walter's Ash. *Buck* 2G 37
Walterston. *V Glam* 4D 32
Walterstone. *Here* 3G 47
Waltham. *Kent* 1F 29
Waltham. *NE Lin* 4F 95
Waltham Abbey. *Essx* 5D 53
Waltham Chase. *Hants* 1D 16
Waltham Cross. *Herts* 5D 52
Waltham on the Wolds. *Leics* 3F 75
Waltham St Lawrence. *Wind* 4G 37
Waltham's Cross. *Essx* 2G 53
Walthamstow. *G Lon* 2E 39
Walton. *Cumb* 3G 113
Walton. *Derbs* 4A 86
Walton. *Leics* 2C 62
Walton. *Mers* 1F 83
Walton. *Mil* 2G 51
Walton. *Pet* 5A 76
Walton. *Powy* 5E 59
Walton. *Som* 3H 21
Walton. *Staf* 3C 72 (nr. Eccleshall)
Walton. *Staf* 2C 72 (nr. Stone)
Walton. *Suff* 2F 55
Walton. *Telf* 4H 71
Walton. *Warw* 5G 61
Walton. *W Yor* 3D 92 (nr. Wakefield)
Walton. *W Yor* 5G 99 (nr. Wetherby)
Walton Cardiff. *Glos* 2E 49
Walton East. *Pemb* 2E 43
Walton Elm. *Dors* 1C 14
Walton Highway. *Norf* 4D 77
Walton-in-Gordano. *N Som* 4H 33
Walton-le-Dale. *Lanc* 2D 90
Walton-on-Thames. *Surr* 4C 38
Walton-on-the-Hill. *Staf* 3D 72
Walton on the Hill. *Surr* 5D 38
Walton-on-the-Naze. *Essx* 3F 55
Walton on the Wolds. *Leics* 4C 74
Walton-on-Trent. *Derbs* 4G 73
Walton West. *Pemb* 3C 42
Walwick. *Nmbd* 2C 114
Walworth. *Darl* 3F 105
Walworth Gate. *Darl* 2F 105
Walwyn's Castle. *Pemb* 3C 42
Wambrook. *Som* 2F 13
Wampool. *Cumb* 4D 112
Wanborough. *Surr* 1A 26
Wanborough. *Swin* 3H 35
Wandel. *S Lan* 2B 118
Wandsworth. *G Lon* 3D 38
Wangford. *Suff* 2G 65 (nr. Lakenheath)
Wangford. *Suff* 3G 67 (nr. Southwold)
Wanlip. *Leics* 4C 74
Wanlockhead. *Dum* 3A 118
Wannock. *E Sus* 5G 27
Wansford. *E Yor* 4E 101
Wansford. *Pet* 1H 63
Wanshurst Green. *Kent* 1B 28
Wanstead. *G Lon* 2F 39
Wanstrow. *Som* 2C 22
Wanswell. *Glos* 5B 48
Wantage. *Oxon* 3C 36
Wapley. *S Glo* 4C 34
Wappenbury. *Warw* 4A 62
Wappenham. *Nptn* 1E 51
Warbleton. *E Sus* 4H 27
Warblington. *Hants* 2F 17
Warborough. *Oxon* 2D 36
Warboys. *Cambs* 2C 64
Warbreck. *Bkpl* 1B 90
Warbstow. *Corn* 3C 10
Warburton. *G Man* 2B 84
Warcop. *Cumb* 3A 104
Warden. *Kent* 3E 40
Warden. *Nmbd* 3C 114
Ward End. *W Mid* 2F 61
Ward Green. *Suff* 4C 66
Ward Green Cross. *Lanc* 1E 91
Wardhedges. *C Beds* 2A 52
Wardhouse. *Abers* 5C 160
Wardington. *Oxon* 1C 50
Wardle. *Ches E* 5A 84
Wardle. *G Man* 3H 91
Wardley. *Rut* 5F 75
Wardley. *W Sus* 4G 25
Wardlow. *Derbs* 3F 85
Wardsend. *Ches E* 2D 84
Wardy Hill. *Cambs* 2D 64
Ware. *Herts* 4D 52
Ware. *Kent* 4G 41
Wareham. *Dors* 4E 15
Warehorne. *Kent* 2D 28
Warenford. *Nmbd* 2F 121
Waren Mill. *Nmbd* 1F 121
Warenton. *Nmbd* 1F 121
Wareside. *Herts* 4D 53
Waresley. *Cambs* 5B 64
Waresley. *Worc* 4C 60
Warfield. *Brac* 4G 37
Warfleet. *Devn* 3E 9
Wargate. *Linc* 2B 76
Wargrave. *Wok* 4F 37
Warham. *Norf* 1B 78
Waringstown. *Cgvn* 5G 175
Wark. *Nmbd* 1C 120 (nr. Coldstream)
Wark. *Nmbd* 2B 114 (nr. Hexham)
Warkleigh. *Devn* 4G 19
Warkton. *Nptn* 3F 63
Warkworth. *Nptn* 1C 50
Warkworth. *Nmbd* 4G 121
Warlaby. *N Yor* 5A 106
Warland. *W Yor* 2H 91
Warleggan. *Corn* 2F 7
Warlingham. *Surr* 5E 39
Warmanbie. *Dum* 3C 112
Warmfield. *W Yor* 2D 93
Warmingham. *Ches E* 4B 84
Warminghurst. *W Sus* 4C 26
Warmington. *Nptn* 1H 63
Warmington. *Warw* 1C 50
Warminster. *Wilts* 2D 23
Warmley. *S Glo* 4B 34
Warmsworth. *S Yor* 4F 93
Warmwell. *Dors* 4C 14
Warndon. *Worc* 5C 60
Warners End. *Herts* 5A 52
Warnford. *Hants* 4E 24
Warnham. *W Sus* 2C 26
Warningcamp. *W Sus* 5B 26
Warninglid. *W Sus* 3D 26
Warren. *Ches E* 3C 84
Warren. *Pemb* 5D 42
Warrenby. *Red C* 2C 106
Warren Corner. *Hants* 2G 25 (nr. Aldershot)
Warren Corner. *Hants* 4F 25 (nr. Petersfield)
Warrenpoint. *New M* 6G 175
Warren Row. *Wind* 3G 37
Warren Street. *Kent* 5D 40
Warrington. *Mil* 5F 63
Warrington. *Warr* 2A 84
Warsash. *Hants* 2C 16
Warse. *High* 1F 169
Warslow. *Staf* 5E 85
Warsop. *Notts* 4C 86
Warsop Vale. *Notts* 4C 86
Warter. *E Yor* 4C 100
Warthermarske. *N Yor* 2E 98
Warthill. *N Yor* 4A 100
Wartling. *E Sus* 5A 28
Wartnaby. *Leics* 3E 74
Warton. *Lanc* 2D 97 (nr. Carnforth)
Warton. *Lanc* 2C 90 (nr. Freckleton)
Warton. *Nmbd* 4E 121
Warton. *Warw* 5G 73
Warwick. *Warw* 4G 61
Warwick Bridge. *Cumb* 4F 113
Warwick-on-Eden. *Cumb* 4F 113
Warwick Wold. *Surr* 5E 39
Wasbister. *Orkn* 4C 172
Wasdale Head. *Cumb* 4C 102
Wash. *Derbs* 2E 85
Washaway. *Corn* 2E 7
Washbourne. *Devn* 3D 9
Washbrook. *Suff* 1E 54
Wash Common. *W Ber* 5C 36
Washerwall. *Staf* 1D 72
Washfield. *Devn* 1C 12
Washfold. *N Yor* 4D 104
Washford. *Som* 2D 20
Washford Pyne. *Devn* 1B 12
Washingborough. *Linc* 3H 87
Washington. *Tyne* 4G 115
Washington. *W Sus* 4C 26
Washington Village. *Tyne* 4G 115
Waskerley. *Dur* 5D 114
Wasperton. *Warw* 5G 61
Wasp Green. *Surr* 1E 27
Wasps Nest. *Linc* 4H 87
Wass. *N Yor* 2H 99
Watchet. *Som* 2D 20
Watchfield. *Oxon* 2H 35
Watchgate. *Cumb* 5G 103
Watchhill. *Cumb* 5C 112
Watcombe. *Torb* 2F 9
Watendlath. *Cumb* 3D 102
Water. *Devn* 4A 12
Water. *Lanc* 2G 91
Waterbeach. *Cambs* 4D 65
Waterbeach. *W Sus* 2G 17
Waterbeck. *Dum* 2D 112
Waterditch. *Hants* 3G 15
Water End. *C Beds* 2A 52
Water End. *E Yor* 1A 94
Water End. *Essx* 1F 53
Water End. *Herts* 5C 52 (nr. Hatfield)
Water End. *Herts* 4A 52 (nr. Hemel Hempstead)
Waterfall. *Staf* 5E 85
Waterfoot. *E Ren* 4G 127
Waterfoot. *Lanc* 2G 91
Waterford. *Herts* 4D 52
Water Fryston. *W Yor* 2E 93
Waterhead. *Cumb* 4E 103
Waterhead. *E Ayr* 3E 117
Waterhead. *S Ayr* 5C 116
Waterheads. *Bord* 4F 129
Waterhouses. *Dur* 5E 115
Waterhouses. *Staf* 5E 85
Wateringbury. *Kent* 5A 40
Waterlane. *Glos* 5E 49
Waterlip. *Som* 2B 22
Waterloo. *Cphy* 3E 33
Waterloo. *Corn* 5B 10
Waterloo. *Here* 1G 47
Waterloo. *High* 1E 147
Waterloo. *Mers* 1F 83
Waterloo. *Norf* 4E 78
Waterloo. *N Lan* 4B 128
Waterloo. *Pemb* 4D 42
Waterloo. *Per* 5H 143
Waterloo. *Pool* 3F 15
Waterloo. *Shrp* 2G 71
Waterlooville. *Hants* 2E 17
Watermead. *Buck* 4G 51
Watermillock. *Cumb* 2F 103
Water Newton. *Cambs* 1A 64
Water Orton. *Warw* 1F 61
Waterperry. *Oxon* 5E 51
Waterrow. *Som* 4D 20
Watersfield. *W Sus* 4B 26
Waterside. *Buck* 5H 51
Waterside. *Cambs* 3F 65
Waterside. *Cumb* 5D 112
Waterside. *E Ayr* 4D 116 (nr. Ayr)
Waterside. *E Ayr* 5F 127 (nr. Kilmarnock)
Waterside. *E Dun* 2H 127
Waterstein. *High* 4A 154
Waterstock. *Oxon* 5E 51
Waterston. *Pemb* 4D 42
Water Stratford. *Buck* 2E 51
Waters Upton. *Telf* 4A 72
Water Yeat. *Cumb* 1B 96
Watford. *Herts* 1C 38
Watford. *Nptn* 4D 62
Wath. *Cumb* 4H 103
Wath. *N Yor* 3D 98 (nr. Pateley Bridge)
Wath. *N Yor* 2F 99 (nr. Ripon)
Wath Brow. *Cumb* 3B 102
Wath upon Dearne. *S Yor* 4E 93
Watlington. *Norf* 4F 77
Watlington. *Oxon* 2E 37
Watten. *High* 3E 169
Wattisfield. *Suff* 3C 66
Wattisham. *Suff* 5C 66
Wattlesborough Heath. *Shrp* 4F 71
Watton. *Dors* 3H 13
Watton. *E Yor* 4E 101
Watton. *Norf* 5B 78
Watton at Stone. *Herts* 4C 52
Wattston. *N Lan* 2A 128
Wattstown. *Rhon* 2D 32
Wattsville. *Cphy* 2F 33
Wauldby. *E Yor* 2C 94
Waulkmill. *Abers* 4D 152
Waun. *Powy* 4E 71
Waunarlwydd. *Swan* 3F 31
Waun Fawr. *Cdgn* 2F 57
Waunfawr. *Gwyn* 5E 81
Waungilwen. *Carm* 1H 43
Waunlwyd. *Blae* 5E 47
Waun-y-Clyn. *Carm* 5E 45
Wavendon. *Mil* 2H 51
Waverbridge. *Cumb* 5D 112
Waverley. *Surr* 2G 25
Waverton. *Ches W* 4G 83
Waverton. *Cumb* 5D 112
Wavertree. *Mers* 2F 83
Wawne. *E Yor* 1D 94
Waxham. *Norf* 3G 79
Waxholme. *E Yor* 2G 95
Wayford. *Som* 2H 13
Way Head. *Cambs* 2D 65
Waytown. *Dors* 3H 13
Way Village. *Devn* 1B 12
Wdig. *Pemb* 1D 42
Wealdstone. *G Lon* 2C 38
Weardley. *W Yor* 5E 99
Weare. *Som* 1H 21
Weare Giffard. *Devn* 4E 19
Wearhead. *Dur* 1B 104
Wearne. *Som* 4H 21
Weasdale. *Cumb* 4H 103
Weasenham All Saints. *Norf* 3H 77
Weasenham St Peter. *Norf* 3A 78
Weaverham. *Ches W* 3A 84
Weaverthorpe. *N Yor* 2D 100
Webheath. *Worc* 4E 61
Webton. *Here* 2H 47
Wedderlairs. *Abers* 5F 161
Weddington. *Warw* 1A 62
Wedhampton. *Wilts* 1F 23
Wedmore. *Som* 2H 21
Wednesbury. *W Mid* 1D 61
Wednesfield. *W Mid* 5D 72
Weecar. *Notts* 4F 87
Weedon. *Buck* 4G 51
Weedon Bec. *Nptn* 5D 62
Weedon Lois. *Nptn* 1E 50
Weeford. *Staf* 5F 73
Week. *Devn* 4F 19 (nr. Barnstaple)
Week. *Devn* 2G 11 (nr. Okehampton)
Week. *Devn* 1H 11 (nr. South Molton)
Week. *Devn* 2D 9 (nr. Totnes)
Week. *Som* 3C 20
Weeke. *Devn* 2A 12
Weeke. *Hants* 3C 24
Week Green. *Corn* 3C 10
Weekley. *Nptn* 2F 63
Week St Mary. *Corn* 3C 10
Weel. *E Yor* 1D 94
Weeley. *Essx* 3E 55
Weeley Heath. *Essx* 3E 55
Weem. *Per* 4F 143
Weeping Cross. *Staf* 3D 72
Weethly. *Warw* 5E 61
Weeting. *Norf* 2G 65
Weeton. *E Yor* 2G 95
Weeton. *Lanc* 1B 90
Weeton. *N Yor* 5E 99
Weetwood Hall. *Nmbd* 2E 121
Weir. *Lanc* 2G 91
Welborne. *Norf* 4C 78
Welbourn. *Linc* 5G 87
Welburn. *N Yor* 1A 100 (nr. Kirkbymoorside)
Welburn. *N Yor* 3B 100 (nr. Malton)
Welbury. *N Yor* 4A 106
Welby. *Linc* 2G 75
Welches Dam. *Cambs* 2D 64
Welcombe. *Devn* 1C 10
Weld Bank. *Lanc* 3D 90
Weldon. *Nptn* 2G 63
Weldon. *Nmbd* 5F 121
Welford. *Nptn* 2D 62
Welford. *W Ber* 4C 36
Welford-on-Avon. *Warw* 5F 61
Welham. *Leics* 1E 63
Welham. *Notts* 2E 87
Welham Green. *Herts* 5C 52
Well. *Hants* 2F 25
Well. *Linc* 3D 88
Well. *N Yor* 1E 99
Welland. *Worc* 1C 48
Wellbank. *Ang* 5D 144
Well Bottom. *Dors* 1E 15
Welldale. *Dum* 3C 112
Wellesbourne. *Warw* 5G 61
Well Hill. *Kent* 4F 39

Wellhouse—West Norwood

Wellhouse. *W Ber* 4D **36**
Welling. *G Lon* 3F **39**
Wellingborough. *Nptn* 4F **63**
Wellingham. *Norf* 3A **78**
Wellingore. *Linc* 5G **87**
Wellington. *Cumb* 4B **102**
Wellington. *Here* 1H **47**
Wellington. *Som* 4E **21**
Wellington. *Telf* 4A **72**
Wellington Heath. *Here* 1C **48**
Wellow. *Bath* 1C **22**
Wellow. *IOW* 4B **16**
Wellow. *Notts* 4D **86**
Wellpond Green. *Herts* 3E **53**
Wells. *Som* 2A **22**
Wellsborough. *Leics* 5A **74**
Wells Green. *Ches E* 5A **84**
Wells-next-the-Sea. *Norf* 1B **78**
Wellswood. *Torb* 2F **9**
Wellwood. *Fife* 1D **129**
Welney. *Norf* 1E **65**
Welsford. *Devn* 4C **18**
Welshampton. *Shrp* 2G **71**
Welsh End. *Shrp* 2H **71**
Welsh Frankton. *Shrp* 2F **71**
Welsh Hook. *Pemb* 2D **42**
Welsh Newton. *Here* 4H **47**
Welsh Newton Common. *Here* 4A **48**
Welshpool. *Powy* 5E **70**
Welsh St Donats. *V Glam* 4D **32**
Welton. *Bath* 1B **22**
Welton. *Cumb* 5E **113**
Welton. *E Yor* 2C **94**
Welton. *Linc* 2H **87**
Welton. *Nptn* 4C **62**
Welton Hill. *Linc* 2H **87**
Welton le Marsh. *Linc* 4D **88**
Welton le Wold. *Linc* 2B **88**
Welwick. *E Yor* 2G **95**
Welwyn. *Herts* 4C **52**
Welwyn Garden City. *Herts* 4C **52**
Wem. *Shrp* 3H **71**
Wembdon. *Som* 3F **21**
Wembley. *G Lon* 2C **38**
Wembury. *Devn* 4B **8**
Wembworthy. *Devn* 2G **11**
Wemyss Bay. *Inv* 2C **126**
Wenallt. *Cdgn* 3F **57**
Wenallt. *Gwyn* 1B **70**
Wendens Ambo. *Essx* 2F **53**
Wendlebury. *Oxon* 4D **50**
Wendling. *Norf* 4B **78**
Wendover. *Buck* 5G **51**
Wendron. *Corn* 5A **6**
Wendy. *Cambs* 1D **52**
Wenfordbridge. *Corn* 5A **10**
Wenhaston. *Suff* 3G **67**
Wennington. *Cambs* 3B **64**
Wennington. *G Lon* 2G **39**
Wennington. *Lanc* 2F **97**
Wensley. *Derbs* 4G **85**
Wensley. *N Yor* 1C **98**
Wentbridge. *W Yor* 3E **93**
Wentnor. *Shrp* 1F **59**
Wentworth. *Cambs* 3D **65**
Wentworth. *S Yor* 1A **86**
Wenvoe. *V Glam* 4E **32**
Weobley. *Here* 5G **59**
Weobley Marsh. *Here* 5G **59**
Wepham. *W Sus* 5B **26**
Wereham. *Norf* 5F **77**
Wergs. *W Mid* 5C **72**
Wern. *Gwyn* 1E **69**
Wern. *Powy* 4E **46** (nr. Brecon)
Wern. *Powy* 4E **71** (nr. Guilsfield)
Wern. *Powy* 4B **70** (nr. Llangadfan)
Wern. *Powy* 3E **71** (nr. Llanymynech)
Wernffrwd. *Swan* 3E **31**
Wernyrheolydd. *Mon* 4G **47**
Werrington. *Corn* 4D **10**
Werrington. *Pet* 5A **76**
Werrington. *Staf* 1D **72**
Wervin. *Ches W* 3G **83**
Wesham. *Lanc* 1C **90**
Wessington. *Derbs* 5A **86**
West Aberthaw. *V Glam* 5D **32**
West Acre. *Norf* 4G **77**
West Allerdean. *Nmbd* 5F **131**
West Alvington. *Devn* 4D **8**
West Amesbury. *Wilts* 2G **23**
West Anstey. *Devn* 4B **20**
West Appleton. *N Yor* 5F **105**
West Ardsley. *W Yor* 2C **92**
West Arthurlie. *E Ren* 4F **127**
West Ashby. *Linc* 3B **88**
West Ashling. *W Sus* 2G **17**
West Ashton. *Wilts* 1D **23**
West Auckland. *Dur* 2E **105**
West Ayton. *N Yor* 1D **101**
West Bagborough. *Som* 3E **21**
West Bank. *Hal* 2H **83**
West Barkwith. *Linc* 2A **88**
West Barnby. *N Yor* 3F **107**
West Barns. *E Lot* 2C **130**
West Barsham. *Norf* 2B **78**
West Bay. *Dors* 3H **13**
West Beckham. *Norf* 2D **78**
West Bennan. *N Ayr* 3D **123**
Westbere. *Kent* 4F **41**
West Bergholt. *Essx* 3C **54**
West Bexington. *Dors* 4A **14**
West Bilney. *Norf* 4G **77**
West Blackdene. *Dur* 1B **104**
West Blatchington. *Brig* 5D **27**
Westborough. *Linc* 1F **75**
Westbourne. *Bour* 3F **15**
Westbourne. *W Sus* 2F **17**
West Bowling. *W Yor* 1B **92**
West Brabourne. *Kent* 1E **29**
West Bradford. *Lanc* 5G **97**
West Bradley. *Som* 3A **22**
West Bretton. *W Yor* 3C **92**
West Bridgford. *Notts* 2C **74**
West Briggs. *Norf* 4F **77**
West Bromwich. *W Mid* 1E **61**
Westbrook. *Here* 1F **47**
Westbrook. *Kent* 3H **41**
Westbrook. *Wilts* 5E **35**
West Buckland. *Devn* 3G **19** (nr. Barnstaple)
West Buckland. *Devn* 4C **8** (nr. Thurlestone)
West Buckland. *Som* 4E **21**
West Burnside. *Abers* 1G **145**
West Burrafirth. *Shet* 6D **173**
West Burton. *N Yor* 1C **98**
West Burton. *W Sus* 4B **26**
Westbury. *Buck* 2E **50**
Westbury. *Shrp* 5F **71**
Westbury. *Wilts* 1D **22**
Westbury Leigh. *Wilts* 1D **22**
Westbury-on-Severn. *Glos* 4C **48**
Westbury on Trym. *Bris* 4A **34**
Westbury-sub-Mendip. *Som* 2A **22**
West Butsfield. *Dur* 5E **115**
West Butterwick. *N Lin* 4B **94**
Westby. *Linc* 3G **75**
West Byfleet. *Surr* 4B **38**
West Caister. *Norf* 4H **79**
West Calder. *W Lot* 3D **128**
West Camel. *Som* 4A **22**
West Carr. *N Lin* 4H **93**
West Chaldon. *Dors* 4C **14**
West Challow. *Oxon* 3B **36**
West Charleton. *Devn* 4D **8**
West Chelborough. *Dors* 2A **14**
West Chevington. *Nmbd* 5G **121**
West Chiltington. *W Sus* 4B **26**
West Chiltington Common. *W Sus* 4B **26**
West Chinnock. *Som* 1H **13**
West Chisenbury. *Wilts* 1G **23**
West Clandon. *Surr* 5B **38**
West Cliffe. *Kent* 1H **29**
Westcliff-on-Sea. *S'end* 2C **40**
West Clyne. *High* 3F **165**
West Coker. *Som* 1A **14**
Westcombe. *Som* 3B **22** (nr. Evercreech)
Westcombe. *Som* 4H **21** (nr. Somerton)
West Compton. *Dors* 3A **14**
West Compton. *Som* 2A **22**
West Cornforth. *Dur* 1A **106**
Westcot. *Oxon* 3B **36**
Westcott. *Buck* 4F **51**
Westcott. *Devn* 2D **12**
Westcott. *Surr* 1C **26**
Westcott Barton. *Oxon* 3C **50**
West Cowick. *E Yor* 2G **93**
West Cranmore. *Som* 2B **22**
West Croftmore. *High* 2D **150**
West Cross. *Swan* 4F **31**
West Cullerlie. *Abers* 3E **153**
West Culvennan. *Dum* 3H **109**
West Curry. *Corn* 3C **10**
West Curthwaite. *Cumb* 5E **113**
Westdean. *E Sus* 5G **27**
West Dean. *W Sus* 1G **17**
West Dean. *Wilts* 4A **24**
West Deeping. *Linc* 5A **76**
West Derby. *Mers* 1F **83**
West Dereham. *Norf* 5F **77**
West Down. *Devn* 2F **19**
Westdowns. *Corn* 4A **10**
West Drayton. *G Lon* 3B **38**
West Drayton. *Notts* 3E **86**
West Dunnet. *High* 1E **169**
West Ella. *E Yor* 2D **94**
West End. *Bed* 5G **63**
West End. *Cambs* 1D **64**
West End. *Dors* 2E **15**
West End. *E Yor* 3E **101** (nr. Kilham)
West End. *E Yor* 1E **95** (nr. Preston)
West End. *E Yor* 1C **94** (nr. South Cove)
West End. *E Yor* 4F **101** (nr. Ulrome)
West End. *G Lon* 2D **39**
West End. *Hants* 1C **16**
West End. *Herts* 5C **52**
West End. *Kent* 4F **41**
West End. *Lanc* 3D **96**
West End. *Linc* 1C **76**
West End. *Norf* 4H **79**
West End. *N Som* 5H **33**
West End. *N Yor* 4D **98**
West End. *S Glo* 3C **34**
West End. *S Lan* 5C **128**
West End. *Surr* 4A **38**
West End. *Wilts* 4E **23**
West End. *Wind* 4G **37**
West End Green. *Hants* 5E **37**
Westenhanger. *Kent* 2F **29**
Wester Aberchalder. *High* 2H **149**
Wester Balgedie. *Per* 3D **136**
Wester Brae. *High* 2A **158**
Wester Culbeuchly. *Abers* 2D **160**
Westerdale. *High* 3D **168**
Westerdale. *N Yor* 4D **106**
Wester Dechmont. *W Lot* 2D **128**
Wester Fearn. *High* 5D **164**
Westerfield. *Suff* 1E **55**
Wester Galcantray. *High* 4C **158**
Westergate. *W Sus* 5A **26**
Wester Gruinards. *High* 4C **164**
Westerham. *Kent* 5F **39**
Westerleigh. *S Glo* 4C **34**
Westerloch. *High* 3F **169**
Wester Mandally. *High* 3E **149**
Wester Quarff. *Shet* 8F **173**
Wester Rarichie. *High* 1C **158**
Wester Shian. *Per* 5F **143**
Wester Skeld. *Shet* 7D **173**
Westerton. *Ang* 3F **145**
Westerton. *Dur* 1F **105**
Westerton. *W Sus* 2G **17**
Westerwick. *Shet* 7D **173**
West Farleigh. *Kent* 5B **40**
West Farndon. *Nptn* 5C **62**
West Felton. *Shrp* 3F **71**
Westfield. *Cumb* 2A **102**
Westfield. *E Sus* 4C **28**
Westfield. *High* 2C **168**
Westfield. *Norf* 5B **78**
Westfield. *N Lan* 2A **128**
Westfield. *W Lot* 2C **128**
Westfields. *Dors* 2C **14**
Westfields of Rattray. *Per* 4A **144**
West Fleetham. *Nmbd* 2F **121**
Westford. *Som* 4E **20**
West Garforth. *W Yor* 1D **93**
Westgate. *Dur* 1C **104**
Westgate. *Norf* 1B **78**
Westgate. *N Lin* 4A **94**
Westgate on Sea. *Kent* 3H **41**
West Ginge. *Oxon* 3C **36**
West Grafton. *Wilts* 5H **35**
West Green. *Hants* 1F **25**
West Grimstead. *Wilts* 4H **23**
West Grinstead. *W Sus* 3C **26**
West Haddlesey. *N Yor* 2F **93**
West Haddon. *Nptn* 3D **62**
West Hagbourne. *Oxon* 3D **36**
West Hagley. *Worc* 2D **60**
West Hall. *Cumb* 3G **113**
Westhall. *Suff* 2G **67**
West Hallam. *Derbs* 1B **74**
Westhall Terrace. *Ang* 5D **144**
West Halton. *N Lin* 2C **94**
Westham. *Dors* 5B **14**
Westham. *E Sus* 5H **27**
West Ham. *G Lon* 2E **39**
Westham. *Som* 2H **21**
Westhampnett. *W Sus* 2G **17**
West Handley. *Derbs* 3A **86**
West Hanney. *Oxon* 2C **36**
West Hanningfield. *Essx* 1B **40**
West Hardwick. *W Yor* 3E **93**
West Harnham. *Wilts* 4G **23**
West Harptree. *Bath* 1A **22**
West Harting. *W Sus* 4F **25**
West Harton. *Tyne* 3G **115**
West Hatch. *Som* 4F **21**
Westhay. *Som* 2H **21**
Westhead. *Lanc* 4C **90**
West Head. *Norf* 5E **77**
West Heath. *Hants* 1D **24** (nr. Basingstoke)
West Heath. *Hants* 1G **25** (nr. Farnborough)
West Helmsdale. *High* 2H **165**
West Hendred. *Oxon* 3C **36**
West Heogaland. *Shet* 4D **173**
West Heslerton. *N Yor* 2D **100**
West Hewish. *N Som* 5G **33**
Westhide. *Here* 1A **48**
Westhill. *Abers* 3F **153**
West Hill. *Devn* 3D **12**
West Hill. *E Yor* 3F **101**
Westhill. *High* 4B **158**
West Hill. *N Som* 4H **33**
West Hill. *W Sus* 2E **27**
West Hoathly. *W Sus* 2E **27**
West Holme. *Dors* 4D **15**
Westhope. *Here* 5G **59**
Westhope. *Shrp* 2G **59**
West Horndon. *Essx* 2H **39**
Westhorp. *Nptn* 5C **62**
Westhorpe. *Linc* 2B **76**
Westhorpe. *Suff* 4C **66**
West Horrington. *Som* 2A **22**
West Horsley. *Surr* 5B **38**
West Horton. *Nmbd* 1E **121**
West Hougham. *Kent* 1G **29**
Westhoughton. *G Man* 4E **91**
West Houlland. *Shet* 6D **173**
Westhouse. *N Yor* 2F **97**
Westhouses. *Derbs* 5B **86**
West Howe. *Bour* 3F **15**
Westhumble. *Surr* 5C **38**
West Huntspill. *Som* 2G **21**
West Hyde. *Herts* 1B **38**
West Hynish. *Arg* 5A **138**
West Hythe. *Kent* 2F **29**
West Ilsley. *W Ber* 3C **36**
Westing. *Shet* 1G **173**
West Itchenor. *W Sus* 2F **17**
West Keal. *Linc* 4C **88**
West Kennett. *Wilts* 5G **35**
West Kilbride. *N Ayr* 5D **126**
West Kingsdown. *Kent* 4G **39**
West Kington. *Wilts* 4D **34**
West Kirby. *Mers* 2E **82**
West Knapton. *N Yor* 2C **100**
West Knighton. *Dors* 4C **14**
West Knoyle. *Wilts* 3D **22**
West Kyloe. *Nmbd* 5G **131**
Westlake. *Devn* 3C **8**
West Lambrook. *Som* 1H **13**
West Langdon. *Kent* 1H **29**
West Langwell. *High* 3D **164**
West Lavington. *W Sus* 4G **25**
West Lavington. *Wilts* 1F **23**
West Layton. *N Yor* 4E **105**
West Leake. *Notts* 3C **74**
West Learmouth. *Nmbd* 1C **120**
Westleigh. *Devn* 4E **19** (nr. Bideford)
Westleigh. *Devn* 1D **12** (nr. Tiverton)
West Leigh. *Devn* 2G **11** (nr. Winkleigh)
Westleigh. *G Man* 4E **91**
West Leith. *Buck* 4H **51**
Westleton. *Suff* 4G **67**
West Lexham. *Norf* 4H **77**
Westley. *Shrp* 5F **71**
Westley. *Suff* 4H **65**
Westley Waterless. *Cambs* 5F **65**
West Lilling. *N Yor* 3A **100**
West Lingo. *Fife* 3G **137**
Westlington. *Buck* 4F **51**
Westlinton. *Cumb* 3E **113**
West Linton. *Bord* 4E **129**
West Littleton. *S Glo* 4C **34**
West Looe. *Corn* 3G **7**
West Lulworth. *Dors* 4D **14**
West Lutton. *N Yor* 3D **100**
West Lydford. *Som* 3A **22**
West Lyng. *Som* 4G **21**
West Lynn. *Norf* 4F **77**
West Mains. *Per* 2B **136**
West Malling. *Kent* 5A **40**
West Malvern. *Worc* 1C **48**
Westmancote. *Worc* 2E **49**
West Marden. *W Sus* 1F **17**
West Markham. *Notts* 3E **86**
Westmarsh. *Kent* 4G **41**
West Marsh. *NE Lin* 4F **95**
West Marton. *N Yor* 4A **98**
West Meon. *Hants* 4E **25**
West Mersea. *Essx* 4D **54**
Westmeston. *E Sus* 4E **27**
Westmill. *Herts* 3D **52** (nr. Buntingford)
Westmill. *Herts* 2B **52** (nr. Hitchin)
West Milton. *Dors* 3A **14**
Westminster. *G Lon* 3D **39**
West Molesey. *Surr* 4C **38**
West Monkton. *Som* 4F **21**
Westmoor End. *Cumb* 1B **102**
West Moors. *Dors* 2F **15**
West Morden. *Dors* 3E **15**
West Muir. *Ang* 2E **145** (nr. Brechin)
Westmuir. *Ang* 3C **144** (nr. Forfar)
West Murkle. *High* 2D **168**
West Ness. *N Yor* 2A **100**
Westness. *Orkn* 5C **172**
Westnewton. *Cumb* 5C **112**
West Newton. *E Yor* 1E **95**
West Newton. *Norf* 3F **77**
Westnewton. *Nmbd* 1D **120**
West Newton. *Som* 4F **21**
West Norwood. *G Lon* 3E **39**

Whitley Heath—Witcham

Whitley Heath. *Staf* 3C **72**
Whitley Lower. *W Yor* 3C **92**
Whitley Thorpe. *N Yor* 2F **93**
Whitlock's End. *W Mid* 3F **61**
Whitminster. *Glos* 5C **48**
Whitmore. *Dors* 2F **15**
Whitmore. *Staf* 1C **72**
Whitnage. *Devn* 1D **12**
Whitnash. *Warw* 4H **61**
Whitney. *Here* 1F **47**
Whitrigg. *Cumb* 4D **112**
(nr. Kirkbride)
Whitrigg. *Cumb* 1D **102**
(nr. Torpenhow)
Whitsbury. *Hants* 1G **15**
Whitsome. *Bord* 4E **131**
Whitson. *Newp* 3G **33**
Whitstable. *Kent* 4F **41**
Whitstone. *Corn* 3C **10**
Whittingham. *Nmbd* 3E **121**
Whittingslow. *Shrp* 2G **59**
Whittington. *Derbs* 3B **86**
Whittington. *Glos* 3F **49**
Whittington. *Lanc* 2F **97**
Whittington. *Shrp* 2F **71**
Whittington. *Staf* 2C **60**
(nr. Kinver)
Whittington. *Staf* 5F **73**
(nr. Lichfield)
Whittington. *Warw* 1G **61**
Whittington. *Worc* 5C **60**
Whittington Barracks. *Staf* 5F **73**
Whittlebury. *Nptn* 1E **51**
Whittleford. *Warw* 1H **61**
Whittle-le-Woods. *Lanc* 2D **90**
Whittlesey. *Cambs* 1B **64**
Whittlesford. *Cambs* 1E **53**
Whittlestone Head. *Bkbn* 3F **91**
Whitton. *N Lin* 2C **94**
Whitton. *Nmbd* 4E **121**
Whitton. *Powy* 4E **59**
Whitton. *Bord* 2B **120**
Whitton. *Shrp* 3H **59**
Whitton. *Stoc T* 2A **106**
Whittonditch. *Wilts* 4A **36**
Whittonstall. *Nmbd* 4D **114**
Whitway. *Hants* 1C **24**
Whitwell. *Derbs* 3C **86**
Whitwell. *Herts* 3B **52**
Whitwell. *IOW* 5D **16**
Whitwell. *N Yor* 5F **105**
Whitwell. *Rut* 5G **75**
Whitwell-on-the-Hill. *N Yor* 3B **100**
Whitwick. *Leics* 4B **74**
Whitwood. *W Yor* 2E **93**
Whitworth. *Lanc* 3G **91**
Whixall. *Shrp* 2H **71**
Whixley. *N Yor* 4G **99**
Whoberley. *W Mid* 3H **61**
Whorlton. *Dur* 3E **105**
Whorlton. *N Yor* 4B **106**
Whygate. *Nmbd* 2A **114**
Whyle. *Here* 4H **59**
Whyteleafe. *Surr* 5E **39**
Wibdon. *Glos* 2A **34**
Wibtoft. *Warw* 2B **62**
Wichenford. *Worc* 4B **60**
Wichling. *Kent* 5D **40**
Wick. *Bour* 3G **15**
Wick. *Devn* 2E **13**
Wick. *High* 3F **169**
Wick. *Shet* 8F **173**
(on Mainland)
Wick. *Shet* 1G **173**
(on Unst)
Wick. *Som* 2F **21**
(nr. Bridgwater)
Wick. *Som* 1G **21**
(nr. Burnham-on-Sea)
Wick. *Som* 4H **21**
(nr. Somerton)
Wick. *S Glo* 4C **34**
Wick. *V Glam* 4C **32**
Wick. *W Sus* 5B **26**
Wick. *Wilts* 4G **23**
Wick. *Worc* 1E **49**
Wick Airport. *High* 3F **169**
Wicken. *Cambs* 3E **65**
Wicken. *Nptn* 2F **51**
Wicken Bonhunt. *Essx* 2E **53**
Wickenby. *Linc* 2H **87**
Wicken Green Village. *Norf* 2H **77**
Wickersley. *S Yor* 1B **86**
Wicker Street Green. *Suff* 1C **54**
Wickford. *Essx* 1B **40**
Wickham. *Hants* 1D **16**
Wickham. *W Ber* 4B **36**
Wickham Bishops. *Essx* 4B **54**
Wickhambreaux. *Kent* 5G **41**
Wickhambrook. *Suff* 5G **65**
Wickhamford. *Worc* 1F **49**
Wickham Green. *Suff* 4C **66**
Wickham Heath. *W Ber* 5C **36**
Wickham Market. *Suff* 5F **67**
Wickhampton. *Norf* 5G **79**
Wickham St Paul. *Essx* 2B **54**
Wickham Skeith. *Suff* 4C **66**
Wickham Street. *Suff* 4C **66**
Wick Hill. *Wok* 5F **37**
Wicklewood. *Norf* 5C **78**
Wickmere. *Norf* 2D **78**
Wick St Lawrence. *N Som* 5G **33**
Wickwar. *S Glo* 3C **34**
Widdington. *Essx* 2F **53**
Widdrington. *Nmbd* 5G **121**
Widdrington Station. *Nmbd* 5G **121**
Widecombe in the Moor. *Devn* 5H **11**
Widegates. *Corn* 3G **7**
Widemouth Bay. *Corn* 2C **10**
Wide Open. *Tyne* 2F **115**
Widewall. *Orkn* 8D **172**
Widford. *Essx* 5G **53**
Widford. *Herts* 4E **53**
Widham. *Wilts* 3F **35**
Widmer End. *Buck* 2G **37**
Widmerpool. *Notts* 3D **74**
Widnes. *Hal* 2H **83**
Widworthy. *Devn* 3F **13**
Wigan. *G Man* 4D **90**
Wigbeth. *Dors* 2F **15**
Wigborough. *Som* 1H **13**
Wiggaton. *Devn* 3E **12**
Wiggenhall St Germans. *Norf* 4E **77**
Wiggenhall St Mary Magdalen. *Norf* 4E **77**
Wiggenhall St Mary the Virgin. *Norf* 4E **77**
Wiggenhall St Peter. *Norf* 4F **77**
Wiggens Green. *Essx* 1G **53**
Wigginton. *Herts* 4H **51**
Wigginton. *Oxon* 2B **50**
Wigginton. *Staf* 5G **73**
Wigginton. *York* 4H **99**
Wigglesworth. *N Yor* 4H **97**
Wiggonby. *Cumb* 4D **112**
Wiggonholt. *W Sus* 4B **26**
Wighill. *N Yor* 5G **99**
Wighton. *Norf* 2B **78**
Wightwick. *W Mid* 1C **60**
Wigley. *Hants* 1B **16**
Wigmore. *Here* 4G **59**
Wigmore. *Medw* 4C **40**
Wigsley. *Notts* 3F **87**
Wigsthorpe. *Nptn* 2H **63**
Wigston. *Leics* 1D **62**
Wigtoft. *Linc* 2B **76**
Wigton. *Cumb* 5D **112**
Wigtown. *Dum* 4B **110**
Wigtwizzle. *S Yor* 1G **85**
Wike. *W Yor* 5F **99**
Wilbarston. *Nptn* 2F **63**
Wilberfoss. *E Yor* 4B **100**
Wilburton. *Cambs* 3D **65**
Wilby. *Norf* 2C **66**
Wilby. *Nptn* 4F **63**
Wilby. *Suff* 3E **67**
Wilcot. *Wilts* 5G **35**
Wilcott. *Shrp* 4F **71**
Wilcove. *Corn* 3A **8**
Wildboarclough. *Ches E* 4D **85**
Wilden. *Bed* 5H **63**
Wilden. *Worc* 3C **60**
Wildern. *Hants* 1C **16**
Wilderspool. *Warr* 2A **84**
Wilde Street. *Suff* 3G **65**
Wildhern. *Hants* 1B **24**
Wildmanbridge. *S Lan* 4B **128**
Wildmoor. *Worc* 3D **60**
Wildsworth. *Linc* 1F **87**
Wildwood. *Staf* 3D **72**
Wilford. *Nott* 2C **74**
Wilkesley. *Ches E* 1A **72**
Wilkhaven. *High* 5G **165**
Wilkieston. *W Lot* 3E **129**
Wilksby. *Linc* 4B **88**
Willand. *Devn* 1D **12**
Willaston. *Ches E* 5A **84**
Willaston. *Ches W* 3F **83**
Willaston. *IOM* 4C **108**
Willen. *Mil* 1G **51**
Willenhall. *W Mid* 3A **62**
(nr. Coventry)
Willenhall. *W Mid* 1D **60**
(nr. Wolverhampton)
Willerby. *E Yor* 1D **94**
Willerby. *N Yor* 2E **101**
Willersey. *Glos* 2G **49**
Willersley. *Here* 1G **47**
Willesborough. *Kent* 1E **28**
Willesborough Lees. *Kent* 1E **29**
Willesden. *G Lon* 2D **38**
Willesley. *Wilts* 3D **34**
Willett. *Som* 3E **20**
Willey. *Shrp* 1A **60**
Willey. *Warw* 2B **62**
Willey Green. *Surr* 5A **38**
Williamscot. *Oxon* 1C **50**
Williamsetter. *Shet* 9E **173**
Willian. *Herts* 2C **52**
Willingale. *Essx* 5F **53**
Willingdon. *E Sus* 5G **27**
Willingham. *Cambs* 3D **64**
Willingham by Stow. *Linc* 2F **87**
Willingham Green. *Cambs* 5F **65**
Willington. *Bed* 1B **52**
Willington. *Derbs* 3G **73**
Willington. *Dur* 1E **105**
Willington. *Tyne* 3G **115**
Willington. *Warw* 2A **50**
Willington Corner. *Ches W* 4H **83**
Willisham Tye. *Suff* 5C **66**
Willitoft. *E Yor* 1H **93**
Williton. *Som* 2D **20**
Willoughbridge. *Staf* 1B **72**
Willoughby. *Linc* 3D **88**
Willoughby. *Warw* 4C **62**
Willoughby-on-the-Wolds. *Notts* 3D **74**
Willoughby Waterleys. *Leics* 1C **62**
Willoughton. *Linc* 1G **87**
Willow Green. *Worc* 5B **60**
Willows Green. *Essx* 4H **53**
Willsbridge. *S Glo* 4B **34**
Willslock. *Staf* 2E **73**
Wilmcote. *Warw* 5F **61**
Wilmington. *Bath* 5B **34**
Wilmington. *Devn* 3F **13**
Wilmington. *E Sus* 5G **27**
Wilmington. *Kent* 3G **39**
Wilmslow. *Ches E* 2C **84**
Wilnecote. *Staf* 5G **73**
Wilney Green. *Norf* 2C **66**
Wilpshire. *Lanc* 1E **91**
Wilsden. *W Yor* 1A **92**
Wilsford. *Linc* 1H **75**
Wilsford. *Wilts* 3G **23**
(nr. Amesbury)
Wilsford. *Wilts* 1F **23**
(nr. Devizes)
Wilsill. *N Yor* 3D **98**
Wilsley Green. *Kent* 2B **28**
Wilson. *Here* 3A **48**
Wilson. *Leics* 3B **74**
Wilsontown. *S Lan* 4C **128**
Wilstead. *Bed* 1A **52**
Wilsthorpe. *E Yor* 3F **101**
Wilsthorpe. *Linc* 4H **75**
Wilstone. *Herts* 4H **51**
Wilton. *Cumb* 3B **102**
Wilton. *N Yor* 1C **100**
Wilton. *Red C* 3C **106**
Wilton. *Bord* 3H **119**
Wilton. *Wilts* 5A **36**
(nr. Marlborough)
Wilton. *Wilts* 3F **23**
(nr. Salisbury)
Wimbish. *Essx* 2F **53**
Wimbish Green. *Essx* 2G **53**
Wimblebury. *Staf* 4E **73**
Wimbledon. *G Lon* 3D **38**
Wimblington. *Cambs* 1D **64**
Wimboldsley. *Ches W* 4A **84**
Wimborne Minster. *Dors* 2F **15**
Wimborne St Giles. *Dors* 1F **15**
Wimbotsham. *Norf* 5F **77**
Wimpole. *Cambs* 1D **52**
Wimpstone. *Warw* 1H **49**
Wincanton. *Som* 4C **22**
Winceby. *Linc* 4C **88**
Wincham. *Ches W* 3A **84**
Winchburgh. *W Lot* 2D **129**
Winchcombe. *Glos* 3F **49**
Winchelsea. *E Sus* 4D **28**
Winchelsea Beach. *E Sus* 4D **28**
Winchester. *Hants* 4C **24**
Winchet Hill. *Kent* 1B **28**
Winchfield. *Hants* 1F **25**
Winchmore Hill. *Buck* 1A **38**
Winchmore Hill. *G Lon* 1E **39**
Wincle. *Ches E* 4D **84**
Windermere. *Cumb* 5F **103**
Winderton. *Warw* 1B **50**
Windhill. *High* 4H **157**
Windle Hill. *Ches W* 3F **83**
Windlesham. *Surr* 4A **38**
Windley. *Derbs* 1H **73**
Windmill. *Derbs* 3F **85**
Windmill Hill. *E Sus* 4H **27**
Windmill Hill. *Som* 1G **13**
Windrush. *Glos* 4G **49**
Windsor. *Wind* 3A **38**
Windsor Green. *Suff* 5A **66**
Windyedge. *Abers* 4F **153**
Windygates. *Fife* 3F **137**
Windyharbour. *Ches E* 3C **84**
Windyknowe. *W Lot* 3C **128**
Wineham. *W Sus* 3D **26**
Winestead. *E Yor* 2G **95**
Winfarthing. *Norf* 2D **66**
Winford. *IOW* 4D **16**
Winford. *N Som* 5A **34**
Winforton. *Here* 1F **47**
Winfrith Newburgh. *Dors* 4D **14**
Wing. *Buck* 3G **51**
Wing. *Rut* 5F **75**
Wingate. *Dur* 1B **106**
Wingates. *G Man* 4E **91**
Wingates. *Nmbd* 5F **121**
Wingerworth. *Derbs* 4A **86**
Wingfield. *C Beds* 3A **52**
Wingfield. *Suff* 3E **67**
Wingfield. *Wilts* 1D **22**
Wingfield Park. *Derbs* 5A **86**
Wingham. *Kent* 5G **41**
Wingmore. *Kent* 1F **29**
Wingrave. *Buck* 4G **51**
Winkburn. *Notts* 5E **86**
Winkfield. *Brac* 3A **38**
Winkfield Row. *Brac* 4G **37**
Winkhill. *Staf* 5E **85**
Winklebury. *Hants* 1E **24**
Winkleigh. *Devn* 2G **11**
Winksley. *N Yor* 2E **99**
Winkton. *Dors* 3G **15**
Winlaton. *Tyne* 3E **115**
Winlaton Mill. *Tyne* 3E **115**
Winless. *High* 3F **169**
Winmarleigh. *Lanc* 5D **96**
Winnal Common. *Here* 2H **47**
Winnard's Perch. *Corn* 2D **6**
Winnersh. *Wok* 4F **37**
Winnington. *Ches W* 3A **84**
Winnington. *Staf* 2B **72**
Winnothdale. *Staf* 1E **73**
Winscales. *Cumb* 2B **102**
Winscombe. *N Som* 1H **21**
Winsford. *Ches W* 4A **84**
Winsford. *Som* 3C **20**
Winsham. *Devn* 3E **19**
Winsham. *Som* 2G **13**
Winshill. *Staf* 3G **73**
Winsh-wen. *Swan* 3F **31**
Winskill. *Cumb* 1G **103**
Winslade. *Hants* 2E **25**
Winsley. *Wilts* 5D **34**
Winslow. *Buck* 3F **51**
Winson. *Glos* 5F **49**
Winson Green. *W Mid* 2E **61**
Winsor. *Hants* 1B **16**
Winster. *Cumb* 5F **103**
Winster. *Derbs* 4G **85**
Winston. *Dur* 3E **105**
Winston. *Suff* 4D **66**
Winstone. *Glos* 5E **49**
Winswell. *Devn* 1E **11**
Winterborne Clenston. *Dors* 2D **14**
Winterborne Herringston. *Dors* 4B **14**
Winterborne Houghton. *Dors* 2D **14**
Winterborne Kingston. *Dors* 3D **14**
Winterborne Monkton. *Dors* 4B **14**
Winterborne St Martin. *Dors* 4B **14**
Winterborne Stickland. *Dors* 2D **14**
Winterborne Whitechurch. *Dors* 2D **14**
Winterborne Zelston. *Dors* 3D **15**
Winterbourne. *S Glo* 3B **34**
Winterbourne. *W Ber* 4C **36**
Winterbourne Abbas. *Dors* 3B **14**
Winterbourne Bassett. *Wilts* 4G **35**
Winterbourne Dauntsey. *Wilts* 3G **23**
Winterbourne Earls. *Wilts* 3G **23**
Winterbourne Gunner. *Wilts* 3G **23**
Winterbourne Monkton. *Wilts* 4G **35**
Winterbourne Steepleton. *Dors* 4B **14**
Winterbourne Stoke. *Wilts* 2F **23**
Winterbrook. *Oxon* 3E **36**
Winterburn. *N Yor* 4B **98**
Winter Gardens. *Essx* 2B **40**
Winterhay Green. *Som* 1G **13**
Winteringham. *N Lin* 2C **94**
Winterley. *Ches E* 5B **84**
Wintersett. *W Yor* 3D **93**
Winterton. *N Lin* 3C **94**
Winterton-on-Sea. *Norf* 4G **79**
Winthorpe. *Linc* 4E **89**
Winthorpe. *Notts* 5F **87**
Winton. *Bour* 3F **15**
Winton. *Cumb* 3A **104**
Winton. *E Sus* 5G **27**
Wintringham. *N Yor* 2C **100**
Winwick. *Cambs* 2A **64**
Winwick. *Nptn* 3D **62**
Winwick. *Warr* 1A **84**
Wirksworth. *Derbs* 5G **85**
Wirswall. *Ches E* 1H **71**
Wisbech. *Cambs* 4D **76**
Wisbech St Mary. *Cambs* 5D **76**
Wisborough Green. *W Sus* 3B **26**
Wiseton. *Notts* 2E **86**
Wishaw. *N Lan* 4A **128**
Wishaw. *Warw* 1F **61**
Wisley. *Surr* 5B **38**
Wispington. *Linc* 3B **88**
Wissenden. *Kent* 1D **28**
Wissett. *Suff* 3F **67**
Wistanstow. *Shrp* 2G **59**
Wistanswick. *Shrp* 3A **72**
Wistaston. *Ches E* 5A **84**
Wiston. *Pemb* 3E **43**
Wiston. *S Lan* 1B **118**
Wiston. *W Sus* 4C **26**
Wistow. *Cambs* 2B **64**
Wistow. *N Yor* 1F **93**
Wiswell. *Lanc* 1F **91**
Witcham. *Cambs* 2D **64**

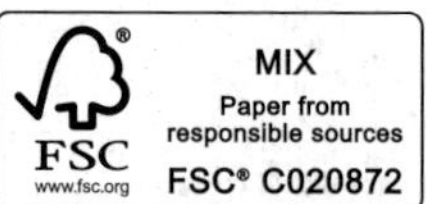